POLITICAL CORRUPTION

POLITICAL CORRUPTION

A Handbook

Edited by

**Arnold J. Heidenheimer, Michael Johnston,
and Victor T. LeVine**

Transaction Publishers
New Brunswick (U.S.A.) and London (U.K.)

Fifth printing 1999
Copyright © 1989 by Transaction Publishers, New Brunswick, New Jersey.

This book is printed on acid-free paper that meets the American National Standard for Permanence of Paper for Printed Library Materials.

Library of Congress Catalog Number: 87-16157
ISBN: 0-88738-163-4
Printed in the United States of America

Library of Congress Cataloging-in-Publication Data
Political corruption.

Bibliography: p.
1. Corruption (in politics). I. Heidenheimer, Arnold J. II. Johnston, Michael, 1949– . III. LeVine, Victor.
JF1525.C66P65   1989   350.9   87-16157
ISBN: 0-88738-163-4

Contents

Preface

In the fall of 1986 a typical weekday issue of the national edition of the *New York Times* contained about a half dozen extensive news articles about political corruption in such political entities as Queens, the Bronx, Manhattan, Boston, Chicago and Mexico. The space devoted to these reports usually exceeded by far that devoted to the entire gamut of political developments in such often unnewsworthy world areas as Europe or Asia.

We leave it to future historians to provide deeper interpretations on this political-cultural phenomenon. Our desire here is to point out that while social scientists have clearly not matched the zeal of the journalists, their publications also reflect a tendency to deal with this subject which has increased considerably over the last decade or two. Perhaps this was partly because there was more corruption occurring; we don't know for sure. But we can ascertain that in a number of countries changes in political climates and the conditions of competition made instances of alleged or proven corruption more visible to political publics.

Recognition that political corruption constitutes a valid and challenging subject for political and social scientists has diffused in a curious way. In the 1960s there was very little research on corruption in the United States or western Europe. Rather social scientists from these areas were investigating corruption in various developing areas to the south of their homelands. In the 1970s and 1980s a predominantly quite different collection of academics have focussed more attention on corruption either in their home countries or in other more developed societies of the northern hemisphere, such as western Europe, the United States and the leading communist systems.

This change of geopolitical focus has probably served to diminish the continuity of the learning process through which social scientists educate each other. Most authors of studies on corruption are primarily "area specialists," either on their native or other political systems. For many of them it goes somewhat "against the grain" to learn lessons derived from other kinds of systems, especially if these are perceived as lower on some implicit developmental scale.

Strengthening the opportunities for intellectual continuity, both conceptually and empirically, has motivated the editors to assemble the materials contained in this volume. Our own areas of interest straddle both the categories of systems mentioned above, as well as the periods in which we became socialized as students of corruption phenomena. Le Vine started on the road to comparative corruption research from an African base, Johnston builds on an American base and is an editor of the recently-founded journal, *Corruption and Reform.*

Some time ago we consulted among ourselves and with other colleagues in the field as to whether it might be opportune to consider editing a volume which could constitute something of a successor to *Political Corruption: Readings in Comparative Analysis,* which Heidenheimer had edited for publication in 1970. We found widespread agreement that the lack of any volume which brought together larger sections of the better more recent literature was a handicap to both research and teaching.

We pondered and rejected the plan of editing a volume which would be constituted solely of material which could not be considered for the 1970 volume, because it was published subsequent to that date. That option might well have militated against the very continuity of research effort and perspective which we felt we wanted to sustain.

We decided that we could proceed best by cross-breeding in a bibliographical sense. In one sense this volume is a new edition of *Political Corruption: Readings,* since a core of the constituent articles are carried over from the earlier volume. But in another sense the volume can be considered a serial successor to its older cousin, since a majority of the selections are unique to the new volume. All of these were either published since 1970, or in some eight cases, were either written or adapted specifically for the present volume.

The articles and excerpts included here were culled from a very much larger pool of potential ones through a sifting and fitting process that went on for several years. Some articles were preeminent candidates because of their evident originality. In making other choices we shared the process of evaluation with both graduate and undergraduate students in our classes; in quite a few cases their ratings helped us to decide which among several candidates was the strongest.

Relating the teaching and editorial tasks also permitted us to experiment in grouping and organizing the materials in different ways. It is in this trial-and-error manner that we shaped the basic units which now appear as "chapters" in the volume. The selections may be regarded as samples of the relevant literature which combine descriptive richness, analytical thrust, conceptual awareness, and contextual articulation in an optimal manner.

New Wine in Old Bottles? We had to decide also to what extent to replicate the format of *Political Corruption: Readings.* This was not much of a problem as the first part of the book is concerned, since our approach stressed continuities in the conceptual context of analysis. But should we continue to classify chapters as to whether they related primarily to corruption in the administration, in the electoral and legislative institutions, or to processes of modernization? Our scanning of the literature indicated that whereas administrative corruption had continued to constitute a focus of attention, the other two categories had somewhat diminished as significant rubrics. So we concluded that it would be in the spirit of exploration, as well as instructive for both ourselves and our readers, to group selections in different ways. These are the results:

Part One deals with problems of conceptualization, definition and historical comparison in the study of political corruption. The authors reflect diverse European and North American backgrounds and include economic historians, political scientists, sociologists, communication scholars, and lawyers. Some new selections are found, but they are most numerous in the section on social perceptions, where some alternative approaches to questions of definition and interpretation are presented.

Part Two examines the incidence of corruption within the conceptual framework of theories of political development and modernization. About half the selections are new to this volume. The focus lies partly on developments in western, and partly on those in developing non-western, countries. The authors also include economists and anthropologists. Temporal references range from the sixteenth century to the present, and there is some emphasis on the experiences of Asian and African countries. Nations whose experiences are more significantly analyzed here than in the preceding volume are Morocco, Ghana, Indonesia, and Israel.

Part Three is conceptually more heterodox and draws significantly on recent scholarship on corruption problems involving the more powerful developed nations, both capitalist and communist. Some selections embrace studies of political corruption in contemporary Soviet Union and China, thus correcting an omission of the preceding volume. Selections on the United States forego representativeness to focus on studies which attempt to examine the American experience in comparative perspective. Other chapters deal with problems of corruption at, respectively, the sub-national and trans-national levels. Included are studies of government attempts to regulate corruption involvements of transnational corporations, a problem that was scarcely alluded to in the pre-1970 academic literature. A majority of the selections in this part are by authors, mainly political scientists, who are post-1970 recruits to the study of political corruption.

In Part IV attention is focussed on the repercussions of corruption under the title, "Distinctions, Reactions and Effects." There we present a variety of ways of responding to the skeptical observer's question, *So what?* Here the institutional frameworks accentuated in the earlier parts are transcended so as to reestablish connections to the perceptions and reactions of individuals. Survey-based studies analyze how elites and ordinary citizens judge and react to various kinds of behavior that might be labelled corrupt. They analyze more carefully the gradients and variations in perceptions of corruptness in various locales. Subsequent chapters deal with complementary means of seeking to control corruption. One deals with how bureaucracies can or have implemented various kinds of disincentives to corrupt practices. In another, authors examine the relationship between corruption and scandals, and examine some results of scandals in different political settings. Many of the selections are drawn from post-1970 work, and several incorporate innovative theoretical and methodological departures. In the concluding selections authors apply various cost-benefits and other matrices to assess the effects of corruptions along a variety of dimensions.

We hope that our compilation of this volume will have a number of effects. The first is pragmatic. Since this literature has grown at a time when library resources have been reduced, we hope that this kind of selective presentation of the literature will reduce the "entry costs" of those seeking an orientation to the field. It should also make it more feasible to consider organizing university courses on this subject. We urge both researchers and teachers to also examine *Political Corruption: Readings*. Many of the selections published there but not here are of high quality and have by no means become superseded.

The second aim is addressed more to our fellow journeymen in the field of research. Perhaps after reading this volume some will perceive more conceptual and intellectual continuity in the research from both periods than might otherwise be apparent. While there has not been any theoretical breakthrough, there has certainly been discourse, dialogue, innovation, and movement. The political and research questions of the 1980s are in part significantly different from those of the 1960s.

Finally, we hope that more of our colleagues will use the opportunities we present to cast their future studies in more explicitly comparative terms. One of the astonishing aspects of the large literature of the past decade is how little has been comparative in the cross-national sense. Thus there has not been any work which has attempted to match the historical and cross-national breadth of James C. Scott's *Comparative Political Corruption*. While many studies of corruption will continue to focus on local or national issues, the existence of an increasingly international literature should make parochial treatment less necessary and sufficient.

Acknowledgments: Completion of work on the preparation of this volume has been facilitated by the assistance of various individuals, groups and institutions. Most important were our publishers, Transaction, which had taken the predecessor volume onto its publication list, and encouraged working out the conditions leading to the preparation of the new volume. Apart from Irving Louis Horowitz, our thanks go to Alex Fundock and Kimberly Jesuele.

Our home institutions were helpful in varying degree. At Washington University our work coincided with a period of lukewarm support of social science research, but we acknowledge a grant of three hundred dollars from the Graduate School Research Fund. Valuable assistance was provided by department secretaries, especially Marilyn Schad, who worked on many sections of the manuscript. Michael Johnston also acknowledges support from the University of Pittsburgh and Colgate University for research and secretarial assistance.

Very important to the project were two helpful spirits in St. Louis, Okun Attah and Emma Dankoski. Mr. Attah provided wise advice in the selection of manuscripts and their editing, and also took the main responsibility for preparing the bibliography. Ms. Dankoski applied her extensive editorial skills to the preparation and editing of articles, and in keeping control over the complex and multi-faceted manuscript.

Students in courses on corruption taught by us were helpful in varying ways. At Washington University we would like to mention especially Ian Haney and Michael Rosenthal.

Among colleagues active in political corruption research we are grateful especially to those who agreed to prepare articles especially for this edition. But we also express appreciation to those who gave reprint rights, or encouraged their publishers to grant them. It is ironic that the exchange value we could offer to authors was so largely non-material in nature, and we and our readers are appreciative of the concessions made on this score.

A number of other colleagues were also helpful in providing information and suggestions, and in facilitating reprint permissions. Among these we would like to mention especially Donald Lien, Linda Levy Peck, Stephen Riley, Wolfgang Schuller, Winfried Steffani, and Gottfried Wewer.

Colleagues associated with the Study Group on Corruption and Political Finance of the International Political Science Association have sometimes provided critical audiences for some of the publications included in this book. All three editors have been intermittently active at the low-profile meetings periodically held by this group. Assistance and support was also given by those associated with the recently-founded journal, *Corruption and Reform*, published by Martinus Nijhoff.

Arnold J. Heidenheimer   Michael Johnston
Victor T. LeVine   *Hamilton, New York*
St. Louis, Missouri

Part I

THE CONTEXT OF ANALYSIS

Terms, Concepts, and Definitions:
An Introduction

Aristotle wrote that "there are three kinds of constitution, or an equal number of deviations, or, as it were, corruptions of these three kinds . . . The deviation or corruption of kingship is tyranny. Both kingship and tyranny are forms of government by a single person, but . . . the tyrant studies his own advantage . . . the king looks to that of his subjects."[1]

Was Aristotle, when he described tyranny as a *corrupt* form of monarchy, using the concept of corruption much as we would apply it today to an official who secretly accepts a bribe to decide a policy issue differently than he otherwise would have?

Carl Friedrich, following Aristotle, holds that both applications derive from the basic core meaning, which he formulates as "deviant behavior associated with a particular motivation, namely that of private gain at public expense" (chapter 1).

However, today this attempt sacrifices clarity to brevity, insofar as it leaves too implicit how or why behavior is deviant from which norms for those whose conceptions are not based on Aristotelian ideal types. Some institutional framework seems a definitional prerequisite. We have less disagreement with Friedrich's formulation that corruption exists, "whenever a power holder who is charged with doing certain things, that is a responsible functionary or office holder, is by monetary or other rewards, such as the expectation of a job in the future, induced to take actions which favor whoever provides the reward and therefore damage the group or organization to which the functionary belongs, more specifically the government."

How prevalent has corruption thus defined been in various countries over recent times? His answer is:

> That corruption is endemic in all government is practically certain. That there are striking differences in the extent of corruption between governments which are formally similar such as Great Britain, Switzerland and the United States, all functioning constitutional democracies, is equally patent.

3

> It is possible that a law could be stated that would say that the degree of corruption varies inversely to the degree that power is consensual.[2]

Switzerland can be taken as an example of a political system where consensual power was maintained into the period of industrialization and mass suffrage, so that in the nineteenth and twentieth centuries, that country has reported very few cases of corruption. The Scandinavian countries of Sweden and Denmark have used different techniques to inhibit corruption, even in recent periods when the same political party has remained in control of local and national power over many decades.

How time-bound are these perceptions? If, for instance, we turn back to the eighteenth century, how were these countries ranked on corruption by Americans in the decades preceding the American Revolution?

We are not surprised to find that eighteenth century Americans regarded the British system of that period as "corrupt." At the time Robert Walpole and his friends ruled Britain by assembling majorities in parliament, which they largely recruited through money payments and the trading of patronage favors. But the traditional English concept of "corruption" on which the eighteenth century writers built related not only to means, but to the ends of politics. It was the encroachment of the executive power on that of the legislature and of the elites it then represented, which constituted the core of the definition of corruption used by many Englishmen as early as 1700:

> The executive possesses means of distracting parliament from its proper functions; it seduces members by the offer of places and pensions, by retaining them to follow ministers and ministers' rivals, by persuading them to support measures—standing armies, national debts, excise schemes—whereby the activities of administration grow beyond Parliament's control. These means of subversion are known collectively as corruption.[3]

In the period in which American protest boiled up to culminate in the revolution, Americans echoed and escalated such charges against George III and his ministers. But how did they rank Sweden and Switzerland, countries not particularly allied with Britain or involved in North America?

Very differently from each other. Switzerland was regarded as a country which had not only maintained local direct democracy usages similar to those employed in New England towns, but had protected its local institutions and effectively resisted the encroachment of potential political centralizers or 'despots.' Denmark and Sweden, by sharp contrast, were seen as systems which had become corrupted because their estates had allowed the powers of their parliaments to be undermined by centralizing monarchs who deprived the nobility and citizens of legislative rights which they had earlier enjoyed. Their people and elites had failed to maintain effective checks on the wielders of power. The Americans believed that it had been lack of vigilance

> that had brought liberty in Denmark to its knees, for there is a corrupt nobility, more interested in using its privileges for self-indulgence than for service to the state, had dropped its guard and allowed in a standing army which quickly destroyed the constitution and the liberties protected by it.[4]

Sweden was a subsequent case in point.

> The colonists themselves could remember when the Swedish people had enjoyed liberty to the full; but now, in the 1760s, they were known to "rejoice at being subject to the caprice and arbitrary power of a tyrant, and kiss their chains."[5]

The concepts of corruption employed by the American colonists partly anticipated the manner in which concepts and terms were employed in some subsequent American crises, but also relate to concepts employed by such founding fathers of western political thought as Thucydides, Plato, and Aristotle. They and some modern political theorists have employed the notion of the "corruption of the bad polity," to characterize situations which they perceived as marked by the decay of the moral and political order. As Friedrich writes about one of them: "Rousseau was deeply concerned with what he believed to be the corruption of his age, and he looked upon himself as the wise man who must raise a warning voice: . . . Rousseau's concern with corruption is primarily with moral corruption, and only indirectly with political corruption, as providing the setting for moral corruption." Another writer notes that, "The arguments about corruption are scattered throughout the Western political tradition but a coherent theory of corruption has never been fully articulated."[6]

As some of the above examples illustrate, there may be some overlap between the broader 'institutional decay' concept of corruption, and the more delineated one which defines corruption in terms of the acceptance of money or money's worth by public officials for misusing official powers. But analytically the two concepts are fairly clearly distinguishable. There will tend to be some "corrupt" public officials in most political systems which are not widely believed to be becoming corrupt in the sense of the decay of their vital moral or constitutional rules of behavior. But by and large even radical critics have come *not* to link the establishment of standing armies and the growth of national debts as indicators of political system corruption in the way that eighteenth century critics did.

At times shocking revelations about the misuse of political, and especially executive powers, have tended to revive the associations and partly archaisized usages linked with the concept of institutional decay. Watergate was a marked instance of that. When it became apparent that President Nixon and his White House aides had boldly abused the powers of their offices to undermine their opponents, the issue of corruption reappeared starkly on the American national scene.

The Watergate revelations revealed clear violations of political rules in the shape of a television drama, which seemed to come, "straight out of the American Christian literary tradition . . . revealing naked ambition, Christian piety, lust for power and tragic betrayal." Americans watching it got the overwhelming impression that "all the president's men were satanic minions, that the president himself was villainy incarnate, and that the highest office in the land had been lamentably stained." (Eisenstadt, chapter 31)

In its drama and consequence the Watergate revelations, leading as they did to the near-impeachment and resignation of the president and the imprisonment of many of his closest advisers, far exceeded both the drama and political import of such "normal" American scandals of earlier days, like Teapot Dome and Credit Mobilier.

Yet the prevailing definitions of political corruption by recent political scientists have fairly consistently defined corruption in terms of transactions between the private and public sectors such that collective goods are illegitimately converted into private-regarding payoffs.

The intrigues and plots which composed portions of the illegal chain in which operatives of the Nixon White House abused executive powers did not clearly conform to such and similar definitions of corruption. By contrast to the typical patterns of bribery, nepotism, patronage, misappropriation of funds, sale of office, and the like, Watergate did *not* involve primarily private-regarding payoffs, the president's tax returns and home remodeling notwithstanding. All the President's Men were not interested in private gain. Watergate thus differed from such cash-oriented scandals as Teapot Dome, Credit Mobilier, or the Agnew affair.

The revelations and reactions to Watergate had significant impact on some American academic authors. Whereas in the early 1970s some important works on political corruption were dropped from publishers' lists for lack of significant sales, the situation altered sharply after Watergate. Political scientists found publishers eager to publish their volumes on American political corruption. Among them were books such as Berg, Hahn and Schmidhauser's *Corruption in the American Political System* (1976), and Benson's *Political Corruption in America* (1978).[7]

These works employ very elastic and expanded definitions. In their sense, political corruption refers to any behavior which "violates and undermines the norms of the system of public order which is deemed indispensable for the maintenance of political democracy" (Berg, et al. 3). Similarly Benson casts his net as widely as possible and employs political corruption as a general term covering "all illegal or unethical use of governmental authority as a result of considerations of personal or political gain." (Benson, xiii)

Many political scientists whose attention to political corruption phenomena antedated the Nixon/Watergate period reacted critically to these proposed, more broadened definitions. We are inclined to agree with a British colleague that

> the looseness of contemporary definitions provides infinite scope for argument. Unethical behavior or behavior which violates "the norms of the system of public order" may include almost anything. The danger here seems to be that clarity and consistency in analysis may have been sacrificed for comprehensiveness. The fundamental weakness of the recent literature on corruption lies in the use of vague criteria and inappropriate perspectives which distort, exaggerate or otherwise over-simply explanations of corruption in the United States.[8]

Varieties of Meanings

A careful examination of what past and present writers seem to have intended when they employed the term *corruption* in political contexts reveals an even broader catalog of usages and potential ambiguities. Some reasons for this become more apparent by referring to the *Oxford English Dictionary* (OED), where we find that only one of nine commonly accepted definitions for the term is applicable to political contexts: "Perversion or destruction of integrity in the discharge of public duties by bribery or favour; the use or existence of corrupt practices, especially in a state, public corporation, etc."

The *OED* categorizes the nine meanings of corruption as follows:

1. *Physical*—for example, "the destruction or spoiling of anything, especially by disintegration or by decomposition with its attendant unwholesomeness and loathsomeness; putrefaction."
2. *Moral*—the "political" definition already given comes under this category. Another definition in this category is: "a making or becoming morally corrupt; the fact or condition of being corrupt; moral deterioration or decay; depravity."
3. *The perversion of anything from an original state of purity*—for example, "the perversion of an institution, custom, and so forth from its primitive purity; an instance of this perversion."

The present usage of the term *corruption* in political contexts has obviously been colored by the meanings in the "moral" category, and in earlier times usage was frequently colored by the meanings in the two other categories, especially by those in the third category. Thus the author of a nineteenth-century encyclopedia article entitled "Corruption in Politics" developed his discussion essentially in terms of meanings derived by way of Montesquieu from Aristotle, who, for instance, conceived of *tyranny* as a "corrupted" variant of monarchy.

Contemporary Social Science Definitions

The variety of definitions employed by contemporary social scientists interested in corruption fortunately does not cover as wide a span as those given in the OED. Among them we can identify usages that seek to define corruption in terms of one of three kinds of basic models or concepts. The largest group of social science writers follow the OED definition and relate their definitions of *corruption* essentially to concepts concerning the duties of the public office. A smaller group develop definitions that are primarily related to demand, supply, and exchange concepts derived from economic theory; while a third group discuss corruption more with regard to the concept of the public interest.

Public-Office-Centered Definitions

Definitions of corruption that relate most essentially to the concept of the public office and to deviations from norms binding upon its incumbents are well illustrated in the work of three authors—David H. Bayley, G. Myrdal, and J.S. Nye—who have concerned themselves with the problems of development in various continents. According to Bayley's definition of the word (chapter 53)

Corruption, while being tied particularly to the act of bribery, is a general term covering misuse of authority as a result of considerations of personal gain, which need not be monetary.

Examining the wording of American statutes relating to bribery, Lowenstein (chapter 3) finds that one of five elements generally mentioned, that relating to the involvement of a public official, is least ambiguous. More open to interpretation are conditions that

   i. the defendant must have a corrupt intent;
  ii. that benefits of value must accrue to the public official;
 iii. that there must be a relationship between the thing of value and an official act; and,
 iv. that the relationship must involve the intent to influence or be influenced in the carrying out of an official act.

J.S. Nye (chapter 55) defines corruption as

> . . . behavior which deviates from the normal duties of a public role because of private-regarding (family, close private clique), pecuniary or status gains; or violates rules against the exercise of certain types of private-regarding influence. This includes such behavior as bribery (use of reward to pervert the judgement of a person in a position of trust); nepotism (bestowal of patronage by reason of ascriptive relationship rather than merit); and misappropriation (illegal appropriation of public resources for private-regarding uses).

Market-Centered Definitions

Definitions in terms of the theory of the market have been developed particularly by those authors dealing with earlier western and contemporary non-western societies, in which the norms governing public officeholders are not clearly articulated or are nonexistent. Thus Van Klaveren (chapter 2) states that

> A corrupt civil servant regards his public office as a business, the income of which he will . . . seek to maximize. The office then becomes a "maximizing unit." The size of his income depends . . . upon the market situation and his talents for finding the point of maximal gain on the public's demand curve.

Also pertinent is the statement by Nethaniel Leff (chapter 24).

> Corruption is an extra-legal institution used by individuals or groups to gain influence over the actions of the bureaucracy. As such the existence

of corruption *per se* indicates only that these groups participate in the decision-making process to a greater extent than would otherwise be the case.

Public-Interest-Centered Definitions

Some writers feel that the first set of definitions is too narrowly conceived and the second set too broadly conceived. They tend to maintain that the embattled concept of "public interest" is not only still useful but necessary to illustrate the essence of concepts like corruption. Carl Friedrich, for instance, contends that

> The pattern of corruption can be said to exist whenever a powerholder who is charged with doing certain things, i.e., who is a responsible functionary or officeholder, is by monetary or other rewards not legally provided for, induced to take actions which favor whoever provides the rewards and thereby does damage to the public and its interests.[9]

Since the concept of the public interest is open to broad interpretation, it has been suggested that determination of whether a political policy-influencing action is or is not corrupt will depend on the observer's judgment as to whether a particular policy is or is not desirable. But Lowenstein argues that acts that "are made according to the wishes of the highest bidder," may be regarded as contrary to the public interest, "without regard to the substantive direction of its influence on public policy." (chapter 3)

In the 1980s there has been a revival of attempts to employ the public interest concept to delegitimate particularly large-scale business financing of political activity by attaching the label of corruption to legal or quasi-legal activities. Accordingly, distinctions are made between 'public interest groups,' which represent 'the community at large' and whose focus is on 'non-pecuniary interests,' and 'special interest groups,' which have a narrow base and represent primarily pecuniary interests. Thus the financial allocations of political action committees have in the American context, been attacked, by Amitai Etzioni as exercising power through so-called 'legalized corruption.'

> Plutocrats in a democracy work by corrupting public life. They seek to turn a government of, by and for the people into one of the wealthy. . . . Political corruption is typically perpetrated by private interests seeking illicit public favors and finding quite willing public officials.[10]

In West Germany, where similar payments evaded disclosure requirements, similar charges have been made by members of the Green party

(See chapter 49). For political analysts this raises the question of whether they should blur the distinctions between exchanges that are implicit rather than explicit, and between those that are channeled through legalized organizations rather than through back-door contacts. Should 'undue influence' become labelled as 'corruption' when the means are used by a group that is seen as working less in the public interest than others? Arguments about whether social scientists should endorse or employ such broadened definitions continue to be vehement in both America and Europe.

Whose Norms Set the Criteria?

The definitions employed in the first and third of the categories just discussed directly raise the question encountered in all normative analysis: Which norms are the ones that will be used to distinguish corrupt from noncorrupt acts? If the definitions are public-office-centered, then which statement of the rules and norms governing public officeholders is to be employed? If the definitions are public-interest-centered, then whose evaluation of the public's interest is to be operationalized? Definitions couched in terms of market theory appear to bypass this problem, but in fact they do not. They too imply that somewhere there is an authority that distinguishes between the rules applicable to public officials and those applicable to businessmen operating in the free market, or that there are certain characteristics that distinguish a "black market" from the free market.

Political scientists of an earlier generation tried to deal with the problem of norm setting with reference to the legal rules provided by statute books and court decisions. Thus behavior was judged by James Bryce to be either permissible or corrupt in accordance with the criteria established by legislators and judges:

> Corruption may be taken to include those modes of employing money to attain private ends by political means which are criminal or at least illegal, because they induce persons charged with a public duty to transgress that duty and misuse the functions assigned to them.[11]

But the author of the article on "Corruption, Political," in the *Encyclopedia of the Social Sciences* argued that "the question of formal legality . . . is not the essence of the concept." The normative judgments that should be used as criteria, he thought, were the judgments of the elite: "Where the best opinion and morality of the time, examining the intent and setting of an act, judge it to represent a sacrifice of public for private benefit, then it must be held to be corrupt."[12]

Senturia's particularistic emphasis would require that this fairly large body of elites serve as a jury for each particular case. Their findings, in effect, would relate only to their society of that particular era. A consensus of the "best opinion" in a time and place, such as Britain in 1960, could presumably establish criteria beyond which private-regarding behavior would be considered corrupt in the contemporary setting. However, it would then be impossible to compare either the extent or the varieties of political corruption between the situations prevailing of Britain in 1960 and in 1860 because of the uniqueness of the suggested definition. This difficulty would apply equally to attempts to compare, say, bureaucratic corruption in nineteenth-century Russia and twentieth-century Chicago.

Is there a term which political scientists could use as a synonym for corruption, which would include the meanings most relevant for them, while screening out some of those that create ambiguity, such as the one associated with the broader meaning linked with system decay? The term *graft* is put forward as one possible candidate by several authors in this volume. V.O. Key (chapter 4) evidently employs it as a synonym for corruption, but one should know that he was writing exclusively about practices prevalent in Chicago and other American cities. Although the exact origins of the term are not known, it is clearly of American origins and was long regarded as an Americanism, as the OED *Supplement* records. When therefore authors like Peter Harris (chapter 30) propose to substitute 'graft' for 'corruption' when discussing the Soviet and Chinese communist systems, they may be inadvertently generating additional problems of cross-language comparability. Terms very similar to corruption have been taken over from Latin into most established languages, and this constitutes an advantage from the comparative perspective. Also, some authors employ the term graft to cover only some forms of corrupt behavior, namely those initiated by the office-holder and not the favor-seeker.

Western Versus Non-Western Standards

If one does not accept the criteria established by law or the norms of a small elite group as delimiting political corruption, how far can one go in delineating the relevant norms with reference to the standards of a more diverse set of reference groups and codes? At present this problem presents itself most directly for those social scientists who have sought to analyze corruption in developing countries where mores rooted in two very distinct milieu govern the standards of political and bureaucratic behavior. David H. Bayley (chapter 53) has outlined the resultant problem posed for the objective investigator:

It not infrequently happens . . . in developing non-Western societies that existing moral codes do not agree with Western norms as to what kinds of behavior by public servants should be condemned. The Western observer is faced with an uncomfortable choice. He can adhere to the Western definition, in which case he lays himself open to the charge of being censorious and he finds that he is condemning not abhorrent behavior, but normal acceptable operating procedure. On the other hand, he may face up to the fact that corruption, if it requires moral censure, is culturally conditioned. He then argues that an act is corrupt if the surrounding society condemns it. This usage, however, muddies communication, for it may be necessary then to assert in the same breath that an official accepts gratuities but is not corrupt.

The problem of applying the concept and standards of corruption to developing countries is exhaustively discussed by Colin Leys (chapter 5), who builds on the analysis of the literature as it had developed by the 1960s, to raise and answer questions both of conceptual and empirical relevance. He criticizes some of the parallels drawn by earlier writers between developments in Britain and Africa. The British ruling class of the Victorian period is seen by him as having a clear if tenuous conception of the public interest and the duty they owed to it through their use of public offices. In Africa, by contrast, "the idea contained in the phrase *noblesse oblige* scarcely applies. There is no previous experience, and so no prior ideology, of the rules of public offices and institutions in relation to the public interest, in terms of which the private exploitation of public office could be rationalized." This illustrates how developing countries, where definitions of corruption were rather peremptorily incorporated into new legal codes, differed from western countries, where changes in the moral and legal connotation of corruption evolved gradually along with other processes of societal change.

Notes

1. *The Politics of Aristotle,* translated and edited by Ernest Barker (Oxford: Clarendon Press, 1946), p. 373.
2. Carl J. Friedrich, "Political Pathology," *Political Quarterly,* 37 (1966), p. 74.
3. J.G.A. Pocock, "Machiavelli, Harrington and English Political Ideologies in the Eighteenth Century," *William and Mary Quarterly,* 3d ser., 22 (1965), p. 565.
4. Bernard Bailyn, *The Ideological Origins of the American Revolution* (Cambridge, Mass.: Harvard University Press, 1967), p. 65.
5. Ibid., p. 64.
6. Patrick Dobel, "The Corruption of a State," *American Political Science Review,* (1978), p. 959.
7. Larry L. Berg, H. Hahn, and J. R. Schmidhauser, *Corruption in the American Political System,* Morristown, N.J.: General Learning Press,

1976. George C. S. Benson, S. A. Maaranen, and A. Heslop, *Political Corruption in America,* Lexington, Mass.: Lexington Books, 1978.

8. Robert J. Williams, "Political Corruption in the United States," *Political Studies,* XXXIX, 1 (March 1981), 126–29.

9. Friedrich, *loc. cit.*

10. Amitai Etzioni, *Capital Corruption: The New Attack on American Democracy* (New York: Harcourt, Brace Jovanovich, 1984), pp. 3–4, 201–203. For a politician's way of employing this approach in public discourse, see Mark Green, "Stamping Out Corruption," *New York Times,* October 28, 1986; see also *New York Times,* October 29, 1986.

11. James Bryce, *Modern Democracies,* II. New York: St. Martins, 1921, 524.

12. Joseph A. Senturia, "Corruption, Political," *Encyclopedia of the Social Sciences,* IV. New York: Crowell-Collier-Macmillian, 1930–1935, 449.

1

Corruption Concepts in Historical Perspective

Carl J. Friedrich

"Any attempt to analyze the concept of corruption must contend with the fact that in English and other languages the word *corruption* has a history of vastly different meanings and connotations."[1] This is very true; but a core meaning readily emerges from an analysis of these different meanings. Corruption is a kind of behavior which deviates from the norm actually prevalent or believed to prevail in a given context, such as the political. It is deviant behavior associated with a particular motivation, namely that of private gain at public expense. But whether this was the motivation or not, it is the fact that private gain was secured at public expense that matters. Such private gain may be a monetary one, and in the minds of the general public it usually is, but it may take other forms. It may be a rapid promotion, an order, decorations, and the like, and the gain may not be personal, but benefit a family or other group. The pattern of corruption may therefore be said to exist whenever a power holder who is charged with doing certain things, that is a responsible functionary or office holder, is by monetary or other rewards, such as the expectation of a job in the future, induced to take actions which favor whoever provides the reward and thereby damage the group or organization to which the functionary belongs, more specifically the government. It is preferable for our purposes to state the concept of corruption thus, rather than as the use of public power for private profit, preferment, or prestige, or for the benefit of a group or class, in a way that constitutes a breach of law or of standards of high moral conduct; for while such breaches constitute some sort of damage, they are not necessarily involved. But

Source: Carl J. Friedrich. *The Pathology of Politics: Violence, Betrayal, Corruption, Secrecy and Propaganda.* New York: Harper & Row, 1972, pp. 127–41. Copyright © 1972 by Carl J. Friedrich. Reprinted by permission of Harper & Row, Publishers, Inc.

there is typically gain for corrupter and corrupted, and loss for others, involved in such a situation.[2]

This kind of corruption is the specific kind related to the notion of administrative service which the modern bureaucracy conceived as meritocracy has fostered.[3] But there is a much broader notion of political corruption which is implied in judgments such as that expressed by Lord Acton in his famous dictum that all power tends to corrupt and absolute power corrupts absolutely.[4] For while the specific kind of corruption may be involved here too, the meaning of Lord Acton is focused on the moral depravity which power is believed to cause in men; they no longer think about what is right action or conduct, but only about what is expedient action or conduct. Such deep suspicion of power has, it would seem, a religious root, and is typically Western and Christian. It harks back to the notion of the two kingdoms and to the contrast between the earthly and the heavenly city.[5] In this broad and imprecise sense, corruption cannot by definition be "functional." For such corruption, being in fact a decomposition of the body politic through moral decay, is a general category to include all kinds of practices which are believed to be disfunctional and hence morally corrupt.

Acton's famous statement touches the paradox of power and morals. Systematically, corruption is a form of coercion, namely economic coercion. Not only the buying of votes and actual monetary rewards, but all the more indirect forms, such as gifts, or otherwise influencing the judgment of those who exercise governmental functions, are instrumentalities in this sphere. Here it is a question of the degree of corruption. For that such corruption is endemic in all forms of government is practically certain. But that there are striking differences in the extent of corruption between governments which are formally similar, such as Great Britain, Switzerland, and the United States, all functioning constitutional democracies, is equally patent. It is possible to state a "law" or general regularity by saying that the degree of corruption varies inversely to the degree that power is consensual. Corruption is a corrective of coercive power and its abuse, when it is functional. Many complications arise from the fact that power often appears to be consensual when it actually is not; or it may be consensual for Anglo-Saxon, Protestant whites, whereas it is not for immigrants or blacks. . . . It would appear that in those situations where a semblance of consent hides the coercive reality, corruption is rife. The power which is believed to be consensual, having to a considerable extent become coercive, lends itself to corruption. Tammany Hall is a sort of example of this situation.[6] As Willie Stark puts it in *All the King's Men*, "Graft is what he calls it when the fellows do it who don't know which fork to use."[7] There is and always has been a tendency on the part of critics of democracy to assert that developments of this kind are typical of democracy. Historical studies have shown that such a judgment is untenable. In monarchial England, Prussia, and Russia corruption was ubiquitous.[8] The real difference is that in open societies corruption is often uncovered by the opposition and brought to public notice by a free press, whereas in autocratic regimes it remains largely hidden. The extensive corruption in totalitarian dictatorships is evident in the now available documents of the fascist and national socialist regimes. Reports from the Soviet Union suggest similar conditions.[9] To give a couple of illustrations let me cite Hermann Goering, Hitler's field marshal: "I have seen terrible things. Chauffeurs of District leaders have enriched themselves to the extent of half a million. The gentlemen know this? It is true? (Assent) These are things which are impossible. I shall not hesitate to proceed ruthlessly." This happened in a meeting on November 12, 1938, and treated such corruption as widespread and generally known.[10] Trotsky reported such corruption on a great scale as proof of his contention that the Soviet Union was utterly bureaucratized.[11] These bits of evidence could readily be multiplied. If it had not been for such corruption, many more would have perished under the terror whom corrupt officials allowed to escape.

Corruption in totalitarian regimes may also be of the broader unspecific kind. Thus the ideology has been undergoing what critics have described as corruption, namely a disintegration of the belief system upon which a particular political system rests. Such corruption will often take the form of a perversion of legal rules by misinterpretation. Such perversion, like a breach, challenges the intended generality of the rule; when exceptions multiply, they become the rule. It is obvious that they may thus become the basis of a revision of a basic ideological position which to the true believer appears as a corruption. There can be little doubt that this sort of "moral corruption" is what concerned political philosophers in the past. Aristotle, and after him Machiavelli particularly, but basically Plato in his theory of the "corrupted" or "perverted" constitutions—democracy, oligarchy, and tyranny—stressed the point that these regimes instead of being guided by the law (we would say the public interest) were serving the interest of the rulers. They were, we might say, exploitative, and thus corrupt. Aristotle followed Plato's notions, but substituted the happiness of the ruled, that is to say their well-being, for the law; such general happiness is, of course, closely akin to what is customarily in modern times referred to as the public or general interest. These fundamental general notions of corruption all practically define corruption as disfunctional; for it is seen as destructive of a particular political order, be it monarchy, aristocracy, or polity, the latter a constitutionally limited popular rule, and thus by definition devoid of any function within a political order.

This classic conception of corruption as a general disease of the body politic persisted into modern times, and is central to the political thought of Machiavelli, Montesquieu and Rousseau. For Machiavelli corruption was the process by which the *virtù* of the citizen was undermined and eventually destroyed. Since most men are weak and lacking in the *virtù* of the good citizen except when inspired by a great leader, the process of corruption is ever threatening. And when *virtù* has been corrupted, a heroic leader must appear who in rebuilding the political order infuses his *virtù* into the entire citizenry. Thus the miserable creatures that human beings ordinarily are or become when not properly guided are thereby transformed into patriotic citizens, capable of sacrifice, self-exertion, and other patriotic virtues. But such a leader must not be a Caesar. Machiavelli was sharply critical of the great Roman. He described him as one of the worst figures in Roman history; for he had destroyed the venerable Roman constitution instead of regenerating it.[12] He was, we might say, himself corrupted. In our time, a similar misunderstanding aided Hitler in seizing power. Instead of proving the heroic benefactor who would reconstitute Germany, he proved to be a corrupted destroyer of the German values and beliefs. The evidence we have on the thought of the resistance brings this out very clearly; men like Pastor Niemoeller offer instances of this original misunderstanding and eventual reversal.

Francis Bacon was generally believed to be a Machiavellian. He certainly shows Machiavelli's influence. Yet he was a corrupt man, perhaps the most famous instance of a high English dignitary brought down by his corruption. As High Chancellor he accepted bribes in order to favor certain parties before the court. The complexities of the case are considerable[13] and they are of no particular interest for our purpose. But what is of interest is that he and his friends essentially defended his case on the ground that he was not doing anything that was not generally done. It is a defense that has persisted to this day; he was the unlucky one who got caught. In the functional perspective, the matter may be stated differently; Bacon's case indicated that corruption had gone too far, that the limit of what might be allowed for purposes of moderating the regime's injustices was here exceeded and caused a reaction. . . .

The Roman Republic also had its trials of corruption, and men like

Cicero who were interested in regenerating the Republic addressed themselves to the task of unearthing and bringing to trial extreme cases of corruption, especially in provincial administration.[14] But these efforts came too late. The Republic's public ethic was already too generally corrupted, and the limits had by that time been greatly transgressed. Corruption had become so general that corrupt practices rather than the strict morals of the forefathers had become the accepted mode of behavior. This Roman case was a primary instance in the theory of Montesquieu.[15] This nobleman and believer in the aristocracy, or a monarchy moderated by a nobility, devoted a major work to *Grandeur des Romains et de leur Décadence,* a work in which he described the process of corruption which he attributed to the imperial enterprise of the Romans. Their *virtù* gave them the victories over the other regimes of the Mediterranean and the extension of their city from *urbs* to *orbs* corrupted their moral fiber and eventually destroyed the constitutional order which had won them the empire. Some may anxiously ask today whether the Americans are not undergoing the same process. Be that as it may, Montesquieu again saw corruption as the disfunctional process *par excellence* by which a good political order or system is perverted into an evil one, a monarchy into a despotism.

This global concept was pushed to its extreme and thereby to its *reductio ad absurdum* by Rousseau, who argued at one point that man had been corrupted by social and political life, and this notion was elaborated by the anarchists of the nineteenth century from Godwin to Bakunin. It is not the corruption of men which destroys the political system but the political system which corrupts and destroys man. Beyond this, Rousseau was deeply concerned with what he believed to be the corruption of his age, and he looked upon himself as the wise man who must raise a warning voice; for he believed that the right kind of guidance could shape public opinion to avoid such corruption. He believed in the manipulation of opinion as it was practiced in Sparta as a proper defense against corruption.[16] Artists, scientists, and literary men are "both the victims and the promoters of social conditions which necessarily caused them to corrupt their fellow men. . . . The *corps littéraire* only cheers on princes when they oppress their peoples."[17] In short, Rousseau's concern with corruption is primarily with moral corruption, and only indirectly with political corruption, as providing the setting for moral corruption. Political corruption is seen by Rousseau as a necessary consequence of the struggle for power, and he could have agreed with Acton that all power tends to corrupt. According to Rousseau, equality is natural and good laws are directed toward maintaining this equality against the corrupting influence of power-hungry individuals.[18]

Although this preoccupation with equality may be reduced and refined to an equality before the law, Rousseau's outloook provides the setting for the modern and specific sense of corruption. The abuse of power, which constitutionalism is primarily concerned with preventing through the application of the rule of law to public officers *(Rechs-staat),* is at the heart of corruption. Corruption was widespread, as mentioned before, under monarchies, absolute and other, and more particularly in England. In fact, the system which Walpole built is perhaps the most striking instance of corruption functioning effectively to transform a political system and establish a new one; for it is well known that the parliamentary system of government in which the ruling party rests upon majority support in the House of Commons was first organized by Walpole. In a celebrated, if somewhat controversial study, Professor Namier has analyzed this system.[19] Each party, but more particularly the Whig party under Walpole and Pelham (1715–1760) sought to secure for itself a solid majority in Parliament; for such a majority greatly facilitated the realization of policies and the enactment of necessary legislation. Walpole proceeded to secure such a parliamentary majority for himself and his cabinet by a carefully worked-out system which to his contemporaries, more especially the leader of the opposition, Lord Bolingbroke, appeared to be a system of corruption. Wraxall tells us in his *Memoirs* that the government under Pelham handed each of its partisans in Parliament from five hundred to eight hundred pounds at the end of a session, the amount varying according to the services rendered. These payments were official enough to be entered on a record kept in the Treasury (which has enabled recent researchers to elucidate the actual practice of corruption involved). These investigations have shown that the Whigs had worked out a very elaborate system of governmental favors, ranging from direct payments to voters and members of parliament, to patronage and the various favors available in foreign trade and the privileged trading companies. All this is well enough known, and was intimately bound up with what caused the Americans to rebel. If they had been better informed, they would have attacked this corruption rather than King George in their Declaration of Independence. In fact, Walpole once remarked that he and Lord Townsend constituted the "firm" to which the king had entrusted the government of the country.[20]

The argument of Bolingbroke and his friends that this system constituted corruption of the old constitution was, of course, sound. It was radically disfunctional in one sense, but in another it actually helped a system which had become antiquated to function and to be transformed into a preferable one. An economist might say that a kind of market of the services of government officials had been substituted for monocratic (monopolistic) control. Such an arrangement was at variance with the requirements of a responsible public service, a rational bureaucracy in which ideally the official is paid from the public treasury for precisely defined legal duties, and must not have any other interests.[21] In Germany, all attempts at bribery on the part of private persons or groups are made crimes and punished. Such bribery is considered the most pernicious crime, an attack upon the very foundations of the state, and comparable to treason, in fact a form of treason. These are views by no means restricted to Germany,[22] but are found also in Switzerland, the Low Countries, and Scandinavia. They are logical consequences of the rationalized bureaucracy as developed in modern government and economics. For a large business concern will just as rigorously insist upon this approach to personal favors as will a responsible government.

Corruption, then, has become a particular form of political pathology rather than a global degeneration. As such it can be defined in behavioral terms, and the activities objected to can be outlawed. Institutions like the Comptroller's Office can be and have been set up in all advanced countries to watch the expenditure of public funds, and civil service commissions and the like have been established to inhibit and prevent patronage outside the official merit system. In this sense, modern bureaucracy spells the end of aristocratic privilege. Under absolutism, it was quite common that offices could be bought and sold. But to speak here of corruption is anachronistic, for the kings were not subject to any legal rules. Such sales were regulated and the proceeds went to the public treasury to be employed for such purposes as the king and his council decided upon. Thus, the sale of public offices was considered a "check on corruption" because it benefited the public weal, instead of some personal favorites of the king.[23] Reform-minded writers, such as Montesquieu and Bentham, openly advocated the buying and selling of offices because the service would thereby be improved. It is remarkable that Bentham of all thinkers should have taken this position: for it was the utilitarians and the reform movement they sparked which put an end to the venality of public offices in Britain. In fact, the process by which the British pulled themselves out of the morass of corruption which had made a Burke defend the "rotten borough"[24] as a sound political institution and developed what is, in the opinion of many, the most thoroughly honest public service ever organized is little short of miraculous. It shows that pathological phenomena are not necessarily destined to go from bad to worse and the corrective for them is often quite readily at hand. By the second half of the nineteenth century what had been considered "normal behavior" had become corruption sharply condemned by the majority of Britons.[25] Similar, though less dramatic, reforms were achieved in Prussia, Bavaria, and France; in all of which a properly trained bureaucracy, a responsible public service, was developed in this period.[26] It is not here possible to explore the problem of "bureaucracy" and its development, to which this transformation in the concept of corruption is linked.[27] The socialist movement, and more especially Marxism, developed their revolutionary ideology without any stress on the corruption of the social and political order they proposed to supersede. Only in recent years have the rulers of the Soviet Union and other socialist states had to acknowledge the growth of corruption in their own regimes, and to seek to combat it by vigorous countermeasures, not especially successfully. In view of the corrupt behavior of the tsarist bureaucracy, notorious at the turn of the century, the original thrust was in the direction of developing an honest public service, thereby catching up with the bourgeois societies of the West. In this connection, these regimes have added yet another dimension to the unfolding concept of corruption. As mentioned above, their conceit is that most corruption in socialist countries is traceable to a preceding ideological corruption of which it is the result. The total bureaucratization which the socialist ideology has tended to promote in practice has made the problem of corruption particularly central to these regimes, and each case is apt to appear as a flagrant case of betrayal of the trust that had been placed in the offending functionary. Thus treason and corruption become intertwined and the language of the Soviet criminal code demonstrates it.[28] . . .

Notes

1. Arnold J. Heidenheimer, ed., *Political Corruption: Readings in Comparative Analysis,* 1970, p. 3.
2. Joseph J. Senturia, "Corruption, Political," *International Encyclopedia of the Social Sciences,* 1968; and Charles Aiken, "Corruption" in *Dictionary of the Social Sciences.*
3. On bureaucracy cf. Carl J. Friedrich and Taylor Cole, *Responsible Bureaucracy: A Study of the Swiss Civil Service,* 1933; Max Weber's classical treatment in *Wirtschaft und Gesellschaft,* 1922, 2d ed., 1925, and the comments in *Reader on Bureaucracy,* Robert K. Merton, ed., 1952 (includes a critique by Friedrich); and Friedrich, *Man and His Government,* 1963, ch. 18, which has extensive further references, as has Friedrich, *Constitutional Government and Democracy,* 4th ed., 1968, ch. 2.

4. The statement is found not in one of Lord Acton's major writings but in a letter in which he criticizes another scholar for "the canon that we are to judge Pope and King unlike other men, with a favorable presumption that they did no wrong." The text of Acton's remark is given in context in John E. E. Dalberg Acton, *Essays on Freedom and Power,* G. Himmelreich, ed., 1948, p. 364.

5. Especially as developed by St. Augustine in *City of God.* Cf. Carl J. Friedrich, *Transcendent Justice,* 1964, pp. 11 ff.; and Herbert A. Deane, *The Political and Social Ideas of Saint Augustine,* 1956; as well as Friedrich, *The Philosophy of Law in Historical Perspective,* 2d ed., 1965, ch. 5.

6. M. R. Werner, *Tammany Hall,* 1928; and V. O. Key, Jr., *Politics, Parties and Pressure Groups,* 4th ed., 1958, ch. 13, gives a scholarly analysis of a phenomenon which Bryce had emphasized in his *Modern Democracies* and *The American Commonwealth;* Werner's is a detailed descriptive account of Tammany's workings at the time, soon to be superseded by the impact of La Guardia's welfare state operations and the New Deal's social security legislation.

7. Robert Penn Warren, *All the King's Men,* 1946, p. 134.

8. Walter L. Dorn, "The Prussian Bureaucracy in the Eighteenth Century," *Political Science Quarterly,* vol. 46, pp. 403 ff.; vol. 47, pp. 75 ff.; and vol. 49, pp. 259 ff., 1931–1932. Lewis B. Namier, *The Structure of Politics at the Accession of George III,* 1929; Norman Gash, *Politics in the Age of Peel,* 1953; Holden Furber, *Henry Dundas, First Viscount Melville, 1742–1811,* 1931.

9. Merle Fainsod, *How Russia Is Ruled,* rev. ed., 1963. For the comparable situation in Hitler's Germany cf. my *Totalitarian Dictatorship and Autocracy* (with Z. K. Brzezinski), rev. ed., 1965, pp. 241 ff., on the intermingling of government and business. A study is in preparation by Assessor Nebelung at Heidelberg which will soon appear, it is hoped. Soviet publications provide ample proof in their own articles against corrupt practices.

10. "Stenographische Niederschrift von einem Teil der Besprechung ueber die Judenfrage unter Vorsitz von Feldmarschall Goering im RLM am 12. November, 1938," to be found in *Der Prozess gegen die Hauptkriegsverbrecher vor dem internationalen Militaergerichtshof Nuernberg,* 1948, vol. XXVIII, p. 502 f.

11. Leon Trotsky, *Die Verratene Revolution (Revolution Betrayed),* 1937, p. 120; cf. also the works cited in note 9, above.

12. Cf. Friedrich, *Introduction to Political Theory,* 1967, p. 138. The discussion on Caesar is found in Machiavelli's *Discourses,* bk. I, ch. 10.

13. C. D. Bowen, *Adventures of a Biographer,* 1946.

14. John Dickinson, *Death of a Republic: Politics and Political Thought at Rome, 59–44 B.C.,* G. L. Haskins, ed., 1963.

15. Montesquieu, *Considérations sur les causes de la Grandeur des Romains et de leur Décadence,* 1734; cf. also the bicentenary collection of papers on Montesquieu edited by Mirkine-Guetzevitch and Henri Puget, *La Pensée Politique et Constitutionelle,* París, 1948.

16. Rousseau, *Contrat Social;* see also the comments by Dita Shklar, *Men and Citizens—A Study of Rousseau's Theory,* 1969, esp. pp. 100, 103, and 110;

Mario Einaudi's interesting *The Early Rousseau,* 1967, does not especially address itself to the problem, but cf. his pp. 114 ff.

17. Shklar, *op. cit.,* p. 111.
18. Friedrich, *op. cit.* (note 12, above), pp. 164 ff. dealing with equality.
19. Namier, *op. cit.* (note 8, above).
20. Friedrich, *Constitutional Government and Democracy,* 4th ed., 1968, pp. 431–432; Namier, *op. cit.* (note 8, above), and more recently Samuel E. Finer, "Patronage and Public Service: Jeffersonian Bureaucracy and the British Tradition," *Public Administration,* vol. 30, 1952, pp. 333 ff. and reprinted in Heidenheimer, *op. cit.* (note 1, above), pp. 106 ff. Cf. also Harvey C. Mansfield, Jr., *Statemanship and Party Government: A Study of Burke and Bolingbroke,* 1965, esp. comments on pp. 66 ff. Concerning Bolingbroke, cf. Isaac Kramnick, *Lord Bolingbroke and His Circle: The Politics of Nostalgia in the Age of Walpole,* 1968.
21. On bureaucracy see the works cited above in note 3.
22. Rotteck-Welcker, the typical liberal progressive (cf. the study by Ursula Herdt [Albrecht] on Rotteck, Ph.D. thesis, Heidelberg), in his *Staatslexikon,* on p. 454.
23. Heidenheimer, *op. cit.* (note 1, above), in his Introduction, p. 13. There references are given to Montesquieu's *The Spirit of the Laws,* 1748, and Bentham's "The Rationale of Rewards," in his *Works,* vol. V, pp. 246–248.
24. For Burke see reference given in footnote 7, ch. 10. Cf. also in general E. and A. G. Porritt, *The Unreformed House of Commons,* 1901, ch. III; cf. also Karl Loewenstein's *Staatsrecht und Staatspraxis von Grossbritannien,* vol. I, 1965, pp. 95 ff. At one point, this author echoes Burke's argument when he writes: "Without the rotten and pocket borough the British parliament would not have been that incomparable gathering of the political and social elite which let England rise to the rank of the leading world power." Who knows? Like all arguments from history, it is inconclusive.
25. This instance incidentally shows how risky it is, and how misleading, to treat such conditions as stable, unalterable features of a "political culture." Cf. Samuel E. Finer's study, *op. cit.* (note 20, above).
26. On Prussia, Hans W. Rosenberg, *Bureaucracy, Aristocracy and Autocracy: The Prussian Experience, 1600–1815,* 1958, is valuable, in spite of its Marxist slant; cf. also Dorn's paper, cited above, in note 8; on France see W. A. Robson, *The Civil Service in Britain and France,* 1956, and Walter R. Sharp, *The French Civil Service: Bureaucracy in Transition,* 1931.
27. Friedrich and Brzezinski, *op. cit.* (note 9, above), chs. 16 and 18 and the literature cited there.
28. Harold J. Berman, *Justice in the USSR: An Interpretation of Soviet Law,* 1950, 2d ed., 1963, and John N. Hazard, *The Soviet System of Government,* 1964, who gives special attention to the legal aspect.

2

The Concept of Corruption[1]

Jacob van Klaveren

In everyday life corruption means that a civil servant abuses his authority in order to obtain an extra income from the public. This conception, however, expresses a value judgment that is altogether temporal and did not always exist. If it were possible to determine the amount of the civil servant's salary by objective measures, that is, by determining the functional value of the civil servant's performance for the achievement of the social product in its broadest sense, then a value-free definition of corruption would be possible. Since such a functional definition of the distribution of income is neither possible for private business nor for administration, this approach leads us nowhere.[2]

Alternatively, one could forget about normative-objective determinants of individual incomes and accept the results of the free-market economy. Provided that every economic subject tries to maximize his gains or his income or both, one could assume that the incomes derived from the free-market accord with functional-economic income. Given a system of free competition, where numerous buyers exchange with numerous sellers, both sides of the market are equally strong, and equilibrium is achieved where the two exchange curves intersect. However, if a monopolistic condition exists on one side of the market, the monopolist does not display his exchange curve but selects the point of maximum profit on the exchange curve of the other market side. Stackelberg correctly describes such a behavior as exploitation.[3]

Although a market economy can only operate under the protection of some public order or government, it is precisely this public sphere

Source: Jacob van Klaveren, "Die historische Erscheinung der Korruption, in ihrem Zusammenhang mit der Staats- und Gesellschaftsstrukur betrachet." *Vierteljahresschrift für Sozial- und Wirtschaftsgeschichte,* 44:4 (December 1957), pp. 289–294. By permission of the publisher, Franz Steiner Verlag. Translation by Peggy Hofmann and Karl Kurtz.

that represents a foreign body within the market sphere. The value of its services, and thus the income of the officials, cannot be determined via the free market mechanism. The establishment of government is an act of the whole society[4] to further the common good; thus, government is not an end in itself but only a means, and officials are only servants of the community, trustees of the common good.[5] The salaries of these civil servants can hardly be derived from their contributions to the national product but must be determined by socioethical and historical considerations.

The line of this argument is based on the ideas of the "social contract," that is, on the ideas of the age of enlightenment, which led to the rise of the democratic states of the nineteenth century. At this point we already touch upon the question of the relationship between constitution and corruption that will be examined thoroughly in the next section. Suffice it to say here that the official who relinquishes this subservience comes to confront the public as an independent power invested with a legal monopoly. If he wishes, he can abuse his monopoly position for exploitation of the public by extorting for each official act the maximum reward that the subject with whom he is dealing is willing to pay. We are thus dealing with a method of exploitation by which a constituent part of the public-order sphere is exploited as if it were part of the market sphere. Thus we will conceive of corruption in terms of a civil servant who regards his public office as a business, the income of which he will, in the extreme case, seek to maximize. The office then becomes a "maximizing unit." The size of his income then does not depend on an ethical evaluation of his usefulness for the common good but precisely upon the market situation and his talents for finding the point of maximal gain on the public's demand curve.[6]

This comparison between the office and the business is particularly apt if, first, the civil servant does not obtain a salary and, second, if he himself has to finance the costs of his administration, an extreme situation, rarely found in modern times.[7] In this case there is also no public treasury, but only the civil servant's private cashbox. The situation becomes somewhat more complicated if a public treasury exists to meet the expenses of the administration, including those constituted by the salaries of the civil servants. Then the official may still act toward the individual members of the public whom he encounters as a maximizer and monopolist; nothing changes in this respect. At the same time there may occur various forms of theft from the public treasury. This also is a form of profit maximization, but it assumes a collective form. The public as a whole is exploited, because the tax payments are only partly used for the purposes of the community.

Whether, in a case like this, the civil service is a one-sided monopolist, or whether the public has a sufficiently well-organized representation so that the struggle becomes more akin to that of a bilateral monopoly, depends on different circumstances, to be discussed later. Provisionally it can be said that corruption is always an exploitation of the public, which can occur only because the civil servants occupy a constitutionally independent position vis-à-vis the public.

To know from which side the initiative for corruption comes is no more important in this case than it was when we examined the relations among free-market parties. Only when corruption is made illegal does this question become important and then mainly from a criminal-law point of view, which is of no interest here. An offer of a bribe that seemingly comes from the public may in reality be due to blackmail on the part of the civil servant. Thus businessmen may be forced to make such offers if they want to participate with success in public tenders. But the previous existence of compulsion, is disguised by the fact that the final award of the contract, and as a corollary the identity of the briber, depends on a quasi-anonymous selection process.[8]

Compulsion, however, takes the form of naked blackmail, if everyone fulfilling certain objective criteria must pay such a fee, even when the initiative seemingly derives from the public. An example would be if all travelers who wanted to cross a frontier had to offer money to [border] officials solely in order to be processed. Hence it is not the initiative that is decisive but the given fact that corruption is rooted in the constitution, in other words, that there are no means to abolish legally these malpracties. Thus the public has to come to terms with letting the officials obtain a larger part of the national income than they are entitled to on the grounds of ethical considerations.

If corruption is illegal, it tends to appear as occasional acts of dishonesty on the part of civil servants, the initiative of which may come from either side, that of the public as well as that of the civil servants. Then the root of corruption lies exclusively in the *appetitus divitiarum infinitus,* the insatiable avarice that is one of the human weaknesses against which battle was already waged by scholastics. This, however, is not a historical problem.

Therefore, if we are talking about corruption, we must always think of the systematic form of corruption that is rooted in the constitution, *la fraude erigée en système,* as it is labeled in a French study. . . .[9]

Notes

1. This article evolved from a habilitation lecture that I delivered to the faculty of economics at the University of Munich on June 20, 1956. Both style and annotations reflect the original lecture form. Unfortunately there is little

material to be found on corruption since the relevant events, naturally, are hardly ever documented. This is true also for those times where corruption was still legally tolerated, as I shall explain below. Much of this should thus be regarded as a tentative first attempt. Only the consideration that this is seemingly the first time that corruption as a phenomenon is examined in context and with regard to its inherent character gave the author the courage to publish this article.

2. See Vilfredo Pareto, *Manuel d'économie politique* (translation). Paris, 1909, p. 196.

3. Heinrich von Stackelberg, *Marktform und Gleichgewicht*. Vienna and Berlin, 1934, p. 39.

4. The foundation of such a society by a "social contract" occurred repeatedly in the area of what is now the United States and was one of the characteristics of the so-called frontier. Probably the "vigilance committees" are most familiar to us from the Western movies. They were voluntary associations of peace-loving citizens who started by hanging the villains; this was called "to stretch hemp." Descriptions can be found in many American history textbooks. See Ray Allen Billington, *Westward Expansion: A History of the American Frontier,* 4th ed. New York, 1954 (1949), p. 621 ff.

5. Fritz Terhalle, *Die Finanzwirtschaft des Staates und der Gemeinden.* Berlin, 1948, pp. 17, 27.

6. In other words, he determines the reward for his services in every case according to the well-known principle of the railways' rate policy, "charge what the traffic can bear."

7. I discussed such a case in my study, *The Dutch Colonial System in the East Indies,* The Hague, 1953, p. 71. The case refers to the Commissioner of Native Affairs of the Dutch East Indian Company, who supervised coffee cultivation in West Java. He paid all costs of office and although he did not draw a salary, the estimated annual income of Commissioner Pieter Engelhardt was 300,000 guilders at the end of the eighteenth century.

8. Contemporaries very well understood these connections. The indictment of Lord Middlesex (1624) mentioned "tribes squeezed from customs farmers" who were "blackmailed into bribery." See R.H. Tawney, *Business and Politics under James I.* Cambridge University Press, 1958, pp. 257, 258.

9. E.W. Dahlgren, *Les relations commerciales et maritimes entre la France et les côtes de L'Ocean Pacifique,* Paris, 1909, p. 33. The question here is the illegal trade of French vessels with Peru. This was only made possible, as Dahlgren correctly understood, because in the Spanish colonies corruption was part of the constitution. The same applied to the Spanish mother country at that time.

3

Legal Efforts to Define
Political Bribery

Daniel H. Lowenstein

It often has been said that social scientists have given too little attention to official bribery and corruption.[1] Whatever may be the sins of omission of the social scientists in this regard, they pale beside those of the legal scholars, who have ignored the subject almost entirely.[2] This neglect cannot be excused on the ground that acts of bribery or prosecutions for bribery are rare. They are not.

One explanation for the absence of legal scholarship may be the widespread view that the crime of bribery covers only the most obvious instances of corrupt conduct. For example, in its famous campaign finance decision, the Supreme Court alluded to bribery laws and stated that they deal with "only the most blatant and specific attempts of those with money to influence governmental action."[3] In the common conception, reflected in this statement by the Supreme Court, the crime of bribery is the black core of a series of concentric circles representing the degrees of impropriety in official behavior. In this conception, a series of gray circles surround the bribery core, growing progressively lighter as they become more distant from the center, until they blend into the surrounding white area that represents perfectly proper and innocent conduct.

The crime of bribery is regarded as having fixed, clear boundaries. These boundaries may be inadequate, in the sense that they do not encompass all improper conduct. On the other hand, they surely do not penetrate far into "grey areas" of conduct regarded as questionable, much less into the white area of clearly proper conduct. In short, the bribery laws are not supposed to be dangerously broad.[4] In particular,

Source: Daniel H. Lowenstein. "Political Bribery and the Intermediate Theory of Politics, *UCLA Law Review,* 32 (1985) 705–806. Copyright 1985, The Regents of the University of California. All rights reserved.

the bribery laws are supposed to require a *quid pro quo*—an explicit exchange of a specific benefit for a specific official action (or inaction)[5]—a requirement that is evaded easily, and is difficult to prove even when it has not been evaded. Thus, the difficulty with bribery laws is supposed to be ineffectiveness rather than uncertainty.[6] Perhaps it is understandable that legal scholars have devoted their efforts to the presumably more difficult intellectual and legal questions to be found in the grey area. Witness, for example, the voluminous amount of legal writing on campaign finance.

This conception of the crime of bribery as narrow and sharply circumscribed may explain the lack of legal scholarship; it cannot serve as a justification, however, because it is false. Most American bribery statutes and many of the judicial decisions interpreting them do not require a *quid pro quo* in the sense described above. More generally, the statutes as interpreted are susceptible of being applied, and occasionally have been applied, to situations that occur on an everyday basis in American politics. Nor are the legal questions necessarily limited to whether an activity is within the "blackness" of bribery or the "dark greyness" of conduct that is still clearly less than proper. In the recent case of *Brown v. Hartlage,*[7] the Supreme Court was faced with the question of whether promises made to voters might consistently with the Constitution be treated as bribery of the voters. The Court described the problem as one of distinguishing "between those 'private arrangements' that are inconsistent with democratic government, and those candidate assurances that promote the representative foundation of our political system."[8] While *Brown v. Hartlage* is atypical in that it deals with bribery of voters rather than bribery of public officials, it illustrates that nice distinctions determining what violates a bribery statute and what does not may not divide shades of grey, but instead may separate the darkest black from the brightest white. . . .

Elements of the Crime of Bribery

Though the wording of American bribery statutes varies considerably, the crime as defined in the federal and most state statutes consists of the following five elements:[9]

1. There must be a *public official*.
2. The defendant must have a *corrupt intent*.
3. A benefit, *anything of value,* must accrue to the public official.
4. There must be a relationship between the thing of value and some *official act*.

5. The relationship must involve an *intent to influence* the public official (or to be influenced if the defendant is the official) in the carrying out of the official act.

Of these five elements only the first, that the person bribed must be a public official, is relatively straightforward.[10] The sections that follow in this part will consider the remaining four elements.

First, however, the elements of bribery should be contrasted with those of a lesser offense that exists in federal law and in some states: giving or receiving an unlawful gratuity.[11] A comparison of the elements of the unlawful gratuity offense with bribery yields the following:

1. The requirement that there be a public official is substantially the same. A transaction involving a former official, however, can be an unlawful gratuity but not a bribe. This is because a bribe must be made in contemplation of a future official act, whereas an unlawful gratuity may be made in contemplation of an act in the future or the past.
2. The offense of bribery must be committed "corruptly." There is no such requirement for an unlawful gratuity.
3. The requirement that a benefit, "anything of value," must accrue to the official is identical for bribes and unlawful gratuities.
4. The requirement of an official act is identical for bribes and unlawful gratuities.
5. For an unlawful gratuity there must be an intent that the benefit pass to the official "for or because of" the official act. Unlike bribery, however, there need be no intent that the official act be influenced by the benefit.

This part will demonstrate that the general bribery statute has an ill-defined but potentially broad scope. Where, as under federal law, there is also a separate unlawful gratuity offense, the definitional difficulties are compounded. Rather than having to define one difficult boundary (between a bribe and a lawful act) it is necessary to define two such boundaries (between a bribe and an unlawful gratuity and between an unlawful gratuity and a lawful act).

Corrupt Intent

The Lack of a "Legal" Definition. To constitute a bribe, the prohibited acts must be performed "corruptly." Most statutory definitions of bribery make this element explicit. Even if the statute does not require a corrupt intent, the courts may require it anyway.

Certainly the bribery statutes are intended to proscribe corrupt activity, but it is not easy to discern what, if anything, the concept of acting "corruptly" adds as an *element* of the crime of bribery. If the other elements are present, a public official is offered, seeks, or accepts an individual benefit that is intended to influence the recipient's official actions. What more is needed to make the offering, seeking, or accepting "corrupt"? If nothing, then the word "corruptly" as used in the statutes is redundant. Its purposeful omission would not be a "cataclysmic" alteration, as one court supposed. To the contrary, such a change would have no significance.

In Part I, in the analysis of a candidate-bribery statute, it was necessary to add the requirement that the acts constituting the offense be engaged in corruptly to save the statute from prohibiting legitimate political activity. The following sections will show that the need is as great in general bribery statutes. Therefore, in this section I shall argue that "corruptly" need not be regarded as a redundancy, but that it functions differently from the other elements, which describe "factual" aspects of actions constituting bribes. The element of corrupt intent requires that the facts described by the other elements be subject to characterization as wrongful, and thus requires the application, implicitly or explicitly, of normative political standards.

In order for the requirement of a corrupt intent to be more than surplusage, meaning must be assigned to the word "corrupt." Conventional legal sources are of little help. No judicial decision that I have found contains a definition or explanation of "corruptly" that adds significantly to the other elements of bribery, and most of the bribery statutes themselves do not attempt to define "corruptly."[12]

Social Science Definitions.   Some social scientists and other writers have proposed to define corruption by describing the types of actions that may be characterized as corrupt. These descriptive definitions typically more or less parallel the descriptive elements of the crime of bribery. For example, W.F. Wertheim has written, "we call corrupt a public servant who accepts gifts bestowed by a private person with the object of inducing him to give special consideration to the interests of the donor."[13] Such definitions support the suggestion that the word "corruptly" in a bribery statute is a redundancy.

Other definitions are broader. For example, Gunnar Myrdal used "corruption" to include "all forms of . . . improper or selfish exercise of power and influence attached to a public office . . .."[14] It might seem that such a definition tends to provide further support for reading "corruptly" in a bribery statute as surplusage. Conduct that satisfies the other elements of the offense will come within such a broad definition of "corrupt," as will much other conduct, such as embezzlement of public funds. Myrdal's definition, and other similarly broad definitions, however, contain a normative element. To be corrupt an action must be wrongful, improper, or contrary to the public interest. Does this save the requirement of corrupt intent in the bribery statutes from redundancy? Can an action satisfy the descriptive elements of bribery without being wrongful? What ethical criteria should be used in applying such a concept, and what should be the source of such criteria?

James C. Scott and other writers, believing that answers to these questions cannot be found, have rejected definitions of "corruption" cast in terms of morality or the public interest.[15] Scott suggests there are two other possible sources of standards for defining corrupt conduct. Scott rejects the first of these, public opinion, because of the difficulty in identifying precisely the "public" whose opinion is to be decisive. Accordingly, Scott joins a number of scholars in defining the normative element of corruption as a deviation from legal or formal norms of official conduct. Such a definition is said to be "operational,"[16] because bribery laws are relatively "precise and consistent," or "generally clear-cut."

It is a central contention of this article that, at least as far as political bribery is concerned, the law of bribery is neither "precise," "consistent," nor "clear-cut." What is curious, however, is that while Scott and the others have insisted on the legally-based definition of corruption because they assert it can be made operational, they have made no visible effort to make it operational. Social science writings on corruption have centered on such issues as the causes and consequences of corruption in various settings and the connection between corruption and other social phenomena, such as economic development. The typical article or book begins with a definition of corruption and then proceeds to the empirical questions without reference to the definition. The writers who insist that a corrupt act must be illegal make no effort to ascertain what the law of bribery actually prohibits.[17]

While no one seems to have noticed the failure of even proponents actually to apply their own legally-based definitions of corruption, such definitions have been criticized on other grounds. For example, Larry L. Berg, Harlan Hahn, and John R. Schmidhauser have argued that legally-based definitions entail a conservative bias because powerful groups are able to influence the content of the law, and are likely to do so to legalize the practices on which their power depends, thus exempting themselves from charges of corruption if the term is limited to violations of law.[18] But even if a legally-based definition should prove useful for some purposes in social science, it can be of no help in the present inquiry, the purpose of which is to elucidate the content of the law itself.

"Corruption" as Harm to the Public Interest. It follows that the lawyer, and perhaps the social scientist as well, must return to the idea of finding the normative element of "corruption" in some conception of being wrongful or contrary to the public interest. This is not a surprising conclusion, in view of the purpose a word such as "corruption" serves in the English language. The descriptive element of the word cannot be isolated by removing the normative element. The word's very function is to group together actions and situations that generally have a certain descriptive character *and* that are regarded as seriously wrong.

The demonstration that the idea of wrongfulness (which I am equating with being contrary to the public interest) is intrinsic to the concept of corruption, even if it is accepted, does not in itself respond to the critics' assertion that the idea of corruption, so conceived, is too general and too controversial to be serviceable. In particular, some writers have argued that if such a public interest definition of corruption is accepted, the determination of whether a particular policy-influencing action is or is not corrupt will depend on whether the direction in which it seeks to influence policy is or is not desirable. Not only will such judgments nearly always be controversial, it is argued, but the whole approach suggests that the end justifies the means, so that what appears to be bribery will be exonerated from the charge of corruption if only the parties can persuade us that the substantive policy they are seeking is in the public interest.

Although applying a public interest definition of corruption is no easy task, this specific objection misconceives the nature of such a definition. To say that a policy-influencing action of a certain descriptive character is corrupt because it is contrary to the public interest can mean either that actions of its type lead to policy decisions that are substantively contrary to the public interest, or that the occurrence of the action is itself contrary to the public interest, without regard to the substantive direction of its influence on policy. The argument stated in the previous paragraph is directed only to the first of these possibilities, and even there it is wide of the mark. Actions of a type that tend to have a bad influence on policy over the long run may be deemed corrupt for that reason. One need not believe that the governmental process as it operates in the United States or in any other democracy is a perfect machine for generating policies in the public interest in order to believe that that process tends in the long run to produce better policies than would a system in which all decisions are made according to the wishes of the highest bidder. If we accept this, it becomes immaterial for purposes of determining whether an action is corrupt that the direction in which it seeks to influence policy is believed to be in the public interest.

The argument that a public interest conception of corruption must be contingent on the substantive policy issue is even less applicable to the second sense in which policy-influencing events can be regarded as contrary to the public interest, which is without regard to the substantive direction in which policy is being influenced. To the extent that policies frequently are formed by processes contrary to the processes sanctioned by the overall political system, the system may break down.[19] If we agree that the system as a whole is preferable to a breakdown of the system, it would then follow that actions seeking to influence policies in ways endangering the system are contrary to the public interest. . . .

Notes

1. Consideration of only those studies containing such an assertion would be nearly sufficient to refute the charge. *See, e.g.,* L. Berg, H. Hahn, & J. Schmidhauser, *Corruption in the American Political System,* 3 (1976); Nye, *Corruption and Political Development: A Cost-Benefit Analysis, in* POLITICAL CORRUPTION: READINGS IN COMPARATIVE ANALYSIS 564 (A. Heidenheimer ed. 1970) [hereinafter cited as POLITICAL CORRUPTION: READINGS]; Peters & Welch, *Political Corruption in America: A Search for Definitions and a Theory,* 72 AM. POL. SCI. REV. 974, 982 (1978); Wertheim, *Sociological Aspects of Corruption in Southeast Asia, in* POLITICAL CORRUPTION: READINGS, *supra,* at 195; The Economist, *Towards a Grammar of Graft, in* POLITICAL CORRUPTION: READINGS, *supra,* at 489.
2. A few student comments are exceptions. Note, *Campaign Contributions and Federal Bribery Law,* 92 HARV. L. REV. 451 (1978) [hereinafter cited as Note, *Campaign Contributions*]; Comment, *The Federal Bribery Statute: An Argument for Cautious Revision,* 68 KY. L.J. 1026 (1979–80) [hereinafter cited as Comment, *Cautious Revision*]; Comment, *Drafting an Effective Bribery Statute,* 1 AM. J. CRIM. L. 210 (1972). The first two of these comments consider only the federal bribery statute, although the second contains references to the major bribery statutes of each state, Comment, *Cautious Revision, supra,* at 1026–27 n.]. An additional study, W. REISMAN, FOLDED LIES: BRIBERY, CRUSADES, AND REFORMS (1979), was written by a lawyer who takes pains to "emphasize that this is not a conventional 'legal' study."
3. Buckley v. Valeo, 424 U.S. 1, 28 (1976).
4. Professor Reisman distinguishes conduct condemned both by the "myth system" and the "operational code" from conduct condemned by the

former but approved by the latter. W. REISMAN, *supra* note 2 at 15. It seems to me that the image in the text of a range of conduct extending from the most corrupt to the most innocent better captures both the complexity of the subject and the way people think about it. "Greyness" may be a function of either an ambivalent view of a practice held throughout the society or approval of a practice by some and condemnation by others.

5. *See* Heidenheimer, Introduction to Part I, *The Context of Analysis,* in POLITICAL CORRUPTION: READINGS, *supra* note 1, at 18: "Bribery . . . creates a very specific obligation on the part of the officeholder."

6. *See* E. DREW, POLITICS AND MONEY: THE NEW ROAD TO CORRUPTION 3–4 (1983).

7. 456 U.S. 45 (1982).

8. *Id.* at 56.

9. The federal statute, 18 U.S.C. § 201 (1982), is representative. The statute defines bribery and acceptance of a bribe, respectively, in subsections (b) and (c):

   (b) Whoever, directly or indirectly, corruptly gives, offers or promises anything of value to any public official . . . or offers or promises any public official . . . to give anything of value to any other person or entity, with intent—

   (1) to influence any official act; or

   (2) to influence such public official . . . to commit . . . any fraud . . . on the United States; or

   (3) to induce such public official . . . to do or omit to do any act in violation of his lawful duty, or

   (c) Whoever, being a public official . . . directly or indirectly, corruptly asks, demands, exacts, solicits, seeks, accepts, receives, or agrees to receive anything of value for himself or for any other person or entity, in return for:

   (1) being influenced in his performance of any official act; or

   (2) being influenced to commit . . . any fraud . . . on the United States; or

   (3) being induced to do or omit to do any act in violation of his official duty;

   . . .

   Shall be fined . . . or imprisoned . . . or both . . . .

10. The boundary between the public and private sectors is sometimes unclear, and there can be difficult questions as to whether officials in entities that straddle the boundary are "public officials" within the meaning of the bribery statutes.

11. The federal statute, contained in the same section of the Penal Code as the main bribery statute, is again representative. 18 U.S.C. § 201 (1982):

    (f) Whoever, otherwise than as provided by law for the proper discharge of official duty, directly or indirectly gives, offers, or promises anything of value to any public official . . . for or because of any official act performed or to be performed by such public official . . .; or

    (g) Whoever, being a public official . . . otherwise than as provided by law for the proper discharge of official duty, directly or indirectly asks, demands, exacts, solicits, seeks, accepts, receives, or agrees to re-

ceive anything of value for himself for or because of any official act performed or to be performed by him;

Shall be fined . . . or imprisoned . . . or both.

Omitted portions make these subsections applicable to former public officials and persons selected to be public officials.

12. An exception worth considering is the California statute. The definition of "bribe" is unexceptional: "anything of value or advantage, present or prospective, or any promise or undertaking to give any, asked, given or accepted, with a corrupt intent to influence, unlawfully, the person to whom it is given, in his action, vote or opinion, in any public or official capacity. . . ." CAL. PENAL CODE § 7(6) (West 1970). However, the same section defines the word "corruptly" as "a *wrongful* design to acquire or cause some pecuniary or other advantage to the person guilty of the act or omission referred to, or to some other person. . . ." *Id.* § 7(3) (emphasis added). Under the California definition of "bribe," the intent to influence an official must be "corrupt." Under the definition of "corruptly," there must be a "design" for the official to receive a "pecuniary or other advantage." But this requirement is expressly set forth in similar language in the definition of "bribe." The word "corrupt" in the definition of "bribe" is redundant, unless we give meaning to the word "wrongful" in the definition of "corruptly." But what meaning?

13. Wertheim, *supra* note 1, at 196. By far the most serious effort in the social science literature on corruption to break the concept down into its elements and to give careful attention to each element is Peters & Welch, *supra* note 1. Unaccountably, however, this otherwise excellent article does not consider as one of the elements of corruption the "intent to influence," or any other connection between the benefit to the public official and the official act. Useful social science inquiries such as that of Professors Peters and Welch unquestionably are impeded by the absence of legal scholarship on the subject of bribery.

14. Myrdal, *Corruption as a Hindrance to Modernization in South Asia,* in POLITICAL CORRUPTION: READINGS, *supra* note 3, at 229.

15. J. SCOTT, COMPARATIVE POLITICAL CORRUPTION 3–4 (1972); *see also* M. JOHNSTON, POLITICAL CORRUPTION AND PUBLIC POLICY IN AMERICA 5–6 (1982); Peters & Welch, *supra* note 1, at 975.

16. Nye, *supra* note 1, at 566. William E. Connolly describes the "doctrine of operationalism" as holding "that each concept in political inquiry must be associated with a precise and definite testing operation that specifies the conditions of its application." W. CONNOLLY, THE TERMS OF POLITICAL DISCOURSE 15 (1974). Professor Connolly goes on to criticize political scientists who engage in an illusory and misleading effort to comply with the doctrine. The unavailing efforts by some writers to establish a legally-based definition of corruption provide excellent support for Professor Connolly's criticism.

17. Admittedly, if any of them made any such efforts, they would find precious little assistance in the law reviews.

In most cases the failure of social scientists to pay attention to their own definitions of corruption has been harmless. But in some cases the confusion engendered has been significant. For example, in G. BENSON, S.

MAARANEN, & A. HESLOP, POLITICAL CORRUPTION IN AMERICA (1978), corruption is defined as covering certain types of "illegal or unethical" conduct. *Id.* at xiii. One page later the authors say that their definition excludes campaign contributions, because although such contributions can resemble bribes, corruption as the authors use the term "is limited to actual illegalities." *Id.* at xiv. The authors apparently assume that as a matter of law campaign contributions cannot constitute bribes, an assumption that the next section reveals as false. *See infra* notes 86–90 and accompanying text. In any event, there is no explanation why campaign contributions that function in a manner similar to bribes are necessarily excluded from a definition that includes "illegal *or unethical*" conduct . . .

Susan Rose-Ackerman also seems to make the incorrect assumption that campaign contributions cannot be bribes. S. ROSE-ACKERMAN, *Corruption: A Study in Political Economy* 7 (197). Her analysis does not contain inconsistencies of the sort just discussed, but her assertion that limiting the size of campaign contributions might increase the amount of corruption by diverting money from lawful means of influencing policy to unlawfulk means, *Id.* at 16, is incorrect if the campaign contributions can constitute bribery and therefore can be regarded as corrupt under her legally-based definition. A more serious problem with her statement is that even if her legal assumption were correct, the statement that regulating campaign contributions could increase corruption would be trivial and misleading since it would be true only because of a truncated definition of corruption.

18. CORRUPTION IN THE AMERICAN POLITICAL SYSTEM, *supra* note 1, at 5. The same point is made, perhaps to the point of exaggeration, by Amitai Etzioni. A. ETZIONI, CAPITAL CORRUPTION 18 (1984) ("the beneficiaries of corruption have managed to legalize most of it"). For additional arguments against a legally-based definition, see Peters & Welch, *supra* note 1, at 974–75.

19. A. ETZIONI, *supra* note 18.

4

Techniques of Political Graft

V. O. Key, Jr.

Graft has been defined as an abuse of power for personal or party profit. It was noted that graft usually involved a relationship between the official exercising the power which is abused and some other individual or individuals and that the techniques of graft are the methods employed in these relationships plus the methods used in cases of graft involving only a single individual.

Bribery to influence official action is the most obvious technique of graft. The name which a particular payment in money or other value for this purpose takes is immaterial. Some campaign contributions cannot be differentiated from bribes.[1] Business and professional relationships may conceal bribery. When a corporation secures its bonds or insurance, for example, from a political leader, it cannot be assumed that this is done because the "boss" sells the best insurance. Any favor secured as a result of such relationships is secured by bribery.[2] Bribery is fundamentally the same whether employed in relation to legislators, administrators, judges, other public officials, "bosses" exercising their power or private individuals acting in agency positions. It is the same on all levels of government and in all functions. The act of bribery, as has been observed from some of the instances recounted, is a matter requiring considerable skill. In the process there is often considerable preliminary negotiation in order to achieve an intimate relationship with the person to be bribed. He is given "good" and plausible reasons for doing what he is being bought to do. Sometimes advantage is taken of his financial needs, and he may be in a way "coerced" to accept. In other cases, of course, bribery is a more or less cold-blooded commercial transaction.[3]

The converse of bribery is extortion, i.e., the abuse or threat of abuse of a power in such a way as to secure response in payment of

Source: V. O. Key, Jr., *The Techniques of Political Graft in the United States*. Chicago, Ill.: University of Chicago Libraries, 1936, pp. 386–401.

money or other valuable thing. This technique is the same whether it is exercised by a legislative coterie through a "sand-bagging" bill or by a building inspector through a trivial "shake-down." In extortion the initiative is clearly with the public official or the person exercising his power. Legislators may hold a "regulator" or a "revenue-raiser" over the heads of persons directly interested in the proposed legislation and subtly intimate that it might be put quietly away by payments to the right persons. A licensing official may threaten revocation of a saloon license if a campaign contribution is not made. A disbursing officer may threaten to delay a payment justly due if some gratuity is not forthcoming. The assessment of public employees usually takes the form of extortion although it is actually carried on with widely varying degrees of subtlety. In all these and other similar situations the behavior pattern involved is the same, although, of course, in making threats and demands for money various shades of bluntness in communication prevail.

In individual instances it may be difficult to distinguish between extortion, solicitation of a bribe and bribery. Businessmen usually claim that all their bribes are "protection" money which they are compelled to pay. Others take the view that there is really no extortion, but that it is all bribery.[4] It seems quite evident that there are both types of relationships.

"State-bribery" is a term which may be applied to those instances where control of various public properties and of the expenditure of public funds is abused—or perhaps more accurately misused—for the purpose of creating power or controlling relationships. Analyzed to the ultimate any instance in which one individual controls another is a power situation or relationship. Thus, state-bribery includes the control of the political organization, its candidates and to some extent its policies, by the control of patronage. A rebellious district leader or ward committeeman may discover that his printing contracts or his fire hose business has been cut off by the men "higher-up" in the organization and that it is too late to mend his ways. Control by state-bribery may extend to electors as in the employment of election officials and the hiring of polling places with the tacit understanding, if not express, that the ballots will be cast "right." This type of control may extend to the political attitudes of community leaders, such as bankers, through the distribution of deposits of public funds. The construction of public works, the distribution of subsidies may be in the nature of state-bribery, to control the electoral behavior of particular groups, territorial or functional. An executive may "buy" a legislator with an appointment. These examples are not intended to exclude others but are merely illustrative. The common element running through all of them is the element of control secured by an abuse—a perversion of the purpose—of the power granted to the official concerned. The object of the control need not be to influence a person with reference to his political behavior, but it generally is. The widespread acquiescence in the practice of various forms of state-bribery does not change their real nature. The relationship is without doubt one of bribery with public funds.

Another fundamental form of graft is political discrimination in the formulation and administration of law or rules of behavior,[5] that is to say, the power to make or administer law. The consideration is a political attitude rather than a payment of money or other value. Law making and law enforcing may be lumped together in this category for when law making is unequivocally employed for this purpose, as in administration, the individual case is dealt with rather than broad interests. The effect of abuse in this category may be to create lines of control within the political organization as when a ward committeeman or a district leader is permitted to operate a gambling house. The boss of the organization is certain of the support of this leader for he can order the police to close the place, if he wishes. In smaller matters the effect of this discriminatory administration of law may be to create "friends" among the electorate, as when tickets for violating traffic ordinances are "fixed." Political discrimination of this sort may come either as the result of the initiative of the official concerned or on petition of the person favored. The relationship may resemble either bribery or intimidation.

Discrimination in the administration of service functions for political purposes is a fifth fundamental technique of graft. The standards set up for the administration of services in individual cases are departed from and the criteria become political. Republicans are discriminated against in favor of Democrats in granting unemployment relief, for example. The Republican party functionary is given preference in the selection of stalls in the public markets. Abuses in the service functions may be differentiated from state-bribery in that abuses in the latter category are usually incident to some appointive or contractual rela-tionship whereas abuses in the service activities are incident to a service relationship between citizen and government. Abuses in ser-vice relationships differ from abuses in the administration of law for in the latter a norm of conduct is applied through penal sanctions.

A final type of technique of graft may be denominated "auto-corruption." In bribery, extortion, state-bribery, and the other types which have been described, relationships between two or more individuals are involved. In auto-corruption the public official or person exercising the power of such official, boss or whatever he may be, in a sense plays the role of both parties in the other situations involving two or more persons. He secures for himself the administrative privilege which would be secured by an outsider by bribery. He awards contracts to himself, perhaps using dummy corporations, which would go to reward a contractor in the organization. He appropriates public property which might be used to reward some other member of the political organization. At times in all types of auto-corruption the gains may trickle into the political organization through campaign contributions and by various other means, but there is a fundamental distinction between this and the other forms of graft. However, in some instances auto-corruption may be a single link in a chain of individual cases which create a "ring" formation of power. The spoils are divided by individuals in their respective official positions, but the series of events bind together all the participants in the political machine. In auto-corruption cases often occur in which the personal gain far outweighs the group or party advantage. Matters of this kind, of course, have no place in the well regulated machine.[6]

In addition to these fundamental techniques of graft there are employed in conjunction with the primary methods various subsidiary or ancillary techniques, which have been described in considerable detail in connection with the various activities of government. The methods of maintaining secrecy, which is essential in most types of graft, are fairly obvious. In the first instance as little evidence as possible is created. When bribes are passed only the giver and the receiver are present, or perhaps the money passes through several hands from briber to bribee.[7] Some of the individuals through whose hands it passes may be more or less ignorant of what the purpose is. The terms of an agreement to give some particular privilege may be vague, indefinite or merely implied. Non-verbal symbols may be employed.[8] As little documentary evidence as possible is created. When payments have to be made from corporate or firm funds, false entries are made. A bribe may be charged as repairs to steamers or roadbed maintenance. Double records—one false, one true—may be kept. Dummy corporations have a multiplicity of uses. Business and professional relationships may conceal bribery. In the maintenance of secrecy much depends on the "right" relations with opposition politicians and with newspapers which might ferret out and disclose unsavory matters.

The various methods of camouflage and counter-propaganda constitute another subsidiary technique. In nearly every instance of alleged graft the accused has an explanation differing from the interpretation offered by the prosecutor.[9] The meanest sort of "steal" is sometimes transformed by the graft artist into a great deed for the promotion of the public welfare or at least a bit of harmless pillaging of the rich for the benefit of the poor. If this cannot be done, sufficient dust may be raised to create confusion and doubt. Foreign wars to allay domestic uprisings is a political theme on which there are many variations. Grafters as well as other political technicians have been thoroughly aware of this principle of politics. We have the spectacle of "Big Bill" Thompson sallying forth to kick King George "on the snoot" after his cohorts had virtually carried away the city hall stone by stone. Grafting political organizations have managed their activities as if public opinion mattered, whether it did or not.[10]

The evasion of legal requirements, such as those in civil service laws and in regulations governing the award of public contracts, is a subsidiary method which varies with the legal regime concerned. Certain types of evasion, however, recur. Legislation cannot anticipate every possible contingency and exceptions to the general rule are usually provided. These exceptions may be utilized to such an extent as to nullify the general rule. Temporary appointees are named under the provisions of the civil service laws providing for emergency appointments. In awarding contracts orders are divided and made under the legal provisions allowing purchases without calling for bids when the amount is less than $1000 or $500. Discretion may be abused. Thus, who is the lowest responsible bidder? General terms may be used to indicate specific things as in the manipulation of contract and purchase specifications. Probably more important than these verbalistic techniques designed to give a color of legality is the outright disregard of legislation governing the administration.

The master strategy of the political machine consists in the political consolidation of the beneficiaries of the graft system together with others who may be brought into the combination by some other appeal. Thus, graft as it has been defined may be either sporadic or systematic. The individual instances are the same in either case, or on any level of government, or in any country, but in any instance it is contended that it is virtually impossible to rule by graft alone. Other techniques must be employed to win the support of persons who do not obviously benefit as a result of graft.[11] At any rate the technique of combination of various interests into a governing bloc is not peculiar to organizations specializing in corrupt political techniques. It consists in welding together all the interests benefiting by the privileges given as a result of bribery, the receivers of state-bribes, and beneficiaries of political discrimination into the most powerful combination in the political life of a jurisdiction. It may include the suppression of opposition by methods often akin to intimidation as by a threat to skyrocket an individual's tax bill. Regardless of the techniques employed this procedure has to be consummated in order to attain and retain power. The aspect of a corrupt power combination which may be peculiar is that the combinations and alliances are effectuated by the application of sanctions and controls with compelling force directly to the individual. When some other types of techniques are employed successful combinations may be effectuated to a greater extent by group appeals. But the sole function of these power techniques is not to place a given set of individuals in power.

The Functions of Graft

A clear distinction has been made between means and ends, between techniques and objectives. The techniques of graft have been regarded primarily as techniques of political control. The function of these political methods is to exert control or to influence somebody—to get something done. The basic techniques are practically the same in different places and at different times, but their function varies with the particular situation in which they are employed. The class of persons utilizing and profiting from the techniques of graft varies from time to time, but the methods are about the same. Thus, in a given city perhaps at one time the street railways were the chief corrupters of politicians; a little later it might be the gas interests; still later, the bus companies. In a state the railroads would run the government for a time and then turn it over to the timber and mining interests who in turn might relinquish control to the electrical utilities. These differences in personnel and objectives, but similarity in techniques and patterns of participants, show what is meant by the distinction between techniques, functions, ends.

The function performed or the end achieved by the use of the techniques of graft varies, of course, from time to time. The same is true for any political method. The Moscow communists may employ essentially the same methods to retain power as the Italian fascists, but for quite different ends. Some of the more frequently appearing functions which have been performed through the instrumentality of the techniques of graft in the United States may be indicated in brief compass.

The patronage system has served, and still serves, as the principal method of consolidating into a cohesive mass the politically effective sector of the population.[12] Within the relatively small group or class constituted of the people of political importance the control of patronage serves as a powerful means of control, of discipline, of direction. Lacking the tradition of a governing class, a socially responsible elite bound together by the ties of tradition and perhaps class interest, patronage serves to integrate the activities of individuals bound together by no other tie. It aids in the creation of class loyalties and simplifies the problem of party discipline. Other factors in the creation of party cohesion are not to be discounted, of course. The patronage system may be credited in a way with the functions performed by political parties for they have been largely financed from the public payroll. It is difficult to see how the functions carried on by parties could have been done on the same scale without some such method of financing. Almost everywhere party organizations have a permanent personnel which is paid for its services, but the funds for this purpose may come from sources other than the public treasury. American parties receive the benefit of a great deal of voluntary service, but a large proportion of the party work is paid for from the public treasury.

Various other functions have been served by the patronage system. It may be true that a bureaucracy will almost inevitably take on the color of the social structure of the nation, but the free and easy distribution of jobs has aided in the nationalizing process in the United States. The western lawyer and politician has always had an open ear to the call to serve his country in the federal service; and many of them responded to the call. Thus, through the federal and other public services has flowed a stream of individuals which, perhaps, has had its influence in creating national cohesion in a continental state surprisingly free from serious centrifugal tendencies. Patronage, of course, has been but one of many factors. The ready access to the public service to members of immigrant groups has doubtless aided in the process of assimilation and in the creation of new national loyalties. Had any successful effort been made to reserve public office for "Nordics," serious difficulties would have in all probability arisen.

Other forms of state-bribery, such as the distribution of contracts, orders, bank deposits, and tax favors in return for political services or support serve precisely the same function as the utilization of patronage to create lines of discipline in a political army. Many party functionaries are compensated for their labors with printing contracts, construction contracts, and various other types of public expenditures. These relationships serve to control, just as jobs do. It is, of course, not to be denied that many of these relationships involve more of fraud, of purely personal profit, rather than group profit, but the aspect of patronage and other forms of state-bribery which stands out vividly is the fact that office, hope of office, or other immediately personal reward serves to solidify a "political" class lacking the tie of tradition or the resources necessary to sustain a benevolent·oligarchy. Whether this is "right," or "just," is a matter for the professors of ethics. The phenomenon is there.[13]

Graft in the proprietary activities of government results in the creation of control relationships within the political machine. It is a means of controlling and rewarding the members of the party organization. Techniques such as bribery serve a different function. They may often be a means of solving provisionally at least conflicts of interest between social groups or between individuals and society. The wholesale bribery of legislatures by railroads in connection with rate regulation and taxation involved a dispute between carriers and shippers. The shippers were victorious in the long pull, but they were checked for years by techniques often of a corrupt character. Thus, bribery may be a means of retaining a privileged position which would otherwise have been lost earlier.[14] In the development of telephone, traction, gas and electric utilities in urban centers bribery was and is employed rather freely in various forms. This involves a conflict between the utility and its customers over rates and services, but in its earlier phases there was a bitter struggle over the issue of whether such services should be monopolistic in character. In the achievement of monopoly bribery and kindred methods played no minor role. Retrospectively monopoly appears to have been inevitable and not wholly undesirable. Thus, bribery may expedite the coming of the inevitable. In the exploitation of forests and minerals, bribery bore down much of what little opposition there was to the activities of the exploiters.

In some cases bribery has served as a technique for the achievement of accommodations between groups with conflicting codes of moral conduct. The stream of puritanism encounters powerful opposition from masses with different standards of behavior and from those who profit by catering to their tastes. Sentiment wavers. The newspapers and the churches "turn on the heat" occasionally. The community as a whole takes a hypocritical attitude. In this state of indecision and conflict the system of police graft makes possible prostitution, gambling, and other practices. It serves in a way to "regulate," control, license, and keep within bounds practices which are beyond the law. They cannot be controlled through the forms of law. Whether these problems could be dealt with without the use of bribery is another question, but there can be no doubt but that bribery has been an important ingredient in the forces eventuating in operating arrangements for these businesses.

In the administration of regulatory ordinances and laws of various types bribery has been a convenient way to avoid legal requirements which may be impracticable of application. Other rules socially desirable and applicable have been swept aside in the same way by business-men too busy and impatient to spend their time in securing the formulation and adoption of more workable standards reconciling their interests and the public welfare in a "fair" manner.

As has been indicated at different points throughout the article various methods of graft serve to control a considerable proportion of the electorate. The political organization usually attempts to dispense all governmental favors through the party hierarchy. At times the governmental officials have become so habituated to action upon the request of party officials that to secure a service involving no departure from the customary rule requires party intervention.[15] The party becomes the government. In its relations with the citizenry in distributing privileges there seems to be a tendency for relations between the political organization and other social hierarchies to be carried on between equals. A "big" business man will see a "big" party man and so on. By this method of administration of favors the party may gain the loyalty of the beneficiaries, although so little is known of the behavior of the electorate that the extent of this influence can not be estimated with any degree of accuracy.

It is not to be denied that the privileges and ends sought by the techniques of graft are almost always immediately selfish in character. Perhaps most ends achieved by political action, regardless of the methods employed, are selfish to a greater or lesser degree, but the ends secured by graft are usually more immediately and obviously so. The various functions of graft have been set forth for the purpose of suggesting that in some instances the immediate ends achieved by specific instances of graft may have more meaning when considered from a broader point of view.

Notes

1. Perhaps the difference arises when parties openly espouse the ends which campaign contributors hope to achieve as a result of their largesse. This occurs only when such ends are for class, group, or public interest, or may be made to appear so, rather than for patently and unequivocally selfish individual interest.
2. Legally the crime of bribery must involve persons possessing the power under the law to give what is sought by bribery. Legal fictions like this must be ignored in any realistic view. A "boss" probably would not have the legal power to grant the desired action, but actually he might have such power.

3. See the brilliant article on "Bribery" by H.D. Lasswell, *Encyclopaedia of the Social Sciences,* Vol. I. New York: Crowell-Collier-Macmillan, 1930, pp. 690–692.
4. See Donald Richberg's remarks: "Frequently they mask their effort by publicly asserting the need for 'protection' from political interference. Indeed, this is such a prevalent disguise for political aggression that doubtless most of the Insulls most of the time feel assured that they only carry a sword for defense and not for attack when they lead a wealth-gathering foray."—"Gold-Plated Anarchy," *The Nation,* CXXXVI (1933), 368.
5. Law is used here in the sense of a rule governing the behavior of the individual or corporate citizen. Administration is used in the sense of the application of such a rule to the individual case rather than in the sense of management.
6. Many political leaders who do not profit in a pecuniary way themselves tolerate and bear criticism for inexpedient grafting by their followers. In the nature of things it is difficult to exercise much control over the illegal activities of the members of the organization in office, once it is agreed that the organization is out to get all it can. The unscrupulous leader must leave it to them to exercise their judgment to do what "will go" and what "won't go." If every plan for graft were submitted to the board of strategy of the organization, some of the less well considered ones would undoubtedly be vetoed. But, then, there are statutes punishing conspiracy which might be effectively applied if such an arrangement could be proved.
7. Compare the aphorism in R.E. Shapley, *Solid for Mulhooly* (New ed.; Philadelphia: Gebbie & Co., 1889), p. 59: "A man who's d––d fool enough to call in witnesses to see him take a bribe deserves the extreme penalty of the law."
8. The conversation of the corporation head and his political lawyer serving as an intermediary "could be heard by all the world and published without harm—so long as the winks, nods, and facial expressions are not shown on the screen."—Frank Kent, *The Great Game of Politics* (New York: Doubleday, 1930), p. 137.
9. The transparent saw, "It was a loan and not a bribe." "I got the money speculating on town lots in Japan." "It came from my tin box, a wonderful tin box." "My uncle, a seafaring man, gave me the money." "I won it on the races."
10. A first rate study could be made of the techniques and functions of deception in politics.
11. Many of the most important techniques of political machines do not involve graft. Thus, many voters cast their ballot in accordance with attitudes inculcated in early childhood. The machine may control the symbols of the Republican party or of the Democratic party through graft, but graft is not necessary to secure the support of the persons who inherited their political beliefs. As long as people are simple there will be somebody to delude them.
12. The concept of the politically effective sector of the population is based upon the hypothesis that a relatively small proportion of the population will operate and be immediately influential in the operation of the government. In so doing the wishes or hypothetical wishes of the masses may

condition their behavior, but the actual power will be left to a relatively few. In a city this group may be the political machine proper and the persons bound to it by close ties often of a material character. In a social aristocracy based on land it may be a relatively few large landowners. In large social units it is of course difficult to define the limits of this group with any high degree of precision.

13. The emphasis here has been on state-bribery as a method of intensifying or creating loyalties and lines of control within the ruling bloc. This method may also be used in warfare between social groups with very real differences as in the use of pensions and places by the court party to control members of parliament in England. This reflected deep seated differences in the nation. See James Burch, *Political Disquisitions, or, An Inquiry into Public Errors, Defects, and Abuses* (London: E. & C. Dilly, 1774–1775).

14. Privilege as used in American politics is a rather vague term. It could be defined as something the other fellow has which you do not have. It may be a profit or a business or financial position or "right" which is in violation of the existing rules of the game or standards of fair play. Or the constant revision of these standards may bring into the category of privilege practices or "rights" once considered legitimate.

15. Compare "deputantism" in France.

5

What Is the Problem About Corruption?

Colin Leys

The "Moralistic Approach"

The systematic investigation of corruption is overdue. There are three main types of literature in English on the subject: historical studies of corrupt practice in Britain; inquisitional studies, mainly of the United States and the English-speaking West African and Asian countries; and sociological studies which deal with corruption incidentally. So far as I know no general study in English has appeared.[1] One reason for this seems to be a widespread feeling that the facts cannot be discovered, or that if they can, they cannot be proved, or that if they can be proved, the proof cannot be published. All these notions seem dubious. There are nearly always sources of information, some of them—such as court records—systematic in their way, and some of them very circumstantial (like privileged parliamentary debates). Many of the people involved are quite willing to talk. And commissions of inquiry have published large amounts of evidence, obtained by unusual powers of compulsion.

I doubt if it would really be as hard to discover the facts about corruption in most countries as it would be to find out the facts about some legitimate political matters which those involved really want to keep secret. One could even find ways of measuring, within broad limits, the scale and economic effects of some forms of corruption. Publishing the results might present difficulties, but these would only be acute if naming persons were essential to the object of publishing, which is not ordinarily the case in scientific inquiry, even in the social sciences. As anyone who has written on contemporary issues is aware, there are adequate conventions which enable events and incidents to

Source: Colin Leys, "What Is the Problem about Corruption?" *Journal of Modern African Studies*, 3: 2 (1965), pp. 215–230. By permission of the publisher, Cambridge University Press.

be described anonymously or obliquely without reducing their credibility or value as evidence.

But so far very few people have approached the subject of corruption in this spirit, aiming to describe, measure, analyze, and explain the phenomena involved.[2] This is curious when one considers the word itself (corruption means to change from good to bad; to debase; to pervert); it denotes patterns of action which derive their significance from the role of value-systems in social behavior. Similar phenomena, such as suicide, crime, or religious fanaticism, have intrigued sociologists greatly. However, the question of corruption in the contemporary world has so far been taken up almost solely by moralists.

The recent book by Ronald Wraith and Edgar Simpkins on *Corruption in Developing Countries* is of this *genre*. They are concerned with "the scarlet thread of bribery and corruption," with corruption which "flourishes as luxuriantly as the bush and weeds which it so much resembles, taking the goodness from the soil and suffocating the growth of plants which have been carefully, and expensively, bred and tended." It is a "jungle of nepotism and temptation," a "dangerous and tragic situation" in which the enthusiasm of the young African civil servant turns to cynicism, and where there are "not the attitudes of progress and development."[3]

They are aware that the "moralizing approach" (their own term) involves a difficulty, namely that their standpoint may differ from that of those who do the things which they regard as corrupt. For instance, they can see that since any African who is so fortunately placed as to be able to get jobs for his relatives is felt (by the relatives at least) to be under an obligation to do so, it is peculiar to call this corrupt: "an act is presumably only corrupt if society condemns it as such, and if the doer is afflicted with a sense of guilt when he does it; neither of these apply to a great deal of African nepotism."[4]

However, they are convinced (no evidence is adduced) that the results of nepotism and all other forms of what they call corruption ("in the strict sense . . . in the context of the *mores* of Great Britain") are serious and bad; and they take courage from the fact that a small minority in most developing countries shares their ethical viewpoint. Consequently they conceive the problem as one of seeking in British history the causes which led to the triumph in Britain of this point of view, with its attendant advantages, in the hope that African and other developing countries might profit from the experience of Britain. (Over half the book is devoted to this inquiry.)

The results are, as they recognize, inconclusive, which is not surprising when one considers that this formulation of the problem ("Why does the public morality of African states not conform to the British?'') contains an obvious enough answer: because they have a different social, economic and political system, and a different historical experience. The approach is not as bad as it sounds, for Wraith and Simpkins have observed the Nigerian scene with discrimination and sympathy. But the basis of the whole book is a simple faith, that corruption is what it is, namely what has been known as corruption in Britain for a long time; and it has at bottom a "simple cause"—avarice: "the wrong that is done is done in the full knowledge that it is wrong, for the concept of theft does not vary as between Christian and Muslim, African and European, or primitive man and Minister of the Crown."[5]

Emotionally and intellectually, this seems to be in a direct line of descent from the viewpoint of those missionaries who were dedicated to the suppression of native dancing. The subject seems to deserve a more systematic and openminded approach.[6]

What is Corruption?

Under what circumstances are actions called corrupt? It seems best to start from some examples.

1. In the spring of 1964 the (Republican) secretary of state of Illinois died. Under the state constitution the (Democratic) governor temporarily filled his place by appointing a young (Democratic) official to the office. Within a few weeks a substantial number of state civil servants appointed by the late secretary of state were dismissed, and their jobs were filled by Democratic party supporters.

2. In Chicago about the same time a controversy was taking place concerning school desegregation. Active desegregationists alleged that they were prevented from attending in force a meeting of the city council as part of their campaign, because all the public seating was filled by council employees who had for this purpose been given a holiday by the city administration.

3. In Kampala, Uganda, in August 1963 the city council decided to award a petrol station site to a majority-party member of the council, who offered the lowest price, £4000; the highest offer was for £11,000. It was alleged in the National Assembly that the successful purchaser resold the plot to an oil company at a profit of £8000.[7]

4. In Port Harcourt, Nigeria, in 1955, there were people in the Town Hall drawing laborers' salaries not provided for in the estimates; they were employed on the personal recommendation of individual councillors.[8]

5. In New York City, in 1951, it was estimated that over $1 million

per annum was paid to policemen (for overlooking illegalities) by a bookmaking syndicate.[9]

6. In Lagos, Nigeria, in 1952, the practice of giving an unofficial cash gift or a fee for services rendered was fairly authoritatively stated to be found

> in hospitals where the nurses require a fee from every in-patient before the prescribed medicine is given, and even the ward servants must have their "dash" before bringing the bed-pan; it is known to be rife in the Police Motor Traffic Unit, which has unrivalled opportunities on account of the common practice of overloading vehicles; pay clerks made a deduction from the wages of daily paid staff; produce examiners exact a fee from the produce buyer for every bag that is graded and sealed; domestic servants pay a proportion of their wages to the senior of them, besides often having paid a lump sum to buy the job.[10]

One thing which all these events have in common is that someone regards each of them as a bad thing. Equally, however, it is clear that at least someone else—i.e., those involved in the acts in question— regards each of them as a good thing. Writers of the moralist school accept this, but they are convinced that such behavior is always against the "public interest." But what is the "public interest"? Some substantial arguments have been put forward to suggest that the public interest may sometimes *require* some of these practices. The most famous of these is probably the American defense of patronage, as in case (1) above, and "honest graft."[11] This argument turns essentially on the view that democratic politics in "mass" societies can only be insured by the integration of a multitude of interests and groups into political parties, capable of furnishing leadership and coherent policies;[12] this involves organization and inducements, both of which cost money; therefore, politics must be made to pay. From this point of view the political role of money is to serve as a cement—"a *hyphen* which joins, a *buckle* which fastens" the otherwise separate and conflicting elements of a society into a body politic; "the greater the corruption, the greater the harmony between corruptor and corruptee," as one candid critic recognized.[13] And Professor Hoselitz has argued that the early years of the life of a nation are dominated by these "persistent integrative needs of the society," and that

> Much of the alleged corruption that Western technical advisers on administrative services of Asian and African stages encounter, and against which they inveigh in their technical reports with so little genuine success, is nothing but the prevalence of these non-rational norms on the basis of which these administrations operate.[14]

This can be taken a stage further. The moralist school of thought may recognize that some of the activities recorded above indirectly serve these broadly beneficial purposes. But they generally assume that the economic price paid is a heavy one. For instance: "The sums involved in some of the proved cases of corruption in Africa would have brought considerable benefits to people for whom "under-privileged" is too mild a word, if they had been properly spent."[15]

But spending public money properly does not guarantee that it will benefit the poor.[16] The Uganda Minister of Information was much criticized for giving a lucrative and unusual monopoly of television set sales to an American contractor, in return for building a transmission station at cut rates: even had corruption been involved, the policy did produce a television station much more quickly and cheaply than the policy adopted in neighboring Kenya.[17] To take another example, one may ask whether the Russian consumer would be better off without the operations of the illegal contact men who derive illegal incomes in return for their aid in overcoming bottlenecks in the supply of materials for production.[18] Even in the case of petty bribery or extortion, it is relevant to ask, What is the alternative? Could an equally efficient and socially-useful administration be carried on if effective means of eliminating perquisites were found and all concerned were required to live on their salaries? Would the pressure for higher salaries be no greater? Could it be resisted? If it could not, would increased taxation fall on those most able to pay and would this, or reduced services, be in the public interest? To ask these questions is to realize that the answers call for research and analysis which is seldom undertaken, and that they are likely to vary according to circumstances. One also becomes aware that near the heart of the moralists' concern is the idea that the public interest is opposed to anything that heightens *inequality*. But we also have to ask how far equality and development are themselves compatible ideals. The régime most committed to both of them—the USSR—found it necessary to postpone its concern with equality in order to achieve development.[19] This is not to say that all kinds of inequality promoted by all kinds of corruption are beneficial from the point of view of development; it is merely to challenge the assumption that they are invariably bad.

But we still have not answered the question, Under what circumstances are actions called corrupt? What is at issue in all the cases cited above is the existence of a standard of behavior according to which the action in question breaks some rule, written or unwritten, about the proper purposes to which a public office or a public institution may be put. The moralist has his own idea of what the rule should be. The actors in the situations concerned have theirs. It may be the same as the moralists' (they may regard themselves as corrupt); or quite different (they may regard themselves as behaving honorably according to their standards, and regard their critics' standards as irrelevant); or they may be "men of two worlds," partly adhering to two standards which are incompatible, and ending up exasperated and indifferent (they may recognize no particular moral implications of the acts in question at all—this is fairly obviously quite common). And in addition to the actors there are the other members—more or less directly affected—of their own society; all these positions are possible for them too.[20]

The Analysis of Corruption

The following questions suggest themselves as a reasonable basis for the analysis of any case in which corrupt is alleged:

1. What is being called corrupt and does it really happen? In the case of the African Continental Bank it became clear that no one was able to formulate a clear enough allegation against Dr. N. Azikiwe showing precisely what was the rule which he had broken.[21] A precise statement is required of the rule and the sense in which it is said to have been perverted. It may turn out, as in the case of the African Continental Bank, that there is really no clear idea of what the rule is; or that there is a clear rule but that it has not clearly been broken (this was Lord Denning's verdict on the Profumo case).[22]

2. Who regards the purpose which is being perverted as the proper or "official" purpose? It may be so regarded by most people in the society, including those who pervert it; or it may be so regarded by only a few people (e.g. state political patronage is regarded as corrupt by only a relatively small group of American reformers).[23]

3. Who regards the allegedly corrupt action as perverting the official purpose? This is not necessarily the same question as question (2) above. For example, in a subsequent debate in the Uganda National Assembly on the petrol station site mentioned above, the Minister of Regional Administrations accepted the principle that the council ought not to accept offers lower than the official valuer's valuation of the property, but held that they were by no means obliged to accept the highest offer and that the council were justified in preferring to give a "stake" in the city to a poor man rather than to a rich one.[24] The opposition took the view that it was the man's politics rather than his poverty which actuated the majority on the council, and that the loss to the public revenue was too high a price to pay for assisting one

individual member of the public. They also took the view that the official object should be to accept the highest bid, unless circumstances of public importance not present in this case dictated otherwise. Thus the nature of the rule was also a matter of controversy, but both sides to the dispute to some extent made the distinction between the rule on the one hand, and the question of what amounted to breaking it on the other.

4. What are the short-term and long-term consequences of the behavior in question, both of each particular case and of such behavior generally? The answer might usefully, if roughly, be broken into two parts: (a) objective consequences, and (b) subjective consequences. Under (a) will come such questions as, What resources are directed from what applications to what other applications? What are the real as opposed to the theoretical opportunity costs of the alleged corruption? What are the effects for income distribution? And what consequential effects are there on the pattern of loyalties, the scope of party activities, the incentives to economic activity? etc. etc. Under (b) will come such questions as e.g., What effect does behaving in this way have on the work of civil servants who regard themselves as behaving corruptly? and, What effect does observing such behavior have on the attitudes and/or behavior of others? etc. etc.

It is natural but wrong to assume that the results of corruption are always both bad and important. For instance it is usually assumed that a corrupt civil service is an impediment to the establishment of foreign private enterprise, which has enough difficulties to contend with without in addition having to pay bribes. This may be clearly the case, but sometimes also the reverse appears to be true. Where bureaucracy is both elaborate and inefficient, the provision of strong personal incentives to bureaucrats to cut red tape may by the only way of speeding the establishment of the new firm. In such a case it is certainly reasonable to wish that the bureaucracy were simpler and more efficient, but not to argue that bribery *per se* is an obstacle to private economic initiative.[25] On the other hand the results may be unimportant from any practical standpoint, even if they are not particularly nice.

From such questions one may go on to pose another which is clearly the central one for the scientific study of the problem: In any society, under what conditions is behavior most likely to occur which a significant section of the population will regard as corrupt? Some obviously relevant points are:

1. *The "standing" of the "official purpose" of each public office or institution in the society.* This involves the diffusion of understanding

of the idea generally, and within particular relevant groups (e.g. civil servants or police); how strongly supported this conception is, generally, and within particular groups; and what effect distance and scale have on both these dimensions. For example, ordinary people in England did not immediately condemn the Ferranti company for wanting to keep over £4 million windfall profits on a defense contract, because it was an incomprehensibly vast sum gained in highly unfamiliar circumstances; but the same people would instantly condemn a local contractor who made a windfall profit of £40,000 on laying a drainpipe for the Rural District Council. And the "standing" of the "official purpose" of anything is also affected by the "standing" of other rival conceptions of its purpose, e.g. the computing moral claims of relatives on a civil servant who is making junior appointments.

2. *The extent to which action which perverts or contravenes such official purposes is seen as doing so*—another complex problem of research into attitudes.

3. *The incentives and disincentives to corrupt the official purposes of an office or institution.* For instance, the size of the profits to be made by bribery, or the losses liable to be incurred by refraining from it, compared with the penalties attached to being caught and exposed.

4. *The ease with which corruption (once defined) can be carried on.* This involves such things as the case of a particular type of corruption,, and the extent to which ordinary people are exposed to opportunities for it (which is among other things affected very much by the range of the activities of the state).[26]

All these aspects clearly interact with each other.

New States and the Concept of Corruption

It is clear that new states are very likely to be the scene of a great deal of behavior that will be called corrupt. Neither attitudes nor material conditions in these countries are focused on the support of a single concept of the national interest or of the official purposes of state and local officers and institutions which would promote that interest. We can consider this under the headings outlined above:

1. The idea of the national interest is weak because the idea of a nation is new. And the institutions and offices of the states are, for most people, remote and perplexing. Even to the civil servants and politicians directly involved in them they are new; they are aware of the "official purposes" which are attached to them by importation, but they scarcely regard them as "hallowed" and hence they do not necessarily regard them as sacrosant.[27] On the contrary their western

origin makes them suspect. To many people the "state" and its organs were identified with alien rule and were proper objects of plunder,[28] and they have not yet been reidentified fully as instruments for the promotion of common interests. Meanwhile to the illiterate peasant the "state" and its organs continue to be the source of a web of largely unknowable and complicated regulations, and hence of a permanent threat of punishment; against this threat it is very reasonable to take any available precaution, such as offering bribes. Some official purposes of public office are challenged by strongly supported counter-conceptions, especially the strong obligations of family, tribe, and district in the matter of awarding jobs, scholarships, or other scarce commodities in the gift of the state. Neither politicians nor civil servants are usually drawn from a class brought up for public service from an early age, or insulated from corrupting pressures by the established aloofness of a mandarin class. And to the extent that the rules of public morality lean ultimately on the strength of the rules of private morality, they are weakened by the hammer blows delivered to all moral rules by rapid social and economic change.

2. The incentive to corrupt whatever official purposes public institutions are agreed to have is especially great in conditions of extreme inequality and considerable absolute poverty. The benefits of holding an office—any office—are relatively enormous; by comparison the penalties for attempting to obtain one by bribery are fairly modest, in relation to the low standard of living of the would-be office holder, or in relation to the pressure of relatives' claims on his existing standard of living. Generally, corruption seems likely to be inseparable from great inequality.

3. Corruption is relatively easy to conceal in the new states. Partly this is because people are generally not too clear about what the official rules are, or what (*really*) constitutes breaking them; or if they are clear, it may be because they do not greatly resent their being broken, and so are not zealous to prevent corruption. Partly it is because the law is ineffectively enforced and the police themselves may not be immune from corruption. And while traditional gift-giving can be distinguished from a bribe of money, it is quite obvious that from the point of view of the giver the one has shaded into the other, so that although the practice has taken on a new significance, as the open gift of a chicken is replaced by a more furtive gift of a pound note, it is nevertheless an established fact of life, in which the precise nature of the rule-infringement is partially concealed by continuity with an older custom.[29]

To say all this is only to explain, however, why there is likely to be much behavior in new states that will be called corrupt. It is not to say anything about the "level" of morality of the citizens of these countries. It is only to say that, poised as they are between the inherited public morality of the western nation-state and the disappearing public morality of the tribe, they are subject to very considerable cross-pressures which make it unlikely that the western state morality, at least in its refined and detailed forms, will emerge as the new public morality of these countries; meantime, however, the criteria of the West have sufficient standing in some quarters to ensure that the accusation of corruption is freely levelled against all behavior which does not conform to them. To go much beyond this is, in the apt words of Lucy Mair, to ignore

> the kind of social pressure that is in fact responsible for the practice of the virtues that are cherished in any given society. Good men do not practice . . . industry in circumstances where this would lead to a reduction in piece-rates.[30]

What Is the Problem in New States?

Of course there are ample grounds for *concern,* if not for moralizing, about corruption in new states. The most important of them can probably be best isolated by making the comparison with Britain again, but from a different point of view.

Wraith and Simpkins tend to present a picture of Britain, for instance, as having been—around 1800—the scene of great corruption, which was then quite remarkably eliminated. However, the prevalence and the robustness, so to speak, of the practices which they, following the Victorian reformers, regard as corrupt, suggests a rather different interpretation; namely that according to the previously obtaining moral code many of these practices were not corrupt, but either had no moral significance, or indeed were actually quite right and desirable. For instance, the average landlord thought it quite natural, and to that extent desirable, that his tenants should use their votes on behalf of his favored candidate and did not hesitate to put pressure on them to this end. Jobbery, sinecures, rotten boroughs, treating, and other colorful political practices of the period were practiced with an openness that shows that they were not regarded as improper by those whose opinions mattered.[31] What is really remarkable is the rapidity and completeness of the reformers' victory during the nineteenth century.

What seems to have happened is that the ruling classes were induced to accept an altered perception of the nature of the public interest and so to redefine the purposes of the public offices and state institutions which remained, during most of this period, still under their control. It was precisely because they already had a clear notion of the public interest that the assertion of the new notion was established with such completeness. What was involved was not the establishment for the first time of a set of ideas about how public offices and institutions were to serve the public interest, but the adaptation of an established set. Britain did not, in other words, pass from a corrupt condition to a very pure one; rather it passed from one set of standards to another, *through* a period in which behavior patterns which were acceptable by the old standards came to be regarded as corrupt according to the new. It is arguable that, at the height of this experience, public life in Britain was not much less "pure" than it is today. Certainly the records of so-called corruption in the early nineteenth century have about them an air of innocence which is largely lacking in the literature on the same subject in America.

Such innocence is also absent from the portrait of corruption in modern Nigeria drawn in the novels of, for instance, Chinua Achebe and Cyprian Ekwensi, and no doubt this partly explains the compulsive moralism of so many commentators on it. In Britain the corruption of public office was by a ruling class who *had* had a clear conception, even if in the end it was rather tenuous, of the public interest and the duty they owed to it by their use of the public offices and institutions under their control, a conception which complemented their frank exploitation of those offices and institutions for personal gain. In the era of reform they eventually accepted a redefinition of the principles governing the use of those offices and institutions and this, together with the other adaptations on their part, in large measure ensured their survival as a ruling class.

By contrast the ruling classes of Africa are new classes, exercising a new rule. Only a minority have been brought up in ruling-class circles. The idea contained in the phrase, *noblesse oblige,* scarcely applies. There is no previous experience, and so no prior ideology, of the roles of public offices and institutions in relation to the public interest, in terms of which the private exploitation of public office could be rationalized. There *is* a prevailing conception of the national interest and dedication to popular welfare. But it is precisely this idea that may be called into question by the way in which public office is actually exploited by those who occupy it. They have publicly accepted, at least by implication, the official purposes officially attached to public offices and institutions by the colonial powers. If their practice is indefensible by any standards which they are publicly prepared to defend, it robs the whole business of any air of innocence, and this is what provoked Dumont's reluctant protest against the creation in Africa of "a bourgeoisie of a new type, which Karl Marx could scarcely have foreseen, a bourgeoisie of the public service."[32]

The contrast between this contemporary phenomenon and the English scene in the early nineteenth century can be exaggerated. But it would not be hard to sharpen it further. Before the era of reform there were, as well as sinecures worth thousands of pounds, exacting civil service jobs which were not paid enough to induce anyone competent to occupy them, and which consequently were made attractive only by perquisites. Government-provided services, too, tended to be needed primarily by the relatively affluent sections of the population. And the idea was broadly accepted that well-born young men had some sort of entitlement to be maintained in one capacity or another in the public service. By contrast, in contemporary Africa public service is not merely paid well, in relation to local income levels, but lavishly;[33] government services affect the ordinary citizen in numerous ways, not as a luxury but as a conventional (or even an actual) necessity; and there is no accepted "natural" ruling élite. In any case, these eighteenth-century ideas do not seem to have been invoked in defense of "corruption" by those engaged in it today.

This is, perhaps, the main reason for the automatic condemnation of these widespread behavior patterns by most contemporary commentators, and it seems rather reasonable. For to the extent that the official public morality of a society is more or less systematically subverted, especially if the leadership is involved in it, it becomes useless as a tool for getting things done, and this is expensive in any society where other resources are scarce. What is involved here is the idea of a "corrupted society."

It seems impossible to declare that a society without an effective public morality *cannot* develop economically. On the other hand, there do seem to be reasons for doubting whether in African conditions this is likely to happen. In the first place, most African states are extremely dependent upon government action for their development. Their development prospects largely depend on attaining the targets chartered in development plans, and by very fine margins. This requires single-minded hard work from all holders of public office. If the top political élite of a country consumes its time and energy in trying to get rich by corrupt means, it is not likely that the development plans will be fulfilled.

Secondly, if this is the pattern of behavior of the élite and if this is fairly well known, it is likely to rob them of much of their authority both with subordinates in the government and with political followers in the countryside. The country will be apt to forfeit whatever benefits can be derived by the output of effort not solely motivated by the hope of personal gain.

Thirdly, the wealth improperly accumulated by the top élite may be modest by world standards, but still large in relation to the level of investment on which the economic development of the country depends. In this case much will turn on how such wealth is redeployed. If political leaders try to buy security by depositing their wealth in numbered accounts in Swiss banks it represents a wholly negative drain on the economy.[34] (But perhaps they will buy farms and make them very productive.) Fourthly, if the top élite flout the public moral code which is cherished by "donor" nations the supply of foreign aid may diminish.

The likelihood of the last two developments seems remote. The possibility which seems most solid and even obvious is the first; there are perfectly plain differences to be seen between one developing nation and another in terms of the amount of public spirit and devotion to duty shown by their élites, and the idea of a society economically stagnating in the grip of a self-seeking and corrupt élite is not a pure fantasy. The line of escape from such a situation is also fairly clear. Typically, a nucleus of "puritans"—drawn from groups such as an independent business class, professional groups, or small farmers— begins to exercise effective pressure to apply the official but disregarded public code of ethics.

By and large this was the experience of the reform movement in America. The moral vulnerability of the ruling groups was very great, and so piecemeal advance was possible. Distinctions were gradually insisted upon which narrowed the area of operation of self-interest and widened that of the public interest; it came to be held, for instance, that "private profit by public servants at the expense of the public welfare was corrupt; but private profit by public servants obtained as a *concomitant* to service in the general welfare was quite proper."[35] (A similar distinction was drawn by Achebe's hero when he took to accepting bribes: "But Obi stoutly refused to countenance anyone who did not possess the minimum educational and other requirements. On that he was unshakeable.")[36] The result in America is a patchwork: the scope of political patronage has been greatly reduced and the cash bribery of higher public servants largely eliminated. At the same time, large areas of public life have so far remained more or less immune to reform, and practices that in one sphere would be regarded as corrupt are almost taken for granted in another.

The question is where the puritans are to come from in the new states, with their prevailing lack of economically independent professional and middle classes and the corresponding weakness of the puritan ethos; and whether the puritans in new states can succeed by gradualist means, rather than by revolution.

Notes

1. The best known English study is perhaps Norman Gash's *Politics in the Age of Peel* (London, 1953). Much of the American literature is reviewed in V.O. Key, *Politics, Parties and Pressure Groups* (New York, 1955), chap. 13, "Party Machine as Interest Group." See also *The Annals of the American Academy of Political and Social Science* (Philadelphia), March 1952, special number on "Ethical Standards in American Public Life." The wide range of reports of commissions of enquiry into colonial malpractice is indicated in the footnotes to Ronald Wraith and Edgar Simpkins' recent work *Corruption in Developing Countries* (London, 1963). While the bulk of this material is from West Africa and deals with local government, there are valuable reports from East Africa, and also from India and Malaya and elsewhere. Unfortunately I have not had an opportunity to study Professor Van Klaveren's series of articles in *Vierteljahrschrift für Sozial- und Wirtschaftsgeschichte* since 1957, referred to in his comments on M.G. Smith's "Historical and Cultural Conditions of Political Corruption among the Hausa," in *Comparative Studies in Society and History* (The Hague), January 1964, pp. 164–198.
2. An interesting and ably-written exception is M. McMullan, "A Theory of Corruption," *A Sociological Review* (Keele), July 1961; pp. 181–201. The author has, however, a rather restricted conception of what corruption is, and a number of unwarrantable assumptions about the results.
3. Wraith and Simpkins, *Corruption in Developing Countries,* pp. 12–13 and 172.
4. Wraith and Simpkins, p. 35.
5. Wraith and Simpkins, p. 45.
6. The authors display a militant ignorance of sociological theory and research, which may be partly a consequence of their reluctance to abandon their ethical absolutism, but seems more a part of the settled philistinism on this matter which is still so depressingly common in Britain. "It is always unwise" (they write of social anthropology) "to argue with exponents of this formidable science, since they have their own vocabulary, which differs from that of the ordinary man, and their own concepts, which are not readily understood" (p. 172), and they proceed to represent the main burden of the social anthropologist's contributions on the subject as being to the effect that all corruption in their sense is the African's idea of a customary gift. One is provoked to echo Campbell-Bannerman's exasperated reply to the outmoded dialectics of Balfour: "Enough of this foolery."
7. *Uganda Parliamentary Debates,* 27 September 1963, pp. 179–200, and 3 October 1963, pp. 411–21. The Uganda government subsequently denied that any such sale had taken place.
8. *Report of the Commission of Enquiry into the Working of Port Harcourt Town Council, 1955;* quoted in Wraith and Simpkins, p. 22.

9. *Third Interim Report of the Senate Committee to Investigate Organised Crime in Interstate Commerce, 1951* (Kefauver Committee), quoted in H.A. Turner, *Politics in the United States* (New York, 1955), p. 412.

10. From the Storey Report, *Commission of Inquiry into the Administration of Lagos Town Council, 1953* (Lagos, 1954).

11. William Turner, "In Defence of Patronage," in *The Annals of the American Academy of Political and Social Science,* January 1937, pp. 22–8, and William J. Riordan, *Plunkitt of Tammany Hall* (New York, 1958). Plunkitt coined the phrase "honest graft" in a famous passage:

> There's an honest graft, and I'm example of how it works. I might sum up the whole thing by sayin': "I seen my opportunities and I took 'em." Just let me explain by examples. My party's in power in the city and it's goin' to undertake a lot of public improvements. Well, I'm tipped off, say, that they're going to lay out a new park at a certain place. I see my opportunity and I take it. I go to that place and I buy up all the land I can in the neighborhood. Then the board of this or that makes its plan public and there is a rush to get that land which nobody cared particular for before. Ain't it perfectly honest to charge a good profit and make a profit on my investment and foresight? Of course it is. Well, that's honest graft.

12. V.O. Key, pp. 395–98.

13. M. McMullan, p. 197.

14. Bert F. Hoselitz, "Levels of Economic Performance and Bureaucratic Structures," in La Palombara (ed.), *Bureaucracy and Political Development* (Princeton, 1963), p. 190.

15. Wraith and Simpkins, p. 172; although previously they do say "The economic effects of all this [corruption] on a country may not be very considerable." McMullan also believes the economic costs are high, but his definition of economic cost appears to be somewhat Gladstonian, "A Theory of Corruption," p. 182.

16. For an interesting discussion of the general question, see C.C. Wrigley, *Crops and Wealth in Uganda* (Kampala, 1959), pp. 70–73.

17. *Uganda Parliamentary Debates,* 8 November 1963, pp. 108–12, and 11 November 1963, pp. 137–42. Corruption was alleged by the opposition.

18. M. Fainsod, *How Russia Is Ruled* (Cambridge, Mass., 1958), p. 437.

19. For a brief but penetrating comment on this see W. Arthus Lewis, *The Theory of Economic Growth* (London, 1955), pp. 428–29.

20. Chinua Achebe provides a fascinating selection in *No Longer at East* (London, 1960), pp. 5–6 and 87–88. See also E.C. Banfield, *The Moral Basis of a Backward Society* (Chicago, 1958), ch. 5.

21. *Report of the Tribunal Appointed to Inquire into Allegations Reflecting on the Official Conduct of the Premier of, and Certain Persons Holding Ministerial and other Public Offices in, the Eastern Region of Nigeria* (London, 1957).

22. *Lord Denning's Report* (London, 1963).

23. Wraith and Simpkins ally themselves with the analogous minority in West Africa whom they identify as "the most eminent and responsible citizens" of these countries, p. 173. It appears that Chinua Achebe should be included among these, and to this extent it is permissible to wonder how typical are the reactions of his hero in *No Longer at Ease,* who has an ultimate and profound revulsion against his own acceptance of bribes.

24. *Uganda Parliamentary Debates,* 27 September 1963, p. 187.
25. McMullan, p. 182, takes the orthodox view: "Investors and entrepreneurs are frustrated and dismayed and may find that the unofficial cost of starting an enterprise is too great for it to be profitable." Another view is that this is one method of reducing excess profits. In the case of extractive industries this has some plausibility. McMullan points out (p. 197) that "a group under harsh disability but still possessed of considerable wealth" provides the "optimum conditions for corruption" and that it is perhaps another "useful" function of corruption to enable economically energetic ethnic minorities to protect themselves.
26. An official study of civil service corruption in Malaya in the 1950s found much more corruption in those departments of government which provide extensive services than in those which do not.
27. Dr. Lucy Mair has put this excellently: "They cast for a play in which the *dramatis personae* are enumerated but the lines are not written. The new African governments are recruited from new men . . . The relationship of the leader with his followers, of ministers with their colleagues, with bureaucrats, with the general public, are new relationships." *The New Nations* (London, 1963), p. 123.
28. Senator Kefauver's comment on the attitude of Americans to colonial administration before the American Revolution: "In a sense the whole populace engaged in the profitable process of mulcting the government— which was after all a hated tyrant—of every possible penny"; *The Annals of the American Academy of Political and Social Science,* March 1952, p. 2.
29. See the interesting and detailed discussion of this in A.W. Southall and P.C.W. Gutkind, *Townsmen in the Making* (Kampala, 1957), p. 189–94.
30. Lucy Mair, pp. 124–25.
31. "In the latter half of the eighteenth century *it was taken for granted* that the purpose for going into parliament or holding any public office was to make or repair a man's personal fortune." R.M. Jackson, *The Machinery of Local Government* (London, 1958), p. 345. (Italics mine.) It seems clear that during this period there was a tendency for this attitude to become more widespread and the consequences more extensive and expensive, and that this in turn aided the development of the reform movement. However, the use of public office for private gain was a recognised public practice going back to a period in English history when these distinctions were still imperfectly worked out.
32. R. Dumont, *L'Afrique noire est mal partie* (Paris, 1962), p. 66.
33. Cf. Dumont's notorious comparison: "A deputy works (?) for three months a year, but receives from 120,000 to 165,000 CFA per month. In six months of salary—i.e. in one and a half months' work—he makes as much as the average African peasant in 36 years, in a whole life of hard labor."
34. See, e.g., Frantz Fanon, *Les Damnés de la terre,* quoted by Dumont, pp. 67–68.
35. Kefauver, Ref. 2, p. 3.
36. Chinua Achebe, *No Longer at Ease* (London, 1910), p. 169.

The Evolution of Public Office Roles: An Introduction

The approach emphasized in Chapter Two centers on the public office concept and attempts to trace how in the process of modernization and bureaucratization in Western societies the holders of public offices came to be subject to norms and rules that were scarcely applicable to their predecessors. The selection of articles is guided by the aim of illustrating how, in the process of modernization, distinct public responsibilities were gradually built into the public-office concept, how earlier property claims to office were gradually disappropriated, and how bureaucratic concepts of the office were introduced in varying ways in European and American political systems.

Public Offices in Prebureaucratic Systems

In framing his definition of the public official's position within modern bureaucratic systems, Max Weber stressed contrasts to practices in prebureaucratic systems, which serve as a key take-off point for this discussion:

> Legally and actually, officeholding is not considered ownership of a source of income, to be exploited for rents or emoluments in exchange for the rendering of certain services, as was normally the case in the Middle Ages. . . . Rather entrance into an office . . . is considered an acceptance of a specific duty or fealty to the purpose of the office in return for the grant of a secure existence. It is decisive for the modern loyalty to an office that, in the pure type, it does not establish a relationship to a person, like the vassal's or disciple's faith under feudal or patrimonial authority, but rather is devoted to impersonal and functional purposes.[1]

Among the varieties of premodern, prebureaucratic systems the most important was that based upon patrimonial domination. The Inca society, discussed by Jacob van Klavern in chapter six, clearly fits into the category. Under patrimonial systems a ruler could legitimately engage in a self- or family-centered distribution of the national income to the extreme of the Inca model, but whether or not he tried to do so, no one could seek to challenge his decision making as illegitimate or corrupt.[2] One can therefore agree with Van Klaveren that "by definition, corruption does not occur" in the Inca and other systems based upon pure patrimonial domination.

In feudal Europe the problem was not that all constitutional and economic power was centralized in one ruler but rather that offices had come to be perceived as properties rather than being associated with assigned duties. As the "appropriation" of offices progressed, the ruler's power fell apart into various powers, which became the property of various privileged individuals. As Weber argued, "Whatever traces of an objectively defined official duty there are disappear altogether with the treatment of the office as benefice or property."[3]

Public Office as Benefice or Property

The appropriation of benefices to officeholders was seen by Weber as characteristic both of the feudal system and of the early modern patrimonial-bureaucratic state. The feudal period was most strongly associated with *landed benefices,* which assigned office land for the incumbent's own use in the manner of a fief, thus giving the benefice holder and his heirs great autonomy from the ruler. Under early modern patrimonialism there was some reassertion of the ruler's control, but this period was characterized by the widespread and continued use of fee benefices, under which the ruler assigned to a favorite or to a purchaser the right to receive certain fees due him from his subjects. Thus the office could also become hereditary in the family of the original favorite or turn into the patrimonial possession of the purchaser.

In the early patrimonial-bureaucratic state the practice of remunerating officials by means of fees had the effect of making the officials' income largely dependent upon his "rapacity and ingenuity." It is thus seen by Koenraad W. Swart (Selection Seven) and others to have been "very irrational" from the perspective of developing a responsible administrative instrument. However, says Swart, "the system . . . had great advantages in a society in which it was difficult to check on local officials because of a widespread dishonesty, relatively large distances, and a primitive administrative technique. In this way much accounting and transferring of money was avoided, and the official was interested in the execution of his duties."

The Growth of a Permanent Officialdom

The Sale of Offices

In many parts of continental Europe the reemergence of a powerful merchant class and the growing importance of a highly developed money economy soon resulted in something like a "refeudalization" of large parts of the career officialdom. For in order to meet pressing financial demands, rulers adopted, to varying degrees, the practice of selling office *(venalitè des offices),* which became objects of trade and exchange. The purchasers of these offices served in them as a matter of right, and thus the king was prevented from choosing his officials on the basis of their ability or reliability.

Royal rulers during this period of absolution were still not subject to any significant constitutional rules that limited their choice of alternative techniques for achieving the goals of the state. Had they been subject to such rules, they would have run as much chance of being accused of corruption for selling judgeships as do contemporary American presidents for appointing large campaign contributors to ambassadorial positions. For once the sale of offices became officially regulated so that the proceeds flowed into the treasuries of the king and the state, they ceased to constitute a drain of public resources toward private-regarding ends. The king used the proceeds from the sale of offices to meet the costs of military campaigns, just as contemporary parties use financial contributions to meet the costs of election campaigns, and both procedures are seen as goals asserted to be related to the public interest.

Van Klaveren perceives that excessive private-regarding resource extraction during this period can be conceived of in terms of "corruption." From this perspective the main question is: Which group of officeholders would tend to be relatively more conscientious and relatively less greedy—those who received their office because they were favorites of the king or those who purchased their office from the king? Montesquieu was one of a number of reform-minded writers of the time who actually supported the sale of public office over other methods of appointment because "change will furnish better subjects than the prince's choice."[4] Thus, whereas today the venality of office is considered a form of political corruption, it was then perceived as a check on corruption. Jeremy Bentham, who saw the British aristocracy as being particularly prone to self-indulgence, also favored the sale-of-office principle, because he believed that it would allow more of the wealthier and more moral middle-class types to have access to high government posts.[5]

Appointments in Exchange for Parliamentary Support

By comparison with contemporaneous practices in France, fewer offices were sold and more were given away by the crown in eighteenth-century Britain. This was primarily due to the fact that the British monarch's ministers had an overriding concern that their French equivalents did not have to face up to: they had to maintain pro-government majorities in an elected parliament. In Britain it was not so much administrative posts as seats in the House of Commons that had acquired a quasi-proprietary character—"they were a valuable inheritance or a costly acquisition from which proper returns were expected."[6] Some members ensured their reelection through tiny electorates by personal favors or family influence; others felt themselves primarily responsible to small cliques of powerful patrons in their respective constituencies. By the early eighteenth century the promise of government jobs had become a main means through which pro-government members of Parliament rounded up marginal voters in their boroughs. By the time of the accession of George III, in many boroughs "few extensive electoral interests could be maintained except with the help of Government patronage lavished at the recommendation of the borough patron."[7] These practices were long legitimatized by "a universal belief that the politically active portion of the community had a legitimate claim to maintenance by the State, just as the medieval knight had a claim to maintenance by the lord."[8]

Public-Office Conceptions in Britain and America

Whereas the Continental code-law countries could easily remodel their legal systems through the adoption of comprehensive codes, norms in the English-speaking countries had to be operationalized in terms of a more complex sequence of legislative and judicial acts and precedents. Thus, even in the twentieth century discussions of public officers and their duties have had to be very circuitous because "the terminology and the precedents relied upon in interpretation developed before public administration had developed its present scope and complexity."[9]

In Britain judicial decisions that serve as important precedent date back to the beginning of the civil service reform movement there, especially a 1783 decision which held that "a man accepting an office of trust concerning the public, especially if attended with profit, is answerable criminally to the king for misbehavior in his office." American and English courts have followed the same rule that the public officer, occupying a position of trust, is bound by the duties of a fiduciary.

Finer's examination (Selection Eight) of the sharply contrasting developments of public service rules in the two countries in the early part of the nineteenth century is highly illuminating. After the successful revolution against the British mother country, with its traditional society and the mutual obligations that it had engendered, the original American public service was spartan and honest compared to "the loaded compost heap of corrupt influence," which was Burke's characterization of its British equivalent. But soon the development of party competition developed in the United States the same incentives that in Britain had triggered the development of the "old" patronage system: administrative appointments had to be used for the purchase of electoral and legislative support. In Britain a two-party system was also developing; but in contrast to post-Jacksonian America, the administrative service became gradually severed from and insulated against party political influences. Helpful to the British reformers was the fact that the phenomenon that became most characteristic of the "new" American patronage, namely the rotation of offices as the "ins" became the "outs," had earlier not been widely prevalent in Britain because the freehold concept of office had made it legally difficult for incumbents to be "expropriated."

How can one compare practices that are illegal in terms of legal standards which non-western countries have imported from the West, with similar behaviors that were tolerated by both legal and moral standards in western countries some centuries ago? This problem is addressed by James C. Scott in an excerpt from a longer study which concentrates on contrasts between corrupt practices in Tudor and Stuart England and contemporary developing countries like Thailand.

He makes a case for comparing practices that are corrupt only by modern standards so as to facilitate inquiry into their causes in different periods and locales, as well as their effect on the composition of elites. "If nepotism or bribery have similar causes and consequences in early France as in contemporary India, that is an important subject for analysis, notwithstanding the fact that legal codes and public standards have changed so much that what was tolerated (not corrupt) in early France is now forbidden by law (corrupt) in India?"

Scott proposes that earlier practices that anticipate behaviors later stigmatized as corrupt be labelled examples of 'proto-corruption.' Such a terminological usage would in some ways parallel the manner in which historians distinguish between the parliamentary factions which are seen as constituting 'proto-parties' in the eighteenth century House of Commons before the conventions of cabinet government led to the development of fully-fledged political parties in the nineteenth century.

Scott's approach to destigmatizing the study of corruption is to regard it as one form of influence among others—including those more legitimately based, such as those based on considerations of ideology and equity. He suggests that enhancing the analytical capacity of social scientists should take precedence over their role as labelling agents on behalf of a particular set of moral values. He argues that his approach highlights "the functional equivalence of a variety of acts of political influence—some of which violate all standards of community ethics and some of which are totally beyond reproach."

Scott also cautions social scientists and historians to be aware of how their attitudes toward regimes in which corruption occurs can affect their implicit attitudes. He points out that present-day observers can find corruption in earlier systems, which involved the subversion of an aristocratic monopoly of government, ideologically less unacceptable than they might in instances of corruption in liberal democratic or socialist regimes, where wealth may be used to undermine egalitarian values which they themselves might be inclined to share.

Notes

1. Max Weber, *Economy and Society,* III, New York: Bedminster Press, 1968, p. 959.
2. Weber, *Economy and Society,* p. 1007.
3. Weber, *Economy and Society,* p. 1040.
4. Charles Secondat de Montesquieu, *The Spirit of the Laws,* New York: Hafner, 1949, p. 69.
5. Jeremy Bentham, "The Rationale of Reward," *Works,* Vol. 5, Edinburgh, 1863, pp. 246–248.
6. Donald Kingsley, *Representative Democracy,* Yellow Springs, Ohio: Antioch Press, 1944, p. 26.
7. Sir Lewis B. Namier, *The Structure of Politics of the Accession of George III,* 2d ed. New York: St. Martin's, 1957, p. 169.
8. Kingsley, *Representative Democracy,* p. 26.
9. Arthur W. MacMahon, "Public Office," *Encyclopedia of the Social Sciences,* VI, p. 665.

6

Corruption as a Historical Phenomenon

Jacob van Klaveren

Corruption as a historical phenomenon is, to the best of my knowledge, a problem that has never been dealt with systematically. The reason probably is that corruption has not been regarded as a problem. This point of view is completely justified as long as corruption is only perceived as a series of accidental acts of dishonesty on the part of civil servants. He who examines this subject more carefully, however, recognizes that the phenomenon occurred much more frequently prior to the French Revolution and that it was almost constitutionally determined. In this paper, too, corruption shall be examined as an [unwritten] part of a political constitution.

Constitutions[1] and Corruption

There are two types of constitutions under which corruption, by definition, does not occur—namely in the case of monarchy when interpreted as absolute one-man rule, and in the case of constitutions built upon the idea of popular sovereignty. Thus in this respect one could say *les extrèmes se touchent.*

First we shall discuss the Inca state as the closest approximation to the model of absolute monarchy. Here all the resources of the country were claimed for an economic plan that served the glorification of the ruler and the sun cult. Since there were no productive factors left untapped, it was impossible for civil servants to divert more revenues than were already allocated to them by the king in the economic plan. The incomes of civil servants and the people were precisely determined according to social position. This even affected nutrition pat-

Source: Jacob van Kalveren, "Die historische Erscheinung der Korruption, in ihrem Zusammenhang mit der Staats- und Gesellschafsstruktur betrachtet." *Vierteljahreschrift f Sozial u. Wirtschaftsgeschichte*, 44:4 (1957), pp. 294–302, 312–318. By permission of the publisher, Franz Steiner Verlag. Translated by Peggy Hofmann and Karl Kurtz.

terns, number of wives, and the quality of the clothes that were distributed. A governor of the Inca caste received vicuña clothes from the public storehouses, while the people's clothes were made from llama wool. The people walked; the Sapa Inca and the high civil servants of Inca origin were carried in sedan chairs.[2] Thus everyone received an appropriate income, and to claim more constituted an offense against the Sapa Inca and the sun cult. This distribution of the national income to the furthering of the commonweal was based on ethical and religious values, but was centripetally oriented toward the glorification of the Sapa Inca and the sun.

It will be intelligible without more ado that this *ex-ante* distribution of the national income by means of an economic plan in a natural economy . . . could be realized rather easily. This task becomes more complicated in a money economy. The presence of money is a symptom of the existence of an exchange economy, which is not to say that an exchange economy could not also exist without money. In an exchange or market economy, quasi-anonymous forces determine the extent of employment and the distribution of the national income. It could only be confirmed afterward, but not regulated in advance whether all productive forces of a nation were really utilized fully and for what ends, and whether every social group obtained the income deemed appropriate on ethical grounds. Only through the techniques of modern economic policy is it possible nowadays to determine in advance not only the size of the national product but its distribution. In this process the market economy is regulated and the functions of money are to a large extent eliminated or at least influenced into a desired direction through a public monetary policy.

These modern possibilities were still unknown at the beginning of the twentieth century and are even nowadays not available for the less-developed countries. Thus if we posit an absolute monarchy existing simultaneously with a money economy, we could assume for the above-mentioned reason that it would be impossible to carry out a patriarchal distribution of income on the Inca model. The monarch could obtain from the people through taxes what he deems necessary for himself and the public civil service, but he would always be lagging behind developments by one phase. Although he is not able to dictate to his subjects what constitutes appropriate income, he can compellingly prescribe the income appropriate to the civil servants and penalize all cases of corruption. To this extent the monarchy has a beneficial effect on the broad mass of the population. This is not to say, however, that the monarch will always act in this manner. It is possible that he might allow his civil servants to maximize their income in dealing with the public.[3] However, this would loosen the relationship between the civil servants and the monarch's decision-making power. The civil service hierarchy would disintegrate into a number of "maximizing units," each with its own interests, and would thus become unreliable for the execution of the national policy.[4] The more developed the monarchy, the greater its corruption-checking tendency, to the point that corruption disappears completely in an absolute monarchy, as in the case of the Inca state.

We shall now discuss the other polar situation. Let us assume that the common good is not found in an almost metaphysical way by a sovereign prince in the sense similar to Rousseau's *volonté générale* but is ascertained by an expression of opinion by the people. Let us assume further that the popular will is genuinely reflected in the nation's policy. Thus there incontestably exists a situation of popular sovereignty, and the civil servants are only executive instruments of the people's will. It goes without saying that it can never be the people's will to be exploited by the civil servants, and this is just the inevitable consequence of corruption. Therefore, the people will precisely prescribe the income appropriate to the civil servants and will not tolerate corruption. As a result corruption can never be rooted in the constitution and can only occur as occasional acts of dishonesty.[5]

What we have described here are two extreme ideal types, which will never be fully realized. However, the contrast between them should make evidence which circumstances determine whether corruption is built into the constitution. Corruption is built on the underlying principle that the people are subjected to the control of officials. Thus there exists a regulating principle, which gives to the officials and other intermediary groups a public existence with a purpose of their own. We divide these intermediary groups into those that are created by the monarch, that is, the public officials, and those which have autonomous origins, that is, the traditional intermediary groups. Among the latter are the landlords but also the urban patricians. Without a monarchy there would be no royal civil servants but only the civil servants who serve traditional intermediary groups. These have, however, been historically less significant than the royal civil servants; therefore, we shall pass them by. Similarly, among the traditional intermediary groups we will consider only the urban patricians.

These intermediary groups have rights of their own. The people exist not only for the king, but also for the intermediary group. The monarch may adjust to letting these intermediary groups claim what they regard as their due portion of the national income. It is obvious that relevant opinions may diverge, in which case tensions may occur. There may ensue a struggle around the distribution of the national income, which takes place in a field encompassed by a conflict triangle whose pillars are the monarch, the civil service, and the urban oligarchy. The intermediary forces tend to nurture corruption, whereas the monarchy tends to check corruption. However, the intermediate groups do not necessarily stick together; on the contrary, quite often the civil service is created by the monarch during the struggle with the traditional intermediary groups. There then tends to ensue a rechanneling of corruption incomes in favor of civil servants and courtiers, although the total amount of corruption incomes may well decrease.

In his study *Deutsches Städteleben in der älteren Zeit (German City Life)* Gustav Schmoller[6] emphasized the corruption-checking effect of the monarchy. However, he exhaustively discussed the tendency of intermediary groups to further corruption only where blame was attached to the city oligarchy. This, of course, is due to the topic of his study but is also significant for his mentality. Corruption by civil servants is only mentioned where an honest historiography cannot avoid it. It is his major concern to correct those historians who, influenced by the Enlightenment, had viewed the "free" cities as "democratic" communities whose character had supposedly been aborted by the encroachment of the Prussian princes. Schmoller is perfectly right to correct this widely prevalent but erroneous idea and to point out that these very cities were breeding places of oligarchic despotism and corruption and had no claim to being considered democratic.[7]

This error is, by the way, very widespread, and is reflected in the title of a study by Pirenne, dealing with *Les anciennes démocraties des Pays Bas* (Paris, 1922). At the end of the eighteenth century there were in the Netherlands several thinkers influenced by the Enlightenment, who praised "grand pensionaries" Johann van Oldenbarneveldt and Johann de Witt, who fell victims to the hostility of the House of Orange, as martyrs in the struggle against tyranny. In reality, however, these proud patricians were the last to be concerned with the promotion of popular influence.[8] Even Cunningham falls into this error in his thorough and learned study *The Growth of English Industry and Commerce,* in which he asserts that democracies are more often corrupt and inefficient than are autocratic governments.[9] This, however, is impossible since democracy—as we have seen—is without corruption by definition. If, on the other hand one recognizes that Cunningham identifies democracy with the rule of parliament, then this statement carries more truth. One sees here that the conception of "democracy" was already completely diffuse by the end of the nineteenth century, although its identifying characteristics can be precisely determined on the basis of an exact analysis of the ideas of the Enlightenment.[10] Therefore, we prefer to avoid this expression as far as possible, and to speak instead of constitutions that honestly reflect the people's will. If one identifies democracy with the government of parliament, as Cunningham does, then the Magna Charta, which the English nobility extracted from John Lackland in 1215, could be regarded as the beginning of English democracy, since parliament was founded then. That would be incorrect. While correcting Cunningham in this regard, one may otherwise agree with him since he is stating only what has been extrapolated above, namely that intermediary groups tend to further corruption. His reference is primarily to the rural squires that were then dominant in Parliament, so that particularly for the period after 1688 one may speak of a "squirearchy." However, for Prussia, which is examined by Schmoller, and with respect to the Netherlands, the city oligarchies are more significant. Schmoller maintains that the kings, by integrating the cities into the Prussian national state, rid them of "oligarchic corruption" and extended to them an "honest and well-regulated administration." However, he feels forced to admit some reservations, particularly for the age of the soldier-king Frederick William I (1730–1740). Schmoller admits that the groups from which the civil service was recruited were not at all "ethically pure," and that a decay of the civil servants' morality must be noted during the reigns of Frederick the Great and Fredick Wilhelm II, although this did not lead back to the nadir marked during the reign of the Great Elector (1640–1688).[11]

We must contradict Schmoller as well if he thinks that his description of the situation explains a gradual transition from an "oligarchic corruption" to the—in our sense—"honest" city regulation of 1808.[12] The later reform is, in our view, rooted in the Enlightenment, which penetrated Prussia after the defeats of Jena and Auerstaedt, even though the intellectual instruments of the reform, the "educated bourgeoisie" which had grown considerably during the eighteenth century, could not participate in the country's government to a great extent until after 1848. Thus it becomes clear that Schmoller's benevolent monarchy and his spontaneous rises and declines of morality will not carry us very far. These are not accidental events; we are concerned with a new epoch of intellectual and cultural history, the age of the Enlightenment, which affected the constitutions of Europe.[13]

Such an optical illusion could not arise with regard to the Netherlands, where the Orange Stadtholder had to flee to England in 1795. The democratic reform party, the "Patriots," had already carried out a type of French Revolution in 1786. However, they were defeated by the hurriedly summoned Prussian forces in 1787, causing their leadership to flee to France. Strongly influenced by Jacobin thought, the exiles returned with the French troops in 1795, took over the government, and established the Republic on modern foundations.[14] One of their leaders, the lawyer Herman Willem Daendels, went as governor to Java and accomplished there what he described as the "sincere and honest political rule of the Netherlands." He established good official salary levels and forbade all forms of corruption, whether at the expense of the state or of the natives. One European civil servant who did not take the sudden reversal seriously and continued to extort from the natives was executed; thus was "honest" administration established.[15]

Monarchy as a Check to Corruption

This section maintains that the tendency of monarchy to check corruption was little developed in Europe during the *ancien régime,* perhaps least of all in England. . . .

The Tendency of the Intermediary Groups to Encourage Corruption

As we have already pointed out, "corruption lay," so to speak, "in the middle."[16] The intermediary groups were the breeding places for corruption. This is generally true for both the traditional intermediary groups and the civil-servant class created by the prince. This distinction gradually disappeared, especially when the civil service was mixed with representatives of the traditional intermediary layers, as was the case in most countries. The only remaining distinction was that the city oligarchies to which we limited ourselves were organized in a collegial manner, whereas the civil servants' underlying structure was hierarchical. Therefore, the internal relations were not quite the same. Of course, the civil servants were quite often organized collegially in "boards," but this was only true for each step of the hierarchy. To begin with we shall overlook the differences and concentrate on the general conditions that are true of both groups.

Every intermediary group has the tendency to set itself apart from the lower ones, thus developing a specific social and economic consciousness. It regards itself as a specific entity of a higher social order that has the right to place itself on a higher economic level than the masses, not on the basis of any specific service to the community but because of its mere existence. But even when its members indulge in notions of their own usefulness to the community, they think of a more or less metaphysically based common good and are inclined to consider their privileged position as a requisite for the divine order. This kind of "service" is not exactly what is demanded by a truly sovereign people.

This was the mentality of Tolstoi's Count Vronsky, who supported the principle of promptly paying a gambling debt to a friend, but thought that one should kick a tailor out the door for his boldness when he time and again appeared to claim payment for his work. He would complain bitterly if this tailor asserted his legal rights; equality before the law was anathema to these strata. In 1768 this same opinion was expressed by the Scottish nobleman who called the businessmen who reclaimed Lady Caithness' furniture "a set of low-lifed creatures."[17]

Of course, these were noblemen, but the intermediary groups of lower origin were no different. The Dutch city patricians were always on the same level as the hereditary nobility, and they were truly convinced that they ruled by divine right.[18] John Evelyn noted with satisfaction in his diary one day that on the previous Sunday the priest had praised the differences of rank and position as being divinely ordered.[19] This mentality is evidenced by many other references. But the remarkable thing is that those civil servants who advanced by virtue of their own skills, but who were not of noble origin, assumed this view. For example, Samuel Pepys[20] succeeded in gradually achieving a more or less equal position among the members of the Naval Board of which he was the secretary. He proudly noted that day when he, like the others, kept his hat on during a conference without any objection from the other gentlemen. Soon he brought himself a sword and a carriage with two beautiful horses.[21]

Thus the intermediary groups were not totally closed, particularly not the civil service, since the work had often to be done by an ambitious member of humble origin like Pepys. Nevertheless, it can be regarded as closed, since such outsiders were assimilated at once. This mentality of the middle groups gradually led its members to believe that they were entitled to a certain conventionally conditioned way of life and the corresponding incomes. It is important for us to note here that the already mentioned standards were rather vague. Even among contemporaries and colleagues there must have been some uncertainty about the rights due to them because of their position. This uncertainty had the effect—and this is what concerns us here—of continuously increasing the demands but never of decreasing them. The tendency of the demands to spiral—and thereby the corruption, too—can be observed among both the civil servants and the city oligarchy. No one wanted to fall behind his colleagues either in his outwardly visible way of life or in the less noticeable size of his income. Thus, even when corruption was thoroughly accepted, there was an astonishing amount of secretiveness, with the result that only little material can be found for these periods as well.

The demands of the intermediary groups were sometimes pushed to a higher level by the shocklike effect of external conditions, for example, by the spread of French fashion during the era of Louis XIV or by the growing acquaintance with Oriental luxury goods. Chinese porcelain, japanned goods, or art objects made out of ivory spread more rapidly the more one believed that he had to keep pace with everyone else. There is no need to emphasize that the women were primarily responsible for this. A comparison between the way of life of the Dutch patricians and the English gentry during the seventeenth and the eighteenth centuries shows a very significant increase of demands as well as of income gained by corruption.[22] On close inspection this would certainly be found to be the case in every country Schmoller[23] has already pointed to an increasing closure in Prussia of the civil service, which became a caste at the same time, as well as an increase in corruption after the death of the simple soldier-king Frederick William I (1713–1740). Undoubtedly, the predominance of French and courtly culture during the reign of Frederick the Great influenced this development. It is clear that the king's way of life had great influence. The courtiers all tried to copy this way of life in miniature, but they had to make sure that they kept their distance, just as it was generally between inferiors and superiors. What was considered an "appropriate" distance was not clear and depended on the superior.[24]

It will be obvious that not even high salaries were a prophylactic against corruption in view of these spiraling demands and the prevailing attitudes. This was particularly true because it was not just *income* that was at stake but the building of a *fortune* in a relatively short period of time in order to allow one's descendants to live the life of gentlemen without having to work.[25] It is hard for us to imagine the high demands made by the intermediary groups of that time. From our point of view, the salaries cannot be considered low. That is, they were rather average by our standards for the lower civil servants; for the higher officials they were nominally almost as high as today's but, of course, much higher in purchasing power.[26] Samuel Pepys made £350 a year. It should be realized that an excellent cook earned £4 a year with room and board, or that a clever widow got by on £6 a year and was still able to give alms.[27] With an income of £350 a year Pepys' fortune increased annually by about £1000.[28] The many figures he notes in his diary show, furthermore, that he was only one of the smaller officials. A high income in itself did not serve the purpose: there had to be some pressure for honesty, which increased at the same rate that the morals and opinions of the time increased in favor of corruption. Only a tyrant could provide order here.

The Forms of Corruption

This section establishes two broad categories of practices: (1) fraud or graft at the expense of the treasury and (2) extortion of the subjects. It is argued that once corruption is tolerated both forms must come into existence. . . .

The Instability of the System of Corruption

This section tries to ascertain how the profits of corruption were divided: (a) between the colleagues of oligarchical bodies and (b) within the official hierarchy. The lack of precise standards led to frictions and generally unstable equilibria of corruptional systems. . . .

Notes

1. Of course, we do conceptualize "constitutions" as referring not only to written constitutions or to those that were framed by a deliberate act of legislation, as many adopted since 1789 have been. Administrative principles are of far more importance, particularly during the *ancien régime,* when they were never developed *ad hoc.* Numerous Asian and Latin-American states today possess written constitutions that tolerate corruption no more than do our own constitutions. Yet corruption in these countries is systematized and goes back to superordinate, unwritten principles of administration. The author had the opportunity to observe the functioning of such a political system during his stay as university lecturer at Chulalongkorn University in Siam in 1950–1953.
2. For a discussion of the Inca state's economic system see particularly P.A. Means, *Ancient Civilizations of the Andes.* New York, 1931, chap. VIII, and Louis Baudin, *L'Empire socialiste des Inka.* Paris, 1928.
3. This tended to be the case in the Muslim states, which is partly explained by the fact that the emirs, the caliphs, and the dignitaries recruited from the upper social classes were Arabs, whereas the people had been conquered by force of arms and had then turned to Islam. However, the distinctions persisted, even though the conquerors, as the result of mingling with harem women of all nationalities, ceased to remain pure Arabs. At any rate, a close union between people and princes proved infeasible, so that the intermediary castes, originally also of Arab origin, were able to prevent the establishment of an absolute monarchy. They formed an intermediary group with a goal of its own, which to a large extent

succeeded in making its offices hereditary but which also fell apart into cliques and parties whom the emir could use for his own purposes. Domestic politics were thus complex and difficult to keep track of. The emir let his governors and civil servants largely go their own ways, but when they had sucked themselves full, he pressed them like a sponge. To illustrate this we refer to a dialogue that took place between Emir Abdur-rhaman II of Cordoba (822–852) and a high official, as noted in an Arab chronicle. Emir: "je voudrais couper la tête de celui qui sais avoir une grosse fortune a notre détriment et qui n'en verse rien au tresor." Mo-hammed-ben-Said (turning pale since he felt that the reference was to himself): "Ma fortune, je l'ai acquise par l'économie!" The outcome was that Mohammed donated part of his fortune to the emir, thus saving his own life. For this interesting dialogue see Louis Bertrand, *Histoire d'Es-pagne*. Paris, 1932, p. 82. These were the prevailing conditions in the entire area from Morocco to Yemen, which can be learned of Dimacqui's vademecum for merchants as well. See G.H. Bousquet, "L'économie politique non européano-chrétienne: L'exemple de Dimachqui," *Revue d'histoire économique et sociale*, 1957, p. 15.

4. One may speak of feudalism as a horizontal decomposition of the state, which disintegrates into a number of quasi-independent territories. Cor-ruption, on the other hand, leads to a vertical decomposition of the civil service, which was created precisely to centralize state powers. The colonial policy of Charles V of Spain provides a good example. Shortly after the Conquest the conquistadores tended to develop into a powerful landed caste, which to a large extent threatened to isolate the native population from the monarch. Charles now endeavored, with more energy than caution, to inhibit the distribution of these estates, the so-called *encomiendas*. This led to the uprising of the Pizarro brothers in Peru in 1544, and the attempt to dissolve the *encomiendas* failed. However, the still undistributed parts of the country now came under the supervision of civil servants, the *corregidores*. Soon the emperor realized that he did not have command over the colonies by these means either, since the *corregi-dores* intercepted the natives' tributes without penalty and blackmailed them in every possible way. To put an end to the thievery from the treasury Charles at last sent royal treasury officials to the colonies in 1550, but they converted themselves as well into quasi-owners of their offices. Thus Charles had to recognize that even with the help of civil servants he was unable to maintain tight control over the colonies. Under Philip II the aggressive policy toward the *encomiendas* ceased altogether. See Silvio Zavala, *La encomienda indiana*. Madrid, 1935, pp. 54, 63, 173, and L. Simpson, *The Economienda in New Spain 1492–1550*. Berkeley, 1929, p. 112.

5. Act XII of the Declaration on Human and Citizen Rights of the French Revolution says: ". . . cette force [publique] est donc instituée pour l'avantage de tous et non pour l'utilité particuliere de ceux a qui elle est confiée."

6. Gustav Schmoller, *Deutsches Städteleben in der älteren Zeit,* Bonn and Leipzig, 1922.

7. Gustav Schmoller, p. 232. See also his *Umrisse und Untersuchungen zur*

Verfassungs-, Verwaltungs- und Wirtschaftsgeschichte. Leipzig, 1898, p. 250.

8. See P.J. Blok, *Geschichte der Niederlande (Ubers.)*. Gotha, 1910, VI, p. 387.

9. See William Cunningham, *The Growth of English Industry and Commerce*, II. 5th Ed. Cambridge, 1912, p. 19.

10. This was brilliantly done by Leonard Woolf in his not-well-enough-known study, *After the Deluge*. London: Pelican, 1937.

11. Gustav Schmoller, *Deutsches Städteleben*, p. 232; Derselbe. *Umrisse und Untersuchungen*, pp. 250, 308.

12. Gustav Schmoller, *Deutsches Städteleben*, p. 232.

13. Likewise, the "honest" administration in Bavaria was only installed after the French successes. See Hans Schmelze. *Der Staatshaushalt des Herzogtums Bayerns im 18. Jahrhundert*. Stuttgart, 1900, p. 186. Schmelze tends to attribute the corruption that was widespread before this time to the nonexistence of an established salary and pension system. But this point of view is a naïve one. High salaries and pensions are in themselves insufficient for the establishment of an honest administration, as shall be shown below. Likewise, Lawrence Stone, who generally has a good understanding for phenomena of corruption does not comprehend this decisive point when he writes about the government of Queen Elizabeth: "Lacking the financial resources or the educational media to produce an honest and efficient bureaucracy." See Lawrence Stone, *Sir Horatio Palavicino*. Oxford, 1956, p. XV. Precisely the higher civil servants, who generally derived the biggest advantages from corruption, normally received pensions the size of which was determined by the king on the basis of varying considerations. Thus Edmond-Jean François Barbier, *Chronique de la Regence*, II. Paris, 1857, p. 16, with respect to such a case: ". . . on retranche a cent pauvres familles des rentes viagères . . .; on donne . . . de pension à gens qui ont été dans grands postes, dans lesquelles ils ont amassés des biens considérables, toujours au depens du peuple. . . ."

14. See I.T. Brugmans, *Sociaal-economische Geschiedenis von Nederland, 1795–1940*. The Hague, 1961, p. 16.

15. Details may be found in the study by the veteran director of the archives of the Dutch East India Company in Batavia. F. de Haan, *Priangan*. 4 vols. Batavia, 1910–1912, particularly Vol. 1, p. 461. See also J. van Klaveren, *The Dutch Colonial System in the East Indies*. The Hague, 1953, chaps. X, XI, XII. In Europe the conversion to "honest" administration cannot be precisely identified; but in the colonies corruption occurred quite openly precisely for the reason that it occurred at the cost of foreign people who had been conquered for exploitation. Hence the conversion was most obvious here. More details and also a summary may be found in my forthcoming textbook *General Economic History 200–1760*, esp. in chap. 25.

16. Wilhelm Roscher, *Naturgeschichte der Monarchie, Aristokratie, Demokratie*, Munich, 1933 (1892), p. 147, describes the aristocracy as "the most self-serving of all three forms of government." It is striking that this important economist never examined the effects the forms of government have on the distribution of income. The above quotation, however, shows

a latent understanding for the relationship. In my view the physiocrats' preference for absolute monarchy can only be explained because they realized the tendency of the intermediary strata to encourage corruption. This fact is generally known, although not yet explained. Sismondi comes close to an explanation when he writes: "Ils révéloient les abus effroyables sous lesquelles le peuple était écrasé; mais en général, plus ennemis des corps privilegiés que de l'autorité royale, ils sembloient, par leurs princi-pes, favoriser le despotisme." See H.C.L. Simonde de Sismondi, *Histoire des Français,* XXVIII. Paris, 1821, 1844, p. 483.

17. We quote this passage at some length because it is so characteristic of the spirit of the *ancien régime:* "My Lady Caithness is harassed in a most barbarous and inhumane way by a set of low-lifed creatures she has had the misfortune to have dealings with. Upon Saturday last her Ladyship's furniture was all sequestrated and carried away by one Pett an upholsterer, for a debt due him." The letter has been published by Leonard Woolf, *After the Deluge,* p. 75.

18. See P.J. Blok, VI, pp. 199, 203 ff.

19. See John Evelyn, *Diary II,* p. 47. Evelyn's opinions were clearly revealed in the following incident. As he was returning from Italy through Switzer-land to the North with a number of gentlemen, a dog belonging to one of his companions killed a goat. When the poor shepherd asked for compen-sation, he was refused out of hand as being ridiculous. However, at the next village the company was stopped and forced to compensate for the loss and to pay a small fine as well. Evelyn called this "an affront" and complained about the "ill-treatment we had received for killing a wretched goat." See John Evelyn, *Diary I,* pp. 231, 233 f. It should be pointed out here that Evelyn had an honest, humane, and even noble character.

20. Samuel Pepys came from a family of estate managers in Cambridgeshire. After the Black Death these "villici" appeared as tenants (farmers). See Sir John Clapham, *A Concise Economic History of Britain.* Cambridge, 1951, p. 115, p. 202. Pepys' father was a tailor in London.

21. See Samuel Pepys, *Diary I,* pp. 128, 132.

22. At the beginning of the seventeenth century the way of life of the Dutch patricians was not much different from that of the petty bourgeoisie. A hundred years later, however, they owned villas, saloons, and gardens in the style of Le-Notre, and often married into the hereditary nobility, who receded in the background. See P.J. Blok, IV, p. 112 and VI, pp. 101, 199. For England we refer to the cases of the Duke of Marlborough and Lord Chancellor Somer, which we will discuss further below. Thus two contra-dictory developments are to be observed: on the one hand an increasing degree of corruption and on the other a significant growth of the educated bourgeoisie, the carriers of the Enlightenment, who insisted on an "hon-est" administration. This inevitably led to a shocklike confrontation which took place during the French period. The transition is difficult to recognize in England, where—from my point of view—it had already taken place prior to the French Revolution during the financial reforms of Pitt the Younger (1784). However, I am still trying to prove this assumption.

23. See Gustav Schmoller, *Deutsches Städteleben,* p. 232.

24. Compare the careful manner in which Samuel Pepys imitated the gentle-men's habits and the satisfaction he got when he succeeded. History noted

some transgression of the proper distance, particularly in the case of important persons. This aroused both the envy of colleagues and the wrath of princes. The "colleagues" ruined Lord Chancellor Hyde, whose magnificent Dunkirk House supposedly caused him to make the prophetic statement: "This house will one day be my ruin." See Samuel Pepys, *Diary II*, p. 233, notation of the editor. In France the splendid palace of the superintendent Nicholas Fouquet invoked the wrath of the young Louis XIV, which led to his own overthrow, although the skids were greased by Colbert.

25. We want to illustrate this with only a few examples. Thus Lawrence Stone, *Sir Horatio Palavicino,* Oxford, 1956, p. 271, mentions that Palavicino had bought the estate Babraham from a Robert Taylor. He was a protégé of Lord Chancellor Burghley (also spelled Burleigh) and "had made a handsome fortune as teller in the Exchequer." John Evelyn, *Diary II,* p. 118, reports that in passing he once visited Viscount Hereford, who had fallen out of favor in Ipswich, and he says, "Whilst he was Secretary of State and Prime Minister he had gotten vastly, but spent as hastily, even before he had established a fund to maintain his greatness." Of Will Hewer, Samuel Pepys' friend and dependent, John Evelyn, p. 323, reports: ". . . Mr. Hewer, who got a considerable estate in the Navy. . . ."

26. This is a widespread phenomenon. See Wilhelm Roscher, *Naturgeschichte der Monarchie, Aristokratie, Demokratie,* new ed. Munich, 1933 (1892), p. 311.

27. For these figures see Samuel Pepys, *Diary I,* p. 352, and John Evelyn, *Diary II,* p. 244. From this it appears that the civil servants' salaries were so high that large amounts could be saved for old-age pensions. Naturally, Pepys did not have to live like a cook. Note, however, that households with an income of £50 or an estate of £600 were classified as "substantial households" according to a census taken in London in 1695. See Roger Mols S.J. *Introduction à la Démographie historique des villes d'Europe du XIVe au XVIIIe siècle,* II. Louvain, 1954–1956, p. 94. However, Pepys was able to make the £600 necessary for a comfortable existence in less than a year because his fortune increased by £1000 annually. We must remember that Pepys, who did not belong to high society, did not have high expenses. Nevertheless, he spent more than his salary, that is, more than £350 per year. Even though the salaries were sufficient to build up considerable reserves while living quite well, the high officials often received lifetime salaries. Thus Admiral Lord Sandwich received £4000 a year for his entire life. Corruption, however, was flourishing among the highest classes. Thus it is clear that high salaries and pensions in themselves are not sufficient to inhibit corruption.

28. John Evelyn's remark in 1703 shows how differently corruption was looked upon then: "This day died Mr. Samuel Pepys, a very worthy, industrious and curious person, none in England exceeding him in knowledge of the navy, in which he had passed through all the most considerable offices . . . all of which he performed with great integrity." See John Evelyn, *Diary II,* p. 371 f. Of course, it must be considered that Pepys insisted on delivery of good quality and correct amounts by the suppliers though he certainly cheated the Treasury by way of padded accounts. This can be discovered from his own notes as well. He deprecated other officers

of the Navy Board who collaborated in the supply of bad materials to the shipyards. John Evelyn, *Diary II,* pp. 152, 167, writes of Sir Stephen Fox, a paymaster general in time of war, who was allowed to keep "a moderate allowance" of the soldiers' pay thanks to the prompt payment ". . . an able and honest man" and describes his fortune of £200,000 as "honestly got"!

7

The Sale of Public Offices

Koenraad W. Swart

Sale of offices was a phenomenon which was common to many countries in Europe, Asia, America and Africa, but which was not prevalent everywhere in the same forms or to an equal degree. Sometimes offices were sold for only a few years, in other cases for lifetime, or even as inheritable property. Offices could be sold by the governments, as in despotic countries, by ministers or other prominent people, as in the English departments, or by the officials themselves, as in the English army. Offices were also sold both by the government and the officials, as was the case in France. In most countries sale of offices was a more or less official institution, but there was a considerable difference between countries, such as France, England and Spain, in which the buyer of an office acquired a piece of property almost as secure as real estate, and states, such as China and the Ottoman Empire, in which every official could be deprived of his office by a caprice of the prince. The legal aspect of sale of offices was most pronounced in France where offices were regarded as immovable property.

In France, sale of offices also penetrated in more departments of government than anywhere else: in Spain, for example, the system was not followed with regard to the more important posts of government; in the Curia Romana, where the highest positions were sold, the total number of offices was small compared with that in France; in China the status of the mandarins bore much similarity to that of the French officials, but offices were normally acquired here by passing competitive examinations, and only in exceptional cases could be bought.

The similarities between sale of offices in the various countries are as important as the differences. The origin of the institution everywhere dated back to the Middle Ages if not to earlier periods. The peak was

Source: Koenraad Walter Swart, *Sale of Offices in the Seventeenth Century*. The Hague: Martinus Nijhoff, 1949, pp. 112–27. By permission of the author and the publisher.

generally reached in the seventeenth or eighteenth century. It was in all countries abolished when modern political institutions became powerful. This historical phenomenon, occurring on a world-wide scale, had everywhere similar causes and similar effects. This will be evident when this institution is examined in its political, social and economic setting.

The most widespread of all factors contributing to sale of offices was the practice of remunerating officials by means of fees, or other payments made by the population. Until recently it was very common for officials to receive no salary, or only a small one. Instead, the judicial official demanded fees, the financial agent imposed taxes, and the military commanders held the population for ransom. The size of the income of the official, therefore, largely depended on his rapacity and ingenuity. He was financially almost independent from the central government.

The system of remunerating officials by means of fees is very irrational. All the proceeds from the offices should be accounted for by the official, and sent to the central government, which pays the official according to the importance of the duties he performs. The system, however, had great advantages in a society in which it was difficult to check on local officials because of a widespread dishonesty, relatively large distances, and a primitive administrative technique. In this way much accounting and transfering of money was avoided, and the official was interested in the execution of his duties.

It is obvious how this system easily changed into farming, or selling offices. If the fees increased, the remuneration of the official would become so large that it was fair that he should pay a part of it to the government or to the person who had nominated him. The only prerequisite was a certain degree of economic prosperity. Offices could not be sold unless people existed who were willing and able to buy them. If trade and commerce flourished, the fees from the offices would increase and this would in its turn, influence the degree of eagerness of the place-hunting. Moreover, people would not be able to pay sizeable sums for offices if a considerable degree of capital forming had not taken place. In societies with a primitive economy, therefore, sale of offices did not develop.

The same conditions were the basis for the system of farming out taxes, which was followed in so many countries in the past centuries. It is not a mere coincidence that in countries in which sale of offices was general, such as France, Spain, Turkey and China, farming of taxes was also a firmly established practice.[1]

In some states, notably in the Ottoman Empire, remuneration of officials by means of fees was the main cause of the sale or farming of offices. In these countries, however, an element was lacking which largely contributed to the development of sale of offices elsewhere, *i.e.*, the conception of public office as private property. Offices could only be considered as freeholds if the official had a more or less permanent status and was independent in a political as well as in a financial respect.

The conception of public office as private property is typical of rather primitive societies,[2] and generally does not develop in bureaucracies, in which the officials are usually dependent on their superiors. However, the societies in which the possibilities of control were limited and aristocratic forces powerful, the officials often succeeded in extending their rights. It was common for officials, who were originally instituted as dependable agents, soon to become appointed for life, and almost independent of the prince. This trend went farthest in the feudal system in which officials developed into sovereigns, but a certain feudal character was inherent in many offices, secular as well as ecclesiastical, which were created by the princes in the later centuries of the Middle Ages. The aristocratic society of this age did not yet draw the distinction between public office and private property as sharply as today.

The officials of a bureaucracy ruled by aristocratic principles were often no longer appointed by the prince. Sometimes the officials themselves had the right to nominate their successors, or their offices had become entirely hereditary. In other cases courtiers or high noblemen had a decisive voice in granting offices, or the patronage of offices belonged to ministers or superiors in office.

Offices of this kind were sought because they brought prestige and honor or because they were very lucrative. True ability was not required for the execution of these offices and the nomination was made according to criteria which had little to do with the merit of the candidates. These offices were often held by deputies and could, therefore, easily be cumulated. These types of officials were not always held responsible for the performance of their duties. Many of them looked upon public service as a commercial enterprise and shamelessly extorted the population.

The freehold conception of public office developed in a combination of bureaucratic and aristocratic forms of government, which was typical of the Western European kingdoms during the later Middle Ages. The civil services of France and Spain, which were organized during a period in which the feudal forces were still powerful, showed all the characteristics of an aristocratic bureaucracy; in England this type of official lingered on well into the nineteenth century. These conditions also existed, to a certain extent, in China, at the moment when the feudal society was replaced by a state governed by officials (300–200 B.C.) and in the Curia Romana at the beginning of the fifteenth century.[3]

If offices are considered as private property, it is natural for them to be sold, but under the rule of aristocracies sale of offices often occurred to only a limited extent, because the number of offices was small and many other forms of jobbery were preferred. The aristocratic bureaucracies, however, in developing the freehold conception of public office, paved the way to the systematic sale of offices by absolute princes.

We have seen how the rise of absolutism was often connected with the introduction of sale of offices: in China sale of offices was embarked upon by the absolute princes of the Ch'in and Han dynasties; in Rome it became firmly established under the despotism of the later Roman Empire; in England it was introduced by the powerful kings of the twelfth century; and above all it flourished during the European absolutism of the sixteenth, seventeenth and eighteenth centuries.

On the other hand, the representatives of the people, the parliament, the Cortes, and the States-General, usually opposed this policy, and in the Dutch Republic and in England, where absolutism did not triumph, sale of offices was practiced on a much smaller scale.

Yet, as has already been argued, absolutism was in principle more opposed to than in favor of the medieval, or aristocratic conception of public office, on which sale of offices was based. Absolute rulers whose policy was more or less consistent, such as Philip II of Spain, Colbert, and King Frederick II, have, therefore, attempted to abolish sale of offices.

Absolute governments exploited an institution, which was in essence incompatible with their ideal of a reliable body of officials, only because of financial or political necessity. Lack of means to defray urgent expenses, especially those in connection with wars, was the main cause leading to sale of offices. In France, sale of offices was introduced during the wars in Italy, and was practiced on the largest scale during the wars of the seventeenth century. In Spain, sale of offices was embarked upon during a war against the Moors and was most frequently resorted to during the many wars against France. One war, that of the Spanish Succession, led to sale of offices in such different countries as France, Savoy, Prussia, Austria and the Dutch Republic. Also in China wars were one of the mainsprings of sale of offices.

The princes would have preferred to use methods less damaging for their authority, but the possibilities which the rulers of the seventeenth century had at their disposal were still very limited. Their greatest drawback was that unlike governments in modern times, they could not issue loans without assigning a special part of their income as security for the interest. The Dutch Republic was probably the only state of the seventeenth century in which public debts in their modern form were already common.[4] In other countries sale of offices was one of the expedients which had to fill this need. The difference was in many cases nominal rather than actual, because the offices had often an entirely honorary character; but people who were not willing to subscribe to loans, were sometimes very eager to buy an office.

In introducing sale of offices as a systematic policy, princes were also motivated by political considerations. Sale of offices put an end to favoritism and intrigue inherent in oligarchies; in fifteenth century Spain, for example, sale of offices was used to restrict the corrupt power of the urban aristocracies and in France, the *Paulette* was said to have been introduced in order to prevent political appointments by the nobility.[5]

The middle classes often supported the royal policy, because they looked askance at the aristocracy granting all offices, and they obtained a fairer share of the spoils of office under the new system. Moreover, offices could never be sold on a large scale without the existence of a rich class who was willing to buy them. In many cases, notably in city governments, the initiative to introduce sale of offices came from this part of the population. They introduced the system into the French, Flemish and Zeeland cities during the Middle Ages, and into Hamburg in 1684. It was the same part of the people who pressed for public sale of offices in the towns of Holland in 1747 and 1748.

Many factors were influential in bringing about systematic sale of offices: a bureaucracy ruled by aristocratic principles, remuneration by means of fees, a flourishing of trade and commerce, a powerful middle class, an absolutist government which had no other means of meeting its financial emergencies than that of resorting to desperate expedients. These circumstances did not exist to the same degree in all countries which I have discussed; in Germany, the middle classes were not powerful and the economic life was only slightly developed; in Spain, the government was not entirely centralized and the economic life was not very prosperous; in the Dutch Republic and in England, the social and economic conditions were favorable to the development of sale of offices, but in these countries absolutism was thwarted and no large bureaucracies existed; in the Ottoman Empire, and to a less extent also in China, the aristocratic principle was not represented.

Only in France were all the factors which furthered sale of offices strongly developed. There existed no other European state of the size of France in which absolutism was so firmly established; on the other hand, as early as the fifteenth century French officials were much less dependent upon the king than elsewhere, even than in an aristocratic country like England.[6] The economic life of France was one of the most prosperous of Europe and the French middle class was rich and numerous. Finally, as a result of the many wars in which France was involved, its financial system was entirely disrupted and all types of financial expedients had to be used. It is, therefore, no wonder that in France sale of offices reached a greater extent than anywhere else.

Whereas sale of offices has come into being under the influence of certain political, social and economic factors, it has, in its turn, also influenced the political, social and economic development. This influence was naturally much greater in countries in which sale of offices prevailed to a large extent (France, the Political States and China) than in states in which the habit was more sporadically indulged in (England and the Dutch Republic). The effects of sale of offices have always been the subject of much speculation by contemporaries. Publicists who condemned sale of offices held it responsible for all sorts of evils, whereas defenders tried to discover wholesome consequences. The passionate point of view of both groups was generally a hindrance to a correct analysis of the question.

One of the most important consequences was hardly noticed by these publicists. This was the weakening of the same royal power which had so greatly contributed to the development of sale of offices. If the king sold offices, he could no longer choose his servants according to their capacities or reliability. In France, for instance, people whose only contact with the university had consisted in the buying of a degree, became judges at a very young age. We have seen that in other countries the inability of many officials also was notorious; in many countries these officials could not be discharged. In introducing sale of offices the princes had called into existence a power which they could not check on.[7] Princes who wanted to retain control of their administration were forced to institute new officials. The French kings created the offices of intendants, officials who had not bought their offices and to whom most of the administrative functions of the *parlements, bureaux de finances* and *baillis* were gradually transferred.[8] Similar dependent agents were appointed by the kings of Spain and Prussia in the eighteenth century.

The strengthening of the independence of the officials has sometimes been considered as a wholesome consequence of sale of offices. It has been pointed out, for example, that in France the judiciary of the *ancien régime* could not easily be influenced by politicians and that the country enjoyed a considerable degree of self-government.[9] The independence of the officials found also expression in the opposition of the *Parlements* against many measures of the government.[10] It should not be forgotten, however, that the many small potentates seldom used their power for the public good. On the whole the officials were conservative and opposed to any reform of abuses which could interfere with their privileges. They were also afraid that by showing too much disobedience to the royal power they would forfeit the valuable property invested in their offices.[11] Sale of offices fostered the revolutionary spirit outside, but not inside the body of officials.

The bureaucratic abuses resulting from sale of offices were numerous; the number of offices multiplied without any relation to the increased task of the government; many of these offices were sinecures, *offices imaginaires;* other offices were held by deputies; some people cumulated many offices; the administration of justice was slow, as the officials could in this way exact more fees. One should beware, however, of attributing all these evils merely to sale of offices. It should not be forgotten that the aristocratic bureaucracies had already suffered under the same sorts of abuses before the systematic sale of offices by the princes had started.

The relationship between political corruption and sale of offices is likewise more subtle than often assumed. Sale of offices is an aspect of corruption as long as it is not officialy regulated and not all the proceeds flow into the treasury of the prince or the state, but this jobbery came to an end when sale of offices had become a legal institution. Sale of offices was defended by writers like Barclay and Montesquieu for the very reason that it had eliminated the favoritism and intrigue of courtiers and ministers.[12] Even a radical thinker like Jeremy Bentham defended his proposal for the introduction of sale of offices by this argument.[13]

Whereas public sale of offices eliminated corrupt practices as far as they concerned the *appointment* to office, the same cannot be said with regard to the *execution* of offices which had been bought. It has always been argued that people who had bought public authority would feel themselves entitled to sell it.[14] This generalization, however, is not true for all officials. There were many who had bought their offices because they wanted to enrich themselves. People who had inherited offices were likewise not much tempted to exploit their offices. The standards of the French judiciary compare favorably with those of England and Spain, although in the latter countries the judgeships never became

freeholds. The most notorious case of bribery in France was committed by a judge who was member of the reformed Parliament of
Maupeou (1771–1774) and who had not bought his office.[15] It was a
different matter if officials regarded the purchase of an office purely as
a commercial enterprise. Extortion, bribery and peculation were the
usual characteristics of their administrations.

Sale of offices also introduced some useful innovations into the
bureaucracies. Elderly officials who were allowed to sell their offices
obtained in this way a sort of old-age pension. The purchase price paid
by financial officials fulfilled at the same time the function of security
for the finances under their control.

The effect of sale of offices on the financial system of a country can
be compared either with that of farming taxes or with that of issuing of
loans. Sale of offices was similar to farming of taxes if the offices were
sold, or rather farmed, for a short period. This method might have been
financially profitable to the government, although it generally increased the tax burden.[16] Sale of offices resembled issuing of loans in
its result if the officials were entitled to transfer the offices to third
persons or if the offices were entirely hereditary. In this case, the
financial problems of the present were solved at the expense of future
generations. Sale of offices, as part of an irresponsible financial policy,
often contributed to the disruption of the financial system of a country.

The effect of sale of offices on the social structure of a country has
not always been the same. Shortly after its introduction, sale of offices
opened the public service to classes which had been excluded under
the rule of oligarchies, and furthered the social mobility. This was the
case in France in the sixteenth and seventeenth centuries, when by
means of purchase of offices the *bourgeoisie* replaced the nobility in
the government of the state. The farming out of offices in the Moham-
medan countries had a similar consequence. This effect disappeared,
however, when sale of offices developed into heritability of offices and
new offices were no longer sold. In the eighteenth century the *noblesse
de robe* in France was as closed to newcomers as any other oligarchy.[17]
Moreover, sale of offices has an undemocratic feature of its own,
because it confines office holding to people of means. The purchase
system in the English army was advocated for the very reason that in
this way the aristocratic selection of officers was guaranteed. By
excluding many capable people from public office, sale of offices called
into being a group of discontented intellectuals who sometimes, as in
France and China, played an important part in revolutionary movements.

The economic development was also affected by sale of offices. In

China, where grain was the medium of exchange, it was argued that sale of offices would promote agriculture, because people would be eager to possess grain with which they could acquire public office.[18] A similar opinion was held by Montesquieu, who maintained that sale of offices would stimulate the economic activity as the possession of money opened the road to honorable positions.[19] Actually, the influence was rather the reverse. Sale of offices stirred up the place-hunting and caused a decrease of interest in commerce and industry. In France a great part of the capital that might have been invested in branches of industry was used for buying offices and the government used the funds which it received in this way not for promoting the economic development, but for waging wars. On the other hand, groups which were excluded from holding office, such as the protestants in France in the seventeenth century, and Jews in general, have often advanced the economic life of a country.

The conclusion from the examination of the causes and effects of sale of offices is that this institution is a product of still primitive forms of administration as long as it occurs in an undeveloped form, but is a mark of decay when it is exploited by absolute, irresponsible governments because of fiscal motives. In this latter form it is a typical characteristic of politically declining societies, such as the Byzantine Empire, the Caliphate of the tenth century, the *ancient régimes* in France and Spain, and China in the nineteenth century. Systematic sale of offices deprived the government of an efficient and reliable body of officials, strengthened the oligarchic tendencies, created a discontented *élite* and disrupted the financial system. The consequence was that the political instability of the country was increased and the outbreak of revolutions furthered.

Only few publicists who discussed sale of offices defended this institution. Among them were some statesmen, such as Richelieu, wanting to justify the course of their policy, and a few financial projectors hoping to profit by the introduction of this system. Other people who upheld sale of offices were distinguished officials, like Montesquieu and Wellington, who pleaded more or less their own cause.[20] Finally, there were critics of the aristocratic society, like Jeremy Bentham, who hoped that the introduction of sale of offices would have a wholesome influence on a political system in which the patronage of offices belonged to an oligarchy.[21]

The great majority of writers were opposed to sale of offices. They can also be divided into different groups. First, the nobility and their spokesmen, who argued that "merit," *i.e.,* gentle birth, and not money, should be the decisive factor in appointments. This opinion was voiced in France by Le Vassor, Boulainvilliers, Fénelon and Saint-Simon,[22] in Spain by Davila and Bovadilla. Most publicists who condemned sale of offices were jurists or literates: Out of the numerous writers I mention only Bodin, Pasquier and Voltaire in France,[23] Francisco de Vitoria, Las Casas and Martínez de Mata in Spain, Edward Coke, Sir Walter Raleigh and Sir Matthew Hale in England, Botero in Italy,[24] Erasmus, Hugo Grotius and Jacob van Heemskerck in the Netherlands,[25] Breckling, Moser and Justi in Germany,[26] Kochi Bey in the Ottoman Empire[27] and Wang Ghi in China. Their opinions were inspired partly by resentment against an institution which had excluded many of them from public office, partly by the conviction that sale of offices was nefarious for the State.

Another category, which had many ties with the preceding one, consisted of dissatisfied officials. They especially denounced a certain aspect of the institution, namely, the sale of new offices by the king, because this measure lessened the proceeds from the existing offices. The representative assemblies were opposed to sale of offices largely because of this consideration, although they sometimes expressed the grievances of lower classes, who suffered more than any other group under the increasing number of officials.[28] A last group of opponents of sale of offices were the princes themselves. Edward VI of England, Philip II of Spain and Frederick II of Prussia are the best known of the monarchs who condemned the institution since it was at variance with their ideal of a reliable body of officials.

This verdict of the overwhelming majority of writers against sale of offices did not achieve any result until the most important factors which had caused sale of offices ceased to exist in the eighteenth and nineteenth centuries. As early as the beginning of the eighteenth century, governments which were in urgent need of money no longer resorted to such expedients as sale of offices, but issued loans. At the same time, the system of remuneration of officials by means of fees fell into disuse as a result of the prevalence of more rational administrative habits. Finally, in the nineteenth century, when the more democratic form of government limited the influence of the aristocracy, and the modern idea of the State came into existence, the conception of public office as private property disappeared. The State became considered as a moral entity and the exercising of public authority as a duty. The official of the *ancien régime,* the *officier,* was replaced by his modern colleague, the *fonctionnaire.* One of the outstanding representatives of the philosophy of this new conception of the state, Hegel, called the sale of government rights the most barbarous trait of a people who constitute a state.[29]

The actual abolishment of sale of offices was the easiest in those states, like the Ottoman Empire where the institution was mainly based on the remuneration of officials by means of fees. In countries where the proprietary rights on offices were firmly established, the abolishment of sale of offices were complicated by the problem of the compensation of the proprietors. At the end of the eighteenth century the following objection was raised, for example, by Edmund Burke against a too hasty reform of the English bureaucracy:

> These places, and others of the same kind which are held for life, have been considered as property. They have been given as a provision for children; they have been the subject of family settlements; they have been the security of creditors. . . . If the discretion of power is once let loose upon property, we can be at no loss to determine whose power and what discretion it is that will prevail at last.[30]

The old system, therefore, often lingered on long after the mainspring of sale of offices had disappeared. In England it was not until the end of the nineteenth century that the *ancien régime* was liquidated. In most countries sale of offices came to an end only after the outbreak of a revolution. It was the French Revolution which abolished sale of offices in France and gave a great impetus to the reform movements of most continental European states (for example, the Netherlands, Savoy, Naples, Rome the Palatinate, Bavaria and Hamburg). Sale of offices in some Oriental states, such as Persia and China, was likewise abolished as a result of revolutionary movements.

Important factors which caused sale of offices in the past have ceased to exist. On the other hand, there are today conditions, unknown to older societies, which may lead to a revival of this institution. The increased power of the State has placed into the hands of officials greater possibilities for abusing the public authority for their own profit than ever before. Naturally the eagerness to hold these offices is great so that many people may be willing to pay for them. Even more important is the increase in power of political parties which are influential in conferring offices in many states. Their position is comparable with that of ancient oligarchies. Sale of offices, if occurring in modern society, would no longer be carried on for the benefit of the State, which has other means of obtaining funds at its disposal, but for that of political parties. In this form it was practised until recently in the United States, where candidates for office often had to pay sizeable "assessments" either to the party treasury or to bosses.[31] On the whole, however, no systematic and legal sale of offices has developed in the modern state. In this respect our society, in which many other forms of political corruption are prevalent, compares favorably with those of the past.

Notes

1. W. Lotz, *Studien über Steuerverpachtung. Sitzungsberichte der Bayerischen Akademie der Wissenschaften,* Phil.-hist. Abt. 1935, 4; W. Lotz, "Revenue Farming," *Encyclopaedia of the Social Sciences,* XIII (1934), 359; K. Bräuer, "Steuerverpachtung, Steuersubmission," *Handwörterbuch der Staatswissenschaften,* 4th ed. VII, 1126; P. Roux, *Les fermes d'impôts sous l'ancien régime* (Paris, 1916); H. Sieveking, *Genueser Finanzwesen. Volkswirtschaftliche Abhandlungen der Badischen Hochschule.* Vol. I, No. 3 (1898), 41.
2. R.H. Lowie, *Primitive Society* (London, 1921), 230–231, 263–265, 310–313.
3. Göller, "Hadrian VI und der Aemterkauf an der päpstlichen kurie," *Vorreformationsgeschichtliche Forschungen.* Suppl. bd., Munster, 1925, 376.
4. W. Lotz, "Staatsschulden," *Handwörterbuch der Staatswissenschaften,* 4th ed. (1926), 824–825; E. Baasch, *Holländische Wirtschaftgeschichte* (Jena, 1927), 188 ff.
5. Richelieu and the Marquis of Fontenay-Mareuil, cited by Ch. Normand, *La bourgeoisie française au XVIIe Siècle,* 34–35.
6. Cf. E.F. Churchill, "The Crown and Its Servants," *Law Quarterly Journal,* XLII (1926).
7. Emperior Anastasius made the Empire into a kind of aristocracy by selling all offices, according to Suidas, *Lexicon,* Ed. by A. Adler (Lipsiae, 1928), s.v. "Anastasius."
8. Godard, *Les pouvoirs des intendants* (Paris, 1902), 439–41.
9. Homais, *De la vénalité des offices sous l'ancien régime* (Paris, 1903), 174–75; G. Pagès, "La vénalité des offices sous l'ancien régime," *Revue historique,* CLXIX (1932), 493.
10. Ch. Normand, 266–69; Göhring, *Die Aemterkäuflichkeit im Ancien Regime* (Berlin, 1938), 88, 290, 306–9; Homais, 47, 125.
11. Loyseau, *Cinq livres du droit des offices,* III, chap. I, no. 101; Ch. Normand, 17–18.
12. J. Barclay, *Icon animarum* (Francofurti, 1668), chap. 3; Montesquieu, *Esprit des lots,* V, 19 (Paris, n.d.) 61–63; Montesquieu, *Cahiers (1716–1755),* B. Grasset, ed. (Paris, 1941), 120–121.
13. *The Rationale of Reward,* II, chap. IX. Works ed. Bowring, II, 246–48.
14. Seneca, *De Beneficiis,* I, 9, Ed. by J.W. Basore in the Loeb Classical Library, CCCX (London, 1935), 30; cf. J. Bentham, and *Constitutional Code,* Works, IX, 31–32, 286 ff.
15. H. Carré, *Le règne de Louis XV (1715–1774) (Histoire de France . . . E. Lavisse, ed., VIII²) (Paris, 1909), 416–17.
16. Cf. places referred to in note 1.
17. Normand, 132; M. Kolabinska, *La circulation des élites en France . . .* (Lausanne, 1912), 95, 104–105, 109–10; P. Boiteau, *Etat de France en 1789* (Paris, 1861), 328.

18. J.J.L. Duyvendak, trans., *The Book of Lord Shang* (London, 1928), 64–65, 236, 253, 304; L. Wieges, *Rudiments: Textes historiques* (Paris, 1905), 421–24.

19. *Esprit des lois,* V, 19.

20. Montesquieu, *Esprit des lois,* V, 19; *Report from Select Committee on Army and Navy Appointments 1833,* 273–74.

21. Among the many words by Bentham concerning his plans of pecuniary competition see especially: *Draught of a Code for the Organization of the Judicial Establishment in France, March 1790.* Works IV, 285 ff., 354; *The Rationale of Reward,* first published in French in 1810. Works V, 246–48; *Constitutional Code,* Book II, chap. IX, section 16, 17, chap. X, section 10, art. 63, Works IX, 271 ff., 380–81; cf. also Works V, 278 ff., 302 ff., 363 ff., IX 31–32; about similar plans by J. Sinclair, see his work *The History of the Public Revenue of the British Empire* (London, 1790), III, 219, 229.

22. Cf. Göhring, 299–304.

23. Cf. Göhring, 69–73, 80–81; Homais, 168–77; ante.

24. G. Botero, *Della ragione di stato libri deici con tre libri delle cause della grandezza e magnificenza delle città* (Venezia, 1589), libro I, cap. 16.

25. Erasmus Encomium morias, LV. P. de Holhac and M. Rat, eds. (Paris, 1936), 142–43; H. Grotius, *Parallelon rerum publicarum, liber tertius; De moribus ingenioque populorum Atheniensium, Romanorum Batavorum* . . . (Haarlem, 1801–1803), II, 8, 9, Johan van Heemskerck, *Batavische Arcadia,* 4th ed. (Amsterdam, 1663), 485.

26. J.H.G. van Justi, *System des Finanzwesens* . . . (Halle, 1766), 528.

27. E. Tyan, *Histoire de l'organisation judiciaire en pays d'Islam* (Paris, 1938), 429–30, 450–51.

28. Cf. Göhring, 61 ff.; Marion, *Dictionnaire des institutions de la France* (Paris, 1925) s.v., "Vénalité."

29. G.W.F. Hegel. *Die Verfassung des Deutschen Reichs. Eine politische Flugschrift.* 1801/1802. G. Mollat, ed. (Stuttgart, 1935), 35.

30. *Works,* II, 101, cited by Holdsworth, *History of English Law,* X, 504.

31. M. Ostrogorski, *Democracy and the Organization of Political Parties* (London, 1902), II, 148, 157, 343–45, 352.

8

Patronage and the Public Service in Britain and America

Samuel E. Finer

British and American Administrative Systems Compared

The United States Begins De Novo

When the United States congress created the American federal administration, 1789–1792, it was neither helped nor burdened by any legacy from the past;[1] it had to work from tiny beginnings: and so it was able to set up a system based on common sense and rationality. It was this which brought on it the praise of Jeremy Bentham.

> In the central government of the Anglo-American United States, the situations in the executive departments are every one of them single-seated. Of the thirteen here [i..e. in the Constitutional Code] proposed sub-departments, some have there no place;[2] the rest are consolidated into four, each filled by a minister, locable and dislocable by president of the state, whose power, in so far, is that of the here proposed prime minister. . . . In the case of the relation between the president, as above, and his immediate subordinates—the power of the superordinate in relation to subordinates is not only as to location, but as to dislocation, absolute: and at the accession of each president the power of dislocation is commonly exercised as to those he finds in office, and that of location, at the same time as to new ones; in regard to each, effectual responsibility is secured by the power expressly given to him to require of each of them a report in writing in relation to all points belonging to their respective offices; and by this arrangement are produced all the good effects, the production of which is professed to be expected from boards. . . . In English practice, this department swarms with boards. . . . Yet for many—seatedness in no one of all the several instances, can there be any necessity or use. . . .[3]

Source: Samuel E. Finer, "Patronage and the Public Service: Jeffersonian Bureaucracy and the British Tradition." *Public Administration,* 30 (1952), pp. 333–53. By permission of the author and the publisher, the Royal Institute of Public Administration.

British Administration in 1780 Dominated by Mediaeval Assumptions and Forms

In sharp contrast the British reformers were faced in 1780 not merely with a going concern, but one that had been going for centuries. The essential thing to notice about this British system is that from the Norman Conquest almost no office or department was ever abolished; but functions often were. By 1780 the structure resembled a coral reef. It was made up of the skeletons of innumerable offices and functionaries which had served their turn; but inside this dead structure new creatures burrowed, made their home, and turned the detritus of ages into some kind of a working instrument.

The King's Government   The key to the system is to be found in the position of the monarch. The legal prerogatives of the king as listed in the *Commmentaries* of Blackstone and the *Constitution* of De Lolme were still very largely the working practice of the eighteenth century. The army and the navy were the *king's* army and the *royal* navy. H.M. ministers were in fact, as well as in law, the *king's* ministers. True, they had to enter into some working arrangement with the House of Commons in order to do the king's business, but it was to the king that their responsibilities lay. Their management of the Commons was an incident to this task. "Cabinets . . . did not depend on popular mandate but poised and turned as of old on a balance, between a royal executive, groups maintained by ministerial influence, and a public opinion not yet drawn up through party systems but scattered, formless and difficult of expression."[4] The nature of the civil list illustrates the same point. On this grant, made to the monarch for his private use, were borne the expenses of ambassadors and judges.

The executive was the king's executive and it lived apart from parliament, controlling its own internal movements, making its own intestinal arrangements—so long only as it could persuade parliament to grant it the funds which it deemed necessary. According to Blackstone

> the king has the sole power of sending ambassadors to foreign states and receiving ambassadors at home. It is also the king's prerogative to make treaties, leagues, and alliances with foreign states and princes. . . . The king has also sole prerogative as to making war and peace. . . . He is a constituent part of the supreme legislative power; and as such has the prerogative of rejecting such provisions in parliament as he judges improper to be passed. . . . The king is considered in the next place as the generalissimo or the first in military command within the kingdom. Another capacity in which the king is considered in domestic affairs is as the fountain of justice and general conservator of the peace of the

kingdom. The king is likewise the fountain of honor, of office and of privilege; he is the arbiter of commerce.[5]

This apparent theorizing of Blackstone was acted on to a very much larger extent in the eighteenth century than is commonly supposed. It was not regarded as parliament's task to control from day to day the affairs of the executive; and for the most part such intermeddling by the Commons consisted largely of calling for reports from time to time, and, every so often, of setting up committees of inquiry; even these being mostly concerned in the first instance with public accounts—a matter which was clearly within the purview of parliament since the Restoration.

The King Lives of His Own Furthermore, the mediaeval notion that "the king lives of his own" still underlay the financial relationship between the legislature and the executive. The civil list was in theory supposed to be the fund by which all the foreign and domestic business of the kingdom was financed.[6] Granted to the monarch for life, once granted it was therefore free from any ordinary parliamentary interference. Of course, it was wholly inadequate to bear the cost of government. From time to time parliament made up additional expenses by extraordinary grants. Military expenses however, and funds to reduce the public debt, were granted by parliament annually and as these represented an overwhelming proportion of the cost of running the kingdom it was through control over these that parliament could in fact, and did in fact, exert a control over royal policy. Yet even in respect of these sums the old mediaeval notion that "the king lives of his own" was maintained in an etiolated sense: for successive parliaments followed the will-o'-the-wisp of creating a self-balancing fund with which to meet the increased expenses of the régime. If, for example, additional sums were needed for the army, an additional customs duty might be laid on Spanish hides sufficient to meet the estimates of the increased cost. The assumption always was that costs would not continue to increase beyond that fixed point, and that therefore the income from this special customs fund could be earmarked in perpetuity for this particular item of expenditure. As a result we find that by 1780 the customs duties were paid into a number of funds, e.g. the General Fund, the Aggregate Fund, the Sinking Fund, the South Sea Fund, while upon these funds were settled the payment of certain specified and recurrent heads of expenditure. Thus, among the services to which the Aggregate Fund was applied we find "To the officers of the Exchequer Bill Offices on their salaries," "To the sheriffs of the several counties of England and Wales for defraying their charges of taking forth their Letters Patent for their respective offices, and passing their accounts, and obtaining their quietus," "For the support of His Majesty's household."[7] This notion that it was possible to strike a balance between the income from certain taxes and the expenditure on certain fixed items so that they should become a self-balancing account, was a mediaeval notion derived from the idea that there was a fixed sum out of which the expenses of the country could and should be defrayed.[8]

Ministries as Private Establishments   Another consequence of the notions that the executive was the king's, and that the king lived of his own, was that the departments were not regarded as public departments. Ministers were the king's ministers: but the departments they managed were (largely) the private establishments of those ministers. For the most part, clerks and subordinates were paid not by salary but by fees exacted in the course of their duties. Where additional clerical assistance was needed in an office there was no reason why the minister should not set aside part of his salary or part of his fees of office for that purpose; or why chief clerks having been appointed and paid in this fashion should not do likewise, setting aside a proportion of the fees which they received in order to pay off additional clerical assistance. There was no reason furthermore, why an officer paid at some very high salary or who received through the course of events inordinately high fees (as, e.g. the fees of tellers of the exchequer were increased enormously through the huge increase of payments during the Napoleonic wars) should not cease to do any work whatsoever and simply engage some hack at a considerably lower sum to do the work for him. When such action was taken the work was said to be performed *"by deputy"* and the original post, e.g. "teller of the exchequer," became a "sinecure."

This notion, that the establishments were the private establishments of ministers, had three important effects. In the first place, a fee system rather than a salary system developed throughout the public services. In the second place, since these fees could not be regarded as a charge on the public accounts they did not come within the generally accepted purview of parliamentary inquiry; and for the same reason neither did the number of individuals of the establishment. And thirdly, obsolete offices were not swept away but in fact tended to multiply; the original post so as to be performed by deputy: then the deputy office became so profitable as to be performed, itself, by deputy; and so on.

Medieval Operating Procedures   Finally, some branches of the public service, and neither the least numerous nor the least important, had been continued in an unmodified medieval form. The best example of course is the exchequer which retained, in 1780, with hardly any substantial modification, the same establishment, organization and procedure as under Edward III. The customs which in 1797 employed some 6,000 officers out of the national total of 16,000 was a particularly glaring example of a mediaeval organization, illustrating how the living organs of eighteenth century administration had to operate within a carapace of obsolete forms. Under Edward I the offices of customer, controller and searcher were created. They were patent offices, originally appointed by the king or his high officers. (From the time of Henry VI the treasurer obtained patronage.) When, as happened from time to time, the collection of the customs was farmed out to private individuals, the patent officers' role shrank to that of merely checking their proceedings. In 1671 negotiations for a new farm broke down, it was decided that the central government itself should once more collect the customs, and the board of customs was created. It might have been thought that the customers, controllers and searchers would now once more perform those duties for which they had been created; but not at all!

The collectors, i.e. the staff of the tax-farmers, were taken over by the Crown to become Crown servants, stationed in all parts of the country, and made completely responsible for collecting the duties and returning money and accounts to the customs office. The controller merely shared with the collector the general superintendence of the ports. The searchers continued to do certain work until, later on, the Board of Customs found that it could be done more usefully by officers called land-waiters and coast-waiters: and then all that remained for the searcher to do was to supervise such goods as went for export. As to the customers, they found themselves without any duties whatsoever. Their work was entirely duplicated by the collector or, at all events, might have been executed by the collector. Yet the numerous brood of customers and searchers continued to be appointed long after they had duties to perform: so that by 1780 there were two sets of officials in the customs service, the working officials (e.g. the collectors and the waiters) and the sinecures or half-sinecure offices (such as the customers and searchers) which had been taken over straight from the Middle Ages. When, in 1798, the 196 sinecure offices in the Customs were abolished, George Rose, not a very fervent friend of reform, had to admit:

> the management in truth, derived great advantage from the suppression of the description of offices here noticed, as the possessors of them, holding by patents, conceiving themselves amenable only to the treasury or the king, sometimes formally disclaimed any responsibility to the

commissioners of the customs to the manifest inconvenience, if not to the loss of revenue.[9]

In the management of the executive branch of British government any reformer had to tackle the dead weight of centuries. The Americans on the other hand, were able to make a clean start and planned their offices on grounds of rational utility. This must be accounted as the first and overriding reason why British administration in the period under review was far more expensive and certainly not more efficient than its American counterpart.

British Administration Sacrificed to Politics

Patronage and Politics in Britain and America

The second reason for the lower standards of public management in Britain was derivative from the first. The mediaeval structure of the administration, the ease with which an establishment could be multiplied, the high degree of independence which its internal processes enjoyed from the observations and control of the legislature—all of these were advantages which the politicians were quick to seize. The administration, to borrow Burke's phrase, was "a loaded compost heap of corrupt influence."

In representative government of the American and British types, there are three conceivable political objects for which the gift or promise of places and offices might be manipulated.

   i. To ensure a public service loyal to the regime.
  ii. To influence the electorate in their choice of representatives.

Here we must distinguish between a situation:
  a. Where the public officials are expected and intended to be partisans, i.e., always to vote for the "friends" who first appointed them, irrespective of the political complexion of the government of the day, and (therefore) the interest of their administrative superiors.
  b. Where the public officials are expected and intended to be ministerialist, i.e., always to vote as told by their administrative superiors, i.e., the government of the day, regardless of the political interests of the "friends" who first appointed them.
 iii. To influence an elected legislature; by detaching members from their private allegiances, in order to support the government of the day.

Now in respect to (i), both the United States and Great Britain, at certain times in the period under review, made loyalty to the regime a prerequisite of appointment to public office. Washington would not appoint former Tories. In Britain also there is evidence of some disturbance in public offices after the accession of George I, to secure adherence to the new order.[10] This kind of discrimination is compatible with a very wide choice of candidates and need not prejudice the quality of the public service. This factor may be discounted as affecting the quality of public administration in either Britain or America.

In respect to (ii[a]) such were the political circumstances of either country at this time that the bartering of public offices for partisan support hardly arose. In Britain, as Feiling points out, "It is indeed a truth, fundamental for our purpose, that organized continuous party existed neither in the seventeenth nor in the eighteenth century.[11] It is equally true that there was no organized opposition until the Napoleonic Wars,[12] nor was there either popular constituency or anything resembling a national party organization. In these circumstances, there was no tendency in eighteenth century Britain for rival groups of politicians to promise the places of their rivals to their own friends in return for electoral support. In the federal sphere of American politics, between 1789 and 1824, circumstances were similarly such as largely to preclude this type of abuse of the patronage system. So long as Washington was in office parties were in abeyance. After Jefferson's first term the Federalist party began to dwindle away and not until 1828 did the two-party system emerge. Had this not been so, however, it is conceivable and even likely that the "rotation of office" would have developed there and then, for the short period of intense party rivalry, 1794–1804, is full of instances where patronage was bartered for political support. The defection of New York to Jefferson in 1800 was the outcome of disappointment felt by Livingstone and Clinton who had been deprived of patronage by Washington and Adams. Again, Jefferson, on acceding to power, carried out a proscription of Federalists in the public service and gave their posts to his own supporters. There is little reason to suppose that if the Federalists had returned to power in 1804 they would have acted like the Rockingham Whigs in 1765 and simply restored the *status quo ante;* the probability is that they would have carried out a counter-purge. But, fortunately, the Republicans stayed in power, and for another twenty-odd years there was one-party control of the federal government. Thus, bye and large, between 1789 and 1828, a situation of political partisanship did not exist in the federal sphere of American politics, and so it was not necessary for Americans to abuse recruitment for electoral purposes.

Patronage could also be manipulated to secure the return of a "ministerialist" legislature, one that would support the administration of the day, i.e. (ii[*b*]). Now under the American constitution this kind of legislature, however desirable, is not strictly necessary; for the president, once elected, is independent and irremovable. Not so in Britain, however; for although the monarch was independent and irremovable, his ministers were not and it was through his ministers that he had to carry out his policies. Consequently it was not merely desirable in Britain but *vital* that the administration of the day should secure—if necessary in advance—an amenable House of Commons. To quote Feiling again

> It was for the king to choose ministers and though he would obviously choose them from groups strong enough to get his business done in the Commons he chose them irrespective of the constituencies. So that the process of our day was actually inverted, ministers being selected not in consequence of, but in order to make, an election; and before 1831 there is no example of ministers, if supported by the Crown, being beaten at the polls.[13]

Finally, once a legislature had been elected, patronage could be used to detach members from the private loyalties and to get them to rally round the administration, i.e. (iii). To this purpose patronage has been put in the United States of today; but we are assured by Professor White that he has found no evidence that it was so used during the Federalist and Jeffersonian period. Such use of patronage might have prevented the frustration of Monroe and J.Q. Adams by congress; but, however desirable, it was not absolutely necessary, because again, once elected the president was irremovable and independent. By the same token, however, the British cabinet being dependent and removable by the House of Commons *had* to make use of patronage in order to make the 1688 settlement work.

If, then, we review these three purposes which patronage could serve (i) did not and would not exercise a marked effect; (ii[*a*]) operated only intermittently in the United States and not at all in Britain; but (ii[*b*]) and (iii) which, however desirable, were not strictly necessary to the American Constitution were both central to the British political system.

Patronage Buys Political Support in Eighteenth Century Britain

Since a compliant House was essential if the British constitution was to work, to this purpose the patronage system was necessarily subverted. Honors could buy such support, contracts could buy such support, commissions in the army and navy could buy such support; but these baskets of loaves and fishes were not enough, by themselves, to keep the constitution working. The public service was a fourth basket of spoils; and, owing to the Gothic nature of the administration it could, up to a point, be expanded at need, to meet the exigencies of a political crisis. This is, in fact, what happened.

Compliant legislatures were returned, kept or made, by (1) the granting of favors, and (2) the nomination to official posts. By "favors" we mean the handing out of pensions, or sinecures or the reversions to those sinecure posts which existed in the public service. These—which were the plums of the public service—were granted for two reasons. They might be granted to individual embers of parliament in order to get them to support a particular measure brought forward by the administration. They were in fact a good method of making a House and of keeping it. Or, they might be used to prepare the way for an electoral triumph. Given the unreformed electoral system of the day the keys to electoral victory lay in the pocket boroughs and the close boroughs. To secure victory the politician must address himself to those individuals who possessed the first, or had what was called "a political interest" (i.e. influence) in the second. To secure the support of these individuals the sinecures, the pensions and the reversions were handed out; and in return MPs who could be relied on to support the administration would be elected. The second class of patronage, i.e. nomination to working posts in the public services, was useful, not for making or keeping a House, but in the electoral process. The electorate was very small at the close of the eighteenth century—about 200,000–250,000. Throughout the century, therefore, the rare individuals who had a right to vote were given preference in appointment to the public service; and as public officials they were expected to cast their vote as their administrative chiefs directed. Thus at any general election there was a large block of voters in a very small electorate, whose tradition it was to vote as they were told. Furthermore, their loyalty was, traditionally, not owed to the individual minister or patron who had secured their admission to the public service, but to the government of the day. In practice some of these public officials were often in a predicament; for sometimes they had to choose between voting for the candidate of their original patron and voting for the candidate of the minister of the day. Thus in the election at Malden in 1763, the excise men were told to votee for one Gascoyn, although they did not in fact do so, but voted against him and returned his rival, Mr. Husk.[14] Similarly, in the Maidstone election of 1761 the Admiralty instructed all the freemen of Maidstone who were employed by them in the Chatham dockyards, to vote for Mr. Northern. Instead, they seem to have voted (as did the customs and excise officials) for a Mr. Fuller. Thereupon Fuller wrote to the Duke of Newcastle (who controlled the treasury patronage) asking him to "protect them from censure and discountenance."[15] But on the whole these revolts seem to have been rare and the public officials who had votes played a very important role in securing the return of government candidates. The Marquis of Rockingham stated in 1782 "That there were no less than 70 boroughs where the election depended chiefly on the votes of revenue officers; the Custom House alone had 5,000 persons belonging to it besides about 2,500 more of extra tides men, etc., and the Excise at least 4,000 more, who were voters . . . The revenue officers, as the law now stood, not only were forced to vote for those they did not approve, but to vote against their own friends and those in particular to whom they were most obliged."[16] In his forecast for the election of 1784, John Robinson mentions the effect upon certain boroughs of the recent disfranchisement of these revenue officers by Crewe's Act of 1782. In Winchelsea, "The revenue officers having been struck off leaves scarce a good voter." In Hastings, Rye and Seaford, he says "The disfranchising bill has made great alterations."[17]

Since the harmony of the executive and legislature rested upon the making of elections and the making and keeping of the House of Commons, there was increasing pressure in the eighteenth century to turn more and more posts to political advantage and to barter public office for the possession of a vote regardless of character and capacity. In her study of the customs system in the eighteenth century, Elizabeth Hoon shows that there was a steady increase in treasury patronage. Early in the century the treasury did little more than alter some of the Customs Board's presentments; only occasionally did it recommend. Later, it recommended more frequently; and sometimes, where there were no available vacancies, it directed persons to be employed in a temporary capacity. In 1757 it ordered that notice of all vacancies must be sent to the treasury immediately; in 1765 that the presentments to vacancies be submitted to them each week. Next the treasury began to create many new offices "by constitution"—a form of establishment which vested complete control of the servant in the Treasury Board; and then, in 1782, they ordered that no deputies to the old patent officers be appointed without treasury consent. Under this regime the standards required from candidates were progressively lowered and the commissioners complained that they were drawn "from county fox hunters, bankrupt merchants, and officers of the army and navy."[18] As to the excise officers, these had been brought under treasury control considerably earlier in the century—between 1729 and 1736. By the later date it was all over: an exciseman with a vote was thereafter expected to cast it as the First Lord of the Treasury directed.

Thus the exigencies of the Gothic constitution led successive governments not only to perpetuate but even to exaggerate the eccentricities and incapacities of the Gothic administration. So long as this method of working the constitution was not under attack—and it was not seriously under attack until after 1780—the structure and organization of the administrative system could not be attacked either. Politics was supported by the nature of the administrative system; the administrative system was supported by the nature of politics.[19]

Thus we have seen first, that whereas the United States was able to start with a clear field and to build a rational structure of administration, Britain in 1780 was loaded with the detritus of ages; and secondly, that whereas the political situation in the United States from 1789 to 1828 was such that the constitution could work without seriously depressing the quality of the public servant, this was not so in Great Britain. It is to these two causes, medieval organization on the one hand and the servitude of efficiency to politics on the other, that we must attribute the superiority of American administration in the first forty years of the life of the Republic.

Probity and Capacity of the Public Officials in America and Britain, 1780–1830

In considering the depression of British administrative standards we must not give too much weight to the fact that in the United States those with the power to appoint had moral standards vastly different from their opposite numbers in Great Britain. It is true that Washington was particularly stern and unbending. As we have seen, "family relationship, indolence and drink" were to him an insuperable bar to public office. John Adams was equally lofty: "I should belie the whole course of my public and private conduct and all the maxims of my life if ever I should consider public authority entrusted to me to be made subservient to my views or those of my family or friends."[20] And, once Jefferson's purge of 1801–1803 was over, "the standards were high," says Professor White. "Their choice fell upon persons from the same reputable social class of gentlemen upon whom the Federalists had depended. We need not allow favors . . . to obscure the standards that

the Republicans announced and generally maintained. Their selections
. . . were made within the ranks of the Republican party, but they were
confined to gentlemen who were men of integrity.''[21]

It is equally true that in contemporary Britain appointments were not
confined to men of integrity and that numerous bad appointments were
made. As late as the period 1836–1854 (by when the situation had
greatly improved), many appointments were still of the very worst
quality.

> I have made out a return of fifty-five persons who were nominated by the
> treasury between 1836 and 1854. Several of them were incompetent from
> their age. I found some perfectly unqualified. . . . One person in that list
> had been imprisoned by the sentence of the court as a fraudulent debtor.
> . . . There was one man whom I was forced to keep in a room by himself
> as he was in such a state of health that he could not associate with the
> other clerks. . . . There was the case . . . in which a gentleman was
> appointed who really could neither read nor write; he was almost an idiot
> and there was the greatest possible difficulty in getting him out of the
> office.[22]

Another example of the low standards in the civil service is to be found
in an analysis of the results of the qualifying examinations instituted in
1855. Of 958 persons *nominated as being fit* for public office, nearly 300
were rejected by the civil service commissioners, and of these rejec-
tions 206 failed in arithmetic or in spelling.[23]

Nevertheless, on a closer examination, the apparent gap between
the two civil services does not appear to be quite as wide as these facts
would suggest. It is commonly said that ''nepotism'' was one of the
besetting sins of the British civil service at this period. Professor
White, quoting Federalist and Jeffersonian presidents, shows that they
were opposed to nepotism; but his evidence also shows clearly that the
senior civil servants (e.g. Nourse, Bradley and Dearbourn) were by no
means averse from bringing their relatives and friends into the public
service.[24] In point of fact, this is only to be expected. Why should not
departmental heads very properly consider that their friends and
relatives were as capable as distant and unknown applicants? Is there
any reason to believe that they might not have been right?

In assessing the standards of personnel in Britain, especially in
relation to the American civil service at this time, it must also be borne
in mind that the collectors of revenue (e.g. the customs officials) were
expected to give a heavy bond before being allowed to take up office
and, furthermore, that even if nominated by the treasury they were
always subject to disciplinary dismissal by their Board. In Elizabeth

Hoon's study there is surprisingly little evidence of defalcation or embezzlement on anything but a very petty scale. As to the Board of Customs itself, it was exceedingly hardworking; and her comment on its record is:

> for the most part administration was sound. . . . The Board made continual attempts to improve the effectiveness of the service by expanding the organization, encouraging officers, bettering the regulation of routine business, and having regard to the danger of patent offices, fees, and the like. The commissioners, however, cannot be entirely freed from the responsibility for the poor condition of many of the ports, for the too-frequent conniving of customs officials in fraud and smuggling and for the indifferent personnel which meant a proportional degree of inefficiency.[25]

Despite the just criticism contained in this paragraph it is manifest that the customs system, in the teeth of the tremendous handicaps to which the inadequate organization and political interference gave rise, was not the weltering sink of corruption, immorality and indolence which we have been conditioned to expect.[26]

Now if we look in any detail at some of the American services during this period we shall find that despite the care in choosing public servants, the officials were not always as efficient or upright as presidential high-mindedness would suggest. For example, after the war of 1812 there was a crop of embezzlements by public agents in the United States. Theoren Rudd, clerk of the district court in New York, absconded with $65,000 of public money and over $52,000 belonging to litigants before the court. John Braham, receiver of public money at Huntsville, Alabama, speculated away $80,000 on the cotton market. Byas Watkins, auditor in the U.S. Treasury, embezzled over $7,000 and ran away.

Professor White comments "that these cases were as exceptional as they were conspicuous,"[27] but the fact remains that it is from isolated incidents like this—such as the Duke of York scandal in 1809 or the Melville scandal of 1805 or the existence of the "subordinate treasuries" in 1780—that the low morality of the British public service of the time has been deduced. It is a major merit of Professor White's volumes, in itself, that he has supplied a standard by which we can gauge the shortcomings of contemporary British administration. It is clear from the examples cited that even in a public service like that of the United States with its high standards of recruitment and high ideals as to public service grave derelictions could every now and then occur. And this should serve as a warning to scholars on this side of the

Atlantic not to judge the eighteenth century British civil service by the more spectacular examples of nepotism, inefficiency and malversation: because it may very well be that if these services were inspected as closely as Professor White has examined the American, the much-paraded examples of inefficiency might turn out to be as untypical of the British public services as he has shown them to be untypical of their counterparts in the United States.

Finally, in assessing the quality of the eighteenth century British public service, one ought never to forget that side by side with the bankrupts, the foxhunters and the illiterates there were such notable as Abbott, Arbuthnot, Barrow, Bickersteth, Finlaison and Deacon Hume, Larpent, Rickman, Stevenson and Sir T. Murdoch: and also an anonymous mass of humbler officials whose integrity and capacity was sufficient to leaven the ineptitude of the ranker political nominations, and to carry the GPO, the customs and the excise to a not altogether inconsiderable measure of success.[28] Indeed any student undertaking to examine the characteristics of the eighteenth century public servant might well adopt, as his starting hypothesis, Sir James Stephen's classification of the Colonial Office of his day. There were, said he, a small minority of first rate intellects, experienced and devoted to the public service: a larger group of men "who performed diligently, faithfully and judiciously the duties to which they were called"; and a third group, in the majority, of those who possessed "only in a low degree and some in a degree almost incredibly low either the talents or the habits of men of business, or the industry, the zeal or the knowledge required for the effective performance of their appropriate functions."[29] A similar state of affairs seems to have characterized the public offices in the eighteenth century.

Pace of Invention and Reform, 1780–1830, in America and in Britain

If we are trying to assess administrative capacity, ought we to judge a system merely by what it is at one point of time: or may we not also judge by reference to what it has evolved from and what it is advancing to? From this standpoint, the British achievements from 1780 to 1830 bear comparison with the American and, indeed, may be deemed to surpass them. It should by now be clear how great was the American advantage in starting with a clear field, and in that her internal politics at this period did not necessitate, as in Britain, a continual subordination of administrative efficiency to the maintenance of political power. Yet from 1801 onwards, as Professor White clearly shows, American administration had reached a plateau; more than that, a good deal of evidence throughout *The Jeffersonians* indicates that in many respects it was already slipping back. In Britain, on the other hand, it is no exaggeration to say that in the years 1780–1834 a revolution was accomplished in the public service. Its Gothic structure was laid in ruins and upon them was reared the massive foundations for a coherent and rational structure which the next generation was to erect.

Developments in America, 1801–1830

Of the United States during this period Professor White remarks:

> The major developments grew out of the crisis caused by war. The embargo left no permanent changes in normal procedures, although it provided some extraordinary precedents, and the depression of 1819–1822 was neither long nor severe enough to leave a mark on the administrative system. The incompetence of the defense departments and of civilian administration revealed by the war with Great Britain was so impressive, however, that it caused the first major reorganization of the federal administrative system. The principal elements will be recalled: the establishment of the army General Staff,[30] the formation of the Board of Navy Commissioners, and the reconstruction of the accounting organization and system of accountability. Other significant reforms and developments also took place after 1815. West Point was reorganized and put on a high professional standard. Ship construction was standardized. A system of inspection of land offices was introduced, the first of its kind. The procedures of the state department were greatly improved by John Quincy Adams. The post office was energized by John McLean.
>
> Of special importance was the establishment of professional assistance to the heads of the two defense departments by means of the General Staff of the Army and the Board of Navy Commissioners. The full significance of this innovation was probably not understood at the time, since each institution was proposed and defended as a means of relieving the head of the department from an impossible burden of detail. The secretaries did benefit to some extent in this respect, although detail kept crowding its way to their desks. Much more important was the availability of professional advice on army and navy affairs, hitherto lacking on any systematic or orderly basis. The navy board was particularly useful in bringing its judgment to bear on naval construction and on the management of navy yards and posts. Both agencies were successful in elaborating a body of regulations for the government of the uniformed forces.
>
> The state department remained throughout the period with no professional officer to assist the secretary. The treasury had enjoyed the services of men above the rank of chief clerk from the beginning: the commmissioner of revenue, the register, and the head of the General Land Office in particular, but like the comptrollers and auditors, they brought no relief to the secretary in the discharge of his own duties. The

post office had two officers of general competence aiding the postmaster general: the first and second assistant postmasters general. These modest advances were significant of later developments.

The Republican years confirmed Federalist ideas about permanent service in the general government. Tenure, although not protected by law, was in fact during good behaviour, both in Washington and in the field. Clerks might end their official work in the same office, indeed in the same position in which they began, but the expectation of life service was high. The army and navy offered somewhat greater freedom of movement than the civilian agencies, but both uniformed services suffered reductions that forced many career officers into civilian life.[31]

"The Jeffersonians in fact," he says, "carried the Federalist administrative machine forward without substantial alteration in form or in spirit for nearly three decades."

But in some respects, the standards of administration were slipping back. The Treasury, after the retirement of Gallatin, ceased to control the estimates of the other departments. The collectors "tended to become careless in the conduct of Custom House business."[32] The State Department had become choked by domestic business which Congress declined to transfer to a separate Department of the Interior.[33] Above all, from 1824 to 1828 the high standards of recruitment hitherto characteristic of the system became subjected to an increasingly intolerable political pressure and finally collapsed with the election of President Jackson.

Developments in Britain, 1780–1830

By contrast, the British system had been almost completely remodelled since 1780, and the Reform Bill of 1832 was to provide a still greater impetus to its reorganization.

Size and functions   In 1828 the British Civil Service (excluding the law courts, the Colonies, and the Household) consisted of 22,900 persons. In 1797 there had been 16,267. The net increase of over 6000 was almost entirely accounted for by an addition of over 5000 in the Customs Service, 600 in the GPO, and 66 in the Taxes Office.

The functions of central government were at this time not greatly dissimilar from those of the U.S. federal government. The primary function was to defend the country and to pay off the national debt; consequently the biggest departments and the most expensive were those of the armed services on the one hand and the collection of revenue on the other. The public service as a whole may be divided into six groups. There was first the treasury group which comprised the Treasury, the Exchequer, the Audit Board, the Land Revenue Board, the Tax Office, the Stamps Office, the Hackney Coach and Hawkers Office, the Board of Customs and the Board of Excise. The Mint, the Board of Woods and the Board of Works may also be regarded as coming within this general group. Next there comes the army group of which the chief offices were the War Office, the Ordnance Office, the Army Pay Office, the Store-keeper's Office and the Commander-in-Chief's Office. Of the navy group the chief offices were the Admiralty, the Navy Office, the Navy Pay Office, and the Royal Navy Hospital Board. Fourth comes a group of departments or offices which we may call the secretariat. They represent the developments, by 1828, of the primal office of the Royal Secretary. By this time they consisted of the Home Office, the Foreign Office and the Colonial Office. The last group, miscellaneous, consisted of such offices as the Council Office and its quondam offshoot, the Board of Trade; the Privy Seal Office; and the Board of Control.

Lack of Coherence   The system as a whole was still largely incoherent. It is true that board management, in appearance the prevalent pattern, was already illusory. (In respect to the Treasury's major functions, the chancellor was in full control. The minutes continued to be read twice weekly to a board at which the junior lords were present; but from 1809 no record was kept of their individual attendance and the matter became more and more a formality. The junior lords were permitted to criticize the wording of the minutes and were sometimes set to research and report upon certain aspects of business; but by 1828 the running of the department was firmly in the hands of the chancellor and his permanent staff.[34] Similarly, the Board of Trade, though technically a board, was, in fact, a department administered by its president and vice-president. The Board of Control was likewise a board only in name.)

In addition, the secretariat, organized from the start on Bentham's principle of single-seatedness, was, between 1780 and 1830, moving into the forefront of administrative activity. Thus six of the departments, and these not the least important, were by 1828 organized on the "single-seated principle" regardless of any formal appearances to the contrary.

Yet though some of the departments were thus acquiring a coherent pattern, the departmental groups, with one big exception, still remained inchoate. The exception was the treasury group, over which the Treasury was beginning to assert much more stringent control.[35] The army and the navy groups, however, were very loosely organized. Thus, the Secretary for War and Colonies was responsible for the size of the force and for controlling its functions abroad during war; but the

Home Secretary was responsible for general military questions when the army was at home. The Secretary at War was responsible to parliament for finance and for the contacts between the army and civilian population, but the Commander-in-Chief was responsible for the discipline of the forces. He had no control over troops abroad, however, and he could not move troops at home without the consent of the Secretary at War: he had no control over the supplies because arms and stores were the responsibility of the ordnance branch, provisions the responsibility of the Commissariat, and clothing the responsibility of the Board of General Officers. All these offices approached each other by formal letter. The incoherence of the system was fully seen by contemporaries. Lord Howick's commission in 1837 produced a comprehensive plan of reorganization, but Wellington, who was Commander-in-Chief, opposed this so firmly that no action was taken and the system continued to muddle along until the disasters of the Crimean War. The Navy was in a similar state; but reforms here were initiated by Graham in 1832.

Finally there was a marked lack of Treasury control over the whole organization—if organization it could be called. The Treasury's control over the estimates of its own "group" were recognized by the law and custom of the constitution, but the other departments preserved their independence jealously. Estimates for the armed services were discussed at the cabinet level before being passed on the Treasury;[36] and in 1783 when Pitt's Public Offices Regulation Bill found its way to the House of Lords it raised cries of alarm from officers who feared that their autonomy would be curtailed. Lord Townshend opposed it because "it would give the Lords of the Treasury greater influence over the Board of Ordnance than they at preseent possessed." Lord Stormont (the Lord President) complained that "it gave most extraordinary powers to the Treasury and diminished the necessary power and the dignity of the other officers, in a manner very inconsistent with the duties which they had to discharge. . . . Several of the great offices of the State had even been distinct and independent; but this Bill gave the Treasury a painful pre-eminence over all of them, and made every one of the rest subject to its control." The Bill was defeated 40 to 24.[37]

Emergence of the Cabinet   Nevertheless, between 1780 and 1834 reform had proceeded continuously on a massive scale. In the first place we must remark the rise of the cabinet as a supreme controlling body; secondly, that the essential preliminary for treasury control had been created; thirdly that the public offices had been largely modernized; and fourthly that there was an increasing divorce of administration from political considerations.

By 1828 the cabinet was beginning to take its modern shape and becoming the coordinator and supervisor of the separate departmental establishments.[38] In 1780 the cabinet had consisted of the cabinet officers, the cabinet officer *"with the circulation,"* and the cabinet officers "with the circulation *and the Post Office."* Under Pitt's premiership a distinction was finally drawn between the efficient cabinet and the titular cabinet; and the latter withered away. Again, with the accession of Pitt, "government by departments," which had become prevalent under North's administration, began to decline. The cabinet began to work as a team and look to the prime minister for its lead. The convention of cabinet unanimity grew up: after enduring public criticism and opposition from his Lord Chancellor for nine years, Pitt insisted on his removal from the cabinet, and this enforced resignation of Lord Thurlow in 1792 marks the beginning of the tradition of unanimity.[39] In 1821 Canning resigned from the cabinet because he did not see eye-to-eye with his colleagues on the affair of Queen Caroline; and Huskisson's resignation over his vote on the East Retford Bill in 1828 further drove home this convention that a minister ought to resign if unable to vote together with his colleagues. It is perfectly true, of course, that owing to the prevalence of "open questions" during this period, cabinets were formed and maintained at that time in a fashion impossible today; but, nevertheless, while 1780 saw the cabinet a mere group of departmental heads, 1828 saw it a collective unity. In this way, the British cabinet was fast becoming an American presidency put "into commission"; or if one prefers it, to become a collective presidency, and the head of the executive branch. What is more, after the Reform Bill of 1832, the cabinet was destined to go far beyond the American presidency in its control of the administrative branch; for whereas the latter became increasingly hampered and plagued by congressional committees and their financial pressure, the procedural changes which followed the Reform Bill in Britain reinforced the leadership of the cabinet over the House of Commons, finally rendering it the undisputed head of the administrative departments.

The Foundations of Treasury Control   In respect to the second great line of reform, viz. the foundations of centralized treasury control, the matter is somewhat more complicated. The reforms proceeded along four lines. To begin with, such control cannot be exercised, unless the public accounts show clearly how much money comes in, how it is appropriated, and how it is being spent. This was quite impracticable under the system of 1780. By this, certain revenues were traditionally assigned to certain funds and from these funds certain payments were traditionally made; furthermore many public servants were paid by fees, not by salaries. The reform of the public accounts was the first requisite of effective budgeting. It began with Pitt's Consolidated Fund Act of 1787. Contrary to popular belief, this act did not operate fully until the close of the whole Napoleonic wars:[40] but by 1828, its intentions were being fully carried out. All income, from all sources, was paid into one single Consolidated Fund; and all expenditure was paid out of it. (Except for "drawbacks," etc., for which see below.) Annual gross amounts of income and expenditure had been placed before the House in 1802 and balanced accounts in 1822. Though an enormous improvement on the 1780 situation, these were still incomprehensible as to detail. It was not until appropriation accounts were introduced in the generation after 1830 that the exact identification of all items of expenditure was accomplished.

A second move in the direction of effective budgeting was the modernization of the system of receipts and payments. In 1780 these were still being effected in the ancient Exchequer by a procedure sanctioned by time and Henry I. In 1783 the old system of giving tally-sticks as receipts was directed to be abolished, and check-receipts to be substituted for them;[41] though the reform did not become effective until 1826. But by 1834 the whole Exchequer had been swept away and replaced by the Comptroller General and his small staff; and it was to him that the legality of payments of public money was now referred; while instead of the physical transfer of treasure in and out of chests kept at the Exchequer offices,[42] payments were made by book transactions on accounts at the Bank of England.

Two more reforms which increased treasury control of budgeting were the steps leading to greater control over estimates and those facilitating greater control of appropriations. The latter was effected by reforms in the method of audit. In 1780 audit was in the hands of the Auditors of Imprest, or, rather, by their deputies, for the auditorships were notorious sinecures. But the system in use was so complicated and cumbersome and slow that in 1780 there were open accounts going back thirty years: there was even one which went back to 1689. In 1785 the Auditors of Imprest were abolished and an Audit Board set up. Incapable of handling the huge sums spent during the Napoleonic War, after 1815 it steadily improved. Furthermore, its accounts were more readily comprehensible to the public. In 1780 the Auditors of Imprest were still keeping their accounts in *Roman* numerals. Now, since it is impossible to add up large sums expressed in Roman numerals with any accuracy or speed, Arabic numerals were written in by the side, and additions and subtractions were made in these; but the result was so to superimpose the Roman and Arabic numerals that neither were easily distinguishable. Furthermore, the receipts and issues were still recorded in the Latin tongue; and this was not the golden Latin tongue nor even the silver Latin tongue, nor even the language of Ulpian, but a barbarous gibberish which had evolved departmentally in the course of centuries, and was impossible for any outsider to read or understand.[43] However, in 1834 the English language and Arabic numerals were at last introduced in the teeth of a protest, "that if those proceedings were directed in future to be made in English, the present records in a few years would be obsolete and unintelligible."[44]

Despite the modernization of the audit system it was not complete. For one thing, the sums paid into the Consolidated Fund by the departments were net sums and not the gross ones; that is to say, departments did not pay in all that they received, but subtracted what were called "drawbacks" (i.e. costs of collection) and the costs of making contracts or sales of property, etc. Consequently it was hard to check whether such drawbacks were justified. In the second place, and far more serious, no departments laid an appropriation account before the House. It was discovered in 1831 that for some years past, sums voted by parliament for one purpose to the Admiralty had been used systematically for quite different purposes. The underlying reasons were

> loose estimates which did not truly represent the financial requirements of the naval service; an incomplete system of accounts, which generally could not exhibit the naval expenditure under the heads of the separate grants of Parliament; tardy examination of accounts, which would have delayed the preparation of audited returns of expenditure to a period when they would have been of no practical value; but, above all, the absence of any returns to the House of Commons upon which reliance could be placed, showing how far the intentions of Parliament had been complied with in the application of the naval grants.[45]

In 1832 the huge sums voted to the Admiralty were expressed in an appropriation account by Sir James Graham: in 1846 the system was extended to the War Office, and in 1861 extended to all other votes.

The last set of reforms which conduced to more effective treasury control was the growth of its control over departmental estimates. In 1780 the items of expenditure were to be found in three groups, viz. in the services' estimates, in certain miscellaneous grants, and in certain charges traditionally borne on the king's civil list. The service estimates do not concern us here as we have seen that they were negotiated at cabinet level before proceeding to the treasury. Treasury control originates in its control over items of civil expenditures. In 1780 this was a minute item compared with the whole, only £80,000 out of a total of over £22 million.[46] The Treasury had controlled these estimates for miscellaneous expenditure, and in some cases had even made them up in its own offices, as far back as the Revolution of 1688, and possibly before. The more extensive control over civil items which developed after 1780 arose from the fact that by successive statutes certain items, e.g. the cost of ambassadors or judges, which had hitherto been borne on the civil list, were transferred to the miscellaneous estimates and so became subject both to the scrutiny of the Treasury and of the House of Commons. The final transfer of the civil items took place in the definitive reform of 1831, as a result of which the civil list was confined to royal household expenditure and all national items were transferred either to the Consolidated Fund or to the annual miscellaneous estimates. Thus, by 1831 the Treasury and the Commons were made responsible for items which hitherto had been concealed in the royal civil list. But in addition to this, the proportion which miscellaneous items bore to the total government expenditure began to rise sharply during the nineteenth century. In 1820 there was something like £2 million out of a total of £57 millions: by 1850 some £4 milion out of a total of £55 million. In this way, after the reform of 1831, Treasury control increased *pari-passu* with the increase of civil estimates.

By 1834 instead of a primitive system of finance incomprehensible either to the public or to the Treasury, reforms had been made without which centralized treasury control of departmental expenditure would have been impracticable; national and departmental accounts were either effective or about to become so; the receipts and payments system had been modernized; the notion of retrospective audit to check appropriations had been evolved at the Admiralty and was to spread to all other departments; and finally, the Treasury control of the miscellaneous estimates had been insured and was to grow with the growth of these estimates in the national budget. The sequel has a certain irony. While the British system of financial control was evolving to its logical terminus in the Exchequer and Audit Act of 1866, the US financial system stood still. The US Treasury became one department among many, exercising neither supervision nor restraint over its partners; each department submitted its own estimates to the appropriation committees of congress; and no effective post-audit of accounts was developed. In 1916 an unofficial commission of three American political scientists examined and reported on the British system; and in 1921, by the Budget and Accounting Act, the essentials of that system were, as far as the Constitution permitted,[47] introduced into the United States. A comptroller and auditor was appointed, and the Bureau of the

Budget set up to collate departmental estimates and present congress with a unified "executive budget."

Modernization of the Departments While the cabinet was fast becoming the effective head of the whole public establishments of the country, and as the Treasury was on the point of becoming the effective co-ordinating head at the departmental level, a third great change took place in the British public service. This was the modernization of the public offices. We have seen that in 1780 a great number of the clerks of these offices were paid by a fee system, and that as a result, internal developments in each ministry occurred outside the public gaze. In 1780, Lord North agreed to set up a commission to examine the public accounts, and this commission which reported between 1782 and 1786 analyzed in detail the system of payment by fees and concluded heavily against it. It recommended that wherever possible they should be replaced by a salary system. There was a subsequent piecemeal development throughout the public offices, some adopting the recommendations and some not. A select committee of 1797 repeated the recommendations of the earlier inquiry; and this report was followed by a treasury circular to defaulting offices. In changing from fees to salaries the system generally adopted was to fund all departmental fees into a common pool from which fixed salaries were then paid out to all persons on the establishment. The difficulty that arose here, was that the fund itself fluctuated from year to year. Were officials to accept cuts in their salaries whenever there was a fall in the fee fund? In 1810 a statute laid it down that any such deficiencies would be made good from the Civil List, but this proved grossly unsatisfactory. In 1816 it was replaced by a statute by which any deficiencies were to be made good by a parliamentary vote. From this point, salaries came within the purview both of the Treasury and of parliament; and what we have hitherto called the public service had made the step which transformed it into the civil service. Quasi-private clerks and officers were now definitely public officers; henceforth parliament's interest in cheap government and efficient government carried the reform movement forward into inquiries about the internal management of the departments and the quality of their personnel. Thus by 1830 the stage was set for the great internal reorganization which was carried through after 1848, and which was stimulated by the gross administrative shortcomings revealed in the Crimean War.

During this period also, the dead wood was swept out of the departments. It has been seen that so long as sinecures existed and so long as politics could make use of them, so long obsolete forms and processes must continue in the public service, e.g. in the Customs or the Exchequer. From 1780 to 1834 the sinecures were eliminated. It is difficult to make an estimate of the total existing in 1780 as very often what was described as a sinecure was, in fact, an office with a very light duty; but the number of total sinecures seems to have been in the order of 600. Burke's Civil List Act of 1782 swept away 134 offices and another 144 were swept away by Pitt in 1782–1783. All these were offices on the Civil List, however. In 1783 the Exchequer Act suppressed the usher, tally cutters, chamberlains, and the second-clerks in the teller's office, and similarly the offices of the auditor and four tellers. In 1798 a further wave of suppressions occurred: 196 offices in the Customs were done away with and three in the Land Revenue. In 1810, there were still 242 sinecures costing roughly £300,000: but by 1834 they were almost eliminated.[48] Thus, partly by the transition from a fee system to a salary system and partly by the abolition of sinecures, the way was at last open to the reorganization and public control of the departments and the civil service.[49]

Increasing Divorce between Politics and Administration

The last of the four major developments in the modernization of the public service, 1780–1834, was the increasing divorce of administration and politics. In 1782 contractors were excluded from parliament, and in that same year the revenue officers were disfranchised. In 1809, following the Duke of York scandal, an act prohibited the sale and brokerage of offices; and another act "to secure independence in parliament," laid down that bribes "of offices, places and employment were contrary to the freedom of election." This last act was made more effective in 1827 by an act which made the *acceptance* of such bribes penal, not only the mere offering of them. These measures together with legislation which regulated and brought under public control the pension list, and others which interfered with the buying and selling of government boroughs had by 1830 destroyed the influence of the Crown. Perhaps the final proof is that Wellington lost the election of 1830.[50] By 1830, although the party in office always endeavoured as far as possible to give jobs to *its* supporters rather than to those on the benches opposite, and although patronage was helpful in ensuring party discipline inside the House, the more flagrant subordination of administrative efficiency to political considerations had disappeared; and, within the next generation, was to disappear completely.

In all these respects, therefore—the emergence of cabinet leadership, the foundations of effective budgeting and treasury control, the modernization of the public offices, and finally, the severance of administration from high politics—the foundations were laid for the remarkable reforms of the mid-nineteenth century which made Britain rather than America the ideal model for administrative reformers throughout the world. If, to resume the thread of our argument, British administrative ability is to be measured by the tendency of the period 1780–1834, it stands up very well against its contemporary in America. For this, after the initial burst of creativity in the Federalist period, had settled down and in some cases had lost pace.

Notes

1. Unless we are to consider the prototype departments set up under the Confederacy; in which case we simply ante-date the construction of the Federal bureaucracy, but in no way mitigate the contrast between the American *tabula rasa,* and the British incubus of tradition. See Jensen, *The New Nation, 1781–1789,* for a strong plea to regard the Confederacy's departments as the real beginning of the American public service.
2. Because they were entrusted by the U.S. Constitution to the individual *states,* and not to the Federal Government.
3. *Bentham's Works,* Bowring, ed., pp. 216–17.
4. *The Second Tory Party, 1740 to 1812,* by K.G. Feiling, p. 143.
5. Blackstone, *Commentaries,* Book I, Chap. 7.
6. Idem. "The expenses defrayed by the Civil List are those that in any shape relate to civil government: as, the expenses of the household; all salaries to officers of State, to the judges and every one of the King's servants; the appointments to foreign ambassadors; the maintenance of the Queen and royal family, the King's private expenses, or privy purse; and other very numerous outgoings, as secret service money, pensions, and other bounties." Cf. Holdsworth, *History of English Law,* Vol. X, pp. 483–485.
7. Appendix 72, 13th Report of the Commissioners of Public Accounts, 1785.
8. By the 18th century it had reduced the collection of customs and the auditing of public accounts alike to a state of complete copnfusion and idiocy.
9. *Observations Respecting the Public Expenditure and the Influence of the Crown,* by the Rt. Hon. George Rose, 1810, p. 10.
10. Cf. E. Hughes, "Studies in Administration and Finance," pp. 274–276. Cf. also pp. 185–188. Hughes shows how very slight the disturbance was.
11. Feiling, p. 2.
12. The first recorded use of the phrase "H.M. Opposition" is in 1826. It was coined—as a jest—by Hobhouse. But in 1804 Fox (in a private letter) talked of "Systematic Opposition"; and it is from this date that the practice, as against the theory, of H.M. Opposition, may be dated.
13. Feiling, p. 3.
14. Sir Lewis Namier, *The Structure of Politics under George III,* p. 116 ff.
15. Namier, p. 142.

16. *The Parliamentary History of England,* Vol. 23, p. 101.
17. *Parliamentary Papers of John Robinson,* Camden Society, 1922, pp. 80–81.
18. *The Organization of the English Customs System, 1696–1787,* Appleton, Chapter VI.
19. The nature of the process has been explored in all its ramifications by Sir Lewis Namier in his *Structure of Politics at the Accession of George III* and his *England in the Age of the American Revolution.* These works are the foundation of our understanding of 18th century politics.
20. L.D. White, "The Federalists," p. 267. It must be added that McHenry did not think that Adams' appointments quite lived up to this high moral line. "Mr. Adams thought it an essential part of the art of government to apply the influence of rewards through the medium of appointments to offices to future elections" ("The Federalist," p. 267).
21. L.D. White, "The Jeffersonians" (New York, 1951), pp. 356; 367–368.
22. Report on the Civil Service, 1860; p. 176.
23. Report on the Civil Service, p. 283.
24. "The Jeffersonians," pp. 358–359.
25. Hoon, p. 78.
26. Indeed, she continues thus: "There was no concerted attempt at the badly needed reform of the system partly perhaps because the Commissioners' hands were tied by the limitation of their powers, *partly because of such immutable institutions as sinecures, fees and customs duties,* and partly also because eighteenth century opinion did not demand reform. . . . That the revenue was as productive as it was *despite the system which had to be enforced,* is evidence of a certain degree of judicious administration . . ." (Hoon, p. 78). The italics are my own.
27. "The Jeffersonians," pp. 419–22.
28. For the G.P.O. see H. Robinson, *The British Post Office* (Princeton, 1948). For the Customs, see E. Hoon, op. cit.; for the Excise, notably the Salt Office, Hughes, op. cit. These three services made up seven-eighths of the public service at the close of the 18th century. The Taxes Office, 1799–1816, is described in A. Hope-Jones, *Income Tax in the Napoleonic Wars* (C.U.P. 1939); it shows an organization as efficient as any described in Professor White's volumes.
29. "Papers relating to the Reorganisation of the Civil Service," 1855, pp. 72–73.
30. Not a General Staff in our modern sense (created in the U.S. in 1903), but an Advisory Board who assisted the Secretary in the housekeeping and management services of the Army.
31. "The Jeffersonians," pp. 554–55.
32. White, p. 161.
33. White, chap. 14.
34. Select Committee on Miscellaneous Expenditure, 1848: . 1260; 1303; 1311: The American War of Independence and the Napoleonic Wars had thrown so vast a burden on the Treasury that Board management became impossible.
35. *Edinburgh Review,* April 1810: Hon. G. Rose's "Observations."
36. Select Committee on Public Monies, 1856: 1173, 2199, 3170, 3174.
37. Parliamentary History, Vol. 23; pp. 1110–14.

38. For a masterly summary of the present state of studies see E.T. Williams, "The Cabinet in the Eighteenth Century," *History,* XXII (1937).
    This essay has been thoroughly revised, and is reprinted in *The Making of English History,* Dryden Press, New York, 1952, pp. 378–91.
39. The resignation of Richmond in 1794 seems to illustrate both the tradition of unanimity and the emergence of the efficient Cabinet, in one and the same case. Richmond was Master General of the Ordnance in Pitt's cabinet of 1784. Ceasing to attend cabinet meetings he was in 1794 finally asked to resign both his post and his cabinet office. The correspondence (Bathurst MSS., HMC, pp. 707–11) indicates:

    1. That both Pitt and Richmond agreed that a Cabinet member was to consider himself as "responsible among others" for Cabinet decisions, and to give public support to them.
    2. Pitt also argued that absence from Cabinet discussions was inconsistent with such responsibility for collective decisions, a view to which Richmond at first demurred, but to which he was willing to assent later.
    3. Richmond excused his absences by arguing that the Ordnance was not "naturally" a Cabinet office, and hinted that he might carry on at his post while resigning the Cabinet; to which Pitt replied that the execution of these important departmental duties was "incompatible with a state that precludes confidential intercourse on *all* the points of public business."

40. Select Committee on Public Monies (Report), 1857: Appendix I, p. 25.
41. A Tally was a stick on which notches were cut indicating the sum received; a large notch meant £1000, a smaller one £100 and so on. When suitably notched it was split in two, endwise, the exchequer retaining one half, the other being given, by way of receipt, to the party who had paid in the money.
42. To be strictly accurate, the procedure up to 1834 was as follows. Sums paid into the exchequer were entered in the teller's book and then sent to a clerk of the Bank of England, who kept them and credited the teller with the amount. Sums paid out of the exchequer were paid on the teller's instructions by this same bank clerk, who debited the teller with the amount. "After one o'clock the bank clerk agrees and settles the accounts with the several tellers, and either pays to or receives from each teller the balance: if a large sum, in exchequer bills of £1000 each and the remainder in cash; otherwise in cash, in bags . . ." This farce was to keep in being the notion that the whole income and expenditure were being physically transferred into and out from the tellers' chests. (Appendix 68, Sixth Report of Commissioners of Public Accounts, 1781).
43. Cf. Select Committee on Public Monies (Report), 1857, Appendix I, p. 469.
44. 22nd Report of the Select Committee on Finance: Appendix E.2, 1797.
45. Select Committee on Public Monies (Report), 1857, p. 31.
46. A very large sum indeed was paid out to maintain the Customs Excise Service and the other treasury boards, but as shown above, this was recovered by these boards in the form of drawbacks and did not appear before parliament; but these drawbacks were controlled and challenged by the treasury, and in this sense were, from the outset, amenable to treasury control in addition to the £80,000 mentioned in the text. In 1854 "draw-

backs" were abolished, and the revenue departments paid their gross revenue into the Consolidated Fund.

47. I say, deliberately, "as far as the Constitution permitted," because the simple fact is that it has not permitted anything but a travesty of the British system to be transplanted. Congressional control of appropriations, and its perennial jealousy of the executive branch have stultified any close approach to the British model. See *The President's Committee on Administrative Management* (U.S. Govt. Printing Office 1937), pp. 169–202; *The Hoover Commission Report,* 1949, (i) "Budgeting and Accounting," and (ii) "Fiscal, Budgeting and Accounting Systems." Also, "Federal Administrative Pathology and the Separation of Powers" by C. McKinley, *Public Administration Review,* Winter 1951.

48. Report of the Select Committee on Sinecure Offices, 1834.

49. This is to ignore the momentous reorganization of certain particular departments, notably the customs, the tax office (1785), the post office (1784).

50. Cf. *English Historical Review,* Vol. LXII, No 245: "The Waning of the Influence of the Crown," by A.S. Foord.

9

Handling Historical Comparisons
Cross-Nationally

James C. Scott

If the study of corruption teaches us anything at all, it teaches us not
to take a political system or a particular regime at its face value.
Corruption, after all, may be seen as an informal political system.
Whereas party manifestos, general legislation, and policy declarations
are the formal façade of the political structure, corruption stands in
sharp contrast to these features as an informal political system in its
own right. Here coalitions that could not survive the light of day,
government decisions that would set off a public outcry, elite behavior
that would destroy many a political career are all located. For a few
nations this hidden arena is only of marginal importance and, although
worthy of study, would not appreciably change an evaluation based on
what takes place in public. For most nations at some point in their
history, and for many nations today, however, the surreptitious politics
of this arena is so decisive that an analysis which ignored it would be
not simply inaccurate but completely misleading. How for example,
could we have adequately explained the rule of Boss Tweed in New
York of the 1890s, the structure of Chiang Kai-shek's Kuomintang
Party, the methods of "Papa Doc" Duvalier in Haiti, or the failure of
the parliamentary system in Indonesia without examining corruption?
These are perhaps dramatic examples but they alert us to the fact that
corruption is frequently an integral part of the political system—a part
which we ignore only at our great peril. . . .

A closely related problem in the comparative study of corruption
involves not so much a question of formal analysis as a question of our
scope of inquiry. As much as possible, we shall try to view corruption
as a special case of political influence—a case that must be seen in the

Source: James C. Scott, *Comparative Political Corruption*. Englewood Cliffs, N.J.:
Prentice Hall, 1972, pp. 2–8, 21–35. By permission of the author and copyright-holder.

context of the distribution of power in society and the character of regime institutions. When we examine specific regimes such as England under the early Stuarts, or India under the Congress party, we will attempt to show how the pattern of corruption is related in each case to the values and institutions of both the elite and the society as a whole. In concrete terms, this means treating an American urban political "machine," in which corruption is commonly rife, *as part of an entire system* of electoral and financial influence in which legal patronage, pork-barrel legislation, and lax regulation of city-based business interests are also important features. Thus, because an adequate understanding of corruption generally requires a grasp of an entire network of influence, we shall try to deal with corruption in a way that embeds it contextually in a broader analysis of a regime's political dynamics.

Comparing Norms

The second, and most serious, difficulty arising from the use of formal norms to define corruption is that it seems to rule out some historical comparisons. An example will illustrate the dilemma. If we wanted to compare corruption in seventeenth-century France with corruption in twentieth-century France, a legal perspective would make our task difficult. The sale of state offices in seventeenth-century France would not come under our definition of corruption, whereas the same act in twentieth-century France—or the United States—would. The behavior seems the same; only the legal context has changed. Nor would the use of a "public opinion" criterion here instead of the legal standard solve the dilemma, inasmuch as the sale of office in seventeenth-century France was neither illegal nor frowned upon, except by the old nobility who resented the nouveau riche office holder. In a similar vein, the alarm among the Dutch at increased corruption in colonial Indonesia in the nineteenth century did not result from a change in what colonial officials were doing, but rather from a shift in the values and public law being applied to such behavior in Holland.

We face the same problem in comparing practices in eighteenth-century Europe with identical practices in new states today. The new states, for the most part, have adopted the full panoply of laws that emerged from the long political struggle for reform in the west. Considering only political patronage jobs, the Indian, Malaysian, or Nigerian politician finds himself denied by law many of the spoils that legally aided the growth of political parties in England and America. The 1964 *Report of the Committee on Prevention of Corruption,* an official Indian report, explicitly recognizes the difficulty of comparing the severity of bureaucratic corruption in India with that of eighteenth-century England because the legal framework under which India operates was not yet established in England at that time. Patronage in contemporary India and in eighteenth-century England may seem to serve much the same purpose but from the legal perspective the former is corruption whereas the latter is not.

The difficulty here simply serves to highlight the fact that much corruption is in a real sense a product of the late eighteenth and nineteenth centuries. Only the rise of the modern nation-state, with its mass participation, broadly representative bodies, and elaborate civil service codes, signaled the transformation of the view of government office, and even kingship, from a private right into a public responsibility.

How, then, can we handle historical comparisons? If, for example, we wanted to compare the practice of bribing to gain appointment to the bureaucracy in traditional England with the same practice in modern England, we could classify such an act as corrupt in the modern period but not in the traditional period, where it often occurred openly and legally. We will want, nonetheless, to compare *practices* that are corrupt only by modern standards and ask what their causes are in different periods, how they affect the composition of the elite, and so forth. If nepotism or bribery have similar causes and consequences in early France as in contemporary India, that is an important subject for analysis, notwithstanding the fact that legal codes and public standards have changed so much that what was tolerated (not corrupt) in early France is now forbidden by law (corrupt) in India. For our comparative purposes, then, we will refer to pre-nineteenth-century practices which only became "corrupt" in the nineteenth century as *"proto-corruption."* This convention will allow us to analyze the comparative causes and effects of similar behavior while recognizing that such earlier practices did not contravene the existing norms of official conduct and thus cannot be considered corruption as we have chosen to use the term. . . .

Means of Persuasion in Different Political Systems

Our central concern here is with the political significance of corrupt actions. Most acts we call corrupt are transactions in which one party exchanges wealth—or more durable assets such as kinship or friendship—for influence over the decisions of government. Whether the "buyer" seeks an honorary title (status), a post of some authority (power), or a large supply contract (wealth), the essential characteristics of the transaction fit this pattern.

Corruption may then be seen as just one of many ways a person can persuade someone who exercises public authority to act as he wishes— that is, as a kind of influence. Other sorts of influence, such as appealing to regulations, to ideology, or to equity, are quite legitimate means of persuasion so long as the power-holder acts within the rules. When we say that influence is corrupt we imply that without the special consideration of kinship, bribery, or friendship the public official could not have made the same decision.

Although not every corrupt act can be interpreted in this fashion, analyzing most forms of corruption in terms of a process of political influence allows us to examine corruption as part of a larger mosaic of political influence. This approach highlights the functional equivalence of a variety of acts of political influence—some of which violate all standards of community ethics and some of which are totally beyond reproach.

Were it not for the fact that a host of government decisions represent valuable commodities to some citizens, there would be little corruption. Nor would there be much corruption if the valuable things a state had at its disposal were simply sold at auction to the highest bidder. No modern government, however, sells civil service jobs or allots public health service and education only to those who can bid highest. Using the price system to allocate such services would violate shared standards or justice and equity. The problem, of course, is that demand for many government dispensations far outstrips their limited supply, and because the state makes no charge, or only a nominal one, the price for such services does not begin to reflect the supply-demand situation. In this context, the effort by many citizens to circumvent government non-price criteria for the award of these valuables takes the form of what Tilman has aptly called a "black-market bureaucracy." Such attempts to influence government decisions are naturally more frequent where state activities are more pervasive. The legitimate influence of political pressure on legislatures, and ideological or ethical appeals compete against the illegitimate influence of wealth, kinship, and "connections."

Three instances of the use of wealth to sway state decisions will illustrate the expressly political perspective of viewing corruption as a form of influence. Each case exemplifies, in a different manner, what is likely to occur when wealth and power elites are separate. All are cases of influence, but in Thailand the political influence of wealth was achieved by corruption, in Japan by quite unexceptionable means, and in seventeenth- and eighteenth-century England by devices that are questionable but not illegal.

In England throughout the seventeenth and eighteenth centuries the lesser, wealthy gentry and the new commercial elite were able to buy positions of political authority either through the purchase of public office and peerages from the crown or, especially later, through the purchase of parliamentary boroughs. In this way, the new classes began to replace the older nobility in the affairs of state. Objections were raised to all these practices but they were not illegal until well into the nineteenth century.

In contemporary Thailand, by contrast, the business elite is largely Chinese, not Thai, and thus for ethnic reasons formal positions of authority are seldom open to them. Instead, members of the Chinese commercial community have established fairly stable relations with individual clique leaders in the Thai military and bureaucracy in order to protect and advance their entrepreneurial concerns. Many of the transactions that provide the cement for this informal coalition are quite illegal, but the relationships are, of course, enormously rewarding for members of the Thai bureaucratic elite who oversee the licensing and taxing of enterprises. Deprived of the privilege of outright office-holding, Chinese businessmen in Thailand have nevertheless managed quite well—albeit through corruption—to share quite fulsomely in the decisions which affect them.

Wealthy business elites in Japan, finally, operating in a very different fashion from Thai entrepreneurs, have also managed to wield great political influence. Working through the factions—particularly the "main current" faction of the Liberal Democratic party (LDP) that has dominated elections in the postwar era—businessmen have provided the lion's share of this party's huge electoral war chest. Rather than having each firm work out its own arrangements, as in the Thai case, Japanese businessmen functioned for a time collectively through an industrywide association that assessed member firms according to their assets and annual profits and passed on these funds to factions of the LDP. Japanese industrialists have thus had a large, and quite legal, hand in determining which clique would prevail within the LDP. The legislative program of the LDP has, of course, consistently reflected the support it has received from large business concerns.

These three illustrations are all cases in which wealthy elites attempt, more or less successfully, to influence government actions. In the Thai case, much of what occurs meets the definition of corruption; the English case belongs in the category of "proto-corruption"; and the Japanese case would be difficult to construe as corruption in any sense. Using divergent strategies in each nation, wealthy elites have achieved strikingly similar ends by bending government actions to their needs. The sale of office and parliamentary seats in Britain made the direct pursuit of office by the nouveau riche a common pattern. The ethnic background of wealthy elites in Thailand severly circumscribe formal avenues to power and thereby promote more corrupt practices. But in Japan the existence of an organized party system allows businessmen to contribute openly and legally to the ruling party in order to gain their policy ends. Such factors as whether a nation has an electoral system, whether wealth elites are organized, whether there are ethnic or religious barriers that prevent wealth elites from formally holding office will thus partly determine the kind or amount of corruption in a political system. Each political system has distinctive routes by which wealth, as a political resource, influences government policies. The availability of some channels for influence and the exclusion of others set boundaries on the channels available to wealthy elites for influencing formal power-holders, thereby affecting both the incidence and style of corruption.

Influence at the Output Stage

Corruption, like other forms of political influence, often arises from the claims and demands people make on government. The study of how claims and demands are made on government in the industrialized west has for the most part focused on interest groups and the process by which such groups affect the content of legislation. If we distinguish between influence at the "input" stage (influence on lawmakers) and influence at the "output" stage (influence on enforcers after rules and laws have been promulgated), we can see that the "input" process has occupied the center of scholarly attention.

Students of politics in the new states of Asia and Africa, however have been struck by the relative weakness both of the interest structures that might organize demands and of institutionalized channels through which such demands, once organized, might be communicated to the political decision-makers. The open clash of organized interests, so common in the west, is often conspicuously absent during the formulation of policy annd legislation in these nations. To conclude from this fact, however, that the public has little or no effect on the eventual "output" of government would be completely unwarranted. Between the passage of legislation and its actual implementation lies an entirely different political arena that, in spite of its informality and particularism, has great effect on the execution of policy.

Much of the expression of political interests in the new states has been disregarded simply because western scholars, accustomed to their own contemporary politics, have been looking in the wrong place. A large portion of individual demands, and even group demands, in developing nations reaches the political system, not before laws are passed, but rather at the enforcement stage.[1] Influence before legislation is passed often takes the form of "pressure-group politics"; *influence at the enforcement stage often takes the form of "corruption" and has seldom been analyzed as the alternative means of interest articulation which in fact it is.*[2]

The peasants who avoid their land taxes by making a smaller and illegal contribution to the income of the assistant revenue officer are as surely influencing the outcome of government policy as if they formed a peasant union and agitated collectively for the reduction of land taxes. In a similar fashion, businessmen who protect their black-market sales by buying protection from the appropriate civil servants are changing the outcome of policy as effectively as if they had worked collectively through chambers of commerce for an end to government price controls. A strong case can be made that it may often be more "efficient" (and here the term "efficient" is used in the sense of minimizing the costs involved in attaining a given objective) to advance one's interests when policy is being implemented rather than when it is still being debated in the cabinet or in parliament. Three typical examples of situations in which corruption may help minimize costs for would-be influencers are suggested below.

1. Where the narrowness of loyalties or the scarcity of organizational skills inhibits the formation of political interest groups, the corruption of law enforcement may be the most efficient means of affecting changes in *de facto* policy.[3] The divisive loyalties of many peasants to their kinship, ethnic, village, religious, or caste groupings create social barriers that may preclude their organizing a common association that would advance their interests *qua* peasants. Given this fact, it is more efficient for the individual peasant to bribe local government officials, and thereby avoid the application of laws that may disadvantage him than for him to attempt to alter those laws.

2. Where legislative acts tend to be formalistic—where the administration of law is so loose and erratic that existing law bears little relationship to administrative behavior—it may be more efficient to make demands known at the enforcement stage than at the legislative

stage. Even though interest groups exist, businessmen in developing nations may realize that the administration of even the most favorable tax laws will have little or no resemblance to what is called for in the statutes. That is, they may have to bribe as much to secure enforcement of a favorable law as to escape the provisions of an unfavorable one. Under the circumstances, then, it may make more sense for each enterprise to quietly "buy" precisely what it needs in terms of enforcement or nonenforcement, rather than to finance an open campaign for a new law that would be as formalistic as the existing one.[4]

3. Where a minority is discriminated against and its political demands are regarded as illegitimate by the governing elite and the general population, its members may feel that open pressure-group action would expose them to attacks from more powerful groups. Therefore, they may turn to the corruption of politicians and/or civil servants in order to safeguard their interests. Throughout much of Southeast Asia and East Africa, a large portion of commerce and small industry is in the hands of Indian or Chinese minority groups which, even if they have managed to acquire local citizenship, are considered as aliens by most of the local population. It would be foolish, even suicidal, for these so-called "pariah" capitalists to seek influence openly as an organized pressure group. A healthy regard for their property and skin alike impels them to rely on payments and favors to strategically placed power-holders.

Each of the three situations described, in which influence at the enforcement stage minimizes costs, are quite typical of the less developed nations.

The relative absence of organized interest-group activity in new nations is in part due to the fact that group loyalties are still centered at the family, village, or ethnic-group level. The peasant thinks of himself first a member of his extended family, then perhaps as a member of his village or tribal/ethnic group; he hardly ever sees himself as a peasant with interests similar to other who work the land. If he has political demands, they are not likely to be demands that embrace the entire peasantry, but instead will center either on his family's needs or on some small group to which he has direct links.

Implicit in this reasoning is the fundamental fact that the nature of most political demands in transitional nations is such that they are simply not amenable to the legislative process. Family-centered demands—e.g., a family's desire to secure a civil service post for its eldest son—are generally not expressible in legislative terms. When demands occasionally are made on behalf of wider groupings, they are likely to refer to ethnic, linguistic, or village units and only seldom can they be given general legislative form.[5] The problem thus lies less with the weakness *per se* of interest structures at the legislative stage than with the very character of loyalties in transitional nations and the kinds of demands fostered by such loyalty patterns. Couched, as it generally is, in universalistic language, legislation is often not a suitable vehicle for the expression of particularistic interests.[6] Influence at the enforcement level, on the other hand, is almost exclusively particularistic. It is scarcely surprising, then, that many of the narrow, parochial demands characteristic of new nations should make their weight felt when laws are being implemented rather than when they are being passed. Appropriate though it may be for organized groups in the modern sector, the modern legislative machinery of new nations is less effective in coping with the host of special pleadings coming from outside the modern sector.

The illustrations given above were, moreover, designed to show how potential political demands might be channeled along corrupt paths *even* in a functioning parliamentary system. For the majority of Afro-Asian nations, however, military rule has meant that interest group pressure on parliaments is no longer an alternative means of gaining political ends. In the absence of such open institutionalized procedures for influence, informal—often corrupt—channels have become all the more decisive.

Seen as a process of informal political influence, then, corruption might be expected to flourish most in a period when the formal political system, for whatever reasons, is unable to cope with the scale or the nature of the demands being made on it. Samuel Huntington, in his analysis of what he calls "political decay" in the new states, views corruption from virtually the same vantage point. Rapid social mobilization—urbanization, politicization, etc.—he argues, has placed an impossible burden on the frail political institutions of new nations, thereby leading to the decline of political competition and to political instability, institutional decay, and corruption.[7] But corruption in this sense not only reflects the failure of the formal political system to meet demands from important sectors, but also represents a kind of subversive effort by a host of individuals and groups to bend the political system to their wishes. Those who feel that their essential interests are ignored or considered illegitimate in the formal political system will gravitate to the informal channel of influence represented by corruption. It is possible, as in the case of the American urban "machine," that while the formal political process may seem restrictive and rigid, corruption and other informal arrangements may add substantial openness and flexibility to ultimate policies. Thus important political interests that seem unrepresented in the formal structure may enter unobtrusively through the back door.

An empirical assessment of the interests served by state action would be inadequate, then, if it stopped at the content of laws or decrees and failed to ask in what direction and to what extent corruption altered the implementation of policy. Table 9.1 represents an effort to distinguish between those groups that usually achieve direct access to the formal political system in new nations and those groups that, for a variety of reasons, enter the competition for influence at a more informal level.

This rather sketchy composite cannot do complete justice to the situation in any single developing nation; it is, however, sufficiently descriptive of the situation in enough cases to alert one to the variety of interests that may seek to gain a surreptitious hearing. Aside from those groups that are blocked from formal participation for ideological reasons—for they are frequently in the modern sector and relatively well organized—the formal political system is *par excellence* the domain—virtually the monopoly—of the modern social sector. Minori-

Table 9.1
GROUPS AND THEIR MEANS OF ACCESS TO THE POLITICAL SYSTEM IN LESS DEVELOPED NATIONS

Generally Easy Access to Formal Political System	Groups Often Securing Access Primarily by Means of Corruption Because Denied Formal Access by Virtue of:		
	Ideological Reasons	Parochial Reasons	Lack of Organization
1. Political elite	1. Indigenous commercial and industrial groups	1. Minority ethnic, religious, or linguistic groups	1. Unorganized peasants and other rural interests
2. Cadre and branches of ruling party	2. Foreign business interests		2. Unorganized urban lower classes
3. Civil servants' associations	3. Political opposition		
4. Professional associations			
5. Trade unions (especially those dominated by ruling party)			

ties and the unorganized are placed at a distinct disadvantage since they face a formal political system that is simply not designed to accommodate them.

While a wide variety of groups may gain access to the political system through corruption, it is clearly those with substantial wealth who have the greatest capacity to bend government policy in their direction. Except for favors done from motives of kinship or friendship, it is the wealthy who are involved in most of the larger "deals" and whose influence is likely to overshadow that of smaller claimants. The reasons such powerful groups may operate corruptly rather than openly will be examined next.

Patterns of Access and Exclusion

Any set of political arrangement creates its own distinct pattern of access and influence. When we call a given regime oligarchic or aristocratic we are essentially making a judgment about the size and nature of those groups in the society which exercise the most influence over public policy; we are describing a particular pattern of access.

The dominant forces in a political system usually have no reason to resort to corruption or revolution to make their influence felt, for the state is institutionalized to serve their purposes. If we look at local government in mid-nineteenth-century Prussia, for example, we find that government was tailored entirely to the needs and interests of local landed elites. Exploitation of the rural lower classes was built into the political system; it was carried on legally and openly through preferential taxation and expenditure of public funds. Being virtually the owners of the state, landed elites had little reason to corrupt local officials.

Groups which may have engaged in bribery to advance their interests may cease to corrupt public officials once they have achieved greater formal access to power. Dutch business interests in colonial Indonesia follow this pattern. Prior to 1920 they tended to bribe colonial administrators in Batavia to secure, on a piecemeal basis, the advantages they desired for their enterprises. Later, however, they became organized and their businesses became profitable enough to achieve many of their goals directly through legislation back in Holland. Thus, throughout the 1920s and 1930s there was no export duty on oil from Indonesia and little or no tax on rubber. The need for colonial financial interests to bribe agents of the state diminished in proportion as their open influence over the state increased.

The pattern of formal access to influence in any political system provides preferential treatment to some kinds of interests while slighting or even excluding others. Occasionally the excluded groups are without resources to back their claims (e.g., small, oppressed minorities such as Indians in the United States, aborigines in Australia) and cannot improve their position without powerful allies. More often, however, excluded groups possess political resources such as wealth, organization, numbers, or armed force that provide them with the potential for enhancing their influence. If the resources of the disadvantaged groups center around organization or armed force, they may well choose to engineer a revolution or coup that would refashion the political structure to give them greater formal power. If, on the other hand, the disadvantaged groups control wealth and property, they may seek an informal adjustment of their influence through corruption.

Broadly speaking, there are two situations in which important and powerful groups are likely to have less access to formal influence than one would anticipate on the basis of the resources they command. First is the common historical case of a pattern of formal access established in the past which has been gradually undermined by rapid social change that has yet to find formal expression in institutional changes or legislation. The formal rules, in this case, no longer reflect the new distribution of potential power in society. This situation was, of course, typical in much of Europe in the early industrial revolution when traditional aristocratic rule made little allowance for the new social forces then emerging. The second situation in which the gap between formal access and informal power potential is likely to be great is when there has been a *sudden political transformation* that diminishes or cuts off the access of groups that still command potent political resources. Recently independent nations with socialist ruling parties fall into this category, inasmuch as the new regime has often formally excluded such powerful groups as commercial and business elites and traditional chiefs and headmen who still command significant resources for influence.[8] The gap between formal access and potential for influence is thus widened both when the pace of social change outruns traditional political arrangements and when abrupt political changes suddenly displace groups that still have some weight to throw around. Excluded groups in both instances are a threat to the regime either by the violence of which they are capable—whether revolutionary or counterrevolutionary—or by their ability to corrupt the agents of the existing order.

To illustrate, we may compare the strains created by the gap betwen formal access and potential for influence in seventeenth-century England and in Ghana after independence. In the former case large landowning families and well-placed nobility enjoyed preferential access to positions of power and influence under the monarchy. The rapid pace of commercialization had even by this time, however, created a commercial elite of considerable wealth whose formal influence did not yet reflect their newly acquired power in the economy. As this new elite had interests that often clashed with those of the older landowning magnates, they employed their wealth to influence state policy informally. Some bought seats in parliament by bribing small electorates or by advancing loans to impecunious notables who controlled a constituency. Other sought, by means of loaning money to the Crown, to assure themselves a lucrative franchise or a strategic post in the king's administration. These activities were not illegal at the time, although older elites complained loudly against the steady infiltration of new men. The commercial elites were not, of course, the only excluded group since both the new urban mass and the increasingly destitute rural wage-laborers had no influence till late in the nineteenth century. But these latter groups had few resources and little organization with which to press their demands save by occasional riots that generally lacked both leadership and direction. Until they acquired the force of organization, their exclusion could be enforced without greatly threatening the system. Wealth elites, by contrast, had the resources to make their way informally to power.

In England at this time, then, we have an example of a formal political system that has not kept pace with momentous changes occurring in the society. A new wealth elite whose resource position is growing steadily more powerful has little formal influence while the older nobility, whose position has declined, still enjoys preferential access. The adjustment, to the extent one has been made, has not taken place formally but has occurred through informal, often corrupt means.

Ghana in 1960 presents a somewhat different situation in terms of formal and informal access. Nkrumah's Convention People's party had become the dominant institution in structuring patterns of access and exclusion. The groups under the umbrella of the CPP that enjoyed preferential access to influence were the new, lower middle class of teachers, journalists, and government clerks, the so-called "veranda boys" representing the young urban unemployed who flocked to the CPP, party-dominated trade union leadership, a large number of petty traders, and, of course, the party branches. A number of other groups, many of which had enjoyed greater access to influence in the colonial order, were placed at a disadvantage under the new regime, although they were not without resources. Wealthy Ghanaian traders and large expatriate firms that dominated the export-import sector were foremost among the groups now largely excluded from formal access. In addition, many of the traditional leaders (particularly in Ashanti areas but elsewhere as well), some smaller, upcountry minority communities like the Tiv, and the older professional and bureaucratic elites were not relatively disadvantaged by the CPP.

The excluded groups each sought to improve its situation with the resources it had at hand. Many wealthy Ghanaian owners of construction firms and traders joined the CPP and contributed lavishly to its coffers and/or bribed administrators or politicians to acquire the needed licenses and permits and to win government contracts. For the expatriate firms the formal difficulties were somewhat greater since such businesses were in a legal sense outside the Ghanaian political system. But if their difficulties were greater, so were their resources for illegal influence. Foreign firms doing business with Ghana quietly contributed 5 to 10 percent of their overpriced supply contracts to the CPP; they did a lucrative business and became the financial mainstay of the party. Thus the interests of foreign business—and the CPP—were amply served by an informal system of highly priced corruption.

Other disadvantaged groups under the new regime—such as the Ashanti, Tiv, and the professional class—by and large lacked the resources to attain their ends corruptly. Consequently, the Ashanti and Tiv regions became hotbeds of opposition activity and incipient revolt that became significant only when the military and the trade unions became alienated from the Nkrumah regime. Much of the professional class was also in opposition, but it lacked the broad following that made the Ashanti and Tiv a more palpable threat.

In Ghana during this period, then, we have an example of a new regime—a sudden political change—that has abruptly displaced groups that had enjoyed formal avenues to influence in the last years of the colonial regime. The formal pattern of access has, in a sense, shot ahead of the rate of social change, pushing aside groups that still have significant political resources. Those groups that control wealth or property have resorted to corruption to repair their position while those without wealth have turned to nonviolent or violent political opposition. . . .

Our feeling about corruption often depends on whether this "uninstitutionalized" influence of wealth is undermining a formal system of which we approve or disapprove. Thus, corruption in eighteenth and early nineteenth-century England seems less contemptible to us than modern corruption since it involves the subversion of an aristocratic or status-based monopoly of government. Corruption in modern liberal democratic or socialist regimes, on the other hand, seems especially damaging since it undermines both the egalitarian assumptions of majority rule and the principles of even distribution of civil and social rights of which we normally approve. Under liberal democratic regimes, corruption represents an additional and *illegal* advantage of wealthy interests over and above the *legal* advantages they ordinarily enjoy by virtue of large campaign contributions, muscle in the courts, and so forth. Wealth, in this sense, is doubly conservative in such regimes. . . .

Notes

1. It seems also that western scholars have perhaps underemphasized the importance of administrative politics in their own political systems, where both particularistic and organized interests can undo the effects of legislation or secure a favorable application of the law in their own case.
2. Although not all corruption occurs at the enforcement stage and not all "influence at the enforcement stage" is corrupt, the empirical referents of the two terms overlap considerably. A striking exception, of course, is the legitimate arena of "regulatory politics" in the west—an area that largely involves contending interpretations of statutes governing private-sector activity.
3. Here we are assuming, of course, that there are few compunctions about corruption and few costs (e.g., probably of arrest) attached to such an act. Whether the bureaucrat "sells" influence—given a fixed reward—depends as well on the probability of his being caught, the penalty if caught, and his scruples.
4. Occasionally politicians even may pass legislation that restricts the private sector so as to maintain the proper ideological stance while, at the same time, permitting private firms to operate unimpeded through corruption in which the politicians may share.
5. "Pork-barrel" legislation catering to regional interests and legislation about languages of instruction in school or about local rule for minorities are exceptions to this statement. India has legislated preferential treatment for its *harijan* castes as has Malaysia for its Malay population.
6. There is a history of "special legislation" and, in England, "private member bills" that attempted to meet particularistic demands or redress specific grievances at the legislative stage. The kinds of demands represented by this type of legislation have tended increasingly to shift to the administrative or judicial arenas.
7. Samuel P. Huntington, *Political Order in Changing Societies*. New Haven: Yale University Press, 1968, pp. 59–71. The frailty of such institutions is often due to the fact that they have been tailored to the demands and requirements of narrow oligarchies.
8. Postrevolutionary France might fit this category too, inasmuch as the nobility was still a powerful force in the countryside despite the formal liquidation of the *ancien régime*.

Social Perceptions:
An Introduction

These selections complement the institutional focus of the preceding one by analyzing how the cultural and social contexts in which the powers of political office are exercised affect perceptions of whether and how much corrupt behavior (as previously defined above) is morally and legally condemned. Altogether these are intellectual exercises in relativity because they develop, from various theoretical perspectives, how dependent is the perception of corruption on various contextual influences. If we ask what is required to reduce or eliminate these ambiguities, the answer probably would be the existence of a universal bureaucracy with total control to impose and adjudicate norms across all societies.

Black, Grey and White Corruption

In the absence of such a universal authority, real-life situations tend rather to reflect differences such as those discussed by Arnold J. Heidenheimer in chapter 10. From the welter of relevant literature he distills four models of community structure found in the contemporary world. He then in an elementary way characterizes how they differ from each other with regard to prototypes for political exchange relations, and the relative strength of family and community regarding norms. Are obligations to sustain and help members of one's family perceived as having a claim on the office-holder that are superior to those of the formal rules that regulate the use of the office? In two cases the answer is yes, and in others it is no, and the reasons for these and similar differences emerge from the descriptive analyses of the four types of communities.

If various forms of behavior classified as corrupt by some universal schema occur more in some types of communities, what does this imply about the degree of severity with which various kinds of corruption are morally condemned by the citizens of these communities? To illustrate a hypothetical answer to this problem, the author lists on one dimension a scale of kinds of political corruption classified, as they might be in a legal code, from petty to aggravated. He then records whether these forms of corrupt behavior are coded tolerantly (white), with some opprobrium (grey), or regarded as severe violations of community moral and legal norms (black). The suggestion is that, as one moves from the traditional to the modern, and from the boss- to the civic-culture based communities, actions and exchanges that are objectively similar come to be more severely coded and often punished.

Attitudes As Bases for Definitions? In chapter 11, Kenneth Gibbons relates the questions of definitions and categories of corruption to attitudinal aspects, which are further developed in his own and other articles in this section. He builds on the preceding article by Heidenheimer to explore interconnections between the intellectual processes of conceptualization, categorization, and explanation. Elaborating on the white-grey-black schema, he argues that the concept of corruption has definable dimensions that are recognized by the public and that permit a more complex analysis to be made in the light of public opinion data. But where Heidenheimer treats the attitudinal component as a dimension to be examined, Gibbons argues for a change in categorization. Building also on the position developed by Peters and Welch (chapter 43), Gibbons makes a case for recognizing that attitudinal- or public opinion-based approaches be recognized as a fourth basic definitional type, supplementing the three types based on office, market, and public interest definitions.

Institutions As Symbolic Environments

The linkages between legal and political institutions, and the symbolic fields upon which public attitudes may be grounded, are explored in chapter 12 by Bruce E. Gronbeck, a scholar of rhetoric and communications. For him its routineness and ubiquity makes political corruption a fascinating object for rhetorical analysis needed to augment the emphasis on legal and institutional contexts, which has been the main focus of political and other social scientists. He does not denigrate the significance of institutions, but encourages the reader to visualize institutions as symbolic environments whose repositories are laws and powers of enforcement.

Institutionally-based concepts such as "public office" possess for him symbolic lives of their own, imbued as they are for the properly socialized citizen with respect, affection, or even devotion. Crimes against the rules governing the office may be seen as offending the culture's basic organizing principles, and may thus evoke frustration and demand for vengeance.

Gronbeck's analysis seems focussed more on the fourth of Heidenheimer's types of communities, and elaborates the symbolic basis that distinguishes the civic culture from those in which particularistic loyalties hold higher priority. He draws attention to effective rhetorical devices used by both the accuser and accused. For the defendants, he points to the manner in which Sir Robert Walpole sought to "deofficialize" his accusers, and denigrate their superior moral claims, by quips that among them "patriots seemed to grow up overnight just like mushrooms." He analyzes the socio-linguistic processes through which relatively "naked" actions become "clothed" in the heinousness of social-political patricide. His rhetorical analyses prepare the reader to understand more of the processes of scandalization.

Because his focus is primarily on rhetoric, Gronbeck does not distinguish sharply between the kind of corruption that focusses on the exchange of official favors for material benefits, and the abuse of public office powers for reasons of power enhancement. He deals at some length with the rhetorical devices employed in the course of the Watergate episode. The fact that the ceremonial process there involved the highest political office in the land helps to explain why the demands for punishment were so strong. But the same response effect is also seen in more mundane urban police corruption scandals described in chapters 50 through 52. From the symbolic point of view, the secrecy of the cabal through which the corrupters exploit their offices not only can be, but must be, responded to publicly via a full-blown rhetoric of meaning attribution in which the populace is involved as the offending party. The outcome of the resulting scandal is seen as analogous to the purgation experience that was seen as an essential attribute of Greek tragedies. It should result in symbolic purgation, and thus provide some form of positive collective gain through which a community and culture retrieves good out of evil.

Dual Normative Structures

Jeanne Becquart-Leclercq, in chapter 13, also concentrates on the tensions developed between two orders of reality, one embedded in social context, the other in political symbolism. As a French social scientist, she builds on the theories of Durkheim and employs contrasts between the American and French political settings to illustrate her analysis. For example, if some corruption is needed to make the wheels turn in the augmented polity of Cook county, what are the functions of corruption in the more centralized and rationally administered French system? The answer seems to be to create "shadowy zones" around the focal points of power, zones that make possible some more flexibility in decision making. She asserts that disguised supplements augment the salaries of French civil servants in ways that might affect their official decisions.

Corruption phenomena are explained by Becquart-Leclercq in terms of the dual normative structure that encompasses social groups in cultural systems. A symbolic dimension encompasses the idealized vision that the society holds of itself, and perpetuates its illusions. On the other hand, the operational or strategic dimension embraces the implicit codes of behavior and de facto accepted tactics. In systems with highly developed idealized images there will tend to be greater gaps between the operational mode and the symbolic ideal. In some societies relationships between the two orders of reality can become ruptured or disconnected, thus leading to a kind of social schizophrenia.

Becquart-Leclercq emphasizes the secret aspect of corrupt relationships, in a manner also related to the emphasis on "paradox" in the title of her chapter. In part secrecy may reflect on the lack of investigative enterprise among French journalists, who don't unwrap many local scandals. But in part the emphasis on secrecy is also related to the nature of continental law enforcement rules and to the varieties of formal proofs needed to pursue investigations. The discretion of members of these relational networks seems to help reduce the likelihood of apprehension. The mobilization of those who are exploited is inhibited by the high level of secrecy, which effectively "blinds its victims."

10

Perspectives on the Perception of Corruption

Arnold J. Heidenheimer

Most actions that are considered corrupt by norm enforcers within or critics outside a political system are basically varieties of exchange transactions. Depending on the technique employed, the transactions create varying degrees of specificity of obligation on the parts of the exchangers. Bribery is the most frequently cited technique of corruption, because it creates a very specific obligation on the part of the officeholder. The more that political exchange transactions engender specific obligations, the more they resemble the prototype of an economic transaction, which rests on a formal contract stipulating the exact quantities to be exchanged. The bribed official typically agrees to undertake or to forego a designated action in return for a designated compensation.

Other kinds of corrupt political exchange agreements are based on obligations that are more vague and that involve less specific quantities.[1] Officials may tacitly agree to extend unspecified forms of future preferment to office seekers or contractors in return for accepting extensive services that have a large but deliberately unspecific value. The more developed the economy, the less specific the benefit is likely to be. A tipoff leading to purchase of stock or real estate holdings that are likely to increase sharply in value will benefit the office-holder much more than will cash presents. Indeed, the more that political exchange resembles social exchange, the more unspecific and the more difficult to classify in terms of corruption it becomes. The more complex the network of social interaction and the more complicated and diverse the ways that tangible benefits can be exchanged, the less likely it is that particular actions can clearly be labelled corrupt. To the

Source: Arnold J. Heidenheimer, *Political Corruption: Readings in Comparative Analysis,* 1970, pp. 18–28.

extent that their exchange transactions tend to be more direct, the citizens of less-developed countries are indeed somewhat one-sidedly exposed to the easy moral judgments of citizens of more developed societies.

Insofar as more politically developed societies are also more highly integrated societies, they tend to socialize their citizens against the temptations of material gain in ways that are organically related to the basic, supracultural definitions of corruption. If their strong civic and other social norms are effectively internalized by their members, they tend to give a greater subjective reality to "community interests" in terms of the preferences of their citizens. Thus sanctions in terms of guilt feelings and social disapproval may constitute costs that under certain circumstances may cause commitment to a proposed exchange relationship to appear irrational rather than rational from the perspective of the individual's self-interest.[2] By contrast, in a community like Montegrano no community interest or norms to enforce it are perceived to exist, hence the value of a bribe received would be discounted neither by guilt feelings nor by fear of moral condemnation.[3] It is expected that an officeholder will accept bribes when he can get away with it, and indeed community lore ascribes corruptibility to officials almost *ex officio*.

Communities at various levels of sociopolitical development may be related to various prototypical types of exchange relations. In a culture that contains a money economy but where most individuals relate only to collectivities like the family or the tribe, exchanges with other groups closely follow the economic exchange model, since there is limited precedent that might have created trust that nonspecific obligations will ever be repaid. Because the gradual expansion of mutual interaction is accompanied by a parallel growth of mutual trust, there will be a tendency to enter into more exchanges that entail unspecified obligations to well-known clients and patrons whose reliability has been established. Trust in neighbors and identification with the community certainly does not increase monotonically with modernization! As the former peasant becomes an immigrant to an urban environment, whether in his own country or abroad, his environment seems very untrustworthy and he seeks relationships resembling those he has known. Gradually, then, he and his children develop greater faith in their neighbors and greater identification with the community, because the processes of social exchange generate trust in social relations through their recurrent and gradually expanding character.[4]

It is from this conceptual background that we may attempt to approach the "central question for the scientific study of the problem of corruption," which Colin Leys suggests . . . should be posed as follows: "In any society, under what conditions is behavior most likely to occur which a significant section of the population will regard as corrupt?" However, because Leys's formulation appears overly ambitious and general at this stage of research and assessment, and the following, more modest form is suggested: "Which of the various forms of behavior that a significant portion of the population regards as corrupt are more likely to be more pervasive in one society than another, and why?"

Four Types of Political Obligation Relationships

Our analysis will be developed in terms of four types of political obligation relationships characteristic of communities. . . . (See Table 10.1). For each type of community we will seek to show:

1. the relative prevalence of varieties of political behavior which are considered corrupt in terms of Western elite norms regarding office-holding and civic participation.
2. the severity or tolerance with which elite and mass opinions in that community regard the varieties of behavior which are corrupt by official definition.

The Traditional Familist (Kinship) Based System

The community that comes closest to illustrating the familist-based system is Montegrano, as described . . . by Edward C. Banfield.[5] The "amoral familists" who populate this community distinguish it from kinship-based systems in underdeveloped countries around the globe in that the absence of the "extended family" traditions emphasizes the especially narrow bases of group interests. Here loyalty to the nuclear family is the only loyalty that counts. In contrast to other Mediterranean communities, upper-class inhabitants avoid entering into patron-client relationships with the poorer families. Families are jealous of their neighbors' good fortune even if it has occurred at no cost to themselves. There is not enough trust to support the kind of "political machine" characteristic of American cities, because the voters do not believe in the promises of potential bosses, and the latter have no faith that bribed voters will stay bought. Among appointed officials there is a decided lack of any sense of duty or calling.

Table 10.1
TYPES OF COMMUNITY AND POLITICAL EXCHANGE

Characteristic	Traditional Familist (Kinship) Based Systems		Traditional Patron–Client-Based System	Modern Boss–Follower-Based System	Modern Civic–Culture-Based System
	Within Families	Between Families			
Archetypal protector	Family head	—	Patron saint	Political boss	State (constitution and courts)
Prototype for political exchange relations	Family obligation	Economic exchange	Social and economic exchange	Economic and social exchange	Social (indirect) exchange
Strength of community-regarding norms	—	Nil	Weak	Weak	Strong
Denotation of "patron"	—	—	Moral ideal, protector, intermediary	Protector, intermediary	Benefactor of community (art and education)

Strong reciprocal basis of obligations between chief patron and client	No	—	Yes	Yes	—
Kinship/friendship network open enough to permit independent "contacts" by client	No	Yes	No (depends)	Yes (depends)	Yes
Collective (family) obligation for favors to its members	—	Yes	Yes	Yes (depends)	No
Clients directly follow patron-chief in political behavior	Yes	—	Yes	Yes	—
Family obligations perceived as having primary claim on officeholder	Yes	—	Yes	No	No

153

The Traditional Patron–Client-Based Systems

Illustrative of the patron–client-based type are the Sicilian and Greek communities studied by anthropologists Jeremy Boissevain . . . and J.K. Campbell . . .. They exist in the twentieth century but are still the captives of belief and authority patterns rooted in the distant past. Protection is sought outside the family; but in the minds of the simpler peasants the powers of supernatural patron saints and of upper-class patrons blur into one another. Ties to powerful protectors are strong, identification with the general community still quite weak. Through the patron–client relationships, which unlike the kinship relationship is based upon voluntary choice of both parties, a strong sense of reciprocal obligation develops. Friendship ties and those to the patron in particular are viewed as the "throwing stick" that gives the extended family greater range when dealing with established authority. Out of reciprocity the family head pledges his own voting support and that of his entire family to the patron's discretion. The client maintains the dependency tie to the patron because he senses a need for protection that neither the family nor the state is able to provide. In terms of social distance the lowest officials of the state are so far above him that he needs to work through the patron in order to establish favorable contact with it.

The Modern Boss–Follower-Based System

Two types of situations illustrate the boss–patronage-based system. The first is the operation of American big-city political machines in normal (that is, not excessively scandalous) times during most periods in the first half of this century. . . . The second situation is that of a chronically corrupt town, Wincanton, as analyzed by John Gardiner[6] . . . where the incidence of "dirty graft" has been a paramount issue for half a century. These communities differ from those in the preceding category by virtue of the fact that they are "wide-open" urban centers based upon highly differentiated economies in which even the greenest immigrant differentiates very clearly between a patron saint and the political boss. Traditionally legitimated social and bureaucratic elites have little direct influence here, for the machine makes the political decisions and the only important question is whether it is headed by a "game politician" or a "gain politician." Nonetheless, many aspects of the boss-follower relationship are modeled on that of the patron-client relationship in the traditional setting. . . . One of the few differences in the client's situation is that, due to the greater diversity of direct links to the larger society, he has somewhat more discretion as to which mediator to attach himself to, although he may have to move to another ward to effect the change. And most importantly, since these communities are "modern," they foster and adapt to change. Thus, whereas in the traditional patron-client setting, political exchange relationships tend to be based primarily on the social exchange model and secondarily on that of economic exchange, in these modern settings it is the more flexible and adaptable economic exchange model that tends to be dominant.

The Civic–Culture-Based System

The civic–culture-based system of political exchange relationship prevails in "clean," medium-sized towns or suburbs in America or Britain. The citizens do not feel they need to work through an influential intermediary in order to get the benefit of the laws and administrative programs. They have developed strong community-regarding norms, which are supported by viable voluntary associations who repay their volunteer activists in tokens of moral satisfaction rather than money or money's worth. Political exchange relations follow a model of diversified and indirect social exchange. Crude political reciprocity in economic terms, such as the bribe, occurs very rarely. Political obligations insofar as they are still undergirded by economic exchange techniques, assume sophisticated and respectable new forms, such as testimonial dinners, lawyer's fees, consultant contracts, and campaign funds. These communities are "clean" because the political leaders are not bound by reciprocity agreements with lower-class followers, which the latter could utilize as channels for forcing their styles of competition on the more "respectable" strata. In this setting the "patron" still exists, but only in a very attenuated and generalized function. The object of his patronage, directly or indirectly, is the community at large. It may benefit directly from his philanthropy or indirectly from his patronage of creative artists, the value of whose work to the community some rank higher than market prices recognize.

Corrupt Behavior Incidence in the Four Types of Communities

All ten types of corrupt behavior listed in Table 10.2 would be defined corrupt by a scrupulous upholder of Western administrative norms and civic behavior rules, and could be prosecuted in almost any North American or European country by an able public prosecutor

Table 10.2
INCIDENCE AND EVALUATION OF CORRUPT PRACTICES

Type of Behavior	Traditional Familist (Kinship) Based System		Traditional Patron–Client-Based System		Modern Boss–Patronage-Based System		Modern Civic–Culture-Based System	
	Incidence	Evaluation	Incidence	Evaluation	Incidence	Evaluation	Incidence	Evaluation
Petty Corruption								
Officials deviate from rules in minor ways for benefit of friends	SOP	W	SOP	W	SOP	W	FI	G
Routine Corruption								
Gifts accepted by public officials (or parties) for generalized good will	SOP	W	SOP	W	SOP	W	OI if collectivized	B collectivized G
Nepotism practices in official appointments and contract awarding	SOP	W	SOP	W	SOP	G	OI if collectivized	B collectivized G
Officials profit from public decisions through sideline occupations (clean graft)	SOP	W	SOP	W	FI SOP: Wincanton	G	OI	B

156

Clients pledge votes according to patron's direction	SOP	W	SOP	W	FI	G	OO	B
Aggravated Corruption Clients need patron intervention to get administrative "due process"	SOP	W	FI	G	OI	B	OO	B
Gifts (kickbacks) expected by officials as prerequisite for extending "due process"	SOP	W	FI	G	OI SOP: Wincanton	B	OO	B
Officials tolerate organized crime in return for payoffs	FI	W	FI	G	OI SOP: Wincanton	B	OO	B
Activists suddenly change party allegiance for pecuniary reasons	FI	W	OI	B	OI	B	OO	B
Officials and citizens ignore clear proof of corruption	FI	W	OI	B	OI	B	OO	B

Key: SOP = Standard Operating Procedure; FI = Frequent Incidence; OI = Occasional Incidence; OO = Rare Incidence, Without Regular Pattern;
B = Black Corruption; G = Gray Corruption; W = White Corruption

who does not mind making enemies or appearing slightly ridiculous among his peers. What we shall attempt to show with reference to these types of corrupt behavior is their varying incidence in the four types of situations, as suggested by a loose form of content analysis of the relevant literature. Behaviors coded SOP are believed to be "standard operating procedure" in the respective locality. Behaviors coded FI are believed to occur with "frequent incidence." Those coded OI are thought to occur with only "occasional incidence." Finally, those coded OO are thought to occur without any regular pattern of incidence, with individual acts of official turpitude being no more frequent than they are in any large organization employing fallible human beings. For convenience in discussion the corrupt behaviors are arbitrarily grouped into three categories, those involving "petty," "routine," and "aggravated" corruption.

Petty Corruption

Petty corruption refers to the bending of official rules in favor of friends, as manifested in the somewhat untruthful reporting of details, the ignoring of cut-off dates, the "fixing" of parking tickets, and so on. It occurs widely in all four settings, although it is not standard practice in the civic-culture town, where it is likely to be frowned upon by purists, but taken advantage of by practical businessmen. In the boss-patronage community it is a widely engaged in practice, even among all recipients of the "newspaper wards."

Routine Corruption

Some of the practices listed in the category of routine corruption do occur to some extent in civic-culture towns, but usually only in forms where they are sanitized through the "collectivization of the receiver." Thus campaign contributors to political party funds may win some degree of preference as contract bidders or appointive office candidates. In the boss-patronage city, on the other hand, most of these practices were either standard or widely practiced operating procedures, with most material benefits accruing to individuals. Thus, . . . the wealth through which many of the Irish elevated themselves to middle-class status in American cities was to a large degree accumulated in construction, trucking, and waterfront industries, in which prosperity was largely dependent upon favoritism in city contracts. Favoritism, or the guarantee of unequal access, is of course the main lever through which the machine generated the stock of resources from which it diverted the "economic" component of the rewards extended to ward leaders and voters. The boss also used patronage powers to . . . pay colleagues for obeying orders and to bribe elected officials to follow leads.

In the *traditional patron-client* settings many of the gifts received by public officials are less clearly related to specific obligations, but are standard practice in the sense that they recur almost seasonally. Thus, some Greek shepherd families give the village president each spring a gift of cheese, butter, or meat in the hope that this may "moderate his general attitude towards them in the coming months." . . . In return for helping them when they are in trouble, the lawyer-patron, who acts in the general role of a professional fixer, is able to promise the political support of his clients during local and national elections. The assistance of patrons is as essential in applying for a government job as it was some decades ago in Chicago, even though there is no party machine. In Sicily a former municipal employee who sought to regain his job had to mobilize two higher-class patrons before his application was given due consideration. In this setting, therefore, all the activities that would be considered "routine corruption" by official Western standards are standard procedures deeply rooted in more general social relationships and obligations.

Of course, all the syndromes noted above are also standard procedure in the amoral *familist* community of Montegrano. Because families in Montegrano are nuclear rather than extended, and because of the lack of the patron as mediating agent, the exchanges are more nakedly specific and the contracts more short-term in duration. A poor peasant votes for the Christian Democrats because the party has given him a "few days work on the roads each year. . . . If it ceased to give him work and if there were no advantage to be had for voting for another party, he would be a monarchist again."[7]

Aggravated Corruption

In the civic–culture-based community instances of aggravated corruption occur very rarely, if at all.

Among boss–patronage-based communities it is precisely the frequency of incidence of aggravated corruption that distinguishes "reform" periods from "scandal-ridden" ones, or "corrupt cities" from "machine cities." Thus, most of the varieties of corrupt behavior occur only occasionally in the better-run "machine cities" of twentieth-century America, but they were standard practice in the town that John A. Gardiner calls Wincanton.[8] Whereas in Chicago crime opera-tors could intermittently purchase toleration from various police officials, in Wincanton the syndicate head controlled the police to the extent that he could use it to run rivals out of town. Corrupt mayors made it a standard practice to demand $75 gifts for the approval of building permits and $2000 kickbacks for the awarding of city contracts. The crooked police chief had to pay the mayor $10,000 for his appointment, and was allowed to recoup through payoffs from organized crime. In Wincanton, therefore, the varieties of "dirty graft" and aggravated corruption were as widespread as in any traditional community, except that the more developed state of the economy caused the amounts involved in the corrupt transactions to be much larger.

The incidence pattern of aggravated corruption in the patron-client society seems to differ in two interesting ways from the same pattern in the two other communities. It differs from the boss-patronage community in that the properly connected client can use it to tap a wider variety of services. It is unlikely that anyone in the Wincanton machine would have been of much help in establishing contact with a particular university professor, who would be far less likely to offer the client a thesis that he could hand in as his own. (In the Sicilian context these acts did constitute *political* corruption.) On the other hand, this setting appears to differ from the familist society in that some of the techniques of aggravated corruption are less widely employed. The Greek shepherds conceded that "eating money" (the acceptance of small bribes) was one of the rights of office that the village president needed to exercise in order to support his family. However, they were cautious about offering bribes to higher officials; and if they pledged their votes to a patron, they usually maintained their agreements for a decent period of time. In Montegrano, on the other hand, most of the inhabitants were sure that not only the local officials, but also those up the line to the national government, were corrupt and completely without a sense of obligation to office. This belief encouraged an almost universal tendency among both officials and citizens to ignore proof of corrupt behavior even when it was directly observed and to undertake no initiatives to cooperate with established authority to invoke sanctions.

The Tolerance and Evaluation of Corrupt Practices

Although behavior fitting into any one of the forty categories in Table 10.2 could be considered corrupt by some citizen who was particularly conscious of official norms, his interpretations would obviously be shared to a very widely varying degree by his fellow citizens. Indeed, it has been argued that if 99 percent of the community disagrees, then, although one's viewpoint is well-grounded in the applicable legal codes, the action is not considered "corrupt" in that community. It is this problem of normative evaluation that we seek to approach in terms of the shorthand notations of black, gray, or white corruption in Table 10.2. The evaluation "black corruption" indicates that in that setting that particular action is one which a majority consensus of both elite and mass opinion would condemn and would want to see punished on grounds of principle. "Gray corruption" indicates that some elements, usually elites, may want to see the action punished, others not, and the majority may well be ambiguous. "White corruption" signifies that the majority of both elite and mass opinion probably would not vigorously support an attempt to punish a form of corruption that they regard as tolerable. This implies that they attach less value to the maintenance of the values involved than they do to the costs that might be generated as the result of a change in rule enforcement.

One of the subtler characteristics of norm patterns in the civic-culture community relates to the "grayness" of attitudes toward petty corruption. The general elite disapproval of favoritism would tend to contain its extent, . . . even though some forms of "giving consideration" persist. . . . This would be in contrast to the boss-patronage city, where even the reform-minded elements would tend to think that practices such as ticket fixing have to be tolerated. Attitudes toward several forms of "routine" corruption might also tend to be "gray" in the civic-culture setting, with the degree of toleration related essentially to important questions of form. The giving of gifts to public officials and nepotism may be regarded as "black," or punishable, if favors are exchanged at the level of the individual official or firm, but their equivalents are likely to be tolerated if the funds in question are "collectivized" through devices such as party campaign treasuries. Investigations often reveal that individual politicians surreptitiously cross the indistinct line differentiating "gray" from "black" behavior. Thus, in 1967, Senator Thomas Dodd of Connecticut was shown to have diverted to private use funds allegedly raised for his campaign treasury, and this revelation was instrumental in causing his colleagues to levy censure upon him.

In boss-patronage communities much of the "grayness" characterizing attitudes toward forms of "routine" corruption is likely to be associated with sharp differences between attitudes in the poorer, or "river," wards and those in the more well-to-do, or "newspaper," wards. Robert Lane and others have found that the attitude of working-class residents of large cities to reports of governmental corruption is "generally speaking a tolerant one, certainly not indignant, not moralistic, possibly insufficiently censorious."[9] Corrupt practices localized in the poorer sections are likely to be tolerated by middle-class opinion and to be strenuously resisted only when they spread into, or more directly affect, the "respectable" areas of the city. In Wincanton, surveys showed that very significant minorities were willing to be tolerant of varieties of favoritism and "clean graft," which were technically illegal; thus 35 percent thought it all right for city officials to accept presents from companies, and 27 percent had no objections if the mayor profited financially from municipal land purchases as long as the price charged was "fair." The "grayness" of attitudes in the boss-patronage city makes possible a higher threshold of enforcement beneath which multiple forms of "clean graft" and favoritism are tolerated. It is when rings of politicians and contractors expand their practices to include forms of aggravated corruption which do run counter to the values of the vast majority of the population that a "clean-up" campaign will sooner or later ensue, as John Gardiner illustrates in the Wincanton case.

In the traditional patronage-client community the attitudes toward the various forms of corruption are several shades "lighter" and more tolerant. Thus, most of the routine forms of corruption regarded as "gray" in the American city setting are viewed as "white," or quite acceptable, in this environment. The strength of informal social obligations is too great to permit significant criticism of the widely prevalent practices of nepotism and the purchase of influence. In the words of a local informant, the perception that "in Sicily all friendships are political," leads to acceptance of the fact of life that all politics involves giving preference to one's friends. There the patronage system, which Boissevain . . . likens to "a parasitic vine," weakens the rule of law to the point where many cases of aggravated corruption are considered as falling into the "gray" rather than "black" area. In Sicily, as in Greece, it is regarded as legitimate for officials to require bribes or patron intervention in order to give the peasant what should be his due according to the law. In contrast to the modern setting, where even lower-class citizens are infused with some measure of egalitarian ideology, the peasants in this kind of community accept the arrogance of officials as an almost legitimate function of their higher social status and regard it as natural that their sympathy can only be aroused through gifts and bribes.

In the familist-based system all of the types of behavior that are considered corrupt by the standards of Western legal norms are considered "white," or acceptable, by the bulk of the population. As effective community-regarding norms are lacking, attitudes will be determined in individual cases in relation to who is doing the corrupting on whose behalf. Since public affairs are conceived to be the exclusive concern of those public officials who are paid to look after them, the latter can expect little citizen cooperation, which would be a prerequisite for norm enforcement. In the face of such total apathy they, too, will incline to ignore evidence of obvious corruption, and thus join the conspiracy of silence that permits most forms of corrupt activity to have a frequent incidence or to become standard operating procedure.

Notes

1. Harold D. Lasswell, "Bribery." *Encyclopedia of the Social Sciences,* Vol. I. New York: Crowell-Collier-Macmillan, 1930, pp. 690–92.
2. Peter M. Blau, *Exchange and Power in Social Life.* New York: Wiley, 1964, p. 258.
3. Edward C. Banfield, *The Moral Basis of a Backward Society.* New York: The Free Press, 1958.
4. Blau, *op. cit.,* p. 94.
5. Banfield, *op. cit.*
6. John A. Gardiner, "The Politics of Corruption in an American City." In Arnold J. Heidenheimer, ed., *Political Corruption: Readings in Comparative Analysis.* New Brunswick, N.J.: Transaction Books, 1978, pp. 167–75.
7. Banfield, *op. cit.*
8. Gardiner, *op. cit.*
9. Robert E. Lane, *Political Ideology.* New York: Free Press, 1962, p. 335.

11

Toward an Attitudinal Definition of Corruption

Kenneth M. Gibbons

. . . In the course of the revivification of the concept of political corruption in Western political science, the concept's definition has become a major concern. This concern goes well beyond mere lexicography; it is one of conceptualization—of connotation as well as denotation. Perhaps due to the underlying "moralism" inherent in the general usage of the term, corruption seems to have generated more than its fair share of definitional debate. Perhaps, too, there are other reasons for this conceptual disagreement, but the point stands nonetheless: agreement as to a reasonable definition of political corruption seems, at best, a distant and improbable goal. Yet, this realization does not permit us, as a discipline, to ignore the need to grapple with the meaning of the concept. It is not necessary to argue from this that all research and analysis of corruption should stand still, awaiting the unlikely appearance of consensus. It does follow, however, that the terminological problem must not be ignored. . . .

The Definition of Political Corruption

Definitions of political corruption have become so numerous as to permit their classification into types. As an example, one might draw on the work of Arnold Heidenheimer, who divided the mass of definitions into three basic types: public-office-centered, market-centered, and public-interest-centered.[1] Other typologies exist, such as that proffered by John G. Peters and Susan Welch,[2] which have both overlapping and distinctive elements, but it is not the purpose here to

Source: Kenneth M. Gibbons, "Towards an Attitudinal Definition of Corruption: Evidence from a Survey of Canadian University Students." Paper given at the 1985 International Political Science Congress, Paris. By permission of the author.

elaborate upon all possible variants. It shall suffice to add a fourth type drawn from the second example: public-opinion or attitudinally-based definitions.

Public-office-centered definitions (what Peters and Welch call legalistic definitions) can be illustrated by reference to the work of J.S. Nye, who defined corruption as "behavior which deviates from the normal duties of a public role because of private-regarding (family, close private clique), pecuniary or status gains, and violates rules against the exercise of certain types of private-regarding influence."[3] This view is consistent with that of James C. Scott who argues against definitions based either on public interest or public opinion. Indeed, he uses Nye's definition explicitly.[4] Unfortunately, Scott may have been too hasty in accepting the merits of legalistic definitions and rejecting those assumed by proponents of otheer types. Heidenheimer contends, and is supported by the views of earlier writers like Robert Brooks and Joseph Senturia, that the legalistic view is too narrow.[5] There are many political phenomena of significance which would be put aside if strictly legal definitions of corruption held sway: defeats of scandal-ridden governing parties, long-term declines in the legitimacy of successive "corrupt" governments, even coups d'etat. Legal definitions have their value, but not to the exclusion of other considerations.

Market-centered definitions would seem to have particular relevance to those who pursue an economic analysis of corruption (though this by no means is meant to imply that economic analyses *must* be market-oriented). One such example is advanced by Jacob von Klaveren, who states that "a corrupt civil servant regards his public office as a business, the income of which he will . . . seek to maximize. . . . The size of his income depends . . . upon the market situation and his talents for finding the point of maximal gain on the public's demand curve."[6] While it might be argued that these definitions are really explanations (i.e., perhaps not definitions at all), the focus on market-orientation implies a definition at least, and this definition inherently replaces "moral" or "public interest" considerations with "profit maximization" as the prime motivator. As such, these definitions (or explanations, if one prefers) suggest that corruption is only another means of acquiring economic resources, thus placing this approach well within the "functionalist" framework to the extent that the definition argues implicitly or explicitly that a necessary social function is served by having such market mechanisms in place. Most will recognize this perspective as having its genesis in the work of Robert Merton.[7] The tautological nature of such arguments is now widely accepted; there seems little need to reiterate them here. Likewise, the shortcomings of functionalist arguments regarding corruption have been frequently discussed.[8]

Heidenheimer's third type is the public-interest-centered definition, which deviates clearly from both of the preceding types, though not so boldly in the case of a comparison to the legalistic view. Public-interest-centered definitions differ from legalistic definitions in that they are broader and apparently assume that there is a public interest which transcends the law itself. Heidenheimer cites examples from the work of Friedrich and of Rogow and Lasswell, respectively.[9]

> The pattern of corruption can be said to exist whenever a power-holder who is charged with doing certain things, i.e., who is a responsible functionary or office-holder, is by monetary or other rewards not legally provided for induced to take actions which favor whoever provides the rewards and thereby does damage to the public and its interest.

> A system of public or civic order exalts common interest over special interest; violations of the common interest for special advantage are corrupt.

The concept of public interest is, in itself, problematic and worthy of a separate and extensive debate. Nevertheless, it is clear that, among many alternative views of what does or does not constitute "the public interest," public opinion is often cited as an integral part of the consideration, even if it is not equated with public interest per se. Hence, it is not unreasonable to argue that public-interest-centered definitions encompass what others might call public opinion or attitudinal definitions. However, if one follows the lead of Peters and Welch, public opinion definitions merit a separate category or type. Indeed, Heidenheimer moves beyond the three types of definitions himself, and employs a public opinion definition having gradations of intensity which he describes as black, grey, and white. Still others, like Graeme Moodie, use a public opinion or attitudinal definition without attaching that label to their work. Moodie contends that the best indicator of corruption is the existence of "scandal," that is, a "hostile and shocked response" to a given action.[10]

It is not necessary to put aside legalistic definitions as unimportant in order to accept the validity or utility (or both) of public opinion definitions. Heidenheimer's conceptualization of corruption as having gradations based upon the agreement between mass and elite opinion bears this point out.[11] These gradations (the aforementioned black, grey, and white) allow a distinction to be made between that which is illegal and that which is corrupt, although a conjunction of these attributes is clearly possible. If one supposes that legal codes are at least an imperfect indicator of elite opinion (at least of legislative elites), then one could argue that Heidenheimer's concept of black corruption—actions condemned by both mass and elite opinion—could be measured by the congruence of mass opinion and the law. By extension, grey corruption is an ambiguous situation where there is no consensus of opinion, but where significant elements—usually elites by Heidenheimer's reckoning—are in favor of proscription. Thus, it might also be argued that grey corruption is illustrated by the lack of congruence between law and public opinion, where laws exist which condemn behavior that is not equally met by public hostility. This does not mean that the law is totally without its supporters, but that the support is not consensual in the community. Prohibition in the United States strikes an interesting example of this "greyness." Finally, there is the white corruption which is free from vigorous opposition within any element of the community and largely, although not completely, tolerated for any one of a number of reasons. From a legal perspective, such corruption is unlikely to become law in the first place, as the necessary consensus exists neither at the elite nor the mass level.

Heidenheimer's "public opinion" approach ignores market-orientation in its definitional context, and the modification to recognize legalistic criteria does the same. However, even market considerations can be accommodated within this conceptualization, but from an explanatory rather than definitional perspective. That is, what both the law and public opinion do is define what is or is not corrupt, but neither effectively or completely explains why corrupt acts continue to occur. While the absence of laws condeming what the public feels is corrupt, or the reverse situation where the law exists but is not widely respected by public opinion, may encourage corrupt behavior, these notions are insufficient. In other words, even where either of these conditions exist, why do some people engage in "corrupt" acts but others do not? While some form of economic-rationalist reasoning may not always explain motivation in this context, it is likely that it has impact in some cases, perhaps where the individual is "psychologically predisposed" to employ pure economic-rationalist models to thinking.

Ultimately, conceptualization (i.e., definition) and explanation are linked in the process of social inquiry. Distinctions between these two processes are not always clear, yet it seems reasonable to argue that conceptualization precedes explanation. Thus, conceptualization is often treated as exploratory or as "clearing away the underbrush" before serious explanation can begin. However, in the pre-paradigmatic state which confronts social (and especially political) science, conceptualization is critical. It is that critical problem to which this paper is addressed. . . . The concern is that the concept of corruption has definable dimension which are recognized by the public (students, voters, elected officials, etc.) and which permit a complex analysis of the concept to be made in light of public (or student, or voter, or elected official, etc.) opinion. From this type of analysis should flow the potential for a better understanding of the concept and its meaning. Further, this understanding is potentially enhanced by the application of various independent variables which may assist in "explaining" why certain views of corruption obtain, i.e., are there regional differences, age differences, etc. which seem to accompany the citizens' definitions or conceptualizations of corruption? If so, how might these differences be explained? The means by which such questions were analyzed will be discussed later.

The components of political corruption consist of concepts which can be used by respondents to "define" what is or is not a corrupt act, what is or is not common or democratic or necessary. These components must not be confused with types of corruption, which constitute sub-concepts of the concept of corruption itself. By that is meant that corruption, being the complex notion that it is, must be seen as having sub-types of sub-concepts which permit a more precise description than the term "corruption" alone could provide. It is even reasonable to argue that the sub-types which seem to exist within the corruption literature are not consistently seen as being corrupt. Indeed, part of the effort at arriving at reasonable conceptualization of corruption is directed at discerning what kinds of activities are deemed corrupt and which are not. To a degree, differences between citizen attitudes and existing legal frameworks allow us to grasp, at least rudimentarily, the underlying assumption of Heidenheimer's "black-grey-white" categorization as it applies to different types of activity.

The various types of corruption which permeate the literature on corruption can be defined in terms of certain dimensions: the scope of involvement in the activity alleged to be corrupt; the status of the actors involved (are the officials targets of the act or initiators or neither?); the types of rewards offered for involvement (power, money, etc.); the selectivity of the inducements (ranging from very selective or particularistic on the one hand to very diffuse on the other, but not universalistic by definition); the location or arena of the activity (electoral, legislative, etc.); and, subject to confirmation by attitudinal analysis, the level of condemnation ascribed to the activity in question (Heidenheimer's "black-grey-white" distinction). While the first five of these dimensions can arguably be assessed by impressionistic means, the last requires empirical testing on both a quantitative and qualitative level. The quantitative analysis applies, for obvious reason, to the aspect of this dimension which reflects public attitudes or opinions. The qualitative aspect refers to the review of legislative statutes which represent, however imperfectly, the views of legislative elites and their reference groups (leaving aside the class nature of legislators' "significant others," to use Goffman's[12] descriptive phrase). Of course, one can use quantitative methods to examine elite (especially legislative) attitudes in a direct way as well. This method has been used by others successfully, including Peters and Welch, Beard and Horn, and Mancuso.[13] . . . However, the study of legislative attitudes rather than legislation per se seems to miss at least part of Heidenheimer's fundamental concern regarding consensus and its congruence (or lack thereof) with law. . . .

Notes

1. Arnold Heidenheimer, "Introduction," in *Political Corruption: Readings in Comparative Analysis* (New Brunswick, N.J.: Transaction Books, 1978), pp. 3–9. See also his first chapter in the same volume for several articles dealing with definitional problems.
2. John G. Peters and Susan Welch, "Political Corruption in America: A Search for Definition and a Theory," *American Political Science Review*, 72 (September, 1978), p. 975. Interestingly, although Heidenheimer's typology does not include public opinion based definitions itself, he employs such an analysis at the end of his "Introduction," *ibid.*, pp. 26–28. Peters and Welch cite Heidenheimer as the best illustration of this approach, p. 975.
3. Heidenheimer, *ibid.*, p. 5.
4. James C. Scott, *Comparative Political Corruption*, (Englewood Cliffs, N.J.: Prentice-Hall, 1972), pp. 3–5.
5. Heidenheimer, *op. cit.*, p. 7.
6. *Ibid.*, p. 5. See also Susan Rose-Ackerman, *Corruption: A Study in Political Economy*, (New York: Academic Press, 1973) for a general application of the market-oriented approach.
7. Robert K. Merton, *Social Theory and Social Structure*, (Glencoe, Ill.: The Free Press, 1957), pp. 72–82. Also reprinted as "Some Functions of the Political Machine," in Jack D. Douglas and John M. Johnson, eds., *Official Deviance: Readings in Malfeasance, Misfeasance, and Other Forms of Corruption*, (New York: Lippincott, 1977), pp. 339–49.
8. On the general problem of the tautological nature of functionalist explanation, see Richard S. Rudner, *Philosophy of Social Science*, (Englewood Cliffs, N.J.: Prentice-Hall, 1966), Ch. 5. For a critique of functionalism as it is applied specifically to the study of corruption, see Gerald E. Caiden and Naomi J. Caiden, "Administrative Corruption," *Public Administration Review*, 43 (March/April, 1983), pp. 146–54.
9. Heidenheimer, *op. cit.*, p. 6.
10. Peters and Welch, *op. cit.*, pp. 974–75; Heidenheimer, *ibid.*, pp. 26–28;

Graeme Moodie, "On Political Scandals and Corruption," *Government and Opposition,* vol. 15 (Spring, 1980), pp. 208–22, and especially p. 219. The distinction btween attitudinal and public opinion approaches is not intended to be merely a preference. Attitudinal seems not only to encompass the more transitory nature of opinion, but to add a deeper and less transitory aspect as well. On this point see Bernard Hennessey, *Public Opinion,* (Belmont, Calif.: Wadsworth, 1965), pp. 101 and 319.

11. Heidenheimer, *ibid.*
12. E. Goffman, *The Presentation of Self in Everyday Life,* (New York: Doubleday, 1959).
13. Peters and Welch, *op. cit.;* Edmund Beard and Stephen Horn, *Congressional Ethics: The View from the House,* (Washington: Brookings Institution, 1975); and Maureen Mancuso, "Attitudes of Canadian Legislators Toward Political Corruption: An Empirical Analysis," unpublished M.A. thesis (Ottawa: Carleton University, 1984).

12

The Rhetoric of Political Corruption

Bruce E. Gronbeck

On Tuesday, 13 June 1967, Senator Thomas A. Dodd of Connecticut was charged in a resolution presented to the United States Senate with a "course of conduct" which is "contrary to accepted morals, derogates from the public trust expected of a Senator, and tends to bring the Senate into dishonor and disrepute."[1] Underlying the Dodd Resolution is a conception of private acts by public officials which, I would argue, has guided democratic deliberations since ancient Greece. That conception of human behavior is encapsulated in the idea of *political corruption*.

The concept "political corruption" includes a set of behaviors which falls within a larger set termed by Friedrich "the pathology of politics." Generally, political pathologies are acts and intentions which violate the laws, procedures, and ideological-cultural expectations of a political system, and include political violence, betrayal or treason, corruption, secret and often arbitrary decision-making, and the distortion of "reality" for political purposes (i.e. propaganda).[2] More specifically, the term "political corruption" encompasses those acts whereby private gain is made at public expense. The personal gain may be purely monetary, as was the case with Verres' rape of Roman provinces in the first century **B.C.**, and Adam Clayton Powell's diversion of public funds for unquestionably private vacations in the 1960s. Or, the monetary gain may be passed to others in the form of patronage, as were rewards under Robert Walpole's tenure as leading minister of England in the first half of the eighteenth century and under Warren Hastings' Governor Generalship of India in the second half. The gains, moreover, need not be monetary: While Richard Nixon certainly was charged with cheating on his income tax, as a society we were more concerned with

Source: Bruce E. Gronbeck, "The Rhetoric of Political Corruption: Sociolinguistic, Dialectical and Ceremonial Processes," *Quarterly Journal of Speech*, 64: 2 (1978), pp. 155–72. By permission of the publisher and author.

his use of presidential power to obstruct justice and manipulate electoral results. . . .

We are here dealing, then, with a range of political offenses which perhaps characterize any government at any time—graft, kickbacks, overzealous promotion through the meritocracy, slush funds which have public effects without public accountability, favors which bypass normal channels. We are dealing, in sum, with those behaviors which many people take as part of the everyday cost of government. Indeed, it is the very *routineness* of political corruption which makes its public airing and treatment so fascinating rhetorically. Its routineness and ubiquity, as we shall see, make it at once farcical and tragic; its exposure often brings out both the Art Buchwalds and the Jeremiahs of a society.

Now traditionally, political corruption has received sporadic attention from political scientists and economists—particularly those interested in comparative international politics. The pragmatic dimensions of the notion have been explored with comparative fullness, as such scholarship has concentrated upon identifying the sources of corruption, classifying the kinds of immoral influence, and tallying the "real" costs and rewards of corruption in various political systems.[3] Little work, however, has pursued its second-level or "symbolic" dimensions. In our attending to corruption within a *political-institutional context,* we have virtually ignored it in a *rhetorical-social context.* We have done little to explain why some instances produce public disillusionment and apathy, even resentment aimed at government generally, and why others are celebrated and hence produce a sense of public optimism and self-satisfaction; why some corrupters are wept over in their disgrace, while others suffer the social equivalent of a public hanging; and why corruption as a social drama can generate both farce and tragedy.

More specifically, in times past the twin notions of prerogative (the rights of political personages) and *raison d'etat* (the right of government to take extraordinary actions suitable to crises) lent compelling assurance that corrupters would be immune to public prosecution.[4] Once, however, the divine right theory waned and parliamentary government waxed, the "people's right" to know, evaluate, and judge seemed to demand the instigation of a public ritual for indicting, exhibiting, and symbolically "killing" the corrupter. Political corruption, I would argue, became more than a matter of institutional housekeeping; it became a matter of public concern, with a people demanding to participate in ritualistic deposition.

The rationale underlying that ritual is undoubtedly complicated, for it must involve (1) a *sociolinguistic process*—verbally "naming" or defining such seemingly minor acts as theft, larceny, lying, and the like as heinous crimes which gnaw at the very footings of democracy; (2) a *dialectical process*—investing those crimes, on the one hand, with "seriousness" by officially constitued role-players or tribunals (who do not want to be viewed as mere vigilantes or political opportunists), and, on the other, with triviality or meanness by the indicted corrupter; and (3) a *ceremonial process*—a public dancing of charges and counter-charges, investigations, trials, and real or symbolic executions, which allow a public (a culture) to participate in the ritualistic purification of the country. In all, these essentially rhetorical processes must guarantee that the public does not react with cynicism or humor in the face of purgative proceedings, for such reactions would stop or misdirect the social catharsis at which the proceedings aim. And they must illustrate the power of the state—its ability to protect a citizenry from devils within.

In this essay, therefore, I seek to explore the rhetorics of political corruption essentially as *sets of social rules,* rules guiding the selection of sociolinguistically potent labels, the constitution of appropriate speaker-roles or postures, and the orchestration through time of socially relevant rituals. . . .

The Sociolinguistic Process

Any attempt to explore the notion of a "rhetoric" of political corruption must almost of necessity involve, first, an understanding of symbols and social reality. Indeed, the concept of "social reality"—vis à vis sensate, scientific, or metaphysical reality—provides the keys to the symbolic consequences of Watergate-like activities. Although it certainly is not the purpose of this essay to offer a philosophical and pragmatic defense of symbolic interactionism, dramaturgical theories of communications, or phenomenological speculation, nevertheless such studies provide ways into cultural environments which allow for pointed rhetorical analysis.

In the raw, the following is predicated on the assumptions that (1) *"Man is the symbol-using (symbol-making, symbol-misusing) animal";* (2) symbols—and the society which invents, promulgates, and sanctions them—are determinative of any individual's perception or apprehension of the world, attitudes, values, and behaviors, i.e. that human beings find "meanings" and "meaningfulness" only in symbolic processes; and, hence, (3) humans are born into, nurtured by, and in large measure controlled through a series of symbolic environments, . . . existing on three levels:[5]

(1) *Level of facticity*. On the most basic level, symbols are "names" with direct reference in sense experience, as any correspondence theory of meaning postulates. This is the level of primary socialization, of understanding basic categories-for-data.

(2) *Level of institutionalization*. Additional, and often more specialized, meanings become attached to some symbols on another level—the institutional level. . . . On the second or institutional level of meanings, we tend to speak of "languages" of economics, politics, manners, love, and so on. These languages are not distinguished sociolinguistically by the fact that different words belong to different languages (for we assuredly, for example, can talk about "transactions" in economic, political, or interpersonal contexts), but, rather, because each language is constrained by special "rules" of usage and expectation. That is, each of these institutional languages attaches special meanings to words, and violations of those meanings produce varied social sanctions. . . . The symbolic environments which constitute institutions, therefore, are given meaning and power by the social-political-economic-theological entities which are their repositories, that is, by the precedents, laws, and powers-of-enforcement which grant those institutions force in human affairs.

(3) *Level of culture*. Finally, some symbols . . . have significations beyond institutions. They represent the fundamental tenets of the society or culture, those sacred beliefs and conceptualizations which define "humanness" in a particular collectivity. . . . Because, then, symbolic environments at this third level are ultimately determinative of what it is to be a *social* being in any given epoch or place, in them reside the primordial gods and goblins of the collectivity; it is only in these environments that we properly can employ such labels as "outrage," "indignation," "horror," "duty," and the like.

In terms of my central concerns here, symbolic environments at these levels function differently. Take, for example, a maxim from English common law—"The king never dies." On the level of facticity, of course, the proposition makes no sense, has no referent. On the institutional level, however, it encapsulates a verbal-behavioral routine—the machinery of succession or heritability. "The king never dies" institutionally because we have mechanisms for keeping the office "alive." But, more importantly, on the cultural level, the maxim has embedded in it all of the hopes and fears we have for political institutions. The natural body of the king can be wracked with disease, infirmity, and old age, but to the antiquarian his political body was timeless—a perfect representation of cultural stability. Humanity's fear of a hostile world and distrust even of itself combine to drive us, almost frantically in what Berger and Luckmann so antiseptically term "marginal situations," to establish, maintain, and vigorously defend our political institutions—in spite of the human frailties which reside in particular leaders at particular times. "The king never dies" culturally for, if he did, central administration would be gone and unknown worlds of internal and external devils would swarm over and engulf the predictable ones.[6]

Such notions of symbolic environments most decisively bring us squarely into the middle of the sociolinguistic thesis of this essay. "Graft," "kickbacks," "public falsehoods," and the like are symbols which may partake of various symbolic environments. On the level of facticity, whenever someone is charged with engaging in such behaviors, factual questions can be (and are) raised: Was someone paid off? If so, how much and by whom? Was a situation misdescribed? If so, what "really" were the "facts"? . . .

Once someone decides that a politically corrupt act—i.e. one which either precedent or statute deems an example of "private gain made at public expense"—has been perpetrated, we move to the institutional web of meanings and significations: Are there appropriate institutional penalties which ought to be applied, and, if so, which penalties or sanctions? Should someone be fired (or allowed to resign, as were Bob Haldeman and John Ehrlichman by Nixon), jailed (as was Billie Sol Estes under the Johnson administration), publicly stripped of power by the offended institution (as were Thomas Dodd by the Senate and Adam Clayton Powell by the House of Representatives)?

And, finally, in some instances a "mere" institutional solution is apparently not enough. In these, a full-blown, society-wide purgation process is engaged. If an indicted corrupter is deemed not simply to have engaged in madadministration but to have assaulted the "office" or the "public trust" or whatever, we enter the third-level symbolic environment. An "office," after all, has a symbolic life all its own; it is imbued with love, respect, rationality, truth, sagacity, devotion, and a host of other fundamental cultural values. Crimes against "the office"—and hence against the culture's organizing principles—are not punished by institutional solutions alone. Such crimes engender, not mere anger or resentment, but frustration, horror, and a demand for society-wide vengeance. Such horror was expressed grandiloquently, for example, in 1788 in the peroration of Edmund Burke's opening speech against Warren Hastings:

> I impeach Warren Hastings, Esquire, of high crimes and misdemeanors.
>
> I impeach him in the name of the Commons of Great Britain, in Parliament assembled, whose parliamentary trust he has betrayed.
>
> I impeach him in the name of all the Commons of Great Britain, whose national character he has dishonored.
>
> I impeach him in the name of the people of India, whose laws, rights, and liberties he has subverted, whose property he has destroyed, whose country he has laid waste and desolate.
>
> I impeach him in the name, and by virtue, of those eternal laws of justice which he has violated.
>
> I impeach him in the name of human nature itself, which he has cruelly outraged, injured, and oppressed, in both sexes, in every age, rank, situation, and condition of life.[7]

Burke's litany of "names" is instructive: Hastings was a servant of a particular parliament, and he violated its institutional rules. By violating its expectations, he demeaned the culturally positive notion of parliamentary government generally. Furthermore, he harmed, not just individual Indian rulers and princesses, but the Indian cultural mores as a whole; he thereby assaulted the core of any society, "eternal laws of justice." Indeed, by the last sentence, Burke argues that Hastings attacked the very adhesive of society—its vision of its structure (hierarchies) and its reasons-for-being. In Burke's charges, Hastings' acts have acquired not only institutional meanings but cultural significations well beyond the harm done to individuals and institutions. Hastings has committed the almost unspeakable offense; he has "cruelly outraged" human nature. He has denied everything it means to be a person. . . .

This sort of analysis of symbolic environments begins to move directly into the foundations of rhetorics of political corruption: (1) Any rhetoric of political corruption must begin with a sociolinguistic process of *attaching symbolic meanings* to thoughts, words, and acts—meanings which outstretch the "everyday" or factual significations of those human modalities. (2) Such a rhetorical process of meaning attribution can occur in *two symbolic environments*—the institutional or the cultural. (3) In the *institutional environment,* political corruption is responded to by the offended institution, which engages its precedential or statutory rules-of-judgment. (4) In the *cultural environment,* political corruption *must* be responded to publicly, via a full-blown rhetoric of meaning attribution in which a populace participates as offended party. Because the actual and the political body of "the kind" (or any other corrupter) are separate-yet-united, the subversion of offices calls forth from advocates and "a people" deep-seated fears of chaos and disorder, which must be alleviated openly to return the culture to a state of routine and quiescence. (5) The primary requisite of any rhetoric of political corruption, in sum, is sociolinguistic transformation, whereby thoughts, behaviors, and words are "named" systematically—i.e. in accordance with the society's rules of conduct—so as to determine a proper arena-for-judgment, and, as we shall see, a proper authority and a proper ritual.

The Dialectical Process

Once a "name" has been given to an act, a dialectical process—unless a perpetrator finds some way to leave quietly—is automatically engaged, as one "person" (or set of attacking personae) confronts another person (or set of defending personae). Normally, such a confrontative process can begin on the factual level—in the basic symbolic universe—as when charges are made and denied. Thus, Ronald Ziegler, as Nixon's press secretary, immediately labeled the happenings of 17 June 1972 "a third-rate burglary," and Nixon's earliest reference to them contained the phrase "a bizarre incident." . . .

It becomes incumbent upon those who wish to pursue crimes of public servants to do so in "serious" ways; that is, they must *officialize* proceedings and cast themselves into roles appropriate to such actions, while those who seek to escape onerous judgments must attempt to abort such efforts at officialization by engaging in a process of "de-officialization." Officialization and deofficialization involve (1) the attribution of "role" or "authority" to indicting and indicted individuals and (2) the employment of proper "places" for waging the battle over such judgments. Simply put, *not everyone* can seriously accuse a public figure of corruption *anywhere*. In a recitation of factors which make for a "good denunciation," for example, Garfinkel includes the following:

> He [the denouncer] must act as a bona fide participant in the tribal relationships to which the witnesses [either the offended institution or the wronged society in our analysis] subscribe. What he says must not be regarded as true for him alone . . . The denouncer must make the dignity of the supra-personal values of the tribe salient and accessible to view,

and his denunciation must be delivered in their name . . . The denouncer
must arrange to be invested with the right to speak in the name of these
ultimate values. . . . The denouncer must get himself so defined by the
witnesses that they locate him as a supporter of these values. . . . Not
only must the denouncer fix his distance from the person being denounced, but the witnesses must be made to experience their distance
from him also.[8]

Attribution of Roles

On an institutional level, a denouncer can acquire the "right" or the
"authority"—i.e. a justifiable rhetorical posture—to level serious
charges of corruption by citing either historical examples (precedents)
or specific statutes (legal foundations) which detail previous actions or
present policies. When Cicero in 62 B.C. urged the Roman Senate to
move against Lucius Sergius Catilina, for example, he cited precedents
from the counsulships of Scipio Nasica (138 B.C.) and Servilius Ahala
(439 B.C.) as well as the Senate's own decree, *decretum ultimum* (21
October 62 B.C.), as ground for his proposed assumption of the
extraordinary powers necessary to the prosecution of Catiline. Armed
with the office, history, and statute, Cicero deemed himself a proper
instrument of retaliation.

If no specific institutional grounds for a charge exist, then, as
Garfinkel suggests above, the denouncer must embrace the roles of
social mores—in *materia* of ultimate terms. In the case of Aeschines
and Demosthenes, no Greek statute forbade the acceptance of a
"crown" even if it were possibly undeserved; Aeschines could not
attack Demosthenes' handling of fortification monies on historical or
legal grounds, and hence had to convince the popular assembly to act
as cultural surrogates . . . by virtue of nature, ethics, and sanctioned
state processes; such a trilogy of legitimizing agencies assuredly officialized the proceedings.

Such an effort at officialization not only insures proper solemnity,
society-wide attention to the pomp, and a worshipful resignation within
a citizenry to the power of justice, but it also, of course, protects the
prosecutors. . . .

Conversely, of course, corrupters likewise must realize that officialization can work to their detriment, and hence must seek to undermine
the rights, motives, and purposes of avenging authorities, and bolster
their own role performances. Thus, Sir Robert Walpole, who regularly
faced systematic opposition for nearly twenty years in the early
eighteenth century, when confronted with a motion addressing the

King to remove him from office, became more impassioned than usual in attempting to de-officialize the charges:

> I must therefore ask the gentlemen, From whence does this attack proceed? From the passions and prejudices of the parties combined against me, who may be divided into three classes, the Boys, the riper Patriots, and the Tories. . . . [After discussing the Tories he goes on to the Patriots:] Look round both Houses, and see to which side the balance of virtue and talents preponderates! Are all these on one side, and not on the other? Or are all these to be counterbalanced by an affected claim to the exclusive title of patriotism? . . . A venerable word, when duly practised. But I am sorry to say that of late it has been so much hackneyed about, that it is in danger of falling into disgrace. The very idea of true patriotism is lost, and the term has been prostituted to the very worst of purposes. A patriot, sir! Why, patriots spring up like mushrooms! I could raise fifty of them within the four-and-twenty hours. It is but refusing to gratify an unreasonable or an insolent demand, and up starts a patriot. I have never been afraid of making patriots; but I disdain and despise all their efforts. This pretended virtue proceeds from personal malice and disappointed ambition. There is not a man among them whose particular aim I am not able to ascertain, and from what motive they have entered into the lists of opposition.[9]

Notice carefully what Walpole has done in an effort to deescalate the rising flood of impeachment sentiment.

(1) He has attempted to appropriate one of the century's principal condensation symbols, "true patriotism," which functioned as the culture's shorthand term for Whiggery and parliamentary virtue; that is, he has tried to take on the mantle of cultural protector for himself.
(2) In addition he has sought also to defuse the words' power in this context by rehearsing the true motives of his detractors, putting them on an equal political ("merely" political) footing with his own supporters and hoping to reduce the conflict to an instance of everyday factious infighting.
(3) And he has striven for the high ground in the controversy by reporting his, the leading minister's, disdain for petty smears and issues of personality; such an analysis presumably, if accepted, would fortify his claim of proper role performance.

Although Richard Nixon's oratorical splendor never quite reached the heights of Walpole's, most will remember his similar attempts to denigrate the procedural purity of his opponents. Only thus, usually, can de-officialization be accomplished dialectically by the defender. . . .

Proper Places

We must note, also, that the dialectical confrontation inherent in institutional or cultural rhetorics of political corruption occurs in some *place*. As Garfinkel suggested, the "place" must function to put a gulf—a distance—between warriors and witnesses, and between everyday political operations and the extraordinary contest which purgative proceedings represent. In the words of Edelman,

> They [settings] are unabashedly built up to emphasize a departure from men's daily routine, a special or heroic quality in the proceedings they are to frame. Massiveness, ornateness and formality are the most common notes struck in the design of these scenes, and they are presented upon a scale which focuses constant attention upon the difference between everyday life and the special occasion when one appears in court, in Congress, or at an event of historic significance.[10]

The gulf or distance, one may surmise, is a rhetorically significant part of the dialectical process because (1) it enlarges the proceedings, making them more "serious"; (2) it formalizes—through the addition of parliamentary or judicial rules-of-conduct—the relationships between prosecutor and defendant; and (3) it adds resonant notes and meanings, via full pomp and spectacle, to the verbal arguments of the combatants. . . . The choice of setting reinforces the cultural significance of the events.

In summary, then, I would argue that while sociolinguistic processes generate the "meanings" rhetors can attach to acts of corruption, the dialectical processes forge the competing analyses by selecting from among all of the possible meanings those useful for attack and defense, by casting the competing voices into officialized (sanctioned) roles, and by enlarging (almost mythically) the context through the selection of a setting for the battle.

The Ceremonial Process

This last observation leads to the final sub-process inherent in rhetorics of political corruption—the full range of acts which comprise the actual institutional or public spectacle. In both the institutional and cultural symbolic environments, a society needs routines which allow it to visualize the complete and final purgation of the offender. "Office," Balandier posits, "necessarily entails ceremonial and ritual elements which, by 'a deliberate and solemn procedure,' effect the accession of its holder and invest him with a 'new social identity.' " . . .

Office not only has a technical aspect; it also has a moral and/or religious character that is obviously accentuated in the case of politico-ritual functions."[11] If a new social identity must be invested ceremoniously, it follows that divestiture likewise must be accomplished through a series of degrading acts, and hence Duncan argues that "the punishment of victims becomes a sacramental act of purification in which the community is purged."[12] At heart, then, rhetorics of political corruption are fully elaborated attempts to remove a political identity through a process which (1) has the blessings of the witnesses, in Garfinkel's idiom, and (2) celebrates anew for those selfsame witnesses the "rules" upon which the process is built. In a phrase, the sort of ritual I am exploring must have characteristics of Burke's "representative anecdote."[13]

By "ritual" or "ceremony" I refer simply to a preordained, sanctioned, regularized dance of action and reaction laid along a temporal continuum, and to the sequence of antiphonal roles played by protagonist and antagonist in a sociodrama. In the case of political corruption, Western societies possess such ceremonies in both the institutional and cultural environments. The Senate's handling of the Thomas Dodd affair is a good example of an institutional ceremony.[14] . . . Space does not permit a full outline of public criminalization and denouncement in any detail, so let me explore only the most generalized pattern, and then consider its important rhetorical aspects. As an example, Nixon's fall from societal grace suffices.

The controversy began, of course, the weekend of 17 June 1972 with news of the break-in of the Democratic National Committee's offices. The first strategy of the Nixon administration was obvious, as we have noted—the attempt to keep discussion on the factual level through the announcements of Ziegler and Nixon himself. Straight denial on that level held back the dam through the campaign, even though Judge Sirica was punching his first small holes in it through October. (All charges of executive duplicity were filtered by the audiences through their sensitivities to the 1972 presidential campaign; institutional or social meaningfulness could hardly be expected in those circumstances.)

The wheels of judicial bureaucracy, however, continued to turn out evidence, half-truths, testimony, and transcripts of petty trials—first Bernard Barker's; then, in January of 1973, those of Virgilio Gonzalez, Eugenio Martinez, and Frank Sturgis; and, finally, others in the resumption of the Daniel Ellsberg-Anthony Russo trial over the Pentagon Papers. Throughout the period of these low-level trials and with the January announcement that Sam Ervin would head a Senate investigating committee, Watergate burbled beneath the surface. Gordon Liddy was found guilty in late January; the Democratic National Committee in February extended its civil suit to cover Jeb Magruder and Herbert Porter of the Committee to Re-Elect the President; Nixon tried executive privilege on for size in March while a federal grand jury continued its search for new evidence; and in April, Magruder, Richard Kleindienst, and John Dean showed signs of breaking. Nixon had to take the counter offensive, which he did on 30 April 1973, announcing the resignations of Kleindienst, Haldeman, and Ehrlichman, and promising that "justice will be pursued, fairly, fully and impartially, no matter who is involved"—and all the while insinuating political motives to his opposition. But Nixon could not stop high-level officialization, and the Ervin Committee was convened less than two months later. Dean planted the charges which could blow open the White House, and Alexander Butterfield, in revealing the taping capacity in the Oval Office, showed the Committee where the match was. Once officialized, now both in the courts and in Congress, the proceedings ground even more relentlessly forward. Nixon's news conferences were filled with impolitic questions, and even his Oval Office messages were instantly analyzed for references (and lacks thereof) to Watergate. As tape after tape unreeled into public view, and as the smoking pistol was found in a tape released on 5 August 1974, Nixon was forced to resign, still protesting innocence.

This bare outline of the ritual—(1) initial factual affirmation and denial, (2) low-level officialization in the courts, (3) high-level officialization in the courts and Congress, (4) high-level confrontation, in full public view, through the House Judiciary Committee hearings, and (5) final resolution by resignation or trial—reveals several points of rhetorical interest:

1. There is obviously a step-by-step extended sociolinguistic process whereby naked "facts" and "actions" become clothed in the heinousness of social-political patricide. On this point I differ with Kenneth Burke, who seemingly argues that the invocation of "myths" automatically elevates a controversy to the level of cultural drama. Rather, I think that a third-rate burglary remains just that until a rhetor invests it with institutional and cultural meanings, and that such a process of perceptual reorientation—the attributions of meaningfulness—takes time. . . . Walpole's detractors worked four years to frame the motion of impeachment, periodically gave up, and could not assemble enough pressure to bring about resignation for another two years; the Hastings Affair ran twelve years. To convert everyday crimes sociolinguistically into constitutional outrages, to change a

leader's image from savior to subverter, takes rhetors skilled with symbols and imbued with patience.

2. It should be obvious, as a corollary, that a variety of rhetorical postures and weapons is necessary for anyone wishing to bring down cultural giants on questions of corruption. The vision of Edmund Burke hearing the early rumors of Hastings' activities in India, then gathering enough evidence to convince an ingroup that prosecution was in order, next assembling a prosecuting team able by virtue of its prestige to stir the House of Commons into action and an indictment, and finally orchestrating trial managers, witnesses, and cross-examiners in an extended seven-year trial in the House of Lords—this vision alone is enough to illumine the point. . . . Faint hearts and lackluster talents cannot win the day, for by now, with a history of impeachments and censures behind us, we all expect a well-played ritual. If the ritual is defective, a culture becomes suspicious, aroused instead to quit the fight, to examine the motives of the accusers, or to laugh at the portrayal of someone getting caught with hands in the till. Harkening back to one of the questions which opened this essay, we may even hypothesize that suspicion, apathy, and knowing chuckles—instead of the anticipated responses in the face of tragedy—result from those ceremonies in which the necessary rhetorical postures are not convincingly assumed. Just as the novice teacher is mocked by students until authority and expertise are demonstrated, so too will a culture refuse to take purgative proceedings seriously until rhetorical roles are played with point.

3. As the foregoing point suggests, the total ritual can be shortcircuited at several points:

a. A ritual can die before it starts if accusers cannot assemble convincing data on the factual level, as frequently happened in the British civil service system.[15] Public attention may not be engaged.

b. Low-level trials, i.e. institutional investigations, similar to those of the "plumbers" in Watergate, may suffice; they did not in that case, but Eschenburg details cases in Konrad Adenauer's West German Republic in which they did.[16]

c. Public satisfaction, however, is probably increased if higher-level personnel are sacrificed in large-scale officialization proceedings, for they tend to involve the culture as a whole more directly. Certainly it seems reasonable to view Nixon's sacking of Haldeman, Ehrlichman, and Kleindienst as an attempt to stop the ritual at this stage; he obviously tried to appease the public's growing anger while simultaneously bolstering his own role performance with his "integrity of the White House" speech of 30 April 1973. The strategy is generally founded on the "evil minister" tradition in Western governmental structures; that tradition dictates that the "king" (or president) can do no wrong personally, but only can receive "bad advice" from his chief administrators.[17] Western cultures, committed to "democratic" ideals, assuredly want blood when faced with public corruption, but they prefer not to have it flow from the veins of foremost leaders, who normally are thought to be as good as the offices they occupy. Hence, sacrificing high-level sources, rather than the leader, fulfills both urges, as Kenneth Burke's analysis of scapegoating (a process of selecting an appropriate vessel into which the sins of society are poured and then destroyed) portrays.[18] . . .

d. On rarer occasions, however, even high-level officialization is not enough; then, a full-blown degradation ceremony must begin, as happened . . . in the Queen Caroline affair of nineteenth-century Britain. As wife of George IV, Caroline's case is especially instructive, because, while she was undoubtedly guilty of private sins among her European entourage, when a move was made in the House of Lords in 1820 to dissolve the marriage and deprive her of a title, the case had to become one involving a public political crime. The trial was the most spectacular confrontation London had seen since the Hastings embroglio, with the populace, the press, Commoners, and Lords all taking sides. The full pomp of a Lords' trial; the assemblage of secret agents, double agents, lovers with "political" connections, deniers, accusers, and seers; and the excitement of a close vote stirred even Sir Thomas Erskine to his oratorical zenith of the century. The resulting social catharsis in this sociodrama was enormous.

e. Some sort of resolution, of course, must follow in the final act. The possible outcomes can include: (1) *Innocence*—victory by the accused party, as in the case of Andrew Johnson, which turns tragedy into melodrama. (2) *Reversal*—not only victory but subsequent repression as well, as happened when Cicero attempted to bring down Marcus Antonius and when Indira Gandhi jailed her detractors. (3) *Guilt with punishment*—e.g. . . . Thomas Dodd's formal censure and removal from senatorial powers. The society is completely purged of evil in this way. (4) *Guilt without punishment*—the outcome of the Queen Caroline affair, in which the Lords by a slim margin voted the divorce, which was never formalized in a bill in Commons because of the closeness of that vote. Social mores were thus reinforced, yet a residue of sympathy for the corrupter remained. (5) *Resignation*—normally for reasons other than the charges in the indictment, as happened in the cases of Nixon (who resigned for "political" reasons) and Spiro Agnew (who pleaded *nolo contendere* to "save" the vice presidency). Again, society's foundational tenets are reaffirmed, but most likely sympathy for the office holder will not be engendered; apathy and cynicism—"politics as usual"—is the more likely public reaction. (6) *Deflection*— the vacating of an office on a completely different issue, as with Robert Walpole, who resigned when he lost a vote on an election petition in 1742.[19] Such a solution is, in effect, a drama without a last act. Neither the society nor the corrupter is vindicated in this outcome; a pragmatic decision such as deflection breeds only confusion.

4. This last point suggests, indeed, that the outcome of rhetorics of public corruption ought to provide some sort of positive collective gain, whereby a culture fetches good out of evil.[20] Except perhaps in instances of deflection, the very presence, engagement, and playing of the full ritual allays social fears by demonstrating that the abstractions we call the "machinery of justice" can ingest and eliminate the evil one, can protect the citizenry. Thus it is, I think, that a country such as this one literally *celebrates* corruption and its public purgation. . . . Purgation has a salutary effect upon a country in its reaffirmation not only of principles but of stately power and office, of the presence of the armament needed to preserve the social order and insure social quiescence. Richard Nixon, in addition to his notable foreign accomplishments, has succeeded in fostering domestic tranquility; his seventh crisis,[21] paradoxically, has had profoundly beneficial effects in his country.

Perhaps, indeed, any society needs to exercise public degradation ceremonies periodically, especially in times of peace. We can rediscover ourselves during wartime with the identification of heroes and villains—positive and negative personifications of social mores. In peacetime, that sort of declaration is more difficult to make. Positively, we can turn to some few rituals-of-celebration, as in inauguration ceremonies, State of the Union addresses, dedications of dams, Fourth of July orations, and the like. Affirmation-by-negation, however, occurs less often. An occasional peacetime spy, some of the character assassination which fills electoral campaigns, trials of mass murderers—these we have. None of them, however, engages a society in quite the same way that a well-played purgation process does; political corruption becomes enshrouded by semantic fields (sociolinguistic processes), role confrontations (dialectical processes), and extended rituals (ceremonial processes) which operate on a much grander scale than the other negative modes of celebration. Thus, a Richard Nixon will take his place alongside Demosthenes, Caroline, the Marquis of Strafford, Walpole, Hastings, Adams, Dodd, Powell, Agnew, and scores of lesser and greater personages—people whose private sins occasioned the resanctification of public virtue and social essences.

Epilogue

This essay has arrived at a point where to go farther requires an assemblage of detailed case studies. I have asserted the importance of examining the social-rhetorical contexts of political corruption; identified the three chief components of rhetorics of political corruption in both their institutional and more generally cultural spheres; outlined a metacritical approach—rooted in concepts found in symbolic interactionism (symbolic environments), ethnography (the idea of rules), ethnomethodology (the use of paradigmatic cases), dramaturgy (the constituents of public rituals), and the like; and baldly asserted some explanatory generalizations regarding the need for destroying evil periodically so as to reinforce cultural identity.

I have, however, really only gotten to the brink of answers to the questions which justified this essay—why a people reacts positively to somme examples and negatively to others, why some corrupters manage to acquire sympathy while others are completely disgraced, why the drama described is sometimes melodrama, sometimes farce, and only occasionally a classic tragedy. If, via case studies, we can answer such questions, then the rhetorical critic will be joining brethren in anthropology, sociology, political science, political ethics, and biography, all searching for generalizations which explain characteristics of macro- and micro-society and its claims upon its members. . . .

Notes

1. U.S. Congress, Senate, Select Committee on Standards and Conduct, *Investigations of Senator Thomas J. Dodd of Connecticut,* 90th Cong., 1st Sess., Report 193, pp. 26–27.
2. Carl J. Friedrich, *The Pathology of Politics: Violence, Betrayal, Corruption, Secrecy, and Propaganda* (New York: Harper & Row, 1972), passim.
3. Such research is offered by Friedrich, as well as Ronald Wraith and Edgar Simpkins, *Corruption in Developing Countries* (New York: Norton, 1963), and especially Arnold J. Heidenheimer, ed., *Political Corruption: Readings in Comparative Analysis* (New York: Holt, Rinehart and Winston, 1970).
4. The protection offered by hereditary prerogatives and Machiavelli's notion of *raison d'etat* is discussed in Friedrich, esp. pp. 1–15.

5. The phrase "symbolic environments" I borrow from students of Lasswell, esp. Morris Janowitz, "Content Analysis and the Study of the 'Symbolic Environment,' " in *Politics, Personality, and Social Science in the Twentieth Century: Essays in Honor of Harold D. Lasswell,* ed. Arnold A. Rogow (Chicago: University of Chicago Press, 1969), pp. 155–70; and from Hugh Dalziel Duncan, *Symbols in Society* (New York: Oxford University Press, 1968), p. 16.
6. On the maxim, see Ernst H. Kantorowicz, *The King's Two Bodies: A Study in Mediaeval Political Theology* (Princeton: Princeton University Press, 1957).
7. Chauncey A. Goodrich, *Select British Eloquence* (New York: Bobbs-Merrill, 1963), p. 363.
8. Harold Garfinkel, "Conditions of Successful Degradation Ceremonies," *American Journal of Sociology,* 61 (1955–56), 423.
9. Goodrich, pp. 36–37.
10. Edelman, p. 96.
11. Georges Balandier, *Political Anthropology,* trans A.M. Sheridan Smith (New York: Pantheon Books, 1970), p. 88.
12. Duncan, p. 34.
13. Burke introduces the notion of the "representative anecdote" in *Grammar,* pp. 59–61, to describe a process whereby a people come to see a connection between their cultural myths and specific pieces of social behavior, especially in order to understand social motives and their consequences.
14. See Wenger's dissertation [Paul E. Wenger, "A Study of Legislative Discourse in the Censure Debate Concerning Senator Thomas J. Dodd," Diss., University of Iowa 1972].
15. See Wraith and Simpkins, Part II.
16. Adenauer's government was scandalized when members of his administration accepted free cars from Mercedes Benz dealers; some opponents tried to bring him down on the issue, but the public was satisfied when a few officials resigned. See Theodor Eschenburg, "The Decline of the Bureaucratic Ethos in the Federal Republic," in Heidenheimer, pp. 259–68.
17. The idea that all parliamentary officers were accountable servants of the Crown had its origins in the dim reaches of medieval political theory; that those officials could give "bad advice"—and hence be removed by the kind—was an equally venerable concept.
18. For Burke's original formulation of scapegoating, see *Grammar,* pp. 336, 406–08.
19. He maintained that his enemies could not attribute his resignation to the earlier censure and impeachment attempts.
20. The notion of "fetching good out of evil" is developed nicely in Ernest G. Bormann, "Fetching Good Out of Evil: A Rhetorical Use of Calamity," *Quarterly Journal of Speech,* 63 (1977), 130–39.
21. For his own account of the earlier six, see Richard M. Nixon, *Six Crises* (Garden City, N.Y.: Doubleday, 1962).

13

Paradoxes of Political Corruption: A French View

Jeanne Becquart-Leclercq

Feelings of dislike, even of disgust, for politics are quite frequent and translate into apathy, or cynicism, or a rejection of politics. These sentiments are ambivalent, because corruption seems inherent to the exercise of power. The link can be fatal: could one do better in the place of those who govern? Is it possible to play politics without dirtying one's hands? Whence the paradox of a kind of latent acceptance of corruption, a legitimation that co-exists with profound feelings of disapproval.

Thus it is that the citizen, by a kind of tacit symbolic complicity, sometimes keeps in office politicians suspected of, even indicted for, corruption. An American mayor was able to get himself reelected while imprisoned in Boston. In the United States, numerous officials are permitted to resume their duties after having been indicted for criminal corruption. In France corruption is less visible and therefore such cases are seen less, but they do occur. The French system of financing political parties, campaigns, and partisan newspapers with funds collected behind the scenes and laundered through various channels do become periodically and ephemerally visible in the form of large and small scandals. But the indignation is usually mild, and the system continues as before with the political class maintaining a conspiracy of silence, a conspiracy that may well be part of a "concensus à la francaise," in which informal "cohabitation" must co-exist with acute partisan cleavages.

In sum, corruption has yielded little to endeavors to suppress it; it is endemic to all regimes and at all political-administrative levels, despite

Source: Jeanne Becquart-Leclercq, "Paradoxes de la corruption politique," *Pouvoirs,* 31 (1984), pp. 19–36. By permission of the author and publisher, Presses Universitaires de France. The translation by Victor T. Le Vine was revised and updated by the author in October 1986.

its well-known negative effects: fiscal fraud and embezzlement, degradation of public services, resources ill-used or misappropriated, lax job performance, degeneration of civic sense, nepotism, favoritism, the political game falsified by hidden resources or by electoral fraud, and the administrative apparatus encumbered by concealed privileges.

These paradoxes are nonetheless the principal threads by which one can grasp the profound sociological reality of corruption, as an integral part of the socio-political system. It is thus from a well-grounded theoretical perspective that we approach the phenomenon of political corruption—the illegal appropriation of public goods—so as to analyze its latent structures from three points of view: (1) Why corruption? This question is posed in a functionalist perspective and leads us to a critical analysis of certain functions of corruption; (2) How corruption? This question leads us to a cross-cultural comparison of the relational networks which underlie the mechanism of corruption; and (3) For whom and for whose profit does corruption take place? A structural approach finally integrates the question of norms and of cultural models of the groups in power, the effects of anomie and of normative disassociation linked to social structure, as well as some attempts to develop a theory of political corruption seen in its relation to civic society.[1]

Why Political Corruption? The Functionalist Argument

This is not the place to analyze the individual motivation of the actors in corruption . . . but to examine a number of systemic effects of corruption, seen in terms of manifest and latent functions.[2] Corruption functions like grease in the gears; it has an important redistributive effect, it is a functional substitute for direct participation in power, it constitutes the cement between elites and parties, and it affects the effectiveness with which power is exercised.

Previous research has shown how implicit relational networks and clientelistic linkages parallel official relationships, more so when the bureaucratic and administrative apparatuses are highly rigid.[3] The unofficial relational system loosens the clogged points in the system, serving as the means for the reappropriation of power for those who have lost it or who want still more of it. The relational network results in cumulating power resources, which assures advantages precisely for those who already dispose of bases of support (such as revenue or education), but it rarely acts to compensate the most disadvantaged. The network supports inequalities of power by attaching itself to power, but remains within the limits of cultural legitimacy and of legality. The relational networks articulate civil society to the political administrative world and vertically link various levels of power. Clientelism and machine politics are particular forms of these networks, and they function as systems of immediate or differentiated exchange. So it is for political corruption. Invariably in this case, the networks are discreet or secret, and overstep the limits of cultural legitimacy, if not of legality.

Political corruption is thus a specific mode—a secret aspect—of the functioning of the relational network. Secrecy permits the arbitrary misappropriation of the monopoly of legitimate violence attached to the power of the state, to the profit of interests whose satisfaction would be blocked without this intervention. It is in this sense that corruption is "normal," thus a crime according to Durkheim, assuring the free "play" necessary for the gears of society. Thus in a decentralized and fragmented system such as the United States, corruption is indispensable for government and for the application of the decisions of public policy; if Chicago functions, if the programs of the New Deal have been applied locally, it is partly thanks to the corruption of politicians and of local bureaucrats (Bollens and Schmandt, 1979, p. 23). What about a centralized system such as France, usually considered as one in which access to power is blocked? Bribes, special privileges, favors, facilities, tolerances, discreet small and large channels—all constitute the inevitable shadowy zones around the strong points of power, zones that assure a certain flexibility in decision-making and the possibility of getting things done. Corruption guarantees certain zones of freedom and of free movement in the face of the totalitarian tendencies inherent in states and political parties.

We will return to a criticism of the functionalist approach, but one can already note that the functional justification of corruption confuses the "necessities of the system" with the interests of some groups. In effect, it places on the same level abstract notions of the system and concrete interests in favor of this or that decision. It overlooks sociopolitical stratification and the differences in the exercise of power between those actors who can "play" the system and those who cannot.

Political corruption has another important function, to redistribute public resources by parallel means accessible to groups that would otherwise be excluded. The political machines of big cities are an example better known in the United States than in France.[4] In France, in the absence of official mechanisms to finance them, unofficial exactions levied on businesses serve to finance political parties. Numerous national and international transactions involve some corruption with the discreet complicity of the fiscal authorities, and systems of more or less disguised and unofficial percentages and supplements augment the salaries of French civil servants. This function of parallel redistribution becomes more important because the sums in question appear to be considerably augmented by thousands of little evasions at all levels. . . .

It is thus difficult to deny the effects of parallel redistribution, but that does not prevent us from asking about the compatibility of this kind of redistribution with democratic values. To what measure do these parallel lines of redistribution escape popular control? Do they confer advantages on those who already benefit from privileged access to the system, or on those who are excluded?

This is precisely one of the functions of political corruption put forward by certain authors: it operates as a "functional substitute" for direct participation in power, enabling those who have been excluded from power to obtain access to resources which they would like to have, but which are forbidden to them. On the other hand, if the rich can attain power through liberal or social-democratic political parties, or through institutionalized pressure groups, the scope of corruption could thus be diminished (Scott, 1972, p. 34). In this view, one can pose the hypothesis that the "cartels of elites" of "consociational" democracies, through their organisms of negotiation at all levels, can be an instrument for the reduction of corruption. At the very least, corruption will be little utilized as a political weapon, because majorities and oppositions tend to protect themselves by developing a concensus about certain political practices.[5]

It is in this sense that one of the functions of corruption is to reinforce the solidarity between political and economic elites in society as well as within the political parties: corruption has been considered as the cement of partisan relationships. For example, when a mayor succeeds in making his position a fiefdom by privileged hiring of his political friends, by using municipal personnel for electoral purposes (Frament-Meurice, 1983), by friendly decisions and certain exactions on businesses, and by purchases through fictional intermediaries (Donneur and Padioleau, 1982), the networks of solidarity become extremely close, because no one can betray anyone since everyone can blackmail someone. At the same time, elected officials or public employees who are obliged (by various means) to return a portion of their salaries to their political parties[6] reinforce solidarity within the party, its militants, adherents, and sympathizers.

In brief, the functional justification for corruption is that it makes the system more effective through the operation of certain unofficial or secret processes that allow the system a margin of flexibility and ease of maneuver, an ability to operate more rapidly, a possibility to be innovative, a certain measure of political solidarity, and a parallel redistribution of the resources pertaining to political power. Such a functional argument rests on a larger and abstract vision of social reality and must be supplemented with another paradigm, that of a relational analysis that sheds light on the structures of political corruption.

How Corruption? The Relational Approach

The functional explanation of corruption as a response to the needs of the system is insufficient because it ignores the interaction of concrete actors, their relational networks, their hierarchies, as well as an understanding of their specific interests, be they divergent or compatible. One must thus understand the relational structure on which corruption rests. This structure is essentially asymmetric because of the inequality of the positions of the actors, even if this implies an exchange . . ., and even if everyone apparently can find satisfaction in it. This asymmetry permits power to be monetized, to be abused, and to be the source of benefits, eventually by implicit or disguised extortion. In the process of political corruption, because of the increasing weight of government (the "state"), he who disposes of governmental resources (funds, decisions, authorizations, jobs, etc.) is in a strong position of power, even if it is the other person who is apparently the "active corruptor."

Moreover, the functionalist approach only encompasses the winners in the game of corruption, the corruptors and those who are corrupt, but forgets an essential actor in any crime: the victim. In fact, the victim is so obscured that he is not immediately apparent to the observer, who must then seek out this forgotten or lost victim.

Let us pick up the functionalist argument again: by its flexibility, corruption unblocks the system. But if one sees it from the relational point of view, it can well be asked if the fact of getting something better and quicker by illicit means does not avoid the need to reform these rigidities, and if these rigidities are not preserved precisely because they are a source of discreet and selective advantage. Moreover, circumventing blockages by corrupt practices tends to benefit those who already dispose of relational resources, which permits them to operate in the subsystem of corruption and to obtain a decision, or a contract, or a job, to their profit. The networks of corruption thus have their beneficiaries (as well as those who are excluded from their benefits), and the solidarity these networks reinforce is always restricted to selective circles. Thus, if a town becomes a fiefdom, only one part of the population has access to the parallel networks of redistribution, that is, that part which belongs to the dominant clientele. Only the replacement of those in power can permit a reshuffling of the cards. Corruption does not compensate for inequalities, but recreates them in other forms. Moreover, its secret character prevents those who are excluded from standing up for themselves, because they are not aware that they are victims—hence the absence of social reaction to corruption. Thus, above all, it is by blinding its victims that secrecy permits the relational structures of corruption to reproduce and perpetuate themselves.

Here one discovers another paradox: the protagonist beneficiary of the corrupt relationship can at the same time be its victim. This paradox appears in interviews with builders or businessmen almost obliged to return part of their contract funds to public officials, be it in the form of an electoral contribution, or a vulgar bribe, or through some more sophisticated process such as with falsified invoices and bills or by spurious costs for studies, gifts, and various services. To be sure, these people get the business they want, but at the same time, they have the feeling that they have been swindled because they know full well where the money comes from: their taxes. Thus corruption presents itself as a kind of parallel tax that contributes to an increase in the state's cash flow, all at the expense of the community, of those who are receiving welfare benefits, of the consumers of public services, and of those who inhabit government housing, etc. The active agent of corruption (here the businessman) is equally the victim of and the contributor to corruption. . . .

One may add that the "victim of corruption" is more visible—is seen more clearly—in the United States than he or she is in France. Taxpayers and consumers organize themselves into lobbies and associations in the United States; by opposing the misuse of public funds, they are an integral part of the relational structure of corruption. Their activity, nonetheless, is not enough to reform the political scene or to avoid the paradoxical reelection of compromised leaders. This paradox is clarified by a structural approach to the social context of corruption in its symbolic and practical aspects.

Contextual Differences in Corruption Mechanisms

A contextual comparison sheds light on other differences in the structure of corruption and the mechanisms at work in France and in the United States. Differences pertain to 1) the role of associations, 2) the opacity of party finance, and 3) the attitude of taxpayers.

Facade and conduit associations

A general practice in France is to subsidize voluntary associations with public funds from all levels of government. Each of the 36,000 municipalities has a special budget to which associations apply for grants-in-aid. This is a legitimate appropriation of public funds which is accepted in the French political culture as part of an inevitable operational mode, while in the United States, it might seem shocking for a special interest group to request a grant from the city. Note that associations obtain private financing more easily in the United States because there are more tax deductions for such purposes, while in France, so far, one can normally deduct only 1 percent of one's income for payments to registered non-profit organization. The consequences are twofold: (1) Associations tend to depend more on governmental money from taxes and less on their own constituency. This reinforces the oligarchic tendencies of such organizations to function with a fragile basis and a hypertrophied narrow circle of leaders at the top. (2) Their funding is often decided by political leaders. Therefore, associations tend to become satellites of partisan networks and branches of political machines. As an indication, in 1985 the budget used by the largest cities in northern France to subsidize associations varied between $200 and $350 per household.

Because they are non-profit organizations, voluntary associations have a facade of respectability and obtain official recognition by registering at the Perfecture under the famous "Law of 1901." This allows them to manage banking accounts, to sue in the courts, to acquire goods, and to hire people and to operate like a corporation, except for the sharing of profit. In so doing, and even if they operate on public funding, they escape the strict rules of public administration and public accounting. Many governmental organizations such as cities or national agencies create and subsidize associations for that very purpose: to have more leeway in spending power. Most of the time, the associations work for legitimate purposes, but sometimes, this opens doors to the misuse of public funds. Subsidization works in a circular pattern with three usual steps: a) a public official grants some subsidies to an association whose board is small and filled with friends; b) the money is used for paying fake bills; and c) the billing person or organization receives the money from the association but returns it in cash to the public official, his party, a campaign fund, etc. (deducting a percentage for expenses).

Periodically, at election time or when a new majority gains power, many examples of such bogus bills are denounced by the press. However, very few people are convicted (for criminal violations).

The scandal connected with the *"Carrefour du Developpement"* association illustrates the role of voluntary non-profit associations in a corruption network. This scandal is a confused maze which came to light during the political change of March 1986, that brought in a right-wing government after five years of socialist power, and opened the doors for the investigation of shadowy transactions at the top level of the Ministry of Cooperation (African affairs and relations with previous colonies). The new Minister of Cooperation discovered that the cabinet of his Socialist predecessor, Christian Nucci, had misused large amounts of public funds. The *chef du cabinet* (principal political advisor), Yves Chalier, was indicted, but before he was arrested he left France for South America, probably with enough money to continue to maintain his mistresses and secretaries in Paris. Two fake associations, the *"Carrefour du Developpement"* (whose president was Chalier) and *"La Promotion Francaise,"* were used to channel more than 50 million francs (official figures without counting the underground money) with bogus bills for an incredibly costly Franco-African summit. Both these associations had some high officials on their boards of directors. The funds were used to buy a special armored luxury car for President Francois Mitterand, who hurried to pay for it a second time as soon as he discovered the possible scandal. Association funds were also used to buy a castle for the personal use of friends of Chalier.

In October 1986, a dozen persons were indicted and a Special Assistant (to President Mitterand) for African Affairs, Guy Penne, was dismissed and replaced by Mitterand's son. The scandal developed further with the revelation of overestimated contracts for $11 million guaranteed by the French government, for an airport on the Caribbean island of Antigua; here, the ex-Minister of Foreign Affairs, R. Dumas, was implicated. (See *Le Monde,* 19 October 1986). The ex-Minister of Cooperation, Nucci himself, appears compromised because many of the phony bills paid by the bogus associations were denounced as extortion by local entrepreneurs, who were asked for cash kickbacks (for example, certain businessmen in Beaurepaire, where Nucci is the powerful mayor). An indicted businessman, Mr. Leroy, broke the conspiracy of silence and accused C. Nucci of having received 500,000 francs in cash to finance his electoral campaigns. Nucci has protested his innocence and invoked parliamentary immunity, since he is at the same time a deputy to the National Assembly and a mayor in the Department of Isere. Whatever else can be said of the Nucci affair, it is clear that growing electoral expenses such as advertising, posters, pamphlets, partisan newspapers and magazines, printing of voting bulletins, etc. make the subsidized associations tempting sources of easily obtained but illicit funds.

The absence of public scrutiny of party finance

The absence of public scrutiny of party finance is another feature of politics which influences corruption mechanisms in France. Political parties are not obliged to disclose either their sources of revenue or their expenses. Everything is veiled with a hypocritical complicity shared even by opposing parties. This situation is periodically denounced and bills are proposed in parliament to oblige more openness, but so far none have been passed.

From the facts in numerous small scandals, one can infer that political parties receive a large part of their funding from private corporations, from kickbacks on salaries of their fulltime elected members, and principally, from a huge network of associations, "research organizations," agencies and other intermediaries that overbill their services and are paid for with public funds. These networks are particularly widespread in local politics and this is sometimes given as an explanation for the increasing importance of local politics and of local elections; they have come to represent important partisan stakes in terms of political resources of all kinds. This fact might also be related to the phenomenon of concomitantly holding several offices at various levels of government, "accumulating mandates," which is still a specific feature of French politics despite its recent limitation with a mild law in 1985. National leaders often try to get a local office by the process of "parachuting" themselves into any constituency, imposing themselves through their parties despite the indignation of politicians with long local roots.

Thus, having a local base procures substantial political resources for national leaders, resources such as leverage on local businessmen eager to work for the city. The case of the "Carrefour du Developpement" shows how a local printer of Baurepaire (a small city whose mayor was the indicted minister, Christian Nucci) probably became an unwitting connection in a circuit emerging at the top levels of the state. Having issued falsified invoices to influential but doubtful customers and put in jail, the printer became a scapegoat for prosecution in the widespread scandal of the "Carrefour du Developpement."

Generally, television programs avoid the topic of corruption. An exception in recent years was a program called "Right to Reply" (Droit de Reponse), in which the topic of corruption and party finance was discussed for one-and-a-half hours late at night in October 1986. Viewers saw a selfmade businessman who revealed how he succeeded in attracting financing for his company to enable it to survive in a decaying area. The process, however, involved returning significant amounts to the Socialist newspaper *"l'Unité"* for inflated advertisement bills (see *"Le Monde"*: "le financement de l'hebdomadaire du Parti Socialiste," Feb. 20, 1986).

The silent taxpayer

In France, the passive, powerless, extorted victim, the silent taxpayer is an essential part of the French system of corruption. For example, municipalities use a significant part of their finances to subsidize local associations without scrutiny or control by taxpayers. Elections take place only every six years: citizen participation is almost nonexistent or extremely low; local referenda are not legal, and recalls of local officials as well as public hearings are unknown. This means that the citizen gives a kind of *carte blanche* to politicians and loses control after electoral periods. Taxpayers' associations are either nonexistent or weak; they have no right of scrutiny, and they share the history of illegality of the other types of associations as well. Most of the time, local officials act to adjust taxes according to their needs, not the other way around. On the whole, and paradoxically, they enjoy much discretionary spending power despite traditional centralization and state tutelage. A taxpayer revolt such as seen in California with "Proposition 13" and in several other places in the United States seems impossible in France for cultural and institutional reasons such as the ones we have indicated here. In comparison with the "civic culture" of the North American middle-class citizens, those who should be more active seem alienated from the political process, more skeptical or cynical. According to polls, most French people think that their politicians are liars. Feelings of powerlessness lead to a broad acceptance of operational modes seen as illegitimate but inevitable. Such a political culture does not help and even counteracts the struggle against corruption. Even when it becomes visible, corruption causes little indignation or (few calls for its) suppression.

Nevertheless, one can discern some signs of change with the increase in stories of corruption in the press, and a few cases of timorous taxpayers' revolts. For example, the mayor of the city of Draguignan (in south France), made himself famous for his nepotism, waste, squandering of funds, speculation, muddle, intrigue, trickery, and underhanded dealings. He publicly compared himself to Richard Nixon, the victim to catch! His wife obtained a highly paid job in an association named "La Régie Provençale de Publicité," which was subsidized with municipal funds. There were incredible bills for drinks, five-star hotels, and expensive restaurants for the mayor. Another subsidized local association, "Draguignan Promotion," paid many of the mayor's personal bills. As a consequence, city coffers were plagued with a huge deficit that had to be paid by taxpayers. This situation created an unseen drama, a kind of "civil war" in Draguignan, with a "jacquerie risé" and a confused demonstration of taxpayers and local people on the city square (they were refused an indoor hall for the meeting). Hundreds of citizens swore to refuse to pay any tax increase. Finally, the city tax collector dispersed them by pointing out the illegality of such a refusal. (See *Le Monde,* October 12, 1986.) The story is unfinished, but it is a significant, though timid indicator of an emerging change in citizens' consciousness, one not yet to be compared with the bold mind of American taxpayers, their strong lobbies, and articulate advocates.

In any case, this change in consciousness, although very real, is nonetheless, not enough to reform the political scene or to avoid the paradoxical reelection of compromised leaders. This paradox is clarified by a structural approach to the social context of corruption in its symbolic and practical aspects.

Anomie and Normative Contradiction: Toward a Theory of Double Normative Structure

The structural examination of a phenomenon consists in seeing it as an ensemble of more or less contradictory or complementary social relations, in seeing the interests and the strategies of the actors involved. In this view, political corruption is analyzed in relation to a composite social structure; it is relative to the norms of the diverse groups that compose it. According to Huntington (1968, p. 59), an act is considered corrupt if it deviates from the norms held by most of the population. It may also be that the "population" is heterogeneous and that opinions diverge precisely on the nature and degree of corruption: the norms of the elites and of the members of the political administrative class can differ from those of the citizens at the roots, given their respective positions in the sociopolitical structure.

The notion of structural position leads Heidenheimer (1978, pp. 26–28) to propose a typology of corruption. If corruption is at the same time defined in a particular way by both the political elites and by the public, this is "black" corruption and involves severe and general disapproval. At the other extreme of the continuum is found "white" corruption, which provokes a generally shared indulgence for the breaking of certain rules, such as "fixing tickets." In the middle, "gray" corruption evokes contradictory attitudes among elites and the population; disapproval or tolerance. "Gray" corruption is most destructive of democratic organization.

This typology describes several aspects of the social reaction to corruption and confronts us with the problem of the ambivalence intrinsic to this reaction, which is essentially contradictory in its movement. Why is corruption at the same time disapproved of and tolerated? Why can corruption, which is at first glance a sign of anomie (everything is allowed) and of exceptional challenge to norms, exercise at the same time a constraining and a normative effect? Enmeshed, the actor is caught in the system and cannot escape it without excessive cost. Furthermore, the contagion of corruption is spiral in effect and thus enmeshment becomes generalized. For example, the businessman who does not "grease" or distribute bribes is quickly condemned to operate without profit because his competitors are less rigorous and moral than he. The same is true of a political party that would content itself with the ordinary dues it gets from its members and refuses unofficial sources of finance. Thus as a "social fact,"[7] corruption imposes itself on the actors involved, and becomes institutionalized by perverting the system itself. Here, then, is the paradox of a social fact that becomes at once illegal and constraining by its double effect of enmeshment and of spiralling inclusion. These paradoxes can be clarified by the theory of the dual normative structure.

The cultural system of all social groups has a dual normative structure involving two kinds of interactions, operating on more or less dissociated levels: the symbolic (order) and the strategic (order).

1. *The symbolic dimension:* This corresponds to the idealized vision a society has of itself. This acts as a "myth" for the group embodied in its official legal rules (Reisman, 1979). By analogy with psychoanalytic concepts of the "superego" and the "idealized ego," this dimension is the "supergroup," and crystallizes the group's values and the ideologies, and the illusions it has about itself. Besides ideologies, this dimension includes the purpose of the laws insofar as they are defined by the legislator, independent of their practical application.

2. *The operational (or strategic) dimension:* This registers concretely the practices of the actors confronted with social reality. . . . It is constituted as an effect of the principle of reality. It comprises the rules of the game as applied, the implicit codes and the accepted tactics, even if the social group tends to ignore them, even if it prevents self-examination in order to protect the group's "superego" and its self-image.[8]

Interactions and Boundaries Between Symbolic and Operational Dimensions: Ambivalence of Feelings and Imaginary Compromise

The two categories interact in various ways. Sometimes the symbolic dimension camouflages reality, increasing the gap between the two dimensions even more and provoking a kind of social schizoid condition. Sometimes these two dimensions act on one another by an adjustment that is translated on the one hand by a rapid evolution of law if it is too distant from practice (common law and jurisprudence), and on the other hand by diffuse social or state control when the behaviors are too deviant with respect to the symbolic dimension. The gulf between the operational mode and the symbolic dimension fluctuates more or less according to the groups involved. The gap is large if the normative structure is highly disassociated; it is narrow when the two dimensions tend to approach, even to merge with one another.

This boundary is not the same for simple citizens as for the elite. According to Plato, only the governors have the privilege, sometimes the duty, of lying to citizens, a conception similar to that expressed by Machiavelli. It is thus that the governors see themselves invested with the duty of applying certain tactical procedures to the end of realizing the objectives of the social group and of maintaining its identity, all in the interest of preserving the other (perfectly) mythical code, the one disassociated from the operational mode. The specialists in the manipulation of power speak thus: "Let's be practical, operational; it's necessary to survive; it's necessary to be effective." Those who deviate with respect to the myth are punished only if the deviation is publicly revealed and evokes moral indignation; otherwise, it is accepted as part of the legitimate operational mode.

The borderline between accepted and illegitimate practice varies according to political cultures, space, and time according to the tolerance of a group or the degree of (il)legitimacy accorded to the operational mode, or according to the needs of some relatively stronger elite group. This borderline evolves over the years through classical processes of social change (internal, external influence etc.). For example, in local French communities, members of zoning boards often own land within the city bounds. . . . Surprisingly, among decision makers, there is hardly any consciousness of the possible perversion by conflicts of interests. Yet, the stakes of such boards are very high because they define the building and construction rights attached to various areas *(plan d'occupation des sols)* and their decisions strongly affect the personal interests of landowners as well as the future of the community. Such conflicts of interests would be strongly denounced in the United States but are largely ignored in France. This lack of consciousness not only veils operational practices, but reinforces a disconnected symbolic dimension; in addition, it permits the social reproduction of the process. Another consequence is the overurbanization and degradation of most beautiful areas.

However, we have observed a few timid signs of change emerging with the protests of environmental groups who denounce such conflicts of interests because they want to protect some beautiful land from urbanization (for example in the peninsula of Saint Tropez, Côte d'Azur). Now, one can wonder why conflicts of interests are not systematically denounced by political opponents in the city? In fact, this rarely occurs because they would behave similarly if they were in power: the normative structure is part of a broad and silent consensus.

How is the symbolic dimension preserved? Political discourse plays an important role in preserving the symbolic dimension and in putting certain policies into action. At the same time, a law that is perfect but cut off from sociological realities contributes to maintaining a symbolic dimension disassociated from practice. There is an equally important role for dogmatic rhetoric and for purely abstract models. This exemplifies the need to substitute a dream for reality, a myth for the violence surrounding the struggle for power, to idealize and to obscure the operational mode. Thus a kind of social schizophrenia installs itself in certain societies and hardens, cutting off and breaking up the two orders of reality. But how can one rationalize such a disassociation? How can one bring about a compromise between the ideal and political reality?

The symbolic dimension functions as an ideology which may create a kind of imaginary world, a substitute for the real one. The illusion can be deliberate, if it involves fooling others; it is unconscious or feigned if it involves telling oneself stories that one only half-believes. The symbolic dimension includes political discourses and the projection of politics into the media. It is the "state" as spectacle, a kind of imaginary sublimation of the culture. The stakes of political competition are the goals: their pursuit necessitates a strategy in the operational mode, but accompanied by an imaginary compromise. This compromise translates into ambivalence, such as that appearing in the same interview of the local elected official who said that "politics are rotten, everybody's been sold," and then added: "one is obliged to swim in compromises and that becomes normal." In brief, our ambivalent attitudes are an imaginary compromise between our desires and the principle of reality.

The Operational Mode As The Cement of An Elite Group

The operational modes are shared by the key members of the political, administrative, and economic network. When their codes become the official symbolic order, deviance is selectively and arbitrarily tolerated, in relation to the status of the deviants, to their objectives, and to the probable repercussions on other organizations and on the larger social system. Adherence to the operational mode is a sign of loyalty and of solidarity with the network. Six corollaries are:

(1) Gratification for the members of the network;
(2) Increased distance between the elites and the average citizen. The techniques of moral compromise end by becoming a norm of the group, one that holds it together, and a barrier that narrows access;
(3) Protection of the universe of values and of symbolic norms; it is sheltered by compromises of principles, it becomes the object of rhetoric; it is cultivated and reinforced, all in good faith, sometimes with a disillusioned or Machiavellian cynicism;
(4) A diffuse and conscienceless guilt sometimes crystallizes around certain scapegoats who pay personally for the corruption of the system;
(5) The conspiracy of silence: it operates particularly between leaders of various political parties, despite their sometimes bitter and violent conflicts; to survive, all must respect the rules of the game, and maintain silence about the rules themselves. For example, in the United States, the two major parties get most of their financing from business. From 1930 to 1970 there was an implicit detente between Democrat and Republican leaders about their sources of finance, which they made the object of a sort of informal division. It was clear that if one of the parties threatened the financial sources of the other, the equilibrium would be shattered;
(6) A contagious effect on people who are "satellites" to the circle of the elite, who copy—well or badly—the rules of the operational mode and, by so doing, threaten the game itself by going beyond certain well known limits set by those who possess the code: "Construction, that's a job for gangsters done by gentlemen . . ." "But if one isn't a gentleman anymore . . . nothing works!" (The owner of a French large construction company, in February 1983). A gentleman understands the limits when he puts his strategies into effect.

The operational mode can include illegal practices, but those generally operate within the limits of legitimacy, with legal guarantees, justifiable camouflages. These are generally related to perfectly respectable activities (industries, construction, social activities, etc.) rather than to illegal activities (drugs, swindles, gambling, currency speculation, etc.), activities that are marginal to the system. Political corruption takes place by a kind of "graft" on normal activity, in which those who have been "grafted" are placed under the vow of silence. This is the politics of the corridors.

The theoretical perspective proposed here includes the effects of coercion, extortion, and conflict for the actors involved in the systems of political corruption. It explains the dilemmas with which the politicians are confronted.[9] These conflicts between groups and actors, this normative disassociation between an operational mode for practical strategies and a symbolic code disconnected from the behaviors, the complicities among actors in the network of corruption who try to make their strategies succeed: are all these complex phenomena signs of a state of anomie?

Corruption and Anomie

This question arises from the theory of deviance, most particularly with respect to institutional and systemic deviance such as the one we are analyzing. Durkheim defines anomie as the absence of norms, an unstructured situation that disorients individuals, sometimes to the point of suicide. It does not seem that the networks of corruption are characterized by a situation of anomie in its strict sense, but more by a contradiction between ends and means, or between two normative structures, one oriented toward the scheme of values and symbols, and the other oriented toward the operational code. This perspective is similar to that made by R. K. Merton, who argued that anomie is a conflict between norms and values.[10] The harmony of the system is thus assured by an ambiguous consensus, a willing ignorance, a half-conscious illusion fostered by the citizens, and by the compromises by which the elite clings to power.

Anomie enters with revolt against the operational code, with popular indignation or the violation of the law of silence, sometimes naive . . . sometimes conscious and organized (such as an electoral battle, for example). The operational mode can thus be challenged without touching the normative structure. The concept of anomie offers an indication, if not an explanation, of the process of institutionalization of systemic corruption. Anomie, the absence of rules of the game, is a kind of individual "free ride," a loss of structure from which some venal individuals will know how to profit.

On the other hand, collective, systemic corruption is not anomie; on the contrary, it introduces rules of the game when norms are absent, rules that are perhaps discreet but in any case constraining, obliging the relevant actors to conform. Thus it is that the head of a construction company could, while denouncing the rackets imposed by governmental agencies, nonetheless qualify the system as being "fair game": "We know where we are going . . ." "At least you know you're on the same footing as your competitors . . ."

In sum, the businessman knows that thereafter he is going to have to pay one percent or more if he is told during the negotiations that some particular intermediary office is involved; but he also knows that his percentage is going to apply to all of his competitors as well, and increase similarly all of the bids for the contract. Indeed, hidden norms regulate corruption. Systemic corruption is thus not anomie, but it does seem like it because the norms are parallel and implicit. These norms, however, are clear to those who are "in" the game. They are the winners—but who loses?

Carried on at the expense of an abstractly defined, diffuse victim such as civil society, political corruption is a hidden misappropriation of public resources. Can it be considered as one of the areas of exploitation in the modern state? Certainly, an increasing proportion of economic "surplus value" is transferred via the state and gives life to an increasingly ponderous political-administrative class. Corruption is the illegitimate appropriation of one part of this flow, an economic form of political alienation in which the losers are repudiated as victims, injured as taxpayers, and swindled as citizens.

Notes

1. The article is based on comparative empirical research conducted in France and the United States. The results were presented in an unpublished paper delivered at a meeting of the European Research Consortium on Political Science, Fribourg, in 1983.
2. Functionalist analysis concentrates mainly on the study of functions of a system, rarely on its disfunctions or perverse effects. Moreover, the distinction is arbitrary and depends on the observer's point of view, his values, or his interests. It is rather in terms of contradictions that we analyze a number of negative effects of corruption in the second part of this article.
3. See the published research of the Center for the Sociology of Organizations directed by Michel Crozier, the work of P. Gremion and J.C. Thoenig. See also Becquart-Leclercq, "Relational network, relational power" ("Reseau relationel, Pouvoir relationel") *Revue francaise de Science politique* (February, 1979), pp. 102–28.
4. In the United States V.O. Key analyzed in detail the techniques of political corruption in Illinois and Chicago, preceded by Brooks (1910). The histori-

ography and sociology of municipal life include studies of corruption (Griffith, 1974, pp. 63–74; Steffens, 1957; Dorman, 1972; Allen, 1974; Ross, 1976; Gardiner, 1977; Beck, 1982, etc.). Research on the police include abundant examples of corruption (Sherman, 1974; O'Block, 1981). There are also numerous studies of corruption on the state level (Wilson, 1966); at the federal level (Clark, 1977; Lasky, 1977; Baker, 1978; Greene, 1981; Berg, 1976; Benson, 1978, etc.). In France, political corruption has been of little interest to social scientists, and there are few empirical research studies on this theme, apart from such journalistic writings as Gros, 1936; Montaldo, 1977 and 1978; James, 1978; Fournier and Legrand, 1975; and a special issue of *Esprit,* 1973 and of *Nouvel observateur,* 13 Sept. 1985. See also Becquart-Leclercq, unpublished (state doctorate) thesis "La democracie locale en Amerique," Paris, 1984, chapter 7.

5. See, in this connection, the hypotheses presented by A. Frognier to the European Research Consortium on Political Science at Fribourg, 1983.

6. For example, the celebrated "2 percent club" can be cited. According to interviews conducted in 1982, this "club" still operates today in Indiana. Following unofficial practice, every municipal employee, in one way or another, returns some small portion of his income to the locality's majority party; state employees are expected to contribute to the governor's party. The practice evades criminal prosecution because it is said to be "voluntary," though, in the view of some justice department lawyers, it appears to be a form of extortion. In France, one can cite unofficial, but obligatory, payments that certain political parties require of those who win office under their (the parties') banner, and which can attain important percentages of official indemnities or salaries. Here again, legislative intent is thwarted because the funds allocated to an elected official to cover his representational expenses and constituent contacts are partially denied him.

7. Durkheim characterizes the *social fact* as at once general and constraining. Cf. his *Rules and Methods of Sociology.*

8. In France there may be discerned a propensity to affirm the *supergroup* by positive feelings of belonging and by national chauvinism. In Italy, by contrast, a devalued group image may be easily perceived, in which individuals stress awareness of the rules of the game. In the United States, it is the law which seems to count heavily in the symbolic and political structure, though it is not accorded the same sacral qualities as in France. However, in France, only a small circle of intellectuals really discuss "the means and ends of the law," while the common view of the law is characterized by such epithets as "the law is meant to be evaded" (la loi est faite pour être tournée).

9. Normative dissociation is involved in the dilemmas that are particularly crucial to local politics, faced by local politicians. Cf. J. Becquart-Leclercq, "Absolute values and practical compromises in local politics: a sociological approach to political values" ("Valeurs absolues et compromis practiques dans la politique locale, un approche sociologique des valeurs politiques"), *Revenue francaise de Science politique* (April, 1982), pp. 233–50. This perspective differs from the clientilistic analysis of corruption, in which actors in corruption are given an aura of respectabil-

ity and which conceals coercive relationships (Cf. McConnel, 1970, p. 46, and Boyarsky, 1974).
10. Cf. Robert K. Merton, *Elements of Sociological Theory and Methodology*. Paris: Plon, 1965, Ch. V.

Bibliography

Allen, Robert S., ed. *Our Fair City*. New York: Arno Press, 1974.

Baker, Robert Gene. *Wheeling and Dealing: Confessions of a Capitol Hill Operator*. New York: Norton, 1978.

Beck, Elmer Axel. *The Sewer Socialists: A History of the Socialist Party of Wisconsin*. Fennimore, Wis.: Westbury, 1982.

Becquart-Leclercq, J. "Reseau relationel, Pouvoir relationel," *Revue francaise de science politique* (February 1979), 102–28.

Becquart-Leclercq, J. "Valeurs absolues et compromis pratiques dans la politique locale, une approche sociologique des valeurs politiques," *Revue francaise de science politique* (April 1982), 223–50.

Becquart-Leclercq, J. "Du reseau relationnel à la corruption politique," Communication au Congres du Consortium européen de Recherche en Science politique, Fribourg, March, 1983.

Benson, George S. *Political Corruption in America*. Lexington, Mass.: Lexington Books, 1978.

Berg, Larry L., et al. *Corruption in the American System*. Morristown, N.J.: General Learning Press, 1976.

Bollens, John, and Schmandt, Henri. *Political Corruption: Power, Money and Sex*. Pacific Palisades, Calif.: Palisades Publishers, 1979.

Bourricaud, Francois. *Le bricolage ideologique: Essai sur les intellectuels et les passions démocratiques*, Paris: Presses universitaires de France, 1980.

Boyarsky, Bill. *Backroom Politics: How Your Local Politicians Work, Why Your Government Doesn't, and What You Can Do About It*. Los Angeles and New York: Hawthorn Books, 1974.

Chambliss, William J. *On the Take: From Petty Crooks to Presidents*. Bloomington, Ind.: Indiana University Press, 1978.

Clark, Marion. *Public Trust, Private Lust: Sex, Power and Corruption on Capitol Hill*. New York: Morrow, 1977.

DeRogy, I., and J. M. *Enquête sur un carrefour dangereux*. Paris: Fayard, 1987.

Donneur, André, and Padioleau, Jean. "Local Clientelism in Post-Industrial Society: The Example of the French Communist Party," *European Journal of Political Research*, 10, (1982), 71–82.

Dorman, Michael. *Payoff*. New York: David McKay, 1972.

Fournier, Nicolas, and Legrand, Edmond. *Dossier C . . . comme Combines*. Paris: A. Moreau, 1975.

Fronment-Meurice, Anne. "Comment faire de sa mairie un fief," *Pouvoirs* (1983), 45–56.

Gardiner, John A. *Decisions for Sale: Corruption in Local Land Use and Building Regulation*. New York: Praeger, 1978.

Greene, Robert W. *The Sting Man: Inside Abscam*. New York: Dutton, 1981.

Griffith, Ernest S. "Public Opinion: From Corrupters to Clienteles," in *A History of American City Government: The Progressive Years and Their Aftermath: 1900–1920,* New York: Praeger, 1974, Ch. 16, pp. 213–46.

Gros, Gaston. *Vingt ans de corruption*. Paris: Ed. Baudiniere, 1936.

Heidenheimer, Arnold J. "Political Corruption in America: Is It Comparable?" in Eisenstadt, ed., *Before Watergate* (New York: Columbia University Press, 1978), pp. 21–34.

Huntington, Samuel. *Political Order in Changing Societies*. New Haven, Conn.: Yale University Press, 1968.

Jannes, Henri. "Le Watergate français." Paris: Ed. RUC, Jannes, 1978.

Lasky, Victor. *It Didn't Start with Watergate*. New York: Dial Press, 1977.

McConnell, G. *Private Power and American Democracy*. New York: Vintage, 1970.

Montaldo, J. *Les finances du Parti communiste*. Paris: Albin Michael, 1977.

Montaldo, J. *La France communiste*. Paris: Albin Michel, 1978.

O'Block, Robert L. *Security and Crime Prevention*. St. Louis, Mo.: C.V. Mosby, 1981.

Reisman, W. Michael. *Folded Lies: Bribery, Crusades, and Reforms*. New York: Free Press–Macmillan, 1979.

Ross, Philip. *The Bribe*. New York: Harper & Row, 1976.

Royer, J.-P., Martinage, R., and Lecoq, P. *Juges et notables au XIX siècle*. Paris: Presses universitaires de France, 1982.

Scott, James C. *Comparative Political Corruption*. Englewood Cliffs, N.J.: Prentice Hall, 1972.

Sherman, Lawrence W., ed. *Police Corruption: A Sociological Perspective*. New York: Anchor Press, Doubleday, 1974.

Wilson, James Q. "Corruption, the Shame of the States," *The Public Interest,* No. 2 (Winter 1966), 28–38.

Part II

CORRUPTION AND SOCIOPOLITICAL DEVELOPMENT

OVERVIEW

One of the principal themes of this volume is that political corruption is best understood *in comparative context*— of the histories, the cultures, the politics, and the particular societies in which it occurs. Such a perspective permits analysis of the ramifications, effects, and consequences of corruption, and of its origins, spread, and growth. This perspective also permits an examination of the relationship between corruption and the complex of changes usually associated with sociopolitical development. The questions that can arise from that examination not only identify possible critical relationships between corruption and development, but often suggest whole research agendas: What role did corruption play in the political development of the British and American democracies? How has it affected the development of the relatively new, "Third World" polities? Is political corruption a home-grown (endogenous) or imported (exogenous) phenomenon? How does corruption affect the economic part of the development equation?

Much of the conceptual language we now use to describe sociopolitical development is itself the product of a post-World War II preoccupation with the problems confronting over seventy new states that emerged between 1947 and 1975. Most of these states had previously been colonies of European metropoles, and almost all of them were very poor by contrast with the industrialized countries of Europe and North America. The new situation called for new ways both to describe the new states' plight and to permit useful generalizations to be made about their social, political, and economic progress.

In the process, it became clear that these analytic tools and perspectives could cast as much light on the *past* of the developed polities of the west, as they could on the present and prospects of the new "developing" states. After all, the United States, Great Britain, France, Italy, and the rest had all undergone their own developmental experiences, crucibles of change in which their present-day political institutions, norms, behaviors, and ideas (as well as their economies) had been formed. At any event, students of corruption, including those who had explicitly or implicitly adopted the developmentalist perspective, began to search the English and American past for clues about the relationship between corruption and the growth of the democratic model. Some of these students, of course, hoped the search would also illuminate the new states' kinds of corruption, and their (the states') hopes for a better future.

Clearly, both in England and in the United States, various forms of corruption affected political development, more often to some general benefit, although not all the authors excerpted here would agree to that conclusion. In Britain, for example, corruption may have eased the transition from royal absolutism to parliamentary rule by helping to secure the political cooperation of the aristocracy during and after the shift. On the other hand, after the eighteenth century, once the focus of corruption had shifted to the electoral arena, corrupt practices undoubtedly retarded, if not prevented, the appearance of the social and economic reforms that had been expected to go hand in hand with the growth of the franchise. In the United States, high electoral competition and mass suffrage gave rise to the political machine, which often grew into massive vehicles for illicit patronage networks and corrupt practices. At their best, however, the political machines provided goods, services, employment, and economic opportunity for masses of people—often immigrants—still at the political and economic margins of the American system. In time, as their clients moved into the American mainstream, the machines outlived their usefulness, although the patterns of corruption they engendered often outlived the machines themselves.

The American and British experiences seem to suggest that certain kinds of benign—white and market—corruption may have helped to open up the two systems at critical points in their development. Whether this has been the case for the newer political systems, and for some of the other, older systems, is a matter of some dispute. For example, where deeply-rooted systems of patronage continue to persist—as in Sicily, Morocco, and Ghana (a "new" nation)—political and economic change occurs slowly, if at all, and ambitious programs of modernization lose their momentum or grind to a halt.

In Sicily, the older systems of patrimonial clientelism, entrenched in social mores and reinforced by a pervasive suspicion of government, has effectively prevented almost all post-World War II Italian governments from implementing various economic and political reforms on the island. It took a massive frontal judicial attack, involving the indictment of literally hundred of Mafiosi chiefs and followers in 1985–1986, even to begin to crack the system's walls. In Morocco, the government of King Hassan dealt with the problem by making official, budgetary provision for bribes and payoffs, and in Ghana, the problem became increasingly intractable after the country's first government effectively converted older forms of patronage into modern patterns of official corruption.

If a negative relationship between systematic patronage-based corruption and political development and modernization seems plausible in some traditional societies, the experience of other new states complicates the issue. One such state, Israel, started out in 1948 with relatively little public corruption; however, as it became increasingly socially heterogeneous (with the arrival of large numbers of Oriental Jews beginning in the 1950s), the old socialist developmental ethos began to weaken, party machines began to make their appearance, and various forms of corruption came to be increasingly condoned. Corruption may well have helped the post-1950 immigrants to enter the national system more rapidly and productively, but the cost to the country—heightened political conflict, mounting political cynicism, decreased support for government—may have been too high.

In the "Third World" new states of Africa and Asia, many of whom were launched with ambitious programs for rapid political and economic development and modernization, systematic political corruption soon made its appearance. Some students of the phenomenon were persuaded that, on balance, some corruption could actually play a positive role in fostering constructive social, political, and economic change where, for example, such change was blocked by bureaucratic sceloris or inertia, governmental inefficiency or incapacity, or regressive social mores. Others argued that the balance tilts in the other direction, that whatever the contributions of corruption to development and modernization, the costs ultimately become too high and destructive.

The debate remains unresolved, but it is clear that such answers as may be had will emerge from empirically based studies, both focussed and comparative, of the continuing developmental experience of both "developed" and "developing," old and new, political systems.

Political Development and Corruption Incidence: An Introduction

In this section, the reader is presented with analyses that show how, when political institutions changed toward the democratic model, the perception and incidence of corruption changed as differing social groups were allowed to participate in the political process. The panorama extends from the sixteenth to the twentieth centuries, focusing on three countries with differing patterns of settlement and citizenship extension—Britain, the United States, and Israel. The comparisons build up various historical and developmental models which attempt to encompass the forces that changed and shaped the party, bureaucratic, and institutional structures within these three countries.

In the first selection, Linda Levy Peck examines how corruption in Britain changed from court-centered corruption in the sixteenth century to parliament-centered corruption in the eighteenth century. At the beginning of this period, public and private interests were intermingled in the royal patronage system, which had more favors to dispense because the state took over functions previously exercised by the church and guilds and because regulatory legislation expanded. Peck shows how social changes in the seventeenth century led to a shift toward market corruption, which caused the monarchy itself to be labeled corrupt in the period leading up to the Puritan revolution. Still later, after the establishment of parliamentary sovereignty in the Glorious Revolution of 1688, corrupt practices came to maintain coalitions between the House of Commons and royal ministers.

Next, John P. King pursues the interrelationship between socioeconomic change and political corruption in England by examining the incidence of corrupt election practices as the franchise was broadened in the course of the nineteenth century. Was it more the newly admitted voters who succumbed to offers of bribes and treating in order to support and sell their support in parliamentary elections, or did corruption continue to be more rife among voters who already had the franchise before the first Reform Act of 1832? Was corruption more prevalent in the more rapidly expanding new industrial towns, or in the communities whose population remained more static? In general, King identifies a negative relationship between development and the occurrence of corrupt practices.

In Israel, the country examined by Simcha Werner, there were also differences between the old voters who had been pioneers in Palestine under the British mandate, and the newer immigrants who entered in particularly large numbers from North Africa and Asia in the 1950s. Lacking democratic traditions and located near the bottom of the social ladder, the newer Oriental immigrants were more dependent upon the party political machines, thus engendering networks of political clientelism. Generally negative attitudes toward bureaucracy engendered toleration and cover-ups for increasing corruption. Some of the ideological factors that had inhibited corruption earlier, parallel to the way they had come to operate in Britain, weakened in the 1970s which led to more pervasive corruption. Werner holds that the condoning of white corruption can encourage more insidious kinds of corruption and allow corruption to become institutionalized as the political system matures.

The American setting is analyzed comparatively by James C. Scott in the next chapter, to contrast the situations under which mass suffrage and high degrees of electoral competition engender political machines. Party machines, as they first developed in American cities around the time corruption was phasing out in Britain, are characterized by their use of particular material rewards as the cement holding together the followers of incumbent leaders. Scott argues that machines develop more during certain phases of development in modernizing and democratizing countries, but that the timing and duration of such phases may vary widely. He distinguishes the factors involved, such as fragmentation of political power, social disorganization, and poverty.

In the final selection, Eva Etzioni-Halevy reexamines the theoretical constructs used in the preceding attempts to explain the rise and decline of corrupt practices in all three countries. Etzioni-Halevy avoids a developmental perspective, but rather examines how various factors adduced to explain corruption do not seem to have led to very consistent cross-national explanatory patterns. Immigration, poverty, education, and other variables are shown not to be consistently correlated with levels of corruption in Britain, America, and Israel at the same or similar periods. From a democratic elitist perspective, she argues that the single most important factor for the control of corruption in twentieth century mass democracies is the insulation of the bureaucracy so as to make its resources unavailable for party-political exploitation.

14

Corruption and Political Development in Early Modern Britain

Linda Levy Peck

If corruption has been the most powerful issue within American politics in recent years, it was even more explosive on the eve of the American Revolution. The most frequent political charge pressed against the British by the colonists was that of moral and political corruption. In 1775, Benjamin Franklin wrote from England:

> When I consider the extreme corruption prevalent among all orders of men in this old rotten state, and the glorious public virtue so predominant in our rising country, I cannot but apprehend more mischief than benefit from a closer union. Here numberless and needless places, enormous salaries, pensions, prerequisites, bribes . . . devour all revenue and produce continual necessity in the midst of natural plenty. I apprehend, therefore, that to unite us intimately will only be to corrupt and poison us also.[1]

After close examination of the extensive elaboration of such charges in colonial newspapers and pamphlets, Bernard Bailyn concluded that to most informed colonists "by 1774, the final crisis of the constitution, brought on by political and social corruption, had been reached."[2]

Yet it is important to note that the practices cited with outrage by the colonists were normal political practice in early modern England, a very part, as Patrick Henry suggested pejoratively, of its system of government.[3] Why was this the case? One answer has been suggested by analysts of corruption in developing nations. Social scientists following the influential writings of Samuel Huntington have created a new orthodoxy in the last ten years, equating corruption with the

Source: Linda Levy Peck, "The British Case: Corruption and Political Development in the Early Modern State," in *Before Watergate: Problems of Corruption in American Society,* Abraham S. Eisenstadt, Ari Hoogenboom, and H.L. Trefousse, eds. Brooklyn, N.Y.: Brooklyn College Press, 1978. By permission of the publisher.

process of modernization.[4] Modernization, the argument goes, is characterized by the development of new forms of wealth that are not encompassed by the traditional norms of society. Corrupt practices provide access and control over resources for groups that have hitherto been excluded from power. Huntington himself suggests:

> Political life in seventeenth-century Britain and in late nineteenth-century Britain was, it would appear, less corrupt than it was in eighteenth-century Britain. Is it merely coincidence that the high point of corruption in English and American public life coincided with the impact of the industrial revolution, the development of new sources of wealth and power, and the appearance of new classes making new demands of government?[5]

Drawing on Huntington's approach, James C. Scott in his examination of corruption in early Stuart England, emphasizes the role of what he calls wealth elites (by which he seems to mean well-to-do merchants), themselves outside the political system, who used corrupt means to gain access to economic privileges and to influence the enforcement of government regulations.[6] The Huntington-Scott view seems to be yet another invocation of the rise of the bourgeoisie, in this instance to explain the flourishing of corrupt practices in a period of political and economic change. This chapter examines corrupt practices in England from the sixteenth to the eighteenth centuries, tracing the fundamental shift from court-centered to parliamentary corruption. The aim is to relate corruption to English political development and to suggest another hypothesis of who benefited from corrupt practices and why. The definition of corruption adopted is "behavior which deviates from the formal duties of a public role because of private-regarding . . . pecuniary or status gains; or violates rules against the exercise of certain types of private-regarding behavior."[7] Although many practices later labeled corrupt were standard practice in the early modern period and might better be labeled proto-corruption,[8] this use of the contemporary Western definition, which includes bribery, nepotism and peculation, does allow comparative analysis with societies in other times and places.

What did early modern English government look like? From the 1530s to the end of the seventeenth century, corrupt practices were centered in the sizable administration of Tudor and Stuart England. In the sixteenth century, beginning with the Henrician revolution, the English state took over the functions previously exercised by church and guild, and the period was marked not only by the expansion of offices but also by an increase in laws regulating all aspects of social and economic life. Such an increase in the regulatory side of the state's activities institutionally allowed for an increase in corrupt activities.[9] But it is crucial to note that the notion of a bureaucracy of civil servants serving the public interest did not exist in the period. Public and private interest were hopelessly mixed in what Max Weber described as the early modern patrimonial bureaucratic state.[10] What did this mean in specific terms? The staffing of the bureaucracy proceeded not by merit but by a patronage process in which kinship and client ties were usually more important than ability to perform the job. Since salaries for administrators were pegged either at centuries-old levels or were nonexistent, officials were paid by those who needed to use their services. In the period of price inflation that marked the sixteenth century, money above and beyond traditional fees was exacted. By the 1640s these informal takings amounted to 40 percent of the government's yearly revenue.[11] In addition, positions on the middle and lower levels of administration carried with them not tenure during good behavior but life tenure, and appointment was often in the hands of middle-level officials. For instance, because England never abolished offices, by the sixteenth century three different royal seals were required for any legal document. The clerkships within these seals' offices were sinecures that offered good pay, little work and the possibility of hiring a deputy. Offices were briskly bought and sold and it was not uncommon to find five or more reversions of interest attached to any one office, sometimes in the names of infants. Royal officials used government property as if it were their own. Thus the two top naval officials used a ship that supposedly accompanied the Lord High Admiral on an embassy to Spain for a private merchant voyage at the king's expense.[12] This was not, however, unusual. After all, Elizabeth's navy had been made up in part of privateering ships in whose ventures the queen participated when England was not at war. It was cheaper than footing the bill for the navy entirely by herself and in addition "deniability," which is thought of as a contemporary phenomenon, was so much easier for Elizabeth when public and private interest merged. In short, bribery, graft and nepotism where characteristic of early modern bureaucracy in England and elsewhere.

These patterns of administrative corruption parallel those in contemporary developing nations, and it is important to cite the positive functions that many social scientists provocatively argue that corruption performs, for similar benefits ensued in early modern England, specifically, increased governmental capacity and national integration.[13] Thus the increased scope of government activity permitted the government to increase its rewards in the form of offices, fees and privileges. The distribution of these spoils served to centralize power, to make the court the center of reward and to integrate those who on the local level were politically important. This was a signal achievement after the disintegrative period of the fifteenth century, the Wars of the Roses and the bane of what contemporaries called "the overmighty subject." The expansion of patronage helped to provide the king with an administrative staff in a period when the monarchy was without the resources to pay its servants. Groups outside the political elite, such as the merchant community, did gain access to power and resources by paying bribes to government officials. Their loyalty was thus assured and, more importantly, their economic resources were made available to the Crown. Given the fact that England lacked a standing army as well as paid local administrators, the allocation of reward was the means by which local elites could be amalgamated to the Crown. In analyzing corruption in Tudor England there can be little doubt that those who benefited from corrupt practices were primarily members of the landed interest and the court itself. Corrupt practices were the cement welding together the Crown and the political elite: the aristocracy, composed of the nobility and gentry.

But in the decades of the seventeenth century before the Puritan revolution, in addition to the administrative corruption endemic to the early modern state, there was a sharp change in corrupt practices, an increase in their extent and variety and the outcry against them. Most important, there was a shift to "market corruption" which tended to generalize the distribution of privileges by putting them within the grasp of those who could pay.[14] Did this mean that corruption now centered on the activities of the merchant community? It did seem as if everything were for sale at the court of James I. Public functions such as taxation and law enforcement were granted to private persons in exchange for cash. Access to economic privileges was granted for money. The customs duties were farmed out and the customs farmers, London merchants, soon became the main source of royal loans. Economic privileges belonging to the Crown, such as patents of monopoly on the manufacture or importation of goods, were granted to favorites and officials who subcontracted them to merchants.

Social privileges too were granted in exchange for cash. In the Jacobean period, knighthoods were sold and later, titles: for £10,000 one could purchase a peerage and have the privilege of sitting in the House of Lords by becoming a baron. Or if that was too expensive, for quite a lot less, £1,095, one could become a baronet. James Scott in his book, *Comparative Corruption*, pinpoints the importance of the rise of an affluent commercial elite that desired influence, protection and status. He suggests that there was a trend under the early Stuarts from decentralized nonmarket corruption to centralized market corruption, "reflecting the growing alliance between the Crown and commercial interests and worked to the disadvantage of the independent aristocratic cliques that had previously controlled much of patronage and spoils."[15] Such a statement seems to be substantially incorrect. It cannot be denied that leading merchants did pay bribes to gain access to monopolies and customs farms, particularly in the Jacobean era. In fact the London financial community became a pillar on which the early Stuart monarchy rested. But it is most important to note that Scott's dichotomy between aristocratic networks and court-merchant relations is not accurate. Most merchants who dealt with the Crown did so through the intercession of those very aristocrats whom Scott is intent on phasing out. In 1604, for instance, in the competition for the letting of the Great Customs, Lords Dorset, Salisbury and Northampton each had his own merchant clients who competed for the farm.[16] Lionel Cranfield, a successful merchant of the period, was brought into government and later became Lord High Treasurer through the intercession of an aristocrat of the Howard family, and continued his career as the client of the Duke of Buckingham. While there was an outcry against the sale of honors, criticism focused not on the sale itself but on who got what. And at the beginning in 1611, baronetcies were sold only to the leading gentlemen in each country. In fact, sales were considered reasonable so long as the price was kept *up*! Those who were most eager to buy were not wealthy merchants but the landed gentry. Indeed gentry, not members of the merchant community, were the principal buyers of government offices.[17]

Historians have the nasty habit of wanting to look at specifics. The court was not without its reformers.[18] In 1608 court officials seeking to rationalize Jacobean administration established a royal commission to investigate corruption in the navy.[19] These were its findings. At the lowest levels of the navy, supplies such as timber, cordage, tar, pitch were diverted into private hands: good wood was used to build private homes and bad wood substituted for the king's ships. At the middle levels, ship's officers, captain, pursers and victualers, would take on supplies for 100 men when there were only 70 and sell the excess. At the top levels, naval officers placed their own liveried followers in office; took kickbacks from all those who provided supplies to the navy, or were themselves the purveyors and passed the cost on to the king; supplied their own ships for merchant voyages at royal expense; and, in appointments, placed "most for Mony, fewe for Meritte, whereby your Navie is made, as your best Ministers depose, a Ragged

Regiment of Tapsters, Coblers and Rogues."[20] This is certainly market corruption, but who were the corrupt? The officials were of impeccably gentle credentials; those who were forced to kick back were small businessmen.

What about the towns, home of the newly well-to-do merchants? Corrupt practices flourished on the local level during the period in the form of loans from town corporation funds, use of public power for personal financial advantage and simple peculation. In large part this was due to the multiplication of offices required for the administration of the Tudor and Stuart regulations of the economy and society, in particular the poor law. Newly wealthy men certainly dominated the government of many English towns in the period, often because they could afford the expenses associated with town office. But it is important to note that the sixteenth century also witnessed an increasing interference by the Crown and local gentry in town affairs. Borough seats in parliament were monopolized by gentlemen who often also took over the position of town clerk, "lynchpin of civic administration." And the Crown's agents were mostly country gentlemen or county lawyers. The result was the reinforcement of oligarchical power, but shared between the gentry and the well-to-do merchants of the town.[21]

Again, in the most notorious corruption case of the reign, the trial of the Earl of Suffolk, son of the Duke of Norfolk (in short, not a new man), the charges against him included extorting kickbacks of 10 percent to 20 percent from those owed money by the Exchequer and using government funds as if they were his own private bank account. Even other departments within the administration were forced to kick back to him in order to secure their budgetary allotments and even then did not necessarily receive their money. Having borrowed £10,000 from the customs farmers, Suffolk arranged for a kickback of £1,500 a year to be applied to his debt.[22] The purpose of the bribe, however, was not to enable those outside political power to circumvent enforcement of irksome regulations, as Scott's argument suggests, but rather to reinforce their status as insiders, as clients of the Lord High Treasurer. Because Scott construes corruption as influence exercised at the enforcement stage, he overlooks those practices. But if not simply the result of wealthy merchants seeking to influence policy, what political function, then, did "market corruption" fulfill in early Stuart England?

To begin with, it provided needed revenue for the king faced by a parliament loath to pass what were, after all, inadequate subsidies. The Crown could do better by selling titles and privileges, could reward its favorites more through licensing than by granting concessions or giving up such practices to a tightfisted parliament.[23] Market corruption also served as a mechanism of allocation in a situation where the increase in the political elite made it impossible to distribute reward as broadly as in the past.[24] If the social structure of Tudor and Stuart England is examined, what is most significant for the question of corruption is the large increase in the size of the gentry and nobility, owing not to the rise of the bourgeoisie (or wealth elite) but to the increasing prosperity of yeomen. Where in 1433 there were 48 gentle families in Shropshire, in 1623 there were 470.[25] In keeping with this, increasing numbers of gentry flocked to the university in the second half of the sixteenth century but there were not sufficient positions in church or state for them. This growth in the political elite had crucial consequences. On the one hand, it meant a greater strain on the Crown's ability to reward and to maintain the Elizabethan balance of patronage. On the other, it meant the need for allocating devices as the scramble for reward intensified under the early Stuarts. In short, market corruption, characteristic of the Stuart period, served to raise revenue for the Crown and its favorites and to allocate rewards in a system in which demand greatly exceeded supply. But while market corruption may have served certain functions, the monopolization of favor by the Duke of Buckingham's faction exacerbated the inadequacy of court rewards to gain the support of all segments of the political elite. In addition, the type of corrupt practices prevalent at the Jacobean court provoked a strong outcry from an important section of the gentry because it affected their vital interests. The indiscriminate sale of honors affected the social structure and threatened the status of the politically preeminent. Bribery formed part of the fiscal grievances of the gentry. The payment of pensions by the Spanish to the most influential courtiers affronted vigilant Protestants. As a result, the court and the king himself were labeled corrupt. In the decades before the English Civil War, as the political elite polarized into factions of Court and Country with differing views on politics and religion, the issue of corruption undermined the legitimacy of the monarchy itself.[26]

What changes did the Commonwealth and Protectorate bring? G.E. Aylmer in the second of his important studies of seventeenth century administration pointed out that there was a massive change in personnel.[27] Where before the Civil War the nobility and gentry had been the principal holders of office, the government of the republic was strikingly less upperclass. There was a considerable change, too, in administrative practices. Salaries were increased, fee-taking was curtailed and offices were not sold on a significant level during the period. The result was a noticeable drop in administrative corruption, but the new elite created by the revolution was unable to entrench itself. With the Restoration, along with Charles II came the restoration of the old elite and the "old administrative system." Aylmer observed that its tenacious continuation into the nineteenth century was due to the victories of oligarchy and constitutionalism in 1660, 1688–89 and 1714, and the later reaction against the French Revolution.[28]

In the period from the Restoration to the American Revolution England experienced great economic growth and a large expansion in government offices which caused changed patterns of corruption too. The "commerical revolution" with increased trade to America, the West Indies and the East, and the development and growth of the home market created new wealth, with the result that the newly well-to-do took power in almosst all English towns great and small. Significantly, this economic growth benefited the landed interest too, offering the gentry a variety of new opportunities for money-making as well as increased reward for agricultural products. Furthermore, the landed were becoming more stable as a group and even more entrenched in the countryside, as evidenced by the increasing size of landholdings and the shrinkage of the land market throughout most of the eighteenth century.[29] Where early Stuart England and the Civil War had seen a polarization of the politically important, the political elite of eighteenth century England, much more broadly based, its focus of attention less on the court and more on Parliament, was characterized by remarkable stability, one important factor of which was a "sense of common identity in those who wielded economic, social and political power."[30] What did this mean for corrupt practices? Certainly corruption played an important role in eighteenth century politics. Yet the cause lay not in wealthy merchants *outside* the political system making new demands for political power. Rather it lay in the alliance of the important landed and mercantile interests in a highly stable oligarchy. In combination with the Crown, this oligarchy ruled England well into the nineteenth century. As J.H. Plumb suggested of the period after 1689,

> what the revolution did was to confirm the authority of certain men of property, particularly those of high social standing, either aristocrats or linked with the aristocracy, whose tap root was in land but whose side-roots reached out to commerce, industry and finance. . . . Their authority was established . . . because they settled like a cloud of locusts on the royal household and all the institutions of executive government.[31]

With the Glorious Revolution, parliamentary sovereignty was finally established, but there existed neither a constitutional mechanism by which the executive related to the legislature nor a means to finance increasingly expensive political campaigns. As a result, the royal ministers devised the informal but very effective means of using governmental patronage to reward the Crown's supporters in Parliament with offices and contracts. The monopolization of political control by the Whigs from 1720 to 1760 meant that division on issues receded and politics revolved around personality. The "influence of the Crown" was thereby augmented and the division of spoils became the lifeblood of the British system.[32]

The patronage at the disposal of the Hanoverians would have been the envy of James I. Late seventeenth and eighteenth century English government underwent a massive expansion, in conjunction with commercial growth, particularly in the offices of the Treasury which included the customs and excise subdepartments. New taxes brought not only increased revenues but also increased sinecures. In 1718, for instance, there were 1,561 customs officers working in the Port of London alone.[33] And the expansion of the number of officials was as much for political reasons as administrative: the increase in governmental patronage increased the number of those who profited from government employment and those who benefited were drawn from the politically active. As Sir Lewis Namier emphasized, the idea that the politically active part of the nation had a claim to maintenance on the state was generally accepted, tantamount to an eighteenth century version of outdoor relief.[34]

The warfare that characterized the century inflated the size of the War Office, and the army and navy. The result was not only a large increase in government positions but an expansion of government contracts to provision the armed forces. The political importance of these contracts as political favors can be calculated from the fact that 37 of the 50 merchants who sat in the parliament of 1761 were government contractors.[35] Government office, government contracts and the nepotism, peculation and malfeasance that came in their wake were used by the Crown's ministers to ensure the loyalty of a majority of the members of parliament and to pay for the cost of their electioneering. These were the indirect means. In addition, the government maintained a secret fund taken from the Treasury for bribes, pensions and payments for electioneering to its friends in parliament and out. In five years, £291,000 was paid out of the Treasury for this purpose.[36] In some sense it might be said the parliamentary gentry of the eighteenth century sold their political gains from the revolutions of the seventeenth century for a mess of patronage.

To the extent that the Crown's sharing of the spoils among a wide range of recipients widened participation in the regime, maintained the support of the politically important and increased the abiilty of the executive to shape policy, it contributed to the political stability of the period. After a century of instability and revolution, this may be deemed political development if considered in terms of the system's needs as opposed to the needs of the populace.[37] The entrenchment of this elite, however, nearly provoked further revolution in the 1830s, as it resisted every movement toward change until unwillingly and under the threat of violence it agreed to share some of its power with other groups. Even the extension of the suffrage, however, did not end the dominance of the landed interest, which continued into the middle of the nineteenth century and later.

To sum up, corruption in England in the sixteenth and early seventeenth centuries tended to be of a nature endemic to a patrimonial bureaucracy. The shift to market corruption under the early Stuarts was due to changes in social structure: the growth if not the rise of the gentry, the shaky finances of the Crown which could more easily be shored up through the sale of titles, patents and licenses, and the tendency of officeholders to maximize short-term gains because of a breakdown in supervision and the monopolization of patronage by one faction. With the development of parliamentary supremacy after the revolution of 1688, corrupt practices were instrumental in maintaining coalitions of interest between royal ministers and the House of Commons, and welded together the aristocracy and major financiers into a single oligarchy. In short, corrupt practices in early modern England served to reinforce the status quo, primarily the interests of the landed aristocracy. Wealthy merchants played their role to be sure, but only in association with the court and later parliamentary aristocracy. Wealthy merchants played their role to be sure, but only in association with the court and later parliamentary aristocracy. They were neither the major initiators of corrupt practices nor the major beneficiaries. Huntington, Scott and other social scientists, bemused by the rise of the bourgeoisie, have not sufficiently taken into account the ability of the English aristocracy to adapt to changing economic and social conditions.

Finally, the role of corruption should be considered in bringing about political change. It has been argued elsewhere that it is the linking of corruption to other vital issues that gives it the power to undermine the legitimacy of a regime. In the decades before the English Civil War, as the nobility and gentry polarized into factions of court and country with differing views on religion and politics, the monarchy itself came to be labeled corrupt. The country opposition thought of themselves as "persons of public spirit, unmoved by private interest, untainted by court influence and corruption—representatives, in short, of the highest good of their local communities and the nation in whose interest they, and they only, acted."[38] With the Restoration such polarization ended and in 1688 there was no such split within the political elite. Although James II was removed from the throne, corruption played little role in the rhetoric of the revolution. While the country ideology continued to exist in England in the eighteenth century, it found its real home in the colonies. In the years leading up to 1776, a good part of the colonists' rhetoric reflected that of the Puritan revolution. Influenced by the circulation of the works of the eighteenth century Commonwealth men, whose ideas reflected those of the country opposition, Americans came to look at the English parliament with the same eyes as the Puritan country gentry had when they looked at James I and Charles I. In Benjamin Franklin's words can be heard the court/country polarization across a gap of 125 years and 3,000 miles, in what J.G.A. Pocock has labeled the "revolution against parliament."[39] Tough-minded social scientists sometimes like to think of corruption as the oil that greases the wheels of the political machine. But emphasis on governmental capacity and stability to the exclusion of popular participation may not provide the best definition of political development. It is important to remember that, while corrupt practices may have reinforced the status quo in early modern England and fostered stability, corruption as a political issue was a dissolvent in the 1640s and in 1776 of the political ties that bind.

Notes

1. Bernard Bailyn, *The Ideological Origins of the American Revolution* (Cambridge, Mass., 1967), pp. 36, 48–49, 130–39.
2. *Ibid.,* p. 132.
3. *Ibid.,* pp. 136–37.
4. Cf. Samuel P. Huntington, *Political Order in Changing Societies* (New Haven, 1968); Nathaniel H. Leff, "Economic Development through Bureaucratic Corruption," José V. Abeuva, "The Contribution of Nepotism, Spoils, and Graft to Political Development," and other selections in Arnold Heidenheimer, ed., *Political Corruption* (New York, 1970), pp. 479–578.
5. Huntington, "Modernization and Corruption," in Heidenheimer, *op. cit.,* p. 492.
6. James C. Scott, "Proto-Corruption in Early Stuart England," *Comparative Political Corruption* (Englewood Cliffs, N.J., 1972), pp. 37–55. Scott uses "wealth elites," "commercial and financial interests" and "bourgeoisie" interchangeably.
7. J.S. Nye, "Corruption and Political Development: A Cost-Benefit Analysis," in Heidenheimer, *op. cit.,* pp. 566–67.

8. Scott, *op. cit.*, p. 4. Scott, who accepts Nye's definition, suggests the use of "proto-corruption" to describe practices of the pre-nineteenth century period which were only labeled corrupt in the nineteenth century.

9. Cf. Joel Hurstfield, "Political Corruption in Modern England: The Historian's Problem," *Hitory,* LII, No. 174 (February 1967), 16–34. Huntington, *op. cit.*, p. 494.

10. Heidenheimer, *op. cit.*, pp. 10–11.

11. G.E. Aylmer, *The King's Servants* (New York, 1961), p. 248.

12. British Museum, Cotton MSS, Julius F III, fol. 15, 26. Julius F III contains the testimony given before the 1608 naval commission.

13. Cf. Huntington, "Modernization and Corruption," pp. 492–500; David H. Bayley, "The Effects of Corruption in a Developing Nation," in Heidenheimer, *op. cit.*, pp. 521–33; J.S. Nye, *op. cit.*, pp. 564–78.

14. Scott, *op. cit.*, pp. 12, 54.

15. *Ibid.*, p. 54. Lawrence Stone, *The Crisis of the Aristocracy* (Oxford, 1965).

16. A.P. Newton, "The Establishment of the Great Farm of the English Customs," *Transactions of the Royal Historical Society,* 4th series, I (1918), p. 150.

17. Scott is incorrect in his statement, "The sale of office provided an important avenue of social mobility for the growing bourgeoisie. . . . As elsewhere the sale of office led to a tacit alliance between the Crown and a portion of the national bourgeoisie," *op. cit.*, pp. 46–47. Cf. Aylmer, *op. cit.*, pp. 263–65, who stresses the upperclass background of most officials: "It can only be maintained that Tudor bureaucracy was staffed by men of predominantly middle-class origin if the gentry are classified with 'the middle classes'." This classification is not accepted by English historians. Cf. J.H. Hexter, "The Myth of the Middle Class in Tudor England," *Reappraisals in History* (New York, 1961), pp. 71–116.

18. Cf. Linda Levy Peck, "Problems in Jacobean Administration: Was Henry Howard, Earl of Northampton, A Reformer?" *The Historical Journal,* 19 Dec. 1976, 831–58; Menna Prestwich, *Cranfield: Politics and Profits under the Early Stuarts* (Oxford, 1966).

19. British Museum, Cotton MS, Julius C III. The commission's report is Public Record Office, S.P. 14, LXI, 1.

20. Trinity College, Cambridge, MS, R. 5. 1.

21. Peter Clark and Paul Slack, *English Towns in Transition, 1500–1700* (London, 1976), pp. 128–34.

22. A.P.P. Keep, "Star Chamber Proceedings against the Earl of Suffolk and Others," *English Historical Review,* XIII (1898), 716–29.

23. Cf. Conrad Russell, "Parliamentary History in Perspective, 1604–1629," *History,* LXI (February 1976), 1–27.

24. For a discussion of this aspect of corruption, cf. Heidenheimer, *op. cit.*, p. 5.

25. Stone, *op. cit.*, p. 67.

26. Cf. Linda Levy Peck, "Corruption at the Court of James I: The Undermining of Legitimacy," forthcoming in *Festschrift* in honor of J.H. Hexter.

27. Aylmer, *The State's Servants: The Civil Service of the English Republic, 1649–1660* (London, 1973), pp. 324, 328, 373.

28. Aylmer, *The King's Servants,* p. 438. Aylmer makes the following points: "The vested interests of the predominantly gentry and lawyer-staffed

administration were perhaps equally at variance with the needs and aspirations of 'Thorough' and of a bourgeois-democratic republic," p. 436; "The Restoration is to be seen above all as an oligarchic victory over any incipient trends either towards 'enlightened absolutism' or towards middle-class democracy," p. 438.

29. J.H. Plumb, *The Origins of Political Stability, England, 1675–1725* (Boston, 1967), pp. 3–10.
30. *Ibid.,* pp. xviii, 18–19.
31. *Ibid.,* p. 69.
32. Cf. Archibald S. Foord, *His Majesty's Opposition, 1714–1830* (Oxford, 1964), pp. 16–19; Sir Lewis Namier, *The Structure of Politics at the Accession of George III* (London, 1963), pp. 16–18.
33. Plumb, *op. cit.,* pp. 116–18.
34. Namier, *op. cit.,* p. 16.
35. *Ibid.,* pp. 45–49.
36. *Ibid.,* p. 234.
37. Cf. Nye, *op. cit.,* p. 566, who defines political development as "growth in the capacity of a society's governmental structures and processes to maintain their legitimacy over time."
38. Pérez Zagorin, *The Court and the Country: The Beginning of the English Revolution* (New York, 1970), p. 37.
39. J.G.A. Pocock, "1776: The Revolution against Parliament," paper delivered at Folger Shaespeare Library conference, "Three British Revolutions," May, 1976. Cf. Caroline Robbins, *The Eighteenth Century Commonwealthman* (Cambridge, Mass., 1959).

15

Socioeconomic Development and Corrupt Campaign Practices in England

John P. King

Some English historians dispute Disraeli's contention that England in the nineteenth century was two nations. It cannot, however, be denied that certain parts of England developed more rapidly than others. Some towns expanded by over 300 percent in population while others stagnated or even declined. In the North and Midlands eighteenth-century villages became towns. Indeed one of the themes of Hanham's study of nineteenth-century politics is the contrast between "the old political world of the counties and small towns which looked back to the years before 1832, and the new world of the big industrial towns."[1] It was in these developing towns that the Anti-Corn Law League, trade unions, and political associations were most active. It was in these developing areas that the rising industrial and commercial classes were most apparent. The purpose of this chapter is to suggest a relationship between development and corruption.

Development is a concept with many aspects. Of course it suggests rapid population increase. More importantly it implies a social and cultural transformation of a town or an area. It is possible to measure the degree of development within a town not only by looking at the size of its population or even merely by examining its growth rate, but also by scrutinizing its class structure. To the extent that attitudes, values, and norms are a product of environment, development has a cultural aspect as well. Almond has defined political culture as a "set of attitude-cognitions, value standards and feelings towards the political system, its various roles, and role incumbents. It also includes knowl-

Source: John P. King, "Socio-Economic Development and the Incidence of English Corrupt Campaign Practices," in A.J. Heidenheimer, ed., *Political Corruption*, pp. 379–90. By permission of author.

edge of, values affecting, and feeling towards the inputs of demands and claims into the system and its authoritative outputs."[2]

It is contended in this article that within nineteenth-century England there were two political subcultures—preindustrial and industrial.[3] The existence of the two political subcultures was a product of the rapid but spasmodic urban, industrial, and intellectual development of the country. It is not argued that these two political subcultures were diametrically opposed. Nor is it argued that the degree of difference between them was as great as that between the three continental political subcultures. Indeed, it may be that one was the logical development from the other. Colin Leys has argued that in nineteenth-century England no new set of ideas or political conduct was introduced, rather an established set was adapted.[4] Nonetheless, it is contended here that there were two different, if related, subcultures, with distinctive attitude differences toward the political system and the actors within it.

The older preindustrial, political subculture encouraged the continuation of certain predemocratic forms of political persuasion. Little emphasis was placed on the need for a dynamic state. There was little point within this subculture, therefore, for the development of the mandate, for the political party possessing a platform, or for program-oriented campaigns. The franchise was a piece of property. The purpose in voting was to satisfy a social better or to acquire a material reward. "According to the previously obtaining moral code many of these practices were not corrupt. Either they had no moral significance or indeed they were actually right and desirable. For instance the average landlord thought it quite natural, and to that extent desirable, that his tenants should use their votes on behalf of his favoured candidate, and did not hesitate to put pressure on them to this end. Treating and other colourful political practices of the period were practiced with an openness that shows that they were not regarded as improper by those whose opinions mattered."[5] It encouraged the continuation of an old style of political persuasion.

On the other hand, the new emerging political subculture, a product in part of the Enlightenment and urbanization, emphasized the creativity of the state. It encouraged the formulation of arguments; it encouraged the discussion of ideas. It implied that elections were occasions during which rational and informed citizens decided between competing programs. The voters' preference was dependent not upon the exertion of pressure or upon the offer of a bribe, but upon an appraisal of party platforms at public meetings or in the seclusion of one's house. It led, therefore, to the emergence of a new style of political persuasion.

During the nineteenth century the socialization of voters into the new political subculture rapidly increased. The process was still not completed, however, at the end of the century. Trade unions, chapels, friendly societies all instilled into their members the virtues of listening, discussing, and voting. Gladstone himself was most impressed by the behavior of the Amalgamated Society of Engineers and the Lancashire Cooperative Society.[6] This period saw, too, a significant increase in the literacy rate. Popular radical newspapers emphasized the use of the vote as a means of gaining social and economic reforms, not as the method of acquiring beer or a £1 note. Many of the newly enfranchised voters in 1832 as well as 1868 had thus already obtained the norms and values of a commercial and industrial century. Wraith and Simpkins argue that this is of considerable importance in explaining the change in the style of political campaigning.[7] Old voters, who voted before 1832 and who lived for the most part in the stagnant areas where the new political subculture had not really penetrated, were only partly socialized into its norms and techniques. They remained familiar with the older political subculture. They had played their parts in the old style of campaigning for many years—as spectators if not participants. They were unlearning the old as well as learning the new. Thus corruption can be expected more frequently in those areas with a high percentage of old voters.

This chapter argues that it was in the most rapidly developing constituencies that elections became the rational choice between competing programs. It is suggested that corruption occurred most frequently in the small stagnating boroughs "uncleansed" by population increase or by the influx of new voters, representative of the emerging industrial and commercial classes.

Source of Data

The statistical analysis is based on the alleged cases of corruption presented in election petitions arising from English borough constituencies, with the exception of London, between 1832 and 1885. All forms of corruption have been included in the general tables. There were, however, insufficient occurrences of the exertion of "undue influence" or the use "of intimidation" to permit individual analysis. Petitions were presented by a losing candidate, either to claim the seat or to force a new election. Sometimes, if both sides had been guilty, no petition was made. Occasionally in mid-century, because of the high cost involved, agreements were made between the parties to withdraw a certain number of petitions. On a few occasions petitions were presented with little evidence, in the hope of persuading the victors to come to a more acceptable arrangement, such as sharing the membership of a two-member borough. Such practices, however, became less frequent as the costs of the petitions became the responsibility of the petitioners. Sometimes the existence of corruption did not lead to a petition since both sides were equally "guilty," and neither could afford the cost of the hearing.

Until 1868, petitions were heard by a five-man committee of the House of Commons. Thus, frequently in giving judgment they split on party lines and were motivated by party consideration. After 1868, petitions were heard by a specially constituted court before an appointed High Court Judge. Even then, the failure of a petition did not necessarily imply that corruption had not occurred. Often it had, but the corrupt influence could not be associated with the candidate. Agency had not been proved. It is probable, therefore, that during the period from 1832 to 1885 the presentation of a petition, rather than its result, indicated the existence of corruption. Petitions as used in this article do not differentiate between extensive and limited corruption.

Despite these reservations, however, and bearing such modifications in mind, election petitions are a suitable corpus of material for an analysis in depth of electoral practices in England. Indeed, if a statistical analysis is to be attempted, petitions are the only suitable material. They do provide, if not a systematic measure of corruption, at least a barometer of the incidence of corrupt practices. They illustrate where such practices were rife and the type of constituency most liable to be affected. Hanham accepts them as the best index of corruption in England.[8] Petitions were a mirror through which was reflected an image of the electoral scene. The absence of corruption reflected the adoption of a more modern style of political persuasion—one in which the vote preference was the result of an association between voter and party and in which the target of the campaign was the group rather than the individual.

Size of Electorate

Although size of the electorate is an indication of development, it is the least satisfactory of those used in this chapter. Some old, well-established cities were very large, such as Bristol and Liverpool; whereas some growing industrial towns, recently merely villages, were as yet of moderate size. Bolton and Blackburn are two examples. However, it has been argued that size was the most important determining factor in the adoption of a style of political campaigning.[9] (See Table 15.1.)

For the earlier period, it is apparent that size had little systematic effect upon the style of persuasion adopted. This conclusion was also reached by Young.[10] Although in part no doubt due to the existence of proprietary boroughs, the tabulated figures indicate nonetheless that factors other than mere size were of more importance in the determination of a constituency's electoral style.[11] Although the revealed pattern is more predictable, such a conclusion is valid for the later period as well. (See Table 15.2.)

Population Growth

During the period from 1832 to 1867, the English borough population increased by 150 percent.[12] However, the increase was by no means consistent throughout the nation. Some towns expanded by as much as

Table 15.1
SIZE OF ELECTORATE AND THE INCIDENCE OF BRIBERY AND TREATING, 1832–1867

Size of Electorate	Percentage of All Constituencies	Percentage of Constituencies Where Bribery Was Alleged	Difference in Proportion	Percentage of Constituencies Where Treating Was Alleged	Difference in Proportion
3000+	13	6	— 7	15	+ 2
1500+	19	28	+ 9	30	+11
550+	33	41	+ 8	25	— 8
0–549	35	25	—10	30	— 5
N		88		39	

SOURCE: The returns in Great Britain, Parliamentary Papers, Vol. 1, LVII (1866).

Table 15.2
SIZE OF THE ELECTORATE AND CORRUPTION, 1868–1884

Size of Electorate	Percentage of All Constituencies	Percentage of Alleged Corrupt Cases	Difference in Proportion	Percentage of Alleged Corrupt Constituencies	Difference in Proportion
5000+	30	26	—4	24	—6
4000+	24	28.5	+4.5	31	+7
0–3999	46	45.5	—0.5	45	—1
N		136		58	

SOURCE: Compiled from Martin, "A Review of the Working of the Representative System," *The Journal of the Royal Statistical Society*, XLVII (1884), pp. 95–103.

400 percent, others even declined. Obviously, population growth has
some merit as an index of development. Industrialization is usually
accompanied by an increase in the birthrate as well as by migration to
the industrializing areas.[13] A rapidly expanding town was more likely to
be indicative of developing England than a stagnating one. Such
growing towns were not merely industrial boroughs. Some were dormi-
tory areas serving the new middle classes; others were coastal resorts,
such as Brighton and Hastings. Consequently, industrialization led not
merely to the development of gloomy and dirty towns, but also to the
growth of suburbia and coastal resorts. All such towns were part of the
developing England. Most had grown from mere villages, others from
out of the plains and valleys. They owed their growth to the new forces
that inspired the Industrial Revolution. Rapidly growing boroughs
were not representative of the rest of stable, stagnant England. Even
towns that had an existence in the eighteenth century, were liable if
growing fast to be transformed by the influx of migrants and the
emergence of the industrial and social classes. It is in towns, therefore,
that the newer style of political persuasion should have taken root.
Hence in them the incidence of corruption should have been minimal.
(See Table 15.3.)

To some extent the hypothesis is supported. The least corrupt
constituencies were those expanding most rapidly. Therefore, it is
probable that a relationship between this aspect of development and
corruption did exist.

Turning to the later period, the results are extremely interesting, and
at first sight a little perplexing. (See Table 15.4.)

The least rapidly expanding constituencies were those affected by
corruption. The existence of proprietary boroughs is no doubt in part
the explanation. It has been shown that such boroughs were for the
most part stagnating or even declining as far as population growth was
concerned.[14] Bearing in mind such important reservations, it is possible to conclude that there was in all probability throughout the years
from 1832 to 1885 a causal relationship between corruption and development as measured by the rate of population growth. However, it is
also probable that population growth was not the aspect of development most significant in the determination of the style of political
persuasion adopted.

Class Structure

From a study of the 1861 census it is possible to compute the class
structure for most constituencies. Part of this census outlined the class

Table 15.3
POPULATION GROWTH AND CORRUPTION, 1832–1867

Percentage of Population Growth	Percentage of All Constituencies	Percentage of Alleged Corrupt Cases	Difference in Proportion	Percentage of Alleged Corrupt Constituencies	Difference in Proportion
85+	19	12	− 7	12.5	− 6.5
20–84	38.5	51	+ 12.5	56.25	+ 17.75
0–19	42.5	37	− 5.5	41.25	− 1.25
N		145		80	

SOURCE: Compiled from Martin, and Great Britain, Parliamentary Papers, Vol. LVII (1866).

Table 15.4
POPULATION GROWTH AND CORRUPTION 1868–1884

Percentage of Population Growth	Percentage of All Constituencies	Percentage of Alleged Corrupt Cases	Difference in Proportion	Percentage of Alleged Corrupt Constituencies	Difference in Proportion
41+	27	32	+ 5.	29	+2
11–40	43	48.5	+5.5	47	+4
0–11	30	19.5	−10.5	24	−6
N		135		58	

SOURCE: Compiled from Martin.

structure of all the Poor Law districts in England, dividing the population into six classes.[15] They were: professional, domestic, commercial, agricultural, industrial, indefinite, and nonproductive. The domestic class included not only domestic servants, but also artisans such as engine drivers. By adding the domestic and industrial categories, it is possible to obtain a percentage of the male population aged twenty and above in the working class. This can be computed for all Poor Law districts. While there is not a complete correlation between Poor Law districts and borough constituencies, the similarity in the boundaries is sufficient to give a reasonably accurate picture of the class composition within each borough. Where the constituencies were predominantly working class, the incidence of corruption should have been less than the normal in other boroughs. A vast majority of the population should have possessed a political subculture that tended to see the state as a vehicle for the transformation of society. Hence, elections should not have been occasions to make a little money out of voting the right way, but opportunities for placing into Parliament members committed to a particular program.

Table 15.5 indicates a trend in the direction expected. It confirms the hypothesis that a particular type of class structure in a constituency facilitated the adoption of the more modern style of electoral persuasion. However, its significance is not such as to warrant the assertion that class determined the style of persuasion used.

Proportion of New Voters

Possibly the most suitable indication of development is the proportion of new voters within a constituency after the 1832 Reform Act and the 1867 Reform Act. Not only is this a socioeconomic measure insofar as it is related to population increase and the class structure, it also has cultural significance. Most of the voters enfranchised in 1832 were from the commercial and industrial middle classes; a few were artisans. The 1867 bill granted the franchise to the majority of the urban working class, certainly to most of the artisans. Socially, as indicated above, these classes were undeniably part of the developing England. They wanted program-focused, issue-oriented elections. Many of the artisan class and "shopocracy" were members of trade unions, cooperative societies, friendly societies, and chapels. Some had read radical newspapers. Some had even participated in, or been influenced by the Chartist movement. Gwyn suggests that, "as this political awakening of the masses took place, and the voter began to value his suffrage as a lever of political power rather than as a privilege for picking the candidate's pocket, corruption became outmoded and gave way to democracy."[16] Most importantly, few of the new voters had gained experience of the old style of political persuasion through participation in elections. Therefore, few had gained direct familiarity with the norms and mores of the old political subculture. Hence, such voters were not torn between the attitudes and values of the developing England, of which they were a part, and those of the older England, to which many old voters irrespective of class or location had become addicted. A large percentage of new electors should have facilitated, then, the adoption of the modern style of electoral persuasion. Those constituencies—still with a large proportion of old voters aware of the

Table 15.5
CLASS STRUCTURE AND CORRUPTION, 1832–1885

Percentage of Working Class	Percentage of All Constituencies	Size 5000 + Percentage of Corrupt Constituencies	Difference	Percentage of All Constituencies	Size 4999 − Percentage of Corrupt Constituencies	Difference
76 +	22	14	−8	10	12	+2
75.9 −	5.5	6	+0.5	62.5	68	+5.5

monetary gains derived from elections—should have remained affected by the techniques of persuasion associated with the old style.

It is apparent from Table 15.6 that there was a significant relationship between the decline of corruption and the proportion of new voters. The exhibit strongly suggests that in those boroughs in which the old electorate was reinforced by a group of new voters possessing different experiences and attitudes, the old political style was replaced to some considerable extent by the new.

Table 15.7 confirms the impression gained from a study of Table 15.6. An influx of new voters unfamiliar with the practices and unaffected by the attitudes and mores of the old political subculture paved the way for the emergence of the new style and for the end of corruption.

The conclusions of these two tables can be reinforced by studying the behavior of those constituencies enfranchised in 1832. (See Table 15.8.) None of these constituencies had been participants in the old political style, although a few of their electors might have voted in the county elections.

Table 15.6
PERCENT OF OLD VOTERS AND CORRUPTION, 1832–1867

Percentage of Old Voters	Percentage of All Constituencies	Percentage of Alleged Corrupt Cases	Difference in Proportion	Percentage of Alleged Corrupt Constituencies	Difference in Proportion
A (50+)	34	54	+20	46	+12
B (25–49)	16	16	0	17	+ 1
C (0–24)	50	30	−20	37	−13
N		149		82	

SOURCE: Great Britain, Parliamentary Papers, Vol. XLIV (1837), as checked against Great Britain. Parliamentary Papers, Vol. XXVII (1833).

Table 15.7
PERCENT OF OLD VOTERS AND CORRUPTION, 1868–1884

Percentage of Old Voters	Percentage of All Constituencies	Percentage of Alleged Corrupt Cases	Difference in Proportion	Percentage of Alleged Corrupt Constituencies	Difference in Proportion
51+	20	27	+ 7	27	+7
31–50	50	56	+ 6	51	+1
30	30	17	−13	22	−8
N		136		58	

SOURCE: Compiled by comparing the electorate in 1865 as found in Great Britain, Parliamentary Papers, Vol. LVII (1866) with the electorate in 1871 as reported in A. Ellis, "The Parliamentary Representation of the Metropolitan, Agricultural, and Manufacturing Division of the United Kingdom with Suggestions for Redistribution," *The Journal of the Royal Statistical Society,* Vol. XLVI (1883), pp. 84–89.

Table 15.8
DATE OF ENFRANCHISEMENT AND BRIBERY, 1832–1867

Date of Enfran- chisement	Percentage of All Constituencies	Percentage of Alleged Cases of Bribery	Difference in Proportion	Percentage of Alleged Corrupt Constituencies	Difference in Proportion
1832	20	8	−12	10	−10
Prior to 1832	80	92	+12	90	+10
N		88		60	

Corruption, then, declined partly as a result of the expanding size of the electorate, partly as a result of population growth, and, most importantly, in proportion to the percentage of new voters in each constituency. However, even in some of the most rapidly developing parts of England corruption tended to linger. Gloucester was a developing city. It was both a port and a railway center. It possessed industry as well, and nonconformity was strong. In many ways it was representative of the developing England. It had long been a city, however, and for many centuries it had been a parliamentary borough. Tradition and growth were combined. Over the years a style of political persuasion had developed in conformity to the norms and values of the old political subculture. So strong was this tradition that, despite nineteenth-century development, corruption remained a feature of Gloucester's elections throughout the century.[17]

Carlisle also was an expanding town and was also predominantly industrial. For many centuries it had been a city of considerable importance. The old and new, therefore, coexisted in Carlisle. Petitions were regularly presented alleging corruption. The coming of the Midland Railway Company merely intensified endemic corruption.[18]

Party Organization

The growth of the political party was itself a factor in the decline of corruption, but not of supreme importance. Indeed, it was both a cause and an effect of the adoption of the new style of political persuasion. The post of party manager became increasingly important in the early years of the Victorian era. During this period, however, the party managers' influence was not exerted against corrupt practices. Their task was to find suitable candidates for each constituency. They were as much concerned with introducing rich men to constituencies of dubious tradition as with finding suitable men for the new industrial boroughs.[19] Moreover, they were not averse to becoming involved in corrupt practices themselves. At Sudbury and Ludlow the liberal manager was proved to have personally bribed voters.[20] In the early period party headquarters did little toward replacing the old style of political persuasion in those areas dominated by the old political subculture. In the larger towns, where registration was so important, it did encourage the local parties to become organized and efficient.

Thirty years later, in 1867, party organizations began again to expand rapidly. With the increase in the electorate, organization both at the center and in the constituencies became more important. Nonetheless, the control of the central office was limited. Feuchtwanger summed up its influence as follows: "The chief scope of the central organization after 1870 lay chiefly in the large towns, while there was little it could do in the counties and smaller boroughs, where the methods of an earlier stage of electioneering still prevailed."[21] However, the 1833 Corrupt Practices Act, with its increased penalties for corruption, led to a more active assertion of central control against corruption. O'Leary suggests that the 1885 election was the first to be dominated by the national and local party organizations.[22] Nonetheless, even in the elections of that year, the effectiveness of the central offices was restricted. In certain areas they could not prevent the continued dominance of local families or industries. Nor could they, therefore, control the style of political persuasion adopted. Pelling has shown that during the last years of the century, corruption continued to dominate political life in at least ten boroughs.[23] Party organization was, then, not so much a vital factor in the elimination of corruption in the old system as a means of facilitating the adoption of the new style in the developing areas.

Candidates, too, exerted some pressure for the elimination of bribery and treating. One estimate of the cost of the 1880 election was that it was twice as expensive as any previous contest.[24] Hence, in Parliament many members were enthusiastically behind suggestions for the reform of electoral practices. The Ballot Act of 1872 introduced the secret vote. Henceforward the briber was less certain of a return on his money. The Corrupt Practices Act of 1883 also contributed to the decline of bribery. By limiting election expenses and increasing the penalties hitherto outlined in the Corrupt Practices Act of 1854 it made bribery less attractive than before. By making the central party organizations responsible for the conduct of elections in the constituencies, it placed the whole weight of the party machines against corruption.

Overall Development and Corruption

Perhaps the best way of further validating the central argument of this article is to compare the incidence of corruption in a constituency with its score on a composite index of development. The three variables—size of electorate, proportion of new voters, and population growth—measure different but nonetheless important and complementary aspects of development. Of the three it was suggested that the sociocultural variable—the proportion of new voters—was the most important. It measured class to some extent and was based on the behavioral or participant pattern of the electors. Hence, in compiling the combined index of development it has been weighted slightly heavier than the other two aspects. Constituencies with the highest proportion of new voters have been awarded four points; those in the middle category, three; and those in the lowest, two. Thus, in the earlier period, Manchester, with almost 100 percent new voters, scored four; Liverpool, with under half the electorate new voters, obtained three; and Bristol, with less than a quarter of its voters newly enfranchised, scored two. In the other two variables the most developed constituencies scored three; the middle group, two; and the least developed, one. The proportion of the electorate in the working class as measured by the 1861 census had not been used in the compilation of the index. It is felt that as class is somewhat involved in the proportion of new voters, to include it as an extra component of the index would be to overweight the class aspect. Thus the index ranges from four to ten. From this it can be seen that the most highly developed constituencies would total nine or ten. In the earlier period, for example, Manchester, Birmingham, and Bradford obtained ten; Leeds and Liverpool scored nine. At the other extreme, Lichfield scored five, and Bridgenorth obtained four. The constituencies scoring the highest totals should be those in which the new style of political persuasion had developed and corruption had declined.

It is apparent from Table 15.9 that for the period from 1832 to 1867 the hypothesis is valid. There is a relationship between the scores on the index of development and corruption. Indeed, a perfect step pattern emerges. This illustrates that the more highly developed the constituency, the less likely it was to be still dominated by the old political subculture and thus addicted to the old style of political persuasion. However, no clear step pattern emerges for the 1868 to 1884 period.

Types of Corrupt Acts

So far, corruption has been considered in general terms. However, corruption took many forms. A necessary refinement in the analysis is to compare the incidence of different types of corruption with the stage of development reached by the constituencies. This is especially

Table 15.9
THE INDEX OF DEVELOPMENT AND CORRUPTION, 1832–1867

Category Score on Index	Percentage of All Constituencies	Percentage of Alleged Corrupt Constituencies	Difference in Proportion
(9 and 10)	10	5	−5
(7 and 8)	32	30	−2
(6)	29.5	30	+0.5
(4 and 5)	28.5	35	+6.5
N	176	80	

	1832–67	1868–85
No. of Petitions	125	99
Bribery	86	49
Treating	39	50

valuable because it can be shown that certain categories of corruption are more compatible with modern democratic practice than others.

Under the Corrupt Practices Act of 1854 bribery was defined as any form of persuasion in which financial gain was suggested by one person to another with the intention of influencing a person's vote.[25] Thus it included not only the payment of a simple bribe, but also the payment of excessive traveling expenses and the payments to excessive election workers. Such cases as these have been excluded from the analysis of bribery in this article but included of course in the overall total of corrupt instances. Payment of excessive traveling expenses was more often than not an action that reinforced an apathetic supporter's intention to vote. Therefore, it was not usually an inducement aimed at changing the voter's vote preference. The same could be argued about the employment of excessive messengers by the parties. The omission of such cases as fall into these categories permits bribery to be accepted as a practice typical only of the old style. In the case of bribery, not only is persuasion income channeled, but the attitude of the voter to his vote preference is commercial. Bribery usually was made possible by the entry of strangers into the borough. Voters would be approached in public houses and at home. They would be offered financial rewards if they voted for the right candidate. Such work was undertaken by strangers to make it more difficult to prove agency. Bribery, too, usually occurred under cover: it was known to be illegal and was considered undesirable. Bribery was considerably facilitated by the open voting system and by the extended duration of the poll.

Bribers could see the voter's choice made; and the voter could delay voting until the last desperate hours. Sir Lewis Namier has argued that the existence of bribery, as distinct from the exertion of undue influence or intimidation, illustrated the independence of the British elector.[26] It might do this, but it was an independence within the old style. Within the new style, independence is revealed by the ability of the voter to make a rational choice between competing programs.

Treating was defined as "the indirect or direct offer, or promise of an offer of any meat, drink or entertainment."[27] It included both the provision of drinks and excessive or delayed contributions to charity. It included, too, the provision of facilities such as slipper baths or clock towers for the constituency as a whole. Much difficulty centered around defining the time prior to an election at which such marginal activities as supporting the local hospital should cease. Hence, some types of treating do not need a small electorate and an open ballot to be effective. Not all forms of treating were aimed at an individual. However, treating does not conform to the norms of the modern style of political persuasion. On the other hand, many members of parliament found treating of a communal nature absolutely essential if they were to retain their seats. Many members, especially from locally well-connected families, believed that contributions to local charities, the poor, and organizations in the locality wre gifts expected from men of their station and not inducements to vote. Thus Parliament was not so hostile to treating during the 1870s as to bribery.

O'Leary noted that election petitions after 1867 increasingly cited treating rather than bribery.[28] From the figures below, taken from petitions arising from English borough constituencies outside London, O'Leary's point is quite clearly substantiated.

	1832–67	1868–85
No. of Petitions	125	99
Bribery	86	44
Treating	39	50

These figures definitely indicate a move in the direction expected. It is apparent that treating was replacing bribery as the more common form of corruption, especially in the more developing parts of the country—the boroughs.

Such a conclusion is reinforced and refined by a comparative analysis of bribery and treating with the Index of Development. (See Table 15.10.)

It is noticeable that the most highly developed constituencies in the

Table 15.10
INDEX OF DEVELOPMENT, BRIBERY, AND TREATING, 1832–1867

Category Score on Index	Percentage of All Constituencies	Percentage of Corrupt Constituencies	Difference in Proportion
	Bribery[a]		
(9 and 10)	10	3	−7
(7 and 8)	32	33	+1
(6)	29.5	28	−1.5
(4 and 5)	28.5	36	+7.5
	Treating[b]		
(9 and 10)	10	5	−5
(7 and 8)	32	28	−4
(6)	29.5	33	+3.5
(4 and 5)	28.5	33	+4.5

[a] N = 88   [b] N = 40

early period (1832 to 1867) were more afflicted by treating than by bribery. Also, the least developed constituencies were more likely to be affected by bribery than by treating.

Conclusion

From the analysis of election petitions arising from English boroughs (except London) it is noticeable that a relationship between development and corruption does exist. In particular, the analysis has shown that the most highly developed constituencies refrained more from corrupt techniques of political persuasion. Electoral campaigns in these constituencies approximated more closely to the norms and values of modern democratic practice. Beneath the highest level of development the pattern is not as clearcut. Except in the most developed areas, the correlation between the campaign practices adopted and development was not so apparent. It must therefore be concluded that other interesting factors were of importance. Of these the participation experience, or past behavior of electors, was of most significance.

At first, the new style of political persuasion was limited to those areas conducive to its growth. Legislation and party could do little to speed its influence into hostile territory. In the last quarter of the nineteenth century, however, the new style increasingly influenced elections, even in the areas least suitable for its adoption. The development of a concerted move to wipe out corruption started after the 1867 Reform Act. Deriving partly from the new political subculture, and partly from the new circumstances created by "development," this movement was responsible for the legislation attacking corruption. More importantly, it was responsible for its vigorous enforcement. By the turn of the century, then, the new political style had become the normative one used in English elections. Corruption was almost extinguished. The new political style had become not merely a part of the developing England, but had increasingly become the style adopted throughout the country. The speed at which it spread, especially after 1868, was quite outstanding.

Notes

1. H.J. Hanham, *Elections and Party Management: Politics in the Time of Disraeli and Gladstone*. London: Longmans, 1959.
2. G.A. Almond and J.S. Coleman, *Politics of the Developing Areas*. Princeton, N.J.: Princeton University Press, 1960, pp. 27–28.
3. Within these two substitutes, there were a variety of attitudes, many of them peculiar to a particular town—London, Liverpool, or Leicester. Hence the existence of borough cultures.
4. C. Leys, "What Is the Problem about Corruption?" *The Journal of Modern African Studies*, 3, 2 (1965), p. 227.
5. C. Leys, p. 226.
6. G.M. Young and W.D. Handcock, eds., *English Historical Documents*, XII. London: Eyre and Spottiswoode, 1956, p. 168.
7. R. Wraith and E. Simpkins, *Corruption in Developing Countries: Including Britain until the 1880s*. London: George Allen and Unwin, 1963, p. 168.
8. H.J. Hanham, p. 262.
9. H. Pelling, *Social Geography of British Elections*. New York: St. Martin's, 1967, p. 428.
10. G.M. Young and W.D. Handcock, eds., p. 114a.
11. For an examination of proprietary boroughs, see H.J. Hanham, p. 411.
12. J.B. Martin, "A Review of our Representative System," *The Journal of the Royal Statistical Society*, 47 (1884), p. 113.
13. A. Redford, *Labour Migration in England 1800–1850*. Manchester: Manchester University Press, 1926, p. 165.
14. John P. King, "An Analysis of Corrupt Campaign Practices in English Boroughs 1832–1884" (Unpublished Master's thesis, University of Florida, 1964), pp. 61–63.
15. Great Britain, "Appendix," *Census Report 1861*, pp. 128–135.
16. W.B. Gwyn, *Democracy and the Cost of Politics*. London: The Athlone Press, 1962, p. 92.
17. Great Britain, Parliamentary Papers, 58 (1880).
18. Great Britain, Parliamentary Papers, 8 (1847–1848).
19. N. Nash, "F.R. Bonham: Conservative Political Secretary 1832–1847," *The English Historical Review*, 42 (October 1949), pp. 511–14.
20. C. O'Leary, *The Elimination of Corrupt Practices in British Elections 1868–1911*. New York: Oxford, 1962, p. 18.
21. E.J. Feuchtwanger, "J.E. Gorst and the Central Organization of the

Conservative Party, 1870–1882," *Bulletin of the Institute of Historical Research,* 33 (November 1959), p. 199.
22. O'Leary, p. 18.
23. H. Pelling, p. 49.
24. T. Lloyd, *The General Election of 1880.* New York: Oxford, p. 128.
25. G.M. Young and W.D. Handcock, p. 145.
26. Sir Lewis Namier, *The Structure of Politics at the Accession of George III,* 2d ed. New York: St. Martin's, 1957.
27. G.M. Young and W.D. Handcock, p. 146.
28. C. O'Leary, p. 202.

16

The Development of Political Corruption in Israel

Simcha B. Werner

The developmental and structural-functional schools in political science of the 1960s gave birth to the revisionist approach to political corruption. The revisionists departed from the traditional school of political thought, which regarded political corruption as an important factor in social decay, and instead classified it as a "functional dysfunction."

Cost-benefit analysis is central to the revisionist approach, and four functional propositions relevant to this discussion have been identified:[1]

(a) *Economic Market Propositions*. Corruption brings with it a wider range of economic choices by encouraging foreign investment and strengthening the private *vis-à-vis* the public sector. It is, therefore, a means of bypassing cumbersome, genuinely hampering, governmental economic regulations.[2]

(b) *The Integrative Function*. Corruption allows citizens access to public officials and thereby fosters the integration of immigrant or parochial groups.[3]

(c) *Institutionalization Initiative*. Either corruption encourages institutionalization and party-building,[4] or an honest merit-oriented and incorruptible bureaucracy hampers the rise of political leadership.[5]

(d) *Administrative Advocacy*. Corruption brings flexibility and humanity to rigid bureaucracies.[6] It may also serve to increase the calibre of public servants because corruption brings with it opportunities for supplemental income which may counterbalance incentives within the non-governmental job market.[7]

Source: Simcha B. Werner, "The Development of Political Corruption: A Case Study of Israel," *Political Studies*, 31 (1983), pp. 620–39. By permission of author and publisher.

The revisionists accepted as axiomatic that corruption is by now restricted to non-western nations undergoing political modernization and development. The corollary of the axiom was that "corruption as it strengthens parties and political institutionalization . . . undermines the conditions of its own existence', and, 'once the process of political modernization is completed, corruption inevitably will wither away."[8]

In the 1970s, research in political science indicated that the phenomenon of corruption was endemic globally. These studies shattered the functionalists' claims about the benefits of corruption to the developing countries, and about the alleged "built-in" self-destruct mechanism of corruption. Instead, it was argued, corruption is an instrument of under-development.[9] In the fully-developed countries of the West, corruption not only manifests dysfunctional aspects, but also permeates a variety of social institutions; it becomes systemic. Thus, this research has led to a post-functional approach to the study of political corruption.[10]

At present, however, this new literature is an inconsistent *corpus* of descriptive studies. New definitions as well as a methodology for comparative analysis were not developed, nor was a theory of corruption. As a result, various dimensions of corruption are still unexplored. One such problem is the lifecycle of corruption. If corruption is not doomed to self-destruct with the completion of the maturation process, then what are the dynamic societal forces that allow it to prevail? If corruption thrives even in developed democratic countries, which proclaim ethical principles and presumably demonstrate rather high levels of political institutionalization, bureaucratization, and civil law and order, then what permits corruption to continue?

Thus, the next stage in the study of political corruption must be to determine what effect, if any, political development and modernization, as well as other societal factors, which are not necessarily developmental in nature, have upon the development of the phenomenon. By such effort, it may be possible to develop a theory which will explain the actual dynamics whereby old norms are transformed and new norms of corruption evolve, and identify what kinds of norms these will be.

It is obviously impossible for a single study to focus upon all aspects of corruption on a global basis. A more prudent course is to concentrate upon the life-cycle of corruption in a country now achieving the final stages of political modernization. Such a country would possess sufficient political institutionalization to evidence corruption while retaining many of the norms of the premodern stage.

Israel provides an excellent example for this study, for it is a country achieving modernization. Moreover, modern Israel history exemplifies relevant political processes. Over the short span of 50 years, political and organizational changes have rapidly occurred as the early Jewish settlers of Palestine—Israel's immediate historical antecedent—have coped first with Ottoman corruption, then British imperial politics and finally their own national government. For these reasons, then, Israel is the focus of this study of the life-cycle of corruption.

Embryonic Corruption: The Period of Foreign Rule

Perhaps the most important characteristic of Ottoman government in Palestine from the middle of the nineteenth century to its final demise in 1917 was the unbridgeable gap between the formal/external outlook of the central administration and its informal/internal practices of the *satraps*. As often as the Turkish sultans initiated reform, local officials prevented its implementation. Not even the Young Turks Revolution of 1908, which succeeded in effecting numerous reforms within Turkey itself, eradicated bureaucratic corruption in the territories.

The Turkish system of government was a "proprietary state."[11] This view of office combined with systemic nepotism and the form of Levantine extortion known as *baksheesh* constituted a way of life. Ottoman Palestine thus bore a distinct resemblance to historical Europe, where capitalism involved "the granting by the state of privileged opportunities for profit."[12] Unprofitable activities were left to indigenous religious and charity organizations, which gradually assumed responsibilities usually reserved for official government by supplying a variety of services to their constituents. Such "limited" government was further limited by the utilization of two unique systems of self-government, namely: the *Millet* and the *Mukhtars*.

Since the middle of the nineteenth century, some non-Moslem entities in the empire were recognized by the Turkish government as a *Millet*. (While in its original Arabic it means a "religious community," in Turkish it usually denotes a "nation.") Such communities were granted considerable autonomy in internal religious and socio-cultural matters. Jews were organized along the lines of the *Millet*, and gradually they extended the principles of religious and cultural autonomy far beyond Turkish intentions. Toward the end of Ottoman rule in Palestine, the Jewish community operated an intensified and diversified set of institutions that delivered a variety of religious, social, cultural, welfare and technical services. In 1909, Jewish Peace Tribunals (Mishpat Shalom Ivri) were created in response to the inefficiency and corruption of Turkish courts.

Contact between the Arab Palestinian villagers and the central government was maintained by a "conveniently undefined and indefinite"[13] network of *Mukhtars*, native elders who represented their rural communities before Ottoman officials.

The combination of the *Millet* system of self-government with that of the *Mukhtars*, not only helped to lessen an already lessened government, but also reduced contact between the official Ottoman authorities and their constituents. The major contacts with the corrupt Turkish officials were left to the representatives of the *Millet* communities and the *Mukhtars*. While a small *baksheesh* was a daily routine for low rank officials, the more black types of bribery were 'reserved' for the respected representatives of the communities. Nepotism and the buying of officials and offices were exclusively reserved for the *effendis*, members of a dominant Arab upper-class, who, being the landlords, possessed both the economic means and the political influence to use the proprietary state to achieve their own ends.

For the early Zionist leaders, confrontation with the corrupt and autocratic Turkish officialdom was niether unexpected nor new. Many of these leaders spent their formative years under similarly corrupt Tsarist Russian and East European regimes where pogroms, social deprivation and prejudice produced hostile conditions of survival that led to circumventing the law. But, in Palestine, their moral dilemma became more acute, for Palestine was, in their eyes, to become again their homeland and was to be turned into a "laboratory of Utopian social experiments."[14]

The bulk of the Zionist new immigrants came to Palestine in pursuit of social equality and idealistic values. They were an élite group: "Instead of the fleshpots of America, they chose the desert . . . Instead of individual escape, they chose the collective ideal . . . Instead of middle-class careers, they chose to become peasants and manual workers."[15] Toward the end of the Ottoman domination of Palestine, the Jewish community became a diverse assortment of various groups (Ashkenazi and Sephardic Jews, Zionist new immigrants and non-Zionists who lived for generations in holy Jewish cities like Jerusalem, Hebron, Tiberia, and Sefat) who, with few exceptions, subsisted on philanthropy. Such an assortment was made homogeneous only by poverty. Thus, idealistic values combined with poverty denied both the wish and the means to corrupt.

In terms of political development, Jewish political parties entered their embryonic stage only when Britain was given the mandate over Palestine in 1922 and mass immigration of Jews began. Party machines were then quickly established to absorb the newcomers. The conditions which would allow patron-client relations to develop were then, for the first time, created in Palestine.

Political Institutionalization, Integration, and Civil Order during the British Mandate

The British governments of Palestine (first military and then civil) were quick to introduce a western model of bureaucracy based on structural hierarchy, formal and impersonal relationships with its clients, merit-oriented personnel administration and an intensive code of laws and regulations, which forbade and punished acts of administrative corruption. Simultaneously, Britain imposed a strong central government in Palestine. Because the Arab Palestinians were slow to develop political institutions at the national level, and because local government was their political stronghold, it is not surprising that Arab Palestinian officials were critical of such centralization policies. They accused the British Mandatory Government of "robbing" the municipalities of many of their prerogatives, of the "abrogation" of municipal powers and of "crippling" their sources of revenue.[16]

The case of the Jewish sector was markedly different. While semiautonomous Jewish organizations were allowed to develop at the local level under the *Millet* system, it was not until Britain was given the League of Nations mandate over Palestine that semi-autonomous Jewish national organizations were encouraged. This was due both to the avowed purpose of the mandate to secure the establishment of a Jewish national home, and to the subsequent increase in Jewish immigration. This led to the evolution of a national administration, the Jewish Agency, deriving its legal authority from Article 4 of the mandate. The Jewish agency gradually assumed increasing responsibilities, often replacing the official British administration in promoting social and economic modernization of the Jewish sector. But the demand for increasing national self-government did not proceed uncriticized:

> The demand for autonomy in every matter carries us too far. It separates us from the life of the state. . . . Thus we proceed to establish institutions which should in reality, be maintained by the government and which we ourselves shall never be able to support, institutions which exist not on the basis of healthy economics of governmental income but on philanthropy. The income of the government, in which our share is very large . . . is being spent for the benefit of the rest of the population . . . The government becomes accustomed to view us as a strange child which needs not to be taken care of.[17]

Political institutionalization assumed a three-tiered structure. An Elected Assembly was constituted by universal suffrage and convened for special purposes; a National Council Plenum served as the framework for a permanent parliament; and a National Council Executive took responsibility for implementing the decisions of the elected bodies.[18]

Until the mid-1930s, none of these developmental activities required corruption as a functional catalyst. This was due in large part to the unique Palestinian Jewish social values and the relatively egalitarian structure of the Jewish community. The Zionist immigrants who continued to arrive during the 1920s and until the mid-1930s were driven by idealistic impulses and were, for the most part, highly educated. A common idea among them was *"avodah shechora"*—hard and dirty labor. Waging a social revolution, teachers, lawyers and physicians paved roads, drained malarial swamps and performed all the functions necessary to rebuild their homeland. Such national aspirations, idealism and egalitarian values inhibited materialistic demands and paved the way for the social and political integration of the *Yishuv* (the Hebrew term for the pre-independence Jewish community in Palestine). Several other factors further fostered integration, rendering corruption unnecessary as an integrative mechanism:[19]

(1) The need for effective representation *vis-à-vis* the mandate government;
(2) The need for national institutions to control the dissemination of resources, capital and personnel;
(3) The recognition of the need to compromise in order to maintain intact the strength of the whole;
(4) The concentration of Jews in cities, which weakened the urban-rural rivalry common to developing countries; and,
(5) The existence of well-organized substructures (*kibbutzim* and *moshavim*; types of collective settlements) which generated social innovations, and served as a source for élite recruitment and political mobilization.

Thus, the revisionist premise that corruption fosters political development and aids the integration of disaffected and potentially excluded parochial groups or immigrants was not evident in the *Yishuv* Jewish polity in the same way it perhaps was in other developing countries.

Advocates of the functionality of corrupt bureaucracy have argued in parallel that an honest, merit-oriented and incorruptible bureaucracy cripples economic development,[20] and hampers the growth of a party system and political leadership of a developing nation.[21] Braibanti[22] suggests that, if Pakistan had not inherited an honest, efficient, and incorruptible British civil service, there might have been a better opportunity for the growth of a political party system. In contrast to other developing countries, the case of Israel is again markedly different for two reasons. First, the evolution of a Jewish polity and bureaucracy took place parallel to, and external from, the British government and bureaucracy, so that functional political growth occurred independently of the dominant British bureaucracy, corrupt or not. Secondly, unlike the British central bureaucracy, the Jewish administrative body evolved on a non-Weberian basis. It did not endeavour to emulate the parallel and external British bureaucracy, which stressed formal regulations and rigid hierarchical structures. The Jewish bureaucracy "coped." It was open and willing to yield to the demands of its clientele. Jewish institutions stressed *"kol Yisrael chaverim"*—all Israelis are friends. In the long run, this spirit gave rise to that brand of Israel borderline corruption known as *"protekzia,"* upon which this study will elaborate in a moment.

The rise of the Nazis prompted a new wave of Jewish immigration to Palestine. Between 1932 and 1939, about 225,000 new immigrants arrived, most of them from Poland and Germany "to give the final stamp of Western character to the new Yishuv of Palestine."[23] Many of them (particularly the German Jews) possessed both financial means and professional expertise which quickly helped to create the nucleus of a private enterprise sector and "laid the foundation for the economic take-off of the Jewish community in Palestine."[24] In the long run, capitalism planted the very first seeds of social polarization and economic inequality which serve as a major cause of corruption.[25]

The new waves of immigrants of the 1930s and the 1940s fostered political institutionalization through party machines. Immigrants made few demands upon central government; rather, they came to rely upon the machines.

> In the pre-state period, an immigrant's first stop upon arrival would often be his local party branch headquarters. He lived in a party-affiliated . . . block of flats. He found employment through the party labor exchange. His children were educated in party-controlled schools. He read the party newspaper. When sick, he lay in a party-dominated hospital, and recuperated in a party convalescent home. He played football on the party soccer team.[26]

As party-client relations intensified on a personal level, so members of the evolving capitalist class came to resort to these machines for influence and subcontracting. But, until 1948, political clientelism still remained embryonic, for the machinery of a national government was not yet available. It was still vested in the hands of the British who, during the 1930s, first implicitly and then explicitly abandoned their support of the Jewish homeland. The effects of such a shift of imperial policies upon security, civil order, and law obedience in Palestine were, apparently, insurmountable.

In his study of the breakdown of public security in Ireland and Palestine, Tom Browden[27] has shown how Arab riots against Jews in 1936 were the immediate cause of a breakdown in civil order. British partisanship in support of the Arabs was displayed even by British judges. This partisanship had severe repercussions on both government and security. On the one hand, Arab *Fellahin* (mass peasants) who were active in brigand bands against the Jews or the mandate interpreted British officials' behavior as a "sympathy with their cause and tactics."[28] On the other hand, British police "had been demoralized by conflicting loyalties."[29] The Arab section of the police had disintegrated almost completely and had become little more than an easy source of supply of rifles and ammunition for the rebels. Circumvention of the law in the name of the national interest also became increasingly flagrant within the Jewish sector as a response to British behavior.

> Although the Jews in Palestine lived in a state of physical insecurity, their self-defense organization was never legalized . . . Similarly, the rescue of Jews from European massacre was made an illegal act. Once again the Jews could only protect their lives and save some of their kin by circumventing the law. British rule, instead of being a school of democracy, became a school of conspiracy.[30]

It is important to note that this patriotic circumvention of the law did not present a moral dilemma to the *Yishuv*, because British law and policies came to be regarded as being both alien and arbitrarily imposed.

In sum, under the Turkish and later under the British, corruption did not play a significant role in the development of the Jewish polity. Rather, as has been demonstrated, the unique characteristics of self-government, idealistic values and socio-economic homogeneity limited corruption. But the changing conditions of the 1930s produced the seeds of political clientelism, *protekzia* and patriotic corruption that survived the transition from Palestine to Israel.

The Development of Corruption: The Period Between 1948 and 1967

Between Independence and the Six Day War, Israel underwent a massive process of modernization and integration. These produced favorable conditions for the development of corruption.

Political Integration, Clientelism, and Protekzia

After the establishment of the state of Israel, new waves of Jewish immigrants altered the more homogeneous Western character of the pre-state Jewish society. Between 1948 and 1962, over half of the 1,100,000 new immigrants to Israel came from Asian and African countries. These Oriental Jews had high birthrates, high levels of illiteracy, unskilled professions and strong kinship ties. It was not unusual for them to continue to perceive themselves, not as citizens, but as subjects, recognizing and not necessarily endorsing a higher authority.[31] They did not have a democratic tradition but, instead one which stressed Middle East bargaining and *baksheesh*.[32]

The announced goal of the state was to convert mass immigration into mass democratization through fostering social, cultural and economic integration. However, the political potential of the new immigrants was quickly discovered by all political parties. Lacking democratic traditions and bureaucratic socialization, and saddled with poor economic standing, poor housing and poor employment conditions, these Oriental immigrants were more susceptible to and more dependent upon the political machines than were the European immigrants. Networks of political clientelism, often bordering on political corruption, thrived between political parties and the immigrants. New immigrant votes became a commodity, transferred to the highest political bidder.

Ben-Dor[33] observed, however, that the patronization of these immigrants did not necessarily lead to their integration within the Israel polity. Access to the centers of influence was monopolized by exclusive small groups, whose members had the means to corrupt and be corrupt. This selectivity increased the alienation of the new immigrants.

Protekzia, which originated in the *Yishuv* and expanded during the 1950s, became accessible to these immigrants as part of the process of assimilation.

Protekzia has been defined as the "management of influence,"[34] a "political tool for bypassing bureaucracy";[35] and the management of informal contacts and exchange of favors to bypass bureaucratic procedures:[36] "In colloquial Hebrew, the concept has been narrowed to exclude all reference to graft, bribery or exchange of money—thus including only the exchange of non-monetary favors and activation of non-normative objectives."[37]

Studies of the socialization of *protekzia* have produced somewhat contradictory results. Danet found in the late 1960s that Jews of North African origin, where the system has been traditionally functional, now attach more negative than positive values to *protekzia*. However, while European Jews still disparage the practice, they nevertheless continue to follow it. A later study done by Nachmias and Rosenblum[38] showed that bureaucratic socialization in Israel is gradually giving rise to the attribution of negative values to *protekzia*. Socializing the Israelis against *protekzia* is slow, not only because of the prevalence of the system and its utility, but also because agents of socialization, such as parents, teachers and leaders, cannot teach values which they themselves have not incorporated. Also, the more society becomes materialistic, the more incentives there are to abuse political and bureaucratic trusts, and the greater the fear that the boundaries of the favors will change.

Administrative Regulation Versus Informal Practices

The immediate needs of the newly established state—surviving the War of Independence, the subsequent reorganization of the Israeli Defense Force, the economic recession and rationing, and the massive waves of new immigration in the early 1950s—all precluded a rational transition from quasi-national organization to national government.

It was not until 1950, two years after the establishment of the state, that the Israel Civil Service Commission was inaugurated under the auspices of the prime minister's office. Three years later, jurisdiction was transferred to the powerful finance ministry. The civil service was immediately confronted by personnel and ideological problems. Although screening procedures were established, a manpower shortage made it necessary to admit into the bureaucracy some workers who had been tainted by corruption while working in the pre-state Jewish Agency administration or in the British civil administration.

During the first few years, various informal practices from the pre-state Jewish institutions had penetrated into the political parties, into local government and, to a lesser degree, into the newly established Israeli civil service. The pre-state Jewish institutions not only used to "cover up" corrupt behavior, but also assumed responsibility for trying, sentencing and punishing the perpetrators, through internal courts regulated informally.[39] This informal system of justice differed from the Soviet and Chinese systems of community justice. In the Communist countries, social pressure was used to rehabilitate the offender. In the Israel model, the offense itself was secondary to the maintenance of organizational prestige. Often, the cover up was a result of yielding to pressures from powerful labour unions.

Idealistic corruption also led to leniency toward pecuniary corruption. Levi Eshkol, the late prime minister of Israel, when questioned about a corrupt official, replied with a quotation from Deuteronomy (25:4): "Thou shalt not muzzle the ox when he treadeth out the corn." Indeed, in Israel, when bureaucratic regulation was introduced, it had only an external resemblance to western standards. Internally, structures and behavior remained informal. It was accepted that Israelis were difficult to govern.

The general disregard of the Israelis for administrative laws, together with a generally negative attitude (although gradually changing for the better) toward state bureaucracy and bureaucratic procedures, are perhaps the key reasons for the poor enforcement of administrative regulations and procedures. For an eastern European Jewish immigrant, a bureaucrat is a *Tchinovnik* (a civil servant under Tsarist regime): "He must be corrupt. He must be hostile. He is the enemy of the people."[40] Similar attitudes developed among Jewish refugees from the autocratic regimes of Asia and North Africa. Survival in such hostile environments necessitated circumvention of the law. This attitude found its counterpart in the belief that certain ideas are superior to law. The attitude was reinforced by Jewish experience that respect for any law was mitigated by weak enforcement mechanisms. Survival and philosophy toward state and law gave rise to the Israeli concept of *"le'histader"*—to take care of yourself.

> *(Le'histader)* is the Israeli password through the maze of authority, the thicket of law, the confines of impersonal regulations. Regulations are 'objective' and thus theoretically just; but the needs of the individual, his private concepts of right and wrong, are superior. The average Israeli recognizes few regulations of universal applicability. In his dealings with the authorities he invariably demands, firmly and loudly, exceptional treatment.[41]

Lack of Consistent Control

Although it is common to attribute to Israeli government machinery a high level of centralization, in practice the public enterprise sector, and also to some degree the local government system, are often free from consistent external control, resulting not only in administrative and economic inefficiencies, but also in cases of irregularities and corruption.

During the 1950s and 1960s, the government enterprise system was rapidly expanded to cope with ambitious economic projects, and the ministry of finance adopted the policy of seeking greater economic efficiency by allowing government corporations a greater degree of commercial and administrative freedom. Soon, these companies acquired sufficient power to be relatively independent of government control. The state comptroller had only limited ability to subject administrative inefficiencies to public and political scrutiny or to impose their correction. Because the state comptroller's office was chronically short of manpower, each state company was subject to controls only once every five years, on average. This gradually contributed to excesses of power in state companies, which after 1967 had been quite often abused for private gains. As a result, a long overdue State Companies Act was passed in 1975 designed to increase the accountability of state-owned-enterprises.

Similarly, in the local government, irregularities and corruption grew, primarily during the aftermath of the Six Day War. A number of reasons contributed to the gradual deterioration of morality and bureaucratic order in the local government machinery of Israel. Amongst these were the weakness of the state comptroller: political and bureaucratic opposition to the introduction of an internal city comptroller; and the one-party dominance of municipalities, which often retarded the formulation and exercise of adequate political and control mechanisms.

Thus, a lack of consistent control is a key reason why the two networks of public enterprise and local government gradually became more vulnerable to the scandals of irregularities and corruption which erupted in the late 1960s and the 1970s.

Deepening of Social Inequality

The influx of Oriental Jews into Israel during the 1950s caused significant changes in the social stratification of the country. Using the Lorenz Index,[42] social inequality in Israel increased from 0.220 in 1950 (as compared, for example, with 0.320 in the United States) to 0.330 in 1959 and to 0.360 in 1967. In 1953, a sample of 450 families living in Jerusalem in a new neighborhood, comprising a heterogeneous population of immigrants, showed that 56 percent of the North Africans and 68 percent of the Iraqis belonged to the lower class as compared with 26 percent of East European immigrants and 18 percent of other European countries. Other contributing factors to the increase of social inequality were non-progressive taxation on products which weakened the effect of progressive taxes; the existence of a special system of fringe benefits available only to white-collar employees and which (until 1975) were not officially included in taxed income; and economic recession and high unemployment during the years 1966 and 1967.

Thus Israel has followed the pattern suggested by contemporary research in that socio-economic or political inequalities have stimulated the development of corruption.

Inhibiting Factors on Corruption: Idealism, Egalitarianism, and National Insecurity

While the previous analysis has pointed to various factors that have helped to create murky political and administrative ethics, idealism, egalitarian philosophy and national insecurity have served as safeguards. The spirit of the early Zionists, drawn from Biblical thought, from the modern Hebrew renaissance and from contemporary East European socialism,[43] blossomed in the years following the War of Independence. Massive efforts at nation building, economic scarcity and rationing during the early 1950s, and a hostile political environment all contributed to a national spirit of idealism, of working for the benefit of all and of denying the material and physical pleasures of life.

The civil service was to become a vanguard of such idealistic notions. In 1964, a government commission (Horowitz Commission) had recommended the creation of a "uniform wage structure" in the civil service, proclaiming the principle of "equal pay for equal work." But changes in the wage structure were soon thwarted by powerful and restless unions that opposed the idea of wage uniformity. They argued that professional uniqueness requires unique compensation structures. Egalitarian values became a myth of the past, and workers waged a war against the artificial imposition of such values. In order to satisfy employee demands, the Israel government gradually formulated policies to bypass the rigid and egalitarian wage system. Improvements *(hatavot)* were introduced to increase the income of professional civil servants. The basic wage structure remained intact. People who never owned a car were provided with vehicle expenses, and office workers received hazardous duty allowances. Unskilled workers were given funds for "professional literature." The government, anxious to avoid bureaucratic unrest, chose to circumvent its own wage structures rather than adapt them to a more materialistic society.

While these changes originated in official policy, civil servants themselves began to emulate them. What apparently began prior to the Six Day War was a white, petty type of administrative corruption, that was rationalized, condoned and allowed to prevail. A few examples will suffice.

One example that borders on corruption is the artificial padding of overtime work. This system prevails primarily in local government, where high officials approve excessive overtime hours for devoted workers, or for workers with large families. The padding of the actual number of overtime hours now characterizes the entire Israeli public sector wage system.

Also, individual civil servants abuse their authority and increase income by padding various reports concerning their expenses (meals, travel allowances and accommodation expenses). The gaps between position and remuneration are also often narrowed by the petty abuse of privileges, by luxurious dinners, presents, vacations, all paid for by contractors seeking "clean bypasses" to influence over official decision-making.

Another example of white corruption that originated in the 1960s and prevails in Israel is petty bribery. The most common illustration of this is the custom of "bottles basket," where civil servants, at all administrative levels, receive a present of a basket of bottles from their clients. The giver sees it as a means of establishing favour or receiving preferential treatment. Today, because of the prevalence of this type of bribery, even the courts have found themselves in an embarrassing position. Although they are aware of the negative side they have difficulty in passing judgment upon such a widely-condoned custom. The Israeli Civil Service Commission, which has again and again emphasized that these "presents" are forbidden by law, has found itself quite helpless in weeding out this practice.

A brief theoretical analysis of the dynamics of the dimensions of corruption now seems both timely and necessary.

Dimensions of Corruption: The Dynamics of White Corruption

In 1970, Heidenheimer[44] introduced a litmus test by which identification of corruption becomes possible. Corrupt behavior can be judged to be black, grey, or white, depending upon the perception by both the public and public officials. Agreement between the two groups that a specific "bad" action would be either condemned and punished, or condoned and unsanctioned, led to the classification of either black or white corruption, respectively, whereas areas of disagreement were classified as grey corruption. Heidenheimer argued that grey corruption is the most destructive to a democratic political system because the public and its representatives are either ambivalent towards corrupt behavior, or unconcerned with its restrictions.

Peters and Welch[45] next categorized a corrupt act according to its four components: the donor, the recipient, the favor and the payoff. Corruption will be perceived as limited when the recipient, if he/she is a public official, acts as a private citizen; when a constituent pays a public official as opposed to the official "putting his hand in the till"; when the favor to be performed is a routine of the job, or benefits the public as opposed to a private interest, or serves a constituent rather than a nonconstituent; and when the payoff is small, long range, general (such as an unspecified, future electoral consideration), or in the form of support rather than money.

These two classification systems of the dimensions of corruption are useful, but they are also too general and static, failing to elucidate the mechanism(s) by which corrupt acts change in intensity.

The salient characteristic of white corruption is its being a petty borderline type, which neither the public nor public officials regard as being punishable. Often it does not clearly and totally violate the law. While every codex of law will define corruption, it also "carries the seeds of its own neutralization"[46] because it does not account for extenuating circumstances.

More than any other type of crime, petty corruption involves a "denial of injury"[47] in that it asserts the pettiness of the act. Within an organization, potential "whistle-blowers" usually remain silent, not because they are intimidated, but because they feel their action would be quixotic. As petty corruption becomes the norm for individuals, the organization itself begins to rationalize and neutralize it.

Because of this rationalization of white corruption, and because of the system's failure to determine when corruption becomes destructive, the formulation and enforcement of control strategies are severely limited. Left unchecked, white corruption becomes a growth industry. When a corrupt act is regarded as being innocuous, that act is removed from previous definitions of corruption. The acceptance of white corruption as being "legitimate" will, in turn, tend to spill over to perceptions of other types of corruption. The grey and black shades become progressively lighter, and a momentum is established.

This premise will now be illustrated by the case of Israel after the Six Day War. As will be shown, the rationalization and trivialization of white corruption, coupled with socio-economic changes that began to crystallize after the Six Day War, combined to allow corruption to mature.

Maturation of Corruption: 1967 to the Present

After the Six Day War of 1967, the euphoria of victory lifted national self-confidence and induced individuals to "turn their attention to personal goals that had long been postponed."[48] The period between

1968 and the Yom Kippur War of 1973 was one of full employment and unprecedented prosperity. It was also a period of boom years for Israeli contractors who capitalized from the vast government expenditures on military build-up and civil settlements in the Sinai, West Bank and the Golan Heights. In the short run, full employment and a somewhat artificial economic boom produced some positive results. The Lorentz inequality coefficient temporarily went down from 0.377 in 1968 to 0.298 in 1972. In the long run, materialism grew. The elders complained about the decline of idealism; past values of *halutziut* (a Biblical term which means "to vanguard") and *hitnadvut* (altruistic voluntarism) faded out and were quickly replaced by materialism and self-serving values.

Between 1967 and 1973, white corruption continued, along with some cases of major scandals in the state enterprises network. In 1969 black corruption in the form of embezzlement and fraud was found in *Netivei Neft*, the government-controlled, oil-producing company in Sinai. The scandal provoked public criticism, which reached its peaks when the then-powerful minister of justice first attempted to nullify public demands for a judicial investigation, and later when the huge legal fees he awarded to the attorney assisting the work of the inquiry were made known. Public outcry made the minister hand in his resignation, "an action unprecedented among Israeli politicians."[49] In 1972, bribery was discovered in the Amidar Housing Company, which is responsible for the distribution of apartments. This case clearly demonstrated how "*protekzia* without remuneration may degenerate into contacts between a briber and bribee . . . and that preferential treatment in return for money or another form of bribe had become a common phenomenon in Israel."[50]

The Yom Kippur War of 1973 itself seemed to be but the harbinger of bad times. National security was again questioned, immigration to Israel decreased while emigration increased, economic problems began to rage, and inflation soared to unprecedented levels. Israeli society became more consumer-oriented and the gap between desire and the means of its fulfilment increased. More white and even black corruption became a means of bridging the gap. Incentives for administrative corruption were particularly enhanced in Israel due to increasing gaps between salary and status, salary and rank, and salary and inflation.

Robert Price[51] introduces the salary-status gap in his study of Ghana's bureaucracy. Price argued that venality in Ghana closes the gap between the strong societal pressure on public officials to possess external symbols of status (as did their colonial predecessors), and the meagre salaries they receive. Although Israelis still expect their public officials to adhere to a traditional Jewish norm of modest behavior, a double standard is being created as the society itself is becoming more materialistic. Indeed, as will be shown, various scandals of the 1970s involving white-collar crime indicate that some adherence to modest behavior is observed domestically, but not when officials go overseas on public business and the predilection for luxury is not socially inhibited.

The salary and rank gap derives from the formation of an Israeli civil service based on an idealistic sense of mission and egalitarianism. Basic salary differentiation between the various administrative ranks is slight. This, and the increasing salary-inflation gap (the inflation rate now surpasses 100 per cent per annum) increase the needs of public officials to look for means of supplementing income. One such means is "moonlighting" which now prevails to such an extent in the Israeli public sector as to constitute a whole system by itself. Another means is petty corruption as well as the willingness to take the risks involved in black corruption. As Israelis continue to expect their public officials to be content with a meagre salary, while they themselves become more materialistic, the double standard that is created tends to erode even further the morality of civil servants.

In the 1970s, unprecedented white-collar crime and corruption ran rampant. Some examples will suffice:

1. In the summer of 1974, the general manager of the Israel-British Bank (IBB) was arrested for investigation for "huge discrepancies"[52] in bank records that eventually led to the collapse of the IBB. The losses, estimated to be over $40 million, had to be covered by the central Bank of Israel. Later, in September 1977, Menachem Begin, the newly-elected prime minister, became the center of controversy when he recommended a pardon for the manager of the defunct IBB. The manager, serving a prison term, had been the financial backer of the ultranationalist movement, which is ideologically close to Likud. On the grounds of severe sickness, Begin stressed forgiveness.[53]

2. In April 1975, a major new scandal erupted involving charges of bribery, price-fixing, falsifying bids and orders, and embezzlement by government high officials and defence contractors. The scandal raised questions about the extent of dubious practices that were prevalent between the 1967 and 1973 wars, boom years for defense contractors.[54]

3. Also in April 1975, the then general manager of Israel Corporation (a government-supported development corporation) was indicted and later on 9 May 1975, pleaded guilty to 14 counts of larceny, bribery, fraud and corruption involving estimated losses of over

$100 million. A vast proportion of the embezzled money was illegally transferred out of the country to the International Credit Bank of Geneva.[55]

4. In October 1976, the Israel political system was shaken by the arrest of the head of the huge Trade Union Sick Fund. The man was also then a nominee of the ruling Labor party for governor of the Bank of Israel. Approximately half a year later, after the charges had been made, the man admitted that real estate kickbacks had gone both to the Labor party's 1973 election campaign and to his own pocket.[56]

5. In April 1977, former Prime Minister Yitzhak Rabin was found to have violated Israel foreign currency regulations.[57] The resultant scandal forced Rabin to step out of the Labor government and resign as a Labor party candidate.

These scandals played a significant role in the defeat of the Labor party during the next election of 1977.[58]

Scandals and black corruption continued under the Likud government during the years 1980 and 1981. Court actions were lenient but public obloquy was intense.

In September 1979, the French government sought extradition of Samuel Flatto-Sharon, Israeli member of parliament who previously, as a French citizen, was allegedly involved in embezzling $60 million in fraudulent real estate deals during the 1960s and 1970s.[59] In the 1977 election, he formed his one-man political party, but later in 1981 was accused of bribing voters, sentenced to imprisonment and suspended from parliament.

In September 1980, the then minister of religious affairs of the National Religious party was summoned for police questioning concerning alleged kickbacks, bribery and corruption in the ministry of religious affairs. In May 1981, a court in Jerusalem acquitted him of charges of accepting kickbacks, but denounced his moral standards in dispensing grants from his ministry.[60] The trial evoked conflicts between the minister and the National Religious party. Subsequently, he established a new Sephardic (Oriental) list, which won three seats in the June 1981 election. In November 1981, as the new minister of immigrant absorption, he stood trial again on charges of theft, fraud and violation of public trust whilst he was serving as Ramle mayor from 1973 to 1977.[61] Later, in early 1982, he was found guilty. While the court was lenient (imposing a fine and a suspended sentence), public outrage led to his resignation as a minister.

These selected cases of corruption not only support the argument about the maturation of corruption in contemporary Israel, but also point to the role of leadership in shaping societal attitudes toward law and order. Leaders, by definition, are the paradigms of the body politic, and by their corrupt behavior they set an example which tends to erode the moral base of law and provides an opportunity for their followers to emulate and rationalize corrupt behavior. In Israel where, due to past developments, public regard for law and order still cannot be taken for granted, the corrupt behavior of leaders is particularly dangerous. Also, as exemplified by Levi Eshkol and Menachem Begin, the failure of leaders to condemn corruption serves to increase the spread of corruption.

Another deleterious aspect of leadership behavior can be observed in the Israeli machinery of local government, namely, local-patriotic corruption. If central government regulation stifles local productivity, then, Israelis reason, these regulations can be circumvented for the good of the locality. Mayors will use their personal influence to build an "important" city project even if, for example, the license or budget is not yet approved by the responsible, but cumbersome, central agencies.[62] In February 1982, the head of a local authority, who was also a member of the Israel parliament, made the following statement which evoked enormous public criticism: "I give bonuses to my employees whom I find performing a good job. I do it under the table. It is perhaps illegal, but that does not concern me."[63]

Patriotic corruption is not new to Israelis: it was committed by Jewish officials during the end of the British mandate, but then it was concealed. It has now resurfaced in Israel's local government and is committed more and more openly. It creates a fear that, if left unchecked, it will become a *modus operandi*.

Reacting to increasing pressures for higher wage compensation, the government itself continued to circumvent its own wage structures. Labor unrest in the air ports administration led to numerous strikes that paralysed Israel's international air communication. Afraid that yielding to the pressure for better salaries would lead to new demands from other unions in the civil service, the Labor government decided in 1976 to act by abusing the concept of the 'public corporation'. It was 'logical' to incorporate the air ports administration and, by doing so, to exclude both management personnel and the wage structures of the newly born Air Ports Authority from the umbrella of the civil service laws and regulation. This blunt policy was heavily criticized by the public. More significantly, it created a craze for incorporation: other professional unions (for example, workers of the Income-Tax Administration) sought incorporation of their relevant departmental agency.

Since 1977, when the Likud came to power, inflation has grown. The government continues to adopt policies designed to prevent the standard of living from falling. The historical peace treaty with Egypt has given the Israelis a new feeling of national security. Materialism has increased, whilst the idealistic values of the past have continued to fade. Artificial salary 'improvements' introduced by the Labor government have been conveniently adopted by the Likud government. The Israelis' disregard of law and order has not changed for the better, and the corrupt behavior of officials of high calibre sets a bad example for the common Israeli.

Nevertheless, the Likud government strives at changing some of the conditions that have allowed civil order to deteriorate. It began by launching an attack against organized crime. It has striven to tame powerful labor unions and to coordinate local government and state enterprises. Indeed, it seeks to become a central government in practice as well as on paper. On the other hand, it is getting more and more involved (after the June 1981 election) in personnel and contract political patronage, as well as in diverting accessible public funds to the religious parties that have the balancing power in the coalition. Because of other priorities, or perhaps because of a fear that the elimination of practices now bordering on white corruption may produce administrative chaos, these practices are left intact.

Furthermore, because of the failure of the system to determine when white corruption becomes destructive, and because of the acceptance of white corruption as being 'legitimate', other types of grey and black shades of corruption become progressively lighter and a further momentum is established. This self-perpetuating nature of white corruption, in addition to the other factors discussed above allow corruption in Israel to mature along with the maturation of the political system.

Conclusion

This study of Israel has demonstrated that political and bureaucratic corruption are not necessarily associated with political modernization. Neither is corruption doomed to destruction as a political system matures. Corruption alters its character in response to changing socio-economic, cultural and political factors. As these factors affect corruption, so does corruption affect them. Significantly, because corruption is in equilibrium, the concept of entropy is not applicable. Simply put, corruption may be controlled through alterations of its character but, most importantly, not destroyed. Corruption carries a dynamic mechanism that allows it to spill over and perpetuate itself. Such a corruptive mechanism is primarily evident in white corruption which is trivialized, condoned, rationalized, and which leads to a general sense of impunity, encouraging more insidious types of corruption.

In the pre-state period in Israel, corruption originated as a necessity. But after independence, corruption manifested dysfunctional aspects. It did not foster the integration of new immigrants and did not assist in economic development. White-collar crime of the post Yom-Kippur War manifested economic dysfunctionality almost entirely. Institutionalization of white bureaucratic corruption not only created an environment in which more serious types of corruption developed, but also blocked the process of bureaucratization. Also, political institutionalization was not necessarily affected by corruption, and corruption of the type of patron-client relations can thrive parallel or external to the level of political institutionalization.[64]

In terms of policy implication, the case of Israel has demonstrated that certain factors can inhibit corruption while political development is still enhanced, or can allow corruption to flourish while bureaucratic performance declines. When these factors are identified, it will be possible to begin to develop a multi-faceted effort to control corruption.

Notes

1. The classification is adopted from S. Werner, "New Directions in the Study of Administrative Corruption," *Public Administration Review*, 43:2 (March–April 1983), 146–54.
2. H.D. Bayley, "The Effects of Corruption in a Developing Nation," *Western Political Quarterly*, 19 (1966), 719–32; N.H. Leff, "Economic Development Through Bureaucratic Corruption," *American Behavioral Scientist*, 8(1964), 10–12.
3. Bayley, "The Effects of Corruption in a Developing Nation"; J. Scott, *Comparative Political Corruption* (Englewood Cliff, NJ: Prentice-Hall, 1972).
4. J.V. Abueva, "The Contribution of Nepotism, Spoils, and Graft to Political Development," *East–West Center Review*, 3(1966), 45–54; S.I. Huntington, *Political Order in Changing Societies* (New Haven, Conn.: Yale University Press, 1968); R. K. Merton, "Some Functions of the Political Machine," in R. K. Merton, *Social Theory and Social Structure* (New York: Free Press, 1957), 72–82.
5. R. Braibanti, "Public Bureaucracy and Judiciary in Pakistan," in J. LaPalombra (ed.), *Bureaucracy and Political Development* (Princeton: Princeton University Press, 1963); W.F. Riggs, "Bureaucrats and Political Development: A Paradoxical View," in J. LaPalombra (ed.), *Bureaucracy and Political Development*.
6. J. Nye, "Corruption and Political Development: A Cost Benefit Analysis," *American Political Science Review*, 61 (1967), 417–27.

7. Bayley, "The Effects of Corruption in a Developing Nation."
8. S. Varma, "Corruption and Political Development in India," *Political Science Review,* 13 (1974), 167.
9. D. Gould, *Bureaucratic Corruption and Underdevelopment in the Third World* (New York: Pergamon Press, 1980).
10. *On political dysfunctionalities* see: G. Benson, *Political Corruption in America* (Lexington: Lexington Books, 1978); S. Dasgupta, "Corruption," *Seminar,* 185 (1975), 194–300; J. Dobel, "The Corruption of a State," *The American Political Science Review,* 72 (1978), 958–73; T. Lowi, "The Intelligent Person's Guide to Political Corruption," *Public Affairs,* 82(1981), 1–6; S. Mamoru and H. Auerbach, "Political Corruption and Social Structure in Japan," *Asian Survey,* 17 (1977), 556–64; N. Marican, "Combating Corruption: The Malaysian Experience," *Asian Survey,* 19 (1979), 597–610; T. Smith, "Corruption, Tradition and Change," *Indonesia,* 71 (1974), 21–40; S. Varma, *Corruption and Political Development in India;* J. Waterbury, "Endemic and Planned Corruption in a Monarchical Regime," *World Politics,* 25(1973), 533–55.

On economic dysfunctionality see: G. Amick, *The American Way of Government* (Princeton, NJ: The Center for the Analysis of Public Issues, 1976); M. Goodman, "Does Political Corruption Really Help Economic Development: Yucatan, Mexico," *Polity,* 7 (1974), 143–62; F. McHenry, "Food Bungle in Bangladesh," *Foreign Policy,* 27(1977), 72–88; S. Rose-Ackerman, *Corruption: A Study in Political Economy* (New York: Academic Press, 1978); R. Tilman, "The Philippines Under Martial Law," *Current History,* 71 (1976), 201–25; H. Warren, "Banks and Banking in Paraguay," *Inter-American Economic Affairs,* 32 (1978), 39–55.

On bureaucratic dysfunctionalities see: G. Caiden and N. Caiden, "Administrative Corruption," *Public Administration Review,* 33 (1977), 301–8; P. Drucker, "What is Business Ethics," *The Public Interest* (1981), 18–36; O. Dwivedi, "Bureaucratic Corruption in Developing Countries," *Asian Survey,* 7 (1967), 245–53; J. Gardiner and T. Lyman, *Decisions for Sale: Corruption and Reform in Land-Use and Building Regulation* (New York: Praeger, 1978); L. Hager, "Bureaucratic Corruption in India: Legal Control of Maladministration," *Comparative Political Studies,* 6 (1973), 179–219; L. Sherman, *Scandal and Reform: Controlling Police Corruption* (Berkeley: University of California Press, 1978); N. Singhi, "Bureaucratic Corruption," *Administrative Change,* 2(1977), 34–47.
11. Scott, *Comparative Political Corruption,* p. 77.
12. Scott, *Comparative Political Corruption,* p. 52.
13. Bentwich, *England and Palestine,* p. 245.
14. A. Koestler, *Promise and Fulfilment* (London: Macmillan, 1949), p. 240.
15. Koestler, *Promise and Fulfilment,* pp. 244–5.
16. Omar Bey Salih Al-Barghuthi, "Local Self-Government—Past and Present," *The Annals of the American Academy of Political and Social Science,* 164(1932), p. 37.
17. D. Ismojik, *Bustna'i (Tel-Aviv Weekly), 15, 22 and 29 May 1929. Quoted in Burstein, Self-Government of the Jews in Palestine Since 1900,* pp. 281–2.
18. D. Horowitz and H. Lissak, *Origins of the Israeli Polity: Palestine Under the Mandate* (Chicago: University of Chicago Press, 1978).
19. D. Horowitz and M. Lissak, *Origins of the Israeli Polity,* p. 41.

20. LaPalombra, *Bureaucracy and Political Development.*
21. Riggs, "Bureaucrats and Political Development: A Paradoxical View."
22. Braibanti, *Public Bureaucracy and Judiciary in Pakistan.*
23. R. Patai, *Israel Between East and West: A Study in Human Relations* (Philadelphia: The Jewish Publication Society of America, 1953), p. 66.
24. Horowitz and Lissak, *Origins of the Israeli Polity,* p. 5.
25. J. Dobel, "The Corruption of a State."
26. Amos Elon, *The Israelis: Founders and Sons* (New York: Holt, Rinehart & Winston, 1971), p. 293.
27. T. Browden, *The Breakdown of Public Security: The Case of Ireland 1916– 1921 and Palestine 1936–1939* (London: Sage, 1977).
28. T. Browden, *The Breakdown of Public Security.*
29. T. Browden, *The Breakdown of Public Security,* p. 233.
30. A. Koestler, *Promise and Fulfilment,* p. 296.
31. D. Elazar, "Israel's Compound Polity," in H.R. Penniman (ed.), *Israel at the Polls: The Knesset Elections of 1977* (Washington, DC: American Enterprise Institute for Public Policy Research, 1979), pp. 28–33.
32. G. Caiden, *Israel's Administrative Culture* (Berkeley: University of California, 1970).
33. G. Ben-Dor, "Schitut, Misud Ve'itpatchut Politit," *Rivon Le'Mechkar Chevarati,* 5(1973), 5–21 Hebrew.
34. D. Elazar, "Israel's Compound Polity," p. 15.
35. D. Nachmian and D. Rosenblum, *Bureaucratic Culture: Citizens and Administrators in Israel* (London: Croom Helm Ltd., 1975), p. 95.
36. G. Caiden, *Israel's Administrative Culture,* p. 60.
37. Danet and H. Hartman, "On Protekzia: Orientations Toward the Use of Personal Influence in Israeli Bureaucracy," *Journal of Comparative Administration,* 3(1972), 407.
38. D. Nachmian and D. Rosenblum, *Bureaucratic Culture: Citizens and Administrators in Israel.*
39. Y. Reuveni, *Ha'Minhal Ha'ziburi Be'Israel* (Ramat-Gan: Massada, 1972). Hebrew.
40. A Statement of a Jewish witness before the *Palestine Royal Commission Report* (London; HMSO, 1937), p. 119. The page number refers to the 1946 reprint.
41. Elon, *The Israelis: Founders and Sons,* pp. 300–1.
42. On the Lorenz Index, absolute equality is indicated by a value of zero, and absolute inequality is indicated by a value of one.
43. *Palestine: A study of Jewish, Arab, and British Policies* (New Haven: Yale University Press, published for ESCO Foundation in Palestine, Inc., 1947), p. 349.
44. A Heidenheimer (ed.), *Political Corruption: Reading in Comparative Analysis* (New York: Holt, 1970).
45. J. Peters and S. Welch, "Political Corruption in America. A Search for Definition and Theory: Or, If Political Corruption is in the Mainstream of American Politics, Why is it not in the Mainstream of American Political Research?," *The American Political Science Review,* 72 (1978), 974–84.
46. D. Matza, *Delinquency and Drift* (New York: John Wiley, 1964), p. 60.
47. G. Skyes and D. Matza, "Technique of Neutralization: A Theory of Delinquency," *American Sociological Review,* 22(1957), 664–70.

48. H. Greenberg and S. Nadler, *Poverty in Israel: Economic Realities and the Promise of Social Justice* (New York: Praeger, 1977), p. 3.
49. Y. Elizur and E. Salpeter, *Who Rules Israel* (New York: Harper & Row, 1973), p. 86.
50. Y. Elizur and E. Salpeter, *Who Rules Israel,* p. 24.
51. R. Price, *Society and Bureaucracy in Contemporary Ghana* (Berkeley: University of California, 1975).
52. *New York Times,* 25 July 1974, 49: 7.
53. *New York Times,* 10 September 1977; 3: 1.
54. *New York Times,* 15 April 1975, 3: 1.
55. On the affair, see: *New York Times,* 9 April 1975, 12: 2; 10 April 1975, 41: 7; 14 April 1975, 1: 4; 8 May 1975, 5: 1; 10 May 1975, 8: 1; 22 May 1975, 4: 6.
56. On the affair, see: *New York Times,* 20 October 1976, 10: 3; 14 December 1976, 6: 3; 15 February 1975, 1: 1; 14 February 1975, 1: 1.
57. *New York Times,* 21 March 1977, 1:4; 8 April 1977, 1:6.
58. See M. Aronoff, "The Decline of the Israeli Labor Party: Causes and Significance," in H. R. Penniman (ed.), *Israel at the Polls* (Washington, D.C.: American Enterprise Institute, 1979), pp. 115–145.
59. *New York Times,* 9 September 1979, III, 3: 1.
60. *New York Times,* 26 May 1981, 5: 1.
61. *New York Times,* 9 August 1981; 2: 1; 23 November 1981, 6: 1.
62. On the mayor of Haifa see, *Ha'aretz,* 1 March 1982, 3; On the mayor of Tel-Aviv see, *Ha'aretz,* 10 October 1982, 8.
63. *Ha'aretz,* 2 February 1982, 9. Hebrew.
64. See Ben-Dor, "Schitut, Misud Ve'itpatchut Politit."

17

Corruption, Machine Politics and Political Change

James C. Scott

. . . Despite formal obstacles, there is one political form that has not only been able to respond to particularistic interests but has thrived on them—the urban "machine," a form that flourished in the United States around the turn of the century. Although now virtually extinct, the machine once managed to fashion a cacophony of concrete, parochial demands in immigrant-choked cities into a system of rule that was at once reasonably effective and legitimate.

The purpose of this study is to outline the contours and dynamics of the "machine model" in comparative perspective and attempt to show that the social context that fostered "machine politics" in the United States is more or less present in many of the new states. This is done by first sketching the general character of "machine politics," (2) then by suggesting a developmental model to account for the machine, (3) and finally by analyzing the decline of the machine in the United States. . . .

The Machine

To abstract the basic characteristics of a political machine obviously does some violence to the great variety of entrepreneurial talent that was devoted to creating this form. Nevertheless, as all but a few beleaguered machines have succumbed to the forces of "reform government" analysis has replaced accusation and the central features of most machines are reasonably clear.[1]

It will be recognized at the outset that the machine form can occur only in certain political settings. At a minimum, the setting of the machine requires:

Source: James C. Scott, "Corruption, Machine Politics, and Social Change," *American Political Science Review,* 63:4 (1969), pp. 1142–59. By permission of publisher.

1. The selection of political leaders through elections
2. Mass (usually universal) adult suffrage
3. A relatively high degree of electoral competition over time—usually between parties, but occasionally within a dominant party

These conditions reflect the fact that since machine politics represents a distinctive way of mobilizing voters, it arises only in systems where getting out the vote is essential to gaining control of the government. While these conditions are necessary for machine-style politics, they are by no means sufficient, as we shall see later.

Always applied to a political party in power, the term *machine* connotes the reliable and repetitive control it exercises within its jursidiction. What is distinctive about the machine, however, is not so much its control as the nature of the organizational cement that makes such control feasible. The machine is not the disciplined, ideological party held together by class ties and common programs that arose in continental Europe. Neither is it typically a charismatic party, depending on a belief in the almost superhuman qualities of its leader to ensure internal cohesion. Rather, it is a nonideological organization interested less in political principle than in securing and holding office for its leaders and distributing income to those who run it and work for it.[2] It relies on what it accomplishes in a concrete way for its supporters, not on what it stands for. A machine may, in fact, be likened to a business in which all members are stockholders and where dividends are paid in accordance with what has been invested.[3]

"Patronage," "spoils," and "corruption" are inevitably associated with the urban machine as it evolved in the United States. As these terms indicate, the machine dealt almost exclusively in *particularistic, material rewards* to maintain and extend its control over its personnel. Although pork-barrel legislation provided inducements for ethnic groups as a whole, the machine did most of its favors for individuals and families. The very nature of these rewards and favors naturally meant that the machine became *specialized in organizing and allocating influence at the enforcement stage.* The corruption it fostered was not random greed but was finely organized and articulated to maximize its electoral support.

Thus the machine is best characterized by the nature of the cement that binds leaders and followers. Ties based on charisma, coercion, or ideology were occasionally minor chords of machine orchestration; the "boss" might take on some heroic proportions: he might use hired toughs or the police now and again to discourage opposition; and a populist ideological aura might accompany his acts. For the machine such bonds were definitely subsidiary to the concrete, particularistic rewards that represented its stable means of political coordination. It is the predominance of these reward networks—the special quality of the ties between leaders and followers—that distinguishes the machine party from the nonmachine party.

Given its principal concern for retaining office, the machine was a *responsive, informal context* within which *bargaining* based on reciprocity relationships was facilitated. Leaders of the machine were rarely in a position to dictate; those who supported them did so on the basis of value received or anticipated. For the most part the machine accepted its electoral clients as they were and responded to their needs in a manner that would elicit their support. The pragmatic, opportunistic orientation of the machine thus made it a flexible institution that could accommodate new groups and leaders in highly dynamic situations. . . .

In the United States, the rapid influx of new populations for whom family and ethnicity were the central identifications, when coupled with the award of important monopoly privileges (traction, electric power, and so forth) and the public payroll, provided the ideal soil for the emergence of party machines. Developing nations can be viewed as offering a social context with many of the same nutrients. New governments had in many cases only recently acquired control over the disposal of lucrative posts and privileges, and they faced electorates that included many poor, newly urbanized peasants with particularistic loyalties who could easily be swayed by concrete, material incentives. The point each writer makes is not only that the machine is a suitable and relatively democratic political form that can manage such a complex environment, but that the social context typical of most new nations tends to encourage the growth of machinelike qualities in ruling parties. For America, Burnham has summarized the argument now being applied to less-developed nations.

> If the social context in which a two-party system operates is extensively fragmented along regional ethnic and other lines, its major components will tend to be overwhelmingly concerned with coalition building and internal conflict management. The need to unite for electoral [broad coalition building] purposes presupposes a corresponding need to generate consensus at what ever level consensus can be found.[4]

Given this sort of social context, so the reasoning goes, the price of effective political cooperation—at least in the short run—involves meeting narrow, particularistic demands, often through the patronage, favors, and corruption that are the hallmarks of machine politics. But why are other forms of association not feasible? What specific changes in the social context promote or undermine different styles of political collaboration? Unless the model is placed in a developmental perspective and considerably sharpened from its presently intriguing but impressionistic form, its explanatory value will remain limited.

Social Context of Political Ties

The schema presented in Table 17.1 focuses on changes over time in the nature of loyalty ties that form the basis of political parties. It is tailored to a bargaining—particularly, electoral—context and is less applicable where force or threats of force are the basis of cooperation. Nothing is intended to be rigidly deterministic about the movement from phase *A* to phase *B* to phase *C*. The phases are, however, largely based on the empirical experience of the United States, England, and the new nations.

Although the phases have been separated for the purpose of conceptual clarity, they are likely to overlap considerably in the empirical experience of any nation. It is thus a question of which loyalty pattern is most common and which less common. Within new nations all three patterns typically coexist: rural villagers may remain deferential to their traditional leaders; the recent urban migrants may behave more as free agents seeking jobs or cash for their votes; and a small group of professionals, trade union leaders, and intellectuals may perhaps be preoccupied with ideological or class concerns. Even fully industrialized nations may contain recalcitrant, and usually isolated pockets where deference patterns have not yielded to more opportunistic modes of political expression.[5]

Prior to fuller treatment below, a brief word is in order about the process of change implied by Table 17.1. Movement from phase *A* to phase *B* involves the shaking loose of traditional deference patterns, which can occur in a variety of ways. For the United States, large-scale immigration by basically peasant populations was often the occasion for this change, while for less developed nations the economic changes introduced by colonial regimes and rapid migration from village to city has provided the catalyst. The social disorganization that resulted was often exacerbated by ethnic, linguistic, or even caste fragmentation, but similar patterns have arisen in Thailand and the Philippines—for example, amid comparatively homogeneous populations. Elections themselves have, of course, played a central role in tis transformation because they placed a new political resource of some significance at the disposal of even the most humble citizens.

Table 17.1

PHASE A[1]	Political ties are determined largely by traditional patterns of deference (vertical ties) to established authorities. Material, particularistic inducements to cooperation play a minor role except among a limited number of local power holders.[2]
PHASE B	Deference patterns have weakened considerably in a period of rapid socioeconomic change. Vertical ties can only be maintained through a relationship of greater reciprocity.[3] Competition among leaders for support, coupled with the predominance of narrow, parochial loyalties, will encourage the widespread use of concrete, short-run, material inducements to secure cooperation. The greater the competitive electoral pressures, the wider the distribution of inducements is likely to be. Influence at enforcement stage is common.
PHASE C	New loyalties have emerged in the process of economic growth that increasingly stress horizontal (functional) class or occupational ties. The nature of inducements for political support are accordingly likely to stress policy concerns or ideology. Influence at the legislative stage becomes more appropriate to the nature of the new political loyalties.

1. The broad lines of this schema were suggested by an analysis of the use of money in elections contained in Arnold Heidenheimer, "Comparative Party Finance: Notes on Practices and Toward a Theory," pp. 790–811 in Richard Rose and Arnold Heidenheimer, eds., *Comparative Studies in Political Finance: A Symposium, Journal of Politics,* 25:4 (November 1963), especially pp. 808–809. Changes in the nature of political ties influence greatly the degree to which monetary incentives are successful in electoral campaigns, and I have thus borrowed from that analysis for the broader purpose of this study.

2. Traditional ties often allow some scope for bargaining and reciprocity; the ability of clients to flee to another jurisdiction and the economic and military need for a leader to attract and keep a sizable clientele provided subordinates with some leverage. The distinctions made here in the degree of reciprocity are relative, not absolute. See, for example, Herbert P. Phillips, *The Peasant Personality,* Berkeley, Calif. University of California Press, 1965, p. 89, or George M. Foster, "The Dyadic Contract in Tzintzunzan, II: Patron Client Relationships," *American Anthropologist,* 65 (1963), pp. 1280–1294.

3. What appears to happen in the transitional situation is that the client is less "locked-in" to a single patron and the need for political support forces patrons to compete with one another to create larger clienteles. For a brilliant analysis of this pattern in Philippine politics see Carl H. Landé, *Leaders Factions, and Parties—The Structure of Philippine Politics.* Monograph No. 6. New Haven, Conn.: Yale University—Southeast Asia Studies. 1965, throughout.

Movement from phase *B* to phase *C* would appear to depend on the process of industrialization as new economic arrangements take hold and provide new focuses of identification and loyalty. As the case of the United States illustrates, however, the presence of sharp ethnic and sectional cleavage—the latter reinforced by constitutional arrangements—may considerably dilute the strength of these new bonds.

The duration of phase B, when the social context is most hospitable to machine-style politics, may vary widely. When the social disorganization accompanying urbanization and economic change is particularly severe and of long duration, when it is compounded by deep cultural differences, and when competitive elections with a universal suffrage are introduced early, the pressures toward machine politics will be vastly greater than when demographic change is gradual and less severe, when it occurs with a minimum of cultural cleavage, and when the electorate is restricted. The historical circumstances of both the United States and most new nations have been, in this sense, quite conducive to the development of machine politics as opposed to, say, the Western European experience.

Inducements and the Nature of Loyalty

Political parties must generally offer inducements of one kind or another to potential supporters. The pressures to enlist adherents is obviously greatest when the party faces a competitive electoral struggle, but in the absence of battles for votes merely the desire to establish a broad following among the populace will create analogous pressures.

The sort of incentives most likely to "move" people is contingent, as the phase model clearly implies, on the kinds of loyalty ties that are most salient to the potential client. In the short run, at least, parties that need supporters are more apt to respond to the incentives that motivate their clientele than to transform the nature of those incentives. Elaborating on this relationship between loyalty bonds (independent variable) and party inducements (dependent variable), Table 17.2 suggests the actual empirical patterns that are likely to occur.

Table 17.2

NATURE OF LOYALTIES	INDUCEMENT
Ties of traditional deference or of charisma	Mostly symbolic, nonmaterial inducements
Community or locality orientation (also ethnic concentration)	Indivisible rewards; public works, schools, "pork-barrel" Communal inducements
Individual family, or small-group orientation	Material rewards; patronage, favors, cash payments, "corruption" Individual inducements
Occupational or class orientation	Policy commitments at tax law, subsidy programs, and soon "general legislation" Sectoral inducements

Parties in the real world commonly confront all four patterns of loyalty simultaneously and fashion a mix of inducements that corresponds to the mix of loyalties.[6] Inducements, moreover, are not unifunctional; public works usually carry with them a host of jobs and contracts that can be distributed along more particularistic lines while patronage can be wielded in such a way as to actually favor an entire community or ethnic group.

With these qualifications in mind, it is suggested that, given pressure to gain support, a party will emphasize those inducements that are appropriate to the loyalty patterns among its clientele. Material inducements are as characteristic of occupational or class loyalties as they are of local or family loyalties; what is different is simply the scope and nature of the group being "bribed" by the party, not the fact of "bribery." In the case of occupational and class loyalties, the inducements can be offered as general legislation (and rationalized by ideology, too), whereas inducements at the individual or family level must often be supplied illegally ("corruptly") at the enforcement stage.[7] The classical machine faces a social context in which community and family orientations are most decisive. Responding to its environment, the machine is thus likely to become consummately skilled in both the political distribution of public works through pork-barrel legislation and in the dispensation of jobs and favors through more informal channels.

Historically, the expansion of the suffrage, together with the rupture of traditional economic and status arrangements, has signaled the rise of particularistic, material inducements. In Robert Walcott's masterful portrait of electoral politics in eighteenth-century England, this transition is vividly depicted in the contrast between the shire constituencies, where traditional landholders still commanded the allegiance of a small electorate, and the larger urban constituencies, where elections

> were notoriously venal and turbulent. Wealthy beer-barons with hireling armies of draymen battled for the representation of Southwark: while the mass of Westminster electors were marshalled out, with considerable efficiency, to vote for candidates set up by the court.[8]

Southwark and Westminster, at the time Walcott describes them, were the exception rather than the rule, and English parliamentary politics revolved around coalitions of clique leaders, each of whom was generally accepted as the "natural" representative of his constituency. The transition, however, was under way. . . .

Changes in modal patterns of loyalty help account for not only the development of machine politics but for its decline as well. In addition to other factors (discussed later), the growth of political ties in which family bonds were less important than before and in which occupational and/or class considerations played a more prominent role undercut the very foundation of the machines.[9] The specific inducements that the machine was organized to supply worked their "magic" on an increasingly smaller proportion of party workers and supporters. Instead, as businessmen and laborers each came to appreciate their broader, more long-run interest as a sector of society, they increasingly required general legislation that met their interests in return for political support. Here and there a social context tailored to the machine style remained; but the machine either reconciled itself to the new loyalties—becoming less and less a machine in the process—or was the electoral victim of social change. Parties still continued to offer palpable inducements to voters, but the new inducements were more typically embodied in general legislation whereas previously they had been particularistic and often outside the law. As Banfield and Wilson summarize the transition.

> If in the old days specific material inducements were illegally given as bribes to favored individuals, now much bigger ones are legally given to a different class of favored individuals, and, in addition, general inducements are proferred in packages to every large group in the electorate and to tiny but intensely moved minorities as well.[10]

Ecology of Machine Coordination

The distinctive style of political coordination embodied in the machine has historically occurred in settings where, in addition to rapid social change and a competitive electoral system, (a) political power was fragmented, (b) ethnic cleavage, social disorganization or both were widespread, and (c) most of the population was poor. Drawn mostly from studies of urban machines in the United States, these features of the environment seem applicable to a large degree to the many underdeveloped nations in which political parties have begun to resemble machines.

Fragmentation of Power

In accounting for corruption and machine politics in Chicago, Merriam lays particular stress on the multiplicity of urban authorities and jurisdictions that existed within the city. He describes eight main "governments," each with different powers, which created so many jealously guarded centers of power that a mayor faced a host of potential veto groups, any one of which could paralyze him.[11] He could secure cooperation with these authorities only by striking informal bargains—often involving patronage, contracts, franchises—and thus putting together the necessary power piece by piece.

Power was fragmented in yet another sense. Party candidates did not face one electorate but several; each ethnic group had its own special interests and demands, and a successful campaign depended on assembling a temporary coalition on the basis of inducements suited to each group. The decentralization of power created by such a heterogeneous environment meant that the "boss's" control was forever tenuous. His temporary authority rested on his continuing capacity to keep rewards flowing at the acceptable rate.

New York in the era of Boss Tweed strikingly resembles Merriam's picture of Chicago. In spite of the prodigious manipulations attributed to him, Tweed was not especially powerful and had little control over party branches that could nominate their own candidates for many posts. What he did manage to do, however, was to create, for a time, a centralized, finely articulated coalition. Carefully assessing the nature of Tweed's feat, Seymour Mandelbaum declares,

> There was only one way New York could be "bossed" in the 1860s. The lines of communication were too narrow, the patterns of deference too weak to support freely acknowledged and stable leadership. Only a universal payment of benefits—a giant payoff—could pull the city together in a common effort. The only treasury big enough to support coordination was the public till.[12] . . .

Social Fragmentation and Disorganization

The immigrants who constituted the bulk of the clientele of the American urban machine came largely from the ranks of the European peasantry. They "required the most extensive acculturation simply to come to terms with urban-industrial existence as such, much less to enter the party system as relatively independent actors."[13] If the fragmentation of power made it advantageous for the politician to offer special inducements for support, the situation of the immigrant made him eager to respond to blandishments that corresponded with his most immediate needs. Machine inducements are thus particularly compelling among disoriented new arrivals, who value greatly the quick helping hand extended to them by the party.

The dependence of machine parties on a clientele that is both unfamiliar with the contours of the political system and economically on the defensive is underscored by the character of the small pockets where vestiges of once-powerful machines still exist. One such example is the Dawson machine (really a submachine) in Chicago. This machine rests squarely on favors and patronage among the Negro population, most of which has come to Chicago from the rural south within the last generation. Deprived of even this steadily diminishing social base, the machine has elsewhere withered as the populations it assisted became acculturated and could afford the luxury of wider loyalties and more long-range political goals.

It is no coincidence, then, that machines flourished during the period of most rapid urban growth in the United States, when the sense of community was especially weak, and when social fragmentation made particularistic ties virtually the only feasible means of cooperation. The machine bound its clientele to it by virtue of the employment, legal services, economic relief, and other services it supplied for them. "For the lower strata, in return for their votes, it provided a considerable measure of primitive welfare functions, personalized help for individuals caught up in the toils of the law, and political socialization."[14] . . .

Poverty

Perhaps the most fundamental quality shared by the mass clientele of machines is poverty. Machines characteristically rely on the suffrage of poor and, naturally, prosper best when the poor are many and the middle-class few. In America, Banfield and Wilson emphasized that "Almost without exception, the lower the average income and the fewer the average years of schooling in a ward, the more dependable the ward's allegiance to the machine."[15]

Poverty shortens a man's time horizon and maximizes the effectiveness of short-run material inducements. Quite rationally he is willing to accept a job, cash, or simply the promise of assistance when he needs it, in return for his vote and that of his family. Attachments to policy goals or to an ideology implies something of a future orientation as well as wide loyalties, while poverty discounts future gains and focuses unavoidably on the here and now.

The attitudes associated with poverty that facilitate machine-style politics are not just confined to a few urban centers in less-developed nations, but typify portions of the rural population as well.[16] In such circumstances, the jobs, money, and other favors at the disposal of the government represent compelling inducements. Deployed to best advantage, these incentives are formidable weapons in building coalitions or electioneering or both. The ease with which votes are bought—individually in many urban areas and in blocs where village or ethnic cohesion is sufficient to secure collaboration—during elections in the new nations is a measure of the power of narrow material rewards in the social context of poverty. . . .[17]

Notes

1. Some of the more successful efforts at careful description and analysis include: V. O. Key, Jr., *The Techniques of Political Graft in the United States*. Chicago, Ill.: University of Chicago Libraries, 1936; Seymour J. Mandelbaum, *Boss Tweed's New York*. New York: Wiley, 1965; Edward C. Banfield and James A. Wilson, *City Politics*. Cambridge, Mass.: Harvard University Press, 1965.
2. Banfield and Wilson, p. 116.
3. This analogy was made by former Liberal party president José Avelino of the Philippines in the *Manila Chronicle,* Jan. 18, 1949. Quoted in Virginia Baterina, "A Study of Money in Elections in the Philippines," *Philippine Social Sciences and Humanities Review,* 20:1 (March 1955), pp. 39–86.
4. Walter Dean Burnham, "Party Systems and the Political Process," pp. 277–307, in William Nisbet Chambers and Walter Dean Burnham, eds., *The American Party Systems: Stages of Political Development,* New York: Oxford, 1967, p. 287. Fragment in brackets mine.
5. In this context, party labels are deceptive. The existence of parties proclaiming an ideology or class position are often found in rural areas where the labels have been appropriated in toto in a continuation of traditional feuds between powerful families and their respective clienteles. The key is the nature of loyalty patterns, not the name of the organization. See Carlo Levi. *Christ Stopped at Eboli.* New York: Pocket Books, 1965.
6. The importance of one or another pattern can, in addition, be amplified or diminished by structural characteristics of the political system; in the U.S. federalism and local candidate selection tend to amplify geographical ties. See Theodore J. Lowi, "Party, Policy, and Constitution in America," pp. 238–276 in Chambers and Burnham.
7. Political systems vary significantly in the extent to which favors and patronage can be carried out within the law. In the United States, for example, the traditional use of postmasterships, ambassadorial posts, and a number of state jobs exempt from normal civil service requirements provides a pool of party spoils denied most Indian, Malaysian, or Nigerian politicians.
8. Robert Walcott, Jr., *English Politics in the Early Eighteenth Century.* Cambridge, Mass.: Harvard University Press, 1956, p. 13. The coincidence between the patterns Walcott describes and contemporary Philippine politics is discussed by Carl Landé, pp. 101–107.
9. Family loyalties are always of significance but in the typical machine case narrow family ties become a central factor in the evaluation of government action. Occupational, much less broad civic, sentiments play a marginal or even negligible role. Most immigrants to the United States, for example, at first "took for granted that the political life of the individual would arise out of family needs. . . ." Richard Hofstadter, *The Age of Reform,* New York: Vintage Books, 1955, p. 9.

10. Banfield and Wilson, p. 340.
11. Charles Edward Merriam, *Chicago: A More Intimate View of Urban Politics*. New York: Crowell-Collier-Macmillan, 1929, pp. 68, 90. Merriam's analysis is especially valuable as he was simultaneously political scientist and politician throughout the period he describes.
12. Seymour J. Mandelbaum, p. 58. See also, Edward J. Flynn, *You're the Boss,* New York: Viking, 1947, p. 21, for a twentieth-century account of New York City politics in which a similar argument is made.
13. Burnham, p. 286.
14. Burnham, p. 286, Merriam calls the precinct worker "something of a social worker not recognized by the profession," p. 173.
15. Banfield and Wilson, p. 118.
16. For a more extended discussion of these attitudes and their origin, see James C. Scott, *Ideology in Malaysia*. New Haven, Conn.: Yale University Press. 1968, chap. 6.
17. Wurfel (p. 763), for example, claims that from 10 to 20 percent of Filippino voters *regularly* sell their votes.

18

Exchanging Material Benefits for Political Support: A Comparative Analysis

Eva Etzioni-Halevy

This chapter presents a comparative study of Britain, the United States, and Israel, focusing on the exchange of private material benefits for political support. Such practices have been dealt with by various scholars under the heading of "machine politics" or "clientelism." Each of these terms, however, has a slightly narrower connotation than the practices discussed here, hence my preference for the above term.

Framework for the Analysis

The comparison is presented in a democratic elitist framework, a well established but recently neglected perspective in the social sciences. Democracy, more than any other regime, restrains elites in the exercise of power by certain "rules of the game," by an institutionalized, constantly recurring threat of replacement and by confronting them in an institutionalized manner with the countervailing power of other elites. However, the effectiveness of these mechanisms varies from one democracy to another. Elites are the ones who chiefly safeguard the rules of democracy (see Dye and Zeigler, 1975). Nonetheless, by the same token they are also the ones who, under certain circumstances, augment their power by obviating or corrupting these rules and thereby the democratic procedures. Thus, when political corruption is at work in a democracy, elites are the ones who *make* it work.

The democratic perspective attempts to integrate elements of elite theory with elements of the pluralist theory of democracy. In this it follows in the footsteps of Mosca (1939), Schumpeter (1966), Keller

Source: By permission of the author.

(1963) and Aron (1968, 1978). Its basic contention is that there is no inconsistency between democracy and elitism: elites are as necessary for democracy as they are for all other political regimes. But the manner in which elites acquire power and exercise it is of the first order of importance.

Furthermore, there is a direct relationship between the various democratic restrains on elite power: when the power of the political elite is effectively countervailed by the power of other elites, its ability to contravene the "rules of the game" and thereby to engage in the corruption of democratic processes is commensurately restricted.

Conditions for Political Corruption and Its Decline

The corruption of the democratic process dealt with here is that of material inducement in return for political support. Such inducements, in turn, may be ordered on a continuum from the collective to the individual. On the collective level this device concerns the creation of overall policies—especially economic policies (e.g., tax cuts)—in accordance with the perceived wishes of the electorate. On the intermediate level it concerns the molding of policies in line with the demands of interest groups, communities, or constituencies. On the individual level it entails benefits to various institutions, firms, small groups, or to families and individuals in return for political support.

Such an exchange may take the form of outright bribing of voters. It may also take more subtle forms such as providing jobs, housing, services, preferential treatment by authorities, contracts, licenses, subsidies and the like, well in advance of election day, on the assumption that beneficiaries will feel an obligation or find it in their interest to support the donors at the polls, to give them general political or financial support, or even to become active on their behalf.

While the use of material benefits by political elites is considered legitimate on the collective level, it is considered increasingly illegitimate as one moves down to the individual level, where it usually contravenes accepted rules of the democratic process and falls under the headings of "political corruption." It is this practice (or malpractice) that is the concern of the present analysis. While the use of material benefits takes place at all times, in all societies at the collective and intermediary levels, present-day societies differ significantly in the extent to which this practice is prevalent on the individual level.

Several theories have been advanced to explain these differences. There are Marxist theories, which endeavor to explain these practices on the basis of ruling class interests and hegemony. There are also what may be called populist theories, which explain the practice on the basis of certain traits of the rank-and-file public, such as large numbers of immigrants not steeped in the political culture of democracy, widespread poverty, or low levels of education. The thesis presented here is that while these may be contributing factors in the development or decline of political corruption in each country, they are of little use in a comparative analysis, and cannot explain the differences between the various countries in this respect.

Rather, it will be shown that these differences can best be explained through the relationships between the political elite and the bureaucratic elite, and the *elite*-political culture that governs them. In particular, it will be shown that where the elite political culture is such that it enables the party-politically elected elite to be intermeshed with the appointed bureaucratic elite or to dominate it, the exchange of tangible benefits for political support flourishes and at times greatly biases the democratic process. Conversely, where the "rules of the game" are such that the bureaucratic elite has had to be separated from the political elite and has gained power independent of that of politicians, this type of political corruption has declined and proper democratic procedures have come into force. To substantiate this thesis, the relevant political experiences in Britain, the United States, and Israel will be briefly characterized and explained.

Factors in an Explanatory Schema

To recapitulate the analysis presented in the preceding selections: In Britain the handing out of material inducements on an individual basis had declined by the turn of the nineteenth century, and since then has not been in existence on any significant scale. In the United States and Israel, on the other hand, the practice has remained prevalent. Although in both countries a certain decline in political machines has recently set in, machine-type political practices are still in evidence.

How can the similarities and the differences among the countries be explained? On the face of it, the legal reforms, especially in Britain, go a long way towards explaining the elimination of corrupt electoral practices. But what needs explanation is why these legal reforms came about in the first place. Also, initially in Britain, and later on in the United States, legal reforms were less than effective because they were circumvented or not properly enforced. Hence, what counts is not so much the stringency of the laws, but rather the effectiveness of their enforcement. This once more raises the question of why such laws should be more effectively enforced in one country, or at one time—

rather than another—so that other explanations must be looked for. One such explanation offered is the Marxist one.

The Marxist Conception: Ruling Class Hegemony

From the Marxist conception it would follow that political manipulation through material inducements would be most likely to prevail where the economically dominant class (the ruling class in Marxist terms) has the clearest leverage over the political system and most clearly dominates the other classes. Thus Graziano (1977) and O'Connell (1980) have suggested that the practice develops and persists where there has been an incomplete development of the capitalist economy and where, therefore, the hegemony of the capitalist class over the working class prevents the latter from organizing and developing class consciousness. In such cases, it is argued, material inducements represent one method whereby the process of class formation on part of the labor force can be resisted.

This theory was originally applied to Ireland and Southern Italy and may well be appropriate for these areas. But it does not explain the cases at hand. In eighteenth- and nineteenth- century Britain, the ruling classes (the aristocracy and later the bourgeoisie as well) had a virtual monopoly over political power. With the development of democratic procedures, this monopoly was maintained (among other things) through the introduction of material inducements into the political process. The further perpetuation of such inducements could thus have served the interests of the ruling classes in maintaining their monopoly. Yet Britain was the first country to largely relinquish the practice, thereby helping to pave the way for the working class's political organization and its participation in the political process.

The United States stands out among Western democracies in its lack of a large-scale labor party. This absence could be taken to indicate underdevelopment of working-class consciousness, and in line with Marxist reasoning could conceivably be used to explain the extraordinary development and tenacious persistence of machine politics in that country. However, a working-class consciousness (as indicated by the large-scale organization of labor) has not been more evident in this country in recent years than it was in previous years; yet the political machine has suffered a partial decline, even though it has by no means disappeared.

To clinch the argument, it must be pointed out that in Israel (both before and after independence) the capitalist class has been relatively weak and subdued. On the other hand, the working class has been highly organized, and its leaders have had a virtual monopoly over political power for almost a half a century. Yet throughout this period, material inducements in politics have flourished. Indeed, it has been the labor movement's leadership that has been most prominent in the perpetuation of this practice (though ably assisted by its coalition partners). When the right-wing *Likud* (a conglomeration of rightwing parties, literally: cohesion) came to power, and under the present widely based government, coalition parties are merely perpetuating (less adeptly) a tradition that was established and nurtured under Labor parties. In general, then, the strength and hegemony of the capitalist class and the lack of working-class consciousness and organization have little to do with material inducements in the electoral process.

The Populist Conception: Characteristics of the Rank and File

According to Scott (1973), machine (i.e., material) inducements in the electoral process may be explained by disorganization (the presence among the public of large numbers of immigrants as yet disoriented in the new society and not yet steeped in the political culture of democracy) and by poverty. These factors may serve to explain some of the developments in some of the countries studied, but neither can serve to explain the differences among them.

Immigration. The diminution of immigration to the United States after the World War I may explain the partial decline of the party machine from the 1940s and onward. Also, the large-scale immigration to Israel in the Yishuv era and in the 1950s may explain the flourishing of material inducements at these times. The decline in immigration later on may likewise possibly serve to explain whatever decline in machine-type corruption took place in Israel in recent years.

On the other hand again, as Johnston (1982) explains, many American cities with large numbers of immigrants have never been dominated by machine politics or shook off that dominance a long time ago. Conversely, there have been "yankee machines" with little immigrant support. Examples are Platt's statewide machine in Newark and Brayton's machine in Rhode Island. Also, in some states like Indiana, where there are small numbers of foreign voters, machine politics have continued to flourish.

Immigration has even less explanatory power when the various countries are compared with one another. In the nineteenth century, for instance, the United States was a country of immigration, and Britain was not. Yet bribery of voters flourished in Britain and matched or surpassed this practice in the United States. It is true that large proportions of the nineteenth-century immigrants to America came from the United Kingdom. Coming from a similar culture, they did not face serious disorientation in the new society. Even so, how can Britain's especially prominent "achievements" in electoral corruption be explained?

A twentieth-century comparison casts similar doubts on the thesis. Britain, no less than the United States and Israel, has had an influx of immigrants in recent years. Yet in Britain, corruption of the type described here is no longer in existence on a significant scale (and certainly has not enjoyed a revival in recent years as a result of immigration), whereas in the United States and Israel the practice still persists.

Poverty.   If immigration cannot account for differences among the countries, can poverty (among immigrants or other inhabitants)? The period in which material inducements were gradually eliminated from the political scene in Britain (the second half of the nineteenth century) was also the time in which a significant rise in the standard of living occurred. real wages rose markedly in the last forty years of the nineteenth century, and this was supplemented by improvements in housing, education, health, and the like. Developments in that country then, would seem to confirm the poverty thesis.

This is not so when a cross-Atlantic comparison is made. In America, as in Britain, the late nineteenth century was a period of rapidly growing real incomes and of improvements in the living environment (Bagwell and Mingay, 1970). There is no reason to believe that the rise in real income and standard of living was greater in Britain than in the United States. Yet Britain far overtook the United States in the elimination of political corruption. On the contemporary scene, it seems the population's general level of affluence (or lack thereof) cannot explain the difference among the countries either. As comparisons of gross national product (GNP) generally show, of the countries dealt with here, the United States is the first in affluence but by no means first in the elimination of electoral corruption.

Perhaps, however, it is not a country's general level of poverty vs. affluence, but rather *pockets* of poverty which account for the exchange of benefits for political support. This contention seems plausible because the recipients of some of these benefits have frequently been the poorer elements in society. Thus, if pockets of poverty are eliminated or contracted, some parts of the public become less vulnerable to certain petty bribes and small-scale favors by politicians. But, again, the pockets-of-poverty theory has little value in explaining intercountry differences.

In the United States, for instance, despite the rise in the standard of living towards the end of the nineteenth century and the beginning of the twentieth century, there remained a mass of poverty and unemployment among the indigenous population. However, the situation in Britain was not greatly different. Despite the general improvement in living conditions towards the end of the nineteenth century, almost one-third of the population in industrial cities was comprised of poverty-stricken slum dwellers who existed at a bare subsistence level (Bagwell and Mingay, 1970).

In the United States there have been pockets of poverty in recent years as well: the proportion of persons living below the poverty line declined from 22.4 percent in 1959 to 12.6 percent in 1970, but has risen to 15.2 percent in 1983 (*Statistical Abstract of the United States, 1985*, Table 758, p. 454). In Israel the Prime Minister's Committee on Children and Youth in Distress reported that from 1968 to 1971 about 11 percent of the urban population (which accounts for about 90 percent of the population) lived in poverty. Since then the situation has worsened, as real wages suffered a cutback of some 20 to 30 percent in the wake of the recent economic crisis. By the same token there has been poverty in recent years in Britain as well. In 1979 7.45 percent of Britons were receiving support from the Supplementary Benefits Commission, and were thus living below the government's own estimate of the poverty line. In 1983 the proportion of the poor by this criterion had grown to 13.44 percent (*Great Britain Annual Abstract of Statistics, 1985*, Table 3.25, p. 60). According to some observers, to this must be added an estimated 4 percent of the population who were eligible for benefits but did not claim them.

It is exceedingly difficult to compare levels of poverty and sizes of populations living in poverty from one country to another, as standards used to demarcate the poverty line vary from country to country. Still, the impression is that the proportions of the population living in poverty are no smaller in Britain than they are in the United States and Israel. Certainly pockets of poverty in Britain have been sufficiently large to have warranted the handing out of petty inducements by party machines, had there been such machines in existence. In their absence, or almost total absence, poverty could not bring them into existence.

Moreover, as Johnston (1982) shows, while political machines in America have usually done well in poor districts, this was only half of the story. Machines have also been successful with wealthy business people who have obtained contracts, licenses, franchises, and weak enforcement of regulatory laws in return for political and financial support to parties and candidates. More recently, the New York city corruption scandals have supplied new evidence of this form of exchange.

There is no reason why the advantages of favors from politicians should appeal only to the poor. Their appeal includes all those who want to do business with government, as well as those whose activities are subject to government regulation—indeed, all those affected by government decisions. Thus "help" shades into "pull". The need for "pull," moreover, increases in proportion to the size of one's dealings with government. And, the ability to use pull increases with the amount of knowledge of the workings of government (in other words, "you've got to know the ropes to pull the strings").

Education. In close conjunction with poverty, low levels of education have also been considered as explaining the exchange of benefits for votes (Sorauf, 1960). In fact, it has been reported that in nineteenth-century Britain, voters open to this type of manipulation were frequently (although not exclusively) at a low level of education. In America, too, the people most vulnerable to certain types of machine politics were the less educated (frequently, immigrants, and poor in the bargain).

In Israel, on the other hand, the situation is more complicated. While many of the immigrants of the 1950s, of whom a great proportion came from Middle Eastern countries, were indeed poorly educated, the situation was different from the pre-state era when large proportions of immigrants belonged to the intelligentsia. Yet the highly-educated immigrants (and old-timers) did not hesitate to accept material benefits from political organizations and to pledge their allegiance to these organizations in return.

Moreover, there seems to be no relationship between the countries' rating on level of education and their rating on electoral corruption. The British system of education has been characterized as an elitist system and the Israeli system fits this title as well; in these countries, changes toward greater equalization are slow and gradual. The American educational system, on the other hand, has been much more mass oriented, and the great majority of American youngsters attain at least a high school diploma.

It may be argued that the American high school diploma cannot be compared with its British counterpart. But it is significant that a far greater percentage of American youngsters (as compared with British ones, for instance) benefit from education up to a higher age. This difference is certainly not reflected in differences in the countries' political corruption through material inducements.

Immigration, poverty, and level of education of the rank-and-file public, therefore, doesn't explain differences among the countries in political corruption. Perhaps this is so because members of the rank-and-file public can make use of the practice (and it certainly helps if they are willing to do so), but they cannot initiate it. Hence the major explanation of political corruption involving material inducements is sought not in the character of the public that is the object of manipulation, but in the character of those who seek to dominate the public through such manipulation, and in the structures of domination they have devised—in other words, in the conceptions and structure of the elites. But if so, what features of the elites account for the practice, its resilience, or its decline?

Elite Culture and Structure: The Politicization of the Bureaucracy

A theory proposed by Heidenheimer (1970) involves the development of the elites' structure and power: according to this theory, electoral corruption and specifically the offering of material inducements arose where electoral assemblies, political parties, or other political instruments of mass mobilization were powerful prior to the development of a centralized, powerful, bureaucratized civil service. Conversely, it was curbed where fully developed bureaucracies antedate political parties. This theory may help explain why political corruption of this kind developed in both Britain and the United States, which fitted the first pattern. But it cannot help explain why it declined and has been largely eradicated in Britain but declined only in part and is still prevalent in the United States.

The present argument is that what counts on the contemporary scene is the independent power of the bureaucracy—not vis-à-vis public, but vis-à-vis the party-political structures (or the polity) or, in other words, the independent power of the bureaucratic elite as against that of the political elite. Where the bureaucratic elite is intermeshed with the political elite or dominated by it to the extent that the interests of top politicians dictate the activities of top bureaucrats in the performance of their duties, the handing out of individual material inducements in the political process is likely to flourish. Conversely, where the bureaucratic elite can countervail the power of the political elite, where the actions of top bureaucrats are dictated by criteria other than those of the interests of top politicians, then the handing out of material inducements in return for political support is likely to decline or be absent.

In this context, two major types of public administration have been distinguished: a politically neutral one and a politically involved one. In the first, the selection, appointment, and advancement of personnel take place without political intervention and are made largely by objective criteria in an open competitive system. Bureaucratic activities are not guided overwhelmingly by party-political criteria. In the second type there is involvement of politicians in senior appointments, and a significant proportion of officials are appointed and promoted by party-political criteria. Since they owe allegiance to their party-political appointers and depend on them for advancement, such officials frequently engage in activities that promote those appointers and their party's interests. As a result, the administration's actions are shaped to a much greater extent by party-political considerations.

It is now generally agreed that no government bureaucracy is totally nonpolitical as the very formulation of policy—in which the bureaucracy is necessarily involved—has political and frequently party-political connotations. Nonetheless, not all bureaucracies are permeated by party-politics to the same extent. Where the bureaucracy is strongly infiltrated by political appointments and political considerations, political corruption flourishes and biases the democratic process. Only a bureaucracy that is relatively independent politically can safeguard fully-fledged democratic procedures.

This thesis fits the cases at hand. At one time (before the second half of the nineteenth century in Britain and America and before the establishment of the state in Israel) politicians and party-politics had a grip on the bureaucracies in all three countries. During the same timespans all three were pervaded by electoral corruption through material inducements. Subsequently, politicization declined at a different pace and to a different extent in the three countries. Political corruption through material inducements followed parallel trends.

In Britain the decline of the bureaucracy's politicization came earlier and was more extensive than in the other two countries. Recently some commentators have seen evidence of politicization in the top Thatcher appointments and promotions (Wass, 1985). Still, these concerns pertain only to a minute number of top appointments, and there has been no basic change in the character of the British bureaucracy in recent years. As Rose (1981) indicates, British higher civil servants are political in the sense of being involved in conflicts concerning policy. Their advice on these matters cannot be neutral and necessarily has political implications. But these civil servants are not party-political except in the sense that they serve the government of the day rather than the opposition.

By contrast, in the other two countries, the politicization of the bureaucracy was maintained much longer, and when it declined, it did so only partially (the United States) or to a small extent (Israel). In the United States civil service reforms led to a situation where only a relatively small top layer of officials in the federal administration can be political appointees. There is a consensus among observers that President Reagan makes as many political patronage appointments as he can to positions not insulated by public service rules, and that he does so to a greater extent than recent presidents. According to Goldenberg (1984) the number of such appointments stood at 709 in 1983—still only less than one tenth of one percent of total direct federal employment.

However, according to Goldenberg, political appointees now have greater leverage over career civil servants than was the case before. Career civil servants now can be more easily relocated even against their will. In 1983 there were 1,100 such relocations. Only a small proportion of these were forced relocations. But career officials quickly realized that forced moves were possible. This has made them more politically compliant. Those who have not taken the hint have had close political supervision imposed on them.

Moreover, on the municipal level politicization of the bureaucracy has remained much more pervasive. Thus in Chicago in the 1970s, despite civil service reforms, there were still some 20,000 patronage positions available to the city government (Guterbock, 1980). In New York City, too, some departments are still packed with political appointments, especially the transportation department, which has been the major focus of recent corruption scandals.

In Israel, as in the other two countries, there have been attempts at political reforms. But their practical results have not been far reaching. As Werner (Chapter 17 in this volume) correctly perceived the situation, despite these reforms, "internally, structures and behavior remained informal." The fact that in recent years the bureaucracy has still been beset by political partisanship is illustrated by the fact that before the 1981 election the Ministry of Religious Affairs was reported to have been the site of hectic electoral activity in favor of two religious parties. Only in February 1986 did new regulations prohibiting political activity on the premises of government offices come into force, and it is not clear as yet what their effectiveness will be.

Moreover, after the 1981 election political appointments continued to be rampant. At that time the Ministry of Absorption passed control from *Likud* to *Tami,* a small religious party. Subsequently there have been reports of *Tami* systematically ridding the ministry of all previously introduced *Likud* personnel. Even more recently my own research on the Israel Broadcasting Authority (a semiindependent but rather typical Israeli bureaucracy) has shown that party-political appointments reach down to the level of heads of units (Etzioni-Halevy, forthcoming). By the account of key informants, the situation is not much different in government departments proper.

It can be seen, then, that in Britain, where the penetration of politicians and party-politics declined earliest and most thoroughly, political corruption through material benefits has done likewise. In the United States, political intrusion into the federal bureaucracy has also declined, although by recent testimony it has increased to some extent under the Reagan administration. Concomitantly, no political machines with a clear implication on federal politics are visible today, although indictments for corruption have been more prevalent under the Reagan administration than under recent administrations. On the municipal level political patronage appointments have remained much more widespread and so has machine-type political corruption. Finally, in Israel both party-political intrusion into the bureaucracy and political corruption have declined only to a small extent and both remain clearly visible on the political scene.

Politicalization of the bureaucracy may explain the use of material inducements in return for political support in several ways. Firstly, such inducements include patronage appointments in the government bureaucracy itself. To the extent that these appointments are used as rewards or inducements for political support, politicalization of the bureaucracy and political corruption coincide. However, as a rule, bureaucratic appointments are only a fraction of the material inducements political organizations or politicians have at their disposal.

Secondly, the introduction of political appointees into the government bureaucracy and its consequent cannibalization by the political ruling elite, make it possible to use that bureaucracy for the handing out of a wide array of additional rewards by political criteria. Since the government bureaucracy is usually in charge of massive resources, the material inducements that may be handed out in this manner are massive as well.

Some observers have seen it as self-evident that where a bureaucracy is party-politicized, it will make its resources available for political contests on a party-political basis. Hence, they argue, the above thesis needs no elaboration or empirical support. However, Marxist and populist theorists endeavored to account for this corruption through factors other than the politicalization of the bureaucracy, namely through class interests and rank-and-file characteristics. Hence, the importance of showing that it is, in fact, the politicalization of the bureaucracy (rather than other factors) that accounts for the practice.

Moreover, some observers who see the tie between political patronage in the bureaucracy and electoral corruption as self-explanatory have, in fact, posited a causal relationship between the two that is widely open to criticism. Thus Scott (1973) conceives of political patronage as an important tool in the hands of the political machine. Rather than viewing it as an outgrowth of the politicalization of the bureaucracy, he sees it as an outgrowth of party-politics. These, in turn, he considers to be decisively influenced by conditions of poverty and disorganization among the public (see above). Hence, the causal chain, according to Scott, leads from the traits of the rank-and-file to the machine and from that to patronage. A similar causal chain has been posited by Sorauf (1960), who argues that the political involvement of the bureaucracy is the outgrowth of large-scale immigration and poverty.

However, in actual fact, the causal chain is the reverse of that posited by these observers. Thus in Britain, since the initial development of its administration, there has been no clear distinction between political personnel and the civil service, between political activities and administrative tasks. This was, initially, the most striking feature of the British administration, and it continued well into the nineteenth century (Parris, 1969).

In America the penetration of party-politics into the administration was in place in the late 1820s and 1830s, although it developed further and reached new heights at the turn of the twentieth century. As Ostrogorski (1902, vol. 2) shows, the evolving parties' political machines' activists pressed heavily on the government to perpetuate this politicalization and employ it in their favor. They would not have been able to do so had not the practice been institutionalized early in the system's development. Also, the politicalization of the bureaucracy preceded the mass immigration from non-English–speaking countries, of immigrants not socialized to the culture of democracy, as well as poverty, which supposedly explain this administrative pattern. Hence, it would be more plausible to regard this pattern as the outgrowth of a tradition that had its roots in the prereform British system, some elements of which were institutionalized in America (Huntington, 1968).

In Israel the politicalization of the bureaucracy had its roots in the prestate *Yishuv* era, when administrative and political roles and structures intermeshed to such an extent as to be practically indistinguishable (Shapiro, 1975). This, in turn, has been explained by the absence of a commonly-accepted state framework. The British government adopted a policy of minimum interference in the *Yishuv* society, and the Jewish community was run by its own internal political authorities. Although this set of institutions, the *Yishuv's* political center, enjoyed a fair degree of autonomy, it had, in the phrasing of Horowitz and Lissak (1971), "authority without sovereignty." Lacking the ultimate force of sanctions available to a sovereign state, the national institution had to base their authority on the recognition of the various existent political bodies (parties and labor organizations). To elicit their cooperation the national institutions were obliged to cede several functions and large-scale resources to them, thereby turning them into political-administrative subcenters. It was largely this situation that gave rise to the fusion of politics and administration. Thus, as successive waves of immigrants arrived, they were confronted with existing, well-established political-administrative institutions that used the large-scale resources at their disposal to facilitate the immigrants' absorption, thereby gaining their political support.

It is thus clear that the causal chain is not as posited by the above observers. Indeed, since all three countries concerned had politically infused bureaucracies at the outset, yet their patterns of immigration varied widely, it is clear that the causal chain cannot proceed from immigration through machine politics to bureaucratic politicalization. It would be more plausible to argue that such politicalization was part and parcel of a tradition of fused, undifferentiated sociopolitical structures that marked the premodern and the initial stages of the modern era. This was clearly so in Britain and in America (which had initially imported the traditional British patterns). In prestate Israel, the leaders who shaped the evolving sociopolitical patterns had immigrated mainly from Russia and Eastern Europe at the beginning of the century. From there they transplanted notions of pervasive political control on all facets of social life, and the fusion of political and administrative structures that these notions implied (Shapiro, 1975). These notions then helped them cope with the situation of authority without sovereignty, as previously described. There was, then, in all three countries, a clear causal chain leading from the traditions of government in general to the politicalization of the bureaucracy, and thence to political corruption through material inducements.

What still requires explanation are the differences among the countries in the decline of party-politicalization of the bureaucracy. The explanation here proposed is in terms of the evolving elite political culture and the concomitantly changing power structures. In Britain the evolving notions of proper political-democratic and administrative procedures served to curb the power of the political elite while favoring the development of a politically independent, administrative elite. The gradual development of such codes of propriety restrained the political elite from encroaching on the administrative elite and separated its stronghold, the bureaucracy, from party-politics. (cf. Sisson, 1971, p. 451). It occurred in the framework of a similar separation of other government institutions (e.g., the judiciary, the crown) from party-politics (Huntington, 1968). It was paralleled by the development of rules of proper administration, at least partly under the influence of Benthamite ideas (Parris, 1960), calling for a public service ethos of professionalism, and strict controls on rewards and benefits—to eliminate corruption (Hume, 1981; Rosen, 1983; Rosenblum, 1978). Once independent public officials had been appointed, they played a leading role in legislation furthering the development of their own power (Parris, 1960).

In the United States and Israel no such clear notions of propriety restraining the power of the political elites developed, and the democratic-administrative "rules of the game" have remained ambiguous. Even where depoliticization of the bureaucracy was called for by formal rules and regulations, these precepts were only belatedly and partially followed in practice. In conjunction with this, the administrative elites never became independent enough to countervail the power and interests of politicians and corruption through tangible benefits in return for political support was not eliminated.

Contemporary support for this explanation comes from the fact that corruption resulting in political benefits is closely related to other types of corruption, resulting in private benefits. Where the elites' notions of propriety have not been explicit and stringent enough to eliminate the one, they have not been clear and strong enough to eliminate the other. Thus, as Schwartz (1979) observed in another context: "If one must falsify for the good of the cause, then why not add a little more for one's self."

Conclusion

Political corruption through material benefits in return for political support depends not on class characteristics and interests, nor on the characteristics and political culture of the rank-and-file public, but on the elite political culture and power structures dominated by the elites.

Its presence depends upon political and bureaucratic elites and power structures being intermeshed, upon politicians and party-politics intruding into the bureaucracy, upon the consequent availability of bureaucratic resources for party-political purposes, and upon an elite political culture that treas such deployment of bureaucratic resources as (at least unofficially) acceptable. Conversely, elimination of this sort of political corruption and the development of (in this sense) proper democratic procedures hinges upon a certain change in the political-bureaucratic rules of the game, upon the bureaucratic elites countervailing the power of political elites, upon bureaucratic structures gaining independence from the intrusion of politicians and party politics, and upon the consequent withdrawal of bureaucratic resources from the party-political contest.

Paradoxically, then, only where the power of a democratically-elected political elite has been restrained and counterbalanced by the power of a non-elected bureaucratic elite, have proper democratic procedures been put into place. In other words, restraint of the power of the elected political elite by a nonelected bureaucratic elite is a prerequisite for a properly functioning democracy. Not surprisingly, the independent power of a non-elected elite is also a source of problems for democracy. However, such analyses are beyond the scope of the present study (see Etzioni-Halevy, 1985).

References

Aron, R.
1968   *Progress and Disillusion*. London, Pall Mall Press.
1978   *Politics and History* (trans. M. Bernheim-Conant). New York, Free Press.

Bagwell, P.S. and Mingay, G.E.
1970   *Britain and America 1850–1939*.London, Routledge & Kegan Paul.

Dye, T.R., and Zeigler, L.H.
1975   *The Irony of Democracy* (3rd edn). North Scituate, Mass., Duxbury Press.

Etzioni-Halevy, E.
1985   *Bureaucracy and Democracy*. Revised, paperback edition. London, Routledge & Kegan Paul.
forthcoming   *National Broadcasting Under Siege*. London, Macmillan.

Goldenberg, E.N.
1984   "The Permanent Government in an Era of Retrenchment and Redirection," in L.S. Salamon and M.S. Lund (eds). *The Reagan Presidency and the Governing of America*.Washington DC, The Urban Institute Press.

Graziano, L.
1977   "Patron-client Relationship in Southern Italy," in L.G. Schmidt, C.
       Lande, and J. Scott, (eds). *Friends, Followers and Factions,* Berkeley,
       University of California Press, pp. 360–78.

Great Britain Central Statistical Office
1985   *Annual Abstract of Statistics 1985.* London, Government Statistical
       Service.

Guterbock, T.M.
1980   *Machine Politics in Transition.* Chicago, University of Chicago Press.

Heidenheimer, A.J. (ed.)
1970   *Political Corruption.* New York, Holt, Rinehart & Winston.

Horowitz, D. and Lissak, M.
1971   "Authority without Sovereignty," in M. Lissak, and E. Gutman (eds),
       Political Institutions and Processes in Israel. Jerusalem, Akademon.

Hume, L.J.
1981   *Bentham and Bureaucracy.* New York and London, Cambridge Univer-
       sity Press.

Huntington, S.P.
1968   *Political Order in Changing Societies.* New Haven, Ct., Yale Univer-
       sity Press.

Johnston, M.
1979   "Patrons and Clients, Jobs and Machines," *American Political Science
       Review,* 73 (June) pp. 385–98.
1982   *Political Corruption and Public Policy in America.* Monterey, Cal.,
       Brooks/Cole Publishing Co.

Keller, S.
1963   *Beyond the Ruling Class,* New York, Random House.

Mosca, G.
1939   *The-Ruling Class* (tr. H.D. Kahn). New York, McGraw Hill.

O'Connell, D.
1980   "Clientelism and Political Culture in Ireland." (unpublished).

Ostrogorski, M.
1902   *Democracy and the Organization of Political Parties.* New York,
       Macmillan (in 2 volumes).

Parris, H.
1960   "The Nineteenth Century Revolution of Government," *The Historical
       Journal,* 3, 17–37.
1969   *Constitutional Bureaucracy.* London, Allen & Unwin.

Rose, R.
1981   "The Political Status of Higher Civil Servants in Britain," paper No. 92,
       Centre for the Study of Public Policy, University of Strathclyde, Glas-
       gow.

Rosen, F.
1983   *Jeremy Bentham and the Modern State,* Oxford, Clarendon University
       Press.

Rosenblum, N.L.
1978   *Bentham's Theory of the Modern State*. Cambridge, Mass., Harvard University Press.

Schumpeter, J.
1966   *Capitalism, Socialism and Democracy*. London, Unwin University Books.

Schwartz, A.C.
1979   "Corruption and Political Development in the USSR," *Comparative Politics*, 11(July) 431–32.

Scott, J.C.
1973   *Comparative Political Corruption*. Englewood Cliffs, N.J., Prentice Hall.

Shapiro, Y.
1975   *The Organization of Power*. Tel-Aviv, Am Oved (Hebrew).
1977   *Democracy in Israel*. Ramat Gan, Massada (Hebrew).

Sharkansky, I.
1986   "Distinguishing 'Corruption' from 'Flexibility' in the Israeli Public Sector." Paper prepared for delivery at the 1986 Annual Meeting of the American Political Science Association, Washington.

Sisson, C.H.
1971   "The Politician as Intruder," in R.A. Chapman, and A. Sunsire (eds), *Style in Administration*. London, Allen & Unwin.

Sorauf, F.J.
1960   "The Silent Revolution in Patronage," *Public Administration Review*, 20, 28–34.

Wass, D.
1985   "The Civil Service at the Crossroads," *Political Quarterly*, 56 (July–September), 227–41.

The Persistence of Patronage Systems:
An Introduction

Patronage systems typically involve patrons–individuals, groups of individuals, or organizations that dispense such things as favors, protection, money, employment, or goods to clients, or people who usually look to the patrons for these benefits and in return give them loyalty, political support, or service. Patronage systems, when they operate outside the law or at the normative margins of society, can engender corrupt exchange relationships. These selections examine how patronage systems, some of them deeply rooted in social mores, continue not only to affect modern politics, but to remain at the core of political corruption in many countries. The selections analyze socio-political contexts in Greece, Sicily, Ghana, and Morocco, countries in which patronage systems are either central to or contribute to political corruption.

In the first selection, Jeremy Boissevain discusses why patronage networks in Sicily became, over time, an essential part of the island's political system. The author describes how the kin/non-kin distinction is central to Sicilian social relations and remains at the core of politics. The definition of the family, central to the key values of obligation and reciprocity, also defines political relationships and the networks of patronage that set the bounds of acceptable political behavior. Although Boissevain does not specifically focus on political corruption, it is clear that this patronage system operates largely in the interstices of the formal government system, which to most Sicilians is alien; but when it can be used or manipulated, it reinforces the patronage system by fostering politically corrupt exchanges.

Chapter 20 by J.K. Campbell examines the relationship between village patrons in Sarakatsan, a mountainous area of Greece, and their clients. Here the patronage system is as deeply imbedded as it is in Sicily. However, unlike Sicily, it is friendship and relationships to key influentials, rather than kinship, that define patronage networks. In the Greek villages, families are isolated in constant struggle with other families, whether in terms of the possibility of bare subsistence or of social prestige. Thus, membership in the mutually reinforcing bonds of patronage relationships determines power, influence, and social prestige. Politics in the Zagori villages operate with and within the local patronage systems, thus embracing both official and unofficial authority relationships.

The third chapter is John Waterbury's description of a political system in which political corruption has so much become standard operating procedure that the government itself allocates resources for bribes and plans operations to include sufficient margins for illicit payments. The author points out that the Moroccan government has little choice in the matter; it cannot eliminate corruption because it has become deeply imbedded in the country's social fabric, and so makes the best of a bad situation by, in effect, "planning" for endemic corruption. Waterbury demonstrates how both modern and traditional patronage relations reinforce and perpetuate the networks of illicit exchanges, thereby making the Moroccan government an open accomplice to widespread political corruption.

The final chapter is drawn from Victor LeVine's monograph on political corruption in Ghana, a country in West Africa. He interviewed in depth some dozen key party and government officials of the regime of ex-President Kwame Nkrumah, deposed in 1966. Attempting to uncover the reasons why his respondents did what they did, the author probed the values that underlie their actions. High among those values were norms associated with both traditional and modern patron-client relationships, particularly those involving family and relations with influentials not unlike those that undergird the Sicilian and Greek local patronage systems.

19

Patronage in Sicily[1]

Jeremy Boissevain

The purpose of this chapter is two-fold. First, it seeks to further our understanding of certain organizational aspects of patronage, an institution which has recently been given considerable attention (Banfield 1961; Boissevain 1962, 1965; Campbell 1964; Foster 1961, 1963; Kenny 1960, 1961; Mair 1961; Silverman 1965; Trouwborst 1961, 1962; Wolf 1966). Secondly, it examines some of its functional aspects and discusses factors which appear to account for its importance in Sicily, the area which provides the ethnographic data for the paper.[2]

Patronage is founded on the reciprocal relations between patrons and clients. By patron I mean a person who uses his influence to assist and protect some other person, who then becomes his "client," and in return provides certain services to his patron. The relationship is asymmetrical, for the nature of the services exchanged may differ considerably. Patronage is thus the complex of relations between those who use their influence, social position or some other attribute to assist and protect others, and those whom they so help and protect.[3] The means by which this relationship is constituted and the form which it takes differ considerably from society to society. It varies from the formal contract in East Africa between members of the dominant class and the peasants, which is usually sealed by a gift of cattle from the former to the latter and entails a series of clearly delineated, institutionalized rights and obligations for each party (*cf.* Mair 1961; Trouwborst 1962), to the less formal relationship concluded between the Mediterranean patron and his client, in which the exact nature of the rights and obligations are not clearly defined culturally. The structure of the system in the Mediterranean is thus much more difficult to analyze, for it is implicit rather than explicit. Nevertheless, common to

Source: Jeremy Boissevain. "Patronage in Sicily," *Man* (N.S.). Vol. 1, No. 1 (March 1966), pp. 18–33. By permission of the publisher, The Royal Anthropological Institute of Great Britain and Ireland.

both the formal and informal systems of patronage is the need for protectors on the one hand, and for followers on the other. Why this should be so, at least in Sicily, is a matter which I discuss later.

Sicilian Society

Before turning to examine patronage in Sicily I shall give a summary of some of the important structural features of Sicilian society. In particular I touch upon the island's recent violent history, the importance of the family, the socio-economic hierarchy and some local moral concepts. Following the unification of Italy in 1860, administrators from the north, notably Piedmont were sent to Sicily to make this region part of the new state of Italy and to enforce its new laws. But their task was greatly complicated by their ignorance of the local dialect and customs, notably the network of kinsmen, friends, friends-of-friends, patrons and clients that bound baron to brigand, rich to poor, and stretched from one end of Sicily to the other, providing a parallel line of communication, and at times, completely paralyzing the attempts of the central government to enforce its laws (*cf.* Franchetti 1925). The corruption and banditry in Sicily became a national problem, and in 1875 the Italian parliament appointed a commission to report on the situation. Moreover, the rural proletariat, including the miners tapping the island's rich mineral deposits, continued to rebel against the appalling conditions under which they worked and lived, and further insurrections exploded before the turn of the century (*cf.* Sonnino 1925; Renda 1956).

After the rebellion of the Sicilian Fasci (1893–1894) had been ruthlessly crushed by the central government, an uneasy peace reigned while the battered workers' movement recovered. Following the 1914–1918 war the bandits, their numbers swelled by deserters from the military forces and discharged soldiers who had no desire to return to the soil, once again held sway in the Sicilian countryside. At the same time, Mussolini's strongarm gangs set off a new wave of violence that the police and the military, in fact the government of the country, made little attempt to contain (Mack Smith 1959: 348). This period of unrest was followed in 1922 by Mussolini's march on Rome, the beginning of 21 years of oppression, poverty and war for most Sicilians.[4]

A period of unrest and violence also followed the end of World War II. Conservative political forces within Sicily, aided by *mafiosi* and bandits, the most famous of whom was Giuliano, sought to obtain the independence of Sicily from Italy and to crush the revived workers' movement and the growing pressure for land reform (*cf.* Maxwell 1956; Pantaleone 1962).

Thus for the last century, Sicily has been a land where revolution and violence have been endemic, where economic exploitation of the proletarian masses by a small upper class composed of the bourgeoisie and nobility, often aided by delinquents, went hand in hand with their control of the local and regional administration, and their manipulation of it for personal gain. In short it was, and to an extent still is, a land where the strong survive at the expense of the weak.

The central institution of Sicilian society is the nuclear family. The rights and obligations which derive from membership in it provide the individual with his basic moral code. Moreover a man's social status as a person with honor, an *omu* or *cristianu*, is closely linked to his ability to maintain or improve the economic position of his family and to safeguard the purity of its women, in whom is enshrined the family's collective honor. A person's responsibility for his family is thus the value on which his life is centered.

Other values and organizational principles are of secondary importance. If they interfere with his ability to carry out his obligation to his family, he combats them with intrigue, force and violence if necessary. In so doing he is supported by public opinion, even though he may be acting contrary to the law. Justice and the rule of law are not synonymous.

Because the system of reckoning kin is bilateral, each person stands at the center of a vast network of persons to whom he is related both through his parents and through marriage. Relatives are expected to help one another. But the help one can expect from, or, reciprocally, the obligation one has to assist a kinsman, diminish as the genealogical distance between the two increases. In general it is extended to blood relatives as far as second cousins, the limit of the range within which the Church prohibits marriage. Effective recognition for purposes of mutual aid and friendship generally goes out only as far as first cousins.[5] It is strongest between members of the same nuclear family, that is between parents and their children, and between siblings. This obligation to the members of one's own natal family diminishes when a person marries and founds his own family.

Thus the Sicilian divides the world around him into kin and non-kin. The former are allies with whom he shares reciprocal rights and obligations of mutual assistance and protection. The latter are either enemies or potential enemies, each of whom is seeking to protect and improve the position of his own family, if need be at the expense of others.[6]

Sicilian society is highly stratified. Away from the few large cities the economy is based upon agriculture. Effective control over land, the traditional basis of local wealth, was until recently held almost exclu-

sively by the rural bourgeoisie composed of professionals, shopkeepers, brokers and artisans, who do not work the land themselves.[7]
These form the *borghesia* or bourgeoisie, for whom most of the
contadini,[8] those who physically till the soil, work. The proportion of
borghesi to *contadini* in Leone,[9] an agro-town of 20,000 in southern
Sicily where I spent seven months in 1962 and 1963, was 16 to 84
percent. Only 15 percent of the *contadini* owns or hold the land they
work under emphyteutical (perpetual) leases. The rest are share crop-
pers or landless laborers; thus they are the dependents of those who
control the land.

An enormous gulf separates those who work the land from those
who do not. Traditionally there tended to be a strong correlation
between wealth in land and education, though expanding public education, though expanding public education, the gradual division of the
large estates[10] and the cash now being sent home by Sicilian migrant
laborers working in norther Europe is rapidly modifying this neat
alignment. In general, high social status attaches to wealth and to
education. Low social status is accorded to those who work the land,
for physical labor, especially agricultural labor, is despised. The
borghesi are better educated and wealthier. Moreover, their sons
become the municipal and provincial civil servants who run the affairs
of rural Sicily. In contrast, the *contadini*, who by and large work for the
borghesi, have an inferior education and often live in grinding poverty.
The contrast between the bourgeoisie and the rural proletariat has thus
been not only between employer and employee, but between wealth
and poverty, between education and illiteracy.

It must not be thought, however, that these broad classes are
organized corporate groups. They are interest groups which are often
opposed. Though the separation between them is marked, there are
many lines of mutual dependence as well as many kinship links which
cut across the indeterminate frontier between the two. Though most
marriages take place between members of the same social class, social
mobility is quite common. Thus many families have relatives in the
other classes located at various levels of the socio-economic hierarchy.

This stratification, when taken in consideration with the overriding
obligation of mutual aid that exists between close kinsmen, has important effects on the political life. Civil servants generally favor their
close relatives, and try to derive a personal advantage from their
position. Since most are members of the *borghesia*, this means that the
upper classes receive preferential treatment. In northern Europe or
North America, civil servants who behave in this way and who are
caught are punished by law and by the pressure of public opinion,

which regards as immoral and contemptible the bureaucrat who betrays the public service ethic of honesty and impartiality. But in Sicily, there is no neat correlation between what is *legal* and *moral*. It is illegal for a brother to murder the person who has raped his sister, yet this, in terms of the local system of values, is a highly moral act. In the same way, it is illegal for a civil servant to let a public contract to a person who gives him a large commission or present. But, seen from the point of view of his relatives, this act is not immoral. On the contrary, by performing it he fulfils his primary obligation to aid his own family and his nearest kinsmen. In practice this means that the civil servant is only impartial to persons who are neither relatives nor friends. Yet these belong to a category of persons whom he mistrusts and, in a very real sense, looks upon as potential enemies. Thus non-kin with whom he deals in his official capacity, unless they are introduced by a third party who is a kinsman, friend, patron or client, receive short shrift. He is not only impartial, he is so detached as to be remote.

Patrons, Clients, and Friends

To an extent, then, every Sicilian feels himself to be isolated in a lawless and hostile world in which violence and bloodshed are still endemic. Not only is he surrounded by enemies and potential enemies, he is also subject to the authority of an impersonal government whose affairs are administered by bureaucrats, each of whom is either trying to derive some personal advantage from his official position or is liable to be maneuvered against him by his enemies. The more one descends the socio-economic ladder, the farther removed people are from kinsmen and friends who wield power and who can therefore control the forces shaping their lives.

Thus the basic problem the Sicilian faces in dealing with the world of non-kin is how to protect himself from his enemies, both known and unknown; and how to influence the remote, impersonal, if not hostile, authorities who make the decisions which control his wellbeing and that of his family, with whom his honor and standing in the community is so intimately bound. Most resolve these problems by seeking out strategically placed protectors and friends, who, together with kinsmen, make up the personal network of contacts through whom the average Sicilian attempts to protect and advance the fortunes of his family.

He often seeks to bind an influential, professional-class patron to himself by persuading him to become the godfather, the spiritual sponsor and protector, of one of his children. This is a relationship that is not lightly entered into since it is a formal contract, solemnized in public and before God, and once concluded not to be broken. Co-godparents, *compari,* are automatically "friends," and a *compare* is supposed to favor his godchild, if not the child's father.

Before turning to an analysis of the operation of the system of patronage, it is necessary to unravel the apparently overlapping statuses of kinsman, friend and patron. I am here concerned primarily with the last two. I believe a conceptual distinction can be made between kinship, on the one hand, and patronage and friendship, on the other, although in the actual operation of the system, they overlap. Their difference lies in the distinction between the obligations of kinship and patronage. An individual is born into a kinship system, and there finds, readymade so to speak, a network of persons with whom he has a series of jurally defined obligations. His position in the system is ascribed. Kinsmen are supposed to help each other. Thus if he asks a close kinsman to put his personal network of contacts at his disposal, this favor is accorded freely, if it is within the means of the relative to do so. By according the favor, the kinsman is not necessarily contracting a reciprocal service. The service he provided does not place the kinsman whom he is helping under an obligation over and above that which exists normally between kinsmen.[11]

In contrast to the ascribed mutual obligations which exist between kinsmen, the relationship between patron and client, or between friends, is entered into voluntarily. A favor or service granted creates an obligation which entails a reciprocal service that must be repaid on more or less a *quid pro quo* basis. If it is not repaid when requested or expected, the relationship is terminated. A person's position in a network of patronage is achieved, not ascribed, generally speaking. It should be noted, however, that the obligation created by a patron in one generation may not be called on until the following generation; hence patron-client relations often exist between families. Thus a patron may place his personal network of kinsmen, friends, patrons and clients at the service of a client or friend, but it is a calculated action which imposes a very definite obligation upon the person soliciting the favor. It is a debt that has to be repaid sooner or later. Among close kin no detailed ledger of services given and received is maintained, while such a social accounting is the basis upon which a system of patronage rests. However, because there is no clear demarcation separating kinship and non-kinship between distant cousins, the greater the genealogical distance between two persons exchanging favors, the more likely it is that an accounting will be kept. Kinship thus shades off into patronage.

While the institution of friendship, *amicizia*, exists in Sicily, it is necessary to see it in its local context in order to free it from the burden of preconceptions the outsider transfers almost automatically to the term. Given the overriding importance of the nuclear family in Sicilian society, and the distrustful attitude a person takes towards non-kin, friendship is an apparent contradiction to the principles presented above. But friendship must be qualified. To begin with, the tie between friends is always subordinate to that between kinsmen. Secondly, it is a voluntary relationship which entails reciprocal services. If these are not granted, it can be broken. Because it is an unstable thing, friendly non-kin often convert their friendship into a binding, formal tie through the institution of godparenthood.

The analysis of friendship in Sicily is further complicated by the fact that the term friend, *amico,* is applied indiscriminately not only to all social equals with whom a person is in contact, but also to patrons by their clients, and to clients by patrons. All are *gli amici*, friends.

The useful distinction which Eric Wolf (1966: 10 sqq.) has drawn between "emotional" and "instrumental" friendship is very much to the point here. Emotional friendship "involves a relation between an ego and an alter in which each satisfies some emotional need in his opposite number" (10). In contrast, in instrumental friendship "each member of the dyad acts as a potential connecting link to other persons outside the dyad." The former is associated with "closure of the social circle," the latter "reaches beyond the boundaries of existing sets and seeks to establish beachheads in new sets" (12). Friendship in Sicily is instrumental. The only friendships that I encountered which might have been described as emotional were between first cousins, but there the members of the dyads used the term *cugino,* cousin, and not *amico,* friend, to address and refer to each other.[12] Actions which are patently return services rendered by a client to a patron are said to be done *per amicizia,* for friendship. In fact an informant once remarked that in Sicily all friendship is political, and quoted the proverb "He who has money and friends holds justice by the short hairs"[13] to emphasize his point. Thus in the Sicilian context, friends are actual or potential intermediaries and patrons. For when a friend is called on to provide protection or assistance—a situation which occurs not infrequently in a society such as that in Sicily in which there is great inequality in the distribution of economic and political power—the friendship becomes asymmetrical and shades off into patronage. (Pitt-Rivers 1954: 154; Campbell 1964: 232 sq.)

The present-day Sicilian normally has more than one patron, and works through the one he deems most useful in a given situation. But should two patrons come into direct competition, he must choose one to the exclusion of the other. However, as social relations become progressively specialized, and the Sicilian moves out of his relatively isolated community to deal with increasingly diverse decision makers—thus requiring functionally specific patrons—the danger of an encounter between two patrons operating in the same social field diminishes. In contrast, in the past, particularly before the first World War, rural communities were more isolated from outside centers of power and the average Sicilian was limited to patrons drawn from the local *élite*. These were persons who were in direct and continuous competition with each other. It was consequently normally not possible for him to have more than one patron.

Up to this point the benefits of a patron-client relationship have been considered only from the point of view of the client. But clients protect a patron's good name and report on the activities of his enemies. It is in their interest to do this, for the stronger their patron is, the better he is able to protect them. Favors such as reports on the maneuvering of an enemy are services which generate reciprocal obligations, thus strengthening the tie between client and patron. In a society where social prestige is measured by the resources a person can command to protect and advance the position of his family, a clientele of persons who owe services of various types is a considerable asset. It enables the patron to perform, in his turn, a large variety of favors for his own patrons and "friends," and makes him more attractive as a patron. Thus an increase of either clients or patrons brings about an increase of the other.

Many of the services that a professional-class patron can claim from his clients are activities that a member of his social class could not perform—either because they are beneath his dignity, or because they are illegal—such as threatening or committing violence on the person or property of a personal enemy, or the enemy of some friend, or some friend-of-a-friend. A *contadino* is sometimes willing to perform unpleasant, if not illegal, services for a social superior, for it places his patron under a heavy obligation that can be turned to good advantage at a later date, possibly to help some "friend," who then becomes a client. A *contadino* with such a patron is in a position both to obtain protection and to command services. If he is astute (and ruthless) he may be able to turn selected contacts into an ever-widening network,[14] which can often be converted into political and economic power, and thus enable him to move up in the socio-economic hierarchy. Many members of the *borghesia* owe their secure middle-class positions as landowners, shopkeepers, or even professionals, to the extralegal activities of an ancestor who started the family on its way up. The life history of the late Don Calogero Vizzini, the so-called *capo-mafia* of Sicily until his death in 1954, provides a well-documented, if extreme, case in point (Pantaleone 1962: 94 sqq.).

There are then in Sicily persons seeking protectors even as there are influential persons seeking followers. The dangers, imaginary or real, which would surround the client should his patron withdraw his support, and the need that a person has for a large and powerful clientele in his competition with his peers, ensure that both patron and client generally meet their reciprocal obligations when called upon to do so.

Patronage in Action

It may now be asked how a system of patronage actually operates. We have examined the structural principles upon which it rests. But what are its organizational elements? Michael Kenny has noted three basic roles in a system of patronage: patron/client, patron/patron and client/patron. A fourth logical possibility, client/client, he rules out, for by definition, as soon as one client offers the other some service, he is no longer a client (Kenny 1960: 23). But if we accept this argument, can we not also say that the role relation patron/patron is a logical impossibility, for if one gives and the other receives, is not the relation asymmetrical at any particular moment? Most persons in fact occupy roles as both patron and client. Patrons, at least in present-day Sicily, do not form a separate social category as landowners or school teachers or municipal administrators, though it is fair to say that in the past those who belonged to these social categories monopolized the links with centers of power outside the community and were thus the most important local patrons.

Relations between patrons and clients involve superordination and subordination. But by superordination I mean greater access to power, not necessarily superior social rank; though as noted, in the past, economic and political power and high social rank coincided. Today the situation is more complex. Persons who are sons of *contadino* families, and who thus have low standing in the local hierarchy of prestige, now not infrequently occupy positions of power in political parties and workers' syndicates. They are consequently able to dispense favors to and intercede on behalf of wealthy landowners who have much higher social standing. Traditional roles are reversed; economic and political superordination no longer coincide.[15]

Though the dyadic sets patron/client and client/patron are the basis upon which the system rests, a system of patronage is more than just the sum total of an almost infinite number of dyadic sets, each of which is cut off from other sets. I shall argue that essential to understanding patron-client relationships as a system is the notion that two dyads can make a triad. The key person in the system is the man in the middle, the broker, who has dyadic relations with a wide variety of persons, and is thus in a position to place two people, possibly unknown to each other, into a mutually beneficial relationship from which he derives a profit. This is the *raison d'être* of the broker, of whom there are a great variety in Sicily as in other Mediterranean countries.

It is at this point that I differ from the formal analysis of patronage presented by Professor Foster (1963). While I agree with him that each individual can be seen as standing at "the center of his private and unique network of contractual ties," I disagree when he argues that the overlap of this personal network with other similar networks has "no functional significance" (1281). On the contrary, it is precisely because this overlap exists that we can speak of a *system* of patronage. The fact that B is a client of a powerful person A is often precisely the reason why C becomes B's client. As Foster notes, there is no dyadic or contractual relationship between A and C. But I suggest he fails to appreciate the importance of the fact that because both the personal networks of A and C include B, C can work through B to come in contact with A. They are friends-of-friends, *amici degli amici*, which in Sicily, and I suggest in other societies in which patronage operates, is an important social category. The undue emphasis that Foster has placed on the dyadic contract, which by his definition binds only two persons (1281), has obscured this. Moreover, the informal dyadic "contact" between two persons is very often converted to a reciprocal relationship between two groups of persons, and is therefore no longer dyadic in Foster's terms.[16]

But to return to the two basic patronage role relations suggested above. Action based upon patronage is varied, and normally involves two other role relations at the same time, namely friend/friend and kinsman/kinsman. While there may be a direct person-to-person trans-action between a client and the patron whom he is trying to influence, the manipulation of the system is not usually that simple. A person seeking to influence an important decision maker who is his social superior, but not his patron, selects a patron in his own network who is close to this person. The relationship is vertical. But his patron, the social equal of the person whom he wishes to influence, moves horizontally, possibly making use of his own kinship network in the process. Frequently a client moves vertically and horizontally by using recommendations, *raccomandazioni*. Where the person seeking a favor must move outside his face-to-face community these recommendations are often the personal calling cards of the last patron warmly recommending his *carissimo amico*, or dear friend, to a relative or a friend farther along the patronage network in the direction the client wishes to move. The person presenting the *raccomandazione* is a friend-of-a-friend, and is helped because of that. Usually the relationship between the person being passed along and those who help him is quite impersonal: he is merely a counter in the social game played between those among whom he is passed.

I should like to give a few examples of patronage in operation. The first is that of the horizontal-vertical approach. Salvatore, a student from Syracuse who had worked in Leone, wished to come into personal contact with a certain professor at the University of Palermo in order to obtain permission to present a thesis, for which registration had closed two months before. He made a special trip from Syracuse to Leone to discuss this problem with *Avvocato* Leonardo, the Secretary of the Christian Democratic Party in the town. Six months before, while he was still in Leone, Salvatore had helped Leonardo prepare a draft of an important memorandum on the town which had been requested by the party's provincial leaders. Salvatore explained his trip by saying, *Leonardo mi doveva questa,* Leonardo owed me this (favor). Salvatore knew the lawyer was in touch with many people in Palermo and felt sure that through him he could come into personal contact with his professor.

Leonardo was willing to help and gave Salvatore a card to his cousin, the personal secretary of a Palermitan official, asking him to help. He also offered to let Salvatore copy his thesis, which he pointed out would save a great deal of bother, since it was a good thesis and had been presented to a different professor a few years before. Salvatore thanked him but replied that he wanted to do his own thesis, for the experience.

Armed with Leonardo's *raccomandazione,* Salvatore set out for Palermo. The following day he met Leonardo's cousin and explained what he wanted. The cousin suggested that he see his brother, who knew many people in the University, and in his turn gave him a card. That evening Salvatore met the brother who said that he knew the professor's assistant, and gave him a card introducing him as his *carissimo amico*. The next day Salvatore called on the assistant with his *raccomandazione* and explained his case in full, asking what he should do. The assistant replied that he could arrange matters with the *Professore* but only on condition that Salvatore make electoral propaganda in Leone and the surrounding area for the *Professore,* who was standing for the Chamber of Deputies in the election the following month. Salvatore understood and pretended to live in Leone, and not in Syracuse, which was outside the elctoral district in which the *Professore* was standing, a fact which made him quite useless. The assistant then telephoned the *Professore* and made an appointment for Salvatore.

Salvatore went to see the *Professore* and explained his wish to present his thesis that June. The *Professore* looked rather doubtful, but Salvatore mentioned that he was impressed with his public spirit, and had already spoken about his candidature to several of his friends in Leone. The *Professore* loosened up at once. He indicated that the thesis should not present a problem. He then wrote a letter for Salvatore to take back to a former student of his in Leone, whom he also asked to help in his campaign.

Salvatore returned to Syracuse, via Leone, where he delivered the letter, and at once began to work on his thesis. Eventually his thesis, which was very good, was accepted and today Salvatore has his degree. The *Professore,* however, was not elected.

In his passage along this patronage network, which was essentially the network of Leonardo who placed it at his disposal, Salvatore of course was momentarily in contact with Leonardo's cousins and his professor's assistant. As he was helped along not for his own sake, but because he had been passed along by a friend or kinsman, his relations with these persons were qualitatively different from the others. Leonardo did not weaken his position with Salvatore by placing his network at the latter's disposal. On the contrary he strengthened it, for thanks to him, Salvatore attained his goal, and in so doing became aware of the efficacy of Leonardo's network. Moreover, should he wish to use the network again, he would have to pass through Leonardo again in order to receive the same cooperation from the next link.

The second example illustrates what may be called the vertical-horizontal approach. Calogero, a small land-broker, wished to become a municipal employee in Leone. He based his case on the fact that he had been employed as a clerk in the town hall before he had emigrated to Argentina, that he was a wounded veteran of World War II (and as such should receive preference), and that he possessed the educational requirements. After a great deal of maneuvering at the local level, he succeeded in getting the Leone town council to propose his name to the Commissione Provinciale di Controllo (CPC), the body that screens the credentials of all candidates proposed for office by town councils in the province and decides whether they shall be accepted. The members of the CPC are normally subject to considerable pressure from political parties and influential persons seeking to have their candidates accepted and those of their rivals rejected. Calogero was afraid that his name would be rejected by the board because of the counter manipulation of enemies in Leone, who had their own candidate. As he had no direct contact with any of the members of the board, he worked through two patrons. The first was a former commanding officer. He explained his fears and asked for help. The major agreed to help his former corporal, and proceeded to contact one of the members of the board whom he knew personally. The second patron was a lawyer in the provincial capital whom Calogero had known for many years. The lawyer was able to contact another member of the board who was a former classmate and a member of the same exclusive social club. The pressure applied by the two patrons effectively countered the move of Calogero's rivals, and he was appointed to the post. It is interesting to note that he had retained the lawyer to represent him in much the way that any professional client might do and had paid him a fee for his troubles. Yet the relation between the two was more complicated than the impersonal market relations based on an exchange of services for cash. Calogero looked upon the lawyer as his patron, his protector at the provincial capital who was able to contact the important decision-makers as an equal and friend. The action of the lawyer was not reciprocated completely by the fee he received, for he retained a claim on the loyalty and services of Calogero, who would be more than willing to defend his name and to provide his services within the more limited social field of Leone, should he be requested to do so.

The final example illustrates the last point as well as the continuing nature of patron-client relations, for as Sicilian families are tightly united, so a service to one member is felt to be given to the group, creating a collective reciprocal obligation. One Sunday *Professore* Volpe discussed certain personal problems with me as we strolled back and forth in the village square. He had been having problems over the education of his eldest son. Both the problems and the methods used to resolve them are rather Sicilian. He suspected that one of his colleagues at the secondary school in the neighboring town where he taught, and where his son went to school, was trying to injure him by failing his son and thus blocking his entrance to the University. This would have damaged the family's position as an important member of the professional class in Leone. He was able to have his enemy followed whenever the latter passed through Leone on his way to the provincial capital or Palermo by certain of his own clients and those of his brother, an important notary in Palermo. He was proud that his brother, who lived on the other side of Sicily, but "who has friends everywhere," was even able to obtain reports, from one of those friends, of conversations held by the suspect at the latter's social club. Both the conversation overheard and the observed contacts in Palermo of his enemy seemed to confirm his suspicion. *Professore* Volpe's brother then moved swiftly to apply counter pressure through a nameless important person in Palermo. This person then placed pressure on his client, the important decisionmaker, regarding the boy's admission to University, who had been previously contacted by the patron of *Professore* Volpe's enemy. As the two brothers between them boasted a wider range of contacts and a more powerful protection than their rival, they were able to resolve the affair to their satisfaction. The son was admitted to the University.

It is of course quite possible that the entire plot to dishonor the family was a figment of *Professore* Volpe's imagination, for it was all based upon intuition and indirect evidence. The suggestions by his brother to his influential friend in Palermo were most certainly couched in allegory and allusion, as was his recital to me in which no names or specific accusations were mentioned. *Professore* Volpe believed it to be true, and acted accordingly, thereby illustrating well several of the points I have tried to make above.

But the story continues. Several months after his son was admitted to the University, *Professore* Volpe was insulted in front of most of his fellow-teachers by his old enemy. He told me that he was so angry that he had to leave the common room, but before slamming the door he had shouted at his enemy that he would have his apology. He had returned to Leone and during his evening stroll the same day met *"uno dei quelli"* ("one of them," an expression often used to allude to a *mafioso*). In telling me this, he pulled his cap down over one eye to indicate to me a *mafioso* in Sicilian sign language. This person was one of those who had helped keep his enemy under observation two months before when he passed through Leone on his way to the provincial capital and Palermo. He mentioned the insult he had received, and his *amico* said, *Ci penso io,* I'll see to it. The *amico* apparently went to the neighboring town late one evening soon after and knocked on his enemy's door. In a courteous but tough voice— which the *Professore* imitated for me—he informed the enemy that it would be better to apologize or there might be unpleasantness. Two days later the *Professore* got a short note of apology by post. When I asked how much he had had to pay his *amico* for all his help, he smiled and replied, "Nothing, of course," and explained that the *amico* was the son of a man whom his own father, who had been an important notary, had helped to keep out of prison forty years before. "He helped me for *amicizia*. Because of our father we have friends all over Sicily. They are not criminals. They are men who make themselves respected. They will help you when you need it, but . . . when they turn to you for help, you give it or . . .," and he made the chopping motion that means the application of violence. "You help them and they help you. They give and you give."

Professore Volpe ended by saying that his son is doing well at the University and thus justified his faith in his ability and intelligence. "But his younger brother is lazy and not very bright," he observed. "He will probably be failed this year. My enemies are busy again. I must see what can be done." And muttering about the many responsibilities of fatherhood, he went off to lunch.

From the foregoing discussion and the three cases we have examined it is evident that while at the analytical level a distinction can be drawn between patronage, friendship and kinship, this distinction has little importance at the operational level. The Sicilian uses all three interchangeably to influence the outcome of decisions which concern him. Of the 18 dyadic sets based on kinship, friendship or patronage which constituted the portions of the networks that Salvatore, Calogero and *Professore* Volpe manipulated to achieve their ends, three were based on kinship, six on friendship and nine on patronage (four patron/client and five client/patron). These are summarized in Table 19.1. It is not possible to give priority to one to the exclusion of others.

Discussion

The system of patronage is seen to be an essential part of the political system in Sicily, for through it individuals and groups influence the outcome of decisions which concern them. It provides a system of communication which is parallel to the official channels of

Table 19.1
SUMMARY OF NETWORKS

Social Basis of Dyads	Salvatore	Calogero	Volpe	Total
Kinship	2		1	3
Friendship	2	2	2	6
Patronage				9
Patron/Chief	1		3	(4)
Client/Patron	1	2	2	(5)
Total	6	4	8	18

importance of patron-client relations.[21] I do not mean to suggest that there is a causal connection between the cult of saints and a system of political patronage, although there may be. But I think it is obvious that religious and political patronage reinforce each other. Each serves as a model for the other.

Thus spiritual patrons join the more mortal patrons, friends, and kinsmen who make up the personal network which individual Sicilians manipulate in order to influence the outcome of decisions and events, both natural and supernatural, which affect the wellbeing of their families.[22] I see the system of patronage as part of a gigantic network in which all Sicilians have a place. The average Sicilian is in contact with many others through whom, following selected strands, he is able to come into personal contact with almost every other person in the same network. He is at the same time the client of a number of patrons, each of whom normally operates in a separate social field, and the patron of a number of clients. Each of his patrons and clients have others who depend on them and on whom they depend. He also has lines which link him laterally to friends with whom he exchanges favors. He is the central point for a number of strands. The most selected strands to influential persons, and especially to persons with many clients, that pass through him, the stronger his position becomes, for his power grows in proportion to the number of appeals made to and through him. Some persons are in contact with only a few people. Others are linked directly with many above and below them as well as with equals, and serve as brokers for various types of services. Yet others, very few to be sure, are immense centers of power from which strands radiate directly to every part of the network. These are persons who occupy key positions in the political structure.

Notes

1. I read an earlier version of this paper at the 1964 meeting of the American Anthropological Association in Detroit and I am grateful for the comments of those who participated in its discussion. Professor F. G. Bailey, Dr. A. Balikci, Dr. A. Blok, Dr. P. and Dr. J. Schneider, Dr. A. Trouwborst and Dr. A. Xibilia kindly read and criticised the manuscript.
2. The field work upon which this article is based was carried out in 1962 and 1963 and was made possible by grants from the Centro Regionale per lo Sviluppo di Communità, the Penrose Fund of the American Philosophical Society (grant 3275) and the Co-operative for American Relief to Everywhere (CARE, Inc.), for which I am most grateful.
3. I have purposely used a very broad working definition of patronage, for as will be apparent from the following analysis, patron-client relations are often relations between friends.

4. The attitude of Sicilians towards the fascist period depends in part upon their present political persuasion and their social position. Many conservative bourgeois who held positions of power under the fascist regime, look back with nostalgia to the Mussolini era. Their more liberal counterparts do not do so, nor does the mass of the rural proletariat, which regards this period as one of oppression and grinding poverty. This does not necessarily mean that they feel Sicily would have been better off economically without the fascists.

5. There is no socially recognized limit, as with the Sarakatsani in Greece, where the limit is set clearly at second cousin (Campbell 1964: 36). The dividing line between kinship and non-kinship for purposes of mutual aid varies with the personal preferences of the individuals concerned, and also with their socio-economic class. In general the wealthier one is the farther out the limits of kinship obligations are extended.

6. Banfield (1958) found that much the same attitude prevailed among the peasants of Montegrano in Lucania, and called it "amoral familism." But it is of course only "amoral" in the eyes of the outside observer. The people of Lucania and Sicily regard it as a highly moral attitude, and consider those who act accordingly as acting morally.

7. Very often the land was, and still is, owned by members of the nobility resident in the cities, who lease their estates *en bloc* to intendents or *gabellotti,* or in smaller parcels under emphyteutical leases (which give perpetual effective control over the land in return for a small annual ground rent) to other prominently placed members of the bourgeoisie. These in turn either employ landless labourers, *braccianti,* to cultivate it for them, or they sublease it to share-croppers, *mezzadri,* who in their turn either cultivate it themselves or employ *braccianti* to help them.

8. Technically speaking *contadini* are those who own land and work it themselves. I avoid the use of the term in this sense and employ it as do most Sicilians, as a social category to designate all those who work on the land.

9. A pseudonym.

10. The gradual application of land reform laws after 1950 has had surprisingly little effect upon this generalised picture (*cf.* Blok 1964; Rochefort 1961: 109 sqq.).

11. Campbell (1964: 99) makes a similar point.

12. *Cf.* Campbell (1964: 101 sqq., 205, 230, 233) for an analysis of cousinage and friendship in Greece, which has many parallels to the situation in Sicily.

13. *Cu' havi denaro ed amicizia, si teni intra lu culu la giustizia.*

14. Banfield (1961) in his interesting study of the operation of patronage ("political influence" in his terms) in Chicago makes a similar point with regard to the trading of political favours. One regrets that he did not display the same political sensitivity in his study of Montegrano (Banfield 1958), where he reduced political activity to voting behavior.

15. Sydel Silverman (1965) gives an excellent account of the evolution of patronage in central Italy. This parallels changes taking place in Sicily, though the replacement of traditional multi-purpose patrons by functionally specific "intermediaries" has not gone as far in Leone as it has in her village of Colleverde.

16. Silverman (1965: 178) makes a similar point.
17. Trouwborst (1959) and Mair (1961) have observed a similar connection between patronage and social mobility in East Africa.
18. *Cf.* Marc Bloch, who sees the fact that the kinship group was not able to offer adequate protection to the individual against the violence and general lawlessness that followed the break-up of the Roman Empire as a primary reason for the development of the relations of personal protection and subordination so characteristic of feudalism. "For the only regions in which powerful agnatic groups survived—German lands on the shores of the North Sea, Celtic districts of the British Isles—knew nothing of vassalage, the fief and the manor. The tie of kinship was one of the essential elements of feudal society; its relative weakness explains why there was feudalism at all" (1961: 142).
19. Kenny also points to this functional similarity in his study of patronage in Spain (1960: 17).
20. For the Maltese version of the same proverb see Boissevain 1965 (121).
21. Wolf (1966: 18), for example, remarks on the absence among the South Tyrolese of the patron-client tie of the type discussed here. In a personal communication he informed me that the public cult of saints there appears to be less important than in the south of Italy. The feast of the Sacred Heart of Jesus was celebrated with far greater pomp than that of the patron saint of the Tyrolese village he studied.
22. In fact what I call the *patronage network* is nothing less, though it does include something more—the importance of the ties between patrons and their clients—than the *personal network* discussed by Barnes (1954: 43 sqq.).

References

Banfield, E.C. 1958. *The Moral Basis of a Backward Society.* New York: The Free Press.
———. 1961. *Political Influence.* New York: The Free Press.
Barnes, J.A. 1954. Class and Committees in a Norwegian Island Parish. *Human Relat.* 7, 39–58.
Bloch, M. 1961. *Feudal Society.* Chicago: University of Chicago Press.
Blok, A. 1964. Landhervorming in een west-siciliaans latifondo-dorp: de bestediging van een feodal structure. *Mens Maatsch.* 39, 344–59.
Boissevain, J. 1962. Maltese Village Politics and Their Relation to National Politics. *Commonwealth Pol. Stud.* 1, 211–27.
———. 1965. *Saints and Fireworks: Religion and Politics in Rural Malta.* (Monogr. Social Anthrop.) London: Athlone Press.
———. 1966. Poverty and Politics in a Sicilian Agrotown. *Intern. Arch. Ethnogr.* (In press.)
Campbell, J.K. 1964. *Honour, Family and Patronage.* New York: Oxford Press.
Foster, G.M. 1961. The Dyadic Contract: a Model for the Social Structure of a Mexican Peasant Village. *Amer. Anthrop.* 63, 1173–92.
Foster, G.M. 1963. The Dyadic Contract in Tzintzuntzan, II: Patron-Client Relationships. *Amer. Anthrop.* 65, 1280–94.

Franchetti, L. 1925. *Condizioni politiche e amministrative della Sicilia*. Franchetti, L. and Sonnino, S. *La Sicilia nel 1876*. (2 vols) 1.Florence: Valecchi.

Kenny, M. 1960. Patterns of Patronage in Spain. *Anthrop. Quart*. 33, 14–23.

———. 1961. *A Spanish Tapestry: Town and Country in Castile*. London: Cohen & West.

Mack Smith, D. 1959. *Italy: A Modern History*. Ann Arbor: University of Michigan Press

Mair, L. 1961. Clientship in East Africa. *Cah. Etud. afr.* 2, 315–25.

Maxwell, G. 1956. *God Protect Me from My Friends*. London: Longmans, Green.

Pantaleone, M. 1962. *Mafia e politica*. Torino: Einaudi.

Pitt-Rivers, J. 1954. *The People of the Sierra*. London: Weidenfeld & Nicholson.

Renda, F. 1956. *Il movimento contadino nella società siciliana*. Palermo: "Sicilia al Lavoro."

Rochefort, R. 1961. *Le travail en Sicile*. Paris: Presses Universitaires de France.

Silverman, S. 1965. Patronage and Community-Nation Relationships in Central Italy. *Ethnology* 4, 172–89.

Sonnino, S. 1925. *I contadini*. Franchetti, L. and Sonnino, S. *La Sicilia* nel 1876. (2 vols) 2. Florence: Valecchi.

Trouwborst, A.A. 1959. La mobilité de l'individu en fonction de l'organisation politique des Barundi. *Zaire* 13, 787–800.

———. 1961. L'organisation politique en tant que système de'échange au Barundi. *Anthropologica* 3, 1–17.

———. 1962. L'organisation politique et l'accord de clientèle au Barundi. *Anthropologica* 4, 9–43.

Wolf, E.R. 1966. Kinship, Friendship, and Patron-Client Relations in Complex Societies. In *The Social Anthropology of Complex Societies* (ed.) M.P. Banton (A.S.A. Monogr. 4). London: Tavistock Publications.

20

Village Friendship and Patronage

J. K. Campbell

[From a study of life in a community of Greek Sarakatsan peasants, which the author believes contains many parallels to society anywhere in the Greek provinces and in other portions of the Mediterranean world.]

Here a brief digression is necessary to consider the nature of friendship in Zagori villages.[1] Between villagers ties of friendship relate persons who are, in principle, equals. All villagers, without discrimination, possess the same legal rights in the local polity. If a man is also honorable in his conduct, a good neighbor, and legitimately born of Zagori parents, he is entitled in the social life of the village to be treated with a degree of consideration that represents a recognition of his social personality. Persons who are equal in these respects must show some concern for each other's social sensibilities by avoiding public rudeness and by a careful and courteous exchange of greetings when they meet.

Friendship begins where one man accepts a favor ($\chi\omega\rho\eta$) from another. The person who gives the favor will assert that he expects no return; it would be insulting to suggest that his act of friendship had a motivation. It is, however, the very altruism of the act, whether this is simulated or not, which demands a counter favor. Default destroys the friendship and provokes accusations of ingratitude. Although liking and sympathy are alleged to be the premises on which friendship between village equals is based, it would be more true to say that villagers who are able to do each other reciprocal favors sometimes discover from this experience confidence in one another. From these beginnings there may grow a relationship of intimacy and warmth. But

Source: J. K. Campbell, *Honour, Family and Patronage: A Study of Institutions and Moral Values in a Greek Mountain Community.* Oxford: Oxford Clarendon Press, 1964, pp. 229–38. By permission of the publisher.

in essence friendship of this kind remains a contractual relation, a form of cooperation in which services of various kinds are exchanged and accounted.

The network of friendships of the president or of other influential villagers becomes in reality a system of patronage. Accountancy is then more difficult because the patron is able to do more material favors for his client than the latter is able to return. But although the character of the relationship is now, in effect, asymmetrical, patron and client, because they are interacting in the context of village community relations where all true villagers are in principle equals, they continue to treat one another as if they were equals in the situation of their friendship as well. Both patron and client claim publicly that the other "is my friend." The patron says that he helps his client simply because it pleases him to help those of his friends who are in difficulties. The client explains that he is the friend of the patron, not simply because he receives benefits from him, but because he is a good man. In short, their friendship exists within the field of village values where behavior is evaluated against the ideals of independence and love of honor.

In the Sarakatsan community the situation is different. There is no cooperation between unrelated families and no established political authority in the shepherd community which might lead to relations of political friendship. A relationship which has many of the aspects of patronage exists between the dominant family and the other associated families in a cooperating "company," but these connections are based on the values of kinship, not friendship. When a Sarakatsanos says "I have him as a friend," he generally means that he has established a relation of mutual advantage with a person outside the community who is most cases is in the superordinate position of patron. The use of the word "friend" by the Sarakatsanos is not here encumbered with any theory of equality or disinterested motives. The fact that in terms of power he is the weaker partner in the majority of his relations of friendship is recognized by the Sarakatsanos but does not immediately concern his pride since these people stand outside his community. On the contrary, the more effective relationships of this kind that a man possesses, the greater his prestige in the community since it proves him to be an able protector of his family and his flocks.

It is by no means certain that a president will accept any Sarakatsanos as his political client. What the president has to offer will be clear enough from the earlier description of the ways in which he can help or hinder. The chief service the shepherd is able to pledge in return is his vote and those of his family and associated kinsmen. But to accept a man as a client commits the patron to protection instead of exploitation, and to that extent it is a restriction on the free exercise of his power. A president generally prefers to assume these obligations only to Sarakatsani with some influence. Naturally, more humble families have vicarious access to his patronage through their influential kinsmen, but the intermediate link which separates them from the president's beneficence makes it less likely that their affairs will be settled with the same dispatch and satisfaction.

The extent to which a president needs to enter these commitments depends, of course, on the balance of the political groupings in his village. In one village the president commanded about three quarters of the village vote, but by his generally uncompromising hostility he had driven the Sarakatsani into the arms of the small opposition party. A month before the election it appeared that he had no Sarakatsan supporters and that his cause was lost. Conveniently the election was held in November, after the Sarakatsani had departed to the plains eighty miles away. The opposition party chartered a lorry to transport, as they had calculated it, an adequate number of Sarakatsan voters to assure their victory. But, in the event, the president skilfully contrived a narrow majority by making secret agreements with two shepherd families. The five members of these families who returned from the plains, ironically enough in the lorry chartered by the opposition, were sufficient to give the president victory and a new term of office.

After the election the two families received a number of favors. In the spring the sheep of one family were short-counted by sixty and the flock of the other, which by right of the customary rotation of grazing areas ought to have gone to an area of indifferent grazing, spent a more profitable summer on the village's best grassland. In the face of the unusual solidarity of the local Sarakatsan group at the time of the election, the action of the two dissident families was described as treacherous. They were branded as "The president's men," with an overtone of meaning which implied that they were puppets dancing at the command of the master, capable even of betraying their own people. Yet as passions cooled and the months passed, evaluations changed perceptibly. At first the members of these families were unequivocally "traitors," but later they were considered merely "cunning" (by no means an entirely pejorative judgement), and eventually one sometimes heard grudging admissions of their "cleverness." For it is recognized that each family is free to seek its own protection and the political friends who can provide it. Indeed, Sarakatsani believe that in the nature of the situation favors and concessions are to be won only by some, not all families. It is, therefore, the duty of each head of family to scheme and intrigue for his own security. Only in the case of a breach of faith between kinsmen is an accusation of treachery seriously considered.

But the friendship which a Sarakatsanos achieves with a village president, or indeed with any other influential person, involves more than the exchange of specific material favors; it establishes, also, an asymmetrical relation of sociability which enhances the prestige of both men. A Sarakatsanos who has friendship with the president boldly sits down with him at the same table when he enters the coffeeshop. The president offers him a drink, he stands him a drink in return. Meeting him in the village square, the shepherd stops to talk for a few minutes about this and that. Were they not patron and client, a curt "good day" from each side would be the extent of their social intercourse. However, it is not a relationship of equals. The shepherd belongs not only to a different community, but to a qualitatively inferior one. While the President will say of a villager who is similarly his client that this man is his friend, he will not say this of a shepherd. If an explanation in his presence is necessary, he may say, "George is a good lad, I help him," but behind his back he will simply say, "He is my man." Yet, although they are his social inferiors, the president gains prestige by being seen publicly with his shepherd clients. If he drinks with other villagers who are his supporters, this is no cause for comment. He merely keeps company with those who are his social equals and natural companions. When he drinks with four or five shepherds, it draws attention to his possession of power, to his ability to hold men who do not waste their time drinking with ordinary villagers whom as a class of persons they detest and despise. The Sarakatsanos accepts his position of inferiority in the relationship because he must. He does not, as most villagers would, address the president by his Christian name; but he is not subservient in his manner. He speaks to him courteously as "president." When another person of importance comes to speak to the president, and it is clear that he is dismissed, he moves to another table, or with a "good health, president," to which the latter replies, he leaves the shop. These are the conventional terms on which these unequal friendships are founded. What is important to the Sarakatsanos in these situations is that other shepherds who do not possess this valued link should see and envy him.

In asymmetrical friendship relations, since it is assumed that the patron has more favors to offer than the client can return, or that reciprocal favors are so dissimilar in quality that accountancy is difficult, there is often greater stability than in friendships between equals, which are very frequently bedevilled by accusations of ingratitude. Yet, even here, there are many complaints, the patron asserting that the client should be more vocal in his gratitude, the client complaining that the patron does very little in relation to the client's worth and needs, and the services he has rendered. In short, the patron wants more honor, the client more benefits.

The third widely practised method of placating or influencing the president is to present him with a gift of cheese, butter, or meat. Some families do this each spring as a matter of general policy without having in mind any particular favor. They hope that the gift may moderate his general attitude towards them in the coming months. More often, families wait until they face some specific difficulty. A gift of cheese or some other produce is delivered to the president's home and then, perhaps two days later, the gift-giver walks into the village office and makes his request. The president may be helpful or he may not. The assumptions of the giver and the recipient of the gift are not necessarily the same. The giver hopes that the gift will arouse some sense of obligation in the receiver. But the latter, if he chooses to feel that the gift was forced on him against his will, may decide that he is not obliged to feel grateful. If he intends not to grant the favor, the refusal is never direct. The many difficulties which stand in the way are elaborated at very great length. He explains that he will see what can be done, he will write to a friend in Jannina, he wants to help. In fact he will do nothing; and the original gift is not returned.

A gift is frequently offered to the president by a Sarakatsanos when he meets with legal troubles. Stratos and a number of his kinsmen were using 20 mules to transport wooden planks from a sawmill to the road below the village where the wood was loaded on to lorries. The area for the grazing of Sarakatsan mules and horses is an hour's climb above the village and this was very inconvenient for Stratos and the other muleteers. They changed their luck and grazed their animals at night in the little-frequented village orchards close to their loading point. On the thirty-ninth night of their operations they were discovered by the agricultural guard who from his examination of the length of the grass and some damage to young apple trees was confident of a very successful case. Stratos was not able to claim that the president was his friend, but since he was a lawabiding careful man his relations with the president had been generally good. He begged for his assistance, explaining the extreme difficulty the group would have suffered if each night the mules had had to be released so far from the scene of operations. He managed also to mention that he would like to help the president in the current rebuilding of his house. It so happened that he had two loads of timber which he did not require. The next day, the president saw the agricultural guard and warned him that, in his opinion, it would only be reasonable to take into consideration the one night when he had actually seen the mules. For the rest, who could say? There had been high winds recently which often damaged trees, and he added that he had noticed one of the agricultural guard's own goats straying one evening in the direction of the orchards. Accordingly, the president received his wood, Stratos and his kinsmen escaped with a small fine, and the agricultural guard's dream of a triumphant case came to nothing.

Two points must be stressed about this method of influencing the president. Gifts must be presented with finesse. A man of honor is not to be crudely bought by social inferiors if he does not wish to lose prestige in the community. The shepherd must give the lamb, butter, or cheese to the president as if it were merely an expression of friendly respect, and in no way tied to the favor he is about to request. Secondly, whether in relation to these gifts of produce, or to other perquisites of his office, the limited dishonesty and corruptibility of a president is not dishonorable. "He eats money" (τρῳει παρῳδε!), others say with envy. But they concede that this is the right of his office. His allowance is not large, he too must live, he also has a family to support. If a favor, even where it is entirely legal, involves trouble beyond the ordinary routine duties of his office, why should he weary himself for a man to whom he is not related in any way, unless that man by a gift, or in some other way, demonstrates the esteem in which he holds him.

We have now discussed in the order of their effectiveness three ways in which the Sarakatsani attempt to influence the president of their summer village—spiritual kinship, friendship, and gifts. In principle, spiritual kinship binds a president to help the shepherd in all situations. Ideally it is a diffuse relation, there is nothing reasonable that cannot be requested, and the right to expect this assistance is sanctioned by the ritual link between godfather and godchild. Friendship of the kind established between a village president and a Sarakatsanos, is a patron-client relationship of some stability over time, and the range of favors which may be demanded is almost as extensive as that between spiritual kinsmen, but the atmosphere of calculation is more pronounced. Confidence which is ritually sanctioned in spiritual kinship is more easily destroyed in the relations of patron and client. Gifts given by a shepherd to the president generally have a specific object in view and each gift is effective for only a short period of time if, indeed, it is effective at all.

The president is not the only man with power or influence in a village; the other members of the council, the schoolmaster, the priest, other villagers of wealth or reputation may have these qualities in varying degree. When the president is particularly severe towards them, the shepherds attempt, by the same methods we have just considered, to attach themselves to other persons in the village who are known to have influence on the council, or personally over the president himself.

When the sheep of Theodoros were dispatched by the president to the poorest area of grazing for the second year because of his active opposition during the elections, Theodoros did not appeal to the Nomarch against this injustice. He went instead to Vlachopoulos. Vlachopoulos is the vice-president of the village, and the president's closest friend. He also owns the older of the two village coffeeshops which is the one more generally patronized by the Sarakatsani both for social gatherings and for the many small purchases which they make. After the bitter feelings aroused by the autumn elections there was a spontaneous boycott of the Vlachopoulos shop by the Sarakatsani and at the time when Theodoros approached him two or three weeks after the shepherds had returned to the summer pasture, only a few Sarakatsan men were to be seen drinking in the old shop. For a week Theodoros assiduously made small purchases in the shop. Finding Vlachopoulos alone one day, he took the next step by remarking that he was not a man to dwell on old scores and that he thought his return to the shop proved this point. It seemed, however, that the president was still governed by his rage and spite. This was surely unjust, and he asked Vlachopoulos if he would not intercede with the president on his behalf. Vlachopoulos agreed to do this. It is a fair assumption that he was especially pleased to see Theodoros who leads a substantial cooperating "company" and has many other kinsmen in the local group of shepherds. It was very probable that if Theodoros returned to his shop to drink, as well as to buy, the boycott would be over. This proved to be the case. Vlachopoulos persuaded the president to rearrange the grazing areas, and after a week or two of further delay to impress upon Theodoros the misguided nature of his opposition in the previous autumn, the president eventually effected the necessary changes.

A Zagori village and the local group of Sarakatsani that is linked to it through rights of citizenship, form a network of friendship relations, some of which are symmetrical and others of the patron–client variety. This network enables a man in many situations to obtain a measure of satisfaction from a person with whom he is in direct opposition. He the government. This is of particular importance in a society such as that in Sicily, which is highly stratified and in which positions of authority are frequently occupied by persons who belong to the upper strata of the socio-economic hierarchy. For in such a society the lines of communication through the formal system are tenuous and difficult to follow because of the social distance between those who wish to make their voices heard on high, and those who control the channels through which such messages necessarily must pass. Those desiring to communicate are faced by the rigid apparatus of a ponderous bureaucratic system. The system of patronage permits a person to contact officials on a personal basis. Campbell has remarked in describing the operation of the patronage system in Greece that "it introduces a flexibility into administrative machinery whose workings are very often directed by persons remote from the people whose fortunes they are affecting" (1964: 247). It means that the *contadini* have some way of controlling the harsh forces that surround them. To some extent then, it gives them a voice in their own destiny. It not only provides protection and facilitates communication, but may also furnish a way of moving upward in a stratified society.[17]

Beyond the individual and family levels, patronage can be seen to link entire villages to the structure of government, for the personal networks of village leaders, while manipulated primarily for personal ends, also provide the lines of communication along which village business moves upward, and provincial, regional and national funds flow downward into the village for public works and other development projects. At this level the patronage system is linked with the structure and operation of political parties (*cf.* Boissevain 1965: 120–33; 1966). This is a subject I shall deal with more fully elsewhere.

A system of patronage can also be likened to a parasitic vine clinging to the trunk of a tree. As the vine saps the strength of the tree, so patronage weakens government. It leads to nepotism, corruption, influence-peddling and, above all, it weakens the rule of law. And, in Sicily, because violence is still part of the social currency, it has led to the persistence of brokers who are specialists in matters of violence, the *mafiosi*. In brief, it leads to and perpetuates the very conditions which have brought it into being, nurtured it, and permitted it to develop to the point where it is perhaps the most important channel of communication.

Why has patronage assumed such social importance in Sicily?

Ties of dependency exist because there is still need for protection that neither the state nor the family is able to provide.[18] The Sicilian requires protection not only from his neighbors, who are trying to protect and advance themselves at his expense, but also from a powerful government which he feels has been imposed upon him and which he regards as corrupt. He also needs protection from the law which he not only believes can be manipulated by his enemies to his detriment, but with which he is also often in conflict because of the differing requirements of the legal system and those of traditional justice. Finally, he needs protection from the violence and exploitation that are a part of Sicilian life. It is obvious that many of the conditions which give rise to the need for protection, and hence patronage, are simply the result of the successful operation of the patronage system. Patronage is, to a very large extent, a self-perpetuating system of belief and action grounded in the society's value system.

Nonetheless, there is another important factor which I believe has favored the persistence of patronage in Sicily. This is the continuing importance of the Catholic religion. Despite rampant anticlericalism, the Roman Catholic religion remains deeply rooted in the life and customs of the people. The many religious processions and feasts for the various patron saints are still among the most important social events of the countryside. I suggest that in such a society there is a strong ideological basis for a political system based upon patronage. There is a striking functional similarity between the role of saints as intermediaries between God and man, and the mortal patron who intercedes with an important person on behalf of his client.[19] In fact, a patron is sometimes called a *santo* or saint, and people occasionally quote the proverb *Senza santi nun si va'n paradisu*, without the help of saints you can't get to heaven,[20] to illustrate the importance of patrons in achieving one's desires. This parallel was drawn for me by the Archpriest of Leone as he sought to explain the spiritual role of saints. He noted that just as you would not think of approaching a cabinet minister directly, but would work through some influential friend who could introduce you to the local deputy who could then state your case to the minister, so too must you not approach God directly. You must work through your patron saint who, being closer to God than you, is in a better position to persuade Him to heed your prayers. The role of patron in Sicily thus receives constant and authoritative validation from the Church through the widespread cult of personal and community patron saints. It is a striking fact that in Catholic countries with a strong cult of saints, such as those in the Mediterranean area and in Latin America, there is also a political system which if not based upon, is at least strongly influenced by patron-client relations. These countries may be contrasted to Catholic societies in the north of Europe where the cult of saints is considerably less pronounced, as is the achieves this by indirect pressure because he is a client, or friend, of the friend of his enemy. Villagers and shepherds are careful to maintain friendship links with opposed political factions and personages whenever this is possible. The implication is that there are often inherent limits on the way in which the president or other influential villagers may use their power against most individuals, since, very probably, in any particular act of victimization they are attacking the friend, or client, of one of their own friends. Only very poor villagers, or Sarakatsani with small flocks who are not attached to the cooperating "company" or more powerful kinsmen, may be treated unjustly without encountering some responding pressure through the system of friendships; for these persons, having little to offer in return, may not have patrons. But in other cases to ignore the pressures received through the system of friendships may endanger important relationships on which a man's influence and prestige largely depend. It is not suggested, however, that a man with strategically aligned friendships is secure from all injustice. On the contrary, Theodoros suffered a considerable financial loss until his friendship with Vlachopoulos rescued him from further punishment.

In the Zagori villages, as in the Sarakatsan community, a dominant feature of the social system is the isolation of the family and its struggle against other families, whether in terms of the possibility of bare subsistence or of social prestige. The more important social obligations are particular to the individual's family, and these stand in direct conflict with the weaker and more general responsibilities of good neighborliness. The notion of service to the community (ενεργεσщα) exists, and is honored. But the service takes a form which honors the individual, his family and the community in equal degree as, for instance, in the foundation of a church or school. Such services are never anonymous. The idea of service to fellow citizens of the same community exists also, but it remains an ideal value which is not realized in a society where familial obligations have an absolute priority. The president and councillors of the village are firstly heads of households and only secondly public servants. A president does not feel under the same moral obligation, even within the sphere of his formal duties, to help equally a close kinsman, a spiritual kinsman, a friend, and a man to whom he is linked only by common citizenship. It is suggested that in this absence, for the most part, of universally applicable values the system of village friendship and patronage in fact achieves a distribution of various facilities which, although it is never equitable, guards most families, even those of the hard-pressed Sarakatsani of Zagori, against complete exclusion. The system of friendship and patronage achieves this, not by upholding any general rights of citizenship, but, in a sense paradoxically, by an appeal to the individual and family interests of a person in authority. For without friends a man loses all power, influence, and social prestige.

Note

1. Friendship in Epirote villages appears to be very similar to the parallel institution in Andalusia. See Cf. Pitt-Rivers, *Mediterranean Countrymen* (The Hague, 1963), chapter 7.

21

Endemic and Planned Corruption in a Monarchical Regime

John Waterbury

Corruption may be defined in a legal or normative sense, and in some societies the two definitions may be coincident. In the legal sense, corruption is self-regarding behavior on the part of public functionaries that directly violates legal restrictions on such behavior. Normatively, a public functionary may be considered corrupt whether or not a law is being violated in the process. A legally corrupt person may arouse no normative reprobation; a person judged corrupt by normative standards may be legally clean. What is common to both definitions is the notion of the abuse of public power and influence for private ends. It can safely be assumed that any society or political system manifests some level of one or the other, or both of these forms of corruption.

We may consider this level (while begging the question of how to measure it) as the amount of free-floating, endemic corruption in a system. In general, analysts of corruption have portrayed it as mostly unwanted (although sometimes convenient), and most often unplanned. It has been seen as a concomitant phenomenon accompanying the politico-administrative process, but only marginally instrumental in the maintenance and vitality of that process. The real or perceived saliency of corruption in the developing countries has generated some rethinking of the functions of corruption in both political and economic development. Again, because of the difficulty of measuring something that may be legally and morally condemned, we cannot be sure if the degree or level of corruption in various developing countries is really higher than in economically advanced nations. Perhaps, because in many developing countries cultural norms are more tolerant

Source: John Waterbury, "Endemic and Planned Corruption in a Monarchical Regime," *World Politics*, 25, 4 (July 1973), 533–55. Copyright © 1973 by Princeton University Press. Reprinted with permission of Princeton University Press.

of corruption as legally defined, and because the laws themselves are
so out of touch with cultural expectations and actual administrative
practice, corrupt behavior, as judged by the outsider, is far more open
than in advanced nations where such behavior is masked by legal
subterfuge and the complexity of the deals.

Whatever the difficulties of measuring and comparing levels of
corruption, the contemporary experience of the developing countries
has provoked considerable speculation as to whether or not corruption
may ultimately prove beneficial to economic growth and political
development. Three authors, who will receive greater attention further
on, have pointed out that corruption may promote national integration,
capitalist efficiency, capital formation, administrative flexibility, and a
shift toward popular democracy.[1] Those speculations must be tested
against empiric evidence, and in this chapter evidence will be drawn
from contemporary Morocco.

Beyond that, the analysis will be carried a step further. Not only
must we consider the possibility that corruption may have certain
beneficial effects on the development process, but, however we appraise these effects, it may be that corruption is far more than an
accompanying phenomenon of the political process. It may be seen as
a planned, cultivated, and vital element in assuring the survival of a
regime. As the case of Morocco would tend to demonstrate, corruption
is not simply an aspect of politics but has displaced and dwarfed all
other forms of politics.

Thus, in Morocco, free-floating corruption is manipulated, guided,
planned, and desired by the regime itself. Although the terms may not
fit with precision, the Moroccan monarchy can be seen as a patrimonial
regime with strong rationalizing tendencies. The elements of rationalization manifest themselves in at least two ways. First, the growing
central bureaucracy is increasingly subject to rational criteria of organization, recruitment, and training. Bureaucrats, in terms of education,
exposure to outside currents of thought, mental outlook, and career
expectations, are *somewhat* removed from the traditionalistic, clientelistic, and particularistic ethos of the patrimonial regime.[2] Moroccan
bureaucrats tend to identify with an exogenous cultural referent that
leads them to condemn morally corrupt behavior which, for the rest of
society, may be corrupt in the legal sense only. Second, although they
condemn corrupt practices, a very substantial part (again the phenomenon defies precise measurement) of the bureaucrats are involved in
them. But because of their outlook and their skills, they have brought
about some rationalization of the system of patronage and of corruption itself. They are willing participants in a particular regime's system,

and are in some ways its accomplices. Their participation has a price which comes in the form of illicit rewards. There is, then, a notion of contract at play here, one that is defined almost entirely in terms of participation on the one hand and payoffs on the other. This represents a straightforward, rational transaction.

The patrimonial aspects of the regime[3] are quite obvious and will be dealt with in detail further on. Suffice it to say for the moment that the monarchy underscores its supremacy within the system by constantly spawning new relations of dependency between itself and various sectors of the society. Dependency is maintained by manipulating access to various kinds of administrative prebends. These may, of course, be seen as part of the distribution system, but they are not subject to criteria of state planning, rational development priorities, or organizational performance. Instead, they are subject to bargaining, threats, influence-trading, and, above all, the judgment and sometimes the whim of the man who has his hand on the tap.

The fact that the Moroccan regime is a monarchy highlights the patrimonial characteristics of the regime, but guided or planned corruption need in no way be confined to monarchies. Keeping in mind that manipulation of a spoils system may be not only useful to a regime but crucial to its survival, we may refer to Ann Ruth Willner's portrayal of Sukarno.

> President Sukarno successfully assumed lifetime tenure, an impressive array of titles, and a style of life that included the entourage, regalia, and rituals customarily maintained by traditional Javanese monarchs. . . . Significantly, he did not maintain his position of supremacy by direct control of a tightly organized and disciplined political, bureaucratic, or military apparatus, commanding either overt or implicit instruments of coercive pressure at his direction. Rather, his strength derived from his adroit command of various strategies of manipulation, negotiation, and bargaining; from bestowal and withdrawal of approval; from appointments and emoluments, and from psychological exploitation of his knowledge of the probable responses of his chief lieutenants and subordinates, their lieutenants and subordinates, and other leaders and contenders for power and position.[4]

It may be that any head of state who wishes to remain in power indefinitely, i.e., permanently, is pushed towards the elaboration of a neo-feudal patronage system. In Mexico, the PRI has avoided one-man rule, but has nonetheless created the problem of the dynastic survival of what James Wilkie calls the "Revolutionary Family." Regime maintenance has come to be founded on an elaborate system of state patronage, the benefits of which are disbursed under the budget heading *erogaciones adicionales*; in any year these may account for 15 to 23 percent of all budgeted expenditures.[5] It must be emphasized that the phenomenon under examination goes beyond mere pork-barrelism and is essential to the maintenance of the regime. In the context of United States politics, the closest analogies are to be found in the city-boss systems where, again, relations of dependency are created and maintained through the discriminatory use of the power and privileges of public office. The vote is simply a convenient way to reaffirm these ties and to measure their extent as well as their cost within the boss's arena.[6]

Characteristics of Endemic Corruption in Developing Countries

To reiterate an earlier point: Any political system, regardless of the nature of its regime, manifests some level of corruption; in turn, this may be incorporated into the lifeblood of those regimes that predicate their survival upon its use. It has already been intimated that corruption may best be seen as a variant of the broader phenomenon of patronage. Patronage is founded upon asymmetrical relations between a powerful person or group of persons and their clients, who seek protection, favors, and rewards from the patrons. At the same time, to an important extent the patron is powerful as a result of the size or nature of his clientele, and is able to protect and reward his supporters because he uses them to strengthen his hand in bargaining for scarce resources.[7] A patron, of course, need not be a public official; he can attract clientele on the basis of his wealth or his control of or access to scarce resources such as jobs, or land, or arms. However, when a patron occupies a public position or extracts favors from those in public positions, patronage and corruption overlap.[8]

In developing societies, which are characterized by material scarcity, both real and perceived, the asymmetry in relations between the powerful and the less powerful is particularly pronounced. Scarce resources are relatively more scarce, and the power derived from controlling them is more extensive and inescapable. The few resources at the disposal of the poor and the powerless can be easily lost or destroyed, and awareness of this fact heightens a general sense of vulnerability and potential disaster, and sets in motion myriads of clients in search of patrons. There is no real escape from the quest until and unless the contextual scarcity is overcome. Networks of dependency, or what Andreski more vividly calls "relations of parasitism," are continually regenerated: "Once a society is pervaded by parasitic exploitation, the choice is only to skin or be skinned. A man may combine the two roles in varying measure but he cannot avoid them: he cannot follow Candide's example and till his garden, relying on hard work for his well-being, because he will not be left alone: the wielders of power will pounce upon him and seize the fruits and tools of his labor."[9]

It has often been observed that the search for protection from nature, violence, and the exactions of arbitrary and predatory governments was a constant theme of social life in socalled traditional societies. Although today the vagaries of nature and the extent of communal violence may be more subject to technological control than they were in the past, the application of technology has become a quasi-monopoly of new state systems. The poor of the Third World may have exchanged one kind of vulnerability for another. The introduction of Mexican wheat may lead to increased yields, but the peasant must somehow obtain credit from the state agricultural credit bank and hope for the best in a market pricing system partially or totally determined by the state. The need for intercessors, protectors, and patrons is no less great now than it was in the past. Moreover, the contemporary power and penetration of the modern state apparatus has in many instances been achieved without any modification of the degree of real or perceived material scarcity. Competition for privileged access to state services or relief from impositions has come to dominate political life; the scope for corrupt patronage has expanded with the state itself.[10]

It has frequently been the case that in polities where class structures range from fragile to nonexistent, access to political power has been the surest means to wealth (rather than the reverse which, according to Marx, was characteristic of the development of capitalist structures). The very notion of a prebend presupposes the use of office as a means to acquire property. In patrimonial and neo-patrimonial systems, passing on access to public office (if not the office itself) from generation to generation has been a more dominant and rational motive than acquiring wealth; in such systems, wealth has usually been subject to the destruction, confiscation, or other predatory actions of the state.

In the contemporary period that motive has been reinforced in many ways. Frequently the governments of the developing countries maintain arbitrary and predatory practices that involve the destruction of resources of real or imagined enemies. Moreover, the technological and administrative means to achieve these ends have been greatly expanded in the twentieth century. At the same time, relatively well-organized and penetrative state bureaucracies have come to intervene in and control large areas of the economic life of their societies. Not only do these bureaucracies regulate and sanction ever wider spheres of social and economic behavior, but they influence and determine the allocation of desired resources on a hitherto unprecedented scale. It is little wonder then that, for the ambitious, access to public power has become more than ever the key to material success as well as to the formation of clientelistic support.[11] For the average citizen, reaching some sort of *modus vivendi* with a state system that affects nearly all aspects of one's life has become a daily chore.

In brief, historical precedent and conditions, combined with the logic of contemporary bureaucratic expansion in the devleoping countries, have fostered the growth of extensive amounts of systemic corruption.

For the most part it is corruption in the legal sense only, for while the political and abuses of patronage may be disliked by the masses, they are not regarded as illicit; in effect, they are seen as a fact of life that one cannot avoid and that had best be mastered. "Corruption," Huntington posits, "is behavior of public officials which deviates from accepted norms in order to serve private ends."[12] But self-regarding or client-regarding activities of public officials do not deviate from accepted norms. Something of the attitudinal ambivalence involved here is revealed by certain findings of a recent mass survey in India. Forty-two percent of an urban and 48 percent of a rural sample thought that the majority of civil servants was corrupt. At the same time, 76 and 89 percent, respectively, of the same samples stated that they would prefer to work for the government as compared with the private sector: "The expectation of dishonesty and corruption in government is high in India and, paradoxically, for the same people who see government service as prestigeful. Government service is apparently seen in two separate images, from two distinct value positions. It is both corrupt and prestigeful."[13] On the basis of this statement, I would suggest that the paradox is more apparent than real, and that the corrupt and prestigeful images of the bureaucracy are in fact reconciled within an ethos founded on asymmetrical relations of dependency and vulnerability.[14] Power and privilege are simultaneously resented and coveted by those who do not have them.

The tolerance of corruption at all levels is predicated upon the basic cynicism of the people with regard to their government. No one is dupe in this game where services and influence are marketable commodities and where buyers and sellers use all their wiles to strike a bargain.

> When, as a supplicant, the peasant tries to bribe a clerk, or to establish a dependent relationship with an official in the idiom of a family relationship or of a courtier at the king's palace, he is in fact trying to coerce the clerk or the official by including him within his own moral community.

He is trying to transform the transaction, which he knows is one of exploitation, into a moral relationship, *because it is in his interest to do so*. In just the same way, when the campaigning politician addresses him as "brother," the peasant sees this as an act of hypocrisy, and looks behind the facade of symbolic friendliness for the hidden interest.[15]

As regards transactions inherent in administrative corruption, we are dealing with the distribution of and payment for services and dispensations. For the masses of supplicants, paying for the service (bribing) is not reprehensible in itself; but when the market value of services becomes too high, moral indignation is aroused. In Morocco, for instance, some evidence suggests that the inflation in the price of corruption has become onerous and resented. Passports and work permits are too highly priced, price-control brigades shake down retailers too often and for too much, entrance "fees" for state examinations have been greatly inflated, and so forth. It is at this point that the indignation of the masses over the excessive prices of needed services may mesh with the professed indignation of the educated elites who condemn corruption regardless of its costs.

Finally, we may note that pervasive administrative corruption at the lower echelons of the bureaucracy is particularly favored by the low level of literacy in many developing countries, as well as by the personalized rendering of administrative services. Where literacy is at a premium, there are very few routine operations that can be performed anonymously between the citizen and the functionary. One must line up, find someone to fill out the forms, locate the intermediary who knows the right office, and then bargain one's way to some sort of solution. The process is on a face-to-face basis, with several possible services to be purchased along the way.[16]

Costs and Benefits of Corruption in Morocco

With virtually no exceptions, the kinds of endemic corruption set forth in the preceding pages are to be found in Morocco. Is it possible to establish some sort of balance sheet as to their costs and benefits to the Moroccan polity and society?

Both Leff and Nye have suggested a number of possible benefits resulting from corruption. Regarding economic development, Nye argues that corruption may encourage capital formation where taxation would inhibit it. Further, illegal purchases of administrative favors may help cut red tape and overcome the rigidity of administrative practices. Finally, corruption may promote efficient entrepreneurial behavior. Leff joins Nye in emphasizing this point. In situations of what he calls "market corruption," the highest bribe wins the contract or favor, and it may be that the most efficient capitalist is the one who can muster the highest bribe; ergo, corruption rewards efficiency.[17]

We may summarize some of the other advantages, particularly as presented by Nye, as follows: corruption (implicitly on a broad scale) may tend to overcome elite cleavages by means of the unobtrusive and clandestine redistribution of spoils. It is perhaps this "function" that Scott has in mind in his remarks about Thailand: "What distribution [of corruption] takes place is intended to cement the ties that bind particular military-civil cliques together and prevent defection to other potential 'coup-groups.' "[18]

In addition, corruption permits access to the distribution system to groups and minorities that might otherwise be frozen out. Ironically, corruption is thus seen as overcoming certain discriminatory practices and as promoting national integration. Along these same lines, corruption—particularly when viewed as a facet of broader patronage networks—may mitigate potential ethnic or class conflict by diverting the attention of spokesmen from the exploitation of grievances to the distribution of spoils.[19] A third political and integrative benefit may derive from the use of corruption to create supporting institutions such as political parties, and to grease the wheels of electoral politics. Moreover, it may be, as Scott argues, that electoral corruption indicates a real spread of popular democracy when a regime can no longer control elections through violence, threat, or fraud, and must pay for votes rather than extract them by force.

We may now try to determine how Morocco scores on some of these dimensions, but a preliminary remark is in order. It is illusory to think that we can actually measure the costs and benefits of corruption in Morocco or in any other country. The reason is simple. Either one is dealing with a country in which some level of corruption is apparent or with a country in which, at least for the sake of argument, no corruption is apparent. On the one hand, a discussion of the benefits of corruption would oblige the observer to make a purely hypothetical guess as to how the system would function without corruption, and on the other, how a noncorrupt system would function with corruption. One can convincingly and legitimately analyze only what actually is going on and what the costs and benefits seem to be. It is very difficult to suggest what the costs and benefits of some hypothetical process might be. The only way out of this bind would be to find (or simulate) two or more governmental systems sharing the same cultural environment and basic socioeconomic configurations and political regimes, one of which is "corrupt" and the other "clean," and then compare the functioning of the two systems in terms of costs and benefits. Unfortunately, no two such comparable units come to mind.

Market Corruption Encourages Capital Formation and
Entrepreneurial Efficiency

Leff's hypothesis regarding the positive effect of corruption upon capital formation is too simplistic and naive. The amount of capital the bidder is able to offer depends on far more than efficiency. The highest bidder may be—and in the Moroccan context frequently is—a talented speculator who made a killing in urban real estate or in import-export. In general, the indigenous native bourgeoisie has accepted and cultivated relations of dependency with the state bureaucracy and semi-public authorities. It is a parasitic bourgeoisie that lives off privileged access to state-controlled resources or the differential application of state regulations. At the same time, individual entrepreneurs may specialize in serving as intermediaries between the Moroccan State and various foreign private investors. Whatever deal they are able to arrange entitles them to a percentage of the investment: As brokers they take a "commission" but invest nothing except their time and influence.[20]

It is true that the biggest bribes in Morocco can be and probably are offered by the French industrial establishment *(patronat)* of Casablanca and other Moroccan cities. It is also true that the *patronat* represents the most efficient industrial and commercial enterprises in the country. Their payoffs, in the form of protection money to avoid discriminatory application of regulations, and in placing influential Moroccans on their boards of directors with high salaries, may be seen as promoting efficient capitalist endeavor. But the relationship is blurred by the existence of protected markets or industries, and the fact that various enterprises (banks, vehicle assemblies, breweries, cement factories, sugar refineries) are branch operations of metropolitan enterprises rather than independent establishments that must sink or swim on their own.

A not unusual scenario involving some of the themes mentioned above might unfold as follows. *X, Y,* and *Z* are prominent Moroccan businessmen with connections in the Palace and, more often than not, close relations or friends in the Ministry of Finance. They approach a thriving French textile plant and propose that they be allowed to acquire a certain proportion of the company's stock, let us say 15 percent of all outstanding shares. It is understood that they will pay nothing for the shares, but that dividends will accrue in their names until they are equivalent to the value of the shares on the day of "purchase." The company can use those dividends as they accumulate, and, depending on the bargain, include interest in the purchase price. In the meantime, *X, Y,* and *Z* will have been "elected" to the board of directors with salary. Without investing a penny, the three entrepreneurs can each pick up a salary and eventually a share of the company's assets. The more influential they appear to be, the more often they can repeat this gambit. In return for what is essentially protection money, they do favors for the company, such as arranging duty-free importation of machinery or keeping the labor inspector from closing the place down for violation of safety regulations.

It should also be noted that Leff's analysis of market corruption does not take into account the use of illegal payments in an ongoing process that Fred Riggs has called "strategic spending."[21] To summarize Rigg's argument, an individual's surplus earnings—be he public official or private entrepreneur—are disbursed in tributes and gifts to safeguard his power position and to maintain his ability to extract tributes and gifts in turn. Wealth is not power; rather, it is spent in the quest for power. As a result, Riggs concludes, strategic spending keeps surplus resources from productive investment and hence leads to "negative development."

In Morocco, and elsewhere, strategic spending may be perfectly legal, but more than likely it will involve trading in privileges and favors dependent upon persons in public office. Private groups may pay protection, good will, or access money as a strategic device, and hope for administrative favors in return. In addition, considerable strategic spending goes on within the administration, including falsified accounts, manipulation of personnel and promotion, differential application of watch-dog and auditing procedures, cost-plus contracting where the work is performed by a public agency, and so forth. All these operations may be carried out as tributes and loans among bureaucratic clans and political power-holders.

This kind of trading, rather than constituting market corruption, seems designed to insulate the participants in a protective web of obligations and expected services that makes every man at once a creditor and a debtor. In an administration whose upper reaches are subject to the whims of the ruler, the unpredictable redistribution of prebends, and the vagaries of clan-infighting, strategic spending leads to some minimal degree of predictability of social security. No one really has much incentive to break away from the web, for, while he may escape his debts, he will also abandon his claims to what is owed him. Investments in this web bear no interest, and some degree of stability is bought at the price of productivity. Finally, flight into the private sector solves nothing: to the extent that it is dependent on the administration, the refugee's web of obligations will follow him.

The notion of protection payments warrants further attention, for it bears directly upon entrepreneurial activity and capital formation. The kind of corruption that is under discussion is a negative transaction between some branch of the administration (and by implication, the regime itself) as one party and any designated interest as the other. In return for political loyalty or apoliticism, the regime offers *not* to apply discriminatory practices. In 1966, for example, an important sugar importer and newspaper owner received word that his connections with a leftist party were well known and unfavorably viewed in higher circles. It was suggested that these connections be terminated lest his warehouses be closed for various violations or his applications for import licenses be turned down. In such a transaction nothing is exchanged; both parties agree to conditions guaranteeing that neither will engage in activities harmful to the other.[22]

Because there is some tendency in Morocco's political system for the palace to view any successful entrepreneur as politically dangerous (he could buy clientele, influence, and a political power base), there is also a tendency to break or domesticate such men, to reassert the links of dependency essential to the regime's survival. Most actors are aware of the possibility of discriminatory sanctions, and this awareness or general expectation is more important than the actual frequency with which sanctions are applied. Anticipatory reaction to this threat motivates entrepreneurs to make short-term speculation and protection payments and to shun strategies of long-term investments. In conclusion: corruption in the Moroccan system does little to contribute to entrepreneurial efficiency or capital formation.

Corruption Promotes Administrative Flexibility

In one respect, the flexibility hypothesis would seem to apply in Morocco. Corruption does, to some extent, promote flexibility in *intra*administrative procedures. These involve skirting, manipulating, or violating civil-service rules for all matters regarding living, promotion, salaries, benefits, expense accounts, and so forth. One quasi-legal device is the contract system *(contrat fonctionnel)*. Access to various levels of the civil service is nominally determined by educational and training qualifications. When Morocco first became independent, there was a severe shortage of Moroccans who could meet French educational standards for various posts. To overcome this, ministries were allowed to negotiate bilateral contracts to meet staffing needs. The same kind of contract could be renegotiated to promote the contractee to a higher post. However, even after the initial shortages were overcome, the practice of using discretionary contracts continued, for they provided a means by which a minister or *directeur* could reward his clientele with coveted posts. In this way the *contrat fonctionnel* became an integral part of the patronage system while at the same time eroding some of the rigidity inherent in the civil service code.

It could be argued that the possibility to milk an office or market administrative services helps attract talented personnel to the administration—personnel that might otherwise be discouraged by the very low salaries paid at all levels. This judgment would apply particularly to the middle and upper reaches of the civil service. Each ministry or agency may contain an internal prebendary system by which service payments at one level are disbursed to the personnel involved while a certain percentage is passed on to the next level. In addition, some ministries or directors within them may be particularly well placed to extract large-scale tributes: Public Works, contracting for road and dam construction; Education, contracting for school construction; and Commerce, contracting for licensing, market inspection, weights and measures, import permits, and so forth. All of these ministries offer a vast potential for kickbacks and protection money. The administrative "entrepreneurs" who seek out appointments as ministers or in key directions all know the relative ranking of these agencies. The prebend is known in the trade (with no offense to David Easton) as the *caisse noire* or "black box." The biggest and most coveted black box is that of the Ministry of Finance which extracts tribute from all other ministries and agencies through the budget and auditing process and the control of the civil-service payroll, *and* from the non-governmental sector through fiscal control. The Minister of Finance and his clients have a finger in every pie and can exact a heavy price for their vital services.[23]

To an important degree, a parallel, non-official, and illegal system of payments and incentives has developed, providing a possibility for high material rewards that the official salary structure precludes. Perhaps talented Moroccans would shun administrative careers without the parallel system. Corruption, it could be argued, serves in this instance to maintain a façade of austerity while at the same time attracting quality personnel to the administration. Yet to the extent that this is true, the benefit is cancelled by at least two major costs. First, budget austerity was originally designed to stabilize the salary structure in the public sector and free state resources for productive investment. For all intents and purposes that objective has been abandoned. Second, the civil-service code was designed to bring stability and predictability to administrative careers, an element notably lacking to date. Moreover, talented personnel is wasted by immersion in the game of manipulating the quasi-illicit procedures that have developed to improve career prospects and earnings. Without reallocating state resources, civil-service salaries could probably be raised across the board and promotion practices standardized without reallocating state resources. But for reasons of political control, the king has been reluctant (at least until July 1971) to put an end to these civil-service games precisely because the ambitious civil servant becomes so preoccupied with them that he has little time left over to think about the "system" as a whole.

The flexibility hypothesis seems misplaced as regards corruption arising between civil servants and the citizenry. In fact, corruption in the form of taking and offering bribes is directly linked to the maintenance of red tape. A service charge is to be expected in every instance that an administrative regulation is applied. The service charge does not permit the payee to *avoid* the regulation, but rather guarantees—sometimes—that the civil servant will expedite the payee's case. The royal gendarmerie inspects trucks and cars for faulty headlights or tires: a flat fee is charged whether or not there is a violation; Moroccans who work in Europe need passports and renewals: a service charge is required before the wheels grind. Virtually any piece of paper issued by local authorities requires a fee or the promise of further services: birth certificates, work permits, death and marriage documents, affidavits that one is destitute, that one has a sick child requiring medical attention, that one has school-age children, that one is an army veteran entitled to a pension, that one is a cripple—all of these have a price. Add to these building permits, trading licenses, property deeds, water rights, zoning regulations, taxes, building and work inspection, and price controls, and it is clear that administrative corruption touches all aspects of the citizen's life, whether rich or poor. The underpaid civil servant renders his career somewhat more palatable, but he is being bribed to perform his normal duties rather than to cut through red tape.

Corruption Mitigates Ethnic or Class Conflict by Diverting Attention to the Spoils System

The mitigation of class conflict is indeed a consciously sought-after objective of the Moroccan spoils system. However, the notion of level is important here. Corruption runs throughout the administration, and the most humble Moroccan can nourish the hope that his son may someday, with a modicum of education, accede to the lower echelons of the civil service. Thus, the opportunity of social mobility may operate against alienation from the system along class lines. Yet, to the extent that this is true, spoils and corruption are not the key elements. The status and salary associated with civil-service employment would be sufficient in themselves to attract the offspring of the poor.

But if it is implied that entire classes or segments thereof can be coopted through systems of corruption, the situation is far different. On the one hand, the regime has actually been creating a dependent *kulak* class through the illegal sale of land taken over by the state from the French. The sales have gone on since 1956, linking the material wellbeing of officials of the Ministry of Interior, army officers, and the rural nobility to the survival of the regime. To some extent, the formation of this quasi-class may serve as a buffer between the growing numbers of landless peasants and the traditional rural land-owning groups. At the same time there is little the regime can do to avert the increase of the landless peasantry and its derivative, the urban unemployed. If there are remedies to the growth of these groups, they do not lie in the expansion of the spoils system. Cooptation through spoils on a class basis may be possible, if at all, only in those developing societies that have exceptional resource bases, such as Iran.

While conventional class cleavages can be partially bridged by corruption, this same phenomenon contributes to the development of an administrative class. In Morocco, the state is by far the largest employer in the country. Civil servants at all levels are relatively privileged and relatively resented. There is a strong tendency for the citizenry to talk in terms of "us and them." While administrative corruption is regarded as normal, it is nonetheless disagreeable and serves to reinforce the cleavage between the masses and the administration.

At the uppermost levels of the civil service, where corruption takes place on a major scale, ethnicity, class, and participation in the spoils system tend to overlap. The merchant-bourgeois elite, drawn disproportionately from families from the city of Fez (hence the appellation *Fassi* for this group) represented, before 1912, a relatively well educated and skilled group that had an initial edge in acceding to privileged positions in the administration and the market economy developed by the French during the Protectorate (1912–1956).[24] The essential point here is that a particularist elite category—the Fassi—overlaps with a nascent class category, the indigenous *haute bourgeoisie*. These groups have taken over the lion's share of high-level administrative posts. At the same time they dominate the private and semi-private sectors of the economy (if one leaves aside the French *patronat*) which depend on the favors and protection of the state. They have, to say the least, privileged access to those public officials who can grease the wheels. Thus, administrative and entrepreneurial elites are really wings of the same group. Not only is there much back-scratching and evidence of joint ventures between the two wings, but also a constant coming and going of personnel. A civil servant, let us say in the Ministry of Industry and Mines, can facilitate the success of an enterprise whose directorship may subsequently be his reward. Of course, these kinds of transactions also take place with regard to the French *patronat*, but there, relations are not so chummy and room to maneuver is somewhat more restricted. After the attempted coup d'état of July 1971, there was much talk that the rebel officers had wanted to clean up the "Fassi Mafia"; to view this group in such terms does not distort reality.

The conclusion that can be drawn here is that high-level corruption has taken place to some extent in a socially closed circuit. Market corruption may allow outsiders to buy their way into the circuit, but it is no easy task. In sum, corruption in Morocco may have contributed to the stratification of resources within a particularist bourgeois elite.

Corruption Affords Access to the Administration for Minorities that Might Otherwise be Excluded

The French *patronat*, either by numbers or by nationality, is a minority that has bought its way into the system. The most obvious, although dwindling, Moroccan minority is that of the Jews. Despite the fact that the Six-Day War of 1967 and the attempted coup d'état of July 1971 accelerated the rate of Jewish emigration, we can make some generalizations about Jewish integration in the system since 1956. Like the Fassi, the Jews enjoyed educational advantages not shared by most of the Moroccans. Under the Protectorate they had become prominent in commerce, manufacturing, insurance and banking, the free professions, and the administration. Several Jews have been, and still are, highly placed civil servants (although only one ever rose to ministerial rank). Quite clearly they traffic in influence and favors as much as anybody, but they must be more careful than the Muslims. A Jewish businessman may have to be more circumspect in offering a bribe, or perhaps pay a higher price. When on the receiving end, the Jewish civil servant may find that he cannot refuse a bribe. Either way, he must play the game while running a higher risk of discriminatory denunciation.

The reason is simple and reflects the peculiar dependency relationships that have long defined the Jews' room for maneuver within the dominant community. Jewish patronage networks are always partially interwoven with Muslim networks, and any Jewish participant must have his Muslim umbrella. In a very real sense, "the umbrella of umbrellas" for the Jews is the king himself who has made efficient use of this protected minority, holding them in thrall by the fear of what his removal would mean to them.

Still, it is impossible to say whether or not the Jews have better access to the system through corruption than they would have without it. Their integration is founded on traditional dependency, supplemented by the modern business, technical, and managerial skills they are able to offer their protectors. What is clear, however, is that the weighing of costs and benefits in this respect is irrelevant because in the coming years the Jewish minority will have *dis*-integrated itself from the system and moved elsewhere.

Corruption in Electoral Politics may Indicate the Spread of Popular Democracy

Constitutionally, Morocco is a multi-party system. Up to 1965, when King Hassan suspended Morocco's first elected parliament, there was at least an outside chance that a competitive multiparty system might actually emerge. But during the 1960's the Palace made a concerted and successful effort to drain all important sources of patronage and spoils away from the parties. By 1970, with a quasi-monopoly on patronage sources, the palace had achieved its objective of keeping up a "liberal" multi-party regime in which the parties could not really compete but only participate. Since 1963 various rounds of local and parliamentary elections and referendums have demonstrated, if anything, only that the carrot may be cheaper than the stick: It is probably less expensive to buy votes than to extract them by force. In Morocco's noncompetitive electoral process, material inducements such as distributing PL 480 American wheat can buy an election for the regime without its having to stuff the ballot box.[25] The incidence of electoral corruption in Morocco says nothing one way or another about the vitality of popular democracy in that country.

Planned Corruption in Morocco

The elements of corruption in the Moroccan system that have so far been described are to be found in all political systems. But only under some regimes are they the ingredients of regime survival and an essential source of its cohesion. Several of the strategies of the utilization of corruption and patronage by the monarchy have been alluded to in the preceding pages. It is now time to try to pull them together.

All systems must provide rewards for those who agree to participate in them. Participation implies something less than the acceptance of the legitimacy of the regime on the part of the participants. Whether or not they actually believe in its legitimacy is not essential to its survival; what is essential is that they continue to play the game. In this sense participation is equivalent to acquiescence; the regime can maintain control of the political arena if strategic groups acquiesce.

The rewards of acquiescence vary from regime to regime. Prestige, power, high salaries, and the satisfaction of serving national or ideological goals may all be involved. But Morocco, as a monarchy, cannot easily handle rewards in the same way as non-monarchist nation-states. To the extent that Morocco is a patrimonial system and the king is ruler for life, rewards, promotions, and demotions within the administrative and military spheres are dependent upon the will of the monarch. Only in this way can he assure his relevance to the system. In general, the king's degree of political control varies directly with the level of fragmentation and factionalization within the system, and inversely with the level of institutionalization among political parties and administrative agencies. The king must always maintain the initiative through the systematic inculcation of an atmosphere of unpredictability and provisionality among all elites and the maximization of their vulnerability relative to his mastery of the situation. With their political and material fortunes always in doubt, he is in a position to exert and maintain the asymmetrical lines of dependency and protection that the elites seek to establish. If at any time (as when the rebel officers struck) the king's mastery is questioned, then the asymmetry of the relations disappears, and his relevance to the system is immediately called into question.

With specific regard to the civil service, what the king has sought to avoid is a psychological disposition among strategic elites that would lead to the notion of a meritocracy. High-ranking bureaucrats must not believe that they have earned their positions; there must always be the recognition that were it not for H.M.'s favor, they ight never have made it.[26] Conversely, they must always be aware that they may rapidly fall from grace despite their professional qualifications. In successfully nurturing this disposition, the king has maintained the initiative; all elites are preoccupied with trying to anticipate or trying to react to the king's moves. Seldom do they have the confidence, and almost never the resources, to take initiatives themselves. They are constantly reminded of their vulnerability by the unpredictable and sometimes arbitrary interventions of the king into the administrative sphere. Rapid and unexplained demotions and promotions and inscrutable policy decisions leave any high-ranking bureaucrat fearful for his future. The participants in this system are thus reduced as much as possible to the role of competent (rational) and obedient (patrimonial) executors of the Royal Will. If they find this too demeaning, they can try to find another game. The king once remarked in an interview, "If one day all my ministers resigned, I would say to my chauffeur, be minister."[27]

Quite clearly, inculcating the mental disposition among the elite that maximizes royal control of the game limits the kinds of rewards the king can offer to his clients. He cannot offer them career stability; nor can he offer them significant influence over the policy-making process. He cannot offer them the satisfaction of devoting themselves to a coherent doctrine of government or of development. Finally, he cannot offer them even the satisfaction of developing and implementing specific programs. Career instability and policy impotence go hand in hand, and Moroccan bureaucrats are aware of this pairing. Even though they may have a sincere interest in the programs of their agencies, there are no institutional guarantees that they will be around long enough to have any effect upon them.[28] Personnel turnover may be no more rapid in the Moroccan administration than in any other,[29] but Moroccan civil servants are aware that, in their case, turnover *could* be extremely rapid. Most of them, at the level of *chef de service* and above, feel at the mercy of the discretionary powers of promotion and transfer vested in the minister and, by derivation, in the king— against which there are no institutional defenses.

The compensation offered to the Moroccan participant is access to the spoils system. Above all else, access is subject to the arbitrary manipulation of the palace, and hence is supportive of patrimonial ties. At whatever level—the policeman who takes a bribe or the minister who builds a chateau on $13,000 a year—access is a privilege which is *not earned* or *merited*. It is a privilege whose ultimate source is always known and which can easily be revoked. Finally, it is a privilege which is always to some degree illicit. The participant runs the risk of exposure by rivals or superiors, of scandals, and of the confiscation of the fruits of his acquiescence and participation. Moreover, it is somewhat degrading to compete for material reward in this way, and success in the competition is not something of which the participant can feel proud. The participant becomes the accomplice of the system. What holds it together is not necessarily loyalty to its master; rather it is the commensal sharing of its spoils. Everyone the master deems of strategic importance is invited or cajoled to join the feast. When the privileges are revoked, the erstwhile participant has no recourse. He must simply keep his silence, for what he knows of the system's corruption he learned through participation in it. The strategy is not foolproof, as the attempted coup of 1971 indicated. The king published the inventory of the rebel officers' ill-gotten gains within forty-eight hours of the coup attempt. It was a hollow gesture, because fear of exposure was supposed to have kept the officers from acting in the first place. But even if the temple had crashed down upon the king's head, he would have had the last word: Few Moroccans would ever have accepted the rebel officers as undefiled builders of a new order; they would still have been seen as self-seeking accomplices of the *ancien régime*.

The preoccupation of all sectors of the elite with governmental spoils has made competition for access to the administration the major form of politics in the country. From the point of view of the palace this development is not only desirable but planned; the politics of patronage are essentially non-ideological. The competition is not among "isms" or programs, a realm in which the monarch is relatively weak and vulnerable, but among patronage groups who vie for material advantage, a process in which the monarch-boss is indeed supreme. De-politicization of the administration (for it was highly politicized from 1956 to 1961) is bought in this manner. Individuals and groups can re-politicize the system only at the risk of police repression ("leftist" plots and subsequent trials were staged in 1963 and 1971; in-between, Mehdi Ben Barka was kidnapped and assasinated) and in face of the artfully manipulated threat that the army would intervene if the politicians became too active. Much to the king's surprise the army did intervene, apparently out of disgust for the patronage system and its own inglorious role in it; but, having survived the intervention, the king is still able to argue that if civilians do not like his game, they will like the army's even less.

In the absence of some major breakdown in the system, the old rules still obtain. Administrative patrons, rotating in and out of various offices, build their own nest eggs in terms of material resources or favors and obligations that they can cash in on later. The politico-administrative ethos that has emerged in the 1960's is strikingly similar to that of the old sultanate before 1912. The sultan turns over a prebend to a "trusted servant" who then farms it as intensely as possible, gaining title to the usufruct but not to the farm itself. An atmosphere of every man for himself and every clan for itself emerges that precludes large-scale coalition-building or politicking in the bureaucracy. Various clans, to the extent that they have any political coloring at all, represent only marginal policy options: X is pro-American, Y pro-French; Z wants six dams instead of eight, and Y wants to introduce hybrid corn, etc.

Whatever the participant amasses he is permitted to keep; but that too is a privilege, not a rule. The artful administrative patron can accumulate, through his office and strategic spending, enough resources to sustain him through thick and thin. The fall from grace is seldom draconian, for the king does not want to alienate ex-participants.[30] Inasmuch as there has been a tendency to maximize the numbers of participants (accomplices) by encouraging the rotation of personnel in and out of the administration, the regime might, by employing harsher methods, risk creating a large class of disgruntled ex-participants. Therefore, title to usufruct is seldom revoked.

Very few Moroccans have any illusions about the game: certainly not the king or the participants, nor, for the most part, the masses. It is for this reason that, although the term "patrimonial" has been used, it is somewhat misplaced: loyalty is not a crucial element in the Moroccan system. There is a general level of cynicism running throughout— the cynicism of the non-participant masses who fall back on the traditional reflex, "government has ever been thus"; the cynicism of the participants who partake of the system individually while refusing any responsibility for it; and the cynicism of the king who plays on the weakness and greed of his subjects.

In this system, corruption serves only one "positive" function—that of the survival of the regime. Resources are absorbed in patronage and are drained away from rational productive investment. Morocco remains fixed in a system of scarcity in which the vulnerable seek protection and thus regenerate the links of dependency and patronage that perpetuate the system. The dilemma for the ruler in such a system is whether, in the short term, his survival can be made compatible with rational administration and economic development, or whether, in the long term, it can be made compatible with planned corruption.

Notes

1. J.S. Nye, "Corruption and Political Development: A Cost-Benefit Analysis," *American Political Science Review,* LXI (June 1967), 417. Nathaniel Leff, "Economic Development through Bureaucratic Corruption," *American Behavioral Scientist,* VIII (November 1964), 8–15; James C. Scott,

"The Analysis of Corruption in Developing Nations," *Comparative Studies in Society and History,* XI June 1969), 315–41. I regret that in the preparation of this article I was unable to consult James Scott's *Comparative Political Corruption* (Englewood Cliffs, N.J. 1972).

2. Cf. James Bill, "Modernization and Reform from Above: The Case of Iran," *Journal of Politics,* XXXII (February 1970), 19–40.

3. See Max Weber, *Theory of Social and Economic Organization,* trans. by Talcott Parsons (Glencoe, Ill. 1947), 313–29.

4. Ann Ruth Willner, "Neotraditional Accommodation to Political Independence: The Case of Indonesia," in Lucian Pye, ed., *Cases in Comparative Politics: Asia* (Boston 1970), 249. Cf. Marvin Zonis, *The Political Elite of Iran* (Princeton 1971), esp. 100–102. The systemic parallels between Morocco and Iran are extraordinarily, although not coincidentally, close.

5. James W. Wilkie, *The Mexican Revolution: Federal Expenditure and Social Change since 1910* (Berkeley and Los Angeles 1967), 5–9.

6. For a relevant analysis, see James C. Scott, "Corruption, Machine Politics, and Political Change," *American Political Science Review,* LXIII(December 1969), 1142–58.

7. For some excellent discussions of what has become the subject of a great deal of study among anthropologists, sociologists, and political scientists, see Jeremy Boissevain, "Patronage in Sicily," *Man: Journal of the Royal Anthropological Institute,* 1 (March 1966), 18–33; René Lemarchand and Keith Legg, "Political Clientelism and Development: A Preliminary Analysis," *Comparative Politics,* IV (January 1972), 149–78; Lemarchand, "Clientelism and Ethnicity in Tropical Africa: Competing Solidarities in Nation-building," *American Political Science Review,* LXVI March 1972), 68–90; Alex Weingrod, "Patrons, Patronage, and Political Parties," *Comparative Studies in Society and History,* X (July 1969), 376–400; James C. Scott, "Patron-Client Politics and Political Change in Southeast Asia," *American Political Science Review,* LXVI (March 1972), 91–113; Richard Sandbrook, "Patrons, Clients, and Factions: New Dimensions of Conflict Analysis in Africa," *Canadian Journal of Political Science,* V (March 1972), 104–19.

8. For a useful discussion of the overlap between patronage and corruption, see Edward Van Roy, "On the Theory of Corruption," *Economic Development and Cultural Change,* XIX (October 1970), 86–110. Scott calls attention to the same overlap when he proposes ". . . that corruption may be viewed as a process of political influence such that similar practices may violate community norms at one place and time and not at another" (fn. 1), 317. I do not concur in the relevance of the distinction between "patron," a person who controls resources, and "broker," a person who controls *access* to resources—a distinction made by both Scott (fn. 7), 96–98, and Lemarchand (fn. 7), throughout. It would seem to me unlikely that any given patron would fail to combine some aspects of both functions, and, after all, connections are resources, as is the number of clients.

9. Stanislav Andreski, *Parasitism and Subversion: The Case of Latin America* (New York 1969), 11; see also Lemarchand (fn. 7), 75, n. 27, citing Ronald Cohen; Scott (fn. 7), 101.

10. Boissevain (fn. 7), develops this theme with reference to Sicily, suggesting that Catholicism, a saint-oriented religion, gives an other-worldly impetus

to the quest for intercession. It may be that saints are part and parcel of belief systems emerging out of situations of real material scarcity. Islam, while hostile to saints, has been forced to tolerate saintly cults most everywhere it has spread. For more on the interrelation of scarcity, state power, and patronage, see Lemarchand and Legg (fn. 6); A. Vingradov and J. Waterbury, "Situations of Contested Legitimacy in Morocco: An Alternative Framework," *Comparative Studies in Society and History,* XIII (January 1971), 32–59.

11. William J. Siffin emphasizes this process with regard to Thailand. See his "Personnel Processes of the Thai Bureaucracy," in Heady and Stokes, eds., *Papers in Comparative Administration* (Ann Arbor 1962), 207–28.

12. Samuel P. Huntington, *Political Order in Changing Societies* (New Haven 1968), 60.

13. See S.I. Eldersveld and others, *The Citizen and the Administrator in a Developing Democracy* (New Delhi 1968), 31–33 (citation from p. 33).

14. It may be hypothesized, although I have seen no systematic test of the hypothesis, that in many developing countries corruption fails to arouse mass moral indignation because the notions of public and private spheres are not highly developed. That is, when we speak of the use of public power for private ends, it is assumed that we can define what is private, and that public power is subject to universalistic criteria. It is also assumed that there is a kind of multiple role specialization whereby a bureaucrat is a "public" figure for eight hours a day and a "private" citizen the rest. In fact, it is common for bureaucrats in developing countries to carry role-playing to extremes by insulating themselves rigidly in the impartiality and rule-conscious role of the public official in order to stave off the importunities of clients who want to force them into the role of dispenser of particularistic favors. Variations on this theme are explored in Fred Riggs, *Administration in Developing Countries: The Theory of Prismatic Society* (Boston 1964); Hahn-Bee Lee, "Developmentalist Time and Leadership in Developing Countries," *CAG Occasional Papers* (Bloomington 1966); and José A. Silva Michelena, "The Venezuelan Bureaucrat," in *A Strategy for Research on Social Policy* (The Politics of Change in Venezuela), I (Boston 1967), 86–119.

15. F.G. Bailey, "The Peasant View of the Bad Life," *Science and Culture* (Calcutta), XXXIII (February 1967), 31–40 (emphasis in original).

16. See the graphic description of one such process in Richard Patch, "The La Paz Census of 1970," *American Universities Field Staff Report* (West Coast Latin American Series, Hanover, N.H., 1970), 7–10.

17. Leff (fn. 1); Nye (fn. 1).

18. Scott (fn. 1), 335; see also Weingrod (fn. 7).

19. Boissevain (fn. 7) sustains this point with regard to Sicily; see also Ernest Gellner, "Patterns of Rural Rebellion in Morocco: Tribes as Minorities," *European Journal of Sociology,* III, No. 2 (1962); Lemarchand (fn. 7), 68.

20. Many Moroccan entrepreneurs combine elements of the Marxist notion of "comprador" as well as the more graphic expletive of "Lumpen-bourgeoisie" used by André Gunder Frank in *Lumpen-bourgeoisie et lumpen-développement,* Maspéro, Cahiers Libres 205–206 (Paris 1971). Omar Ben Messaoud, former attaché in the Royal Cabinet and go-between between Pan American and the Moroccan Ministry of Finance, is exemplary of the

Moroccan bourgeoisie, although his arrest indicates that he overplayed his hand. See Waterbury, "The Coup Manqué," *American Universities Field Staff Report*, North African Series, xv, No. 1 (1971).
21. Riggs (fn. 14), 141–42.
22. In this instance, sanctions were applied. The businessman's newspaper was temporarily closed down by order of the minister of interior, just long enough for the shipping companies that published their schedules in it to transfer their advertising and notices to another newspaper. The "leftist" newspaper went out of business. Its publisher, after having mulled over his fate for a while, was put at the head of an important state investment body.
23. There are so many operations going on within the ministry of finance that it is hard to know which are the most profitable. One steady source of income to the ministry's black box comes from the processing of all governmental claims for overtime payments. A fixed percentage of whatever total is approved by finance for a given agency is retained for finance's black box. A threat that finance can always use vis-à-vis other ministries is to refuse to budget their unfilled slots; as much as 25 percent of all funded slots in the civil service may go unfilled, allowing one man to draw two salaries. Finance holds the key to this practice.
24. See Waterbury, *The Commander of the Faithful: The Moroccan Political Elite—A Study in Segmented Politics* (New York 1970), chaps. 5 and 6.
25. At the time of writing, Morocco was awaiting new parliamentary elections in the wake of the attempted coup of July 1971. It may be that the opposition parties will participate in the elections, and, because the king needs their participation, the elections may be relatively unrigged. But the parties do not have many material rewards to attract voters; they must rely on the appeal of their programs and the rewards they can offer *if* they win a majority of parliament.
26. So too, senior army officers, most of whom served in the French army at the time King Hassan's father, Mohammed V, was sent into exile by the French authorities in 1953. That these officers wound up in command of the Moroccan armed forces after 1956, rather than being tried as traitors, is attributable only to the will of the Moroccan monarchs. Both Mohammed V and Hassan II never let them forget that fact—which is all the more testimony to their desperation in trying to overthrow Hassan II in July 1971 and again in August 1972.
27. From an interview in *Réalitées*, No. 250 (November 1966).
28. Interviews with ninety high-ranking bureaucrats revealed that only a few ventured to predict what job they would have a year hence. It is not pure hyperbole to note that one of those who did predict was shot and killed at Skhirat a year later. It is also important to note that the rebel officers were allegedly partially motivated by their unhappiness with unstable careers and political marginality.
29. Over a period of twelve months, 25 percent of an initial sample of 160 high-ranking bureaucrats changed posts at least once, some of them three times.
30. Since the attempted coup, some ministers have been actually been put on trial for corruption—up to then an unheard-of punishment. At the same time, a minister who was fired in the fall of 1970 amid rumors of malfeasance has been made minister of interior.

22

Supportive Values of the Culture of Corruption in Ghana

Victor T. LeVine

One element of any political culture is the structure of supportive values and orientations that define, among other things, what is politically legitimate in society and what is not. In Ghana, the development of an incipient culture of political corruption was accompanied by an evolving structure of values that had the effect of rationalizing, if not legitimizing, corrupt behavior. Between December 1970 and June 1971, the author had the opportunity to interview in depth a dozen men who were actively involved in the widespread corruption of the Nkrumah regime, and to explore at length the values and attitudes that underlay their behavior. The interviewees are not identified in this study since all were promised absolute anonymity, but it can be reported that all were officials either in the Nkrumah government or in the Convention People's party. One was a junior minister, two held high party office, and the rest operated at various official and semiofficial levels of the regime. By the time they were interviewed, most of them had gone into business and several were dealing regularly with the current government. Only two were technically unemployed, but even these admitted they had stable sources of income, in both cases deriving in part from investments and contacts made during their terms in office.

The author explored the twelve respondents' political values in four main areas: (1) general attitudes toward authority, authority figures, and government; (2) perceptions of political efficacy; (3) parameters of obligation and individual responsibility; and (4) retrospective attitudes concerning their own corrupt behavior and the like behavior of others. It must be emphasized that the interviews were conducted informally, although the respondents were told in advance what predetermined themes were being explored. Thus, expressions of political values

Source: Reprinted from *Political Corruption: The Ghana Case* by Victor T. LeVine with permission the Hoover Institution Press. © 1975 by the Board of Trustees of the Leland Stanford Jr. University.

often emerged in discussions of other matters, and of course not always in the sequence in which the four themes are noted above. A few quotations from the interviews illustrate some representative patterns within each area.

General Attitudes toward Authority

> The only man who ever could tell me what to do, and who I respected, was my father and sometimes my uncle K_____. The chief, he was a big thiefman. My father listened to him, but I only did because I had to . . . Nkrumah too was thiefman; he said big things, but everyone knew he liked pretty woman too much, posh cars and money. (Mr. *D*; Interview D-6)

> Government always promise more than it gives; only if the smart men get together can we get what we need. (Mr. *K*, Interview K-2)

> R (Respondent): Any man who believes what the chief or the DC [District Commissioner] or a minister tells him is a fool. Sometimes you have to do what they tell you or be put in jail; but if you go to jail, you are not very wise.
> I (Interviewer): But do you obey only if you are afraid of going to jail?
> R: Sometimes. But most you obey if it is better to obey than to disobey. But it is better to avoid having to make the choice whether to obey or not obey. (Mr. *B*; Interview B-5)

> All government is bad. English, Nkrumah, NLC, Busia—all cannot be trusted, at all, at all! ["At all!" is a Ghanaian colloquialism signifying an emphatic negative] I do well under English [and] Nkrumah, because I know that only if you are a big man you can get what you want. This is the Ghanaian way. (Mr. *G*; Interview G-6)

These comments reflect, if nothing else, a high degree of generalized political cynicism, as well as a sharp awareness of the personal, instrumental aspects of politics. There is no hard evidence that all or most Ghanaians shared these views of politics and authority, but certain qualified observers, such as Maxwell Owusu (whose views are cited later in this chapter), suggest that these attitudes are far more prevalent than hitherto suspected. Certainly the comments cited accurately represent the views and values of the twelve interviewees concerned in the immediate analysis, and if these men are at all representative of those involved in politically corrupt dealings in Ghana—as we suspect they are—it is reasonable to infer that their views reflect those of the larger group.

Perceptions of Political Efficacy and Competence

As the term is generally used in political science, "political efficacy" refers to an individual's ability to influence political outcomes. It implies, for most purposes, the individual's concept of his own "political competence," that is, his perception of the extent to which he can effect political outcomes favorable to himself or to those with whom he identifies.[1]

The twelve respondents all professed to understand what made the Ghanaian polity work. Each in his own terms named the key levers of authority and influence as he saw them, and each could describe at length the means by which he obtained what he wanted from the system. Not unexpectedly, the levers named and the methods described tended to be those of indirection, usually operating through informal rather than formal channels.

It was not that the respondents were unaware of formal structures and channels, or of the norms that circumscribed the conduct of official business: indeed, most of them could still, after four or five years out of office, cite chapter and verse of the regulations that governed their positions. Rather, they tended to pursue these regular channels in conducting what one called "ordinary business"—that is, for transactions in which they had little personal interest, or which involved matters of routine. However, once their self-interest was engaged or some important social or political obligation was involved, they preferred to operate through informal channels and by informal methods. Finally, in light of such attitudes and behavior it is hardly surprising that the respondents all claimed to know the "right" people, that is, those who could be relied upon to do their bidding or advance their cause, or with whom mutually profitable exchanges could be initiated and maintained. On any scale of perceived political efficacy, then, the twelve respondents would rank very high indeed. A few of their comments highlight these observations:

> I: If you wished, for example, Government to accept your tender or a contract rather than someone else's, how should you—or anybody else—go about it?
> R: I could always, or almost always, get my friends' tenders considered first. Now they do not heed me because they are afraid of Busia. Some day it will be changed again. But any smart man who has friends or family in the right place can get what he wants—if you do not forget to "dash" [bribe, or gift] proper. (Mr. *C*; Interview C-7)

> Ask and you shall receive. But do not ask too much, or too big man. But even a small, small man can get a favor from a big man if his gift is right, or if his uncle asks for him. . . . We say, "mouth smile, but money smile better." (Mr. *K*; Interview K-4)

> It is all a matter of knowing where to go and whom to see. Once you learn the men in power, who their friends are, and their family, there are always ways to receive favorable treatment. . . . I never had any

difficulty securing my way once I had learned my lessons. (Mr. *E*; Interview E-5)

You know Ghana saying, "Monkey de work, baboon de chop." [The wise man profits from the fool's labors.] I am always baboon! (Mr. *D*; Interview D-3)

Parameters of Obligation and Responsibility

In the absence of reliable hierarchies of trust, political and social intercourse becomes impossible. Both social structures and political structures function partly to provide precisely such hierarchies of trust, the one through bonds of natural or simulated consanguinity, the other through symbols and institutions that seek to replicate the ties of the social structure and bind men to common tasks and objectives. Such structures in varying degrees make it possible to predict human affairs; the looser or weaker the structures, the less predictable the social and political outcomes, and the tighter or stronger, the more predictable. Despite evidence that primary group loyalties have undergone serious erosion in modern industrialized societies, the primary group remains the prime focus of trust in most developing nations. The family, the clan, the village, even the ethnic group, encompasses those people who are most apt to be trustworthy, or at least those with whom social intercourse is likely to be possible with minimal friction. Correspondingly, certain obligations—of reciprocal trust, loyalty, service, and perhaps obedience—are embedded in each circle of affiliation, becoming specific or generalized according to the expectations of the group.

It has been widely asserted that the "modern men" of Ghana, because of their involvement in political groups and institutions beyond the primary group, have adjusted their hierarchies of trust to accommodate their broader involvements. At the very least, it is claimed, those operating within governmental institutions have experienced the sorts of conflicts of role and loyalty that afflicted Lloyd Faller's Busoga "Bantu bureaucrats."[2] These assertions may be generally accurate; there is scant empirical evidence on the subject, and Faller's study has not been replicated in Ghana. But if they are accurate, then the dozen men interviewed for this study, all admittedly "modern men" in the sense that their political and economic behavior suggests strongly held instrumental or secular values, somehow depart from the legal norm in terms of their loyalties, and hence their perceived obligations. Their observations indicate that broadened loyalties did not necessarily attend their involvement in the national political arena.

I see first my mother, my uncles, my father, my brothers, my country-man and I help them first. I know them, but do I know Ghana govern-ment, or Ghana court? (Mr. *H*; Interview H-2) [In Ghanaian colloquial usage, "brother" refers not only to a blood brother but to any male member of the extended family except one's father or uncles, and often even to any male from one's own village or area. It indicates membership in a primary group. "Sister" is often used in the same way. The colloquial "countryman," (or "countrywoman") may refer to someone from the same village or the same area as the speaker, or it may simply refer to someone from the same ethnic group. It usually implies coethnicity except when used by Ghanaians abroad, when it may simply refer to another Ghanaian.] The politicians, the ministers, the MPs, even the civil servants with their regulations said much at first about working for Ghana's good. We were all proud to bring Ghana to democracy and to do better than the English, who only wanted to exploit us. Nkrumah said so, and we believed him. Then everybody started to chop money, chop cars, chop stores, and those who didn't chop and said it was unlawful were soon sacked. So I learned by lessons and chopped without worry, for myself and my brothers. (Mr. *J*; Interview J-7) ["Chop" or "chap" is a widely used west African pidgin word meaning generally "to eat," or simply "food." Ghanaian colloquial usage gives it the additional meaning "to take," or more crassly "to steal." "Chop" is also used to mean "strike down" or "hit," as in the phrase, "A de chop um good," which means "I hit him hard."]

I: But don't the regulations forbid trading in official favors? And if a civil servant does that, don't his acts hurt the country?
R: No. If government doesn't help the people, then civil servants are right in helping them. And if I am posted to K_____, I help my family and countrymen first, because they know me and would be angry if I did not. (Mr. *C*; Interview C-4)

Retrospective Attitudes

The A_____ Commission of Enquiry found I had exceeded my income by £ _____, and I had to pay that. But I am not sorry; I used the money wisely. (Mr. *G*; Interview G-3)

When Busia is gone, I will be back in Service. And unless the soldiers stand by my desk, I will do what I did before, because no one can stay in office unless he prefers those who serve him well. (Mr. *A*; Interview A-5)

Do you want me to feel guilty about what happened? Guilt is for pastors and priests. If I give drink gift to the chief, a gift to a big man is also the Ghana way. (Mr. *K*; Interview K-4)

The above quotations represent but a small sampling of the retro-spective attitudes expressed by the twelve respondents. Nevertheless, they incorporate the general themes and values common to all their conversations in the same vein.

All respondents admitted violating the formal norms; moreover all suggested that rules against corruption apply only to the losers in the zero-sum game of Ghanaian politics, while those on top, the winners, can conveniently disregard them.[3] Everyone flouts the rules, they said; anyone who might insist on their literal application could not survive politically.[4]

Most of the respondents saw their current out-of-power, out-of-office situation as temporary, a result of political bad luck which the future could well reverse to their renewed profit.

The respondents were on the whole a thoroughly unrepentant lot, contemptuous of the Busia regime in particular and of government in general. So far from exhibiting guilt or remorse over their alleged misdeeds, they argued that they had acted as they did out of necessity, in order to reduce the uncertainty of what they perceived to be a sort of Hobbesian world in which every man's hand, if not set against his neighbor, was at least groping in his pocket.

All respondents articulated extremely high levels of political cynicism, ascribing self-seeking motives not only to most of their colleagues during the Nkrumah era, but to officials in the Busia regime as well. It was only with respect to the military, who ousted them, that they exhibited any ambivalence; four conceded that most of the members of the (military) National Liberation Council were honest and uncorrupted, although three others pointedly recalled the resignation of NLC Chairman Gen. Ankrah (for privately collecting of money to finance his presidential aspirations) as proof that "moral" soldiers are not immune to corruption.

The respondents could be adjudged as perfect a set of economic men as any that economists postulate in theory. They appeared to be wholly rational in their actions, wholly calculating, and genuinely convinced that their admittedly illicit behavior was justified by reason of their loyalties to kin, friends, clients, and ethnic brethren. What is more, they apparently were prepared to do it all again if given the chance.

They also displayed a sense of political efficacy that was unexpectedly positive in light of their current situations. Not only did they profess to a thorough knowledge of how to get around the system; they were wholly convinced that given the proper settings and opportunities, they could once again manipulate men and events to their own ends. This attitude would not have been so startling had it been expressed by only a few of the respondents; in that case one might feel tempted to dismiss it as wishful thinking. But every single one of this forceful, generally realistic group appeared to share the feeling, and thus it is difficult not to give some credence to their claim.

Finally, the twelve respondents were wholly parochial political men whose politics seemed invariably circumbscribed by the range of their pragmatic interests. They showed no reluctance to identify themselves as Ghanaians, to be sure, but for most it appeared that this identity implied little of operational consequence. A generalized ordering of their socio-political hierarchy of identification—and hence of their hierarchy of trust—could be set out as follows (in order of importance):

1. Nuclear family and/or extended family
2. Close friends/"countrymen"/co-ethnics
3. Business associates
4. "Old boys" (school classmates)
5. Clients/supporters (usually persons in categories 1, 2, 4)
6. Professional/official colleagues
7. Persons in superior/superordinate official and social positions
8. The country (the government and/or its institutions)

The categories set out above need some explanation, as does their ranking. First, the categories are not mutually exclusive. It is likely, for example, that all of those in category 1 (kinsmen) could also be included in category 2 (coethnics and close friends), that some of those in categories 1 and 2 would be included in category 5 (clients and supporters), and so on. The categories and their ranking emerged in part from sets of questions designed to probe three dimensions of trust and identification: (a) the persons to whom a respondent would turn when in difficulty; (b) the persons or institutions with whom a respondent preferred to deal in most official and social matters; and (c) the persons, groups, or institutions to whom a respondent felt he owed obligations and loyalties. The categories and the order in which they are ranked constitute a generalized sum of the respondents' answers and to those that dealt with more general attitudes to authority, obligation, and the like. Each category, therefore, represents a collective statement concerning relative *levels* of trust and identification. Thus, category 3 could be read as follows: "Business associates tend to be trusted more than 'old boys,' clients and supporters, official colleagues, or persons in superior positions, unless any of the latter happen to be coethnics or kinsmen."

Second, the categories assume that trust implies identification, and vice versa, because in practice, the persons, groups, and institutions with whom one most closely identifies, are also those most likely to be objects of considerable trust. In our set of categories, number 6 (the country) is the only depersonalized object listed; it is ranked last precisely because the respondents saw institutions of government as objects of last resort. Political and social relations in Ghana tend to be personalized in the extreme, and when Ghanaians think of transactions within or with the formal polity, they do so in terms of relations with individuals or discrete groups of individuals rather than with institutions. Trust is given to specific persons or groups with familiar, non-threatening attributes. Institutions rank lowest on the scale of trust and identification because their impersonal nature makes them—in the Ghanaian situation—both unpredictable and arbitrary.

A final note on the interviews. The author concedes that the respondents did not in any sense constitute a statistically valid sample of the corrupt officials of the Nkrumah regime. (Indeed, there appears to be no way to estimate that population reliably; respondents' estimates, for example, ranged all the way from 20 to 75 percent of *all* Ghanaian office-holders.) Conceivably, then, what is generalized above from twelve sets of interviews may be largely unrepresentative of the values held by most of those involved in corrupt practices. Moreover, by any criterion of selection the twelve respondents were members of Ghana's former political elite, and it is possible that bureaucrats and functionaries who served at the lower levels of government and the party might hold generally different values. But analyses by other observers, Ghanaians and non-Ghanaians alike, indicate that our respondents were indeed representative in their attitudes, representative not only of the larger population of persons involved in politically corrupt dealings, but in some degree of most politically aware Ghanaians. For example, Margaret Field, whose classic ethno-psychiatric study of rural Ghana remains one of the most insightful analyses of the Ghanaian psyche, notes that one of the prime characteristics of the Akan social and political structure (i.e., of southern and central Ghana) is "the absence of hide-bound rigidity." This condition, Field asserts, proceeds from the following attitudes and values:

> Class hardly exists; rank does exist but its attainment is the reward of individual merit. Institutions were made for man. Nothing is immune from criticism. Justice is more than law. The spirit of the law is more than the letter.[5]

"Of course," she notes, "this adaptability and flexibility cut both ways: the self-seeking opportunist has no hampering scruples."[6]

The last word on the value structure that supports the political culture of Ghana belongs properly to a Ghanaian. We have noted how our respondents conveyed the image of nearly perfect economic men, how they depicted the system as a sort of Hobbesian jungle in which illicit behavior was justified in the interests of political self-preservation and fulfillment of obligations to kinship or to other primary ties.

Maxwell Owusu, in his excellent study of local politics in Agona-Swedru (again, south-central Ghana), persuasively argues a view of Ghanaian politics in which

> The exercise of power, chiefly, colonial, and party, was seen as a major means of achieving, protecting, and advancing individual, family, and status-class or group economic and other material advantages and interests. The struggle for power . . . was primarily a struggle in relation to the possession of wealth and its distribution and consumption to achieve high social status, prestige, and social privilege.[7]

Thus, "Changes in power relations tend[ed] to reflect, to a very large extent, changes in the control, distribution, and generalized consumption of wealth."[8]

> What is often forgotten or not realized [Owusu points out], is that the political development in Ghana, particularly between 1950 and 1966 . . . was characterized by a political process in which individuals and groups in various local areas supported and voted for this or that group or political party in terms largely of instrumental values expressed by individual opportunism and careerism. . . . Other techniques in the political process were "crossing the carpet," bribery, corruption. . . .[9]

Owusu does not, it should be noted, advance an analysis based on a Ghanaian variety of economic determinism; rather, he asserts there has been an "economization" of political relations, so that political transactions are colored and often dominated by economic interest. From his perspective, what we have here called "political corruption" is seen as but one of a large variety of self-serving political modes that are instrumental in determining the important questions of who rules, what political resources are distributed or consumed, and who will benefit from the exercise of public authority. If Owusu is correct, the values expressed by the twelve respondents may be even more generally held than the interviewees themselves suggested. And if that is indeed the case, the source of support for a Ghanaian culture of political corruption seems obvious.

The cut-off date for Owusu's discussion of Swedru and Ghana is 1966, and it might be argued that his comments therefore do not apply to the post-coup period. The author's own first-hand observations, however, indicated that Owusu's propositions were equally applicable during the Busia period; the same conclusion seems to have been reached by three Progress party MPs during parliamentary debates in 1970 and 1971:

Mr. E. K. Addae (PP—Ashanti–Akim North): during the old regime there were reports of embezzlement of state funds, laziness on the part of some public employees, malingering and sorts of dubious deeds leading to the loss of public funds. All these evils are prevalent in our society today and they have to be eradicated; else the progress we talk so much about today will never come to pass.[10]

Mr. George Oteng (PP—Asiakwa–Kwaben): The idea of everybody in Ghana trying to get rich quick, building a house at the expense of others, especially of the government, is what is ruining the country. This idea inherited by Ghanaians is taking firm root.[11]

Mr. M. Archer (PP—Wasa East): Any time I stand up and say that people are corrupt, Members in this House think I am joking. I am not joking at all. I say that with all seriousness. What we saw and what we listened to during the deliberations of the Public Accounts Committee is evidence of the fact that people in this country—in fact many of them— are corrupt. . . . One thing that I should like to say is that many people in this country think that it is only politicians who are corrupt. . . . But those who are most corrupt are civil servants and people in the public corporations. . . . Only Heaven knows how much we are losing in this country through the practice of corruption.[12]

Notes

1. For a discussion of concepts associated with efficacy, political competence, and civic competence, see Gabriel A. Almond and Sidney Verba, *The Civic Culture* (Princeton, N.J.: Princeton University Press, 1963), pp. 180–84. Applications of these concepts are discussed in the same work, pp. 184–257 *passim*.
2. Lloyd Fallers, *Bantu Bureaucracy* (Chicago: University of Chicago Press, 1965).
3. A Ghanaian political scientist, F. K. Drah, argues that this view has traditional roots. In support of this contention, he cites the example of "destoolment" (divestiture) of chiefs:

   What is not in doubt . . . is the fact that if and when a chief was destooled or "overthrown," the whole of his lineage was involved in his downfall. Those of them who happened to be stool office-holders were not seldom stripped of their offices *and* their titles, resulting in a whole redistribution of power. Extreme punitive and vindictive measures against the members of a defeated royal lineage were not uncommon: "You lose, I win and I take all." Without a scintilla of exaggeration, this "zero-sum" view of politics has been a powerful undercurrent of Ghanaian politics—at both the local and the central levels—up to the present. It was no new practice to, and was not initiated by, the C.P.P. nationalists and rulers.

   "Political Tradition and the Search for Constitutional Democracy in Ghana: A Prolegomenon," *Ghana Journal of Sociology* 6, no. 1 (February 1970), 10.
4. A conspicuous case in point is that of Mr. Kwabena Owusu, who in 1961 was named acting manager of the Ghana Distilleries Corporation. Mr.

Owusu objected to the inflated prices charged by a London firm—Duncan, Gilbey, and Matheson—which was then paying kickbacks to NADECO; as a consequence, he and members of his family were arrested and humiliated, and he was finally dismissed from his position in January 1962. (Azu Crabbe Commission, pp. 43–44.) In the kingdom of the corrupt the honest man could hardly get near the throne, much less become king; the usual fate of one who refused to become corrupt was to be made an outcast, or suffer other social and economic penalties. Ayi Kwei Armah's vivid novel about corruption in Nkrumah's Ghana, *The Beautyful Ones Are Not Yet Born* (New York: Colliers-Macmillan, 1969), makes this point with great force.

5. Margaret J. Field, *Search for Security: An Ethno-psychiatric Study of Rural Ghana* (London: Faber and Faber, 1960), p. 26.
6. *Ibid.*
7. Maxwell Owusu, *Uses and Abuses of Political Power: A Case Study of Continuity and Change in the Politics of Ghana.* (Chicago: University of Chicago Press, 1970), p. 325.
8. *Ibid.*, p. 326.
9. *Ibid.*, p. 248.
10. Ghana, *Parliamentary Debates, Official Report*, Second Series, vol. 5, no. 4 (13 November 1970), col. 107.
11. *Ibid.*, vol. 6, no. 9 (8 March 1971), col. 300.
12. *Ibid.*, col. 301.

Modernization, Corruption, and Economic Development: An Introduction

Since the mid-1950s, one of the main foci of comparative politics has been questions of political development, usually conceived in terms of political democracy, development and nationalism, and modernization. The impetus for this concern was the post-World War II emergence of well over seventy new states, most of them former colonies. "Modernization," then, meant becoming like the countries of the capitalist or socialist west, and "economic development" was advanced as one of the primary means of getting there. The authors of the chapters in this section all share these assumptions, and address the issue of the relationship between modernization and economic development, and corruption. Does corruption help or hinder the processes of development, or does it have little or no effect either way?

Samuel Huntington, in the first selection (drawn from his widely acclaimed book on political development), offers the thesis that when modernizing countries buy rapid social modernization at the price of the decay of political institutions, corruption and violence become alternative means of making demands upon the system. While violence poses the greater and more direct threat to the system, corruption may simultaneously satisfy demands in ways that violence cannot. "Those who corrupt a country's police officers," argues the author, "are more likely to identify with the system than those who seize its police stations." In this sense, then, corruption can fulfill a useful function as a lesser among evils common in developing countries.

Nathaniel Leff, the economist author of Chapter 24, is an analyst of economic development who ascribes positive functions to corruption as a regulatory instrument for the informal allocation of scarce resources such as licenses and public services. Bureaucracies in developing countries are seen as often afflicted with excessive personnel, inefficiency, sluggishness, and general hostility to entrepreneurial activity outside the scope of their jurisdiction. Corruption helps unblock the system by providing incentives necessary to mobilize the bureaucracy for more energetic action on behalf of the entrepreneurs. It can reduce uncertainty and increase investment, open the door to economic innovation, stimulate efficiency by catalyzing bureaucratic energies, and act as a hedge against bad policies.

Gunnar Myrdal, unlike Huntington and Leff, finds little to praise in corruption. In Chapter 25, drawn from his study into the causes of poverty in Asia, he asserts that the levels of public corruption in most Asian countries have risen rather than declined after the accession to independence. He attributes the growth of general cynicism to the unwillingness of post-independence governments to raise the issue lest in so doing they stimulate it further, thus strengthening sociocultural patterns that encourage corrupt practices. The net effect, Myrdal argues, is to hinder rather than encourage the processes of modernization.

The last selection, by Theodore M. Smith, includes results of surveys and interviews with Indonesian lower-and middle-level bureaucrats. The officials almost overwhelmingly deplored corruption in their ranks; they agreed that such practices damaged economic development; they clearly identified the social and structural factors that led to corruption. Yet they suggested that they could not change their behavior unless the causal circumstances (including low pay) were ameliorated. The author concludes that on the whole, corruption in Indonesia is less of an economic problem than a recurring political one; its net effect is to reduce bureaucratic efficiency and undermine support for government among middle- and lower-level elites in the country.

23

Modernization and Corruption

Samuel P. Huntington

Corruption is behavior of public officials which deviates from accepted norms in order to serve private ends. Corruption obviously exists in all societies, but it is also obviously more common in some societies than in others and more common at some times in the evolution of a society than at other times. Impressionistic evidence suggests that its extent correlates reasonably well with rapid social and economic modernization. Political life in eighteenth-century America and in twentieth-century America, it would appear, was less corrupt than in nineteenth-century America. So also political life in seventeenth-century Britain and in late nineteenth-century Britain was, it would appear, less corrupt than it was in eighteenth-century Britain. Is it merely coincidence that this high point of corruption in English and American public life coincided with the impact of the industrial revolution, the development of new sources of wealth and power, and the appearance of new classes making new demands on government? In both periods political institutions suffered strain and some measure of decay. Corruption is, of course, one measure of the absence of effective political institutionalization. Public officials lack autonomy and coherence, and subordinate their institutional roles to exogenous demands. Corruption may be more prevalent in some cultures than in others but in most cultures it seems to be most prevalent during the most intense phases of modernization. The differences in the level of corruption which may exist between the modernized and politically developed societies of the Atlantic world and those of Latin America, Africa, and Asia in large part reflect their differences in political modernization and political development. When the leaders of military juntas and revolutionary movements condemn the "corruption" in

Source: Samuel P. Huntington, "Modernization and Corruption," *Political Order in changing Societies*. New Haven, Conn.: Yale University Press, 1968, pp. 59–71. By permission of the publisher. Copyright © 1968 by Yale University.

their societies, they are, in effect, condemning the backwardness of their societies.

Why does modernization breed corruption? Three connections stand out. First, modernization involves a change in the basic values of the society. In particular it means the gradual acceptance by groups within the society of universalistic and achievement-based norms, the emergence of loyalties and identifications of individuals and groups with the nation-state, and the spread of the assumption that citizens have equal rights against the state and equal obligations to the state. These norms usually, of course, are first accepted by students, military officers, and others who have been exposed to them abroad. Such groups then begin to judge their own society by these new and alien norms. Behavior which was acceptable and legitimate according to traditional norms becomes unacceptable and corrupt when viewed through modern eyes. Corruption in a modernizing society is thus in part not so much the result of the deviance of behavior from accepted norms as it is the deviance of norms from the established patterns of behavior. New standards and criteria of what is right and wrong lead to a condemnation of at least some traditional behavior patterns as corrupt. "What Britons saw as corrupt and Hausa as oppressive," one scholar has noted of northern Nigeria, "Fulani might regard as both necessary and traditional."[1] The calling into question of old standards, moreover, tends to undermine the legitimacy of all standards. The conflict between modern and traditional norms opens opportunities for individuals to act in ways justified by neither.

Corruption requires some recognition of the difference between public role and private interest. If the culture of the society does not distinguish between the king's role as a private person and the king's role as king, it is impossible to accuse the king of corruption in the use of public monies. The distinction between the private purse and public expenditures only gradually evolved in Western Europe at the beginning of the modern period. Some notion of this distinction, however, is necessary to reach any conclusion as to whether the actions of the king are proper or corrupt. Similarly, according to traditional codes in many societies, an official had the responsibility and obligation to provide rewards and employment to members of his family. No distinction existed between obligation to the state and obligation to the family. Only when such a distinction becomes accepted by dominant groups within the society does it become possible to define such behavior as nepotism and hence corruption. Indeed, the introduction of achievement standards may stimulate greater family identification and more felt need to protect family interests against the threat posed by alien ways. Corruption is thus a product of the distinction between public welfare and private interest which comes with modernization.

Modernization also contributes to corruption by creating new sources of wealth and power, the relation of which to politics is undefined by the dominant traditional norms of the society and on which the modern norms are not yet accepted by the dominant groups within the society. Corruption in this sense is a direct product of the rise of new groups with new resources and the efforts of these groups to make themselves effective within the political sphere. Corruption may be the means of assimilating new groups into the political system by irregular means because the system has been unable to adapt sufficiently fast to provide legitimate and acceptable means for this purpose. In Africa, corruption threw "a bridge between those who hold political power and those who control wealth, enabling the two classes, markedly apart during the initial stages of African nationalist governments, to assimilate each other."[2] The new millionaires buy themselves seats in the Senate or the House of Lords and thereby become participants in the political system rather than alienated opponents of it, which might have been the case if this opportunity to corrupt the system were denied them. So also recently enfranchised masses or recently arrived immigrants use their new power of the ballot to buy themselves jobs and favors from the local political machine. There is thus the corruption of the poor and the corruption of the rich. The one trades political power for money, the other money for political power. But in both cases something public (a vote or an office or decision) is sold for private gain.

Modernization, thirdly, encourages corruption by the changes it produces on the output side of the political system. Modernization, particularly among the later modernizing countries, involves the expansion of governmental authority and the multiplication of the activities subjected to governmental regulation. In Northern Nigeria, "oppression and corruption tended to increase among the Hausa with political centralization and the increase of governmental tasks." All laws, as McMullan has pointed out, put some group at a disadvantage, and this group consequently becomes a potential source of corruption.[3] The multiplication of laws thus multiplies the possibilities of corruption. The extent to which this possibility is realized in practice depends in large part upon the extent to which the laws have the general support of the population, the ease with which the law can be broken without detection, and the profit to be made by breaking it. Laws affecting trade, customs, taxes plus those regulating popular and profitable activities such as gambling, prostitution, and liquor, consequently become major incentives to corruption. Hence in a society where corruption is widespread the passage of strict laws against corruption serves only to multiply the opportunities for corruption.

The initial adherence to modern values by a group in a transitional country often takes an extreme form. The ideals of honesty, probity, universalism, and merit often become so overriding that individuals and groups come to condemn as corrupt in their own society practices which are accepted as normal and even legitimate in more modern societies. The initial exposure to modernism tends to give rise to unreasonable puritanical standards even as it did among the Puritans themselves. This escalation in values leads to a denial and rejection of the bargaining and compromise essential to politics and promotes the identification of politics with corruption. To the modernizing zealot a politician's promise to build irrigation ditches for farmers in a village if he is elected seems to be just as corrupt as an offer to pay each villager for his vote before the election. Modernizing elites are nationalistic and stress the overriding preeminence of the general welfare of society as a whole. Hence in a country like Brazil, "efforts by private interests to influence public policy are considered, as in Rousseau, *inherently* 'corrupt.' By the same token government action which is fashioned in deference to particular claims and pressures from society is considered 'demagogy.' "[4] In a society like Brazil the modernizing elements condemn as corrupt ambassadorial appointments to reward friends or to appease critics and the establishment of government projects in return for interest group support. In the extreme case the antagonism to corruption may take the form of the intense fanatical puritanism characteristic of most revolutionary and some military regimes in at least their early phases. Paradoxically, this fanatical anticorruption mentality has ultimate effects similar to those of corruption itself. Both challenge the autonomy of politics: one substituting private goals for public ones and the other replacing political values with technical ones. The escalation of standards in a modernizing society and the concomitant devaluation and rejection of politics represent the victory of the values of modernity over the needs of society.

Reducing corruption in a society thus often involves both a scaling down of the norms thought appropriate for the behavior of public officials and at the same time changes in the general behavior of such officials in the direction of those norms. The result is a greater congruence between prevalent norms and prevalent behavior at the price of some inconsistency in both. Some behavior comes to be accepted as a normal part of the process of politics, as "honest" rather than "dishonest graft," while other, similar behavior comes to be generally condemned and generally avoided. Both England and the United States went through this process: at one point the former accepted the sale of peerages but not of ambassadorships, while the latter accepted the sale of ambassadorships but not of judgeships. "The result in the U.S.A.," as one observer has noted, "is a patchwork: the scope of political patronage has been greatly reduced and the cash bribery of higher public servants largely eliminated. At the same time, large areas of public life have so far remained more or less immune to reform, and practices that in one sphere would be regarded as corrupt are almost taken for granted in another."[5] The development within a society of the ability to make this discrimination is a sign of its movement from modernization to modernity.

The functions, as well as the causes, of corruption are similar to those of violence. Both are encouraged by modernization; both are symptomatic of the weakness of political institutions; both are characteristic of what we shall subsequently call praetorian societies; both are means by which individuals and groups relate themselves to the political system and, indeed, participate in the system in ways which violate the mores of the system. Hence the society which has a high capacity for corruption also has a high capacity for violence. In some measure, one form of deviant behavior may substitute for the other, but, more often different social forces simultaneously exploit their differing capacities for each. The prevalence of violence, however, does pose a greater threat to the functioning of the system than the prevalence of corruption. In the absence of agreement on public purposes, corruption substitutes agreement on private goals, while violence substitutes conflict over public or private ends. Both corruption and violence are illegitimate means of making demands upon the system, but corruption is also an illegitimate means of satisfying those demands. Violence is more often a symbolic gesture of protest which goes unrequited and is not designed to be requited. It is a symptom of more extreme alienation. He who corrupts a system's police officers is more likely to identify with the system than he who storms the system's police stations.

Like machine politics or clientelistic politics in general, corruption provides immediate, specific, and concrete benefits to groups which might otherwise be thoroughly alienated from society. Corruption may thus be functional to the maintenance of a political system in the same way that reform is. Corruption itself may be a substitute for reform and both corruption and reform may be substitutes for revolution. Corruption serves to reduce group pressures for policy changes, just as reform serves to reduce class pressures for structural changes. In Brazil, for instance, governmental loans to trade association leaders have caused them to give up "their associations' broader claims. Such betrayals have been an important factor in reducing class and trade association pressure upon the government."[6]

The degree of corruption which modernization produces in a society is, of course, a function of the nature of the traditional society as well as of the nature of the modernizing process. The presence of several competing value systems or cultures in a traditional society will, in itself, encourage corruption in that society. Given a relatively homogeneous culture, however, the amount of corruption likely to develop during modernization would appear to be inversely related to the degree of social stratification in the traditional society. A highly articulated class or caste structure means a highly developed system of norms regulating behavior between individuals of different status. These norms are enforced both by the individual's socialization into his own group and by the expectations and potential sanctions of other groups. In such a society failure to follow the relevant norms in intergroup relations may lead to intense personal disorganization and unhappiness.

Corruption, consequently, should be less extensive in the modernization of feudal societies than it is in the modernization of centralized bureaucratic societies. It should have been less in Japan than in China and it should have been less in Hindu cultures than in Islamic ones. Impressionistic evidence suggests that these may well be the case. For Western societies, one comparative analysis shows that Australia and Great Britain have "fairly high levels of class voting" compared to the United States and Canada. Political corruption, however, appears to have been more extensive in the latter two countries than in the former, with Quebec perhaps being the most corrupt area in any of the four countries. Consequently, "the more class-polarized countries also seem to have less political corruption."[7] Similarly, in the "mulatto" countries (Panama, Cuba, Venezuela, Brazil, Dominican Republic, and Haiti) of Latin America, "there appears to be greater social equality and much less rigidity in the social structure" than in the Indian (Mexico, Ecuador, Guatemala, Peru, Bolivia) or *mestizo* (Chile, Colombia, El Salvador, Honduras, Nicaragua, Paraguay) countries. Correspondingly, however, the relative "absence of an entrenched upper class means also the relative absence of a governing class ethic, with its sense of noblesse oblige" and hence "there seems little doubt that it is countries in this socio-racial category in which political graft reaches its most flagrant heights. Pérez Jiménez in Venezuela, Batista in Cuba, and Trujillo in the Dominican Republic all came from non-upper-class backgrounds and all became multimillionaires in office. So also, "Brazil and Panama are notorious for more 'democratic,' more widely-distributed, graft-taking."[8] The prevalence of corruption in the African states may well be related to the general absence of rigid class divisions. "The rapid mobility from poverty to wealth and from one occupation to another," one observer has noted of Africa, "has prevented the development of class phenomena, that is, of hereditary status or class consciousness."[9] The same mobility, however, multiplies the opportunities for and the attractions of corruption. Similarly, the Philippines and Thailand, both of which have had reasonably fluid and open societies with relatively high degrees of social mobility, have been characterized by frequent reports of widespread political corruption.

In most forms corruption involves an exchange of political action for economic wealth. The particular forms that will be prevalent in a society depend upon the ease of acess to one as against the other. In a society with multiple opportunities for the accumulation of wealth and few positions of political power, the dominant pattern will be the use of the former to achieve the latter. In the United states, wealth has more commonly been a road to political influence than political office has been a road to wealth. The rules against using public office to obtain private profit are much stricter and more generally obeyed than those against using private wealth to obtain public office. That striking and yet common phenomenon of American politics, the cabinet minister or presidential assistant who feels forced to quit office *in order* to provide for his family, would be viewed with amazement and incredulity in most parts of the world. In modernizing countries, the reverse situation is usually the case. The opportunities for the accumulation of wealth through private activity are limited by traditional norms, the monopoly of economic roles by ethnic minorities, or the domination of the economy by foreign companies and investors. In such a society, politics becomes the road to wealth, and those enterprising ambitions and talents which cannot find what they want in business may yet do so in politics. It is, in many modernizing countries, easier for an able and ambitious young man to become a cabinet minister by way of politics than to become a millionaire by way of business. Consequently, contrary to American practice, modernizing countries may accept as normal widespread use of public office to obtain private wealth while at the same time taking a stricter view of the use of private wealth to obtain public office. Corruption, like violence, results when the absence of mobility opportunities outside politics, combined with weak and inflexible political institutions, channels energies into politically deviant behavior.

The prevalence of foreign business in a country in particular tends to promote corruption both because the foreigners have less scruples in violating the norms of the society and because their control of important avenues to economic wellbeing forces potential native entrepreneurs to attempt to make their fortunes through politics. Taylor's description of the Philippines undoubtedly has widespread application among modernizing countries: "Politics is a major industry for the Filipinos: it is a way of life. Politics is the main route to power, which, in turn, is the main route to wealth. . . . More money can be made in a shorter time with the aid of political influence than by any other means."[10] The use of political office as a way to wealth implies a subordination of political values and institutions to economic ones. The principal purpose of politics becomes not the achievement of public goals but the promotion of individual interests.

In all societies the *scale* of corruption (i.e. the average value of the private goods and public services involved in a corrupt exchange) increases as one goes up the bureaucratic hierarchy or potential ladder. The *incidence* of corruption (i.e. the frequency with which a given population group engages in corrupt acts) on a given level in the political or bureaucratic structure, however, may vary significantly from one society to another. In most political systems, the incidence of corruption is high at the lower levels of bureaucratic and political authority. In some societies, the incidence of corruption seems to remain constant or to increase as one goes up the political hierarchy. In terms of frequency as well as scale, national legislators are more corrupt than local officials; high level bureaucrats are more corrupt than low level ones; cabinet ministers are the most corrupt of all; and the president or top leader the most corrupt among them. In such societies the top leader—the Nkrumah, Sarit, San Martín, Pérez Jiménez, Trujillo—may make off with tens if not hundreds of millions of dollars. In such a system corruption tends to accentuate already existing inequalities. Those who gain access to the most political power also have the more frequent opportunities to gain access to the most wealth. Such a pattern of top-heavy corruption means a very low level of political institutionalization, since the top political institutions in the society which should be most independent of outside influences are in fact most susceptible to such influences. This pattern of corruption is not necessarily incompatible with political stability so long as the avenues of upward mobility through the political machine or the bureaucracy remain open. If, however, the younger generation of politicians sees itself indefinitely excluded from sharing in the gains of the older leaders, or if the colonels in the army see little hope of promotion and the chance to share in the opoortunities open only to generals, the system becomes liable to violent overthrow. In such a society both political corruption and political stability depend upon vertical mobility.

The expectation of more corruption at the top is reversed in other societies. In these societies the incidence of corrupt behavior increases as one goes down the political or bureaucratic hierarchy. Low-level bureaucratic officials are more likely to be corrupt than high-level ones; state and local officials are more likely to be corrupt than national ones; the top national leadership and the national cabinet are comparatively free from corruption, while the town council and local offices are deeply involved in it. Scale and incidence of corruption are inversely related. This pattern would seem to be generally true for highly modern societies, such as the United States, and also for at least some modernizing societies, such as India. It is also probably the dominant pattern in communist states. The crucial factor in this type of society is the existence of fairly strong national political institutions which socialize rising political leaders into a code of values stressing the public responsibilities of the political leadership. National political institutions are reasonably autonomous and differentiated, while lower-level and local political individuals and organizations are more closely involved with other social forces and groups. This pattern of corruption may directly enhance the stability of the political system. The top leaders of the society remain true to the stated norms of the political culture and accept political power and moral virtue as substitutes for economic gain. Low-level officials, in turn, are compensated for their lack of political standing by their greater opportunity to engage in corruption. Their envy of the power of their leaders is tempered by the solace of their own petty graft.

Just as the corruption produced by the expansion of political participation helps to integrate new groups into the political system, so also the corruption produced by the expansion of governmental regulation may help stimulate economic development. Corruption may be one way of surmounting traditional laws or bureaucratic regulations which hamper economic expansion. In the United States during the 1870s and 1880s corruption of state legislatures and city councils by railroad, utility, and industrial corporations undoubtedly speeded the growth of the American economy. "Many economic activities would be paralyzed," Weiner observes of India, "were it not for the flexibility which *bakshish* contributes to the complex, rigid, administrative system."[11] In somewhat similar fashion, during the Kubitschek era in Brazil a high rate of economic development apparently corresponded with a high rate of parliamentary corruption, as industrializing entrepreneurs bought protection and assistance from conservative rural legislators. It has even been suggested that one result of governmental efforts to reduce corruption in societies such as Egypt is to produce additional obstacles to economic development. In terms of economic growth, the only thing worse than a society with a rigid, overcentralized, dishonest bureaucracy is one with a rigid, overcentralized, honest bureaucracy. A society which is relatively uncorrupt—a traditional society for instance where traditional norms are still powerful—may find a certain amount of corruption a welcome lubricant easing the path to modernization. A developed traditional society may be improved—or at least modernized—by a little corruption; a society in which corruption is already pervasive, however, is unlikely to be improved by more corruption.

Corruption naturally tends to weaken or to perpetuate the weakness of the government bureaucracy. In this respect, it is incompatible with political development. At times, however, some forms of corruption can contribute to political development by helping to strengthen political parties. "The corruption of one government," Harrington said, "is the generation of another."[12] Similarly, the corruption of one governmental organ may help the institutionalization of another. In most modernizing countries, the bureaucracy is overdeveloped in comparison with the institutions responsible for aggregating interests and handling the input side of the political system. Insofar as the governmental bureaucracy is corrupted in the interests of the political parties, political development may be helped rather than hindered. Party patronage is only a mild form of corruption, if indeed it deserves to be called that at all. For an official to award a public office in return for a payment to the official is clearly to place private interest over public interest. For an official to award a public office in return for a contribution of work or money to a party organization is to subordinate one public interest to another, more needy, public interest.

Historically strong party organizations have been built either by revolution from below or by patronage from above. The nineteenth-century experience of England and the United States is one long lesson in the use of public funds and public office to build party organization. The repetition of this pattern in the modernizing countries of today has contributed directly to the building of some of the most effective political parties and most stable political systems. In the later modernizing countries the sources of private wealth are too few and too small to make a major contribution to party building. Just as government in these countries has to play a more important role in economic development than it did in England and the United States, so also it must play a more important role in political development. In the 1920s and the 1930s, Ataturk used the resources of the Turkish government to foster the development of the Republican Peoples Party. After its creation in 1929 the Mexican Revolutionary Party similarly benefited from governmental corruption and patronage. The formation of the Democratic Republican Party in Korea in the early 1960s was directly helped by the use of governmental monies and governmental personnel. In Israel and India, governmental patronage has been a major source of strength for Mapai and Congress. The corruption in West Africa derived in part from the needs of the political parties. Of course, in the most obvious and blatant case of all, communist parties, once they acquire power, directly subordinate governmental bureaucracies and governmental resources to their own purposes.

The rationale for corrupting the bureaucracy on behalf of the parties does not derive simply from a preference for one organization as against another. Corruption is, as we have seen, a product of modernization and particularly of the expansion of political consciousness and political participation. The reduction of corruption in the long run requires the organization and structuring of that participation. Political parties are the rpincipal institution of modern politics which can perform this function. Corruption thrives on disorganization, the absence of stable relationships among groups and of recognized patterns of authority. The development of political organizations which exercise effective authority and which give rise to organized group interests— the "machine," the "organization," the "party"—transcending those of individual and social groups reduces the opportunity for corruption. Corruption varies inversely with political organization, and to the extent that corruption builds parties, it undermines the conditions of its own existence.

Corruption is most prevalent in states which lack effective political parties, in societies where the interests of the individual, the family, the clique, or the clan predominate. In a modernizing polity the weaker and less accepted the political parties, the greater the likelihood of corruption. In countries like Thailand and Iran where parties have had a semilegality at best, corruption on behalf of individual and family interests has been widespread. In the Philippines where political parties are notoriously weak, corruption has again been widely prevalent. In Brazil, also, the weakness of political parties has been reflected in a "clientelistic" pattern of politics in which corruption has been a major factor.[13] In contrast, it would seem that the incidence of corruption in those countries where governmental resources have been diverted or "corrupted" for party-building is on the whole less than it is where parties have remained weak. The historical experience of the West also reflects this pattern. The parties which at first are the leeches on the bureaucracy in the end become the bark protecting it from more destructive locusts of clique and family. Partisanship and corruption, as Henry Jones Ford argued, "are really antagonistic principles. Partisanship tends to establish a connection based upon an avowed public obligation, while corruption consults private and individual interests which secrete themselves from view and avoid accountability of any kind. The weakness of party organization is the opportunity of corruption."[14]

Notes

1. M.G. Smith, "Historical and Cultural Conditions of Political Corruption Among the Hausa," *Comparative Studies in Society and History,* 6 (Jan. 1964), 194.
2. M. McMullan, "A Theory of Corruption." *The Sociological Review,* 9 (July 1961), 196.
3. Smith, p. 194: McMullan, pp. 190–91.
4. Nathaniel Leff, "Economic Development Through Bureaucratic Corruption," *American Behavioral Scientist,* 8 (Nov. 1964), 132; italics in original.
5. Colin Leys, "What Is the Problem About Corruption?" *Journal of Modern African Studies,* 3 (1965), 230.
6. Leff, p. 137.
7. Robert R. Alford, *Party and Society* (Skokie, Ill.: Rand McNally, 1963), p. 298.
8. Needler, *Political Development in Latin America,* chap. 6, pp. 15–16.
9. Peter C. Lloyd, "The Development of Political Parties in Western Nigeria," *American Political Science Review,* 49 (Sept. 1955), 695.
10. George E. Taylor, *The Philippines and the United States: Problems of Partnership* (New York: Praeger, 1964), p. 157.
11. Myron Weiner, *The Politics of Scarcity* (Chicago: University of Chicago Press, 1962), p. 253. See in general Joseph S. Nye, "Corruption and Political Development: A Cost-Benefit Analysis," *American Political Science Review,* 61 (June 1967), 417–27.
12. James Harrington, quoted in George Sabine, *A History of Political Theory* (rev. ed. New York: Holt, Rinehart & Winston, 1950), p. 501.
13. See Leff, pp. 10–12.
14. Henry Jones Ford, *The Rise and Growth of American Politics* (New York: Macmillan, 1898), pp. 322–23.

24

Economic Development Through Bureaucratic Corruption[1]

Nathaniel H. Leff

The bureaucratic corruption of many underdeveloped countries has been widely condemned both by domestic and foreign observers. Apart from the criticism based on moral grounds, and the technocratic impatience with inefficiency, corruption is usually assumed to have important prejudicial effects on the economic growth of these societies.[2]

Corruption is an extralegal institution used by individuals or groups to gain influence over the actions of the bureaucracy. As such, the existence of corruption *per se* indicates only that these groups participate in the decisionmaking process to a greater extent than would otherwise be the case. This provides information about the effective— as opposed to the formal—political system, but in itself, tells us nothing about the content and development effects of the policies so determined. These depend on the specific orientation and interests of the groups which have gained political access. As we shall see, in the context of many underdeveloped countries, this point can be crucial. For example, if business groups are otherwise at a disadvantage in articulating their interests to the government, and if these groups are more likely to promote growth than is the government, then their enhanced participation in policy formulation can help development.

Furthermore, our discussion is limited to corruption of a particular type: namely, the practice of buying favors from the bureaucrats responsible for formulating and administering the government's economic policies. Typical examples are bribery to obtain foreign exchange, import, export, investment or production licenses, or to avoid

Source: Nathaniel H. Leff, "Economic Development through Bureaucratic Corruption," *American Behavioral Scientist*, 8:3 (November 1964), pp. 8–14. By permission of the publisher, Sage Publications, Inc.

paying taxes. Such bribes are in the nature of a tax levied on economic activity. These payments have not been legitimized by the correct political process, they are appropriated by the bureaucrat rather than the state, and they involve the subversion of the government's economic policies—hence the stigma that attaches to them. The question for us to decide is whether the net effects caused by such payments and policy redirection are likely to favor or hinder economic development.

We should also distinguish between bureaucratic corruption and bureaucratic inefficiency. Corruption refers to extralegal influence on policy formulation or implementation. Inefficiency, on the other hand, has to do with the success or failure, or the economy of means used by the bureaucracy in attaining given goals, whether those of its political directors, or those of the grafters. Empirically, inefficiency and corruption may appear together, and may blend into each other. Both as a policy problem and for analytical purposes, however, it is important to distinguish between two essentially different things.

Who Condemns Corruption?

Before proceeding to our analysis of the economic effects of bureaucratic corruption, it may be useful to make a brief detour. Any discussion of corruption must contend with the fact that the institution is almost universally condemned. Insofar as this criticism is based on moralizing—explicit or latent—self-interest, or ideology, it can be a formidable obstacle to rational analysis. Consequently, in order to gain a degree of perspective on the subject, I would like to consider the sources of the widespread prejudice against corruption. Identifying the specific sources of bias, and breaking down generalized censure to its component parts should help us to evaluate each argument on its own merits. For this purpose, let us consider the origins of the critical attitude held by such groups as foreign observers, government officials, and entrepreneurs, and by intellectuals, politicians, and businessmen in the underdeveloped countries themselves.

Foreigners living in the underdeveloped countries have been persistent critics of corruption. First, they have resented the payments of graft to which they are often subjected in the normal course of their business. Secondly, they have condemned corruption on moral grounds, and criticized it as both a cause and a characteristic of the backwardness of these countries.

A more sophisticated, and recent version of this argument derives from the new interest in promoting economic development. As economists and observers of economic development have grown aware of the enormous obstacles to spontaneous growth, they have come to assign an increasingly important role to the governments of the underdeveloped countries.

First, there has been an emphasis on the need for entrepreneurs, coupled with the fear that the underdeveloped countries may lack indigenous sources of entrepreneurship. Secondly, recent economic theory stressed the importance of indivisibilities, externalities, and other structural features that may prevent an underdeveloped economy from breaking out of a low-income equilibrium trap. In addition, there was the realization that the flow of private capital and technical skills was insufficient for promoting large-scale growth. With the ensuing flow of inter-governmental transfers, came the need for the governments of the underdeveloped countries to assume responsibility for the resources they were receiving.

Because of these reasons and political pressures, the governments of the underdeveloped countries have come to occupy a very prominent place in most visions of economic development. In a sense, economists have collected their problems, placed them in a box labelled "public policy," and turned them over to the governments of the underdeveloped countries.

In order for the governmental policies to be effective, however, the bureaucracies must actually implement them. Hence it becomes crucial that officials not be influenced, through graft, to deviate from their appointed tasks. The logic of this argument goes as follows: development—bureaucracy—efficiency—probity. This chain of reasoning is central to the whole critique of corruption, and we shall examine it carefully in the next section. Before going further, however, let us note a few important points about this argument.

First, it confuses bureaucratic inefficiency and bureaucratic redirection through dishonesty and graft. Secondly, transferring these problems to the governments and bureaucracies is hardly enough to solve them, for these institutions may not be at all likely to promote growth. Rather than leading the development process, the governments and bureaucracies may be lagging sectors. Finally, the argument implies that because the bureaucracy is so strategic an institution, an attack on bureaucratic corruption deserves high policy priority, offering relatively cheap and easy gains.

Foreign aid missions seem to have been particularly prone to draw such conclusions, for understandable reasons. The bureaucracy's performance will determine the success or failure of many other projects. Moreover, in contrast with some of the other problems facing foreign development specialists, reform of the civil service may seem a relatively straightforward matter. furthermore, whereas in other development efforts foreign specialists may feel hampered by the lack of well tested doctrine and procedures, in restructuring the bureaucracy, they can rely on the expertise of public administration and management science. Therefore, it is not surprising that so much foreign development attention and activity have been directed toward the reform of the bureaucracies of underdeveloped countries.

In the underdeveloped countries themselves, much of the condemnation of graft has also come from interest in economic development, and from the apparent cogency of the development/bureaucracy/efficiency/probity logic. Here, moreover, the special ideological perspectives and interests of powerful and articulate groups have reinforced the criticism. Let us consider the specific perspectives that intellectuals, politicians, and businessmen in the underdeveloped countries possess.

The attitudes of intellectuals and of politicians toward corruption overlap to a certain degree. As members of the same rising elite, they condemn corruption because of the idealistic streak which often pervades radicals and reformers. Contemporary intellectuals in underdeveloped countries often emulate the Jacobins in their seeking after virtue. Moreover, as Shils has pointed out,[3] they frequently attribute sacral value to the governmental sphere: hence their hostility to the venality that would corrupt it. More generally, they may see graft as an integral part of the political culture and system of the *ancien régime* which they want to destroy.

Furthermore, they also have a direct interest in discrediting and eliminating corruption because of its functional effects. In most underdeveloped countries, interest groups are weak, and political parties rarely permit the participation of elements outside the contending cliques. Consequently, graft may be the only institution allowing other interests to achieve articulation and representation in the political process. Therefore, if the ruling elite is to maintain its exclusive control of the bureaucracy, it must cut off or control this channel of influence.[4] Such considerations apply especially when the politically disadvantaged group consists of an ethnic minority or of foreign entrepreneurs over whom the elite would like to maintain its dominance.

Entrepreneurs in underdeveloped countries have also condemned bureaucratic corruption. This is understandable, for they must pay the bribes. Moreover, because of certain economic characteristics of graft, the discontent that it arouses probably goes far beyond the cost of the bribe alone.

It is important to realize that most of the objects of corruption are available only in fixed and limited supply. For example, at any point in time, there is only a given amount of foreign exchange or a given number of investment licenses to be allocated. Consequently, when the number of favors is small relative to the number of aspirants, entrepreneurs must bid against each other in what amounts to a clandestine and imperfect auction. With competition forcing prices up, the favors will tend to be allocated to those who can pay the highest prices. In the long run, the favors will go to the most efficient producers, for they will be able to make the highest bids which are compatible with remaining in the industry.

Marginal firms, on the other hand, will face severe pressures. Either they accept sub-normal profits, or they must make the effort to increase efficiency, so as to muster the resources necessary to bid successfully. If they drop out of the contest, they are placed in a weakened position *vis-à-vis* the other firms, which are now even more intra-marginal because of the advantages given by the bureaucratic favor.

This sort of situation, where the efficient are able to outdo the inefficient, is not generally appreciated by businessmen. It is likely to be the less popular in underdeveloped countries where—in deference to the prevalence of inefficiency, and to local ideas of equity—the more usual practice is to tax efficient producers in order to subsidize the inefficient. Moreover, as we have seen, corruption may introduce an element of competition into what is otherwise a comfortably monopolistic industry.

Furthermore, in their bidding for bureaucratic favors, businessmen may have to give up a substantial part of the profits from the favor. The economic value of the favor is equal to the return expected from the favored position it makes possible. This value constitutes the upper limit to the bids made by entrepreneurs. The actual amount paid is indeterminate, and depends on the relative bargaining skills of the bureaucrats and the businessmen. The competitive bidding between businessmen, however, may force the price to approach the upper limit. In such a case, the bureaucrat captures the lion's share of the profits expected from the favor. Competitive selling by different bureaucrats may strengthen the bargaining position of the businessmen, but in general they are probably forced to pay out a relatively large portion of their expected gains. Hence, it is not surprising that they dislike an institution which deprives them of the fruits of their enterprise.[5]

The foregoing discussion suggests that many of the negative attitudes toward corruption are based upon special viewpoints and interests. We should also realize that the background material available on the subject is both scanty and one-sided. Those who engage in corruption maintain secrecy about their operations, so that the little data available comes from declared opponents of the institution. Moreover, those who profit from corruption may themselves have no idea of the socially beneficial effects of their activities.

The widespread condemnation of corruption has come to constitute a serious obstacle to any reexamination of the subject. Indeed, the criticism has become something of a ritual and symbol-laden preamble accompanying policy discussion and statements in the underdeveloped countries. As such, it is cherished for the modicum of consensus it provides to otherwise antagonistic groups.

Positive Effects of Corruption

The critique of bureaucratic corruption often seems to have in mind a picture in which the government and civil service of underdeveloped countries are working intelligently and actively to promote economic development, only to be thwarted by the efforts of grafters. Once the validity of this interpretation is disputed, the effects of corruption must also be reevaluated. This is the case if the government consists of a traditional elite which is indifferent if not hostile to development, or of a revolutionary group of intellectuals and politicians, who are primarily interested in other goals. At the same time, the propensity for investment and economic innovation may be higher outside the government than within it.

Indifference and Hostility of Government

In the first instance, the government and bureaucracy may simply be indifferent to the desires of entrepreneurs wanting to initiate or carry on economic activities. Such a situation is quite likely in the absence of effective popular pressure for economic development, or in the absence of effective participation of business interests in the policymaking process. This is especially the case when entrepreneurs are marginal groups or aliens. More generally, when the government does not attribute much value to economic pursuits or innovation, it may well be reluctant to move actively in the support of economic activity.

Even more important, the bureaucracy may be hostile to entrepreneurs, for it dislikes the emergence of a competing center of power. This is especially the case in colonial economies, where a large domestic middle class has not emerged to challenge traditional power-holders.

Governments Have Other Priorities

The foregoing relates to societies where although lip-service may be paid to the importance of economic development, the government and bureaucracy are oriented primarily to maintaining the *status quo*. It is also relevant in countries where a successful revolution against the *ancien régime* has occurred. There, the government may be proceeding dynamically, but not toward the promotion of economic development. Other goals, such as an increase in the military power available to the elite, or expansion of its control over society, may be justified in terms of economic development, however "ultimate." At the same time, the immediate effect of such policies is to impede growth.

Typically the bureaucracy plays an extensive interventionist role in the economy, and its consent or support is a *sine qua non* for the conduct of most economic enterprise. In such a situation, graft can have beneficial effects. First, it can induce the government to take a more favorable view of activities that would further economic growth. The policies or freedom sought by the entrepreneurs would help development, while those they subvert are keyed to other goals. Secondly, graft can provide the direct incentive necessary to mobilize the bureaucracy for more energetic action on behalf of the entrepreneurs. This is all the more important because of the necessity for bureaucratic help in so many areas—e.g., licenses, credit, and foreign exchange allocation—in order to get anything done.

Corruption Reduces Uncertainty and Increases Investment

Corruption can also help economic development by making possible a higher rate of investment than would otherwise be the case.

The investment decision always takes place in the midst of risk and uncertainty. As Aubrey has pointed out,[6] however, these difficulties are very much compounded in the economic and political environment of underdeveloped countries. The basic estimates of future demand and supply conditions are harder because of the lack of data and of the sharp shifts that can occur during a period of economic change. The dangers of misjudging the market are all the more serious because of the lower elasticities of substitution at low income levels.

Aside from the problems of making such economic estimates, the potential investor also faces a major political unknown—the behavior of the government. The possible dangers arising from the government's extensive role in the economy are increased because of the failure of representative government to put an effective check on arbitrary action. The personalist and irrational style of decisionmaking, and the frequent changes in government personnel and policies add to the risks. Consequently, if entrepreneurs are to make investments, they must have some assurance that the future will not bring harmful intervention in their affairs. We can see an illustration of these difficulties in the fact that in periods of political uncertainty and crisis, investment shrinks, and economic stagnation occurs. By enabling entrepreneurs to control and render predictable this important influence on their environment, corruption can increase the rate of investment.

Corruption and Innovation

The would-be innovator in an underdeveloped society must contend with serious opposition from existing economic interests. Unable to compete economically with the new processes or products, they will usually turn to the government for protection of their investments and future returns. If the bureaucracy supports innovation and refuses to intervene, the innovation can establish itself in the economy. In the more usual case, however, existing economic interests can depend on their long-standing associations with bureaucratic and political compadres for protection.

In this situation, graft may enable an economic innovator to introduce his innovations before he has had time to establish himself politically.[7] Economic innovators in underdeveloped countries have often supported oppositional political cliques or parties. Corruption is another, less radical way of adjusting to the same pressures of goals.

Corruption, Competition, and Efficiency

As we have seen in the previous section, bureaucratic corruption also brings an element of competition, with its attendant pressure for efficiency, to an underdeveloped economy. Since the licenses and favors available to the bureaucrats are in limited supply, they are allocated by competitive bidding among entrepreneurs. Because payment of the highest bribes is one of the principal criteria for allocation, the ability to muster revenue, either from reserves or from current operations, is put at a premium. In the long run, both of these sources are heavily dependent on efficiency in production. Hence, a tendency toward competition and efficiency is introduced into the system.

Such a pressure is all the more important in underdeveloped countries, where competition is usually absent from many sectors of the economy. In the product market, a high degree of monopoly often prevails. International competition is usually kept out by quotas, tariffs, and overvalued exchange rates. In the factor market, frictions and imperfections are common. Consequently, we can appreciate the value of introducing an element of competition, if only through the backdoor.

Corruption as a Hedge Against Bad Policy

Corruption also performs the valuable function of a "hedge" and a safeguard against the full losses of bad economic policy. Even when the government of an underdeveloped country is proceeding actively and intelligently to promote growth, there is no assurance that its policies are well conceived to attain its goals. In effect, it may be taking a vigorous step in the wrong direction. Corruption can reduce the losses from such mistakes, for while the government is implementing one policy, the entrepreneurs, with their sabotage, are implementing another. Like all insurance, this involves a cost—if the government's policy is correct. On the other hand, like all insurance, it is sometimes very welcome.

An underdeveloped country often stands in special need of such a safeguard. First, even when policy goals are clearly specified, competent counsel may well be divided as to the best means of achieving them. For example, the experts may differ among themselves on such basic issues as export promotion vs. import substitution, or other intersectoral priorities. Consequently, if the government has erred in its decision, the course made possible by corruption may well be the better one, supported by a dissenting segment of expert opinion. Moreover, the pervasive effects of government policy in an etatistic economy compound the effects of poor decisions, and increase the advantages of having some kind of safeguard against the potential consequences of a serious policy mistake. Corruption provides the insurance that if the government decides to steam full-speed in the wrong direction, all will not be lost.

Some illustrations may help clarify this point. For example, the agricultural producers whose graft sabotaged Peron's economic policies were later thanked for having maintained Argentina's capacity to import. Another example shows in more detail how this process can operate. An important element in the recent Latin American inflations has been the stagnation of food production, and the rise in food prices. In both Chile and Brazil, the governments reacted by freezing food prices, and ordering the bureaucracy to enforce these controls. In Chile, the bureaucracy acted loyally to maintain price controls, and food supplies were relatively stagnant. Inflation rose faster, supported in part by the failure of food production to increase. In Brazil, however, the bureaucracy's ineffectiveness sabotaged the enforcement of price controls, and prices received by producers were allowed to rise. Responding to this price rise, food production also increased somewhat, partially limiting the course of the inflation.[8]

In this case, we see the success of entrepreneurs and corrupted officials in producing a more effective policy than the government. Moreover, subsequent economic analysis justified this "decision," by emphasizing the price elasticity of agricultural supply, and the consequent need to allow the terms of trade to turn in favor of rural producers.

These points are perhaps strengthened when viewed with some historical perspective. As John Nef has remarked, the honesty and efficiency of the French bureaucracy were in great measure responsible for the stifling of economic innovation and progress during the eighteenth century.[9] By way of contrast, the laxity of the British administration permitted the subversion of Colbertism, and allowed new economic processes and activities to flourish.

Alleged Negative Effects of Corruption

Most of the arguments concerning the negative effects of corruption are based on the assumption that development can best proceed through the policies of an uncorrupted government and bureaucracy. As noted in the previous section, this assumes that the government really wants economic development, and that its policies would favor growth more than the activities of an unregulated private sector. Actually, the economic policies of the governments of many underdeveloped countries may be predicated on priorities other than global economic development. Even in countries where there has been a successful revolution against the colonial *ancien régime*, policy may aim primarily at advancing the economic interests of the ruling clique or of the political group on which it bases its dominance. Although the economic policies of some countries may be foolish or catastrophic from the viewpoint of development, they may be well conceived for implementing these other goals.[10]

Impeding Taxation

One version of this argument focuses on taxation. Specifically, it asserts that bureaucratic corruption may hamper development by preventing the government from obtaining the tax revenues necessary for developmental policies.

This argument probably attributes to the government an unrealistically high propensity to spend for development purposes. Economic development usually has a less compelling priority among the elites of these societies than among the westerners who observe them. Even if the dominant groups are aware and sensitive to the situation of the lower classes, they may be reluctant to bear the costs of development. Hence, the actual level of taxes collected, and their allocation in the budget may represent the decision of the ruling group as to how hard they want to press forward with economic development. In these circumstances, it is misleading to criticize the bureaucracy for the effects of its ineffective tax collection on economic growth. Of the revenues they might have collected, only a part would have gone for development rather than for the many forms of nondevelopmental expenditure. Moreover, when the entrepreneurs' propensity to invest is higher than the government's, the money saved from the tax collector may be a gain rather than a loss for development.

Usefulness of Government Spending

Furthermore, there is no reason to assume that the government has a high *marginal* propensity to spend for developmental purposes, based on a high income elasticity of demand for development. Without changes in the factors determining the average allocational propensities, increases in governmental revenue may well go for more lavish satisfaction of the same appetites. For example, as budgetary receipts rise, the military may be supplied with jet aircraft rather than with less expensive weapons.

Cynicism

Another argument has emphasized the social effects of corruption as an impediment to development. For example, it has been claimed that immorality and selfseeking of bureaucratic corruption may cause widespread cynicism and social disunity, and thus reduce the willingness to make sacrifices for the society's economic development.

This argument can be criticized on several points.

First, insofar as the disillusion is engendered among the *lower* social orders, the effects on development may not be an important as assumed. Because of economic and social conditions, these people are probably being squeezed as much as is possible, so that with all good will, they could not sacrifice any more.

Secondly, if the cynicism caused by bureaucratic corruption leads to increased selfseeking in the rest of the society, this may not be a completely bad thing for economic development. Many of the wealth-creating activities which make up economic growth depend on such atomistic egoism for their stimulus. Consequently, if cynicism acts as a solvent on traditional inhibitions, and increased selfseeking leads to new ambitions, economic development may be furthered.

Moreover, this argument also exaggerates the extent to which economic growth depends on a popular rallying-around rather than on many individual selfish activities. The implicit picture seems to be that of an "all-together" social effort, perhaps under etatistic direction. Once stated explicitly, such a model appears more like a fantasy of intellectuals rather than an accurate guide to how economic development takes place.

More generally, we should recognize that there are very good reasons for the incivism and unwillingness to make sacrifices that are often characteristic of underdeveloped societies. Mutual distrust and hostility usually have much deeper roots in cultural gaps, inequitable income distribution, and long experience of mistreatment. Rapid change, dislocating existing institutions and values, also disrupts social solidarity. In such circumstances, reduced bureaucratic corruption would make only a marginal contribution to improved public morale.

Corruption as a Policy System

The foregoing analysis and perspective may also be helpful in dealing with bureaucratic corruption as a policy problem.

First, we should be clear as to the nature of "the problem" that policy is attempting to solve. As we have seen, much of the criticism of corruption derives from the political, economic, and ideological interests of particular groups. Presumably the elimination of corruption is a problem only insofar as we share their specific conerns.

Aside from these special interests, however, let us consider corruption from the point of view of its effects on economic development. As we have seen, under certain conditions, the consequences of corruption for development are not as serious as is usually assumed. At the same time, it may have important positive effects that are often overlooked. Consequently, to the extent that reality approaches the conditions of our model, corruption of the type discussed in this paper may not be a problem at all. This will depend on specific conditions, and will vary between countries and between sectors.

When the conditions of our model do not obtain, however, corruption will be an important barrier to development. To the extent that corruption exists as a policy problem, it is probably wise to accept it as a particularly intractable part of an underdeveloped country. On a superficial level, we should recognize that corruption creates its own political and economic interests that will resist efforts at its eradication. More important, corruption is deeply rooted in the psychological and social structure of the countries where it exists. On the psychocultural plane, corruption will persist until universalistic norms predominate over particularistic attitudes. Socially, the elimination of corruption probably requires the emergence of new centers of power outside the bureaucracy, and the development of competitive politics. Such changes will come, if at all, only as the result of a long period of economic and social development.

Bureaucracy the Lagging Sector

Two conclusions emerge from this discussion. first, we should realize how illusory is the expectation that bureaucratic policy can intervene as a *deus ex machina* to overcome the other barriers to economic growth. In many underdeveloped countries, the bureaucracy may be a lagging rather than a leading sector. Secondly, it should be clear that direct policy efforts against such deeply rooted psychological and social conditions cannot hope for much short-term success. As Braibanti concludes,[11] powerful investigatory commissions may have a limited success, but one should expect the problem to be improved "more by time than by effort."

Despite the pessimistic prospects for the usual direct-action policies against corruption, certain possibilities do exist for dealing with it indirectly. The problem is perhaps best conceptualized in terms of the need to economize in the use of a particularly scarce and important resource—honest and capable administrators. Indeed, for several reasons, this shortage may be more serious than others more often cited, e.g., the lack of capital. Because of political reasons, this input into the development process cannot be imported on a large scale. Furthermore as we have noted, available domestic supplies cannot be expected to increase for a long time in most underdeveloped countries. Finally, this input is all the more crucial because of its importance for the successful deployment of other resources. If we view corruption as a problem in the allocation of scarce administrative resources, two solutions are immediately suggested.

Two Techniques

First, the available resources should be concentrated in areas where their productivity in promoting development would be greatest. Such budgeting of administrators would avoid dispersion of honest and able personnel, and make them available only for tasks of the highest priority.

A second way of economizing in the use of this scarce resource would be the use of alternative production techniques to achieve the same development results. In our context, this would mean employing measures to achieve the goals of policy without reliance on direct administration and bureaucratic regulation of the economy.

In many cases, the desired effects could be achieved either by market forces, or by indirect measures creating the necessary incentives or disincentives—i.e., with much less direct government intervention, and the consequent need to rely on the bureaucracy. For example, a government which wants to keep down the domestic price level can either institute a cumbersome system of price regulation, or it can permit a measure of competition from imports. Similarly, a straightforward currency devaluation can have many of the beneficial effects achieved by an administration-intensive regime of differential exchange rates. Admittedly, such policies may have some undesired consequences and side-effects that ideally would be avoided by more sophisticated government management of the economy. The point is, however, that when policy alternatives are evaluated, it would be better to take explicit account of how bureaucratic corruption will affect the direct management policies contemplated. This would lead to a more realistic choice between the means which can accomplish similar goals. Perhaps the best procedure would be to select a mixture of direct and of indirect management policies, taking account of the bureaucratic resources available.

By way of contrast, the more usual practice is to choose the policies that would be best *if* the whole bureaucracy were dependable, and then to deplore its corruption, and condemn it for the failure of the policies chosen. Following the procedure suggested here, however, governments would accept corruption as an aspect of their societies, and try to optimize policy-making within this framework.

Finally, we should note that preoccupation with corruption can itself become an impediment to development. This occurs if the focus on corruption diverts attention from other political and economic deficiencies in the society, and from the measures that can be taken despite corruption. To avoid the losses from such misdirection, re-thinking of the sort suggested here may be helpful.

Notes

1. I am grateful to Richard Eckaus, John Plank, Lucien Pye, and Myron Weiner for their comments on an earlier draft of this paper. They bear no responsibility for the remaining deficiencies.
2. But see V.O. Key, *The Techniques of Political Graft in the United States,* privately printed, 1936. Robert K. Merton, *Social Theory and Social Structure,* New York, 1959, pp. 19–85. Harold Lasswell, "Bribery," in *The Encyclopedia of the Social Sciences,* vol. 2, New York, 1930. Cf. especially, F.W. Riggs, "Bureaucrats and Political Development: A Paradoxical View," paper prepared for the Social Science Research Council Committee on Comparative Politics, Conference. January 29–February 2, 1962.
3. Edward Shils, "Political Development in the New States," *Comparative Studies in Society and History,* 1960, p. 279.
4. Cf. Riggs, pp. 28–30.
5. These processes are nicely brought out in Alexandre Kafka, "The Brazilian Exchange Auction." *The Review of Economics and Statistics,* October 1956.
6. H.C. Aubrey, "Investment Decisions in Underdeveloped Countries" in *Capital Formation and Economic Growth,* National Bureau of Economic Research. Princeton, 1955, pp. 404–15. Also cf. the finding of Y. Sayigh (*Entrepreneurs of Lebanon,* Cambridge, Mass. 1962, p. 117) that political conditions constituted the greatest unknown facing the entrepreneurs surveyed.
7. Cf. Lasswell, p. 671.
8. I am indebted to an eminent expert in Latin American economic development for this observation.
9. *Industry and Government in France and England: 1540–1640.* Cf. also, J.J. Spengler, "The State and Economic Growth—Summary and Interpretations," p. 368, in H. Aitken, ed., *The State and Economic Growth,* N.Y. 1959.
10. Cf. Frank Golay, "Commercial Policy and Economic Nationalism," *Quarterly Journal of Economics,* 1958, and B. Glassburner, "Economic Policy-Making in Indonesia, 1950–1957," *Economic Development and Cultural Change,* January 1962.
11. Ralph Braibanti, "Reflections on Bureaucratic Corruption," *Public Administration,* Winter 1962, p. 370, and p. 372.

25

Corruption as a Hindrance to Modernization in South Asia

Gunnar Myrdal

The term "corruption" will be used in this chapter in its widest sense, to include not only all forms of "improper or selfish exercise of power and influence attached to a public office or to the special position one occupies in public life" but also the activity of the bribers.[1]

The significance of corruption in Asia is highlighted by the fact that wherever a political regime has crumbled—in Pakistan and Burma, for instance, and, outside South Asia, in China—a major and often decisive cause has been the prevalence of official misconduct among politicians and administrators, and the concomitant spread of unlawful practices among businessmen and the general public.[2] The problem is therefore of vital concern to the governments in the region. Generally speaking, the habitual practice of bribery and dishonesty tends to pave the way for an authoritarian regime, whose disclosures of corrupt practices in the preceding government and whose punitive action against offenders provide a basis for its initial acceptance by the articulate strata of the population. The Communists maintain that corruption is bred by capitalism, and with considerable justification they pride themselves on its eradication under a Communist regime.[3] The elimination of corrupt practices has also been advanced as the main justification for military takeovers. Should the new regime be unsuccessful in its attempts to eradicate corruption, its failure will prepare the ground for a new putsch of some sort. Thus it is obvious that *the extent of corruption has a direct bearing on the stability of South Asian governments.*

Source: Gunnar Myrdal, "Corruption—Its Causes and Effects," *Asian Drama: An Enquiry into the Poverty of Nations,* Vol. II. New York: Twentieth Century, 1968, pp. 937–51. By permission of the publisher.

A Taboo in Research on South Asia

Although corruption is very much an issue in the public debate in all South Asian countries, as we shall demonstrate . . . [later], it is almost taboo as a research topic and is rarely mentioned in scholarly discussions of the problems of government and planning. With regard to research conducted by Americans, the explanation might seem, at first glance, to lie in the fact that public life in the United States, particularly at the state and city levels, is still not as free of corruption as in Great Britain, Holland, or Scandinavia. But this explanation does not take us far, as social scientists in the United States, particularly in an earlier generation, never shied away from exposing corruption in public administration, politics, and business, nor were their inquiries censored. Moreover, scholars from the Western European countries mentioned have shown no greater interest than Americans in studying corruption in South Asia. Neither does the fact that Western enterprises are in league with corrupt elements in South Asia on a large scale explain the disinterest of Western scholars in the problem of South Asian corruption, for business has not been that influential in guiding research; many studies with conclusions unfavorable to Western business interests have in fact been made. For reasons we shall set forth later, the lack of investigation cannot be attributed, either, to the difficulty of finding an empirical basis for research on corruption.

Instead, the explanation lies in the general bias that we have characterized as diplomacy in research. Embarrassing questions are avoided by ignoring the problems of attitudes and institutions, except for occasional qualifications and reservations—which are not based on even the most rudimentary research and do not, of course, alter the basic approach. South Asian social scientists are particularly inclined to take this easy road, whether they are conservatives or radicals. The taboo on research on corruption is, indeed, one of the most flagrant examples of this general bias. It is rationalized, when challenged, by certain sweeping assertions: that there is corruption in all countries (this notion, eagerly advanced by students indigenous to the region, neglects the relative prevalence of corruption in South Asia and its specific effects in that social setting); that corruption is natural in South Asian countries because of deeply ingrained institutions and attitudes carried over from colonial and pre-colonial times (this primarily Western contention should, of course, provide an approach to research and a set of hypotheses, not an excuse for ignoring the problem); that corruption is needed to oil the intricate machinery of business and politics in South Asian countries and is, perhaps, not a liability given the conditions prevailing there (again, this mainly Western hypothesis about the functioning of the economic and social system should under-line rather than obviate the need for research); that there is not as much corruption as is implied by the public outcry in the South Asian countries (this claim needs to be substantiated, and if it is true, the causes and effects of that outcry should be investigated). These ex-cuses, irrelevant and transparently thin as they are, are more often expressed in conversation than in print. That the taboo on any discus-sion of corruption in South Asia is basically to be explained in terms of a certain condescension on the part of Westerners was pointed out in the Prologue [not reprinted here].

In our study we have not attempted to carry out the necessary research on corruption in South Asia, or even a small part of it; we had neither the time nor the facilities for an empirical investigation on this scale. The main purpose of this chapter is thus to explain why the taboo should be broken. In the course of the discussion we venture to sketch a theory of corruption in South Asia by offering some reason-able, though quite tentative, questions to be explored and hypotheses to be tested.

The "Folklore" of Corruption and the Anti-Corruption Campaigns

The problem of corruption, though not a subject of research, is, as we have said, very much on the minds of articulate South Asians. The newspapers devote much of their space and the political assemblies much of their time to the matter; conversation, when it is free and relaxed, frequently turns to political scandals. Periodically, anti-cor-ruption campaigns are waged: laws are passed; vigilance agencies set up; special police establishments assigned to investigate reports of misconduct; sometimes officials, mostly in the lower brackets, are prosecuted and punished and occasionally a minister is forced to resign.[4] Occasionally committees are appointed to deal more generally with the problem of counteracting corruption,[5] following the practice established in colonial times, particularly by the British. In India and Ceylon especially, but also in other South Asian countries, the authori-ties have, from the start of the independence era, tried to prevent corruption, and these efforts have, on the whole, been increasing. Yet the articulate in all these countries believe that corruption is rampant and that it is growing, particularly among higher officials and politi-cians, including legislators and ministers. The ostentatious efforts to prevent corruption and the assertions that the corrupt are being dealt with as they deserve only seem to spread cynicism, especially as to how far all this touches the "higher-ups."

Two things, then, are in evidence: (1) what may be called the "folklore of corruption," i.e., people's beliefs about corruption and the emotions attached to those beliefs, as disclosed in the public debate and in gossip; and (2) public policy measures that may be loosely labelled "anti-corruption campaigns," i.e., legislative, administrative, and judicial institutions set up to enforce the integrity of public officials at all levels. Both are reactions to the fact of corruption, and they are related to each other in circular causation. A study of these phenomena cannot, of course, provide an exhaustive and entirely accurate picture of the extent of corruption existing in a country—the number involved, the positions they hold, and what they are doing. But it is nevertheless true that *the folklore of corruption embodies important social facts worth intensive research in their own right.*[6] The beliefs about corruption and the related emotions are easily observed and analyzed, and this folklore has a crucial bearing on how people conduct their private lives and how they view their government's efforts to consolidate the nation and to direct and spur development. The anti-corruption campaigns are also important social facts, having their effects, and they are just as easy, or even easier, to record and analyze.

A related question worth study is the extent to which the folklore of corruption reflects, at bottom, a weak sense of loyalty to organized society. Is there, in other words, a general asociality that leads people to think that anybody in a position of power is likely to exploit it in the interest of himself, his family, or other social groups to which he has a feeling of loyalty? If so, people's beliefs about the corruptibility of politicians and administrators would be in part a reflection of what they would like to do, given the means.

If corruption is taken for granted, resentment amounts essentially to envy of those who have opportunities for private gain by dishonest dealings. Viewed from another angle, these beliefs about corruptibility, especially the belief that known offenders can continue their corrupt practices with little risk of punishment, are apt to reinforce the conviction that this type of cynical asocial behavior is widely practiced. The folklore of corruption then becomes in itself damaging, for it can give an exaggerated impression of the prevalence of corruption, especially among officials at high levels. It is certain that fear of bolstering that impression influenced Henru consistently to resist demands for bolder and more systematic efforts to cleanse his government and administration of corruption. "Merely shouting from the house-tops that everybody is corrupt creates an atmosphere of corruption," he said. "People feel they live in a climate of corruption and they get corrupted themselves. The man in the street says to himself: *'well, if everybody seems corrupt, why shouldn't I be corrupt?'* That is the climate sought to be created which must be discouraged."[7]

The first task of research on corruption is thus to establish the ingredients of the folklore of corruption and the anticorruption campaigns. These phenomena are on the surface of social reality in South Asia and therefore lend themselves to systematic observation. The data, and the process of collecting them, should give clues for the further investigation of the facts of actual corruption. Analysis of the interplay of folklore, action, and fact and of the relationship of all three to the wider problems of national consolidation, stability of government, and effectiveness of development efforts must necessarily take one into murkier depths of social reality.

The Facts of Corruption

With public debate quite open and gossip flourishing, the facts in individual cases of wrongdoing should not be too difficult to ascertain. The true research task is, however, to establish the general nature and extent of corruption in a country, its incursion upon various levels and branches of political and economic life, and any trends that are discernible. In this section we shall make a start on this task, but our contribution should not be considered as more than a very preliminary sorting out of problems for research. What is said is based on extensive reading of parliamentary records, committee reports, newspapers, and other publications dealing with the subject, and even more, on conversations with knowledgeable persons in the region, including Western businessmen, as well as on personal observation. The fact that in the United States corruption has for generations been intensively and fruitfully researched should counter the notion that nothing can be learned about this phenomenon.

Concerning first the general level of corruption, it is unquestionably much higher than in the Western developed countries (even including the United States) or in the Communist countries. It serves no practical purpose, and certainly no scientific interest, to pretend that this is not so. This judgment will gain support when in the next section we turn to the causes of corruption; they are clearly much stronger in South Asia than in the other groups of countries mentioned. The relative extent of corruption in the South Asian countries is difficult to assess. There is more open discussion of corruption in the Philippines, where, in the

American tradition, the press is particularly free and outspoken than in, say, Pakistan, Burma, and Thailand under their present regimes. In India, where a moralistic attitude is especially apparent, greater concern is expressed than in Ceylon, for instance. Whether the amount of public discussion reflects the real prevalence of corruption is doubtful. On the basis of scanty evidence, India may, on balance, be judged to have somewhat less corruption than any other country in South Asia. Nevertheless, a commonly expressed opinion in India is that "administrative corruption, in its various forms, is all around us all the time and that it is rising."[8] The findings of the Santhanam Committee as to the prevalence of corruption in different branches and levels of responsibility will be reported below, in the text and in footnotes.

If a comparison is made with conditions in the colonial era, the usual view of both South Asian and Western observers is that corruption is more prevalent now than before independence and that, in particular, it has recently gained ground in the higher echelons of officials and politicians. This view, too, will gain support from our subsequent discussion of the causes of corruption. We know on the authority of J. S. Furnivall, moreover, that the Netherlands Indies was practically free of corruption in colonial times, unlike Burma where corruption was rampant except at very highest level;[9] but in present-day Indonesia corruption seems to be at least as much a fact of life as in any other South Asian country.[10] In the Philippines corrupt practices at all levels of business and administration were common in colonial times, but it is generally assumed that they have increased substantially since then.[11]

There is said to have been much petty corruption in British India on the lower level where indigenous or Anglo-Indian officials were almost exclusively employed, though in most instances Europeans were served promptly and without having to pay a bribe. On the other hand, it is commonly asserted—not only by British observers—that the Indian Civil Service was largely incorrupt. Not all Indian intellectuals agree; some maintain that in later years, and especially during the Second World War, corruption tended to spread even to this select group, including British officials.[12] In the princely states corruption was often unchecked and infested the courts of the maharajahs and the higher echelons of administration. What has been said about British India holds broadly true even for Ceylon. The French administration in Indo-China was probably never as clean as its British counterpart in India and Ceylon, but it is generally acknowledged that corruption has increased very rapidly in the successor states.[13] Thailand was always corrupt in its peculiar fashion and is thought to have become more so of late.

There seems to be rather general agreement that in recent years corruption in South Asia has been increasing. The Santhanam Committee Report speaks of "the growth of corruption" and of the need to arrest "the deterioration in the standards of public life," the assumption that the recent trend of corruption in India is upwards is implicit in the whole report. In Pakistan and Burma the military takeovers in the late 1950's undoubtedly brought major purges in their wake, but many observers—both Westerners and nationals in these countries—are found who believe there has been a resurgence of corruption, particularly in Pakistan, though the bribes have to be bigger because of greater risks.

Statements such as these should be tested by research that could either confirm or refute them; even if broadly confirmed they need to be made much more specific. As for the different branches of administration in the South Asian governments, it is generally assumed that the public works departments and government purchasing agencies in all of the countries are particularly corrupt,[14] as are also the agencies running the railways, the offices issuing import and other licenses, and those responsible for the assessment and collection of taxes and customs duties.[15] More generally it is asserted that whenever discretionary power is given to officials, there will tend to be corruption.[16] Corruption has spread to the courts of justice, and even to the universities.[17]

The spread of corruption among minor officials is understood to be consequent on a deterioration of the morals of some of the politicians and higher officials.[18] Both as cause and effect, corruption has its counterpart in undesirable practices among the general public. The business world has been particularly active in promoting corrupt practices among politicians and administrators, even if it be granted that it is difficult or impossible to carry on business without resort to such practices when corruption is widespread. As the Santhanam Committee Report points out:

> Corruption can exist only if there is someone willing to corrupt and capable of corrupting. We regret to say that both willingness and capacity to corrupt is found in a large measure in the industrial and commercial classes. The ranks of these classes have been swelled by the speculators and adventurers of the war period. To these, corruption is not only an easy method ot secure large unearned profits but also the necessary means to enable them to be in a position to pursue their vocations or retain their position among their own competitors. . . . Possession of large amounts of unaccounted money by various persons including those belonging to the industrial and commercial classes is a major impediment in the purification of public life. If anti-corruption

> activities are to be successful, it must be recognized that it is as important to fight these unscrupulous agencies of corruption as to eliminate corruption in the public services. In fact they go together.[19]

Our comments concerning the importance of corruption in various branches of the economy are necessarily cast in vague, qualitative terms, as are the judgments expressed in the Santhanam Committee Report, from which we have quoted so extensively. One important question on which the report of that Indian committee is silent is the role played by Western business interests competing for markets in South Asian countries or embarking on direct investments in industrial enterprises there, either independently or in joint ventures with indigenous firms or with governments.[20] Western business representatives never touch on this matter publicly, but, as the writer can testify, in private conversation they are frank to admit that it is necessary to bribe high officials and politicians in order to get a business deal through and to bribe officials both high and low in order to run their businesses without too many obstacles. They are quite explicit about their own experiences and those of other firms. These bribes, they say, constitute a not inconsiderable part of their total costs of doing business in South Asian countries. Although hardly any foreign company can make it an absolute rule to abstain from giving bribes, it is apparent that there is a vast difference in regard to the willingness to bribe, not only between companies but also between nationalities. Among the Western nations, French, American, and, especially, West German companies are usually said to have the least inhibitions about bribing their way through. Japanese firms are said to be even more willing to pay up. On the other hand, the writer has never heard it alleged that bribes are offered or paid by the commercial agencies of Communist countries. These widely held opinions are part of the social setting in South Asia, as are all the elements that make up the folklore of corruption; to what extent they mirror actual business practices should be established by the research we recommend.

There is one specific difficulty facing researchers in their attempts to establish the facts about the taking and seeking of bribes, particularly on the part of higher officials and politicians. Bribes are seldom given directly; usually they go to a middleman, whether an indigenous businessman or an official at a lower level. In particular, a Western firm, operating in a South Asian country, often finds it convenient—and less objectionable—to give a negotiated lump sum to a more or less professional briber, an "agent," who then undertakes to pay off all those whose cooperation is necessary for the smooth conduct of production and business. More generally, when a business transaction is to be settled, an official somewhere down the line of authority will often inform the Western businessman that a minister or a higher official expects a certain sum of money. Even an indigenous business-man is occasionally placed in such an indirect relationship to the bribe-seeker. As the whole affair is secret, there is often no way of knowing whether the middleman is keeping the money for himself. Indeed, he may be using the weight of an innocent person's name to sweeten the deal and increase his take. This is, of course, one of the ways in which the folklore of corruption may exaggerate the extent of corruption at the higher levels.

In research designed to establish the facts of corruption, the role of Western business interests in the spread of corruption could be investi-gated best by Western researchers since they would in most cases have easier access to the confidence of the bribers, while the nationals in the several countries would probably meet fewer inhibitions and obstacles in carrying out the more general study of the spread of corruption in South Asia. But more important than such a division of labor is the researchers' seriousness of intent and their willingness to cooperate with one another.

The Causes

The folklore of corruption, the political administrative, and judicial reverberations of these beliefs and emotions in the anti-corruption campaigns, the actual prevalence of corruption in theseveral countries at different times, and the present trends—all these social facts must be explained in causal terms by relating them to other conditions in South Asia.

When we observe that corruption is more prevalent in South Asia than in the developed Western countries, we are implying a difference in mores as to where, how, and when to make a personal gain. While it is, on the one hand, exceedingly difficult in South Asia to introduce profit motives and market behavior into the sector of social life where they operate in the West—that is, the economic sphere—it is, on the other hand, difficult to eliminate motivations of private gain from the sector where they have been suppressed in the West—the sphere of public responsibility and power. In South Asia those vested with official authority and power very often exploit their position in order to make a gain for themselves, their family, or social group. This is so whether that position is the high one of a minister, a member of the legislature, or a superior official, whose consent or cooperation is needed to obtain a license or settle a business deal, or the humble position of a petty clerk who can delay or prevent the presentation of an application, the use of a railroad car, or the prompt opening of the gates over the tracks. Certain behavioral reactions generally held to be outside profit considerations in the West are commonly for sale in South Asia; they have a "market," though certainly not a perfect one in the Western sense of the term.

The two differences are complementary and, to an extent, explain each other. Indeed, they are both remnants of the pre-capitalist, traditional society. Where, as often in South Asia, there is no market for services and goods or only an imperfect and fragmented one, and where economic behavior is not governed by rational calculations of costs and returns—and this is true not only in subsistence farming and crafts but to a degree also in the organized sector—"connections" must fill the gap. These "connections" range all the way from the absolute dependence of attached labor in agriculture and the peasants' relations with moneylenders and landlords, which are determined by custom and power, to the special considerations that lead to nepotism even in big business. In such a setting a bribe to a person holding a public position is not clearly differentiated from the "gifts," tributes, and other burdens sanctioned in traditional, pre-capitalist society or the special obligations attached to a favor given at any social level.

In pre-colonial times officials had to collect their remuneration themselves, usually without much regulation or control from above. As Furnivall points out in speaking about Burma:

> The officials drew no fixed salary. Some were paid by allotment of the revenue of a particular district, but for the most part their emoluments were derived from a commission on revenue collected, or from fees paid by the parties to a case. One great source of revenue was from local tolls on the transport or sale of goods.[21]

A situation then became established that one Westerner viewed as follows:

> In nearly all Asian countries there has always been a tradition of corruption. Public office meant perquisites. Officials were not well paid and had to make ends meet. The well-timed bribe—which was often almost a conventional fee—was the emollient which made the wheels of administration turn more efficiently.[22]

Even where the colonial powers in later years were able to establish a higher civil service, which was honest, well paid, and manned by both colonial and indigenous personnel—as the British, in particular, succeeded in doing—they still found it difficult to enforce rigid standards at the lower levels of administration.[23]

Traditionally, the South Asian countries were "plural societies," in the meaning given to the term by Furnivall, and under colonial rule became increasingly so. In the present context this implies above all a fragmentation of loyalties and, in particular, little loyalty to the community as a whole, whether on the local or the national level. Such wider loyalty, backed by firm rules and punitive measures, is the necessary foundation for the modern Western and Communist mores by which certain behavior reactions are kept apart from considerations of personal benefit. In South Asia the stronger loyalty to less inclusive groups—family, caste, ethnic, religious, or linguistic "community" (in the South Asian sense), and class-invites the special type of corruption we call nepotism and tends in general to encourage moral laxity. The prevalence of corruption is, moreover, one aspect of the "soft state," to which we have often referred, it generally implies a low level of social discipline.[24]

When explaining the presence of corruption in South Asia, this legacy from traditional society must be taken into account, mainly as part of social statics. But to explain the increase in corruption that is commonly assumed to have taken place in recent times, we must view the social system in dynamic terms. Many of the changes that have occurred have afforded greater incentives as well as greater opportunities for corruption. The winning of independence and the transition from colonial status to self-government were preceded and accompanied by profound disturbances. In all South Asian countries the goal of development was accepted, while the attainment of that goal was made more difficult by the accelerated growth of population, the deterioration of the trading position, and other trends. Independence greatly increased the role of the politicians. At the same time the repatriation, following independence, of a large number of officials from the metropolitan countries left South Asia few competent administrators with the stricter Western mores.[25] This scarcity was much greater and more damaging in Indonesia, Burma, and even Pakistan than in the Philippines, India, and Ceylon.

. . . [T]he extensive—and generally increasing—resort to discretionary controls is apt to breed corruption;[26] the spread of corruption, in turn, gives corrupt politicians and dishonest officials a strong vested interest in retaining and increasing controls of this type. Another contributing factor has undoubtedly been the low real wages of officials, especially those at the lower and middle levels.[27] There is also, quite generally, a circular causation with cumulative effects working within the system of corruption itself. As we have indicated, it acts with special force as people become aware of the spread of corruption and feel that effective measures are not taken to punish the culprits, particularly those who are highly placed.[28] Among the sophisticated the situation may become rationalized in the idea that corruption, like inflation, is an unavoidable appendage of development.[29] The effect of this is to spread cynicism and to lower resistance to the giving or taking of bribes.

Notes

1. See India, Government of Ministry of Home Affairs, *Report of the Committee on Prevention of Corruption*, New Delhi, 1964, p. 5; see pp. 11 ff. This committee is usually referred to as the Santhanam committee, after its chairman; we shall cite its report as the Santhanam committee report hereafter.

2. A few years before the military *putsch* of 1958 in Pakistan, Tibor Mende reported that: "Probably no other symptom of Pakistani public life has contributed more to the demoralization of the 'common man' than corruption." Illicit practices had reached such proportions that "their effect is likely to wipe out whatever benefits new economic projects might have secured for him." Some measures were taken by the government in response to "widespread demand for action" and "a few minor officials" were dismissed, but "they were the small culprits." (Tibor Mende, *South-East Asia between Two Worlds*, Turnstile Press, London, 1955, p. 227.)

3. "In the disorders in China since 1911 the scale of corruption had increased in a monstrous way, and reform was very much needed. The surprising achievement of the communists was to be able to induce among their party members, who were after all thoroughly Chinese, a militant and puritanical hatred of the old system. Here was one of the outstanding instances of ideas and institutions being able to change people's character. The communist party set out to hunt the corrupt; it disciplined its own members savagely if it caught them; it developed a steady pressure against corruption in all the administration—incidentally attaching charges of corruption to all of whom it disapproved upon other grounds." (Guy Wint, *Spotlight on Asia*, Penguin Books, Middlesex, 1955, p. 91.)

   The present writer's observations confirm the view that what has impressed the South Asian intellectuals most about China's communist revolution has been the establishment of a strong, disciplined state, one that is scrupulously honest by South Asian standards.

4. In India the number of vigilance cases reviewed is steadily increasing. See Santhanam committee report, Section 3, pp. 14 ff. Although the report places the statistics under the heading "extent of corruption," it makes clear (p. 14 *et passim*) that the statistics themselves do not indicate the actual amount of corruption in various branches of administration, or its recent trend.

5. The Santhanam committee report is the latest and the most ambitious South Asian study of corruption. The committee gives certain general

judgments about the prevalence of corruption in India to which we shall refer below, but directs its main attention to establishing in considerable detail the various possibilities for corruption afforded by established administrative procedures in India, particularly in the central government, and to working out a system of reforms that would decrease corruption.

6. In the study of race relations it is the beliefs about race and the institutional and attitudinal systems of segregation and discrimination related to those beliefs that are important, not racial differences as such (see Gunnar Myrdal, *An American Dilemma,* Harper & Row, New York, 1944, p. 110 and throughout). Something similar is true about corruption, though not to the same extent, as undoubtedly the corruption practices are important, independent of what is believed about them or done to combat them. . . .

7. R.K. Karanjia, *The Mind of Mr. Nehru,* George Allen & Unwin Ltd., London, 1960, p. 61.

The Santhanam committee report states: "It was represented to us that corruption has increased to such an extent that people have started losing faith in the integrity of public administration. We heard from all sides that corruption has, in recent years, spread even to those levels of administration from which it was conspicuously absent in the past. We wish we could confidently and without reservation assert that at the political level, ministers, legislators, party officials were free from this malady. The general impressions are unfair and exaggerated. But the very fact that such impressions are there causes damage to the social fabric" (pp. 12, 13). "The general belief about failure of integrity amongst ministers is as damaging as actual failure" (p. 101).

8. *The Economic Weekly,* December 21, 1963, Vol. XV, No. 51, p. 2061.

9. J.S. Furnivall, *Colonial Policy and Practice: A Comparative Study of Burma and Netherlands India,* Cambridge University Press, London, 1957, p. 269 and throughout.

10. In fact, a decade ago an Indonesian statesman, Mohammad Hatta, wrote: "Corruption runs riot through our society; corruption has also infected a great many of our government departments. . . . Workers and government employees, whose wages and salaries are no longer adequate for their daily needs, are being exploited by enterprising adventurers who want to get rich quickly. . . . This is why all businessmen who remain faithful to economic morality are constantly being pushed backward. Bribery and graft have become increasingly common, to the detriment of our community and our country. Each year the government loses hundreds of millions of rupiahs in duties and taxes which remain unpaid as a result of fraud and smuggling, both illegal and 'legal.' " (Mohammad Hatta, *The Co-operative Movement in Indonesia,* Cornell University Press, Ithaca, 1957, pp. 84–85.)

The situation has certainly not improved since this was written. . . .

11. An American congressional study group reported: "Those members of the study mission who had visited the Philippines previously on one or more occasions were startled and shocked to find an increase in lawlessness and of government corruption that was more than hinted at." *(Report of the Special Study Mission to Asia, Western Pacific, Middle East, Southern Europe and North Africa,* GPO, Washington, 1960, p. 22.)

12. This view is also expressed, obliquely, by the Santhanam committee:

Till about the beginning of the Second World War corruption was prevalent in considerable measure amongst revenue, police excise and public works department officials particularly of the lower grades and the higher ranks were comparatively free from this evil. The smaller compass of state activities, the 'great depression' and lack of fluid resources set limits to the opportunities and capacity to corrupt or be corrupted. The immense war efforts during 1939 to 1945 which involved an annual expenditure of hundreds of crores of rupees over all kinds of war supplies and contracts created unprecedented opportunities for acquisition of wealth by doubtful means. The war time controls and scarcities provided ample opportunities for bribery, corruption, favoritism, etc. The then government subordinated all other considerations to that of making the war effort a success. Propriety of means was no consideration if it impeded the war effort. It would not be far wrong to say that the high watermark of corruption was reached in India as perhaps in other countries also, during the period of the Second World War (pp. 6–7).

Any implication that corruption was more widespread among higher officials during the Second World War than now is probably groundless, however, and is gainsaid by the committee in other passages; see below.

13. About developments in North Vietnam we have no specific information; that communist regimes ordinarily stamp out corruption was pointed out before.

14. For India the Santhanam committee report states: "We were told by a large number of witnesses, that in all contracts of construction, purchases, sales, and other regular business on behalf of the government, a regular percentage is paid by the parties to the transaction, and this is shared in agreed proportions among the various officials concerned. We were told that in the constructions of the public works department, seven to eleven percent was usually paid in this manner and this was shared by persons of the rank of executive engineer and below down to the ministry, and occasionally even the superintending engineer might have a share" (p. 10).

   "During the Second Plan period the total expenditure on construction and purchases was of the order of Rs. 2800 crores. . . . If it is assumed that even 5 percent . . . is accounted for by such corrupt practices, the total loss to the excheqer is about Rs. 140 crores" (p. 18).

15. On these the Santhanam committee report observes: "In the railways, besides the above [constructions and purchases], similar practice in connection with allotment of wagons and booking of parcels particularly perishables, is said to be in vogue" (p. 10).

   "We were told that corruption and lack of integrity are rampant in transactions relating to obtaining of quota certificates, essentiality certificates, licenses and their utilization" (p. 254).

   "It is common knowledge that some portion of the tax avoided or evaded is shared by many including the assessing officers." (p. 19) This practice has wider effects: "Tax so evaded and avoided is kept as unaccounted money and one of the many uses to which it is put is for corrupting public servants" (p. 271).

16. Says the Santhanam committee report: "Where there is power and discretion, there is always the possibility of abuse, more so when the power and discretion have to be exercised in the context of scarcity and controls and pressure to spend public money" (p. 9).

17. The same report notes:
    "Though we did not make any direct inquiries, we were informed by responsible persons including vigilance and special police establishment officers that corruption exists in the lower ranks of the judiciary all over India and in some places it has spread to the higher ranks also. We were deeply distressed at this information" (p. 108).
    "It is a matter of great regret that in some universities, conditions are far from satisfactory for the admission of students, recruitment of lecturers and professors and the general management of university funds" (p. 109).
18. In India, according to the report on which we have been drawing, "There is a widespread impression that failure of integrity is not uncommon among ministers and that some ministers who have held office during the last 16 years have enriched themselves illegitimately, obtained good jobs for their sons and relations through nepotism, and have reaped other advantages inconsistent with any notion of purity in public life. . . . We are convinced that ensuring absolute integrity on the part of ministers at the center and the states is an indispensable condition for the establishment of a tradition of purity in public services" (pp. 101–102).
19. Santhanam committee report, pp. 11–12.
20. Of a somewhat different character is the corruption connected with grants and aid offered by western governments. That a considerable amount of the American aid to countries like Laos, South Vietnam, and even the Philippines has been dissipated in large-scale corruption is common knowledge and, in the frank American tradition, has been reported in congressional inquiries and in the press. The writer has not heard similar allegations in relation to foreign aid given India or Pakistan. Apparently the World Bank, the International Monetary Fund, and, more generally, the intergovernmental agencies within the United Nations family have on the whole been able to avoid playing into the hands of the corrupt, except that when aid is rendered in the form of commodities—as, for instance, powdered milk given by UNICEF—part of the deliveries tend to appear on the market instead of reaching their intended destinations. The World Bank, in particular, has increasingly exerted its authority to see that its loans are used to preserve fair competition among suppliers.
21. *Colonial Policy and Practice*, pp. 14–15. Cf. the Santhanam committee report's characterization of "primitive and medieval societies": "So long as the officials were loyal to the existing regime and did not resort to oppression and forcible expropriation, they were free to do as they liked. If through tactful methods, they amassed wealth for themselves or advanced their other material interests they were praised rather than censured. Often offices were hereditary and perquisites which would today amount to bribery were con-growth of the currently accepted standards of integrity" (p. 6).
22. Guy Wint, *Spotlight on Asia*, p. 91.
23. A remarkable exception to the general rule was the Netherlands Indies. The lack of corruption there was commented on above. It resulted from cultivating incorruptibility in the higher brackets of civil service and from leaving the old village organization as undisturbed as possible. Furnivall, after stating that corruption was practically unknown in Java, explains:

The absence of judicial corruption can easily be understood. Petty cases are settled by arbitration either out of court, or before a bench of notables with a senior and well-paid official as chairman; or they go before a civil servant or judicial officer with long service and on high pay. Moreover, the penalties imposed are so trivial that it is cheaper to be punished than to bribe a policeman or magistrate to escape punishment. Serious matters go before a bench containing at least three high judicial officers as well as laymen of good standing. It would be difficult and dangerous to bribe the whole bench. In civil cases the decision purports to follow customary law, and the people can know whether it is right; the court must justify itself to popular opinion and not to higher judicial authority. In these circumstances there is little scope for bribery. (*Colonial Policy and Practice*, p. 269.)

24. The conditions referred to so far in this section are reflected in the South Asian quest for a higher level of "morals" in business and public affairs—an improved "social climate" in which behavior patterns are judged in terms of the modernization ideals.

"In the long run, the fight against corruption will succeed only to the extent to which a favorable social climate is created. When such a climate is created and corruption becomes abhorrent to the minds of the public and the public servants and social controls become effective, other administrative, disciplinary and punitive measures may become unimportant and may be relazed and reduced to a minimum. However, change in social outlook and traditions is necessarily slow and the more immediate measures cannot be neglected in its favour." (Santhanam committee report, p. 101.)

25. The dynamic factors hinted at in this paragraph are touched on in several places in the Santhanam committee report; see, in particular, pp. 8 ff.

26. The Santhanam committee report in various contexts makes this point; see footnote 2, p. 945 above. "There is scope for harassment, malpractices and corruption in the exercise of discretionary powers" (p. 45). "It is necessary to take into account the root causes of which the most important is the wide discretionary power which has to be exercised by the executive in carrying on the complicated work of modern administration" (p. 209).

27. "We have found that low-paid government servants are entrusted with . . . matters like gradation of commodities, inspection of mines, supervision of implementation of labour laws and awards, various kinds of licensing, passing of goods at customs etc. While the general increase in the salaries of government servants is a matter to be decided in the light of national economy and the tax paying capacity of the people, it may be worthwhile in the country's interest to examine whether the categories of officials who have to exercise considerable discretion in matters relating to taxation, issue of valuable permits and licenses, or otherwise deal with matters which require [a] high degree of integrity, should not be given special attention regarding status and emoluments." (Santhanam committee report, p. 46.)

28. "Complaints against the highly placed in public life were not dealt with in the manner that they should have been dealt with if public confidence had to be maintained. Weakness in this respect created cynicism and the growth of the belief that while governments were against corruption they were not against corrupt individuals, if such individuals had the requisite

amount of power, influence and protection." (Santhanam committee report, p. 8.)

29. "A society that goes in for a purposively initiated process of a fast rate of change has to pay a social price, the price being higher where the pace of change excludes the possibility of leisurely adjustment which is possible only in societies where change is gradual." (Santhanam committee report.)

26

Corruption, Tradition, and Change in Indonesia

Theodore M. Smith

In January 1970 Indonesian student organizations took to the Djakarta streets to protest corruption in their government. It was the strongest anti-corruption outburst in the 25-year history of the Republic and threatened to upset the political stability which President Suharto had sought to establish as a basis for national economic growth. Special troops from the army handled the immediate challenge, but as a longer term palliative the president appointed a special Commission of Four *(Komisi IV)* to review the problem and make concrete suggestions for improvement.

For several months the Commission held hearings in executive session and sifted through charges and evidence pertaining to corrupt practices while the press, students, and national political figures expressed their own views.[1] Subsequently, in his annual Independence Day speech to the nation, the president reviewed the recommendations of the Commission and boldly stated that, "There should no longer be any doubts about it. I myself will lead the fight against corruption."[2]

This personal statement partially succeeded in defusing the issue, enabling the regime to turn its resources away from shortrun political problems and back to longer-run economic policy considerations. But given the pervasive nature of the problem, corruption is certain to be a recurring issue. This chapter attempts to explain Indonesian corruption and in so doing, to review the kind of demands it makes on a regime preoccupied with the primary objectives of staying in power and promoting economic growth.

As applied here, the term "corruption" refers to the use of public resources for private purposes. This definition covers not only conven-

Source: Theodore M. Smith, "Corruption, Tradition, and Change," *Indonesia*, 11 (1971), 21–40. By permission of the publisher.

tional monetary, but also political and administrative corruption as well. An administrator who exploits his position to extract unofficial payments from investors (either foreign or domestic) is using a public resource—his official position, prestige, status, and/or authority—for personal profit. Likewise, an official who appoints family and friends to lucrative government positions regardless of their abilities is using a public resource for private gain.

Corruption can be categorized in various other ways. One type of classification might use scale, starting with large manipulations at the top and descending to "speed money" and gifts of cigarettes at the bottom.[3] This could lead to a useful qualitative distinction between high level and low level corruption, both within a single government organization and across various levels of the governmental system— national, provincial, district, sub-district and village.

A second kind of classification might distinguish types of resource diversion according to the method employed by the perpetrators. There are some officials who directly divert funds which are under their control, while others use their official authority to command unofficial payments from private parties seeking special privileges or governmental assistance. The former is stealing and constitutes a direct loss of state financial resources. The latter is bribery and represents the loss of a different kind of resource, the government's legitimacy, particularly in the eyes of some critical elite groups such as professionals, academics, students, and civil servants. Bribes may account for significant financial losses to the state as well, since they frequently represent private payments in lieu of official tax or licensing obligations. In their present anti-corruption campaign, Indonesia's leaders seem to favor this distinction, and their statements indicate that they are primarily concerned with the first kind of deviation. At first glance this choice appears to be a case of misplaced priorities, but administrative convenience and "reach" probably governed the choice: far fewer people are involved in outright stealing than in bribery.

A third system of classification deals with the targets of corrupt practices. Table 26.1 lists kinds of corruption as reported by regional economic planners from all of Indonesia's 26 provinces. This last classification is especially useful for two reasons. First, officials are interested in this classification and are willing to discuss it, thereby eliminating a major methodological problem for research. Second, such a breakdown can inform policymakers of the kinds of problems troubling particular constituencies, thus clarifying possible decision areas for government leaders.

Table 26.1
RESPONSES OF 54 REGIONAL ECONOMIC PLANNERS TO THE
QUESTION: "WHAT KIND OF CORRUPTION IS MOST
DAMAGING TO ECONOMIC DEVELOPMENT?"

Type of Target Identified	Planners Noting Kind	
	Number	Percent
Monetary corruption (including commissions)	28	55
Corruption of time	14	28
Misuse of government authority or position	14	28
All kinds of corruption	9	18
"Stealing" or unauthorized use of government equipment and materials	9	18
Corruption at high levels	4	8
Other kinds of corruption	5	10

The data are based on the author's survey of provincial economic planners in August 1969.

Causes of Corruption

Historical Variables

Furnivall has written that the Netherlands or Indies was practically free of corruption.[4] While this view is corrobated by many Indonesians living today who are prone to credit the Japanese occupation government with introducing corruption, there is a wealth of evidence to show that it is incorrect. Prior to 1800, the Dutch East India Company offered Indonesians flagrant examples of corrupt behavior. In the words of Clive Day, the men of the company "were underpaid and exposed to every temptation that was offered by the combination of a weak native organization, extraordinary opportunities in trade, and an almost complete absence of checks from home or in Java. . . . Officials became rich by stealing from the company. Some forms of theft came in time to deserve a less harsh name, as they were so current and open that they could be regarded as legal."[5]

From the writings of Raffles and the numerous colonial reports cited by Day, it is clear that the demise of company rule and the arrival of the Dutch governor general at the turn of the nineteenth century resulted in an unavoidable widening of illicit practices. As colonial regulation and control expanded, both European and native officials indulged in obvious abuses, enjoying not only the specified percentage which was their right, but also a portion of most resources passing through their hands. When traditional services and payments due the native aristocratic officials were abolished in favor of Dutch-paid salaries, native officials had no alternative but to use illegal means if they wished to maintain the state of life to which they were accustomed.[6] Other aristocratic *(prijaji)* Javanese bribed their way into remunerative positions dispensed by Dutch officials.[7] And with the expansion of Dutch taxation on the land and its produce, native officials as low as village headmen and their assistants took advantage of new opportunities for profiteering. In Java, "Some *bekel* (tax farmers) raised twenty-fold what they paid to their superiors. Their devices for extortion were innumerable."[8] In West Sumatra, village *adat* (customary law) leaders "frequently had to be dismissed for fraud."[9] Just as stealing from the Dutch East India Company in the eighteenth century came to be overlooked, so too, minor forms of extortion by native officials grew to be tolerated. "The little man never makes open complaint," said a native witness when asked about gross abuses during an 1850 investigation.[10]

Part of the difficulty in reaching agreement on the incidence of corruption during the colonial period is definitional. For example, the use of tax revenue for personal purposes, which may have been much commoner in pre-independence times, did not wholly violate the prijaji conscience. Soemarsaid Moertono, writing about statecraft in the later Mataram period (sixteenth to nineteenth centuries), provides good clues as to the type of administrative culture which the Dutch encountered in Java:

> The maintenance of a department, office, or institution was left wholly to the ability and moral considerations of the office-holder, a fact quite in harmony with a state organization in which personal authority played such a dominating role.

And further:

> The finance system of later Mataram can be called "salary-financing," for out of the salary which the official earned (entirely in the form of appanages called *lungguh*) he was expected to pay all the expenses entailed in the performance of his tasks and duties.[11]

In short, traditionally there was little differentiation between public and private money.

But subsequently, particularly with the rise of nationalism and the achievement of an Indonesian state, claims to state resources increasingly became public claims and the private use of what were now "public" funds became "corruption." Thus, the expansion of corruption in Indonesia, as in other new states, constitutes, in part, a new definition of corrupt practices rather than a change in traditional behavior. In the well-chosen words of Wertheim," a kind of public conduct hitherto considered normal was now looked at with other, more critical eyes."[12]

Another link between corruption and nationhood stems from revolutionary leaders' perceptions of the function of the state. In nearly all cases, and particularly in the case of Indonesia during the Guided Democracy period (1958–1965), the government's role in society—political, economic, and administrative—expanded very considerably. With this expansion came many new possibilities for corruption and bribery involving public officials.

These two points which link the rise of corruption as an issue with the early years of nationhood are not earthshaking, but they provide a corrective to Myrdal's uncritically gloomy assertion that corruption in post-independence Asia is increasing.[13] Points of reference are important. For example, relative to the growth in personnel and functions which national bureaucracies have undergone, corruption may not in fact be "increasing."

Cultural Variables

For hundreds of years much of Java was effectively ruled by aristocrats who, as representatives of the kings, enjoyed patrimonial privileges not unlike those found in feudal Europe. Princely and regency offices were often hereditary and a percentage of crop yields was due their incumbents, as were domestic services known as *pantjen*. Daendels' attempt to instil the Napoleonic concept of government in Java faltered under the impact of the Java War (1825–1830), but eventually made headway at the end of the nineteenth century when many traditional privileges were reduced at all governmental levels, except at the base of Javanese civil administration, the village. Here no distinction was made between money that went to the treasury and that which did not; non-salaried village headmen collected taxes, paid themselves whatever they felt they deserved and used the remainder for the village needs. This practice was completely in harmony with patrimonial values.

In many Javanese villages this pattern has changed only slightly since independence. This means that for the villager who rises to the level of district or subdistrict officer today, traditionally accepted behavior and values suddenly become legally corrupt behavior and values. Since a majority of today's Indonesian civil servants were born and raised in villages and undoubtedly carried (and still carry) many of these traditional values into office with them, this normative conflict has an important bearing on bureaucratic behavior.[14]

Because a clear majority of a representative sample of regional officials were born in and grew up in villages, there is a strong potential link with the patrimonial value-system described so well by Geertz.[15] While there is no good comparative data to show differences in Indonesian rural and urban values, powerful residues of patrimonial value structures can be found in most multi-generation urban dwellers. Thus the lack of congruence between civil servant values and legal-rational bureaucratic norms may be even more general than the data on place of birth and childhood suggest.

While the explanations presented above are not intended as an apology for corruption, they do go far to explain the dilemma faced by many government officials. Schooled in traditional village values, many of them entered the government directly at the time of Independence without benefit of value-changing higher education. Today they are either burdened with (sustained by?) these traditional values or else find themselves in a situation of increasing moral disorientation.

An understanding of the continuing significance of the traditional value system in Java also helps to explain why anti-corruption drives rarely proceed very far. Java's administrative culture is built around "a very intense concern for status: for smooth, constrained, hyperpolite behavior."[16] To make direct charges of corrupt practices against individuals engenders a disagreeable, open conflict situation. It threatens a man's livelihood and status, that of his family, his staff, and possibly that of his organization. It may even go beyond that. Like a thread that begins to unravel, the exposure of malpractices by one official may lead to the order-shattering implication of several others not even under suspicion. David Mitchell has suggested that most officials in the district which he studied were complicit in each others' corrupt practices (*tahu-sama-tahu*), and a recent case in the central Java regency of Wonogiri offers a clear example of how this system sometimes works.[17] For the typical Javanese, the psychic costs of direct interpersonal conflict and the dangers involved in leveling charges of corruption appear too high to encourage much of the aggressive behavior that is a *sine qua non* for successful anti-corruption drives.[18]

Economic Factors

In the late 1950s, Dr. Hatta observed that, "Workers and government employees, whose wages and salaries are no longer adequate for their daily needs, are being exploited by enterprising adventurers who want to get rich quickly. . . . Bribery and graft have become increasingly common, to the detriment of our community and country."[19] Since early colonial times, insufficient salaries for Indonesian officials have been a continuing problem. Table 26.2 illustrates the current gap between basic government salaries (including official supplements in rupiahs which may run as high as 100 percent for senior officials) and

Table 26.2

**A COMPARISON OF MINIMAL MONTHLY SALARY NEEDS
AND OFFICIAL BASIC MONTHLY INCOMES BY
CLASSES OF CIVIL SERVANTS**

Type of Regional Official	Stated Minimal Monthly Needs (Average)	Official Basic Monthly Income (Average)[a]
Economic planners (54)	Rp. 15,132	Rp. 8,514
Higher level (157)	20,028	11,268
Lower level (146)	16,434	7,050
Subdistrict officers (226)	15,361	7,050

a. To reach this figure the following allowances were added to the basic salary (*gadji pokok*): implementation allowance (*tundjangan pelaksanaan*), 20 percent; "responsibility" allowance (*tundjangan djabatan*), 20 percent; a rice allowance of approximately Rp. 40 per kilogram at 10 kilograms per family member; a spouse allowance of 5 percent; and 2 percent for each child under 18 years of age. There is then a 10 percent standard deduction in the basic salary for health insurance and pensions.

Only a minority of officials receive the "responsibility" allowance, the maximum number being limited to 25 percent of the total employees in each department. The supplement is given to those in leadership positions, such as section and bureau heads. All officials, except for the lowest ranking (Salary Group I) receive the implementation allowance.

As an example of the monthly salary computation, here is the case of an official who is a bureau head in the governor's office (South Sulawesi), has a master's degree, ten years of government service, a wife and five children.

Basic salary	Rp. 5,040
Implementation allowance (20%)	1,008
"Responsibility" allowance (20%)	1,008
Rice allowance (70 kilograms × Rp. 40)	2,800
Wife allowance (5%)	252
Children allowance (2% × 5)	504
Gross income	Rp. 10,612
Health/pension deduction (10%)	− 504

Total government income Rp. 10,108 =
$26.95/month

Officials in the Department of Finance receive a *premi* each month (100 percent of their basic salaries) which adds about one-third to these figures and some departments have attached personnel incentives to their development projects—foremost among them being the Department of Public Works. The figures presented do not include housing and vehicles which are provided for a small minority of high-level officials.

All of the data were gathered in the period October 1969 to April 1970.

minimal monthly rupiah requirements of various groups of civil servants. The figures demonstrate that, practically speaking, there is not a single official who can live by his government income alone.

The data show that official income amounts to approximately half of essential monthly needs. Actual monthly *expenditures*, a more accurate indicator of perceived needs, run somewhat higher but cannot be precisely determined. However, there is a disparity between officials' government income and their expenditures. Salaries and bonuses currently amount to about one-third of the amount most officials say they need to sustain their families' standard of living.

More than anything else, these figures reflect the disastrous effects which inflation has had on salaried government officials between the years 1958 and 1968. (In 1966 the rate of inflation was over 600 percent.) Although there have been occasional salary increases, the latest being a 50 percent raise in April 1970, compensation levels still lag far behind price increases. While the data presented are not as "hard" as one might wish, they do illuminate the dilemma faced by government officials who are compelled to find additional sources of income. The figures become still more significant if the general lack of incentives for correct behavior by government officials is considered. Salary increases are very difficult to obtain and truly meaningful increases may be impossible for the government to provide at this time. Rapid promotions are rarely possible. Government housing and vehicles are limited to a small fraction of all government employees. Travel and training opportunities are severely limited, particularly so for officials working outside Djakarta.

In addition to the shortage of incentives, applicable sanctions are also in comparatively short supply. Cultural norms effectively preclude punitive denial of the perquisites, however minor, that attend each position. Salary increases and promotions are all but automatic and it is difficult to remove someone from office. In fact, the common procedure for dealing with officials whose corrupt practices become open knowledge is to transfer them to new jobs before their activities gain wide attention.

Key Variables Identified by Indonesian Bureaucrats

The survey data indicate that Indonesian officials view low salaries as the prime factor behind corrupt practices. But the responses indicate that they are introspective and self-critical of their own government's performance. About 50 percent of those surveyed blamed corruption on weak administration and a lack of effective government controls. Almost as many said civil servant mental attitudes were responsible. This last variable is not easy to unravel since the "mental attitude" *(sikap mental)* response encompasses such different concepts as traditional values, the lack of a public service ethic, greed, and dishonesty. Table 26.3 provides a breakdown of their responses.

Structural Variables

There are obvious limitations on the reforming policymakers' capacity to affect the abovementioned variables. They cannot change the history and culture of Indonesia, and aside from tariff, licensing, and direct tax regulations, they have few alternatives in the economic field under present conditions. However, there may be a close link between corruption and the kind of governmental structure which Indonesia has today. If this is true, then perhaps the options of government leaders are not as limited as they might at first appear to be.

Deductive reasoning suggests that a highly centralized governmental

Table 26.3
"IN YOUR OPINION, WHAT FACTORS CAUSE CORRUPTION?"

Province (Number of respondents)		Corruption Causes Identified by Regional Officials				
	Low Salaries	Civil Servant Mental Attitudes	Generally Poor Economic Conditions	Weak Admin. and Lack of Controls	Other	No Answer
West Sumatra (74)*	51 69%	53 72%	26 35%	44 57%	11	6
South Sulawesi (125)*	69 55%	50 40%	39 31%	58 46%	12	12
Central Java (104)*	51 49%	35 34%	35 34%	43 41%	17	11
Totals (303)	171 56%	138 46%	100 32%	145 48%	40 13%	29 10%

*These figures refer to the number of officials in each provincial sample. Multiple responses account for percentages which total more than 100.

The response of a higher level official working in the Ministry of Home Affairs in South Sulawesi was not atypical. He suggested four reasons for corruption:
1. There are good opportunities for corruption.
2. It results from the general condition of the economy and low government salaries.
3. Our own administration weaknesses facilitate corruption.
4. There is a lack of firmness by those who are charged with carrying out laws against corrupt officials with the result that corruption becomes a general phenomenon or a normal thing *(jang biasa sadja)*.[20]

structure may not only make corruption possible, but necessary. Five elements of this argument are outlined below.

First, extremely limited numbers of decisionmaking centers place a premium on the ability of the public to draw attention to their problems and to get decisions from top leaders. Decisionmakers have a seller's market. The demand for decisions, many of them minor in nature, is much greater than they can supply. Money can be, and is, used to make particularistic demands more effective. This is rational in some senses—payment for performance—but disparities in purchasing power ensure that unequal treatment will be given to different publics.

Second, centralization leads to the issuance of more control regulations since top leaders cannot personally supervise the activities for which they are responsible. The multiplication of "preventive", controls through regulations establishes additional gatekeepers—officials who can extract a price at each gate. In sum, the more gates, the more widespread the need to use speed money.

Third, centralization lessens the likelihood that second and third-level regional governments will take initiatives in combatting corruption. They may not have the right to issue general corrective regulations, and, as our survey evidence indicates, perceived corruption at the center of government is itself a strong psychological deterrent to positive steps at lower levels.

Fourth, the results of a series of interviews by the author indicate that Indonesia's top decisionmakers do not know with any precision the degree of corruption prevailing at lower levels nor do they fully appreciate its impact on the general public. This is a result of the extent to which the upward flow of accurate information and frank reporting is discouraged within the government. With only vague notions of the degree and impact of corruption below them, they cannot readily be expected to take positive action.

Finally, the centralized revenue policy of the Indonesian government does little to enhance the responsibility of regional officials as they (the officials) perceive it. Figures for fiscal year 1969–1970 indicate that local and regional governments received 52.6 percent of their budgets in the form of subsidies, 39.5 percent from revenue collections carried out by central government agencies in regions, and only 7.9 percent from their own efforts.[21] It might fairly be hypothesized that the less governments are responsible for financing themselves, the less concern their officials and local publics will show in seeing that funds are carefully handled. Stated another way, one tends to take better care of one's own money than that of someone else. It therefore seems highly probable that decentralization of rights to raise revenue would be followed by increased regional and local responsibility in the use of funds.

These points may be important in a policy sense because they suggest that limited steps toward the decentralization of decisionmaking could reduce the need for certain kinds of corruption. The contrary view, that increased local autonomy might, by reducing central control, actually result in increased corruption, has some plausibility. But there is a measure of irony here, since it is precisely some of those centralized controls which increase the need for corrupt behavior in the regions. Moreover, this argument rests on the unproven assumption that local controls would be less seriously enforced than central controls.

Political Party Factors

Political parties, particularly new political parties, have financing needs which have been only fitfully met in most low-income countries. Their organizational investments and their purchase of support require a great deal of money, and often the only available means to obtain such working capital is to syphon it off the state. In narrow rational-bureaucratic terms this kind of corruption represents a serious loss. But in a broader perspective it may represent unofficial investments in the political infrastructure (party development) which will open new, or strengthen established channels of interest articulation. Indonesia's last general elections in 1955 witnessed successful attempts by several parties, particularly the Partai Nasional Indonesia-National Party (PTI), to divert state resources to their own campaign funds.[22] The line between civil service and political party activity has never been sharply drawn in Indonesia. Government Regulation No. 6 of 1970 prohibits members of the armed forces, officials of the Defense Department, judges, public prosecutors, and the state bank governor from joining political organizations, but the bulk of the civil service is free to join. Moreover, civil servants standing for election need not resign their positions until they are elected and accept membership in a legislative body (Presidential Decision of October 26, 1970). Although some officials are troubled that the civil service should be involved in partisan politics, a series of interviews with provincial officials indicated that a majority of them will participate actively in the July 1971 general elections. . . . In many cases this participation will mean the providing of office equipment, supplies, vehicles, and money to the political organizations supported by the official.

Beyond election needs, there are the day-to-day routine expenses which are required to keep a party functioning. Party leaders in Indonesia have sought and won extralegal commercial privileges and the use of government facilities to serve their income needs, and they are likely to continue this practice; military organizations follow the same strategy with even greater success.[23]

Costs and Benefits of Corruption

Full credit should be given to J. S. Nye for attempting to take the problem of corruption out of its moral context by suggesting a kind of analysis that might be useful to government leaders.[24] Making use of his and some additional criteria for measurement, one can begin to assess the impact of corruption on development in Indonesia. Most of the tentative conclusions presented are impressionistic, but some data on elite attitudes toward corruption in the Indonesian government provide substance for an evaluation of political costs.

Potential Benefits

Higher level corruption may be one means of accumulating capital. Assuming the possibility of this kind of corruption in Indonesia, the crucial question to be asked is whether or not this capital is being reinvested in Indonesia or being sent abroad. It is obvious that much of the capital is being reinvested in Indonesia. How much? We simply do not know, though one might be able to obtain some rough indicators through bank officials.

Limited enforcement of present business tax laws may allow businessmen to accumulate the necessary funds for new capital investment. Papanek notes in the case of Pakistan: "In practice, only 10 percent of actual industrial profits were collected in taxes, thus providing the spur and capital for industrial enterpreneurship."[25] The Indonesian system of tax bargaining (tawar-menawar) which is carried on between tax officials and private businessmen clearly leaves some unofficial margin for the businessmen, but how much is uncertain. Informed Indonesian academics estimate that those larger indigenous companies which do pay taxes pay roughly 10 percent to 40 percent of what the assessed tax should be according to law. With the possible exception of many trading enterprises, much of this windfall is apparently being reinvested in Indonesia, particularly in urban housing and enterprises.

The selling of services at lower governmental levels represents an exchange of goods and services which in most cases actually permits a civil servant to perform his government function. Not only is this practice in harmony with traditional rural norms, but it allows low-salaried officials to remain on the job. Certainly at the subdistrict and village levels the practice of paying for services rendered continues in full force. Usually the payments are in kind and the proximity of the subdistrict officer's house to the local market facilitates the exchange. There seems to be little resistance to this practice, though some was encountered at the village level in West Sumatra.

The use of "speed money" may facilitate more rapid foreign investment. Forced to work through normal bureaucratic channels, it may take several months or longer for foreign enterprises to get the necessary agreement and permission to establish factories. Unofficial incentives may hasten the process with the result that operations begin considerably sooner, benefitting both Indonesia and the foreign investor. It appears that competition among Indonesian agencies for the privilege of negotiating or approving investment offers is so great that all benefits of using "speed money" are lost—and along with them, many of the offers and potential offers. However, once investment agreements have been signed, it seems probable that this form of bribery pays dividends in getting production going.

Potential Costs

Capital accumulated through high-level corruption may be wasted. There is considerable evidence from Latin American dictatorships and more recently from Vietnam that much of the accumulated capital in those areas finds its way to West European banks, a practice not entirely unknown in the United States. In such cases the loss for the country involved is obvious. As noted above, very little can be learned about this phenomenon in Indonesia. However, if there is a direct correlation between the flight of such capital and the instability of a country's government (as we might reasonably suspect there is), Indonesia's present degree of political stability provides some basis for optimism.

Investment may be channeled into sectors such as construction, not because of economic profitability, but because it may thus be easier to hide corruption.[26] It is probably indisputable that construction contracts permit some "sharing" of resources, but it is almost impossible to begin to measure the amount of resource diversion caused by this. A careful review of building permits issued by offices of the public works department would provide clues, but not firm answers. The results of interviews carried out with several budgetary officials suggest that

departments consistently attempt to hide increased personnel allocations in construction projects, but it seems overly rigid to regard this
routine strategy as corruption.

Corruption may squander the important asset of political legitimacy
which most governments seek to preserve and build on. One of the
major tasks of any regime is the building of its own legitimacy, a
resource which will enable it to gain more easily the support and the
assistance of the public in connection with development (at the expenditure of fewer economic and political resources). It may or may
not be true, but many Indonesians in the Outer Islands *believe* that
most of the corruption in Indonesia is located in Djakarta. The fact that
they believe this and that few serious steps have been taken to control
corruption tends to reduce the legitimacy of the central government in
their eyes.[27]

Corruption may tend to destroy some of a new nation's greatest
potential assets, the enthusiasm, idealism, and sympathy of its youth
and students.[28] In the event that the idealism and enthusiasm of the
younger generation turns to cynicism, not only political stability but
long run economic development efforts are bound to be affected. The
students will be the future political leaders and economic modernizers.
The Djakarta demonstrations of January 1970 indicate the reality of
this concern in the capital. Some preliminary data from university
students in Sumatra, Sulawesi, and Java suggest that most Indonesian
students are aware of the problem and critical of corruption in the
government.

In a recent study involving 554 university students, 447 (80.7 percent) indicated that they had discussed the problem of corruption with
someone. One hundred one students (18.2 percent) replied no (six no
responses). When asked, "In your opinion does corruption constitute
an important problem in connection with economic development?",
529 (95.5 percent) answered, "Yes." Eleven (2 percent) replied no, and
seven each either didn't know or had no response. Students seem to
discuss corruption, and they seem to be concerned about its impact on
economic development. In response to another question in which they
were asked to identify the main problems facing Indonesia today, a
surprising number mentioned the problem of corruption first.[29]

Corruption may alienate civil servants and cause them to reduce
their efforts and support for the government's policies. The loyalty and
enthusiasm of capable, government officials is a desirable resource for
any regime to have. But such loyalty is never guaranteed and the
literature on bureaucracy suggests that bureaucracies, as distinct sec-

tors of the polity, can sometimes be very effective in their demands. How does corruption in Indonesia's government affect its civil servants? There are no good measurements of the support which Indonesian civil servants give to their government, but again some data suggest that corruption is a matter of much concern to them. Of 357 regional civil servants who were asked, "Have you ever discussed corruption with anyone?", 253 (71 percent responded, "yes." Ninety-three (26 percent) responded, "no or not yet," while 11 (3 percent) had no response. Response to the question, "In your opinion does corruption constitute an important problem in connection with economic development," was strongly positive. Of the respondents, 334 (94 percent replied, "yes," 11 (3 percent replied no; and 72 respondents (3 percent) either didn't know or has no response.

Though not shown here, the data are consistent across the three provinces of West Sumatra, South Sulawesi, and Central Java. Nearly all officials are unhappy with present levels of corruption; some are angry that stronger measures have not yet been taken to lessen the frequency and amount of corruption. The data also suggest that there is general receptivity to increased control mechanisms should they be introduced.

Conclusion

Contrary to the views of Furnivall and others, corruption (by its current definition) was widespread in the Netherlands Indies. The legal system imposed by the Dutch left traditional patrimonial relationships largely untouched. For the Dutch to have destroyed them through attempts at direct rule would have resulted in chaos. Thus the "abuses" of the patrimonial system persisted through the colonial period and because social norms do not change as rapidly as statutory law, many of them continue today.

Given these traditions, the stimulus of low salaries, and expanded government functions, it is obvious that major investments would be required if a decision were to be made today to eradicate corruption. What kind of investments? Direct investments in governmental salaries, legal institutions, political parties, education, control mechanisms, and possibly even structural changes in the bureaucracy. The magnitude of these investments can best be understood by isolating one variable, that of government salaries and benefits. A doubling of salaries and benefits would require a total personnel expenditure in the neighborhood of Rp. 400 billion—considerably more than total domestic revenues at present.[30] Even if salary increases of this magnitude were feasible, there are many other important variables affecting the incidence of corruption and only part of the problem would be solved.

On the whole, corruption in Indonesia appears to present more of a recurring political problem than an economic one. It undermines the legitimacy of the government in the eyes of the young, educated elite and most civil servants. In the case of the latter, it is assumed, but cannot be proven, that certain types of corruption substantially reduce bureaucratic productivity. Furthermore, scores of interview responses indicate that corruption reduces support for the government among elites at the province and regency level. Finally, the survey data suggest that concern over the problem of corruption runs much deeper than is superficially apparent.

The Suharto government has adopted a low-cost strategy to cope with the problem. High civilian and military officials must now list their personal wealth annually;[31] new anti-corruption laws have been proposed; selected state organizations are being investigated; and the president has obligated himself to "lead the fight" personally. The strategy is a realistic one which is designed to meet immediate political demands and short-range objectives.

But corruption will continue to recur as a political issue, requiring additional investments by the government. Because much of the indigenous concern over corruption in Indonesia is at present latent or unexpressed, there is good reason to believe that with the further development of political parties, the press, and associational interest groups, investments to limit corrupt practices will need to be larger in the future.

Notes

1. The presidential adviser to the Commission, former Vice-President Hatta, was quoted as saying that "corruption has become an Indonesian art," and that it is a "part of the culture." *Indonesian Observer,* July 2, 1970, p. 1. Half-humorously, a columnist for the *Djakarta Times* suggested that the ministry of education and culture establish a division for corruption, presumably in its directorate general for culture. July 3, 1970, p. 1.
2. "Address of State by the President of the Republic of Indonesia Before the House of Representatives on the Eve of the 25th Independence Day," August 16, 1970, Djakarta, p. 28.
3. "Speed money,"—or "lubricating money" *(uang semir)* as it is called in Indonesia, is a small bribe offered on the assumption that some permission or necessary governmental action will either be waived or disposed of more quickly.
4. J.S. Furnivall, *Colonial Policy and Practice: A Comparative Study of*

Burma and Netherlands India (London: Cambridge University Press, 1957), p. 269.

5. Clive Day, *The Dutch in Java* (London: Oxford University Press, 1966), pp. 100–103.
6. *Ibid.*, pp. 299–300.
7. See John Smail's sections on Indonesian history in David J. Steinberg, ed., *In Search of Southeast Asia: A Modern History* (New York: Praeger, 1970), p. 147.
8. Day, *Dutch in Java*, p. 33.
9. B. Schrieke, *Indonesian Sociological Studies* (The Hague: W. Van Hoeve, 1955), I, p. 137.
10. Day, *Dutch in Java*, p. 307.
11. Soemarsaid Moertono, *State and Statecraft in Old Java: A Study of the Later Mataram Period, 16th to 19th Century* (Ithaca: Cornell Modern Indonesia Project, 1963), pp. 90 and 134. Many of these tasks and duties were social ones, and present cultural norms dictate that they still be performed today. But in modern, rational-legal terms, the use of government money for these functions is often considered corruption. Only a very few top officials receive budgetary subsidies for this purpose.
12. W.F. Wertheim, "Sociological Aspects of Corruption in Southeast Asia," in *East-West Parallels: Sociological Approaches to Modern Asia* (The Hague: W. Van Hoeve, 1964), p. 111. This point has been elaborated upon by James C. Scott in, "The Analysis of Corruption in Developing Nations," *Comparative Studies in Society and History,* 2, No. 3 (June 1969), pp. 318–319.
13. Gunnar Myrdal, *Asian Drama* (New York: Pantheon, 1968), II, p. 944.
14. B. Soesarso, *Korupsi di Indonesia* (Djakarta: Bhratara, 1969), especially Chapter 10, "Redefinition of Morality."
15. Clifford Geertz, *The Religion of Java* (New York: The Free Press, 1960), Chapter 17.
16. Clifford Geertz, *The Social History of an Indonesian Town* (Cambridge: MIT Press, 1965), p. 79.
17. "Wanokalada: A Case Study in Local Administration," *Bulletin of Indonesian Economic Studies,* July 1970, p. 83. For a review of events in Wonogiri, see "Sidang Korupsi 5 Pedjabat di Wonogiri," *Kompas,* September 9, 1970, p. 2.
18. Part of this general argument can also be found in the published conclusions of a seminar on "Corruption and Development" held in Djakarta and sponsored by the Student Council of the University of Indonesia, August 10–12, 1970. "Inventarisasi Pendapat peserta Panel Diskusi Tentang 'Korupsi dan Pembangunan' " (mimeo). Seminar panelists explained the failure of the Indonesian public openly to criticize officials who are widely known to be involved in corrupt practices as follows: "The people have extraordinary respect for someone in authority. He is thought of as a superior and they do not want to take a critical attitude toward anything that he does. This seems to be the reason why this social stratum does not react to cases of corruption."
19. Mohammad Hatta, *The Co-operative Movement in Indonesia* (Ithaca: Cornell University Press, 1957), pp. 84–85.
20. Interview, December 1969.

21. These problems are explored in much greater depth in R. Stafford Smith and Theodore M. Smith, "The Political Economy of Regional and Urban Revenue Policy in Indonesia."

22. Herbert Feith, "Dynamics of Guided Democracy," in Ruth McVey, ed., *Indonesia* (New Haven: HRAF Press, 1963), p. 315.

23. Bintoro Tjokroamidjojo, Sudjoko Prasodjo, and Bambang Trijoso, "Masalah Korupsi" (Djakarta, March 1970, mimeo), p. 14.

24. J.S. Nye, "Corruption and Political Development: A Cost-Benefit Analysis," *American Political Science Review*, 61 (June 1967), pp. 417–28.

25. Gustav Papanek, *Pakistan's Development: Social Goals and Private Incentives* (Cambridge: Harvard University Press, 1967), pp. 110 and 193.

26. Nye, "Corruption and Political Development," p. 421.

27. Based on interviews with government officials in West Sumatra and South Sulawesi.

28. Ronald Wraith and Edgar Simpkins, *Corruption in Developing Countries* (London: Allen and Unwin Ltd., 1963).

29. The student interviews were divided evenly among three provincial universities: Andalas (West Sumatra), Hasanuddin (South Sulawesi), and Diponegoro (Central Java). Third-year students from the faculties of medicine, economics, law, agriculture, and the social sciences were selected as respondents. The responses are all the more significant in that most of them were given prior to January 1970, when corruption became a national political issue.

30. Revenues for fiscal year 1969–1970 were Rp. 309.4 billion, or about $818.5 million. A doubling of government salaries would provide a college-educated bureau chief with an increase to only $80 from the present $40 per month. Most civil servants and military personnel would receive much less. Data on revenues were obtained from "Pelaksanaan Tahun Pertama Repelita," an appendix to the President's National Day speech, August 16, 1970, p. 72.

31. Presidential Decision, Number 52, August 3, 1970.

Part III

VULNERABILITY TO CORRUPTION —VARIATION AMONG SYSTEMS

OVERVIEW

While corruption has occurred in political systems of all sorts in all ages, a number of factors can influence the types and frequencies of corruption to be found. Ideology and form of economic organization; centralization or fragmentation of power, and the basis for such power relationships (elements of formal structure, such as federalism, versus underlying cultural and social variations); and the number and kinds of participants in important decision-making processes, can all affect a system's vulnerability to corruption.

Communist systems present a complex interplay of governmental and economic institutions, ideologies, and traditional political cultures. Perhaps their most clearly distinguishing feature is a virtually all-encompassing public sector. In this setting, the definitions of "political corruption" can include not only the realm of government officials, but also the dealings of shop clerks. Indeed, in the Soviet Union both could be prosecuted for corruption under the same section of the law—"crimes against socialist property." In addition, many more aspects of life are exposed to the system's control processes, be they the provisions of central planning or the more immediate but no less pervasive interpersonal and group sanctions found in China. The result is a more pervasive tension between otherwise "private" interests and official norms, and considerably more stress upon stated procedures, than would elsewhere be the case.

Of similar importance are the sheer scope and internal problems of the planning apparatus, particularly in systems like the Soviet type. Complex industrial processes involving hundreds of interdependent enterprises are regulated at every turn by inflexible plans and allocation procedures. Production problems which in market systems might be alleviated by price or production changes can spill over from one part of the planned economy into many others. Enterprise managers often have little choice but to use illicit influence and the efforts of illegal "contact men" to obtain labor and raw materials, or to "persuade" planners to ignore shortcomings in production. Fundamental remedies to such problems, which might serve as issues for the

443

opposition in more open systems, are in a single-party hegemony more likely to be viewed as disruptions. Party and planning leadership thus often "wink" at corruption, particularly if it finesses bottlenecks of production.

The party, moreover, will often be the locus of significant corruption in its own right. Top leadership is immune to exposés and reprisals from below, and can thus engage in self-serving behavior. Those episodes in which revelations of corruption are allowed to surface and punishments are meted out, and the kinds of treatment afforded "whistleblowers," correspond more closely to the political agendas of the leadership than to the actual incidence or importance of corrupt conduct. Perhaps paradoxically, corruption itself can serve similar ends: access to illegitimate benefits and perquisites can, for a faction leader, keep one's followers loyal, or be useful for higher leadership in punishing some factions and rewarding others.

Another important concern is the consequences of corruption in such systems. In some ways, corruption is an innovative and adaptive force, creating an unofficial price system, opening up informal avenues of influence for citizens and enterprise managers, and finessing problems of supply and production in industry. In other ways, however, corruption may inhibit change, not only by postponing more fundamental reforms, but also by providing illicit incentives for current leadership to retain its hegemony.

In other places, where power is less centralized and extensive, and political participation more open, the dynamics of corruption are altered. In the United States, for example, the public sector is relatively limited in scope compared with the overall size of the economy. Where Soviet citizens must resort to various forms of "covert participation," all levels of American government are legitimately the target of many kinds of pressures emerging out of an individualistic, entrepreneurial culture and economy. If the penetration of the state into what would elsewhere be regarded as "private" activities is a defining aspect of communist systems, the problem in the market-oriented systems has been rooted more in the difficulties of "insulating" government from the private-regarding dynamics of its cultural and economic setting. This problem was compounded, in the American case at least, by a cultural suspicion of government power which produced a system of federalism, extensively fragmenting power among and within levels of government. These arrangements have succeeded, on the whole, in inhibiting the use of public power; but they may also have contributed to its abuse by multiplying the avenues of access available to private power and interests.

Thus, much of the corruption story in the United States has taken place at the state and local levels. Those governments, in turn, are embedded in varying social and sub-cultural settings which not only help shape standards of conduct in state and local politics but can also affect national politics as well. The case of Vice President Spiro Agnew can be viewed as an extension of the norms of Maryland politics. Federal policy can in turn affect state politics; changes in the interpretation of federal anti-bribery laws have profoundly altered the ground rules of influence at the state and local levels. Decentralization affects reform as well: protection of budgets and institutional autonomy are often more important than corruption as concerns for administrators. Such decentralization is but one of a number of factors making the American case both more intriguing and more difficult to compare with others. It also is a reminder that social and economic contrasts (and conflicts) within nations may produce distinctive patterns of vulnerability to corruption.

Fragmentation of power is found to an even greater degree in dealings among nations, and between national governments and multinational corporations. It is difficult to say how much of this sort of corruption occurs, but the growing cost and complexity of the goods on the market—weapons systems and jet aircraft are but two examples—and the increasing interdependence of nations in the world economy make this sort of corruption a most important concern. In the arena of international business bribery, jurisdictions are unclear, standards of behavior are only poorly defined, and there may be no party involved with an interest in, or responsibility for, ensuring that such standards as do exist will be enforced. So large and complex are the stakes that conventional rules and restraint may matter very little. Unlike corruption within states such as the Soviet Union or the United States, international business enterprises may possess far more resources and options than the governments and officials with whom they deal.

Attempts in the past decade to regulate the conduct of American businesses in their international dealings do draw upon some long-standing conceptions of business ethics. But they also reflect a complex and partially contradictory mix of motives and purposes and rely upon uncertain mechanisms of detection and enforcement. Corruption in this international arena represents a relatively new challenge to scholars, and a complex one as well. Not only do we confront the usual problems of definitions and a pervasive lack of hard evidence; systematic comparisons will be difficult as well, for the universe of cases to be studied is relatively small, and idiosyncratic factors such as personalities may make each case unique in important respects.

Corruption in Communist Systems: An Introduction

Not only is political corruption universally proscribed in communist systems, but it may as in the Soviet Union be punishable under the laws defining "economic crimes" and can incur draconian punishments, including execution. Despite communist theory that corruption cannot occur in a genuine socialist state the reality is that corrupt practices in the Soviet Union operate outside a relatively inflexible and sluggish formal political system. Illegal or corrupt exchanges perform highly useful redistributive functions, so that they have become widely tolerated by both public and government alike. But when corruption becomes blatant, or when it overtly challenges the aims and policies of the state, it becomes the object of official concern and suppression in the Soviet Union and China.

In Chapter 27 John M. Kramer presents what is known about the levels, incidence, and typical practices of political and economic corruption in the Soviet Union. He describes the various ways the Soviet state tries to suppress and minimize corrupt practices, and the kinds of laws and punishments used to those ends. It is apparent that corruption in the Soviet Union is not only pervasive, but that it even permits parts of the public sector to operate more efficiently and effectively than it could in the absence of the informal transactions that have become standard operating procedure throughout the country.

The second selection, by diFranceisco and Gitelman, is based on interviews with over 1,000 Soviet emigres. These provided insights into the attitudinal and behavioral aspects of elements in the Soviet political culture which nurture and encourage widespread corruption in Russia. The authors' findings suggest that the dominant social ethos is one of private self-interest, and that experience appears to have dictated a preference for informal access and influence on bureaucratic individuals and a general disdain for formal and legalistic procedures and norms. Thus, *blat* (bribes and other kinds of side payments) and *protektsiia* (personal cultivation and use of influential people) are considered normal ways of extracting preferences, favors, or even ordinary services from the official system.

Alan P. Liu, in the third selection, draws upon the mainland Chinese press for his description and analysis of corruption in communist China. He identifies some 300 cases of corruption, almost all dealing with the activities of local and rural officials, and usually involving acts commonly defined as corrupt elsewhere but some which reflect a wider definition. As in the Soviet Union, the Chinese authorities apparently take formal notice of corrupt practices when they can no longer avoid doing so. Liu also reports that the Chinese themselves have devoted considerable effort to "theorizing" on the causes of corruption. Some of his discussion seems to confirm propositions on the subject found in western literature, while some aspects stress uniquely Chinese circumstances (such as certain characteristics of the PRC system) as causal factors. Thus both clientelism and special Chinese political-cultural factors find a place in the Chinese "theorizing." The author addresses the question of vulnerability in comparison with Chinese communities in places like Singapore.

The fourth selection, by Peter Harris, focusses on the common characteristics of what the author calls "socialist graft" as it is practiced in mainland China and the Soviet Union. According to the author, the term encompasses a whole range of practices commonly lumped under the name "corruption," but which are treated with special official opprobrium because they occur in "socialist" countries, at least theoretically on the path to freer and more just futures. In his comparison of the two systems, the author pays particular attention to the Soviet "second," or informal, economy, in which a wide variety of uncontrolled economic exchanges take place outside, or within the interstices, of the formal (and government-controlled) economy. He concludes that, in socialist societies, resource scarcities and bureaucratic inefficiencies engender corrupt practices that develop special privileges for some.

27

Political Corruption in the U.S.S.R.

John M. Kramer

Soviet commentators traditionally have associated political corruption with public officials in decadent capitalist systems. The "New Soviet Man," they assert, is a dedicated public servant who would never pursue private gain to society's detriment. Such commentators generally attribute instances of corruption among Soviet officials today to "vestiges of the past" that will wither away as the socialist system becomes ever more firmly established. Yet, an examination of political life in societies as disparate as ancient Rome and the contemporary United States indicates that none of them, including the U.S.S.R., has been entirely free from political corruption.

Certainly enough public officials throughout history have been sufficiently tempted to pursue private gain at public expense to suggest that defects in the human character are an important cause of corruption. Indeed, Alexander Hamilton in *The Federalist Papers* writes that "man is vindicative, ambitious, and rapacious," and that it has been "invariably found that momentary passions and immediate interests have a more active and imperious control over human conduct than do general or remote considerations of policy, utility, or justice." While the notion that human nature is base may explain why all political systems have experienced corruption, it does not explain why some officials engage in corruption while others do not, nor why some political systems seem to have more corruption than do others. The opportunities and incentives for corruption within and among political systems help explain these differences. An analysis of such factors in the U.S.S.R. suggests that, despite Soviet claims, they are similar in kind if not degree to those found in many other societies.[1]

The following analysis examines the scope, incentives and opportunities for, and efforts to combat, corruption in the U.S.S.R. The

Source: John M. Kramer, "Political Corruption in the U.S.S.R.," *The Western Political Quarterly,* 30, No. 2 (June 1977), 213–24. By permission of the publisher and author.

study defines corruption as the behavior of public officials which diverges from the formal duties of a public role to serve private ends.[2] Three aspects of the definition require brief elaboration.

First, a public official must be involved in a corrupt act. Thus, while a private Soviet citizen who steals merchandise from a government warehouse and sells it on the black market commits an illegal act, it is not one that this study would term corrupt. If, however, a public official colludes with the private citizen in these illegal activities, then the official is guilty of corruption.

Second, the definition's conception of corruption as behavior diverging from the formal duties of a public role does not necessarily mean that large segments of the population condemn such behavior. In fact, a divergence between official and private conceptions of acceptable public behavior is often an important factor fostering political corruption in a society.

Finally, although public officials engage in corruption for private gain, their activities may also benefit society. Therefore, many contemporary students of corruption, rejecting the traditional view that usually saw corruption as an evil to be eradicated, now assert that it may perform important functions not provided by the formal political system.[3]

Types of Corruption

Most corruption in the U.S.S.R. falls within two broad categories: (1) corruption for private gain; (2) corruption for bureaucratic gain. The former involves illegal acts by public officials to provide themselves and/or others with government goods and services. The latter entails corrupt practices committed by officials to enhance organizational performance and efficiency to the benefit of the organization's employees.

Corruption for Private Gain

Bribery, embezzlement, and speculation are the most common forms of corruption for private gain in the U.S.S.R. Although no precise data exist on the extent of this corruption, it is apparent from Soviet media reports that these practices are widespread. Thus, an *Izvestiia* article in 1974 acknowledged that "instances of embezzlement and irresponsible attitudes toward material goods are still quite common," while a plenary session of the U.S.S.R. Supreme Court noted that bribery "represented a major social danger and required decisive measures to eradicate it." In 1970 a Soviet criminologist reported that economic crimes such as bribery and embezzlement accounted for almost one quarter of all crime in the country, and in Georgia, where a number of scandals involving public officials have erupted in recent years, "such antipodes of our society as money grubbing, bribery, extortion and other crimes that are nourished by the private ownership tendency," constitute almost 40 percent of all reported criminal offences.[4]

Corruption for private gain is especially prevalent in the housing sector. The U.S.S.R. currently faces a serious housing shortage, particularly in urban areas. As a result, many public officials have used illegal means to acquire housing for themselves and for others. Often these officials embezzle materials from the state for the construction of their own private homes. Madame Ekaterina Furtseva, the recently deceased U.S.S.R. Minister of Culture and the only woman ever to serve on the Politburo, was one of the latest, and certainly the most famous, officials accused of such activity. In a scandal somewhat reminiscent of former President Nixon's controversial expenditures on his San Clemente estate, Madame Furtseva was charged with using almost 60,000 rubles in government funds to help defray the cost of a weekend dacha that she was building outside of Moscow.[5] (The sum is equivalent to approximately 40 years' salary for the average Soviet worker.)

While Madame Furtseva is undoubtedly the most well known official accused of housing abuses, she is by no means the only one. In Georgia, for example, the republic party newspaper alleged that among many Georgian officials an "active competition" existed as to who could build the most extravagant home. All of the homes were built with embezzled materials, and many of them, according to *Pravda*, were "truly Tsarist." Further, *Pravda* charged that this occurred with the "direct connivance of the Central Committee of the Communist Party of Georgia and the republic Council of Ministers."[6]

Officials often devise elaborate schemes to acquire new housing or expand the size of existing dwellings. For example, when an invalid was rushed to the hospital, an enterprising member of the local soviet used forged documents to acquire her vacant apartment. Many officials in Tbilisi have erected private dachas on land allocated for collective gardening under the pretext of building garden sheds. The former Georgian Minister of Trade is said to have "committed the grossest violations in the distribution of apartments." This minister exchanged his three-room apartment for one of five rooms, which was created by combining the space that five separate apartments had previously occupied. The minister's son, who lived with his father but also had his own home, joined a housing cooperative after having submitted false documents on the size of his family and having made a down payment of over 12,000 rubles (approximately $16,000), although his monthly salary was only 105 rubles.[7]

Finally, corrupt officials often take advantage of the housing shortage by accepting bribes for the allocation of new apartments. Although many people are legally entitled to a new apartment, they pay bribes to "ensure" that they will get it. Examples abound of officials extorting substantial sums from families in desperate need of new housing. Thus in a seven-year period officials of one housing construction cooperative extorted more than 600,000 rubles ($800,000) in bribes. The cooperative was originally formed to build several housing units, but "through criminal means," it quickly became "a powerful construction organization planning the erection of 16 high-rise housing blocks."[8]

Widespread shortages of consumer goods and agricultural products make many Soviet officials behave in a manner that confirms Proudhon's famous dictum that "property is theft." Officials often "plunder socialist property," which they then manufacture into highly sought after consumer goods, and sell for substantial profits on the black market. Such illegal operations often involve the most unlikely groups. Thus, corrupt officials of the Armenian Choral Society established their own manufacturing complex where, with embezzled materials, they produced over nine million rubles worth of consumer goods, "everything from varnished materials to aluminum pans and women's apparel." Perhaps the most notorious case of this type of corruption occurred in Georgia where a large group of embezzlers appropriated over one million rubles in state property. The group had its own underground manufacturing plants and an extensive retail network where it sold such scarce items as plastic raincoats and beach slippers. Reportedly, the group enjoyed protection from officials in the highest echelons of the Georgian Communist party.[9]

Considerable corruption has also accompanied the arrival of the automobile age in the U.S.S.R. Although the Soviets have ambitious plans for expanding automobile production, prospective buyers must still frequently wait two to three years, and in some cities even ten years, to purchase a new car. Therefore, many buyers hasten the delivery of their cars by bribing officials with amounts at times exceeding the car's purchase price. Corrupt officials also help car owners overcome their many service and maintenance problems. Hence, the acute shortage of spare parts has fostered a "nutrient medium for speculation and all sorts of machinations and stealing" whereby car owners can acquire desperately needed items. The difficulty in purchasing gasoline (Moscow in 1971 had over 250,000 privately owned automobiles, but only 12 service stations) has led to the enormous theft of state-owned fuel for sale on the black market. An *Izvestiia* article recently indicated that in 1972–73 more than one-third of Soviet motorists were driving on state-owned gasoline, and a Western source estimates the annual amount of this illegally acquired fuel at 150 million gallons worth approximately 60 million rubles.[10]

Illegal trade in agricultural products is also a profitable undertaking for many officials. Again, it is in Georgia, a republic which grows many fruits and vegetables not ordinarily obtainable in much of the Soviet Union, that such practices are particularly prevalent. There, many officials steal fruits and vegetables from canneries, load the produce onto illegally obtained trucks, bribe militiamen to permit the trucks to leave the republic, and sell their valuable cargo in the markets of Moscow and Leningrad. Commenting upon these practices, one article noted that "the ancient legend of the quest for the Golden Fleece has been given new meaning in the Soviet Union. Today's argonauts are truck drivers and the Golden Fleece has become the golden fruit of Georgia—tangerines, persimmons, and pears.[11]

Illegality in higher educational institutions (VUZy) provides a final example of corruption for personal gain. Competition is fierce for admission to such institutions, because official policy restricts enrollment to approximately 20 percent of high school graduates, almost all of whom wish to pursue higher education. Hence, many parents attempt to enhance their children's admission prospects by pressuring VUZ administrators through illegal means. Admission officers at a Moscow VUZ explained that they had to admit an otherwise unqualified applicant, because "his father will fix us up with plots of land on the Black Sea Coast." Professors at another institution suddenly acquired Moskvich automobiles when they admitted the daughter of a prominent official. Many press accounts seem particularly concerned with such illegalities. Their result is that the sons and daughters of proletarians and peasants are often substantially underrepresented among university students, since important party and government officials usually have far more influence with admission officers than do ordinary workers. This circumstance is particularly dangerous for a regime that claims to be the "vanguard of the proletariat" and the true representative of the interests of the toiling masses.[12]

Corruption for Bureaucratic Gain

Corruption for bureaucratic gain, as noted, is designed to increase organizational effectiveness to the benefit of the organization's employees. Such corruption especially manifests itself in Soviet production units in two ways: (1) use of illegal influence; (2) false reporting of enterprise data.

To understand this corruption, one must first appreciate the milieu in which production personnel function. First, they often confront great uncertainties not only because plan targets are sometimes changed during the plan period, but especially because of the frequently erratic flow of supplies to the enterprise. Second, these officials are under heavy pressure to increase enterprise production and efficiency. Soviet planners usually apply the "ratchet principle" in formulating plan targets; that is, new targets must always be raised above previous performance levels. While this tends to be a universal planning principle, the elite's emphasis on economic growth may make its impact especially felt on Soviet production personnel. Finally, planners often employ quantitative criteria (e.g., the number of units produced) to evaluate an enterprise's success. Thus, enterprise officials may be able to simulate plan fulfillment simply through the manipulation of production data.

Production personnel respond to such problems as the erratic flow of supplies through the use of *blat* and *tolkachi*. *Blat* is the use of personal influence to obtain certain favors to which production units are not legally entitled. While *blat* may be based on personal acquaintance, it also frequently involves a *quid pro quo* difficult to distinguish from bribery. Thus, state farms supplied the head of the secretariat of the U.S.S.R. Ministry of Agriculture with a house, free food, and a television in exchange for needed equipment. As a *Pravda* article explained, "the principle 'I give to you and you give to me' (and all at the state's expense) operated without a hitch."[13] Joseph Berliner, in his classic study of Soviet managerial behavior, found *blat* pervasive throughout the Soviet economic system. As one of his informants commented:

> There is *blat* everywhere. There is leather *blat*, shoe *blat*, etc. People with different kinds of *blat* get together. Everybody who has some power over goods has a supplementary income based upon *blat*.[14]

The premier practitioner of *blat* is the *tolkach*. He is the plant's representative who travels the country searching for needed supplies or unsnarling bureaucratic bottlenecks. Some officials are so proficient at the art that they become "professional" *tolkachi* and simultaneously represent several firms. Since the continuation of plant production often depends on the success of the *tolkach*, it is not surprising that he may resort to illegal inducements to accomplish his mission. As one enterprise manager exhorted his *tolkach* before sending him out for needed supplies: "Keep your eyes open, don't be caught napping, act according to the situation. If you have to offer someone a bottle don't be shy. We will cover all expenses. But I warn you: don't come back empty-handed."[15] The consequence of so many *tolkachi* is that enterprises producing commodities widely needed by other plants become inundated with them. At such locations, the *tolkachi* even maintain fulltime offices and staffs.

Ideally, the Soviet planning system should function without *blat* and *tolkachi*. In effect, their existence testifies to imperfections in the planning process. As such, they may perform important functions (e.g., cutting red tape) not performed by the formal system. Higher authorities appear ambivalent toward such illegality. They seem to recognize that these informal mechanisms may be useful, and they may therefore grudgingly tolerate their existence. Yet *blat* and *tolkachi* may also complicate the tasks of higher authorities, because when they operate successfully they can impede the realization of elite objectives. This may occur, for example, when a *tolkach* diverts supplies from a high priority plant to one of lower priority. In fact, this often happens, because the latter, discriminated against in the allocation of supplies, equipment, and other necessities, is more likely to need recourse to these measures than the former.

Soviet production personnel have a number of incentives to falsify enterprise performance data.[16] First, this may provide a hedge against unforeseen developments that endanger plan fulfillment. For example, higher authorities may unexpectedly order an enterprise manager to lend some of his personnel to a nearby farm to assist it in gathering in the harvest; if the manager has had the foresight to overstate his manpower requirements, this request will not preclude the plant from fulfilling the plan. The enterprise manager might also overstate the plant's requirements for various raw materials. In this way, the plant accumulates a stockpile that its *tolkach* can use in trade with other enterprises (which have stockpiles of other goods) when supply shortages suddenly develop.

Second, the enterprise manager has an incentive to understate the plant's true production capacity. Although he wants higher authorities to accept his estimate of the enterprise's capacity and thereby present him with a plan that he can easily fulfill, he will be careful not to overfulfill the plan so much that the succeeding plans contain targets that actually are difficult to achieve.

Third, since plan fulfillment is the road to bonuses, premiums, and promotions, and failure to fulfill the plan has numerous unpleasant consequences, managers may simply falsify enterprise performance data when such performance falls below planned levels.

The foregoing analysis has examined the various types of corruption in the Soviet Union. Although the absence of quantitative data makes it impossible to specify their precise dimensions, they are undoubtedly extensive. Judging from published reports, one might conclude that corruption for personal gain is far more prevalent than corruption for bureaucratic gain in the Soviet Union. Yet the relatively smaller number of media reports devoted to the latter may simply reflect the regime's appreciation that it often performs important systematic functions, and therefore should not be as vigorously exposed as the former.

Opportunities and Incentives for Corruption

A public official must have both opportunity and incentive to engage in corruption; the absence of either makes corruption impossible. Soviet society creates conditions whereby both of these conditions frequently exist.

Thus, the Communist party's reliance on the state as the principal instrument of societal change has enormously increased the scope of governmental activity in the U.S.S.R. and concomitantly the opportunities for corruption. Since corruption entails deviant behavior by public officials, the opportunities for corruption (although not necessarily its extent) are greater in a system where the state is the primary agent for employment, production, and regulation than where it is not. The Soviet pattern follows that found in many developing nations. As James Scott observes:

> Foremost among the structural factors that encourage corruption in new states is the tremendous relative importance of government in these nations as a source of goods, services, and employment. An appreciation of the pivotal role of the public sector in the less developed nations contrasts with the pattern in the United States and is essential to an account of corruption.[17]

It is precisely because the state is the dispenser of such sought-after goods and services as the allocation of housing or admittance to higher educational institutions that Soviet officials have the opportunity to engage in numerous illegalities involved with their dispensation; such opportunities would not exist in a system where private entrepreneurs performed these tasks.

Public officials have great incentives to seize these opportunities. First, they possess a strong financial incentive to meet through illegal means the many consumer needs of the Soviet people. The regime's traditional stress on the priority of the military and heavy industrial sectors has left comparatively few resources for the production of substantial quantities of high-quality consumer goods.[18] Hence, there exist considerable shortages of these goods from frying pans to passenger cars. Further, the Soviet consumer, now provided at least with life's necessities, increasingly demands higher quality and more attractive goods, a demand that partly accounts for the phenomenon of substantial inventories of unsold goods in great demand.[19]

These circumstances provide a propitious setting for the widespread black market activities of Soviet officials. As one Western observer commented, "It is safe to suggest that virtually everyone who holds a managerial position in the Soviet retail trade network breaks the law almost daily."[20] In fact, some officials even auction off jobs to the highest bidder, because the positions offer such rich financial opportunities. For instance, the head of a wholesale consumer goods trust in Tashkent in Soviet central Asia customarily started the bidding for the position of warehouse chief at 5,000 rubles (approximately $6,500). The official forced the winning bidder to swear on a wafer of bread that he would never betray his benefactor and that he would share with him half of the proceeds from his illegal activities. Elaborating, *Pravda* explained that "by Moslem custom an oath taken on a wafer of bread is as sacred as an oath sworn on the Koran."[21]

The strong financial incentive of officials to engage in black market activities is unlikely to diminish in the foreseeable future, despite the leadership's recent concern to raise consumer welfare. Indeed, the leadership set this as the "main task" of the Ninth Five Year Plan (1971–75), and scheduled for the first time in a five year plan a faster rate of growth for industrially produced consumer goods than for producer goods. Further, the Politburo reportedly twice rejected drafts of the Tenth Five Year Plan (1976–80) because they called for too little growth in the consumer sector, and party leader Brezhnev at the recently completed party congress harshly attacked those who have been unable "to surmount completely the attitude [that] the production of consumer goods [is] something secondary and ancillary."[22] Yet the leadership's plans are encountering considerable difficulties. Not only were the consumer targets of the Ninth Five Year Plan not met, but its successor, despite the leadership's intervention, again calls for a faster rate of growth for producer than consumer goods.

Second, the plethora of administrative regulations in the highly centralized Soviet system provides an incentive for corruption. Some ministries have issued as many as 20,000 instructions for their employees, and annually they promulgate hundreds of orders and other normative acts. Therefore, lower level administrators are continually confronted with a bewildering variety of regulations that, if faithfully adhered to, would make it impossible for them to function efficiently. One commentary reported that many officials argue "it is impossible to lead according to legal norms; a good manager must inevitably go around the law."[23]

Third, many groups and individuals with little input into policy formulation may engage in corruption to frustrate the implementation of elite specified policies contrary to their interests. This is certainly the case with the manager of a low priority plant who, when confronted with high plan targets and a shortage of resources to fulfill them, uses various illegalities to acquire the needed supplies. In this sense, corruption acts as an informal means for partially redistributing power in the system so that low priority groups and individuals have a better chance of competing with more powerful actors for society's goods and services.[24]

A fourth incentive is that many officials attach no moral stigma to acts the regime considers corrupt. This circumstance simultaneously reflects contradictions in and a rejection of official values. Thus, the party elite's stress on rapid economic growth conflicts with its emphasis on legality, because the former has fostered an attitude among many production personnel that almost any illegalities committed for plan fulfillment are justified. A *Pravda* commentary complained, for example, that many "presumptious economic managers seem to feel that a triumphant plan report makes fraud, bribery, and other acts permissible."[25]

This circumstance also represents a serious breakdown in socialization. Hence, the official claim that bribery and graft are alien to socialist man conflicts with the prevailing popular attitude that there is nothing wrong with officials who practice what Russians commonly call *vzyatka* (literally "the take," a bribe or graft).[26] Further, the regime has largely failed to inculcate within people a "communist attitude toward property" that treats property as belonging to the entire Soviet people. As a convicted embezzler commented:

> You know it's like it [public property] doesn't belong to anybody. If you don't latch onto it, then nobody gets it. It'll fall between the cracks somewhere at the bottom of the government trough.[27]

Finally, for many officials the potential benefits of corruption far outweigh the possible costs because of the relatively small chance of detection and severe punishment. The following section elaborates upon this.

The preceding analysis indicates that, despite official claims, the opportunities and incentives for corruption in the U.S.S.R. are similar to those in many non-socialist states. Indeed, an extensive state sector, excess demand for government goods and services, a plethora of administrative regulations, politically weak groups seeking to influence public policy, a sharp divergence between public and private conceptions of illegal official behavior, and the unlikelihood of harsh punishment impel many officials, regardless of the political system, to seek private gain at public expense. Naturally, the precise mix of these factors varies by country, and determines the extent of corruption within a given polity.

Combatting Corruption

Combatting corruption entails changing the opportunities and/or incentives that foster it. The Soviets have attempted this primarily through coercive measures that seek to raise the cost of corrupt behavior by increasing the certainty and severity of punishment. They have particularly combatted corruption for personal gain and certain forms of corruption for bureaucratic gain, especially falsification of enterprise data. They have not placed nearly the same stress on combatting such corruption as *blat* and the illegal activities of *tolkachi*.[28] This may reflect elite perceptions that these forms of corruption often perform vital systemic functions.

Legal sanctions and decrees predominate among the coercive measures. The Party Central Committee, the U.S.S.R. Council of Ministers, and the U.S.S.R. Supreme Court have all issued anticorruption resolutions. In particular, the Party Central Committee in 1972 issued a sharply worded resolution condemning corruption and inefficiency in the Tbilisi party organization of the Georgian communist party. The resolution clearly was aimed not only at Tbilisi but at the entire Georgian party as well. In addition, the Soviets have prescribed harsh punishments for corruption. Persons convicted of repeated and/or serious acts of bribery or embezzlement are subject to prison terms of eight to fifteen years and even to the death penalty in certain circumstances. Soviet courts on occasion have invoked these penalties, including sentencing several bribe-takers to death.[29] One source reports that from mid-1970 to mid-1975 the authorities executed eighteen persons for economic crimes.[30] Interestingly, legal regulations do not subject *tolkachi* engaging in illegal procurement activities to the death penalty, and a review of the Soviet press since 1961 does not reveal any *tolkachi* executed for these activities.[31]

Finally, the regime has purged many corrupt officials from their posts, and the communist party has expelled a number of them from its ranks as well. The most extensive purge has occurred in Georgia, where approximately 25,000 officials, including several members and candidates of the central committee of the Georgian communist party, the ministers of justice and trade, the deputy minister of internal affairs, and the secretary of the Tbilisi party organization were removed from office in the last several years for abuse of official positions.[32]

The regime has also launched an intensive propaganda campaign among the public to gain popular adherence to the law. Hopefully, this will reduce corruption, because public officials will then voluntarily adhere to a code of behavior that they perceive as legitimate. In recent years, surprisingly frank media accounts have detailed the corrupt acts of public officials, condemning their behavior as un-Leninist and alien to socialist society. The arts have also played a role in this effort. For example, the Georgian ministry of culture has been instructed to include plays sharply criticizing bribe takers and other law breakers in theater repertoires.[33]

The propaganda campaign has complemented the regime's coercive measures. Thus when a district court in Azerbaidzhan sentenced a group of embezzlers to death, the authorities broadcast the sentence live over the district radio network. Further, media reports of corruption usually attempt to demonstrate that crime does not pay by specifying the severe punishments meted out to corrupt officials.[34]

There is ample evidence that the regime is concerned with the anti-corruption campaign's effectiveness. Higher authorities have expressed dissatisfaction especially with the legal system. For example, an *Izvestiia* article pointed out that in 1971 there were no court cases in the republics of Lithuania, Armenia, and Estonia involving officials accused of falsification of enterprise data: "Can it be that there was no padding here?" the article asked, "Alas, the basis for such an assertion is dubious."[35]

The courts are also often criticized for not dealing harshly enough with corrupt officials. Thus, almost 50 percent of the officials convicted of embezzlement under aggravating circumstances receive sentences that do not even include deprivation of freedom, although the law provides far harsher penalties for these acts.[36] An article in *Zaria Vostoka* was blunt in its criticism of courts in the Georgian republic:

> They [the courts] do not wage a decisive battle against embezzlement . . . bribery, and other socially dangerous heinous crimes, do not punish bribe takers, plunderers of the peoples' property harshly enough, do not take effective measures to compensate fully for the material loss to the government.[37]

Finally, the courts and the procuracy, the agency charged with carrying out the preliminary investigation and the prosecution of alleged illegalities, often content themselves with punishing only officials directly caught in some corrupt act, and frequently fail to expose the officials who have actually organized the activity. This usually arises when powerful Communist party members are involved in illegalities, because the subordination of the legal agencies to the party often makes them reluctant to challenge these officials.[38]

The purge has also proved ineffective, because many dismissed officials manage to be reappointed to important positions where they again engage in corruption. A recent *Pravda* article charged that "taking people . . . who have been dismissed from their posts and promoting them to responsible positions has become a phenomenon . . . which is by no means exceptional," while another article complained that this circumstance happens with "astounding frequency."[39] This occurs because corruption often enters the cadre selection process itself. For Georgia, it is said, "corruption, graft, bribery, and lack of principle" frequently characterize personnel policy. It has even become possible to "order" the post of head of a ministry.[40]

Why have the Soviets encountered these difficulties? Ideally, the regime's reliance on legal sanctions should deter others from emulating corrupt officials by severely punishing them. However, deterrence is only as effective as the system's ability to expose these officials and bring them to justice, and this has proved difficult.

One might normally expect the Soviet system to prove reasonably adept at exposing corruption, because of the party's substantial coercive apparatus and its elaborate system of monitoring the behavior of public officials. However, Soviet officials charged with exposing corruption frequently collaborate in perpetrating and/or concealing it. The Soviets recognize this circumstance and give it such labels as "krugovaia poruka" (mutual involvement) or "semeistvennost" (familyness).

Officials have a number of incentives to collude in the concealment of corruption. First, lower level officials are responsible for ensuring that production units meet plan targets and observe legal norms. The tasks, however, are frequently incompatible, because production units must often resort to corrupt practices to fulfill the plan. Hence, lower party organs, as Jerry Hough notes, frequently seek to achieve plan fulfillment "by compelling administrators to break the law."[41] In effect, they usually assume that higher authorities are far more concerned about plan fulfillment than about adherence to legality.

Second, paradoxical as it seems, officials may not pursue corruption too vigorously because higher authorities might interpret this as laxity in permitting the corruption initially to occur. This is especially true when the party organization appoints an official to a post who then becomes corrupt. If the party organization reveals the abuses, it may be criticized for its cadre selection policy. The party organization is far more likely to cover up the corruption and thereby avoid, in the words of the Georgian First Party Secretary, "washing its dirty linen in public."[42]

Finally, officials often accept bribes in return for their silence or are themselves directly involved in the corrupt activity. The Soviet press contains many accounts of such circumstances. Thus, as Keith Bush, in another context, once commented, in the Soviet system often "the poacher is appointed gamekeeper."[43]

The Soviet political elite is undoubtedly concerned about the extent of corruption in the U.S.S.R. Sharply worded anti-corruption resolutions and decrees testify to its apprehension. Again, the absence of quantitative data makes it difficult to measure the effectiveness of these efforts. Yet, the numerous press accounts detailing their shortcomings strongly suggest that they have fallen short of elite expectations. Ultimately the increasing affluence and greater availability of consumer goods in Soviet society may be among its most effective weapons against corruption by reducing the financial incentive to engage in it. The elite has exhibited growing concern for consumer welfare, but its plans have not yet been sufficiently realized to make corruption less profitable.

Conclusion

Commenting upon the seeming universality of political corruption, the British satirist Jonathan Swift once remarked that "I will venture all I am worth that there is not one human creature in power who will not be modest enough to admit that he proceeds wholly upon a principle of corruption." While Swift's comment surely exaggerates, corruption seems an integral component of most political systems. Despite ideological claims to the contrary, the U.S.S.R. has not been spared from political corruption. Indeed, sufficient evidence exists to support the observation of one Western commentator that "corruption may be as integral to Soviet life as vodka and kasha."[44]

It is difficult to assess corruption's overall impact on the Soviet system. Undeniably, corruption has made important contributions to its efficient functioning. Thus, many Soviet enterprises could not meet production targets unless they utilized *blat* or the services of *tolkachi*. Yet the political elite may well regard these actions as inimical to its own interests, because the unauthorized transfer of goods and services to low priority groups and individuals complicates elite efforts to impose its priorities on society.

The Soviets in fact realize that some types of corruption may be functional while others may not, for they have often extended a *de facto* toleration to the former while combatting the latter. The following quotation clearly indicates the regime's assessment that corruption may be dysfunctional.

> Not only are bribes detrimental to society in a material sense, but they inflict great moral damage as well. In selling their soul for a ruble and letting their self-respect go at a discount, some people grow accustomed to living beyond their means and sneering at the generally accepted rules and standards of life. Bribery leads to drunkenness, depravity, personal corruption; it provides opportunities for the perpetration of other crimes. The struggle against the briber and the extortionist is the concern of all society.[45]

Finally, the regime's intensive anti-corruption campaign reflects the deep concern of Soviet political leaders about the prevalence of corruption. Resolutions condemning corruption, stiff punishments for corrupt officials, and a propaganda campaign to gain acceptance of the regime's view of proper public behavior have all been utilized in the fight against corruption. However, these efforts have encountered serious difficulties. Indeed, the U.S.S.R.'s experience appears to confirm the observation of Thomas Jefferson that "the time to guard against corruption . . . is before it shall have gotten hold of us. It is better to keep the wolf out of the fold than to trust to drawing his teeth and talons after he shall have entered."

Notes

1. For general treatments of political corruption see Samuel Huntington, *Political Order in Changing Societies* (New Haven: Yale University Press, 1968), pp. 59–71; James Scott, *Comparative Political Corruption* (Englewood Cliffs: Prentice Hall, 1972).

2. For definitions of corruption that closely parallel the one used here see Huntington, *Political Order,* 59, and Joseph Nye, "Corruption and Political Development: A Cost-Benefit Analysis," *American Political Science Review,* 61 (June 1967), 419.

3. See, for example, David Bayley, "The Effects of Corruption in a Developing Country," *Western Political Quarterly,* 19 (December 1966), 719–32; Nye, "Corruption," pp. 417–27. For a recent analysis that examines the validity of this argument see Gabriel Bendor, "Corruption, Institutionalization, and Political Development: The Revisionist Theses Revisited," *Comparative Political Studies,* 7 (April 1974), 63–83.

4. *Izvestiia,* June 11, 1974; ibid., July 10, 1970; *Zaria Vostoka,* June 18, 1972. *Washington Post,* May 23, 1975, A24, cites the data of the Soviet criminologist.

5. *Washington Post,* June 19, 1974.

6. *Pravda,* November 13, 1973.

7. *Bakinskii Rabochii,* June 26, 1973; *Pravda,* October 19, 1972; *Zaria Vostoka,* June 26, 1973.

8. *Pravda,* June 16, 1972; *Zaria Vostoka,* February 22, 1974.

9. *Izvestiia,* August 21, 1973; *Washington Post,* March 29, 1973.

10. *Pravda,* November 13, 1972; *Izvestiia,*November 20, 1973; ibid., January 1, 1975; Hedrick Smith, *The Russians* (New York: Quadrangle Books, 1976), pp. 82–83. Radio Liberty is the Western source for the amount of illegally acquired fuel.

11. *Pravda,* January 10, 1974.

12. *Izvestiia,* September 2, 1969; *Bakinskii Rabochii,* December 12, 1973.

13. *Pravda,* August 16, 1972.

14. Joseph Berliner, *Factory and Manager in the USSR* (Cambridge: Harvard University Press, 1957), pp. 191–92.

15. *Pravda,* February 25, 1972.

16. For a discussion of these incentives see *Izvestiia,* June 11, 1974.

17. Scott, *Comparative Political Corruption,* p. 12.

18. Several figures illustrate the traditional higher priority of the military and heavy industrial sectors. According to Central Intelligence Agency estimates, the Soviet Union now spends about 35 percent more on defense than does the United States, even though its GNP is approximately 60 percent of ours. *New York Times,* February 23, 1976. Of the funds devoted to industrial investment, the consumer goods sector has usually received relatively little. Hence, the U.S.S.R. Ministry of Food and Light Industry, the primary producer of consumer perishables for years, received only about 10 percent of total annual industrial investment. Finally, heavy machinery plants produce the majority of consumer durables as secondary production in addition to their primary products. On the low priority of consumer goods production see Gertrude Schroeder, "Consumer Problems and Prospects," *Problems of Communism,* 22 (March–April 1973), 10–24.

19. In 1970 inventories in retail trade were 2.2 billion rubles above plan. Schroeder, "Consumer Problems," p. 12.

20. Dimitri Simes, "The Soviet Parallel Market," *Survey,* 21 (Summer 1975), p. 49.

21. *Pravda,* February 18, 1972.

22. *New York Times,* March 3, 1976.
23. *Izvestiia,* January 15, 1975.
24. For a discussion of corruption as a form of power see Scott, *Comparative Political Corruption,* pp. 21–35.
25. *Pravda,* November 16, 1971.
26. For an interesting discussion that in part examines popular attitudes toward corruption see Smith, *The Russians,* pp. 81–101.
27. *Komsomolskaia Pravda,* December 16, 1973.
28. Of course, this does not mean that the regime has never severely punished officials guilty of such corruption. For examples see *Izvestiia,* March 24, 1973.
29. The resolutions appear in *Sovetskaia Iustitsiia,* No. 11, July 1973, and *Pravda,* March 1, 1972. The texts of the decrees providing the penalties for corruption are in *Izvestiia,* May 7, 1961, and *Vedomosti Verkhovnovo Soveta SSSR,* February 21, 1962, pp. 221, 222. *Bakinskii Rabochii,* February 13, 1974, provides several examples of harsh penalties meted out to corrupt officials.
30. Cited in the *Washington Post,* May 23, 1975, A24.
31. Steven Staats, "Corruption in the Soviet System," *Problems of Communism,* 21 (January–February 1972), 43.
32. Peter Reddaway, "The Georgian Orthodox Church: Corruption and Renewal," *Religion in Communist Lands,* 3 (July–October 1975), 15.
33. *Zaria Vostoka,* December 8, 1970.
34. *Vyshka,* January 15, 1974.
35. *Izvestiia,* February 18, 1973.
36. *Sovetskaia Iustitsiia,* No. 11, July 1973.
37. *Zaria Vostoka,* December 5, 1970.
38. Pravda, June 16, 1973.
39. Ibid., August 16, 1972.
40. *Zaria Vostoka,* July 31, 1973.
41. Jerry Hough, *The Soviet Prefects: The Local Party Organs in Industrial Decision Making* (Cambridge: Harvard University Press, 1969), p. 253.
42. *Partiinaia Zhizn,* No. 8, April 1973.
43. Keith Bush, "Environmental Problems in the USSR," *Problems of Communism,* 21 (July–August 1972), 28.
44. Staats, "Corruption," p. 47.
45. *Pravda,* January 29, 1971.

28

Soviet Political Culture and Modes of Covert Influence

Wayne DiFranceisco
and Zvi Gitelman

. . . If Soviet political relationships are as we shall describe them, then conventional notions of Soviet political culture need to be revised. Neither the "parochial-subject-participant" trichotomy developed by Almond and Verba (1963), nor the idea of a "subject-participatory" (Barghoorn, 1972, p. 25) political culture, where structures are designed for participation but the operative culture seems to treat the citizen as a subject, apply accurately to the Soviet case. This is not a subject political culture marginally affected by participatory institutions because there is a meaningful form of participation, but it takes place either outside the nominally participatory institutions because there is a meaningful form of participation, but it takes place either outside the nominally participatory institutions or within those institutions but in nonprescribed ways. But because this participation is limited to affecting political outputs that concern the individual directly, it would be misleading to equate the Soviet kind of political culture with those that are conventionally thought of as largely participant. Moreover, the Russian-Soviet case (like others, especially in the Third World) demonstrates that there is no ineluctable progression from parochial to subject to participant political cultures. The Soviet system, like many others, is syncretic, adapting traditional clientelist modes to what appear to be institutions for democratic participation.

One might expect a radical revolutionary regime not to adapt but to eliminate completely traditional political modes. But as Jowitt (1974) points out, Marxist-Leninist elites are induced by their ideology to

Source: Wayne DiFranceisco and Zvi Gitelman, "Soviet Political Culture and 'Covert Participation' in Policy Implementation," *American Political Science Review,* 78, 3 (1984), 603–21. By permission of the authors and publisher.

select a set of system-building institutions which, ironically, reinforce traditional values and orientations toward politics. Jowitt cites three of these structural components of communist system building and their ramifications for political beliefs at the mass level. The first component, the "dictatorship of the proletariat," with its stress on discipline, coercion, and party control of both public and private sectors of the society, preserves much of the essence of traditional authority relationships—a bifurcation of society into the elite and a mistrusted populace. The second element involves the Leninist-Stalinist "commanding-heights" formula for development and a phenomenon that Jowitt (p. 1175) labels "revolutionary laissez-faire." Under this rubric, the emphasis is on rapid economic progress and mobilization such that the regime focuses on a rather limited set of priority areas, leaving vast segments of the society untransformed. "In return for performance in priority sectors . . . members of society are 'allowed' to manipulate non-priority sectors for their private benefit." This lack of development in nonpriority sectors allows, as we shall see in the Soviet case, for the perpetuation of traditional clientelistic orientations toward officials, i.e., the use of *blat* (pull) or *sviazy* (connections) or even bribery. It is this pattern of interactions with public officials and institutions that we label covert participation.

A third component of Leninist system-building regimes is the elites' production mentality. The leadership believes that political culture change will inevitably follow transformation in social and economic spheres, which in practice means that the party tends to deemphasize cultural issues except where its primary goals of socioeconomic development are affected. Of course, the Soviet Union has long passed the system-building stage, and its intensive and extensive efforts at political socialization have narrowed the gap between political structures and political culture. (Even among our sample of emigres described below, 47 percent acknowledge that they read agitation-propaganda material in the USSR, at least some of the time.)

Our observations on the nature of political participation and its implications for Soviet culture are based on Soviet writings and on our interviews with recent Soviet emigres. These observations lead us to conclude that the way Soviet people relate to the political administrative system is to go through the motions of participation in the nominally democratic process of making decisions, but to put far more serious effort into trying to influence the way decisions are implemented. Thus the view of Soviet political culture as subject or subject-participant is misleading. Soviet political culture is neither a democratic nor a subject one, but an amalgam of traditional, pre-revolutionary modes of citizen-state relations and a superstructure of participatory institutions that superficially resemble those of Western democracies in many respects.

Sample and Method

A group of 1,161 ex-Soviet citizens who left the USSR from 1977 through 1980 were interviewed during 1980–1981 in Israel ($n = 590$), the Federal Republic of Germany ($n = 100$) and the United States ($n = 471$). The sample was drawn as a quota, nonprobability sample, in line with hypotheses that led to a certain distribution of age, sex, education, nationality, and republic of residence. On some variables, such as age and sex, the proportions in the sample approximate those in the Soviet adult population rather closely. On the other hand, nearly half the respondents have had higher education (approximately 40 percent of all Soviet immigrants to Israel and the United States have come with higher education), 38 percent had secondary education, and only 15 percent had grade school education or less. Seventy-seven percent, or 889 people, had been registered as Jews on their internal Soviet passports, 129 as Russians, 98 as Germans, 18 as Ukrainians, and 27 as other nationalities. . . .

Men and women are quite evenly distributed in age and regional categories, but men dominate blue collar and women white collar occupations, despite very similar educational levels. (Among the sample, 48 percent of the men and 46 percent of the women have higher education.) Educational levels are highest among those from the RSFSR, and, from the ethnic groups, among the Russians; 69 percent of the former and 72 percent of the latter have some higher education. The lowest educational levels are found among people from Central Asia (only 18 percent have higher education) and from Moldavia (23 percent). These people were interviewed in Russian or Georgian by native speakers. There were remarkably few refusals to be interviewed, although the average interview lasted between two and three hours. In addition to the standard questionnaire administered to the entire group, nearly 60 in-depth interviews were conducted with people who had been employees of the Soviet government agencies we inquired about, or who seemed to have unusually extensive knowledge about how citizens and government agencies operated in their respective republics.

The Problem of Bias

It cannot be claimed that the results obtained from any emigre sample are generalizable to the population in the Soviet Union, because not only are the emigres demographically different from the population as a whole, but presumably their attitudes and assessments are different as well. Having chosen to leave the USSR, it is reasonable to assume that they were less pleased with the system than those who stayed behind. While accepting the inadmissibility of generalizing easily from the emigre to the original population, the assumption of emigre bias can be exaggerated. . . . Lacking any reliable data on the Soviet population's attitude toward the system, it cannot be assumed that the attitudes of the emigres are significantly more hostile, and in our sample, at least, we see that alienation from the political system was by no means the primary motivation for leaving it. Moreover, as in other emigre studies, our respondents demonstrated considerable support for many Soviet institutions and practices. One can also assume that whatever biases may be present in the sample as a whole, they are distributed fairly uniformly across population subgroups. Therefore, we anticipate that any differences observed across the subgroup strata are similar to those characterizing the same groups within the Soviet population. . . .

In any case, even alienated citizens have no choice but to participate in many ways. They are not able to avoid some of the ritualistic forms of participation, such as voting, attending meetings, joining trade unions and, usually, the Komsomol. Because the state controls so many basic necessities, they must resort to official agencies, if only for the satisfaction of their private needs. The crucial question for us then becomes not whether they participate, but how they do so, and in this there seems no prima facie reason for thinking that they differ substantially from those who did not leave the country. . . .

The data presented in Table 28.1 further illustrate the unique aspects of Soviet political activity and hint at the widespread persistence of clientelism in the political culture. Table 28.1 lists the responses of the emigres to a question about "the best way to influence a Soviet government decision." Despite the inclusion of the word "group" in the question, fewer than 10 percent mentioned forming an interest

Table 28.1
Best Way to Influence a Government Decision ($n = 1,161$)

Connections	Letters	Group	Party	Protest Demonstration	None	NR
35.5	4.5	9.9	5.9	3.4	25.8	15.2

Text of question: If a group of Soviet people were trying to influence some government decision, which way would be most effective?

group as a viable option. The combined frequencies for officially sanctioned methods of interest articulation—"writing letters to officials" and "exerting influence through the Party"—account for only 10.4 percent of the respondents. The modal response is "personal or family connections *(sviazy),*" at 35.5 percent. It seems likely that these individuals interpreted the phrase, "government decision," in terms of its implementation or output aspects—for example, the disposition of an individual case—and not in the much broader sense of policymaking, a conversion function, for which *sviazy* would be inappropriate. These findings fit the proposition stated above, that the Soviet citizen tends to avoid or denigrate cooperative activity and formal channels of interest articulation. Where he does participate he orients himself toward a specific individual or agency in an informal, and often covert, manner.

Politics on the Output Side

Thus far we have discussed two types of participation: ritualistic participation and citizen-initiated contacts with people who hold positions in policymaking institutions. In neither case is there much expectation of input into policymaking, but in the second there is some hope that action will be taken to benefit the individual, just as in the United States a congressman is asked to render constituency service without trying to influence legislation. Soviet citizens are more oriented toward the administrative side of the system. They are "subject competent," but not in the way described by Almond and Verba, that is, trying to get legally prescribed, proper treatment. According to Almond and Verba (1963, p. 162), the competent subject obeys the law, does not help shape it, and "if he is competent, he knows the law, knows what he must do, and what is due him." In the Soviet system, however, the "competent subject" is not content to demand fair play and the universal application of the law, for he does not expect that of the system. Rather he takes matters into his own hands when he is convinced that the routine workings of the system will not automatically confer upon him the benefits he desires. He does this by approaching those who implement policy, not those who make it, and by following traditional ways of handling administrators, adapted to the modern Soviet political system. "Thus a premium is placed on informal adaptive mechanisms . . . that allow for some stability and certainty in response to what is often perceived as an arbitrary and threatening regime." These mechanisms "obstruct the development of a political culture based on overt, public, and cooperative relationships. Instead they reinforce the traditional community and regime political cultures with their stress on covert, personalized, hierarchical relationships involving complicity rather than public agreements" (Jowitt, 1974, p. 1183). It may well be that the Soviet development process has actually reinforced clientelistic cultural patterns. By raising society's overall level of education to facilitate modernization, by focusing on heavy industry to the detriment of the individual's standard of living, and by failing to develop meaningful citizen participation and emotional attachment to the policymaking process, the communist leadership has created a large number of "socialist entrepreneurs" who are highly capable of and heavily predisposed toward working nonpriority public sectors for their own benefit. Our data suggest that Soviet citizens are open to entering into informal or even illegal interactions with officials. For example, we find that three-quarters of our respondents believe that at least half of the Soviet officials "derive material benefit from citizens who approach them for help," and 60 percent believe that a bribe could persuade a policeman to overlook a minor traffic violation. Bribery is not a last resort or an activity limited to society's marginal elements, but seems to be accepted by a large number of people as a common way of handling difficult situations. We posed an open-ended question to our respondents: "If a government official clearly lied to you or refused to give what you had coming to you, what would be the best way of making him tell the truth or giving you what was due you?" The modal response was to "offer him a gift," with 46 percent of the total sample mentioning this, and only 31 percent—the next largest group—suggesting an appeal to the official's superior. A second open question was, "What is the main precondition for success in life in the USSR?" Two responses were coded, with 42 percent and 64 percent mentioning it either first or second. Clearly, informal, and even illegal, means are those that immediately suggest themselves to Soviet people who have to interact with the state bureaucracy.

Working the Output Side

How Soviet citizens attempt to influence actively the implementation of policy seems to vary according to two factors: their own education and the particular agency involved. Regional differences are not as great as might be supposed. Sex and age are not important in differentiating styles of confronting and dealing with the bureaucracy. The influence of education is seen in responses to the question, "Which type of government official would you prefer—the one who treats everyone equally regardless of circumstances or the one who treats each case individually, taking account of its special characteristics?"

The preference of the most educated people for a case-by-case differentiation is striking. As an engineer from Kharkov expressed it, "Taking each case on its own merits means that the opportunity to use *blat* (pull) or *znakomstvo* (connections) is present, and that's the only way to survive in the USSR. In the United States, on the other hand, I prefer that state employees treat everyone the same." In the country of immigration, in other words, the engineer felt disadvantaged vis-à-vis the rest of the population and no longer had confidence in his ability to swing things his way in bureaucratic encounters. But in the Soviet Union educated people may think their education gives them status greater than that conferred on the bureaucrat by his position. It also gives them *savoir faire*, which they can use to their advantage. Less-educated people have no such illusions. They defer to the status conferred on the official by his position, making no judgments about the person. The more educated look at the individual and figure they can handle him because they are better educated; the less educated look at the position and are not prepared to challenge it.

However, this does not mean that they will meekly accept whatever fate, speaking through the bureaucrat, will ordain. Many people, irrespective of their educational background, try to influence the implementation of policy and the decisions of administrators, although the more educated are more likely to take an activist posture even in rigid bureaucracies such as the armed forces.

But the tactics of the more and less educated differ. Less-educated people are more inclined to bribery, whereas more-educated ones will use personal connections to extract what they want from a bureaucracy. Obviously, the highly educated are more likely to know people in high places, how to get to them, and how to approach them. This tactical difference has probably been the pattern in Russia and elsewhere for centuries; the best that the peasant could do to gain the favor of the all-mighty official was to bring him a chicken or some moonshine, whereas the educated and the wealthy were more likely to mix socially with the official and, probably, his superiors.

It is also quite clear that different agencies evoke different kinds of behavior on the part of the clients, probably not because of differences in the structure and personnel of the agencies so much as differences in the availability and nature of the services they provide, and in the importance they have been assigned by the regime.

In this study we found three categories of administrative agencies.

Table 28.2
Bureaucratic Style Preferred by Education ($n = 1,113$)

	Grade School %	Secondary %	Higher %
Equal treatment	21.9	14.8	5.9
Sometimes equal, sometimes differentiated	30.9	24.7	17.4
Differentiated	36.5	55.7	73.8
Don't know, no answer	10.7	4.8	3.0

The first category includes bureaucracies toward which citizen initiative is either unnecessary, because the agency will most likely produce the desired output without special efforts by the client, or it is useless, because the agency will not be responsive to such efforts. The great majority of respondents who had personal experience with pension agencies *(gorsobes, raisobes)* did not find it necessary to undertake any extraordinary initiatives in order to receive their pensions (although some "improved" their pensions by various means). Asked what a person should do if he did not receive a pension to which he was entitled, more than half the respondents said that a letter to a higher authority should suffice. Another 20 percent recommended that the person simply wait patiently, for he would surely get the pension. There was also widespread agreement that in the armed forces it would be useless to try to change one's assignment and to get around orders.

Housing falls into a second category. Although some accept the routine workings of the official housing agencies, others try to influence those workings by illegal means, and still others choose to ignore the official agencies and opt for private, legal solutions to their housing problems.

The third category of agency includes admissions committees in higher educational institutions, hiring departments of enterprises, and *raspredelenie* commissions, whose job it is to assign higher education graduates to their first post. In these institutions, it is widely felt, the routine workings of the system were highly unlikely to produce the desired result without a special "push" by the citizen which might involve semilegal or illegal measures. Thus, two-thirds of the respondents suggested bribery or using connections *(sviazy)* to avoid an undesirable job assignment, and three-quarters suggested the same tactics for gaining admission to a university or institute of higher education.

We arrived at this categorization partially on the basis of a battery of five open-ended questions consisting of hypothetical situations that asked what a (third) person could do in response to a negative decision by each of five Soviet institutions. Paraphrased versions of these questions are listed below.

Soviet Army: How could a Soviet Army officer in 1980, stationed in a good staff position in Leningrad, avoid being transferred to a unit headed for Afghanistan?

Pensions: What should a person do if he is entitled to a pension, has not received it, and is told by officials to "be patient"?[1]

Raspredelenie (assignment commission): What should a person do if he is assigned to work in a remote area after graduating from an institution of higher education?

University Admissions Committee: What should a woman do who wants to get her mediocre son into the mathematics department of a university?

Zhilotdel (local housing authority): What should a person do to get a better apartment, if the one he has is, by legal standards, large enough?

We observed that few respondents felt it advisable to resort to manipulative tactics in dealing with the army, but a large proportion suggested covert measures in dealing with job assignments, university admissions, and housing. Moreover, approximately 80 percent of the respondents were in the "active" range of the three variables, suggesting that regime control of these sectors is relatively lax and more willing to tolerate flexibility in them. (As we shall see, there are legal alternatives for those who fail to obtain satisfactory housing, which explains the relatively low proportion of responses in the covert range regarding housing.)

The final portion of our data analysis illustrates the combined impact

Table 28.3
Actions Suggested by Respondents (%) ($n = 1,161$)

	Bribery	Connections[a]	Legal or Semi-Legal	Other	Nothing/ Passive[b]
Soviet army	2.9	11.1	10.2[c]	3.6	72.2
Raspredelenie	19.6	37.6	10.5[d]	11.6	20.6
University admissions committee	29.4	32.7	13.8[e]	3.5	20.6
Housing authority (zhilotdel)	18.4	14.1	39.5[f]	5.3	22.7

[a]Includes both *protektsiia* (patronage) and *sviazy* (connections).
[b]Those who responded that one could do nothing, or who could not think of anything to do.
[c]"Threaten to resign from the army" or "plead illness or family problems."
[d]"Marry someone with the right of residence in one's home town" or "find a medical excuse."
[e]"Appeal to the committee," "apply to a different school," or "engage a private tutor."
[f]"Enter a cooperative," "exchange apartments with someone," or "buy a private apartment."

of structure and education on the preferred strategy of the respondents. The findings in Table 28.4 follow fairly closely from our predictions. First, the higher one's education, the greater his or her sense of competence and resulting activity vis-à-vis Soviet allocative structures. This can be discerned from a glance at the column headed "passive": in every administrative setting there is a uniform decline in passivity with increasing levels of education. However, the results clearly indicate that the more powerful and strategically located is the institution, the less is the perceived opportunity to influence that institution by any means, regardless of one's social status. This is indicated by the contrast between the frequencies for the military and those for the other bureaucratic agencies.

There is ample evidence to confirm our hypothesis that the modern Soviet system has tended to reinforce traditional clientelistic orientations toward the structures of government. Soviet citizens defer to the status or power of an official and his agency as much for pragmatic as for normative reasons. Where a bureaucratic encounter can be exploited for private gain, the "competent" Soviet citizen, particularly if he or she is highly skilled and educated, will attempt to do so. There appears to be less confidence in legal rules and procedures as a means of extracting services from the state, as demonstrated by the fact that for every institution in Table 28.4 except the housing authority, to

Table 28.4
Actions suggested by Respondents, by Education (%) ($n = 1,161$)

	Bribery	Connections	Legal/ Semi-Legal	Other	Nothing/ Passive
Soviet army					
Primary or less	2.2	6.7	5.1	2.2	83.7
Secondary	3.7	8.2	8.2	3.9	76.0
Some college	2.2	14.9	13.4	3.9	65.3
Raspredelenie					
Primary or less	22.5	18.5	8.4	6.2	44.4
Secondary	22.1	37.7	9.6	8.2	22.4
Some college	16.7	43.9	11.9	16.1	11.4
College admissions					
Primary or less	34.8	15.7	6.2	4.5	38.8
Secondary	32.2	33.6	11.0	3.2	20.1
Some college	25.3	37.6	18.5	3.5	15.0
Housing agency					
Primary or less	19.7	9.6	34.3	7.3	29.2
Secondary	18.5	11.6	41.6	5.9	22.4
Some college	18.0	17.6	39.6	4.0	20.7

which legal alternatives exist, the proportions of respondents suggesting covert tactics (bribes and connections) are higher than any other type of approach. It should be also pointed out that all of the legal avenues suggested in regard to housing were private (enter a cooperative or exchange apartments) rather than public solutions.

The data also confirm that, although covert forms of participation appeal to all social classes in the Soviet Union, different educational groups have different preferences for strategies of influence. Bribery is (of necessity) the chosen method of the less educated, whereas *blat* is the favored instrument of the intelligentsia. In fact, for every institution, the college-educated typically outdistanced the low-status respondents in all spheres of specified activity *except bribery*. This finding confirms our hypothesis about the higher level of skills and resources available to upper-status individuals and their more expansive repertoires of tactics for pulling the right strings in their dealings with the bureaucracy.

One must exercise caution in interpreting these data, since some of the hypothetical stories we presented to the respondents more often than not involve a character who is trying to get something to which he or she is not legally entitled in the first place. One could argue that, as such, they almost force the respondents to suggest illicit and unethical activities. On the other hand, the high rate of passive responses toward the military, in contrast to the willingness of the emigres to recommend covert and manipulative tactics with respect to the other institutions, supports the decision to utilize these variables in the analysis. Furthermore, in a total of 4,644 responses to the four questions, there was not a single instance in which a former Soviet suggested that the character in the situation attempt individually or in a group to effect a change in the policy or procedure, thus corroborating the previous evidence that Soviet citizens concede that policymaking itself is a foregone conclusion. They are inclined instead to concentrate their efforts at political influence in the appropriate output sectors.

We turn now to the actual tactics used by citizens to extract their desiderata from the institutions, and observe how the nature of the institution influences the ways in which citizens will approach it. The agencies we investigated included those dealing with housing, employment, pensions, admission to higher education, the police and armed forces. Soviet sources provide ample evidence that the pension agencies are plagued by poorly trained personnel and inefficient procedures,[2] and yet we find that our respondents evaluate the agency and its personnel favorably, and that the great majority see no need to resort to any special tactics in order to receive their pensions. The apparent paradox is explained by the fact that almost all who are entitled to pensions receive them, whereas the housing problem is perhaps the most difficult one in the daily life of the Soviet citizen. Even though the USSR has been building 2.2 million housing units annually since 1957, in the mid-1970s the average per-capita living space in urban areas was only 8 square meters (10 in Moscow). An estimated 30 percent of urban households still shared apartments, and it is not uncommon for people to wait as long as 10 years to get an apartment (Morton, 1980, pp. 235–236). Even getting on the list is a problem, as only those with less than nine square meters of living space (a minimum standard set in the 1920s) are eligible. Twenty percent of our respondents had been on a waiting list for an apartment.

The scramble to obtain housing is fairly general, and not a few short stories, feuilletons, and even novels have been written on the subject.[3] Small wonder that the most imaginative tactics are devised to obtain even the most modest apartments. An informant who worked in two housing administrations in Moscow in the late 1940s and 1950s, when housing was especially short, notes that bribery to obtain an apartment was so widespread that "people did not ask each other 'did you give' but only 'how much.' " Party officials, those with "responsible posts," those who had other favors to trade or simply had relatives and friends working in the housing administration were advantaged in the struggle for a dwelling. Although the situation has improved markedly in recent decades, nearly two-thirds of our respondents report that they tried to advance their position on the waiting list, either through appealing to a higher Soviet organ or, less frequently, using illegal tactics. The intervention of one's supervisor at work is often sought. Of those who went through the appeal process ($n = 129$), just over half reported that the appeal was successful and they obtained the apartment. Those who do not appeal successfully use other tactics and enter what Morton (1980) calls the "subsidiary housing market" (private rentals, cooperatives, exchanges of apartments and private houses). Exchanging apartments is the remedy most often prescribed by our respondents for those who have been unsuccessful in getting one from the official lists, but bribery is the second best. The official list is quite "flexible," as Soviet sources explain. "Too often the decisive factor is not the waiting list," *Pravda* commented, "but a sudden telephone call [after which] they give the flats to the families of football players and the whole queue is pushed back."[4] Even to purchase a cooperative apartment involves waiting lists.

A Bukharan Jewish woman from Tashkent whom we interviewed grew up in an eight-room private house with her own room. After marriage, she applied for a co-op because all her mother's children and grandchildren were registered as living in the big house, making it look like crowded conditions. The Uzbek clerk could not read Russian well and asked her to fill out the application for the co-op and then have it typed. "When I brought the typed version I put a bottle of vodka on the desk. He didn't take money, only vodka. Uzbeks don't take money. They are very humane people. He took vodka because, as an Uzbek, he is not allowed to drink. He can't go into a store to buy vodka because the clerks are Uzbeks and it would be embarrassing. So they get vodka from us, the 'foreigners.' "

Getting a pension rarely involves this much chicanery, although the press reports numerous instances of bureaucratic snafus connected with pensions, and there are occasional reports of pension officials making money from "dead souls" in the Gogolian tradition (*Trud*, 1980). But some pensioners also monkey with the system, especially since many pensions are very low. (We have reports from Central Asia of pensions as low as 24 rubles a month, and many instances in the European USSR of pensions of approximately 60 rubles, the latter being roughly one-third the average urban wage in the 1970s.) A bookkeeper from a small town in Moldavia explained that since pensions are based on average salary in the last years of employment, "sometimes to help out a worker who was going on pension the administration would promote him to a vacancy with a higher pay scale, even if he was not qualified for the job." Bonuses and overtime pay would be calculated into the figures for average salary in order to inflate the pension. All of this, she claimed, was assumed to be legal.

Getting into an institution of higher education is a far more complicated matter, especially for Jews, in the periods from 1945 to 1958 and from 1971 to the present. Although some respondents indicate that *blat* rather than bribery is used to gain entrance to higher education, two former members of admissions committees recall the widespread use of bribery, and one woman from the Ukraine frankly said that she was admitted only because her mother paid a 3,000 ruble bribe. Another person who was on the admissions committee of a polytechnic in Leningrad reports that in his institute the bribes ran about 500 rubles, but were into the thousands for the pediatric faculty and the First Medical Institute in Leningrad. But other forms of chicanery are more prevalent. A Georgian Jew tells how he paid 100 rubles in Kulashi to have his nationality changed from Jew to Georgian so that he would be admitted to the pediatric institute in Leningrad. This trick having worked, he returned as a pediatrician to Kulashi. But when he went to change his nationality back to Jew—"everyone knew me there and it was silly to be registered as a Georgian"—"the boys" demanded 200 rubles, for, they explained, because the Jews were getting out of the country, it was now worth more to be a Jew! Our Leningrad informant, who was himself helped in getting into the school of his choice because he was a basketball player, tells us that athletes and residents of Leningrad were favored for admission, as were children of faculty. Admissions committee members in Leningrad got written instructions not to admit anyone to the journalism faculty without recommendations from the party *raikom*. Certain specialties even in the philological faculty were explicitly closed to Jews. In such cases, bribery, connections, and other tactics will not work, except very rarely, and people learn quickly to give up on these institutions.

The other side of this is an "affirmative-action" program designed to increase the number of natives in the republic's higher educational institutions. Two Soviet authors assert that "It is understood that in socialist societies objectively there can be no discrimination against any national group. Soviet educational practice knows no such examples." At the same time, they say that, "It must be assumed that the more the proportion of a nationality in higher education corresponds to its proportion in the population as a whole, the more the system of higher education lives up to the democratic ideal of equal educational opportunity for all people irrespective of nationality." To achieve this "one can permit . . . conditional influence of a variable such as the nationality of an individual" on admissions decisions (Prikhodko & Pan, 1974, pp. 70, 61). Indeed, informants from two cities in Moldavia reported independently that in the 1970s they were told quite openly not to bother applying to Kishinev Polytechnical Institute because that was being reserved for ethnic Moldavians. Central Asian respondents portray admissions officials desperately trying to fill ethnic quotas. One woman draws a perhaps exaggerated picture of Uzbek officials scouring the countryside for young Uzbek women who could be persuaded to attend a pedagogical institute training music teachers for elementary schools. Other informants report that in the Ukraine and Moldavia, at least, rural students were favored for admission to institutes and were eagerly recruited, and this is confirmed as policy by official sources.

For those departments and schools that are realistic possibilities for Jews, the way in is not always a direct one. A common practice is to hire a tutor for the applicant, not so much to prepare the applicant as to prepare the way with the admissions committee. Often, the tutor is a member of the faculty, and he will see to it that his student gets in, sometimes by turning over some of his fees to his colleagues (reported in Moscow, Kharkov, Leningrad). One operator told parents: "I'll get your child into the institute for 1,000 rubles. Give me 300 now and the rest only if he gets in." The advance would be used to bribe clerks to put the child's name on the list of those admitted, bypassing the admissions committee, and then the rest was pocketed by the fixer. One admissions committee member admitted frankly that he gave higher admission grades to students who had been tutored by his friends.[5]

If citizens and members of admissions committees fool with the system, so, of course, does the party. A woman who taught in several pedagogical institutes reports that at the final meeting of the admissions committee a representative of the party *raikom* and another of the *obshchestvennost* (usually someone working with the party) would come and express their opinions freely. They would insure that certain ethnic distributions were achieved and that certain individuals were admitted or turned down. In Kharkov, it is claimed, there are three lists of applicants: those who must be admitted, those who must not be, and the rest. In the Kharkovite's experience, the party did not directly participate in the admissions process, but did so indirectly by approving members of admissions committees, making up the above-mentioned lists, and providing written guidelines for admission policies.

The Soviet press does not hide the fact that the struggle for admission to higher education is a fierce one, and that all kinds of means are employed in it. "Every summer when the school-graduates boom starts and the doors of *vuzy* (higher educational institutions) are blocked by lines of applicants, ripples of that wave sweep over editorial staffs as well. Parents and grandparents of school graduates call up and come in person (the person who failed the exams never comes). With great inspiration they tell what profound knowledge their child has, how diligent he was, how well he replied to each question, but the perfidy of the examiner was beyond all expectations." The writer notes, however, that "the majority of complaints are quite just" (Loginova, 1980, p. 11).

The intelligentsia is especially anxious to have its children gain higher education. In Azerbaijan none other than the first secretary of the republic Party organization, now a member of the All-Union Politburo, Gaidar Aliev (1981, p. 10) complained that in the law faculty of the local university, "We discovered that the overwhelming majority of the students are children of militia, procurators, judges, law professors and employees of Party and state organs. . . . We were concerned with the threat of nepotism and 'heredity' within the administrative organs." He complained also about the fashion of the 1960s, when senior officials "arranged" to receive higher degrees, commenting sardonically on a popular saying that, "A scholar you might not be, but a *kandidat* you surely must become."

If one gets into the institute or university and then graduates, a *raspredelenie* commission will normally assign the graduate his or her first job. Very often this is an undesirable position in an even less desirable location. For example, it is common practice to assign teachers or physicians, many of whom are single women, to rural areas in Siberia and Central Asia. To avoid such assignments, some will simply take a job outside their field, others arrange fictitious marriages with spouses who have residence permits in desirable locations, and many will appeal the decision and try to get a "free diploma," that is, one without a specific job assignment, leaving them to their own devices. In only one instance were we told of a bribe being used (in the West Ukraine) to get a good assignment. Several informants report being assigned to jobs in Central Asia, only to find upon arrival that there was no need for them, that the local institutions had not re-quested them, and the local authorities were not eager to have non-natives take jobs there. Despite the inconvenience, such *contretemps* were welcomed because they freed the person from the assignment. In 1979 nearly 30 percent of assigned jobs were not taken (*Uchitel'skaia gazeta,* 1980, p. 2), and in some rural areas the proportion of those who did not show up to their assignments was higher.[6] Of course, some graduates try to use *blat*, to try and pull strings with the job assignment commission, and this is reported to work fairly well. The other use of *blat* is to get some big boss to request the graduate specifically as an employee of his institution.

The Use of Blat and Protektsiia

Since *blat* and *protektsiia* are so commonly used, they are frequently commented on by the Soviet press. One detailed analysis raised both principled and pragmatic objections to *protektsiia*. It is said to be objectionable because it violates the socialist principle of "from each according to his capabilities, to each according to his work." On the practical level, *protektsiia* is said to reward the incompetent, discour-age hard work and initiative, allow people to make buying and selling favors their profession, and promote calculations of self-interest "in-compatible with communist morality." The resort to *protektsiia* arises, it is suggested, because social norms are not well defined and because of the "underdevelopment of certain branches of our economy." The law is said to be too vague for curbing the use of *protektsiia*. Unlike bribery, using *protektsiia* is not generally considered a crime except if "substantial harm is done to state or public interests, or to the rights of individuals" (Kiselev, 1981, p. 152).[7]

As this argument implicitly acknowledges, the use of *protektsiia*—and in some areas and under certain circumstances, even of bribery—is socially acceptable and not discouraged by law or custom. It is in line with age-old traditions in many areas of the USSR. A Georgian author shows how traditional birthdays, weddings, mourning rituals, the departure of young men to the army, and even funerals are occasions for trading influence and subtle forms of bribery (Dzhafarli, 1978, p. 72; see also Verbitskii, 1981, p. 2). Soviet authors decry "survivals of the past" which are said to contradict "socialist morality and way of life." Some Western observers see not just survivals but a Soviet failure to resocialize the population to Marxist-Leninist norms. One student of Soviet political culture asserts that " 'New Soviet man,' in short, does not yet exist; Soviet citizens remain overwhelmingly the product of their historical experience rather than of Marxist-Leninist ideological training" (White, 1979b, p. 49). This is an exaggeration—there as been successful resocialization in many areas of life—but it is true that prerevolutionary styles and practices survive in certain spheres, even among third and fourth generation Soviet citizens. The relationship between the government official and the citizen closely resembles pre-communist forms in the USSR and other socialist countries. Jowitt's (1974, p. 1176) argument that traditional attitudes and behavior patterns survive the communist revolution—and are even reinforced by it—is borne out by our investigation.

The prevalence of *blat* should not be attributed to some mystical staying power of pre-revolutionary political culture. Rather, it is supported by present-day structural factors which are themselves continuations of tsarist practices. The highly centralized and hierarchical administrative structure of tsarist days has been continued and reinforced by its heirs, so the kind of tactics used to ameliorate the harshness of tsarist administration are well suited to the present day as well. In the light of weak rational-legal authority and of interest groups in both historical periods, the average citizen is without influence over policymaking and has little legal protection against administrative arbitrariness or even the mindless application of what is construed as the law. He is left to devise individual strategies and tactics which will not change the making of the law, but will, he hopes, turn its implementation (or non-application) in his favor. Each person, then, is reduced to being a special pleader, and not with those who make the rules but with those who are charged with applying and enforcing them.

Conclusion

. . . Our findings repeatedly suggest that the dominant social ethos of Soviet citizens vis-à-vis their government is one of private self-interest. Furthermore, they display clear preference for informal access to and influence on bureaucratic officials and a general disdain for formal and legalistic procedures and norms. This observation leads us to think of the Soviet political culture (or at least the dominant subculture) as covert-participant. The covert-participant individual is oriented toward system outputs, but he exhibits few of the deferential, passive attributes of the classic subject. Rather, he participates in (or more precisely, attempts to manipulate) the implementation process in whichever institutions he can, utilizing a varied repertoire of assertive, creative, and illegal methods to secure his private welfare from the extensive Soviet public sector. Our research also indicates that covert orientations are to be found in every stratum in the USSR, but that different educational groups prefer different manipulative strategies, and these variations are probably rooted in both tradition and in the structure of the confrontation between citizens and the state. In a critique of *The Civic Culture,* a distinguished Polish social scientist who has considerable firsthand experience with the workings of his country's political system notes that "Some social groups feel . . . that their chances of performing effectively within the system are minimal or nil; in this case political apathy may be interpreted in terms of the critical evaluation of the existing system rather than in terms of the psychological characteristics of inactive citizens" (Wiatr, 1980, pp. 116–117). He suggests that Almond and Verba err in their "tendency to explain discrepancies between normative standards of democracy and political reality in terms of psychological deficiencies rather than structural conditions within the system." Though Wiatr makes these points with regard to Western democracies, they seem equally applicable to the Soviet Union and other socialist countries. Rational political behavior in the USSR should involve pro forma participation in the system's rituals, occasional contacting of approved agencies in approved ways in order to influence policy implementation in individual cases, and more frequent transactions with officials charged with policy implementation for the same purpose. Ritualistic participation is rational, not because it influences policy, but because it protects one against charges of nonconformity and antisocial attitudes, and for some it may provide emotional satisfaction. For others, however, the effect is to emphasize the gap between rhetoric and reality and to reinforce political cynicism.[8] Despite the Khrushchevian rhetoric of the "state of the whole people" succeeding the "dictatorship of the proletariat," only the formal franchise has been broadened in the last decades. The Soviet citizen participates politically in several ways, but, except for a small elite, his (and especially her) ability to influence policy decisions, even indirectly, is practically nil. The citizen does have some ability to influence the implementation of policy. But this can be done only on an ad hoc and ad hominem basis, so that no systemic effects and changes are felt. Despite the expansion of opportunities for formal participation and the grudging increase in opportunities for expressing opinions, the Soviet system remains fundamentally directed from above. As Verba and Nie (1972, p. 113) comment in their analysis of political participation in America:

> Particularized contacts can be effective for the individual contactor but they are inadequate as a guide to more general social policy. . . . The ability of the citizen to make himself heard . . . by contacting the officials . . . represents an important aspect of citizen control. Though such contacts may be important in filling the policy gaps and in adjusting policy to the individual, effective citizen control over governmental policy would be limited indeed if citizens related to their government only as isolated individuals concerned with their narrow parochial problems. The larger political questions would remain outside popular control. Therefore, though electoral mechanisms remain crude, they are the most effective for these purposes.

For the foreseeable future the "larger political questions" will remain the domain of the *verkhushka*. Our respondents appear to be much more interested in private benefits than in democratic institutions. We infer from our analysis of respondents' evaluations of Soviet bureaucracies and their dissatisfaction with its operations, that much of the Soviet population would probably be more interested in increasing levels of performance by the present system than in fundamental systemic change. Until such time as either of these comes about, the citizen is left to grapple as best he can with those small questions of daily life that he and those who administer the system must solve together.

Notes

1. Since the question concerning attitudes toward pension agencies was asked only of those who had actually received a Soviet pension, the data could not be incorporated into Exhibit 29.3. However, the responses fell within the predicted range. For example, more than 72 percent of those who answered advised patience or writing a letter of appeal.
2. See, for example, Azarova (1979). She notes that more than two-thirds of

district and city social security inspectors in the Russian republic have neither higher nor secondary specialized education. She strongly criticizes red tape, "illegal acts of employees," and the appeals process, whereby citizens are supposed to get a hearing on the size of their pensions. She goes so far as to imply quite clearly that the administration of pensions in the USSR is inferior to that in other socialist countries, citing specific examples.

Other articles along these lines are Tarasova (1976) and Tosunian (1981). The latter describes some of the pension officials: "Often the nature of the bureaucrat does not depend on his appearance. For some, rudeness and caddishness are the way they treat all visitors. Others are polite, well-mannered, speak softly to everyone, but they are nevertheless capable of confusing the simplest cases. Many experienced employees are well versed in the nuances of their job, but they use their knowledge, however strange it may sound, not to benefit but to harm their clients."

3. Examples include Plekhanov, "Order na kvartiru," *Literaturnaia gazeta,* July 25, 1979, p. 12; Ia. Ianovskii, "O sudebnoi praktike po grazhdansko-pravovym sporam mezhdu grazhdanami zhilishchnostroitel'nymi kooperativami," *Sovetskoe gosudarstvo i pravo* No. 1, 1967; "Fiancees with Dowries," *Pravda,* January 20, 1979, translated in *Current Digest of the Soviet Press* 31, 3 (February 14, 1979): "Discussing an Urgent Problem: An Apartment for the Newlyweds," *Sovetskaia Rossia* February 14, 1979, translated in *CDSP* 31, 8 (March 21, 1979). A well-known novel on the subject is by the recently emigrated Vladimir Voinovich, *The Ivankiad* (New York: Farrar, Straus and Giroux, 1977).

4. Cited in Morton (1980, p. 250).

5. Corruption is involved in admissions even to military schools. *Krasnaia zvezda* reports a case where a general got his relatives admitted despite their poor grades and admits this is not an isolated case. "When applications to the military school are being considered the admissions committee is besieged with phone calls. . . . There are really two competitions for admission: the regular competition and the competition of relatives" (Filatov, 1980, p. 2).

6. In Orel province in 1979 only 179 of 323 graduates of agricultural institutes showed up to their assigned jobs, some " 'signed in' only to vanish immediately afterward. . . . In all fairness it must be said that not all farm managers create proper conditions under which young specialists can work. . . . In other cases, they simply 'forget' to provide them with apartments . . . leave them on their own to solve all the problems of everyday life." See Troyan (1980).

7. See the frank article by the first secretary of the Georgian writers' union, Tengiz Buachidze (1975, p. 12).

8. Unger's (1981, p. 122) interviews with 46 former Soviet political activists of the party and Komsomol lead him to conclude that "they did not believe their own participation to be effective. . . . The combination of compulsion and formalism which characterizes participation in the Komsomol and party arenas clearly provides no scope at all for the development of a sense of efficacy. Indeed, one may well hypothesize that it has the opposite effect, that the induction of the individual into the 'spectacle' of Komsomol and party activities produces not a sense of efficacy but of inefficacy, not subjective competence but subjective incompetence."

References

Aliev, G. Interview. *Literaturnaia gazeta,* November 18, 1981, p. 10.

Almond, G.A. The intellectual history of the civic culture concept. In G.A. Almond & S. Verba (eds.), *The Civic Culture Revisited.* Boston: Little, Brown, 1980, 1–36.

Almond, G.A., and Verba, S. *The Civic Culture.* Princeton, N.J.: Princeton University Press, 1963.

Azarova, E. O zashchite pensionnykh prav grazhdan. *Sovetskoe gosudarstvo i pravo,* 1979, *2,* 44–49.

Barghoorn, F.C. *Politics in the USSR* (2nd ed.). Boston: Little, Brown, 1972.

Bennett, W.L. "Culture, communication, and political control." Presented at the annual meeting of the American Political Science Association, Washington, D.C., August 18, 1980.

Bialer, S. *Stalin's successors.* New York: Cambridge University Press, 1980.

Brown, A., and Gray, J. (eds.), *Political culture and political change in Communist states* (2nd ed.). New York: Holmes and Meier, 1979.

Buachidze, T. Protektsiia. *Literaturnaia gazeta,* January 8, 1975, p. 12.

Connor, W.D., & Gitelman, Z. (eds.), *Public opinion in European socialist systems.* New York: Praeger, 1977.

Dzhafarli, T.M. Izuchenie obshchestvennogo mneniia—neobkhodimoe uslovie priniatiia pravil'nykh reshenii. *Sotsiologicheskie issledovanie,* 1978, *1,* 69–75.

Falkenheim, V. Political participation in China. *Problems of Communism,* 1978, *27,* 18–32.

Filatov, V. Plemianniki: k chemu privodit protektsiia pri prieme v voennoe uchilishche. *Krasnaia zvezda,* November 12, 1980, p. 2.

Friedgut, T.H. *Political participation in the USSR.* Princeton, N.J.: Princeton University Press, 1979.

Gitelman, Z. Becoming Israelis: political resocialization of Soviet and American immigrants. New York: Praeger, 1982.

Gray, J. Conclusion. In A. Brown and J. Gray (eds.), *Political culture and political change in Communist states* (2nd ed.). New York: Holmes and Meier, 1979, 251–72.

Hasenfeld, Y. Client-organization relations: a systems perspective. In R. Sarri and Y. Hasenfeld (eds.), *The management of human services.* New York: Columbia University Press, 1978, 184–206.

Hasenfeld, Y., and Steinmetz, D. Client-official encounters in social service agencies. In C. Goodsell (ed.), *The public encounter: delivering human services in the 1980s.* Bloomington: Indiana University Press, 1981, 83–101.

Hough, J. Political participation in the Soviet Union. *Soviet Studies,* 1976, *28,* 3–20.

Hough, J., and Fainsod, M. *How the Soviet Union is governed.* Cambridge, Mass.: Harvard University Press, 1979.

Inkeles, A., and Bauer, R. *The Soviet citizen.* Cambridge, Mass.: Harvard University Press, 1961.

Jowitt, K. An organizational approach to the study of political culture in Marxist-Leninist systems. *American Political Science Review,* 1974, *68,* 1171–91.

Katz, E., and Danet, B. *Bureaucracy and the public.* New York: Basic Books, 1973.

Kiselev, V.P. O povyshenii deistvennosti prava v bor'be s protektsionizmom. *Sotsiologicheskie Issledovanie,* 1981, *1,* 151–54.

Loginova, N. Chervi kozyri. *Literaturnaia gazeta,* January 23, 1980.

Morton, H. Who gets what, when and how? Housing in the Soviet Union. *Soviet Studies,* 1980, *32,* 235–59.

Odom, W. A dissenting view on the group approach to Soviet politics. World Politics, 1976, *28,* 542–67.

Odom, W. *The Soviet volunteers.* Princeton, N.J.: Princeton University Press, 1973.

Oliver, J. Citizen demands and the Soviet political system. *American Political Science Review,* 1969, *62,* 465–75.

Prikhodko, D.N., and Pan. V.V. *Obrazovanie i sotsial'nyi status lichnosti: tendentsii internatsional-izatsii i dukhovnaia kultura.* Tomsk: izdatel'stvo Tomskogo Universiteta, 1974.

Sadowski, C. The fragile link: citizen voluntary association and polity in People's Poland. Unpublished doctoral dissertation. Department of Sociology, The University of Michigan, 1979.

Schulz, D., and Adams, J. *Political participation in communist systems.* New York: Pergamon Press, 1981.

Sharlet, R. Concept formation in political science and communist studies: conceptualizing political participation, *Canadian Slavic Studies,* 1967, *1,* 640–49.

Skilling, H.D., and Griffiths, F. *Interest groups in Soviet politics.* Princeton, N.J.: Princeton University Press, 1971.

Tarasova, V.A. Okhrana subiektivnykh prav grazhdanin v oblasti pensionnogo obespecheniia. *Sovetskoe gosudarstvo i pravo,* 1976, *8,* 133–36.

Tosunian, I. Vot dozhivem do pensii. *Literaturnaia gazeta,* September 30, 1981.

Troyan, S. They never arrived for their assigned jobs. *Izvestiia,* June 11, 1980, *3.* Translated in *Current Digest of the Soviet Press.* July 9, 1980, *32,* 16–17.

Trud, October 16, 1980, p. 4.

Uchitel'skaia gazeta, January 15, 1980, p. 2.

Unger, A. Political participation in the USSR: YCL and CPSU. *Soviet Studies,* 1981, *33,* 107–24.

Verba, S., and Nie, N. *Participation in America.* New York: Harper and Row, 1972.

Verbitsky, A. Vziatki, vziatki, vziatki. *Novoe Russkoe slovo,* August 4, 1981, p. 2.

White, S. *Political culture and Soviet politics.* New York: St. Martin's Press, 1979.

White, S. The USSR: patterns of autocracy and industrialism. In A. Brown and J. Gray (eds.), *Political culture and political change in Communist states* (2nd ed.). New York: Holmes and Meier, 1979, pp. 25–65.

Wiatr, J. The civic culture from a Marxist-sociological perspective. In G.A. Almond and S. Verba (eds.), *The civic culture revisited.* Boston: Little, Brown, 1980, pp. 103–23.

29

The Politics of Corruption in the People's Republic of China

Alan P.L. Liu

Since 1977 there have been numerous reports, official or unofficial, about widespread corruption in the People's Republic of China (PRC). Reports by law enforcement authorities ("Report of Supreme," 1980), editorials in the Chinese press ("Concerning Party Style," 1981), readers' letters to newspapers ("To Change Social," 1980), novels and short stories (Li, Y. 1980), and foreign correspondents (Biannic, 1977; Butterfield, 1979; Fraser, 1979), all testify to the seriousness of political corruption on mainland China.

Probably the strongest indication of the extent of corruption in the PRC is the establishment, in 1978, of the Central Discipline Inspecting Commission under the Central Committee of the Chinese Communist Party (CCP). In contrast to the former Party Control Commission, which was for overall supervision of party members, the present commission is set up specifically to deal with corrupt behavior of the members of the CCP. Apparently the work of the Central Discipline Inspecting Commission has not been enough. So, at the time of this writing, topmost Chinese leaders such as Deng Xiaoping are threatening the cadres of the CCP with a great purge in order to control corruption ("Peking Press Implies," 1982; Wren, 1982a, b).

This study of the politics of corruption in the PRC is based on 275 reports that I have collected from the press on mainland China from 1977 to 1980.[1] These reports are certainly not a random sample that may be used for national projection, but they do represent to some degree the media reports in the PRC. As the agent of the political authority responsible for shaping public opinion, the mass media in the PRC, as a rule, do not comment on events damaging to the communist

Source: Alan P.L. Liu, "The Politics of Corruption in the People's Republic of China," *American Political Science Review,* 77 (1983), 602–623. By permission of the author and the publisher.

system unless they become pervasive. As the chief editor of *Renmin Ribao* (People's Daily), organ of the Central Committee of the CCP, explained in a speech at the Higher Party Institute in Peking in 1979, the self-criticism in the press aims at a generalized problem, a "current of thought" or a prevailing style of work (Hu, 1980). A senior Chinese journalist told an American teacher in Peking: "We see nothing gained in playing up sensational material like murder cases, *unless it becomes a major problem. Of course, crime is bad, but it is not so important as other news. When a criminal act in itself becomes a warning sign that there is a deeper general malaise, then something should be done in the press"* (emphasis added) (Aronson, 1980, p. 48). In other words, corruption must be widespread in China, otherwise the media would not have reported it. But the above official statements should not lead one to conclude that the press on mainland China is always and completely objective. Behind every Chinese press campaign one can often detect partisan motives. For example, the subsequent discussion will show that the cases of corruption reported in the Chinese press in 1977–1980 were blamed mainly on "the system" left behind by the late Chairman Mao. It is only after 1980 that the press in China began to report more and more cases of corruption that were the results of the present Chinese leaders' policy of opening trade with the West. It may be that this reporting reflects the political strategy of Deng Xiaoping: First deal with the "radical left," then clean up Deng's own house. All this is highly plausible, but the most important point is that the Maoist system *did* in fact leave behind widespread corruption as testified to by many former residents of mainland China. The cause of partisanship is served best when it coincides with a "right" and "real" political issue, just as personalistic factors in politics have maximum impact when they are combined with the appropriate political climate.

Moreover, the 275 media reports are interesting and informative for their internal variation, which may shed light on both the politics and dynamics of corruption in China. First I will define corruption, that is, the types of corruption and the characteristics of corruptors; then, I shall present the Chinese media's and leaders' own analyses of the genesis of corruption and its correspondence to some of the sociological and political science analyses of corruption in American scholarly literature. Finally, I will discuss the measures taken by Chinese leaders to control corruption.

Phenomenology of Corruption: What and Who

Table 29.1 presents sixteen types of corrupt acts described in the 275 media reports of our sample. Compared with corruption in other

Table 29.1
A SAMPLE OF MEDIA REPORTS OF CORRUPTION IN THE PEOPLE'S
REPUBLIC OF CHINA, 1977–1980

Type of Corruption	Number	Percentage of Total
Housing irregularity	49	16.11
Illegitimate feasting	46	15.13
Embezzlement	28	9.21
Bribe or extortion	25	8.22
Appropriation of public goods	23	7.56
Hiring irregularity	22	7.23
Sexual abuse of women	20	6.57
Illegal imprisonment and torture	18	5.92
Obstruction of justice	14	4.60
Reprisal against informers	13	4.27
Cheating on school examination	13	4.27
False models	8	2.63
Feudal rites	8	2.63
Irregularity in residence permit	7	2.30
Illegal trade of public goods	7	2.30
Irregularity in party membership	3	0.98
Total	304	99.93%

Source: See Note 1.

nations, the sixteen types can be grouped further into three: the first group comprises corrupt acts, such as embezzlement and bribes, which are commonplace among nations having a political system to speak of; the second group, such as appropriation of public goods, illegal trade, and housing irregularity, results from a breakdown in the central allocation system and is commonplace among socialist nations. (In other words, a subterranean free market operates under the facade of a command economy.) But the third group of corrupt acts is rather peculiarly Chinese communist, e.g., illegitimate feasting, feudal rites, false models, and illegal imprisonment and torture. The first two, illegitimate feasting and feudal rites (cadres' staging lavish, traditional style weddings and funerals), concern what is known in the PRC as *dongfen* or style of work of a communist party member. Those acts violate the ideal that a communist cadre ought to be a revolutionary ascetic. The corruption of this ethos points to a central contradiction between the formal ideology of Marxism, to which the CCP subscribes, and the social base of the CCP, which is rooted in the countryside. On the one hand Marxism demands the purest type of secularism and public spirit, but, on the other hand, most Chinese communist rank and file have been recruited from poor peasantry and are still under the sway of traditional familism, ancestral worship, and feudal rites. The mixture of Marxist virtue, based on advanced industrialism, and Confucian ethos, rooted in the small rural community, at times creates confusion in norms and contributes to corruption.

One corrupt act that is uniquely Chinese communist is the false model, which refers to fraudulent models, such as model farms, model worker, and model deeds. As part of its mass mobilization, the CCP employed numerous "emulation campaigns" in which certain "model persons" or "model units" were singled out for nationwide emulating. As later accounts revealed, there was much rigging in some of the models so as to make them more persuasive. Model farms often received extra funding either from national or local authorities, as in the case of the discredited Dazhai model (Zhou, 1981). A party leader whose unit has been declared to be a model can count on quick and dramatic promotion, such as the case of Chen Yonggui of Dazhai (Baum, 1975). What the false models demonstrate is that in a highly structured and hierarchical system like the PRC, the normal route of upward mobility is slow and uncertain. Advancement by making up a model enables a lower cadre in the PRC to rise from rags to riches in a short time.

Another unusual form of corruption (Table 29.1) is illegal imprisonment and torture by many lower cadres. Although the terrorizing of common people by petty bureaucrats is not unheard of elsewhere, impressionistic evidence from the Chinese communist press suggests that both in number and degree of atrocity, Chinese cases are rather extraordinary (Zhu, 1980). Since 1978, the use of the third degree by lower-echelon party cadres has been singled out for denunciation by several top-rank party leaders (Zhao, 1978). To bring nationwide attention to this matter, a cause celebre, that of the cadres in Xunyi county of Shaanxi province, was publicized in 1978. The majority of party leaders in this county had resorted to beatings and torture of peasants, which had resulted over the years in death, suicide, mental breakdown, and disablement ("Carry Out," 1978). This corruption illustrates several aspects of the Chinese communist political system. First, since 1950 arbitrary detention and abuse of persons or groups designated as the object of a particular campaign have been an established practice in many mass campaigns. Second, the current widespread nature of this violence is a direct result of the political disorganization after the Cultural Revolution. Third, it speaks of the weakness of accountability of cadres in the PRC.

Who is responsible for these corrupt acts? Table 29.2 presents a breakdown according to their administrative level of party cadres who have been accused of corruption of one kind or another. It is important

Table 29.2

TYPE OF PARTY CADRES IN EACH CATEGORY OF CORRUPTION

Type of Corruption	Administrative Level of Cadre									Cadres in Each Category of Corruption
	National Party/State	Provincial Party/State	District Party/State	Municipal Party/State	County Party/State	Commune Party/State	Military Officers	State Firm	State Factory	
Housing irregularity		7	2	20	13	3	4			49
Illegitimate feasting	3	5	1	8	10	5	3	1	7	40**
Embezzlement		3	2	5	5	5	1		7	28
Bribe or extortion				4		4	1	6	6	21
Appropriation of public goods				4		1		5	11	21
Hiring irregularity	2	2		2	7		2	4	3	22
Sexual abuse of women		3	1	7*	1	6	2		2	21
Illegal imprisonment		1		6	6	7				17
Obstruction of justice	1	4			1		2			14
Reprisal against informers		1	1	3	3				4	12
Cheating on school examination					7	1	1			12
False model or reports		2	1			4		1	2	8
Feudal rites	1	1			5					7
Residence permit irregularity			1	1			2			7
Illegal trade					3			1	5	6
Illegal party membership					2		1			3
Total cadre in each administrative level	7	29	9	60	63	36	19	18	47	288
Percentage of cadre in each administrative level	2.43	10.07	3.13	20.83	21.88	12.50	6.60	6.25	16.32	100.0

*Sons or relatives of municipal party leaders.

**The discrepancies between some of the numbers on this column and the number of cases in Exhibit 30.1 are due to the number of general commentaries on some categories of corruption. The general commentaries, of course, do not as a rule name names.

to emphasize that the data are rough; for example, reports of irregularities in issuing residence permits or hiring often refer to the entire provincial or county party committee, each of which would consist of twenty to thirty members, but in Table 29.2, a reference to the entire unit is counted as one entry. Thus the data in the table understate the actual count of persons involved in the reported incidents.

Table 29.2 shows that corruption exists at every level of the political system on mainland China and among the military as well. The higher authorities in China apparently focused their anti-corruption drive at the local level, particularly from the municipal level down. The cadres at municipal, county, and commune levels account for 68.4 percent of total corrupt cadres. The largest percentage is the county cadres, county being traditionally the breaking point of Chinese bureaucracy. Now, even with the unprecedented mobilizational power of the Chinese communist party, the county remains a worry in the minds of Chinese national leaders.

In contrast to the great attention to corruption among local leaders is the relative inattention to national leaders. Of the seven reports on corruption by national leaders, only two named specific individuals; the other five cases were referred to vaguely in the press as "high cadres" ("Communique of Central," 1980; "Li Goucai Cheats," 1980). Corrupt acts of national leaders more often than not circulate only in the rumor network (Butterfield, 1979). The press in the Soviet Union also publicizes corruption among regional officials but ignores corruption among national leaders (Staats, 1972). Apparently the national leaders of China and the Soviet Union are sensitive to the danger that lower bureaucrats may become the feet of clay of totalitarian states in the double sense that the lower bureaucrats might deprive national leaders of their monopoly of all resources, and the misdeeds of lower functionaries might bring disrepute to the whole establishment.

Table 29.2 also indicates, to a limited extent, the spread of various forms of corruption. Table 29.3 identifies the 16 types of corruption as occurring primarily in rural or urban settings or both.

What is most striking in Table 29.3 is the incidence of rural corruptions, which points to two rural characteristics: tradition and lack of access to modern amenities. The feudal rites and illegal imprisonment represent traditional values and rural despotism which were common in old China. Cheating on school examinations refers specifically to fraud in taking the unified national college and university admission examination, which was reinstated in 1977 after 12 years of suspension. The rural areas were clearly in a disadvantaged position in this exami-

Table 29.3
URBAN OR RURAL CENTEREDNESS OF CORRUPTION

Urban and Rural	Urban	Rural
Housing irregularity	Bribe and extortion	Illegal imprisonment
Illegitimate feasting	Appropriation of goods	Cheating on school
Embezzlement	Obstruction of justice	examination
Hiring irregularity	Reprisal against	False models
Sexual abusement	informers	Feudal rites
	Illegal trade	Residence permit
		irregularity
		Illegal party
		membership

nation, which is, in principle, based on universalistic standards. The acts of false model, irregularity in obtaining residency permit (i.e., *urban* residency), and illegal party membership reflect the lack of access of rural cadres to a higher standard of living.

The urban-centered corruptions are, as expected, associated with the buildup of industry and enterprises after 1950, e.g., appropriation of goods and illegal trade. These forms of corruption, together with "obstruction of justice" which involves, in most cases, children of high-rank party officials, also testify to the existence of a new privileged class in the PRC. Unlike the rural cadres, the high cadres have acquired access to modern amenities; their corruption is a result of "accessibility with impunity."

The analysis so far has shown that underneath the reported cases of corruption is a mixture of political and socioeconomic factors. Political consideration, for example, accounts for the importance that the CCP attaches to lower-level cadres, their style of work and distributive justice. Social and economic factors are germane to the urban-rural nature of certain corruptions. Furthermore, some types of corruption, such as false models, illegal trade of goods, and illegal imprisonment, seem to be closely related to the way the political system operates in the PRC. To explore these dynamic factors underneath corruption, we look into the provincial base of the reports on corruption. . . .

Corruption and Press Reports

A complex mixture of political, social, and economic factors account for the variation in the Chinese press reports of corruption in various places of China. My central point is that there is no direct or simple correlation between actual instances of corruption and frequency of press reports on corruption of an area. It has been suggested that the Chinese press anti-corruption drive may have more to do with efforts to remove opponents from positions (e.g., "remnant elements of the Gang of Four") than with actual levels of corruption. This hypothesis of "total partisanship" is, strictly speaking, not testable since no one, not even Deng Xiaoping, could identify *fully* who the "remnant elements of the Gang of Four" are, which partly accounts for the CCP's sluggish campaign to rid itself of those "elements." Second, very often one finds that a deep penetration by the Gang of Four and corruption form a developmental sequence; that is, where the radicals were successful, political disorganization such as factionalism became extensive, and as a result, corruption rose. . . . Third, the total partisanship hypothesis is too simplistic. Chinese communist leaders like Deng Xiaoping and Hu Yaobang also have broad, long-range, and strategic considerations on their minds. We find, for example, that Fujian province was known to be a center of Gang of Four influence, but that the Chinese press reports on the corruption in Fujian are relatively scant. We suggest that this probably results from Fujian's strategic location vis-a-vis Taiwan. What is even more convincing than the Fujian example is the significant rank order correlation in the Chinese press reports of corruption in various regions in the 1950–1951 and 1977–1980 campaigns. No Gang of Four and their remnant elements were involved in the 1950–1951 campaign. Yet in both periods we find that the Chinese press reports on the anticorruption drive concentrated on northeast, north and east China. To the extent that political vengeance (ridding the PRC of the remnant elements of the Gang of Four) was involved in the 1977–1980 campaign, it must coincide with legitimate aims, be it the control of certain strategically important regions or "cleaning up" areas of aggravated corruption. Moreover, the Gang of Four did not act randomly; they penetrated into strategic regions such as north China, northeast China, east China, or cities like Shanghai and Tianjin, or the provinces of Henan and Zhejiang. In most of these areas, the influence of the Gang of Four and the severity of corruption are intrinsically related to a developmental sequence. Where, as in the municipalities of Shanghai and Tianjin, the influence of the Gang of Four and corruption do not seem to be positively correlated, the Chinese press reports in 1977–1980 accurately represented that fact. As we mentioned, although Shanghai and Tianjin were known to be the two most important centers of the power of the Gang of Four, the Chinese press reports did not concentrate reporting of corruption on the two cities.

The Genesis of Corruption

That the Chinese press reports do reflect widespread corruption in the PRC is further evidenced in the high instance of "theorizing" in the Chinese mass media on the causes of corruption. We are interested in the Chinese theorizing of corruption for three reasons. First, much Chinese discussion on corruption confirms numerous propositions on the causes of corruption in the social science literature of the West. Second, Chinese analysis of corruption also suggests some unique aspects of corruption in the PRC which have not been emphasized in the general discussion on political corruption. Third, Chinese conceptualization of corruption has heuristic value for general analysis of corruption. Because of space limitation, subsequent discussion can only be brief.

A considerable portion of Chinese theorizing on corruption deals with the nature of the political system in the PRC. The best and most succinct analysis is one that is provided by none other than Deng Xiaoping himself:

> Our various leading organs have run many things that they should not have run, did not run well, or could not run them. Many of the things would have been handled well if they were delegated to lower units such as enterprises, professional or social bodies if only we had established rules and adhered to democratic centralism. Once all things were handled by the party and the state at the center then we run into difficulties. No one is so efficacious as to manage well so many complex things. This may be regarded as the root of the peculiar bureaucratism that we have at the present. Another cause of bureaucratism is that our party, state and enterprise, for a long time, lacked a set of rules and a system of individual responsibility. There was no stipulation on the scope of one's function or authority. So a majority of our officials could not handle problems independently and spent their time in writing reports and passing on documents. With respect to some people whose sectarian spirit is strong, they evade responsibility and struggle for benefit. Furthermore, concerning the cadres, we do not have a system of appointment, promotion, demotion, retirement, dismissal and circulation. Regardless of a cadre's performance, his job is secure. A logical result of all this is a bloated organization, having numerous layers, a large number of subsidiary and superfluous positions. A bloated organization promotes bureaucratism. This system must be changed in a fundamental way . . . (Staff, 1981, pp. 118–119).

In one brief passage Deng manages to name all the system characteristics that are known to be conducive to corruption: centralization

(Rose-Ackerman, 1978; Staats, 1972), monopoly (Rose-Ackerman, 1978), lack of functional division (Rogow & Lasswell, 1963) and accountability (McMullan, 1970; Rose-Ackerman, 1978). Other Chinese writers attribute corruption and "bureaucratism" to the fusion of the communist party and the state in the PRC (Jing, 1980).

An expected result of combining central planning, collectivization, and the big push for industrial development in the PRC is the concentration of resources in public-owned enterprises or institutions. The Chinese in the PRC have given these collectivized enterprises a name, "social entities" (*shehui jituan*), whose purchasing power and practice have come under public censure in the PRC. It is reported that in 1979 the funds at the disposal of the "social entities" were two times the state revenue of 1950 (Commentator, 1979). Some of the corruption, such as feasting, appropriation of goods, and illegal trade, has its roots in the wealth of "social entities" ("Take Effective Measure," 1979). The government of the PRC also blamed the purchasing practice of institutions for shortages of consumer goods in the market.

The disparity between the wealth of public institutions, especially those in heavy industry, and the generally low living standard of society in the PRC results in a condition peculiar to China: numerous exactions on an enterprise by the surrounding community. Under the pretext that "a socialist enterprise is not solely for production," a Chinese factory or enterprise is often called upon to undertake extraordinary tasks, such as transporting provisions for employees and their dependents, participating in settling youth in the countryside, managing civil defense, birth control, and school administration, training of militia, operation of stores and hospitals, and, sometimes, even taking care of public security affairs ("Key Enterprises Have," 1978; "The Out of," 1979; "Too Many Miscellaneous," 1979). That this sort of "diffusion of function" of a public institution is highly conducive to corruption is self-evident. Interesting also is the resemblance of the multiple requirements of a Chinese enterprise to traditional practice. As pointed out by social anthropologists, in a traditional society social acts are seldom for a single interest but, more often than not, for multiple interests. Hence, a productive activity not only has an economic function but also social, religious, and political functions. This traditional ethos of multiple functions of a social act not only contributes to "corrupt" actions in a modern industrial state, but it also impedes change. Hoselitz writes:

> Hence, if different forms of productive activity are proposed, they will prove acceptable (without strong external compulsion) only if they also

fulfill in one form or another, all or most of the other objectives fulfilled by the activity to be replaced. The prevalence of many folk-like elements in the productive relations of non-industrialized societies accounts for some of the serious obstacles to economic and technical change that have been experienced there (1966, p. 12).

There is little doubt that some of the problems of Deng Xiaoping's "four modernizations" in the PRC today are rooted in the multifunctionality of many PRC institutions. A Chinese article with a revealing title, "Eliminate Feudal Vestige in Economic Work," states:

> Many of our enterprises do not like to engage in specialized production, share our work and cooperate with each other. They hope to undertake everything in the production process themselves. This is also a manifestation of the influence of the feudal manorial system and small production (Qian, 1980, p. 17).

An aspect related to the multifunctionality of Chinese enterprises is that the stress on collectivism has caused a serious blur in the minds of the people over the distinction between public and private goods. "Everyone eats from the socialist pot!" goes a popular saying on mainland China. Several types of corruption listed in Exhibit 30.1, such as housing irregularity, illegitimate feasting, appropriation of public goods, and hiring irregularity, can be attributed to the unclear distinction between public and private domain. In the name of "taking care of the welfare of the masses," factories often distributed their goods first to their own employees at a discount or even free of charge. Sometimes, private distribution of public goods is simply another form of bribe, as when factory heads used goods to buy their employees' silence about the former's corrupt deeds. Some public policies unwittingly aggravated this confusion over the public-private boundary, as in the permission given to children to take over the positions vacated by their retiring parents.

Another system characteristic that is conducive to corruption in the PRC is the overall "aging" problem, pertaining not just to the age of cadres, but also of institutions and their output. The mainland Chinese press talks often of old and sick cadres' lack of interest in change. Chinese economists speak about obsolescence of machinery and output (Commentator, 1981). Rogow and Lasswell (1963), for example, have suggested that corruption is associated with the life-cycle of an institution. Once an institution has passed its pioneering period and becomes just another bureaucratic establishment, its early idealism loses appeal, and corruption tends to increase.

Next to the discussion on system characteristics, the Chinese communist analysis of corruption deals also with numerous stresses and dislocations in the economy and society. There are, for example, dislocations caused by excessive central planning. Often central ministries assign an output quota to enterprises without providing the required materials, funds, or equipment. In the PRC this is referred to as "leaving gaps in planning." Consequently, each enterprise sends out groups of purchasing agents to roam the nation for materials and equipment. Corrupt deeds such as bribery, illegal exchange of goods, and even speculation grow partly out of this breakdown in central planning. Furthermore, each enterprise engages in the hoarding of materials in order to anticipate future needs, which creates more shortages in the society and encourages more bribe and illegal trade of materials (Tian and Liang, 1978).

In a centralized and collectivized economic system like that in the PRC, the central ministries take all the profit from enterprises for centralized redistribution and absorb all the losses. Since the state receives all the goods produced and absorbs all the losses, there are many inferior and unwanted goods. To dispose of an accumulated inventory of unwanted goods, some enterprises resort to institutionalized extortions; that is, in some cases Chinese customers are required to purchase "attached merchandise" along with the merchandise that they want to buy ("The Current of," 1978). Those enterprises producing goods in heavy demand receive institutionalized bribes from state commerce agencies who give "extra-payment" to factories producing television sets, blankets, sewing machines, bicycles, and other popular items ("The Practice of," 1979).

Last, corruption in China is significantly related to the severe shortage of consumer goods. The prevailing shortage of consumer goods in the PRC is readily admitted by Chinese officials; Song Jiwen, Acting Minister of Light Industry, reported in 1981 that in the twenty-year period from 1958 to 1978 the ratio of state investment in light to heavy industry is 1:10.4 (Song, 1981a, b). In 1980, with the Chinese population standing at close to 1 billion, China yearly produced 12.6 million bicycles, 7.2 million sewing machines, and 21 million watches (Tian, 1980). Folklore in China testifies to the shortage of consumer goods. A certain kind of cigarette is known as "machine gun" and some brands of liquor as "hand grenade," meaning that the bribe power of these goods are like weapons ("The Fraud of," 1980). That housing irregularity ranks first in our sample of corruption in China is not surprising; according to a survey in 1978, the average living space for a Chinese in the People's Republic of China was 3.6 square meters.

The comparable figure of living space for a Japanese is 7.3; French, 13; West German, 16; and American, 18. Moreover, 3.6 square meters represents a decline from 4.5 square meters of living space for a Chinese in 1952 (Zhou & Lin, 1980).

Scarcity, years of poverty, and the examples set by privileged party cadres combine to perpetuate, among the masses of China, the traditional attitude of regarding public property as legitimate loot. The Chinese press has reported several instances of mass looting of factories that were ordered to shut because of poor management ("Baoshan Iron Works," 1980; "The Chemical Fertilizer," 1981; "Lushan Steel Mill," 1980; "Must Learn a," 1981).

A third aspect of Chinese self-criticism touches on the cultural or ideological basis of corruption. In general, in a time of social stress numerous ideologies arise in society to explain the causes of problems and offer solutions. Since the 1970s the PRC has manifested the classical syndrome of an ancient regime in a time of severe social and economic stress, which often leads to a revolution. A clear sign of this condition is the circulation of homespun theories on social, economic, or political crises. The Chinese press refers to a number of these ideologies. For example, one of the most popular indigenous ideologies that has been spreading on mainland China since the days of the Cultural Revolution is the theory of a bureaucratic class (*guanliao jieji*), which has provoked a new round of official denunciation (Lin & Shen, 1981; "On 'Opposition to,' " 1981). But even officially sanctioned writers have to address the reality of privileges and corruption among cadres by the use of the concept of "alienation of power" (Commentator, 1980).

Whereas the ideologies of bureaucratic class come mostly from the dissenters in the PRC, Chinese official statements testify to the existence of a culture of corruption. The latter is represented by folklore circulating among Party cadres, such as: "Building Socialism is too difficult; realizing Communism is too remote; remote ideals are empty; concrete benefits are real" (Zhang, C., 1980, p. 8). The Chinese official media openly admit "a crisis of confidence (or trust)" in socialism or the communist party among cadres, and youth in particular (Lei, 1980; Li, H. 1980). A rich folklore also exists on mainland China concerning the practice of seeking connections and favoritism. For example, "Learning geometry or physics is not as useful as learning 'connectionology' " (Qi, 1980, p. 8), or "The learning of 'connectionalism' is endless" (Yu, 1980, p. 3). These sayings should not be dismissed as mere anecdotes, for there are some survey data to corroborate them. Like East European nations in the mid-1950s (after de-Stalinization),

Chinese communist authorities have rediscovered the usefulness of sociology and opinion polls which had been suspended for 30 years. That polls (limited) are being taken in the PRC itself testifies to the authorities' alarm over public morale. In each poll, whether among students, workers, or "youth," there is a strong antipathy toward the special privileges of party cadres and significant apathy toward communism. The 1980 poll taken at Fudan University in Shanghai is typical in its results:[2]

> One of the most interesting results came from the question "What is China's biggest social problem?" Fifty-five percent replied that it was the special privileges of communist party cadres. Some 23 percent said unemployment. Another question simply asked the students to name what they believe in. Only one-third answered "Communism," a surprisingly low figure considering the intense indoctrination of youth for the past 30 years. Nearly a quarter of the students said they believed in fate, a tiny fraction named capitalism. A significant 25 percent offered a chilling answer, "Nothing at all." ("What Students Believe," 1980, p. 57).

An officially approved "poll," supposedly of approximately a thousand "youth" in the provinces of Fujian and Anhui, found that 30.2 percent of respondents maintain that "the superiority of socialism is not great" or "the superiority of socialism is not evident" (Huang, Z., 1981, p. 5). This finding is interesting not only because of its correspondence with the poll at Fudan University, but also because Fujian and Anhui are known for their poverty and rural nature, whereas Fudan University is located in the most modernized city in China.

The "culture of corruption" described so far creates a "climate of corruption" in the PRC that, in turn, encourages "mass participation" in bribes and extortion ("Current of Deviation," 1979; "With Gifts Everything," 1977) and subjects a few honest officials to isolation and public ridicule ("What Does the," 1981).

Just as any mass practice has both a cultural and organizational base, so does the corruption in the PRC. In its analysis of the genesis of corruption, the Chinese communist press attributes part of the blame to the existence of cliques or clientelism inside the party and state bureaucracy. Since 1977 almost every case of "aggravated corruption" publicized by the Chinese press in the mainland unearthed an extensive network of vertical (clientelist) and horizontal (dyadic) personal networks. Most of the former grow out of formal association, whereas part of the horizontal alliance is based on "rebel associations" during the Cultural Revolution. Owing to limitation of space, we can present only three cases here. First, there is the embezzlement of flood relief funds by a deputy party secretary of Henan province which has already been discussed before. The expose of this case reveals a clientelist relationship between national, provincial, and county party leaders as illustrated in Table 29.4. The clientelism of Henan begins at the national level. Jiang Qing, leader of the Gang of Four and widow of Mao Zedong, had become the patron of several members of Henan Provincial Party Committee, promising them new positions in the future in return for the latter's mobilizing the resources of Henan to denounce Jiang's chief opponent, Deng Xiaoping. A deputy party secretary named Wang, being one of Jiang's clients, had in turn become the patron of the subordinate district party committee at Chumadian. The relationship between Wang and the district party committee was based on the exchange of goods in which Wang supplied Chumadian with needed goods and services and granted promotion to several members of the Chumadian Party Committee in return for the latter's enriching Wang with an assorted group of luxurious consumer items such as a refrigerator, television, and liquor ("Deputy Party Secretary," 1978; "The People of," 1976). An append-

Table 29.4
THE CLIENTELIST RELATIONSHIP OF HENAN PARTY COMMITTEE

Patron	Jiang Qing (widow of Mao Zedong)	
Client	Wang Weichun of Henan Provincial Party Committee	Patron
Patron	Chumadian District Party Committee First Party Secretary Su Deputy Party Secretary Yang Chairman of Planning Commission Zhao Chief of Provincial Finance Su (Clique based on formal association)	Client
Client	Nine County Party Committees (Cliques based on formal association)	Patron
	Commune Party Committee (Clique based on formal association)	Client
	Informal alliance Formal relationship	

age to the clientelist relation is nepotism. Wang's son was made a commune party secretary and became the patron of his commune, using his position and his father's connections to obtain for his commune automobiles, tractors, steel, and chemical fertilizer and using his commune's resources to deal in "illegal trade" to enrich himself.

The second case of clientelism with national patronage concerns the Communist Party committee at the city of Luda in Liaoning province. The chief figure is the first secretary of Luda municipal party committee, Liu Decai, who held the concurrent positions of the chairman of the Municipal Revolutionary Committee (i.e., mayor), Commander of Luda Garrison District and Deputy Commander of Shenyang Garrison Command. Thus Liu exemplifies the principle of concentration of power and functions in the Chinese communist political system. Liu had organized a horizontal dyadic alliance with his former colleague named Xuan Shimin, Secretary of Party Committee. Xuan in turn was a member of a horizontal dyadic alliance, based on a "rebel group" in the Cultural Revolution, which included two leaders of Municipal Public Security Bureau (police) and the staff of several factories. But Liu had a powerful provincial and national patron—Mao Yuanxin, nephew of Chairman Mao and *de facto* head of Liaoning province to which the city of Luda belongs. The patron-client relationship of Liu is shown in Table 29.5. The result of this linkage between vertical and

Table 29.5
PATRON-CLIENT RELATIONSHIP BETWEEN LUDA MUNICIPAL PARTY COMMITTEE AND NATIONAL LEADERSHIP

National patron: Mao Zedong

(Kinship tie)
Provincial patron: Mao Yuanxin   Vertical dyadic alliance

(Patron-client)
Luda Municipal Party Committee

Liu Decai   Xuan Shimin
First Party Secretary   Party Secretary

Municipal Public
Security Bureau   Party Secretaries in
                             municipal firms

Horizontal dyadic alliances based on formal organizational linkage and also "rebel group" association horizontal dyadic alliances was "aggravated corruption," as Liu and his company embezzled public funds, extorted contributions from other oganizations, and employed free prison labor to build 64 unauthorized buildings, including 28 club houses and a score of office buildings, theatres, and department stores. When the various organizations asked Liu how to report the expenses they incurred to build Liu's projects, the latter was said to have replied, "Put them on the account of the revolutionary line of Chairman Mao" ("The Responsible Person," 1978, p. 4).

The third case of clientelism involves subnational patronage. The cause celebre involves a woman named Wang Souxin, manager of a county fuel company in the province of Heilongjiang. Wang was a cashier in the company when the Cultural Revolution began. During that time of disorganization, the *de facto* power of Wang's county was in the hands of a military representative known as Commissar Yang, who became Wang's patron. The latter then formed a "rebel group" and seized the managership of the fuel company. Using the supply of coal to various organizations, factories, and households as a political resource, Wang soon established connections with all party officials in the county. After Wang's initial patron, Commissar Yang, was promoted to a provincial post, Wang extended her connections to the provincial party establishment. Wang offered to place the sons and daughters of high provincial party leaders in her fuel company so the former would not have to be exiled to the countryside, in exchange for valuable goods from provincial leaders such as cement, chemical fertilizers, and tractors. In other words, Wang became the link between the county and the province. To her employees, Wang was their patron. She supplied them with coal, food, and clothing. When Wang was arrested for embezzlement in 1979, she had declared, "You go to the county and inquire about me. You will learn that I, Mrs. Wang, always have the welfare of the masses as my chief concern" (Liu, 1979, p. 29).

Chinese communist self-analysis thus confirms studies by Roth (1968) and LeVine (1975) that "personal rulership" and "informal polity" are an important contributory cause of widespread corruption.

Although Chinese writers and journalists recognize that corruption is rooted in the system of the PRC, they also view the Cultural Revolution of 1966–1969 as the precipitant cause of the present situation in corruption (Zheng, 1979; Commentator, 1980). Former residents of the PRC confirmed the official diagnosis. The Cultural Revolution destroyed much of the PRC's institutionalized rules and eliminated the only internal judiciary of the communist party—the Party Control

Commission (forerunner of the present Discipline Inspecting Commission). The terror of the Cultural Revolution promoted the personal alliance network. The mass expose of the high living of party leaders in the numerous tabloids published by the Red Guards during the Cultural Revolution undermined popular respect for the communist party and its ideology. Owing to the power struggle between the radicals and the established party machine, many new members, often unscrupulous ones, were admitted into the party and state structure, albeit at lower levels. Overall, the Cultural Revolution fundamentally tarnished the image of the communist party of China both among the party's rank and file and the public at large.

Coping with Corruption

Perhaps the most interesting aspect of the foregoing Chinese communist analysis of the causes of corruption is that the various underlying factors form a "system." Moreover, the components of this "system of corruption" coincide with Smelser's (1971) conceptual scheme of "collective behavior": structural conduciveness, structural strain, spread of generalized belief, precipitating event, mobilization of participants for action, and loosening of social control. The strategy of the present Chinese administration is to break the system of corruption at some crucial point.

The first and foremost action undertaken by Deng Xiaoping and his colleagues to weaken the "system of corruption" is strengthening the "social control" mechanism through the establishment of the Central Discipline Inspecting Commission. At the same time the state judiciary has also been resurrected. Since its inception in 1978, the Discipline Inspecting Commission has launched a vigorous drive to prosecute cases of corruption. The Commission, however, is handicapped by several things. First, there is the problem of credibility of doubts in the minds of cadres on the viability of present administration's policy and program. Owing to past incessant changes and reversals of policy, Chinese communist party cadres have cultivated a deep suspicion on the permanency of any public policy. Consequently the Discipline Inspecting Commission does not always obtain the cooperation that it needs to uncover corruption. Second, owing to a combination of the credibility problem, the destruction of many party establishments during 1966–1976 and the prevalence of cliques, the Discipline Inspecting Commission has difficulty in acquiring information on cases of corruption. The Commission often has to rely on letters from ordinary people to detect even obvious cases of indiscipline (Zhang, L., 1980).

That is why, together with the anticorruption drive, the Chinese press has also launched a campaign of letter-writing from the public to inform the party higher-ups on the misdeeds of party officials. Third, the existence of cliques in the party and state bureaucracy makes it very difficult for the Discipline Inspecting Commission to establish clear accountability. In almost every case a cadre under the investigation of the Commiission is able to find a patron-protector to intercede for him. As one writer puts it, the cliques and personal connections in the party "reduces a big case into a small one and a small case into dust" (Zhang, 1982, p. 5). Finally, both the Discipline Inspecting Commission and the state judiciary on mainland China seriously lack trained personnel to handle investigation and prosecution. A 1980 report states that only 6 percent of the employees and staff of the state judiciary have had some education in legal matters. From 1953 to 1979, the law schools in China graduated 20,000 students, a mere 0.6 percent of college graduates (Zhao, 1980).

In publicizing cases of corruption and encouraging people to report cases to the party authorities, the present Chinese communist leaders mobilize public opinion, which is another form of increasing "social control" on the system of corruption.

Lately, Chinese communist leaders have also embarked upon the stupendous task of streamlining the party's bloated bureaucracy. If successful, this will reduce the "structural conduciveness" of corruption. The latest twelfth Communist Party Congress (September 1, 1982) declares its intention to screen the credentials of 39 million party rank and file in order to rid the party of the corrupt members. In carrying out these awesome tasks, the CCP will face the same difficulties that the Discipline Inspecting Commission has already experienced.

As another way of reducing the "structural conduciveness" and "strains" in the system of corruption, since 1978 the CCP has reordered its economic priority by increasing state investment in consumer industry and construction of housing. Small-scale private enterprises have been allowed to open in order to reduce state monopoly over commerce and services. In the countryside the power of rural party officials has been significantly reduced as peasants are now permitted to do contract farming instead of being forced to work on communized land. Reducing monopoly and increasing the supply of necessary goods will weaken incentives for corrupt behavior.

All these will not, of course, eliminate corruption on mainland China. As we mentioned earlier, Deng's new policy of decentralization and modernization also causes corruption, for the control of corruption is like what James Madison said about the control of factions; one can limit its effect but not be rid of its cause. Ultimately, the prospect of controlling corruption in China depends on overall social and economic development. The historical experience in Europe and England has shown that corruption is not an isolated phenomenon that could be dealt with in an *ad hoc* manner. Eugene and Pauline Anderson, for example, write about nineteenth-century Europe: "Where the economy, education, and other aspects of society showed creative activity, the bureaucracy tended to be efficient; where they continued sluggish and indifferent to public welfare, officials shared these characteristics" (1970, p. 105). Impressionistic evidence from other Chinese communities such as Singapore and Taiwan where corruption has been brought under a degree of control amidst rapid economic and social change suggests that the Andersons' remarks on nineteenth-century Europe may be equally applicable to mainland China.

Notes

1. The 304 cases are based on 275 press reports (some reports contain more than a single type of corruption or involve more than a single party cadre). The majority of the reports, 221 out of 275, are from the most authoritative paper *Renmin Ribao* (People's Daily), which is published by the Central Committee of the Chinese Communist party. The remaining 54 reports are drawn from news agencies or regional newspapers that are excerpted in the *Ming Pao Daily News* in Hong Kong, which has a page in every issue that selectively publishes reports from the Chinese press.
2. For other reports on polls in the PRC, see Sterba (1980) and Butterfield (1980).

References

Anderson, E.N., and Anderson, P. Bureaucratic institutionalization in nineteenth century Europe. In A.J. Heidenheimer (ed.), *Political corruption: readings in comparative analysis*. New York: Holt, Rinehart and Winston, 1970.

Aronson, J. By your pupils you'll be taught. *Columbia Journalism Review*, 1980, *1*, 44–48.

Baoshan iron works of Zhengzhou Railway Bureau looted after being deactivated. *RMRB*, November 14, 1980, p. 3.

Baum, R. *Prelude to revolution*. New York: Columbia University Press, 1975.

Biannic, G. AFP correspondent reports on 'corruption' in Peking. *Daily Report—People's Republic of China*. June 26, 1977, p. E1.

Butterfield, F. Peking prepares a drive against corrupt officials. *The New York Times*, August 1, 1979, p. A5.

Carry out the good tradition of the Party; transform cadres' style of work. *RMRB*, August 3, 1978, p. 1.

The chemical fertilizer plant of Faku County left without care. *RMRB*, March 5, 1981, p. 1.

Commentator. Strictly control the purchasing power of social entities. *RMRB*, January 4, 1979, p. 2.

Commentator. Build up spirit to manage well economic work. *Hongqi*, 1981, *19*, 13–16.

Communique of central discipline inspecting commission criticizing commerce minister. *RMRB*, October 17, 1980, p. 1.

Concerning party style of work. *RMRB*, February 28, 1981, pp. 1, 3.

The current of "attached purchase" should be stopped. *RMRB*, August 12, 1978, p. 3.

Current of deviation as seen in a small incident. *RMRB*, March 2, 1979, p. 3.

Deputy party secretary of Henan Wang Weichun led in indiscipline and illegality, *RMRB*, November 13, 1978, p. 1.

Fraser, J. Even some top Communists pull rank in China. *The Christian Science Monitor*, September 26, 1979, p. 7.

The fraud of Zhang Liangchun. *RMRB*, August 6, 1980, p. 3.

Hoselitz, B.F. Main concepts in the analysis of the social implications of technical change. In B.F. Hoselitz and W.E. Moore (eds.), *Industrialization and society*, Mouton: UNESCO, 1966.

Hu, J. On hitting "flies" and "tigers," *Ch'ih Shih Nien Tai*, 1980, 5, 30–35.

Huang, Z. Just how should one appraise this generation of youth. *RMRB*, February 24, 1981, p. 5.

Jing, D. The Party should not take the place of the State. *Hongqi*, 1980, *21*, 5–8.

Key enterprises have too many bosses. *RMRB*, December 6, 1978, p. 2.

LeVine, V.T. *Political corruption: the Ghana Case*. Stanford, Calif.: Hoover Institution Press, 1975.

Li Guocai cheats, falsifies, and tyrannizes. *RMRB*, September 25, 1980, p. 5.

Li, Y. Chinese reality as reflected in new literary works. *Ch'ih Shih Nien Tai*, 1980, *6*, 28–33.

Lin, B., and Shen, Z. On the so-called "opposition to the bureaucratic class." *Hongqi*, 1981, *5*, 12–18.

Liu, B. Between human and monster. *Ch'ih Shih Nien Tai*, 1979, *12*, 22–38.

Lushan steel mill of Henan looted before and after closing. *RMRB*, November 14, 1980, p. 3.

McMullan, M. Corruption in the public services of British colonies and ex-colonies in West Africa. In A. J. Heidenheimer (ed.), *Political corruption: readings in comparative analysis*. New York: Holt, Rinehart and Winston, 1970.

Must learn a lesson. *RMRB*, March 3, 1981, p. 2.

On opposition to the bureaucratic class. *RMRB*, February 11, 1981, p. 4.

The out of ordinary burden of our enterprise is too heavy. *RMRB*, April 5, 1979.

Peking press implies a purge of party may be imminent. *The New York Times*, February 6, 1982, p. 2.

The people of Henan angrily denounce the "Gang of Four." *RMRB*, December 7, 1976, p. 2.

The practice of extra-payment by commerce agency to enterprises must be stopped. *RMRB*. February 5, 1979, p. 2.

Qi, C. Random thoughts on employment. *RMRB*. April 7, 1980, p. 8.

Qian, J. Eliminate feudal vestige in economic work. *Beijing Review*. 1980, *52*, 15–17.

Report of supreme people's procuratoracy. *RMRB*. September 17, 1980, p. 2.

Resolve to overhaul financial discipline. *RMRB*. September 16, 1978, p. 2.

The responsible persons of Luda City party committee seriously violate rules of finance. *RMRB*. April 6, 1978, p. 1.

Rogow, A.A. The definition of corruption. In A.J. Heidenheimer (ed.), *Political corruption: readings in comparative analysis*. New York: Holt, Rinehart and Winston, 1970.

Rogow, A.A., and Lasswell, H.D. *Power, corruption and rectitude*. Englewood Cliffs, N.J.: Prentice-Hall, 1963.

Rose-Ackerman, S. *Corruption: a study in political economy*. New York: Academic Press, 1978.

Roth, G. Personal rulership, patrimonialism, and empire-building in the new states. *World Politics*. 1968, *2*, 194–206.

Smelser, N.J. *Theory of collective behavior*. New York: Free Press, 1971.

Song, J. On a great increase in the production of consumer goods. *Hongqi*. 1981, 6, 8–12.

Song, J. A great increase in the production of consumer goods is an important task of the party. *RMRB*. July 1, 1981, p. 6.

Staats, S. J. Corruption in the Soviet system. *Problems of Communism*. 1972, *1*, 40–47.

Staff. Teng Hsiao-ping's speech to the party central political bureau enlarged conference. *Chungkung Yenchiu*. 1981, *7*, 104–39.

Take effective measure to control the purchasing power of social entities. *RMRB*. August 19, 1979, p. 2.

Tian, J. and Wensen, L. Planning should not leave gaps. *RMRB*. December 13, 1978, p. 3.

Tian, Y. More consumer goods. *Beijing Review*. 1980, *47*, 20–28.

To change social ethos requires the mobilization of the entire society. *RMRB*. November 1, 1980, p. 3.

Too many miscellaneous taxation and contributions required of factories and mines. *RMRB*. May 2, 1979, p. 4.

What does the fate of two superior party members testify. *RMRB*. April 24, 1981, p. 3.

With gifts everything can be done; to give or not to give gifts. *RMRB*. December 13, 1977, p.3.

Wren, C.S. Chinese try to allay rumors that Deng's power is fading. *The New York Times*. February 9, 1982, p. A4.

Yu, Y. A prevailing thought of sordid merchants. *RMRB*. December 17, 1980, p. 3.

Zhang, C. The ideals and practice of a communist party member. *Hongqi*. 1980, *13*, 8–11.

Zhang, L. Restrain the current of protecting deviation. *RMRB*. January 29, 1982, p. 5.

Zhao, C. Talk at the forum on legal establishment. *RMRB*. October 29, 1978, p. 2.

Zhao, Y. Education of law should expand greatly. *RMRB*. October 10, 1980, p. 5.

Zheng, T. On Madame Curie's refusal of patent right. *RMRB*. July 10, 1979, p. 4.

Zhou, J. Appraising the Dazhai brigade. *Beijing Review*. 1981, *16,* 24–28.

Zhou, S., and Lin, S. On the housing problem. *RMRB*. August 5, 1980, p. 5.

Zhu, W. Oh, my brothers and elders! *RMRB*. November 8, 1980, p. 5.

30

Socialist Graft: The Soviet Union and the People's Republic of China

Peter Harris

The concept of socialist graft requires some preliminary explanation. Socialist graft is a phenomenon which may puzzle if not actually offend some people. As a rule socialism does not draw undue attention to its possible failings. Indeed, such weaknesses as exist are seen as those inherent in capitalism, not to be found in the theory and practice of socialism. The emphasis in socialist literature is on the iniquities of the alternative, and on the benefits of socialist social engineering.

The objective of this paper is to point out that graft may exist in a socialist order. A gap exists between socialist rhetoric and human fallibility. Socialist graft exists. The term itself of course may require explanation. To take the adjective 'socialist' first, the reference to 'socialist' refers to 'a politico-economic system' where the state controls, either through planning or more directly, and may legally own, the basic means of production. Socialism is a whole system which distinguishes it in large measure from (bourgeois) liberalism.

The term 'socialist' may be preferred to 'communist,' because the former allows the observer to consider states which see themselves as being in a transitional state towards some as yet undefined more perfect end. All the classical writings on socialism postulate a goal whose moral core is strong, unsullied by baseness or human degradation. Indeed, corrupt societies are explicitly associated with capitalism and China has never ceased to denounce the capitalist West, frequently as a source of 'spiritual pollution.'

As for the term 'graft,' this might well be preferred to possible alternatives such as corruption and 'bribery.' The term 'corruption' itself causes considerable problems in a number of languages. In

Source: Peter Harris, "Socialist Graft: The Soviet Union and the People's Republic of China—A preliminary survey," *Corruption and Reform*, 1 (1986), 13–32.

Russian it is *blat,* in Chinese it is *fubai* or *tanwu*. In English, the term 'corruption' is very broad, and carries considerable moral connotations. Thus we may speak of a corrupt society as a 'sick' society without any evidence of overt 'bribery.' We know that power corrupts, but not necessarily in the legal sense. The term bribery, (in Chinese *hui lu),* is perhaps regarded by students of corruption as an excessively narrow and legalistic term, referring to the passage of money from hand to hand. Bribery may of course lead to (moral) corruption and to the erosion of the legitimacy of the state apparatus itself.

As an alternative, the term 'graft' may be helpful, as it could be described as an 'intermediate' term, carrying connotations both moral and financial. In any case the term 'graft' is well-known and well-understood but may perhaps deserve wider currency than it presently enjoys in the general literature on corruption.

Socialist graft includes many things. Among these may be included bribery, corruption, embezzlement, the black market, the pace of rank and influence, even careerism and unscrupulous behaviour generally. Socialism is not immune from the frailties of human nature. We need not however go as far as Milovan Djilas to argue that "the Communist economy is perhaps the most wasteful economy of human society."[1] We might however agree with Djilas that: "The use, enjoyment and distribution of property is the privilege of the party and the party's top men."[2] Whatever our stand, there is little room to doubt the existence, at least, of socialist graft.

The Marxian Millennium: A Society Without Graft

> The statements of Karl Marx are like bats. From one angle they resemble birds, while from another view they look like mice. You see what you want to see, uninhibited by what is actually there.
>
> Vilfredo Pareto
> *Les Systemes Sociales (Paris, 1902) II p. 332*

Logically, there is no graft in a monastery (unless the monks have a father superior who would organize work and praying schedules for bribes or other considerations) and there is no graft in an anarchist commune (because having removed the state apparatus cooperation has replaced coercion). In a communist state, the position, while less obviously clear than in the above two examples, nevertheless presupposes a graft-free network of human relationships. Marx was very concerned with materialism in one sense, the philosophical view that materialism had supplanted idealism as an explanation of the philosophical order. Marx was not particularly concerned with materialism in the other sense of low and base material values, filthy lucre. As a man who willingly accepted poverty for himself and his family (at times even surviving, though not able to go out, without shoes) Marx would not have seen graft as a special case of human weakness. The economic interpretation of history does not for him ever become a history of bribery.

The invention of money he saw as a progressive factor permitting the "development of all forces of production, material and mental." Naturally greed will be present as his *Grundrisse* suggests but such a concept is too 'unscientific' for Marx. The driving force of money is both progressive and impersonal. Marx believed that he had discovered "the economic laws of motion in modern society." He shows us the spirit of capitalism working its way out in the open as it were according to objective historical economic laws. The final social outcome arrives when 'society can inscribe on its banners: from each according to his ability, to each according to his needs,' to refer to the words of the *Critique of the Gotha Programme.* Marx implies at times that the evil of private property is eradicable: '*Communism* is the *positive* abolition of *private property,* of human self-alienation.' Now the implication here is that when the 'government of persons' is replaced by the 'administration of things,' human lives can be ordered, in the classless state, according to the highest principles. The future as he sees it is one devoid of alienated humanity. Men will no longer be tempted. They will be delivered from evil.

One of the large assumptions of Marx and Engels is that for socialists there is no particular problem in bribery. While accepting that vulgar material desires are feasible, even possible during the period of primitive capital accumulation, we see nothing to suggest that bribery, corruption, and graft are likely at all to flourish under socialism. Indeed the persistence of graft into the post-revolutionary epoch would entail a further set of economic laws which included bribery. Such an acceptance of bribery in post-revolutionary times would suggest that there were certain human constants irrespective of the relative constraints of class. In short Marx may have 'omitted' from his analysis the universal law of corruption. This omission has led to socialist graft.

The 'philosopher' of bribery who abandoned Hegelianism for materialism is probably Feuerbach. Feuerbach asserted that our 'symbolic dreams,' for example the precepts of religion, offer no effective explanations but that philosophy is the study of man as defined by experience. The notion that 'man is what he eats' is logically at the heart of a philosophy of graft. Hence the party official in, for example, a socialist state who accepts bribes cannot be explained by Marxist tenets; he can be explained however in Feuerbachist terms.

Marx himself however cannot envisage the proletariat as animated by brutish materialism. Corruption in all senses of the word is no part of the proletarian future as envisaged by Marx. Rather the future is one of fraternity and class solidarity.

Marx inveighed against capital in an excessively purple passage, but one which Lenin learned by heart. "If money, as Augier says, 'came into the world with a congenital bloodstain on one cheek,' then capital comes dripping from head to foot, from every pore, with blood and dirt."[3] These given attributes of capital somehow disappear with the realization of socialism. Unless money is abolished then its continuation into a socialist society is likely to pose problems.

Yet Marx was utopian in respect to any idea of graft. Under socialism people would willingly exchange roles without the intervention of restrictive practices: "in a communist society where nobody has one exclusive sphere of activity, but each can become accomplished in any branch he wishes, society regulates the general production and thus makes it possible for me to do one thing today and another tomorrow, to hunt in the morning, fish in the afternoon, rear cattle in the evening, criticize after dinner, just as I have a mind, without ever becoming hunter, fisherman, shepherd, or critic."[4]

Under these conditions no one should in the ideal socialist state be tempted to use a special knowledge or special position to make money. Indeed, in a socialist society the distribution of benefits proceeds along well-known lines. Under true socialism "the distribution of burdens" should depend on abilities, while the "distribution of benefits" should depend on needs: 'from each according to his ability, to each according to his needs.' Men shed their selfishness and contribute towards the general good of all without any thought of personal gain. Socialism envisages men working contentedly to receive what they need, not what they have earned or merited and certainly not what they can 'squeeze' out of their fellowmen.

Of course distinctions are made between socialism and communism. In the former, distributive justice means that people are rewarded according to their work, which implies a form of merit. Hard work will be rewarded. In the final communist state people will be allocated benefits as they need them, and not as they merit them.

Both under socialism and communism private benefits are, at most, taboo. There is surely no ground in a socialist society for the existence of graft which permits persons to arrogate private benefits from the public weal. Ideally, graft should not exist under socialism. To possess a special advantage from the public ownership of the means of production must be contrary to the theoretical justification of socialism. Yet graft is in the empirical world as opposed to the ideal world of contemporary socialism, deeply embedded in the current practice of communist states, and examples are constantly cited in the press in various states which notionally owe allegiance to the 'ideals' of Marxism. Two particular cases will be examined, the largest socialist states today, namely the Soviet Union and the People's Republic of China. There are necessarily many exclusions in our analysis, such as the states of Eastern Europe, Africa and the rest of Asia, other than China. However the choice of the Soviet Union and China in themselves account for almost 1.3 billion people. From even a cursory examination of these two socialist states we are afforded an opportunity to examine some aspects of the relationship between socialism and graft.

Socialist Graft: The Soviet Case

The road to socialism in the Soviet Union is paved with good intentions. The official Soviet orthodoxy in the U.S.S.R. suggests that the Soviet Union is a class-free society of equals in which all would benefit from the selfless leadership of the communist party. The promise of 1917 is still the official promise of the 1980s. There is also a Soviet dream. The words of the preamble to the 1977 Constitution offer the official picture in glowing terms: "The Great October Socialist Revolution, made by the workers and peasants of Russia under the leadership of the communist party headed by Lenin, overthrew capitalist and landowner rule, broke the fetters of oppression, established the dictatorship of the proletariat and created the Soviet state, a new type of state, the basic instrument for defending the gains of the revolution and for building socialism and communism. Humanity thereby began the epoch-making turn from capitalism to socialism."[5]

The preamble further states: "After achieving victory in the Civil War and repulsing imperialist intervention, the Soviet government carried through far-reaching social and economic transformation, *and put an end once and for all* [my italics] to exploitation of man by man, antagonisms between classes, and strife between nationalities." The virtues of socialism so described are beyond question. In Chapter 2 of the Constitution under *The Economic System* we read: "No one has the right to use socialist property for personal gain or other selfish ends." In short, socialist graft is prohibited by the Soviet Constitution.

The distinction is made between private, i.e. personal property, and state property. Article 13 states that: "Property owned or used by citizens shall not serve as a means of deriving unearned income or be employed to the detriment of the interests of society." This stipulation offers us a more difficult idea, namely that property advantages should not lead to income which has not been earned (we might wonder whether stock market-type dealings in capitalist societies are here envisaged) or which society might as whole see as 'detrimental.'

Concern is also expressed for state property. In Article 61, we read: "It is the duty of the citizen to combat misappropriation and squandering of state and socially-owned property and to make thrifty use of the people's wealth. Persons encroaching in any way on socialist property shall be punished according to law." The basic difficulty which faces the student of corruption is whether such a moral society exists in the U.S.S.R., and to what extend the rhetoric is at variance with the reality.

Some enthusiasts, and not always all fellow-travellers, have seen the Soviet Union as above reproach. 'Like Pericles in his *Funeral Oration at Athens*,' the Soviet citizen could say with truth: "Our citizens attend both to public and to private duties, and do not allow absorption in their own various affairs to interfere with their knowledge of the City's. The U.S.S.R. was far from the perfect society or the perfect life as yet—but it was moving *faster* [his italics] in its improvement than any previous community in history."[6]

In fact the place of corruption in private dealings in Soviet society is well-established. It is possible to ruin the beautiful theory of Marxism-Leninism with the ugly fact of socialist graft. Opportunities for graft were early presented to socialist revolutionaries and were undoubtedly taken.[7] The nature of the economy in early Soviet history (i.e. in the 1920s) presented opportunities for corruption largely because of difficulties regarding the supply of materials. As late as the 1950s we gather that "the use of *blat* is most important as a means of expediting the supply of materials. The Soviet manager faces the perpetual threat that promised materials will neither be delivered on time nor in the right quantity and quality . . . he turns to the use of *blat*. "But of course," says Brumberg, "there are varieties of *blat;* there is 'leather blat' and there is 'coal blat.'[8] To find the correct specialist one needs to find a 'pusher,' 'fixer' or *tolkach*. The *tolkach* knows which officials can be fixed. Even K.G.B. officers are known to have a soft spot for extra-curricular bottles of vodka or a few pairs of shoes to forget particular charges.[9]

Attention has also been paid to *strakhova* which signifies 'insurance' or 'security.' Officials can be paid '*strakhova*' money to guarantee planned output at a level below that possible. Thus coal, paper and cotton production levels can be set below capacity; or at the other extreme, requirements for raw materials can be pitched at levels far above those necessary to complete the task.

Examples of near-corruption quoted by Brumberg appear to be related to the nature of the socialist system. Falsification and manipulation of data often "solve" problems. On paper there may be no actual difficulties. A sum of money can change hands to keep the records straight and the statistics favorable. The successful manager fulfills or over-fulfills his plan. People can be persuaded to cooperate—for a bribe. To realize the plan (even on paper) people may have to be persuaded to "look the other way." Malenkov himself believed that "such situations ordinarily lead to corruption and degeneration."

Once Stalin saddled that Soviet people with the first so-called 'command economy,' the over-bureaucratization of the economy as well as excessive centralization and confusion in decisionmaking promoted temptation. Those who had power have undoubtedly used it to profit themselves. Indeed even before the first five-year plan was introduced elements of a black market emerged. Graft emerged from the earliest days after the revolution. The peasants did not wish to cooperate with those who appropriated their produce so they sold grain on the side—for a profit. At the same time, war communism made money suspect. Workers even stole metal, made lighters (essentially consumer goods) and sold them for food.[10] The response to such unsocialist attitudes was the development of a characteristic Stalinist terror.

The 'realist' approach to Soviet politics does envisage corruption in large measure in Soviet society. However there is a long line of opponents of the Soviet state from Trotsky through, for example, Djilas and a variety of modern critics internal as well as external, who see a dark thread of corrupt practices. This approach, at its most controlled and dispassionate would say: "The heroic era of communism is past. The epoch of its great leaders has ended. The epoch of practical men has set in. The new class has been created."

One of the most useful analyses is contained in Hedrick Smith's book *The Russians,* and this analysis takes *blat* as the standard Soviet idea on corruption. *Blat* is defined as "influence, connections, pulling strings." Smith argues that: "In an economy of chronic shortages and carefully parcelled out privileges, *blat* is an essential lubricant of life." Smith speaks of '*na levo,*' which literally means "on the left," and implies an undercover payment. This may be in kind. On January 1,

1975, *Izvestia* revealed that more than one-third of the Soviet private motorists were driving on state petrol. The value of such petrol was estimated at 60 million roubles.[12]

Soviet citizens describe corruption as "creeping capitalism," and it is estimated by Andrei Sakharov to involve about 10 percent of the gross national product—a figure of about 50 billion roubles ($66 billion). There are no figures on the level of corruption in the Soviet economy but 10 percent could be a fair estimate based on the British economy.[13] There is a Russian saying, *'blat silnee sovnarkoma'* ('blat is higher than Stalin') which argues that influence is stronger than the government. The usurpation of legitimate government organizations and state norms by corrupt practices is widespread. A particular example is in *defitsitny* or deficit-goods. When scarce goods arrive at a shop, assistants secrete these away and supply them to those prepared to pay a large discount. The *Beryozka* shops "are an open invitation to black market profiteering." Only persons with properly gained and permitted hard currency may shop there, but products on sale for 4 roubles may reach 40 roubles on the street.

There is little information regarding large and influential syndicates. Smith refers to a corrupt syndicate in textiles and fabrics in Lithuania, another dealing in fruit juice in Azerbaijan and a third dealing with gems in Moscow. A network involving Tadzhikstan products (by which products were systematically undervalued to the profit of one Mikhail Laviyev) brought the death sentence for the man involved.

Soviet Georgia has a particular reputation for corruption, and appears to be particularly resistant to purges. The first secretary of the Georgian party, Vasily Mzhavanadze, was believed to have been involved in large-scale corruption, including Mafia-style drug syndication.[14] In June 1981, Y.A. KobaKahidze was executed for housing graft in Georgia.

Blat is part of influence and is a Russian (and Soviet) device. Solzhenitsyn offers a picture of bribery in the judicial sector which has led one writer to comment that "breach of the law is an integral part of the Soviet economy."[15] "It may seem strange to us now, but it is a fact that in those thunderous years bribes were given and taken just as tenderly as they had been from time immemorial in old Russia and as they will be in the Soviet Union from here to eternity."[16]

Solzhenitsyn states that "bribery was particularly rife in the judicial organs." The Cheka (Counter Revolutionary organ) "often depended upon bribes." The sums involved were considerable. Solzhenitsyn discusses the power of gold. "But if you had gold, you could determine the extent of your torture, the limits of your endurance and your own fate." He argues: "If in fact you had no gold, then your situation was hopeless."[17] Of course the early part of Soviet history just after the Revolution differed in that some persons might still have family gold to bribe their gaolers. However Solzhenitsyn is inclined to offer a picture of the moral corruption of power rather than dwell excessively upon the more petty aspects of simple bribery. The object of Gulag was, as Solzehnitsyn saw it, the total degradation of human beings, who were the objects of what was euphemistically called the Sewage Disposal System.

In spite of everything, corruption has flourished. The role of *wziatka* (as baksheesh is known in the Soviet Union) is central. At low levels it is rampant but at the highest levels information is less forthcoming. As already mentioned, the first secretary of Georgia, Vasili M. Mzhavanadze (and a member of the political bureau in Moscow) was fired for corruption, but nothing of this matter was revealed in the Soviet press, even though 50,000 people were arrested in the subsequent police investigation. Mzhavanadze was replaced by Edward Schevarnadze, his former K.G.B. head. Little was revealed of the misdeeds of Ekaterina Furtseva formerly minister of culture who quietly retired after having built a luxurious *dacha* for herself, using state materials and labor costing about 120,000 roubles. In Azerbaidzhan, the chief executive of a textile plant and his accomplices, including a justice ministry inspector and a public prosecutor, were found guilty of transforming a textile plant to private use and embezzling 2 million roubles (about $3 million).

The "Second Economy" of the Soviet Union

Below the 'first economy' is the 'second economy' in the command state of the U.S.S.R. The second economy is private, outside the rigid central plan of the public or state sector. Gregory Grossman believes of the second economy that closely tied to it is widespread corruption of officialdom.[18] The second economy fulfills at least one of the two tests following. Firstly it is directly for private gain and secondly it significantly contravenes existing law.

There are many examples of the second economy, and they are given in the press in profusion. Typical examples include the payment of higher differential fees for professional services on the part of medical men or dentists. A whole state enterprise may in fact be engaged in private production or the provision of services, such as the repair of cars. The second economy will naturally link into the general area of the purchase of influences and other favors which only members of the *party* bureaucracy (or to a lesser extent the *state* bureaucracy) can provide.

In 1982 a very significant case, involving Brezhnev's family itself, was reported on 4 March 1982 in *Pravda*.[19] On 29 December 1981, diamonds were stolen from the home of a female liontamer with the Moscow circus. These were discovered to be in the home of a singer in the choir of the Bolshoi Theatre, Boris Buryatiya, who was believed to be the "close friend" of Galina, Brezhnev's daughter.

Galina's husband was Lt. Gen. Yury Churbanov, first deputy head of the MVD (Ministry of Internal Affairs) police which investigated the robbery. Buryatiya was arrested on 29 January by the K.G.B., whose tasks include the control of speculation and bribery in valuables and hard currency. Semen Tsvigun, first deputy head of the K.G.B., committed suicide apparently because he was reprimanded by Suslov, who also died of a stroke late in January 1982.

The nature of the corruption involved was related to the department for visas and registrations. Those who travel abroad have reputedly had to pay 3500 roubles rather than the official rate of 350 roubles and the illicit funds have found their way back to Buryatiya who could indulge a flamboyant life style in consequence, as well as some degree of immunity from arrest given his protectress who was the daughter of Brezhnev.

The scandal was only the tip of a very large Soviet iceberg, at the bottom of which are found innumerable examples. In 1970, a quarter of all alcohol consumed in the U.S.S.R. was produced and also supplied through the second economy. In 1972 about 500 liters of petrol were stolen and recycled into the black market. Information from Jewish emigres suggests that the second economy provides 10 percent of earnings with particular areas of interest in service industries such as appliance repairs, hairdressers and beauty shops. Russians earn 175 roubles per month on average; they are excluded from ownership of precious stones in consequence.

The market does not allocate resources in such a system; this is the task of officials. But a cash economy exists and so does the trade in diamonds and precious metals. It is therefore no surprise to learn that diamonds in large quantities were discovered in the homes of those with important connections.

Western goods are in great demand. In a Moscow radio program we learn that Soviet-made jeans costing 60 roubles a pair (when obtainable) are resold at 200–250 roubles, and an attractive dress bought at 40 roubles can fetch 200 roubles.[20] Shoes, ornaments, rings, earrings, necklaces and other trinkets are sold at "monstrous profits" on the black market. The use of vodka *na levo* is virtually an institution, whose side effect is part of the subculture of Soviet alcoholism. Arising from the fact that corruption is now "endemic in every layer of society," we need to offer some generalizations about the consequences of this all-pervasive graft. First, graft in the Soviet Union has become a part of the political succession battle. Accusations of graft are a handy means of denigrating one's opponents. Whether true or not, an accusation of graft is always a potential means of undermining opponents in a power struggle. A second aspect of Soviet socialist graft lies in the light which it sheds upon the bureaucracy and the inefficient conduct of the Soviet Union's planned economy. Whatever the merits or demerits of the planned economy, in practice it has offered many examples of graft largely because administrative dysfunctions prevail. Penalties do not appear to have much impact. All Soviet citizens know that the death penalty can be given for corruption. In September 1981, the criminal code was altered to increase the penalty for corruption more generally. In November a confidential letter was apparently read (according to western journalist Leopold Unger) at local party meetings held *in camera*. In January 1982, the head of the anti-corruption department, Boris Zabotin, was reported as having been assigned to the department of the Interior. The new post was raised to deputy minister status by an announcement by Lt. Gen. Yuri Churbanev, the chief minister of the Interior Ministry police, the husband of Galina, daughter of Brezhnev. Hence graft, nepotism and intrigue are found closely associated in Soviet life. The London *Times* indeed refers to an "atmosphere of Byzantine intrigue and scandal," in its assessment of the Galina scandal.

The Soviet Union has shown clear evidence of what might be called 'degenerate commandism.' In other words, the Soviet machinery of planning performs badly and is prone to graft. During the long Brezhnev years (1964–1982) it was widely believed that the command economy had on available evidence degenerated. After Brezhnev's death, the short-lived rule of Andropov was associated with tentative reforms at both the organizational and personnel level.

Andropov's supposed 'liberalism' was taken up by Gorbachev when he became General Secretary in March 1985 after the death of Andropov's successor, Chernenko. Gorbachev appeared to envisage that he could retain the command economy albeit as a cleansed economy. The 1986 budget plans, for example, saw a 4 percent growth increase largely through improved labor productivity. In short, Gorbachev thought that socialist graft could be eliminated without a structural change in the economy.

The problem is that there is a command economy in the Soviet Union and there is also graft. Are the two related? One commentator, K. Simis, argues that the present Soviet system is a necessary condition for the emergence of socialist graft. Simis believes that the heart of the people is good. The system is the cause of all problems. He argues: "The Soviet government, Soviet society, cannot rid itself of corruption as long as it remains Soviet. It is as simple as that." Socialist graft is deepseated. Simis is in no doubt: "Corruption permeates the life of *Homo sovieticus.*" Gorbachev, by contrast, sees the matter of socialist graft (even if he admits of its existence) as a cleansing operation only. Sceptics think that graft must continue in the Soviet Union as long as the structure exists. Both agree however to the extent that opportunities do exist for misbehavior. Both agree that the Soviet economy does not provide goods required in sufficient quantities. In consequence, people seize the opportunities provided to develop networks of graft. But, we only know about breaches of the rules because these may be recorded in *Pravda* or in organs of the press. We are likely to hear reports of isolated instances of graft rather than be able to probe networks of graft. Syndicated graft is more difficult to prove than isolated examples.

If there were such a thing as 'pure' socialism, it may well be that graft would not develop in socialist states. Parallel to the concept of imperfect competition in the West, there is, in socialist states, a concept of imperfect socialism. In practice, to use one of Mao Zedong's favorite words, there are many 'contradictions' in present-day Soviet society. The continued existence of socialist graft is one of them.

Socialist Graft: The Case of China

Lenin and other Russian Marxists at the turn of the century had the task of reconciling their understanding of Marxism with the reality of Russia. Marx gave some attention to the Asian (or Asiatic) mode of production, noting the relationship between oriental despotisms and control over water, which was elaborated in detail by Wittfogel in his concept of a hydraulic society.

Resource allocation is naturally associated with politics in a debate over the control over the means of production. The worker may have nothing to sell except his labor. The Chinese tradition of graft is very deep-rooted. In prerevolutionary imperial times, corruption was entrenched in the mandarinate. The 'long-fingernailed mandarins' always creep back and so does bureaucratic corruption. In place of the imperial bureaucracy the bureaucracy of the party has given us its version of graft.

For a number of years, the extent of bureaucratic graft has been concealed. Mao's long years in power were seen as years of rigorous austere proletarian morality. Yet in the years since Mao's death, graft has taken firm hold of many sectors of Chinese society. Chinese understanding of graft is exceedingly broad. In particular it encompasses the idea of embezzlement which itself implies misappropriation of socialist property, which itself is a moral notion. A survey of graft in China in a number of Hong Kong newspapers in February 1982 lays particular stress on embezzlement. In a socialist society embezzlement is of particular concern; in a capitalist society, embezzlement is a private vice, and the main loser is the capitalist. In China, embezzlement is equated with graft.

The revelations have been in the correct sense of the word, sensational. "Rarely has any Communist country provided such sensational information about illegal goings-on inside its ruling party."[21] There is "a well-publicized campaign to crack down on corruption, abuse of position and what looks like a near-epidemic of organized crime by ranking officials."[22]

This vigorous anti-corruption drive took place in the period following the removal of Hua Guofeng in 1980. Laws were introduced which provided heavy penalties for graft, including the possible use of the death penalty. Many party articles inveighed against the deterioration in moral standards.

A typical example came from the *New China News Agency* dated April 13, 1982. The Agency argued that the struggle for "communist integrity" and against "corruption" is "vital." In the past two or three years, the article said, "activities in smuggling, bribery and theft have increased sharply, causing serious economic damage." The culprits were to be punished and those "very few" organs of the bureaucracy responsible "which are really rotten to the core must be reorganized or dismissed."

The People's Daily (8 December 1981) revealed the existence of widespread graft in Wuxi with 1532 cases of bribery reported. In Xinhua the China Daily paper reported the prosecution of 20,000 economic criminal cases, and a 10 million yuan tax evasion, including "smugglings, speculation, graft, embezzlement, bribery and tax evation." In Shenzhen, a number of party officials were punished and the assistant director of the city post and telegraphs was dismissed for misappropriating renminbi totalling 50,000 yuan (US $29,410). He built a house with the proceeds. Shenzhen is one of four so-called special economic zones in China which is permitted certain trading relations with the outside world. Smuggling and embezzlement of course are likely to be bedfellows with graft.

A veritable torrent of cases appeared late in 1981 and in 1982. The *People's Daily* announced a web of corruption involving 130 offices, departments and factories for the illegal selling of over 1300 motor vehicles. The *People's Daily* exposed electric power supply corruption in which officials embezzled enough to start their own "treasury" with assets of 1.5 million yuan (about US $1 million). Investigators were frustrated at every turn. The electricity supply bureau in Anhui province, Hao county, was known to the local people as the 'electric despot.'

Telecommunications in Guanhou (Canton) gained a reputation for being 'corrupt.' A husband and wife syndicate bought up television sets, watches, and electric calculators and sold them as far as Shangtung province in the North. In Fujian province the Xiang Nan party leader declared war on graft and related economic crimes, arguing that "corruption is a two-way struggle." Beijing itself reported 9853 smuggling cases and 223 cases of corruption in the capital in 1981.[23] Party officials in Anhui were in trouble as well as in Hainan Island. Hainan Island's graft was particularly noteworthy, where the head of the Bureau of Supplies was expelled from the party for the second time for offences involving graft.

In Liaoning province, one swindle led to the "bankruptcy" of seventeen factories. Party officials were involved (Ma Xinguang and Lin Yung) and the factories closed down. Ma received five years. In Shanghai serious swindling and profiteering took place, involving 26 officials. Bad accounting as well as deliberate swindles were encountered in Wenzhou, 250 miles south of Shanghai. One rationale advanced for these practices by the *People's Daily* was that city leaders had misinterpreted national policy on the loosening of restraints on the economy to mean 'money above all.' They "gave the green light to speculators and swindlers." "Some leaders of these units," said *People's Daily,* "provide the criminals with nearly everything they needed—capital, titles, letters of introduction, work permits and blank but validated contract forms by the thousands." A massive campaign against bureaucratic corruption was instituted by Deng personally. Early in 1982 Deng appeared to think that the proliferation of bureaucrats in the state and party had gone too far. He set out to trim the over-weight structure of the bureaucracy. The suggestion was that bureaucratic corruption (i.e., graft which stems from bureaucratic practices) is the major enemy.

Graft in China has moved from administrative organ to administrative organ, from the state to the party to the shop floor.[24] Factories have entered into systematic conspiracies to evade taxes. Industry has suffered. Members of the party regularly use public funds for private houses and cars. Bank employees embezzle funds on a large scale. Even disaster relief money has been misappropriated. In the first eight months of 1981 the electricity power industry "lost" US $8 million worth of transmission equipment. A leading official in Beijing, Jiang Shaoyan, who headed a rectifier factory, took 9,600 yuan (US $6000) in bribes. He had previously refused to release the money due to a certain factory giving as his reason that its products were defective.

Countering graft in China has proved to be extremely difficult. In stimulating enterprise and individual initiative (as opposed to ideological fervor), a genie had been let out of a bottle. The *China Daily,* quoting Qinynian Bao, pointed out that "individualism cannot exist without personal gain but personal gain does not necessarily mean individualism." The official Chinese press fulminated against the selfish attitudes of people who had been undermined by the "silver-coated bullets of bourgeoisie." Indeed one person dismissed for graft, Lin Jinyi, was daring enough to comment that "if you report me, I'll complain to the capitalist press."[25]

Red Flag (Honggi) stated that it was wrong to see corruption as a small matter. "Backdoor dealings, favoritism, seeking of privileges and other bad practices," these cause discontent among the masses, tarnish the image of the party and lower its prestige.[26] The writer, Wang Renzhog, was a director of the propaganda department under the Central Party Committee. The sugar-coated bullets of the bourgeoisie had influenced all persons and all ranks in Chinese society, judging by the mass of evidence coming forward.

A discipline inspection committee or central commission on inspecting discipline, appears to be the body charged with surveillance of graft. Graft is however apparently deeply entrenched, and while the leadership believes that graft can be eradicated by resolute means, it also recognizes that graft is not easily eradicated. A decision on the severe punishment of serious and harmful economic crimes was passed by the standing committee of the Fifth National People's Congress in February 1982.

Now the difficulty with evaluating Chinese graft lies in the overall general conception of graft which is comprehensible in Chinese thinking on the matter. Graft is to be seen as more than just bribery, and corruption in China suggests a moral element as well as a minor peccadillo resulting from understandable human weakness. The Chinese would not easily differentiate between forms of bribery, speculation, fraud, embezzlement and smuggling. As in most socialist societies there are economic crimes, and as the means of production are supposed to be publicly owned, embezzlement is perhaps the most common. The embezzler misappropriates resources which properly belong to the state. This is contrary to the Criminal Code, Article 155. Yet the embezzler will be likely to be involved in the giving and taking of bribes because bribes are required to sustain the mechanics of the system. Bureaucratic corruption frequently depends upon syndicates which control the allocation of scarce resources.

The student of graft in China has ample raw data on which he can draw. Examples of graft running into hundreds of millions of yuan have been noted from the following areas: Anxiang (Hunan), Baotau, Beijing, Changde, Datong, Guangzhou (Canton), Hainan, Heilongjiang, Jiangsu, Jilin, Liangsui, Nanyang, Oizhou, Shanxi, Sichuan, Tienjian, Wuhan, Xinmin, Yanshan, Yuling, Zgabghian, Wuhan, Xinmin, Yanshan, Yuling, and Zhangjiang. The categories into which these examples fit will vary. They may relate to bribery or embezzlement in some cases, or to fraud, and even to speculation.

In Chinese eyes, graft is involved in all these. However, if it is accepted that all property belongs to the state, then in embezzlement further complication arises in that western notions of private property do not fit Chinese property theories; even in classical China, family, rather than individual ownership is important. Certainly the private misappropriation of public goods should not be tolerated.

Socialist graft is interpreted in China in a number of ways. Some people such as Chen Yun see the huge volume of graft cases as the result of some defects in economic philosophy. Too rapid a move in the direction of economic liberalism can, Chen Yun appears to believe, only unsettle China, giving rise to graft and other evils.

Deng Xiaoping believes that as long as it catches mice, it does not matter whether a cat is black or white. The economic philosophy may not be so worrying, within certain political limits, as long as the economy performs well. Deng appears to see the problem of graft more as a fault of poor organization—or bureaucratism. Deng's position is not far from that of Gorbachev. If the currently inefficient bureaucrats were to be removed, then the position would be much healthier. But whatever the interpretation, the numbers of cases investigated in China run into the millions. The pages of *Renmin Ribao* offer numerous examples of continuing socialist graft. Particularly bad cases receive the death penalty.

Corruption in China is a moral issue and transcends the existence of mere bribe taking. In China moral imperatives, whether Confucian or Maoist, have been placed before the population as ideals. With the demystification of Mao in the late 1970s, economic, rather than political, objectives were emphasized. Modernization became a surrogate ideology, but it was a vision of a richer state in which economic growth was stressed. With the loss of Maoist moral fervor, a reaction appeared to set in. Materialism, so long theoretically unacceptable, became a tenable part of the theory of modernization because the latter stressed the economic benefits of modernity in China. On May 8 1982, *Xinhua* stressed that corruption might be curtailed by a proper understanding of those parts of the writings of Lenin and Mao which warn communists against 'degeneration,' and seek to 'maintain the communist purity and not permit corruption or moral laxity.'

Yet in China, as with the Soviet Union, friction within political leadership and faction-fighting have frequently been associated with accusations of graft. Those groups who are frequently depicted as 'corrupt' are described as such as part of a campaign of political intrigue. Since 1980 China has been inundated with many accusations of corruption. Previously cases of graft would be concealed or covered up because to reveal such cases would be to reveal that a socialist system had certain moral deficiencies. The period of Maoist rule was marked by a moral intensity which admitted of no failings in the superiority of proletarian morality. A curious paradox existed with a mass psychology coexisting with a God-like man of destiny. Morality was the gift of the Great Helmsman. Suggestions of any deviation from the path of righteousness were rarely entertained.

The contrast with the present situation of laxness in public life is all the more remarkable. The leaders of China see the problem as one of straightforward bureaucratic graft. Hence Zhao Ziyang, prime minister of the P.R.C., told a standing committee at a meeting that the top echelons of the bureaucracy within the state apparatus would be cut by almost one-half, from 98 ministries to 52 with a staff reduction of about one-third. The number of ministers would be cut from about 1000 to 35. Vice-premiers would be removed and lower-level bureaucrats, which have offered comfortable sinecures to men long into their eighties, would be cut in half.

In China, unlike the U.S.S.R., corruption is not only openly admitted, but is seen to be a problem of immensely serious dimensions. The contrast is pointed out between the poverty of the masses and the riches of the party mandarinates. In the Soviet Union no such admissions are made. Graft in China is confessed, *Mea culpa, mea maxima culpa;* in the Soviet Union occasional peccadilloes are shamefacedly admitted. The extent of graft in the Soviet Union as in many Eastern European states is hard to discern because the matter will most frequently be covered up. But the self-perpetuating oligarchies which all so often pass for socialist states ensure the continued prosperity of those who benefit from party control.

Socialist graft is obviously part and parcel of the panoply of irresponsible socialist power structures. Party officials effectively control the politics, economy and lives of the people over whom their power is uncontrolled. The arrival of 1984 (Orwell's nomenclature) has already been noted by *apparatchiki* who call black/white according to their will. When in China the ration vouchers arrive, the party secretary in the locality gives them to his cronies.[27] The new party bosses are installed with gifts. Advantages and perquisites are built into the system. Socialist graft is the graft of poverty; its capitalist counterpart shares relatively a greater degree of affluence. Socialist graft is a double failure; a bureaucratic failure (as its leaders argue) but also a moral failure (which its leaders could never admit).

Conclusion

There can be little doubt that graft is likely to exist within modern socialist states. Socialism confers no immunity upon its practitioners in their confrontation with graft. Yet, the point further arises whether socialist states (i.e. states controlled by communist parties) are in fact *more* prone to the temptations of graft than are non-socialist states. There are a number of reasons why socialist states in fact demonstrate greater opportunities for graft than do non-socialist states.

1. Socialist states are hierarchical, even at times 'feudal,' in their structure. To please a superior becomes an imperative. There are no alternative constituents. The temptations for graft readily manifest themselves under such circumstances.
2. Socialist states are most frequently self-perpetuating oligarchies. Power is bureaucratically structured in such a way as to inhibit the inflow of new talent. Such talent may be able to advance only through illegal and extralegal means. Bribery may be the best way forward to a career. *Blat* therefore flourishes.
3. Persons outside the charmed circle of power unable to channel their activities into the prescribed pattern of political activities, principally through the party structures, may seek alternative outlets in graft. Eastern Europe, including Czechoslovakia, Poland, and Rumania provide graphic examples.
4. Socialist states justify their existence by reference to an all-embrac-

ing ideology. Yet the gap between the rhetoric of the ideology and the reality of political struggle places enormous strains upon citizens. Socialist states carry the encumbrance of an unquestioned political theology which promotes Orwellian double-think.

5. Most socialist states see their development as bound up with, if not dependent upon, socialist planning. Planning in practice however demands a new code of ethics from its practitioners. Instead of accepting the selfish stimuli of the price mechanism, planners need to understand that logic is not always perceived or acted upon. There is falsification, diversion of resources and inadequate false or improper accounting in a very large number of cases. Graft all too easily becomes an inescapable part of the economy in a socialist state. Examples are forthcoming only when, as for example in the case of contemporary Poland, conditions of extreme inefficiency are revealed.

6. Most socialist states are in the less developed category and glimpses of apparent capitalist affluence often tantalize even the most devoted socialist administrator. Goods perceived as necessities in affluent states are often unimaginable luxuries in states which set themselves high-minded socialist principles. High-minded socialist principles are not, in a realistic world, adequate compensation for lack of consumer goods. In the Soviet Union for example, it has been said that "good food and especially meat (are) the yardstick by which most Russians measure their own prosperity."[28] Such a notion is perhaps more 'cultural' than 'ideological.' Chinese measure their prosperiity in terms of rice and family, a somewhat different concept but instinctively seen in terms of consumer benefit.

Officially in socialist states graft is seen as a temporary aberration. Officially only capitalism is sick: socialism is healthy. Where graft persists in socialist states, the apologists contend, it can be attributed to the 'sugar-coated bullets' of the bourgeoisie. The bourgeois mentality alone promotes graft according to socialists. Yet they fail to account satisfactorily for the prevalence of graft in socialist societies. The main factors are bureaucratic inefficiency, linked to inherent scarcity of resources and arbitrariness, supported by an entrenched acceptance of special privileges for party, self, and family. No socialist would be happy in admitting socialist graft, but fewer still are inclined to accept that socialist graft is a direct product of socialism.

Capitalist graft is of course the particular manifestation of graft in North America, Europe or Japan.[29] No doubt it is difficult to make moral distinctions as between the one and the other. However socialism finds particular difficulties in its claim of moral superiority over capitalism *per se*. Graft develops under socialism because of a serious divergence between supply of goods and services and the demand for these. Shortages may be worsened by bureaucratic ineptitude or cynicism regarding the ability of the system to produce or allocate resources. Graft may, under such circumstances, become institutionalized at the moment when expectations of a higher living standard have been generated. Socialist leaders must therefore resign themselves to the existence of graft and to acceptance of it as natural and normal, provided it offers no serious challenge to the system. Paradoxically therefore, socialism is supported by graft and *vice versa*.

Notes

1. Milovan Djilas, *The New Class: An Analysis of the Communist System*. Praeger, 1957, p. 118.
2. Op. cit., p. 60.
3. Op. cit. in Robert Payne, *The Life and Death of Lenin*. (W.H. Allen), Pan Books, 1964, p. 148.
4. K. Marx and F. Engels, *The German Ideology*. See Lewis S. Feuer, *Marx and Engels*, Basic Writings on Politics and Philosophy. Fontana Classics, Collins, 1969, p. 295.
5. Constitution of the Union of Soviet Socialist Republics, October 7, 1977, Novosti Press Agency Publishing House, Moscow.
6. Andrew Rothstein, *A History of the U.S.S.R.* Penguin Books, 1950, p. 379.
7. Some studies on Soviet graft were made by Joseph Berliner, "Blat is higher than Stalin." in Abraham Brumberg (ed.), *Russia under Khruschev*. New York: Praeger, 1962. Paul R. Gregory and Robert C. Stuart, *Soviet Economic Structure and Performance*. Harper, 1981. Hedrick Smith, *The Russians*. London: Time Books, 1976. K. Simis, *USSR: The Corrupt Society*. New York: Simon and Schuster, 1982, is a major, if over-committed, source.
8. Berliner in Brumberg, op. cit., p. 156.
9. Brumberg, op. cit., p. 160. According to Simis, the K.G.B. uses black-market networks in order to trap and blackmail foreigners, Simis, op. cit., pp. 195–199.
10. Alec Nove, *An Economic History of the U.S.S.R.* Penguin, 1976 (Revised) p. 137.
11. Djilas, op. cit., p. 53.
12. Smith, op. cit., pp. 82–83.
13. In Britain, one assessment puts the black economy at 6 percent to 8 percent of the economy. This would amount to £15,000 million. *Times*, Feb. 1 1982. See also the *Sunday Times*, "Cheats at Work: An Anthropology of Workplace Crime," January 31 1982. The latter was a summary of the book by Gerald Mars of the same name (1982, Allen & Unwin). In the United States, it could be as high as $428 billion (U.S. Treasury estimates). Britain and the United States are covered respectively by Alan Doig, *Corruption and Misconduct in Contemporary British Politics*. (Har-

mondsworth: Penguin) 1984 and Michael Johnston, *Political Corruption and Public Policy in America* (Monterrey, CA: Brooks-Cole) 1982.

14. Soviet Georgia's legendary reputation for graft is particularly noted amongst diplomats in Moscow (see Simis, op. cit., p. 53). Executions for corruption in Georgia were reported early in 1982. Edward Shevarnadze commented: "Once the Georgians were known throughout the world as a nation of warriors and poets; now they are known as swindlers."
15. Simis, op. cit. p. 53. Berliner in Brumberg op. cit., p. 173.
16. Alexander Solzhenitsyn, *The Gulag Archipelago*. Collins & Fontana, 1974, p. 311.
17. Op. cit., p. 53.
18. Gregory Grossman, "The Second Economy of the U.S.S.R.," *Problems of Communism*. Sept. 1977, pp. 25–40. More generally, see Stuart Henry, *The Hidden Economy: The Context and Control of Borderline Crime* (Martin Robertson) 1978.
19. See also the *Times* and *Sunday Times*, 4 March 1982.
20. Moscow Radio, 30 September 1979.
21. *Time*, March 15 1982, p. 17. See also David Bonavia, "Mandarins on the Make," *Far Eastern Economic Review*, Hong Kong, June 18 1982 which argues that graft has reached epidemic proportions in China.
22. *Time*, op. cit., p. 17, February 7, 1982.
23. *South China Morning Post*, 15 April 1982 quoting New China News Agency. *People's Daily* February 8, 1982.
24. *Economist*, December 17, 1981. See also John P. Burns, "Reforming China's Bureaucracy, 1980–1982," *Asian Survey*, June 1983.
25. *South China Morning Post*, February 15, 1982.
26. *China Daily* quoting *Red Flag*, March 6, 1982.
27. Philip Short, B.B.C. correspondent, *Listener*, 15 April 1982.
28. Michael Binyon, *The Times*, 19 February 1980, and November 12, 1982, where Binyon described the 'second economy' as "so entrenched as to be ineradicable."
29. Arnold J. Heidenheimer, "Political Corruption," in *Readings in Comparative Analysis*, New York: Holt, Rinehart and Winston 1970 pp. 3–6, explores market graft. See also Susan Rose-Ackerman, *Corruption: A Study in Political Economy*, Academic Press, 1978. Non-socialist graft in a comparative context is examined by James C. Scott, *Comparative Political Corruption*, Prentice-Hall Inc., 1972.

The United States:
How Special a Case?
An Introduction

These chapters address not only the question whether the United States is particularly vulnerable to corruption but also whether the United Sates is in fact a special case, which would impede comparison of its experiences with those of other countries. Among the issues explored are what could be called the political-cultural nexus of American corruption, relevant differences in American and European political development, and an examination of the relationship between ordinary politics in the United States and political corruption. All the authors agree, explicitly or implicitly, that the United States does constitute a special case when it comes to corruption, but there are differences on how this makes the United States more vulnerable depending on how the criteria for such a judgment are applied to the American case.

In Chapter 31 A.S. Eisenstadt uses the Watergate scandal as a point of departure to ask whether corruption inheres in the American system in a peculiar way. Was the response to Watergate only the latest swing in a long American cycle of corruption and reform? He argues that through all periods there has been a group that decries corruption and demands reform; that group is the American "gentility," an Eastern establishment of prominent people steeped in the traditions of "bourgeois morality" and genteel reform. The author also asserts that there is an American idea and way of corruption derived from the ideas and practices of American democracy, the norms and ways of American sectarian Christianity, and the operation of the American entrepreneurial ethos.

In Chapter 33, Walter Lippmann argues the provocative thesis that corruption and politics may in fact be inseparable, and that corruption may well be an improvement in politics because it permits the peaceful buying and cooperation of opponents when, formerly, they were disposed of by brutal means. If the exchange of favors is an essential element of politics, argues the author, then the common American assumption that corruption represents a lapse from the original contract written by the founding fathers with posterity, is both naive and unrealistic.

Jacob van Klaveren, in Chapter 32, wonders why, given the enlightened ideas of the American founding fathers, corruption is still systematically practiced in the United States—particularly since it seemed by his perception to have practically disappeared in Europe. The answer, he suggests, lies in the peculiarities of American political development, including (among other factors) a lack of consensus on the desirability of honest government, the fact that suffrage became universal "too early," the cosy relationships between big business and politicians, and the possibility that the United States, compared to the European states, was late in becoming a nation.

In Chapter 34, Arnold J. Heidenheimer argues that cross-cultural study of corruption is both possible and desirable as a way of overcoming the various barriers to American scholarship on the subject. Among the impediments to be coped with in comparative analysis are that American institutions differ sufficiently from European ones to make comparison difficult; and that American corruption, particularly at the local level, is much more visible than in Europe. He thinks American analysts tended to cram too much under the corruption umbrella, and that the machine politics paradigm has had the effect of putting conceptual blinders on American analysts.

31

Political Corruption in American History

Abraham S. Eisenstadt

The questions that Watergate presents to the historian analyzing American political corruption are clear enough. To what extent does the Watergate phenomenon inhere in American politics? Is Watergate a uniquely American adventure? Or is it yet another act in the universal drama of man transgressing? If so, is American political corruptibility beyond reformation? Is the response to Watergate, no less than the episode itself, part of a recurrent cycle of American corruption and reform?

If the reform phase of the cycle is now in progress, what are its antecedents, and how does it relate to earlier drives for restoring American politics to honesty? Is today's reform a latter-day expression of what the Puritans of the 1630s stood for when, as Thomas Shepard put it, they proclaimed "the necessity of reformation of the church" and "in zeale of the Truth preached or professed against the corruptions of the times"?[1] Is it a variant form of the colonists' declaration of independence from Britain, which, in John Adams's hopes, would "inspire us with many virtues, which we have not, and correct many errors, follies, and vices," affording Americans, "who were addicted to corruption and venality," "a purification from our vices, and an augmentation of our virtues"?[2] Is it comparable to the reform movements of the antebellum age, when, as Horace Greeley saw it, "the perilous conflict with Wrong and Woe is our most conclusive evidence that Wrong and Woe shall yet vanish forever"?[3] Or is it like the Progressive movement, which, in Theodore Roosevelt's words, sought to "drive the special interests out of politics," and which regarded "executive power as the steward of the public welfare"?[4]

Source: Abraham S. Eisenstadt, "Political Corruption in American History: Some Further Thoughts," in Abraham S. Eisenstadt, Ari Hoogenboom and Hans L. Trefousse (eds.), *Before Watergate: Problems of Corruption in American History*. Brooklyn, N.Y.: Brooklyn College Press, 1978. Copyright © 1979 by Brooklyn College, CUNY. Reprinted with permission of publisher and author.

That Americans are now in a surge of reform is richly evident. In the past few years, forty-nine states have passed new campaign finance laws. The American congress is drafting a strict code of ethics, senators arising in turn, like Roman censors or French Girondins, to call for ever greater probity. But how far can reform carry? Laws do not create morality: if anything, they testify to its absence. Senator Sam J. Ervin of North Carolina, the patriarch who called Richard M. Nixon's sinners to justice, knew better than most the true nature of their sin. "The presidential aides who perpetrated Watergate," he said, "were not seduced by love of money, which is sometimes thought to be the root of all evil. On the contrary, they were instigated by a lust of political power, which is at least as corrupting as political power itself."[5] But if Senator Ervin was right, how can one legislate against another Watergate? How would laws be passed limiting the corruption of lusting for power, to say nothing of the corruption of possessing it? And what should one suggest if he turns from the president's aides to the president himself? Nixon Agonistes was the central figure in the Watergate drama. How could one hope to contain by law the psychic needs that drove a Nixon, knowing that the men who rise high in American politics are, by their nature, far more likely to be natives of Egocentralia than travelers from Altruria?

Granted at once that political corruption is not a uniquely American disease, it would be well to begin by defining it in general terms and then see how far those terms are applicable to American experience. Political corruption means that a public official has perverted the office entrusted to his care, that he has broken a public trust for private gain. To discuss corruption in a polity is, then, to discuss the standards of right and wrong in that polity. To say that the acts of officials holding public office are corrupt is to do two things: obviously, it is to blame them for subverting the moral standards governing the way they conduct their office; but no less importantly, it is to speak of the moral rules by which the community operates and, in effect, to look beyond the public office to the nature and purposes of the polity. It is, thus, to say what one considers to be the ends to which the polity is dedicated and the means by which those ends are to be achieved.

Each polity in every age has its own ideas of what the good society should be, of what role the public official should play in achieving the good society, and therefore of what misplaying of his role can validly be called corruption. When one talks about corruption in American politics, he must therefore refer the concept of corruption to the particularities of the American system: that is, to the premises, values and institutions that form the essence of the American polity. For that reason political corruption in the United States can best be understood if it is seen in a comparative perspective: if American democracy is contrasted with European, and particularly with British, aristocracy. For this perspective, one must consult America's most intelligent foreign visitors, particularly Alexis de Tocqueville and James Bryce. It was the concluded sense of both that America's best men did not go into politics. Did this mean that America had a politics of mediocrity or did it mean, as Andrew Carnegie suggested, that it had settled political institutions over which there was no longer any controversy?[6] Carnegie's suggestion offers another clue to the problem of American political corruption. It is fair to say that American parties and politics have expressed a contest not over ideologies but over alternatives, not between classes but between blocs of interests. The system itself has not been called into question, but only the corrupt way it is said to have been run. Thus the system is safeguarded, put beyond discussion. The system has not been called corrupt; instead the accusation is shifted onto those entrusted with conduct of the system. . . .

In every American age, there has been a group that has sounded the cry of corruption: the cry that political values are being debased, the political system subverted, public officials bought out. This group is the American gentility. It is they who have articulated the republic's ideals, who have denounced corrupt men and corrupt practices. Who are they, and what do they believe? They are neo-Puritans, descendants, in variant forms, of John Winthrop. The gentility has had its spokesmen in every American generation: its Cottons, its Mathers, its Hutchinsons, its Galloways, its Ticknors, its Fenimore Coopers, its Parkmans, its Adamses, its Cabots and Lodges, its Eliots and Morisons. They have always constituted an Eastern establishment. New England was their initial habitat but, as they migrated or as groups in other regions took up their outlook, their influence exercised an expanding dominion. They command America's prestigious divinity schools, prestigious schools of higher learning, prestigious journals and newspapers. They believe in private property, an ordered society, civic and moral education, a respect for institutions, good character as the essence of good leadership, and, of course, the claims of status and genealogy. The code they subscribe to is one summed up in the phrase "bourgeois morality." They stand for an adjustive conservatism and have perennially been America's genteel reformers. They stand for civic virtue, high-mindedness, a respect for the past, a disinterestedness in public affairs: they stand, in a word, for themselves. What they have decried as corrupt practices were, in some measure, actions that were not done their way. Those they decried as corrupt were not infrequently men they had lost out to. The gentility's cry of corruption has been, again in measure, a heart-rending lament over losing their superintendence of American politics. . . .

America's gentility believes that wealth corrupts and democracy is corruptible, that America needs a class of public philosophers or philosopher-kings to give civic lessons to the people and superintend the conduct of the *nouveaux riches*, and that they themselves—men of genteel origins and education—are precisely the class that could best satisfy these needs.[7]

Having said that the American idea of political corruption is particular to the United States, I should like to consider some of the principal factors in American society, factors that have generated political corruption and determined the way Americans perceive it. These factors are American sectarian Christianity, American democracy and law, and the American entrepreneurial ethos. Because the concept and practice of corruption are peculiar to a given polity, it is basic that American political corruption can be properly assayed only if it is compared with that of another polity. Accordingly, where feasible, the American model will be opposed to a European one. . . . In seeking points of reference for analyzing American political corruption, the author has been instructed above all by the intelligence of the man who instructed Hartz, and indeed a whole generation, and who is still the best guide to a comparative study of American institutions and ideas—Alexis de Tocqueville.

America is a Christian commonwealth. The founding of its polity was an incident in the drama of the European reformation. To say that Americans are a Christian people is at once to define their perception of corruption and the role it has played in their history. Christianity informs their public life with a type of moral code; the degree to which their officials fulfill the code determines the Americans' sense of the officials' probity or corruption. The early growth of Christian sectarianism in English North America meant that the Americans were to follow a different route in church-state relations from the Erastian one taken by most European polities. The dominant role of the state in Europe since the Reformation meant that morality in politics was whatever the state's governors said it was. In this way, the concept of corruption in a European polity has been, in some measure, an expression of its concept of *raison d'état*. In America, the triumph of Protestant sectarianism led, paradoxically, not only to the separation of church and state but also to the rule of a Christian ethos in the conduct of public affairs. In an Erastian order of politics, the question of corruption is to a considerable extent foreclosed. But in an essentially sectarian order, the question is not only not foreclosed, it is constantly open.

America's religion has shaped its politics: America's politics is, in a basic way, its religion. Both facts help explain the American view of political corruption. With Americans politics serves a triple function: it is the agora of democracy, wealth-seeking, and religion; in the American polity, the three are inseparable, indeed almost indistinguishable. In the absence of an established faith, the many sects joined a community of belief in the American political system. Participatory democracy was a translation of participatory communion. The relation between church and state in America originated in the fact that *raison d'état* had very often been synonymous with *raison de foi*. Far from a sharp demarcation between church and state, or more accurately, between churches and polities, there was an interplay between them where God was politicized and politics deified.[8] G. K. Chesterton described America as "a nation with the soul of a Church."[9]

It has thus been long understood that politics in America has been a form of civic faith, in which one may find secular variants of special providences, epiphanies and Feasts of Fools, indeed the whole panoply of political sacraments, including extreme unctuousness, double crosses, and the worst sin of all—venality. In the morality play that American politics has been, it was inevitable that the cry of corruption should be so frequently sounded and the prosecution of corruption so zealously pursued. Francis Grund, an Austrian who settled in the United States during the Jacksonian period, spelled out the impact of religion on public office. To violate morality, he said, is to violate religion and, in effect, "to subvert the political institutions of the country." Proof of "the high premium at which morality is held in the United States consists in its influence on the elections of officers." In Europe, said Grund, the statesman's "wanderings are forgotten" in the face of the good he has done for his nation. But

> no such compensation takes place in the United States. Private virtue overtops the highest qualifications of the mind, and is indispensable to the progress of the most acknowledged talents. . . . The moment a candidate is presented for office, not only his mental qualifications for the functions he is about to assume, but also his private character are made the subject of criticism. Whatever he may have done, said, or listened to . . . is sure to be brought before the public.[10]

Corruption is the other side of virtue. Americans hear the perennial cry of corruption because theirs is the land of the perennial reformation. It is basic to their ideology that life is a constant struggle for sanctification, that grace is theirs not by right but, at the very best, by achievement. When Americans say that the Puritan idea of election is made universal, they are saying that the possibility of access to grace is extended to all members of the community. But, by that very token, the struggle for sanctification also becomes universal, and the dangers of corruption become more widespread. The growth of the democratic ethos is at once religious and political, so that in talking of American political corruption, it is almost impossible to draw a line between the democratic and Christian concepts of value, however much the concepts are redefined from one age to the next. Where the ways to grace are thrown open, and the ways to wealth multiply, indeed where the acquisition of wealth becomes a sacrament, then the corruptibility of men becomes a central feature of American life. To the degree that Americans are the people of the perennial reformation, it is part of their ethos that they must constantly struggle to purge politics of evil men and evil ways.

In this quasi-religious drama of politics, the gentility have served as the keepers of the American conscience. They have measured their ideas of political conscience against the tenets of their belief: in a rationalized Christianity, in faith tempered by law, in divinity housed in institutions, in devotion enclosed by science, in godly ways approximated to bourgeois habits. . . .

Their Christianity has, in sum, been an important factor in Americans' perception of political corruption. These things have been noted: that Christianity has informed the Americans' politics, that it stands for them as a civil religion, that it has given them the moral calculus for measuring the good and the bad in their political lives, that their perennial political creed is perennial moral reformation, that the superintendents of their political ethic have been the genteel keepers of their conscience, and that the latter, more than any other single group, have led American reform movements, which have undertaken to restore the morality of a world seemingly lost. Watergate, it is true, had a dimension that cannot simply or directly be referred to the religious terms just presented, a dimension involving the struggle for power between two parties and the genuine fear of a power that corrupts and a corruption that empowers. But one misses a significant aspect of Watergate if he does not *also* see it as a Christian morality play, a struggle between the antinomians and those who insist upon fulfilling the moral law, and a contest between the fundamentalism of the Sun Belt and the rationalized Christianity of the Eastern Establishment.

How far has the American idea of political corruption been shaped by the fact of American democracy? To put the problem another way:

which was more given to corruption, a democratic society or an aristocratic? This question, a vital one during the first century and a half of American history, usually involved a contrast between American and Britain. For the larger part, it was the sense of the principal British and American commentators that corruption was more characteristic of democracy than of aristocracy. True enough, the Founding Fathers decried British political corruption and hoped to install, at home, a republic of virtue; but they were all too familiar with the failures of human nature[11] and, having created a national government based on democracy, they sought nothing so much as to restrain it. In the Jacksonian era, the Reform Bill of 1832 undertook to shift the locus of power in the British constitution and to do so, in significant measure, by reducing the element of corruption in the British electoral process. At the same time, it impressed Tocqueville that European aristocracy was far less susceptible of corruption than American democracy.[12] James Fenimore Cooper, who had begun in the 1820s by refuting British criticisms and by citing the virtues of life in the United States, came to the point in the 1830s where he was largely preoccupied with the vices of American democracy.[13] Charles Dickens went to Washington, D.C., with no great expectations, to put it mildly; but his tale of one city showed the hard times the English democrat suffered on witnessing the moral level of American public life. With his usual flair for understatement, he described the American Congress:

> Despicable trickery at elections; underhanded tamperings with public officers; cowardly attacks upon opponents, with scurrilous newspapers for shields, and hired pens for daggers; shameful trucklings to mercenary knaves, whose claim to be considered is, that every day and week they sow new crops of ruin with their venal types, . . . aidings and abettings of every bad inclination in the popular mind, and artful suppressions of all its good influences: such things as these, and in a word, Dishonest Faction in its most depraved and unblushing form, stared out from every corner of the crowded hall.[14]

Half a century later, Bryce, who found so much to praise in the United States, saw municipal corruption as a major blemish in American institutions. The American gentility agreed with him very largely, calling for civil-service reform to restore politics to honesty. It seemed to commentators on both sides of the Atlantic that British government, still strongly in the hands of the aristocracy, was far more principled and reputable. Half a century after Bryce, Pendleton Herring, then a professor of political science at Harvard, found that corruption was far more prevalent in America than in Britain. He ascribed this continuing difference to two factors: that America had failed "to reconcile the inequalities of private wealth with democratic doctrines of political equality" and that the British parties paid off their wealthy supporters with honorific titles.[15]

To say, from looking at Britain and America, that the politics of aristocracy is cleaner than the politics of democracy is to make the contrast too convenient. There is very likely nothing inherently pure or corrupt about either form of government, except for the minor consideration that both are run by men and men are something less than angels. If corruption inheres in man rather than in types of government, then the problem becomes one of finding the forms of venality that are particular to a given type. Andrew Carnegie believed that American and British leaders were both open to bribery, the first selling out for money, the second for titles.[16] For those less inclined than Carnegie was to acclaim the virtues of American democracy, it may appear that, during the age from Waterloo to Watergate, the Americans showed a greater proclivity to political corruption than the British. The reason may be that purchasing men with a peerage or knighthood is not only part of a spectacular ritual but actually fulfills the aristocratic idea, whereas purchasing men in a democracy by any means violates the democratic idea. It is important too that, in the nineteenth and twentieth centuries, British aristocrats, *malgré eux,* had both to superintend the democratization of their polity and to defend their own interests. The circumstance left them little opportunity for practicing the old-time corruption. Their formula, worked to a fine art by Sir Robert Peel, Lord Palmerston and William Gladstone, was to practice some democracy and to preach much morality. At the time of America's Tweed Ring, its Crédit Mobilier, its robber barons and its great barbecues, Gladstone was running the British government on the premise that godliness was next to financial cleanliness.

To judge how far American democracy has been a factor in American political corruption, it would be well to return to the subject of Watergate, which stands as the emblem of American corruptibility. Seen as a product of its time and place, Watergate signifies not so much a democracy that is endemically corruptible as an executive leadership that has been exotically altered. Those who occupied the White House after the Second World War were, as they are now called, imperial presidents. The course of events had thrust the United States into the center of world conflict and had, inevitably, invested its president with a responsibility and power which he alone could handle but for which his office was not designed. The imperial presidency contradicted the office which the Founding Fathers had contrived and the nation had for almost two centuries lived with. From having served largely domestic purposes, it became significantly international; from having been a check on democratic power, it became an instrument of quasi-autocratic power; from having been an office open to public light, it became one that often could function best behind closed doors. Of course, the actual uses of his power would depend on the person of the president. But whoever the occupant of the White House has been, America's imperial presidents have expressed some of the essential qualities of American democracy: the Americans' sense of mission, their belief that their polity is a model worth emulating, their almost paranoid fear of foreign threat, their malaise about coexisting with alternative political ideals. Thus it is fair to say that, to some degree, Watergate inheres in the structure and ideas of American democracy. It is not merely that American presidents have, for the larger part, been plain men, if not necessarily men from Plains. The question posed by an age of American world power is whether the responsibility of empire can be discharged without having an imperial president, or, to put it another way, whether in retreating from the imperial presidency Americans may not also be retreating from the responsibilities of empire, responsibilities which are at once military and moral.

One cannot ask about the importance of democracy as a factor in American political corruption without also asking about the importance of American law. American constitutionalism and jurisprudence form the centerpiece of American democracy. To understand the history of the American polity, one could find no better source than the history of American law. It is a commonplace that law frames social institutions; law and society are virtually synonymous. Law expresses the polity's mores and defines its goals. New societies, new laws; as a society changes, so do its laws; and as the laws change, so does the society. From the writing of Roscoe Pound, Morris Raphael Cohen, J. Willard Hurst, and indeed, Oliver Wendell Holmes, Jr., Americans have long understood the adjustive vitality of their legal system. For parallel appraisals of English law, recourse for many a decade has been to the dazzling, breathtaking exegeses of Frederic William Maitland. From these scholars it has been learned that laws are not per se corrupt but that they are a society's moral code and that, accordingly, one society's probity is another's corruption.

What are the particularities of American society that its laws would express? American constitutionalism bespeaks the premises of a liberal bourgeois polity. It embraces the ideals of private property and of written laws as their best guarantee. To say that America is a polity of laws and not of men is to record the Americans' quest for protection against what they regarded as the arbitrariness of the monarch, his ministers, and the High Court of Parliament. But, at bottom, the insistence on the primacy of laws over men begs the question, for it is men who make laws and interpret them. Charles Evans Hughes uttered the famous words: "The Constitution is what the judges say it is." Henry Steele Commager's was the brilliant perception that the Supreme Court has long been sitting as a continuous constitutional convention. J. Willard Hurst said that "the most creative, driving, and powerful pressures upon our law emerged from the social setting." All understood the theme that America is a polity of the men who superintend its laws and that the Americans' sense of corruption varies with the precepts of their legal superintendents and of the mores to which the latter subscribe.[17]

America has been the paradigmatic liberal polity. Its citizens have formulated constitutions that delimit the scope of public power. But an empire of liberty is also an empire of corruptibility. The positive law governing public power can, as has been noted, be drafted and interpreted to satisfy the interests of influential individuals and groups. It is hardly necessary to cite a long catalog of those who have questioned the probity of American laws, but the spectrum of opinion is wide, and one can start by citing Henry Steele Commager, Thurman Arnold, Herbert Marcuse, John Kenneth Galbraith, Gunnar Myrdal and John Rawls.

American law is, like all others, essentially the law of property relations. In a polity that is not authoritarian or aristocratic, lawyers have played a role that is, as Tocqueville well understood, quasi-aristocratic. They discharge functions elsewhere performed by dispensers or superintendents of justice based on legal codes, *droit administratif,* or His Majesty's equity and common law—codes, in effect, that derive from the superiority and the exclusivity of a central jurisdiction. The primary function of American lawyers is to serve the interests of property by defending them in court or by making the laws that govern the disposition of property. It is nothing fortuitous that, in this republic of property, the lawyers are also the politicians. They serve in American legislatures, on all levels; they staff the administrative agencies; they staff the judiciaries. They make the laws, they superintend the laws, they interpret the laws. They go from America's best law schools into its most important administrative agencies and they are purchased from the agencies by the highest salaries that the corporations running the American economy can offer. It takes a narrow definition of corruption to say that their activities fall outside the definition. In a liberal bourgeois polity such as America's, they are, as a group and as servants of powerful private interests, probably the most prominent purveyors of corruption.

This is hardly to say that all lawyers are corrupt. It is merely to suggest that the function of law in a polity like America's—to defend the interests of private property—makes laws and lawyers particularly open to corruption. In choosing between the service of public and private interest, it is hard to resist the temptation of money. It is easy to cover one's perception of both interests with a thick cloud of Bernard Mandeville and Adam Smith and to say that in promoting private property one may also advance public causes. And indeed, in some respects, one may. But relatively few lawyers either study their philosophy or probe their conscience. For every Louis D. Brandeis, America has a thousand ambulance-chasers, petty-claims pettifoggers, land conveyancers, business barristers and, of course, corporation lawyers. For some sense of the topography of this world, one would have to look into the edifice complex of the Wall Street law firms, the plushly carpeted offices of their Washington, D.C., unindicted coconspirators, and the far from fictive society of Louis Auchincloss. It would be too simple to call this world a Sodom of corruption. In a polity where the key maxim is that money talks, it is not easy to say just where the talkers and what they say have crossed the line of corruption.

Keepers of the American conscience, the gentility has had a decided sense of the impact of democracy, as a type of government, on political corruption. For more than a century after the War of 1812, the gentility believed that to be rid of corruption democracy had to be revitalized and the civil service staffed with competent men. Outlawing the spoils was a program for supplanting vice with virtue. Revitalizing democracy meant, for the gentility, that elections had to be freed from purchase or covert control and that government officials had to be made responsive to the public interest. Jacksonian reformers and Progressives alike invented a variety of devices whereby the people could speak their voice. To the genteel reformers, it seemed clear that men with special interests, above all the *nouveaux riches,* had subverted the political process. Two steps had to be taken to restore the conduct of government to probity: fully disclosing the political activities of the special interests and restoring to public affairs the direct role of the people. These ideas persist. Reformers have in recent years sought to control campaign contributions, to publicize the influence of industry and industrialists on politics, to unlock the grip of bureaucracy on civic life, to give localities and communities what is uncharmingly called in computerized jargon "an input into the decision-making process." What also persists, with even greater emphasis than before, is the gentility's sense that democracy is a delicate mechanism, that educating the citizen, while necessary, may not be enough to keep the mechanism from being misused, that the American political world has to be made safe not only from plutocracy but also from democracy, and that the best guarantors of America's political probity are its philosopher-kings, its gentility.

No less than religion and democracy, the entrepreneurial ethos has been a factor in American political corruption. It was a regular lament of European observers, that America's most qualified citizens were largely absent from its government. The sociology of talent is surely germane to a discussion of political corruption. When Bryce said that America's best men did not go into politics, he was merely being polite. Other British visitors—Basil Hall, Frances M. Trollope, Frederick Marryat, even Charles Dickens—had said that its worst men went into politics. Why was American government an art for men of secondary talents? The reason is not hard to find. The best men went into money, either to amass it or to preserve it. Where possible, they used their talents and their money to influence the less talented and less affluent men who went into politics.

In any polity, talent seeks its own level. What that level is depends of course upon social ideals and mores. This phenomenon has been studied by Max Weber and Joseph Schumpeter.[18] It was, in one form or another, well understood by earlier political philosophers, including Tocqueville, Montesquieu, Aristotle and Plato. The failure of the revolutions of 1848 in the German states offers a classic example, commented on by several historians, including A. J. P. Taylor, of the forced diversion of talent from politics to economics. The thesis here is that the defeated German bourgeois liberals, men of education, drive and ability, turned their energies from government to production, rapidly making the expanding Prussian polity the principal European industrial power.[19] French history had earlier offered another version of the same principle; that talents are energized by social ideals and that they conform to the prescriptions of power within a given polity. France, the prime revolutionary nation of continental Europe, extended two guiding ideals to its sister polities of the early nineteenth century: the first, that of a *carrière ouverte aux talents,* coming out of the 1790s, was political and democratic; the second, the exhortation of *enrichissez-vous,* coming out of the regime of Louis Philippe, was economic and bourgeois. Both meant a breaking-down of the barriers that had hitherto confined social energies; both meant that France had moved from an aristocratic to a bourgeois democratic age; and they also meant that these energies would be evident in newer pursuits, consonant with the change of public law and social ideals.

American energies and talents went into enterprise. American politics was part of the domain of American entrepreneurship. This of course reversed the continental concept, in which political authority dictated to enterprise under maxims of *raison d'état* and civic needs. The English revolution of the seventeenth and eighteenth centuries marked something of a departure from this concept, bringing about a rough equation of civism and individualism, of free politics and free enterprise. English America was one of the by-products of this revolution. It was fundamental to its polity, as Tocqueville emphasized, that America had become a democracy without having had a democratic revolution. But, by the same token, it was hardly less fundamental that the Americans had become a nation of entrepreneurs without having had a capitalist revolution. Almost from the beginning, the business of America was entrepreneurship and the business of entrepreneurship was self-promotion.

The bourgeois liberal democratic form of polity that France largely achieved and that Germany largely failed to achieve had long been the central fact of American experience. This surely is what Bernard Bailyn urges as the essential nature of the American Enlightenment and the American Revolution.[20] . . .

In analyzing the impact of economic factors on political corruption, the prime concern is with the struggle between the entrepreneurial ethos and the social ethos, between individuality and community, between the demands of the ego and the restraints of the superego. What promoted the entrepreneurial ethos also promoted the tendency to political corruption. What restrained the entrepreneurial ethos also restrained the tendency to political corruption. The concern at this point is to say just what is meant by the American entrepreneurial ethos, to consider the factors that have promoted it, and then to consider the factors that have restrained it. The key argument here will be that the growth of American society generated forces that undid the restraints upon entrepreneurship and that, in consequence, the tendencies to political corruption were enhanced. . . .

The idea of entrepreneurship was a counterpart to the idea of community, both belonging to a larger complex of premises to which the Europeans who settled seventeenth and eighteenth century English America subscribed. The conditions in the American environment promoted the rapid, luxuriant growth of the entrepreneurial ethos. But no less important in promoting that growth was the dissolution of the complex of premises to which the entrepreneurial ethos belonged. As these related ideas lost meaning and vitality, the idea of entrepreneurship lost its confinements. Because the composite of ideas added up to a moral code, its transformation signified the advent of a new morality. The sins of the fathers were not only *not* visited upon the sons, they became, in many respects, the son's redeeming virtues. The rules of the game had changed: yesterday's usurer and purveyor of false goods was today's captain of industry and financial wizard. To use a simple Freudian analog: the older superego no longer stood sentinel upon the ego. The decline of the older values liberated the entrepreneurial ethos for a freewheeling political playmanship. It was a far cry indeed from John Winthrop's General Court to Nelson Aldrich's Senate. . . .

Perhaps the most important single factor altering the entrepreneurial ethic was the growth of a continental industrial economy and the decline, in relative importance, of the local economy. An immediate contact between producers and consumers depended on an immediate morality. Local government responded to the interpersonal relations of the locality. As markets widened, contacts between producers and consumers widened into a long chain of impersonal relations. With the emergence of a national market economy, political control passed inevitably into the hands of the national legislature. James Madison's tenth paper in *The Federalist* could never have conjured up the industrial and financial faction that later regularly tried, and often managed, to corrupt the American congress. Not even Alexander Hamilton could have anticipated the growth of a massive bureaucracy, on all levels of government, so susceptible of economic influence that one could hardly say whether government superintended industry or was merely another of industry's many activities. There is no need to go through the litany of Populist and Progressive indictments to understand that the entrepreneurs of the age were the first beneficiaries of the new nationalism and the new freedom and that, having this legacy to stand on, they brought buying and selling public officials to a fine art.

In considering how far economic factors have produced political corruption, the following observations have been made:

- That what is called political corruption is part of the way a polity looks at itself and thus part of the polity's mores and ideology;
- That American political mores and ideology, however continuous their language and symbols, are continuously being redefined;
- That the prime force in American economic life is what is called here the entrepreneurial ethic;

- That American economic life has always rested on two sets of moral imperatives or ethical codes, the entrepreneurial and the communal;
- That the entrepreneurial and the communal ethic, however piously regarded as coordinate and complementary, have generally been antithetical forces, with the ascendency of the one signifying the decline of the other;
- That the entrepreneurial ethic, as a drive for personal gain, is a perennial source of political corruption;
- That the triumph of the entrepreneurial ethic was favored by America's geography and its vast natural resources;
- That the triumph was guaranteed by the dissolution, in successive American generations, of that complex of older, essentially European, mores in which entrepreneurship had been only one major component;
- That the entrepreneurial ethic emerged as the most important single force in American political life during the years after American independence, and particularly after the end of the War of 1812. . . .

So far the argument here has been that political corruption in America has had its own essential nature, one that has been determined in the main by three principal factors: American sectarian Christianity, American democracy and law, and the American entrepreneurial ethos. It has been contended that each society has a particular concept of political virtue, and the aim has been to define the concept that is uniquely American by comparing the American polity with European models. Merely to discuss episodes of American political corruption per se is to discuss them *in vacuo,* without referents, without plottings and ultimately, then, without definition.

Two questions remain to be considered. How is the recurrence of periods of pronounced political corruption in American history to be explained? And how, in the light of some of the suggestions already offered, is the American response to Watergate to be assayed? With regard to the first question, corruption has been defined as the breaking of the rules of the game of the polity. It is axiomatic that rules are always being broken. The problem is to understand why the breaking of rules proliferates so much that corruption becomes a predominant aspect of a period. It is safe to say that widespread corruption signalizes a deeper strain in the polity. To put it in general terms, the political institutions can no longer accommodate the newer economic and social actualities of the nation. Political mores are in conflict with the altering conditions of society. Indeed, what is called corruption is in no small measure the moral charge that the older political codes are not being observed, that the older political prescriptions are not being fulfilled.

Moreover, when speaking of corruption in American political history, may one not be speaking of the faulty way politicians are handling functions they were not meant to perform? The history of American politics is, in many ways, the story of the expanding functions of government and of the increasing role of the national government. America's ever-changing economy and society throw up new needs. At every point of American history, there is a wide gap between these needs and the effectiveness of politics and politicians in serving them. The lack of service is described as delinquent and morally wrong. And whatever service *is* performed is perforce *ad hoc,* inconsistent with accepted institutions, extralegal if not quite illegal, and in any event censurable. In such times, therefore, official acts of omission and commission evoke charges of corruption. One ought then to consider how far what is called corruption is to be found in the differential between existing political forms and newer social needs. In every epoch, the discrepancy between the two has to be corrected. The attack on the discrepancy marks an era when the government is attacked for its inefficiency and confusion, when moral outrage is voiced, when the cry of corruption becomes loud and widespread. The resolution of the discrepancy marks an era of reform, of reconstructing the bureaucracy, making government more responsive to social needs, and coordinately sounding the high moral purpose of fulfilling the American democratic ideal.[21]

To be more specific, look more closely at the Gilded Age. By all odds, it is the age that is considered to have been one of the most corrupt in American history. What then was there about those decades that might explain the comparatively high incidence of political corruption? The suggestion is that the new society and the modes of conduct it created were being judged in terms of the older political mores. Radical changes were shaping a new America. . . .

The second question is how, in terms of some of the ideas advanced, is the American reaction to Watergate to be perceived? This question invites a second question: What was Watergate? It was, in fact, at least two events: an actual violation of the political rules and a television drama. To some degree, the wide public airing of Watergate amplified the enormity of the corruption and insured strong corrective measures. As a television spectacle, Watergate was an engrossing political soap opera about the lives of Richard Nixon. It was stupendous public theater, a morality extravaganza played on the hippodrome of a million TV screens. As democracy's *Everyman,* it simplified reality almost to the point of transcending it. It came straight out of the American Christian literary tradition—out of the Puritan jeremiads and Michael

Wigglesworth, Nathaniel Hawthorne, Herman Melville, Lewis Wallace and Charles M. Sheldon.[22] Which playwright could have written a drama so full of naked ambition, Christian piety, lust for power and tragic betrayal as the daily episodes of "As the Watergate Turns"? Watching it with fascinated revulsion, Americans could not but feel that all the president's men were satanic minions, that the president himself was villainy incarnate, that the highest office in the land had been lamentably stained, and that strong spiritual cleansing was called for.

As an actual violation of the rules of politics, Watergate had of course major consequences. Nixon's sins could not be ignored—they were cardinal, even for politicians, men hardly distinguished for acts of selfless virtue; they were Nixon's, a president so lacking in charisma or even confidence that his office had become a fortress of unsplendid isolation; they were Republican, and Democrats would have been fools to let their smashing national defeat in 1972 go unchallenged, without at least imputing to the opponents the charge that dirty tricks and tricky Dick had done them in. And the sins, finally, were too public to be passed over. Reforms were called for and they were made. Measures were taken to curb the imperial presidency. Campaign finance laws were almost universally enacted. Legislators were put under stricter ethical codes. It is too early to say just how far this neoprogressive movement will go.

And yet, as some commentators have noted, the movement does not seem to be going very far at all. Congressmen are balking at limitations on their earnings. They are reluctant to offer the electorate a full disclosure of their assets. Little, if anything, will be done to answer Lowell Weicker's charge that men of wealth now dominate the Senate. There is remarkable foot-dragging on probing the allegation that forty congressmen were in the pay of the South Korean Central Intelligence Agency, which, if true, could send one-tenth of the American House of Representatives to prison. Joseph Crangle has fumed at Senator Daniel P. Moynihan's recommendation that three Republican federal prosecutors be permitted to finish out their terms, because the recommendation meant that party patronage would have to yield, at least for a while, to proven official competence. No action is being taken to curb the powerful influence of politically connected lawyers who, as Frank Lynn puts it, "constitute almost a hidden government." David Broder, of the *Washington Post,* says that "the changes wrought by recent electoral reforms were not as extensive as the furor created by Watergate might have indicated." In the view of Professor Joel L. Fleishman of Duke University, there are distinct limitations to recent reforms. The abuses continue. Indeed, some of the great gurus of America's Eastern gentility are warning that, in responding to Watergate, Americans may be going too far the other way. Says Anthony Lewis, the spirit incarnate of pious liberalism: "There is in fact a real danger of overreaction by congress to the executive sins of recent years."[23] . . .

Can it be sensibly expected that political abuses will not continue? No human polity is addicted to virtue, and the American polity, the product of the special factors that have shaped it, has its special way both of practicing corruption and of raising the cry that corruption is being practiced. It is not unfair to suggest that, meanwhile, back at the ranches of American political life, on the municipal, county, state and federal levels, the corruption, however tempered, goes on with impressive vitality. The men running the political show can only hope that idiocies like the break-in at Watergate will either not recur or not be handled so ineptly; that another wild bit of vaudeville like the act put on in 1971 and 1972 by the crazies of the Oval Office will not soon hit the boards of the Presidential Palace; and in particular that a man with such obvious paranoid strains as Richard Nixon will either not become president or, since some of America's best paranoiacs are presidents, will never have to go through the drama of public exposure with his moralities all the way down. In a sense, this could mean that the purgation of trial by television served not so much to preclude future Watergates as to make it possible for them to continue in quieter, more fragmented, less flagrant, more covert ways. And should it surprise anyone if they did continue? No less than other polities, democracy in America has its inherent flaws. And the men who superintend the American democracy are, as the Founding Fathers well understood they would be, far, far less than angels.

Notes

1. "A Defence of the Answer," in Perry Miller and Thomas H. Johnson, eds., *The Puritans* (rev. ed.; 2 vols.; New York, 1963), I, 118.
2. Charles F. Adams, ed., *The Works of John Adams* (10 vols.; Boston, 1850–56), IX, 417–20.
3. *Recollections of a Busy Life* (New York, 1868), p. 527.
4. William E. Leuchtenburg, ed., *The New Nationalism* (New York, 1961), pp. 27, 36.
5. Peter Lisagor, "From Triumph to Tragedy," *The 1975 World Book Year Book* (Chicago, 1975), p. 62.
6. *Triumphant Democracy or Fifty Years' March of the Republic* (New York, 1886), pp. 471–73.

7. The role of the gentility in American life has long been recognized. Foreign and domestic commentators (Tocqueville, Grund, Hall, Chevalier, Fenimore Cooper, to name but a few) were fully aware of this role. The gentility has been the subject of particular study during the past two decades. Richard Hofstadter emphasized their centrality in the Progressive movement in *The Age of Reform* (New York, 1955). Stow Persons, *The Decline of American Gentility* (New York, 1973) is the most important recent book on the subject. Other valuable contributions include John Tomisch, *A Genteel Endeavor: American Culture and Politics in the Gilded Age* (Stanford, 1971); Barbara Miller Solomon, *Ancestors and Immigrants* (Cambridge, Mass., 1956); and John G. Sproat, *"The Best Men": Liberal Reformers in the Gilded Age* (New York, 1968).

8. The transformation and secularization of American Christianity (and particularly American Puritanism) are discussed in Perry Miller, *The New England Mind from Colony to Province* (Cambridge, Mass., 1953), pp. 464–85; Charles A. Barker, *American Convictions, Cycles of Public Thought 1600–1850* (Philadelphia, 1970), pp. 111–15, 180–84; Alan Heimert, *Religion and the American Mind from the Great Awakening to the Revolution* (Cambridge, Mass., 1966), Chap. V; Gordon S. Wood, *The Creation of the American Republic 1776–1787* (Chapel Hill, 1969), pp. 114–18; Rush Welter, *The Mind of America 1820–1860* (New York, 1975), Chap. X; and Robert T. Handy, *A Christian America: Protestant Hopes and Historical Realities* (New York, 1971), Chap. II.

9. Cited by Sidney E. Mead in Russel E. Richey and Donald G. Jones, eds., *American Civil Religion* (New York, 1974), p. 45.

10. *The Americans in Their Moral, Social, and Political Relations* (New York, 1837, 1968), pp. 165–67.

11. Roy P. Fairfield, ed., *The Federalist Papers* (Garden City, N. Y., 1961). As notable examples of their view, see in particular Papers 10, 15, 16, 17, 31 and 51.

12. *Op. cit.*, I, 225–26.

13. In 1838, Cooper published two of his strongest indictments of American political mores: *The American Democrat,* a tract of "censure" and "instruction," and *Home as Found,* a novel less censorious or angry.

14. *American Notes* (Gloucester, Mass., 1968), pp. 141–43. The original edition appeared in 1842.

15. *The Politics of Democracy: American Parties in Action* (New York, 1940), pp. 345–47.

16. *Op. cit.*, p. 481.

17. Cited in my prefatory comments to a very illuminating essay by John P. Roche, included in my *American History: Recent Interpretations* (rev. ed.; New York, 1969), II, 51.

18. See Weber's lecture, "Politics as a Vocation," in H. H. Gerth and C. Wright Mills, eds., *From Max Weber: Essays in Sociology* (New York, 1946), pp. 83f. On Schumpeter, see his *Theory of Economic Development* (Cambridge, Mass., 1934), pp. 74–94, and also "The Creative Response in Economic History" in Richard C. Clemence, ed., *Essays of J. A. Schumpeter* (Cambridge, Mass., 1951), pp. 216–26.

19. A.J.P. Taylor, *The Course of German History* (New York, 1946), pp. 88–89, 110–11.

20. "Political Experience and Enlightenment Ideas in Eighteenth-Century America," *American Historical Review,* LXVII (January 1962), 339–51.
21. In formulating this suggestion, I am drawing on some of the ideas offered by Arthur M. Schlesinger, Sr., in "The Tides of National Politics" in his *Paths to the Present* (rev. ed.; Cambridge, Mass., 1964), pp. 89–103. In that essay, the older Schlesinger argued that there have been alternating currents of conservatism and reform in American political history. Arthur M. Schlesinger, Jr., has excellently amplified his father's thesis, using it to explain the sources of the New Deal in *Columbia University Forum,* II (Fall 1959), 4–12.
22. For a brief survey of the vogue of popular religious literature in the United States, see Frank Luther Mott, *Golden Multitudes* (New York, 1947), Chaps. 3, 26, 28.
23. *The New York Times,* March 10, 1977; March 6, 1977; Oct. 17, 1976; April 7, 1977; Jan. 23, 1977.

32

Corruption: The Special Case of the United States

Jacob van Klaveren

. . . The Northwest European development [of political corruption] is a unique, historically-based phenomenon. We know that the political systems of the so-called underdeveloped regions still remain in the stage of systematic corruption, and there are good reasons for this which we cannot go into here. For simplicity's sake, let us say that the Age of Enlightenment has not yet, in a relative sense, occurred there, which is not too surprising considering the low educational level.[1] But the more difficult question is why in the United States, despite its independence due in part to the enlightened ideas of the colonists, corruption is systematically practiced even today.[2]

This is a well-known fact among those studying American history, yet it is difficult to obtain more specific explanations and information from American scholars. Particularly the present conditions are left unstudied.

Corruption is a delicate subject, and the dependent position of the American professor[3] is not conducive to the systematic study of this subject. However, during my stay in Siam, it was an American guest, strangely enough, who made an open statement on corruption in the United States today. Yet, this was meant to comfort the Siamese, who are accused to be treated scathingly by the Europeans because of the state of corruption in their country.[4] Yet in the past many American authors and journalists have discussed corruption in their country much more frankly than today. One can only infer from this that the United States became increasingly embarrassed about and correspond-

Source: Jacob van Klaveren. "Die Historische Erscheinung der Korruption: Die Sonderentwicklung in den Vereinigten Staaten," *Vierteljahrsschrift für Sozial- und Wirtschaftsgeschichte*, 46:2 (1959), pp. 204–212. By permission of the publisher, Franz Steiner Verlag. Translated by Peggy Hofmann and Karl Kurtz.

ingly sensitive to this phenomenon. But even the nineteenth-century journalists rarely tried or were able to explore the specific basic causes. Considering all these reasons it may be plausible and acceptable for a European to concern himself with these truly American conditions. Perhaps this can be justified by the fact that the origins can only be explained by comparative observations beginning with the central European development.

Anyone who reviews American history must wonder why the corruption that was so common in the *ancien régime* and among English colonial officers never disappeared from the American scene in either the period of property requirements for suffrage or during the period of universal male suffrage. Occupants of countless offices, who are appointed by public authority in Europe, were selected in local elections in the United States, so that there were ideal guarantees for an honest administration. The key to understanding this lies in the fact that the majority of the population of the United States did not place any value on an honest administration, or at least they never collectively manifested this. This leads us again to the fact that the United States was not yet a "true" nation, as we will show later. It first had to become unified into a nation, a process that was frequently interrupted by the increasing number of immigrants, and which maybe has not yet reached its goal. Another factor may be that suffrage became universal too early. This seems like a contradiction within our system, but this is not the case, as we can prove by the European constitutional development. We shall refer to this later.

However, this does not say anything about corruption shortly after the Revolution, when immigration was still limited and suffrage was based on property rights in the majority of the original states. Proof that corruption existed is provided by the unsparing criticism [leveled at the United States] by the English in the early nineteenth century.[5] First we shall discuss the period when ownership of property was required for the suffrage.[6]

The Age of the Colonial Aristocracy and of Census Suffrage

The Age of Enlightenment was decisively important in Europe for the development of an honest administration. But it was also important for the American revolt. England's strongest adversaries were the petite bourgeoisie and the artisans of New England, among whom the "Sons of Liberty" arose. These groups had been very heavily influenced by the Enlightenment. It is amazing to see the thirst for knowledge with which these common people sought out the theories of the

Encyclopedists, how they worked to improve their education with evening courses . . . and all sorts of other subjects.[7] Benjamin Franklin was probably the most famous representative of these groups, although he emigrated to Philadelphia as a youth. The further south one went, the less important was this group. The colonial aristocracy, which was represented in the colonial assemblies, also toyed with enlightened, French ideas, but they became meaningful there only when they were related to the colonists' right of self-determination in relation to the mother country. Later it was discovered that many phrases in the Constitution had never been thoroughly thought through. Thus, in 1857 the Supreme Court determined that Negroes could not be citizens of the United States according to its constitution.[8] Undoubtedly the majority of the framers of the Constitution were conservative representatives of the colonial aristocracy with little esteem for democracy.[9] In most of the original states only a minority, approximately one-eighth of the adult male population, had the right to vote.[10]

Thus it is understandable that the members of the colonial aristocracy, who usurped all power after the War of Independence, took over the positions of the former English civil servants and also demanded for themselves the revenues that belonged to those positions. These revenues derived to a high degree from the sale of public land.[11] The majority of the framers of the Constitution were interested in real estate speculation, and therein also lies an important reason for the rebellion. When the French had been driven out of the hinterland between the Mississippi and the Appalachians during the Seven Years' War and the big land business could get started, the English government forbade the distribution of land west of a so-called proclamation line generally coinciding with the western border of the Appalachians. This did not mean that territories could no longer be distributed but that land concessions had to be secured from London instead of from the colonial administration. This inroad into the profits of the colonial administrators was eliminated by the rebellion, and, whereas corruption disappeared in England after 1784, it continued in the United States with double the strength.

Just a brief comparison of the different development of the United States and its former mother country will be provided here. In England the old upper classes had remained in office, but now they were controlled by the bourgeoisie. In the United States the old rulers had disappeared and the colonial aristocracy had stepped into the offices, but there was no bourgeois controlling group, particularly in the southern states.[12] The colonial aristocracy gained primarily through the distribution of territories, but not all states were enlarged with parts of the hinterland. The representatives of the "have-not" states had no share in these benefits, so they wanted to make the land distribution a job for the federal government in which they were represented. When Georgia, in 1802, became the last state to agree to this, a considerable part of the land had already been sold, but from then on the big land business was done on the federal level, and the representatives of all the states got a part of the benefits gained through speculation based on the continuous westward settlement. This settlement led to the creation of additional states with equal rights whose representatives were opposed to the old colonial aristocracy. The continuous settlement, which benefited the colonial aristocracy, was eventually to tear away its power in the country.

The West and Universal Male Suffrage

Universal suffrage was introduced in the United States much earlier than in Europe. It was an option of the individual states. The new Western states introduced universal male suffrage in principle at once, and the original states followed suit during Andrew Jackson's presidency (1829–1837). This action on the part of the West is understandable. Marked inequalities in the distribution of property, on which a property discrimination for suffrage might have been based, were still unknown in the West, so almost all of the settlers were qualified to vote. In addition, the free frontiersmen would not tolerate such an obvious discrimination. Thus, since all of them had the right to vote, they could have eliminated corruption if they had wanted to.

The people of the West were not only lovers of liberty, they were also uneducated and outspokenly individualistic. Everyone had his own best interests at heart and did not think about the wider societal implications. Almost all of them went west with the one thought of enriching themselves by means of the land rush, and basically the pioneers were no different from the big land speculators who snapped up the best land. With a slight variation on the technique known as "catch-as-catch-can,"[13] we can characterize this spirit with the expression "grab-as-grab-can." Everyone snapped up as much as he could,[14] and naturally the politicians did likewise. The Westerners understood this but did not consider the deeper consequences. They had little education, and the number of semiliterates or illiterates was frighteningly high. This was particularly true for those parts of the West settled by "native" Americans, which was the rule until approximately 1850. The Westerners were outspokenly hostile to intellectuals, and candidates who were identifiable as intellectuals did not have any chance to be elected in the West.[15] In particular the members of the old colonial aristocracy, who were naturally unable to hide their identity, could not take a leading role in the West. When the number of Western states increased, the influence of the West on the federal government rose too, and even the presidency had to go to the West. This jeopardized the employment of the colonial aristocracy in the federal offices. The introduction of universal male suffrage in the original states dates from the presidency of the Indian fighter from Tennessee, General Jackson (1829–1837); at the same time the old upper class disappeared from positions of political leadership in the country.[16]

This in itself was not so disastrous since, unlike the lords and gentry in England, the American upper class had not yet made an honest administration a part of their common life style. Therefore, there was no basic change with the influx of Westerners into federal offices. Only the preconditions for the distribution of land, and therefore for speculation and corruption, were changed. Of course, the Westerners forcefully demanded from their representative a land policy that limited the large-scale speculation by reducing the minimum size of lots, thus giving the settlers the possibility of purchasing such lots at low prices, and preferably, in installments direct from the local land offices. Under the pressure of these demands the Homestead Act, which stated that every settler could get a quarter section, or 160 acres, for free, was enacted in 1862. This applied only as long as there was land available, so the smart politicians had provided themselves with a loophole of which they made abundant use.

As early as 1851 the erection of railroads had been subsidized by grants of land. The grants of land lay on both sides of the projected railroad track and formed a band whose width was proportionate to the size of the subsidies. One must imagine the landscape divided along meridians and parallels in blocks of one square mile (one section) alternately colored black and white, just like a chessboard. The railway was only able to obtain alternate sections of one color, either black or white. If several sections were granted in one mile, the grants just stretched farther into the land. The size of the subsidy, that is, the width of the band,[17] was decided by the politicians in Washington, where relations between railroad companies and senators or representatives were established by lobbyists, wives, nieces, and so on. In this manner half of what was the most valuable land because it was situated close to the railroad was given to the railroads themselves, that is, to the big speculators. The legislators in Washington were quite good at inventing new excuses for giving public land to the big speculators, since these transactions were very profitable, unlike the distribution of land to the settlers. Even to the extent that the land was distributed to the settlers it fell partly to the speculators with the help of dummy buyers since the politicians had made the homesteads salable. These manipulations gave the civil servants from the local land offices their chance, too, since the sale could not take place without their cooperation. It follows that the settlers received only a small portion of the available land. They were thoroughly misled by their own politicians even when the politicians gave the appearance in public of representing the people's interests.[18]

The railways and "big business" gave the politicians new chances for personal gain, which they preferred to representing the interests of the electorate. The monopolistic exploitation of the public by big business (by which the railroads were primarily meant at this time) is closely tied to the political exploitation of the public by means of dealings between corrupt politicians and big business. This connection thoroughly confused the farmers. They confused cause and effect and fought primarily against big business—particularly against railway and grain elevator companies—and regarded corruption of the civil servants and politicians almost entirely as a consequence of the domination of capital. For this reason, the fight of the farmers' associations against corruption was only secondary in nature and not of primary concern. Generally, the policy of the farmers' associations must be regarded as a result of the "Big Depression" of the period 1873–1896.

The Struggle Against Big Business and Corruption

. . .[Taussig] rejects the frequently held opinion that big business is the cause of corruption . . .[and] seeks the reason among the dishonest politicians, whereby the identity of the initiator is unimportant.[19] The question of initiative is unimportant, because politicians and civil servants had always been corrupt long before big business developed. . . . Corruption is always extortion of the public, even if it is initiated and perpetuated by the interposition of businessmen. Hence it is incorrect to identify the question of initiative with that of "extortion or bribery," as Taussig does.[20] The question of initiative is only relevant if the administration itself is honest; even then it is important only from the standpoint of criminal law. It is possible that the initiative for many dubious manipulations in the United States came from big business, but the success of these maneuvers is only due to the fact that corruption already existed. For the entrepreneurs always had to pay, even for the fulfillment of the normal formalities, even if only *one* company applied for the right of way to one particular railroad franchise. If several railroad companies were trying to outdo one another, they had to compete in the size of the "bribes." Yet these were not real bribes because from the beginning it was understood that a concession could not be obtained without such special payments. Only the size of the payments differed, depending on whether and how many entrepreneurs and civil servants were in competition with one another. In any case, civil servants, judges, and politicians regarded the economy as an object for extortion. This can be learned from the correspondence of famous railroad magnates, which has been edited by Thomas C. Cochran. In general, the politicians were regarded by the magnates as parasites who accepted and promised everything but never kept their word or who took money from all of the competitors and decided in favor of the highest bidder without returning the losers' money.[21] Others drafted antirailroad bills if they were not given any free rides or bribes.[22] The opinion of President Cass of the Northern Pacific Railroad, writing in 1873, is interesting: "Wise and good men get corrupt in congress."[23] It is clear that the railroad companies would rather have kept their money than pay it to a judge or politician.

This is not to say, however, that railroad entrepreneurs handled their own offices in an unobjectionable manner. However, corruption was less widespread within the railroad companies than among civil servants and politicians, since it was not tolerated among the employees. The beneficiaries were primarily the boards of trustees ("directors"), who are less important in Europe but who, in America, made the entrepreneurial decisions. Besides, the "managers" were also allowed to share the profits. Prior to the great railroad crisis in 1873 the profits were secured by diverting the company's capital into the pockets of the executives. The directors, a few influential stockholders, and some managers usually formed a "construction company" to build the railroad line at much too high a price.[24] After 1873 the European public, which had to provide the capital, became more alert. However, functionaries still obtained revenues out of a variety of so-called sidelines, this is, projects that they bought out along the railroad line, often after having forced the previous owner to sell by charging high freight rates.[25] Of particular importance, however, was the land speculation close to the railroads.

They tried to cut off the lower railway officials from all benefits. In this they were quite successful since they could control employment and dismissals.[26] This was impossible in the civil administration, where many offices were elective. Thus Taussig's argument that the direct election of the civil servants was one of the reasons for the corruption of the civil servants becomes understandable.[27] Precisely those provisions that could have guaranteed the honesty of the civil servants led to just the opposite effect in the United States, because, as Taussig put it, "a community of good character, intelligence and conduct was lacking." Hence, the responsibility belonged to the public itself: "A good electorate will choose honest and capable officials, a debased and indifferent one will tolerate demagogues and thieves."[28] Thus the question is shifted to the "low level" of the American public. However, this is neglected by Taussig and almost all other students.

[The author then elaborates this delicate aspect of the problem and reaches the opinion that an incipient improvement was followed by a setback by 1900.]

Notes

1. A warning is in order here. An opposition is bound to arise as soon as the number of intellectuals and semiintellectuals (e.g. students) considerably exceeds the number of positions of profit with which they could be accommodated. Thus, in Southeast Asia I was able to observe that the lower civil servants, who were largely excluded from the benefits of corruption, took a hostile position toward corruption, as did the businessmen. Also compare the hostile attitude taken by the late president of the Philippines, Ramón Magsaysay, who had been victimized by corruption as a bus company owner in Manila before the war. Strong resistance is to be found in Indonesia, where the honest Dutch administration is not yet totally forgotten. Besides, it is hard to imagine that the purpose of "national" revolution could have been to enrich the revolutionary leaders at the expense of the people. Much agitation, however, is traceable to envy alone. As a rule, the influence of the few opponents of principle has been watered down by universal suffrage.
2. Nothing needs to be said about the cities' administrations. Corruption on the federal level—shortly before new presidential elections—has become known to the public through the mutual accusations of the parties. Read the press report on Eisenhower's assistant, Sherman Adams. The president has not been saved either. See articles by Don Iddon in the Amsterdam newspaper *De Telegraaf* from June 18 and June 26, 1958. Iddon points out in several examples that the opponents are basically just the same. Therefore he regards the Adams scandal as a Washington scandal and not just a White House scandal.
3. It seems almost unnecessary to prove this observation. See, for example, N.F. Hofstee, *Organisatie en bestuur van de Universiteit*. Diss Groningen, Assen n.d. (1949 or 1950), p. 77.
4. There Americans are also correctly considered as Europeans "since they have a white face as well."
5. Merle Curti, *Das amerikanische Geistesleben* (translated). Stuttgart [1947 (1943)], p. 327 f.
6. I do not intend to prove in detail these well-known facts, which can be found in any good textbook on American history.

7. The detailed discussions in Carl Bridenbaugh, *The Colonial Craftsman.* New York: New York University Press (1950), are extremely interesting. For their activities as Freemasons and their courses in electricity, mathematics, and so on, see pp. 165, 166. 175.

8. This refers to the case of the emancipated Negro slave Dred Scott. See Ray Allen Billington, *Westward Expansion: A History of the American Frontier.* New York [1954 (1949)], p. 604. Compare the text of the Declaration of Independence: "We hold these truths to be self-evident, that all men are created equal; that they are endowed by their creator with inalienable rights. . . ." Of course, the Declaration was mainly concerned with laying down principles, so the judges had to find information in the commentaries and proceedings.

9. On this point see the thorough treatment of Leonard Woolf, *After the Deluge: A Study of Communal Psychology.* London: Pelican Books [1947 (1931)], p. 168.

10. See Harold U. Faulkner, *American Political and Social History.* New York (1937), chap. VII.

11. The revenues began with the building of the Capitol, the symbol of national independence. According to the reports, the expenditures for the building were estimated at $12 million, but $27.2 million more were needed. See Mark Twain. *The Gilded Age: A Tale of Today,* 2 vols. New York, (1873) 1:263 f.

12. The New England states differ from the Southern states on this. They had no hinterland available for land speculation, so they were not hurt by the proclamation line. Despite the fact that the tightening-up of the navigation laws bothered them, the Northern upper class, which was a merchant aristocracy, remained loyal to the mother country, whose gentry they regarded as an example to be followed. Therefore, most of them had to leave the country along with the English. Those left behind, however, replenished the ranks by admitting the descendants of the numerous new rich, who made good profits from the newly opened trade with China and, particularly, as neutrals during the French War. The rise of the merchant aristocracy has been described well by Bernard Baylin in *The New England Merchants in the Seventeenth Century.* Cambridge, Mass. (1955).

13. The Westerners were very familiar with this way of fighting. See R. A. Billington. p. 481.

14. We deliberately overemphasized this. Ernest L. Bogart and Donald L. Kemmerer, *Economic History of the American People.* New York (1942), p. 549, say it in different words: The public was "too much absorbed in private affairs" to complain about it. F.W. Taussig, *Principles of Economics,* II. New York [1921 (1911) Revised 1938], p. 415, sees the cause in the mentality of the American people. Corruption was regarded as something natural, general morality was low, and the larger implications were unknown.

15. In the widely spread settlements illiteracy led to crass ignorance and the practical apostasy of the Christian faith. Therefore, numerous churches and sects tried to send their preachers to the West. There were illiterates among the preachers as well, but this was regarded favorably because it helped in establishing contact with the rough pioneers. Read Curti's interesting discussion. By the way, one must consider that France had

approximately 60 percent illiteracy in 1830; however, they had no influence because of the property requirements for voting.

16. Merle Curti, p. 345, and E. Digby Baltzell, *Philadelphia Gentlemen; The Making of a National Upper Class*. New York (1958), p. 188.

    At this time the difference between Washington "society" and that of the East coast developed and was interpreted by Mark Twain in *The Gilded Age,* p. 220: "It doesn't need a crowbar to break your way into society there as it does in Philadelphia."

17. If a railway company obtained 10 sections for each mile of the track, railway land reached 10 miles deep on each side of the track.

18. Other laws that made possible the distribution of land to speculators were the Timber Culture Act (1873), Desert Land Act (1877), and the Timber and Stone Act (1878). The result was that 80 million acres were distributed to farmers—part of whom were still dummy buyers—but 521 million acres went to speculators. See Billington, pp. 696–701. Bogart and Kemmerer, p. 496, call the land offices "centers for the distribution of the plunder." When Theodore Roosevelt (1901) cleaned out the land offices, the disaster had already occurred.

19. F.W. Taussig, II, p. 431 f.

20. F.W. Taussig, II, p. 432.

21. H.R. Smith, p. 316, provides a striking example. Once, the rivalry between Vanderbilt and Jay Gould led Vanderbilt to pay an important member of the New York legislature $75,000. The same politician accepted $100,000 from Gould later. When the issue came up, the politician voted for Gould but kept Vanderbilt's $75,000.

22. See H.R. Smith, p. 315, and Thomas C. Cochran, *Railroad Leaders 1845–1890*. Cambridge, Mass. (1953), p. 195.

23. T.C. Cochran, p. 190.

24. Prior to 1873 this was normal. See T.C. Cochran, p. 111. The first transcontinental line was built by a construction agency with the beautiful name Credit Mobilier. But it probably had nothing to do with the bank of the same name of the Péreire brothers, which was liquidated in 1866. Out of its immense profits it also had to reward the politicians who had voted for the subsidies. See H.R. Smith, p. 316, and Franklin M. Reck, *The Romance of American Transportation*. New York, Crowell, 1938, p. 141.

25. These included wheat silos, wheat mills, hotels, and so on. Consider, though, that the standards for an honest administration in the business world had not yet been determined, whereas they were already laid out in great detail for the civil servants.

26. Thus, Vice-President Oakes of the Northern Pacific Railroad ordered some employees to nullify their purchases of land or else face being fired. See T.C. Cochran, p. 216. It was impossible to control the freight departments since the tariffs differed from day to day and from customer to customer. It was the age of secret freight rates.

27. F.W. Taussig, p. 431.

28. F.W. Taussig, p. 431.

33

A Theory about Corruption

Walter Lippmann

It would be impossible for an historian to write a history of political corruption in America. What he could write is the history of the exposure of corruption. Such a history would show, I think, that almost every American community governs itself by fits and starts of unsuspecting complacency and violent suspicion. There will be long periods when practically nobody except the professional reformers can be induced to pay attention to the business of government; then rather suddenly there will come a period when every act of the administration in power is suspect, when every agency of investigation is prodded into activity, and the civic conscience begins to boil.

It is a nice question whether a period of exposure signifies that politics has recently become unusually scandalous or that an unusually efficient prosecutor has appeared on the scene. The current revelations about the Walker-Tammany regime in New York City, for example, relate to events that took place two, three, and four years ago. That they have come at this particular time is due largely to the ingenuity of United States Attorney Tuttle who within the last few months has discovered that a comparison of federal income tax returns with transcripts of bank accounts may provide useful clues to the hidden transactions of politicians. Mr. Tuttle's success in cracking the polished surface of the Walker administration was due to the invention of a new political weapon. He may not be the original inventor, but he has certainly developed the invention remarkably. As a result, he is the first man in a long time who has penetrated the defenses of Tammany.

The contest against political corruption in America is very much like the competition among designers of naval armaments. At one time the

Source: Walter Lippmann, "A Theory about Corruption," *Vanity Fair*, 35:3 (November 1930), pp. 61, 90. By permission of the author and publisher. Reprinted from *Vanity Fair* (now *Vogue* incorporating *Vanity Fair*); copyright 1930, © 1958 by The Conde Nast Publications Inc.

reformers have a gun which can pierce any armor plate; then a defense against that gun is developed. I do not think it is a too cynical view of the facts to say that the traffic in privileges, which is what corruption is, has never long lacked men smart enough to find ways of defeating the ingenuity of the reformers. I do not mean to say that American cities are not better governed today than when Bryce said nearly forty years ago that they were the one conspicuous failure of the United States. They are much better governed. They are governed by men who often take a considerable pride in doing a good job. That is true today in New York City under Tammany.

Nevertheless, the fact remains, I think, that the ultimate power over appointments, nominations and policies is in the hands of professional politicians who in one way or another make the public business more profitable to themselves than any private business in which, with their abilities and opportunities, they might engage. I have heard, here and there, of a district leader or even of a boss who remains a poor man, and I am not forgetting men like the late Chief Magistrate McAdoo who, after a lifetime in politics, died in poverty. I am not forgetting rather high officials in Tammany about whose integrity there cannot be the slightest doubt. Yet it cannot be denied, I think, that the mainspring which moves the whole complex human organization behind the public government of New York is private advantage.

It certainly is not undiluted patriotism. District leaders are not primarily interested in the administration of justice when they insist on naming magistrates. They insist on naming the magistrates, in some and perhaps in many cases, because the candidate pays for the appointment; in all cases they insist because they wish to control the favors that a magistrate can dispense. The power of the district leader over the voters depends upon his ability to dispense favors. He is recognized as a political leader, not because of his views on public questions, but because he is able concretely to demonstrate day after day that his word is law. Because he controls government, he controls votes and because he controls votes he controls government: because he has power he is cultivated by those who have favors to give, and leaving out all items of bribery, he occupies a place where he has, so to speak, a multitude of business opportunities. If he is a lawyer, he has law cases which require his political influence rather than his legal ability. He is remembered by real estate syndicates and by corporations that are affected by government. In short he capitalizes, most often nowadays, I think, in accordance with the strict letter of the law, the political power he possesses.

The prosecuting agencies, when spasmodically they set to work, can deal only with the crudely overt features of political corruption. Anyone who has observed closely a prosecutor's office on the trail of a political ring knows how enormous is the gap between scandalous political conduct and specifically indictable offenses; in my time I have seen case after case of politicians who could not be indicted, or, if indicted, convicted, though they were guilty as Satan, because the development of conclusive legal proof was lacking. The truth of the matter, I think, is that an entirely objective view of political life at its base where political organization is in direct contact with the population, would show that corruption in some form is endemic. I do not mean that everybody is bribed. I do mean that the exchange of favors is the elemental and essential motive power which operates the semi-private machinery inside the political parties which in their turn operate the official machinery of government. It is, I think, literally true that if the exchange of favors were suddenly and miraculously abolished, there would be a wholesale voluntary retirement of petty politicians to private life, for they would lack then the incentive to stay in politics and the very means by which they maintain their political influence. The best proof of this is that the reformers who operate only with ideals and indignation never really make a party which lasts; they soon discover, when they deign to get down to the base of politics, that the motives they appeal to are unsubstantial.

If it is true that the exchange of favors is an essential element of politics, then the common American assumption about political corruption is naive and misleading. The assumption, inculcated through patriotic text books, is that in the year 1789 a body of wise men founded a new government in a new world, and that corruption is a lapse from this contract to which all their decendants automatically subscribe. Almost all of us feel, I think, that Tammany, for example, is a kind of disease which has affected the body politic. There it is, to be sure; it has been there a long time, and the counterpart of it is to be found in virtually every American community. Nevertheless, we feel that it is not supposed to be there, and that if only we had a little more courage or sense or something we could cut away the diseased tissue and live happily ever after. The implications of this notion seem to me to be false, and I believe that our political thinking would be immensely more effective if we adopted an entirely opposite theory.

That theory would hold that organizations like Tammany, which bind together masses of people in a complex of favors and coercions, are the ancient form of human association. They might be called natural governments. Our modern, artificial constitutions were superimposed upon them partly by coalitions of the stronger factions and partly by compromises of interest. The natural governments are not abolished when this happens. They continue to a decisive degree to operate through the artificial government. When the conflicts between these natural associations become too momentous the constitutional government breaks down in civil war or it is swept aside, as it has been in all of Eastern Europe, by a dictatorship of one of these associations. In many countries it is only too plain that the constitutional system is a mere façade behind which the real exercise of power depends upon the barter of privileges and the use of violence.

My point is that Tammany is not a disease, but simply the old body politic in its more or less natural state, and that the American ideal of government as a public trust to be carried on by disinterested men represents not the actuality but a long step ahead in the evolution of man. The very conception of a public trust has not yet been heard of by the mass of mankind. It has been a recognized public ideal in Europe even among the most advanced thinkers for not much more than a few hundred years. It is a very difficult ideal to attain, and I know of no public man even in America and even in our time who has felt able to be completely loyal to it. The best test is the appointment of judges, for surely if there is a public trust more imperative than any other it is the task of the president or the governor to insure the highest possible quality in the courts. Does anybody know a president who has been guided solely by merit in his selection of judges? I doubt it. The best of presidents is as virtuous as he dares to be, but at some point or other he must for political reasons knowingly violate his conscience.

The difficulties increase as one descends in the political scale. Presidents, governors, perhaps even mayors, move in a realm where ideal motives may be effective, for their acts are subject to the verdict of the more sensitive minority and to the judgment of history. They are likely, moreover, to be exceptional men who have passed beyond the struggle for existence, to be educated men, and to appreciate the immaterial glories of the state. But down among district leaders, and second deputy commissioners, and clerks of court, the larger rewards, the larger issues, the intrinsic obligations of power, simply do not exist. These office holders are recruited from men who have to struggle to exist, who must hold on grimly to what they can get, who never have any feeling that they are public men making the history of their time. Men of genius have risen now and then from such political beginnings, but for the few who rise there is a multitude who know they never will. What can public office give to them except a job at a meagre salary, an opportunity to prosper a little on the side, a sense of importance in their neighborhood, and the excitement of working for the winning team? At the base of the political structure there are no adequate motives to give meaning to the conception of public office as a public trust. It is not surprising that this relatively new and high conception, which has so little ground in the instinctive life of man, should take hold slowly.

As a matter of historical fact we are justified in going a step farther to say not only that what we call political corruption is the ancient and natural political process, but that corruption in the form of jobbery represents a decisive step upward in political life. I think it could be shown from the history of the Mother of Parliaments itself and demonstrated today in certain politically backward countries that corruption is the practical substitute for factional wars. In the eighteenth century the civil wars in England came to an end and the habit of political violence dissolved finally in the organization of a thoroughly corrupt but peaceable parliament. There are places in the world today where corruption is progress. I once heard the president of a Latin-American republic explain that he was consolidating his régime at home by making ambassadors, with extra large grants for expenses, out of his most dangerous political enemies. It had been the custom to shoot them.

I fear that my theory of corruption will seem fantastic to many and a justification for a lazy tolerance to others. It seems to me the serious truth, and conceivably a useful truth. For if it is true that corruption is not a disease, but on the contrary a natural condition which civilized modern man is seeking to surmount, the knowledge that this is so might very well provide us with a clearer idea of what our periodic scandal-chasing is all about, a better appreciation of the realities with which we are dealing, and even a stronger resolve to keep slogging at it. For we should then know that the campaign against corruption on behalf of the ideal of trust is no mere repairing of something perfect that has broken down, but the implanting of a new habit of acting in the ancient consciousness of man.

34

Problems of Comparing American Political Corruption

Arnold J. Heidenheimer

Any discussion of political corruption is by nature deeply grounded in values and much of the problem of potential analysts has consisted of disentangling the value systems manifested and expounded by the actors, intermediaries, monitors and observers of the actions deemed corrupt. As soon as transactions are labeled corrupt, they engender rhetorical and ideological descriptors that tend to remain only loosely linked to the actors accused of the questionable relationships. Analysis of the monitors' claims to moral superiority or the prosecutors' partisan motivations may elicit greater interest than the nature and value of the material advantages that were illicitly traded. Since many of these components seem so tied to culture and situation, some may seriously question whether evidence of corruption can be effectively gathered and analyzed over time and compared across political cultures.

These obstacles are not insurmountable, however, and analysis of the incidence of various kinds of corrupt transactions *can* be pursued both through varying historical periods and potentially also across national and even broader cultural boundaries. At least for the modern period, since the duties and obligations of public office have become legally and otherwise institutionalized in Western countries, it is possible to attempt an objective definition of political corruption that can be applied transnationally and, properly adjusted, also through time. Such a definition might state:

> Corruption is behavior which deviates from the formal duties of a public
> role because of private-regarding (family, close family, private clique)

Source: Arnold J. Heidenheimer, "Political Corruption in America: Is It Comparable?" in *Before Watergate: Problems of Corruption in American Society,* eds. Abraham S. Eisenstadt, Ari Hoogenboom and H.L. Trefousse. Brooklyn, N.Y.: Brooklyn College Press, 1978. Copyright © 1979 Brooklyn College, CUNY. Reprinted by permission.

pecuniary or status gains; or violates rules against the exercise of certain types of private-regarding influence. This includes such behavior as bribery; use of a reward to pervert the judgment of a person in a position of trust; nepotism (bestowal of patronage by reason of ascriptive relationship rather than merit); and misappropriation (illegal appropriation of public resources for private-regarding uses).[1]

Historians and social scientists who choose to utilize such a definition have for some time had the opportunity to compare the occurrence of corruption in American settings with its incidence elsewhere, particularly western Europe. However, an extensive examination of the literature has indicated that very few writers have succeeded in realizing that potential. European scholars have often looked in vain to their American colleagues for good descriptive studies they could build on. Thus Jacob van Klaveren complained that it was "a well-known fact among those studying American history" that "corruption is systematically practiced even today . . . yet it is difficult to obtain more specific explanations and information from American scholars." Elsewhere Colin Leys characterized most writing on American corruption as being "inquisitional" in nature, in contrast to the more solid historical studies of the eclipse of corrupt practices in Britain.[2]

A contemporary frame of reference will be used here to examine some of the reasons that have impeded the comparative analysis of American corruption.

Students of political corruption need to be intensely concerned about the problem of comparing different phenomena, say bribery and inefficiency, if for no other reason than that they are included by some under an overarching label of corruption. Careful lexicographers, such as those who edit the *Oxford English Dictionary,* identify a dozen or more definitions of corruption in past and present usage.[3] In America the range of practices to which the term is applied by publicists and even scholars has tended to vary more with cycles of public equanimity and arousal than in Europe. In periods of more intense and widespread concern with the morality and legitimacy of government, the variety of practices labeled corrupt tends to multiply. Thus Robert Brooks noted for the Progressive period that scholars, journalists and reformers displayed little discrimination in using the term to stigmatize "transactions and conditions of very different kinds."[4] He warned that the constant repetition of unclearly applied concepts tended to blur the popular conception of corruption. In the post-Watergate period the number of meanings which writers encompass under the corruption label seems to have expanded again. Typical of the broadened concept urged by some is one that calls for "the need to widen the conceptual approach to the study of corruption" by including a wide variety of actions and relationships that in one way or another "comprise a threat to the constitutional order and to the values of the democratic society."[5]

Even if researchers could agree on transnationally applicable definitions of political corruption, they still face problems of applying them to varying political jurisdictions. American national political institutions differ from European ones. To think of the powers of U.S. congressional committees or the discretionary power of U.S. regulatory agencies is to suggest contextual differences crucial to corruptibility that find only limited counterparts in European capitals. From many perspectives, as well as the simple matter of scale, American state systems might most fruitfully be compared with European national and regional governments. It can be appreciated how greatly the incidence of corruption at the state and local level varies between and within regions. It would therefore matter a great deal whether a researcher undertook a comparison of Belgian corruption with corruption in Louisiana or Oregon. Students of the mores of state legislatures can distinguish fairly evident gradations in the incidence of corruption: in the Midwest, for example, most would expect corruption to increase as they moved from Madison, Wisconsin, to Jefferson City, Missouri, to Springfield, Illinois. These variations in the tolerance of corruption at the subnational level are surely much greater than within the larger European countries, both the centralized ones like Britain and the federal ones like West Germany. In fact it is quite possible that an American state like Minnesota might be distinguished from other U.S. states by virtue of the low incidence of corruption almost as much as a European nation like Sweden might be distinguished from the nations and regions of western and southern Europe as a whole.

Another impediment to measuring corruption comparatively may be attributed to the greater visibility of much American corruption, especially at the local level. In America it is highly likely that information about corrupt arrangements will sooner or later come out not just in corridor gossip but also in public print and possibly in subsequent investigation. There are many interrelated reasons for this. In Europe bureaucracies are more tightly knit and insulated, and much medium-level official malfeasance may be discovered and punished without the general public ever becoming aware of it. The exposure of inefficiencies and corruption constitutes a vital theme of American local newspapers, more so than in Europe with the greater predominance of national media there. American journalists were more enterprising in this respect than their European equivalents even before the New

Journalism turned them into superferrets. Typically they have inside information sources, such as the challengers who want to upset incumbents in primary elections, or the candidates for elected district attorneys and judges, for which there are few equivalents in Europe. The appointed jobholder in many American local and state governments, more used as he is to frequent job changes, is also probably more willing to divulge incriminating information than a European equivalent loath to endanger a lifelong career in his civil service. Once aspersions and accusations are public, there are in America half a million individually elected local and state politicians, who can hope to enhance both their personal reputations and the public interest by calling for or expanding investigations. An American writer claimed in 1910 that the combating of more political corruption in the democratic, decentralized American setting implied the existence of greater political virtue than it did in Prussia of that day, where "the local government of the country is kept closely in the leading strings of the state."[6] Some of that difference has remained.

Toward the end of the period of "normalcy" that preceded Vietnam and Watergate, some observers believed that, when all the factors making for escalation of talk of corruption had been discounted, the United States was actually going through "a period of unexampled honesty in public administration." These were the words of a dean of the Stanford Law School, who was particularly concerned lest tightened conflict-of-interest statutes were keeping able corporate executives and lawyers from accepting government positions. The prototypical political outs, he held, had continued to blow up isolated instances of impropriety so that they appeared to illustrate massive, pervasive political corruption, causing "yesterday's peccadillo to become today's enormity." Conflict of interest had for him become "a modern political obsession" because of the American proclivity toward "morality escalation." In an era of unparalleled honesty he saw Americans indulging in the luxury of worrying about harms that were only potential.[7]

Bayless Manning's concern for the restraints on the mobility of American political elites might well be different after the experiences of the Lyndon Johnson and particularly the Richard Nixon administrations. The numerous and disastrous instances of malfeasance, misfeasance and abuse of power, particularly by officials in the White House, the intelligence agencies and the military complex, have certainly destroyed many illusions about the functioning of institutional controls. But neither the cause of social science nor of reform is well served by including all these offenses indiscriminately under an expanded umbrella definition of political corruption. On the contrary, the enormity of some of these abuses can too easily be lost from view if they are labeled as only one variety of a large family of corruption techniques. Corruption charges should continue to be restricted to those who have abused their offices of public trust for the purposes of direct or indirect material enrichment. Fresh analyses of the systemic implications of the revelations of the past decade would be instructive but those who undertake them should distinguish the incidence of the standard forms of corrupt practice from other abuses of public office.

Comparative research or, in the absence of good data, comparatively oriented thinking or even speculation can be helpful in this respect. For instance, suppose a really probing European American study of the incidence of corruption had been sponsored by a foundation in, say, the late 1950s, a period of relative normality and fairly stabilized concepts among both elites and masses. What such a survey would have shown would have depended very much on how questions were asked and responses translated. It would have been fairest then as now to include all of the present European Economic Community together with Scandinavia and other reasonably competitive political systems such as those of Austria and Switzerland. In other words, a Europe extending from Narvik to Syracuse would have been matched against a United States extending from Bangor and Key West to San Diego and Tacoma.

Making some educated guesses what such a survey would have revealed would constitute a sporting proposition, since the Jersey Cities and St. Pauls of America would be matched with the Gothenburgs and Palermos of Europe. Especially since no one will soon develop the technology needed to prove them, the findings of such a survey can be revealed on the basis of intuition. They might well show:

- Press mentions of the incidence of political corruption would be several score times more frequent in the United States than in Europe.
- Knowledge that there was "considerable or extensive" corruption in American state and local, and European national and local, government would vary widely in both settings: it would be more sharply polarized on a north-south dimension in Europe than in the United States.
- The identification of petty corruption would take different forms, such as traffic-ticket fixing in the United States and petty administrative bribery in Europe, but would be more uniformly reported from around the United States than in Europe, where it would rarely have been reported from northern urban areas.

- The pervasiveness of more serious forms of police corruption, as indicated for such cities as New York and Chicago, would not be widely ascertainable in Europe.
- Vote-buying and other forms of electoral corruption would be more widely reported in interviews with older Americans, while their European equivalents would more frequently report memories of other forms of electoral intimidation.
- Where financial contributions by business were believed to have swayed policies corruptly, American reports would usually mention individual firms while European ones would mention more industry and business associations.

The canons of scholarship do not presently punish aggravated historical fabrication much more severely than simple one-shot cases of supposition, so historians could also hypothesize about how the incidence of corruption has developed over time on both sides of the Atlantic. Suppose a data repository containing roughly comparable surveys since the late nineteenth century had been found. The shape of the curves of corruption incidence in Europe and America as they developed in the last three generations can be imagined.

What would these curves look like? Would they be similar, for instance, to the curves of car ownership, with the American incidence ratios higher at the start but with the Europeans gaining to narrow the difference over time? Or would they be more similar to the curves reflecting rates of infant mortality, with both American and European rates declining over time, but with the European rate declining more rapidly, so that almost all West European countries now have lower infant mortality rates than does the United States? Or maybe they would be cyclical in shape, somewhat akin to unemployment rates, with a tendency toward lower levels and lesser oscillation in the more recent periods. A set of curves closer to the infant mortality model seems most likely.

While the honest historian will reject the above extrapolations, the behavioral social scientist may claim that they unfairly malign Americans. The higher American rates of incidence of corruption, they may say, can still mean that a larger proportion of Americans than Europeans have over time virtuously forgone corruption opportunities. They will be thinking of the countless petty and large-scale bribers and favor-exchangers among businessmen, home owners, taxpayers and middlemen, department chairmen and other components of the large unwashed masses of corrupters. Corruption, they will say, can meaningfully be measured only as a proportion of opportunities to corrupt that were taken advantage of.

They have an arguable point. More Americans have probably had more opportunities to corrupt officials than have Europeans. In Germany civil servants traditionally displayed such disdain for the favors of other classes that in one German scholar's words, businessmen "did not even dare to offer any favors."[8] In the Netherlands the citizens' opportunity to bribe the police is limited by the pervasive way in which policemen live up to the legal provisions that forbid them to accept even cigarettes as gifts.[9] The American citizen's more direct involvement in administration gives him more opportunities for evading or breaking the rules. Thus the "tax morality" of most individual American taxpayers has to be evaluated differently, for our system of having the income-tax-payer figure out his own assessment is different from the practice followed in Europe, where the assessments are made by tax officials on the basis of documents submitted by the taxpayer. Faced by a more disciplined and professionalized bureaucracy and fewer opportunities to interpret rules for themselves, most Europeans may indeed face fewer opportunities to engage in corruption.

Are there, for instance, any European countries or regional jurisdictions where the knowledgeable businessman faces as few impediments to bribery to achieve his ends as in Chicago and Illinois, to take a state toward the top of the corruption scale? There the citizens found in the course of a recent six-year period that there was scarcely a single state or city elective office where the incumbent was not on the take. The governor took $300,000 from the racetrack interests. The secretary of state took from so many donors that his apartment overflowed with payoff envelopes. The Cook County clerk was convicted of receiving kickbacks from voting-machine manufacturers and numerous Chicago aldermen were convicted of extortion, embezzlement and conventional bribe-taking in zoning cases. State legislators, metropolitan district commissioners and appointed officials were shown to have formed numerous syndicates to take and distribute bribes. Thus in one five-year period alone several hundred public officials were convicted in more than 100 individual cases.

If a determined opposition party had won control of the Italian justice ministry, would it have racked up so vast a record even in Sicily? Possibly, though it is doubtful whether even there it would have been as sweeping. Elsewhere in central and northern Europe there has been no approximation to the incidence of corruption on this scale. There are, of course, regions there where the get-rich-quick opportunities of a commercial metropolis occasion successful attempts at corruption. Perhaps the state of Hesse with the metropolis of Frankfurt is a close approximation to Illinois in this respect. There, too, insiders greased the way for favorable action on contract bids for city and airport-building construction and concessions. But the scale of influence-buying did not touch all levels of the political and administrative hierarchies as it demonstrably did in Illinois. The scale of corruption payments in some notorious British cases would have aroused interest with difficulty in even the cleaner American states. Thus the main culprit in the Lynskey Tribunal case in the 1940s was shown to have been influenced by gifts of several dozen bottles of wine, a suit of clothes, a gold cigarette case and a week's hotel hospitality. To one American it "seems surprising that so much excitement was aroused in England about so little."[10]

The decline of Tammany in New York apparently reduced certain techniques of favor-buying in New York City politics but it evidently did not diminish the proclivity to bribe-taking of large sections of the New York police, as subsequently documented by the Knapp commission. The vast publicity given to its revelations produced a public scandal of the type that has forced reluctant administrators in many cities to shake up their departments to reduce corruption. The cyclical nature of attempts to reduce administrative corruption seems to be pronounced in American cities, even those lacking dominant party machines. The pattern seems to work as follows. Prior to the scandal corruption may reach pretty far up the police ladder, with assistant chiefs and inspectors joining captains and sergeants in taking corrupt payments. The reform administration then uses various devices, including dismissals from the force and incentive pay increases, to try to eliminate corruption at least at the higher and middle levels. During such phases promotion can be won by reporting bribe offers to superiors. But once the cleanup wave ebbs, there is a tendency to return to the pre-reform pattern of behavior, and the readiness to accept bribes or to sell protection once again rises up the command level within the police force.

What are the major reasons why attempts to compare the scale and nature of American corruption must remain so predominantly based on guesswork and piecework? The paucity of good-quality analyses of corruption cannot be explained entirely by the lack of encouragement from governmental and private research organizations. Rather it seems as though political phenomena that have embraced corruption have been largely ignored as research topics by recent generations of social scientists and historians. Relevant contributions from historians seem to have seldom surmounted the limited frameworks provided by focusing on particular organizations, bosses and eras. The contributions from legal scholars have been limited to the point of nonexistence. A perusal of work in political science, sociology and economics shows that at least some scholars have realized that there were big and important questions to be explored from both empirical and theoretical perspectives. In these disciplines corruption has never been anything like a mainstream research favorite, but at least there have in each decade been several people who tried to mount reasonably ambitious individual research projects.

These initiatives have stimulated rivulets of academic interest, but perhaps in no area less than that of American politics above the level of the ethnic ghetto or the city ward. In the 1930s V. O. Key devoted his Ph.D. dissertation to an interesting attempt to develop an analysis of corruption in America.[11] It largely sank from public view and he treated the subject only peripherally in his subsequent career as one of the most widely recognized scholars of American parties and elections.

In the 1940s and 1950s sociologists like Robert K. Merton and Daniel Bell opened new perspectives which remolded academic views by purporting to demonstrate the positive functions of corruption and patronage from the standpoint of social integration. In the 1960s there was a relative profusion of studies, many of them more comparative and incorporating much new material derived from the study of politics in developing non-Western countries. Many of these studies applied theoretical constructs, derived from the study of machines and patronage, with more insight and in more convincing ways than similar work being done on earlier or contemporary American politics. But very few scholars made any reasonably ambitious or comprehensive attempts to treat the nature and scope of American corruption comparatively. The very few article-length efforts at comparative treatment in historical contexts were written by European and not by American scholars.[12]

A striking characteristic of most of the writing on American corruption by both historians and political scientists of the past several decades is how predominantly it has been linked in particular to the rise and fall of urban party machines. The development and employment of this machine paradigm has no doubt been fruitful, serving as a vehicle for linking the concepts of several disciplines and schools, but it has also inhibited the progress of research in a number of ways.

First, it has served to perpetuate a synecdochic research focus, in which the part looms bigger than the whole. Even as their middle-class inhabitants were fleeing to the suburbs, city machines were being subjected to much more searching and interesting analyses than were the politics at the state capitol or the shifting coalitions of national party coalitions. Historians argued over whether New Deal welfare programs helped or hurt the city machines. The ward was infinitely more closely scrutinized than the corporate board room; the boodle traditions of Philadelphia and San Francisco became much better known than the practices of the steel and construction industries.

Secondly, concentration on the machine paradigm perpetuated a kind of technological lag among social scientists. While they argued over how much of the exactions of party organizations constituted "dirty" or "clean" graft, or induced inefficiency rather than corruption, they were failing to keep abreast with newer, more subtle, indirect forms of favor-exchanging. These techniques typically involved the exchange of highly technical information at the interface of public and private economic spheres. Such newer forms of favor-trading operated much more characteristically between company officials and bureaucrats outside the relatively stagnant cities. If social scientists were as surprised as Republicans that a nice suburban politician like Spiro T. Agnew had to resign to avoid impeachment, it was partly because so much of their attention was focused on whether Mike Royko would ever be able to incriminate Mayor Richard Daley.

Finally, concentration on the machine model has focused attention one-sidedly on how manpower based on patronage and support-channeling has imposed coordinated policies within a given political market across only one particular set of jurisdictional boundaries. It was long thought that the interests that procured acquiescence among some scores of governmental boards in a single American metropolitan area faced unique challenges. Revelations about supranational corporations have demonstrated that companies like Lockheed have been treating national governments around the world much as a turn-of-the-century traction magnate treated local governments. But what differences are there behind these similarities? It used to be held that lack of data prevented an assessment of the global behavior of international companies, when they were challenged by critics like Gunnar Myrdal.[13] Now, rather suddenly, there are plenty of data. But, partly because our "machine" tools do not seem applicable, the conceptual apparatus to process them is generally lacking.

The increments in objective perspective that can be gained by relativizing cultural biases through cross-cultural examination are especially important to a value-laden research topic like corruption. That is why students of American corruption are well advised to become knowledgeable about the definitions and incidence of political corruption in other places and other times. If such analyses are pursued, invaluable insights will also be gained into the costs of corrupt practices relative to other social goods and evils. Thus the arguments that in certain situations the toleration of corruption by the few can in the long term lead to economic benefits for the many is certainly worth considering.

More than seventy years ago Henry Jones Ford derided Lincoln Steffens by claiming that future cultural archeologists might praise America for its willingness to accept corruption. "Most assuredly," he wrote, they would "rejoice" that "men of affairs in our time corrupted government in securing opportunities of enterprise," because "slackness and decay are more dangerous to a nation than corruption."[14] Today many are more likely to agree with Max Weber that America has flourished economically not because, but in spite of, its toleration of lax political and administrative morality. "A corruption and wastefulness second to none could be tolerated by a country with as yet unlimited economic opportunities."[15] As the limits earlier visible in Europe have become more evident also in this country, the drain of corruption becomes more critical.

Part of the wisdom the student of corruption needs to develop will also relate to considering how corruption as a social evil relates to other social evils. Is it occasionally preferable as a lesser evil to the more widespread incidence of societal violence? Scholars like Huntington and Friedrich argue that the two phenomena may indeed be mutually substitutable. The conservative may be willing to tolerate patterns of police corruption as an alternative to attempts to storm and seize police stations. Even the tender-hearted liberal might accept the bribing of concentration-camp guards if it might lessen the death or mutilation toll of the political or ethnic deviants who may constitute the bulk of camp inmates.

Fortunately such trade-offs need not be given prime consideration in an essay comparing corrupt patterns in the postindustrial societies of Europe and North America. But if one attempts to answer the larger question of "what difference" the supposed higher levels of United States corruption make in terms of the dominant goals of these political systems, he should attempt to perceive how the widespread toleration of corruption affects the manner in which governments are able to approach their larger social goals as implemented in their social welfare programs. Even the New Deal might not have been able to break through the resistance to social legislation, had it not included the big city machines within its coalition. These machines in turn would not have delivered crucial congressional votes if the do-gooders had not been tolerant of a certain level of corruption at local and state levels.

Postscript: Under both the Nixon-Ford and Reagan administrations Federal prosecutors became quite active in bringing corruption indictments against local and state officials in many states, most of whom were Democrats. Even when these charges led to convictions, it often did not handicap other Democratic incumbents or candidates very significantly. While the Illinois prosecutions in the 1970's led to a period of Republican control of the governorship there, in other states like New York successful prosecutions in 1987 of scores of local Democrats failed to generate scandals which might have undermined the positions of Mayor Edward Koch or Governor Mario Cuomo.

Some scholars have argued that at the national level Republican administrations have been more vulnerable to both more corruption and more scandalization than Democrats. William Leuchtenberg has asserted that for the century since the 1880's, the overwhelming share, or as much as ninety percent, of the political corruption in national administrations has occurred under Republicans.

Referring to indictments of prominent Reagan administration officials, Richard Neustadt has argued that Republican appointees often bring with them a disdain for government that translates into lack of respect for intricate conflict of interest rules. Since some Republicans believe the "Horatio Alger stuff" they preach, Presidential aides are encouraged to strike out on their own for their personal benefits. Also seen as relevant is that recent Republican Presidents like Eisenhower, Nixon and Reagan tended to delegate more power to White House chiefs of staff drawn from careers in private business. This weakened the network of informal controls which Democratic Presidents had developed through the utilization of more high-level personnel who had extensive experience and socialization in Federal-level political and bureaucratic positions.[16]

Notes

1. This definition is employed by Joseph S. Nye in "Corruption and Political Development: A Cost Benefit Analysis," *American Political Science Review,* LXI, No. 2 (June 1967), 419, and is cited in Arnold J. Heidenheimer, ed., *Political Corruption: Readings in Comparative Analysis* (New York, 1970), pp. 566–67.
2. Jacob van Klaveren, "Corruption: The Special Case of the United States" in Heidenheimer, *op. cit.,* p. 269; Colin Leys, "What Is the Problem about Corruption?" *Journal of Modern African Studies,* III (1965), No. 2, 215–24.
3. Heidenheimer, "Definitions, Concepts and Criteria," in Heidenheimer, *op. cit.,* pp. 3–9.
4. Robert C. Brooks, "The Nature of Political Corruption," in *ibid.,* p. 56.
5. Larry L. Berg *et al., Corruption in the American Political System* (Morristown, N.J., 1977), pp. 7, 80.
6. Henry Jones Ford, "Municipal Corruption: A Comment on Lincoln Steffens," *Political Science Quarterly,* XIX (1904), 673–86.

7. Bayless Manning, "The Purity Potlatch: Conflict of Interests and Moral Escalation," *Federal Bar Journal,* XXIV, No. 3 (Summer 1964), 243–49.
8. Theodore Eschenburg, "The Decline of the Bureaucratic Ethos in the Federal Republic" in Heidenheimer, *op. cit.,* p. 259.
9. H.H. Brasz, "Administrative Corruption in Theory and Dutch Practice" in *ibid.,* p. 247.
10. Madeline R. Robinton, "The British Method of Dealing with Political Corruption" in *ibid.,* p. 254.
11. V.O. Key, Jr., *The Techniques of Political Graft in the United States* (Chicago, 1936).
12. Cf. Samuel E. Finer, "Patronage and the Public Service: Jeffersonian Bureaucracy and the British Tradition" in *ibid.,* pp. 106–27; Van Klaveren, *op. cit.*
13. Gunnar Myrdal, "Corruption: Its Causes and Effects," in *Asian Drama: An Enquiry into the Poverty of Nations* (New York, 1968), II, 937–51.
14. Ford, *op. cit.*
15. Max Weber, *Politics as a Vocation* (Philadelphia, 1965), p. 108.
16. The references in the last two paragraphs are drawn from a journalistic survey article, Gerald F. Seib, "From Grant to Reagan, Scandal Seems To Hit Republican Presidents," *Wall Street Journal,* July 16, 1987.

Regional and Subnational Systems: An Introduction

While much research on corruption focuses upon misconduct in national governments, it is often at lower levels in government, party and other political organizations that corruption is most common. There, central control and public scrutiny tend to be less thorough, and anti-corruption measures less thoroughly developed and implemented, even though significant decisions and benefits are at stake. In the eyes of national officials, subnational corruption can thwart the implementation of central policy, or (alternatively) can provide informal incentives for weaving potential dissident factions and areas into the national political fabric. For the analyst, regional cases of corruption not only necessitate greater care in generalizing about whole nations, but also offer opportunities to study corruption in light of center-periphery relationships, and to "control" for some national system characteristics while studying the significance of regional contrasts. In this section three authors discuss variations in corruption among regions and levels of government in the United States, and a fourth focuses upon the particularly intriguing case of Yucatan, in Mexico.

In Chapter 35 James Q. Wilson's observations on the persistence of corruption in state governments, made in the context of Massachusetts politics twenty years ago, remain valid today. Municipal reformers did much to reduce outright boodling and theft in American cities. But many of the preconditions of corruption which attracted their concern decades ago—high political stakes, ineffective safeguards and public oversight, and a political value system conducive to favoritism and thievery—are alive and well in the statehouse. Administrative reforms may be sufficient remedies for some corruption in state governments, but others are reactions to a pervasive fragmentation of power: having something to bargain with may be the only way governors can get things done. Thus, reformers should take care that in fighting abuses of patronage, they do not make it impossible for state officials to accomplish worthwhile goals.

Characteristics of state politics can carry over to the national scene, as Bruce L. Payne argues in Chapter 36. In his analysis of the case of

Spiro T. Agnew, the emphasis is upon the analysis of character. To that end he argues that the values and political perspectives of key figures have at times been mistakenly overlooked in favor of institutional structures and processes. Character is developed in a social context, however, and Agnew's taking payments and gifts can be viewed as an extension of some of the routine modi operandi of Maryland politics. A national government may seek to enforce a certain set of ethical standards, but particularly in a federal system, where lower levels of government are politically vital and where state political systems have an effect upon the makeup of national governments and institutions, differences and occasional conflict over standards of political conduct will be almost inevitable.

Federal prosecution of state and local corruption cases can cause other sorts of problems, according to Charles Ruff. Judicial reinterpretation of the Hobbs Act over the past two decades, he argues, has produced a new judicially created category of crime, has virtually eliminated the distinction between bribery and extortion, has greatly increased federal prosecutors' ability to intervene in cases of corruption at lower levels of government. These changes, along with more aggressive enforcement of laws such as the Travel Act, have allowed more extensive federal investigation and more corruption convictions. But they can also threaten the vitality of state politics: the Hobbs Act as now applied has become so vague that it is hard to say where some necessary parts of politics such as fund raising end, and corruption begins. Given the formidable resources of federal prosecutors, the decision to intervene is a sensitive one, Ruff argues; often it is better that prosecution, and demands for reform, emerge from within state and local political systems.

Margaret Goodman's study of the consequences of corruption in Yucatan in Chapter 38 underscores the importance of understanding regional economic and political arrangements. When national policymakers reorganized important sectors of Yucatan's agricultural economy, these new arrangements created economic problems and an upsurge of corruption. In this sense corruption could be seen as an adaptive response within one region to changes imposed from without—an adaptation which, Goodman points out, had important costs. But the particular type of response reflected the structure of political and economic power in the region, and in turn had important effects upon subsequent development. In Mexico there are many political arenas which only partially overlap; an understanding of corruption and its consequences requires an understanding of politics at the regional level.

35

Corruption: The Shame of the States

James Q. Wilson

The best state legislatures, observed Lord Bryce over half a century ago, are those of the New England states, "particularly Massachusetts." Because of the "venerable traditions surrounding [this] ancient commonwealth" which "sustain the dignity" of its legislature and "induce good men to enter it," this body—called the General Court—is "according to the best authorities, substantially pure." About the time that Bryce was congratulating the representatives in the Massachusetts State House, these men were engaged in a partially successful effort to regulate the government of the city of Boston on the grounds that city hall was becoming a cesspool of corruption owing, in no small part, to the fact that the Irish, led by Mayor John "Honey Fitz" Fitzgerald, had taken over. The chief instrument of state supervision over the suspect affairs of the city was to be the Boston Finance Commission, appointed by the governor to investigate any and all aspects of municipal affairs in the capital.

Now, a half century later, the tables have been, if not turned, then at least rearranged. While no one would claim that the Boston city hall is "pure," the mayoralty of John Collins (an Irishman) has aroused the enthusiastic backing of the city's financial and commercial elite. Many leading Brahmins work closely with the mayor, support him politically, and—most importantly—stand behind him in many of his often bitter fights with the governor and the state legislature. In contrast, the legislature has been plagued with endless charges of corruption and incompetence, the most recent of which have emerged from the work of the Massachusetts Crime Commission.

This commission, created by the (reluctant) legislature in July, 1962 and appointed by Republican Governor John Volpe (who had recom-

Source: James Q. Wilson, "Corruption: The Shame of the States," *The Public Interest,* 2 (1966), 28–38. By permission of the author and the publisher. Copyright © 1966 by National Affairs, Inc.

mended its formation in the first place), was composed largely of the sort of men who used to be *in* the legislature rather than critics of it. In a state where the principal politicians are Irish and Italian graduates of (if anything) Boston College or the Suffolk Law School, the commission was woven out of Ivy. The chairman was Alfred Gardner (Harvard '18), senior partner in the austerely respectable law firm of Palmer, Dodge, Gardner and Bradford. Of the other six members, three were graduates of Harvard, two of Princeton, and another of the Harvard Law School. (Although at least one Irishman got onto the commission, he was an investment consultant and retired brigadier general, and is probably more Yankee than the Yankees.) The American melting pot has obviously not changed the popular belief that, while the Irish are experts on politics, and the Jews experts on money, the Yankees are experts on morality.

The bad repute of Massachusetts government might seem an exaggeration to the casual reader of the recently published comprehensive report of the commission. Except for a brief section on the Massachusetts Turnpike Authority, there are no juicy stories of boodle and skulduggery, nor any inciting accounts of the testimony. The legislature had taken pains to insure that it would not make the same mistake the United States Senate did when it created the Kefauver committee. Public hearings were explicitly forbidden. All testimony was taken in secret sessions; as interpreted by the commission, this restriction also forbade it from publishing the names of witnesses, direct accounts of their evidence, or details of allegations. If it suspected wrongdoing, the commission was to turn its information over to regular law-enforcement agencies. And when the life of the commission expired this year, the legislature made certain that its files were locked away in a vault, secure against further scrutiny.

But if the report is dull, the results were not. Attorney General Edward Brooke, on the basis of information furnished by the commission, brought indictments against fifty-three individuals and fifteen corporations. About two dozen of the individuals were (or had been) state officials, and they included the former Speaker of the House, a former governor, the public safety director, two present and two former members of the governor's council, the chairman of the state housing board, and several former state representatives. One can be reasonably confident that much the same results could be produced by similar commissions in many other states, particularly industrial states of the Northeast such as Pennsylvania, Ohio, and the like. Many of these states would never have been described as "pure" by Lord Bryce at any stage of their history (he singled out New York and

Pennsylvania as having legislatures that were "confessedly among the worst"); about all that seems to have happened in the last fifty years is that, on the whole, their governors have become more respectable and their political parties more disorganized, thereby transforming what once was well-organized, machine-like corruption into disorganized, free-lance corruption.

Three Theories of Corruption

Why should so many state governments seem so bad? The Massachusetts Crime Commission did not try to answer that question (it said it did not know whether corruption was worse in its state than in others), nor did it address itself to the more fundamental questions, "What is corruption?" "Why does it occur?" In short, the commission did not develop a theory of corruption. This is not simply an academic deficiency (I am not trying to grade the commission's report as if it were a term paper in a political science seminar); rather, it is a practical problem of the greatest importance, for without a theory of corruption there cannot be a remedy for corruption unless by happy accident.

There are at least three major theories of government corruption. The first holds that there is a particular political ethos or style which attaches a relatively low value to probity and impersonal efficiency and relatively high value to favors, personal loyalty, and private gain. Lower-class immigrant voters, faced with the problems of accommodation to an unfamiliar and perhaps hostile environment, are likely to want, in the words of Martin Lomasney, "help, not justice." If such groups come—as have the Irish and the Sicilians—from a culture in which they experienced a long period of domination by foreign rulers the immigrant will already be experienced in the ways of creating an informal and illegal (and therefore "corrupt") covert government as a way of dealing with the—to them—illegitimate formal government. The values of such groups are radically incompatible with the values of (for example) old-stock Anglo-Saxon Protestant Americans, and particularly with those members of the latter culture who serve on crime commissions. Whatever the formal arrangements, the needs and values of those citizens sharing the immigrant ethos will produce irresistible demands for favoritism and thus for corruption.

The second theory is that corruption is the result of ordinary men facing extraordinary temptations. Lincoln Steffens argued that corruption was not the result of any defect in character (or, by implication, in cultural values); rather, it was the inevitable consequence of a social system which holds out to men great prizes—power, wealth, status—if only they are bold enough to seize them. Politicians are corrupt because businessmen bribe them; this, in turn, occurs because businessmen are judged solely in terms of worldly success. The form of government makes little difference; the only way to abolish corruption is to change the economic and social system which rewards it. (Steffens admired Soviet communism because it was a system without privilege: "There was none but petty political corruption in Russia," he wrote after visiting there. "The dictator was never asked to do wrong.") A less Marxist variation of this theory is more familiar: men steal when there is a lot of money lying around loose and no one is watching. Public officials are only human. They will resist minor temptation, particularly if everyone else does and someone is checking up. They are not angels, however, and cannot be expected to be honest when others are stealing (no one wants to be thought a fink) and superiors are indifferent. The Catholic Church, having known this for several centuries, counsels the young in its catechisms to "avoid the occasion of sin." The solution to this sort of corruption is, obviously, to inspect, audit, check, and double-check.

The third theory is more explicitly political and has the advantage of seeking to explain why governmental corruption appears to be more common in America than in Europe. Henry Jones Ford, writing in 1904, observed that in this country, unlike in those whose institutions follow the British or French models, the executive and legislative branches are separated by constitutional checks and balances. What the Founders have put asunder, the politicians must join together if anything is to be accomplished. Because each branch can—and sometimes does—paralyze the other, American government "is so constituted that it cannot be carried on without corruption." The boss, the machine, the political party, the bagmen—all these operate, in Ford's view, to concert the action of legally independent branches of government through the exchange of favors. The solution to corruption, if this is its cause, is to bring these various departments together formally and constitutionally. This, of course, is precisely what the National Civic League and other reform groups have attempted by their espousal of the council manager plan for municipal government, and what advocates of strong and responsible political parties have sought with respect to state and national government. If the chief executive, by virtue of either his constitutional position or his control of a disciplined majority party, is strong enough to rule without the consent of subordinates or the intervention of legislators, then no one will bribe subordinates or legislators—they will have nothing to sell. The leader himself will rarely be bribed, because his power will be sufficiently great that few, if any, groups can afford his price. (This is how Ford explained the lesser incidence of corruption in American national government: the president is strong enough to get his way and visible enough to make bribe-taking too hazardous.)

Crime commissions and reform groups in this country have at one time or another adopted all these theories, but at least one has now become unfashionable. Fifty years ago the Brahmins were quite candid about the defects they found in the Boston Irish politicians. These "newer races," as James Michael Curley called them, were considered to be the carriers of corruption. In 1965, the Massachusetts Crime Commission—perhaps out of politeness as much as conviction—begins its report by finding "no basis for saying that corruption in Massachusetts is the peculiar attribute of any one party or racial or religious group." This commendable tolerance is perhaps a bit premature: it is at least arguable that the various ethnic groups which make up our big cities and industrial states differ with respect to their conceptions of the public interest as much as they continue to differ with respect to style of life, party affiliation, and place of residence. The structure of government in many states of the Northeast is quite similar to that found in the Far West, yet the incidence of corruption appears to be significantly greater in the East. The historical reasons for this may include the differing values of the populations involved. While one can understand the reasons a public body might wish to avoid commenting on this, the result is that one theory of corruption is discarded *a priori* and all reforms are based on the other theories.

What Happened to the Cities?

The curious fact about all theories of corruption, however, is that they could apply equally to American cities as to American states, and yet it is the states (and to a considerable extent the counties) rather than the cities which are notorious for corruption. Although some corruption probably is to be found in almost all cities, and a great deal in a few, the most important fact about American municipal government over the last twenty years has been the dramatic improvement in the standards and honesty of public service. In no large city today is it likely that a known thief could be elected mayor (how many unknown thieves are elected must be a matter of speculation); a few decades ago, it would have been surprising if the mayor were *not* a boodler.

The reasons for this change are thought to be well-known—the reduction in the demand for and tolerance of corruption, owing to the massive entry of voters into the middle class; the nationalization and bureaucratization of welfare programs that once were the province of the machine; the greater scrutiny of local affairs by the press and civic associations; and the rise of forms of government—the council-manager plan and nonpartisanship—which make party domination difficult.

But if these changes in American society have had profound consequences for city politics, why did they appear to have so little effect on state politics? To be sure, known thieves are probably not often elected governor, but few people outside the states of the Far West are under much illusion as to the standards of public morality which prevail in and around state legislatures and cabinets.

There are at least two reasons for the difference. The first is that the degree of public scrutiny of government is not the same at the state as at the city level. Big cities have big newspapers, big civic associations, and big blocs of newspaper-reading, civic-minded voters. State capitals, by contrast, are usually located outside the major metropolitan centers of the state in smaller cities with small-city newspapers, few (and weak) civic associations, and relatively few attentive citizens with high and vocal standards of public morality. The cosmopolitan, in Robert Merton's language, seeks to escape the small city and get to the big city; the locals who remain behind typically place a higher value on personal friendships and good fellowship than on insisting that government be subject to general and impersonal rules. (The Massachusetts state capitol is an obvious and embarrassing exception: it is located in Boston but seems unaffected by that fact. Perhaps this is because Boston newspapers are so poor and its civic life is so weakly organized.)

The other reason is that anyone interested in obtaining favors from government finds the stakes considerably higher at the state level. With the exception of urban renewal and public housing programs, the city government administers services rather than makes investments. These services are often controversial but the controversy is more about who is to manage them, how they are to be financed, and whether they are fairly and adequately administered. Education, public welfare, street cleaning, and police protection are important services but (with the exception of police tolerance of gambling) they are not likely to make many people very rich. States, on the other hand, disburse or regulate big money. They build roads and in so doing spend billions on contractors, land owners, engineers, and "consultants." They regulate truckers, public utilities, insurance companies, banks, small loan firms, and pawnbrokers; they issue paroles and pardons, license drivers, doctors, dentists, liquor stores, barbers, beauticians, teachers, chiropractors, real estate brokers, and scores of other occupations and professions; they control access to natural resources, and supervise industrial safety and workmen's compensation programs. The stakes are enormous.

At one time, the stakes in city politics were also high. In the late nineteenth and early twentieth centuries, big cities were making their major capital improvements—in the form of subways, traction lines, utility systems—and the value of the contracts and franchises was huge. Local government was formally weak—it had been made so deliberately, in order to insure that it would be "democratic"—and thus it was possible (indeed, almost necessary) for a boss or a machine to control it in order to exchange privileges for boodle.

Prohibition, and later organized gambling, extended the rewards of municipal corruption beyond the time when rapid capital formation was at an end. Organized crime remains a legacy of Prohibition which is still very much with us, but on different terms. There are no longer any Al Capones. The gamblers continue to corrupt the police but, except in the smaller towns—Cicero and Calumet City near Chicago, Newport and Covington near Cincinnati—they rarely manage (or even try) to take over the entire political structure of a city. And even these famous "sin towns" are rapidly being closed down. By the time urban renewal came along—a program of capital improvements potentially ripe for corruption—the coalitions of businessmen and mayors which governed most big cities and which were most interested in renewal as a "progressive" program to "save the city" were not inclined to allow the success of the program to be threatened by stealing. More importantly, urban renewal is far smaller in scale than the highway program; the opportunities for "windfall profits" are not vast; the program is surrounded by sufficient public controversy to make it very difficult to transact many deals under the table; and the federal government supervises local renewal much more closely than it supervises highway construction.

Unreconstructed State Government

Ironically, the very things which made matters better in the big cities may have made them worse in the states. The preoccupation with urban affairs and the attendant close scrutiny of the conduct of those affairs has diverted public attention from state affairs. If it was true that state capitols were ignored in the past, it is doubly true today. The civic-minded businessman wants to save the central city; the liberal cosmopolitan wants to improve urban race relations and end urban poverty; the federal government, especially the White House, seeks closer and closer ties with the big cities—in part because that is where the voters are and in part because federal officials are increasingly desirous of establishing direct relations with their city counterparts in order to bypass what they often consider to be the obstructionism of the state bureaucracy.

The various governmental innovations—at-large elections, nonpartisanship, the council-manager form—which have made entry into municipal politics attractive to, and possible for, the non-party civic "statesman" have meant that increasingly the more traditional politician has felt uncomfortable in and disadvantaged by city politics. Elections for state office, which continue to be conducted under party labels in relatively small districts, are a more familiar and congenial experience. Success here can still come to the man with strong neighborhood ties, clubhouse connections, a proven record of party loyalty, and a flair for tuning the ear of his ethnic compatriots to the ancestral voices.

In short, if government is more corrupt in the states than in the cities, it is because all three theories of corruption (and perhaps others) apply with greater force to the states. The ethnic style of politics is weakening in the cities but not in the states; more boodle is lying around with no one watching in state capitols than in city halls; and state governments continue to be badly decentralized, with formal authority divided among a host of semi-autonomous boards, commissions, and departments. The states have rarely been subjected to the kinds of reforms which over the years have gradually centralized formal authority in the hands of a professional city manager or a single strong mayor.

The last point deserves emphasis. Governors are not "little presidents." Their power of appointment and removal is sharply circumscribed. Duane Lockard estimates that only slightly more than half the 730 major administrative posts in state government are filled by gubernatorial appointments; the remainder are filled by election or by appointments made by the legislature or special boards and commissions. Nor does the governor generally have the full power of removal normally assumed to be the prerogative of the president. Only five governors can appoint their own superintendents of education; only half can choose their own men to run state departments of agriculture. Of equal or greater importance is the typical governor's weak position within the party and the interest groups which elect him. A governor who is the principal leader of his party and who has in addition a strong and popular personality may do well with little formal authority;

lacking these, all the formal executive authority in the world may not suffice, if for no other reason than that the governor must still deal with an independent legislature.

The Massachusetts Crime Commission was not unaware of such problems but—perhaps because it was a crime commission rather than an "effective government" commission—it did not really come to grips with these issues. It was preoccupied with corruption that, in its view, could be attributed largely to the "occasion of sin" theory of wrongdoing. Dealing with such forms of larceny is relatively easy: employ well-qualified administrators selected on their merits to implement high professional standards. This, supplemented by careful inspection and audit procedures, will reduce or eliminate corruption in the letting of contracts, hiring of consultants, issuance of licenses, and regulation of conduct by such agencies as the Registry of Motor Vehicles, the Department of Public Works; the Massachusetts Turnpike Authority, and the Department of Banking and Insurance.

Recognizing that bookkeeper reforms alone are insufficient because they provide no ultimate checks on the behavior of the bookkeepers, the commission sought to give elective officials clear authority over the behavior of their subordinates and clear responsibility to the electorate. Thus, many of the commission's recommendations are designed to strengthen the formal powers of the chief executive—the governor and his principal subordinates—so that someone has the power and responsibility for weeding out corrupt underlings. The commission follows a well-marked tradition: reformers, at least during this century, have favored strong executive authority. In this, of course, they have sometimes undone themselves: reformers correctly believe that a strong executive is less likely to tolerate or encourage corruption than a weak one, but they often forget that in the United States a strong executive is also likely to pay close attention to the demands of the masses. Legislatures, though more likely to be corrupt, are also more likely to be conservative. Reformers often secure cleanliness at the price of conservatism.

But because no attention is paid to the third cause of corruption—the need to exchange favors to overcome decentralized authority—the sort of executive-strengthening recommended by the Massachusetts commission, while admirably suited to eliminating the occasion of sin, is not so well suited to dealing with legislatures or other independent bodies. The governor must not only be strong in his own house, but in the legislature's house as well. Otherwise, the executive branch may be pure, but only out of impotence.

The Uses of Patronage

Unless we are willing to adopt a parliamentary form of state government (and I take it we are not), then the way in which a governor can get important things done (at least in a state like Massachusetts) is by having something to bargain with that both the legislature and the party value. There are several such resources: for one, his own popularity with the voters; and for another, favors and patronage. The latter the commission rejects and, I suspect, ill-advisedly. Certainly, patronage abuses should be curtailed (in large part because, as the commission notes, such abuses lower the morale of public employees). Furthermore, the cumbersome Massachusetts civil service system in its present form probably serves the interests of neither the reformers nor the politicians. (For example, the legislature frequently passes statutes "freezing" certain employees into their jobs. This not only protects some incompetents, it also makes it impossible for the governor to use these positions for patronage purposes of his own.) But I believe that patronage itself should not be eliminated entirely.

The commission was of course aware of the fact that patronage is often used to induce legally independent officials to act toward some desirable goal. The Massachusetts Turnpike Authority under the leadership of the late William Callahan raised to a fine art the use of jobs, contracts, and insurance premiums for political purposes—but the Massachusetts Turnpike got built, and on time. The commission faces the issue squarely:

> The methods [the chairman of the Authority] used to get results have had no small part in bringing about the deterioration in the moral climate of our state government. This deterioration in moral climate is of far greater importance to every man, woman and child in Massachusetts than the ease and comfort with which it is now possible to drive the length of the state on a multi-lane highway.

Perhaps, I suspect, however, that this is a question on which the people of Massachusetts might have some differences of opinion. It may well be that a deterioration in the moral climate of government and a concomitant weakening of the respect in which citizens hold their government are serious costs of corruption. But these costs, like all others, are matters of degree; hopefully, ways can be found to reduce them without a more than equivalent reduction in benefits.

What is clear is that the strengthening of the governor cannot be achieved by formal means alone, particularly if Massachusetts, like most states, needs two strong and highly competitive political parties.

If the commission goes too far in some directions, it does not go far enough in others. The most serious cause of the corruption of law enforcement officials is organized crime; recognizing this, the commission calls only for stronger laws, stiffer penalties, and a "reorganized" state police. "Bookmakers are not entitled to lenience." But raising the penalties against betting will not necessarily eliminate organized crime; it may only raise the price. Because more will be at stake, the police and the politicians are likely to demand bigger bribes and the criminals will be more disposed to use violence to protect their monopoly profits. At a time when the mayor of New York City is advocating offtrack betting, it would seem that some attention might be given in Massachusetts to lowering, rather than increasing, the incentives gamblers have to corrupt the government. (To be sure, in some states and cities vigorous police action has reduced gambling to a bare minimum, but these are states—like California—with very different histories and populations; unless one is prepared to reject entirely the "ethos" theory of corruption, one should not be too quick to conclude that equally good results can be obtained in any state.)

With respect to campaign contributions, the commission confesses the limitations of its recommendations, which by and large follow a familiar pattern: better reporting systems, the removal of unrealistic and unenforceable limits on dollar amounts, and so forth. Such methods are not likely to deter the favor-seeking contributor, though they are likely to deter perfectly respectable contributors who feel that reports, inspections, and publicity involve too much trouble and possible embarrassment to justify giving anything at all. The commission "leaves to others" a study of fundamental changes in methods of campaign finance. Unfortunately, calls for "more research" are likely to go unheeded.

It is, of course, easy to criticize crime commissions and to adopt a faintly patronizing tone toward reformers. This would be a mistake. The commission has turned a number of highly-placed rascals over to the attorney general and the courts; and other, lesser rascals are likely to take heed—for the moment. But it would also be a mistake to make corruption (defined so broadly as to include "good" as well as "bad" patronage) the central issue. The central issue is that many states—Massachusetts is one—are badly governed in the sense that certain goals that should be sought are not, and others that should not be, are. The central problem is the problem of power—how can it be used responsibly but effectively for socially desirable ends? Power is hard to find and harder to use wisely, in great part because in many states we are destroying its informal bases (favors, patronage, party discipline) faster than we are building up its formal bases (legal authority). The result increasingly is that, with the states unable to act, they are being bypassed by cities (where the most visible problems are to be found) seeking the assistance of the federal government (where the power is). To the extent that the recommendations of the Massachusetts Crime Commission and its counterparts elsewhere can strengthen the legal capacity of a state to govern, they will have been worthwhile. To the extent they are used only for piecemeal attacks on the more titillating and exotic forms of public corruption, they may do more harm than good.

36

Spiro Agnew and Maryland Customs

Bruce L. Payne

For the Elizabethan generation "policy" meant actions which, although required by reason of state, were wicked as well as expedient.[1] In modern usage the term has shed its connection with cunning and dissimulation, and has come to mean more neutrally the government's course of action. The change reflects alterations in our philosophy of government and in our ideas about sin and virtue. Utilitarianism, the dominant moral framework of this age, has undermined the distinction between good acts and expedient ones, for both our private and our public lives.

The same period of time has brought with it much less development in our notion of political corruption. Now, as in the early seventeenth century, this phrase means illegal or irregular acts by public officials, motivated by their own pecuniary or political self-interest, and at odds with prevailing conceptions of the public interest.[2] A suggestion of individual moral decay has remained a more-or-less constant correlative over the whole period. . . .

This chapter argues that a direct concern with character is helpful in understanding political corruption and in reducing its incidence. Without undue optimism about human nature, it nevertheless may be possible to find ways of encouraging the good and decent motives in officials and citizens, and of inhibiting those coexisting vices with which humans are also variously endowed.

Since Tudor days Anglican congregations have confessed that "We have followed too much the devices and desires of our own hearts. We have offended against thy holy laws." The prayerbook view was that the proper remedy for sin is repentance, combined (God willing) with

Source: Bruce L. Payne, "Devices and Desires: Corruption and Ethical Seriousness," in Joel L. Fleishman, Lance Liebman and Mark H. Moore (eds.), *Public Duties: The Moral Obligations of Government Officials.* Cambridge, Mass.: Harvard University. © 1981 by the President and Fellows of Harvard College. By permission of the publisher.

forgiveness and atonement; and the church threatened on the authority of St. Paul "no less pain than everlasting damnation to all disobedient persons" who followed "man's devices and instinct" rather than "God's wisdom, God's order, power and authority."[3]

These notions were largely rejected by the eighteenth-century thinkers, like Hume and Madison, of whom we are the heirs. They believed that men's predispositions might indeed be evil, but that human devices of law and agreement could use desire to control desire. Ambition was to be set against ambition, faction against faction, interest against interest, and earthly punishments and rewards arranged so as to keep self-interest from threatening the order.

These thinkers thought that private interest, the "pursuit of happiness," was ultimately much safer than those more apparently elevated ideals of righteousness and honor, ideals they thought had been productive of so many murderous wars. They hoped that men who looked to private needs and wants might be induced to moderate their striving for power and glory, that the promise of profit or the expectation of risk or loss would tend on the whole to favor peace and social harmony. Society was to be refounded on self-interest.[4]

The American constitutionmakers, in particular, saw in legislative and judicial self-interest the tools whereby executive corruption might be limited. And they planned more broadly that the potential for corruption throughout the governmental system could be limited by a pattern of checks and balances, and by requirements that governmental powers be shared.[5]

It is, then, hardly to be wondered at that American political scientists see the problem of political corruption as they do. But the very predominance in our society of the egoistic, mechanical, and legal approach of thinkers like Madison suggests we might look elsewhere for solutions to problems that remain unsolved. This is to say that the problem of corruption is not simply to be met by the development of more effective devices, that reform may require psychological insight and moral inquiry, and that it may be helped by the recovery of some older ways of thinking about wrongdoing.

Character and Corruption

It seems obvious that personal honesty plays a great role in opposing corruption and in maintaining the integrity of governmental processes.[6] Sanctions against corrupt behavior are notoriously weak, and penalties of any kind are low. Most corruption is probably undetected and unpunished; the great tides of reform have always revealed long-established patterns of corruption. Yet governmental officials in many jurisdictions and at many levels have reputations for personal integrity that seem for the most part well deserved.

There is no attempt here to assess the degree to which character is the determining factor in the incidence of political corruption. It strikes me as in principle impossible to isolate effects of character from those of law and governmental structure. Groups or governments that are serious about integrity will support it with organizational and personal incentives and with sanctions against misbehavior. The important thing to note is that many or most of those who have the opportunity for corrupt advantage do not seize it; only some who are tempted succumb. I think reflection and analysis can help us to see why some do and others don't, and can help us to identify ways in which the contribution of individual character to governmental honesty and reform may be strengthened.

More specifically, my purposes in examining the relation between character and corruption are these: (1) to promote more effective self-scrutiny by officials, and thus to encourage a deeper awareness and a higher degree of conscientiousness about problems of corruption, as well as about the whole range of moral dilemmas faced by officials; (2) to identify ways in which moral leadership in the face of corruption or temptation can be exercised by governmental superiors and subordinates alike; and (3) to consider what kinds of policy choices, whether about corruption or other problems, have beneficial or harmful effects on the characters of individual officials.

Before going on it may be important to enter a sort of disclaimer. I intend no special or technical meaning for the word character. As I understand ordinary speech, character refers to both psychological and moral characteristics—independence, greed, insecurity, confidence, virtue, aggressiveness, passivity, malice, untruthfulness, and the like. I suppose that using the word implies we can know someone—not fully perhaps (even Hobbes says of motivation that only God "searcheth hearts")—that we can say with some confidence of a person we know well what he or she is "really like."[7] . . .

The story on which I want to comment is about Spiro Agnew accepting bribes for engineering contracts when he was governor of Maryland. It is in a way a case of old-fashioned garden-variety corruption, and it has the advantage of being the subject of a very good book by Richard M. Cohen and Jules Witcover, *A Heartbeat Away*.[8] Other tales might reveal something about other aspects of our subject, but the carefully considered insights and judgments of Cohen and Witcover provide a rich source for thinking about character.

The Agnew story has a certain helpful clarity. For reasons of personal profit, and in order to have the status and accoutrements of status he craved, Governor Agnew continued and refined a system whereby engineering firms were obliged to pay thousands of dollars to the governor and some of his associates, secretly and in cash, as kickbacks on the contracts they won for state work.

If this seems a simple and traditional case of crime and greed, one lesson may be that greed and illegality are rarely without complexity. Agnew's self-interested corruption was angrily upwardly mobile, and while he built a career on moralism, he seems to have been more than ordinarily obtuse about his own moral choices. Nor are Agnew's crimes unconnected with his conservative but strangely abbreviated ideology. In weighing the meaning of Agnew's crimes, one needs as well to consider the patterns of corruption endemic to Maryland politics. Agnew's claim that he did nothing unusual in taking illegal payments is a significant, if partial, truth. . . .

Greed and Need

Spiro Agnew wanted more than money, but his pecuniary aspirations were not small. By corrupt means he managed to increase his income dramatically, though by how much remains unclear. He is known to have received $50,000 in cash while governor from one engineering firm, and an additional $10,000 from the same firm was delivered to him in his vice-presidential office. He received more than $50,000 in cash from another firm, $28,000 of that after he became vice-president.[9] Even if the well-documented bribes are larger than most of the others, it is clear the total was substantial. What was all this money for?

The answer seems to be that it offered an opportunity to live extremely well, to buy expensive clothes and meals, to maintain the social position to which Agnew somehow felt entitled. Scorning politicians for the most part, Agnew associated primarily with wealthy businessmen. He lived on their level, and imitated their ways. Cohen and Witcover see him as the authentic embodiment of "middle-class values, hopes and fears" of the "silent majority," a "creature of suburbia" who "seized upon politics as a vehicle to lift him out of mediocrity and obscurity."[10]

These unremarkable aspirations are, in the absence of countervailing ideals, motivation enough for Agnew's extraordinary greed, and his unusual success in getting what he wanted owed at least as much to chance as native talent. What is puzzling is the feeling of entitlement: Agnew's evident conviction that he deserved his illegal gains. My guess is that the only way to make any sense of this is to give ample recognition to the self-righteous anger that was evident in so much of Agnew's public life.

I am suggesting that Agnew's sense of his own unlimited right to rise, to reach a high position, was fueled by resentment, and not by the Horatio Alger hopes, hard work, and luck that can help in accounting for some successful careers. I say resentment because that is what I remember hearing in his voice, and because it makes sense in terms of the values by which he seems to have lived.

The point is that narrow and principally economic self-interest offers a less than satisfactory basis for making one's peace with the world. Assume that a person interprets social life mainly in terms of the restless striving of economic man, as mirrored in himself. Then ask what will happen when such a person meets patterns of distribution that leave him unhappily stuck near the bottom end of society while others, less restless and striving, attain far higher positions. Anger, settled and deep, is not an unlikely reaction. Something like this seems to have been Agnew's condition.

One can of course deal with the various and unequal ways in which property and income are distributed as John Winthrop did, explaining that God in his wisdom has ordained, in order to manifest the necessity of Christian love and social harmony, that at all times some must be rich and others poor.[11] Or one can believe (as I do) that many and diverse values and principles are important, and that in the face of injustice, different sorts of cures or compensations are available. There are also more systematic views: Marxists, for example, angrily decry the injustice of the whole scheme and urge its transformation. For one who is a capitalist, a materialist, and an individualist, the main available option would seem to be directing one's angry energy toward the task of moving up.

Agnew's ire at effete liberals and independent students may have other explanations, and surely the psychological roots of such attitudes are deep. My concern here is not to uncover the sources of personality, but merely to indicate an important connection. The anger, the ambition, and the feeling that taking bribes was somehow justifiable, all fit reasonably with a belief in the primacy and the rightness of economic motivation. The broad support that exists for this belief in our society is part of the culture in which bribery grows. So too, though perhaps less obviously, is the resentment of those whose economic striving seems to them inadequately rewarded. The angry self-righteousness of Agnew and many of those to whom he was a hero is a narrow and genuinely pathetic substitute for larger hopes or selves.

Conscience

Even at the end Agnew's self-righteousness was evident, but from the beginning it was coupled with a remarkable insensitivity about conflicts of interest or other ethical problems.[12] I think, as I have said, that it was associated in special ways with resentment, and with a narrowly economic view of life. I also believe it owed more than a little to deep feelings of insecurity, though I lack adequate material on which to ground any careful psychological analysis. Such inquiries, well supported biographically, can be instructive; but it is also important to ask about what was not there, and how it might have been. For this some less individualized analytic tools will serve.

What Agnew most obviously lacked was conscience. There is no evidence he felt guilty about what he did, no sign of inner turmoil, of any interior ethical code. A joiner who accepted the moral attitudes of those around him, Agnew never seems to have indulged much in moral questioning or conscientious scrutiny of his own motives. Socrates' constant theme, the Delphic injunction to know oneself, was hardly any part of Agnew's life.

Here again Agnew reflects an important aspect of our political culture. Action is regularly prized over introspection, and not alone by politicians. Academic analysts have often pointed to the dangers of self-doubt and the tormenting conscience, suggesting for example that Franklin Roosevelt's ability to put aside his scruples is preferable to the morally introspective approach of Woodrow Wilson. If effective action is indeed inhibited by an overcareful conscience, must we inquire after ways to a moderated conscientiousness? I do not think so. The notion of conscience need not suggest a kind of moralistic strait-jacket that keeps us from the moral risks of political choice. It can mean instead a kind of internalized moral judgment that provides both strength and self-criticism for political action. Let me try to sketch a portrait of conscience seen this way.

The first word is an old one: sin. Whether we use it or not, the word denotes a common aspect of our experience. We do wrong, we have done wrong, knowingly, and willingly. Our own acts are judged by the moral feelings and standards we have developed. Sometimes we are only tempted, and avoid wrong or even manage to do right. But our sense of sin, our knowledge of willful wrongdoing, shapes our consciences.

Moral feelings are part of conscience. We feel the pull of others' needs, and must explain the reasons—to ourselves, at least—when we fail to respond. We see wrong and want it righted, we hear crying and believe it should be comforted. When we've hurt others, we have a desire for forgiveness and reconciliation, and in a more internal way our crimes demand expiation before they can be forgotten, or our rightness with the world restored.

These feelings come to us naturally and gradually, though not with similar power and effect to each. Likewise, we all grow up promising and being obliged to act by the commitments we undertake, for all that some feel the pull of obligation less keenly than do others. My own view is that being moral means, in part, owning these feelings, taking them seriously, and weighing our choices and our reasons in their light. . . .

Public Debate and the Public Interest

Agnew seemed to have lacked a very developed sense of the public interest. He spoke about it, of course, but one always had the feeling the rhetoric was not quite serious. I think that feeling was justified, that much of Agnew's conservative, anti-big-government, pro-business, law-and-order ideology was adopted opportunistically, and that it functioned partly as a mask for his rather simpler belief in economic self-interest. This view may be unfairly skeptical; some of Agnew's commitments may have been held more deeply and sincerely than I am willing to believe.

His approach to debate is less subject to uncertainty. Agnew was sure of his own position and scornful of his enemies. More than most participants in the public controversies of our time, Agnew seemed not to feel the weight of the opposing arguments, the pull of the values represented by the views he was attacking. Part of this was surely tactical; many other politicians believe similarly that if they admit to some virtues in the opposition's argument they will weaken their own case. But Agnew's confidence in his own views was unusual enough to earn him an almost unequaled reputaton for forthrightness, and among some groups, integrity. In a world of equivocations and howevers, Agnew spoke out clearly.

Those who like their controversy sharp tended to admire Agnew's candor even when they disagreed with his views; to others, Agnew's forthrightness seemed a fraud long before the admissions of corruption. His attacks on reporters showed no sense of the role and importance of a free press, and his law and order stance was hostile to the constitutional guarantees of fair judicial processes. Nor did he exhibit any care, in his attacks on the vices of big government, for the pressing human needs somewhat assuaged by machinery of the welfare state. These omissions were more than rhetorical. He wanted to score debating points, to win support, to further his strategic aims. If he cared about some values, they were few in number, and they were seen simply. About others, there is no evidence he cared at all.

Single-issue candidates and small-range ideologies have their uses in our political order. Sometimes the case must be made emphatically or even unreasonably if it is to become a matter of broad public concern. Nor can one hope to argue effectively or clearly if all the relevant values are always taken into account. But the dangers of partial political argument are real enough. Inured to oversimplifications, we often fail to demand from the parties in our debates any allegiance to the public interest.

By this last phrase I mean at minimum a willingness to have one's arguments and claims tested by some standard of the public good, a willingness to defend one's interests in terms of broader aims and aspirations present in society. I am not claiming there is agreement about what the public interest is, only that in a democracy those involved in politics must admit in principle that their interests are not unlimited, that they are properly adjudicated according to standards that refer to the good of the larger society. It should be evident that such a view ordinarily functions as a bulwark against corruption.

Agnew's narrow views of the meaning of good government are evident in his recurrent explanations of the bribes he accepted. It was important, he kept claiming, to realize that only qualified firms actually got engineering contracts from the government of the state of Maryland, and thus that there was nothing really wrong with the payments he accepted.[13] In such a claim other crucial values are utterly ignored: among them respect for the law, fairness and freedom from favoritism in governmental action, and the reputation for probity of government officials.

Corruption is presumably far more likely in an atmosphere where political ideology does not shape policy goals, and where commitment to the public interest is weak. We may not expect politicians to be moral philosophers, but we ought to demand of them some measure of commitment to principled objectives. And this duty of thoughtfulness, like other duties, should be greater as the position in government is higher. For more is always at stake—at the highest levels, even sometimes the legitimacy of the regime. It seems somehow particularly damning that Vice-President Agnew accepted bribe payments in the White House.

At his worst Agnew appealed to fear and anger, and skirted the edge of racist demagoguery. These are common tactics of narrowly self-interested opportunism; emotional appeals for the most part are too briefly effective to support a long-term program or an enduring party organization. Individuals intent on winning can regularly benefit from such a course, though only at the price of unacceptable risks to the stability and decency of the public order.

Morality and Milieu

Agnew's principal defense was predictable, and predictably unconvincing. He said the practices followed established custom, and proof is readily available that he was right.[14] Agnew added the novelty of an antimachine governor, with a reputation for integrity, accepting bribes; and it may be also that the level of his greed exceeded precedent. While few would agree that conformity to enduring practice excuses Agnew's acts, the pattern of corruption is worth the attention of anyone interested in reform.

One of the dimensions of the story, as Cohen and Witcover tell it, is a drama of lost faith, the confidence of Agnew's supporters in his uprightness and probity shattered by the revelations and the eventual resignation.[15] Their implicit message is the wise admonition of a long tradition in political journalism: pay attention to substance and not to style. Agnew's supporters were bamboozled, but they need not have been so surprised as they were. The defense of selfishness and the narrow moral horizons were evident in the public Agnew, for anyone who cared to look.

The bribers also have stories, as Cohen and Witcover make clear. They were mostly successful businessmen, respected in their communities, and there were quite a lot of them. Some appear to have been a bit victimized by the extortionate tactics of the politicians; others were evidently corrupters; and all benefited from bribery, at the expense of other businessmen and of the public at large. Lincoln Steffens long ago told the essential story of the interconnection between business power and political power, and in some ways the corruption of the business world made him angrier, because the businessmen then seemed the bigger hypocrites.[16] In the Maryland case the choice is more difficult, but it may be worth noting that there seem to be at least as many deeply corrupt businessmen as politicians in the story.

Reformers, on the other hand, are scarce in politics, and even rarer in business. The most worrisome thing about the Maryland political scene is the lack of any true reform movement. There were and are politicians never tainted with or even accused of corruption, but in the face of widespread knowledge about practices of bribery and other official illegality, it is noteworthy that no constituency for reform was ever built. The Agnew case emerged in a large-scale investigation of Maryland corruption, instituted not by state authorities, but by the office of the U.S. Attorney.

While Agnew's defense was transparent, it should perhaps be noted that the pervasiveness of corruption in a system can sometimes excuse, on rare occasions even justify, certain categories of corrupt acts. If laws are rarely or differentially enforced as a matter of course, for example, or if activities like gambling and prostitution are legally proscribed for symbolic reasons—enunciating values of a dominant group or stigmatizing activities without any real commitment to enforcement—then corruption of police agencies is to be expected. When changing these laws seems impossible, modest levels of bribery may even be tolerable, though a *policy* of official toleration for low-level corruption is likely to encourage worse crimes as well.

Illegal payments accepted, but not demanded, by police or other officials in return for routine and legal favors may be even less harmful. Christmas tips to the mailperson, for instance, may have such sanction in custom that they are not seen as criminal, even when accepting such gifts is formally prohibited. Most gratuities, however, are designed to secure more favorable treatment by officials—as when police are encouraged (bribed) to spend extra time looking out for the property of the giver. In such circumstances other citizens must be less favored, so that this kind of corruption will ordinarily be unfair, and indefensible.

Some defensible bribes can of course be found—a bribe to German or Austrian authorities for exit visas paid by a Jewish family in 1938, for example. Here the law is wrong, and no safe way to change or even to oppose it is available. But only *paying* the bribe is morally justified. An official's reasoning that accepting it serves a good end would not be persuasive: the end can be accomplished without requiring the payment. The distinction is more important than it may seem. Official illegality may always be discovered, and a principled defense of it can—in most regimes—encourage change, or foster other acts of resistance. Such a defense is less effective and less valuable when officials are shown to have acted for private gain. In a bad regime, however, an official might be justified in participating in *organized* corruption that would protect or aid the victims or potential victims of unjust acts. Here accepting bribes might be necessary, both to screen one's more decent motives, and to sustain the ability to offer aid. Such cases are obviously rare in a regime like ours.[17]

Exemplars—Class and Character

The Agnew story is unusual in that the heroes are almost as interesting as the villains. The officials who brought Agnew to justice are worth studying, both for the dilemmas they faced and for the examples they meant to set.

The five prosecutors were all hard-working lawyers, and for the most part they stayed within the established rules. Three were relatively low-level figures—assistant U.S. attorneys, one of whom, Barney Skolnik, had considerable experience in prosecuting cases involving the bribery of public officials. The two major figures were well-off and socially prominent politically appointed officials: the Brahmin U.S. Attorney General Elliot Richardson, and George Beall, U.S. attorney for Maryland, brother of a U.S. senator and son of a former senator.

The story of the prosecution is in some ways reassuring. Effective at fighting corruption and devoted to official honesty, these attorneys were nonetheless sensitive to competing claims of the public interest. A particular concern was the damage that might result from Agnew's accession to the presidency, and they devoted real care as well to the protection of his constitutional rights as a defendant. (One aspect of prosecutory practice I found disturbing was the conferring of "use immunity" on unwilling witnesses at an early stage of the investigation.[18] Prosecutors have some responsibility to use the available tools if courts have found them constitutional—but they have sufficient discretion to refrain when they believe the courts have been unwise.)

Beall and his assistant Skolnik had suffered political interference during John Mitchell's tenure as attorney general;[19] in the Agnew case they and the others tried hard to reduce the potential for politically imposed limitations on their investigation. One may judge that in the end the culprit got off too lightly, but one can hardly doubt the sincerity of the prosecutors' judgment that Agnew's resignation was the most urgent priority. I remain critical of the prosecutors at this point— Richardson in particular could have been stronger in the plea bargaining—but Cohen and Witcover offer persuasive evidence that the major decisions were thoughtfully made and honorably motivated.[20]

The prosecutors were not without human and lawyerlike failings;

they were occasionally affected by selfish considerations or pride, poor judgments were sometimes made, and lies were regularly told the press.[21] But on the whole the record is an admirable one. The deep and vigorous debates in the attorney general's office can serve as models for a careful weighing of the moral stakes of official choice. Richardson's willingness to take seriously the ideas and objections of subordinates was studied, but impressive—here was a public official genuinely concerned to meet the diverse obligations he faced.

There is, for all this, a disturbing thread running through the tale. Though the prosecutors came from moderately diverse backgrounds, three of the five most involved (Beall, Richardson, and Beall's assistant Baker) were members of prominent and wealthy families. Agnew, by contrast, was both arriviste and Greek, with educational attainments in the law and otherwise notably inferior to those of any of his foes.

The motives of reformers, and especially well-off ones, have often been attacked. Arguments have been advanced that the anticorruptionists, drawn from older elites anxious about questions of relative social decline, are simply trying to enforce the norms of their class against interlopers.[22] On this basis it may be thought that corruption is not chiefly a moral or legal problem, but rather principally a symptom of conflict between opposing social groups.

Now it may be true that it is easier to have high ethical standards when one is secure, and it is surely the case that many of the great American fortunes were built with the aid of massive illegality and corruption. Before such arguments can function as a justification for corruption or even an excuse for bribers, however, some further claims must be advanced. It needs to be shown, for example, that other avenues to the advancement of particular groups are indeed highly restricted, and further that the benefits of corrupt practices actually reach excluded groups. These benefits must, moreover, outweigh the interests of the public at large, and also of deprived groups, in more honest government.

In modern American politics such a case could be made only rarely and with difficulty. It is true that money can and does command political power, that WASP elites have retained much of their money and portions of their former social and economic clout, and that the slowness of actual social mobility contrasts sharply with prevailing social myths. No one has demonstrated, however, that the advancement by means of corrupt methods of some able persons, from relatively deprived groups, is anything like an optimum strategy for promoting the interests of those groups, or for increasing the opportunities open to their members. Noncorrupt strategies—lawsuits, pressure group politics, social movements of various kinds—are all likely to have greater effects on larger numbers of people. Corruption is, in fact, more often directed against such efforts at equalizing opportunity than it is at accomplishing broad gains for the weak.

In this, as in so much else, Agnew's corruption was typical. Greek Americans won some symbolic gains from his success (and presumably suffered similar losses in his disgrace). But Agnew and the bribers—ethnically diverse, but all well off—got away with the money.

The prosecutors were honest and serious public officials, angry and sometimes sickened by the illegality they discovered. While explanations of their attitudes in social class terms finally make little sense—plenty of people similarly placed in American society have behaved very differently—neither are wholly individual explanations adequate. While these lawyers do reflect values of their families and friends, it seems more important that the Maryland attorneys were part of an office with a reformist tradition. . . .

Other Stories

Many of the great moral stories in literature have a satisfying completeness about them. Some characters, at least, know their sins, and by repenting of them embark upon a path of virtue (always to be distinguished from innocence). Occasionally virtue may even be attained: witness Hester Prynne at the end of *The Scarlet Letter*. The Agnew story, by comparison, leaves one with a sense of disquiet. Agnew has been vastly diminished but in no way transformed, and while some of the businessmen are disturbed by their complicity in crime, in only one or two cases is it suggested that any real changes have happened in their lives.

This failing could owe something to the fact that journalists and historians lack the omniscience of novelists: they do not know, and cannot know, for sure. But I am prepared to assume the transformations really did not happen—not to Agnew, not to most of the others. Nor were they likely to. Among other things, these men lacked the social support, the expectations on the part of relevant others that their lives might be transformed.

This may suggest a role for renewed religious concern (can we believe that conversion has re-formed Charles Colson?), but it argues more directly for a revivification of language and a recovery of experience. What is needed is more, and more serious, conversation about the moral dilemmas of official life, thoughtful talk informed by criticism and interpretation, by ethical examinations of particular circumstances, by moral connoisseurship—the informed appreciation of ethical differences.

In literary portrayals of corruption, like *All the King's Men* (1946) or Henry Adams' *Democracy* (1880), attention is given to moral failings other than bribery, and especially to the moral blindness that can result from a self-righteous, or merely unthinking, confidence in the decency of one's own motives. Such stories do not serve to defend corruption, but they do argue that there are other forms of iniquity, some of them far worse, and that temptation is ubiquitous. Novels like these can also suggest more readily than can journalism or most academic writing the ways by which character is formed or altered.

Biography offers similar advantages, and one recent book is unusually edifying with regard to corruption: Robert Caro's *The Power Broker*,[23] a study of the public career in New York city and state of Robert Moses. Although Moses received no personal financial benefit from his dealings as parks commissioner (or any of the many jobs he often held simultaneously), the highway, public housing, park, and other projects he conceived are portrayed by Caro as a kind of fountain of corruption. All this was, of course, in the service of ends Moses believed to be decent and necessary, and he has been, if anything, less penitent than Agnew. A fair-minded observer, however, would probably conclude that Moses' "good-government" image served to shield many actions that never should have been tolerated, and that Moses often chose to work with corrupt individuals and groups in order to avoid procedural and democratic constraints. . . .

Maintaining Integrity: Laws and Ideals

We need to use what we learn about character in fashioning laws and governmental changes, and in shaping anticorruption efforts in the context of broader policy aims. Those who would speak only of personal qualities risk the charge of ineffectuality and even hypocrisy, and anyone who means to encourage individual virtue, at least in situations other than small groups, must admit that the support of law and governmental regularity are necessary. A few individuals behaving badly with impunity can weaken the commitment of many others to moral principles, or to conscience, or to habits of generosity. Nor are societies divided so easily into better and worse citizens or officials. We know laws are needed from the strength of our own desires, even if it happens that we ourselves have the means to control them.

There are counterproductive laws, as well. "Reforms" can easily be discovered that have had no real effect on reducing corruption, and which have at the same time increased official hypocrisy. While it will not be possible to inspect the whole arsenal of techniques that have been advocated or adopted in fighting corruption, it should be possible to ask about the likely effects on characters, and on official wrongdoing, of some of the major strategies.

There are many varieties of corruption,[24] and more-or-less effective strategies have been designed against each. The Australian ballot, secret voting, registration laws, and some of the legislation about campaign finance have, for example, vastly reduced the scope of electoral corruption. Nor should it be forgotten that America has for the most part succeeded in limiting corruption to venality; that scandals like Watergate, in which laws were violated to augment political power, are relatively rare, owes much to the strength of our institutional arrangements. Thus, the focus here is on venality. Which approaches have been effective against corruption and supportive of integrity in the lives of officeholders, and which have not?

Ordinary Devices

When Agnew took office as Maryland's governor in 1967, the prospects for corrupt advantage were inviting. Decisions about engineering contracts involved relatively few people in state government, and the governor had broad discretion in awarding contracts, discretion not subsequently reviewed by any other authority. Interest in the possibilities of high-level corruption was faint in the press, and among most of Maryland's prosecutors and law enforcement establishment. Many of the usual controls, advocated for decades by reformers, did not exist. The result was a political order in which corruption was widespread, even, perhaps, expected. In such a situation three general types of anticorruption strategies seem called for: procedural reforms, investigations, and the reduction of unnecessary discretion. Each of these approaches has its distinct advantages, and each is likely to incur some costs.

The most important procedures in fighting corruption are those that ensure that an official's acts will be reviewed by others. Some reviews are appropriately conducted by supervisors. Opportunities for dishonesty are reduced when each decision must be explained and justified, when complaints can be heard, and decisions reversed, by higher authority. Reviews can also be carried out by auditing agencies, or by inspectors general, or by the courts. The expectation of regular review will tend to lower the likelihood of the discoverable forms of graft.

Other procedural matters are also important. Dishonesty is made more difficult when government documents are accessible to investigating agencies and to the public at large. Requirements of financial disclosure by officials increase the difficulties in making use of illegally gained funds. There are costs here, organizationally in the greater delays and enlarged disputes occasioned by openness, and personally in the reduced financial privacy of officials; but these costs seem, on the whole, acceptable. Secrecy must sometimes be maintained for reasons of national security; when the justification is merely administrative efficiency, however, the values of governmental integrity, to say nothing of democracy, must ordinarily be convincing on the side of openness.

Investigations perform a function similar to review, but they are more narrowly focused on the possibilities of criminal behavior, and they are usually conducted by outsiders, by law enforcement agencies—police, the FBI, district attorneys, or special prosecutors—or by legislative bodies, or by the press. Techniques of investigation that encourage mistrust or risk unjust accusations may do more harm than good, but these cautionary considerations are no argument against well-run and even frequent investigations, occurring both regularly and randomly over time. . . .

Corruption is likely to be further hindered when the reduction of official discretion accompanies increased review and investigation. Competitive bidding can be instituted for contracts, and merit systems can replace discretionary hiring and firing. Civil service, the great hope of the nineteenth-century reformers, has largely fulfilled its promise as an anticorruption device. The merit system may give too much job security to some whose merit is small, but it has protected the great body of government officials from arbitrary demands and from the application of political tests for employment. Relative financial security has weakened once strong economic incentives to peculation, and has removed the economic necessity of loyalty to party or political organizations.

More detailed laws of various kinds can reduce discretion still further, so that officials lose their powers to make exceptions, or to alter or adjust policy without recourse to the legislature, but there are obvious costs, in morale and governmental flexibility, of going further along this road. . . .

More laws and rules, more hierarchy, more bureaucratization, may indeed reduce corruption, but how much money and organizational effort is this goal worth? What are the costs in democratic values, in organizational morale, and in character, of pursuing these anticorruption strategies more vigorously?

The extent of corruption is vast, and the monetary costs of it are large. The Knapp Commission reported that in 1971, in New York City, "police corruption was . . . an extensive, department-wide phenomenon, indulged in to some degree by a sizable majority of those on the force."[25] Levels of corruption rise and fall, of course—New York's reputation has improved decidedly in recent years—but similarly high levels have been characteristic of many cities in the recent past.[26] Recent scandals, like earlier ones, have revealed corruption in all levels of government—state and local and federal agencies—and in many fields—agriculture, foreign aid, the purchasing of office supplies, immigration, etc. It is evident that corruption is widespread; it seems fair to assume that it involves enormous sums of money. No one has estimated the costs for the corruption revealed in the recent GSA scandals at anything less than several billion dollars.

Thus it seems possible that any successful anticorruption efforts will survive the simpler tests of cost-effectiveness. The more difficult question is whether such strategies will affect morale and character and governmental effectiveness adversely. Clearly they will not, if they are only compared to the alternative of doing nothing; unchecked corruption is demoralizing, and it will probably eventuate in scandals that profoundly disrupt an agency's functioning. The problem is rather to determine which effective methods are least likely to have severely damaging collateral effects. . . .

The Agnew case shows what can be done by U.S. attorneys who are energetic in opposing bribery. While other important types of criminal investigations compete for the attention of their staffs, U.S. attorneys should probably be more involved than they are in probes of officials and agencies. The attorney general would be well advised to encourage or even to require greater efforts in this direction.[27] Nor should the potential of special prosecutors be ignored. From Charles Evans Hughes, whose investigations of New York's insurance companies were the springboard of a long and valuable public career, to Archibald Cox, special prosecutors have been among the more effective reformers.[28] That regular prosecutors resist such appointments as encroachment or reproach is not surprising, but special prosecutors can ordinarily, in fact, bring greater resources of money and staff to bear, with less cost for other anticrime work.

Investigations are essential for the serious work of reforming, or even for maintaining such governmental integrity as exists; but like punishment, their effects are primarily negative. Some processes of review, like audits, are similarly designed to deter dishonesty. Others, however, can more directly encourage probity, and foster commitment to values associated with democracy and the public service.

The expectation that one's decisions will be reviewed by a superior, or by one's colleagues, does not necessarily provoke anxiety. Whether review means hostile snooping and implicit opposition to bureaucratic independence and creativity, or generally constructive criticism, depends very much on how it is conducted. As with investigations, review that is recurrent and expected will have a less damaging effect on morale than the occasional supervisory interventions occurring in response to outside attacks.

Review by peers or by higher authorities can serve to open a discussion of the moral stakes evident in particular decisions, and procedures of review—including those of formal complaints and hearings and appeals—can serve as forums for moral talk that might revive commitment to the animating ideals of an agency, or to the personal standards that guard against dishonesty. Too many bureaucrats try to think and act as if official misbehavior was inconceivable within their precincts, and then, in the face of scandal, are left with nothing more convincing than President Harding's lament, that he was unknowingly betrayed by his "God-damn friends."[29]

Agency chiefs and other high officials are in fact well placed to affect the culture of discussion in the government. It is not enough that they have integrity, however; they must also exemplify it and find ways of encouraging it. One means might be a kind of moral inquest or "grand rounds," an examination of the ethical aspects of some problematic case recently faced by the agency or by individual officials.[30] Even in ordinary reviews subordinates are taught the operative standards, learning whether or which rules and laws are to be respected, and how seriously conflicts among values are to be taken. A more formal process, for a few decisions that seem especially interesting, might have very great advantages in encouraging ethical seriousness.

One benefit of this kind of procedure is that moral commitments and attitudes will at least occasionally be expressed directly, and by those in authority. One of the consequences of the "toughminded" and "hard-nosed" school of decisionmaking in the 1960s was the repression of moral discussion at high levels within the national administration. Although deep and largely unvoiced moral commitments were present, they were not available as tools of inquiry, nor helpful in questioning some of the assumptions of our policy in Vietnam.[31]

Many other promising approaches to reform are advocated. Some of these aim at reducing the price of bribery by organizational alterations, or at otherwise changing the structure of corrupt incentives.[32] Others would increase the penalties for corrupt acts, especially ones involving large sums of money, in order that large bribes might be as effectively deterred as small ones (and also, one supposes, so that the punishment might more nearly fit the crime).[33] As government grows more complicated, and as new ways of accomplishing its objects are developed, fresh opportunities for illegitimate gain arise. It seems only prudent to consider such remedies as modern analysts have devised.

Nevertheless, my own doubts about the efficacy of technical solutions remain strong; and they are indeed somewhat confirmed by the fact that the most recent and most advanced study of the political economy of corruption ends with a discussion of morality—albeit in terms that tend to reduce morality to one rather narrow version of democratic theory.[34] Democratic theory *is* relevant here; rule by the people is impossible when public choices are made corruptly. But other values must also have their place in any full consideration—among them justice, legitimacy, and equity.

Ideals in the Public Service

As a member of a U.S. Forest Service family, I grew up around people committed to the ideals of conservation and multiple use, the management of natural resources aimed at the greatest good for the greatest number in the long run. Those ideals, along with the thorough-going professionalism that supported them, were adumbrated by Chief Forester Gifford Pinchot in the administration of Teddy Roosevelt, and they have remained prime supports for the institutional integrity of the Forest Service, and for the enviable reputation of honesty and public-spiritedness that agency has maintained over the years. From my own observations I have no doubt that idealism, coupled with pride in expertise and public service, strengthened the habit of serious talk about the public interest, and supported the deep conscientiousness and honesty of the Forest Service officials I have known.

Conservation was for Pinchot and his fellow Progressive reformers a part of the gospel of efficiency in the development of the use of natural resources.[35] As an ideal it has had its critics. Partisans of the free market have argued that the kind of efficiency it envisages is less than optimal, and preservationists have maintained an enduring skepticism about its bias toward use. Conservation and the doctrine of multiple use have, however, retained their authority for Forest Service personnel, though not without the adoption of some preservationist goals.

That Forest Service idealism about conservation has been helpful in preventing corruption is instructive. The ideal is not so vague as to be shared by everyone, and it is not merely rhetorical; it is believed in and applied by a large number of officials across a broad range of problems. In public debate and in relation to concrete cases the ideal is given specific reference, and it serves as a guide in assessing those particulars relevant to a certain version of the public interest in the area of natural resources. It should be apparent that this is an ideal capable of contributing to the kind of ethical discourse that has been advocated throughout this essay. It supports a thoughtful weighing of the values at stake in a choice, and it fosters awareness of the public interest in the decisionmakers themselves. . . .

That ideals, and the rhetoric that supports them, can be extraordinarily dangerous is news to no one.[36] The greatest crimes of the century have come out of the passionate hopes of fascism and communism and nationalism. All ideals, even the worst, transcend narrow self-interest. What we need is not idealism per se, but decent ideals, visions of the public interest, that are not destructive of our most important and essential values.

Reform itself can be such an ideal at times when corruption seems of overwhelming importance. "The principle of my reform," said Lord Grey in 1830, "is to prevent the necessity for revolution." Had he not secured passage of the Great Reform Act, the manifest unfairness of the pre-1832 system of parliamentary representation would almost certainly have led to major political upheaval in England.[37] In the face of extraordinary municipal corruption in America, a Progressive movement was built in the early part of this century that played a crucial role in ending the power of corrupt machines in the cities.[38] The Progressive ideal of reform was accomplished, at least in part, by effective candidacies and by campaigns of exposure and political pressure. The structural reforms of Progressivism included some poorly chosen strategies seemingly aimed against politics of any sort; among these the initiative and referendum, the nonpartisan law, and the attacks on political parties seem the most conspicuous failures.[39]

Many other values—including ecology, equity, and (more strongly) justice—function as ideals for those in the public service. Nor are those now planning careers in government bereft of decent aspirations for the common good. But it must be admitted that government is increasingly dominated by habits of thought and methods of analysis that seem to have little room for such hopes. Values of all kinds must be fitted into models and analyses in which the terms of comparison are fundamentally economic.

This represents something of a triumph of rationality, and it embodies the utilitarian faith that desires for pleasure and the avoidance of pain make all human goods commensurable. As a framework for analysis, and for the justification of policy choices, the idea of utility has obvious advantages. Benefits and costs can be analyzed across wide areas of policy, and outcomes in the marketplace or in politics can be seen as the result of consumer or citizen preferences, aggregated in ways that reflect the intensity of preferences. Ultimately policy resulting from a mixture of market forces, political pressures, and benefit-cost analysis can be seen as roughly reflective of the choices of an imaginary omniscient utilitarian decisionmaker—not an invisible hand, rather a kind of invisible digital computer.

In all this the pull of ideals seems almost irrelevant. While utilitarianism, like any good ethical theory, can surely accommodate them in some way, it does not call attention to them, or show us very clearly that they are needed, or even helpful.

With its focus on substantive ends, its individualism, and its compatibility with democratic principles, utilitarianism in some mode or fashion will no doubt continue to guide our public choices. It need not constrain our minds. Other ways of thinking about conscience, or character, or civic virtue may be better able to suggest the missing moral questions, or the goods or ends the analysts can include but are unlikely to discover.

For thinking more deeply and broadly about the problem of corruption, there are several places we can turn. One valuable recent study, for example, has traced the theory of corruption in some of the great political philosophers, arguing that unjust inequality is seen by thinkers as diverse as Thucydides, Plato and Aristotle, Machiavelli and Rousseau to be a fundamental cause of corruption.[40] The same study claims that the theory of corruption they share argues for educational efforts, broad political participation, and limits on the accumulation of great wealth as efffective supplements to particular laws and structures.[41]

Traditional theorists were also concerned with character, and Plato was not alone in illustrating his thinking with specific persons. His portrait of Socrates remains near the center of any of our ideas about civic virtue. In the long run, the study of particular stories is preferable to any abstract analysis of character or virtue, though it may take much more time.

If we are serious about limiting corruption in the public service, we are going to need more than the devices of law and bureaucratic or economic incentives. We need to learn about the shape of honesty and integrity, as well as about the sources of vice. To study strength and weakness of character, or how civic virtue might be fostered, we could do much worse than starting with the Greeks. But we might do even better to look first at Americans, modern figures and old ones too. One good choice would be James Madison, whose whole labor of constitutional design was animated, and guided, by a deep and personal faith in the ideal of liberty.

Notes

1. George L. Mosse, *The Holy Pretence* (Oxford: Basil Blackwell, 1957), p. 14. Hotspur contrasts "base and rotten policy" to the loyalty of "noble Mortimer." Shakespeare *I Henry IV* I, iii.
2. Joel Hurstfield, "The Political Morality of Early Stuart Statesmen," *History,* 56 (June 1971), 235ff. Well before the seventeenth century "corrupt" had referred to acts, and persons, "perverted from uprightness and fidelity in the discharge of duty; influenced by bribery or the like; venal" *(OED)*. Modern scholars writing about political corruption, however, rely more on law than on norms of "uprightness and fidelity"; hence my insistence that corrupt acts be both illegal *and* self-serving. . . . My own view is that corruption should chiefly mean official, self-regarding, illegal acts or procedural violations; but some reference to the public interest must logically remain part of the concept. Corruption is a strong term, too strong for at least some minor self-interested violations of law or rules. Welfare officials might, for example, omit tedious but legally required paperwork. If this harms their clients or otherwise evidently injures the public interest, we may call such practices corrupt. Absent any harm to the public weal, the term could not apply.
3. *Sermons or Homilies Appointed to Be Read in Churches in the Time of Queen Elizabeth of Famous Memory* (London: C. J. Rivington, 1825), p. 118, "The Sermon on Obedience."
4. Compare the account of Albert O. Hirschman, *The Passions and the Interests: Political Arguments for Capitalism Before Its Triumph* (Princeton: Princeton University Press, 1977).
5. Richard Bushman, "Corruption and Power in Provincial America," and Edmund S. Morgan, "Royal and Republican Corruption," in Richard B. Morris and others, *The Development of a Revolutionary Mentality* (Washington, D.C.: Library of Congress, 1972).
6. The Knapp Commission report on police corruption, in a section headed "Factors Influencing Corruption," says this: "The most important of these [factors] is, of course, the character of the officer in question, which will determine whether he bucks the system and refuses all corruption money; goes along with the system and accepts what comes his way; or outdoes the system, and aggressively seeks corruption-prone situations and exploits them to the extent that it seriously cuts into the time available for doing his job." *New York City Commission to Investigate Allegations of Police Corruption . . . Commission Report, December 26, 1972* (New York: George Braziller, 1973), p. 67.
7. James David Barber, *The Presidential Character: Predicting Performance in the White House* (Englewood Cliffs, N.J.: Prentice-Hall, 1972), . . .

Barber's work can assist the sort of self-scrutiny I am urging. Hobbes's comment appears in the introduction to *Leviathan* (London, 1651).

8. Richard Cohen and Jules Witcover, *A Heartbeat Away: The Investigation and Resignation of Vice President Spiro T. Agnew* (New York: Bantam, 1974).
9. Ibid., pp. 97–99, 136.
10. Ibid., pp. 16, 17, 32.
11. John Winthrop, "*A Modell of Christian Charity*," written on board the *Arabella*, 1630, in Perry Miller and Thomas H. Johnson, eds., *The Puritans* (New York: Harper and Row, 1963), I, 195. This sermon owes much to the "Sermon on Obedience," cited in n. 3.
12. Cohen and Witcover, *Heartbeat*, pp. 23, 28–29.
13. Cohen and Witcover, *Heartbeat*, p. 22.
14. Ibid., p. 40.
15. Ibid., p. 33.
16. Lincoln Steffens, *The Shame of the Cities* (New York: McClure, Phillips, 1904).
17. But not impossible. Consider the morally wrenching difficulties faced by low-level immigration or public health officials who deal with undocumented aliens, illegally doing needed work in our country.
18. Cohen and Witcover, *Heartbeat*, p. 66.
19. Ibid., pp. 62–63.
20. See esp. ibid., pp. 313–16.
21. Ibid., p. 82. The defense for these lies, concerning whether the vice-president was under investigation, is that they served the important goal of helping to protect the early stages of the investigation from high-level political interference. This is only partially adequate. It may well be that the mutually advantageous relationship between press and prosecutors had in this case made the ordinarily ethically preferable "no comment" tantamount to admission. But surely some careful thinking in advance about the needs of reporters and prosecutors could have reshaped the pattern. That lying is a regular and rather casually acccepted necessity for prosecutors is disturbing—there is great potential for abuse, and potential damage as well to the social strength of ordinary rules supporting truthfulness.
22. See, for example, William F. Whyte, "Social Organization in the Slums," *American Sociological Review,* 8 (February 1943), 34-39. "Politics and the rackets have furnished an important means of social mobility for individuals, who, because of ethnic background and low-class position, are blocked from advancement in the 'respectable' channels," Quoted in Robert K. Merton, "Some Functions of the Political Machine," pp. 72–78, in *Social Theory and Social Structure* (New York: Free Press, 1957), reprinted in Jack D. Douglas and John M. Johnson, eds., *Official Deviance: Readings in Malfeasance, Misfeasance, and Other Forms of Corruption* (Philadelphia: J. B. Lippincott, 1977), p. 345.
23. Robert Caro, *The Power Broker: Robert Moses and the Fall of New York* (New York: Alfred Knopf, 1974).
24. Among them bribery, extortion, conflict of interest, election fraud, direct theft of public funds or property, stigmatized by Plunkitt as "dishonest graft." Other types are suggested by the illegal acts of the Watergate drama

directed against political opponents apart from the electoral process, and by related crimes committed to conceal earlier illegal acts.

25. *Knapp Commission Report*, p. 61.
26. Sherman, *Scandal and Reform*, p. xxx. Sherman comments that "six years after the Knapp Commission hearings, corruption no longer appears to be widespread."
27. See Wayne Barrett's disturbing account of the weak anticorruption record of the office of the U.S. attorney for the southern district of New York. "Freedom to Steal: Why Politicians Never Go to Jail," *New York, 13* (February 4, 1980), 26–32.
28. Robert F. Wesser, *Charles Evans Hughes: Politics and Reform in New York, 1905–1910* (Ithaca: Cornell University Press, 1967), pp. 40–48.
29. Francis Russell, *The Shadow of Blooming Grove: Warren G. Harding in His Times* (New York: McGraw-Hill, 1968), pp. 560, 571. Russell's book is another valuable story about character and corruption.
30. This plan was suggested by the "grand rounds" of the great teaching hospitals. There, cases are selected, often one each week, for full-scale discussion by leading members of the staff. Other members of the staff, and students, are an occasionally participating audience. Cases of all kinds are examined in this way, and in recent years they have focused occasionally on the ethical dimensions of the cases in question.

    Another means of promoting ethical seriousness would be to encourage good writing about morally troubling decisions. Historians and scholars of the bureaucracy might well be encouraged to prepare short case studies available for reading within the agency and, eventually, by others.
31. On this point see David Halberstam, *The Best and the Brightest* (New York: Fawcett Crest, 1973), esp. pp. 87–88, 497, 595.
32. Rose-Ackerman, *Corruption,* pp. 221–28. Note especially her discussion of overlapping jurisdictions and competition, among low-level bureaucrats, to reduce bribe prices while maintaining some official discretions (pp. 137–66, 221).
33. Ibid., pp. 219–20.
34. Ibid., pp. 228–34.
35. Samuel P. Hays, *Conservation and the Gospel of Efficiency: The Progressive Conservation Movement, 1890–1920,* 2d ed. (New York: Atheneum, 1969), pp. 27–48.
36. Joan Didion notes one type of danger eloquently: "When we start deceiving ourselves into thinking not that we want something or need something, not that it is a pragmatic necessity for us to have it, but that it is a moral imperative that we have it, then is when we join the fashionable madmen, and then is when the thin whine of hysteria is heard in the land, then is when we are in bad trouble." *Slouching Towards Bethlehem* (New York: Dell, 1968), p. 163.
37. Michael Brock, *The Great Reform Act* (London: Hutchinson, 1963), p. 336.
38. It has been said that FDR and the New Deal destroyed machines and the corruption that went with them by federalizing relief and taking over many of the old functions of the machines. This seems unlikely. See Lyle Dorsett, *Franklin D. Roosevelt and the City Bosses* (Port Washington,

N.Y.: Kennikat Press, 1977), pp. 3–5, 117n, who cites several studies that offer impressive arguments against this thesis. . . .

39. Grant McConnell, *Private Power and American Democracy* (New York: Vintage, 1970), pp. 38–50.

40. J. Patrick Dobel, "The Corruption of a State," *American Political Science Review,* 72 (September 1978), 958–73.

41. Ibid., p. 972.

37

Federal Prosecution of Local Corruption

Charles F. C. Ruff

In exercising his discretion, a prosecutor typically seeks to distinguish among cases on their special facts or among defendants by their special circumstances; he also seeks to make the most effective use of his limited resources. For the federal prosecutor, however, an additional element is involved. Frequently, he will be confronted with facts establishing clear violations of both state and federal law, and the decision whether to retain jurisdiction or to turn the case over to local authorities involves close questions of law as well as fine judgments about the employment of the resources of both sovereigns. How he resolves these questions will affect not only the prospective defendant but, more importantly, the delicate relationship between the federal and state governments. His decision to retain jurisdiction in cases where the federal violation is less clear and his eagerness in pressing for expansive interpretations of federal jurisdiction show the extent to which he is prepared not merely to supplement but to supplant local law enforcement. Yet in this vital area, having ramifications beyond the administration of criminal justice, the legislative and administrative controls over the exercise of the prosecutor's discretion are the weakest. . . .

A Case

A policeman walking his beat stops in at the corner candy store to talk to the owner about a rash of shoplifting by some local teenagers who come into his store every day after school. The storeowner asks the policeman if he can arrange his schedule to be in the neighborhood

Source: Charles F. C. Ruff, "Federal Prosecution of Local Corruption: A Case Study in the Making of Law Enforcement Policy," *Georgetown Law Journal* 65, 5 (June 1977), 1171–1228. Reprinted with the permission of the publisher, © 1977 The Georgetown Law Journal Association.

of the store when school lets out, but the officer tells him that such a rearrangement of his normal schedule will be very difficult to accomplish and will delay him in getting back to the station in time for the end of his shift. The storeowner replies that he is willing to make it worthwhile to the officer and gives him $10, promising a similar sum each week.

After several weeks of this arrangement the officer decides that his services are worth more than $10 and suggests to the storeowner that an additional $5 will enable him to provide the kind of protection the store needs. The storeowner is distraught that he must pay such an exorbitant sum for a public service and decides to complain to the authorities. . . .

Having read about federal investigation into police corruption in the city, the storeowner decides to visit the local United States attorney's office and finds himself telling his story to a young assistant.

"I think we may be able to do something for you, sir," says the prosecutor. "We're always looking for a good corruption case, and it sounds as if this policeman has been extorting you."

"But," says the owner, "he never threatened me or threw rocks through the window or anything like that."

"Don't worry about a thing. First, we have to prove he obstructed interstate commerce. You get your candy bars from out of state, right?"

"Yes."

"And you paid the cop money when you didn't have to, right?"

"Yes."

"Then, that's all we need. I'll let you know when we want you to come down and testify."

Eventually, a federal grand jury returned an indictment charging the police officer with violating section 1951 of title 18 of the United States Code [the Hobbs Act], in that he did "knowingly and willfully obstruct, delay, and affect commerce by extortion, to wit, by obtaining the property of another, with his consent induced by wrongful use of actual and threatened force, violence, and fear, and under color of official right."[1]

The Expansion of Federal Jurisdiction over Local Corruption: A Crime Is Born

Like its predecessor, the Antiracketeering Act of 1934,[2] the Hobbs Act prohibits the obstruction of interstate commerce by extortion or robbery.[3] It was passed in response to the Supreme Court's exclusion of labor-related activity from the coverage of the 1934 statute. Nowhere in the legislative history of either statute is there any indication of congressional intent to reach corrupt demands for payment by local officials, or even a discussion of the problem.

Judicial interpretation of the act indicates a willingness to permit expansion of its prohibitions to the limits of the underlying jurisdictional base. With respect to obstruction of interstate commerce, for example, the statute is not limited to conduct that directly and immediately obstructs a particular movement of goods; all that need be shown is the commission of an act, the natural and probable effect of which would be delaying or affecting the movement of goods in commerce.

The obstruction prohibited by the statute must be accomplished by robbery or extortion, with the definitions of both terms taken from contemporary New York penal law.[4] Prosecutions under the robbery provision have been less frequent than those under the extortion provisions, and judicial interpretation of the definition of robbery remains well within the bounds of the common law offense. Interpretation of the definition of extortion, on the other hand, has developed along the same expansive lines as has the law of obstruction. The property obtained may be tangible—money—or intangible—the right to solicit business. The fear used by the extorter may range from fear of personal injury to fear of economic loss, whether engendered by threats of labor union interference with construction projects, withholding of a contractor's permit to construct a plant, or strict police enforcement of parking laws outside a bar.

"Under Color of Official Right"

In seeking to apply the act to cases of local corruption, federal prosecutors encountered only one substantial hurdle. In *United States v. Kubacki*[5] the mayor of Reading, Pennsylvania, was charged with extortion under the Hobbs Act and bribery under the Travel Act[6] but was acquitted of the extortion charge by the district court judge on the theory that the two offenses were mutually exclusive. . . . As a result, some federal prosecutors felt that they faced an impossible task in deciding, on any given set of facts, whether to charge a local public official with obtaining a "victim's" property by use of fear or with being the recipient of a voluntary payment made by one seeking official favor.

Although the Hobbs Act had received an extraordinarily expansive interpretation in every respect, and particularly with regard to its jurisdictional base, prosecutorial efforts to extend the reach of the act's prohibitions at least had been limited by the basic premise that these prohibitions represented the federal equivalent of well recognized, larceny-type state offenses which were punishable under a wide variety of titles but had in common the element of duress. Every indictment thus alleged that the defendant obtained property through the use of fear—conduct that seemed to warrant the act's potential twenty year prison sentence.

As prosecutors delved deeper into local corruption, however, they encountered a level of sophistication in the making and receiving of illicit payments which promised substantial difficulty in establishing the commission of extortion by duress. As evidenced by the prosecution of the mayor of Newark, New Jersey,[7] there existed in that city and elsewhere an understanding, difficult of proof, between contractors and officials concerning the need for payment in exchange for government contracts. To meet these problems of proof, the United Sates attorney for New Jersey attempted—unsuccessfully at first—to expand the previously well-marked boundaries of the Hobbs Act offense.

These boundaries were successfully expanded, however, in the prosecution of John V. Kenny, political "boss" of Hudson County.[8] Count I of the indictment against Kenny charged him and other county officials with conspiracy to obstruct commerce by obtaining from businessmen seeking contracts with Jersey City or with Hudson County a percentage of the contract price in return for the privilege of doing business with either government. It alleged that the property was obtained with consent induced by "the wrongful use of fear *and* under color of official right." Count II of the indictment charged the defendants with conspiracy to violate the Travel Act by using the facilities of interstate commerce in aid of unlawful activity—bribery *and* extortion in violation of New Jersey law. The court submitted the first count to the jury with instructions that they could find the defendants guilty of conspiracy to obstruct commerce if they determined that extortion had been committed either by wrongful use of fear or under color of official right. The court defined that latter as follows:

> Extortion under color of official right is the wrongful taking by a public officer of money not due him or his office, whether or not the taking was accomplished by force, threats or use of fear. You will note that extortion as defined by federal law is committed when property is obtained under color of official right, and in either instance the offense of extortion is committed.[9]

Only one of the five appellants objected to this disjunctive definition of extortion, but the Court of Appeals rejected his contention, concluding that the act "repeats the common law definition of extortion, a crime which could only be committed by a public officer and which did not require proof of threat, fear or duress." . . .

The Federal Offense After Kenny

In the first case after *Kenny* to rely on the official right theory, *United States v. Staszcuk*,[10] a Chicago alderman was charged with receiving $9,000 from a zoning consultant in return for a promise not to oppose zoning amendments affecting property within the defendant's ward. One transaction involved a plan to build an animal hospital on land within the ward barred from such use. The builder paid $5,500 to the consultant because the latter had the reputation of being "the man to see," and the consultant, in turn, persuaded the defendant to introduce the necessary amending ordinance before the city council. On the date for public hearings on the proposed zoning variance, the consultant paid $3,000 to Staszcuk, who at least implicitly supported the proposal, and the ordinance was passed.

The indictment charged that the consultant "feared he would be unable to procure a zoning change . . . unless he compensated defendant to refrain from objecting to such a change as a member of the Chicago City Council." Assuming the validity of the government's theory, the Court of Appeals concluded that the prosecution had made a sufficient showing of an alderman's official influence over the zoning process, and stated that:

> The payments were made to defendant to influence his exercise of the political power he held as alderman over zoning applications. To accept money in return for an agreement not to oppose such applications—in effect to suspend independent judgment on the merits of such zoning changes—constitutes obtaining property from another, with his consent, induced under color of official right.

This language bears a striking similarity to that which would normally describe a bribery. The facts clearly established that the individuals seeking advantage initiated the contact with Staszcuk. . . .

If Staszcuk had used an interstate facility, or if interstate travel had occurred in making the payment in violation of Illinois bribery laws, the government could have charged Staszcuk with violation of the Travel Act. In the absence of such an interstate connection, however, it was necessary to convert the bribery to an extortion in order to obtain federal jurisdiction. That this was the motivation behind the extortion charge is suggested by the government's argument on appeal that there is no distinction between a public official accepting a bribe and extorting a payment under color of official right. . . .

The theory of the Newark prosecutions was that an atmosphere of coercion had been created and that it was unnecessary for the officials to threaten the victims. Undeniably, situations of such pervasive corruption do exist, in which it is difficult for the government to establish the existence of implicit coercion. The solution to this problem is not, however, the judicial creation of a federal offense that eliminates the element of duress. . . .

In *United States v. Hathaway*[11] the court sustained the extortion conviction of one Baptista, the executive director of the New Bedford, Massachusetts, Redevelopment Authority, for having taken payments from one Graham, the president of an engineering company, in exchange for the awarding of contracts by the Authority. Graham, the victim of the extortion who was described by the court as having "a striking and, one might say, colorful history of paying off officials," had initiated the payments to Baptista after being told by another contractor that such payments would be necessary to obtain a contract. On appeal Baptista sought to characterize his conduct as bribe receiving rather than extortion, but the court found that Baptista had manipulated the situation "to play upon Graham's fears of missing out on the contract," and concluded that the initiative in an extortion need not come solely from the public official.

The court's theory that Baptista had knowingly used a preexisting atmosphere of coercion reasonably felt by Graham was well within the bounds of earlier Hobbs Act cases, but it is doubtful that the evidence, at least as reported in the court's opinion, supported a jury finding to that effect. The situation in New Bedford seems to have been similar to that which had prevailed in Newark—a well-known practice of bribery willingly engaged in by payor and payee alike.

Admittedly, it is in cases like this that it is most difficult for the prosecution to establish the elements of a larceny-type extortion. But if a businessman is willing to do whatever needs to be done to ensure success in bidding for a government contract, and also reasonably believes that if he is not so willing others who are may deprive him of the award, it stretches the meaning of extortion beyond recognition to place before a jury the payor as the victim and official as the coercive villain. This is especially so where the sole purpose of this scenario is to permit the trial of the case in a federal court. In the case of a bribe, both parties are guilty, and the prosecutor will be faced with the choice of which party to charge and which to use as a witness—a choice usually premised on a first-in-first-out theory—but in an extortion, whether common law or larceny-type, only the recipient is guilty of an offense. Whatever the legitimacy of charging an extortion where some aspect of the daily life of the payor is at the mercy of the public official who directly or indirectly takes steps to elicit an improper payment, it cannot be legitimate to so characterize a transaction in which the payor searches for fertile soil in which to sow his bribe, finds it, sows, reaps, and then claims that he acted out of fear. . . .

In *United States v. Trotta,*[12] the defendant Commissioner of Public Works was charged with demanding from a firm of consulting engineers two contributions to the local Republican committee. Although it alleged that Trotta had authority over contract awards and that the firm reasonably understood that he had the power to take action adverse to their interests, the indictment did not charge that there had been any adverse action, any threat of action, or, indeed, any relationship between the demand for the contributions and any contract awarded by the defendant. The district judge dismissed that indictment on the ground that, by merely tracking the statutory language, it did not give the defendant sufficient notice of the offense with which he was charged. The court noted that the indictment failed to charge that the defendant had demanded the payments under color of his office but alleged only that the payor's consent was induced by the defendant's ability to take official action. Pointing out that the indictment did not allege facts sufficient to demonstrate a violation of the comparable extortion statute applicable to federal officials, which carries a maximum penalty of only three years' imprisonment, the court rejected the government's contention that the mere passive receipt of money accompanied by the payor's reasonable focus on the requestor's official status could invoke the twenty year imprisonment provided for under the Hobbs Act.

The United States Court of Appeals for the Second Circuit reversed, finding that the indictment "makes it clear that Trotta is charged with using the power of his office over . . . engineering contracts to induce payments of money." Judge Anderson did not view the existence of any connection between the demand for payment and an identified official action as crucial to the offense and quoted with approval the opinion of the Seventh Circuit in [*United States v.] Braasch,*[13] which asked only whether "the motivation for the payment focuses on the recipient's office."

An extortion by fear exists regardless of whether the payment demanded goes to the extorter or to some third party, and presumably the same would be true of extortion under color of public office. Yet if a public official who asks for a political contribution from one who does, or may do, business with the government can be prosecuted on proof of those facts alone, then the Hobbs Act has become an extraordinary mechanism for controlling political activity on the state and local levels. It is a federal offense for an organization with federal government contracts to make a contribution in connection with a federal election, or for any person to solicit such a contribution. Conviction carries a maximum punishment of five years in prison and a fine of $25,000. If the *Trotta* opinion means that a local government official commits extortion by soliciting a contribution from an organization that has or might have contracts with his agency, and is thereby liable to be imprisoned for twenty years, one may well ask whether a governor who attends a fundraising dinner and solicits contributions from the businessmen present has committed a felony.

A Case Revisited

There is little doubt that the Hobbs Act conviction of the greedy policeman in the hypothetical [case] would be affirmed on appeal. . . . The demand for an additional $5 would fall well within the boundaries of the newborn Hobbs Act offense, and it is only slightly less certain that the proffered and accepted $10 payments would as well. Although the amounts involved might strike the average person as minimal and consequently might affect the willingness of the jury to convict or the severity of the sentence imposed, the size of the payoff would not affect the validity of the conviction as a matter of law. At common law, or in a state that has enacted the common law offense, the policeman would have accepted under color of his office a payment not due him and, typically, would be subject to a maximum of one year in prison. In [most federal circuit courts] he would have obstructed interstate commerce by obtaining the property of the candy store owner under color of official right and would be subject to a maximum of twenty years in prison. . . .

The Making of Federal Law Enforcement Policy

. . . The principal justification for federal jurisdiction over offenses not impacting directly on primary federal interests is the need for investigative and prosecutorial facilities that can respond to modern, sophisticated, national or international crime beyond the reach of local police and district attorneys—a role characterized by an earlier writer as "auxiliary to state law enforcement."[14] But once Congress has provided the statutory framework for that role, a substantial amount of criminal conduct capable of being dealt with by the states inevitably will end up being prosecuted in federal courts. Federal and state prosecutors have not been able to draw a line beyond which federal law enforcement agencies will serve only in advisory and supportive capacities; protection of informants, access to "buy money," and an understandable desire for personal or agency image enhancement continue to breed competition between federal and local law enforcement officers. Similar considerations lead to similar competition at the prosecutorial level, although, in theory, this form of combat is more controllable.

. . . [E]ven with the best motive on both sides, the realities of criminal investigation and prosecution give the federal establishment a virtually insurmountable advantage. Information about criminal activity is fed into the federal law enforcement system from an endless variety of sources: Internal Revenue agents conducting civil or criminal tax investigations, bank auditors, investigators from the regulatory agencies, and forms filed with the government pursuant to any of hundreds of registration and disclosure schemes, in addition to the law enforcement agencies themselves—the FBI, the Drug Enforcement Administration, the Bureau of Alcohol, Tobacco and Firearms, the Customs Service, and the Secret Service. The information is then funneled to a prosecutor whose caseload is only a small percentage of that carried by the typical district attorney and who has, in many districts, special units assigned to handle only large narcotics conspiracies, or frauds, or organized crime. Most importantly, the federal prosecutor has at his command the power of the grand jury—the most effective vehicle for investigation of complex criminal operations, but one which is available to and used by only a small number of local prosecutors, even in the most sophisticated metropolitan jurisdictions.

With this marked advantage in both investigation and prosecution, the United States attorney is often the first to obtain usable information concerning public corruption and the only prosecutor with the wherewithal to conduct the necessary investigation. Equally important, he is likely to have the motivation to act against individuals whom his state or local counterpart may be reluctant to challenge. Although this motivation is generally laudable, it would be unrealistic to deny that in a few cases it is colored by personal or partisan ambition. Nevertheless, the United States attorney is viewed as the protector of public integrity at both the federal and state levels, and his image of personal incorruptibility is an important asset in any investigation or prosecution of high-ranking officials. . . .

A rational policy governing federal intervention in cases of local corruption should be founded on an appropriate balancing of three factors: the capacity of the federal prosecutor to manage both the investigation and prosecution effectively; the capacity of the local prosecutor, with or without federal assistance, to do so; and the adverse social consequences that would flow from the failure of both to take action. Because the only likely barrier to federal involvement is jurisdictional and that, as earlier discussion indicates, is hardly impenetrable, the balance in most cases will be tipped initially in favor of intervention. The capacity of the local prosecutor will vary from case to case, depending on the size and efficiency of his office and the availability of adequate police support; his desire will also vary from case to case, but the absence of motivation will be substantially more difficult to ascertain.

If the problem were only logistical, federal cooperation with local agencies would seem to be a reasonable solution, but two hurdles stand in the way. First, federal investigators are reluctant to turn over relevant information, either because they suspect their local counterparts of corruption or because they are simply unwilling to disclose the nature and identity of their sources. Secondly, federal law enforcement agencies are reluctant to devote their energies, except in such cases as kidnapping or bank robbery, to the investigation of matters that will not necessarily become federal statistics. If the problem is one of initiative, federal agencies can do little, but the question remains whether a decision by local authorities not to act because of political or even venal motives justifies federal assumption of the local enforcement role. Assuming that the basis for the local prosecutor's refusal to act is obvious—and in many cases it will not be—the justification for federal intervention depends on the weight to be given the third element: whether inaction would be so detrimental to societal interests that the federal prosecutor should move against what normally would be an offense of purely local impact.

Implicit in this formulation of the issue is a belief that local corruption is not a matter of federal concern unless it impacts directly on a primary federal interest. Although it is difficult to stand by while an offense goes unprosecuted if there is a jurisdictional predicate for action, the federal prosecutor should recognize that the existence of jurisdiction is not a mandate to federalize all forms of state crime but is, rather, intended to be auxiliary to state enforcement. If, as a matter of policy, a state's failure to enforce the law were a sufficient justification for federal intervention, it would be difficult to distinguish between police inability to solve a robbery and police inability to solve a bribery. Only certain robberies, however, are matters of legitimate federal interest, and the same should be true of bribes. The legislative decision to create federal jurisdiction does not necessarily include a decision to take over the field. Even where interstate travel occurs in aid of a bribe, it ought still be asked whether federal prosecution is appropriate. Both the prosecutors and the courts should be skeptical of efforts to expand the jurisdictional base beyond the expressed congressional intent.

Granting that it is detrimental to the interests of the citizens of a state for their elected or appointed officials to breach the trust reposed in them, these interests would be served better by effective state enforcement than by reliance on the federal government for remedial action. There rarely will be the demand for such effective enforcement so long as an outside agency is available as an alternative. Further, when that agency acts there is a substantial risk, with potential impact on jury deliberations, that it will be viewed as an interloper, and that, even if successful in the individual prosecution, the long term effect will be minimal because reform will not have come from within or from the demand of the electorate. . . .

Notes

1. The foregoing account is entirely fictional and is not based on any specific events or persons, but it could happen anywhere.
2. Act of June 18, 1934, ch. 569, 48 Stat. 979.
3. 18 U.S.C. 1951.
4. N.Y. Penal Law app. SS 850–51, 2120.
5. 237 F. Supp. 638 (E.D. Pa. 1965).
6. 18 U.S.C. 1952 (1970) (forbidding interstate and foreign travel in aid of racketeering enterprises).
7. *United States v. Addonizio,* 451 F.2d 49 (3d Cir. 1971), *cert. denied,* 405 U.S. 936 (1972).
8. *United States v. Kenny,* 462 F.2d. 1205 (3d Cir.), *cert. denied,* 409 U.S. 914 (1972).
9. *Ibid.* at 1229.
10. 502 F.2d 875 (7th Cir. 1974), *aff'd in relevant part en banc,* 517 F.2d 53, *cert. denied,* 423 U.S. 837 (1975).
11. 534 F.2d 386 (1st Cir.), *cert. denied,* 97 S. Ct. 64 (1976).
12. 396 F. Supp. 755 (E.D.N.Y.), *rev'd,* 525 F.2d 1096 (2d. Cir. 1975), *cert. denied,* 425 U.S. 971 (1976).
13. *United States v. Braasch,* 505 F.2d 1096, 1100 (7th Cir. 1974), *cert. denied,* 421 U.S. 910 (1976).
14. L.B. Schwartz, "Federal Criminal Jurisdiction and Prosecutors' Discretion," 13 *Law and Contemporary Problems,* 64, 70, 73–77 (1948).

38

Preserving Privilege in Yucatan

Margaret Goodman

Political scientists have recently taken a new look at corruption in developing nations and have tried to analyze the role that this almost ubiquitous force has upon overall political and economic development. Rather than condemning nepotism, spoils, and graft, per se, scholars are using an instrumental approach to such practices, tending to view them as complementary to particular stages of development.[1] Samuel Huntington, for example, sees its extent as "correlating reasonably well with rapid social and economic modernization" and as a product of the new norms which are being established as a consequence of a new distinction being drawn between public welfare and private interest.[2] Other pro-corruption arguments are that bribery leads to efficiency because in the long run the entrepreneur who can best afford the price of a large bribe is the one who runs his business most efficiently. Thus the efficient are rewarded as they would be under any freely competitive system.[3] Others state that corruption may force intransigent bureaucracies to move, and even perhaps move in a better direction, as there is no assurance that the unimpeded choices of government bureaucrats and politicians are any more rational than those of the corruptors. The institution of the "payoff" may also be helpful to new groups, such as unpopular minorities, who might not get a fair hearing under traditional systems of class or caste. In such cases, the almighty dollar (or pesos, or yen, etc.) serves as a force for democracy because anyone who can pay gets representation, regardless of race, creed, or country of national origin. Corruption may also make the system "human" in traditional terms, may facilitate compromise between opposing ideologies, and may reduce the harshness of an elite conceived plan for development.[4]

Source: Margaret Goodman, "Does Political Corruption Really Help Economic Development?: Yucatan, Mexico," *Polity,* 7, 2 (Winter 1974), 143–62. By permission of the publisher and author.

Under these non-normative standards of political morality, nepotism and the spoils systems are viewed as forms of social security and a type of national employment service. Since such services usually accompany economic development, which is viewed as a positive goal, any immorality must be tolerated.

Two premises seem to underlie these apologies for political and bureaucratic corruption.[5] One premise assumes that these forms of corruption belong to some transitional stage in a nation's development, where impersonal standards of merit have not been substituted for ascriptive standards and where the objectives of national welfare have not yet become sufficiently differentiated from personal prerogatives. This argument implies that once this transitional stage has passed, the levels of corruption will turn significantly downward. No matter how corrupt the mobilizers, once people have been brought into the political process, they will with time automatically throw the rascals out and institute more honest procedures.[6] Likewise, in the economic sphere, bribery and nepotism will survive only so long as the economy is relatively closed. As the "payoff" convinces staid bureaucrats to open up new markets to new groups, the job market and the economy will become sufficiently broadened so that these practices will no longer be necessary, and thus no longer acceptable.

The second, and more crucial assumption, because it invariably underlies the first assumption, is that some sort of a competitive bidding system exists, both in the political realm and in the realm of government jobs and contracts. Thus, James Scott, in his study of "Corruption, Machine Politics and Political Change," writes that "At a minimum, the setting of the machine requires, 1. the selection of political leaders through elections, 2. mass (usually universal) adult suffrage, and 3. a relatively high degree of electoral competition over time . . . usually between parties but occasionally within a dominant party."[7] Without these elements the political machine, as it existed in England and the United States, could not function, of course, since its main strength lay in a comparatively free electoral system which permitted mobilization of groups or classes which had previously been disenfranchised. These "machines" then, with their politician-citizen corruption, became the instruments for increased electoral participation and competition.

Arguments that state that business-government corruption will increase efficiency because only the most efficient enterprise will be able to support this added cost, assume that some free market exists within these developing countries, with no monopolies, trusts, or even protective tariffs. New groups are seen as influencing the bureaucrats who in turn, are neither politically committed to one party nor ideologically committed to one person, family, or group. These bureaucrats are viewed as free wheeling entrepreneurs who always accept the offer which benefits them the most, using purely monetary standards.[8]

The fact is, though, that these two assumptions, of an existing competitive political and economic system, and of the transitory nature of corruption, are patently false in many of the developing nations today. In many of these countries there is little or no political competition and the lack of competition in the political realm reinforces monopolistic conditions in the economic sphere. The Soviet Union, China, and Cuba are, of course, obvious examples of countries where neither political nor economic competition exists. Less obvious, and less extreme, are countries such as Mexico and Brazil, Greece and Spain, where authoritarian political systems strictly regulate economic life.

The one-party phenomenon in Mexico and the no-party phenomenon in Brazil are both ways of controlling rather than mobilizing mass support. In Brazil, the masses are told not to participate. In Mexico, the masses participate in support of elite chosen candidates. Mexico, to be sure, does have an extensive political apparatus, but it serves more as a device to bolster an authoritarian regime than as a "machine" serving some transitional function of mobilizing an apolitical electorate until it is sufficiently sophisticated to act on its own.

Bureaucratic corruption in a freely competitive society could conceivably work toward some concept of "survival of the fittest" although it still remains doubtful whether some other factors such as family or school tie, etc., might not alter the market to the benefit of incumbent elites. However, in most of the developing countries today, no such thing as a free market exists. Modernizing authoritarian political elites strictly limit the organizational activities of the economically active population. State monopolies or private monopolies supported by the political apparatus are often created to protect infant industries and resources. Businessmen look naturally to the government to limit competition rather than to foster it. Instead of open bidding and competition, coupled with a free press to expose violations, there are only a few organized sectors, operating in controlled rather than open economies.

This lack of competition places theories about the transitoriness of the corruption stage in serious doubt. Without the cleansing force of competition, either for votes or for markets, there does not seem to be any apparent reason why corruption should either be exposed or should become less prevalent. Particularly in developing societies where class inequalities are great and where the existence of a large lower class is a constant threat to a privileged middle and upper class, the natural tendency would seem to be collusion between the upper two classes rather than exposure of one by the other in front of the lower classes.

Since the conditions described above exist in many of the developing nations today, it would be salutary to explore the effects of corruption where competition in the political and the economic realm is strictly limited to see what the long term effects upon the country's development are. This chapter makes several hypotheses about the effects of corruption upon economic development in modernizing, authoritarian regimes. The hypotheses are:

1. Rather than being a transitory stage in a nation's development between the time when particularistic interests are superseded by more universalistic norms, corruption in modernizing authoritarian societies may inhibit this evolution by encouraging the notion that the state exists to serve particularistic desires.
2. Rather than benefitting the efficient producer, the institutionalization of corruption in modernizing authoritarian societies may protect the incompetent and reward the inefficient. Likewise, rather than insuring that new groups will get a hearing, the institutionalization of corruption may insure that the same groups get profits and new groups are kept out.
3. Rather than forcing intransigent bureaucrats to move, corruption in modernizing authoritarian societies will simply limit options and prevent optimal development planning.
4. Rather than making the system "human" to the more traditional elements of the society, the institutionalization of corruption in modernizing authoritarian societies breeds cynicism even among those who are doing the corrupting for they are fully aware of the lack of public commitment among public servants. For those who are not in a position to corrupt, the advantage that money holds in the system can only be seen as a further limitation on their already circumscribed ability to participate.
5. Rather than building party loyalty, corruption in a modernizing authoritarian society promotes an efficient rather than an effective loyalty to the system. It promotes the idea that the system is only good as long as it produces for the individual rather than providing for the society in general.
6. Rather than working as an expansive force, the institutionalization of corruption in modernizing authoritarian societies works as a conserving force, allowing for some economic development without any great need for extensive distribution of wealth; since only the

wealthy can bribe, only a very small portion of the population is in a position to demand economic satisfaction.

7. The institutionalization of corruption in modernizing authoritarian regimes may provide a very stable climate of investment for knowledgeable entrepreneurs and bureaucrats. So long as they know that nepotism, bribery, and graft are usable expedients in the market of government favors, they probably see little need for Swiss bank accounts.

Over the last fifty years, the state of Yucatan, Mexico, has had some amount of development and a great amount of corruption. Since the state exists within the framework of the modernizing authoritarian structure which Mexico has had since the Revolution of 1910, it may meet the criteria necessary for testing our hypotheses.

The political apparatus of the state of Yucatan, as in the rest of Mexico, is controlled by the Partido Revolucionario Institucional (PRI). Enough has been written about the Mexican one-party system so that a detailed description of it is unnecessary here.[9] Suffice it to say that all important state offices in Yucatan are held by PRI officials. Even when the opposition wins, the PRI controls. In 1968, the mayor of Merida, the capital city of Yucatan, was elected from the Partido Accion Nacional (PAN), the main opposition party in Mexico. This was mainly the result

Table 38.1

Person	Prior Political Positions	Money from Sale
Party A	Director, Henequeneros de Yucatan; Presidente Municipal of Merida; Board of Directors Cordemex	$ 9,465,300.00 pesos
Party B	Chief of the Commercial Department, Henequeneros de Yucatan; Board of Directors, Cordemex	$21,764,325.81 pesos
Party C	Governor of Yucatan	$ 7,547,325.81 pesos
Party D	Director, Henequeneros de Yucatan; Board of Directors, Cordemex	$44,165,560.00 pesos
Party E	Family of Lorenzo Manzanilla Arce, who was also a Director of Henequeneros de Yucatan; Board of Directors, Cordemex	$13,957,847.32 pesos
Party F	Board of Directors, Cordemex	$22,349,200.00 pesos
Party G	Board of Directors, Cordemex	$14,385,600.00 pesos
Party H	Board of Directors, Cordemex	$10,909,835.00 pesos
Party I	Board of Directors, Cordemex	$ 9,995,520.00 pesos
Party J	Board of Directors, Cordemex	$ 7,721,200.00 pesos[21]

of a political scandal which stirred up so much anti-PRI feeling among the middle classes that the normal stuffing of the ballot boxes in favor of PRI did not take place. The governor of the state, a PRI man, immediately made it clear that PRI would still control the city, however, by severely limiting the tax base upon which the mayor depended and by removing the control of the city police from him. The mayor then was left with practically no patronage and favors to dispense.[10] Needless to say, in 1970, the mayoralty reverted to a PRI member.

Not only are traditional public offices such as governor, mayors, and congressmen elected from PRI, but the PRI is so organized that it encompasses the main interest groups in the state within its highly regimented wings. Thus, labor, peasant, and middle-class interests are all incorporated into PRI sector organizations. Even intraparty competition is closely regulated so that only party members in good standing with state and federal elites may win party office. It can be said, then, that Yucatan fits the category of a noncompetitive political system.

Economically too, the state is highly controlled. Since the late 1800s the economy has been dependent upon the production and export of henequen, a sisal plant.[11] First the state and then the national government have regulated the henequen industry, in order to compete with foreign markets and to insure domestic taxes. Since Cardenas, the industry has also served as a source of political propaganda for PRI, as the public distribution of henequen lands held in large haciendas has been one of the main tenets of PRI ideology. Lately, with the decline of the henequen industry, bureaucratic decisions determining the extent of the industry which will remain and the rate of changeover to new products have also determined what economic forces would survive in Yucatan, and at what level of affluence. There has been then in Yucatan a noncompetitive economic system in recent history.

There has also been a lot of corruption, and everyone in the state, from the highest government officials, to the richest merchants, to the lowest peasants, is fully aware of this. On any day of the week the newspapers are filled with political and bureaucratic scandals. The government, in fact, sometimes announces its own scandals. In 1955, for example, the relations between the rich factory owners and the poor *ejidatarios* (collective farm workers) became particularly volcanic. The secretary of agriculture came to Merida and made public denunciations. He said that the owners of the henequen processing plants and the state bureaucrats (often the same people as we shall soon see) were enriching themselves at the expense of the workers, and also at the expense of the federal government because of the great losses of the federal credit lending institutions. Although no one was arrested, and no one paid any restitution, a governmental reorganization did take place amid much publicity.[12]

This tendency of the national government to create its own scandals seems to be a pattern in Yucatan when rising discontent threatens the stability of the state. By moving personnel around, the government hopes to appear clean. Since the investigators are controlled by the same people who control the accused, punishments can be limited to banishments and then a new position in another state, a small price to pay for the continuation of a system which has afforded many privileges to those on top.

The state of Yucatan is uncompetitive and corrupt, then, and so an ideal testing ground for the hypotheses stated above.

Hypothesis one: Rather than being a transitory stage in a nation's development between the time when particularistic interests are superseded by more universalistic norms, corruption in modernizing authoritarian societies may inhibit this evolution by encouraging the notion that the state exists to serve particularistic desires.

The history of particularism is long in Yucatan and shows no signs of abating. Even before the revolution, the governors of the state, who were heavily involved in the henequen industry themselves, passed favorable tax regulations for the growers and exporters. Beginning in 1912, the governor of Yucatan instituted the first of many state monopolies of the henequen industry to control the sale of the fiber. This was necessitated by the failure of the growers themselves to unite to keep prices up or to respond to foreign competition. From that point on, the henequen industry has always been carefully regulated by either the state or the federal government to insure profits for growers and merchants and tax sources for the state. The constant contact which the regulated had with the regulators afforded much opportunity for access and influence not available to outside interests.

At the time of the revolution, the Indians, who made up approximately 80 pecent of the population, were either working as serfs on the large haciendas, or living in a semibarbarian state in the outlying areas of the state. Although they were freed by the military governors who occupied the state after 1914, their living conditions changed very little because the land owners, through the contacts with state and federal officials, were able to put off land reform until 1937.[13] After land reform finally was accomplished under Cardenas, it encountered the problems that most reformist projects do at first, such as lowered production and some administrative chaos.[14] The old hacienda owners, who had theoretically lost their power through land distribution, were able to convince state officials to intervene for them at the federal level. The outcome of these negotiations was the establishment of a state run monopoly, Henequeneros de Yucatan, which was administered by the ex-hacienda owners along with the prerevolutionary politicians who had gradually regained favor with federal officials after the first reformist days of the revolution were over. These hacienda owners *(hacendados)* turned bureaucrats then proceeded to buy into the burgeoning processing industry which turned raw henequen fibers into binder twine and cord. The monopoly was run so that the managers of the state run farms bought the fibers from the *ejidatarios* and sold them to the factories. Since they were literally buying and selling to themselves, they could easily sell on the black market or at credit, because they were paying the *ejido* workers such low prices that healthy profits could still be made. The industry prospered greatly during the henequen-scarce war years of the 1940s and early 1950s.[15]

When the entire henequen industry declined, because of the development of synthetics which began to replace the natural fibers, these same *hacendado* bureaucrats were able to use the connections they had made through years of government contacts plus bribes in the right places, to sell their factories to the federal government at an inflated price. They were then able to enter into new industries.[16]

There is no indication throughout this recital of instances of government partiality that the particularistic norms were being replaced by anything more universalistic. In fact, one might postulate that success in the first venture encouraged trying again: continued success only reinforced old values. The absence of political competition, of course, allowed politicians and bureaucrats much leeway in permitting such favoritism.

Hypothesis two: Rather than benefitting the efficient producer, the institutionalization of corruption in modernizing authoritarian societies may protect the incompetent and reward the inefficient. Likewise, rather than insuring that new groups will get a hearing, the institutionalization of corruption may insure that the same groups get profits and new groups are kept out.

After surviving land-reform, first by becoming state bureaucrats, and then entrepreneurs of the booming processing factories, these most flexible of men were again threatened by ruination when the development of synthetics threatened the entire industry. The number of processing factories had expanded during the profitable war years of the 1940s and early 1950s from a handful of factories in the 1930s to more than 200 improvised factories and fifty well equipped factories. These sold their products cheaply, often at credit. To further stimulate production and eliminate competition between the factories, Nacional

Financiera, a government-owned development corporation, loaned the factory owners (cordelerios) $150,000,000 pesos to guarantee and unify the factories in a society called Cordemex, S.A. This became a semipublic corporation with the secretaries of finance and commerce serving on the board of directors.

During the war years, the factories had produced so furiously that plants were plucked before they were ready and the plantations were reaped without any regard to conservation. By the early 1960s the fields lay in a state of decay, while the Yucatecan henequen producers found themselves with a bad reputation vis-à-vis Brazilian and Philippine planters. Attempts to modernize factories in the face of downward spiraling prices threatened the industry itself.[17]

In 1961 the *cordelerios,* faced with bankruptcy, began making advances to the federal government towards the end of having the latter purchase Cordemex. They also offered the Fondo Nacional de Fomento Ejidal the option of buying 50 percent of the company's stock.[18]

Various members of the group that eventually sold Cordemex delight in retelling the tale of how friends and relatives had laughed at first over the idea of "dumping" this outmoded industry onto the federal government. Not only was the machinery antiquated, but the entire industry itself was being overtaken by synthetics, particularly polypropylene, a product of Kodak, Inc. Friends must have laughed in amazement then, when in July, 1962, the president of Mexico announced that it was not permitted to install new plants in the textile industry of henequen or add to or substitute the equipment then in existence without obtaining the previous authorization of the secretary of industry, because steps were being taken for a major reorganization of the industry to benefit the workers.

A negotiation was finally made that was considered a veritable coup on the part of the factory owners. The plants and their future business potential were evaluated at $250,000,000 pesos. The corporation, Cordemex, borrowed $125,000,000 from a bank in the United States with a Mexican federal government guarantee to pay back the loans. This money was distributed to the factory owners as half the worth of the plant and used to pay back creditors. The other 50 percent of the corporation's worth was given in paper stock in the Cordemex corporation to the federal government. After one year the government took over the loan (which it was generally conceded, the private owners could never have repaid) and paid the owners an additional 62.5 million pesos for their half of the stock. The figure of $250,000,000 pesos was dropped from actual calculations.[19]

Why did the government buy the plants? There are probably several reasons. The henequen industry is the major industry in the state of Yucatan. The federal government had to do something when the major industry of a state that was already deep in a depression was in danger of failing. It may have been in hopes of gaining fuller control of the entire industry if it handled both the planting stage (through the Banco Agrario, the federal bank which gives credit to *ejidos*) and the manufacturing end. There were also pressures from *campesino* and labor groups who were in hopes that any profits from the manufacturing side would filter down to them if the government owned the plants. The take-over would also give the federal government one more place to employ loyal party members and family friends. This is borne out to some extent by the fact that the first federal director of Cordemex was the brother-in-law of the secretary of finance, although the new director had no experience in the field. How much of the decision to buy Cordemex was based on the fact that a healthy profit could be made by all involved in the sale can only be left to speculation.

Why did it pay so much? The general estimate is that the government paid at least double the factories' worth and some estimates range as high as ten times the value. No one, not even government officials and ex-*cordelerias*, denies that the price was too high. The director of Cordemex said that generosity was the price for getting rid of the old owners; large payments left him relatively free to run his own industry.[20] There is no question that if this was the reason, there has been at least partial success: the *cordelerias* do not interfere in the Yucatecan henequen industry directly. However, many of them still own processing factories in other states and so at least indirectly affect the enterprise.

The main reason seems to lie in the fact that the *cordelerios* were well connected in Mexico City and could use influence where it counted. A glance at the people who made the most money out of the negotiation with the government and their political positions prior to the sale is very informative.

The men [involved . . .] have had continuous contact with government officials, some for as long as thirty years, when Henequeneros was formed during the Cardenas administration. All of them were on the board of directors of Cordemex where they had opportunities to talk with the secretaries of finance and commerce and industry, who also served. Rather than being *nouveau riche* families, many were from some of the oldest families in the state who have managed to hold on to money and/or power through various phases of revolutionary and counterrevolutionary zeal in Mexico. The first person on the list is now the president of the largest private bank in the Yucatan, the Banco

Nacional del Sureste. Others are safely reinvested in extensive ranch-
ing and farming interests outside of the state. One is even part-owner
of the Pepsi Cola Company in Yucatan. Several federal officials have
stated that the money was to be reinvested in the state itself, but there
does not seem to have been much effort made to enforce this.[22]

Did the purchase of Cordemex benefit the efficient producer? In this
case the government bought out producers who were neither efficient
nor experimental. From the very first, these ex-*hacendado*-enterpre-
neurs demanded government protection in their endeavors. As far
back as the 1870s they reaped profits through cheap labor rather than
through their business acumen. They allowed their machines to become outmoded and did not experiment with new products when world
markets for their primary product, binder twine, moved downward. In
truth, their main efficiency was that they knew the right people and
knew how to act in a political rather than economic context.

Did corruption insure new groups an opportunity? In Yucatan, just
the opposite took place. If there was ever a time when the old
hacendado and commercial class would have gone down, it was during
the period after the Korean War when their primary means of support
was failing. (Immediately after the revolution, PRI organization was
really too weak to depose them. It was only after land reform in 1937
and the prosperity of the 1940s and early 1950s that the PRI had
sufficient organization among the laborers and peasants actually to
dethrone this group without entirely disrupting the social fabric of the
state.) One can imagine some member of the lower middle class buying
a decorticating factory from one of the bankrupt owners at a modest
sum, and thus beginning his own climb up the entrepreneurial ladder,
to be sure, at a more modest scale. Instead, federal officials insured
that the old upper class would continue by buying them out of economic ruin and allowing them to go into other, more profitable ventures.

Hypothesis three: Rather than forcing intransigent bureaucrats to
move, corruption in modernizing authoritarian societies will simply
limit options and prevent optimal development planning.

By the late 1950s the federal government in Mexico was well aware
that something had to be done about the Yucatecan economy. Through
its agricultural lending institutions, the federal government was heavily
subsidizing the peasants who never earned enough to pay back the
loans (this was partially due, of course, to the fact that the peasants
were paid so poorly when they sold their henequen leaves to the
factories). The federal government finally chose to take over the entire
industry rather than use the huge sums that were paid to finance this

venture on other projects, such as irrigation of the dry Yucatecan soil, which could have made the land more suitable for growing other crops. The government could have invested money in the fledgling cattle and fish industries and let the henequen industry subside of its own accord to a part of the state's economy that the internal and international market could have supported.

Whatever it could have done as an overall development plan for the state became secondary when the decision to buy the factories was made, thus pledging even more government support and commitment to a dying industry. In fact, in 1965, little over a year after the purchase, the new director of Cordemex began building a new factory which was to combine most of the business handled previously in the decentralized Cordemex, thus throwing out most of the equipment so expensively purchased. If there was any question about the worth of the machines before, this action would seem to put the lie to any pretentions of value. The new factory, of course, represented a tremendous investment, which has, as of today, kept the peasants producing henequen at twenty-five pesos a week to support its machines, thus continuing an outmoded and impoverished way of life.

Hypotheses four and five, dealing with corruption as a dehumanizing force, rather than a humanizing force in modernizing authoritarian systems, and leading to cynicism rather than building party loyalty, can really be combined, since "the system" and "the party" are so closely linked together that any "humanizing" of the system would probably reverberate in increased party loyalty while any disillusionment with the system would be inseparable from decreased party allegiance.

In Yucatan the pervasiveness of corruption at the state level has disillusioned citizens about the efficacy of national politics since the distinction between the state and federal politics is not clearly drawn, nor should it be. Several factors have contributed towards a general disillusionment with the government, on the part of the peasants, who still constitute over 50 percent of the population. First, there is an ever increasing debt which each *ejido* incurs through the subsidies which it receives from the government. Since the Mexican government insists that these subsidies be handled as loans, rather than welfare, it is not unusual to find *ejido* organizations with debts mounting to two and three million pesos. To the peasant who earns twenty-five pesos a week, this sum is totally unreal and is seen, quite correctly, as a burden which keeps him in thralldom to the politicians, rather than a legal debt to be repaid.[23]

Second, revolutionary rhetoric has promised the peasant much.

When he realizes that he has received little or nothing from the revolution he is bound to be disillusioned. These frustrations with official authority are compounded by PRI officials who blame the corruption of their predecessors for the state in which the peasants find themselves presently. The government has, in many ways, harmed itself, for now when bureaucrats try to initiate new programs, the peasants are markedly unenthusiastic.

The upper class, of course, is more aware of the realities of corruption, for they themselves are the corruptors. While they will often vote for the PRI because their economic futures depend on it, they are openly cynical about the party among themselves.

The upper, middle, and lower classes have, in fact, been atomized by the high level of corruption in the state. Because contacts are so important and because the civic culture is so full of cynicism about the motives of political and bureaucratic leaders at all levels, there is much intraclass fighting. Members of the upper class are still bitter about the 1964 transaction with the federal government because they feel that some owners did much better than others. The middle class tends to withdraw into itself rather than participate in politics or civic activities. Even the peasants fight with each other on their *ejidos*. Rather than viewing some idealized vision of peasant life when one visits a Yucatecan *ejido*, one is often faced with warring camps of *ejido* dwellers, each supporting different members for elections to *ejido* office, and thus access to official favors. Such an atmosphere does not inspire books about "nationalism" in Yucatan. The most famous recent book about the state was entitled, "Genocide in Yucatan."[24]

Hypothesis six: Rather than working as an expansive force, the institutionalization of corruption in modernizing authoritarian societies works as a conserving force, allowing for some economic development without any great need for extensive distribution of wealth; since only the wealthy can bribe, only a very small portion of the population is in a position to demand economic satisfaction.

Some development has taken place in Yucatan. Government investment, particularly in tourism, has expanded the state's economy. In 1970, 65 percent of the state was urban, 35 percent rural, while in 1960, 59.8 percent was urban, 40.2 percent was rural. In 1970, 73.8 percent of the population was literate, while only 69.6 percent were literate in 1960. In 1970, 41.7 percent of the houses had water available either inside or outside of the houses (the figure ran to little over 16 percent in 1960) and 29.7 percent of the houses had sewage facilities in 1970 as against 17.6 percent ten years previously. In 1970, 20.4 percent of the homes had radio and television and 44.9 percent of the homes had only radios. The figures in 1960 were 0.1 percent of the homes with radio and television and 24 percent of the homes with radio.

Nevertheless, emphasis on the tourist industry has failed to change the basic economic structure of the state, since much of the capital for this has come from international hotel associations with little commitment to overall Yucatecan development. The problem of poverty still remains the major problem of the state. According to the 1970 census, 36.9 percent of the workers made less than 200 pesos a month, while another 34.5 percent earned 200–500 pesos a month. This means that 71.4 percent of the population are barely earning a living (more than one member of a family may work, of course, which undoubtedly brings the family income up higher).[25] Sixteen point five percent of the population earned 500–900 pesos, 5.7 percent 1000–1499, 3.2 percent earned 1500–2499, 1.8 percent earned 2500–4900 pesos, and 0.7 percent earned 5000–9900 pesos, and 0.7 percent earned 10,000 pesos or more. Of the group earning 199 pesos or less, 79.2 percent were in agriculture, 7.8 percent in services, and 5.4 percent in manufacturing industries. Of the group earning from 200–500 pesos a month, 63.3 percent were in agriculture, 9.6 percent in manufacturing, and 8.9 percent in services. At the opposite end of the scale, of the group earning over 10,000 pesos, 32.7 percent were in agriculture (a surprising figure for a state which theoretically underwent a vast land reform), 21.9 percent were in manufacturing. These figures indicate that in both agriculture and manufacturing there is a large group of very poorly paid workers, and a very small group of wealthy owners.[26]

More graphic still are the figures on the eating habits of the Yucatecans: 15.9 percent of the state's population had not eaten any meat during the week before the 1970 census was taken, 20.6 percent had eaten meat once; 19.8 percent of the population had consumed no eggs, 15.6 percent had eaten eggs once; 52.8 percent of the population had consumed no milk, 7.9 percent had had milk once during the previous week; 56.8 percent of the population had eaten no fish, 28.8 percent had eaten fish once.

The evidence from the wage structure and consumption patterns seems to indicate that there is still a hard core of perhaps 50–60 percent of the population who are very poor, a group for whom figures on radios and televisions are irrelevant.[27] This group comes mainly from the agricultural areas. Although the federal government has indicated that it wishes to change the agricultural base of the henequen zone to vegetables, fruits, and cattle raising, it had, until 1970, spent nothing on irrigation. The most that the federal government has done so far in this area is to give credit to individual *ejidos* to build underground wells *(cenotes)* and to provide seeds for planting, often from international organization donations. They have also provided some amount of technical assistance. All of these measures have been only the smallest percentage of what is actually needed.

As far as demanding economic satisfaction, the peasants receive much more rhetoric than material goods and seem to be unable to organize on their own behalf at this time. Those few peasants who are more ambitious can usually attain some party office, either in the *ejido* itself, where they may accept small bribes from other *ejido* members when they are distributing the work load within the collective farm, or they may attain some minor party office in the Merida offices of PRI, which gives them the longed-for status over other members of the *ejido*. The lower middle class can also be silenced with minor bureaucratic jobs, while middle-class businessmen are often frightened into submission. It is really only the small upper class, with previous knowledge of privilege, and a few "upstarts" that have demanded larger profits as the price for co-optation. The demands on government for more effective administration are therefore quite limited and particularistic, and it is able to meet them without fundamentally changing the social or economic system.

Hypothesis seven: The institutionalization of corruption in modernizing authoritarian regimes may provide a very stable climate of investment for knowledgeable entrepreneurs and bureaucrats. So long as they know that nepotism, bribery, and graft are usable expedients in the market of government favors, they probably see little need for Swiss bank accounts.

The profits that were made from the sale of Cordemex have been reinvested in the Mexican economy rather than spent in Europe or deposited in banks. The Mexican businessman seems confident in the future and ready to invest in Mexico.[28] Much of the money, however, left the state itself and was reinvested in neighboring states where labor and climatic conditions as well as general economic opportunities were better.

Did corruption work as a force for economic development? If economic development is defined as the "better use of natural and human resources, changes in the structure of an economy, and the enhanced capacity to increase production through the savings and investment process"[29] the selling of Cordemex and distribution of profits to those who already had money does not better utilize natural or human resources, although it may change the structure of the economy eventually by adding more industry through reinvestment. It is a fact, though, that new industries are often capital rather than labor intensive and that the problems of unemployment and underemployment are not solved by taking capital from a labor intensive industry like henequen cultivation and reinvesting in mechanized bottling plants. In this regard, only the federal government can really take the responsibility of switching out of the henequen industry to yet another labor intensive industry, which in Yucatan will probably mean a more profitable cash crop, such as tropical fruits or vegetables.

To conclude, it is a mistake to view corruption as a temporary stage along the road to development, or as a social service agency, or as benefiting the most efficient, in countries where organized public opinion is low and organized political competition either nonexistent or severely limited. Under the latter conditions, the persistence of political corruption reinforces the unequal distribution of political and economic power within the society. Through a network of personal connections and bribes, old elites become new elites and members of the disadvantaged classes either stay where they are born or, as happens to the more ambitious individuals, are co-opted by the upper classes into a cynical use of the political process for personal rather than group gains.

Scholars who argue that the economy must expand in order to keep the country from exploding underestimate the force of inertia and divisiveness on the part of the poor and the ability of an even half-developed economy to keep 20–30 percent of the country living comfortably. Indeed, Mexico has one of the highest growth rates in Latin America, yet "those families in the bottom two or three deciles have clearly lost ground relatively, and perhaps absolutely, since the beginning of the Mexican 'miracle.' "[30]

There is no trickle-down theory in countries without the gravitational pull of economic and political competition. In a political system such as Mexico's, wages and social services will only be improved by conscious decisions on the part of government officials. The persistence of corruption inhibits such decisions from being made.

Notes

1. Although there are many definitions of "corruption," Rogow and Lasswell's definition of corruption as referring to "behavior in office that is motivated by a desire for personal material gain," or Huntington's "corruption is behavior of public officials which deviates from accepted norms in order to serve private ends," are broad enough to cover the general institutions of nepotism, spoils, and graft which will be referred to here. Arnold A. Rogow and Harold D. Lasswell, *Power, Corruption and Recti-*

tude (New Jersey: Prentice-Hall, 1963), p. 2; Samuel P. Huntington, *Political Order in Changing Societies* (New Haven: Yale University Press, 1968), p. 59.

2. Huntington, ibid.

3. Nathaniel H. Leff, "Economic Development Through Bureaucratic Corruption," *American Behavioral Scientist,* VIII, 3 (November, 1964), 10–12 passim.

4. David H. Bayley, "The Effects of Corruption in a Developing Nation," *Western Political Quarterly,* XIX, 4 (December, 1966), 726–29. Bayley also lists negative effects of corruption such as a rise in the cost of administration, a failure to achieve the objectives that the government sought when it established criteria for decisions of various classes, and a lowering of respect for constitutional authority (pp. 724–26). His article is more a balance sheet on corruption than an article approving it. Huntington, on the other hand, comes out as far more tolerant of corruption.

5. A distinction should be made between the effects of political corruption and the effects of bureaucratic corruption. Political corruption, in the form of the buying and selling of votes, the letting of patronage, and the doing of favors, usually has the end of building party cadres and political machines which will, in turn, support ambitious politicians in their search for power and, perhaps, glory. Bureaucratic corruption, or the passing of bribes or favors from private hands to public hands in order to obtain a governmental prerogative for private gain, does not have a political purpose at all, but is for the enrichment of the corruptor and the corrupted at the expense, usually, of the public. While political corruption may actively involve the public in voting or other activities, bureaucratic corruption tries to exclude the general public to the greatest degree possible.

6. In this connection, John King's article on the vote in England provides a fascinating example of how standards of civic duty gradually replaced the old manorial prerogatives in England. John King, "Socioeconomic Development and the Incidence of English Corrupt Campaign Practices," in Arnold Heidenheimer, ed., *Political Corruption* (New York: Holt, Rinehart and Winston, Inc., 1970), p. 385.

7. James C. Scott, "Corruption, Machine Politics, and Political Change," reprinted in *Political Corruption,* op. cit., p. 551.

8. Carl Friedrich asserts that corruption in authoritarian regimes has the effect of creating what an economist might say is a kind of market for the services of government officials where a monocratic (monopolistic) control has existed before. Carl Friedrich, *The Pathology of Politics* (New York: Harper and Row, 1972), p. 135.

9. For example, Roger Hansen, *The Politics of Mexican Development* (Baltimore: Johns Hopkins Press, 1971); Frank R. Brandenberg, *The Making of Modern Mexico* (New Jersey: Prentice-Hall, Inc. 1964).

10. Hansen, op. cit., pp. 122–23. Also, Interview with Victor Cervera Pacheco, present mayor of Merida, July 17, 1971.

11. In 1960, Yucatan had 614,000 inhabitants, 59.8 percent of the population living in cities of over 2500, 40.2 percent living in rural areas. The high urban percentage is partially due to the draw which Merida, the capital city, with 170,834 inhabitants has for the rest of the state. In 1960, the breakdown of the economically active population was: primary sector 59.8

percent, industry 15.5 percent, commerce 9.5 percent, transportation 2.9 percent, services 8.5 percent, and others 3.6 percent. Although the value of industrial production in Yucatan almost doubled in current prices from 1950–1960, the number of persons employed by industry actually declined from 27,461 in 1950 to 24,014 in 1960. During this ten-year period the value of industrial production in the rest of Mexico almost trebled and the number of persons employed in industrial activities rose by 45 percent. It is evident, therefore, that Yucatan has fallen behind in comparison to the rest of the country in terms of industrial development.

The main product of the state is the cultivation and manufacture of henequen and its by-products. Henequen is a type of cactus from which a fiber can be extracted which is then manufactured into such products as binder twine and other cord products. It is well suited to the dry rocky climate around Merida and what is designated by the Mexican Labor Bureau as Economic Zone no. 109, "Yucatan Henequenero." (Merida and Progresso are designated Zone 108, while the agricultural-forest zone is Zone 110). In 1969, 70.6 percent of the state's population resided in Merida and the henequen zone. The cultivation of henequen represented 98.2 percent and 87.8 percent of the value of all agricultural production in these areas respectively, while the defibrication and cleaning of the plants as well as the production of by-products from henequen represented over 65 percent of the total industrial production there, and over 57 percent of total industrial value for the entire state. The only other industry of any export importance was wood products from the forest zone of the state. (Comision Nacional de los Salârios Minimos, *Descripciones Geograficas Economicas de las Zonas,* Mexico, 1964, pp. 608–65.)

12. Enrique Manero Suarez, "La Anarquia Henequenera de Yucatan," *Diario de Yucatan,* July 3, 1966.

13. Between 1920 and 1930, the Comision Nacional Agraria in Mexico City passed over 200 resolutions dividing the land of Yucatan. At one time, more than 35,000 hectares in the henequen zone were scheduled for division. At the special request of President Ortiz Rubio, this measure was put aside until further studies had been made. In the meantime, organizations of the henequen dealers bombarded the government with alternate plans of ways to distribute the land. This turbulent period of history led to a general decadence in production as the agrarian laws which were passed by the federal government were spasmodically enforced and profits fell due to competition from fibers grown in Africa, Java, and Brazil. In 1916, 300,000 hectares of land grew 1,000,000 pacas of henequen on 1,000 haciendas employing 60,000 workers. By 1937 only 600 haciendas were left. These employed 25,000 workers on 130,000 hectares and produced only 60,000 pacas of henequen. (Suarez, op. cit.)

14. In 1937 Cardenas enacted his far-reaching land reform which left no more than 150 hectares of henequen land to the old *hacendados* and also expropriated their defibricating machinery and railroads. The latter was used to transport the henequen leaves from the interior of the plantations to the defibricating machinery which would then take the necessary fiber from the leaves. The railroads and machinery were to be acquired by the *ejidos* (communally held farms) which were formed from the old haciendas. Cardenas projected that 74 percent of the land would be distributed in

the form of *ejidos* and 24.5 percent for the *pequenos proprietarios*. The system failed, however, mainly because of the inequality of the holdings given to the *ejidos*. Some were already producing henequen while others needed large sums of money to rectify the decadence that had set in previous to the distribution or to hold them over until the plants began the producing stage of their seven-year cycle. In the meantime, the Supreme Court of Justice rendered a decision in favor of the *hacendados* who had sued on the grounds that land reform should not include movable property. The latter were returned to the original owners who charged the *ejidatarios* so much money for processing their leaves that the prerevolutionary class system stayed much the same. State authorities did not regulate the prices charged for these services at the time. (Suarez, op. cit.)

15. Mario Menendez Rodriguez, *Yucatan o el Genocidio* (Mexico: D.F. Fondo de Cultura Popular, 1964), passim.
16. Op. cit.
17. Lic. Alfredo Patron Arjona, *Diario de Yucatan,* July 27, 1962.
18. The Fondo Nacional de Fomento Ejidal is a national development corporation for the *ejidos*.
19. Interview with Lic. Nicolas Gutierrez Pinkus, Director of the Departamento Administrativo, Cordemex, July 21, 1967.
20. Interview with Miquel Enriquez Olea, Director of Cordemex, July 20, 1968.
21. Mario Menendez Rodriguez, op. cit. pp. 209–300. Also, Mario Menendez, "El gram Fraude Agrario," *Sucesos* (March 4, 1967), p. 17.
22. Field Research in Yucatan, 1968 and 1970.
23. Field Research, 1970.
24. On the same theme, a study of the political life in the city of Jalapa, Mexico, concludes that "those who have actually had contact with politics and public officials are the most negative of all" (about the ability to effect government decisions). "This is not a dynamic that leads one to be optimistic about the part played by participation in forming positive orientations toward the political process." Richard Fagen and William Tuohy, *Politics and Privilege in a Mexican City* (Palo Alto, California: Stanford University Press, 1972) p. 114.
25. The 24,014 persons employed in industrial activities in Yucatan in 1960 received a total of 123.2 million pesos as wages and as salaries. The average monthly remuneration for industrial workers in the state was therefore 428 pesos. This compared with an average monthly remuneration of 824 pesos for industrial workers throughout Mexico. A report of the Mexican government Minimum Wage Commission states that the minimum salary was insufficient to meet even basic necessities. Outside of Merida, agriculture becomes the prime mode of existence. In the henequen zone, 86 percent of the people were employed in agricultural pursuits. The average monthly pay for these workers was 245 pesos a month, well below the national average of 675. In the agricultural-forest zone, 77.5 percent of the population were employed in agriculture. The average monthly earnings for these people was 336 pesos. (Comision Nacional de los Salarios Minimos, *Descripciones Geograficas Economicas de las Zonas,* Mexico, 1964, pp. 608–65.)
26. These and other statistics on Yucatan were gathered from the following

sources: (1) Estudio Economico de Yucatan y Programa de Trabajo, Yucatan, Mexico, 1961; (2) Censo General de Poblacion, 1960, Estados Unicos Mexicanos, Secretaria de Industria y Comercio, Direccion General de Estadistica; (3) Censo General de Poblacion, 1970. Estados Unicos Mexicanos, Secretaria de Industria y Comercio, Direccion General de Estadistica.

27. It is difficult to divide Yucatan by classes in exact numbers, but it can be safely said that the upper class is extremely small. Using a cost of living index composed by the national commission on minimum salaries, based on a 2,000 calorie diet, and minimum standards of housing and clothing, the minimum daily expenses per family in 1961 came to 14.72 pesos although the nominal minimum wage in 1961 was only 13.25 pesos. Basing estimates on a minimum wage of 13.25 which is unrealistic since this is rarely paid in the countryside where there is high unemployment and the minimum wage is not usually enforced, times 31 days in a month, monthly costs for a minimum standard of living comes to 410.75 pesos. From the figures above, it can be said that outside of Merida, probably 80 percent of the people are not earning this amount, whereas in Merida, perhaps 50–60 percent are not. Judging from salary levels quoted and statistics on such amenities as sewage, electricity, and television, it can be judged that perhaps 70–80 percent of the population belong to the "popular class," another 15–20 percent to the middle class, and no more than about 5 percent to the upper class.

28. Martin Greenberg, *Bureaucracy and Development* (Lexington, Massachusetts: D. C. Heath and Co., 1970) states much the same theory. One of the functions of bureaucracy in Mexico, according to his analysis, is to serve as potential capital investors (pp. 52–55.)

29. Hansen, op. cit., p. 43.

30. Hansen, op. cit., p. 83.

Business, Governments, and Transnational Corruption: An Introduction

Corruption in international business became an important concern during the 1970s. The international activities of corporations such as Lockheed and Gulf Oil, to name but two, contributed to significant scandals in western Europe and Japan. These and other episodes raised fundamental questions about the ethical aspects of international business in an age of increasing interdependence among nations. Compounding the problems were recent developments in international business. The deals at stake are increasingly large, and the goods being traded are more and more expensive and sophisticated (as in the case of weapons, for example) and indispensible to continued economic growth (as in the case of strategic commodities). Technology and competition have increased the pace of business dealings manyfold; stock, currency, and commodities markets are in effect open twenty-four hours a day, working at computer speeds.

The issue of just who can and should police international trade is a complex one as well: multinationals operate in many countries at once, moving capital and operations more quickly than policymakers and regulators can act. The list of nations involved includes many poor and developing countries which can be critically dependent upon, and politically and economically weak compared to, huge multinational enterprises. Moreover, many "businesses" are in fact extensions of state-owned and subsidized productive enterprises; attempts to regulate their behavior by invoking the power of the state amounts to a request of the participants in international trade that they somehow regulate and restrain themselves.

In the first selection, Susan Rose-Ackerman argues that public sector and private sector corruption ought not be considered as if they existed in separate contexts. Rather, analysis which disaggregates the complexities in both areas—for example, a focus on organizational behavior and opportunities and incentives for corruption—can suggest whether the two sectors are similar, or not. There may be situations where, unlike those faced by high-level government officials, executives in private firms may find low-level corruption will benefit both managers and share-holders. In such cases, the executives may close their eyes to the corrupt activities, and even organize their firms to take advantage of them. Where, however, private sector corruption involves conflicts of interest between owners and managers, or high- and low-level employees (situations analogous to some aspects of legislative and bureaucratic corruption), the firm's responses may vary according to the degree to which it has institutionalized mechanisms of control and accountability. Public bodies and officials, being more accountable to voters, constituencies, and the law, may not have that flexibility.

Victor LeVine, in chapter 40, begins with an analysis of the upsurge in international bribery over the past fifteen years. Despite some long-standing standards of ethics, international trade has always gone on in an environment of high stakes and few rules. But LeVine identifies some of the more recent developments which have exacerbated the international bribery problem, including the entrance of new actors on the international scene such as a host of new states and multinational corporations, the appearance of super-valued commodities (armaments, oil, etc.), and a climate of extraordinary competition in the international marketplace. The result was a series of embarassing transnational political scandals implicating presidents, prime ministers, royalty, and other high personages. The US government not only sought to curb the corrupt activities of the US MNCs—through the federal Foreign Corrupt Practices Act (FCPA)—but to persuade other states to follow suit with respect to *their* multinationals. Though the FCPA generated no foreign analogs, the whole series of episodes did have a chastening effect on the international marketplace and its participants.

Michael Rosenthal augments LeVine's analysis by discussing the origins of FCPA. A diverse group of participants brought the law into being, Rosenthal argues, and their motives and methods were partially conflicting and contradictory. The result is legislation which is at times vague, and whose implementation and enforcement are uncertain. The law also drew its political impetus from the post-Watergate era, when corruption in international trade was seen as a particularly significant problem. But only a few years after the law's enactment, that climate had changed: corruption as an issue attracted considerably less attention. In its place was a deep concern over American competitiveness in the world economy, and a political mood which offered much less support to governmental interference into the doings of business. FCPA legislation, and other efforts to fight international bribery, thus face an uncertain future.

39

Corruption and The Private Sector

Susan Rose-Ackerman

While political scientists have not hesistated to use moral convictions, patriotism, and devotion to duty to explain the behavior of government officials and private citizens, economists have often assumed that the behavior of private firms can be explained without appeals to "higher" values. Even economists who recognize serious market failures and inequities in the distribution of income and wealth tend to seek structural solutions or changes in government taxing and spending policies, rather than reforms of the educational process or modifications of cultural values. My study of corruption, for example, has been concerned with corrupt *opportunities* and with ways to change structures to reduce *incentives*. More generally, economists are uncomfortable with public programs that exhort consumers to make private sacrifices for collective goals or call on businessmen to recognize their social responsibilities.

Despite this discomfort, the profession commonly works with models that assume that law abiding behavior is the norm. Although the responsibility of profit-seeking organizations has long been recognized in the literature of industrial organization and public finance, it is generally assumed that if a law is passed regulating behavior, no one will violate its provisions (for exceptions see Buchanan and Tullock, 1975; Roberts, 1976). Government intervention may distort behavior, but the simple expedients of corrupting the inspector or juggling the books are seldom part of the analysis.

Research on crime (Becker, 1968; Stigler, 1970), fraud (Darby and Karni, 1973), smuggling (Bhagwati, 1974), organized crime (Schelling, 1967), and corruption make clear, however, that illegal behavior will often be in the interest of both individuals and profit-making firms.

Source: Susan Rose-Ackerman, *Corruption: A Study in Political Economy*. New York; Academic Press, 1978, Chapter ten. By permission of author and publisher. Copyright © 1978 by Wellesley College.

Similarly, it will not always be in an individual's interest to follow the rules laid down by superiors. Research on the problems of control in large organizations has emphasized the frequent conflicts of interest between managers and employees or principals and agents (Alchian and Demsetz, 1972: Lebenstein, 1966; Williamson, 1967). Thus it is only necessary to juxtapose research on the economics of crime with analyses of the problems of organizational control to generate an inquiry that threatens the legitimacy of the private business corporation. It is easy to see that corporations single-mindedly concerned with profit maximization will choose an "optimal" amount of fraud or corruption (Banfield, 1975; Darby and Karni, 1973). Some illegal behavior will be encouraged because it increases profits, and other behavior will be tolerated because it is too costly to eliminate. Furthermore, since the illegal behavior of agents, employees, or top management will generally impose external costs on others, it is unlikely that the firm's optimizing decision will be socially optimal under anyone's definition of social welfare. If the opportunities for illegal behavior are widespread in modern business firms, the corporation may only be justified if peopled by individuals who do not take advantage of all opportunities to benefit at the expense of shareholders, top managers, or the public. It follows that economists cannot afford to look askance at those social scientists who are concerned with individual values. The economist's own models are deeply embedded in a set of often unstated assumptions about human values, and many of the normative claims for the market are fundamentally dependent upon the assumption that economic actors will not break the law.

Fortunately, I can discuss the limits of market institutions without having to develop a completely new analytic structure. My models of organizational behavior and of the opportunities for corruption in government can be modified to apply to a study of the private sector. To see this, I look at two aspects of corporate behavior. First, . . . I will consider cases where, unlike high-level government officials, executives in private business firms face situations in which low-level corruption will further the aims of both top management and shareholders. Executives and owners may want to save face and escape legal liability by avoiding direct knowledge of corruption, but they may wish to organize their firms to facilitate its occurrence. Second, [I will] consider other forms of private-sector corruption that involve a conflict of interest between owners and directors or managers, or between high- and low-level employees. There are, nevertheless, some important differences caused by the fact that stockholders and voters do not have identical means of controlling officials whom they elect and by the distinction between competitive pressures and the accountability of bureaucrats.

Private Firm Organization and Corruption

Beginning with the first theme of "profitable" corruption, one can easily see that although a company's stockholders and managers will wish to prevent situations where employees or agents *accept* bribes in return for price discounts on sales or price premiums on purchases, they may not wish to know about cases in which their sales personal *pay* bribes to obtain lucrative deals.[1] This corruption, of course, need not necessarily involve the bribery of government officials. As many wholly private activities produce corrupt incentives analogous to those which exist in the public sector.

A firm's internal organization may reflect the desire to facilitate low-level corruption. Executives may delegate responsibility and avoid close monitoring in order to create an environment hospitable to corruption.[2] They may satisfy legal mandates by issuing directives that exhort employees to obey the law,[3] but fail to follow these orders up with surveillance activities or with promotion policies that reward law-abiding behavior. Instead of monitoring the day-to-day activity of subordinates, managers may simply use output measures such as sales, market shares, or profit margins to evaluate their inferiors.[4] Indeed, a firm may go further and purchase the services of independent entrepreneurs to do the firm's dirty work rather than hiring them as employees. The outsider provides specialized contacts with decision makers or expedited service through a government bureaucracy, and the seller asks no questions about how the service was performed. The use of agents illustrates the role of market transactions in *reducing* information flow, a factor ignored in standard economic discussion, which typically assume that managers always benefit from more accurate information.[5]

Agents are commonly used as buffers in international business (Jacoby, Nehemkis, and Eells, 1977: Weiss, 1975:66–67). For example, the Northrop Corporation used the Economic Development Corporation [EDC], established by a Northrop consultant, to promote the sales of Northrop aircraft to Iran. "Northrop agreed to pay EDC a commission equal to a percentage of all aircraft sales to Iran, and later extended the agreement to cover sales to other countries. According to a report prepared by Northrop's auditors, 'the company is not interested in knowing how EDC operates, and who they are in touch with, but can only measure the benefit of EDC by sales that occur' [quoted in

Weiss, 1975:67]." Similarly, in New York City the construction industry uses agents as expediters to obtain government permits and inspections (*New York Times,* June 27, 1972); and shipping company executives avoid knowledge of payoffs made to the International Longshoremen's Association by using outside agents. The president of a shipping company told a reporter "We have no direct dealings with labor at all. We have a contractual price with certain companies to load and unload our cargoes. What they do with the money is their business, not ours [*New York Times,* September 1, 1977]."

The use of outsiders can also be beneficial for reasons unrelated to their ability to isolate businessmen from unpleasant truths. Professional middlemen are likely to have more bargaining power vis à vis bureaucrats than individual firms. Indeed, individuals engaged in what is often called organized crime are sometimes used as middlemen because of their willingness to use violence if politer forms of criminal behavior are unsatisfactory.[6] The level of bribes may be reduced by threats of violence while legitimate businessmen isolate themselves from both the corruption and the violence and earn high profits as a consequence. The cost in this case is the fear that the threats may be turned against businessmen who try to extricate themselves from their underworld connections. Even more genteel outside agents, however, may be superior to employees. Officials who demand high bribes can be told by the middlemen that they will bring no further business if concessions are not forthcoming, and a bureaucrat who threatens to report a corrupt offer can be deterred by the professional's threat to expose the official's previous indiscretions. Thus there appear to be "economies of scale" in bribe paying that favor its production by a few specialists.[7]

A firm which isolates itself from its salesmen by making them independent entrepreneurs rather than employees, however, may increase a second type of risk—the risk that agents will not serve their client's interests. On the one hand, the salesman may demand high fees, claiming that they are needed to pay bribes, when in fact these payments are simply pocketed by the middleman.[8] On the other hand, the salesman may sell out to the firm's customers through reverse bribery, agreeing to a low selling price for the firm's product in return for a direct payment from the buyer. Empirical work is needed, however, to determine whether outsiders are in fact more difficult to control than insiders. One suspects that the nature of a firm's business will be more important than its formal relationship with its salesmen in determining the ease of monitoring.

Because of the costs of control, business executives will often be placed in the awkward position of trusting agents to engage only in those illegal activities that benefit the company. Yet in order to assure performance of the corrupt bargain, agents on both sides may well develop close personal relationships, especially if they meet frequently to transact business. Thus agents might, under these conditions, decide to collude to favor themselves at the expense of both principals. Firms may have to put up with some counterproductive cheating in order to avoid having to monitor and punish corruption which benefits the organization.

There is one important case, however, where firms will not have to worry about corruption that damages their profit position. When a firm faces a monopolistic seller or a monopsonist buyer, it knows that an honest transaction will be on terms unfavorable to the company. Management expects that honest transactions will imply high input prices or low output prices. Since honest transactions are likely to be costly to the firm, corruption has at least some chance of improving the firm's position. Firms in this situation are therefore very similar to those trying to obtain a favorable place in line from a single official. . . . The firm's agents have nothing of value to provide except for a bribe or kickback which can induce the monopolist's agents to soften their demands. It follows that in this situation *competitive* firms have a stronger incentive to facilitate low-level corruption than those with market power.[9]

A striking case, which illustrates this point as well as the danger that agents will exploit their positions for personal gain, came to light in the New York City supermarket industry. The industry faces a monopsonistic supplier of labor—the Amalgamated Meat Cutters and Retail Food Stores Employees Union. Supermarkets are reported to have made payments to a middleman who in turn paid union officials to assure labor peace.[10] Some unknown proportion of these funds was kept by the middleman. More important, however, this agent apparently used his influence within the union as a way of inducing supermarket chains to use him as their meat wholesaler. Those who did not buy meat through him were threatened with labor troubles. His ability to blunt the monopoly power of one input (labor) permitted him to obtain monopoly power over another input (meat). He further cemented his monopoly position by paying kickbacks to supermarket executives who bought meat through his company. Finally, his control over meat wholesaling in New York permitted him to obtain payoffs from suppliers of beef. One large Middle Western beef processor paid large sums to this agent in return for being able to sell in the New York area without incurring union opposition. The company wished to carry out many butchering activities in the Middle West, thus reducing the shipping costs of the beef but also reducing the work available to New York butchers. While this might seem a classic case of compensating those who lose from a technological innovation, there is no evidence that the butchers themselves received any benefits (*Wall Street Journal,* September 10, 11, 1974; *New York Times,* March 14, 26, and October 8, 1974).

Such complex systems of kickbacks and payoffs, however, appear to be relatively uncommon. Instead, in a wide range of situations, management is likely to believe that the possibility of disloyal agents or the risk of scandal is high. They may then respond to the problem of corruption in a radically different way: They may try to reorganize their business so that no corrupt incentives exist. [It has been] suggested that bribery in government contracting could be eliminated by direct public production of a good or service that had been purchased corruptly in the past. This strategy of vertical integration can also be used by private firms. They may do this by merging with corruptible organizations or by hiring the individuals offering corrupt inducements or demanding bribe payments. Thus nursing homes have eliminated the kickbacks paid for pharmaceuticals by merging with druggists (U.S. Congress, Senate, 1975), and firms can hire people with inside information about competitors (Henn, 1970:460) instead of paying for their services. Labor union demands, such as those faced by supermarket owners, cannot be solved by merger, however. The only alternative for a firm may be to move to a part of the country where corrupt unions are not as powerful. This is, of course, not possible for industries dependent upon large concentrations of population (like supermarkets) or particular geographical or geological features (like ocean shippers or the mining industry).

Many instances of corruption by business firms, however, involve payments to government officials in return for favorable regulatory treatment, tax relief, or direct transfer payments or loans. Full legal merger between a firm and a government agency as a substitute for obtaining special favors amounts to nationalization of the company. So long as the firm's owners can affect the level of compensation paid by the government, mergers of this type may be sought by unprofitable business firms.[11] In other cases, however, less extreme strategies that amount to a partial and short-run merger of a firm and a government are possible. Thus there are many examples of key executives holding political offices that help them aid their firms' fortunes. In Latin America some politicians are directly involved in the illegal drug trade, and in the early days of railroading, executives obtained government financing and assistance for their firms by serving as public officials.[12] Today it remains common in the United States for local politics to attract building contractors and merchants with a stake in city decisions.[13] Similarly, executives may seek to establish friendships with key bureaucrats either by having friends or relatives appointed or by establishing personal ties with those already in office. This strategy could be so successful that officials perform favors out of friendship rather than for monetary gain. Conflict-of-interest laws and civil service reforms prevent the most flagrant examples of mergers of this type, but cases can still be found of federal contracts awarded to firms that have members of Congress as part owners or of politicans favoring family business interests.[14]

The Corruption of Corporate Boards and Top Managers

[It has been] assumed that a firm's managers wished to maximize profits and that toleration of low-level corruption might be one way to accomplish that goal. There is no need, however, to assume that mangements and boards of directors are single-mindedly interested in furthering stockholder interests. Just as legislators may sell out voters, corporate directors may sell out stockholders; just as corrupt top bureaucrats may exploit the discretionary power given them by non-market forms of regulation, so too may private managers exploit imperfections in the market mechanism that generate corrupt opportunities. Thus, many of the factors that were important in explaining legislative and high level bureaucratic corruption may have close parallels in the activities of private firms and nonprofit organizations.

To begin at the highest corporate level, boards of directors are often elected by a group of voters more numerous than many political constituencies. It is generally believed, however, that the election of directors by shareholders is not much of a constraint on board behavior.[15] There are several reasons for this. First, most shareholders have little incentive to amass large amounts of information about corporate performance. Any individual with a diversified portfolio will not be damaged much by the poor performance of a single company. Second, even if a shareholder did uncover evidence indicating that the board was not furthering shareholders' interests, obtaining support from other owners is likely to be costly and difficult. It will usually be a better strategy to keep one's knowlege secret and sell the stock before anyone else finds out. Third, even if shareholders are willing to act, the legal rights of shareholders to control directors' actions appear to be fairly limited. In fact, current doctrine holds that directors should not be thought of as agents or representatives of shareholders but rather as "fiduciaries" whose duties are primarily to the corporation itself.[16] The meaning of this responsibility has, however, never been carefully defined.

From the perspective of corporate democracy, then, the incentives for corruption[17] appear to be high except in closely held corporations where a few shareholders have a major stake in company performance.[18] While accepting kickbacks and profiting personally at the expense of the corporation are clearly not proper actions for a fiduciary,[19] it may be difficult for shareholders to detect such behavior, and very few have an incentive either to undertake the search or to reveal their findings.

There is, however, a second critical check on the corruption of corporate boards not present in government legislatures. Stockholders, unlike voters, need not rely on the ballot box if they are dissatisfied with company policy. They can simply sell their stock; and if potential buyers can also evaluate company performance, the price of the stock will fall. Corruption may be deterred not by the threat of electoral defeat but by the fear of a fall in the market value of the firm followed by a takeover bid from a new group of investors.[20] While similar factors are at work in the public sector, e.g., the fall of New York City bond prices in the face of a threat of bankruptcy,[21] the pressures imposed by fiscal constraints appear generally to be lower for elected representatives than for board members.

In both cases, however, a well-informed public is a critical check on corruption. The major difference here is the ability of legislators and board members to control the flow of information for corrupt purposes. Recall that if politicans had some control over the information provided to voters, they might present blurred and ambiguous stands on the issues, even in the absence of offers of financial support from special interest groups. Creating a rhetorical fog could be the vote-maximizing strategy of an honest legislator, as well as that of one who accepts bribes or campaign contributions from wealthy groups. The same point does not apply in the private corporate sector. The basic reason is that investors do not have widely varying preferences with respect to firm performance. While they may weigh the factors differently, ceteris paribus, everyone wants higher profits, more capital gains, and higher dividends. Thus the board of a firm operating in competitive input and output markets cannot be seriously corrupt since the firm's performance can always be evaluated by comparing it with that of others in the industry. Any loss produced by corruption will cause investors to transfer their money to more profitable operations.

And if a corporate board tries to hide corruption by revealing few facts about company operations, it is unlikely to gain investors, since the suppression of data will be taken as an indication of poor performance. To be successful, then, corruption in a competitive industry may have to be associated with fraud in a way which is often unnecessary in the political sphere.[22]

Turning from private, quasi-legislative bodies like corporate boards, I continue the search for private analogues by looking briefly at the corrupt incentives faced by top executives. Their position is similar to that of the agency heads. . . . High-level managers are restrained from building up personal fortunes, not by the budgetary choices of a political body but by the profitability and growth of the firms under their administrative control. Managers may be fired by corporate boards and their future careers jeopardized if their actions either are illegal or can be associated with a deterioration in the firm's profits. The ease with which corporate boards can evaluate managers' performance conditions the directors' ability to check executives' behavior.[23] Managers will have considerable freedom of action in just those industries where corporate boards are relatively immune from the oversight of market investors. Of course, just as in the political case, the board and the firm's executives may be able to collude for their mutual benefit in the face of a generally poorly informed public. Many cases exist, for example, in which executives and board members have siphoned off funds from failing companies into other business ventures in which they had interests, and bank failures are often caused by risky loans made to bank officials or to their families and friends.[24] A similar situation prevails in the nonprofit sector. If the public has difficulty evaluating the performance of a nonprofit organization, then the board of trustees is likely to have a similar difficulty controlling their executive appointees. Alternatively, collusion between managers and trustees is also possible and seems at least as difficult to control as the analogous problem arising in profit-making businesses.

Market Failure as a Cause of Corruption

While the delegation of authority creates corrupt incentives all the way from boards of directors down to low-level salesmen, some firms will be more corruption prone than others because of the nature of their products. The familiar market failure categories provide a useful way to organize a discussion of how a firm's business produces corrupt opportunities. Thus, scale economies, products which are heterogeneous and technically difficult to evaluate, production or consumption externalities, as well as government regulations can all produce corrupt incentives.

Scale Economies

Simple monopoly power caused by nothing more esoteric than scale economies may provide corrupt incentives. In this case, if corporate boards or managers make deals that benefit themselves at the expense of stockholders, profits do not fall to zero. Returns may still be high enough to attract investors. For example, although evidence is cloudy on the profitability of the Credit Mobilier, the construction company for the Union Pacific Railroad in the 1880s,[25] one of its purposes may have been to divert railroad profits from the Union Pacific to railroad executives (and key politicians) who owed a controlling interest in the construction company (Smith, 1958; White 1895:22–23). Furthermore, if the firm's rate of return is controlled by a regulatory commission, corruption or self-dealing which inflates the rate base will simply increase profits. This may take the form of the purchase of inputs at inflated prices from companies controlled by executives or from firms who pay bribes. . . . Since the inputs must be ones whose true market value is difficult to calculate, real estate rentals and design or research contracts are obvious sources of corrupt incentives. Similarly, large firms under surveillance by the Justice Department for possible anti-trust violations may try to avoid prosecution by keeping profits down. While this may easily lead to inefficient and stagnant operations instead of more vigorous competition, it could also give board members an incentive to convert some of the firm's profits into kickbacks or personalized benefits.

Vagueness, Access, and Inspections

Products are often either one of a kind or of uncertain quality. Here corruption can flourish because no one has a reliable way of measuring a firm's performance. This general characteristic ties together all those who, for instance, do classified work, carry out research, provide artistic or creative products, or run job training programs or nursing homes. Vague standards can also generate corruption on the input side of the market, even for firms producing standardized outputs. A firm may delegate the task of choosing the "best qualified" workers to a personnel director or a trade union official. Those who want jobs may pay to receive employment, and an employee's receipt of a bribe may pass undetected if the rules are vague and general or if all applicants for jobs or access are, in fact, fungible. In the building trades, for example, "walking delegates" used to control the labor supply of their craft. Sam Parks, one such walking delegate, is quoted as saying to a union member in 1903, "I don't care a damn for the union, the president of the union, or the laws of the country. You can go back to work when you pay Sam Parks $2,000 [Hutchinson, 1970:30]." Furthermore, firms themselves may pay union officials to obtain labor at rates below the standard union wage (Hutchinson, 1970, Rottenberg, 1960). A 1952–1953 inquiry in New York showed that officials of the Internationanl Longshoremen's Association distributed jobs on the basis of kickbacks from men and payoffs from employers (*New York Times,* February 13, 1977).

Similarly, many employees—from private guards to executive secretaries—control access to a corporation's buildings and top personnel.[26] Other employees monitor the performance of lower level empoyees or franchisees. Their inspection tasks are little different from those of government housing code or meat inspectors. Thus, employees of Chevrolet who distribute new cars to franchised dealers and oversee warranty work face numerous corrupt incentives. Dealers presented gifts of liquor, turkeys and gift certificates to establish good will and justified their payoffs as a way to obtain some freedom of action. "A guy who went strictly by the book could give you a hell of a time," one dealer lamented (quoted in the *New York Times,* June 15, 1975; the discussion here is based on this article). Other Chevrolet employees, also engaged in large-scale corrupt practices. Fictitious billings for warranty work were certified by Chevrolet inspectors, who were paid bribes or sold automotive parts at large discounts. When these activities came to light, Chevrolet fired all the employees involved. Most of them, however, were quickly hired by sympathetic dealers at increased salaries.

Vagueness and the Nonprofit Sector

In the private sector, corruption is not the exclusive prerogative of profit-oriented business firms. Many nonprofit organizations almost perfectly fit the model of a firm whose outputs are vague and difficult to measure. Charity, hospital care, education, research, and culture all have poorly defined quality and quantity dimensions. It has been argued, however, that where information on outputs is hard to obtain the nonprofit label is used as a way of indicating that high-quality services are, in fact, being provided by a selfless, altruistic group of people.[27] There are two difficulties with this inference. On the one hand, altruism may not be sufficient to produce high-quality output. Benevolence can easily be associated with inefficiency or ignorance. On the other hand, the nonprofit form is not a guarantee that an organization's founders are altruistic. Whenever production functions are difficult to observe, those in control of an organization have an incentive to extract corrupt benefits. By taking advantage of a popular presumption that the non-profit label implies benevolent trustees, an organization may instead permit kickbacks or self-dealing schemes that enrich individuals in charge of allotting the organization's funds.[28] The advantage of the nonprofit firm seems to rest on the rather slim reed of trust and on the notion that entrepreneurs select profit-making firms if they are narrowly self-seeking and choose nonprofit organizations if they have altruistic temperaments.

Furthermore, nonprofit firms may also be susceptible to corruption since they are probably less likely to use market signals in choosing inputs or dispensing outputs. For example, admissions committees of private clubs, schools, and colleges determine which applicants to accept; and boards determine who is qualified to receive particular university degrees or occupational certifications.

Externalities

Firms that produce positive or negative externalities in their ordinary course of business may create corrupt incentives if the externalities impose high levels of costs or benefits on a small group or on a single individual or firm. Of course, in these small-numbers cases, where freerider problems are not serious, we might expect a legal negotiated settlement. Even so, if a firm's low-level employees have some independent control over the level of externalities produced, then bribery of these indivduals may substitute for a legal high-level approach. Furthermore, in some businesses the alternative of reaching a high-level bargain may be explicitly prohibited by law or by managerial directives.

Excellent examples of situations where low-level bribery may be used to control externalities are found in the market for information. Although it is frequently bought and sold in private market transactions, information has many of the characteristics of services provided by governments. While the product is one whose technical characteristics cause extensive positive and negative externalities, it is nevertheless provided in private markets operating with widely varying amounts of government regulation. Private entrepreneurs have made a series of compromises in the production and sale of these information services that reflect its complex character. It is, however, not surprising that corrupt incentives are created whenever private firms either "privatize" a good with important external effects or refuse to sell a good for which others are willing to pay.

For example, employees in some portions of the information market are very similar to bureaucrats who control access to a benefit or who can impose costs on selected individuals. Information provided at minimal cost by journalists, disc jockeys, and television reporters to the general public often imposes substantial private benefits and costs on small groups of individuals or firms. Both muckraking accounts of alleged corruption and the free favorable publicity given to some individuals and firms and not to others impose external costs. Nevertheless, the preservation of the freedom of the press implies that a public, negotiated settlement between the media and those they benefit or harm is out of the question.[29]

Some industries are peculiarly dependent upon free publicity to advertise their products. For example, the record industry relies upon the record-playing decisions of radio stations to promote its new releases. Record companies compete for scarce radio time just as customers of a government agency may compete for a bureaucratic output. Recording studios therefore have an incentive to internalize the externalities of broadcasting by merging with radio stations. An alternative to merger, however, is the use of gifts and money to influence radio station employees directly. Thus, four record company officers have been given prison terms for a variety of offenses including payoffs to disc jockeys, music directors, program directors, and other employees (*New York Times,* June 25, 1975, April 13, 1976).

Of course, much of the free publicity provided by the media and by individuals with access to the media is unfavorable. Hence corruption can be used to suppress critical stories. In fact, one could imagine unscrupulous journalists writing exposés in order to extort payoffs. This use of monopoly power is similar to that possessed by the police and administrators of coercive programs. . . . Alternatively, the risk of offering a bribe may be high in these situations because of the risk that the bribe offer will be made part of the unfavorable publicity. Hence, the option of attempting to implicate the muckrakers themselves in scandals in order to discredit their information may be the chosen alternative. Of course, the fear of extortion might here serve the useful purpose of deterring scandalous activities just as effectively as the actual release of news stories. False news may, however, be nearly as damaging as true reports. Since controls on the veracity of news in the United States must confront constitutional guarantees of freedom of the press, extortion can only be effectively checked by the professional ethical codes of journalists.[30] In fact, the failure of journalists to take advantage of the corrupt possibilities offered by their jobs may be a sine qua non for the preservation of the constitutional guarantee.

Secret inside information is analytically close to free publicity. In both cases, an employee of one organization has access to information which can benefit or harm outsiders. While media employees are not supposed to provide information to the *public* on the basis of third party payments, employees with access to research data and trade secrets are not authorized to sell their information to *competitors*. In this latter situation, however, the firm's managers could decide that it was in their interest to license their patents to other firms. Legal, high-level agreements are possible, but are likely to be expensive for licensees. Furthermore, even if licenses are either unavailable or very costly, a firm can avoid outright bribery by hiring employees with inside information. Nevertheless, even given these alternatives, firms may choose to pay insiders for expert knowledge without asking them to change jobs. The hiring alternative will be preferred if the information is not simply a page of formulas but requires knowledge gained from on-the-job training. Corruption may be favored, in spite of its illegality, if the bribing firm expects to use their spy over and over again to communicate the new discoveries of their competitor.[31]

Government Regulation

Finally, payments from one private individual or firm to another can be used to circumvent government regulations. No public official is involved, but the existence of legislation which restricts private transactions creates payoff opportunities. The most common examples of these practices are the black markets and kickbacks which typically accompany price controls and rationing (Schmidt, 1969). It will often be important to distinguish between payoffs to a firm for favored treatment and payoffs which are given to the firm's agents. Thus, on the one hand, government regulation of shipping rates has led shippers with excess capacity to offer illegal rebates to customers. The kickbacks were paid directly from one corporation to another and were equivalent to a price cut (*New York Times,* September 14, 1976). On the other hand, kickbacks paid to purchasing agents are apparently common in the beer and liquor industries. Laws that forbid retailing and wholesaling practices common in other business are circumvented through payoffs. Here agents have often pocketed the payoffs instead of their employers (*Business Week,* March 8, 1976).

The first case has few direct parallels in the public sector and is not even *corruption,* since no agents are involved. It is equivalent to a situation where a firm pays the government treasury for the privilege of supplying a good at a legislatively determined price. The second, is similar to the low-level corruption of government bureaucrats. . . . The main difference is the attitude of the agent's superiors. In contrast to many public sector applications, the employer of the agent who takes a bribe will be no worse off with low-level corruption than if the agent had obeyed the law. Although the purposes of the government regulation are obviously being subverted, neither of the organizations directly involved in the transaction are damaged.

Conclusion: Corrupt Incentives in the Public and Private Sectors

In this chapter I have tried to break the link between corruption and government that mars even some scholarly analyses of the subject. Once this link is made, it is often easy to imagine that one may eliminate corruption simply by ending government involvement in one or another area of economic life. But this point of view idealizes the private sector in an entirely illegitimate way. While it is true that *perfect* competition in *all* markets will prevent corruption, deregulation will almost never lead to the resumption of a market resembling the competitive paradigm. Indeed, many of the market failures that justify government intervention are the very same conditions that generate corruption in the absence of intervention. Thus scale economies, externalities, and products which are unique or of uncertain quality all create incentives for employees to enrich themselves at company expense. Deregulation may simply mean the substitution of a corrupt private official for a corrupt public one. It is not at all obvious that this is much of an achievement.

Indeed, even if the destruction of a governmental program *will* produce a competitive industry, this will not necessarily lead to a reduction in overall corruption. Competition on only one side of the market will not be sufficient to eliminate corrupt incentives if either suppliers or customers have market power. While the discipline of the market will prevent individual employees from benefiting at the expense of the company, a competitive firm might organize itself to facilitate the corruption of the agents of buyers or sellers. In these circumstances, competition may create corrupt incentives that would be absent if the industry could merge into a single firm. The individual firms might bribe for the purpose of making a sale[32] or obtaining a scarce input while a monopoly firm could transact its business through legal market power without the need to pay bribes. In short, the results are in the general tradition of second-best analysis. If the economy is fully competitive, then no corruption can occur. If some of the competitive conditions are violated, however, then changing one condition to make it closer to the competitive ideal may increase the level of corporate bribery.

Market pressures, however, are not the only factors to consider in comparing corrupt incentives in the public and private sectors. Also important is the ability of top managers and agency heads to supervise lower level officials. While observers like Banfield (1975) argue that private oligopolistic firms will be much better at ferreting out bribery than government agencies, there is neither systematic empirical nor theoretical support for this view. Although Banfield asserts, for example, that firms have clear hierarchies, while government bureaucracies tend to be disorganized and fragmented, this difference cannot be clearly linked with anything essential to the nature of governments and firms. Indeed, many modern firms are very decentralized (Williamson, 1975) while many governmental units are exceedingly hierarchical. Furthermore, to the extent that decentralization is required by the nature of the government task—e.g. law enforcement, education— shifting these activities to the private sector would not importantly reduce corrupt incentives. Banfield, however, seems to be on firmer ground in emphasizing the threat of bankruptcy or takeover if corruption is carried too far. Similarly, disciplining corrupt employees may be more difficult for governments constrained by civil service regulations than it is for private firms, at least for those that need not deal with powerful unions (Banfield, 1975:597). Counteracting the profitability constraint and the more flexible personnel policies of private business, however, is the lesser effectiveness of legal remedies. Commercial bribery is not a criminal offense in many states and is seldom a major concern of prosecutors (Anonymous, 1960).

Even more important than the *ability* of high-level officials to oversee low-level employees is their *willingness* to engage in monitoring. While Banfield recognizes that private managers may have goals other than profit maximization for the firm (p. 591), he does not develop the possibility that they may seek instead to maximize their private incomes. Thus he envisions firms as balancing the costs and benefits of corruption and permitting only the amount of bribery that maximizes profits. In contrast, Banfield asserts that government officials generally have no clear organization objectives and so are unwilling to engage in systematic efforts to end corruption. This contrast, however, lacks strong empirical and theoretical foundations. First, competitive pressures are not powerful enough in many industries to prevent high-level corruption by top executives and board members. Thus, many businessmen have incentives to structure the organization under them to facilitate personal payoffs. Similarly, in industries where slack is possible because of the absence of strong competitive pressures,[33] simple laziness may open the way for low-level corruption.

Second, many government bureaucracies are neither disorganized nor immune from legislative or public review.[34] While it is obvious that both voter and legislator oversight of executive agencies has often been weak and ineffective, the revelation of a scandal frequently leads to budget cutbacks, personnel reshuffles, and the termination of programs. Politicians in many political jurisdictions do react strongly, if sporadically, to evidence of bureaucratic corruption, particularly if pressed by an active media campaign.[35] In short, rather than talking about the public sector and the private sector as if they were monolithic entities, a far more complex and disaggregated approach is needed to grasp the varieties of structure that generate corrupt incentives.[36]

Notes

1. Jacoby, Nehemkis, and Eells argue that the stock prices of firms which disclosed "political payments" abroad did not suffer a long-term decline (1977: 51–57). Shareholders, however, may prefer to be uninformed about these payments particularly since it is generally illegal for them to approve such actions (Henn, 1970:380). Thus in one company 99 percent of those stockholders who voted said that they did not want further information on questionable payments (the case is from a speech by Roderick Hills reprinted in *Yale Law Report,* 23 (Fall 1976), 4–5, quoted in Jacoby Nehemkis, and Eells, 1977:57).
   Gulf's current top management and board of directors denied knowledge of Gulf's political payments (McCloy, Pearson, and Matthews, 1976: 8–15; 224–76). Of course, as the report points out, the actual extent of their knowledge is difficult to document.
2. This practice is not limited to legitimate business firms. Rubinstein and Reuter (1977:20) report that individuals high in the numbers racket in New York City have organized their operations to facilitate low-level payoffs to the police.
3. See the codes of conduct reprinted in an appendix in Basche (1976). Basche gives no evidence, however, on companies' enforcement policies.
4. There is a close analogy here to executives who use similar output measures to evaluate division managers in a competitive environment in which antitrust violations can improve a division's performance. See Herling (1962) and Smith (1963) for a discussion of top management's role in the electrical equipment price fixing conspiracies of the 1950s. Company presidents combined a high pressure drive for profits with moves toward

decentralization of the company hierarchy. Divisional managers were given authority to set prices for the products they produced, and they responded to the pressure for profits by engaging in illegal collusion. Top management appears to have been ignorant of these illegal activities for a decade (Smith, 1963, Chapters 5 and 6).

Although the courts have not taken a clear position, top management cannot always escape criminal liability through this device. Kriesberg (1976) writes that

> The courts have failed to delimit precisely the "responsibility" of corporate employees. . . . Frequently . . . there is no evidence of explicit direction to transgress the law, and the liability issue is whether a corporate employee who assented to, acquiesced in, or failed to halt illegal conduct by others is criminally responsible. In these situations of passive participation, courts usually have approved penal sanctions only when the applicable statute imposed an affirmative managerial duty and the employee charged was a corporate executive [pp. 1097–1098, footnotes omitted].

5. For a modern discussion of the internal organization of the firm which assumes that information always has positive value see Williamson (1975).
6. For example, in New York City doctors processing large numbers of Medicaid patients are reported to use underworld figures both to collect bills due them from the city government and to prevent the entry of competitors (*New York Times,* June 3, 1977).
7. The benefits to specialization will be particularly large in societies where the government bureaucracy is especially large, complex, and hard to understand.
8. Milbrath (1963) in his study of Washington lobbyists cites one lobbyist as saying: "They [a client] came to me with the idea that we had to do something under the table or something dirty to get what they wanted. They asked, 'Where do we put the fix in?' Such persons are often taken in by unscrupulous lobbyists who probably pocket the money they have been given to bribe officials [p. 282]." Similarly, firms dealing with Saudi Arabia through agents have little idea how much of their payments are passed on to government officials and how much agents keep for themselves (*New York Times,* July 3, 1977, Section 3).
9. Banfield (1975) makes a similar point. He writes that "One would expect the tendency to corrupt other organizations to be the strongest among those profit-maximizing businesses which must depend upon a small number of customers or suppliers . . . and whose profit margins in the absence of corruption would be non-existent or nearly so [pp. 594–95]."
10. Similar payments by the building trades industry at the end of the nineteenth century are reported by Hutchinson (1970: 26–27).
11. Before the bankruptcy of the Penn Central Railroad, its executives were seeking not only loan guarantees but also nationalization of passenger service (Daughen and Binzen, 1971:259). The authors report that a finance committee member told them, "We believed that although the reports of losses would scare some investors and might dry up private sources of credit, it would hasten government help. We wanted to alert the government so that it would stay in and help us and maybe even take over the railroad, or at least the unprofitable parts of it [p. 261]."

12. *New York Times,* April 21, 1975 and Cochran (1953).
13. For a discussion of this phenomenon, see Margolis (1974).
14. Representative Robert Sikes, for example, had an interest in a Florida land development project when he pushed legislation beneficial to an adjacent project (*New York Times,* July 27, 1976).
15. Eisenberg (1969) cites a number of authors who share this viewpoint. Among these is Manning (1958), who writes: "Managements are almost never reprimanded or displaced by the shareholder electorate; shareholders remain stubbornly uninterested in exerting control [p. 1487]." Eisenberg also mentions some evidence to the countrary; some institutional investors, in particular, take shareholder voting seriously. Empirical work on the separation of ownership from control and its consequences for performance began with Berle and Means (1932). While the phenomenon is well documented, its consequences for firm performance have not been clearly demonstrated empirically. See Clark (1977) for a summary of recent work.
16. Henn (1970: 415–16).
17. Many private sector transactions that are analytically similar to illegal corruption are not, in fact, illegal: and those which are illegal are often not treated as criminal offenses. A law journal note (Anonymous, 1960) documented the fact that in 1960, 25 states had no statute making commercial bribery a crime. The author also presents a table summarizing state law at the time. Thirteen states had general statutes and 17 (including 5 of the original 13) had special statutes making it a crime to bribe particular people such as purchasing or hiring agents or common carrier personnel (pp. 849, 864, 866). There is no general federal statute making commercial bribery a crime (p. 849). The Federal Trade Commission is authorized to prevent "unfair methods of competition," a phrase which includes commercial bribery, but their enforcement powers are limited to cease and desist orders (pp. 849–50). This legal situation apparently continues to the present day. In New Jersey, a state listed in 1960 as having no criminal statute, commercial bribery is a misdemeanor and does not carry a prison sentence (*New York Times,* November 30, 1976). In Pennsylvania, the offense is a misdemeanor and carries a fine of up to $500 or a jail term of up to 1 year or both (*Pennsylvania Code,* Vol. 18, Sec. 4667, 1963).
18. Clark (1977), however, argues that even in closely held corporations the incentives for managers to benefit at the expense of owners may still be high.
19. Henn (1970) lists six ways in which fiduciary duties can be violated: "(a) competing with the corporation, (b) usurping corporate opportunity, (c) having some interest which conflicts with the interest of the corporation, (d) insider trading, (e) oppression of minority shareholders, and (f) sale of control [p. 458]." These categories are not, however, meant to be exhaustive.
20. Takeover bids however, can be costly. Clark (1977) cites several studies that estimate these costs.
21. See Gramlich (1976).
22. In failures of banks and insurance companies, a combined strategy of corruption or self-dealing and fraud has frequently been uncovered. Fraud is less often given as a cause of regular business failures. The evidence is

presented in Clark (1976:12–13), who mentions the difficulty of interpreting these results (p. 77). Bank failures may, for instance, often be associated with fraud simply because there are so few other reasons why banks might fail.

23. Even if a manager's performance can be quite easily evaluated, Clark (1977) points out that executives might still engage in corruption or other forms of illegal behavior if they are close to retirement and do not care much about their future career prospects. The opportunity for private gain could be so large that the possibility of losing one's pension rights might not be an important deterrent. The executive close to retirement is similar to the corruptible lame duck legislator.

24. See Henn (1970:465–70) and Clark (1976) for examples.

25. Fogel (1960) argues that promoters reaped profits "two to five million dollars greater than the 'reasonable' amount [p. 85]." He goes on to demonstrate, however, that "the charge that profiteering was the root cause of the financial enervation of the Union Pacific was based on a compound of errors that included the overestimation of the profit of the promoters, the underestimation of the cost of construction, and the omission of the element of risk. The railroad would have tottered on the brink of bankruptcy even if the promoters had scrupulously limited their profit to the amount 'justified' by the risk they had borne [p. 86]."

26. Individuals charged with determining access are more easily corruptible if the consequences of the bribe are not obvious. Ticket takers who let people enter baseball stadiums without tickets are unlikely to be caught, while executives are likely to notice if their secretaries schedule appointments on the basis of willingness to pay. Similarly, in admissions decisions, bribes, contributions to the alumni fund, or good connections can help borderline cases more than they can help those with poor qualifications.

27. The view is expressed in several of the articles in Phelps (1975) and Weisbrod (1977).

28. Both nonprofit and for-profit nursing homes were involved in scandals arising under Medicaid and Medicare according to Mendelson (1974, Chapter 9).

29. The equal time doctrine applies only to legally qualified candidates for public office. Broadcasting stations are not required to provide equal time, however, if the publicity is part of a newscast, interview, news documentary, or on-the-spot coverage of a news event. However, these other activities are subject to the "fairness" doctrine which requires broadcasters "to afford reasonable opportunity for the discussion of conflicting views on issues of public importance." (See 47 U.S.C. 315 [1952]). In *Red Lion Broadcasting Co. v FCC.* 395 U.S. 367 (1968) the Supreme Court upheld a Federal Communications Commission regulation which gives individuals or groups the right to use a broadcaster's facilities to respond to "personal" attacks. This regulation, however, does not permit individuals or groups to respond either to favorable publicity given to a rival or a competitor, or to critical comments that do not reflect on their "honesty, character, integrity, or like personal qualities."

30. While many individual journalists undoubtedly have strong ethical beliefs, "there is no universally accepted code of professional ethics to guide and

judge the behavior of newsmen or their editors [Kampelman, 1975:91]."
Kampelman reports on a proposal by the Twentieth Century Fund to
create "a newspaper council to receive and air complaints against the
press by aggrieved persons [p. 91]." The proposal, modeled after a similar
British institution, was opposed by the *New York Times* and the *Washington Post.*

31. Compare Schmidit (1969). Inside information is frequently used in stock
    market purchases. If the tip has been obtained through bribery, two crimes
    have been committed: corruption and the use of inside information to
    determine stock market investments. Henn (1970:470–74) provides examples.

32. The competitive oligopolists in the arms industry have frequently paid
    bribes to obtain contracts. For a Lockheed executive's attempt to justify
    himself in terms of the strength of the competitive pressures he faced, see
    "Kotchian Calls Himself the Scapegoat," (*New York Times,* July 13, 1977,
    Section 3). He said, " 'I may have been wrong. But I thought I was doing it
    in the best interests of the company, its employees and its shareholders. I
    think any manager of a large enterprise has a responsibility to look after his
    employees, and the only thing you can do to keep them working is to sell
    your product, and that is what I tried to do.' "

33. The problem of organizational slack is examined by Leibenstein (1966) and
    Williamson (1967).

34. While Banfield recognizes the deterrent effects of monitoring and unfavor-
    able publicity (1975: 598–99, 600–601), he does not believe that they
    provide effective checks. In concluding his paper, he states that "every
    extension of government authority created new opportunities and incen-
    tives for corruption [pp. 603–604]."

35. A redirection of housing aid occurred in response to the revelations in 1972
    and 1973 of widespread scandals combined with high levels of defaults on
    subsidized mortages (*Business Week,* August 25, 1973). The troubled
    programs were suspended, and in 1973 President Nixon called for the
    development of new policies. The Department of Housing and Urban
    Development then carried out a national housing policy review (U.S.
    Department of HUD, 1973). The report does not explicitly discuss corrup-
    tion although it does mention "abuses and fraud" in home ownership
    programs Section 235 (p. 4–43). Instead, the authors locate other difficul-
    ties which limited the efficiency and equity of the suspended programs.

36. Roberts (1975), in a study of public and private electrical utilities, confirms
    this general perspective. He was unable to find any important interorgani-
    zational differences that could be attributed to type of ownership.

Works Cited

Alchian, Armer, and Demsetz, Harold. "Production, Information Costs, and
Economic Organization." *American Economic Review* 62 (December 1972):
777–795.

Banfield, Edward. "Corruption as a Feature of Governmental Organizaiton."
Journal of Law and Economics 18 (December 1975): 587–605.

Becker, Gary. "Crime and Punishment: An Economic Approach." *Journal of
Political Economy* 76 (January/February 1968): 169–217.

Berle, Adolf, and Means, Gardiner. *The Modern Corporation and Private Property*. New York: MacMillan, 1932.

Bhagwati, Jagdish, N., ed. *Illegal Transactions in International Trade*. Amsterdam and New York: North-Holland-American Elsevier, 1974.

Buchanan, James, and Tullock, Gordon. "Polluter's Profits and Political Response: Direct Controls versus Taxes." *American Economic Review* 65 (March 1975): 139–147.

Clark, Robert. "Market Controls." New Haven: Yale University, 1977. Manuscript.

Darby, Michael R., and Karni, Edi. "Free Competition and the Optimal Amount of Fraud." *Journal of Law and Economics* 16 (April 1973): 67–88.

Daughen, Joseph R., and Binzen, Peter. *The Wreck of the Penn Central*. Boston: Little, Brown and Co., 1971.

Eisenberg, Melvin. "Legal Roles of Shareholders and Management in Modern Corporate Decisionmaking." *California Law Review* 57 (January 1969): 1–181.

Fogel, Robert W. *The Union Pacific Railroad: A Case in Premature Enterprise*. Baltimore: Johns Hopkins Press, 1960.

Gramlich, Edward. "The New York City Fiscal Crisis—What Happened and What Is to Be Done?" *American Economic Review—Papers and Proceedings* 66 (May 1976): 415–429.

Henn, Harry. *Handbook of the Law of Corporations*. 2d ed. St. Paul, Minn.: West Publishing Co., 1970.

Herling, John. *The Great Price Conspiracy: The Story of the Antitrust Violations in the Electrical Industry*. Washington: R. B. Luce, 1962.

Hutchinson, John. *The Imperfect Union*. New York: E. P. Dutton and Co., 1970.

Jacoby, Neil; Nehemkis, Peter: and Eells, Richard. *Bribery and Extortion in World Business*. New York: MacMillan Publishing Co., 1977.

Kampelman, Max. "Congress, the Media and the President." In *Congress against the President: Proceedings of the Academy of Political Science* 32 (1975): 85–97.

Kriesberg, Simon. "Decisionmaking Models and the Control of Corporate Crime." *Yale Law Journal* 85 (July 1976): 1091–1128.

Leibenstein, Harvey. "Allocative Efficiency vs. 'X-Efficiency.' " *American Economic Review* 56 (June 1966): 392–415.

Manning, Bayless. Review of *The American Stockholder* by J. A. Livingston. *Yale Law Journal* 67 (July 1958): 1477–1496.

Margolis, Julius, "Public Policies for Private Profits: Urban Government." In *Redistribution through Public Choice,* edited by H. Hochman and G. Peterson. New York: Columbia University Press, 1974.

McCloy, John; Pearson, Nathan: and Matthews, Beverly. *The Great Oil Spill: The Inside Report: Gulf Oil's Bribery and Political Chicanery*. New York: Chelsea House, 1976. (The report was originally entitled "Report of the Special Review Committee of the Board of Directors of Gulf Oil Corporation.")

Mendelson, Mary Adelaide. *Tender Loving Greed*. New York: Alfred A. Knopf, 1974.

Phelps, Edmund S., ed. *Altruism, Morality and Economic Theory*. New York: Russell Sage Foundation, 1975.

Roberts, Marc. "An Evolutionary and Institutional View of the Behavior of Public and Private Companies." *American Economic Review Papers and Proceedings* 65 (May 1975): 415–427.

Rottenberg, Simon. "A Theory of Corruption in Trade Unions." In *Series Studies in Social and Economic Sciences*. Symposium Studies Series No. 31. Washington, D.C.: National Institute of Social and Behavioral Science, January 1960.

Rubinstein, Jonathan, and Reuter, Peter. "Numbers: The Routine Racket." New York: Policy Sciences Center, April 1977. Manuscript.

Schmidt, Kurt. "Zur Ökonomie der Korruption." *Schmollers Jahrbuch* 9 (1969): 130–149.

Smith, Howard R. *Government and Business.* New York: The Ronald Press, 1958.

Weisbrod, Burton, "What is the Non-Profit Sector?" Institution for Social and Policy Studies Working Paper. New Haven: Yale University, 1977.

Weiss, Elliott. *The Corporate Watergate.* Special Report 1975-D. Washington D.C.: Investor Research Center, 1975.

White, Henry Kirk. *History of the Union Pacific Railway.* Chicago: University of Chicago Press, 1895.

Williamson, Oliver. *The Economics of Discretionary Behavior: Managerial Objectives in a Theory of the Firm.* Englewood Cliffs, N.J.: Prentice-Hall, 1967.

40

Transnational Aspects of Political Corruption*

Victor T. LeVine

Until the mid-1970s, with very few exceptions, analyses of political corruption focussed on the specifically national and sub-national aspects of the phenomenon, though in several instances, due note was taken of the contributions of foreign business interests to domestic official corruption.[1] Gunnar Myrdal indicated—though without providing much data—the fact that bribery of local officials by foreign business concerns was common throughout South Asia;[2] this writer detailed the institutionalized nature of such arrangements in Nkrumah's Ghana;[3] Eugene Burdick devoted an entire book to the massive corruption that took place in Vietnam, most of it inspired and promoted by private and public American entrepreneurs;[4] similar activity was remarked in the Africa by Bretton,[5] Andreski,[6] Price,[7] Gould,[8] and others. However, save in the congressional hearings reports devoted to Vietnam, or to multinational corporations, defense contractors, and other large private concerns doing business abroad, there was little description or analysis of what can be legitimately styled large-scale "transnational corruption."[9] By 1975, the picture had changed. Once the United States Securities and Exchange Commission began to produce its series of sensational revelations in the wake of the Watergate affair, once the details of the ITT-Chile and Eli Black-United Brands scandals had become public, and once the Congress began considering legislation that eventually became the Foreign Corrupt Practices Act of 1977, the popular and scholarly literature on the subject grew at an almost exponential rate.[10]

Bribery, extortion, and other dealings across national frontiers, whether practiced by governments, private individuals, or corporate bodies, or by combinations of the three, are of course nothing new in international affairs. They have been common throughout history, endorsed by near-universal practice, even sanctioned by political necessity. To those who had the necessary leverage, the available resources, a sufficiently flexible set of supportive values, and the means to do so, transnational corruption became simply another way of achieving international political or economic objectives. To be sure, sovereigns and governments were the principal initiators of these activities, but that changed by the end of the nineteenth century when large-scale commercial, financial, and industrial enterprises began to enter the international economic arena as full participants. In any event, these activities did not stimulate a separate scholarly literature simply because they were generally considered standard, if unsavory, operating practice in international relations. Most informed people were probably aware that such things went on, but since they usually happened away from public view, were done discreetly, and had little visible effect on normal international intercourse, they were tolerated, if not condoned. The few really spectacular pre-World War II international scandals such as those associated with the Credit Mobilier, the Belgian Congo, and the like, tended to underscore their exceptional character. Further, the international ethic of Hugo Grotius (and even more to the point, that argued by Suares[11]) has, during the past hundred years or so, come to be accepted by all states in principle, if not always in observance. International duplicity, diplomacy by the "Italian method," state-sponsored transnational bribery and subornation, have all come to be considered as aberrations rather than the norm in international relations. Evidence to the contrary not withstanding, the international rule is *pacta sunt servanda,* with the twentieth century witness to the exponential growth of a jungle of interstate agreements. In addition, the structure of international trade, predicated on ever-widening circles of interdependence, on the need for predictability, and on the search for market and production stability, has come to rest on a host of public, quasi-public, and private agreements that exclude as illegitimate large-scale informal commercial arrangements, be they concluded by governments with one another or with international entrepreneurs. In any case, governments are now expected to show suitable restraint in their economic dealings with one another, and to control their agents and commercial nationals in international trade.

Why then the shock and excitement over the allegedly "corrupt" activities of various multinational corporations, all epitomized by the Lockheed "scandals"?[12] If, as has been frequently contended and increasingly documented,[13] informal trade in official favors is virtually standard operating procedure in such countries as Saudi Arabia, Morocco, Indonesia, the Philippines, and Haiti, and is not uncommon in

Italy, the Netherlands, and other "Western" countries, then the expressions of dismay over the revelations provided and/or compelled by the United States congress and the United States Securities and Exchange Commission sound somewhat disingenuous. Certainly, the revelations have had serious political repercussions in France, the Netherlands, Korea, Iran, Honduras, Germany, and Japan (where "Lockheed" and "Lockheed shokku" became common epithets).

Also, all but the most moralistic accept the proposition that bribes and payoffs, or sophisticated versions of such practices, are often the only way by which foreigners can conduct business in some countries. Failure to do so may, in fact, entail consequences ranging from loss of revenue to expropriation.[14]

Clearly, the source of most of the excitement and much of the outrage was the United States. Michael Rosenthal, in his essay in this collection, argues that the Watergate affair, which triggered the Securities and Exchange Commission's investigations and revelations, triggered a resurgence of long-dormant sentiment about public ethics and morality. That sense of outrage, which led to the disgrace and resignation of President Nixon, lasted long enough in the congress to find legislative expression in the Foreign Corrupt Practices Act (FCPA) of 1977. It turns out that foreign countries affected by the scandals were more embarrassed than outraged; thus, the FCPA remains, to date, the only piece of recent national legislation specifically to confront transnational corruption. (We consider this fact in the last section of this essay.) The United States, in effect, had opened a Pandora's box which much of the world—particularly those countries most affected by the revelations—would have preferred to have remained closed. On the other hand, the new transnational corruption, once revealed, had to be recognized for what it was—a new and dangerous challenge to the stability and predictability of the international market. That the United States, whose multinationals had pioneered the new transnational corruption, should take the lead to curbing their excesses, and that various foreign countries were willing to undergo the embarrassment of politically damaging scandals, is evidence that the United States and the others had in fact recognized the seriousness of the threat. It also testifies to the recognition of the reality that the international economic and political scene had radically changed since the end of World War II, and that this changed environment had provided fertile breeding ground for the new transnational forms of corruption.

What was involved was the parallel appearance of several new elements on the international scene—factors to which the older predicates of international relations simply did not apply, whose coming was unanticipated, and whose effects were generally underestimated. They are listed in no particular order: (1) The appearance of the multinational corporation or enterprise (MNC of MNE) as a quasi-autonomous actor—a "near sovereign"—on the international scene; (2) the entrance onto the international economic stage of a large number of states relatively unsocialized to contemporary international trading norms; (3) the introduction of new, highly politically volatile, and immensely expensive goods to the international market; and (4) intense, relatively unrestrained competition among governments and MNC's for access to new markets and/or production sources. In combination, these elements appear to have created conditions in which the new transnational corruption took easy root; each, therefore, deserves separate comment.

MNCs as International Actors

This is not the place to trace the rise of the MNCs or MNEs or detail the scope of their activities; what is germane to our discussion are three points: the MNEs are largely a phenomenon of the last thirty years, being one of the principal vehicles for direct foreign investment now totalling well over $250 billions;[15] some MNEs dispose of economic resources that rival or surpass most states;[16] around 50 percent of the MNEs are United States-based (ca. 38 percent are based in Europe);[17] increasingly, the MNEs are organizing so that regional and global, rather than national objectives and activities are advanced—more and more MNEs are seeking true transnational status, in which ownership and management transcends national boundaries.[18] It goes without saying, therefore, that the MNEs were and are extremely difficult to control at best, particularly those approaching the "transnational" mode. Some of the larger MNEs do not, in effect, have a true home, and like most of the world's merchant ships, sail under a "flag of convenience." Ford Motors, for example, in its American activities is a United States company; in its MNC guises it is also Canadian, British, German, French, Japanese, South African, etc. companies. To call it "American" is merely to label its origins, not its real scope of activity. Thus, many MNCs are able to survive even the ultimate forms of national control, expropriation and nationalization. Robert Barnes' study of sanctions taken against international oil companies concludes, on the basis of convincing analysis, that "the effect of wealth deprivation by governments has not been negative to the point of preventing a satisfactory and improving performance and growth (of the oil companies) during the past half-century."[19] Barnes included not only nationalization and expropriation among his factors of "wealth deprivation"; he also listed such things as currency restrictions, confiscatory taxes, punitive tariffs, and penalties due to war. One is tempted to reach for the hydra metaphor: the large MNCs can have one or more heads cut off, but still manage to survive comfortably in other parts, even to regenerate elsewhere. It hardly surprises, then, that it became possible to speak of the "international relations" of MNCs.[20] They appear almost as autonomous actors on the international scene, "near-sovereign," difficult to control and largely unaccountable; in short, they resemble states, particularly in the latter two aspects.

What this all means is that given (relative) unaccountability, the (relative) absence or impotence of national and/or international controls, MNCs soon began to conduct their international relations like states, using time-tested methods of transnational corruption when these seemed appropriate to the situation, or the ends desired, or both.

Other New International Actors

The last thirty years witnessed the appearance on the international economic scene of a variety of states to whom the common predicates and constraints of the contemporary system of international trade never applied because they were never fully part of that system, save in highly marginal ways, or in most cases, by colonial or economic proxy. These include states of the so-called "fourth world," that is, those formerly classed as Less Developed Countries (LDC's) but which suddenly became wealthy because they produced some raw material commanding high prices and in short supply. Practically all the members of the Organization of Petroleum Exporting Countries (OPEC) qualify under this rubric, notably Saudi Arabia, Iraq, Iran, Kuwait, the United Arab Emirates, Libya, Algeria, Indonesia, Nigeria, and Venezuela. Also eligible for inclusion are such states as Morocco (which now produces 4/5 of the world's phosphates), Zaire (copper and other minerals), and eventually, providing the price of copper holds up, Zambia. The OPEC countries were in the system by proxy so long as the major oil companies owned and controlled their production; once the governments concerned began taking both ownership and control of their oil, these states entered the system in their own right. The "new" actors also include, though on a lesser scale and with correspondingly smaller impact, a variety of LDC's in Africa, Asia, and Latin America, some of which became independent after World War II, others of longer standing. All the above shared a common condition of political and/or economic dependence, by virtue of which their participation in world trade and finance was organized through a colonial metropole, large foreign economic interests, or a foreign political or economic protector. What many of them still have in common, however, are polities and economies in which older traditions of highly personalized, informal exchange still prevail, particularly at the highest levels of the society.

Again, this is not the place to examine causes, or to detail the particulars of conventional, or systematic, or endemic political corruption in various countries. Suffice it for our purposes to note that it is common in many states and that in some countries political corruption is so pervasive that it has become a planned and regulated governmental activity. John Waterbury has described the Moroccan system in these terms, and official corruption in the Philippines, Indonesia, and Haiti approached similar levels.[21] Evidence from over a dozen other countries suggests a pattern of highly informal dealing in which even presidents, princes, and prime ministers act as brokers or agents in the foreign commercial activities of their countries and/or their governments.[22]

In all, the evidence now indicates that combinations of new-found or newly exploited wealth (oil, phosphates, copper, uranium, etc.), patterns of informal political and economic exchange, and the international activities of some MNEs, have been associated with international bribery on a massive scale.

The New Goods

In one sense, what we have called the "new" goods in international trade are not new at all; there is certainly nothing novel to international trade in armaments, oil, and strategic minerals, or to international transfers of investment capital, financial equities, and other intangibles, be these conducted by governments, by consortia of governments and private enterprises, or by MNEs and large corporations. What is new is the extraordinary scale of some of this trade and the fact that much of it appears often to operate *outside* the accepted international constraints affecting the conventional trade in such things as automobiles or agricultural commodities. Even in such transfers, however, it almost seems that when the value of such trade increases, the usual constraints diminish in salience. In any case, a prime example of the new situation is trade in armaments, now a multi-billion dollar affair, with the United States, France, Great Britain, Canada, mainland China, West Germany, countries of East Europe, Sweden, Israel, etc. in competition for burgeoning markets in the Middle East, Africa, and

Latin America.[23] The United States Arms Control and Disarmament Agency estimates the net value of all world trade in arms between 1964 and 1973 at about $57.9 billion, and between 1973 and 1984 (deliveries only) at $249.5, of which over 65 percent went to developing countries. The major suppliers (1964–1984) were the United States and Soviet Union, which together had cumulative exports amounting to 57 percent of the world total. In 1963 the estimated value of worldwide arms exports was about $4.4 billion; by 1973 it more than trebled to $13.2 billion, and by 1983, it had reached $35 billion (transfer deliveries only). During the 1973–1984 period, the Middle East (principally Libya, Egypt, Israel, Saudi Arabia, Iran, Iraq, and Syria) accounted for about 38 percent of all arms purchases; the 1979–1983 total for the Middle East was $65.3 billion, of which about $40 billion went to three countries: Iraq ($17.6 billion), Saudi Arabia ($12.1 billion), and Syria ($10.5 billion).[24]

To be sure, the international trade in arms is usually carried on under license annd strict national controls, but the fact remains that for all intents and purposes, national defense ministries (or other agencies) assist arms-makers in Western countries in making foreign sales, and on occasion, act as brokers in the transactions. And, of course, where arms-making is a government enterprise, government officials themselves become front-line arms salesmen. Thus, defense contractors were among the most prominent participants in the new transnational corruption. These include (among the American companies) such giants as Lockheed, Boeing, McDonnell-Douglas, Vinnel, Raytheon, FMC and Northrop, Rockwell International, aided and abetted by officials in the countries where these MNCs sold their wares.

The basic point needs no belaboring: the international trade in arms is largely unrestrained, treaties or national regulations to the contrary notwithstanding. Under the circumstances, it is hardly surprising that competitors for the new markets frequently offer, or are asked for, bribes or payoffs to secure contracts.

While the arms trade may have stimulated some of the most egregious examples of the new transnational corruption, the disclosures indicate that large-scale dealings in such goods and/or commodities as commercial airplanes, bauxite, oil, and even bananas also occasioned huge bribes or payoffs.[25] Again, it is the scale and value of the transactions that is new on the international scene; while a billion dollar arms deal would once have been considered highly unusual, today even larger deals create little stir. In 1972, oil trade at the posted price of $2.59 per barrel, with production and distribution largely in the hands of the "Seven Sisters," was conducted under relatively "clean" conditions. Once the posted price had risen to and beyond the $11 per barrel mark, and production control (as well as ownership) has passed to the OPEC states, oil transactions not only jumped in dollar value by a factor of four, but increasingly involved both buyers and sellers in informal, corrupt relationships. Again, American oil companies led the way: the Securities and Exchange Commission disclosures revealed payments by such firms as Ashland, Exxon, Gulf, Phillips, Standard Oil of Indiana, and Occidental.

The New Circumstances

The testimony of Daniel J. Haughten, Lockheed's chairman of the board, before the Senate Banking, Housing and Urban Affairs Committee in August 1975 contained recurrent mention of the highly competitive nature of his firm's international dealings.[26] In the relatively controlled environment of the United States Lockheed could, apparently, compete reasonably well with the other major aerospace industries. (Federally-organized loan guarantees also helped.) Abroad, Haughton argued, Lockheed had to do what its American and foreign competitors did—deliver bribes, payoffs, and kickbacks—in order to get its share of the available business. Executives of McDonnell-Douglas, Northrop, and Grumman have also admitted to such practices, and for much the same reasons. It appears that French, British, German, and other non-American aerospace firms were involved in similar practices. Common to all these cases is the assertion that the enterprises concerned operated in an unusually super-charged, unrestrained, competitive international market.

Admittedly, international competition between dealers/producers of important goods is nothing new, just as there is nothing new in cutthroat tactics by the competitors. Yet, the history of international trade—at least during the past fifty years or so—suggests that governmental and private trading organizations more rapidly move to curb competition when it threatens participants in international markets, or the markets themselves. Thus, formal and informal cartels, international trading agreements, reciprocal tariff pacts, and the like, all serve to moderate damaging competition. Even OPEC, at the height of its power, served as a mechanism that not only squeezed the market for all it could bear, but also operated—to be sure with the unwilling help of the "Seven Sisters" and the consuming states' governments—to keep the petrochemical market from collapsing. However, the vast scale of the new trade in armaments, aerospace goods, and strategic commodities, coupled with the elements described above, may in fact have produced a competitive situation little amenable to control by the standard mechanisms of market restraint. This is not to suggest that such controls may not be developed in one way or another—the new OECD-MNE code is a first, albeit hesitant step in that direction—but that the argument for a new, hyper-competitive environment has at least *prima facie* validity.

The new competition exists partly, as was suggested earlier, because the international market now contains some new actors in which a culture (or strong sub-culture) of political corruption obtains. It must be added, however, that some of the more blatant examples of the new transnational corruption have occurred in countries whose officials, traders, and agents presumably had been socialized to the general international trading moralities. This latter list includes Dutchmen, Swedes, (West) Germans, Italians, Frenchmen, and even Japanese, once the most moral of international traders (former ambassador Reischauer points out that the last major public bribery scandal in Japan occurred in 1914).[27]

In all, then, the evidence for a partial explanation of the new transnational corruption seems to lie in a combination of elements associated with what can only be styled a new set of international trade patterns grown recently alongside the older, more regular and controlled structures.

Nor are the new patterns associated only with international capitalism. The conventional image of the MNE is that it is wholly a phenomenon of the capitalist world; insofar as the MNEs prime objectives center on profits and returns to investors the image is correct. However, Soviet, Czech, Romanian, Polish, and other communist state companies have operated on the international scene using skills, tactics, and strategies usually attributed mainly to their capitalist competitors. (One need hardly be reminded that Soviet agents mastered the intricacies of the American grain market to such an extent that they were able to make huge deals on extraordinarily generous terms.) The evidence is scant, but there is enough to suggest that the socialist states have not hesitated to offer bribes and make payoffs and kickbacks in order to gain their ends. Again, political, rather than financial goals might be the principal consideration involved, but it is here that the difference ends. Some buyers of war planes may, for example, find it easier to acquire MIGs than Mirages, but the exchanges tend to follow the same paths. Iranian generals, private brokers for the Saudi royal house, and African ministers of state have dealt and will deal as readily with Soviet arms purveyors as with McDonnell-Douglas—and on similar terms.[28]

Effects, Consequences, and Reactions

It was clear, from both the American and foreign reactions to the 1975–1976 revelations, that the governments concerned, and ultimately the MNCs and MNEs themselves, recognized that the new patterns, for all their amorphous character, already carried multi-billion dollar loads. At least, insofar as they had to carry heavy surcharges of transnational corruption, as they tended to destabilize international exchanges, and above all, as they began to make international trading increasingly risky and unpredictable, the new patterns were bound ultimately to erode the older, stabler structures of trade as well. The official American reactions unfolded mainly at the federal level. In February, 1976, President Ford ordered a high-level investigation of the overseas practices of American corporations, which he confided to a task force headed by Commerce Secretary Eliot Richardson. In August, 1976, the administration, relying on the task force's report, submitted to congress legislation to require companies to disclose payments, "whether proper or improper," that they had made to foreign officials to foster sales abroad. Failure to make the disclosures could entail criminal penalties. Disclosure, argued the administration (and the Securities and Exchange Commission) would be punishment enough for the MNCs and would permit their stockholders and the public to monitor their overseas activities. The Internal Revenue Service was also put on the trail. The congress took a different tack. Stimulated by the revelations of the Church committee's investigations of the activities of the MNCs, as well as by the Securities and Exchange Commission disclosures, a variety of legislative proposals made their way through congress, resulting in the Foreign Corrupt Practices Act of 1977, which not only made disclosure of corrupt payments mandatory for American firms operating abroad, but also imposed criminal penalties on the companies' officers and agents found guilty of making them. It should be added that for all the uproar over the disclosures no American company officer or agent underwent persecution in the United States for bribing a foreign official, though substantial purges of top management did take place as a result in such companies as Lockheed, Gulf Oil, and Northrop. (Several companies were also charged with fraud under existing United States statutes, and the Internal Revenue Service ultimately levied substantial penalties on a number of firms that had concealed taxable income through questionable payments abroad.)

The foreign reactions were much more spectacular, since the revelations implicated officials already covered by their countries' fraud, extortion, and bribery statutes. The Lockheed disclosures were so damaging, for example, that official investigations and, less often, prosecutions were pursued in a number of countries with more or less vigor. Lockheed-related investigations were launched in Belgium, Holland, West Germany, Turkey, Japan, Colombia, Italy, and Australia, but it was only in Holland, Belgium, Japan, and Italy that matters went as far as prosecution and trial. Two of the fishes netted, however, were big ones: the Prince Consort of the Netherlands, Bernhard, who was ultimately stripped of all his official functions because of his activities on behalf of Lockheed and other arms dealers, and former Japanese Prime Minister Tanaka, who (along with several other notables) was indicted and convicted for accepting Lockheed's bribes. Lockheed, of course, was only one of the nearly 600 American companies which confessed or were shown to have paid bribes abroad, though it did have the dubious distinction of having distributed more questionable money than any of the others.[29] Again, in many of the latter cases, the initial foreign reaction was official investigation, and in still fewer instances, prosecution and trial of the most flagrant offenders. All of the investigations, prosecutions, and trials, however, took place under existing national law; the initial reaction was to utilize mechanisms in place to handle the short term political and juridical problems posed by their bribe-taking officials. None of the countries most directly affected by the scandals, or for that matter any other country, appear to have followed the United States in attempting to regulate the behavior of their business people overseas. Some, such as West Germany, deplored corporate bribes as morally repugnant, but explicitly argued that they were good for business and ought therefore to be tolerated: "West Germany has taken the position that allowing German companies to deduct foreign bribes on their tax returns is morally indefensible. If its laws were changed its firms would be unable to compete."[30] France has a ministry that pays "commissions," and French, British, West German, and Swedish arms contractors are not required to disclose any information about fees and commissions paid to local agents, or whether they used agents as conduits for political payments.[31]

Nations other than France and West Germany have generally been more circumspect, some entering into a series of symbolic international or bilateral agreements following the scandals. The United Nations, the Organization for Economic Cooperation and Development (OECD), and the Organization of American States (OAS), all issued declarations, established committees, and formulated guidelines for multinationals. In the United Nations at least two attempts were made (in 1978 and 1979) to produce international agreements that would have mandated criminal sanctions—under national law—for transnational bribery; despite strong American urging, both were killed before reaching the General Assembly.[32]

In any case, the United States failed to persuade other countries to follow its legislative lead on the issue, or to support international sanctions against transnational corrupters. No international prohibition passed any forum. The only partial responses came in Italy and Iran: in Italy, a new law forbids corporate political contributions unless these are authorized by appropriate corporate action and recorded in the company's books; and in Iran, corporations doing business with the state must now file affidavits guaranteeing that payoffs will not be used to obtain government contracts.[33] The former law appears more symbolic than substantive, and the latter, a reinforcement to existing law.

The lack of foreign enthusiasm for measures to control or penalize transnational corruption notwithstanding, it may well be the case that the 1975–1977 revelations and scandals, coupled with the deterrence embodied in the 1977 FCPA, have considerably lessened both the incidence and the magnitude of corrupt activities by American and foreign MNCs and MNEs. It may also be the case that the concatenation of international patterns which helped give rise to the events of 1975–1977 have also altered appreciably; in 1986, for example, oil is no longer the super-charged commodity it was during the middle to late 1970s. In any event, it is not improbable that the MNCs themselves have come to recognize that their survival depends crucially on two factors: international market stability and a friendly international environment in which to operate. If they overstep the bounds, embarrass their hosts, or indulge in excessive capital transfers, they become vulnerable to national retaliation. As indicated earlier, the MNEs seem capable of weathering a good deal of deprivation, but in the final analysis, that can hardly help them do business under optimal conditions. The new OECD code is again a case in point: it is based on the assumption that even if national governments are reluctant to restrain themselves, the MNEs must do so to avoid fouling their own nests.

We are not likely now to witness the dawn of a new international commercial morality. The massive public and official corruption in some countries will continue to invite informal arrangements by other governments, corporations, and semi-official and private entrepreneurs. It is possible, though probably unlikely, that simple self-interest may ultimately help correct the situation; an unpredictable, unregulated international market will eventually tend to hurt both buyers and sellers, whatever their values, ideologies, politics, or nationality.

Notes

*An earlier version of this article was presented to the Edinburgh Congress of the International Studies Association, August, 1976. I have not included a formal definition of "political corruption" in this short study because I am prepared to use the term in its conventional, generally understood sense. "Transnational" corruption, then, refers to a variety of transactional behaviors in which at least one of the principals is a national of another country. It includes, for my purposes, the range of activities recently associated with the revelations concerning over 600 American "multinationals," as well as similar activities conducted by enterprises, officials, and agents of a variety of other countries. I include such things as bribery, payoffs, kickbacks, extortion, and the like.

1. See, for example, the essays by Myrdal and others in this volume.
2. Gunnar Myrdal, "Corruption—Its Causes and Effects," *Asian Drama: An Enquiry Into the Poverty of Nations,* Vol. II (New York: Twentieth Century Fund, 1968); in Heidenheimer, *Political Corruption: Readings in Contemporary Analysis* (New Brunswick, NJ: Transaction Books, 1978), pp. 234–35.
3. Victor T. Le Vine, *Political Corruption: The Ghana Case* (Stanford, Ca.: Hoover Institution Press, 1975).
4. Eugene Burdick, *A Nation of Sheep* (New York: Harpers, 1963).
5. Henry L. Bretton, "Covert Uses," *Power and Politics in Africa* (Chicago: Aldine, 1973), pp. 119–31.
6. Stanislas Andreski, "Kleptocracy, or Corruption as a Form of Government," *The African Predicament* (New York: Atherton, 1968), pp. 92–109.
7. Robert M. Price, "The Social Basis of Administrative Corruption," *Society and Bureaucracy in Contemporary Ghana* (Berkeley: University of California Press, 1975), pp. 140–65.
8. David J. Gould, *Bureaucratic Corruption and Underdevelopment in the Third World: The Case of Zaire* (New York: Pergamon, 1980).
9. For example, U.S. Senate, "Lockheed Bribery," *Hearings Before the Committee on Banking, Housing, and Urban Affairs . . . August 25, 1975* (Washington: U.S. Government Printing Office, 1975).
10. Much of that growth, it should be noted, occurred in the pages of legal and business journals, particularly as the implications of proposed federal anti-corruption legislation was debated in Congress, in the universities, and in affected professional circles. The Securities and Exchange Commission revelations and the questions surrounding transnational corruption were widely discussed in the leading American newspapers and periodicals, and partisan and polemical arguments appeared in such business journals as *Fortune, Business Week,* and the like. Two general books on the subject are worth noting: Neil H. Jacoby, Peter Nehemkis, and Richard Eells, *Bribery and Extortion in World Business* (New York: Macmillan, 1977), and Yerachmiel Kugel and Gladys X. Gruenberg, *International Payoffs: Dilemma for Business* (Lexington, Mass.: Lexington, 1977). Kugel and Neal P. Cohen have also brought together a variety of legislative documents relating to the Mexican aspect of the problem in a three-volume work, *Government Regulation of Business Ethics: U.S. Legislation of International Payoffs* (Dobbs Ferry, N.Y.: Oceana, 1978).
11. "The Spanish Jesuit, Suarez, in a classic passage of his treatise *De legibus*

ac Deo legislatore, published in 1612, insisted clearly that the states of the world, although independent in their national life, were nevertheless members of the human race and as such subject to a law of conduct: a law based, he said, chiefly upon natural reason, but also in part upon human custom." Charles G. Fenwick, *International Law* (New York: Appleton-Century-Crofts, 1934), pp. 50–51. Suarez did not limit his comments only to "Christian" states.

12. U.S. Senate, "Lockheed Bribery," and see the several excellent articles about Lockheed in the *Wall Street Journal:* July 30, November 17, December 12, 1975; February 9 and March 1, 1976. The Japanese aspect of the situation is well-covered in Jerome Alan Cohen, "Japan's Watergate, made in U.S.A." *New York Times Magazine,* November 21, 1976, pp. 37, 104–19.

13. By (for example) James C. Scott, *Comparative Political Corruption* (Englewood Cliffs, N.J.: Prentice-Hall, 1972).

14. Jerry Landauer and Carol Falk, "Rollins Inc. Plans to Continue Payments Abroad: Other Company Says It Resisted," *Wall Street Journal,* March 3, 1976, p. 1. William H. Jones, "Haitians Demanded Bribes," *Washington Post,* March 3, 1976, p. 4.

15. The base figure is from Stefan H. Robock and Kenneth Simmonds, *International Business and Multinational Enterprises* (Homewood, Ill.: Richard D. Irwin, 1973), p. 44.

16. Ralph Andreano reproduces, in his reader *Superconcentration/Supercorporation* (Andover: Warner Modular, 1973, pp. 331–46, a table from *War/Peace Report* indicating that in 1967–68, eight of the forty biggest economic entities were corporations. General Motors' net sales for 1966, for example—$20.2 billion—was larger than each of the 1966 GNP's of Argentina, Belgium, Switzerland, Czechoslovakia, South Africa, Denmark, Turkey, Austria, Philippines, Finland, Venezuala, Norway, Greece, Colombia, and New Zealand. New Zealand, by the way, had a GNP of $5.5 billion.

17. Robock and Simmonds, *op. cit.,* p. 45.

18. David H. Blake and Robert S. Walters, "The Multinational Corporation," *The Politics of Global Economic Relations* (Englewood Cliffs, N.J.: Prentice-Hall, 1976), pp. 85–88; also Joan E. Spero, *The Politics of International Economic Relations,* 2nd ed. (New York: St. Martin's Press, 1981).

19. Robert Barnes, "International Oil Companies Confront Governments," *International Studies Quarterly,* 16, 4 (Dec., 1972), p. 460.

20. J. Boddewyn and Ashok Kaspoor, "The External Relations of American Multinational Enterprises," *International Studies Quarterly,* 16, 4 (Dec., 1972), pp. 433–53.

21. John Waterbury, "Endemic and Planned Corruption in a Monarchical Regime," *World Politics,* 25, 4 (July, 1973), 533–55; see also Scott, *Comparative Political Corruption, op. cit., passim.* The revelations that followed the downfall of both the Marcos regime in the Philippines and the Duvalier regime in Haiti left no doubts that massive looting of the public treasury had occurred in both countries. By mid-1986, no final reckoning of the amounts involved had yet been revealed in either state.

22. Among those involved in various recent acts of transnational corruption are the following: former Prime Minister Tanaka of Japan, Prince

Bernħard of the Netherlands, President Bongo of Gabon, President Park of Korea, former Prime Minister Busia of Ghana, and the late President Arrientos of Bolivia, the Shah of Iran (and many members of his family), former President Marcos of the Philippines and his wife, former President Duvalier of Haiti and his wife etc. A full list would fill several volumes.

23. That competition has even been responsible for the manufacture of an American fighter plane specifically designed for export, the Northrop F-5E. At a cost of $2 million per plane, it is literally the "better mousetrap" of modern fighters, and has been sold to the air forces of Malaysia, Taiwan, Brazil, Jordan, Iran, Saudi Arabia, Switzerland, and Korea. Joseph P. Albright, "How to get a new plane (and its maker) off the ground," *New York Times Magazine*, February 8, 1976, p. 13.

24. These dates are drawn from U.S. Arms Control and Disarmament Agency, *World Military Expenditures and Arms Transfers* (Washington, D.C., 1985). See also "Arms Sales: A Thriving Bazaar," *The Middle East*, 6th ed. (Washington, D.C.: Congressional Quarterly, Inc., 1986), pp. 67–80.

25. United Brands Company admitted paying a $1,250,000 bribe to a former president of Honduras in return for a reduction in the banana export tax. Shortly before the disclosure, United Brands' chairman, Eli Black, leaped to his death from the 44th floor of the Pan Am Building in New York. *New York Times*, February 15, 1976.

26. U.S. Senate, "Lockheed Bribery," *op. cit.;* for discussions of the problem of competition in relation to transnational corruption, see the following: Milton S. Gwirtzman, "Is Bribery Defensible?" *New York Times Magazine*, October 5, 1975, p. 19: James M. Shevis, "The Web of Corporate Corruption," *AFL/CIO American Federationist*, October, 1975, p. 5; Walter Guzzardi, Jr., "An Unscandalized View of those 'Bribes' Abroad," *Fortune*, July, 1975, p. 118.

27. Edwin O. Reischauer, "The Lessons of the Lockheed Scandal," *Newsweek*, May 10, 1976, p. 97.

28. Gunnar Myrdal, *loc. cit.*, claimed that officials from communist countries were free from the taint of corruption. I was unable to find documentation about such activity, but my own research in Africa revealed several instances in which Soviet officials not only provided "commissions" to African government officials to secure trade deals, but freely dispensed such gifts as scholarships to officials' sons, trips to Moscow and the Black Sea resorts, cases of vodka, automobiles, cameras, and drawing rights on foreign exchange accounts in Swiss banks. I was also informed by an Iranian official visiting St. Louis that Czech, Soviet, and Polish officials and trade agents could and did draw on special funds for informal payments to Iranian officials.

29. For a full description of the revelations of 1977, see Lester A. Sobel, ed., *Corruption in Business* (New York: Facts on File, 1977).

30. F. Lessery, comment in *University of Michigan Journal of Law Reform* (Fall, 1979), p. 191.

31. Lessery, p. 191: Jacoby et al., 1977, pp. 10, 32.

32. Lessery, p. 192; Slade, Comment in *Harvard International Law Journal*, 22, 1 (Winter, 1981), p. 129.

33. Kugel and Gruenberg, p. 135.

41

An American Attempt to Control International Corruption

Michael Rosenthal

The Foreign Corrupt Practices Act of 1977 (FCPA) represented an attempt to curb the growth of 'questionable payments' made by U.S.-based multinational corporations to foreign government officials. Much of the controversy surrounding the bill results from its explicit attempt to enforce American political and social morality abroad, and in the years since its passage, the bill still serves as one of the first national legislative responses to international bribery and corruption. Consequently, it provides an interesting case study in attempts to control corruption.

As Le Vine points out, the FCPA is thus far unique in world legislative annals.[1] Though all countries have laws proscribing official bribery, and though several international agreements attempt to deal with financial improprieties of multinational corporations, the national laws in question do not criminalize bribery committed by its corporate citizens in the course of their foreign activities (as does the FCPA), and the international agreements are largely hortatory in nature.[2] The very existence of the FCPA, then, demands explanation. It will be argued here, first, that the convergence of a unique set of socio-political circumstances (Watergate, the international corporate bribery scandals of the 1970s, the advent of a national administration—that of Jimmy Carter—committed to a foreign policy explicitly based on moral predicates, plus the consequent reactivation of more general American sentiments about public morality and corruption) all played a critical role in securing the passage of the FCPA. Second, we argue that a set of perceptions about the economic (and political) effects of international bribery and corruption, based on the reality of a radically changed international economic order, as well as the defensive reactions of the MNCs and their allies, also contributed to the final passage and form of the act.

701

It should be added that our focus is not the provisions of the FCPA itself, though reference to some of those provisions occurs in the discussion. Rather, by looking through the lenses of its champions and detractors, we stress the circumstances, the contexts, within which it was drafted, passed, and put into effect.

The legislative justifications for the FCPA—almost every bill reported to the floor of the houses of congress is accompanied by a committee report in which "need for the legislation" is set out—provide a starting point here. These justifications generally summarize key arguments made by the members of the reporting committee, and by the witnesses heard by it. All the committees which worked on drafts of the FCPA (one House, two Senate, and one conference committee) agreed that the legislation prevents, or at least attempts to prevent, morally reprehensible conduct by American multinational corporations. Corruption and bribery in the specific, American frame of reference, are viewed as inherently dirty, evil and wrong. As Robert Brooks observes, "Even when it is distinctly qualified as political or business or social corruption, the suggestion is subtly conveyed of organic corruption and of everything vile and repugnant to the physical senses which the latter implies."[3] This perspective is further reinforced by the legislative definition of the word "corruptly" as it is used in the law. Witherspoon, citing one of the Senate reports, notes that "corruptly" is used to describe payment made to "induce the recipient to misuse his official position in order to wrongfully direct business to the payor or his client" and that a necessary condition for this (in the committee's own words) is an "evil motive or purpose."[4]

Corruption becomes even more evil when it undermines capitalism. The hearings record and the committee reports contain numerous references to corruption as eroding the ideal of competition, and the view was frequently expressed that bribes would replace the work ethic. This too strikes at the core of the American political and business ethos. Though this justification seems on its face economic, it was more often treated as a moral argument. Witherspoon, for example, argues the moral ramifications of corrupt trade on capitalism: "From a social perspective, business transactions that generate the payment of questionable or illegal payments are morally repugnant; such transactions are thought to corrupt not only the recipient but the giver as well."[5] By extension, it could be argued—and so it was in congress—that corrupt payments would taint both the multinationals and their hosts. Senator Proxmire, one of the original sponsors of the FCPA, is to the point:

The image of our government abroad is tarnished and the effectiveness of our foreign policy diminished. Bribery undermines fair competition between American firms. Price and quality no longer control the market. The growth, profitability and employment levels of firms operating in such circumstances are distorted. There's just no disagreement on these principles or on the venal effect of bribery, that it is wrong.[6]

The moral argument as justification is thrown into even clearer focus when it is viewed in the context of the American political scene during the mid-1970s. There is little question that at the time, American political attitudes were shaped, at least partially, but in this case substantially, by the Watergate affair. Watergate represented a watershed for American perceptions about corruption. The country's highest elected official had become involved in an affair which (at least) the media was willing to call corrupt, and which evoked perhaps uncritical but certainly widespread appreciation of the implications of corruption. As Michael Johnston notes, "Watergate was also a political turning point. It shook many people's faith in government and politics and spawned a host of efforts at reform."[7] Using Heidenheimer's schema, it can be argued that given Watergate, corruption in general was more readily condemned in America, and thus, some corruption which had previously been viewed as "grey" became "black" corruption. As Heidenheimer explains, "The evaluation of 'black corruption' indicates that in that setting that particular action is one which a majority consensus of both elite and mass opinion would condemn and would want to see punished on grounds of principle. 'Grey corruption' indicates that some elements, usually elites, may want to see the action punished, others not, and the majority may well be ambiguous."[8] After Watergate, as Johnston indicates, Americans became more sensitized to corruption and (hence) much more skeptical about the behavior of those in power. Thus, there was a shift in opinion which predisposed condemnation of corporate bribery, which had played a key role in Watergate. As Romaneski notes, "The Watergate scandal heightened the public's sense of political morality and raised concerns about high level corruption in both the public and private sectors. The FCPA was born in this morality oriented post-Watergate atmosphere."[9]

Watergate, of course, also triggered the revelations and scandals which ultimately led to the FCPA. The Watergate investigation uncovered the fact that many corporations had made illegal contributions to the Committee to Re-Elect the President (CREEP) through foreign connections, and this in turn led to further investigations of these corporations' international financial dealings. The revelations apparently surprised some people, since the scope of bribery and corruption in international and domestic trade had not been evident up to that point. As former Securities and Exchange Commission (SEC) Deputy Direcctor Wallace Timmeny noted, "We at the Securities and Exchange Commission were watching the Special Prosecutor and were intrigued by the devices the corporate community had used to get the funds for the contributions out of the corporate arena, away from corporate books."[10] What ensued was a set of full scale SEC investigations, including a 'voluntary' disclosure program, which persuaded corporations governed by the SEC to reveal their 'questionable payments' abroad. The investigation disclosed large-scale payments ultimately involving as many as 600 firms. The payments ranged in value from $6,000 to over $100 million (by Lockheed); in view of the amounts and the number of firms involved, it was clear the problem was neither new nor an isolated one.[11]

Adding to this aura of distrust were disclosures leading to several major bribery scandals involving the business community. Two were particularly painful. The first was the suicide of Eli Black, chairman of the board of United Brands. Black, by common repute a stable and respected individual, committed suicide without an apparent motive. A standard SEC investigation unveiled the fact that Black had recently authorized payment of bribes to the Honduran government and had not reported one of the payments to the board of directors. As Greanias and Windsor explain, "Black had apparently first offered a bribe to the president of Honduras, who appears to have rejected the offer; United Brands was then approached by the (Honduran) economics minister. The bribe was paid to a Swiss bank account. A second payment of the same amount was never made. Black did not report the bribe to his board of directors. Company books were falsified."[12] A second scandal, the Lockheed affair, drew even more publicity. Lockheed was shown to have paid out massive amounts of bribe money over a seven-year period in several countries, and in doing so had almost driven itself to bankruptcy. Among the recipients were former Japanese Prime Minister Tanaka and Prince Bernhard of Belgium.[13] These and other scandals, combined with Watergate, provided an environment hospitable to anti-bribery and anti-corruption measures such as the FCPA.

Further strengthening the drive for morality was the foreign policy pursued by the Carter administration. Carter had campaigned for a foreign policy based on human rights, not economic domination, and legislation such as the FCPA fitted his vision. In the Carter view, American business should pursue profit only by moral means, and any other path would be counterproductive to our foreign policy objectives. Corrupt business practices could only pollute American foreign policy. Witherspoon epitomized the Carter position:

> From an American political perspective, corrupt practices adversely affect the foreign policy interests of the United States; corrupt practices embarrass the United States and the recipient countries and create strains in the United States' relations with friendly foreign nations."[14]

Carter envisioned businesses and businessmen as American ambassadors of goodwill throughout the world. Given that business and government had to a considerable extent become partners, Carter felt the partnership could be put to productive use in the arena of foreign policy in what Greanias and Windsor describe as a proconsular relationship:

> Business, once an agglomeration of private concerns for the most part run privately, has moved toward the epicenter of the public sector. This movement has not been wholly voluntary, but it has nonetheless taken place. The business enterprise no longer simply operates subject within a political environment. It has itself become a political institution, subject to many of the diverse pressures brought to bear on any public institution. It has also become a conduit for government action, summarized in the concept of the corporation as government proconsul.[15]

Thus, if American business was to play its supportive, proconsular role in foreign policy, its corrupt activities abroad would have to be sharply curtailed. And if American MNCs could not do so on their own, they would need legislative assistance to that end. The revelations of international corruption during the 1970s suggested that precisely such restraints were needed. In the FCPA, then, business morality and the moral imperatives of foreign policy could be joined as one. Noonan underlines the point: "America's ambassadors—that is, its businessmen—were to show American purity throughout the globe. Secular requirements had never so comprehensively embraced and extended the bribery ethic."[16]

The fact that the FCPA won unanimous approval in Congress demonstrates the extent to which the issue was tied to moral considerations. As Noonan points out, "Like a vote against obscenity in the nineteenth century, a vote against bribery in 1977 was certain of public approval in America. No member of Congress cared to stand as the champion of corruption at home or abroad."[17] It should be added that Congress' reponse had no echo in legislatures elsewhere, even in those countries most affected by the 1970 scandals, perhaps because issues of public morality become national issues much more frequently in the

United States than elsewhere. Europeans were generally amazed and dumbfounded by Richard Nixon's "I am not a crook" speech during the Watergate affair; Americans might have reacted with skepticism, but they understood it in the context of an historical American preoccupation with official probity.

Unquestionably, a general resurgence of popular concern about official and corporate ethics, the former catalyzed by Watergate and the latter by the revelations of corporate bribery abroad, plus the renewed stress on the moral aspects of foreign policy, all helped to make the FCPA possible. These are only part of the explanation, however, necessary but not sufficient causes of the unique event the FCPA turned out to be. Other factors, both contextual and immediate to the arguments made about the proposed law, contributed to the final product.

The record of the FCPA's legislative history reveals two general economic arguments on its behalf. One speaks to the need for stability and predictability in the international marketplace, conditions which (presumably) cannot be maintained if bribery becomes the basis of international business competition. In principle, bribery generalized would make normal business extremely difficult, if not impossible, and could lead to a Hobbesian economic world ruled by the most financially powerful, or to the elimination of entrepreneurial risk-takers, or, at worst, to the collapse of the market itself.

The other is the position originally taken by the SEC, which argued that it was important for shareholders to know what their company was doing so as to be able to monitor potential profitability. Disclosure of 'questionable' payments, according to the SEC, would not only accomplish this goal, but would also discourage American multinationals from overstepping the bounds of corporate propriety or venturing too far into uncharted—and hence dangerous—commercial seas. (The argument is analogous to that made by proponents of campaign finance disclosure, who assumed that candidates shown to have taken dirty money would be punished at the ballot box. It doesn't appear to have worked out that way for campaign finances, but there is no evidence that the SEC considered the analogy or doubted the effects of disclosure on improper corporate activity.)

The first economic argument is based upon the self-evident need for a stable world trading economy. In order for world trade to operate efficiently, there must be a high degree of stability and predictability in the international marketplace. Since there is no ultimate enforcement mechanism in world trade, the traders themselves must guarantee the fairness of their exchanges. This is especially true for the multinationals, who despite their enormous economic power remain vulnerable to the political power of host states. As Le Vine notes, "Their survival depends crucially on two factors: international market stability and a friendly international environment in which to operate. If they overstep the bounds, embarrass their hosts, or indulge in excessive capital transfers, they become vulnerable to national retaliation."[18] Thus, by imposing a measure of stable restraint on the foreign operations of American firms, the FCPA would in the long run prove beneficial to the corporate economy.

Witherspoon is again to the point: "Viewed from an economic perspective, payments made for purposes of obtaining or retaining business are so contrary to the notion of a free enterprise system that the marketplace is undermined. In such situations, price, quality, the fundamentals of fair competition, no longer control, and business is directed not to the most efficient producer, but to the most corrupt."[19]

It must be added that this argument in turn rested on the perception of an international economic order radically transformed in several key aspects since the end of World War II. The new environment included an exponential increase in world economic interdependence, which in turn boosted the importance of the foreign trade sector in virtually all countries; the emergence or appearance of a variety of new international economic and political actors, including over 100 new sovereign states (most of them poor and inexperienced in world trade), as well as the multinationals themselves, the majority of which were not only American but almost quasi-sovereign in their operations; and the creation of a new set of markets for super-valued goods such as oil, strategic minerals, and military hardware. The point is that a world of economic opportunity—and temptation—opened to multinational entrepreneurs and national officials operating in the new environment.[20] It is clear that the FCPA's proponents were very much aware of both the new international situation and the dangers it posed for American trade and traders in the international market. Their intent, given scandals and revelations of the period, was to pull American traders and the country from the edge of further harm and to restore, in the proponents' terms, the integrity of American business activity abroad. The scandals and revelations had already substantially damaged American political and economic interests on the international scene; it was time to put on the brakes.

Under the circumstances, it is hardly surprising that the United States took the lead in attempting to persuade other countries to curb corrupt dealings by the MNCs, whatever their origin. Moreover, since the United States is home to the largest number of MNCs and MNEs and is one of the leaders in world trade, any deterioration of the world economic order due to international corporate corruption would be bound to hurt American interests abroad, particularly if widespread exposure of such activity operated to erode American firms' competitive positions.

At any event, though it proved difficult to persuade other countries to go much beyond hortatory statements such as the OECD's code of conduct for MNCs, the increase in the number of in-house codes restricting corporations' ability to engage in corrupt activities strongly suggests the MNCs took the matter seriously. Evidently the MNCs recognized that their self-interest required them to "bite the bullet" of control at least insofar as their own rules were concerned. Leyton-Brown describes these standards and the context of their adoption:

> There is a widespread belief in the American business community that measures by companies to 'clean up their own act' would be far more effective in curbing improper foreign payments and restoring public confidence than governmental or intergovernmental enforcement. One of the most prominent of these internal measures is the adoption of a formal code of conduct specifying practices to be avoided by the company and its employees. These codes may be adopted voluntarily by management, or introduced as a result of shareholder resolution.[21]

While it is possible that in some cases such standards were drawn up to avoid governmental regulation, it seems clear that the majority of American MNCs understood the implications of corporate bribery abroad and the effect it could have on international trade. They also understood that revelations of bribery could ruin their reputations, as well as invite possible retaliation by the host governments. Windsor and Greanias contend that "the statistics seem to indicate that the bribery revelations were the principal motivating force behind the decision to publish such documents."[22] Moreover, it cannot have escaped the notice of the MNCs officers and boards of directors that the revelations themselves frequently led to loss of business or profits, or both. Braithwaite points out, for example, that one of the immediate consequences of the Lockheed disclosures was the loss of a $130 million contract in Japan: "In the years subsequent to the revelations (the company) almost certainly lost some important contracts because governments feared the risk of being (unfairly) accused of corruption because they were buying from Lockheed."[23]

The other economic argument presented was that advanced by the SEC. The SEC saw hidden payments and questionable practices as important information for actual and potential investors, since such practices reflected the companies' policies and financial stability. Timmeny explains the SEC's reasoning:

> The investor had a right to know if the company's books were tampered with; it seemed clear, we thought, that the investor had a right to know that there was a possibility of dishonest accounting. We also thought that an investor had a right to know if management was using his money to violate either U.S. or foreign laws. We also believed that an investor had the right to know when and how management was obtaining significant lines of business through bribery, or was subjecting the company to risks of losing significant lines of business if the bribery activities of the company were discovered. Finally, we believed an investor had a right to know of management stewardship of corporate assets if that stewardship involved the outlay of millions of dollars to consultants with no accountability for the consultants' use of the funds.[24]

Thus, the SEC felt it had to act to protect stockholders rights; thus, under pressure from the SEC and the corruption scandals, the corporations adopted the policy statements, at first with some reluctance, later freely and without further prodding.

Like the moral argument, however, justification based on economic interest fails to provide sufficient explanation for passage of the FCPA. Still more was at work. The FCPA contains two sets of general provisions, one dealing with disclosure and the other with criminalization. If the FCPA was created only to deal with the market problems involved in bribery, then there would have been little need for the criminalization codes. This, in fact, was the original position of the Ford administration on the question of federal legislation to deal with the problem of corporate bribery and payments abroad. Disclosure, it argued, would allow the economic community to be aware of bribes paid, and thus, host governments and investors could react as they saw fit. Disclosure would add stability in that it would deter bribery and would also allow nations to avoid dealing with corrupt companies. *The University of Michigan Law Review* discusses the way in which disclosure would (potentially) operate:

> There may be a basic loss in favorable public relations for the company. More direct consequential costs could include civil and criminal prosecutions under the tax laws, loss of significant amounts of potential future business, law suits seeking contract damages, removal of responsible corporate officers, criminal prosecutions in the foreign countries involved, shareholder suits against directors responsible for the payments, expropriation or nationalization of corporate assets located in the foreign countries, and perhaps most damaging liability under the securities laws for omission or misrepresentation of material facts in any disclosure document.[25]

Though the article goes on to argue that disclosure would not be wholly effective because the benefits of bribery might outweigh these costs, the opinion of many officials was that disclosure could solve (at least) the economic problems. The Ford administration, through the Richardson task force report, enunciated the benefit of disclosure: "It would offer a means to give public reassurance of the essential accountability of multinational corporations."[26] Richardson himself argued that "criminalization . . . would represent little more than a policy assertion," though he conceded, in open testimony and in the task force report, that disclosure by itself might not be enough to do the job.[27] Evidently, the congress felt that such an assertion was necessary, and thus included a criminalization measure in the FCPA; and it is just as evident that there must have been more than economics at stake in the question.

Disclosure also relates to a second argument against a strictly economic rationale for the FCPA. One advantage of using disclosure as the sole or primary means of policing the MNCs is that companies would still be able to compete, through bribery, in nations where bribery was acceptable and legal. Criminalization would forbid this practice (though not such things as "grease" payments, designed to facilitate ongoing negotiations).[28] As Murray Weidenbaum notes, failure to pay such bribes can have dire effects upon certain business relations: "The practice of funneling cash into the hands of government officials or their representatives is long-standing and is defended by many business executives as the only way they can compete effectively abroad. One businessman in Africa said in an interview, 'You have to pay small bribes, called 'dash,' to get anything done.'"[29] Though it is possible to argue that the government was only interested in long-term economic policy, this seems a bit far fetched given the fact that the FCPA locks the American firms into a position of relative disadvantage with regard to (foreign) firms which are able to bribe. As Witherspoon notes, there was a tacit trade off between economics and morals: "In its congressional hearings on the various bills, congress specifically considered and anticipated the negative result that the act would have on U.S. competition and exports. Despite this forseeable negative impact on U.S. exports, Congress decided that U.S. companies should be at a competitive disadvantage if their only means of competing is through the payment of bribes."[30]

The balancing act to which Witherspoon alludes perhaps provides the final key to an understanding of what led to the Foreign Corrupt Practices Act. In effect, a convergence of the moral and economic interests involved resulted in a call for action against corporate improprieties. Though the means which they chose were very different, the forces which wanted to control corporate bribery managed to agree upon a single goal. The ambiguity and dual enforcement measures of the FCPA—both disclosure and criminalization—can be explained by this collision of interests. While those in favor of curbing bribery for economic reasons wanted only a disclosure bill, the political context in which the debate took place forced them to make concessions to the moralist position. Thus, the resulting law reflected both positions, embodied in a section dealing with disclosure and another with criminalization. This compromise, while seemingly giving each side language that satisfied its aims, did little to clarify the larger ambiguities surrounding the two alternatives. If the disclosure section in fact operated to provide full exposure of corporate expenditures abroad, then so much greater would become the incentives to find ways to circumvent the law. And the criminalization section, if examined carefully, appeared to place nearly insurmountable evidentiary requirements in the path of successful prosecution.[31] The record is silent on whether these possible consequences were considered by the authors of the FCPA; it is more than likely that each side, in its anxiety to have its language incorporated in the law, chose to accept ambiguity as the price of compromise. The ambiguities in the bill also result from a lack of clear agreement on motives. The MNCs and those arguing the economic perspective tried to blunt as much as possible the restrictions on business which the moralists attempted to impose upon the corporations.

An analysis of proposed amendments to the FCPA also highlights the conflicting goals of its sponsors. Since the passage of the FCPA in 1977, there have been several attempts to remove some of the restrictions imposed upon corporations by the law. The most publicized of these was the Chaffee amendment, which passed the Senate in 1981, but was never able to get past the House. The Chaffee amendment tried to remove the element of a moral crusade from the FCPA by allowing (what under the terms of the FCPA would be illegal) gifts and payments in countries where such transactions are allowed. The amendment "includes one general exception to its anti-bribery provisions, allowing any payment or gift 'which is lawful under the laws and regulations of the country' of the recipient foreign official. This would override any other anti-bribery provision in the (law) whenever the laws of the recipient's country authorize the payment."[32] The Chaffee amendment had administration support, a clear sign that the government had moved from the strict moralist position.

What seems to have permitted this decline in the moralists' position is a change in public perceptions and goals. With the coming of the Reagan administration and its laissez-faire policies, most Americans became less concerned with questions of public morality. Moreover, though Watergate still played a role in coloring public political perception, as it began to fade into the background, it ceased to be the paramount measure by which the public judged official actions. Finally, there was also the growing perception that we were not competing effectively with the Japanese, among many others, and that this was due to (largely unspecified) government interference. This perception, in the context of a growing recession, made for a much more hospitable climate for freer-wheeling corporate activity.

Did the FCPA fulfill its objectives—and the expectations of its authors? Clearly, as their testimony indicates, the proponents of the law both expected it to restrain improper American corporate activity abroad, and to act as a model and (perhaps) a goad for the adoption of similar legislation elsewhere. A circumstantial case—albeit a weak one—can be made for the proposition that the law did restrain the American MNCs. Though the MNCs have devised various ways of sidestepping the FCPA, and though bribes are apparently still being offered by the MNCs—and accepted by foreign officials—nothing on the scale of the 1970s scandals and revelations has surfaced since.[33] Evidence that the MNCs have at least accepted the reality of the law lies in the fact that many of them have transformed some of the law's provisions they had earlier denounced into company policy. It is also possible that the open market the MNC's always claimed to espouse may have become more of a reality with the FCPA in place; at the very least, the new rules (augmented by a heightened sensitivity abroad) no longer give an automatic competitive edge to those American firms able to pay the largest bribes. Almost certainly, the shock of the events which led to the FCPA, as well as the presence of the law, has had some restraining effect on the MNCs and their international behavior. On the other hand, the FCPA did not become a model law for other countries, or stimulate much more legislative response than for example, the hortatory MNC "code" of the EEC. Clearly, the Congress of the United States, granting its good intentions. could not legislate business morality for the world. The actions other countries took in response to the MNC scandals of the 1970s never reflected either the intensity of American moral concerns at the time, or the MNCs own self-conscious attempts to cleanse their escutcheons by confessing their sins. Rather, usually there was embarrassed prosecution and/or chastisement of their own officials caught in the guilty spotlight, and an oft-expressed hope that the issue would soon fade from the headlines.

Thus, the FCPA still stands alone, but that may be because it did in fact, all things considered, help to control—though not overcome—the problem which called it into being in the first place.

Postscript

Since the adoption of the Foreign Corrupt Practices Act of 1977, the U.S. Department of Justice has brought fourteen prosecutions under this law. Only one actually came to trial; the others were disposed of by plea bargains, or under pleas of guilty or *nolo contendere*. The 1981 prosecution of McDonnell-Douglas corporation's executives for corrupt practices was under pre-1977 law. (Personal communication from Barbara E. Nicastro, Chief, Litigation Branch of the Fraud Section, Criminal Division, U.S. Department of Justice, Dec. 22, 1986.)

Notes

1. Le Vine, *supra* in this volume.
2. Fejfar, pp. 43, 50-51.
3. Brooks, p. 57.
4. Brennan, p. 65.
5. Witherspoon, p. 533.
6. Windsor and Greanias, p. 60.
7. Johnston, p. 109.
8. Heidenheimer, pp. 26-27.
9. Romaneski, p. 407.
10. Timmeny, p. 235.
11. See Sobel, pp. 99-161, for details.
12. Windsor and Greanias, p. 26.
13. The Lockheed scandal, in addition to shaking the Lockheed corporate structure to its foundations, had even more serious international repercussions. As a direct consequence of the Lockheed revelations, former Japanese prime minister Tanaka and several other powerful political and business leaders were indicted and prosecuted, the prince consort of the Netherlands (Bernhard) was publicly disgraced and forced to surrender his official positions, and several other countries (Italy, Germany, Turkey, Mexico, Columbia), were driven to prosecute officials known to have accepted questionable payments from Lockheed, or suffered acute embarrassment as a result.
14. Witherspoon, p. 532.
15. Windsor and Greanias, p. 43.
16. Noonan, p. 680.
17. Noonan, p. 313.
18. Le Vine, 1976, p. 8.
19. Witherspoon, pp. 533-4.
20. See Le Vine 1976, and *supra* in this volume, p. *00*.
21. Leyton-Brown, p. 11.

22. Windsor and Greanias, p. 109.
23. Braithwaite, p. 137.
24. Timmeny, p. 236.
25. "Foreign Bribes," p. 1248.
26. Windsor and Greanias, p. 54. See also Message from the President, 1976.
27. Windsor and Greanias, p. 52.
28. In the Conference Report, at p. 12. The committee clarified "the scope of the prohibition against (illegal) payments by requiring that the purpose of the payment must be to influence any act or decision of a foreign official (including a decision not to act) or to induce such official to use his influence to affect a government act or decision so as to assist an issuer in obtaining, retaining or directing business to any person." In the Act itself, the relevant sections are #103 and #104. Excluded from these provisions—by omission—are payments made to officials to permit the cutting of red tape or to speed up a licensing process, for instance. Such payments are commonly known as "grease" payments.
29. Weidenbaum, p. 256.
30. Witherspoon, p. 219.
31. Braithwaite, p. 131.
32. Duncan, p. 219.
33. "Anti-Bribery Law: Difficulty in Complying," *St. Louis Post-Dispatch*, April 23, 1979, p. 8A.

References

Beswick, Albert L. "Corporate Compliance With the FCPA" *Syracuse Journal of International Law and Commerce* (Fall 1982), pp. 315–23.

Braithwaite, John. "Transnational Corporations and Corruption: Towards Some International Solutions," *International Journal of the Sociology of the Law*, 1979:7, pp. 125–42.

Brennan, Bartley A. "Amending the Foreign Corrupt Practices Act of 1977: 'Clarifying' or 'Gutting' a Law?," *Journal of Legislation*, Winter 1984, pp. 56–89.

Brooks, Robert. "The Nature of Political Corruption," in Heidenheimer, Arnold (ed.), *Political Corruption: Readings*, pp. 56–61.

Duncan, John W. "Modifying the Foreign Corrupt Practices Act: The Search for a Practical Standard," *Northwestern Journal of International Law & Business*, Spring 1982, pp. 203–25.

Fejfar, Mary A. *Regulation of Business by International Agencies*. St. Louis: Center for the Study of American Business, Washington University, 1983.

"Foreign Bribes and the Securities Acts Disclosure Requirements," *Michigan Law Review*, May 1976, pp. 1222–42.

Greanias, George, and Windsor, Duane. *The Foreign Corrupt Practices Act: Anatomy of a Statute*. New Brunswick, NJ: Transaction, 1978.

Heidenheimer, Arnold J., ed. *Political Corruption: Readings in Comparative Analysis*. New Brunswick, NJ: Transaction Books, 1978.

Johnston, Michael. *Political Corruption and Public Policy in America*. Monterey, California: Brooks/Cole, 1982.

Le Vine, Victor T. "The Bribe Goes Global: Preliminary Reflections on the

New Transnational Aspects of Political Corruption," paper presented at the Edinburgh Congress of the International Studies Association, August, 1976.

Leyton-Brown, David. "Controlling American Corporate Political Payments Abroad," paper delivered at the Edinburgh Congress of the International Studies Association, August, 1976.

Message from the President of the United States (to the congress) urging enactment of proposed legislation to require disclosure of payments to foreign officials. August 3, 1976. Washington, D.C.: Government Printing Office, 1976.

Noonan, John T., Jr. *Bribery*. New York: MacMillan, 1985.

Romaneski, Mark. "The Foreign Corrupt Practices Act of 1977: an analysis of its impact and future," *Boston College International and Comparative Law Review,* Spring 1982, pp. 405–430.

Sobel, Lester A., ed. *Corruption in Business*. New York: Facts on File: 1977.

Timmeny, Wallace. "An Overview of the FCPA," *Syracuse Journal of International Law and Commerce*, Fall, 1982, pp. 235–44.

United States Senate. *Foreign Corrupt Practices, Conference Report (To accompany S.305)*, December 6, 1977. Washington, D.C.: Government Printing Office, 1978.

Weidenbaum, Murray L. *Business, Government and the Public*. Englewood Cliffs, New Jersey: Prentice Hall, 1981.

Witherspoon, Ruth Aurora. "Multinational Corporations—Governmental Regulations of Business Ethics Under the Foreign Corrupt Practices Act of 1977: An Analysis," *Dickinson Law Review*, Spring 1983, pp. 531–93.

Part IV

DISTINCTIONS, REACTIONS, AND EFFECTS

Part IV

Distinctions, Reactions and Effects

OVERVIEW

Thus far we have considered the evolution of the concepts which give the notion of corruption its various meanings, the relationships between corruption and the development and change of political systems, and the factors which make those systems more or less vulnerable to particular forms of corruption. It remains for us, now, to consider the consequences of corruption: how elites and ordinary citizens judge, and react to, various kinds of behavior; the ways in which those reactions aid or impede anti-corruption efforts; and the effects of corruption on the political and economic systems in which it occurs.

Social perceptions of right and wrong are critical links between corruption and its broader consequences. As episodes in several countries have shown, even relatively minor instances of misconduct can produce far-reaching political disruption and change if significant numbers of people see the actions involved as seriously wrong. Citizens judge elite activity and public policy in terms of norms and distinctions of their own, derived from religious beliefs, political culture, and everyday experience. Legal and social definitions of corruption will thus often diverge, for at the level of mass perceptions and reactions, "corruption" means what people think it means, and exists where they think they see it. Where there is meaningful mass political participation, such perceptions and judgments can set the effective boundaries of acceptable elite behavior. Elites, too, judge the ethical aspects of situations in terms of informal norms and standards that reflect their own backgrounds and the political cultures within which they live. Nations may reflect several such political cultures or subcultures based on contrasts of social class, religion, ethnicity, or region, to name but a few possibilities.

Thus corruption and scandal are two different things; we may encounter either in the absence of the other. Scandal can be spontaneous, difficult to channel, and unclear in its consequences. But in other cases, a widely shared sense of scandal can be mobilized and channeled by proponents of reform, to provide important political momentum for official responses to corruption. Anti-corruption policies come in many shapes and sizes, and vary from country to country in response to structural and political factors. The most successful strategies will frequently involve both reactive and proactive initiatives, including proscriptive legislation, vigorous investigations, and the promulgation of clear standards of conduct. The content and success of such policies will also frequently depend upon their "fit" with their cultural context.

The utility of reform efforts must be balanced against the costs and benefits of corruption itself—an issue which has spawned a literature and a debate all its own. For a long time, analysts of corruption saw many costs and virtually no benefits. Corruption, in this view, is a major impediment to political and economic development, has few if any beneficiaries beyond the ranks of its immediate practitioners, and must bear the blame for a major share of the problems of developing nations. Others argue in terms of contingencies: while in many cases the costs of corruption will be sizeable, a number of intermediate factors must be taken into account. These include the levels at which corruption takes place, the types of stakes and behavior involved, and the general political and developmental setting. In at least a few cases, the probable benefits of corruption outweigh its costs.

Different varieties of corruption can have different consequences, particularly if we assess their effects not in terms of overall system development, but rather in the ways various forms of corruption strengthen or weaken the linkages between and among various strata in society. Viewed in this light, some corruption links people together into lasting patterns of reciprocal exchange, while others are sharply disruptive and amount to little more than the illicit exploitation of some people by others. In any event, instead of assuming that politics and policy would be orderly and efficient without corruption—a position which decides the issue of consequences *a priori*—corruption must be compared to its genuine, imperfect alternatives. We may at times conclude that while corruption entails significant costs and waste of scarce resources, there are few real assurances that its absence would have resulted in better policy and politics.

Public Conceptions and Corruption Distinctions: An Introduction

Any discussion of the political consequences of corruption must take into consideration the perceptions of both elites and ordinary citizens, and must recognize that their judgments—while often vague, contradictory, and at variance with more formal standards—will influence what is regarded as unacceptable behavior, and what responses (if any) are likely to occur in specific instances. Three studies present these social conceptions of corruption, analyzing the judgments of American elites and ordinary citizens and comparing those judgments to results of similar research in Canada.

In the opening chapter of this section, John G. Peters and Susan Welch present the results of a survey of legislators in several American states. Like the people they represent, these officials perceive many shadings and gradients of right and wrong. While their judgments are influenced by the legality or illegality of a hypothetical action, a variety of other considerations are taken into account as well—some of which, of course, reflect these elites' greater experience in politics. However, even for these politically experienced individuals, there are many "gray zones" of behavior, and many kinds of misconduct which are seen as more or less "wrong" than others depending upon characteristics of situations and of the people involved.

Subtly shaded judgments are also found in Michael Johnston's survey of ordinary citizens in a major metropolitan area. No clear boundary between right and wrong emerges in judgments of a diverse set of hypothetical actions. Instead, there is a spectrum of finely graded relative judgments, with formal standards being tempered by common-sense rationalizations, equivocations, and standards of fairness learned in everyday life. Judgments of misconduct tend to cluster into perceived categories of wrongdoing, with different class-status groups varying significantly in their reactions to them.

In the third chapter, Kenneth M. Gibbons surveyed students in several regions of Canada. His data, too, reveal complexities in judgments of misconduct and wrongdoing. Individuals' evaluations of several different political "scenarios" do take formal standards into account, as people understand those standards, but also introduce a range of qualifications and relative comparisons. These judgments were in turn linked to more general political attitudes, such as party loyalties and some measures of political alienation. As in the American case, age is a strong factor as well: the older the individual, the stronger her or his condemnation of misconduct is likely to be. Gibbons also suggests that reactions to particular kinds of behavior interact with attitudes toward politics in general: We may conclude, on the basis of a few illicit actions, that politics is an inherently corrupt game, and this may lead us to judge subsequent cases in more demanding terms.

Latin America represents a particularly important case for study. We might point to the region's important resources, its economic problems, and its dependent relationship with respect to important world markets as critical aspects of the economic picture. On the political side are the lack of open political competition in many Latin American states, clientelistic followings which can help an ambitious politician take power (but which must be rewarded and held together when power has been won), and political instability, which creates an incentive for ruling elites to take as much as they can as quickly as they can, since a prolonged period in office is by no means a sure thing. Laurence Whitehead's emphasis is upon presidential graft, which can take root quickly in such a setting: whether the focus is upon internal expenditures, foreign trade and arms purchases, or illegitimate trade such as drug dealing, opportunities abound. Whitehead does identify contrasts among Latin American nations, however, and provides a useful comparative backdrop to our knowledge of such processes in the United States and other parts of the world. Presidential graft, like other kinds of corruption, raises troubling questions about future trends in economic and political development in Latin America.

42

Gradients of Corruption in Perceptions of American Public Life

*John G. Peters and
Susan Welch*

Though corruption has been an everpresent part of American political life (cf. Tocqueville, 1861), analysts of American politics have not
studied it systematically (for exceptions, see Greenstein, 1964; Gardiner, 1970; Wolfinger, 1972). This chapter offers a conceptual scheme
which circumvents definitional problems that have posed such a
roadblock to the systematic study of corruption. We also provide some
attitudinal data about corrupt acts gathered from state senators across
the United States and show how our scheme contributes to the analysis
of this data. Finally, some reasonable future research directions for the
study of corruption are briefly discussed.

Definitions of Political Corruption

The attention devoted to a serious examination of corruption in
America occurs largely at those times when particularly venal acts
have been exposed. Thus, the post-Watergate period has brought with
it a renewed interest in the study of political corruption, especially
among political scientists (cf. Rundquist et al., 1977; Scoble, 1973;
Gardiner 1970, Berg et al., 1976). In all of these studies it becomes
immediately apparent that no matter what aspect of American politics
is examined, the systematic study of corruption is hampered by the
lack of an adequate definition. What may be "corrupt" to one citizen,
scholar, or public official is "just politics" to another, or "indiscretion"
to a third. Several definitions of political corruption have been pro-

Source: John G. Peters and Susan Welch, "Political Corruption in America: A Search for
Definitions and a Theory." *American Political Science Review,* 78 (September 1978),
974–84. By permission of the publisher.

posed and generally can be classified according to three criteria: definitions based on legality, definitions based on the public interest, and definitions based on public opinion (Scott, 1972).

The definition of political corruption based on legalistic criteria assumes that political behavior is corrupt when it violates some formal standard or rule of behavior set down by a political system for its public officials. Perhaps the clearest statement of this definition has been given by J.S. Nye when he stated that a political act is corrupt when it "deviates from the formal duties of a public role (elective or appointive) becaue of private-regarding (personal, close family, private clique) wealth or status gains: or violates rules against the exercise of certain types of private-regarding influence" (Nye, 1967, p. 416). While such a definition of corruption is useful to the researcher in that it is generally clear-cut and can be operationalized, when the behavior in question allegedly deviates from a legal norm or standard which is not tied to a specific statute or court ruling, this definition of political corruption becomes less useful as the formal duties of office or the appropriate rules of influence become ambiguous. Moreover, this definition suffers from being simultaneously too narrow and too broad in scope; all illegal acts are not necessarily corrupt and all corrupt acts are not necessarily illegal.[1]

Definitions of political corruption based on notions of the public or common interest significantly broaden the range of behavior one might investigate. Consider the definition proposed by Arnold Rogow and Harold Lasswell: "A corrupt act violates responsibility toward at least one system of public or civic order and is in fact incompatible with (destructive of) any such system" (Rogow and Lasswell, 1966, pp. 132–33). While this definition focuses our attention on any act or set of acts which threaten to destroy a political system, the researcher has the responsibility of determining what the public or common interest is before assessing whether a particular act is corrupt. The possibility exists that a behavior may be proscribed by law as corrupt but be beneficial for the common good, such as "fixing" the papers of an illegal alien who contributed his labor and skills to a rapidly expanding economy. Furthermore, this definition enables a politician to justify almost any act by claiming that it is in the public interest.

A third approach to the definitional problem suggests that a political act is corrupt when the weight of public opinion determines it so (see, for example, Rundquist and Hansen, 1976). This conception of political corruption harbors the same limitations as the public interest focus. Studies of public opinion have revealed that on many issues public sentiments are either ambiguous (significant portions of the public hold no opinion or hold those of low intensity) or are divided in their opinions. Additionally, a definition of corruption based on public opinion must consider the differences which may exist between the public and political elites in their assessment of appropriate standards of public conduct.

This approach to political corruption is probably best illustrated in the work of Arnold J. Heidenheimer (1970). In his view the corruptness of political acts is determined by the interaction between the judgment of a particular act by the public and by political elites or public officials. According to this scheme, behavior is judged particularly heinous or corrupt if *both* public officials and the public judge it corrupt *and* both wish it restricted. This type of behavior is referred to as "black" corruption. An act such as "a public official involved in heroin trafficking" would most likely fit this category in that both groups find the act reprehensible and would demand punishment for the guilty public official. At the other end of the corruption spectrum might be categorized political acts judged corrupt by both public officials and the people, but which neither feel are severe enough to warrant sanction. Quite possibly such acts of "white" or petty corruption as a city council member fixing a parking ticket for a constituent fall into this category. Between these two extremes of corruption acts lie the forms of behavior which are the most difficult to define and detect, and consequently are potentially most destructive to a political system organized along democratic principles. Heidenheimer refers to these political acts as "gray corruption" when either public officials or the people want to see an action punished, while the other group does not, or it may well be that one group is intense about the issue and the other ambivalent or unconcerned.[2] Heidenheimer's work in this area, therefore, points to the existence of a scale or dimension of corruption that can be used to classify political behaviors according to their degree of corruptness from "black" to "gray" to "white." It does not, however, account very well for those acts seen as corrupt by only one group, nor does it seek to explain *why* some groups may see an act as corrupt but other groups see it as less corrupt. Although this conception of political corruption is based on the criterion of opinion (both public and elite), the assessment of a specific political act may rest on violation of a legal norm or a threat to the public interest. In other words, definitions of corruption are not mutually exclusive: elements of the public interest and public opinion criteria are embedded in legal norms which sanction certain political behaviors as corrupt.

Although the Heidenheimer scheme enables us to classify politically corrupt acts in a general way, a more detailed scheme seems required if we are to classify adequately the many variations of corrupt acts, and if we are to develop an explanation of why some acts are judged corrupt and others not. We propose to analyze potentially corrupt acts according to the component elements apparently involved with every political act or exchange. We believe this process can meaningfully be partitioned into the "public official" involved, the actual "favor" provided by the public official, the "payoff" gained by the public official, and the "donor" of the payoff and/or "recipient" of the "favor" act. Although at this early stage in the development of a theory of political corruption it would be too much to claim to be able to specify the exact nature of each of these components and its relation to the others, we do believe that examining acts of political corruption in this manner might hold the key to a better understanding of why public officials perceive some acts as corrupt and others as "just politics," and why public officials and the public may differ in their assessment.

When discussing the subdimensions of each component of a potentially corrupt act, we will be stating some propositions about what acts will be seen as corrupt. Those propositions will be discussed in some detail later. When examining a "public official" involved in an alleged act of corruption, we are particularly interested in whether the act was entered into in the performance of the official's *political* duties. Presumably, an act which is considered malfeasance, misfeasance, or nonfeasance of public duty is *more* corrupt than a behavior engaged in outside of one's official political role. In other words, misusing one's political office for private gain is more objectionable than engaging in questionable behavior outside of one's official duties.[3]

A second characteristic of the public official that seems to determine whether behavior is to be judged corrupt is the political nature of the public official's role. If a public official is in a judicial or other nonpolitical post, certain acts are more likely to be seen as corrupt than if the public official holds a political post. For example, judges have traditionally been held to higher standards with regard to conflict-of-interest situations than legislators. With the new congressional actions to regulate conflict of interest, it is possible that this situation may be changing at the national level, however.

The second component of a politically corrupt act is the "donor" of the payoff or "recipient" of the political favor. It is most important to determine if the "donor" is a *constituent,* broadly defined, or a nonconstituent. If the donor is a constituent, then a "favor" given is more likely to be perceived as *less* corrupt than if the favor is rendered to a nonconstituent. The reason is obvious: acts which are performed under the rubric of "constituency service," no matter how questionable, have a certain legitimacy. Of two similar, potentially corrupt acts, the odds are that the constituency-related act will be judged less corrupt than the service rendered to the nonconstituent. Beard and Horn (1975) offer two examples supporting this proposition. In one case, members of congress were asked about the legitimacy of putting favorable articles about campaign donors in the *Congressional Record,* as a "thank you" to donors. This was seen as more legitimate if the donor were a constituent rather than a firm outside the district. A second example involved accepting rides to and from one's congressional district on a national firm's private plane. If the firm had ties to the constituency, accepting such favors was seen as more legitimate than if the firm had no such ties. Probably the most corrupt situation is when the donor is the public official himself. If the public official can directly enrich himself by tapping the public till, he himself is the donor. Examples of this include padding the expense account, using public funds for personal travel, using money allocated for office expenses for personal activities, and so on.

Another characteristic to be considered is whether the "donor" of the payoff (recipient of the "favor") is more than one private individual or firm. We argue that the single donor will be perceived as making an action more corrupt than if the donor is a large group of individuals or firms.

A third component to consider is the "favor" provided by the public official. We can surmise that the corruptness of the favor will vary in some ways as does the nature of the donor. Private favors and nonconstituency favors will be seen as more corrupt than those with large public benefit or those done for a constituent.[4] Finally, if the favor is done in routine performance of duty rather than extraordinary activity, it is less likely to be seen as corrupt. For example, a member of congress who makes a routine phone call to a federal agency to check on a federal contract of a firm whose officers supported the congress member in an election campaign is less likely to be viewed as performing a corrupt act than one who makes threats or acts in a way that the federal bureaucrat perceives as non-routine.

The fourth component of a potentially corrupt act, the "payoff" given to the public official, is possibly the most important determinant of its perceived corruptness. The obvious fact to consider is, of course, the size of the payoff. It should come as no surprise that the larger the payoff, the greater the perceived degree of corruptness in the act, although as we shall see later on, just what is "large" can be difficult to agree upon. The payoff can also vary according to the long- versus short-range nature of the benefit to the public official. We would assume that a short-range benefit would be perceived as more corrupt than a payoff that will yield benefits at a much later date, because the long-range payoff is separated in time from the favor done. Consider, for instance, an official of a regulatory agency who takes a lucrative position in a regulated corporation after leaving government service. Presumably the official looked with some benevolence on the activities of the corporation while in public office; if that official had been given an immediate tangible payoff, for example a gift of money, we think most people would charge corruption. But the later payoff probably is seen by many as legitimate.[5]

In a similar vein, the payoff can be distinguished as to whether it is specific or general. If a payoff takes specific form, such as money or a service rendered, it will likely be perceived as more corrupt than a general payoff, such as future electoral support or good will. Although this is a rather special case of payoff, it is also important to determine if a gift is related to a political campaign. Payoffs in the form of campaign contributions have a legitimacy not rendered to other forms of material payoffs. A $1,000 cash donation to a campaign is perfectly acceptable, while an equal amount offered as a personal gift to a public official subjects the donor and official to possible legal penalties.

In Table 44.1, we have summarized the basic components of a politically corrupt act, and indicated the dimensions in each component which can vary according to perceived corruptness. In outlining these components and their salient characteristics, we have articulated a large number of testable propositions about the conditions under which an act can and will be viewed as corrupt. We have only outlined propositions at the first level, i.e., dealing with each subdimension singly, and have not defined propositions dealing with more than one subdivision at a time. Certainly an act having most or all of the characteristics listed on the left side is considered more corrupt than one having only characteristics on the right. Which components are most important in determining corruptness is a researchable question not answered here. Yet taking a broader view, our rudimentary scheme offers a conceptual framework for analyzing and comparing potentially corrupt political acts. This framework allows us to circumvent the definitional problems surrounding the meaning of "corruption."

The Study Design

Our study was designed specifically to ascertain information on attitudes about corruption held by a large group of public officials. We mailed questionnaires to all 978 state senators in 24 states.[6] After three mailings, 441 senators had responded with completed questionnaires.[7]

Response rate by state ranged from only 21 percent in California to over 78 percent from North Dakota. Generally, response rate was slightly higher in the rural states than in the industrialized ones.[8]

The major focus of the questionnaire was a series of items concerning ten actions by public officials that might or might not be considered corrupt. As sometimes happens, we have since found problems and lack of clarity in some of the items. These problems will be discussed later. The items are as follows (in the order listed on the questionnaire):

1. A presidential candidate who promises an ambassadorship in exchange for campaign contributions (AMBASSADOR);
2. A member of congress using seniority to obtain a weapons contract for a firm in his or her district (WEAPONS);
3. A public official using public funds for personal travel (TRAVEL);
4. A secretary of defense who owns $50,000 in stock in a company with which the Defense Department has a million-dollar contract (DEFENSE STOCK);
5. A public official using influence to get a friend or relative admitted to law school (LAW SCHOOL);
6. The driveway of the mayor's home being paved by the city crew (DRIVEWAY);
7. A state assembly member while chairperson of the public roads committee authorizing the purchase of land s/he had recently acquired (LAND SALE);
8. A judge with $50,000 worth of stock in a corporation hearing a case concerning that firm (JUDGE);
9. A legislator accepting a large campaign contribution in return for voting "the right way" on a legislative bill (RIGHT WAY);
10. A member of congress who holds a large amount of stock (about $50,000 worth) in Standard Oil of New Jersey working to maintain the oil depletion allowance (OIL).

We omitted items on which we felt there would be near total consensus, either because they were so serious or because they were so trivial: at one extreme, for example, a public official engaging in heroin traffic, and at the other, a policeman taking a free cup of coffee from a local cafe. We asked several questions about each item, with five degrees of response. In this article we will examine responses to the question as to whether the act was believed to be corrupt or not.

Findings

We do not have enough items to explore systematically a number of propositions that could be generated by our work, but we will use these data in ways that indicate the usefulness of our scheme in analyzing corruption. We first ranked the items according to the proportion agreeing that the act was corrupt or very corrupt (Table 42.1). In Table 42.2 we have sketched the most salient characteristics of each act, according to our fourfold scheme; we have also outlined the characteristics of a hypothetical act in which a member of congress in a district with a large percentage of minority population votes in favor of the civil rights act (CIVIL RIGHTS). In return, members of civil rights groups in the district support the member of congress in a reelection bid. We judge that few would see anything corrupt in this sequence of events.

The first conclusion from Table 42.3 is that the acts considered corrupt by most people have many characteristics starred (where starred characteristics indicate more corrupt features, i.e., features on the left-hand side of Table 44.1). Clusters of stars are particularly apparent in the "payoff" boxes. Acts considered by few to be corrupt

Table 42.1
COMPONENTS OF A POTENTIALLY CORRUPT ACT AND SOME SALIENT CHARACTERISTICS

Component	More Corrupt	Less Corrupt
Public official		
Type of position	"Nonpolitical," i.e., the official is a judge	Political
Role when act performed	Public role, i.e., act is done as part of official's public duties	Private role, i.e., act is performed by public official acting as a private citizen
Donor's relation to public official	Nonconstituent pays official Public official pays self	Constituent pays official
Favor rendered by public official		
Type of benefit	Private	Public
Type of recipient	Nonconstituent	Constituent
Nature of act providing favor	Nonroutine, i.e., official departs from normal routine to provide favor	Routine, i.e., favor is performed as routine part of job
Payoff		
Size	Large	Small
Time when benefits accrue to donor	Short-range benefit	Long-range benefit
Substance	Specific	General
Relation to campaign	Noncampaign	Campaign

Table 42.2
CHARACTERISTICS OF TEN POTENTIALLY CORRUPT ACTS

Act	Public Official	Donor	Favor	Payoff
DRIVEWAY	Political, public role*	Self*	Private*	Large (?)* Specific* Short-range* Noncampaign*
TRAVEL	Political, public role*	Self*	Private*	Large* Specific* Short-range* Noncampaign*
LAND SALE	Political, public role*	Self*	Private*	Large* Specific* Short-range* Noncampaign*
RIGHT WAY	Political, public role*	Unclear ?	Unclear ?	Large* Specific* Short-range* Campaign
JUDGE	Nonpolitical,* public role*	Unclear ? (in part)* Self	Unclear Potential Private* Routine act	Indeterminate size Specific* Long-range Noncampaign
AMBASSADOR	Political, public role*	Constituent	Private* Constituent Routine act	Large* Specific* Short-range* Campaign
DEFENSE STOCK	Political, public role* (?)	Unclear, in part self*	Unclear Potential Private* Routine	Indeterminate size Specific* Long-range Noncampaign*
OIL	Political, public role*	Unclear, in part self*	Unclear Potential Private* Routine	Indeterminate size Specific* Long-range Noncampaign*
WEAPONS CONTRACT	Political, public role*	Unclear, possibly constituent	Unclear, possibly nonroutine*	Small Nonspecific Long-range Noncampaign
LAW SCHOOL	Political, unclear	Unclear, possibly constituent	Unclear, possibly nonroutine*	Small Nonspecific Long-range Noncampaign
CIVIL RIGHTS	Political, public role*	Constituent	Routine Constituent Public	Small Nonspecific Long-range Possibly campaign

*More corrupt.

Table 42.3
PERCENT AGREEING ACT IS CORRUPT

	Percent of Respondents Viewing This Act as Corrupt	Percent of Respondents Believing Most Public Officials Would Condemn This Act	Percent of Respondents Believing Most of Public Would Condemn This Act
Driveway	95.9	92.2	97.5
Travel	95.2	80.4	96.5
Land Sale	95.1	92.1	97.5
Right Way	91.9	82.2	94.3
Judge	78.8	82.3	91.0
Ambassador	71.1	44.5	81.2
Defense Stock	58.3	62.1	84.4
Oil	54.9	55.1	81.2
Weapons Contract	31.6	20.9	34.4
Law School	23.7	15.5	35.9

have few stars; CIVIL RIGHTS has only one. Those acts whose corruptness is most disputed have an intermediate number of characteristics starred. We can also immediately see that any one attribute, in isolation, probably does not determine corruptness. For example, an act performed in one's public role may lead to corruption, but simply knowing that an official performed an act as part of a public role tells us nothing by itself. Unfortunately not enough information was given to classify fully some of the acts on our four components. Greater specificity may have changed the public officials' responses, and would also have made the pattern of classification clearer.

Four acts were perceived as corrupt by over 90 percent of our sample: RIGHT WAY, DRIVEWAY, TRAVEL, and LAND SALE. While two of these acts involve minor sums of money, all are illegal and all result in personal financial gain for the public official. In terms of our four components we can say that three of the four acts are characterized by the merger of the donor and the public official role. That is, in the cases of DRIVEWAY, TRAVEL, and LAND SALE, the public official is in the position of personally ensuring direct financial gain. Of our ten examples, these are the only three where such a merger is the case, and are the instances of highest consensus. The fourth case perceived as corrupt by over 90 percent is RIGHT WAY. Here the donor is not the public official but an unspecified second party. However, the payoff is very direct and immediate, though in the context of a campaign contribution. We assume that if a campaign contribution were not involved, almost all would have seen the act as corrupt. RIGHT WAY might be compared with another example, OIL, where the payoff from voting a certain way is much more indirect and long-range (i.e., the possible increase in the value of the legislator's stock), and fewer see this type of payoff as corrupt. In sum, from these four examples, we infer that these illegal acts are judged highly corrupt because of the merger of the donor and public official role in three cases, and because of the direct and monetary gain in exchange for a vote in the fourth.

At the other end of the continuum, less than 40 percent of the sample found LAW SCHOOL and the WEAPONS examples corrupt. These acts might be characterized as rather minor forms of influence peddling. In both cases, the payoff is indirect and long-range: good will that perhaps increases the possibility of future campaign support. In both cases the donor is presumably a constituent. The acts themselves obviously are seen by most as routine kinds of favors that public officials try to do for constituents, and thus only a minority are willing to call the acts corrupt.

Our fourfold typology also sheds some light on why there is some ambiguity about these acts. While the payoff is long-range, and the donor a constituent, it is implied that doing the favor takes the legislator outside the narrow performance of legislative duty. While the question is unfortunately silent about some aspects of the transaction, it can be presumed that the legislator is calling the law school dean or members of the admissions committee in the one instance, and perhaps putting undue pressure on a bureaucrat in the other. These acts would be considered by some to be overstepping the normal scope of a legislator's activity, but by others as routinely trying to provide a constituent service. Perhaps a clarification of the item would allow a better interpretation.

The acts where there is the least consensus are conflict of interest activities: OIL, DEFENSE STOCK, JUDGE, and AMBASSADOR. In each case, public officials are in the position of furthering personal financial interests while making a decision in their public role. In the case of DEFENSE STOCK, OIL and JUDGE, public officials are in the position of performing a favor (i.e., casting a favorable vote or awarding a contract) for which the payoff is an increase in the value of their own stock. Unlike the DRIVEWAY, TRAVEL or LANDSALE instances, legislators are not the sole donors, although they are in the position of being past donors. Public officials, by their acts, cannot convert favors directly into payoffs. Other events might have an impact on the stock's value, regardless of a public official's favor. And, the payoff is much less direct than a cash grant or immediate service rendered. The government contract, the favorable court ruling, the increased oil depletion allowance may or may not increase stockholders' dividends. On the other hand, the payoff is more tangible than the generalized "good will" engendered by the WEAPONS or LAW SCHOOL acts.

Other factors are also involved in comparing conflict-of-interest acts to the others previously discussed. The size of the payoff as well as its immediacy influences an official's perception of corruption. We cannot demonstrate that with our data, as all involve $50,000 worth of stock. Beard and Horn (1975), however, offer a relevant example. More congress members believe it more corrupt for a legislator to cast a vote for benefits to the savings and loan industry when the legislator owns $100,000 worth of stock rather than only $5,000 (1975, p. 22). In our own data, several people indicated that if instead of owning $50,000 of stock, the secretary of defense were a "major" stockholder, then the taint of corruption might be greater.

Finally, in these four items we can see that the nature of the public office is also relevant. The conflict of interest involving a judge was believed more odious than that involving either a bureaucrat or a member of congress. A judge, in a nonpolitical role, is held to higher standards than are legislators.

The AMBASSADOR items differ from the OIL, DEFENSE and JUDGE acts. The payoff, a campaign donation, is much more immediate. The donor, however, is providing a campaign contribution rather than funds to be used simply for personal enrichment. To us, the AMBASSADOR and RIGHT WAY cases seem parallel. In one case, the favor is a vote, in another, an appointment. Why the former is seen as more corrupt is undoubtedly because the "spoils system" of appointment has a residue of legitimacy that the practice of "voting for pay" has not.

Our typology of corrupt acts helps explain why these conflict-of-interest behaviors are often ambiguous. As the payoff becomes more and more long-range, and the donor and favors are constituency-oriented, it is easy to argue that an act is not corrupt. Most public officials hope that all acts have some positive payoff for them, principally reelection (Mayhew, 1975), and doing constituency-oriented favors is one way to increase the probability of reelection.[9] When the "favor" done for a constituent coincides with personal enrichment, then the charge of conflict of interest is relevant. Clearly our sample is ambivalent and divided about the propriety of these acts.

In sum, the simple rank ordering of our ten examples shows at one end of the continuum a clustering of acts that are clearly illegal or represent a direct financial gain, at the other, acts that are minor influence peddling, and in between a set of acts representing a variety of conflict of interest situations. A Guttman scaling procedure revealed that this set of acts was unidimensional. They scaled in the same order as discussed, and produced a coefficient of reproducibility of .95, as shown in Table 42.4.[10]

Our categorization of the components of a corrupt act aided in pinpointing some of the reasons for differential perceptions of the corruptness of various acts. The nature of the favor, the donor, the public official, and particularly the payoff were all useful in analyzing these perceptions. Acts more perceived as corrupt tended to have different characteristics from those few perceived as corrupt. And, where there was near-unanimity about the corruptness of an act, more components of the act were regarded as corrupt than where there were divided sentiments. Using only these ten acts, it could not be determined which (if any) components, or combinations of components, were crucial in influencing perceptions. More research on that point is necessary. We have only explored reasons why some acts are perceived as more corrupt than others; we have not yet tried to analyze why there are intergroup differences in perception of corruption, particularly differences between elites and the public.[11]

Discussion

Political corruption has not been subjected to the sort of rigorous analysis received by other phenomena in American politics. In large measure, the difficulty of defining "political corruption" accounts for this neglect. The present analysis develops a fourfold classification scheme composed of what we consider the essential ingredients of every act of political corruption. While this scheme is not a "theory," it does offer a conceptual framework helpful in comparing and analyz-

Table 42.4
CORRELATION MATRIX OF PERCEIVED CORRUPTION ITEMS

	TRVL	LDSL	RTWY	JUDG	AMB	DFST	OIL	WPNS	LAWS
Driveway	.19	.28	.28	.06	.12	.13	.02	.03	.09
Travel	—	.29	.35	.07	.15	.08	.10	.10	.10
Land Sale		—	.33	.16	.15	.16	.06	.08	.10
Right Way			—	.16	.20	.14	.10	.14	.06
Judge				—	.16	.45	.31	.11	.20
Ambassador					—	.19	.23	.15	.22
Defense Stock						—	.46	.07	.18
Oil							—	.12	.12
Weapons Contract								—	.12

ing potentially corrupt acts. In doing that it allows us to avoid the definitional pitfalls which have stalemated the study of corruption for so long. These problems can be avoided because the components of our conceptual scheme allow one to analyze acts classified as corrupt according to any of the corruption definitions described earlier: the public opinion, public interest, and legalistic definitions.

The scheme, for instance, renders the "public opinion" definition more usable by refining it in such a way as to allow gradients of corruptness in an act and to assist in finding reasons why public officials and elites hold similar or divergent beliefs about a particular corrupt act. This can be accomplished by systematically varying each component of our scheme over a wide variety of acts. The result should enable researchers to pinpoint differences between elites and the mass public, and thus to infer why there are divergent areas—"gray areas of political corruption." Might it be because the two groups view the "payoff" differently: what is seen as small or petty by public officials may be viewed as large and serious to citizens? Or, does the divergence lie in the perception of what is extraordinary in the act providing the favor? Many similar explanations could be posited and tested.

Moreover, the opportunity now exists to explore possible differences in corruption perceptions based on social class and other subgroups in the population such as race, region, and sex (see Welch and Peters, 1977b). Corruption may also be related to psychological or attitudinal predispositions. For example, "private" vs. "public-regarding" distinctions sometimes used to explain corrupt behavior can be encompassed within our scheme. For instance, are citizens and elites whose approach to political life is considered "private-regarding" inclined to be less severe in their condemnation of certain political acts than those displaying a "public-regarding" disposition? In this manner, the study of political corruption can be integrated into the broader propositions about the social and attitudinal bases of political behavior.

The scheme can also be related to the definitions of corruption based on "illegal acts" or violations of the "public interest." Are all corrupt acts viewed similarly which are proscribed by law because they deviate from the formal duties of public office for personal gain? If so, the explanation for the common belief may lie in the components of illegal acts such as the payoff, favor, public official or donor. One can view acts considered to be against the public interest or order in a similar way. An act of political corruption may or may not be viewed by all public officials and citizens as violating a responsibility to maintain civic order or as destroying a political system. Given the wide and varying opinions about the "public interest," one would expect they would not. And the four elements, public official, donor, favor, and payoff, allow us to compare and analyze a wide variety of political acts, whether their potential corruptness is based on illegality, violation of the public interest, or condemnation by public opinion. Our approach is also compatible with the "systemic view" of political corruption. If a large part of political corruption in the United States can be attributed to inherent weaknesses in certain offices, situations, or processes, then more honest government will only come about when those weaknesses are identified and eradicated by public officials and concerned citizens. Thus an understanding of individual attitudes is important even when considering the systemic view of corruption.

Inherent weaknesses are difficult to identify. But once exposed they can be analyzed according to our conceptual scheme. Patterns may emerge which would help one predict those offices, institutions or processes susceptible to political corruption. In this manner the sources of political corruption can be systematically identified.[12]

Our approach to defining corruption, then, is offered as a way to integrate research on corruption with the mainstream of research in American politics, a way of integrating theories about corruption to a well-grounded literature in American political beliefs and behavior. This approach also offers a way to study political corruption from the comparative and international perspective. Again the four components are common to every potentially corrupt act. Different hypotheses might be suggested in the cross-national or international study of corruption, but our scheme offers a framework for such a study. For example, a hypothesis might specify that one type of political culture views a certain type of payoff as a routine part of a public official's perquisites, while another culture views the payoff quite differently. Thus our understanding of differential views toward potentially corrupt acts is enhanced. The citizens of one country may condemn a specific political act as corrupt because it violates the norms of public office holding, while the citizens of another country condone the same act because it does not. The scheme can help us understand why the leaders of a foreign country consider it proper to expect monetary kickbacks from large U.S. corporations in exchange for a government contract, or to offer bribes to key members of the U.S. congress in exchange for favorable treatment. Moreover, it may well be that stages of economic development, modernization, social infrastructure, and so forth, bear systematic relationship to the components of our conceptual framework. It provides us with another way of demonstrating how political corruption is related to political development.

This approach can also be linked to the more traditional approach of studying corruption only when a significant local or national scandal has occurred. One can monitor public and elite attitudes over time in an attempt to link public attitudes to the situational context.

For too long the systematic study of political corruption has been neglected by serious students of American politics. That this should be so is understandable, considering not only the imposing conceptual problems but also the lack of intellectual respectability about the concept itself. But it has become increasingly evident to citizens, public officials, and scholars alike that "corruption in politics" is just too prevalent a phenomenon not to be subjected to rigorous study. Our chapter has attempted to demonstrate one approach, but by no means the only approach, to the systematic study of political corruption.

Notes

1. Berg, Hahn, and Schmidhauser (1976, p. 170) discuss seminars being conducted for large campaign donors on how to use the loopholes in the new campaign fund laws.
2. Harry Scoble (1973) refers to the situation (gray corruption) where public officials tolerate a corrupt act or practice and citizens are unaware or ignorant of the act but would condemn it if they knew about it as "systemic corruption." Moreover, this view of political corruption is useful and important in that it leads to an emphasis on the basic defects and weaknesses in the political system which may be responsible for corruption (see Berg, Hahn, and Schmidhauser, 1976). Therefore, rather than attributing such phenomena as "Watergate" to the weaknesses and foibles of individual political actors, the "systemic view" of corruption would lead to a search for the sources of "Watergate" in the defects of the political process itself.
3. The recent example of Congressman Allan Howe's (D-Utah) alleged solicitation of a prostitute might be a good example. He committed an illegal act, but it would hardly be called the misuse of public office. This is not to say that the voters in his district judged him any less harshly. The other recent "congressional sex scandal," that of Congressman Wayne Hayes, who allegedly put Elizabeth Ray on the payroll only because she was his mistress, more rightly fits into the misuse of public office category, and thus would be judged more potentially corrupt.
4. Even though the dimensions of "favor" are similar to those outlined for the "donor," there are some differences. For example, it is conceivable that a private donor might pay for a favor having public benefit.
5. President Carter, however, has extracted pledges from his high-level appointees that they will not take jobs with firms doing business with or regulated by their agency for a period of two years.
6. All of our mailings, sent in October, December and January, 1975–76 were sent to the senators' home addresses, in order to minimize the possibility that the senator would delegate filling out the questionnaire to a staff

member or legislative intern. The states surveyed were ALABAMA, California, Connecticut, Florida, Georgia, Illinois, IOWA, Kansas, Kentucky, Maine, Massachusetts, MICHIGAN, Minnesota, MISSOURI, Nevada, New Jersey, New York, NORTH DAKOTA, Oregon, PENNSYLVANIA, TEXAS, Utah, West Virginia, and Wyoming. These states were picked randomly, with a few substitutions to assure geographic dispersion (after our initial random selection, we had eight southern states but no states from the industrial Middle West). Only some of the nonrespondents, those from the states listed in capital letters, were sent a third-wave questionnaire.

7. For a discussion of the rationale behind the shorter, third-wave questionnaire, see Welch and Peters (1977a).

8. In addition to California, only New York (25 percent) had a response rate of less than 30 percent. Three more had response rates of less than 40 percent: Massachusetts (30 percent), Illinois (32 percent), and Minnesota (32 percent). On the other hand, eight states had a response rate of more than 50 percent: North Dakota (78 percent), Utah (62 percent), Iowa (62 percent), Alabama (60 percent), Maine (58 percent), Kansas (53 percent), Wyoming (53 percent), and Oregon (53 percent).

9. Jack Anderson commented on this point in a recent "expose" of congressional misbehavior: "Favors are part of a politician's stock in trade. He is expected to produce government jobs, public works projects, appointments to military academies and government contracts which can be arranged within the constraints of the law and ethics. But some legislators are not content to wait until election day to bask in the gratitude of the voters."

10. This correlation matrix of the ten items partially confirms the clustering into three groups though the correlation between the two influence-peddling items is very small.

11. We have no public opinion data to test hypotheses about elite-mass differences. We do, however, have data on how our respondents think citizens feel about these acts. While the rank ordering or legislators' perceptions of citizens beliefs of corrupt acts is similar to the respondents' belief that most citizens would see every conflict-of-interest act as corrupt (Exhibit 44.3). The only acts the majority of our respondents believe citizens would not condemn are the WEAPONS and LAW SCHOOL acts. Unfortunately, these data do not test our propositions. They are only suggestive. The respondents' views of citizens' reactions to these potentially corrupt acts also form an acceptable Guttman scale, with a CR of .94 and with no items having more than than 10 percent error.

One study that surveyed public opinion about corrupt acts was that of John Gardiner (1970), who assessed the attitudes of citizens about political corruption in their community. While he examined tolerance of corruption as it related to several socio-economic attributes, he did not compare public and elite attitudes. He did find, however, that more educated people were less tolerant of corruption than those with less education.

12. In our own sample, 35.5 percent believed that there were no specific offices particularly susceptible to corruption; rather, it was a few susceptible individuals (the "rotten apple" view). Of the remaining 64.5 percent, there was little apparent agreement as to which offices were more suscepti-

ble to corruption. Most frequently mentioned were offices handling a lot of money, named by 7.3 percent.

References

Anderson, Jack (1976). "A Citizen's Committee is Needed to Crack Down on Congressmen who Cheat." *Parade,* 1 November 1976, 4–5.
Banfield, Edward and James Q. Wilson (1963). *City Politics.* New York: Vintage.
Beard, Edmund and Stephen Horn (1975). *Congressional Ethics: A View from the House.* Washington: Brookings.
Berg, Larry L., Harlan Hahn, and John R. Schmidhauser (1976). *Corruption in the American Political System.* Morristown,N.J.: General Learning Press.
Cohen, Richard M., and Jules Witcover (1974). *A Heartbeat Away.* New York: Viking.
Edelman, Murray (1964). *The Symbolic Uses of Politics.* Urbana: University of Illinois Press.
Elazar, Daniel (1966). *American Federalism: A View from the States.* New York: Crowell.
Gardiner, John (1970). *The Politics of Corruption.* New York: Sage.
Getz, Robert S. (1966). *Congressional Ethics: The Conflict of Interest Issue.* Princeton, N.J.: Van Nostrand.
Greenstein, Fred I. (1964). "The Changing Pattern of Urban Party Politics." *Annals of the American Academy of Political and Social Science* 353:1–13.
Heidenheimer, A. J., ed. (1970). *Political Corruption: Readings in Comparative Analysis.* New York: Holt.
Lippman, Walter (1970; first published 1930). "A Theory about Corruption." In Arnold Heidenheimer (ed.). *Political Corruption.* New York: Holt, pp. 294–97.
Nye, J. S. (1967). "Corruption and Political Development: A Cost-Benefit Analysis." *American Political Science Review* 61:417–27.
Pinto-Duschinsky, Michael (1976). "Theories of Corruption in American Politics," paper presented at the annual meeting of the American Political Science Association, Chicago, 1976.
Rogow, Arnold A. and Harold Lasswell (1963). *Power, Corruption and Rectitude.* Englewood Cliffs, N.J.: Prentice-Hall.
Rundquist, Barry S. and Susan Hansen (1976). "On Controlling Official Corruption: Elections vs. Laws." Unpublished manuscript.
Rundquist, Barry S., Gerald S. Strom and John G. Peters (1977). "Corrupt Politicians and Their Electoral Support: Some Theoretical and Empirical Observations." *American Political Science Review* 71:954–63.
Scoble, Harry (1973). "Systemic Corruption," a paper presented at the annual meeting of the American Political Science Association, New Orleans, September, 1973.
Scott, James (1972). *Comparative Political Corruption.* Englewood Cliffs, N.J.: Prentice-Hall.
De Tocqueville, Alexis (1961). *Democracy in America,* Vols. 1–2. New York: Schocken.
Welch, Susan and John G. Peters (1977a). "Some Problems of Stimulating

Responses to Mail Questionnaires: Controllable and Non Controllable Aspects." *Political Methodology* 4:139–52.

—— (1977b). "Attitudes of U.S. State Legislators Toward Political Corruption." *Legislative Studies Quarterly* 2:445–64.

Wilson, James Q. (1966). "Corruption: The Shame of the States." *The Public Interest* 2:28–38.

Wolfinger, R. E. (1972). "Why Machine Politics Have Not Withered Away and Other Revisionist Thoughts." *Journal of Politics* 34:365–98.

43

Right and Wrong in American Politics: Popular Conceptions of Corruption

Michael Johnston

> A great part of both the strength and weakness of our national existence
> lies in the fact that Americans do not abide very quietly the evils of life.
> We are forever restlessly pitting ourselves against them, demanding
> changes, improvements, remedies, but not often with sufficient sense of
> the limits that the human condition will in the end impose on us.
> —Richard Hofstadter, *The Age of Reform[1]*

Political corruption and ethics in public life were important concerns
during the "age of reform" of which Hofstadter wrote. They remain so
today. But what do Americans consider to be corrupt? How do people
apply or withhold their judgments of right and wrong in politics? My
purpose here is to examine important political perceptions which, as
Gunnar Myrdal once observed, constitute the "folklore of corruption."[2] This inquiry is based on a 1983 survey of the greater Pittsburgh
metropolitan area in which respondents were asked, among other
things, to describe their reactions to perceived corruption, and to judge
the "corruptness" of a set of hypothetical examples of behavior.
People apply the term "corruption" to a wide variety of activities; their
reactions range from anger to amusement to cynicism and resignation.
Judgments are complex and seemingly contradictory: on one hand,
they involve the invocation of values and traditions deeply rooted in
the American political culture; on the other, they include processes of
rationalization, equivocation, and attribution of motives, growing out
of everyday problems and experience. The result is not a set of clear-
cut distinctions, but rather a spectrum of finely-graded judgments
reflecting multiple standards of right and wrong.

Social conceptions of corruption and misconduct in politics are of

Source: Michael Johnston, "Right and Wrong in American Politics: Popular Conceptions
of Corruption." *Polity XVIII, 3 (Spring 1986), 367–91. By permission of the publisher.*

interest for several reasons. They have much to do with popular trust (or distrust) of elites and institutions, and they also affect one's own choices as to participation or nonparticipation in politics. Moreover, anyone undertaking reforms would be well advised to consider popular standards of right and wrong before devising anticorruption measures or asking for political support. This line of inquiry also has implications for the study of corruption itself, for there has been much debate over "objective" versus "subjective" definitions of corruption.[3] Do social perceptions of corruption offer standards and distinctions sharp enough to be built into basic analytical definitions? Or do they produce subtle judgments, categories differing only by small degree, and norms that apply to various situations in different, even contradictory ways? If the latter is the case, we might best treat popular conceptions of corruption as factors influencing political responses (or non-responses) to it. I will return to this issue in the concluding section. . . .

Policymaking is typically a time-consuming and complex process, characterized by stiff (and often expensive) competition over important decisions and valuable public goods. Opportunities and incentives to short circuit established rules and procedures through the use of corrupt influence will frequently be present in such circumstances, both for public and private participants. Thus it is not surprising that corruption has proven such a persistent political phenomenon, nor that ethical issues have been an important continuing theme in American politics.[4] But the emotions which corruption elicits derive in part from the fact that perceived corruption runs contrary to some of the fundamental ideals and myths in our political culture. In this idealized picture, the United States is a republic in which power flows from the governed. Elites are merely temporary trustees; short terms and the principle of rotation in office suggest an officialdom made up of citizen-politicians, not of political careerists. Politics is supposed to be an endeavor of service, not a game of self-enrichment. Even when this "government of commoners" does not act on the policy demands of citizens, it is expected to abide by their basic values and rules. Closely related to republicanism is a fear of concentrated power, be it elite power or the clout of runaway majorities. The Constitution, and especially our federal system, were devised to fragment power, making it hard to win and even more difficult to hold. Lord Acton's often-misquoted observation that "power tends to corrupt, and absolute power corrupts absolutely," may not hold true as a positive proposition,[5] but as a statement of widely held political apprehensions, it retains great appeal.

It is clear that perceived corruption is difficult to reconcile with this idealized image: one does not expect a government of citizen-trustees to abuse public roles and resources for their own enrichment. Corruption can also be seen as a way to amass power despite the checks and balances of our institutions. Political wrongdoing can conflict with ideals of equality. Those who abide by the rules may be angered when they see others rise in the world through less legitimate channels; indeed, they may conclude that most of those who succeed do so through corrupt means. As Tocqueville once cautioned:

> what is to be feared is not so much the immorality of the great as the fact that immorality may lead to greatness. In a democracy, private citizens see a man of their own rank in life who rises from that obscure position in a few years to riches and power; the spectacle excites their surprise and envy, and they are led to inquire how a person who was yesterday their equal today is their ruler. To attribute his rise to his talents or his virtues is unpleasant, for it is tacitly to acknowledge that they are themselves less virtuous or less talented than he was. They are therefore led, and often rightly, to impute his success mainly to some of his vices; and an odious connection is thus formed between the ideas of turpitude and power, unworthiness and success, utility and dishonor.[6]

Revelations of scandal, or the belief that wrongdoing is common even if it never comes to light, can upset one's general image of the way politics works, of who wins and loses and how, and of one's own ability to influence government. While idealized pictures of American politics have never fully corresponded with reality, they can still be matters of great emotional investment. This is not to say that everyone starts out with these ideals in mind, only to suffer some loss of political innocence later. But for those who hold at least a few of these perceptions, corruption can strike a heavy blow.

Public Rules, Private Equivocations

Idealized pictures of the political process are not the only influences upon a "social definition" of corruption. Politics and policymaking are, after all, complex, distant and unfamiliar worlds to most people. It is unlikely that most citizens have a clear or consistent idea of the rules governing these activities. Indeed, when questionable deeds come to light, they may fall back upon everyday experience and home truths in forming their judgments. A belief that government should be made up of "people like us" may make them willing to relax their judgments in cases where the behavior in question seems understandable in terms of exigencies of everyday life.

Chibnall and Saunders have discussed these concerns in connection with cases of corruption in Britain.[7] They observe that both elites and ordinary citizens engage in the "social construction of reality,"[8] devising their own conceptions of political ethics. These incorporate not only notions of legality, but also such concerns as the secrecy of an action, exchanges of gifts and favors, the actor's intentions, and whether or not an action has become general practice. Not surprisingly, Chibnall and Saunders conclude that private citizens' "rules" differ markedly from those of elites. Citizens, they suggest, are apt to see secrecy as evidence of wrongdoing ("why keep it a secret if you have nothing to hide?"), while elites defend secrecy as a necessary part of policymaking. Gifts and favors are likewise seen by citizens as evidence of corrupt dealings, while elites claim a right to develop private friendships with people they encounter in public life. Elites are more willing to accept the notion of breaking the rules in pursuit of worthwhile goals, and to defend an action with the argument that "everyone else does it," or that while an action is forbidden in public life it has become routine in private business.

The survey data at hand do not include a sample of elites, so we cannot put these contrasts to a direct test. Chibnall and Saunders' study does suggest, however, that popular conceptions will not conform to formal definitions of corruption. Those definitions employ relatively strict formal rules of behavior, and draw important distinctions between public and private roles, resources, and relationships. We can lay the groundwork for some hypotheses about social conceptions of corruption by examining the ways these two aspects of formal definitions—rules, and distinctions between the public and the private—might be translated into popular perceptions.

Rules and Rationalizations

Stuart Henry's study of the sale of stolen goods in Britain's "hidden economy" tells us much about the fuzzy nature of social rules.[9] He describes the elaborate "excuses and justifications" people offer for their own actions, and for those of others like them. These include mitigating circumstances—that one's wages are low, or that one is in need, at least temporarily; that others have much more, or that one is constantly being tricked and "done" by big business and government. Finally, there is the oldest justification of all—"everyone else does it."[10]

Accompanying these mitigating claims are a set of equivocations that serve to "neutralize" formal standards of behavior. A person selling stolen radios, for example, would never explicitly describe them as such. Instead, the goods would be offered as "something cheap," which "fell off the back of a lorry," or as damaged goods, leftovers, or part of a "bulk purchase." These terms provide "neutral" reasons for offering goods informally and at low prices; all avoid explicitly labeling the goods as "stolen."[11]

These private equivocations are of interest to us because of their implications for the process of rationalization itself.[12] We would expect social judgments of corruptness to reflect a variety of rationalizations, equivocations, and attributions of motives—the more so if the situations and persons involved are familiar in everyday life. Smigel suggests that most people's ethical systems are better suited for judging familiar, private dealings, than they are for judging public situations, because moral systems, and the religions upon which they were often based, developed in small communities at times when great impersonal organizations did not exist.[13] As far as possible, people will judge the corruptness of public actions, as well as that of private deeds, in terms of "social ethics" worked out in everyday life. This notion helps account for Chibnall and Saunders' suggestion that citizens use such criteria as secrecy and gift-giving, in addition to, or even instead of, less familiar legal notions, to judge official conduct. It also suggests that while we might expect public figures to be judged more harshly than private citizens, we should not expect to find clear-cut and consistent distinctions between what is considered public, and what is private.

Hypotheses

It follows that we should not expect to find a sharp social distinction between corrupt and noncorrupt actions. Instead, we will find fine gradations of judgment, reflecting a variety of equivocations, mitigating circumstances, and attributed motives. But we can still compare more- and less-harshly judged examples of behavior in order to understand the implicit distinctions among them, and to draw inferences about general social conceptions of corruptness. Specifically, we might expect the following contrasts to emerge:

1. Actions which are clearly corrupt by more formal definitions will be judged as more corrupt than those of more doubtful status.
2. (a) The larger the stakes or "take," the more harsh the judgment;
   (b) similarly, the more direct the method of "taking," the harsher the judgment.
3. Actions by public figures will be judged more harshly than those of private citizens.

4. (a) Mitigating motives and circumstances will reduce the severity of judgments;
    (b) this effect should be greater when the mitigating factors fit into the realm of private equivocations than when they do not.
5. Social distance, and the contrasts between public standards and private rationalizations, will mean that judgments will depend upon the nature of the perpetrator, and that of the victim.[14] Specifically,
    (a) when a prominent person takes from a large organization, judgments should be relatively harsh;
    (b) when a prominent person or organization takes from ordinary citizens, judgments should also be harsh;
    (c) when ordinary citizens take from a large organization, judgments should be more lenient.

The survey data will not conclusively settle the question of what Americans regard as corruption, but with these hypotheses in mind it should yield an understanding of some of the important distinctions people make in applying, mitigating, or withholding their judgments of corruptness.

The Data

. . . The questionnaire included several types of items. After a series probing general political attitudes, we asked respondents whether they were typically surprised or angered by revelations of corruption, and how serious a problem they felt corruption posed for the nation. Then came a set of twenty hypothetical examples of behavior, drawn from both public and private life, in which some kind of rule-breaking was arguably taking place. Respondents were asked to judge each of these actions as extremely, somewhat, slightly, or not at all corrupt. Six political information questions came next, followed by questions on the respondent's own political participation, media use, and personal characteristics. This analysis will focus primarily upon the respondents' judgments of the twenty examples of behavior.

Conceptions of Corruption

Our respondents were concerned about corruption. Some 61.8 percent responded that corruption is an "extremely serious" problem in America today, and another 35.3 percent saw it as a "somewhat serious" problem. To some extent, corruption seems to have become a part of politics as usual: only about a third responded that they were "very surprised" (2.9 percent) or "somewhat surprised" (30.7 percent) at revelations of corruption. Still, corruption can be upsetting: 45.2 percent responded that corruption tended to make them "very angry," and another 49.4 percent described their reactions as "somewhat angry." Corruption thus seems to be an important concern, and the notion that perceived corruption can engage one's emotional investment in politics receives some support.

As I have already pointed out, "corruption" in this sense is what people think it is. Thus, we need to describe the major components of their judgments of corruptness in order to understand just what it is about which they are (or are not) getting angry. We can turn to the hypothetical examples of rule-breaking to see how respondents tended to apply or withhold the label of corruption.[15] Exhibit 45.1 presents these twenty items, rank-ordered in terms of the severity with which they were judged.

Our respondents' notions of corruption do encompass most of what would be defined as corrupt by an analyst. Rule-breaking by public officials was judged rather harshly: the mean judgment for actions initiated by public figures was 2.314 on a zero-to-three scale, versus a mean of 1.580 for private citizens' actions ($T = 21.56$; $p = .000$). So was behavior involving money or tangible benefits. Moreover, there seemed to be strong consensus regarding the five most corrupt actions, as suggested by their small standard deviations. Analysts and citizens seem to agree that clear-cut abuse of a public role for private benefit is corruption.

But the social definition of corruption also includes behavior which most analytical definitions would not. As shown in Exhibit 45.1, five actions were seen as clearly more corrupt than the rest, while another cluster of eight were regarded as at least moderately corrupt. A supermarket's raising prices on welfare-check days ranked in the first cluster. While such an action is reprehensible, and in some places illegal, it would not be corrupt by most formal definitions. Similarly, a purchasing agent's accepting gifts, and an individual's bouncing a check, are included in the second, "moderately corrupt," cluster. So too is a public official's false claim of holding a management degree, an action which (as Chibnall and Saunders might point out) involves secrecy and deception. While this would certainly be dishonest in a public role, it is not clearly corrupt in the sense implied by a definition such as Nye's.

The Hypotheses Revisited

Table 43.1 thus reveals no precise division between corrupt and noncorrupt actions. Comparisons among items, however, can shed some light on our hypotheses (all inter-item comparisons below are statistically significant at at least the .01 level, unless noted otherwise).

Table 43.1
MEAN JUDGMENTS OF EXAMPLES OF BEHAVIOR
(RANK—ORDERED BY SEVERITY OF JUDGMENT)

0 = "Not at all corrupt"
1 = "Slightly corrupt"
2 = "Somewhat corrupt"
3 = "Extremely corrupt"

Grand mean for all examples: 1.930

	Mean	Std. Dev.
Treasurer embezzles $10,000	2.967	.240
Official keeps 5 percent cut for self	2.892	.361
Treasurer embezzles $500	2.795	.489
Official takes 5 percent cut, gives to party	2.591	.705
Higher supermarket prices on welfare days	2.529	.828
Official falsely claims management degree	2.227	.851
Driver offers cop $20	2.121	.914
Officer asks driver for $20	2.117	.890
Official takes 5 percent, pays child's hospital bills	2.029	1.025
Purchasing agent accepts gifts	1.870	1.000
Councilman gives city job to political supporter	1.776	1.002
Long-distance calls on office phone	1.733	.957
Person bounces a check	1.644	1.002
Councilman gives city job to son	1.463	1.022
Concealing remodeling from tax assessor	1.418	.991
Bouncing check to buy kids' clothes	1.343	1.008
Employee calls in sick, goes to game	1.180	1.036
Offer trash collectors $20	1.155	.930
Babysitter asks for cash	.882	.995
Free food for cops	.632	.893

NOTE: Missing observations were deleted on an item-by-item basis; one item had five missing observations, two had four, and all others had three or less.

1. *Formally corrupt actions should be judged as more corrupt.* This hypothesis is supported: actions involving theft of public resources, in the view of our respondents, are definitely corrupt. Even where such an action is accompanied by rather strong mitigating circumstances (an official's taking a "cut" in order to pay a child's hospital bills), the mean judgment was more harsh than the mean for all twenty cases. But the issue does not seem to be illegality alone; in fact, the two "least corrupt" actions—a babysitter's asking for cash, and a cafe owner's giving free food to the police—are violations of federal, and of state and local laws, respectively. Perhaps many people are not aware that the cafe owner is breaking the law; the data cannot tell us about that. It seems more likely, though, that the most corrupt actions involve an element of public trust (and/or social distance) in addition to illegality.

In the private realm, by contrast, there seem to be some illegal actions which are not "really wrong."

2.a. *The larger the stakes or "take," the more harsh the judgment.* This hypothesis is supported as well. A public official's embezzlement of $10,000 was regarded as significantly more corrupt ($p = .001$) than an embezzlement of $500, and all of the five most corrupt actions in Exhibit 45.1 involve at least moderate sums of money. Similarly, cases in which the tangible stakes are small are clustered toward the bottom of the table (a possible exception being the "city job" which a councilman gives to a supporter, or to a son). Also, as expected in hypothesis 2.b., direct forms of "taking" are judged as more corrupt than indirect forms. This holds true, not just in cases of clear-cut theft (embezzlement, for example), but also in more subtle ways. The cafe owner who gives free food to the police is spending more, even in the course of a few days, than the motorist who offers $20 in order to "beat a ticket"; but the motorist is proposing a direct *quid pro quo*, and his action is seen as more corrupt. Likewise, cash-only payments for services such as babysitting defraud the government of significant tax revenues, but the connection between one person's cash dealings and the wider "underground economy" is indirect.

3. *Actions of public officials will be judged more harshly than those of private citizens.* This hypothesis receives strong support. The mean judgment for actions initiated by public role holders was significantly higher than that for privately-initiated actions, as noted earlier. A private citizen's concealing remodeling work from the tax assessors is clearly illegal, and can involve at least moderate sums of money in avoided taxes. But this action was seen as much less corrupt than a public official's falsely claiming to hold a degree in management, an action involving little or no money. Similarly, petty "office crime" by a state employee—making long-distance calls—was seen as more corrupt than "an employee calling in sick and going to a ball game," even though the value of a missed day's labor may well be greater than that of a few telephone calls. The telephone calls, on the other hand, may be seen as a more direct form of "taking."

4.a. *Mitigating motives and circumstances will reduce the severity of judgments.* Table 43.1 shows strong support for this hypothesis: the judgment of a person's "bouncing" a check, for example, is significantly relaxed when it is added that he or she did so in order to buy clothing for children. An official's taking a cut of a contract was seen as slightly less corrupt ($p = .000$) if he gives the money to his political party instead of keeping it for himself, and as much less corrupt if he uses the money to pay his sick child's hospital bills.

While these results are not necessarily surprising, they do point to clear divergence between formal and social conceptions of corruption. In a court of law, the central issue would be whether or not the official took the money, not what he did with it. Indeed, the "hospital bills" item draws upon an actual case in which a highway official in a southern state took kickbacks in order to pay such expenses, and still went to prison, convicted of a felony under federal law. People may judge officials and other prominent, socially distant figures according to more demanding standards than they apply to others seen to be like themselves. But they may also be willing to relax those standards significantly if motives can be attributed that make the officials seem "more like us."

It may be useful to recall here Chibnall and Saunders' conclusions about the ways elites and citizens differ in their judgments of corruptness. Consider the much larger mitigation effect in the "hospital bills" situation than in the case in which the cut is given to a political party. In Western Pennsylvania, the transfer of such funds to one's party has frequently been represented as a mitigating consideration, or even as the basis for a plea of innocence, by state and local officals charged in kickback cases. This argument is not accepted by all officials, but the frequency with which it has been offered suggests that it is construed as a genuinely mitigating factor among at least a segment of the elite stratum. For the public, however, it is a much less valid rationalization than the "hospital bills" motive, which falls closer to the realm of private equivocations discussed by Henry. When the excuse offered is understandable within this day-to-day context, people seem more willing to relax their judgments.

These differences may help make sense of another interesting comparison in Table 43.1—the relatively harsh judgment applied when a councilmember gives a city job to a political supporter as compared to when he gives it to his son. My expectation was that the latter would be judged more corrupt; it qualifies as nepotism, and would be an illegal practice under many circumstances. But the respondents saw the rewarding of a supporter as significantly more corrupt ($p = .000$). Perhaps they perceived this reward as a *quid-pro-quo* "payoff," even though this is not as clearly a violation of formal rules. In Western Pennsylvania, at least, many jobs—particularly those in youth programs—are exempt from civil service requirements, but are still covered by nepotism laws. Here again the motives attributed to an official who gives a job to his son are familiar and acceptable in everyday life, while those involved in rewarding one's political backers are not.

5. *Judgments of rule-breaking behavior will vary with the nature of the perpetrator and that of the victim.* Smigel suggests that such

factors as the size of the "victim" organization affect popular judgments of acts of theft.[16] While not all possible variations on this notion were put to a test in the survey, Table 43.1 shows support for hypotheses 5a, 5b, and 5c. They suggested that:

   5 (a)   when a prominent person takes from a large organization, judgments should be relatively harsh;
   5(b)   when a prominent person or organization takes from ordinary citizens, judgments should also be harsh; and
   5(c)   when ordinary citizens take from a large organization, judgments should be more lenient.

Prominent persons' thefts from large organizations, such as embezzlement and cuts from contracts, are the four "most corrupt" actions in Table 43.1. Similarly, a large organization's taking from a little person—a supermarket's raising prices on the days welfare checks come out—receives strong condemnation. The "ordinary person" in such a case is the welfare recipient, or possibly the taxpayer; either way, this action—again drawing upon actual events—was judged as seriously corrupt.

When the ordinary citizen takes from large organizations, reactions appear to be quite different. A homeowner who conceals remodeling work, an employee who calls in sick and goes to a ball game, a person who pays the trash collectors to take away items they are supposed to ignore, and a babysitter who asks for payment in cash are all "taking" from large organizations. One might argue that the cafe owner who offers the police free meals is trying to "buy" extra protection, but evidence suggests that this does not actually materialize. But if cafe owners *think* they get extra protection, or that they would get less if they did not treat the police, they too could be regarded as "taking." The material stakes of most such actions are of course small compared to embezzlements from the public purse. But some—unreported remodeling, for example—involve at least moderate sums of money and indirectly increase the tax bills of others. Still, actions in which an ordinary person gets back at a large organization receive some of the most lenient judgments in Table 43.1—a result consistent with Smigel's findings.

Not only are the situations familiar ones, open to the full range of private rationalizations already discussed; the "victims" are large, socially distant, and perceived as powerful and as possibly exploiting ordinary people. The types of "taking" involved, and the connections between the actions and their wider social costs, are indirect. Indeed, it is not altogether unlikely that the notion of large organizations' "taking" from ordinary citizens includes such routine actions as taxation in the public sector and price increases in the private, in addition to actual rulebreaking. The condemnation of that sort of "taking," together with tolerance of the "little guy's" getting back at large organizations, may then reflect strong feelings of inequality and alienation.

Social Class and Perceptions of Corruption

So far, we have discussed some of the distinctions people employ in judging the corruptness of others' actions. But given the importance of everyday experience as a source of their criteria of judgment, we would expect different segments of the population to see things in different ways. And in our sample of respondents, perceptions of right and wrong do indeed vary with social class.

For the analysis which follows, I excluded all respondents who had withheld judgment on any of the twenty examples of behavior. This listwise deletion reduced the sample from 241 to 207 cases, but it allowed a more thorough statistical analysis, and yielded comparisons based on a common population. In any event, the cases deleted in this manner did not come disproportionately from any class-status group. I then divided the sample into rough social class categories by summing each respondent's scores on ordinal measures of occupational status and educational attainment, and then dividing the resulting distribution into groups representing about one fifth *of the range of scores*. This procedure produced five class-status groups, labeled "low" (7 respondents), "lower-middle" (51), "middle" (75), "upper-middle" (42), and "upper" (32). It is important to remember that these terms refer to segments of the distribution of class attributes, and are not necessarily the identifications which our respondents might volunteer themselves. Still, this rough measure is based on two important components of the general concept of social class—occupation and educational attainment—and should yield valid comparisons among class-status groups.

If there are class differences in perceptions of corruption, however, they do not emerge in terms of overall severity of judgments. Table 43.2 presents respondents' mean judgments across all twenty examples of behavior—ranging from 0 ("not at all corrupt") to 3 ("extremely corrupt")—broken down by class-status group. No consistent relationship between class and the severity of judgment emerges in Table 43.2. Indeed, none of the intergroup differences come close to being statistically significant. Very similar results appeared when behavior examples were grouped into categories of public- and private-sector actions.

As noted earlier, when people judge corruptness, they employ

Table 43.2
RESPONDENTS' MEAN JUDGMENTS OF TWENTY BEHAVIOR
EXAMPLES, BROKEN DOWN BY SOCIAL CLASS GROUPING

	Social Class Grouping:				
	Low	**Low-Middle**	**Middle**	**Upper-Middle**	**Upper**
Mean	1.850	1.879	1.857	1.768	1.912
Std. Dev.	.707	.523	.437	.373	.502
N	7	51	75	42	32

Range of Judgments: 0 ("Not at all corrupt") to 3 ("Extremely corrupt")

Grand Mean = 1.853
Std. Dev. = .466

Analysis of Variance: $F = .5174$ $p = .7230$
Test of Linearity: $F = .0212$ $p = .8844$
F (deviation) $= .6828$ $p = .5635$

standards and categories of their own devising. Many factors which influence these judgments—everyday experience, complex rationalizations, and attributions of motives—should vary significantly across class lines. Thus, the most important class-related differences might well be qualitative, not quantitative: while people in various social strata may not differ greatly in the strength of their reactions to a whole range of rule-breaking actions, they might well perceive, and react most strongly to, different kinds of wrongdoing. To examine this possibility, I employed a factor analysis of respondents' judgments of the twenty examples of behavior [Table 43.3]. The analysis yielded five factors, four of which are worthy of discussion. These rotated factors can be thought of as categories of wrongdoing inferred from the respondents' judgments. While naming factors is in some ways as much an art as a science, I have labeled factors 1 through 4 as "personal taking," "official theft," "misrepresentation," and "favoritism," respectively. Some caution is in order in discussing the results, since a list of only twenty examples of rule-breaking behavior might omit types of wrongdoing important to our respondents. Still, these factors allow us to begin to discuss the categories of wrongdoing people perceive in the world around them.

The strength of the "personal taking" factor is particularly interesting in light of our emphasis upon everyday situations, problems, and rules. It seems that these considerations figure most strongly in popular judgments of corruptness. Most people, after all, will be much more familiar with the kinds of situations posed by these items than they are with questions of official conduct and wrongdoing. The "official theft"

Table 43.3
FACTOR ANALYSIS OF JUDGMENTS OF THE
TWENTY BEHAVIOR EXAMPLES

Varimax Rotation (only first four factors presented)

	Factor 1 "personal taking"	Factor 2 "official theft"	Factor 3 "misrepresentation"	Factor 4 "favoritism"
Officer asks driver for $20	.278	.174	.396	−.093
Official falsely claims management degree	.014	−.127	.687	.247
Offer trash collectors $20	.695	−.165	.199	.206
Councilman gives city job to son	.249	−.182	.156	.689
Conceals remodeling from assessor	.748	−.088	.030	.075
Long-distance calls on office phone	.648	.237	.127	.189
Purchasing agent accepts gifts	.546	.117	.141	.164
Treasurer embezzles $10,000	−.047	.156	.031	−.093
Free food for police	.106	.236	−.005	.650
Official keeps 5 percent cut for self	.182	.629	−.194	.151
Employee calls in sick, goes to game	.580	.196	.341	.232
Treasurer embezzles $500	−.069	.623	.183	.074
Person bounces a check	.446	.095	.556	.258
Official takes cut, gives to party	.022	.709	.113	.128
Bouncing check for kids' clothes	.398	.243	.589	.084
Higher prices on welfare days	.158	.173	.206	.376
Councilman gives job to political supporter	.248	.168	.193	.665
Babysitter asks for cash	.731	.134	.108	.069
Official takes cut, pays hospital bills	.179	.650	.355	−.128
Driver offers officer $20	.314	.378	.565	.042
EIGENVALUES	5.623	2.028	1.341	1.172
Percent of variance	28.12	10.14	6.71	5.86
Cumulative percent of variance	28.12	38.26	44.96	50.82

factor, while less important statistically than factor 1, represents another major category of judgments, a finding consistent with our earlier suggestion that popular conceptions of corruption will include the kinds of behavior specified by formal definitions. It is interesting to note that while factors 1 and 2 do reflect an apparent distinction between public- and private-sector wrongdoing, the personal taking factor also includes a public-sector case—that of a state employee's personal telephone calls.

The "misrepresentation" and "favoritism" factors are considerably less important in statistical terms, but are interesting for the kinds of behavior they encompass. Both point to perceived types of wrongdoing separate from personal taking or official theft; neither category is clearly public or private in nature. In both public and private life, people encounter situations in which they face temptations to misrepresent themselves or to cover up their actions (factor 3). The "favoritism" factor is interesting in light of our earlier comments on perceptions of corruption and inequality. Giving and getting unfair advantages, apparently, is another kind of wrongdoing which people perceive in both public and private life.

The relative strength of these factors lends support to our contention that in judging the behavior of others, people will frequently fall back upon everyday situations. This seems all the more likely to be true when the behavior in question does not fit other categories of wrongdoing. Perhaps these factors help us understand why, during the Watergate episode, many people were much more upset by Richard Nixon's tax evasion and use of public funds to renovate his own home, than by the much more serious (but less easily understood) kinds of official wrongdoing that came to light.

It still seems likely, however, that various kinds of wrongdoing will matter much more to some people than to others, as suggested above. Therefore, factor scores for each of the four categories of wrongdoing were broken down by social class; the results are presented in Table 43.4.

All four of our factors represent important categories of perceived wrongdoing. But as Table 43.4 shows, some of them vary considerably in their importance to different social classes, while others do not. Cases of official theft, for example, are much more the concern of middle- to upper-status respondents than of lower-status groups. The former scored significantly higher on the survey's six-item political information scale, which may mean that they have a more complete grasp of what constitutes wrongdoing in public settings, and are more familiar with the public misconduct that does come to light. They also ranked higher on an "input political efficacy" item;[18] perhaps higher-status individuals see official misconduct as a threat to the orderly operation of governments which would otherwise be responsive to their needs.

Class variations in scores for "personal taking," by contrast, are rather weak. This may be taken to mean that the rules and expectations governing personal conduct are shared across class lines to a greater extent than are conceptions of public ethics. The same might also be the case with the "misrepresentation" category. It is interesting to

Table 43.4
FACTOR SCORES BROKEN DOWN BY SOCIAL CLASS GROUPINGS

"Personal Taking"

Class Groupings:	Low (7)	Low-Middle (51)	Middle (75)	Upper-Middle (42)	Upper (32)
Mean	.551	.115	−.207	−.031	.162
Std. Dev.	1.248	.943	1.007	.894	1.187

Analysis of Variance: F = 1.6699 p = .1583
Test of Linearity: F(lin) = .0697 p = .7920
F(dev) = 2.2034 p = .0889

"Official Theft"

Class Groupings:	Low	Low-Middle	Middle	Upper-Middle	Upper
Mean	−.148	−.401	.173	−.024	.198
Std. Dev.	.940	1.298	.812	.973	.715

Analysis of Variance: F = 3.0899 p = .0169
Test of Linearity: F(lin) = 5.2562 p = .0229
F(dev) = 2.3678 p = .0719

"Misrepresentation"

Class Groupings:	Low	Low-Middle	Middle	Upper-Middle	Upper
Mean	.360	.023	−.035	−.130	.054
Std. Dev.	1.069	.925	1.182	1.182	.805

Analysis of Variance: F = .4501 p = .7722
Test of Linearity: (lin) = .2446 p = .6214
F(dev) = .5186 p = .6699

"Favoritism"

Class Groupings:	Low	Low-Middle	Middle	Upper-Middle	Upper
Mean	−.406	.210	.150	−.292	−.227
Std. Dev.	1.010	.900	1.062	.972	1.039

Analysis of Variance: F = 2.5763 p = .0388
Test of Linearity: F(lin) = 4.1691 p = .0425
F(dev) = 2.0454 p = .1087

note, however, that both "personal taking" and "misrepresentation" received their strongest condemnations at the extremes of the class continuum. Perhaps lower-status individuals are the most frequently victimized by personal taking and misrepresentation, and upper-status groups have the most to lose to such practices. But the weak statistical significance of the breakdowns, and the exceedingly small size of the lowest-status group, mean that significant relationships between class distinctions and reactions to the above categories of misconduct cannot be asserted at this time.

The most interesting class-related contrasts emerge in the breakdown of "favoritism" factor scores. Setting aside the very small low-status group, we see a strong tendency for lower-middle and middle-status persons to resent cases of favoritism, and for upper-middle and upper-status respondents to be tolerant of them. This is especially striking for the "upper" status group, whose judgments of all three other categories of wrongdoing were stronger than the group mean. Higher-status individuals are probably more accustomed to expect and receive special privileges than are others. But there is more at stake than this, for here we see the intersection between notions of corruption and perceptions of inequality which Tocqueville pointed out 150 years ago. It may well be that what lower- and middle-status people regard as illegitimate favors and advantages are seen by higher-status groups as merely the fruits of merit and expertise. For lower-middle and middle-class persons, favoritism could certainly be seen as a threat to one's hopes of advancing through hard work, or as an explanation for the failure of such hopes in the past. Moreover, lower-status individuals are less likely to occupy roles in which they can give sizeable favors to others, while higher-status persons may have done so, or may at least regard the giving and withholding of favors as part of the routine authority of managers and decisionmakers—people with whom they may have much in common. The legitimacy of special favors and privileges, it seems, has much to do with whether one views them from above or below.

Right and Wrong in American Politics

. . . While public perceptions must be an important aspect of any analysis of corruption as a political issue, it would be most difficult to build those perceptions into basic definitions. Table 43.1 does show that many actions which are corrupt by formal definitions are also recognized as such by the public. But social perceptions of corruption are most intriguing and politically significant in the broad middle range of Table 43.1, where they diverge from formal definitions. This part of the spectrum of judgments is the turf upon which issues of right and wrong in politics are contested. And here, gradations of judgment are fine, and levels of consensus are comparatively low. Definitions or typologies based on these judgments are likely to be unacceptably "soft" at their boundaries, or they will contain an unmanageable number of categories based on unstable distinctions.[19]

A better approach is to use a formal analytical definition to identify corruption, to posit social conceptions of corruption as an important factor affecting political response (or non-response) to corruption, and then to examine the divergencies between the two outlooks. This strategy, rather than attempting somehow to merge two fundamentally contrasting conceptions of corruption, preserves the differences between them, and focuses our attention upon those contrasts as interesting political questions in their own right. Instead of using public opinion to decide whether or not patronage practices in a given system, for example, should be studied as corruption, why not ask the much more interesting political question as to why corrupt practices elicit, or fail to elicit, particular political responses—or, why citizens might perceive massive corruption in a government which, from an analytical perspective, seems to have little of it? Corruption and scandal, after all, are different things; we may find one without the other.[20]

This sort of analysis will be complex, involving many other factors beyond public opinion. But it can turn a difficulty into an advantage: the subtleties and contradictions of public judgment become not a problem to be somehow overcome in the construction of typologies, but rather indicators of important stresses and linkages between state and society, mass and elite.

Notes

1. Richard Hofstadter, *The Age of Reform* (New York: Vintage, 1955); see also William J. Crotty, *Political Reform and the American Experiment* (New York: Crowell, 1977).
2. Gunnar Myrdal, "Corruption: Its Causes and Effects," in G. Myrdal, *Asian Drama: An Enquiry into the Povery of Nations,* vol. 2 (New York: Twentieth Century, 1968). pp. 937–58.
3. Michael Johnston, *Political Corruption and Public Policy in America* (Monterey, Calif.: Brooks-Cole, 1982), ch. 1; James C. Scott, *Comparative Political Corruption* (Englewood Cliffs, N.J.: Prentice-Hall, 1972), pp. 3–9; Arnold J. Heidenheimer, "The Context of Analysis," in A. J. Heidenheimer, ed., *Political Corruption: Readings in Comparative Analysis* (New Brunswick, N.J.: Transaction Books, reprinted 1978). pp. 3–28.
4. Johnston, *Political Corruption,* ch. 2.
5. Arnold A. Rogow and Harold D. Lasswell, *Power, Corruption, and Rectitude* (Englewood Cliffs, N.J.: Prentice-Hall, 1963).
6. Alexis de Tocqueville, *Democracy in America,* vol. 1 (New York: Vintage, 1945), pp. 234–35.
7. S. Chibnall and P. Saunders, "Worlds Apart: Notes on the Social Reality of Corruption," *British Journal of Sociology,* 28 (June 1977): 138–54.
8. Peter L. Berger and Thomas P. Luckmann, *The Social Construction of Reality: A Treatise in the Sociology of Knowledge* (Garden City, N.Y.: Doubleday, 1967).

9. Stuart Henry, *The Hidden Economy: The Context and Control of Borderline Crime* (London: Martin Robertson, 1978).
10. Ibid., pp. 48–52.
11. Ibid., pp. 52–60.
12. Donald R. Cressey, *Other People's Money* (New York: Free Press, 1953); Erwin O. Smigel, "Public Attitudes Toward 'Chiseling' with Reference to Unemployment Compensation," in Erwin O. Smigel and H. Laurence Ross, eds., *Crimes Against Bureaucracy* (New York: Van Nostrand Reinhold, 1970), pp. 29–45; Donald M. Horning, "Blue-Collar Theft: Conceptions of Property, Attitudes Toward Pilfering, and Work Group Norms in a Modern Industrial Plant," in Smigel and Ross., eds., *Crimes Against Bureaucracy*, pp. 46–64; Jason Ditton, *Part-Time Crime: An Ethnography of Fiddling and Pilferage* (London: Macmillan, 1977); Gerald Mars, *Cheats at Work: An Anthropology of Workplace Crime* (London: George Allen and Unwin, 1982).
13. Erwin O. Smigel, "Public Attitudes Toward Stealing as Related to the Size of the Victim Organization," in Smigel and Ross, eds., *Crimes Against Bureaucracy*, p. 7.
14. Ibid.
15. One objection to this format might be that corruption, as a formal concept, refers to actions affecting public roles and resources, while these items invite respondents to label essentially private actions as corrupt. But the distinction between public and private is not precise, as noted above; and the ways in which people apply the label "corruption" to a variety of actions, both in and out of the public sphere, is part of the process of judgment at issue here. In any event, those who do apply a public-private distinction were given the opportunity to label actions by private individuals as "not at all corrupt."
16. Smigel, "Public Attitudes Toward Stealing," passim.
17. Smigel, "Public Attitudes Toward Stealing."
18. "Input political efficacy" refers to one dimension of the general concept of political efficacy—the belief that one can effectively make one's views and values an "input" into decisionmaking processes. See, for an application of this concept, David Lowery and Lee Sigelman, "Understanding the Tax Revolt: Eight Explanations," *American Political Science Review* 75 (December 1981): 963–74. The "input efficacy" item used in that study as well as this one, was: "Sometimes politics and government seem so complicated that a person like me can't really understand what's going on" (disagreement: high efficacy). Source: Stephen C. Craig, "Measuring Political Efficacy," unpublished manuscript, University of Florida, 1980, as cited in Lowery and Sigelman.
19. Michael Johnston, "Right and Wrong in American Politics," paper prepared for the annual meeting of the American Political Science Association, Chicago, September 1983.
20. Graeme C. Moodie, "On Political Scandals and Corruption," *Government and Opposition* 15 (1980): 208–22.

44

Variations in Attitudes Toward Corruption in Canada

Kenneth M. Gibbons

This chapter has as its purpose the furthering of our understanding of the concept of political corruption. It is hoped that the use of survey research techniques which allow one to identify how citizens (approximated here by a sample of university students) define corruption and—to the extent made possible by the inclusion of questions of sociological, economic, psychological and political nature—why they define corruption as they do. For reasons that will soon be discussed, the analysis of the definition of corruption used here is an empirical one, though based on certain normative assumptions to be addressed. The thesis of the paper is that citizens can define corruption, that they define corruption in terms of relatively complex dimensions, and that there are patterns to the definitions which suggest explanations (i.e., the "why" aspect) for those definitions which are consistent with more generalizable social science literature. In order to come to grips with this thesis, exploratory as it is, certain underlying issues must be addressed. . . .

Under the rubric of political corruption, at least nine different types of corruption can be identified.[1] One of these is patronage or the hiring of government employees or the letting of government contracts according to partisan consideration rather than virtue of merit. Another is vote-buying which constitutes the attempt to influence the vote by virtue of monetary inducements or their equivalent or by "buying" irregularities in the voting process such as "stuffing the ballot box" or impersonation. There is also pork-barrelling, which is the attempt to sway the support of a constituency (rather than an individual or

Source: Kenneth M. Gibbons, "Towards an Attitudinal Definition of Corruption: Evidence from a Survey of Canadian University Students." Paper given at the 1985 International Political Science Congress. By permission of the author.

individuals) by the promise of some public works project such as a new highway or a school. It differs from patronage in that the reward is very diffused, in that all within the constituency will benefit (theoretically) from the project. The reason that it has been considered corrupt, at least by some, is that it distorts priorities in a way which do not immediately suggest that the "public interest" is included in the calculation. Only partisan gain enters the equation for spilling the contents of the public purse. The act of bribery almost needs no definition. It is the act of trying to influence an official to make a decision he or she would not otherwise make, by offering a monetary reward or other such inducement. Graft represents the same phenomenon with the exception that the official initiates the action, rather than the citizen. Nepotism parallels patronage in terms of hiring and letting of contracts, but the motivation is not partisan advantage but kinship or friendship. Influence-peddling is a variant of conflict of interest (or, conceivably, of bribery). However, where conflict of interest refers to an individual official making decisions which are seen (in reality or only potentially) to be unduly influenced by his or her private interests, influence-peddling complicates matters by either having the official attempt to influence others in government or even by having an intermediary play the same role, even if that intermediary is not an official. Thus, influence-peddling increases the scope of involvement over the more atomistic conflict of interest behavior. Finally, "corrupt" campaign finance suggests that contributions to the campaign fund of a party or a candidate are seen as compromising, or potentially compromising, the integrity of the party or the candidate. (Some acts which were listed as related to vote-buying, i.e. electoral "dirty tricks", might just as easily be categorized here as well).

Each of these types of corruption or, to be more precise, potential corruption can be distinguished in terms of the dimensions discussed earlier. (Potential corruption is more precise because it is assumed that public attitudes must be known before such acts can be said to be corrupt). This relationship between types of corruption and the six dimensions is summarized in Table 44.1. . . .

Methodology

Public attitudes about corruption have been approximated in this study by the use of what might be called either a purposive or convenience sample. In fact, the sample is really both of these, and thus constitutes a non-probabilistic sample in any event. While it is true that such samples are hindered by limitations they create for generalizability, they are widely accepted as a necessity for exploratory research or, as Selltiz *et al.* put it, for developing "ideas."[2] The convenience of the sample stems from the fact that the respondents were a captive audience of university students in political science courses. The purposive nature of the sample is highlighted by two realizations. First, the techniques for probing the respondents' understanding of corruption were possibly too complex for a more representative sample, at least as a first attempt. Second, by using such a sample, time and cost restraints which normally plague social science research of this type would not prevent the questionnaire from being distributed to a regionally sensitive sample. In fact, students at five universities, one in each of Canada's recognized major regions, were surveyed. Those familiar with Canada's political nature will understand how significant the concept of region is for the country's attitudinal matrix.[3]

The sample consists of 297 students at various levels of study. The breakdown by campus (and, in effect, region) is shown in Table 44.2. There is no correspondence between the proportion of the sample and the proportion of the general population drawn from each region. The Atlantic provinces are overrepresented substantially, and Quebec is significantly underrepresented; otherwise no proportions are seriously affected. . . .

The questionnaire consisted of eight pages, including the cover page with its instructions and anonymity clause. While many of the questions (particularly in part three, the "background" items) were relatively standard, part two represented a new technique for investigating the concept of corruption. This part included nine scenarios describing political and administrative behaviors which are included in corruption literature. The one exception was a scenario which related an incident of party discipline, a feature of parliamentary (especially Canadian) politics which many students had challenged as being of dubious ethicality in many of the author's political science classes in previous years. Moreover, given that pretests had indicated a fatigue problem with the scenarios—each of which was accompanied by 13 semantic differentials employing concept pairs like "corrupt-not corrupt", "common-rare", "necessary-unnecessary", etc.—two of the original ten scenarios which had corresponded to the vote-buying and graft types noted earlier were dropped. These scenarios were thought expendable because of their overlap with others and because it was posited that there would be very little variation in responses to them. . . .

The use of scenarios depicting dubious activities is not, in itself, a

Table 44.1
Types and Dimensions of Political Corruption

Types of Corruption	Scope of Involvement	Status of Actors	Type of Reward	Selectivity of Inducement	Location (Arena)	Level of Condemnation
Patronage	broad as a rule, narrow in specific cases	political actors are official and initiators	power for political actors and income for others	moderately selective	legislative, administrative, judicial	mixed or "grey," laws are disregarded
Vote-buying	broad	political actors are official or competitive and are the initiators	mostly power for political actors, income for others	not very selective due to secret ballot	electoral	very strong or "black," both in law and opinion
Pork-barrelling	broad	political actors are competitive or official and initiate	power for political actors, public works with monetary value for constituency	very diffuse	electoral or legislative	weak or "white," in opinion, no laws
Bribery	very narrow	political actors are official and targets	income for officials, income or power for others	very selective	legislative, administrative, or judicial	very strong or "black" in law and opinion

Graft	either broad or narrow	politicals are official and initiate	income for officials, income or power (access) for others	either selective or diffuse	legislative, administrative, or judicial	strong or black
Conflict of interest	very narrow	actor(s) are official and initiate, no target because there is no exchange	income	very selective	legislative, administrative, or judicial	mixed or "grey," both in law and opinion
Nepotism	very narrow in specific case—may be broad as a principle in some cultures	political actor is an official and initiates act though others apply pressure	social for official, income for other	very selective	mostly administrative but with legislative influence	mixed or grey in opinion, black in law though not always applied
Influence-peddling	very narrow	normally, official is target, but can be an intermediary	income for official, income or power for intermediary or initiator	very selective	usually legislative, on occasion administrative	black in principle both in law and opinion, but might be rationalized as systemic in specific case
Corrupt campaign finance	broad	political actor may be competitive or official, may be target or initiator	power or income for either side of exchange	moderately selective except in some cases	electoral	black in law, grey in opinion

Table 44.2
Distribution of Sample by University (region)

University	Region	Respondents	% of Total
Memorial (Nfld.)	Atlantic provinces	68	22.9
Laval	Quebec	33	11.1
Carleton	Ontario	72	24.2
Winnipeg (Man.)	Prairies	84	28.3
British Columbia	British Columbia	40	13.5
		297	100.0

novel methodological exercise.[4] However, the inclusion of the 13 semantic differentials is a new effort at discerning the various components of the evaluation or definition of corruption. In addition to the three word or concept pairs mentioned in the previous paragraph, word pairs also included: important-unimportant, provincial-federal, local-provincial, federal-local, democratic-undemocratic, American-Canadian, Progressive Conservative-N.D.P., Liberal-Progressive Conservative, N.D.P.-Liberal, and English Canadian-French Canadian. (An additional differential was used in both British Columbia and Quebec in order to tap unique provincial partisan considerations caused by the existence of regional parties.) The justifications for using these components as differentials will be discussed in the course of the analysis of the findings.

The background variables employed in the study were typical of those normally employed in survey research, and included such notions as age, gender, province of residence, urban or rural residence, parents' and respondents' social class (both subjective and objective), level of parents' education, party preference and intensity, a four item series of alienation measures using the Likert format, and items on level of respondents' university study and the number of political science courses they had taken.

Other background items related specifically to the concept of corruption. One of these was a listing of ten political issues in the order of their importance to the respondents. This cued approach was thought necessary, given that open-ended questions on issues seem to generate relatively few responses and thus limit one to examining "standard" issues such as inflation or unemployment.[5] Indeed, recent Gallup polls had shown that with open-ended responses, 80 percent of all respondents chose those two standard responses. Thus, issues are rarely subjected to "deeper" analysis which might uncover primary, secondary, or even tertiary issues. Corruption, for example, rarely rates mention as one of the three most important issues confronting voters, and almost never seems to be the single most important issue. Hence, at best, corruption is of secondary importance. Yet, even this might be of some significance when compared to the range of issues beyond inflation and unemployment. Indeed, the results of the closed-ended analysis showed corruption to be seventh out of ten issues, well behind inflation and unemployment but ahead of separatism, bilingualism and abortion, all of which had been drawing much media attention in Canada. Unfortunately, the ranking of corruption as an issue had very modest impact at best on the students' evaluations of the corruption scenarios.

The other corruption-based background items included a series of 14 Likert-style items rating the trustworthiness of various institutions and groups (many of which were political) in society; and a series of 13 items asking respondents to indicate whether they had "heard of" any of the events listed. This was followed by a probe series which drew out some indication of the respondents' knowledge about those events that they had indicated as being known to them. These items permitted the creation of a political knowledge index with a special "corruption" twist. The trust scales had little impact.

The statistical analysis combines the use of simple percentages (plus means, etc.) for descriptive purposes with two measures of association (Cramer's V for nominal level data and gamma for ordinal level) and, despite the non-probabilistic nature of the sample, a test of significance (chi square). Two caveats are in order. First, Cramer's V is used for comparative purposes only, as it does not have "operational meaning" in the same sense that gamma—with its "meaning" of reduction of error—has. Second, the test of significance is also offered here merely as a comparative tool. No attempt is made to suggest that the chi-square test permits this analysis to generalize to the population as a whole given the limitations of the data set.

One brief note on the legal status of the types of corruption contained in the scenarios is needed. A review of Canadian legislation at both the federal and provincial levels revealed at least 68 statutes in place for the 11 governments which had at least some minimal connection to the concept of corruption. Some of these statutes had extensive elements devoted to issues of corruption, even to the point of being specifically designed to address a given issue in corruption, e.g., acts regarding conflict of interest. Others contained only fleeting mention of a relevant issue in the midst of a statute designed for completely different purposes, e.g., provisions for conflict of interest in an act devoted to the operation of school boards or even a horse racing commission. Though a full, detailed description of this research is not germane to this chapter, suffice it to say that the evaluations of the legal status of the various types of corruption is supported by this research.[6] With these methodological points, both quantitative and qualitative, having been made, let our attention now turn to the findings themselves.

Findings: Defining Corruption

Perhaps the most significant aspect of the research, from a descriptive perspective only, is the evaluation of the nine different scenarios [see Appendix]. . . .

By referring to Table 44.2, one can see that when the scenarios are rank ordered according to means for each differential, the party discipline scenario was ranked as the fifth most corrupt scenario out of nine possibilities. It was also ranked as the most important. . . .

Considering each scenario on an individual basis, what can be said of the way each behavior is defined? Regarding nepotism, we have an activity which is "defined" by the respondents as very corrupt, common, unnecessary, important and very undemocratic. It is more a local phenomenon than provincial, and more a provincial phenomenon than

Table 44.2
Rank-Orderings of Corruption Scenarios Comparing Semantic Differentials, According to Means

Comparing Means	Scenarios:	1	2	3	4	5	6	7	8	9
Corrupt-not corrupt		2	6	7	1	9	3	8	5	4
Common-rare		5	1	2	9	4	6	7	3	8
Necessary-unnecessary		9	2	4	8	1	6	5	3	7
Important-unimportant		5	4	7	2	8	3	9	1	6
Provincial-federal		2	7	1	3	9	6	4	8	5
Federal-local		9	5	6	8	2	3	7	1	4
Local-provincial		1	6	5	2	8	7	3	9	4
Undemocratic-democratic		1	6	8	2	9	3	7	4	5
American-Canadian		5	4	8	2	1	3	7	9	6
PC-NDP		8	9	7	6	1	2	3	5	4
Liberal-PC		2	4	7	3	8	5	9	1	6
NDP-Liberal		1	3	2	4	9	8	7	6	5
Liberal-PQ (Laval only)		1	8	8	3	1	4	5	6	7
Socred-NDP (UBC only)		3	6	5	7	2	1	8	9	3
English Can.–French Can.		9	6	7	8	1	2	4	5	3

Note: Rank-order is in terms of the mean score closest to the term on the left side of the differential. E.g., on the "corrupt-not corrupt" differential, scenario number 4 was scored as the most corrupt by the respondents.

a federal one. In terms of other, less salient components (salience in this case being a reference to the meaningful, non-neutral responses), nepotism is seen as more closely associated with the Progressive Conservative Party than with the New Democratic Party (NDP), but more with the Liberals than with the Conservatives. While this might be seen as a result of an "ins-vs.-outs" problem (relevant in 1982) in that one might be inclined to associate nepotism with the party in power, the evidence from Quebec seems to discount this. For Quebec, nepotism is seen as more a Liberal phenomenon than a Parti Quebecois (PQ) one, despite the fact that the PQ were in power at the time the survey was conducted in 1982. Finally, consistent with what has been thought to be a popular view of North American politics as far as Canadians were concerned, the sample saw nepotism as more an American phenomenon than a Canadian one. This view was popular during the time of the Watergate crisis in the United States and has even been supported by American writers.[7] Interestingly, given a long-standing reference to French-Canadian attitudes toward corruption, about 75 percent of the sample either gave a neutral response or no response at all when asked whether nepotism was an English-Canadian or French-Canadian phenomenon.[8] Indeed, every other scenario was even less salient than nepotism in terms of this ethnically-based component. For that reason, it is best left undiscussed in other examples.

The patronage scenario was evaluated somewhat differently from the nepotism example. First, while regarded as corrupt, it was thought far less so on the average. Further, it was also perceived as modestly necessary, yet still somewhat undemocratic (again, far less so than nepotism). It was the second most necessary activity after the campaign finance scenario, but near the middle of all scenarios in terms of being democratic. Both of these components, but especially that regarding necessity, seem to confirm the notion that there is a functional side to some forms of corruption.

Pork-barrelling was seen as modestly corrupt (and seventh overall), and quite common. In sum, there are no startling findings regarding any of the components of this type, except to note that it was the most likely of the scenarios to be viewed as a provincial phenomenon. However, caution is required in this regard as the use of the highway example creates a bias in that highways are essentially a provincial jurisdiction. It should be noted also that other scenarios have similar problems with bias which should be reexamined in future research. For example, the use of the term "legislator" in two scenarios also creates a provincial bias in that the term need not be interpreted in its generic sense by the respondents. That is, the term tends to be associated with provincial politics, even by political science students.

Bribery is an especially corrupt type of activity according to student opinion. It is the most corrupt, the least common, the second most unnecessary and so on. Of special interest is the finding that this most corrupt of activities is also one of the least associated with upper levels of government. Had this been a discernable pattern for all the more "serious" scenarios, it would have confimed the notion that upper level governments—especially national governments—were thought to be less corruption prone because they were the bulwarks against less democratic practices at lower levels.[9] Unfortunately, no such pattern did develop.

The only scenario to be seen as not corrupt was that regarding campaign finance. This was true even for students from the Ontario university where provincial law would hold such an act to be illegal. This represents a clear case of the lack of agreement between law and opinion, notable especially because in this one instance the law is thought to go too far, if this measure can be interpreted broadly. In other cases where the law and student attitudes are inconsistent, the pattern identified is one where the law is seen as being too lax. However, the indirectness of the measure makes this less clear than it could be. The consistency between the concepts of corruption and democracy (i.e., an inverse relationship) is most clear in this case; the only scenario which is thought not corrupt is also the only scenario thought to be at least very modestly democratic. As we shall see later, there was a sharp split along regional lines on this matter. Interesting also is the realization that the respondents found this scenario the second least important.

Legislative conflict of interest was modestly more corrupt than its bureaucratic variant, and both were more corrupt than the average case. The legislative variant was slightly more common and slightly less unnecessary than the bureaucratic type. It was also thought to be considerably more undemocratic. The degree of condemnation directed at the bureaucratic conflict of interest scenario is perhaps mildly surprising, given that the scenario does not indicate that the officials in question used government's time, money, or other assets in their consulting business. Had this been the case, the scenario would have likely engendered an even stronger condemnation. Further, the legislative conflict of interest scenario permits a comparison to be made against the attitudes of American state legislators and Canadian members of parliament. If we assume, for the sake of argument, an equivalence between the three scenarios used in this study, the study by Peters and Welch and that by Mancuso, we find that the Canadian students were the most critical. Approximately 75 percent of the Canadian student sample saw this scenario as corrupt, while 54.9 percent of the American state legislators and only 42.4 percent of the Canadian members of parliament felt the same way.[10]

The example of influence-peddling noted in the seventh scenario was intended to register a mild reaction, given that far more blatant cases could be envisioned.[11] Even so, the scenario was seen as corrupt. In this scenario, another opportunity for a reasonable comparison exists in that the Beard and Horn study of United States congressmen noted earlier uses a scenario which was modified for this survey's influence-peddling item. The United States congressional study scored the item almost exactly neutral (neither ethical nor unethical), and the Canadians students rated this scenario as the closest to neutral of any of the nine they encountered.[12] Nevertheless, this scenario was viewed as unnecessary and undemocratic, though no worse than average on these counts.

The party discipline scenario, as noted earlier, was partly included as a response to repeated concerns on the part of undergraduate students over the past number of years. They seemed to find the strict party discipline practiced in Canada (which exaggerates British tradition in this regard) offensive. Also, it seemed methodologically sensible to include a scenario which was not treated as corrupt in the literature on political ethics as a "control" element. As it turned out, this scenario ranked fifth in its "corruptness"; it was also thought to be the most important and, as a counterpoint to its modest unethicality, it was seen as somewhat less unnecessary than all but two other scenarios. This scenario was also an interesting indirect measure of political knowledge in that it was the only one to be perceived as a Canadian rather than American phenomenon.

In summary then, a view of political corruption in general emerges from these observations. First, all scenarios except that dealing with campaign finance were seen as corrupt, a vindication of sorts for the literature on this subject, but a cause for some incongruence relating to the legal status of these acts. The campaign finance scenario is already deemed illegal in one province, and other governments might well follow. On the other hand, an act like pork-barrelling is roundly condemned attitudinally, but the likelihood of any law being passed to curb it is almost nil. In some cases, like nepotism, there seems to be an agreement in both attitude and law, but the law is either restricted in its application or interpretation. Hence, such practices continue despite what might be described as the taint of "black" corruption, using

Heidenheimer's classification. Of course it is debatable as to whether the violation of both attitude and law regarding nepotism is merely the isolated act of a small number of unethical persons or a more systemic social behavior.

In other regards, these scenarios are generally thought to be common, unnecessary, important, and undemocratic. Distinctions are made between levels of government, but these vary according to the specific type of behavior in question and are possibly confounded by the wording of the scenarios. Distinctions based on partisan concerns are also possible, but variable, and salient only to a minority of respondents. This problem with salience was also noted in the American-Canadian component and especially in the case of the English Canadian-French Canadian distinctions. However, all scenarios other than that dealing with party discipline were decidedly American phenomena in the students' view. The smugness of Canadians which was apparent during the Watergate era has not yet faded.

Findings: Influences on Corruption Ratings

Although a total of 29 independent variables was employed in the original analysis of the influences on the way people evaluated the corruption scenarios, only a few such variables had consistent impact on these evaluations: region (whether as province of residence or in terms of the university attended); federal party preference; the score on one particular item in the alienation series; provincial party preference; an index of political knowledge based on awareness of past "corrupt" events; and age. These impacts, which are noted only when both the significance level of .05 and an appropriate level for the measure of association (.15 for V or +/-.15 for gamma) are present, are discussed below as they relate to the "corrupt-not corrupt" component.

Despite the observation by Mancuso, region remains a very strong determinant of attitudes toward corruption, at least for those who are not part of the political elite. Mancuso's argument was wisely hedged by reference to the homogenizing effect of membership in parliament, so the contrast between students and members of parliament should not be considered too critical.[13] Region had an impact upon the evaluation of three scenarios (where the impact of "university" and province of residence was consistent) in terms of the corrupt-not corrupt component. For example, leaving aside other cases where differences which existed did not meet the stated criteria for "acceptance", only nepotism, patronage, and campaign finance were dramatically affected by region. (Region did have much more noticeable impact on the evaluations based on levels of government, however). These impacts are summarized in Table 44.3. Most interesting is the inconsistency between Quebec and the predominantly English-speaking regions, especially on the finance scenario.[14]

The impact of federal party preference was felt on the corrupt evaluation for patronage, campaign finance, and the two types of conflict of interest scenarios, although this was most evident for bureaucratic conflict of interest when intensity, rather than mere

Table 44.3
Influences on the Corruption Ratings

Region:	ATL.	QUE.	ONT.	PRA.	B.C.	Assoc.	Sign.
Nepotism:							
% corrupt	83.8	64.5	95.8	86.9	87.2	V = .18	.005
% not corrupt	10.3	9.7	1.4	7.1	10.3		
Patronage:							
% corrupt	66.1	48.4	38.6	46.6	53.8	V = .17	.01
% not corrupt	23.5	25.8	38.6	39.3	28.2		
Campaign finance:							
% corrupt	25.4	53.3	20.5	32.1	35.0	V = .16	.05
% not corrupt	64.2	30.0	53.0	54.8	57.5		

Federal Party Preference:	LIB	PC	NDP	OTHER*		Assoc.	Sign.
Patronage:							
% corrupt	44.0	55.4	51.6	52.4		V = .17	.05
% not corrupt	40.0	30.5	25.0	33.3			
Campaign finance:							
% corrupt	33.0	22.6	38.6	23.8		V = .16	.05
% not corrupt	50.0	67.9	36.9	47.6			
Leg. conflict:							
% corrupt	78.2	77.1	72.9	60.9		V = .17	.05
% not corrupt	13.9	14.4	13.6	26.1			
*Bur. conflict:***							
% very corrupt	(23.8)	(18.1)	(40.0)	(28.6)			
% corrupt	75.4	71.1	73.3	76.2		V = .20	.0005
% not corrupt	22.7	21.7	16.7	19.0			

Provincial Party Preference:	LIB	PC	NDP	PQ	SC	NONE	Assoc.	Sign.
Campaign finance:								
% corrupt	29.5	22.0	36.5	60.0	16.7	33.3	V = .17	.05
% not corrupt	56.8	66.0	44.6	28.0	75.0	46.7		

direction, was taken into account. In a general sense, there is very little pattern to discern here, although the social democratic NDP supporters seem slightly more censorious overall than the remaining party supporters. This seems true also in the case of provincial party support, except that the Parti Quebecois supporters (also social democratic) are even more censorious than NDPers on the campaign finance scenario.

Age is a factor in two scenarios, both times reflecting a much higher level of condemnation on the part of the older (30 plus) students. The scenarios where this difference reaches statistically relevant proportions are campaign finance and bureaucratic conflict of interest. In the latter case, the older students simply manifest a stronger intensity than others, but for campaign finance there is also a modest shift in the direction of opinion.

The linkage between political knowledge and evaluation of corruption becomes clear in regard to legislative conflict of interest, party discipline, and bureaucratic conflict of interest. In the first case the difference is merely one of intensity. While this is also true in the second instance, the difference is much more dramatic, and the direction of change is the reverse of the first case. The reason for this seems to be that the assessment of party discipline apparently includes the underlying impact of one's knowledge of parliamentary politics (e.g., responsible government, etc.) as well as one's knowledge of past "scandals" which form the basis of the political knowledge index. In the third case, the direction follows the first example, but the difference in intensity is more obvious. The more knowledgeable (about past corruption at least) are more censorious in the case of either type of conflict of interest.

Finally, alienation—as measured by a Likert-type item asking for agreement or disagreement with the statement "Politicians don't care what people like me think"—is dramatically linked with five of the nine scenarios in terms of the corrupt-not corrupt component. The general pattern is very clear and consistent: those who are more alienated are also more censorious; that is, they are more inclined to evaluate the scenarios as corrupt. This realization raises the classic causality question about chickens and eggs. It is possible that the alienated citizen tends to perceive politics as a corrupt game, i.e., that alienation breeds the corrupt evaluations. It is equally possible that the alienated citizen becomes alienated because of the corruption he or she sees in political life.

That the corruption scenarios are affected by certain independent variables is no revelation. Indeed, the question might be asked: With all the possible combinations of scenarios and independent variables, why were there not more instances of statistically relevant influences noted? The reason may be that the sample size was too small or the categorizations used for contingency table analysis could have been rearranged. These are methodological considerations which should receive attention. But it is also possible that the relatively low degree of influence factors (i.e., relative to the mathematical possibilities or even expectations) could reflect a certain homogeneity of attitude or opinion about corruption. In other words, perhaps there are few great differences to be found, and views of corruption may transcend such social-economic-political distinctions. The evidence from the relationships which failed to meet our criteria for inclusion suggest that the answer might be a bit of both.

Conclusion

Most exploratory studies conclude with suggestions that further research is required before certain questions can be said to have been given their due. This chapter is not going to break the tradition of academic "hedging of bets", because the tradition of caution is reasonable. Nonetheless, certain points can be made (with such caution, of course) about the research discussed above.

First, people seem to be able to make discerning evaluations about the complex concept of corruption. They see differences in types of corruption; they perceive some types as more corrupt, more common, etc., and the components employed in the survey seem to have meaning to people in most respects. Further, by discovering patterns which appear for all or most types, one can begin to get a picture of how people conceptualize corruption generally, that is, beyond distinction between types. Generally, people see corruption as common, unnecessary (a direct rebuke, often, to functionalists), important, and ultimately undemocratic. They may define some activities as corrupt which are not treated as such by law or by academic literature, but they may also do the reverse. This realization makes Heidenheimer's perspective that much more useful.

Second, the patterns of influences on the corruption evaluations display some variations brought about by some rather typical (to social science inquiry) independent variables, but these were not as extensive as they might have been, or indeed expected to be. This suggests a degree of homogeneity in terms of the evaluation of corruption, but this perspective must be entertained with care. Most clear among the relationships between influencing factors and evaluations of corruption is the obvious linkage between alienation and censoriousness. This relationship is also, potentially, the most troubling for democratic systems and has been used as a justification for much of the research which has previously taken place in this area. It now appears that the justification has some, albeit indirect, empirical validity.

Appendix

Nine Corruption Scenarios

1. A civil servant is in a position to hire a new worker in his office. He decides to give the job to his relative rather than to another person who is better qualified. (NEPOTISM)
2. When party A won the last election, it removed a number of people from their government jobs and replaced them with loyal party A supporters. (PATRONAGE)
3. During a recent election candidate X announced that the government would build a new highway in the riding that the constituents had wanted for years, but only if the party and candidate X win the election in the riding. (PORK-BARRELLING)
4. Mr. X, an average citizen, wants to get a favorable ruling from a civil servant in the government, so he offers to buy the official a television. (BRIBERY)
5. A wealthy man, Mr. Y donates $50,000 to the campaign fund of candidate B and B accepts. (CAMPAIGN FINANCE)
6. A legislator owns $25,000 worth of stock in a large mining company. He votes for a bill giving tax concessions to the mining industry. (LEGISLATIVE CONFLICT OF INTEREST)
7. Mrs. X, a legislator, often makes reference in the legislature to businesses in her constituency while speaking during question period. These businesses contribute to her campaign fund. (INFLUENCE-PEDDLING)
8. Mr. X, who has made known his intention to vote against his party on an upcoming bill, is told by his party caucus to vote with the party or lose its support for his nomination and campaign funding at election time. (PARTY DISCIPLINE)
9. A group of officials in a government department use their knowledge and contacts to establish a part-time consulting firm which gives advice to private clients. The officials are still employed by the government. (BUREAUCRATIC CONFLICT OF INTEREST)

Notes

1. The discussion which follows is drawn from two earlier works by the author: "Student Attitudes Toward Political Corruption in Canada," (Ottawa: Carleton University, Department of Political Science, 1984), ch. 3; and "The Study of Political Corruption", in K. M. Gibbons and D. C. Rowat, eds., *Political Corruption in Canada: Cases, Causes and Cures* (Toronto: McClelland and Stewart, 1976), pp. 8–14.
2. Claire Selltiz *et al.*, *Research Methods in Social Relations*, rev. (New York: Holt, Rinehart and Winston, 1959), pp. 55–59 and 537–45.
3. The term attitudinal matrix is taken from Michael S. Whittington, "Political Culture: The Attitudinal Matrix of Politics," in J. H. Redekop, ed., *Approaches to Canadian Politics* (Scarborough, Ont.: Prentice-Hall, 1978), pp. 138–53.
4. As examples, consider Edmund Beard and Stephen Horn, *Congressional Ethics: The View from the House* (Washington: Brookings Institution, 1975); Maureen Mancuso, "Attitudes of Canadian Legislators Toward Political Corruption: An Empirical Analysis", unpublished M.A. thesis, (Ottawa: Carleton University, Department of Political Science, 1984); and John G. Peters and Susan Welch, "Political Corruption in America: A Search for Definition and a Theory," *American Political Science Review* 72 (September, 1978), p. 975. However, none of these studies pursue more than two evaluative dimensions. For example, Beard and Horn asked their respondents to merely evaluate the scenarios in two ways: (1) a judgement of the practice as ethical or unethical, and (2) a judgement as to the extent of the practice.
5. *Gallup Report*, February 7, 1983. A national election survey conducted for the 1974 election found that many could not name three important issues; indeed 30 percent could not name even *one*! See Harold D. Clarke *et al.*, *Political Choice in Canada* (Toronto: McGraw-Hill Ryerson, 1979), pp. 244–46.
6. Gibbons, "Student Attitudes . . .," *op. cit.*, ch. 5.
7. On the Canadian view, see *inter alia*, Maurice Cuter, "Watergate: Could it Happen Here?," *Business Quarterly*, 38 (September 1973), p. 11 *et passim*. On the American perspective, see George C.S. Benson, *Political Corruption in America* (Lexington, Mass.: Lexington Books, 1978), pp. 3–5.
8. James C. Scott, *Comparative Political Corruption* (Englewood Cliffs, N.J.: Prentice-Hall, 1972), p. 156.
9. Ibid.
10. Peters and Welch use the following scenario (p. 978): "A member of congress who holds a large amount of stock (about $50,000 worth) in Standard Oil of New Jersey working to maintain the oil depletion allowance." 54.9 percent of the state legislators surveyed saw this as corrupt and 81.2 percent felt the public would condemn such an act (p. 981). Mancuso modified this scenario, replacing Standard Oil with Gulf Canada and the allowance with the National Energy Policy. She found that only 42.4 percent of the MPs saw this as corrupt and only 48.1 percent felt that the public would condemn it (pp. 34, 55).

11. This scenario is a revision of one in Beard and Horn (p. 30). More blatant examples are available, such as a case in Nova Scotia where party fund raisers requested contributions from distilling companies in order to get their products on the shelves of government liquor stores. See "Jury Convicts N.S. [Nova Scotia] Bagmen," *Winnipeg Free Press*, May 13, 1983, p. 1.
12. The wording in Beard and Horn was: "A legislator has ten contributors from different industries and labor organizations in his constituency who raise most of his campaign funds. During the session, the legislator puts one or two articles or speeches about each industry and labor organization in the *Congressional Record* as his way of thanking them for their support." This item received a score of 2.52, where 2.5 equals neutral.
13. Mancuso, *op. cit.*, pp. 94–102, 178–79, argues that regional impact, while evident, is weaker than one expects in Canada.
14. The population of Quebec, of course, is predominantly French-speaking, thus a French version of the questionnaire was distributed at a French-language university.

45

On Presidential Graft: The Latin American Evidence

Laurence Whitehead

Why Focus on Presidential Graft?

To focus on the way heads of state use their office for illicit personal (or family) enrichment may seem to trivialize and sensationalize the much more serious and widespread phenomenon of political corruption. A critic might object that whether or not an individual president was personally venal must be quite accidental—what matters for the country as a whole is whether or not the political machinery under his care operates to any significant extent under the incentives of graft. It is not difficult to find examples of personally incorruptible rulers who select and manipulate their subordinates by appealing to their greed— after all, to become a president normally requires great dedication and single-mindedness, so that the selection process can be expected to favor those with an appetite for power rather than merely a lust for money. Forced to choose between the certainty of future wealth and the possibility of continued power, most heads of state are likely to opt for the latter (although one or two apparent exceptions, such as Batista in 1958, have occasionally clouded this generalization). Surely, a chapter on political corruption, which narrows the focus to purely presidential graft, leaves out too much and reduces the subject to the level of mere anecdote and journalistic polemic?

Certainly if one consults the standard reader on *Political Corruption* (an excellent compilation edited by Arnold J. Heidenheimer) only six of the fifty-eight articles included therein encompass presidential graft as part of their subject matter, and even these mostly concentrate on

Source: Laurence Whitehead, "On Presidential Graft: The Latin America Evidence," Michael Clarke (ed.), *Corruption: Causes, Consequences and Control.* London: Pinter, 1983. pp. 163–89. By permission of author and publisher.

the more elusive and diffuse topic of "low-level corruption." Although many of these articles are informative and suggestive, such an approach raises many difficulties which need not arise in the discussion of presidential graft. For example, with "low-level corruption" there is the problem of encountering a suitable objective definition—some writers shuddered at the thought that they might be imposing values derived from Western industrial society on conduct which was perceived quite differently in a "non-Western" context. However, in the case of flagrant personal enrichment by Latin American rulers, this problem does not arise to the same extent; those not enjoying the spoils are just as likely to resent the illicit privileges of their top leaders in Latin America as people in the United States of America, even though their opportunities for protest and redress may be fewer. Of course at the margin there are still problems of definition about what constitutes abuse of office, but I am little troubled by this objection since so few of the individuals discussed in this chapter operated anywhere near the margin. I would also claim that in the case of presidential graft the problem of marshalling reliable and representative evidence, although substantial, is more manageable than in the case of low-level corruption. Furthermore, the causes and consequences of, and the alternatives to, political corruption (generally nebulous and uncertain in the literature on the low-level variant) seem clearer and more specific in the case of presidential graft.

But is the evidence on presidential graft really sufficiently accurate and comprehensive to justify such claims? There are obvious motives both for exaggerating and understating the scale of graft committed by any individual president, and where possible both a high and low estimate are given. Most of the argument would hold just as well whether the numbers were halved or doubled. The most likely source of inaccuracy would be if a large number of presidents had engaged in extensive peculation without yet being discovered or denounced. Fortunately there is detailed information on enough cases to show that the phenomenon is widespread and involves huge sums, and to explain how it operates. Likewise it may seem an omission to exclude personally honest presidents who tolerate corruption among their subordinates, but even without cases of this kind (which are, of course, difficult to interpret objectively), there is enough material to work on.

But how can one be sure that the slanderous accusations so frequently made against Latin American ex-presidents are not partisan fabrications? It is, in all probability, this fear of taking gossip for fact (and thereby insulting named individuals who may still have a large political following) which to a large extent explains why academics have focussed chiefly on low-level generalized corruption, rather than on presidential graft. Imperfect though they may be, the sources used here are sufficiently varied, serious and specific to uphold a fairly substantial general argument. Naming names on the basis of second-hand reports has obvious drawbacks but also some compensating advantages. By *personalizing* corruption one can clarify motives and bring into sharper focus the usually inconclusive debate about consequences and alternatives. Unlike imprecise forms of low-level corruption, for example, it cannot be claimed that presidential graft is good for society because it "softens the rigidities of the bureaucracy" for poor citizens, or represents socially desirable "speed money" for circumventing red tape. Even in their general form such arguments evade the likelihood that a bureaucracy which profits from rigidity and red tape will tend to reinforce these characteristics. If the president chooses to profit from rather than curtailing them, there can be little ambiguity about the cause of these social ills or the possibility of an alternative to them.

In fact in Latin America the office of the presidency generally concentrates so much power and responsibility in the person of a single leader that an accurate analysis of political corruption must personalize and must devote special attention to the chief executive. Indeed, in a significant number of extreme cases, the head of state has harnessed the whole apparatus of state power to the task of advancing his own personal enrichment until it seems as though the first aim of political activity in certain countries (especially around the Caribbean area) is to facilitate the systematic 'extraction of surplus' on his behalf. The massive implications such an abuse of office can have for the distribution of property, level of investment and overall economic policy of certain relatively small poor economies should be made apparent below. Such cases can provide an unusually clear demonstration of the ultimate supremacy of politics over economics that is possible in determining the allocation of resources when no internal checks and balances are left in operation. Fortunately Somoza's Nicaragua is not typical of Latin America as a whole, and there are other republics in which well established institutions and procedures regulate the interaction between political and economic elites. But even in the most advanced republics, institutional defenses against high-level corruption are characteristically weak, and hence Somoza-like practices intermittently arise in privileged enclaves of the state bureaucracy. Limited corruption can always occur despite presidential vigilance, of course, but on a large-scale systematic basis it normally must require at least his tacit acquiescence and, more likely, his personal supervision.[1]

Incidence of Presidential Graft

Not all presidential graft is hidden from the public. Some rulers have chosen to be quite brazen about what they were doing. For example, after President Trujillo, the "benefactor" of the Dominican Republic (1930–61), took over the country's only shoe factory, there was no secret about the ensuing decree forbidding anyone in the capital from going barefoot. Visiting American journalists reported with enthusiasm that the country was less poverty-stricken than they had expected—e.g. everyone wore shoes—but domestic opinion cannot have been deceived. Likewise President Zayas of Cuba (1921–25) made no secret of his attitude towards the national lottery: "his wife notoriously always drew the first prize and his daughter the second—both without shame" (Braden, *Diplomats and Demagogues*, p. 292). For every one such instance, of course, there are a dozen uncheckable rumors. Excluding such instances for lack of evidence, how many heads of state either paraded their corruption, like Zayas [who in 1925 signed a $2.7 million government contract with the statement that he had 300,000 good reasons for doing so (Thomas, *Cuba, The Pursuit of Freedom*, p. 572)] or were effectively exposed? Table 45.1[1] (referring to the twenty-one republics of the western hemisphere, including the USA) gives my provisional estimate.

A significant proportion of western hemisphere republics seem to be involved and this tentative estimate indicates no tendency for the number of countries involved to fall. Only Nicaragua appears in all three periods, however; Cuba and Venezuela, both of which appear in 1932 and 1952, are not included in 1972, and the reverse is true for the United States. Table 45.1 is, however, a very crude indicator of the incidence of presidential graft, for it puts Richard Nixon's $576,000 tax fraud on the same basis as Rafael Leonidas Trujillo's grandiose achievements, which his biographer values at $500 million.[2] An alternative indicator of the probable scale of president corruption is given in Table 45.2 which is drawn from evidence about the twenty Latin American republics in the decade before the Alliance for Progress. This time the United States is omitted, since its economy is so much larger and the scale of its political graft is so relatively small. It

Table 45.1
STRONG EVIDENCE OF PRESIDENTIAL GRAFT

1932	1952	1972
5	6	6

Table 45.2
REPORTED FORTUNES OF SOME PRESIDENTS OUSTED BETWEEN
1952 AND 1961

Ousted	Name	Country	Estimated fortune ($m.)	Comments	External public debt ($m.)
1952	Aleman	Mexico	500–800	Includes top cronies	509 (1950)
1955	Peron	Argentina	500–700	Least documented	442
1958	Perez Jimenez	Venezuela	over 250	add $100m. for his ordinance chief	227
1958	Batista	Cuba	100–300	Higher figure more likely	about 800
1961	Trujillo	Dominican Republic	500		6
Total			1,850–2,650		

Sources: Lieuwen, *Arms and Politics in Latin America,* pp. 149–50, for Aleman, Peron and Perez Jiminez, also allegations against Arbenz, Magloire and Rojas Pinilla, all "gleaned from a variety of newspaper reports" (Lieuwen probably also had access to confidential US government sources.) On Aleman's personal fortune, see below. Thomas, op. cit., p. 1027, quotes Batista's ex-press secretary as estimating his master's personal fortune in 1958 at $300 million (Batista was a sergeant when he first entered politics in 1933). See also Crassweller, *Trujillo,* p. 279. For corruption under Kubitshek see Gerassi, *The Great Fear in Latin America,* p. 385, according to whom the governor of one state (Governor Lupion of Parana) was accused of embezzling over $100 million. Sir George Bolton estimated that by 1963 the Latin American capital invested outside the continent exceeded $5,000 million in total (*Annual Review of BOLSA,* 1962–63, quoted by Thomas, p. 1184).

presents figures for the reported fortunes of five presidents ousted between 1952 and 1961. Even the most well grounded of these estimates (that concerning Trujillo) is subject to a large margin of error. In addition there is a more serious source of distortion in the cases of Aleman and Peron. In the first case the figures refer to the amounts allegedly "deposited in foreign banks" by Aleman "and the high officials of his administration" between 1946 and 1952 (*New York Times,* as reported in Lieuwen, *Arms and Politics in Latin America,* p. 150); and although Lieuwen's figure of $700 million for Peron supposedly refers to the amount he "escaped with" in 1955 (ibid., p. 149), if it is accurate it must surely include the funds appropriated by his subordinates over the preceding decade.[3] But if these two items tend to overstate the total value of strictly presidential graft in the period, Table 45.2 suffers from an offsetting distortion, which may well exert an equally powerful effect on the total, in the opposite direction. It makes no allowance for the personal fortunes of at least five other presidents who were ousted over the same period and who are sometimes alleged to have enriched themselves on a substantial scale in the process. Balancing up these considerations it is not unlikely that the presidential fortunes which "matured" in Latin America over the 1952–61 decade totalled somewhere around $2,000 million. If Trujillo, with over one-third of his money in foreign banks, was representative[4] then, on fairly cautious assumptions, capital flight attributable to presidential graft would have totalled around $700 million. This bears comparison with the $795 million received by Latin America as a whole over the same decade in the form of much publicized "official grants" to promote the economic development of the continent. It can also be compared with the size of the external public debt of the republic in question at the date of the ouster (see the last column in Table 45.2), which indicates the macro-economic significance of this degree of presidential graft.[5]

If we take a longer time horizon, can we identify any trend in the incidence of presidential graft? Certainly if we follow Samuel P. Huntington's analysis of the correlates of political corruption in general we should expect its incidence to fluctuate over time. He considers that: "Corruption may be more prevalent in some cultures than in others but in most cultures, it seems to be most prevalent during the most intense phase of modernization" (Heidenheimer, p. 492). In the context of twentieth-century Latin America it is not easy to give these categories such as modernization a clear empirical content. When were the basic values of, say, Mexican or Venezuelan society "traditional"? When did Brazil or Cuba undergo their "most intense phase of modernization"? The onus must rest with the modernization theorists to demonstrate the applicability of their categories. There is, however, sufficient information about purely presidential graft in twentieth-century Cuba, Mexico and Venezuela to demonstrate that it persisted on a large scale for at least half a century. Indeed it could be encountered in a variety of different contexts including the fast-rising prosperity of Cuba (up to 1925); the economic and social stagnation or retrogression of the same island from 1925 to 1958; the political and economic disaster that was Mexico for a generation after 1910; the essentially peasant society that was Venezuela under Gomez and the sophisticated urban society of Brazil in the 1950s.

Consider the record of presidential graft in *Cuba, 1909–58* extracted from *Cuba: The Pursuit of Freedom* by Hugh Thomas (which gives exhaustive further details).

President Gomez 1909–13: "known as the Shark . . . he ended his presidency a millionaire after having entered it quite poor" (p. 504).

President Menocal 1913–21: "was understood to have possessed $1 million in 1913 when he became president; when he left in 1921 he had perhaps $40 million" (p. 524).

President Zayas 1921–25: in 1923 "14 members of his family obtained advantageous or strategic positions. Not only the rest of the loan [a foreign loan of $50 million] but in addition the annual revenue of $81 million was used up before further employees could be paid, and bogus bridges were once again provided for in lavish maintenance grants, as in Menocal's day" (p. 555).

President Machado 1925–33: "the president and his friends absorbed a graft equivalent to a fifth of the national product [Thomas must mean national budget] or $10 million a year" (p. 581).

Fulgencio Batista, strongman 1933–40, president 1940–44: in 1953 Fidel Castro denounced Batista (newly returned to power) as "not content with the $40 million that crowned his first regime" (p. 489). Obviously such an estimate by Castro may be considered suspect, but deals of specific rakeoffs to Batista identified by Sprille Braden, US Ambassador to Cuba 1942–45, confirm its plausibility. One instance of a $2 million bribe, of which Batista received $400,000, is quoted in Braden's memoirs, Diplomats and Demagogues, p. 293.

President Grau 1944–48: in February 1949 the ex-president "was forced to appear before the courts, accused by the government of having misappropriated $174 million" (p. 761). However "on July 4th 1949 the court in which his case was being heard was broken into by six masked men who . . . stole 35 files of documents relating to the proceedings" (p. 764). Eventually in March 1951 "Grau was finally indicted with ten of his ex-ministers (two existing congressmen among them) for the theft of $40 million" (p. 768).

President Prio 1948–52: on 10 March 1953 President Batista publicly "accused Prio and his brother of stealing $20 million from the treasury: they replied from Mexico that it had been lent to them" (p. 801).

President Batista 1952–58: "it is of course obscure to what extent Batista enriched himself. His press secretary in exile and one who was for a time youth leader of his party estimated his fortune in 1958 as $300 million, mostly invested abroad in Switzerland, Florida, New York or Mexico (p. 1027, which also contains a footnote giving the more modest alternative of more than $100 million).[6] If intense "modernization" was going on in Cuba over this fifty-year period, it was surely proceeding in slow motion. But, it might be objected, Cuba was a notorious exception, distorted by the overpowering United States influence in the island since 1898. (The only other major country with a comparable history of such protracted United States predominance is the Philippines, where by many accounts even more lavish political graft has flourished for an even longer period.) How about the trend in *Venezuela* over the same half century?

President Gomez 1910–35: "it seemed as though the only beneficiaries of the Gomez system, besides the oil firms, were himself, his family, the military officers, and his Tachira friends in high government positions. Gomez ran the nation as the private preserve of his own family and the army. Through various kinds of graft, particularly peculation in dealing with oil concessions, and through confiscating the property of his opponents, he became the nation's largest landholder. His accumulated fortune in cattle, coffee plantations, industrial plant, and real estate was estimated at over $200 million" (Lieuwen, *Venezuela*, p. 49).

President Lopez Contreras 1935–41 and President Medina Angarita 1941–45: "each during his term of office made off with about $13 million, then following the 1945 revolution retired in New York" (Andreski, *Parasitism and Subversion: The Case of Latin America*, p. 76).

President Perez Jiminez 1952–85: "Perez Jiminez is estimated to have accumulated a fortune of over $250 million during his entire tenure of office, his ordinance chief Colonel Palido Barreto over $100 million (largely through transportation and parking meter concessions), while lesser officials made away with additional millions" (Lieuwen, op. cit., p. 98).

The evidence of these two countries and similar evidence of presidential graft in Mexico over the first half of the twentieth century, which I shall omit for reasons of space, might cast doubt on the precision with which any meaningful indicator of "intense modernization" can be expected to correlate with gross presidential graft in Latin America. However, the passage quoted by Huntington also hinted at an alternative explanation of the distribution of corruption, which might seem to fit the record better. "Corruption may be more prevalent in some cultures than in others," he wrote, and further on he expands this line of argument (drawing on the authority of Needler, *Political Development in Latin America*, Ch. 6) as follows:

> in the 'mulatto' countries (Panama, Cuba, Venezuela, Dominican Republic and Haiti) of Latin America 'there appears to be greater social equality and much less rigidity in the social structure' than in the Indian (Mexico, Ecuador, Guatemala, Peru, Bolivia) or *mestizo* (Chile, Colombia, El Salvador, Honduras, Nicaragua, Paraguay) countries. Correspondingly, however, the relative 'absence of an entrenched upper class means also the absence of a governing class ethic with its sense of

noblesse oblige' and hence 'there seems little doubt that it is countries in this socio-racial category in which political graft reaches its most flagrant heights'. [Heidenheimer, op. cit., p. 496.]

There are, in fact, no grounds whatsoever for the supposition that political graft has been less flagrant in "Indian" Mexico under Miguel Aleman (1946–52) or "Indian" Bolivia under General Rene Barrientos (1964–86), nor that these countries could be characterized by a governing class with a sense of *noblesse oblige*. It might be countered, however, that these two regimes both arose in countries where a social revolution had shattered the old ruling class and, in any case, perhaps the generalization is more well grounded in the case of the countries Needler has rather oddly classified as *mestizo*? General Anastasio Somoza (effective ruler of Nicaragua 1932–56) completed his education in Philadelphia in the twenties, while General Alfredo Stroessner of Paraguay (1954–present) still cherishes relatives in Hof, Bavaria. These two rulers are neither mulattos nor revolutionary upstarts and may indeed pride themselves in their sense of *noblesse oblige*. But for all that, the higher forms of political corruption are integral to their systems of government (which have sometimes been labelled 'sultanistic').

Consider Stroessner's regime: "Since the early sixties the contraband traffic has replaced the public sector as the major source of finance for the purchase of equipment by the Paraguayan armed forces," a journalist reported in *Latin America Newsletter*, 19 November 1971. This report continued:

> Arms for the armoured divisions, which were previously paid for by siphoning funds from the state alcohol monopoly (APAL), are now financed out of the profits from the traffic in contraband cigarettes, which is controlled by the chief of the *Caballarria*—General Andres Rodriguez. Traffic in scotch whisky has likewise replaced funds from the state water board (CORPOSANA) in the case of Stroessner's own crack *Regimiento Escolta*. And the traffic in heroin has replaced the customs department as the major financial support for the counter-insurgency Regimiento group—R114—whose chief, General Patricio Colman, is one of the organizers of the heroin smuggling.[7] General Rodriguez handles re-export by air with old DC-4's belonging to the government, and also his own private fleet of Cessnas. River borne contraband is handled by Rear-Admiral Hugo Gonzalez.

It is on this basis that President Stroessner has retained the backing of the Paraguayan military for his almost thirty years of personal dictatorship.

The evidence is clear that presidential graft in Latin America is widespread, has persisted over long periods of time and can often involve very large magnitudes in relation to the scale of overall economic activity. A more detailed review of the literature would demonstrate that its occurrence is not confined to the smallest republics, nor to the poorest republics, nor to dictatorships, nor to countries where the population has any particular racial or social characteristics, nor is it limited to the "intense phase of modernization," whatever that may be; nor to highly regulated economies. Perhaps these may seem rather obvious and negative findings, but they do contradict some common assertions and they serve to indicate that presidential graft is an important phenomenon in its own right, not to be subsumed under vague culturally defined notions of a diffuse propensity towards corruption.

This section has provided some concrete descriptions of important instances of corrupt behavior, which are necessary before one can realistically assess the consequences of political corruption, or the alternatives to it. These are the questions to be considered below.

Consequences and Alternatives

Most of the explicit discussion of the consequences of political corruption has been by American political scientists. Although there is, of course, no consensus, these writers have tended to adopt what might be termed a *realpolitik* stance on the issue, determined not to condemn the phenomenon out of hand, in a way which would once have been instinctive to all right-thinking liberals. A conscious effort is made to avoid such "moralism" and instead to draw up a balance sheet showing the social costs and benefits of political corruption. In some societies, at some stages in their history, it would seem political corruption is a lesser social evil than the alternatives.[8]

In this section I shall briefly assess two of the main types of social benefit, which, it is sometimes suggested,[9] could justify some forms of political corruption. In the light of my evidence limited to presidential graft in Latin America, this concluding section assesses one economic argument (that it may be good for efficiency, the rate of accumulation and therefore the rate of growth); and one political argument (that it provides a way of resolving political disputes and integrating disaffected groups, which substitute for violence and upheaval). Since no assessment of either of these supposed benefits can be made without also implying some opinion about the alternatives available, this section also considers one major alternative to gross presidential corruption that has been potentially available in Latin America.

It will be apparent that this alternative is one which successive US governments (and some prominent US wealth-holders with Latin American connections) have consistently considered even less desirable than political corruption. Their reasons, however, have been quite different from those proposed by the *realpolitik* school of American political scientists.

First let us consider the alleged economic benefits that some forms of political corruption may bestow. The "speed money" argument, as we saw earlier, only works (if at all) for low-level corruption; Latin American presidents generally have alternative methods of corruption at their disposal if they wish to rush specific measures through the bureaucratic machine. It is thus the "accumulation" argument on which the supposed economic benefits must depend, and to make this clear Nye distinguished between insecure corrupt rulers (who will tend to send their money to Swiss banks) and secure corrupt rulers (who may reinvest the surplus they have illegally extracted from consumers, in which case presidential graft might accelerate the rate of economic growth).[10] Nye writes:

> Too great insecurity means that any capital formed by corruption will tend to be exported rather than invested at home. In Nicaragua, for instance, it is argued that the sense of security of the Somoza family encouraged them in internal investments in economic projects and the strengthening of their political party, which led to impressive economic growth and diminished direct reliance on the army. [Heidenheimer, op. cit., p. 574.]

So let us examine the example of Nicaragua. General Anastasio Somoza (senior) became head of the National Guard in 1932, while US Marines still occupied the country.[11] According to the *Financial Times*, 12 May 1972, after forty years of family rule, the current Somoza's business interests, variously estimated to be worth between $150 and $200 million, stretch into the national airlines, LANICA, the country's only shipping line, MAMENIC, cattle and meat packing, fishing, rum and beer, hotels, banking, cement, radio, television and newspapers. And the president is also the local agent for Mercedes Benz. (Nicaragua's GNP was $800 million, to be divided among a population of two million.) Then on 23 December 1972 an earthquake caused damage estimated by the same newspaper (10 May 1973) at $845 million, and left 250,000 homeless. The *Latin American Newsletter* reported on 9

February 1973 that "because of the now desperate shortage of foreign exchange, there will for some time be few imports of expensive cars, liquor, cigarettes and luxury goods, whose passage round the customs posts was so beneficial to national guard officers. Another lucrative prize, especially for officers just before retirement, has been control of brothels, bars and gambling houses; but of course in Managua these are now mostly rubble, and provincial cities are heavily engaged in looking after refugees."

When offers of help and emergency supplies poured in,

> From the very first, General Somoza demanded that all food and medical supplies should be made over to his government for distribution through the canton or neighbourhood system, which is virtually identified with his Nationalist Liberal party ... A senior member of the Spanish embassy saw his relief supplies pilfered by the authorities at Managua airport and was insulted when he protested (etc.) ... Last week in Managua a reliable foreign eyewitness recounted to me how at Christmas he had seen senior officials, charged with the suppression of looting, dividing among themselves goods looted from the damaged stores in the disaster zone ... General Somoza, as he told me himself last Friday, has no worries at all about getting all the money he needs from the United States. The US embassy, fearful of any change in the government ... is likely to spend $100 million a year for the next two years on aid to the government ... [Yet] as one relief worker in Managua remarked, the Somoza family, which with 22,000 employees is a larger employer than the state, could afford to pay all the damage itself, and still not be poor. [*Financial Times*, 10 May 1973.]

Thus the Nicaraguan example appears to confirm that, given sufficient political security, it is possible in a small country to found a dynasty based on presidential graft and so reinvest the surplus thereby extracted that the economy as a whole can eventually be converted into a personally owned fiefdom. Whether or not this produces a socially optimal level and pattern of investments is more debatable, since even from a narrowly economic point of view this degree of monopoly power can be expected to distort all the supposedly normal market mechanisms. If the definition of social welfare is broadened to include such variables as the distribution of income and wealth, the case becomes still weaker; and "moralistic" though it may seem, many observers might hesitate to classify economic growth policies that require the systematic subjugation and even degradation of an entire population group in the interests of an all-powerful dynasty as socially desirable.

The other supposedly beneficial consequence of political corruption concerns its possible contribution to the non-violent resolution of social conflicts. In what follows, two strands of this argument are identified and two relevant case studies considered. Firstly, if a country seems threatened by violent conflicts, can its people opt for an appropriate amount of presidential graft, just sufficient to stifle the violence and no more? The Dominican Republic example is considered. Secondly, where extensive presidential graft has become established, can it be relied upon to substitute for violent conflict, or may it in fact generate further violence? Batista's Cuba provides a suitable case study. This example brings us naturally enough to the question of whether there is a connection between political corruption and social revolution, and if so, of what kind.

Two opposing hypotheses have been proposed concerning the connection between corruption and political instability: *The Economist* has suggested that the average costs of corruption may diminish over the life of a regime as it becomes more secure, whereas a Singapore minister of foreign affairs has restated the old maxim that "l'appétit vient en mangeant,' *The Economist* of 15 June 1957 quoted a comment about one South American dictator as follows: "it is cheaper for the country that he should be president for life, because he has made his fortune and is satisfied. When we changed presidents every few years the cost of presidential fortunes used to ruin us" (in Heidenheimer, op. cit., p. 491). The foreign minister of Singapore put the opposite view:

> it is, I think, in the very nature of kleptocracy to progressively increase the size of its loot. For one thing, the kleptocrat can stay in power only by bringing more and more supporters to his side, and this means that the size of his loot must increase. As the years go by he must win over all the instruments of state power—the army, the police, the entrepreneurs, and the bureaucracy. If he must loot then he must allow his subordinates from the permanent secretary to the office boy to join in the game. [Ibid., p. 548.]

Generalissimo Rafael Leonidas Trujillo holds the record as the longest-lasting life president in twentieth-century Latin America. This self-styled "benefactor" ruled the Dominican Republic for thirty-one years, so his case provides a suitable test of these rival contentions. His biographer tells us that as early in his career as 1939 "estimates of family income ran to more than $2,000,000 annually. A more heady estimate, from a bank source in this same year, put Trujillo's personal income as high as $200,000 a month." But it seems his acquisitiveness was never dimmed by satiation, and indeed by the 1950s he had proceeded to take over much of the republic's sugar industry, where he reportedly "made every technical mistake in the operation of this industry that it was possible to make, and on a cash-flow basis the entire operation lost money" (Crassweller, p. 259). Even at this stage he was still keenly interested in adding to his assets, as Harry Kantor's account makes clear:

> On practically every transaction by the government Trujillo got a 10 percent cut. This was brought into the open in 1957 when a committee of the US senate was investigating a corporation that deducted a $1.8 million bribe to Trujillo as a legitimate expense from its taxable income. The US Internal Revenue commissioner, justifying the allowance of the deduction, states 'Bribes are an ordinary and necessary business expense to do work in the Dominican Republic' [Kantor, *Patterns of Politics and Political Systems in Latin America*, p. 320].[12]

Thus the Dominican Republic example runs counter to the hypothesis suggested by *The Economist*. On the contrary it would seem that, given long enough, an unrestrained system of presidential graft can expand far beyond the limits that could possibly be justified by terms of the supposed need for corruption in order to "resolve conflicts" without upheaval.

This brings us to a final aspect of the argument that corruption can be socially desirable—namely, the claim that in some circumstances and in suitable amounts it can be an alternative to large-scale violence, rather than an extra source of social upheaval. However, in the words of the Singapore foreign minister quoted above, the successful kleptocrat will always need to protect his position. Furthermore, most of the benefits of such high-level graft accrue to a rather small number of highly visible public functionaries, while almost invariably the costs are borne by a far larger number of people who would therefore be very likely to turn against the rulers if they had the information and the opportunity. Hence large-scale kleptocrats, like those named above, are obliged to use extensive violence in order to deny their subjects such information and such opportunities. To demonstrate that presidential graft is a substitute for violence, it is not sufficient to show that in the short run it averts political upheaval. For thirty-one years there was no political upheaval in the Dominican Republic, yet in a single notorious episode of Trujillo's rule (October 1937) he ordered a massacre in which, according to his biographer, a "reasonable estimate" of the deaths would be 15–20,000 (Crassweller, p. 156). Far fewer died in the "political upheaval" of 1961 which followed the dictator's assassination and even the tragic "civil war" of 1965 (itself in many ways a delayed reaction to the legacy of Trujillo's corruption) was less bloody than that year of kleptocratic "political stability," 1937. Nor is it sufficient to claim that the country would have been just as violent under an incorruptible president: the claim that presidential graft is socially desirable requires that in its absence there would have been even more violent conflict and/or that the violence would be more futile. Considering the amount of violence usually associated with presidential graft, this would be a difficult claim to establish at all convincingly.

Pre-revolutionary Cuba provides an appropriate conclusion to this discussion both of political violence and of presidential graft. This extreme case demonstrates that at least in some circumstances these two social evils can get entirely out of hand, and feed on each other. Taken in conjunction with the recent experience of Nicaragua, the Cuban example strongly suggests that such "sultanistic" regimes may have extreme difficulty in curbing their excesses or in preserving a minimum basis of social support. Consequently they may be highly vulnerable to challenges from revolutionary partisans, and if they collapse the resulting scope for drastic social changes may be unusually large.

Despite Nye's general scepticism on the subject,[13] the Cuban example in fact suggests that large-scale corruption may well be a major factor contributing to the outbreak of social revolution. Here is the interpretation given by James O'Connor:

> Under Batista's last government, the corruption system was extended and more elaborate, and elevated to an everyday system of business. A confidential business report service described the system: 'The "collector" is an important man on the island. Everybody doing business, from the cabbie to a hole-in-the-wall shop must pay to the regime's and the machine's ambulatory cash register. Veritable scales have been set for anything from street vendors to big businessmen ... [graft] probably has never risen to such heights (or dropped to such depths), nor has it ever been so efficient, as under Batista ... In the years preceding the revolution, the average amount of graft in public works (alone) cost as much as the works themselves. About three-fifths of the budget of the public health ministry was stolen, and about one-third of the education ministry budget ... it was common for teachers and school inspectors to sell their positions for one half or less of their salaries. Successive regimes failed to clean up the education racket, graft in the ministries ... and the systematic corruption in the armed forces. These interests, particularly the latter, had to be respected in order to maintain the consensus. Thus ... segments of all classes profited by the system, yet at the same time the system thwarted the aspirations and plans of all classes' [quoted in Bonachea and Valdés (eds), *Cuba in Revolution*, pp. 71–3].

O'Connor therefore argues that "Cuba's system of corruption and bribery was at once one way in which Batista maintained a consensus of support, and one source of his downfall; its inequities, irrationalities, and hardships helped to win for Castro's 26th of July movement allies in all layers of society" (ibid., p.70). Confirmation of this judgement can be found in the work of Mesa-Lago, who argues that the anti-corruption theme in Castro's campaign caused many rival property owners to welcome his triumph, and that in early 1959 even urban capitalists willingly paid back taxes on a massive scale in the hope that under an honest regime there could be a return to economic expansion. Even among such wealthy groups, he claims, the confiscation of property from Batista's henchmen was not disliked (*Revolutionary Change in Cuba*, pp. 357–58 and 364–66).

In short, at least in Cuba gross corruption engendered additional violence and political alienation, and indeed paved the way for a sweeping and puritanical social revolution. To say this is not to romanticize the Cuban revolution (which has uprooted at least half a million Cubans), but merely to state that it offers an alternative to the types of political corruption discussed above. Obviously the alternative is more attractive to some groups and interests than to others, but since those who attempt a cost-benefit analysis of political corruption are bound to make counter-factual assumptions, they would do better to consider at least one of the alternatives to political corruption that has in fact now been adopted in two Latin America republics formerly plagued by presidential graft (Cuba and Nicaragua). Naming these two instances may indicate why Washington policymakers so often regard political corruption a "lesser of evils." It also suggests what the *realpolitik* school of political scientists were really about (perhaps unwittingly) when they stamped an imprimatur of academic respectability on the notion of "socially beneficial forms of corruption."

Notes

1. In the largest republics, state governors may exercise a substantial degree of autonomy, at least on routine matters, and the central executive may decide to tolerate a corrupt state governor because the political costs of overturning him may seem too high. Various states within the Brazilian and Mexican federal structure are larger and potentially more lucrative to govern than many Caribbean republics.

    Consider a couple of Mexican examples from the notoriously vice-ridden states which border on the United States and attract huge influxes of 'tourism'. President Aleman (1946–52) sponsored Governor Montones of Chihuahua (1950–55), who was finally forced out by a vast protest movement. "Many people asserted that the governor controlled prostitution in Ciudad Juarez and that the money collected from medical inspections and licensing of prostitutes was being siphoned into his personal accounts rather than into the public treasury," D'Antonio and Form, *Influentials in Two Border Cities: A Study in Community Decision-Making* [sic], p. 164.

President Ruiz Cortines (1952–58) appointed Governor Maldonado Sandez of Baja California (1953–58). He too was forced out after scandal concerning prostitution in Tijuana "where more than 8,000 whores were exploited for the profit of the governor and his friends, and which helped to pay for a front organisation called the Committee for Destitute Children that was headed by the governor's own wife" ('Por Que?' quoted in Johnson, *Mexican Democracy: A Critical View*, pp. 134–35).

In the last few years the state oil monopoly, PEMEX, has acquired a reputation for corruption that could only occur with presidential acquiescence.

2. On 8 November 1974 a Mr. Edward Morgan pleaded guilty before the US special prosecutor of "wilfully and knowingly" preparing affidavits for Nixon, which officially donated his vice-presidential papers to the US National Archives. "The law that would have enabled the former president to claim tax deduction for his gifts was abolished in July 1969: Mr. Morgan, it transpired today, made up, and had the president sign, affidavits a year later, but then had them backdated so as to appear they were filed before the expiry of the law." The effect of this was to swindle the Internal Revenue Service of $576,000. One journalist has asserted that "since Mr. Morgan acted solely on Mr. Nixon's behalf, it is almost inconceivable that the former president could have failed to know about the backdating" (*Guardian*, 9 November 1974). According to Crassweller (*Trujillo: Life and Times of a Caribbean Dictator*, p. 279), by the 1950s the income of the Trujillo family ... "as estimated by a competent source, was approximately equal to the combined national expenditure for education, public health, labour, social security and public works. The factories owned by him in one way or another now employed about 60,000 workers. The value of his sugar interests could be estimated at $150 million. Another $100 to $200 million had been invested or secreted abroad, mostly in New York ... If one were to venture a rough guess as to the total value of Trujillo's holdings in the Dominican Republic and abroad, $500 million would be as plausible a figure as any."

3. The low ($500 million) estimate for Peron's "loot" comes from *Time*, 3 June 1957 (quoting 'an authoritative source'). The information about Peron is much more open to doubt than the rest.

4. Aleman seems to have ploughed back most of his wealth into Mexico, but few ex-presidents feel that secure from retaliation. Unlike Trujillo, all the other ousted presidents had sufficient advance notice to make their dispositions.

5. In the light of these comparisons it is rather puzzling to read Andreski's assertion that "Like their American counterparts, the upstart Latin American politicians usually try to make fortunes rapidly, but they cannot squeeze very much out of the powerful hereditary rich. As the latter, moreover, in their capacity of landlords and financiers appropriate the greater part of what can be squeezed out of ordinary people ... the

proportion of wealth which remains available for embezzlement ... must be smaller in Latin America than in tropical Africa," (Quoted in Heidenheimer, op. cit. p. 356.)

If Andreski were right, the wealth of tropical African rulers would be very great. But the figures given by First, *The Barrel of a Gun*, pp. 101–4, are not large by Latin American standards. For example, Sir Albert Margai of Sierra Leone was apparently asked to repay £771,037 after his fall from power and ex-President Maurice Yameogo of Upper Volta was charged with embezzling £1,212,000. These are small, poor countries of course. But are the magnitudes involved in Nigeria, Zaire or Kenya really sufficient to uphold Andreski's argument?

6. Totting up the total of these eight rulers it seems not unlikely that this cumulative personal theft from the Cuban state over forty years reached $400 million, which would make an average of $10 million a year. Very crudely this would approximate to $2 per capita of the Cuban population each year, in a country where the average income per head over most of the period was around $500 (with many living at only a fraction of that level).

7. In a later number the same newsletter added (25 August 1972) the following obituary of Colman which indicates the personal wealth of this particular general: "Stroessner originally granted Colman his smuggling franchise (restricted to cigarettes and whisky in those days) in 1960 after the general had led a successful campaign of repression against FULNA guerrillas ... He later expanded his activities to channel heroin through from Europe to its destination in North America ... His personal rule extended over vast tracts of Paraguay and he operated private airstrips for smuggling on his private cattle ranches in strategic spots such as Pilar and Santa Helena ..."

8. In principle this hypothesis must imply that even in the United States and even in the present and in the future the same might be true, but curiously this is not an aspect of their position that such writers have been inclined to stress, at least up to now.

9. Writing in the *American Political Science Review* in 1967, J.S. Nye provided a clear example of the cost-benefit approach and concluded that "it is probable that the costs of corruption in less developed countries will exceed its benefits except for top level corruption involving modern inducements and marginal deviations and except for situations where corruption provides the only solution to an important obstacle to development" (quoted in Heidenheimer, op. cit. p. 578).

10. One example of a country in which this principle has been consciously applied is Mexico. After the excesses of the Aleman period mentioned above, President Ruiz Cortines inherited the task of rehabilitating the economy (including devaluing the peso) while preserving political stability. According to Frank Brandenberg he "informed *alemanistas* who had pilfered the public treasury that exchanging any more of their 'investments' into dollars for purposes of taking capital out of Mexico would prove extremely unwise; this capital was to remain in Mexico and to contribute to economic developments." (*The Making of Modern Mexico*, p. 111.)

11. "The English he had learned ... in Philadelphia enabled him to become one

of the interpreters between the Nicaraguan officials and the military and civilian officials of the US occupying forces. ... [The Marines withdrew in 1933 and in June 1934 a US arms salesman wrote to Mr. Monaghan, export manager of the Remington Arms Co. He] suggested that Monaghan communicate with Mr. Nichols of Colt's and tell him to write to General Somoza offering to sell direct to him. "I would suggest that in this quotation he should include a 10 percent commission for General Somoza." Remington was naturally anxious to have Colt's supply the guns, for which they could then supply the ammunition. The guns had to come first. It takes only a few deals like this before one has enough money to start buying up plantations, airlines etc., which in their turn pour more money into the bank. Somoza's income was estimated at $1 million a year and his assets at about $100 million ... Somoza put every relative he had on the public payroll; soon after his grandson was born, the baby was made a captain in the army with full pay and privileges." (Kantor, *Patterns of Politics and Political Systems in Latin America*, p. 167.)

12. As a result, after Trujillo's assassination in 1961, "official sources revealed that Trujillo's share of the national wealth had amounted to the following: bank deposits 22 percent; money in circulation 25 percent; sugar production 63 percent; cement 63 percent; paper 73 percent; paint 86 percent; cigarettes 71 percent; milk 89 percent; wheat and flour 68 percent; plus the nation's only airline, its leading newspapers, and the three principal radio and television stations. According to the Swiss daily (Basle) *National Zeitung,* the Trujillo family had deposited no less than $200 million in Swiss banks ... [Also] the dictator owned 10 percent of the productive land and 10 percent of the cattle industry; 45 percent of the nation's active manpower was employed directly in Trujillo enterprises; a further 35 percent was engaged in the armed forces and the government-operated banking, hotel and electricity systems" ('Hispanic American Report' quoted in Horowitz *et al.* (eds), *Latin American Radicalism*, p. 254).

13. Nye wrote that "it is not clear that corruption of the old regime is a primary cause of social revolution. Such revolutions are comparatively rare and often depend heavily on catalytic events (such as external wars)" (Heidenheimer, op. cit., p. 571).

References

Andreski, Stanislav. *Parasitism and Subversion: The Case of Latin America.* London: Weidenfeld and Nicolson, 1966.

Bolton, Sir George. *Annual Review of BOLSA.* London: Bank of London and South America, 1962–63.

Bonachea, Rolando E. and Valdes, Nelson T. (eds.). *Cuba in Revolution.* New York: Doubleday, 1972.

Braden, Spruille. *Diplomats and Demagogues.* New York: Arlington House, 1971.

Brandenburg, Frank. *The Making of Modern Mexico.* Englewood Cliffs, N.J.: Prentice-Hall, 1964.

Crassweller, Robert D. *Trujillo: Life and Times of a Caribbean Dictator.* New York: Macmillan, 1966.

D'Antonio, William V. and Form, William H. *Influentials in Two Border Cities:*

A Study in Community Decision-Making. Notre Dame: Indiana University Press, 1965.

First, Ruth. *The Barrel of a Gun.* Harmondsworth, Middx.: Penguin, 1970.

Gerassi, John. *The Great Fear in Latin America.* New York: Macmillan, 1963.

Heidenheimer, Arnold J. *Political Corruption: Readings in Comparative Analysis.* New York: Holt, Rinehart and Winston, 1970.

Horowitz, Irving Lewis *et al.* (eds). *Latin American Radicalism.* London: Cape, 1969.

Johnson, Kenneth F. *Mexican Democracy: A Critical View.* New York: Praeger, revised edn., 1978.

Kantor, Harry. *Patterns and Politics of Political Systems in Latin America.* Chicago: Rand-McNally, 1969.

Lieuwen, Edwin. *Arms and Politics in Latin America.* New York: Praeger, 1961.

——. *Venezuela.* Oxford: Oxford University Press, 1961.

Mesa-Lago, Carmelo. *Revolutionary Change in Cuba.* Pittsburgh, Penn.: University of Pittsburgh Press, 1971.

Needler, Martin C. *Political Development in Latin America.* New York: Random House, 1968.

Nye, J. S. *American Political Science Review.* 61 (1967) 417–27.

Thomas, Hugh. *Cuba: The Pursuit of Freedom.* London: Eyre and Spottiswoode, 1971.

Corruption Control Strategies: An Introduction

The history of governmental attempts to control corruption is a long and not particularly auspicious one. More frequently than not, the anti-corruption agencies and groups set up to investigate and combat corruption within the public services have themselves proved corruptible. Nevertheless the search for means and devices for identifying, controlling, or at least discouraging corruption, continues. Since the universe of corrupters is hard to identify and characterize, the focus has been more on potential corruptees—particularly among the bureaucracy. Theorists have analyzed different models of administrative structure to discern which ones might lessen susceptibility to high-level or low-level corruption. Attention has also been focused on some national or local governments which have had favorable longer-term records of sustaining their anti-corruption activities. These chapters present several theoretical and empirical analyses with directly remedial intent. But they also include a more "revisionist" chapter, which critically assesses the aura of incorruptibility attached to one national bureaucracy, and suggests that by some definitions corruption has been more prevalent than previous analysts have acknowledged.

Susan Rose-Ackerman begins this section by examining how bureaucratic structures, and an official's place in that structure, determine both the individual's cost of accepting a bribe as well as his discretionary power. Her attempt to analyze how various structures can affect the occurrence of corruption builds on analyses of fragmented, sequential, hierarchical and disorganized models of bureaucracy. She identifies reciprocal relations between structure and opportunities for corruption, and suggests how policy makers might choose among the various models. She considers the occurrence of tradeoffs among institutional designs and emphasizes that cost considerations should embrace all stages of the bureaucratic process.

John A. Gardiner and Theodore R. Lyman examine patterns of influence, decision-making, and corruption in the area of land-use policy. Land-use decisions are among the most important that American local communities can make, and the stakes are among the highest.

Even when more than one level of government takes part, lines of conflict and conceptions of appropriate conduct can be rooted in peculiarly local political accommodations and realities. Corruption control in such a context is an extremely touchy task; in many instances public officials must consider not only the issue of misconduct and what to do about it, but also the ways reforms could undermine their agencies' budgets and autonomy. Moreover, many important decisions and processes take place out of the public eye, and necessarily involve a significant range of discretion. Thus, a strong note of realism must be part of any workable strategy for corruption control.

Next, John S. Quah, who lives and teaches in Singapore, examines the reasons for his state's successful campaign against bureaucratic corruption. He argues that the combination of a personally incorruptible and zealously honest leadership, a geopolitically manageable polity, legal and institutional tools to reduce both the opportunities and incentives for corruption, plus an effective and honest enforcement mechanism, have permitted the government of Prime Minister Lee Kuan Yew to make Singapore an exemplar of clean government in Asia.

In the final chapter, Ulrich von Alemann undertakes a reexamination of Germany's reputation for having been relatively free of corruption. He finds that the lack of a developed concept of corruption and other blinders led historians to underinterpret the evidence. Using a deliberately more broadly cast definition, he alleges that the Bismarckian Reich knew more high-level corruption than was acknowledged by those who saw it through Weberian spectacles. More recently, the wide credibility given corruption charges against ministers and even the chancellor of the Federal Republic seemed to belie West Germany's reputation for having achieved techniques of coping with a wide range of political problems. Alemann takes strong issue with the author who discussed German corruption in the previous edition of this volume. While granting that low-level corruption has been infrequent, he suggests that various factors impeded recognition of high-level corruption among both bureaucrats and politicians.

46

Which Bureaucracies Are Less Corruptible?

Susan Rose-Ackerman

Bureaucrats [do] not [necessarily] operate within a complex organizational environment. They may either be at the bottom of the agency, dealing directly with contractors and clients and constrained by criminal laws and the guidelines of superior officials, or they may be agency heads with no problems of internal organization and with monopoly power vis à vis the outside world. To enrich our view of the incentives for corrupt bureaucratic behavior, however, I need to move beyond these models to ask how the structure of the bureaucracy and an official's place in it will determine both his or her discretionary power and the expected costs of accepting a bribe.

While this chapter concentrates upon organizational reform, agencies can often use other techniques to control corruption. Thus an agency may increase the use of outside and inside auditors and inspectors, or appeal for the help of law enforcement agencies. The increased risk of detection which these methods entail may be coupled with stiffer disciplinary actions against those caught taking bribes. Furthermore, it may be possible to redefine bureaucratic tasks so that corrupt incentives are reduced simply by removing discretion or increasing the publicity of agents' actions. Finally, the bureau may seek individuals who have high standards of personal honesty or who subscribe to codes of professional conduct. If such individuals are unavailable, the government department might seek to create them through an educational and indoctrination program. Superiors may try to instill norms of honesty and attempt to control corruption through peer pressure.[1] Changing norms is likely to be difficult, however, and

Source: Susan Rose-Ackerman, *Corruption: A Study in Political Economy*. New York: Academic Press, 1978, chapter nine. By permission of author and publisher. Copyright © 1978 by Wellesley College.

peer pressure can promote as well as retard corruption. Discussions of police corruption, for example, show that a willingness to take bribes may be a way to earn the friendship of fellow officers (Broadus, 1976; Rubinstein, 1973; Sherman, 1974b). Clearly, in any actual reorganization proposal, the personal scruples of employees and the relative merits of the other strategies would have to be weighed in an evaluation of the organizational possibilities presented here. This chapter, however, neglects these tradeoffs and considers instead how alternative bureaucratic structures will themselves affect the incidence of corruption.

In attempting this task, it would be desirable, of course, to draw upon a well-developed theory of bureaucracy, modifying standard models to capture the peculiarities of my subject. Unfortunately, however, a powerful positive theory of bureaucracy simply does not exist.[2] As a consequence, I have had to develop my own models of bureaucratic organization as part of the analytic effort. Instead of constructing an exhaustive theory for all bureaucratic structures, however, I examine four organizational forms which describe many situations in which corruption has been observed. For simplicity, I shall label these forms: the *fragmented,* the *sequential,* the *hierarchical,* and finally, the *disorganized.* In order to concentrate upon organizational features, I stylize the interaction between government agencies and the private sector. Since the incidence of corrupt transactions is my main concern, each official is envisaged as approving or rejecting an application for a "license" or "exemption"—and not as negotiating over the terms of the agreement.

Turning to the four formal constructs, the fragmented and the sequential models lack the hierarchical process of delegation and review that is often assumed to be a necessary prerequisite for bureaucracy to exist at all. In a search for positive models of government, however, these cases must be considered because many actual procedures seem closer to these models than to a hierarchical one. The *fragmented* case is the simplest to describe. An applicant must have each of several parts of an application approved; but each approval procedure is independent of the others, and the applicant can have the portions approved in any order. Each bureaucrat has particular powers, unreviewable except by law enforcement agencies,[3] and each decision-making node may be organized differently.

The *sequential* model is identical to the *fragmented* except that applicants must have the portions of their petition approved in a particular order. No bureaucrat in the sequence, however, ever reviews the choices made by officials who have already acted. These two models, then, best describe procedures in which each functionary behaves like an independent, specialized expert.

The *hierarchical* model is a traditional bureaucracy where the behavior of low-level officials can be reviewed by higher level ones. Authority over some portions of the approval and implementation process is delegated to bureaucrats at different hierarchical levels, but any low-level decisions can, in principle, be overruled by a higher official. The scarce time and imperfect information available to top bureaucrats, however, limits their ability to review subordinates' actions.

While distinguishing these three models facilitates analysis, it is nevertheless true that many actual application approval procedures combine several types. Thus businessmen operating in a regulated industry must often obtain approval from several independent government agencies, each of which is organized hierarchically. In other circumstances, however, it is impossible to characterize the organizational structure of the government. Consequently, the chapter concludes by considering a *disorganized* model, where the official chain of command is unclear and constantly shifting and the decision-making criteria are similarly arbitrary and unknown.

In explaining and comparing these bureaucratic models, I shall locate the opportunities for corruption in each and consider the extent to which reforms in bureaucratic organization have potential as anti-corruption devices. The discussion of fragmented and sequential models locates the corrupt incentives in models without centralized direction, and the hierarchical model considers whether hierarchical forms have greater potential for controlling corruption. . . . The contrast between hierarchical and nonhierarchical forms using some simple formal models to compare the corrupt incentives under alternative systems [is discussed next]. Finally, the section about disorganized bureaucracies examines a question that has concerned students of corruption in other disciplines—what is the role of disorganization and uncertainty in fostering or deterring bribery?

The Fragmented and Sequential Models

High-level review is missing from many government procedures. Different bureaucrats are tied together simply by the requirement that each gives approval to a particular part of an application before the entire proposal is permitted to proceed. For example, a developer seeking to build a structure in an urban region must obtain approval from the zoning board,[4] the building code administrator, and the fire marshal, to name only the most obvious.[5] Any portion of the approval process may be either competitive or monopolistic, i.e., several officials may be able to grant approval, or a single bureaucrat may be in charge of some portion of the application procedure. When bureaucratic tasks have been fragmented in this way, even obtaining honest bureaucratic approval may be a costly and time consuming activity for clients, requiring them to "walk their applications through" in order to avoid delay and caprice.

. . . The presence of competitive officials at some point in a *fragmented* process may sometimes deter corruption at that stage, [and] granting officials monopoly power over other aspects of the application may permit them to extort bribes.[6] Thus the applicant may face a situation similar to that of a developer seeking to assemble a large parcel of land. Some officials may wait until others have acted and then try to extort a large portion of the client's surplus. In situations where a holdout can make large corrupt gains, moreover, each official may try to be the last one to give approval. As a consequence, fragmented bureaucracies may suffer from long delays, generating pressure on bureaucrats to cartelize to present a united front to applicants.

This result obtains, of course, only in the fragmented case—where the order in which bureaucratic tasks must be performed is not specified by law. Quite often, however, the *sequential* model applies, and applicants must approach bureaucrats in an ordered sequence. If applicants must follow a predetermined path, with no competition between officials at any particular level, then only one corrupt official in each path is needed to produce a situation in which a high proportion of the program's benefits to the applicant can be appropriated by bureaucrats. If several in the sequence are willing to take bribes, the corrupt official who must be approached first has an inherent advantage. Corrupt officials who follow, however, might attempt to obtain bribery receipts by threatening to turn down anyone unable to bribe them.[7]

In other situations, applicants may be able to choose to approach any one of several different officials at a particular stage in the ordered sequence. The choice of a particular official may, however, also determine the future list of officials the applicant must approach, with the sequence of subsequent contacts differing from official to official. Each competitive official is, then, associated with a different, uniquely specified chain of other officials who must also grant approval. The choice of an initial bureaucratic contact thus can lead to a series of subsequent bilateral monopoly situations.[8] Given this structure, competition between corrupt officials may not do much to reduce the level of bribery receipts, since, . . . these bureaucrats are selling a differentiated product. Thus if the competitive stage is fully corrupt, applicants who are *legally* qualified will pay more to be served by officials with honest bureaucrats behind them than to be served by those where the officials next in sequence will also demand payment. This result stands in sharp contrast to the case where applicants want *illegal* services at each step in the organizational sequence. Those who want illegal benefits at each official decisionmaking node will pay more to a competitive official if subsequent contacts are also corrupt since the likelihood of a successful final outcome is greater. Cleaning up corruption at the final stages of the application approval process will therefore only deter corruption at earlier stages if bribes are paid to obtain illegal government benefits.

A bureaucratic situation where low-level officials assign applicants to one or another higher level bureaucrat is closely related to the sequential case—so long as higher level officials have no authority to review low-level choices. For example, clerks may be able to assign building plans to particular examiners or cases to particular judges. If honest officials are also competent, then applicants who want an honest evaluation from higher level officials may bribe clerks for favorable assignments. Similarly, those with poor claims will pay to be assigned to dishonest officials.[9] If, however, speed is the service being purchased, even those who have done nothing illegal may pay clerks to assign them to officials willing to provide expedited service in return for bribes.[10] This variant of the sequential model thus has two distinctive features. First, the low-level clerks' assignment responsibilities gives them the power to extract bribes from all applicants, whatever the legal status of their claims. Second, the elimination of corruption at the later stages *does* eliminate it in the earlier stages as well if the honest high-level bureaucrats are all equally competent. If some are honest but lazy, however, clerks may still be bribed to send applications to those high-level officials who work quickly.

Therefore, in assessing the normative significance of these positive models, neither the fragmented nor the sequential model of bureaucratic organization appears to be a very promising organizational means of deterring corruption. On the one hand, if applicants can approach officials in any order, corrupt holdouts can cause delays in their attempts to appropriate the program's surplus. On the other hand, competition at some stage in a sequential process may not deter corruption, even in that stage, if each official is linked to a chain of others with monopoly power. Thus, while a distribution of authority to a series of expert agencies may be justified by other objectives, it does not generally seem to have independent benefit in terms of the speed or honesty of the procedures. Furthermore, if those first in the sequence can assign applicants to particular officials at the next stage in the sequence, then corruption of the later stage creates corrupt incentives at the earlier stage. As we shall see, however, more centralized systems of bureaucratic control create different possibilities for abuse. The task for reform, then, is not to search for a universal remedy but to prescribe an organizational form that seems least subject to abuse, given the facts of particular cases.

The Hierarchical Model

Corruption and the Right to Appeal

The critical difference between a hierarchical bureaucracy and the first two models is the existence of internal review procedures distinct from the outside investigative and prosecutorial powers of the criminal law. Low-level officials are nominally delegated the power to approve applications but may be subject to high-level review. While agency heads have ultimate authority, they may choose not to exercise it.[11] Honest high-level officials can use their power to ferret out corruption. Dishonest ones can use it to buy off subordinates.

Corrupt incentives in a hierarchical bureaucracy depend upon the procedures under which low-level decisions are reviewed by superiors. If applicants have the right to appeal an unfavorable decision, those who are *legally* entitled to benefits will pay little or nothing to low-level officials with *honest* superiors, unless appeal is costly or superiors are lazy and unpredictable. This result contrasts with the sequential case where an applicant seeking a legal benefit would pay *more* to a corrupt official if subsequent officials were honest than if they were dishonest. The market power of low-level officials is enhanced, however, if applicants have no right to appeal or if the probability of appeal can be affected by the actions of low-level bureaucrats.

If superior officials are *dishonest,* however, then legally qualified applicants may be willing to pay high bribes to inferior bureaucrats. Subordinate officials can use the greater greed of their superiors as an argument for paying off at a low level. Naturally, this threat of subsequent higher payments will succeed only if the bribe buys both approval and a lowered probability of appeal. Applicants will pay little to dishonest low-level officials if the likelihood of review is equivalent for both positive and negative decisions and if the next level's decision is independent of subordinates' recommendations.

Turning to applicants who are *not legally qualified,* however, the honesty of superiors now has an ambiguous impact on low-level corruption. On the one hand, it increases the risk of the corrupt transaction, since even if high-level review does not detect corruption, it may detect the bureaucrat's approval of an illegal application. On the other hand, the honesty of potential reviewers gives subordinates some monopoly power, since only they will accept bribes. Their power to extort bribes is further enhanced if they can also reduce the probability of appeal. The result once again contrasts with the sequential model when the honesty of subsequent officials *lowers* the bargaining power of the first official approached.[12] Thus while *dishonest* superiors may give low-level bureaucrats bargaining power over qualified applicants, *honest* superiors give them bargaining power vis-à-vis the unqualified.

High- and Low-Level Corruption: The Pitfalls of Reform

When corruption is uncovered at one hierarchical level, reformers often recommend a change in structure to give that level less discretion. Piecemeal reform will often fail, however, since reducing corrupt incentives at one level in a hierarchy may simply increase them someplace else. Thus, much has been made of the fact that police officers on the beat, and on-site inspectors of housing, construction, grain shipments, restaurants, etc.,[13] operate essentially alone without direct supervision by superiors. These jobs are conducive to corruption both because bribes can pass unobserved and because officials have broad discretion to make case-by-case determinations that cannot easily be checked by superior officials. Restricting the discretion of inferior officials may not, however, reduce corruption. Instead, its locus may simply shift to higher levels of the organization.[14] In fact, high-level bureaucrats in a tightly supervised hierarchy may have just as many unsupervised contacts with applicants as low-level employees have in organizations that allow considerable discretion to those at the bottom.[15] Moreover, personal friendships between high-level officials and clients are common, especially if officials are former employees of the clients' firms. The practice of bureaucrats and regulatory commissioners accepting jobs in the industries they regulate further links the two groups.[16]

The main difference between high- and low-level officials, then, appears to be neither the amount of discretion nor the opportunity for private, personal contact, but the greater visibility of decisions at higher levels of government. The decision of a cabinet secretary is often newsworthy, that of a low-level civil servant is seldom so. When the cost of organized opposition is high, however, publicity may not in and of itself be much of a deterrent to officials. In fact, regulatory commissions and government agencies may not even need outright bribes in order to favor clients. Previous arguments for the superior bargaining power of clients vary (see Noll, 1971; Wilson, 1974) but do not depend on outright bribery, although implied job offers are often cited to explain official behavior. Bribes may be less important at high bureaucratic levels because clients dealing with top government officials generally have a plethora of legal means of influencing the officials' decisions, means not open to the individual facing an isolated police officer or inspector. . . .

Furthermore, centralization of authority may not deter corruption if it produces a bottleneck at the top. When low-level bureaucrats simply pass data and applications upward without a conscious attempt to sort and evaluate information, the agency head often faces a tradeoff between a speedy decision and an informed one. Larger and larger quantities of data may make a decision harder instead of easier. Corruption can then become a substitute for thought. The greater the volume of work the agency head faces and the poorer the quality and the larger the volume of the information available, the greater the incentive to let bribes determine outcomes.[17] The organization of the bureaucracy may mitigate or exacerbate this tendency. On the one hand, if in the journey up the hierarchy an application is competently interpreted and simplified at each stage, then the taller the hierarchy the easier the top bureaucrat's job and the lower the incentive to accept bribes. On the other hand, if each layer loses and distorts information,[18] then the taller the hierarchy the more difficult the agency head's job, and corruption may then be used to simplify the bureaucrat's decision-making tasks. Of course, an agency head may not know which type of hierarchy lies beneath, since even incompetent and corrupt underlings may pose as competent technocrats. Whatever the truth of the matter, if a top official does not trust subordinates to behave competently, he or she will be unwilling to delegate authority and will therefore also be likely to face strong incentives to take bribes.[19]

Thus far the analysis has assumed that centralization was imposed on a bureaucracy by an honest legislature concerned with corruption. It is also possible, however, that honest top bureaucrats may take a similar course of action when they think that inferiors are incompetent or corrupt and providing poor or biased information. Paradoxically, however, the centralization that results from this initial distrust may produce a situation where once conscientious bureaucrats succumb to the corrupt opportunities they have created. For a decision must somehow be made, and while flipping a coin may be one response to untrustworthy information provided by subordinates, bribery is a more lucrative option.

Moreover, on the other side of the potential corrupt transaction, the longer the delays and the more unpredictable and arbitrary the top official's choices, the greater the incentives for applicants to pay bribes to the agency head. Even if the top decision makers do not succumb to the temptations of corruption, however, there is a final difficulty with centralization that is often ignored in the standard anticorruption reform. With the agency head overloaded with work, any lower level official with the power to channel the flow of petitions or to select information is automatically in a powerful position.[20] The "gate-keeper" increases in power the less room there is for applicants inside the gate. The very scarcity of the agency head's time implies that, like it or not, some authority must be delegated even if it is only the power to fill in an appointment calendar or pile up papers in some order on the top official's desk. In some systems, however, the privileged gatekeepers may not be bureaucrats at all but outside expediters,[21] lobbyists or agents[22] who are well connected with top officials. Their ability to obtain access can be used to earn high fees.

Implementation of an Agency Head's Decision

In the discussion thus far, low-level officials either made decisions on their own, subject to high-level review, or else passed information up to the ultimate decisionmaker at the top of the hierarchy. This view of bureaucracy, however, is only a partial one, since once a top official makes a decision, it must be implemented by low-level officials. Therefore, corrupt agency heads may have to share their bribery receipts with numerous subordinates. The potential deterrent effects of having multiple underlings depends on whether the bribe is paid to obtain a benefit to which the petitioner is legally entitled or to obtain an illegal service. In this second case, the higher level official must use some of the bribe money to buy silence from subordinates if their assistance is necessary to deliver the illegal benefit. A police sergeant, for example, may have absolute power to assign officers to particular beats, but may be incapable of inducing them to protect gamblers without offering a cut of the graft.[23] In this case, the smallest total bribe required to obtain the government service will be higher than when only a single official must be bribed, since subordinate officials will demand an amount that covers their moral costs and the expected costs of arrest and conviction. Moreover, the existence of corrupt practices will be difficult to conceal from outside investigators as the number of conspirators increases. Of course, if subordinates can be kept in ignorance, bribery may still be costly if top officials can hold out for most of the private surplus generated by their administrative power. However, the amount of surplus open to negotiation between the applicant and the top bureaucrat is larger, and more likely to be positive, the fewer the number of other people that must be bought off, ceteris paribus.

The Impact of High-Level Corruption on Bureaucratic Structure

Since bureaucratic structure will help determine the volume of corrupt gains available to agency heads, corrupt top bureaucrats will often have strong incentives to alter bureaucratic structures in order to facilitate corruption. On the one hand, they may try to have as few people as possible administering a program.[24] On the other hand, they may create a tall hierarchy to produce delays and then sell favorable positions in the queue to high bidders. When corrupt incentives are not generated by bureaucratic *procedures* (red tape) but by bureaucratic *outputs* (exemptions from law enforcement), corrupt agency heads will wish to have a short hierarchy to minimize the number of middlemen who must be paid off. Similarly, in making hiring decisions, top officials will stress loyalty to superiors rather than competence, efficiency, or honesty. Indeed, where delay produces corruption, inefficiency will be valued positively; and where the corrupt service is illegal, low scruples will be a strong recommendation. In short, corrupt high-level bureaucrats not only may distort their agencies' purposes by allocating benefits on the basis of willingness to pay, they may also organize their agencies inefficiently in an effort to maximize their own income.[25]

Choosing the Least Corrupt Form of Bureaucracy

We are faced, then, with an unattractive range of choices. A fragmented bureaucracy may generate extensive delays as corrupt officials hold out for large bribes, a sequential bureaucracy may be permeated with corruption even though officials have overlapping jurisdictions, while a corrupt bureaucrat at the top of a hierarchy may transform the entire administrative structure into an engine for the maximization of corrupt receipts. However, it should be clear that the control of corruption is only one of the goals of bureaucratic design. Considerations of cost and expertise often imply that one form is preferable to another. The analysis can then suggest the corrupt incentives to be anticipated as a result of the pursuit of these other policy objectives. Nevertheless, there are times when the control of corruption *is* a central policy goal, and one would like to compare the differing organizational forms systematically. This section, then, considers how a policymaker concerned with minimizing the expected proportion of corrupt transactions might analyze the choice of bureaucratic form in very simple situations. While any real-life applications would, of course, be much more complex, nonetheless even a few simple cases will allow me to make some basic points. Abstracting from the possibility that corruption may be reduced by increased monitoring or law enforcement activity, this section concentrates on the interaction between personnel policy and structure.

Assume, then, that an organizational designer can classify job applicants on the basis of the probability that they will be corrupt, β_i, and that the β_i are given exogenously. Job applicants can be classified so that $\beta_1 <, \ldots, < \beta_n \leq 1$. Only one individual of each kind exists.[26] In contrast to Chapters 5 through 8, the size of the bribe has no role in the analysis. If an official is corrupt a briber can always find a satisfactory positive bribe. The β_i are given independently of the size of the bribe paid. My task will be to show how the designer might think about the choice among three simple organizational options under the assumption that the level of expected sanctions is independent of the bureaucratic form. The baseline is a bureaucratic structure in which each official is given monopoly power over a certain share of the applications, without any effort being made to review the flow of low-level decisions. This *independent* structure is then compared to the *sequential* and *hierarchical* alternataives already discussed.

To keep the problem simple, suppose the designer decides that two officials with corruption probabilities β_1 and β_2 must be hired to handle the agency's work and that if these two officials are honest, it is equally efficient either to give each of them *independent* power over half the workload or to give them *sequential* decision-making authority over all the applications. For example, if the policymaker is charged with designing a system for issuing building permits, then if everyone is honest it makes no difference whether one official enforces the building code and the other the fire regulations or whether each carries out complete inspections. Furthermore, corruption has no direct impact on efficiency. Unlike the queuing models . . . bribery neither slows down nor speeds up performance.

Assume, finally, that the policymaker is concerned only with the problem posed by an official forcing applicants to pay for a benefit to which they are *legally* entitled. In this case, the use of independent officials is always superior to the sequential alternative. While this can be demonstrated formally,[27] the basic intuition is simple. In the case of an independent official, even if one official is corrupt, some applicants will not have to pay bribes if the other agent is honest. In contrast, in the *sequential* case, all applicants must pay bribes so long as one corrupt official exists. If, in addition, independent officials can compete with one another, the presence of one honest official may eliminate all corruption. . . . [28]

When the bureaucracy is organized *sequentially*, the results are different when *illegal* benefits must be provided at *each* stage in order for an unqualified applicant to succeed. Since an application cannot be divided up into independent legal and illegal sections, corruption at the first stage is useless unless both officials are corrupt. Similarly, an illegal application will never get to the second stage unless the first official is corrupt. Thus, the conclusions must be reversed. If bribery buys illegal benefits, a sequential system is superior to one with independent officials,[29] since no corruption occurs unless *both* officials are corrupt.

Turning now to a hierarchical organization, let us compare it first to an independent bureaucracy, where corruption is used to obtain a *legal* benefit. Assume that the highest level of the agency reviews all decisions. Hierarchical review thus eliminates low-level corruption. If a bribe is demanded by the low-level official, the applicant resists the corrupt pressure and appeals to the agent's superior. Of course, the conclusions here would have to be modified if, as is often the case, review is not certain or if low-level bureaucrats can use the information under their control to skew higher level outcomes. Nevertheless, if these difficulties are not important, the expected proportion of corrupt transactions is $ß_1$ so long as the most honest official is placed at the top. This is obviously superior to a system of independent officials where the expected proportion is $(ß_1 + ß_2)/2$.[30] Similarly, it is easy to see that hierarchy is also superior to independence in the *illegal* benefit case. So long as inferior officials are not able to turn their superiors in, the probability that an illegal application will be approved is $ß_1$. This is less than the chance, $(ß_1 + ß_2)/2$, in the independent official case.[31]

The last comparison to be made is between hierarchy and sequence. When the benefit is *legal,* the superiority of hierarchy follows immediately from the previous arguments showing that hierarchy (H) is superior to independence (I), and that independence is superior to sequence (S). Therefore, H is preferable to S. When bribes are paid in return for *illegal* benefits, a sequential system dominates a hierarchical one, however, since illegal applicants, turned down at the first stage, cannot appeal to the next level.[32] This conclusion, of course, depends critically upon the assumption that honest officials never approve illegal applications and that low-level bureaucrats do not report the illegal actions of their superiors. In short, for legal benefits, H is better than I which dominates S; while for illegal benefits, S is better than H which dominates I.

Before turning to the final, disorganized, case, it is worthwhile to suggest an interesting way to extend the present analysis. One of the most restrictive assumptions was the exogenous nature of $ß_1$, the probability of taking a bribe. . . . [Often] the official's willingness to be corrupted was not exogenous but depended upon the size of the bribe and the expected penalties levied. For example, if no official will accept bribes lower than some minimum determined by the fixed and variable costs of corruption,[33] this fact will work in favor of a sequential organization in the illegal benefit case. If illegal benefits are provided at each stage in the sequence, then the minimum total payoff equals the sum of the reservation prices of each official. The longer the sequence, the higher the minimum payoff and the greater the possibility that it will exceed the briber's maximum willingness to pay.

Disorganized Bureaucracies

Thus far, I have been dealing with ideal types. Under each model, the route to bureaucratic approval was clearcut, even if neither the probability of a successful outcome nor the length of procedural delays was known. Even in a fragmented bureaucracy, a land developer knows that official X is in charge of granting building permits, offical Y must approve the sewers, and so forth. Some actual bureaucracies, however, can only be described as chaotic: Members of the public have difficulty discovering which officials are legally authorized to deal with their problems or what kind of bureaucratic review they are entitled to demand.

This pervasive uncertainty has two very different impacts upon corrupt behavior. First, the uncertainty of legal procedures makes applicants willing to pay bribes in return for a higher probability of actually obtaining the government benefit.[34] Therefore, the payment of bribes may be undertaken more readily by risk-averse applicants than by those who like to take chances. The probability of arrest on charges of corruption may be so low that the risks associated with following honest procedures are greater than the risks associated with paying bribes. In fact, the very disorganization of the bureaucracy may lower the risk of detection since there may be no clear standard of honest behavior. This first effect of chaos, however, may be offset by a second. While corrupt bureaucrats may be willing to accept bribes, applicants cannot be sure that officials have the power to perform their side of the bargain.[35] Chaotic legal procedures increase the *demand* for more certain illegal ones, but if the disorganization of government is far advanced, no bureaucrats may be able to *supply* the requisite certainty even when offered a monetary incentive.

Curiously, past writing on this subject has failed to distinguish between supply and demand in a disorganized bureaucracy. Thus one group of authors associates chaos with corruption by concentrating upon the demand for illegal bureaucratic services in a disorganized government.[36] V. O. Key (1936), for example, links corruption to a world in flux—where rapid changes in society overwhelm an outdated government structure so that only cash has any chance of accomplishing anything and there is no trust and no set of established institutional procedures. In contrast, a second group emphasizes the *supply* side and advocates the introduction of uncertainty as a means of preventing bribery.[37] Proponents of this latter position, however, do not go so far as to advocate chaos. Instead they generally envisage a basically stable, well-organized bureaucracy within which personnel are constantly rotated, e.g., rotating the beats of police officers, given an honest and well-run police department, or electing a reform mayor who is willing to institute controls on bureaucrats and police officers. The aim is to prevent the development of close, trusting bonds between bureaucrats and clients. Both sets of authors tend to draw overly strong conclusions. Those who advocate the introduction of change stress the impact of this policy on *supply,* forgetting that *demand* may increase. In contrast, observers of corruption in underdeveloped countries notice the high level of *demand,* often neglecting the frequently low levels of *supply.*

Instead of taking the degree of disorganization as fixed, consider also the possibility that corruption itself can play a role in transforming a chaotic bureaucracy. These changes may not be desirable from the perspective of organization theory, but they may have important consequences for both legal and illegal government operations. Paradoxically, corruption, arising in response to the disorganization of the bureaucracy, may generate clear hierarchies where none existed before.[38] Low-level officials who try to collect bribes may find that higher bureaucrats, who would have ignored their honest behavior, now try to exert authority over them to appropriate their corrupt gains. This possibility depends, of course, upon a theory of bureaucratic organization in which the officials themselves play a critical role in establishing an agency's structure. Under this hypothesis, individuals in nominally superior positions do not bother to assert their authority over those below them unless given an incentive to do so. If the usual legal incentives—such as the desire for promotion, the love of power, or personal devotion to the agency's goals—do not operate in a disorganized world, only the hope of extracting some of another's corrupt receipts can induce one bureaucrat to exercise authority over another. It is possible, of course, that once corruption creates *some* kind of bureaucratic order out of chaos, the resulting structure might be more easily reformed than its disorganized counterpart. A shift in personnel may be sufficient to establish legal routes to bureaucratic approval and hence, over time, reduce the demand for corrupt benefits.

Conclusion

One of the most common responses to a scandal is piecemeal institutional reform in which new bureaucratic structures are proposed to guarantee that the scandal will not be repeated in the future. However understandable this response, the basic lesson of this chapter is that policymakers who concentrate on a single stage of the bureaucratic process are unlikely to achieve lasting reform. Thus, perhaps the most common response to the corruption of low-level officials—such as building inspectors or cops on the beat—is the creation of a stronger hierarchy with more review and less delegation of authority. Yet in a given organizational context, this step may simply push the corruption upstairs. Similarly, the reaction to a high-level scandal may be a call for the decentralization of authority. Yet this may only lead to different abuses that will generate a call for more centralized control. Thus both *independent* and *hierarchical* organizational forms place great pressure on personal honesty; *fragmentation* breeds hold-outs, and *sequences* may sometimes permit a few strategically placed corrupt officials to benefit from others' honesty. Furthermore, if central control is really abdicated, the whole system may degenerate into the disorganized case.

All these scenarios, of course, are not equally likely under all conditions. The analysis does suggest, however, the necessity for a hard-headed scrutiny of alternative systems with an awareness that each one is vulnerable to exploitation by unscrupulous officials. Moreover, having identified the critical points in each system, reformers must move on to propose more particularized structures—closer monitoring, higher pay, nonvested pension rights, and so forth—that will increase the expected costs of peculation at the critical soft spots.

Beyond providing a general framework for reform, the chapter also generates some more specific lessons. The most important point emphasizes the existence of a previously ignored tradeoff in institutional design. On the one hand, one may take institutional steps to prevent bureaucrats from forcing applicants to pay bribes for benefits to which they are *legally entitled*. On the other hand, one may prevent *legally unqualified* applicants from bribing their way onto the roles of beneficiaries. But it will not generally be possible to design institutions which achieve both goals at once.

My task is not to resolve such tradeoffs but to demonstrate that they must be confronted by serious reformers. Thus I have specified a set of conditions under which a *sequential* system will dominate a *hierarchy* as a means of reducing corruption if bribes are paid in return for *obviously illegal* actions. In contrast, if officials provide *legal* services in return for bribes, I have specified a simple model in which *hierarchy* dominates both a series of *independent* officials and a *sequential* system. This means that a policymaker will generally be forced to ask some hard questions before recommending a particular institutional structure. Which, for example, is more important—eliminating the bribes paid by legally qualified public housing tenants or making it impossible for unqualified people to obtain subsidized units?

The analysis also permits a refinement of the proposal . . . to introduce competition between officials as a check on corrupt incentives. In both the *sequential* and *hierarchical* models, if subsequent bureaucratic contacts vary in their willingness to accept corrupt payments, competitive officials are really selling a highly differentiated product, and one that is valued differently depending upon whether or not the applicant is seeking a legal or an illegal benefit. In a *sequential* bureaucracy, those who are legally qualified will pay more to an official who gives the applicant access to a sequence of honest officials, while those who want an illegal service will pay more to those who provide access to corrupt officials. In contrast, in a *hierarchical* system, legally qualified applicants will pay only relatively small sums to officials with honest superiors. Nonetheless, even imperfect competition will tend to reduce the dollar value of bribery and, less surely, its incidence as well.

Aside from its use as a tool for reform, the analysis also reveals a reciprocal relation between structure and corruption. Just as structure may influence the level of corruption, so the desire for corrupt returns will influence structure. Corrupt top bureaucrats in public agencies will seek to replace disorganized procedures with rationalized ones that centralize authority. Once in control of an agency, however, corrupt bureaucrats will wish to establish arbitrary and slow-moving legal procedures, either by hiring incompetent underlings or by promulgating complicated regulations. Their ability to use these devices to extract bribes will, of course, depend upon the existence of private market substitutes or alternatives in other areas of government. Thus a corrupt agency head might also try both to outlaw private substitutes and to absorb competing public agencies or independent government jurisdiction. Chaos will be replaced by order, yet this organization may produce, not speed, but agonizing deliberation.

Notes

1. Ward (1967:108) shows how indoctrination into group norms is used as a control device in the Jesuits and the U.S. Navy. Janowitz's (1960:125–49) study of the professional soldier discusses the United States military academies' efforts to develop a commitment to the military profession and a sense of "military honor."

   In some applications nepotism may be a substitute for indoctrination. Agency heads might hire their relatives because they can be trusted to carry out orders. Relatives, however, may be otherwise poorly qualified for government jobs. In fact, nepotism aside, honest high-level officials may often have to trade off the objective skills of job applicants against their level of personal honesty.
2. For a review and critique of recent work, see Nadel and Rourke (1975) and Warwick (1975, chapter 10).
3. This model is closest to the model of legislative behavior . . . where no representative was responsible to any hierarchical superior. The model could also be extended to a discussion of federal government structure, where each level of government has independent unreviewable authority over certain issues. (Riker, 1975, defines federalism as a system where this condition holds for at least some issues).
4. Zoning boards are, of course, composed of more than one official. Therefore, some of the considerations raised . . . would apply to this stage in the application approval process.
5. The example in the text is actually a mixed system, since the officials at most decision nodes are each at the bottom of an independent hierarchical system.
6. Gardiner's (1970:7–12) discussion of Wincanton, Pennsylvania, suggests that the fragmented model was a reasonably accurate paradigm for much of the town's corruption. No group exercised overall control, and the graft itself was not used to enforce centralization. Wolfinger's (1972) description of a decentralized political machine is also similar to the fragmented model, except that many of the officials in his analysis are politicians who face a reelection constraint.
7. In New York City, the prevailing bribe-price for a certificate of occupancy, the final permit required for a new building, was higher than the bribe required on various intermediate permits (*New York Times*, June 26, 1972).
8. A similar situation exists when an applicant can choose what jurisdiction to apply in. For example, the unique chain of officials one must deal with may be important in the locational decisions of firms.

9. For example, maneuvering by New York lawyers to obtain particular corrupt judges has been alleged (*New York Times,* March 26, 1974 and January 28, 1976).
10. In New York City an expediter hired to get building plans approved indicated that his initial strategy was to get the plan assigned to an examiner whom he knew was corrupt. This could be arranged by bribing the clerk who assigned plans to particular examiners (*New York Times,* June 27, 1972).
11. Moore's (1977:33–35) description of the organization of the New York City police who enforce the drug law implies that their department is a hierarchy of this type where superiors have only imperfect control over lower level police officers.
12. This conclusion, of course, depends critically upon the assumption that illegal applicants demand illegal services from everyone in the sequence. If, instead, they are able to request illegal services of corrupt officials and legal services of honest ones, this distinction breaks down.
13. The National Advisory Commission on Criminal Justice Standards and Goals, *Community Crime Prevention,* (Washington, D.C.: U.S. Government Printing Office, 1973), excerpted in Gardiner and Olson (1974:236–46), attributes administrative corruption to decentralized and poorly supervised procedures. In particular cases, the incentives for low-level corruption are documented in Sherman (1974b) and Wilson (1968), for the police: *New York Times,* May 20, June 25, 1975, for grain; *New York Times,* June 26, 1972, November 5, 1974, for the New York City construction industry; *New York Times,* December 3, 1971, for housing inspection; *New York Times,* December 7, 1977, for restaurant inspections.
14. Broadus (1976) argues that the lack of enforcement of the Kentucky strip-mining law can be blamed, in large part, upon the coal companies' influence on high-level state politics. While some low-level corruption occurred, large payments were unnecessary because of the companies' influence over the central organization.

    Students of American municipal government have found that the shift from centralized political machines to more decentralized forms does not necessarily reduce corruption (e.g., Wolfinger, 1972). Edward Costikyan, in *Behind Closed Doors* (New York: Harcourt, Brace and World, 1966), excerpted in Gardiner and Olson (1974:205–15), contends that today's civil servants are no less corruptible than past political bosses.

    The New York City police department, however, seems to have realized that centralization was not sufficient. In response to the Knapp Commission's revelations of corruption, they centralized vice enforcement but also instituted other reforms. They engaged in corruption control activities and reports, reduced personnel in the vice division, and instituted a policy of making fewer arrests and giving vice enforcement low priority (Rubinstein and Reuter, 1977:67–68).
15. The close relationship between top regulatory agency personnel and executives of the industries they regulate has been frequently documented. See, for example, Wilson (1974).

    The informality of regulatory agency processes can be contrasted with the formality of judicial proceedings, where explicit limits are placed on the contact between decision makers and those with whom they deal. The contacts are formal and public, and both life tenure for judges and the random selection of juries are designed to isolate these individuals from the interests of petitioners. All contact is part of the public courtroom record, and strict rules limit the types of information and the kinds of statements lawyers are permitted to present. Judges and potential jurors are expected to refuse to hear cases in which they have a personal interest. The major exception is plea bargaining, which sometimes involves the judge (for example, in the case of Spiro Agnew, *New York Times,* October 11, 1973). Criticism of plea bargaining, in fact, concentrates upon its departure from judicial norms of formality and publicity.

16. Defense contractors employ many former military and civilian defense department workers. Over 2,000 retired military officers with the rank of colonel and above worked for the 100 largest defense contractors in 1969 (Yarmolinsky, 1971:60). In a recent example, a high level defense department official in the Ford administration accepted a position with Hughes Aircraft and received offers from two other defense contractors (*New York Times,* February 15, 1977).

    Noll, Peck, and McGowan (1973:123) report that while many commissioners and high level staff officials of the Federal Communications Commission "have had experience in the communications business, the data mainly demonstrate that for most a high-level FCC job is an entry into a career in the industry." Common Cause reports that 75 percent of the top employees of the Energy Research and Development Administration were formerly employed by companies holding ERDA contracts. A study of regulatory agencies showed that 48 percent of regulatory commissioners who left government between 1971 and 1975 went to work for regulated companies or their law firms. Of commissioners appointed during that time, 52 percent were previously employed by regulated companies or their law firms. (*In Common,* Winter, 1977, vol. 8) A U.S. Senate study (1977:40) concluded that: "In our detailed considerations of appointment and reappointment of thirty-eight regulators in four agencies over a fifteen year period, we uncovered few instances of an actual financial conflict of interest. The single, most serious situation concerned negotiations for future employment while in office."

17. ... foreign officials who lack technical expertise have sometimes relied on competitive bribery as a decision-making device when purchasing defense products.

18. Montias (1976:178) writes that "whether information has been obtained from samples or aggregated from exhaustive reports, in transferring it from each tier [in the hierarchy] to the next losses and distortions in content and delays remain unavoidable."

19. J.M. Montias, in a private communication, has also stressed the importance of geographical distance and poor communications as factors reducing the efficiency of a hierarchy and increasing the incentives for using extrabureaucratic means of expediting decisions.

20. In India, Monteiro (1966) and Palmier (1975:579) both report that clerks who send files up for decision by senior officers are bribed to ensure that a case goes forward rapidly or is not forgotten.

21. Expediters are commonly employed, for example, by managers of Soviet enterprises. Some of their work is similar to lobbying, but a certain amount

of outright bribery and gift giving is indicated by journalistic reports of their activities and by data on their high levels of "travel" expenses (Berliner, 1952:356–58; 1959:361–62, 366–76).

22. The use of sales agents by American firms in overseas sales is reported in *New York Times,* June 22, July 6, 27 (Section 3), 1975; "Payoffs: The Growing Scandal," *Newsweek,* February 23, 1976, pp. 26–33; and Jacoby, Nehemkis, and Eells (1977).

23. Gambling syndicates commonly bribe police officials at many levels. Gardiner (1970) reports that in Wincanton (Reading) the head of the gambling syndicate used two basic strategies: "to pay top personnel as much as necessary to keep them happy (and quiet) and to pay *something* to as many as possible, thus implicating them in the system and keeping them from talking [p. 24]." Low-level officials had little recourse against the gambling syndicate, however, because of its close ties with high-level politicians and the lack of effective outside law enforcement activity by the state or the F.B.I. In other cases, say the police department in a large city where other portions of the city government are not corrupt, lower level police officers may have more bargaining power. See also Rubinstein (1973) and Rubinstein and Reuter (1977).

24. Thus state politicians in Maryland apparently centralized the disbursement of capital funds for public works projects as a means of centralizing the graft (Edsall, 1974).

25. Corrupt agency heads would also consider the impact of corruption on their honest returns. Thus, . . . agency heads would take legislative responses into account in deciding on the level of bribery receipts. Organizational structures that facilitate bribery will be rejected, even by a corrupt bureaucrat, if they imply too great a sacrifice of agency performance.

26. Instead of a fixed applicant pool with known β_i one might assume that the executive branch believes that there is a function, $\beta = f(w)$, where w is the wage rate and $f(w) < 0$. This function can be interpreted in either of two ways. Either it implies that as w increases more honest people apply for government jobs or it implies that the more civil servants are paid the less likely they are to be corrupt.

27. The probabilities of the four possible alternatives are

two	one	
	corrupt	honest
corrupt	$\beta_1\beta_2$	$\beta_2(1 - \beta_1)$
honest	$\beta_1(1 - \beta_2)$	$(1 - \beta_2)(1 - \beta_1)$

The expected proportion of corrupt transactions with two independent bureaucrats is $(\beta_1 + \beta_2)/2$, and with a sequential system it is $1 - (1 - \beta_2)(1 - \beta_1)$. Thus, $(\beta_1 + \beta_2)/2 \gtrless \beta_1 + \beta_2 - \beta_1\beta_2$ or $2\beta_1\beta_2 \gtrless \beta_1 + \beta_2$. Dividing by $2\beta_1$, $\beta_2 \gtrless \frac{1}{2}[1 + (\beta_2/\beta_1)]$. Since $\beta_2 > \beta_1$, this implies $\frac{1}{2}[1 + (\beta_2/\beta_1)] > 1 \gtrless \beta_2$. Thus, a system of independent officials is superior.

28. This result depends upon how congested the honest official becomes. If the presence of one honest official prevents the other from obtaining any

bribes, then the expected proportion of corrupt transactions is $\beta_1\beta_2$, which is less than $(\beta_1 + \beta_2)/2$.

29. The chance that an illegal application will be approved is $(\beta_1 + \beta_2)/2$ for an independent system and $\beta_1\beta_2$ for a sequential method of organization. Since $\beta_1\beta_2 < (\beta_1 + \beta_2)/2$, the sequential organization is preferable.

30. If independent officials can compete, and if no congestion exists, then the expected probability is $\beta_1\beta_2 < \beta_1$, and the independent case is preferable.

31. The minimization of the expected proportion of corrupt applicants is not the only plausible objective function, however. For instance, if applicants are obtaining benefits to which they are legally entitled, the policymaker might want to maximize the chance that at least one applicant obtains the service honestly. (If the benefit is illegal, this alternative objective function is, of course, not a very sensible one.) The policymaker might be willing to sacrifice something in terms of the *proportion* of transactions decided corruptly in order to reduce the chance of having a *completely* corrupt system. Given this objective, an independent system will dominate a hierarchy, since the probability of one honest applicant getting through is 1 $- \beta_1$, with a hierarchy, and $(1 - \beta_1\beta_2) > (1 - \beta_1)$ with independent bureaucrats.

32. In symbols, $\beta_1\beta_2 < (\beta_1 + \beta_2)/2$, by the argument in note 27.

33. . . . [In some cases] only low bribes were acceptable.

34. The Italian bureaucracy provides an example. Jacoby, Nehemkis, and Eells (1977) write that "within the vast bureaucracy, no one knows for certain which laws are valid and what some of them really mean [p. 77]." Only expediters with plenty of bribe money can overcome "the chronic chaos, buck-passing, indecision, and extortionate rulings [p. 37]."

35. Wraith and Simkins' example (1963:24–25) of the Nigerian tailoring contract . . . also applies here. Examples can also be drawn from recent western experience in Saudi Arabia where firms often do not know who has authority to make decisions. One prominent agent has amassed a fortune handling the affairs of multinational companies who wish to deal with the Saudis (*New York Times,* July 3, 1977).

36. Ford (1904), Key (1936), Huntington (1967), Jacoby, Nehemkis, and Eells (1977), and LeVine (1975:96). Jacoby, Nehemkis, and Eells also mention that in a chaotic regime bureaucrats may wish to supply more corrupt benefits but fail to note that they may be incapable of doing so.

37. The Pennsylvania Crime Commission (1974) recommends that in enforcing drug laws the Philadelphia police department should "rotat[e] undercover personnel so that undercover assignments last no longer than 18 months or a certain number of arrests [p. 839]." The New York City police department rotated police officers every four years in a special gambling control unit and frequently changed the unit's organizational form "to keep people off balance [Kornblum, 1976:11–12]." Rotation does not always work, however. In the New York City police department, corrupt clerical officers of plainclothes units checked on the "reputation" of officers who were transferred in order to maintain the corrupt system in spite of rotating assignments (Rubinstein and Reuter, 1977:66). Police involved in drug traffic in Latin America sold lists of corrupt contacts when they were transferred (*New York Times,* April 21, 1975).

38. The government would then be similar to that analyzed by Johnson (1975).

Waterbury (1973), for example, describes Morocco as a place where "corruption is manipulated, guided, planned and desired by the regime itself [p. 534]." Corruption in Indonesia has come under attack, in part, because of its increasing concentration at high levels. A local observer is quoted as saying "Corruption by itself may not be so bad, but corruption without sharing is selfish (*Wall Street Journal,* December 8, 1977)." Banfield (1975) explains that a "boss" who has gained control of a previously decentralized agency "will invest heavily in the dependability of his principle subordinates (one 'comes up through' a machine by demonstrating loyalty over time), regulate the breadth of their discretion, maintain an incentive system that motivates machine workers (especially job patronage, legal fees, the purchase of insurance, construction contracts, etc.), and monitor them to check unauthorized corruption [pp. 601–602]."

Bibliography

Banfield, Edward. "Corruption as a Feature of Governmental Organization." *Journal of Law and Economics* 18 (December 1975): 587–605.

Berliner, Joseph S. "The Informal Organization of the Soviet Firm." *Quarterly Journal of Economics* 66 (August 1952): 342–365. Reprinted in *Readings on the Soviet Economy,* edited by Franklyn Holzman. Chicago: Rand McNally, 1962.

Berliner, Joseph S. "Managerial Incentives and Decisionmaking: A Comparison of the United States and the Soviet Union." In U.S., Congress, Joint Economic Committee, Subcommittee on Economic Statistics, *Comparisons of the United States and the Soviet Economies* (1959), Pt. I, pp. 349–376. Reprinted in *Readings on the Soviet Economy,* edited by Franklyn Holzman. Chicago: Rand McNally, 1962.

Broadus, James. *The Economics of Corruption.* Ph.D. dissertation, New Haven: Yale University, 1976.

Edsall, Thomas B. "State Politics and Public Interests: Money and Morality in Maryland." *Society* 11 (4) (May/June 1974): 74–81.

Ford, Henry Jones. "Municipal Corruption." *Political Science Quarterly* 19 (December 1904): 673–686.

Gardiner, John. *The Politics of Corruption: Organized Crime in an American City.* New York: Russell Sage Foundation, 1970.

Gardiner, John A., and Olson, David J., eds., *Theft of the City.* Bloomington: Indiana University Press, 1974.

Huntington, Samuel. "Political Development and Political Decay." In *Political Modernization: A Reader in Comparative Political Change,* edited by Claude Welch, Jr., pp. 207–241. Belmont, Calif.: Wadsworth Publishing Co., 1967.

Jacoby, Neil; Nehemkis, Peter; and Eells, Richard. *Bribery and Extortion in World Business.* New York: Macmillan Publishing Co., 1977.

Janowitz, Morris. *The Professional Soldier.* Glencoe, Ill.: Free Press, 1960.

Johnson, Omotunde E. G. "An Economic Analysis of Corrupt Government with Special Application to Less Developed Countries." *Kyklos* 28 (1975): 47–61.

Key, V. O., Jr. *The Techniques of Political Graft in the United States*. Chicago: University of Chicago Libraries, 1936.

Kornblum, Allan N. *The Moral Hazards*. Lexington, Mass.: D. C. Heath, 1976.

LeVine, Victor T. *Political Corruption: The Ghana Case*. Stanford, Calif.: Hoover Institution Press, 1975.

Monteiro, John B. *Corruption*. Bombay: Manaktalas, 1966.

Montias, John Michael. *The Structure of Economic Systems*. New Haven: Yale University Press, 1976.

Moore, Mark Harrison. *Buy and Bust*. Lexington, Mass.: D. C. Heath, 1977.

Nadel, Mark V., and Rourke, Francis E. "Bureaucracies." In *Government Institutions and Processes: Handbook of Political Science,* edited by F. Greenstein and N. Polsby, 5:373–440. Reading, Mass.: Addison-Wesley, 1975.

Noll, Roger; Peck, Merton, J.; and McGowan, John. *Economic Aspects of Television Regulation*. Washington, D.C.: Brookings Institution, 1973.

Palmier, Leslie. "Corruption in India." *New Society* 32 (June 5, 1975): 577–579.

Riker, William H. "Federalism." In *Government Institutions and Processes, Handbook of Political Science,* edited by F. Greenstein and N. Polsby, 5:93–172. Reading, Mass.: Addison-Wesley, 1975.

Rubinstein, Jonathan. *City Police*. New York: Farrar, Straus, Giroux, 1973.

Rubinstein, Jonathan, and Reuter, Peter. "Numbers: The Routine Racket." New York: Policy Sciences Center, April 1977. Manuscript.

Sherman, Lawrence. "Becoming Bent: Moral Careers of Corrupt Policemen." In Sherman (1974: 191–208).

Ward, Benjamin. *The Socialist Economy*. New York: Random House, 1967.

Warwick, Donald. *A Theory of Public Bureaucracy*. Cambridge: Harvard University Press, 1975.

Waterbury, John. "Endemic and Planned Corruption in a Monarchical Regime." *World Politics* 25 (July 1973): 534–555.

Wilson, James. "The Politics of Regulation." In *Social Responsibility and the Business Predicament,* edited by James McKie, pp. 135–168. Washington, D.C.: Brookings Institution, 1974.

Wilson, Robert. "On the Theory of Syndicates." *Econometrica* 36 (January 1968): 119–132.

Wolfinger, Raymond. "Why Political Machines Have Not Withered Away and Other Revisionist Thoughts." *Journal of Politics* 34 (May 1972): 365–398.

Wraith, Ronald, and Simpkins, Edgar. *Corruption in Developing Countries*. London: George Allen and Unwin, 1963.

Yarmolinsky, Adam. *The Military Establishment*. New York: Harper and Row, 1971.

47

The Logic of Corruption Control

John A. Gardiner and Theodore R. Lyman

Corruption is an integral part of policy making and implementation, at least in some programs in some cities. As a result, it is rarely feasible or productive to consider steps to control corruption in isolation from consideration of the programs, agencies, and political systems in which it occurs. We cannot attempt [here] to sketch the characteristics of ideal land-use or building regulation systems, or public administration practices; textbooks abound on both subjects, and we lack expertise to add to them. We can, however, suggest characteristics of policies, programs, and structures which will tend to encourage or discourage corruption. The suggestions which follow must be regarded as general and tentative, since we were only outside and usually after-the-fact observers in the cities studied, and since no controlled experiments have been conducted to measure the impact of the types of policies we will discuss. We hope, however, that they will serve both to stimulate experimentation by citizens and officials and to guide further research.

The analysis of patterns of corruption in land-use regulation indicates that while individual wrongdoers can be found in many settings, the probability of corruption will be increased where there are incentives for developers to evade regulations, where regulators have incentives and opportunities to make decisions favoring developers' interests, and, where, for both developers and regulators, the benefits of corruption less its costs exceed the benefits of noncorrupt behavior less its costs. Accordingly, strategies to prevent or reduce corruption must reduce incentives and opportunities for corrupt behavior and the costs of noncorrupt behavior, and increase incentives and opportunities for noncorrupt behavior and the costs of corrupt behavior. Be-

Source: John A. Gardiner and Theodore R. Lyman. *Decisions for Sale: Corruption and Reform in Land-Use and Building Regulation.* New York: Praeger Publishers, 1978, pp. 183–95. Copyright © 1978 Praeger Publishers. Reprinted by permission of Praeger Publishers.

cause of the complexity of the corruption problem, a variety of control strategies must be considered, each of which addresses opportunities and incentives in different ways.

Before describing these control strategies, however, we must recognize that several factors will affect the design and implementation of programs to alter incentives and opportunities for corruption.

First, for both regulators and regulated industries, "corruption" and "integrity" rarely surface as discrete policy choices, but more frequently are minor parts of more complex decisions. For developers tax and interest rates, alternate investment opportunities, and so forth, create an economic framework within which payoffs may be only minor offsets to large profits.[1] Similarly, peer pressures within regulatory agencies create social relationships and work patterns which may encourage or condone payoffs. Under these conditions, even greatly increased prointegrity influences or costs of corruption may fail to change individuals' orientations.

Second, in many communities and organizations, corruption and integrity are not issues of high visibility and salience. Except in those situations where revelations have produced "scandals,"[2] citizens, officials, and regulators are usually thinking about other issues. In the absence of scandal, proposals to prevent corruption are viewed in terms of their impact on other policy goals and priorities: Will stricter enforcement practices attract or repel potential developers (who might bring higher land values or lower tax rates to the community), upgrade existing properties or just put slum dwellers out on the street? Will conflict-of-interest regulations keep otherwise valuable job applicants from accepting regulatory positions? Will time and material investments in monitoring integrity jeopardize "getting the job done?" To the extent that officials who wish to implement anticorruption programs must also consider these other issues, they will be less free to expend resources on integrity goals. We cannot specify when officials should reduce policy goals from point C to point B in order to raise integrity from point D to point E; we can only ask that they recognize the relationships and tradeoffs between the two issues. In general, officials should be willing to "invest" in controlling corruption amounts equal to the damage which corruption can do to the organization, although in practice it is difficult to estimate either the costs of control strategies or the organizational costs of corruption.[3]

Third, many factors which create opportunites or incentives for corruption are beyond the control of individuals or groups seeking to control corruption. Change in local or national economies will affect building markets, tax and interest rates, and the structure of competition in the development, construction, and building management industries.[4] The local tax base and tax rates affect city land-use policies (Broward County, for example, was actively seeking new development while Arlington Heights and Fairfax County sought to control growth) and the pay scales which might attract city employees. Personnel practices, whether stressing patronage appointment of political supporters or "merit" appointment through civil service examinations, influence the types of individuals assigned to regulatory positions and how closely supervisors can control them. (The case studies have shown corruption among both patronage and civil service regulators, so we cannot assume that one system is necessarily preferable to another; our point is that recruitment and job security policies will affect employees' reactions to control strategies.) A reform-minded head of the building department may have to work with policies set by the personnel and finance departments. Zoning decisions may be made by officials answerable only to the electorate. Civil service laws and the statutes governing both corruption and land-use regulation are often set at the state level, and prosecutors and judges are rarely under the control of local officials. These factors will affect opportunities and incentives for corruption, yet are unlikely to respond to the types of programs which can be implemented at the local level.

Fourth, the corruption we have discussed involves many different types of acts and actors, including $10 payoffs to building inspectors on code violations, and $50,000 payoffs to city councilmen on zoning changes. Some of the participants (both regulators and regulatees) may participate in only one transaction while others may engage in corruption routinely over a period of years.[5] Thus we must consider at least four types of corruption, as suggested in Table 47.1. It is likely that policies to prevent a single large payoff ($50,000 on a rezoning case, as in cell B) would differ from those aimed at recurring small payoffs ($10 to the building department clerk or inspector, as in cell C). And perhaps nothing can be done to wipe out all small single transactions

Table 47.1
SCALE AND DURATION OF CORRUPTION

		Scale	
		Small	Large
Duration	Isolated Incidents	A	B
	Repeated Pattern	C	D

Source: Compiled by the authors.

(cell A); to the extent that the participants in type A transactions are amateurs in corruption, however, they may respond best to the deterrence policies we will propose.

Within the limits set by these factors, several strategies can be used to reduce opportunities and incentives for corruption. Some strategies confront corruption directly by increasing supervision over decision making and penalties imposed on wrongdoers; others operate indirectly, providing incentives to perform tasks properly by withdrawing the anticipated benefits of corruption or simply by increasing the visibility of government activities.[6] The direct strategies may be most appropriate for dealing with specific and known targets, while the indirect strategies will affect broad audiences, only some of whom may be likely participants in corruption. Somewhat arbitrarily, since their effects will overlap, these strategies are discussed under the headings of reducing opportunities for corruption, increasing the costs of corruption, and reinforcing expectations of integrity.

Reducing Opportunities for Corruption

In most forms of crime, it is easier to take small sums of money than large sums; possessors of large sums of money usually have the foresight and resources to guard their assets closely. In land-use and building regulation, the opposite situation exists: the building code decisions which generate small-scale payoffs are tightly structured while the planning and zoning decisions which are worth thousands or millions of dollars rest on discretionary judgments about the "public interest." Building inspectors and office clerks are likely to be recruited and supervised through civil service systems, but planning and zoning commissioners are usually appointed on a part-time basis by the city council, and the councillors who react to their recommendations are directly chosen by the electorate.

Where regulatory systems are used to achieve land-use and building goals,[7] opportunities for corruption can be reduced through procedures which make the process and content of decision making more visible. Policy makers can rarely spell out all the factors to be considered in development, construction, and housing decisions. Yet, clear policy goals will tell implementing officials what they should be doing and will identify deviant actions which might involve corruption. On the other hand, policies that are too complex (or even self-contradictory[8]) will force officials to negotiate compromises, providing opportunities for corruption. Official discretion, in other words, is a two-edged sword; it provides both working space for officials to adapt policy goals to specific situations and room for officials and applicants to negotiate corrupt compromises. The best arrangement, of course, would balance clarity of policies with freedom to develop consistent applications of those policies in specific cases.[9] In the case studies, the land-use plans developed during Fairfax County's PLUS program and the building codes used in Arlington Heights contrast sharply with the vagueness of Hoffman Estates' early "residential" zoning classification or the archaic building codes in force in Chicago and New York City.

Similarly, regulatory procedures can be modified to raise the visibility of decisionmaking. In Fairfax County, conflicts over planning goals were aired through extensive and well-attended public meetings. When applications for land-use changes must include data related to specified decision criteria (housing density, access to transportation, public facilities, and so on), a decision inconsistent with those criteria (for examples, allowing high-rise apartments in a single-family neighborhood) would more quickly raise a suspicion of corruption. Where decision procedures require the regulator to record his decision (for example, formal votes on zoning applications or written statements by an inspector that a structure meets code requirements or that requirements have been waived for specified reasons) or set time deadlines (a building permit application will be approved within X days, a zoning application within Y months), deviations will be both more identifiable and more attributable to specific persons.

In addition to strategies which increase the visibility of specific decisions, communities can adopt policies which provide greater information about the individuals assigned to regulatory positions. Arlington Heights, Fairfax County, and Hoffman Estates, for example, require officials to file financial disclosure statements listing sources of income and outside employment, identifying real or potential conflicts of interest.[10] These communities have also required applicants to specify the owners of the land proposed for development. As they reduce perceived opportunities for corruption, these strategies also raise the costs of potential corruption (by raising the probability of detection) and encourage noncorrupt behavior (by showing that the organization condemns corruption).

Strategies which reduce the number of persons in positions to make sensitive decisions and which subject decisions to review can also reduce opportunities for corruption. In Hoffman Estates, the reform village board separated the functions of planning and zoning and insisted on reviews of development proposals by affected school, park, and sewer districts to prevent any recurrence of the Barrington Square type of problem. Arlington Heights and Fairfax County utilize a team approach to provide reviews of development proposals by planners and representatives of environmental, engineering, transportation, and legal offices. Gathering facts about the impact of a new development is thus separated from deciding whether to approve the project. At later stages in a project, responsibility for reviewing plans is organizationally separated from the responsibility to inspect construction in progress. A number of communities have utilized supervisors or "superinspectors" to check the work of inspectors; Chicago has begun to require inspectors to work in teams and to file proposed itineraries, assuming that inspectors will be less likely to take bribes in the presence of others or when their bosses can check up on their work.

Several other forms of reorganization might be mentioned briefly. First, agency reviews can be organized in "parallel" rather than in sequence: if an applicant can turn to more than one permit clerk or plan examiner, he may be less subject to extortion for approval of a legitimate request. Second, managers might consider systems to rotate assignments among officials: if plan examiners and building inspectors are periodically reassigned to different geographic areas, or at least to different projects, the chance that a single official will form close contacts with an individual developer, contractor, or landlord will be reduced (although it may also reduce the information which he utilizes to make decisions).[11] Finally, we might note the unsuccessful attempt in New York City to permit larger developers to by-pass inspectors by means of a certificate from an architect or engineer that a building complies with code requirements.

Raising the Costs of Corruption

We have said that many of the positive incentives to corruption, the profits applicants derive from evading regulatory requirements, are beyond the control of local governments. The costs imposed by regulatory procedures (forms, supporting data, time delays, and so on) and the standards set by regulations (permitted land uses, construction quality, and so forth) influence the profitability of development and building ownership and set up tradeoffs between regulatory goals and inducements to corruption. Incentives can either be reduced—by setting lower construction standards and permitting the most profitable land uses—or increased—with high standards and limited uses. When communities pursue their land-use goals with regulatory systems consonant with probable growth patterns, up-to-date construction codes, competent management, and efficient paper proccessing arrangements, incentives will be reduced; when communities use land-use policies and procedures which create incentives to corruption (for example, by banning high-density housing or setting high construction standards), however, they can reduce *net* incentives by raising the costs of corruption.

The risk posed by engaging in any criminal act combines both the probability of detection and the penalties of being caught. A prevention program must insure that the net costs of corruption exceed the gains it promises, and corruption must be less attractive than legitimate alternatives. The first factor implies that higher risks must be posed where corruption promises high payoffs; even a small penalty (a fine, reprimand, or brief suspension) might outweigh the small bribes paid to inspectors, but more serious sanctions are needed against the zoning commissioners and city officials involved in land-use decisions where payoffs can exceed several years' salary. Designing sanction systems involves a delicate balance; sanctions must be tough enough to deter corruption but not so harsh that enforcers will overlook the offense rather than subject violators to "excessive" punishment.[12]

While these steps make it more *possible* to detect corruption, there may be a greater need to establish organizations which are trying to detect it. In New York City, for example, the Department of Investigations is actively seeking to identify corruption problems. The investigations team and management audits used by the Cincinnati city manager serve similar functions on a smaller scale, and the Office of Professional Review recently established in Chicago may develop into an active corruption investigation agency. In some areas, state and federal prosecutors both respond to complaints about corruption and conduct extensive investigations.[13] Where city officials and prosecutors are inactive, investigative journalists and citizen watchdog organizations can provide an alternative mechanism to search out corruption.[14] Research on other forms of illegal behavior suggests that steps which raise the likelihood that corruption will be detected are likely to have a greater deterrent impact than policies which simply increase the severity of the sentences meted out to those who are detected.

Defining and Reinforcing Integrity Expectations

Applicants and regulators bring to their current roles a lifetime of experiences which shape, with varying degrees of clarity, definitions of corruption and expectations about the consequences of corrupt and noncorrupt behavior. The influence of these past experiences will persist. Yet, they can be counteracted by current experiences which illustrate the agency's definitions of prescribed and proscribed behaviors and the rewards and punishments which will follow from conformity and nonconformity. Definitions and expectations are likely to be learned through contacts with both organizational superiors and peers, from official policy directives and training sessions, and from the word-of-mouth folk wisdom of "those who have been around." To the extent that goal consensus can be built through group participation—through discussion among those who will be affected by the goal statements and implementing policies—it is likely to have a greater influence on behavior than goals announced by the unilateral fiat of supervisors.[15] In Cincinnati, for example, the city manager asked his Middle Management Board to develop a new code of ethics, concluding that a staff-generated code would be more readily accepted by city employees than a code issued from his office. In Arlington Heights, officials established committees representing both regulatory agencies and the construction industry to develop regulatory policies.

Whether evolving unilaterally as an edict from the agency leader or collectively as a peer norm, a crucial part of an anticorruption program is a clear *definition* of what is meant by corruption. Unless the agency spells out the kinds of things that employees should and should not do, it cannot assume that they will know that a specific activity is improper, or that it will be punished. Three steps are involved: the organization must issue clear statements of permissible and impermissible behavior, the consequences of violations must be announced, and these definitions should be consistently reinforced.

As the case studies have indicated, definitions of corruption become fuzzy in many "gray areas." All would agree that a regulator should reject a cash payment from someone he regulates, but what about a free meal (for example, a contractor taking the inspector to a cafeteria, or a developer taking the city council to a supper club "so we can get to know each other").[16] What about a low-interest loan from the developer's bank? Tickets to the Super Bowl? A bottle of liquor at Christmas? A contribution to the mayor's reelection campaign?

It is hard to draw a line that will distinguish expressions of friendship from compromising obligations. Officials and applicants alike will always say "[the gift, the bank loan, the campaign contributions] never entered our minds—of course we were dealing with each other at arm's length when [the subdivision application, building permit, fire inspection] came around." It may well be that no single point divides the harmless from the harmful; one official may bend the rules for the person who gives him a bottle of Scotch at Christmas while another will go by the book even with the banker/developer who holds his mortgage. The relevant guideline may not be defined by objective characteristics of the gratuity but rather by community perceptions: if local residents feel that the inspector who has a hamburger with the builder has "sold out," the political costs to officials may be as great as if cash had changed hands. As a result, many city officials take the safe way out—they forbid anything that either is improper or gives the appearance of impropriety, even knowing that this strict a guideline may prove unenforceable.[17]

Having decided where to draw the line, the next task is to inform both officials and the applicants they deal with about these policies. Arlington Heights, Cincinnati, and Fairfax County, for example, issue formal ethics codes to every new employee, and cover ethical issues in training sessions. Such formal strategies are likely to be viewed as either irrelevant or hypocritical unless indications are frequently and clearly given that "official" policies will be "real" policies. In Arlington Heights, the fact that the village prohibited the acceptance of gratuities from firms doing business with the city probably mattered less than the fact that the village manager enforced the policy. He regularly reminded insiders and outsiders of the policy, and anticipated the Christmas present problem by sending to all businesses dealing with the city a letter stating, "We would be embarrassed if you thought of us with more than a card." Gifts sent by businessmen who didn't get the message were returned by city policemen, employees' outside jobs were terminated when they conflicted with city duties, and so forth. Fairfax County had officially discouraged fraternization between inspectors and contractors for years; the policy was routinely ignored until an assistant county executive threatened to fire anyone caught attending the contractors' Christmas parties. He sent each inspector a copy of the official personnel rules, with the message "This means, in simple terms, that no employee may accept any gift from any person or firm that he is involved with in the line of duty. Any violation of these rules is considered unacceptable conduct and requires that it be dealt with severely."[18]

While setting definitions is an important first step, subsequent enforcement may be more important in affecting regulators' behavior; indeed, official policies which later go unenforced may suggest to subordinates that not even supervisors take the matter seriously. Reinforcement systems can utilize both positive and negative sanctions, and can focus on both corruption/integrity and the substantive policies regulators are to implement.

Designing reinforcement systems appropriate to specific situations depends highly on the leader's familiarity with the work and staff involved—knowledge of their character, the temptations they will encounter on the job, cross-pressures they will face, and idiosyncratic matters such as their family situations, debts, gambling habits, and so forth. Obvious positive sanctions include salaries,[19] pay raises, bonuses, promotions, work assignments, and public awards; negative sanctions can range from a private "chewing out" to reprimands, suspension without pay, dismissal, and prosecution. The availability of these sanctions may vary with budgets, local civil service laws, administrative requirements for promotion and demotion, and so on. More importantly, the effectiveness of these sanctions varies greatly; if the supply of positive sanctions is limited, employees may learn when no further rewards are available, and the targets of negative sanctioning may learn the techniques of evading detection or "wearing the boss down." Depending on the ingenuity of regulators and the requirements of courts or civil service hearing examiners, the costs of a negative sanction strategy may finally exceed benefits in terms of deterrence.[20] Finally, supervisors should be conscious of the virtues (and lower costs) of informal sanctioning strategies, including the simple word of praise to those who get the message and the skeptical look at those who don't. As these examples suggest, sanctioning strategies can be as complex or simple as the behaviors they modify.

One further factor which contributes to the effectiveness of programs to reinforce integrity expectations concerns the scheduling of reinforcements. Experimental research suggests the importance of recognizing and acting upon behaviors early: if the supervisor catches the new employee in a minor indiscretion, a skeptical look may be enough to induce change; similarly, early praise for proper performance will reinforce training session homilies. When employees are being conditioned to handle new activities, reinforcements should be continuous; thereafter, supervisors should intervene intermittently to maintain desired responses. Since the effectiveness of specific reinforcers may decline over time, supervisors should also be alert to the necessity of changing their approaches.

Transforming these positive and negative sanctions into reinforcements for integrity is a complex art greatly dependent on an understanding of the current predispositions of the personnel involved and probable corruption opportunities. A supervisor creating a new department has the luxury of recruiting subordinates who share his values or are at least amenable to beginning with his groundrules; a supervisor working with a group generally supportive of integrity can capitalize upon those feelings to ostracize the occasional deviant. Where such sentiments are not present or where many of the regulators condone or participate in corruption,[21] the task is harder. A necessary first step may be to make compliance possible, protecting those who wish to comply from retribution or further contamination by peers. The compliant group can then be expanded through allocations of formal and informal rewards, showing that integrity is both accepted and rewarding. To the extent that the supervisor can implement positive sanction strategies first (which may be impossible under scandal conditions, with public officials and the press demanding immediate action), he will be able to focus his negative sanctions on that segment of his work force which will not respond to positive approaches. Applying negative reinforcements can be as delicate as using positive reinforcements; negative reinforcements and/or punishments may change the behavior of most problem cases. Totally rotten apples should, if possible, be dismissed; where that is precluded by civil service protections, they can only be isolated from other personnel to minimize contamination. In all of these steps, it is essential that the supervisor build upon whatever latent or manifest support for integrity exists within the group, selling integrity as a collective goal rather than as an ultimatum delivered from on high.

In conclusion, we can say that to some extent, this analysis has assumed that supervisors *want* to reduce corruption in their departments, that city officials *seek* to keep their governments clean, and that they have the *resources* they need to engineer reform.

Notes

1. Special problems in the use of criminal statutes to control *corporate* behavior are discussed in Sanford H. Kadish, "Some Observations on the Use of Criminal Sanctions in Enforcing Economic Regulations," *University of Chicago Law Review* 30 (Spring 1963)423–49; Robert E. Lane, *The Regulation of Businessmen: Social Conditions of Government Economic Control* (New Haven: Yale University Press, 1954); Harry V. Ball and Lawrence M. Friedman, "The Use of Criminal Sanctions in the Enforcement of Economic Legislation: A Sociological View," *Stanford Law Review* 17 (January 1965): 193–223; Comment, "Increasing Community Control over Corporate Crime—A Problem in the Law of Sanctions," *Yale Law Journal* 71 (December 1961): 280–306; Christopher D. Stone, *Where the Law Ends: Social Control of Corporate Behavior* (New York: Harper and Row, 1975); and Michael Riesman, *Folded Lies* (New York: Free Press, 1978).
2. Where scandals have surfaced, however, public officials usually find that high investments in fighting corruption (or at least in appearing to do so) are essential for political survival.
3. Gary S. Becker and George J. Stigler, "Law Enforcement, Malfeasance, and Compensation of Enforcers," *Journal of Legal Studies* 3 (January 1974): 1–18; and Edward C. Banfield, "Corruption as a Feature of Govern-

mental Organization," *Journal of Law and Economics* 18 (December 1975): 587–605. More broadly, Robert C. Ellickson argues that systems to control land use must be evaluated in terms of nuisance costs (the harmful impact of a land use on neighboring properties), prevention costs (steps taken by landowners to prevent nuisance costs), and administrative costs (public and private expenditures to enforce rules); where prevention and administrative costs exceed nuisance costs, Ellickson argues, regulatory systems become socially inefficient. See "Alternatives to Zoning: Covenants, Nuisance Rules, and Fines as Land Use Controls," *University of Chicago Law Review* 40 (Summer 1973) 681–781.

4. While economic conditions may create incentives for corruption, they may also stimulate municipal reforms. The fiscal problems of New York City led to budget cuts and improvements in personnel and accountability systems, and the recession in Broward County led to increases in property taxes to compensate for a sharp decline in building permit fees. Though neither change arose out of concerns for corruption problems, both may lead to changes in the conditions which produced them.

5. Cf. the taxonomies of police corruption in New York City offered by the Knapp Commission (Commission to Investigate Allegations of Police Corruption and the City's Anti-Corruption Procedures), *Commission Report,* (New York, 1972), distinguishing "meateaters" and "grasseaters"; and by Lawrence W. Sherman in *Police Corruption: A Sociological Perspective* (Garden City, N.Y.: Anchor Books, 1974), pp. 6–12, distinguishing "rotten apples and rotten pockets," "pervasive unorganized corruption," and "pervasive organized corruption."

6. Eugene Bardach, in "Reason, Responsibility, and the New Social Regulation," a paper presented at the 1977 annual meeting of the American Political Science Association, argues that regulatory systems in the United States have shortsightedly tended to concentrate on enforcement approaches without providing incentives to perform in the desired manner.

7. . . . Proposals to change the structure of zoning regulations are analyzed in Judith Getzels and Charles Thurow, *Corruption in Land-Use and Building Regulation: Volume IV. An Analysis of Zoning Reforms* (Menlo Park: SRI International, 1978).

8. The temptations to corruption created by the inconsistent obligations imposed upon police officers are discussed in Jonathan Rubinstein, *City Police* (New York: Farrar, Straus, and Giroux, 1973). See also Banfield, "Corruption," p. 599.

9. The general problem of official discretion in legal systems is analyzed in depth in Kenneth Culp Davis, *Discretionary Justice: A Preliminary Inquiry* (Baton Rouge, Louisiana State University Press, 1969).

The National Advisory Commission on Criminal Justice Standards and Goals concludes: "The greatest single cause of corruption in government operations is the availability of excessive discretion in decisions involving significant sums of money. Vague and improperly stated decision guidelines invite attempts at manipulation and fraud and are certainly indicative of sloppy management. Questions of honesty aside, it simply is not in the public interest to have important community decisions made on an ad hoc basis by inadequately briefed or insufficiently trained public officials."

Community Crime Prevention (Washington, D.C.: U.S. Government Printing Office, 1973), p. 259.

Anthony Downs points out three kinds of situations differentially suitable to the development of rules: some are too trivial to justify making rules; some involve repetitive or routine situations which can be covered under rules; and some are so important or complex that review by high authorities is essential before decisions are made. *Inside Bureaucracy* (Boston: Little, Brown, 1967), p. 61.

10. Conflict of interest, financial disclosure, and campaign finance regulations are discussed at length in George Amick, *The American Way of Graft* (Princeton: Center for Analysis of Public Issues, 1976); and Herbert E. Alexander, *Financing Politics: Money, Elections and Political Reform* (Washington, D.C.: Congressional Quarterly Press, 1976), p. 181. Alexander observes, "The line between outright bribery and campaign contributions may often be a thin one, but where there is no accounting whatever of campaign funds or of sources of income, it is easy to rationalize that one was meant to be the other. Statutory disclosure brings at least some discipline to transactions involving money and elected public officials."

11. See Susan Rose-Ackerman, *Corruption: A Study in Political Economy* (New York: Academic Press, 1978), ch. 9.

12. Donald T. Campbell and H. Laurence Ross, for example, found that Connecticut policemen refused to cite many traffic offenders when penalties were raised to the point where speeders were likely to lose their licenses. See "The Connecticut Crackdown on Speeding: Time Series Data in Quasi-Experimental Analysis," *Law and Society Review* 3 (August 1968): 33–53.

13. Problems and opportunities in investigation and prosecution of corruption cases are reviewed in Robert W. Ogren, "The Ineffectiveness of the Criminal Sanction in Fraud and Corruption Cases: Losing the Battle Against White-Collar Crime," *American Criminal Law Review* 11 (Summer 1973): 959–88. Corruption cases handled by United States attorneys are discussed in James Eisenstein, *Counsel for the United States: U.S. Attorneys in the Political and Legal Systems* (Baltimore: Johns Hopkins University Press, 1978).

14. The structure and activities of Chicago's Better Government Association are detailed in Peter Manikas and David Protess, *Corruption in Land-Use and Building Regulation; Volume V: Establishing a Citizens' Watchdog Group* (Menlo Park: SRI International, 1978).

15. See Downs, *Inside Bureaucracy,* chs. 18 and 19, ...

16. Entertainment practices by U.S. defense contractors have been surveyed by the Joint Committee on Defense Production of the United States Congress, *Defense Contractor Entertainment Practices* (Washington, D.C.: U.S. Government Printing Office, 1977).

17. On the problems involved in setting official definitions of corruption, see Herman Goldstein, *Police Corruption: A Perspective on its Nature and Control* (Washington, D.C.: Police Foundation, 1975), pp. 28–30.

18. At times, a supervisor may simply not recognize the situations which his employees regard as opportunities for criminality. Anthropologist Edward T. Hall tells the story of an Aramco subsidiary in Saudi Arabia which was

losing money. An Arab who bought the company then set up a complex system to reward drivers for *not* stealing oil, parts, and so forth; his operating costs dropped by two-thirds. Elizabeth Hall, "Hopis, Anglos, and Tagalogs: A Sketch of Edward T. Hall," *Psychology Today* 10 (July 1976):68–74.

19. Edward C. Banfield argues that the significance of higher pay scales lies not in their ability to attract more competent personnel but rather in the greater loss which would be caused by dismissal: the more an employee is paid, the more he may lose. "Corruption," p. 600.

20. The economic relationships between the benefits of corruption to participants, its costs to society, penalties imposed on convicted participants, and the costs of prevention or enforcement programs are estimated in Becker and Stigler, "Law Enforcement," and Rose-Ackerman, *Corruption*.

21. See Erwin O. Smigel and H. Laurence Ross, eds., *Crimes Against Bureaucracy* (New York: Van Nostrand, 1970).

48

Singapore's Experience in Curbing Corruption

Jon S. T. Quah

In some countries like Singapore corruption is a fact of life rather than a way of life.[1] Put differently, corruption exists in Singapore, but Singapore is not a corrupt society.[2] This does not mean that Singapore is entirely free from corruption, as was contended by Lord Shawcross of Britain in 1977.[3] Now and then there are incidents of corrupt behavior in Singapore, which usually receive extensive coverage in the local newspapers. However, such cases are the exception rather than the rule and are examples of individual rather than systemic corruption.[4] Furthermore, those found guilty of corrupt behavior are punished according to law, regardless of their position or status in society. In short, corruption is incidental but not institutionalized in Singapore.

This chapter analyzes how Singapore's political leadership has managed to curb the problem of corruption through the formulation and implementation of effective anti-corruption measures. Indeed, corruption is incidental and not institutionalized in Singapore because the incumbent People's Action Party (PAP) government, which has been in power since June 1959, is committed to the eradication of corruption in the city-state. Needless to say, Singapore's success in combatting corruption has attracted a great deal of attention around the world. In a special issue of the *Far Eastern Economic Review* devoted to "Corruption: The Asian Lubricant," a survey of the problem in ten Asian countries indicated that Singapore is "the least corrupt of all Asian states" and is reputed to be the "Mr. Clean" of Asia.[5] However, not too many scholars have ventured in this area because of the sensitive nature of the topic and the difficulties in getting access to relevant data. The reason for focusing on Singapore's experience in combatting

Source: The above article has been written specially for this volume.

corruption is also to identify the lessons that can be learned by other countries concerned with solving the problem of corruption.

Incentives and Opportunities

What are the causes of corruption? If corruption is defined as deviant behavior by an individual or individuals to obtain some socially and/or legally prohibited favors, then an individual is more likely to indulge in corrupt behavior the greater the incentives and opportunities to do so. The personal incentive to be corrupt may depend on the following factors: The individual's virtue (or character), the personal virtue of his colleagues (especially that of his superiors), his monthly salary, the strength of his familial loyalties and the values influencing his decision-making, and the general societal attitude towards corruption. The individual's incentive to be corrupt will be great if his personal virtue is low, if his colleagues are corrupt, if his familial loyalties override his loyalty to his organization and country, if his monthly salary is low or insufficient to meet his needs, and if his society tolerates corrupt behavior. Conversely, his incentive to be corrupt will be minimal or absent if he is of strong moral character, if his colleagues are not corrupt, if he is more loyal to his organization and country than to his family, if his wages are adequate, and if corruption is not condoned in his society.

However, the incentive to be corrupt does not by itself result in individual corrupt behavior. The individual must also have the opportunities to be corrupt, which in turn depend on the extent his official activities are controlled by others, the frequency of his contacts with the public, and his position in his organization. In short, an individual is likely to become corrupt if both the incentives and the opportunities to do so are great enough. Accordingly, attempts to eradicate corruption must be designed to minimize or remove the conditions of both the incentive and opportunities that make individual corrupt behavior irresistible.

Singapore's Anti-Corruption Strategy

The fact that corruption is not a way of life in Singapore is an indication of the effectiveness of the anti-corruption strategy adopted by the PAP government after it assumed power in June 1959. However, it should be noted that corruption was a way of life during the colonial period in Singapore, especially after World War II. The rampant inflation during the Japanese occupation gave rise to widespread corruption because the civil servants found it difficult to live on their fixed salaries. Conditions deteriorated after the war and contributed to a further increase in corruption. The low salaries and rapidly rising cost of living during the post-war period accounted for the bureaucrats' incentive to be corrupt and the inadequate supervision of civil servants created many opportunities for corruption on their part with little probability of being caught. In his 1950 Report, the Commissioner of Police pointed out that graft was rife in government departments.[6]

The newly elected PAP government was determined to eradicate corruption in Singapore in general and in the civil service in particular. With this aim in mind, the PAP government amended the Prevention of Corruption Ordinance in 1960 and replaced it with a new ordinance which was more comprehensive in scope and gave the government wider powers of enforcement. In moving for the second reading of the Prevention of Corruption Bill in the Legislative Assembly on February 13, 1960, the then Minister for Home Affairs, Mr. Ong Pang Boon, elaborated on the *raison d'être* for the bill:

> The Prevention of Corruption Bill is in keeping with the new government's determination to stamp out bribery and corruption in the country, especially in the public services. The government is deeply conscious that a government cannot survive, no matter how good its aims and intentions are, if corruption exists in its ranks and its public services on which it depends to provide the efficient and effective administrative machinery to translate its policies into action.
>
> . . . Therefore, this government is determined to take all possible steps to see that all necessary legislative and administrative measures are taken to reduce the opportunities of corruption, to make its detection easier and to deter and punish severely those who are susceptible to it and engage in it shamelessly.
>
> Therefore, in this bill, the government is asking for new and wider powers to fight bribery and corruption. As stated in the Explanatory Statement, the object of this bill is to provide for the more effective prevention of corruption by remedying various weaknesses and defects which experience has revealed in the existing Prevention of Corruption Ordinance. The bill, while directed mainly at corruption in the public service, is applicable also to corruption by private agents, trustees and others in a fiduciary capacity.[7]

The PAP government's strategy of dealing with the problem of corruption emphasizes the necessity of reducing *both* the opportunities and incentives for corruption. These twin strategies will now be described in detail.

Reducing Opportunities for Corruption

The PAP government relies on the Prevention of Corruption Act (POCA) and the Corrupt Practices Investigation Bureau (CPIB) to spearhead its anti-corruption strategy. The aim of the POCA and CPIB is to curb corruption by reducing the opportunities for corruption and by increasing the penalty to be paid for corrupt behavior if one is caught. The POCA was first enacted in December 1937 to ensure "the more effectual prevention of corruption." Fifteen years later, in October 1952, the CPIB was formed as the first autonomous anti-corruption agency outside the jurisdiction of the police because of the inability of the Anti-Corruption Branch of the Criminal Investigation Department of the police to curb the rising incidence of corruption in the country.[8] However, before 1960, both the POCA and the CPIB were ineffective in curbing the problem of corruption. Consequently, as was mentioned above, the PAP government amended the POCA by increasing its scope and its powers for dealing with corrupt practices. The definition of corrupt behavior was specified and the penalty for such behavior was increased to imprisonment for five years and/or a fine of S$10,000[9] in order to increase the POCA's deterrent effect. Furthermore, the CPIB was given a new lease on life by the 1960 amendment of the POCA as the latter identified for the first time the CPIB and its director and the additional powers entrusted to them for performing their anti-corruption duties.[10]

In 1960 the POCA was amended to give CPIB officers the power to require the attendance of witnesses, and to examine such witnesses. This was done to reduce the difficulty in getting witnesses to appear before CPIB officers to help them in their investigations. In 1963 two further amendments were made to strengthen the POCA. First, according to section 28, a person could be found guilty of corruption even though he did not actually accept the bribe. The intention on his part to commit the offense would provide sufficient grounds for his conviction. Second, section 35 states that Singapore citizens would be liable for corrupt offenses committed outside Singapore and would be dealt with as if such offenses had been perpetrated within Singapore. This amendment was directed at those Singaporeans working for the Singapore government in embassies and other government offices abroad. In other words, no Singaporean, regardless of whether he resides within or outside his country, can be immune from the "tentacles" of the POCA.[11] The most recent amendment was introduced in parliament by the Minister for Law, Mr. E. W. Barker on October 23, 1981. The purpose of this amendment was to increase the deterrent effect of the

POCA by requiring those convicted of corruption to repay all the money received besides facing the usual court sentence. Those who are unable to make full restitution will consequently receive heavier court sentences.[12]

The CPIB is the anti-corruption agency which enforces the provisions of the POCA. When the POCA was amended in 1960, the CPIB had only eight officers. In 1986 the CPIB had a total staff of 71 persons and a budget of $4.33 million.[13] From 1955–1970 the CPIB came under the jurisdiction of four different government agencies: the Chief Secretary's Ministry (1955–1959); The Ministry of Home Affairs (1960–1963); the State Advocate-General (1964); and the Ministry of Law and National Development (1965–1969). These shifts in jurisdiction of the CPIB can be attributed to its difficulty in getting cooperation from other government departments and to the constraints faced by it in investigating corrupt behavior among civil servants within its own ministry or department. However, the CPIB had been under the wing of the prime minister's office since 1970, and has remained there ever since. This ensures that the CPIB is able to obtain the necessary cooperation from all the ministries and statutory boards, and is thus able to function effectively in spite of its small staff.[14]

In addition to the role played by the POCA and CPIB in reducing the opportunities for corruption, the ministry of finance issued a circular in July 1973 to all permanent secretaries instructing them to review and improve the measures taken to prevent corruption among their officers by minimizing the opportunities for corrupt practices. The permanent secretaries were asked to make their officers aware of the PAP government's serious efforts to eradicate corruption and to advise them to report any case of corruption. They were also requested to take appropriate anti-corruption measures in those departments particularly exposed to corruption. Such measures included the following: improving work methods and procedures to reduce delay; increasing the effectiveness of supervision to enable superior officers to check and control the work of their staff; rotating officers to ensure that no officer or group of officers remain too long at a single operational unit; carrying out surprise checks on the work of their officers; making the necessary security arrangements to prevent unauthorized persons from having access to a department's premises; and reviewing the anti-corruption measures taken once in three to five years with the aim of introducing further improvements.[15]

Why has the CPIB been effective in spite of its small size? This question is pertinent as countries with better staffed anti-corruption agencies (such as the Independent Commission Against Corruption in

Hong Kong) have not been as successful as Singapore in combatting corruption. Two reasons can be suggested here. First, Singapore's small size and well-developed infrastructure have been a boon to the CPIB's efforts in checking corrupt behavior among Singaporeans. Second, the CPIB, being under the jurisdiction of the prime minister's office, is able to obtain the necessary cooperation from all government departments and statutory boards.

However, the CPIB is not perfect and has been criticized on various occasions for its treatment of those accused of offenses under the POCA. During the corruption trial of a former government naval architect and two shipyard directors in April 1971, various complaints were made by the accused of the treatment given to them by the CPIB officers. The naval architect was not allowed to consult his solicitors before making statements to the CPIB officer who was questioning him.[16] One of the shipyard directors claimed that he had to wait for an hour in a "square, air-conditioned room" which was "very cold" before he was questioned by a CPIB officer. He further alleged that he was threatened by the officer, who said that he would be jailed if he did not cooperate.[17] Furthermore, the counsel for the directors claimed that his clients were not accorded the same treatment by the CPIB as that given to the naval architect, who was an "educated, professional man" and knew his rights.[18]

Several months later, an ex-warrant officer of the Singapore armed forces alleged in court that he was tortured by CPIB officers when he refused to write a statement demanded by them. He was arrested by CPIB officers for dishonestly retaining 35 pairs of combat boots. He claimed that after his arrest he was "put in a room with the lights switched off and then tortured by the officers."[19]

In November 1973 a clerk alleged that he was assaulted by CPIB officers after his arrest on July 2 of the same year for receiving S$5,000 from a businessman. According to him, he was punched twice on the back and once on his right side by three CPIB officers standing behind him.[20] A former acting architect and planner of the Urban Renewal Department, who had been charged with corruptly receiving S$5,000 from a company director, claimed in January 1974 that CPIB officers threatened to put him in a "cold room" if he did not cooperate with them.[21] In November 1976 a subcontractor accused of bribery told a district court that a CPIB special investigator threatened to detain him under the Criminal Law (Temporary Provisions) Act if he did not cooperate to implicate a police inspector.[22]

Finally, a district judge, Chandra Mohan, criticized the investigation methods of the CPIB when he acquitted a police sergeant charged with accepting a S$250 bribe. He rebuked CPIB officers for being "over-zealous" in their attempts to investigate "complaints of alleged corruption made against public persons, by persons who are themselves under investigations for alleged offenses, or against whom some administrative or enforcement action has been commended." According to him:

> An honest man who discharges his law enforcement duties without fear and without being influenced by the character of a person who is under investigation ought not to be placed in a situation where he has to constantly look behind his shoulders for overzealous CPIB officers, who have been made to spring into action by false allegations of vindictive complainants.[23]

While it is true for the most part that those who have accused CPIB officers of misbehavior have been *unable* to substantiate their allegations, nevertheless the frequency of such complaints indicates that CPIB officers must be extremely careful in performing their investigations. The continued success of the CPIB depends to a great extent on the support and cooperation it is able to obtain from the population at large in Singapore. Overzealousness or misbehavior on the part of CPIB officers would not only create tension between them and members of the public but also undermine the favorable reputation and public image of the CPIB.

Reducing the Incentives for Corruption

Apart from reducing the opportunities for corruption, the PAP government's anti-corruption strategy relies on reducing the incentive to be corrupt among civil servants by constantly improving their salaries and working conditions. I assume that corruption becomes a serious problem in a country where the civil servants are generally paid very low salaries and where there is an unequal distribution of wealth.[24] In other words, a civil servant might be forced by financial reasons to indulge in corrupt acts if he is not earning enough to support his family. The linkage between low salaries and corruption is best illustrated in Indonesia, where civil servants' salaries are among the lowest in the world.[25]

The salaries of Singaporean civil servants are quite high by Asian standards because the PAP government has to compete with the attractive private sector by offering comparable salaries and fringe benefits. Since March 1972 all civil servants and employees of statutory boards have received a thirteen month non-pensionable allowance, which is comparable to the bonus in the private sector. In 1973 the salaries of the senior officers were increased substantially to narrow the gap with the private sector.[26] Two further salary revisions in the civil service were made in May 1979 and April 1982 to stem the drain to the private sector by minimizing the salary differential between the public and private sectors.[27] More specifically, the PAP government substantially revised the salaries of those in the administrative service and other professional services in April 1982. As a result of the latest salary increase, which has been the most substantial so far, the top three grades in the administrative service command monthly salaries of S$21,700 (or S$25,112 including allowances) for Staff Grade III, S$18,800 (or $21,756 including allowances) for Staff Grade II, and S$15,900 (or S$18,400 including allowances) for Staff Grade I. This salary revision raised the PAP government's annual wage bill by S$274.7 million, which meant an increase of 26.8 percent compared to the previous year's expenditure on salaries.[28]

Perhaps the most eloquent justification of the PAP government's approach to combatting corruption by reducing the incentive for corruption by raising the salaries of its political leaders was provided by Prime Minister Lee Kuan Yew in parliament on March 22, 1985, when he explained why the salaries of the cabinet ministers had to be increased. He contended that political leaders should be paid the top salaries that they deserved in order to ensure a clean and honest government. If they were underpaid, they would succumb to temptation and indulge in corrupt behavior. The prime minister began his speech by asking this question: "How is Singapore to preserve its most precious assets?" His answer to this question deserves quoting at length because of its relevance to our discussion:

> An administration that is absolutely corruption-free. A political leadership that can be subject to the closest scrutiny because it sets the highest standards. It is not easy, because if we lose this, then our reason for our existence, our *raison d'être* . . . will disappear. Why does this island survive? Why does it attract banks, computer software, financial services, information services, manufacturing, in preference to so many countries better endowed with natural resources, manpower, and markets? Any traveller knows that, because from the moment you hit the airport to the time you get into the taxi, you travel on the road, you know the difference, whether a place works on rules or it bends rules. . . . How do you ensure that a fortuitous, purely accidental group of men who came in in 1959 and after 26 years of office . . . have remained stainless? . . . Every member knows that there is no easy money on the take. That's the way we are. Nobody believes that we spent money to get into this House. . . . I'm one of the best paid and probably one of the poorest of the Third World prime ministers. . . . There are ways and ways of

doing things. And I'm suggesting our way, moving with the market, is an honest, open, defensible and workable system. You abandon this for hypocrisy, you'll end up with duplicity and corruption. Take your choice.[29]

In short, Singapore's anti-corruption strategy consists, on the one hand, of the combined use of the POCA and CPIB to reduce the opportunities for corruption, and, on the other hand, of the periodic upward revision of the salaries of civil servants and political leaders to reduce the incentive for corruption.

Learning from Singapore's Experience in Curbing Corruption

What lessons can be learned from Singapore's experience in curbing corruption? Eliminating corruption is not an easy task, especially in countries where corruption is a way of life. Indeed, a detailed analysis of the extent of bureaucratic corruption in the five ASEAN countries and how their respective governments have tackled this problem has shown that (1) there are two patterns of implementing the anti-corruption measures; and (2) the five countries vary in the effectiveness of their anti-corruption strategies. The first pattern indicates that an anti-corruption law is enacted first, followed later by the creation of the first anti-corruption agency. The second pattern occurs when the reverse happens: the first anti-corruption agency is created before the first anti-corruption law is enacted. The first pattern can be observed in Malaysia and Singapore, while the second pattern applies to Indonesia, the Philippines and Thailand.[30]

An anti-corruption strategy is deemed to be effective if the anti-corruption measures are adequate to deal with the problem and if the political leaders are strongly committed to wiping out corruption in their country. Of the five ASEAN countries, only Singapore and Malaysia have effective anti-corruption strategies. The Philippines has an ineffective anti-corruption strategy because the Marcos government was not committed to eradicating corruption in spite of a vast array of anti-corruption measures available in the country. Indeed, the investigations by the Aquino government after the downfall of the Marcos regime revealed the full extent of their corrupt activities and the plundering of their country's wealth. The anti-corruption strategies of the Indonesian and Thai governments are "hopeless" because the anti-corruption measures are inadequate and their political leaders are not committed to wiping out corruption in their countries.[31]

However, the Singapore case illustrates that it is possible to minimize, if not eliminate, the problem of corruption. Accordingly, countries which are interested in making corruption a fact of life rather than a way of life should take note of the following lessons to be learnt from Singapore's anti-corruption strategy:

The most important lesson is the need for the political leadership to be sincerely committed to the eradication of corruption. This obviously implies that they must demonstrate exemplary conduct (including, perhaps, a modest life-style) and should not indulge in corrupt behavior themselves. Furthermore, anyone found guilty of corruption must be punished, regardless of his position or status in society. If the rich or powerful are protected from prosecution for corrupt behavior, the anti-corruption strategy is defective because it permits a double standard in the enforcement of the anti-corruption laws.

The second lesson to be drawn is the importance of adopting a comprehensive rather than a piecemeal or incremental approach to the problem. Corruption is a serious problem which may require major surgery, not a minor operation. Anti-corruption measures must be comprehensive to prevent loopholes and must be constantly reviewed for the purpose of introducing further amendments whenever necessary.

The third lesson is the precondition that the anti-corruption agency must itself be incorruptible. It must be controlled or supervised by a political leader who is himself incorruptible. Care must, of course, be taken to recruit and select competent and honest men and women as staff of the anti-corruption agency. To keep the size of the anti-corruption agency's staff manageable, all government departments and ministries should be directed by the incumbent government to provide assistance and cooperation for the anti-corruption agency's efforts in combatting corruption. Obviously, any member of the anti-corruption agency's staff who is guilty of corruption must be punished and removed from the civil service.

The fourth lesson is the necessity of reducing the opportunities for corruption. Those government departments which are usually vulnerable to corrupt activities (such as customs, immigration, internal revenue, and traffic police) should review their procedures periodically in order to reduce opportunities for corruption. Those found guilty of corrupt acts should be promptly punished in order to deter others bent on such behavior.

The final lesson is the importance of reducing the incentive for corruption by keeping the salaries of civil servants and political leaders competitive with the private sector. If a civil servant's salary is low, he is more vulnerable to corruption. Of course, salary revision tends to be costly and will depend on whether the government concerned can afford to do so. In the long run, however, if the salaries remain low, capable civil servants will leave the civil service to join the private sector for higher salaries; the less capable—and most vulnerable—will remain in the civil service out of necessity. For them, the temptation to indulge in corrupt activities to supplement their meager salaries may become irresistible.

In sum, Singapore has succeeded in minimizing the problem of corruption because its anti-corruption strategy is characterized by the following features: (1) *commitment by the political leaders,* especially Prime Minister Lee Kuan Yew, towards the elimination of corruption both within and outside the public bureaucracy; (2) adoption of *comprehensive anti-corruption measures* designed to reduce both the opportunities and need for corruption; and (3) creation and maintenance of an *incorrupt anti-corruption agency* which has honest and competent personnel to investigate corruption cases and to enforce the anti-corruption laws. Singapore's experience in tackling corruption demonstrates the importance of having incorruptible political leaders who are committed to wiping out corruption by enacting comprehensive anti-corruption legislation and by establishing an incorrupt anti-corruption agency to enforce such legislation. The combined weight of these three factors was required to erode the problem of corruption. Otherwise, corruption would have remained a way of life instead of a fact of life.

Notes

1. This distinction was introduced by Gerald E. Caiden in his article, "Public Maladministration and Bureaucratic Corruption," *Hong Kong Journal of Public Administration,* 3, 1 (June 1981), 58–62.
2. S. Rajaratnam, "Bureaucracy versus Kleptocracy," in Arnold J. Heidenheimer (ed.), *Political Corruption: Readings in Comparative Analysis* (New York: Holt, Rinehart and Winston, 1970), p. 547. Rajaratnam was the minister for foreign affairs when he wrote this article. He is now senior minister in the prime minister's office in Singapore.
3. "No Corruption in Singapore and China," *New Nation* (Singapore), November 2, 1977, p. 4.
4. Individual corruption refers to those cases where individuals stray from the prevailing norms of official public behavior. Systemic corruption is "a situation where wrong-doing has become the norm, and the standard accepted behavior necessary to accomplish organizational goals according to notions of public responsibility and trust has become the exception not the rule." Gerald E. Caiden and Naomi J. Caiden, "Administrative Corruption," *Public Administration Review,* 37, 3 (May/June 1977), 306.
5. Peter Jordan, "The 'Mr. Clean' of Asia," *Far Eastern Economic Review* (September 6, 1974), 23.

6. Jon S. T. Quah, "Bureaucratic Corruption in the ASEAN Countries: A Comparative Analysis of Their Anti-Corruption Strategies," *Journal of Southeast Asian Studies,* 13, 1 (March 1982), 161–62.

7. State of Singapore, *Legislative Assembly Debates,* First Session of the First Legislative Assembly, Vol. 12 (Singapore: Government Printing Office, 1960), 13 February 1960, cols. 376–77.

8. For more details, see Jon S. T. Quah, "Administrative and Legal Measures for Combatting Bureaucratic Corruption in Singapore," (Singapore: Department of Political Science, University of Singapore, Occasional Paper No. 34, 1978), pp. 14–15.

9. The 1986 exchange rate is S$2.2 = US$1.

10. For example, section 15 of the POCA gave CPIB officers powers of arrest and search of arrested persons. They did not have such powers during the CPIB's first eight years of operation. Section 17 empowered the Public Prosecutor to authorize the CPIB Director and senior special investigators to examine "any bank account, share account or purchase account" of any person suspected of having committed an offense against the POCA. Section 18 provided for the inspection by CPIB officers of a civil servant's banker's book and those of his wife, child or agent, if necessary. *Ibid.,* pp. 11–12.

11. *Ibid.,* p. 13.

12. *Straits Times* (Singapore), October 26, 1981, p. 1.

13. Republic of Singapore, *The Budget for the Financial Year 1986/87* (Singapore: Singapore National Printers, 1986), pp. 551–52.

14. Quah, "Administrative and Legal Measures for Combatting Bureaucratic Corruption in Singapore," p. 15.

15. Government of the Republic of Singapore, *Instruction Manual No. 2 Staff,* Section L, "Conduct and Discipline," paragraphs 120–24; Finance Circular No. 25/73 (Try S9/4–005), "Measures Recommended to Prevent Corruption for General Observation and Compliance by Departments," dated 24 July, 1973.

16. "Architect told: talk to your lawyer after you leave CPIB," *Straits Times* April 8, 1971, p. 8.

17. "Shipyard chief tells of CPIB 'threats'," *Straits Times,* April 27, 1971, p. 6.

18. " 'Different CPIB treatment' claim," *Straits Times,* May 1, 1971.

19. " 'I was tortured by CPIB' charge by ex-warrant officer," *Sunday Times,* August 15, 1971, p. 7.

20. "Weeping witness tells court of alleged assault," *Straits Times,* November 16, 1973, p. 24.

21. "Accused tells of 'cold room' threat," *Straits Times,* January 31, 1974, p. 11.

22. "Man tells of detention threat by CPIB officer," *Straits Times,* November 19, 1976, p. 17.

23. Saw Puay-Lim, "Rebuke for over-zealous CPIB officers," *Straits Times,* November 27, 1976, p. 8.

24. Ralph Braibanti, "Reflections on Bureaucratic Corruption," *Public Administration* (London), 40 (Winter 1962), 357–72.

25. The basic salary of the most junior civil servant (a newly appointed junior clerk) in Indonesia is Rp. 12,000 (US$19.50) per month, while the most

senior civil servant (a senior administrator with twenty-four years of experience) receives a monthly salary of Rp. 120,000 (US$195). See Cyrus Manurung, "The Public Personnel System in Indonesia," in Amara Raksa-sataya and Heinrich Siedentopf (eds.), *Asian Civil Services* (Kuala Lumpur: Asian and Pacific Development Administration Center, 1980), p. 162.

26. Peter Y. S. Tan, "Recruitment for the Civil Service," *Kesatuan Bulletin,* 12 (July 1973), p. 5.
27. See *Straits Times,* February 14, 1981, p. 1 and *Sunday Times,* February 21, 1982, p. 1.
28. Ministry of Culture, *Singapore 1983* (Singapore: Information Division, Ministry of Culture, 1983), p. 40.
29. *Straits Times,* March 23, 1985, pp. 14–16.
30. Quah, "Bureaucratic Corruption in the ASEAN Countries," pp. 173–74.
31. *Ibid.,* pp. 175–76.

49

Bureaucratic and Political Corruption Controls: Reassessing The German Record

Ulrich von Alemann

Corruption—an Alien Term in Germany?

Until recently, corruption seemed to have died out in German politics and to be unknown in German political science. None of the specialist dictionaries—even not latest editions—carries entries on corruption or bribery. No German introduction to political science considers corruption as being worth mentioning, and none of the recent textbooks on the political system of the Federal Republic has dealt with corruption. Has the Federal Republic really advanced to a European model democracy? A few years ago the book *Germany Transformed: Political Culture and the New Politics* advertised that: "A new Germany has come of age, democratic, sophisticated, affluent, and modern."[1] Its citizens are also portrayed as cleancut, participatory and deeply democratic in the international comparisons of data in *Political Action*.[2] Has the Federal Republic ascended to become a model prototype of democratic polity?

In the mid-1980s—only a few years after the publication of the above books—German newspapers are full of revelations of financial affairs and political scandals that focus on illegal donations to parties, tax evasion, and suspicion of corruption. Representatives of the industrial group Flick, at the time one of the largest private companies in the Federal Republic, have been shown as ingratiating themselves by means of cash payments to politicians and parties in Bonn for decades. Two former ministers of economics have recently had to appear in courts under suspicion of corruption. In Berlin, legal proceedings carried out by courts and special commissions have linked offenses such as attempted murder, prostitution, tax evasion, arson, and black-mailing with dubious donations to parties and political corruption.[3]

Scandal literature prospered, with book titles such as: *The Corrupt Republic, The Purchased Republic, The End of Morality in Commercial Society,* or *Corruption in World History.*[4] Only recently have two serious books concerning this topic been published in the Federal Republic.[5] In general, Austrian literature has been more fruitful; Fleck and Kuzmics, the editors of one ambitious volume that can be considered the best German language social science publication on political corruption, are Austrian.

This lack of treatment requires explanation. This paucity can neither be attributed to the nonexistence of corruption during the first three decades of the Federal Republic, nor to lack of expertise in political science.

Of the senior scholars in German political science in the post-1945 period, two gave special attention to corruption. Theodor Eschenburg demonstrated and examined factual findings of corruption in the first period of the Federal Republic, although more in newspaper articles than in his political science books.[6] Thus Eschenburg remained a serious critic and steadfast moralist rather than an analyst of corruption. The second great scholar examining political corruption was the German-American Carl J. Friedrich, whose *Pathology of Politics* was translated into German, but curiously made little impact on German political science, whereas his earlier works enjoyed widespread reception.[7]

In the 1980s corruption has been a topic of "muck-raking" by committed journalists and by a few academic outsiders but not by political scientists—regardless of whether they are empiricists or institutionalists, critical theoreticians or affirmative apologists of the system, radical or conservative. To explain the paradox between the hot debate on political corruption in the German public on the one hand, and the weak interest of the professional scientists of politics on the other, it is necessary to give a description of the forms of political corruption in Germany. This chapter seeks to contribute by clarifying concepts and questions, outlining the historic development of corruption in Germany, and relating the most important cases and types of political corruption of recent times.

Concepts and Questions

Corruption is a term of dispute in the German language, blocking conceptual precision and engendering political controversy. This makes an analysis in the field of political science rather difficult. It is not a term for legal proceedings, because the proper term of the German *Beamtenrecht* (civil service law) is not corruption, but 'bribery.' Under the entry of corruption, the largest German encyclopedia refers the reader to entries on the legal definitions of bribery. In fact, political corruption seems to be a term without indigenous root in the German language.

The civil service law—having its origins in the predemocratic period of the Prussian monarchy—stylized the pride of the incorruptible civil servant to an ideal type of the rational legal rule of bureaucracy: "its ideal is to decree 'sine ira et studio,' without any influence of personal motives or emotional influence, free of arbitrariness and incalculabilities, especially 'without regard to the person' in a strongly formalistic way according to rational rules and—where those fail to be applied—according to 'factual' consideration of expediency."[8]

Correspondingly, the civil service law stipulates heavy penalties within the criminal code. An act of bribery is committed when an office holder is offered, promised, or granted an advantage (not only money) in return for an action which has already been carried out or is to be expected. Moreover, a civil servant risks punishment should he derive advantage by linking an official duty with a service in return, even though he fulfills his duty correctly. Consequently, civil service bribery is graded according to its severity as follows: (1) Accepting advantage *(Vorteilsannahme)* is punishable, if a civil servant demands advantages, accepts the promise of advantage, or accepts advantage for an otherwise official duty which is left at his discretion. Conversely, someone commits an offense if he offers an advantage to a civil servant *(Vorteilsgewaehrung)*. This offense of simple bribery can be punished with a maximum imprisonment of two years. (2) Corruptibility (passive bribery) of a civil servant occurs if he demands advantage, accepts the promise of advantage, or accepts advantage for a breach of duty—even if the action will not be carried out. Conversely, offering a bribe to a civil servant is also punishable. This severe type of bribery is generally sanctioned with imprisonment of between three months and five years.

However, civil service bribery cannot be equated with the concept of political corruption. Indeed, criminal acts as described above very rarely result in indictments. Even if investigated by the prosecuting attorney, the criminal acts rarely lead to formal charges. Criminal acts such as granting advantage and bribery range at the tail end of the statistics in regard to the frequency of preferral of charges.[9]

Having the option of choosing between narrower or wider definitions, I will adopt an intermediate position. An extremely narrow definition seems unsuitable to me for the recent German discussion and the political situation. It is not the juridical fact of bribery in the form of a civil servant being handed a bank note by a private person in return for a certain act which is primarily interesting for us. The interdependency of corruptive acting is much more important, irrespective of whether the initiative is taken by a private person or a civil servant. Not only the civil servants but especially the politicians—as deputies, party politicians or members of government—must be considered.

Among recent definitional attempts that of David Bayley appears to be a reasonable one. According to his definition, "corruption while being tied particularly to bribery, is a general term covering misuse of authority as a result of considerations of personal gain, which need not be monetary."[10] Consequently, bearers of state authority can be addressees of as well as participants in political corruption. Based on this concept of political corruption, the main theses and questions of this contribution are to be formulated.

Theodor Eschenburg's depiction of political corruption in the Federal Republic published in 1959 began with the sentence: "The Germans, spoiled by an extremely honest public administration for more than a century and a half, are sensitive to charges of corruption even today."[11] I claim exactly the opposite. To my mind, German civil servants and politicians have not been "extremely honest" in the course of the last 150 years, nor has the general public been "very sensitive" toward political corruption—especially not in recent years. Both theses need to be proved.

Disputing Theodor Eschenburg does not at all imply a questioning of his merits as one of the most severe critics of bribery, nepotism, and the spoils system in the Federal Republic. His problem is, however, that he adheres too strongly to the ideal type of German *Berufsbeamtentum* (civil service with tenure) in the sense of Max Weber, when, for example, he concludes that, "Thanks to the good tradition of the German civil service which is still effective even today, bribery, the real corruption, has become comparatively rare."[12]

Political Corruption in German History

"The Germans have always nurtured a faith that theirs is one of those nations that has proved to be most resistant to corruption."[13] Nonetheless, a few examples will illustrate that political corruption has occurred under all German regimes, even though certain forms of voting bribery and buying one's way into office through corrupt party machine politics have only rarely occurred in German history in the past 150 years.

The German Reich 1871–1918

Low-level corruption of government officials was much less frequent in Germany than in the Austro-Hungarian monarchy or in imperial Russia. However, this is a tribute less to the professional ethics of the German civil servants than to the fact that they were paid according to the "principle of maintenance" *(Alimentationsprinzip)* which provided a reasonable standard of living.

But numerous cases of top level corruption did occur. Otto von Bismarck, admired by conservative historians as an incarnation of German statesmanship, mixed money and politics very extensively. Even the foundation of the empire and the coronation of the German emperor in 1871 were based on bribery: After the Prussian-Danish war, the fortune of the Hanoverian royal court and all payments made in compensation for the abdication were confiscated by Prussia and seized by the Prussian prime minister for a secret fund. This secret fund, which had originally been called *Welfenfonds* and was renamed later on as the "reptile fund," could be spent by the Prussian prime minister, and later Reich Chancellor Bismarck, without any parliamentary control "in order to defeat and ward off activities aimed against Prussia."

The most spectacular use of funds—which was only revealed decades afterward and the authenticity of which has been questioned by some pro-Bismarck historians—was the bribing of the Bavarian King Ludwig II. This extravagant potentate received approximately 4.7 million Reichsmark in the course of some years to support the coronation of Wilhelm I as emperor, even though the eccentric Bavarian king detested the idea of a Prussian emperor. Needing money for his costly castles, the king had no other choice but to accept Bismarck's political blackmailing in order to avoid bankruptcy.

In the course of the years Bismarck's reptile fund fed a remarkable number of secret financial activities: a secret central news agency at the Prussian prime minister's office was financed to procure political information on socialist and anarchist forces; journalists were paid to influence parties and public opinion in accordance with Bismarck (if the desired effect did not occur, complete newspapers and news agencies were bought); and politicians of the conservative, liberal, and Catholic center parties, and even the socialists, were bribed if it served the policy of alliances.

Under Bismarck's successors after 1890, rapid industrial expansion caused intensive conflicts involving the interests of the heavy industry, the consumer goods industry, the big landowners, and the export industry. The big corporations, especially Krupp—which was very active in the field of armaments—carried out intensive corruption of civil servants, politicians, and journalists, by means of (among others) a "disposition fund for industrial purposes" run by the director of the board of Krupp. The first cartels, especially the *Centralverband Deutscher Industrieller* (CDI), not only intervened in the personnel policy of the liberal and conservative parties, but also financed election campaigns, bought influence on the press and not rarely bribed civil servants. The election funds of heavy industry increased year by year. During the last decade before World War I, approximately 4 million Reichsmark flowed from the CDI to 120 candidates of sympathetic parties.

Weimar Republic and National Socialism 1918–1945

Systemic and structural conditions for the specific German forms of political corruption were not completely different after the change in regime in 1918. A secret fund which existed up to the 1930s and was called the "big pot" was filled by the big companies in order to finance briberies, with the purpose of supporting activities of radical right-wing groups and "volunteer groups" against the democratic state during the initial years of the republic. Even the attempted coups d'etat by Kapp in 1920 and Hitler in 1923 were supported by money coming from the big companies Stinnes and Thyssen. From 1928 onward a secret fund of the Rhine-Westphalian heavy industry, the *Ruhrlade,* in which such companies as Krupp, Thyssen, and Kloeckner were represented, bribed the conservative and liberal parties.

Much has been speculated and written about the role of corruption in the process of Hitler's rise being financed by big industry. Certainly the Weimar Republic did not perish merely because big industry made hidden payments to Hitler. It was only shortly before his *MachtUbernahme* in 1933 that Hitler gained the full approval of big industry and access to its circles. Before that he had been financed by individual industrialists such as Thyssen, Kierdorf, and Flick. It is certain, however, that the funds of big industry had intensely supported all anti-republic and anti-democratic groups from the very beginning, and thus had helped to undermine the establishment and stabilization of the first German democracy.

Many examples of top-level corruption can be seen throughout the Third Reich. The leaders of the Reich, especially Hermann Goering, made money for themselves by taking donations from industry: "The Nazi leaders, whose corrupt behavior was an open secret to many people, utilized protection of a state which was non-democratic and non-liberal. Even justified criticism of office holders was forbidden. Consequently the breeding-ground for corruption was ideal."[14]

The most macabre cases of low-level corruption took place in the concentration camps and the extermination camps, in which members of the SS and other squads on guard received the prisoners' properties in exchange for promises to spare them, or in which the prisoners themselves bribed the squads on guard.[15]

Drawing an interim conclusion of this historical survey, we can conclude that the Germans were neither spoiled by the absence of corruption, nor did they react especially sensitively to it. The special professional ethics which had been upheld by Weber and later on by Eschenburg did indeed reduce low-level corruption in the administration and police. However, it did not prevent political corruption at the top-level, either in the empire, in the Weimar Republic, or during National Socialism.

Corruption in the Federal Republic

Two essential conditions for the analysis of political corruption remained unchanged in the transition from the Third Reich to the Federal Republic: an economic system based on private industry, and a traditional civil service. Apart from that, however, many things have changed. The "belated nation" has caught up with other nations in terms of solid democratic structures and institutions, societal and social change, as well as stabilizing economic success.[16] Despite the democratic transformation of West Germany there are still symptoms of crisis, institutional weaknesses, and ideological encrustings.

The Civil Service

Although the percentage of civil servants sentenced for corruptness is extremely low—in 1956 2.6 out of 100,000 civil servants are said to have been sentenced for bribery[17]—the ideal image of the incorruptible civil servant shows gaps. In the period of the early Federal Republic, comparatively harmless incidents were vehemently discussed, focusing on minor advantages such as a car lent to a civil servant free-of-charge. Especially by the criticism of Theodor Eschenburg, the "Kilb case" has become part of the literature. That this became a topic of discussion resulted from the fact that the chancellor himself was aware that advantage had been granted. "With or without approval, a civil servant in Kilb's position simply cannot afford to do anything that is not permitted to other civil servants. His bad example can undermine the good morals of the others."[18]

Several proceedings against employees and officers of the army's supply office in Koblenz were more serious. In the course of the rearmament of the Federal Republic after 1954, there was great temptation for German industry to influence the expanding military needs. More than 100 proceedings on bribery were taken against employees and civil servants of the procurement agency. The dimensions of these small scandals appear to be insignificant compared with the larger international cases of military corruption, such as the Lockheed affair, in which the Federal Republic's peculiar involvement has never been clarified. The affair about the infantry tank HS 30 of the Swiss company Hispano-Suiza, which was ordered by the army in 1957 and proved to be completely unsuitable, has never been resolved. As in the Lockheed case, millions in bribe money are said to have flowed to civil servants, and the former minister of defense, Franz Josef Strauss, is said to have been involved in both cases.[19]

Beyond these speculative incidents which were revealed by the critical press, especially by *Der Spiegel*, there have been many opportunities for corruption and civil service bribery at the local and regional levels. The construction industry in the communes has been especially susceptible to corruption. There are numerous examples of corruption of communal office bearers by construction companies in regard to building enterprises and property speculators. In the cities of Frankfurt, Berlin, Hamburg, or the Ruhr district, some of the cases gained a broader publicity and political explosiveness. In smaller towns the main feature of corruption is generally even more effective: corruption grows in places hard to find.

The most recent phenomenon of the 1980s was the uncovering of a large nest of corruption within the police that was heretofore hardly imaginable in Germany. Entire departments of the highway police had regularly demanded that truck drivers hand over goods; in return the police refrained from doing their routine checks. The public was baffled by such incidents of corruption among civil servants and was not sure whether to draw parallels to medieval robber barons or to highwaymen of the Wild West in the United States.

Members of Parliament

According to a federal law of 1949, bribery of members of parliament has not been punishable since 1953. Especially since the 1970s there has been intense juridical discussion, but it has not led to legal regulations.[20] There is no incompatibility between private income and mandate, as can be found in many other countries. Since the "code of honour" decree for deputies in 1972, there has only been a very restrictive obligation for making private income transparent to the public. All additional income has to be declared to the president of the Bundestag, but not to the public. Since 1980 consulting contracts with private firms have also been covered. The following regulation has agreed upon in the Bundestag: "A member of parliament is not permitted to enter legal obligations for which payment is given to him, not for rendering particular services but only with the expectation of using his mandate to represent the payer's interests in the Bundestag, and—if possible—to successfully promote these interests."[21]

Bribery of members of parliament is a particularly difficult grey area, overlapping with the lobbying and pressure politics of the business interests. Can a member of parliament who wants to obtain an industrial enterprise for his constituency be called corrupt if this company gives donations to his election campaign? What if this member of parliament is a member of that company and has professional advantages? Not all policies or interests must necessarily be corrupt despite the fact that advantages were willingly granted. The grey area of corruption begins only when illegal or unethical advantages are granted and hidden from the public.

Money given to a few representatives of the small Bavarian party is alleged to have played an important part as early as 1949 in the course of the decision to make Bonn rather than Frankfurt the Federal capital. This party was finally ruined by the "gambling casino scandal," in which individual Bavarian politicians accepted high bribes to issue concessions. Some of them were given considerably severe prison sentences—in fact, this was the only case in the history of the Federal Republic in which a party politician was sent to prison for corruption.[22]

The most serious cases of bribery of representatives have occurred after the change of government in 1969. Especially in the years of the active *Ostpolitik* between 1970 and 1972, the social-liberal coalition had to accept that about a dozen deputies of the ruling parties changed allegiances to the opposition. The narrow majority of the government in the Bundestag faded away. FDP representative Geldner, for example, was offered a safe seat in the next Bundestag as well as a consulting contract with a company for DM 400,000. Geldner only pretended to accept the offer and revealed this attempt at bribery, although the participants denied their activities.

In 1972 a backbencher of the CDU faction, Steiner, maintained having received DM 50,000 in cash from the parliamentary whip of the

SPD faction, Karl Wienand, in order to try to foil the attempt to bring down Chancellor Willy Brandt.[23] In 1983 another case of alleged corruption in the Bundestag concerned Rainer Barzel, the same CDU leader who tried in vain to take Brandt's place as chancellor in 1972. Ousted as CDU chancellor candidate, he was made president of the Bundestag. He resigned in 1984 when it was made public that the industrial group Flick had given him a consulting contract for DM 1.7 million, evidently to help persuade him to relinquish the position of CDU chancellor candidate sooner rather than later.

Bribery of members of parliament remains one of the most complicated cases of political corruption. As opposed to American frankness, there exists a prudish inhibition among Germans to make the income of politicians sufficiently transparent by disclosure. Only a few representatives of the SPD as well as of the Greens reveal their income and expenditures.

Ministers and Parties

Only twice in the history of the Federal Republic have federal ministers been accused of involvement in corruption. The first was Franz Josef Strauss. When he was in office between 1956 and 1962 as minister of defense, at least four affairs were connected with his name: the HS-30 affair, the Lockheed affair, the Uncle Aloys affair, and the FIBAG affair. In all cases corruption concerning military supply was affected—infantry tanks, Starfighters, tank chains, and army barracks. However, F.J. Strauss or his party, the CSU, could never be proved to have accepted money in order to achieve personal or political advantages. When he had to resign in 1962, it was not for reasons of corruption but rather for being accused of not having told the truth in the *Spiegel* affair.[24] Since 1978 Strauss has been the chief minister of Bavaria.

The second affair on political corruption hit the headlines for the first time in the late 1970s and has been going on since. It is the Flick affair, which is tightly interwoven with the entire complex of illegal donations to parties and corruption of members of parliament and civil servants. This scandal is put at the end of this survey on political coruption in the Federal Republic because government offices and even the federal cabinet were involved in it.

The Flick affair is a "large network" of political corruption, not an isolated case.[25] It has a historical as well as a current dimension. By studying the historical dimension, it can be shown how a conglomerate has been systematically supporting conservative political groups with large and regular payments of money throughout the Weimar Republic, National Socialism, and the Federal Republic.[26]

From 1969 until 1980 . . . the Flick Corporation made donations to the CDU, the CSU, the FDP, and the SPD as well as to politicians of these parties, amounting to DM 26 million in total. These were apportioned as follows: The CDU/CSU were allotted DM 15 million, the FDP DM 6.5 million, and the SPD, DM 4.5 million. None of these funds has ever been accounted for in any party reports, as they ought to have been according to legal regulations, nor have they been declared to tax authorities. In many cases the money was personally slipped in plain envelopes to top-level politicians such as Helmut Kohl and F.J. Strauss by the Flick representative, von Brauchitsch.

Apart from legal investigations, a Bundestag commission was appointed to clear up the Flick affair. This commission was set up in May 1983 and gave its final report in February 1986. Most members of a parliamentary commission belonged to the ruling parties, who probably wanted to downplay political scandals. The Greens' representative in the commission criticized sharply in a dissenting report that even the SPD opposition had not contributed actively enough in the process of clearing up the factual findings. The final report as well as separately published testimonies and dissenting reports by the SPD and the Greens remain impressive and alarming documents of political corruption in the Federal Republic. The summary of the critical evaluation made in the SPD report charged that the CDU and CSU party leaders, Helmut Kohl and Franz Josef Strauss, have severely offended principles of political culture by accepting large sums of money. It concluded that the treasurers of the CDU, the CSU, the FDP, and the SPD had not offended party law by covering up the origin of the donations. But it also stressed that politicians of the CDU, the CSU, the FDP, as well as the SPD had made themselves too accessible to the requests of the Flick Corporation.[27]

In 1983 party financing was put on a new basis by an amendment of the party law. According to this law, tax-deductible donations to parties of up to DM 100,000 annually can be made by persons and enterprises. This law, however, also stipulates that large donations which are not made public according to the existing regulations will be punished more severely. The basic law was changed to the effect that parties must give public account not only about their incomes, but also their expenditures. Surprisingly, this law was by and large accepted in 1986 by the federal constitutional court, which earlier had practiced more restrictive interpretations. Two judges of the federal constitutional court, however, evaluated the decision in their dissenting opinions as follows: The constitutional court has smoothed the way for individuals or groups having specific interests and big capital to exert influence on the development of political opinion in combination with tax-relief."[28] Does this mean that political corruption as a means of financially promoting the development of political opinion is being made socially acceptable once and for all?

Otto Schily, a deputy of the Green party, was the only one to use the term "political corruption" for his overall evaluation of the influence of the Flick Corporation in the report of the investigating commission:

> "The most important instrument used by the Flick Corporation to gain and secure political influence on parties and politicians was to make donations in the amount of millions of Deutschmarks according to patterns which had proven to be efficient hitherto. By means of donations the Flick Corporation has gained fields of influence systematically, so that it must be stated that political corruption on a large scale is involved, regardless of whether the punishable act of bribery or corruptibility has been realized in one or another case. By means of the conspiratorial money distributed by the Flick Corporation, the benefitting parties gained a remarkable financial advantage compared with their political competitors. The fact that these donations were concealed from the public is a massive intervention into the process of the formation of political opinion."[29]

Both these reports precisely point out the central problems of the political corruption carried out by the Flick Corporation. Meanwhile the Flick Corporation no longer exists. Friedrich Karl Flick, heir of the Flick Corporation and sole proprietor, surprisingly sold the company in 1986. The Flick affair, however, will long outlive the corporation.

Political Culture and Political Corruption

Both of the assumptions made by Theodor Eschenburg—first, that the Germans have been spoiled by an extremely honest administration for 150 years, and second, that they have been especially sensitive to the charge of corruption—are hardly tenable. In particular, the political sensitiveness toward political corruption leaves a great deal to be desired. Those parties, namely the CDU/CSU and the FDP, which profited most from illegal party donations were able to win the federal parliamentary elections with a distinct majority at the climax of the scandal in spring 1983, and have been ruling since then without any contest. Only a minor critical part of the public reacted in a sensitive and alarmed way. Does that mean that the Federal Republic is a "Republic for Sale" or a "Corrupt Republic," as the relevant scandal literature has tried to convey? Or has the Federal Republic even turned into a state which incurs "political corruption as a means of self-destruction"?[30]

However, scandals revealing political corruption do at least indicate the existence of a capacity of coping with political problems, a capacity not present in all systems. Neither the scandal itself nor the factual finding of political corruption are symptoms of decay; the chances of uncovering and clearing up these scandals are the decisive factors.

Political corruption is almost inevitable in a political culture—and that is exactly what must be learned by the political public and taught by political scientists. As long as the chance of revealing and clearing up such scandals is maintained, the social system will not be destroyed by political corruption. Consequently, when political corruption can be scandalized publicly, this cannot directly be considered a symptom of the decline of political morals and decay, as insinuated by scandal literature.

German political science has so far faced political scandals and corruption rather helplessly.[31] However, this shady side of power must be allocated much more attention—not only by research in the fields of political culture, but also in the fields of parliamentarism, parties, interest groups, and political and constitutional theory.

Notes

I thank Göttrik Wewer, Ralf Kleinfeld, and Ingeborg Voss for their helpful comments on drafts of this article.
1. Kendall L. Baker, Russell J. Dalton, and Kai Hildebrandt, *Germany Transformed: Political Culture and the New Politics* (Cambridge MA: Harvard University Press, 1981).
2. Samuel H. Barnes, May Kaase, et al., *Political Action: Mass Participation in Five Western Democracies* (Beverly Hills: Sage, 1979).
3. Michael Sontheimer, "Das ist der Berliner Sumpf," *Die Zeit*, No. 6 (Jan. 31, 1986), 12–16.
4. Siegfried Bluth, *Die korrupte Republik: Ein politisches und wirtschaftliches Sittengemälde* (Esslingen: Fleischmann (1983); Hans Werner Kilz, and Joachim Preuss, *Flick: Die gekaufte Republik* (Hamburg: Rowohlt 1983); Hans-Peter Wadrich, *Von wegen weisse Weste: Das Ende der Moral in der Kommerzgesellschaft* (Freiburg: Dreisam 1985); and Alfred Sturminger, *Die Korruption in der Weltgeschichte* (München/Wien: Langer-Müller, 1982).
5. Paul Noack, *Korruption: Die andere Seite der Macht* (München: Kindler, 1985); Christian Fleck, and Helmut Kuzmics (eds.), *Korruption: Zur Soziologie nicht immer abweichenden Verhaltens* (Königstein: Athenäum, 1985); and Christian Brünner (ed.), *Korruption und Kontrolle* (Wien: Böhlau, 1981). The best short review of the recent German literature on

corruption is given by Richard Albrecht, "Politische Korruption," *Politische Vierteljahresschrift-Literatur*, 27, 1, (1986), 36–43.

6. Theodor Eschenburg, "The Decline of Bureaucratic Ethos in the Federal Republic," and "German Attempts at the Legal Definition of Parliamentary Corruption," in Arnold J. Heidenheimer (ed.), *Political Corruption: Readings in Comparative Analysis* (New York: Holt, Rinehart and Winston, 1970), pp. 259–65, 404–408; cf. his books *Ämterpatronage* (Stuttgart: Schwab, 1961); and *Staat und Gesellschaft in Deutschland* (Stuttgart: Schwab, 1956).

7. Carl J. Friedrich, *The Pathology of Politics* (New York: Harper & Row, 1972) and *Pathologie der Politik: Die Funktion der Missstände: Gewalt, Verrat, Korruption, Geheimhaltung, Propaganda* (Frankfurt: Herder & Herder, 1973).

8. Max Weber, "Die drei reinen Typen der legitimen Herrschaft," in J. Winckelmann (ed.), *Soziologie, Weltgeschichtliche Analysen, Politik* (Stuttgart: Kröner, 1964), p. 152.

9. Bluth, p. 180. The federal minister of the interior, Gerhard Schröder, calculated a quota of one in 1,000 civil servants susceptible to corruption in 1959, cf. Noack, p. 129.

10. See, Introduction to Chapter One.

11. Eschenburg, in Heidenheimer (1970) p. 259.

12. Eschenburg, in *Staat und Gesellschaft* (1956), p. 699.

13. Noack, p. 113.

14. Leo Menne, "Korruption," *Kölner Zeitschrift für Soziologie und Sozialpsychologie*, 1, (1948), 144–88.

15. Cases of corruption in the Nazi-SS are reported by Heinz Höhne, *Der Orden unter dem Totenkopf: Die Geschichte der SS* (München: Goldmann, (1978), p. 354.

16. Ralf Dahrendorf, *Society and Democracy in Germany* (Garden City: Doubleday, 1967).

17. Noack, p. 135.

18. Eschenburg, in Heidenheimer (1970), p. 262f.

19. Bluth, p. 118f.

20. Cf. the earlier discussion in Eschenburg [in Heidenheimer (1970), p. 404–408]; Jörg Detlef Küne, *Die Abgeordnetenbestechung* (Frankfurt: Athenäum, 1971).

21. Klaus Troltsch, "Der Verhaltenskodex von Abgeordneten in westlichen Demokratien," *Aus Politik und Zeitgeschichte*, No. 24/25 (1985), 14.

22. Konstanze Wolf, *CSU und Bayernpartei: Ein besonderes Konkurrenzverhältnis 1948–1960* (Köln: Verlag Wissenschaft und Politik, 1982), p. 205.

23. Noack, p. 144.

24. Bluth, pp. 118–20.

25. Noack, pp. 160–78; more details on the Flick scandal are provided by Kilz/Preuss; Wagner; and Rainer Burchardt, Hans-Jürgen Schlamp, Flick-Zeugen, *Protokolle aus dem Untersuchungsauschuss* (Reinbek: Rowohlt, 1985). Despite some attempts at window dressing the investigation of the Bundestag committee provides a very interesting documentation of the Flick case: cf. Deutscher Bundestag, Drucksache 10/5079.

26. Ulrike Hörster-Philips, *Im Schatten des Grossen Geldes: Flick-Konzern und Politik* (Köln: Pahl-Rugenstein, 1985).

27. Deutscher Bundestag, *op. cit,* p. 297.

28. Ulrich von Alemann, "Grenzen für das Geld der Parteien," *Das Parlament,* Sept. 19, 1986, p. 18.

29. Deutscher Bundestag, Abweichender Bericht des Abgeordneten Schily zum Bericht des 1. Untersuchungsausschusses, Drucksache 10/5079, Anlage 1, p. 19.

30. Noack, p. 179.

31. Göttrik Wewer, "Parteienfinanzierung und Rechtspflege—einige Thesen zugleich eine Aufforderung an die Politikwissenschaft mitzudiskutieren," *Politische Vierteljahresschrift* 25 (1984), p. 320; Ulrich von Alemann, "Politische Moral und politische Kultur in der Bundesrepublik—vergiften oder reinigen Skandale die Politik?" *Gewerkschaftliche Monatshefte,* 36, 5 (1985), 258–69.

Scandals: An Introduction

Leaders of anti-corruption efforts have powerful symbols and appeals at their disposal. This section addresses the political logic of responses to corruption, with a particular emphasis upon scandal and its political uses. If an active sense of scandal can be harnessed, directed and sustained by anti-corruption forces, then their reforms have a better chance of being enacted, and of being vigorously enforced. Whether or not these reforms are appropriate and soundly constructed is another question; scandal may give rise to "quick fixes" which cause their own sets of problems. In any event, an active sense of public scandal may be difficult to create, and even harder to control once it has come into being.

Graeme Moodie, in the opening chapter, is aware of these complexities, and he argues that while corruption and scandal may seem to naturally go together, they are in fact two quite different things. Corruption may occur without ever coming to light, or may elicit little mass response if it does become known. In other cases, the public may perceive serious wrongdoing where none exists, or where misconduct has been modest by formal standards, and may make a serious issue of it. The labeling of behavior as scandalous thus involves many complexities over and above the specific rules and conduct involved. Scandal may indeed be a powerful weapon in long-standing disputes among factions, parties, or communal groups—again, whether or not "corruption" as formally defined has actually occurred.

In the next chapter, Lawrence Sherman, who has extensively studied the politics of police corruption in American cities, gives us examples of the way scandal can be put to use. Simply to allege serious misconduct is not enough; successful mobilizations of a public sense of scandal entail careful political and public-relations tactics. Moreover, scandal must be sustained, for short-lived reactions, however sharp, will not provide the continuing political backing necessary to remove politically entrenched figures and to implement new policies. For these reasons, the cast of players in a corruption-scandal-reform cycle can be large and diverse, and these players' motives and agendas will not always coincide. No two cases will be alike, but Sherman's analysis points to the political difficulties and opportunities confronting anyone hoping to mount a political effort against corruption.

Erhard Blankenburg, Rainer Staudhammer and Heinz Steinert then examine applications of corruption labels in the context of scandals that emerged from abuses in the West German system of party financing. Building on labelling theory, they perceive inherent relationships between corruption incidence and scandalization, while granting that they can vary independently of each other. The corruption charges they deal with grew out of under-the-table financial donations given particularly by the Flick Corporation to leading German ministers and politicians, but also by other donors who sought to avoid legal rules for disclosure. The framework is contests between parties and judges about the constitutionality of legislation that both regulated and subsidized political parties. They show how changing judicial definitions affected scandalization potential, which in turn affected perceptions of corruption.

50

On Political Scandals and Corruption

Graeme C. Moodie

Scandal and corruption are customarily thought of in much the same ways as pigs and whistles; they go together. Strangely, however, academic studies of corruption seem to pay little attention to scandal.[1] It is strange if only because in societies like this corruption tends to be obscure, a condition in which its participants wish it to remain, and it is to the occasional scandal that we are indebted for what knowledge is generally accessible. This is particularly true in Britain where the major scandals have usually been followed (sometimes illuminated) by official inquiries; certainly that has been the practice in this century from the Marconi shares scandal in 1913 to the Poulson scandal 60 years later which spawned both a committee and a royal commission.[2] A closer look at the incidence of political scandal, this chapter will suggest, is an additional tool for the study of corruption and perhaps particularly so for comparative studies. A more fundamental (and more widely canvassed) problem, however, is to define corruption so as to facilitate reliable comparisons across temporal and cultural boundaries. We will first discuss that problem.

Current writing about political corruption tends to leave aside that wide notion of corruption as deterioration or decay which, for example, preoccupied Plato and Machiavelli; it is concerned more commonly with a narrower range of transgressions by holders of office. Heidenheimer suggests that virtually all the definitions encountered in the modern literature can be grouped under one or other of three headings: public-office-centered, market-centered and public-interest centered. The emphasis is behavioral in all cases, and there seems to be a near consensus round the public-office kind of definition. One example is the definition put forward by J.S. Nye as: 'behavior which deviates from the normal duties of a public role because of private

Source: Graeme C. Moodie. "On Political Scandals and Corruption," *Government and Opposition,* 15, 2 (Spring, 1980) 202–22. By permission of the publisher.

regarding . . . , pecuniary or status gains; or violates rules against the exercise of certain types of private-regarding influence. This includes such behavior as bribery . . . ; nepotism . . . ; and misappropriation. . . .'[3] Similar, but incorporating an allusion to the public interest, is Friedrich's usage. In discussing the core meaning of the term he says that corruption occurs 'whenever a power holder who is charged with doing certain things, that is a responsible functionary or office holder, is by monetary or other rewards, . . . induced to take actions which favor whoever provides the reward and thereby damage the group or organization to which the functionary belongs'.[4] Despite the proper warning that 'the search for the true definition of corruption is, like the pursuit of the Holy Grail, endless, exhausting and ultimately futile'[5] it is still necessary to devote more space to the pursuit of a serviceable one.

The main problem is that definitions like Nye's seem to be too culture-bound to permit comparative studies either across time (Britain today and in the eighteenth century, for example, when many of the practices he instances were not considered corrupt) or across cultures (in particular, Western and many developing countries where, for example, 'nepotism' is an obligation or a small bribe is no more corrupt than a tip is thought to be in the average European restaurant). There is much to be said for operating only with local standards—defining corruption as what is thought to be so in any given society. But this option seems to impede comparative studies of corruption and it is evidently difficult to eschew evaluations of some of the practices encountered or to avoid intruding a more constant element in ideas of corruption. Thus, in a well-known article,[6] Colin Leys stresses the relativity of norms, but also suggests that 'the idea of a society economically stagnating in the grip of a self-seeking and *corrupt* elite is not a pure fantasy' (emphasis not in the original), which seems to imply a more universal meaning to the term. Somewhat similarly, R.J. Williams, in the article from which I have already quoted, first suggests that, in contradistinction to the United States, 'in most African states, it is the pursuit and possession of political power which enables its wielders to acquire private wealth', an activity he seems to hold is not corrupt (i.e. by the relevant local standards), and then proceeds to suggest that 'in the African context at least, a politically indoctrinated bureaucracy may be a better safeguard against corruption than an allegedly impartial one.' Whether to use 'corruption' in a completely relative sense or in a more stable and transcendent one is, it seems, a very sharp dilemma.

The problem exists, of course, within societies as well as between them. George W. Plunkitt's distinction between honest and dishonest graft is well known.[7] The key to his distinction may thus be paraphrased (somewhat euphemistically): any public worker, contract, or real estate development will provide some private individuals and groups with jobs, windfall profits or other accidental benefits. 'Honest graft' ensures that such inevitable private benefit is deliberately and not accidentally channelled in particular directions. Dishonest graft would also involve cheating, short-changing, stealing, adulteration of service or such other conventionally immoral behavior. One does not need to go all the way with Plunkitt to agree that corruption is not always particularly immoral any more than it is always illegal. "One does not condemn a Jew for bribing his way out of a concentration camp," to take a particularly clear example.[8]

Motive, intention and context thus enter into our judgments even about domestic corruption. Generally, too, they seem to affect the ease or difficulty with which we draw the line of acceptability between various practices: between (say) contributing to Nixon's secret campaign funds in 1972 in return for the dropping of an anti-trust law case and a British trade union's increased contribution to the Labour Party's election fund in 1974 because it agreed with Labour policy towards industrial relations legislation; between filling civil service posts with one's kith and kin in West Africa, appointing other former pupils of one's exclusive school to positions in a British cabinet, and using one's children as aides-de-camp (as Churchill and F.D. Roosevelt did) or as roving presidential ambassadors (as Carter does); or between giving a statesman the pen with which he signs a treaty, giving a standard discount to all buyers,[9] and winning a contract for the sale of aircraft by massive and selective bribery at the highest levels of government and public office.

The problem of relativity can, however, be overstated. It need not vitiate comparative studies provided only that care is taken with the terms of the comparison. One approach, suggested by David H. Bayley,[10] is to stick to the customary denotations of the term as used in the West, namely, bribery, nepotism and misappropriation. He defends this usage because many Third World elites tend to think of corruption in the same terms and because, unlike purely relative definitions, this does not muddy communication. Unfortunately he still is culture bound in continuing to regard all these practices as examples of corruption. One relatively simple solution for the comparative student is to drop that assumption and to inquire into the incidence and significance of nepotism, 'bribery' or other specific *practices,* and only consequently into whether they ought to be or are judged corrupt (and by whom).[11] Another possible tack is adopted by Friedrich, and that is to retain the conventional Western tests, but to acknowledge that the crucial question may be whether corruption, in any particular setting, is functional (i.e. tends to serve some public end) or is disfunctional and therefore reprehensible.[12] The effects of certain practices are clearly relevant to one's attitude to them, but this does not solve the difficulties of deciding which functional or disfunctional practices can usefully be labelled 'corrupt' in a variety of settings. The basic issue remains that of finding criteria or tests by which to decide whether some act should be deemed corrupt.

Let us therefore return to the public-office type of definition with its suggestion that the core meaning is the abuse or misuse of an office of trust for private gain (not necessarily of a monetary kind). On consideration, there seem to be certain key conditions, analytical or empirical, for corruption of this kind to take place. It is worth listing them and noting the relationship of those conditions to the problem of corruption in developing countries. But first we must dispose of one red herring. Nye refers to 'rule-breaking' in his definition and Lord Bryce tied his discussion of corruption to illegality. In this country and America much of what is deemed corrupt has been made illegal and it is common to encounter arguments that the law should at least seek to encompass all corrupt acts,[13] but few pretend it always does. In much of the Third World illegality may be even less useful as a test of corruption. The same activities as here may be illegal, but in much of Africa and Asia the law will often reflect alien, i.e. colonial power, conceptions of what is corrupt or lack force for having been part of an alien package of ideas and rules. Legal prohibition is thus not a necessary condition for the existence of corruption, though any relevant legal rules must clearly form part of its study. The first positive, and obvious, requirement is that some official or ruler has room to manoeuvre. Formal discretion and lax supervision or control are among the sources of that space, just as low penalties or a low probability of discovery are encouragements to make use of it. The extent of that space obviously varies with the nature of the government, the checks on its powers, the openness of its activities, the range of its jurisdiction and the availability of alternative rulers, but so might it vary with the kind of loyalties that politicians are obliged to hold while in office—to kin in West Africa or to party in the United States for example. (It is worth noting that nepotism can limit scope for the sale of offices and that some limit is set to both by a rigorous 'spoils system' especially if it is operated by a doctrinaire or messianic political party.) There must, secondly, be some accepted distinction between a ruler's public and private personality, a version of the 'Becket rule'[14] which separates role from occupant. If office and power are part of the man (his own private property), money-grabbing or the use of office for profit is no more corrupt than taxation, however immoral it might be.[15] This crucial distinction is not generally or clearly established in all parts of the Third World. Associated with it, thirdly, there must be some concept of the role (of ruler, official, etc.) as constituting an 'office of trust', and criteria for recognizing perversions, lapses, breaches, or abuses. In virtually all societies there seem to be some expectations and norms about ruling behavior, but those expectations differ not only in content but also in, for example, the detail in which expectations are specified or in the ambiguity of the language. The lack of a clear and precise definition of an official role, it may be noted, is both a factor blurring any concept of corruption and, according to Waterbury, one element in a package of circumstances favorable to the maintenance of patronage between strong and weak.[16] The expectations do not, moreover, relate only to the absence of 'corruption' unless that term is extended to cover every kind of error or short-coming.[17] There must therefore, finally, be evidence that any particular lapse was for the reasons, with the purposes, or under the circumstances that put it under the sub-heading of a corrupt lapse.[18]

If we are to attempt comparative studies of corruption, this breakdown of the formal conditions for its existence may help make the project manageable. For if an investigator looks at each of them he can leave room both for the recognition of cultural variety, for the relativity of 'corruption' and, without recourse to a mere list of activities stipulated as corrupt, yet preserve a central notion round which to organize discussion. This is to say that the conditions listed also constitute categories or factors which lend themselves to comparison across time and space. Only if one attempts to compare societies by reference to a single general category of 'corruption', it may be suggested, does confusion normally arise, and it arises largely, one suspects, because writers have been loathe to sacrifice the element of moral disapproval inseparable from the word itself.

Two other approaches also promise escape from a purely relative concept. The first of these 'stable' notions (as they might be labelled) derives from consideration of the effects of an extensive practice of bribery, nepotism and misappropriation. *The Economist* insists that, in the end, 'Trains really do not run to time' and refers to 'the impotence of a corrupt regime'; and Gunnar Myrdal points out that 'where corruption is widespread, inertia and inefficiency, as well as irrationality, impede the process of decision-making'; and a member of the

Singapore government warned (in 1968) that a society unscandalized by corruption (a 'kleptocracy') 'will steer itself into more and more corruption, and finally into economic and political chaos'.[19] Regardless of the standards prevalent in a particular society the effect of what we in Britain would label corrupt behavior is real and far from relative—something between economic stagnation and general chaos. Extending this argument it might then be suggested that any practice which frustrated government might be labelled 'corrupt'—a test that is in principle capable of general application. This is tempting, but there seems no reason to use the label 'corrupt', for governments can be frustrated, economies stagnate and societies collapse for many reasons other than bribery and corruption as we conventionally understand the terms; as we have already suggested, there is more than one way of being 'disfunctional'.

The second stable conception takes us into that 'wider' meaning of the term mentioned at the start of this chapter and involving the ideas of disintegration and decay or, specifically, the idea of a corrupt society. Dobel has suggested recently[20] that the crucial element is the breakdown of civic virtue and the disappearance of the capacity for loyalty to the common welfare or common ends of the state. This condition is followed by factionalism (the existence of 'objective centers of power and loyalty' that are laws unto themselves and are related to the community only by negotiation and for the sake of convenience); and it is the product of, above all, permanent and massive inequality. This is not the place to enter into a full discussion of a theory which is claimed by its author to derive from Thucydides, Plato, Aristotle, Machiavelli and Rousseau. But one must note the resemblance of Dobel's picture not only to certain aspects of contemporary British and American[21] society but, above all, to those developing countries whose 'corruption' (in the narrow sense) has most struck Western European observers. On the other hand it might well be argued that 'corruption' (in this wider sense) is an inappropriate term to apply to a Third World state which, so far from decaying, suffers from the weakness consequent upon novelty, artificiality, or (to use the older phrase) underdevelopment. Nevertheless, if it be accepted that to talk of political corruption at all is to use the term metaphorically or by reference to some ideal or goal and not to an actual historical past, then it may be acceptable to use the term to refer to a condition analogous to 'decay' or 'perversion' regardless of whether a particular state is passing through it, so to speak, on the way up or the way down. Although one might expect 'corrupt practices' in the narrow sense to form part of this condition, they are not a necessary part (if there is no agreed conception of public purpose, for example). This is therefore best regarded as a use of the term quite distinct from any of the others we have been considering.

Returning, therefore, to my suggestion that comparative studies might usefully attend more to the conditions for corruption, it may readily be granted that to do so would not obviate the need also to look at the relevant details in whatever society or societies are under discussion. One must still deal with uncertainties about the local criteria of corruption, and about the nuances of conduct and circumstance associated with any particular activity. Gifts may be taken as an illustration. Clearly a gift to an official may be a token of personal friendship, a ritual courtesy, an expression of unsolicited and spontaneous gratitude, a bribe, or a contribution extorted by the official, to list a number of possibilities ranging, in order, from the innocents to the tainted. But where should the line between innocence and taint be drawn and, for example, regardless of its degree of innocence, into which category should a tip be placed, and how big a sum can change hands and still be a tip? More generally, what distinguishes a privilege from a perquisite and the latter from misappropriation? In many societies there may be fairly stable and consistent answers obtainable from any reasonably sophisticated group of citizens—from 'the man-of-the-world on the Clapham omnibus' as it were. But there may not always be a consensus about a particular activity, or the existence of the activity may not be widely enough known. It is at this point that scandals can sometimes provide answers—both about the incidence of a practice and about its acceptability. In any event, part of the story of corruption in any society is the story of how, unless it is all-pervasive and obvious to all, it becomes known and how that knowledge is received. Scandal may once again provide the answer. In itself and for students scandal may therefore be valuable, and not least because looking at scandal involves looking also at much else in any given society.

In referring to scandal here I have in mind not so much the ordinary and enjoyable retailing of scurrilous stories about colleagues and notables but rather those complexes of deviant behavior, revelation and public reaction that together make up a historical event like 'Watergate'. For such a scandal to occur there must be more than mere wrongdoing. There are at least three major requirements: an exposer or informer, channels through which to communicate the message, and an audience or public which finds the information to be scandalous. Each deserves comment, if only to indicate where the study of scandal can lead.

First, then, there has to be an 'informer': someone has to 'grass' or 'sneak' to some appropriate 'outsider' (journalist, policeman, or MP for example) except in those cases where wrongdoing is epidemic and blatant. The slang terms are deliberately used as a reminder that the proverbial 'honor among thieves' often extends much more widely. Part of the full history of any scandal is why and how the disclosure came about, and often why, especially, it was for so long delayed. In the north east of England, for example, the Labour Party seemed to have the support of the National Executive in trying to avoid a public inquiry or even much serious public discussion of the allegations of corruption widespread in the 1960s and early 1970s—as Eddie Milne, the Member for Blyth, discovered to his ultimate cost. In Glasgow local politics, too, the old hands used to say that it was impossible to persuade the City Labour Party to institute its own 'house-cleaning' operations. In both cases the argument commonly put forward was that even to admit that there might be a problem was to play into the hands of other parties. To take a very different example: Martin Woollacott, writing about Hong Kong (in *The Guardian* of 22 September 1973) said that 'it is the classic case of the corrupt city: at one end of the scale those few who talk are afraid that their livelihoods and even their lives might be in danger. And at the other, among affluent British and Chinese professionals, while they may not fear physical attack, they are reluctant to upset the modus vivendi that even honest men have arrived at with the system'. There, as in New York City before the Knapp Commission (which reported in 1972) or in parts of Scotland Yard before Sir Robert Mark took over, information was probably also withheld because of the general belief that the police themselves were so deeply involved that to tell them was at best a waste of time.[22] Sheer administrative failure must also be listed. Thus in the Profumo case it seems that ample information had been available in different parts of the Whitehall machine but had neither been brought together nor reported to a relevant minister at an early enough stage to avert the security risks and political disruption that ensued.

Conversely, it is sometimes worthwhile noting why certain scandals did 'break' at all. In this country accident seems typically to be the explanation. In 1948 a lender pressed Sidney Stanley for the repayment of a loan—and by October the Lynskey Tribunal was set up to investigate gifts of whisky and holidays to a member of the government and other more lurid allegations.[23] 'Watergate' owed much, not only to such general factors as the American tradition of investigative journalism and distrust of authority and to the relative freedom of comment on public persons and events, but also to such specific factors as the already flourishing vendetta between Nixon and the press and the resentment of congress at the exceptionally bullying methods of Nixon's White House staff. Other factors include the existence of political conflict so that some groups have a strong positive interest in uncovering scandalous matter about, for example, the 'Gang of Four' in China, or dealings in marconi shares in Britain before the First World War, let alone alleged-dealings in land by close associates of Harold Wilson. Money for certain kinds of story from certain kinds of newspaper is another obvious link betwen scandal and particular social institutions.

The second pre-condition for the existence of a scandal, access to effective channels for public communication, requires less comment. Obviously the more famous scandals have been those publicized in the press, novels, pamphlets, wall-newspapers, or 'underground' broadsheets, and nowadays by broadcasting. The so-called 'Muldergate' scandal was a testimony to some remaining freedom in South Africa as well as to that country's desperate need to 'win friends and influence people'. All channels are in some degree selective and it is often suggested that British law would have muzzled any local equivalent to the *Washington Post's* 'Watergate' revelations. In war-time Britain, too, no publicity was given to the refusal, in 1941, of Zenith to 'complicate post-war business' by altering its contract with Bendix of the USA and Siemens of Germany so as to permit the British air ministry to manufacture increased numbers of aircraft carburettors.[24] Even in peacetime one expected few scandals in the Colonels' Greece or Franco's Spain. On the other hand, a private press avid for circulation may also serve to create a market for scandalous information almost without reference to its reliability, as Lord Denning emphasized on the final page of his report on the Profumo affair[25]—a state of affairs that can lead all too easily to possibly unfounded contempt for politicians or an erosion in the standards of behavior expected of public men.[26]

For there to be a scandal, finally, there must be a public ready to be shocked or scandalized and not merely entertained or titillated by political sensationalism. This requirement is not such a straightforward one. To begin with, it is a compound of, first, the events as reported (the reports may or may not be reliable) and, secondly, a censorious judgment passed upon them by, thirdly, a relevant public (those in a position to do something about the events or actions in question).[27] Further complications arise from the mutual dependence of the elements involved. If the events described or known about are sufficiently outrageous, for example, they can mobilize new groups into political activity and thus transform the nature of the relevant public—which seems to have been one factor in the recent revolution in Iran. Similarly, as we have already suggested, it may only be as a result of a hostile and shocked response that a particular type of behavior is recognized to be scandalous or, if appropriate, corrupt. Clearly, however, the revelation of what behavior is considered to be offensive and by whom is a necessary aspect of any scandal and may also be a key to identifying corruption.

An essential function of scandal (in the sense of 'defamatory talk'), it has been argued, is precisely to strip off the impersonal masks donned by those in authority as part of their role.[28] It is concerned, that is, with revealing the humanity and especially the human frailty of others—and in politics that means mainly of rulers, representatives, and administrators. This may, in Bailey's phrase, be both a gift and a poison: it may serve to liberate or at least to constitute salutory criticism, but it may also serve merely to make a given society virtually ungovernable. And there are other respects in which scandal may be only a limited blessing either to a society or to the academic student of corruption.

An obvious limit is that political scandals do not deal exclusively with corruption; they may well center rather on inefficiency, imcompetence, or mere carelessness which owes little or nothing to the pursuit of private gain or any other private purpose. (The Crichel Down scandal may well be a case in point.) In extreme cases, too, either of oppression or of a populace that universally participates in a corrupt state, widespread corruption may be accompanied by a complete absence of scandal—but in an oppressive regime, it may be noted, scandal (followed by some remedial action) might well benefit ruler and ruled alike. In other situations scandal is limited, often, by being so much at the mercy of chance and accident (as we have already noted about Britain). It may also serve to divert public attention from issues that, to the moralist or political activist, are of greater importance.[29] But none of these limitations affect the positive attributes for which this chapter has argued.

To note the multiple sources of scandal may provide a useful reminder that the purposes of public office may be betrayed for a variety of different reasons and that at least some people would not wish to label them all as corrupt (in any of the normal meanings of that term). 'Betrayal' thus can stem from arrogance, self-righteousness[30] and other motives which should perhaps be considered as corrupt in some very wide sense of the term, but conscience, treason for purely ideological reasons, fear, or stupidity must surely fall outside any useful category of corruption. In some situations of conflicting loyalties or trusts, it may not be clear which should be given preference.

Democrats, moreover, rely on officials to disobey orders that, for example, put democratic government itself in peril for partisan advantage—and if disobedience were encouraged by bribery, many would regard that as only 'technically' corrupt (or, in other language, as being 'functional' corruption). Scandals, including any associated debate or inquiry, again may help to sort out the ambiguities and uncertainties.

Much of the interest in corruption, even academic interest, seems morally inspired, which, as already suggested, is the source of some at least of the confusion to which I have referred. In this chapter I have tried to detach the argument from moral preferences, but it is by no means morally irrelevant. For one thing, the approach here advocated makes it easier to accept the fact that corruption in politics is not necessarily the worst of conditions or evils and, by insisting on a distinction between particular practices and the core meaning of 'corruption', to recognize the positive value of venality in some circumstances. Thus for those with something to give (money, sexual favors, or whatever) such corruption may be the only way to blunt the edges of tyranny or introduce an element of control into an otherwise completely arbitrary and hostile system.[31] To the moralist, too, my analysis may suggest that scandal should not be shunned—to encourage it should, indeed, be the moralist's aim. The important point, however, is that moral judgments about particular actions or situations should form the conclusion and not the premise of the argument.

This chapter has, for the most part, been couched in somewhat general, abstract and possibly academic (in the pejorative sense) terms. In conclusion, therefore, I will indicate, briefly and somewhat abruptly, certain concrete and practical proposals for dealing with political corruption, in the conventional and rather narrow sense, to which my arguments lend support (as distinct from either proving or inventing). The requirements for there to be corruption point, for example, to the importance of that 'wider loyalty (to the community), backed by firm rules and punitive measures' which forms 'the necessary foundation for the modern Western and communist mores by which certain behavior reactions are kept apart from considerations of personal benefit', to quote from Myrdal.[32] The pre-conditions for scandal suggest not only that more open government, organized opposition and a free press are desirable but also that more heed should be given to the case for a permanent investigating body independent of both government and police.[33] To stress the dependence of corruption on context and intention and to recognize that it is only one category of shortcoming is both to suggest that it be seen as only a special case of the general problems involved in securing good and efficient administration, and to leave one sympathetic to Plunkitt's view that 'Higher salaries is the cryin' need of the day . . . You can't be patriotic on a salary that just keeps the wolf from the door . . . But, when a man has a good fat salary, he finds himself hummin' 'Hail Columbia' . . .'.[34] In so far, however, as the approach acknowledges a variety of impulses to corrupt and of forms of corruption, it tends to be pessimistic about the likelihood that to abolish capitalism, or communism, or any other system would do much more in the long run than change the nature, not the existence, of the problem.[35] There will thus always be a need for scandal, whatever may be the case about the opportunities for it.

Notes

1. For example, I have noticed very few mentions and no discussion of it in that invaluable pioneering compendium, Arnold J. Heidenheimer (ed.), *Political Corruption: Readings in Comparative Analysis*, Holt, Rinehart & Winston, 1970.
2. The Radcliffe-Maud Committee on Local Government Rules of Conduct which reported in 1974 and the Salmon Commission on Standards of Conduct in Public Life which reported in 1976.
3. Heidenheimer, *op. cit.*, pp. 1–10. See too the brief survey in S. Riley, 'Teaching Political Corruption,' *Teaching Politics*, 8 (1979), 71–78.
4. C.J. Friedrich, *The Pathology of Politics*, Harper & Row, 1972, p. 128.
5. Robert J. Williams, 'The Problems of Corruption: A Conceptual and Comparative Analysis', a paper delivered to a Public Administration Committee Conference in York, 1976, p. 2.
6. "What is the Problem about Corruption?" *Journal of Modern African Studies*, 3, 2 (1965), 215–30. Most is reprinted in Heidenheimer, *op. cit.* pp. 31–37 and 341–45. In my view insufficient attention has been paid to his recommendations about how to study corruption.
7. See William L. Riordon, *Plunkitt of Tammany Hall* (1st ed., 1905). In the Dutton, 1963, edition see, in particular, pp. xxii, 4–5, 30–32, and 37–40.
8. Susan Rose-Ackerman, *Corruption. A Study in Political Economy*, Academic Press, 1978, p. 9. This is a particularly valuable study for anyone interested in the conditions favorable to corruption and thus with its 'cure'.
9. According to Martin Woollacott, *The Guardian*, 22 September 1973, "leading European buyers routinely take cuts from the manufacturing houses [in Hong Kong, 1973] . . . to whom they give their orders. The normal rate is half per cent of the value, paid into a Swiss bank annually."
10. In his "The Effects of Corruption in a Developing Nation," *Western Political Quarterly*, December 1966; reprinted in Heidenheimer, *op. cit.*, pp. 523–33.
11. I take this to be part of what Leys meant by his 'central question' for the study of corruption: "In any society, under what conditions is behaviour most likely to occur which a significant section of the population will regard as corrupt?" See the article cited above.
12. See his whole discussion of political corruption in *op. cit.* pp. 127–41.

13. See, for example, Michael Roberts's discussion of the place of interested individuals who may attend local authority party group meetings that make policy for a council of which they are not members and who thus need not declare their interest. "Conduct in Local Government—Situating the Redcliffe Maud Report," *Public Administration Bulletin,* 18 June 1975, pp. 39–48, at p. 43.
14. It was the absence of this at Henry II's dinner table, so legend has it, that misled his knights into thinking it was the king, and not merely the temporarily irate and frustrated individual, who wished to be rid of Thomas a Becket.
15. See, for example, Heidenheimer, *op. cit.,* chap. 2.
16. See John Waterbury, "An attempt to Put Patrons and Clients in their Place," in Ernest Gellner and John Waterbury (eds.), *Patrons and Clients in Mediterranean Societies,* Duckworth, 1977, p. 329–42.
17. There is, of course, biblical precedent for regarding all lapses as evidence of human corruption since the Fall, but it is surely politics itself that results from the Fall, with political corruption a perverted or at least special sub-category thereof.
18. John G. Peters and Susan Welch (see their "Political Corruption in America: A Search for Definitions and a Theory," *American Political Science Review,* 72, 3, (September 1978, 958–73) offer an interesting analysis of the components of corrupt acts and the use of those components for a comparison of various acts and the degrees to which they are corrupt. This analysis is conducted explicitly within the American context, but is a good example of how a detailed breakdown can help analysis.
19. See the relevant excerpts in Heidenheimer, *op. cit.,* at, respectively, pp. 489–91, 540–54, and 564–68. See, too, the comment by Colin Leys quoted earlier in this chapter (see above, fn. 6).
20. J. Patrick Dobel, "The Corruption of a State," *American Political Science Review,* 72, 3 (September 1978), 958–73.
21. Cf. Theodore J. Lowi's analysis in his *The End of Liberalism* (New York, W.W. Norton, 1979).
22. For the reference to the Knapp Commission I am indebted to Michael Pinto-Duschinsky, "Corruption in Britain," *Political Studies,* XXV, 2 (June 1977), 274–84. In this review of the *Report of the Royal Commission on Standards of Conduct in Public Life,* Cmnd. 6524 of 1976, a strong case is made for setting up some permanent civil inspectorate to assist in obtaining information about corruption.
23. M.R. Robinson, "The Lynskey Tribunal," *Political Science Quarterly,* March 1953, reprinted in Heidenheimer, *op. cit.,* pp. 249–58.
24. James Stewart Martin, *All Honorable Men,* Little, Brown, 1959, p. 11.
25. "True or false, actual or invented, it can be sold. The greater the scandal the higher the price it commands. If supported by photographs or letters, real or imaginary, all the better," Lord Denning's *Report,* Cmnd. 2152 of 1963, p. 114.
26. See the comments on the situation in early twentieth-century America in Robert C. Brooks, "The Nature of Political Corruption," in Heidenheimer, *op. cit.,* pp. 56–61.
27. See Heidenheimer's interesting distinctions between 'black', 'gray' and 'white' corruption depending on whether a practice is condemned or

condoned by one or both the elite and the masses in a particular society, *op. cit.*, pp. 26–28.

28. See F.G. Bailey, *Gifts and Poison: The Politics of Reputation,* Blackwell, 1971, for a social anthropological discussion.
29. See Rose-Ackerman's observation that the fragmentation of authority to deal with corruption (venality) may lead merely to "a strategy of following the scandals rather than a broader look at the range of alternatives available"; *op. cit.,* p. 225n.
30. Self-righteousness, one of the motives that seems to have informed aspects of the Watergate cover-up, for example, has the great advantage that it brings a continuous 'pay-off' in self-satisfaction.
31. Compare Friedrich, *op. cit.,* p. 129: "Corruption is a corrective of coercive power and its abuse, when it is functional."
32. See his *Asian Drama: An Inquiry into the Poverty of Nations,* Penguin, 1968, Vol. II, pp. 949–50.
33. See the case made in Pinto-Duschinsky, *op. cit.,* pp. 281–84.
34. *Op. cit.,* p. 56; and see Rose-Ackerman's infinitely more sophisticated analysis of the political economy of corruption cited above.
35. See Friedrich again, at p. 141: "Corruption in the historical perspective appears to be ever present where power is wielded."

51

The Mobilization of Scandal

Lawrence W. Sherman

On closer examination, the making of almost any scandal seems to be far more deliberate than accidental. Scandals do not just happen; they are socially constructed phenomena involving the cooperation and conflict of many people.

This chapter analyzes the mobilization of scandal over four corrupt police departments.[1] It shows why the scandals happened when they did and why they were a successful form of mobilizing external social control. The chapter begins by considering the general characteristics of scandal that distinguish it from other forms of social control. The structure of four recent American police corruption scandals is then described in terms of the principal stages of development and roles played in the making of scandal. Finally, the developmental process of the scandals is examined by identifying the conditions associated with scandal moving from one stage to another, especially to the final stage of the police department being labeled a deviant organization.

Scandal as Social Control

Dictionaries and colloquial usage define "scandal" in two very different ways. According to one definition, scandal *is* deviant behavior. According to the other definition, scandal is a social *reaction* to deviant behavior, a reaction of disapproval and outrage. The first definition is used, for example, when reporters are described as "uncovering" or "revealing" a scandal. The second definition is used, for example, when an official is said to have resigned under the pressure of a scandal. The ambiguity of a term that means both crime

Source: Lawrence W. Sherman, *Scandal and Reform: Controlling Police Corruption.* Berkeley: University of California Press, 1978, pp. 59–91. (c) 1978 The Regents of the University of California, used by permission of the University of California Press and the author.

and punishment must be resolved for purposes of analysis. This study adopts the second definition, using "scandal" to refer only to public *reactions* to disclosures of police corruption, and not to police corruption itself.

The definition of scandal as a negative public reaction to deviance is more useful for this study because such reactions can constitute social control: a punitive sanction designed to deter future deviance. Not all deviance, however, is scandalous. Neither are all scandals punitive. Certain conditions seem to be required in order for police corruption to be scandalous and for police corruption scandals to be punitive.

Conditions of Scandalous Deviance

Scandal differs from other social reactions to deviant behavior in three important respects. First, the social reaction that constitutes scandal is one of intense outrage and anger, rather than of mere disapproval.[2] Second, the deviance that is subjected to a scandalized social reaction is usually a surprise to the group reacting to the deviance, something that is not part of their assumptions about what is normally likely to occur. A third characteristic of scandal is perhaps most important in differentiating it from all other forms of social control. Scandal is generally a social reaction to deviance committed by an occupant of a role invested with social *trust*.[3] The socially trusted role of the deviant explains both the intensity of the disapproval and the surprise that the deviance could ever occur. For a trusted actor to break important rules is a "breach of faith," a betrayal of trust that those investing the trust expected not to occur.

Violations of *personal* trust occur with predictable frequency in our society. Spouses commit adultery, bank tellers embezzle, and children lie to their parents. When these violations of personal trust are discovered, the reaction of those who had invested the trust in the trust violators is similar to that of a scandal: outrage, surprise, and a feeling of betrayal. Spouses, bank supervisors, and parents may all display a scandalized reaction as individuals to violations of their personal trust in other individuals. At the societal level, however, such personal trust violations are not surprising, nor do they produce social reactions of outrage and feelings of betrayal. Personal trust violations are not scandalous, precisely because the nature of the trust violated was personal, not social. Scandal is a social reaction to a violation of socially invested trust in an institution or role.

Societies seem to invest more trust in those roles and institutions closer to the center of the society.[4] Such central institutions as a society's law, government, and religion symbolize the identity of the society itself. Deviance in these central positions suggests something negative about the entire society, something the society may be unwilling to accept. It suggests that the society itself is deviant from its own standards of conduct. The unacceptability of this suggestion may be the source of the social outrage that is scandal.

Collectivities, of course, may differ in their standards of conduct. In American society, there is substantial variation across different regions, states, and cities in the "real" standards of conduct that the collectivities hold for their own behavior, often regardless of what the relevant laws establish as appropriate standards.[5] These standards apply by implication to those roles and institutions at the center of the collectivities. And just as they differ across communities at the same point in time, these standards of conduct may differ within communities at different points in time. Behavior is not inherently scandalous. Scandalous behavior is that which a collectivity so labels. What is scandalous in New York may not be so in Chicago. What is scandalous one year may not have been scandalous the year before.

As representatives of the law, a central symbol of society itself, the police arguably occupy a central place in the collectivities they serve. Unlike such public officials as judges and legislators, however, the police occupy their position of trust as an organization rather than as individuals. The deviance of one lone judge has often caused a scandal, but the deviance of one police officer generally produces little social reaction in any but the smallest communities. Police corruption per se is generally not scandalous, because it is merely an individual form of deviance by those whom the collectivity does not invest trust in as individuals. A corrupt police department, however, *is* scandalous, because the collectivity does invest trust in the police department as an organization.

In order to be labeled corrupt, of course, a police department must be shown to be in violation of its collectivity's standards of conduct. This is a problem of both evidence and definition. The problem of evidence centers on the status of those who charge a police department with being corrupt, as well as on the extent of the evidence offered. The problem of definition is more difficult, because collective standards of conduct are often unclear or unarticulated. The attempt to make a scandal over police corruption is often a process of defining exactly what a collectivity's standards of conduct are. Indeed, the making of scandal may even change the standards of conduct, as the currently frequent references to a "post-Watergate morality" suggest. Attempts to make a scandal produce not only a conflict over whether the rules have been broken, but they may also produce a conflict over what the rules should be.[6] In a community that has never objected to police being paid not to arrest prostitutes, a scandal over such corruption may create a new standard against police collusion with prostitutes, as well as demonstrating that the police organization is deviant in relation to an ex post facto application of the new standard.

The most difficult condition to achieve for making police corruption scandalous may be the interpretation of police corruption as organizational rather than individual behavior. In the four cities studied, this condition was satisfied by the discovery of evidence that the police department had failed to police itself properly. When presented with evidence or allegations that police officers had committed corrupt acts, either as individuals or as part of an organized arrangement, superior officers in all four police departments failed to investigate the charges thoroughly enough to satisfy the public. A central aspect of the social trust invested in the police as an organization is that no social resources are routinely allocated to check on police behavior externally. Police departments are trusted organizationally to control the conduct of their members. Failures of internal control are betrayals of that trust.[7] If the organization does not show any interest in controlling its members' deviance, then the organization itself appears to be corrupt.

Conditions of Punitive Scandals

Attempts to make a scandal over deviance, like other ways of attempting to punish deviance, do not always succeed. In order for a scandal to be punitive, it must succeed in creating a collective definition of the deviance as scandalous. To be punished by scandal, deviance must not only satisfy the conditions of being scandalous, it must also be subjected to widely shared agreement that the conditions have been satisfied.

Scandal is a public act of labeling an actor's identity, a ceremony of status degradation. The label that scandal attempts to apply to its subject is a new identity, a morally inferior status unworthy of trust. The new identity is applied by an unmasking of the old identity, a revelation that the deviant's identity has not been what he claimed it to be, but has really been deviant all along.[8] Rather than saying the deviant is *now* unworthy of trust, the scandal shows how the deviant has in fact not been worthy of trust for some time. A scandal over police corruption is an attempt to show that the police department has long been breaking rather than enforcing laws, creating crime rather than controlling it.

A scandal is punitive when the new identity is successfully applied, when the label of deviant is made to "stick." The label sticks in the sense that people generally respond to the deviant in terms of the label.

The more people respond to the deviant in terms of the label, the more punitive the label is. The degree to which scandal stigmatizes its subjects depends on the degree to which the stigma is behaviorally applied to the subjects by other people. The behavioral application need not always be focused directly on the subjects of scandal; families of the subjects may also be the targets of the stigma. At the height of the Knapp Commission hearings in New York, for example, the police commissioner was told that many police officers were keeping their children home from school because of the ridicule they received from fellow students—jokes and taunts about the dishonest occupation of their fathers.[9] Similarly, wives of the subjects of scandal have committed suicide in response to the stigma applied to them.[10] Yet many of the business executives convicted of crimes related to the Watergate scandal or the subsequent wave of scandal over corporate bribery abroad have apparently retired without stigma, living comfortably in terms of their social relations as well as material comforts.[11] For those who have resources to avoid people who would treat them as stigmatized, stigma can be avoided almost entirely.

Scandals come in different sizes. There are several senses in which the size of a scandal varies, but perhaps the most consequential is the variation in the number of people who acknowledge the stigma directed by scandal at its subjects. A little scandal, in this sense, is one that creates very little stigma, one that results in very few people acting as if the subject of scandal had been labeled deviant. A big scandal is one that produces a widely shared definition that its subject is deviant. A little scandal, therefore, is hardly punitive at all, while a big scandal is very punitive. All four police departments studied here experienced a little scandal about two years prior to the big scandal that led to reform. The little scandals met all the conditions for creating a scandalized reaction to disclosures of police corruption, with one major exception: they all failed to demonstrate the organizational nature of the deviance. In some instances, there were even allegations to the effect that corruption was fostered by the organization. But merely claiming that deviance exists is not sufficient for creating a big scandal. Satisfying the conditions for deviance to be scandalous and for scandals to be punitive depends not only on the nature of the information about the deviance that is publicly disclosed, but also on the structure and process of scandal as collective behavior.

The Structure of the Scandals

The scandals over police corruption, both big and little, shared a common structure in relation to both the stages of development and the key roles in the making of scandal. The stages of development corresponded closely to the division of labor, with one key role dominating each stage. The stages and the roles provide the structure within which the process of scandal takes place. The timing of each stage's appearance and the recruitment of people to fill the roles seem to have an important effect on the final outcome of the process of scandal.

Revelation

The first stage of the scandals was the revelation of facts showing that police corruption existed as an organizational form of deviance. The information revealed at this stage was new to the public record, exposing behavior that had generally been kept secret. The revelations may have been no surprise to people knowledgeable about police practices, including everyone from cab drivers to honest mayors. Some facts had even been alleged before in recent years. But as public fact, the revelations and their supporting documentation created a window in a wall of secrecy and suggested that there were even more facts to find.

The revealers were both internal and external to the police department. In New York and Central City, the decision to reveal corruption was a cooperative action by officers in the zealot fringe, four in New York and almost thirty in Central City. In Oakland and Newburgh, the decision to reveal corruption was made by victims of corrupt acts perpetrated by the evil fringe in those police departments. In Newburgh, the victim was a large corporation, Sears, Roebuck and Company. In Oakland, the victim revealing corruption was a lone individual, a local merchant widely known for his drinking habits.

New revelations were made after the initial ones in all four cases. Additional facts were often brought to light at strategic times in the conflict over whether the organization was deviant. The scandals varied in the extent to which subsequent revelations occurred. The revealer role in the subsequent revelations was usually filled by someone other than those who had made the initial revelations. But without the initial revelation, the scandal process would not have begun in the first place. The explanation of the initial revelation, then, is one of the most important problems in understanding the process of scandal.

Publication

Revealers do not usually have the resources to make their revelations known to the general public. Those in control of the news media do have the required resources, and it is their decisions that dominate the publication stage. It was not necessary in all four cities for revealers to go to the news media in order to have their revelations published for the view of the general public. In Newburgh, the victim revealing corruption went directly to the state police, whose investigation led to criminal indictments. The indictments were reported as news, and those reports were the first publication of the victim's revelations of police corruption. But in the other three cities, publication preceded any prosecution. Indeed, publication was often sought as a means of creating pressure for prosecution.

Publication decisions can theoretically be made by any mass communications medium, including radio and television as well as newspapers. Yet the three decisions to publish revelations that preceded prosecution were all made by newspapers, and not by the electronic media. In fact, only one police corruption exposé of which I am aware was "published" through the medium of television.[12] Whether the primary role of newspapers in this stage reflects the muckraking tradition of the print media or the bias of television news for more visual events, it is clear that the newspapers were the only medium to show much interest in the revealers' willingness to talk.

It is important to distinguish editorial decisions from decisions made by reporters. The revealers generally made contact with reporters, but it was the editors who decided whether the revelations would be made public. The reporters in two cases played a key role in pressing for publication, but the editorial decisions always dominated the publication stage. Editorial decisions, in turn, may have been constrained by the publishers' role in the community, relationships to political officials, and other factors. The editorial page's political positions were also a possible constraint upon the news editor's judgment. But whatever the constraints may have been, the decisions to publish revelations seem to have rested with the news editors. As in the case of the revelations themselves, publication of revelations usually occurred more than once. After the first publication decision was made, however, the subsequent decisions to report revelations appear to have been fairly routine, subject to whatever standards of verification had been established for publishing police corruption stories.

Defense

The defense stage usually appeared immediately after the publication stage. The defenses of the police departments against attempts to label them corrupt followed various strategies, from denial of the charges to attacks upon the motives or reliability of the revealers. A less public form of defense was the attempt to prevent any more revelations, either by silencing the revealers (through physical violence in some cases) or by scaring any potential new revealers from joining in the revelations. A successful defense at this stage might have terminated the scandal, preventing further revelations and minimizing the stigma of the revelations already made.

The defender role can be filled publicly by almost anyone who has access to news media. The public figures who played the defender role varied on a continuum of personal interest to disinterest in the police department's reputation. The chief police executive, the police union president, and high police officials all played the defender role in at least one of the cities, but their close personal interest in the department was always clear. Mayors and prosecutors had somewhat less stake in the police departments' reputations, but enough so that their defense of the police could have appeared to have been self-interested. More disinterested actors playing the defender role were city council members and leaders of civic groups, although the political party affiliations of even these disinterested actors often affected the credibility of their defense. Like most of the stages of the scandal, the defense stage usually appeared numerous times.

Dramatization

A dramatization is a public interpretation of the published revelations of police corruption as serious cause for public concern. No new information was introduced at this stage, but the already known facts were dramatized as evil. The known facts may have implied that the police department was organizationally corrupt, but the dramatizations explicitly interpreted the facts in this fashion. Dramatizations lend extra weight to revelations in labeling the police departments as deviants.

The dramatizer role was filled by the same kinds of people who filled the defender role, with the usual exception of police officials. Mayors, prosecutors, city council members, and civic group leaders each played the dramatizer role in at least one of the scandals.

Prosecution

The prosecution stage is the consideration by a prosecutor and grand jury of the evidence revealed by the scandal for possible criminal indictments and trial. The decision to prosecute or not, and how many charges to bring against how many people, was generally made by the local prosecutor himself; federal prosecutors were almost entirely uninvolved in the four scandals. The local grand jury's domination by the prosecutor even became an issue in the Central City scandal, but public criticism did not alter the prosecutor's complete power to decide whom to prosecute.

Prosecution decisions are, however, constrained both by the legal standards of evidence and by the prosecutor's political alliances. Prosecutors in Central City and Newburgh were members of the political elite dominating the police department. Such alliances made extensive prosecution of police corruption seem unlikely, but they did not prevent the prosecution of Newburgh police officers. The prosecutor there did resign halfway through the investigation, but he never attempted to block the prosecution of the cases developed by the state police. If he had, he might have been investigated himself. Moreover, there is a certain amount of political risk in failing to prosecute police corruption. The prosecutor in Central City who scorned the evidence of police corruption was defeated at the polls six months after the scandal, ending a twelve-year career.

In New York and Oakland, the prosecutors were not politically allied to the elected officials responsible for the police. They were, however, operationally allied to the police in the performance of their routine tasks—tasks vital to their own political survival. The prosecutor in Oakland was less dependent on the police for making big cases because he had his own staff of non-police investigators. But the five district attorneys in New York all relied heavily on police officers to conduct their investigative legwork. Both before and after the scandal, the claim was made that the district attorneys in New York would never be eager to prosecute police officers as long as they depended so greatly on police cooperation.[13] Even so, the district attorneys there did prosecute some cases developed from revelations made in the scandal.

Labeling

Attempts to label the police departments as corrupt and attempts to thwart the application of the label were made at every stage of the scandals. Labeling was the final stage of the scandals, the stage at which the label had been successfully applied. The key role in the labeling stage was one that had been important but passive in every prior stage: the audience. The audience for a police corruption scandal was the general community that each department served. Revelations were directed at that community, publications were read by it, defenders and dramatizers sought to persuade it, and prosecution occurred in its name. The labeling stage was the community's verdict, the judgment of the audience about the meaning of the morality play of scandal. If the labeling stage had not appeared, the implicit verdict would be not guilty: the police department is not a deviant organization. But since the audience generally seemed to agree that the police department was corrupt, the label was successfully applied. The organizations were stigmatized, and the scandals were punitive. Whether scandals over police corruption ever reach this final stage may depend on the process of scandal—that is, on the conditions affecting the transition of scandal from one stage to the next.

The Process of the Scandals

While the four scandals all had common stages of development, the exact order in which the stages appeared and reappeared varied from city to city. The recruitment of key public figures into the various roles also varied. Despite the differences, however, there did seem to be some general conditions common to the appearance of each stage of scandal, conditions that comprised the process by which the scandals developed from revelations to labeling.

Conditions of Revelation

The revelation stage of scandal is the one most often interpreted as accidental, explained as a "mistake" in the organizational strategies for controlling information about deviance. But in the four police corruption scandals studied here, the conditions of the appearance of the revelation stage were firmly rooted in the social organization of the corrupt police departments. All four disclosures can be linked to structural failures of internal control, failures associated with conflict over organizational goals. In Central City and New York, the failure of internal control lay in not controlling the zealot fringe. In Oakland and Newburgh, the failure of internal control lay in not keeping the "evil fringe" within safe limits. In all four cases, the failures of internal control were associated with either internal or external conflict over whether the police department should be corrupt.

The zealot fringe in both New York and Central City became alienated from the departments only after a four-year process of trying to work for change from within. In both cities, the alienation of the zealots may have been speeded up by the apparent increase in police corruption related to narcotics sales. But there was also a failure of the "system" in both cities to "cool out" the zealots' complaints. Instead of trying to pacify the zealots by, for example, assigning them to such corruption-free units as the police academy, the response of the two departments was to punish the zealots for making trouble. By rejecting the legal standards for police conduct that the zealots supported, the upper levels of the two departments made the zealots all the more dedicated to those standards, and all the less dedicated to the police departments' norms of silence.

The role of the newspaper reporters was important to the revelations occurring in New York and Central City, quite apart from the reporters' role in the publication stage. In New York, a *New York Times* police reporter had taken an interest in police corruption and had let his police contacts know that he would be interested in doing a story on any revelations police officers might make. The reporter was also gathering evidence from other sources, particularly those who paid bribes to police. One of the reporter's police contacts was a friend of Frank Serpico, the officer who had taken his complaints of corruption to numerous police officials without obtaining satisfaction. The reporter's interest served as a basis for the friend to persuade Serpico and two other officers to make revelations to the reporter. Whether the revealers would have sought out the reporter if he had not announced his interest is unclear.[14]

A team of investigative reporters in Central City played a similar role in seeking out the revealers. The revealers—twenty-eight of them at first, and more later on—were ready to talk, but they had not taken any initiative to do so. Some of the zealots' actions (such as the federal arrest of a police-protected bootlegger in 1972, initiated by a police zealot) had stimulated the reporters' interest in police corruption, so the revealers cannot be seen as entirely passive in making their revelations. Nor can internal conflict alone account for all of the initial revelations in Central City. Discussions of merging the city and county police departments had created friction between the two organizations since 1970, and since 1972 the county police had been raiding vice establishments corruptly protected by the city police. After the investigative reporters contacted the county police about city police corruption, the county police actively interrogated the prisoners of city police housed in the county jail. A number of revelations of police corruption came from the prisoners, who were allegedly promised more lenient sentences by the county police in exchange for information about police corruption, real or invented. But despite the reporters' initiative and the interest of the county police in having the city police labeled as deviant in order to discourage the merger, it is probably fair to say that the revelations of the city police zealots were the most crucial factor in mobilizing the scandal. Without the inside story of the zealots, the other revelations did not constitute evidence that the police department was organizationally corrupt.

The revelations in Oakland and Newburgh were initiated by victims of police corruption, but the police departments themselves made the victims' revelations almost inevitable. If the two departments had kept the evil fringe from engaging in forms of corruption that created victims who knew that the police were their victimizers, then there would have been no victims to make revelations. While it is true that the Newburgh police did not confront their burglary victims directly, the sheer frequency of the Newburgh police burglaries relative to the size of the city probably made it impossible for the victims not to discover the identity of the burglars. The Newburgh police did confront directly the narcotics dealers they shook down, but probably assumed that the criminal status of those victims would keep their accusations from being taken seriously. In the context of the respectable burglary victim's complaints, however, the testimony of the narcotics dealers was eventually taken quite seriously.

The "accident" that led to the initial revelation of police corruption in Newburgh was a result of the poor information control strategies characteristic of an evil fringe led by the chief himself. One of the several police burglaries at Sears had been camouflaged by a police radio broadcast that a "normal" break-in had occurred there. An officer uninvolved in the corrupt activities and working in a different part of town heard the radio message before going into a diner for supper. He commented to a friend that "they're really ripping off Sears." A Sears saleswomen overheard the remark and drove right over to the store, only to find police officers carrying out merchandise. She notified the Sears security force the next day. The security force asked the police chief for an investigation. When the chief did nothing, Sears mobilized a state police investigation of the burglary and then of the entire department.[15] Corrupt officers made revelations in exchange for leniency, and other victims of police corruption contributed further revelations. The implication of the chief in any one of the corrupt acts was sufficient evidence that the department was incapable of policing itself and organizationally in violation of its public trust.

Revelations of police corruption in Oakland were made several times in the early 1950s.[16] All of the published revelations, however, were met with at least a token response by police managers showing some effort to control police misconduct. But the revelation in 1955 of the police department's failure to investigate a brutal extortion and kidnapping by police officers was the first evidence suggesting that the Oakland Police Department was organizationally corrupt. The victim of the corrupt acts by members of Oakland's evil fringe told his experiences to several people, one of whom told a reporter. Although the victim had been threatened with violence by police if he did not keep his story quiet, the victim did confirm the story to a reporter. The reporter then contacted the new city manager, who also took on a revealer role, focusing the facts provided by the victim.

The city manager called a press conference to announce the facts that the victim had revealed. In announcing the facts, he stressed the seriousness of the failure to investigate the charges properly, rather than just the seriousness of the charges themselves. The manager chose that public occasion to reprimand the police chief for not having notified the city manager's office of the case.[17] In announcing his order that all complaints of police misconduct be forwarded immediately to the city manager's office, the manager implied that the police department was incapable of policing itself. The victim may have revealed police corruption, but it was the manager who revealed the evidence suggesting that the department was organizationally corrupt.

The manager's actions stemmed from a conflict over organizational goals for the police department. An Oakland native, the new Oakland manager had been the highly successful manager of nearby Richmond, keeping its shipyard-based economy from dying in the changing national economic conditions after World War II. When a long-term "caretaker" city manager in Oakland died, the new manager was hired to undertake an active approach to developing Oakland's own faltering economic base. What the city council may not have known when it hired the new manager was that he had plans to reform the police department, to make it more honest as well as more efficient. He could not undertake drastic changes without strong justification, however, so he waited for an opportunity to create a justification. The extortion case and its improper internal investigation gave the manager just the opportunity he was waiting for: evidence for labeling the police department as deviant and in need of reform.[18] In the conflict between his own goals for the police department and the existing goals of the dominant coalition of politicians and police officials, labeling the police department as deviant was a weapon the manager used to win the conflict.

Similar conflicts of goals seem to have fueled the revelations in the other cities. The Newburgh revelation stemmed from a conflict between Sears, Roebuck and the police department about the purpose of the police: preventing burglaries or committing them. The Central City and New York revelations stemmed from conflict within each department over the character of the police organization and the implications of that character for the identity of its individual members. Moreover, in all four cases, the conflict over goals widened after the initial revelations were made. More and more actors participated in the conflict, and their participation often came in the form of new revelations. The Knapp Commission in New York, for example, was not created until some time after the zealots made their revelations. But it was the revelations of the Knapp Commission, and not the revelations of the zealots, that ultimately provided the facts (as well as the dramatizations) that led to the final stage of successful labeling. In both the initial and the subsequent revelations, then, the central condition for the occurrence of the revelations seems to have been conflict. The more intensive the conflict over police organizational goals, the more likely it seems that revelations will occur.

Conditions of Publication

Publication of the revelations of organizational police corruption in Oakland, New York, and Central City was linked in every case to some involvement of newspaper personnel in the conflict over police department goals. This involvement in the conflict began before the making or the publication of the revelations. The personnel involved in the conflict ranged from a reporter in New York to an editor in Central City to a publisher in Oakland. In each case, some participant in the internal decisionmaking of the newspaper was predisposed to see the police department labeled as corrupt in order to have new police organizational goals adopted. No employee of a Newburgh paper seems to have been involved in the conflict over police goals, and the publication stage appeared there purely as a result of the prosecution stage. The Newburgh newspapers made no independent decision to publish revelations of police corruption unconnected to ongoing legal processing of the revelations.

The involvement of the publisher of the *Oakland Tribune* in the conflict over police department goals was sought out by the new city manager. The publisher had a strong interest in the manager's program for economic development, and was one of the manager's strongest behind-the-scenes supporters. He had committed himself to providing supportive press coverage for any of the manager's efforts to revitalize the city. When the manager joined in the mobilization of a scandal over police corruption, the *Tribune* supported the effort with extensive press coverage. The manager asked that *Tribune* reporters be assigned to play a revealer role, seeking out new facts about police corruption, and even about general administrative problems of the police department. Stories as routine as friction between the patrol and detective branches of the police department were turned into front-page news. When there was nothing new to report, the facts that had been revealed already were restated as an overview story. The problems of the police department made headlines almost every day for three weeks. As the city manager later said, "If the story had gotten off the front pages, I never would have been able to change the police department."[19] When the story did slip off the front page in the second week of the scandal, the scandal was revitalized by a reporter's new revelation of corruption in the elite detective branch, additional evidence that the problem of corruption was organizational rather than individual.

The involvement of the managing editor of the major Central City newspaper in the conflict over police organizational goals was stimulated by the interests of four of his best reporters, and perhaps by the climate of investigative journalism created in the aftermath of the recent successes of *Washington Post* reporters Carl Bernstein and Bob Woodward in uncovering the Watergate story.[20] The publisher of the newspaper had been and remained a strong supporter of the mayor, but the newly hired managing editor was guaranteed a free hand in setting news policy. One of his first acts was to allow four reporters to undertake long-term investigations of major problems in the city, in order to produce more complete coverage of the problems than is possible on a day-to-day basis. Freeing the reporters from their normal assignments, the editor approved the team's request to work on police corruption, an area that the little scandal had made to look promising. When the initial inquiries began to show results, the managing editor allowed the team to work almost fulltime on the police corruption story for over six months. By the conclusion of their investigation, the team had gathered enough information for a copyrighted series of front-page stories lasting almost two weeks. Followup stories and new revelations stimulated by the stories kept police corruption in the headlines for almost a year. Curiously, the editorial page took little notice of the stories, even though the stories themselves portrayed the department as thoroughly corrupt. The involvement in the conflict over police organizational goals appeared to be limited to the middle levels of the newspaper, and did not extend, as in Oakland, to the top of the news organization.

The involvement of the *New York Times* in the conflict over police organizational goals was located even further down in the hierarchy of the newspaper. The principal police reporter had decided on his own to look into police corruption after doing a series of stories on police "cooping" (sleeping on duty).[21] When he found the zealot police officers willing to make revelations, he arranged a meeting between his editors and the revealers. The editors were not enthusiastic about publishing the revelations. They told the reporter and the police revealers how delicate the subject was and that "there would be enormous difficulties in publishing such a story."[22] The revealers brought along a high middle-management police official to confirm their statements, without whose presence "nothing would have happened," according to the reporter. In the end, the editor approved the story but decided not to print it until a "hook to hang it on" developed. Only when the reporter seized the publication role was the story published: he dropped hints to a top aide in the mayor's office that a "block-buster" story on police corruption was about to be published (which was untrue), and the mayor appointed an investigative committee in order to steal the thunder of the *Times* story. The zealots' revelations finally were published two days later, along with the additional information gathered by the reporter.

The decision to publish revelations of organizational police corruption is more than a yes-or-no choice. Once a decision is made to publish the story, a number of additional decisions must be made. How much newspaper column space to devote to the story, where in the newspaper to place the story, what tone to adopt, whether to draw conclusions from the facts, and whether to run follow-up stories are all decisions that can have major consequences for the outcome of the scandal process.[23] Each of those decisions may yield a greater or lesser quantity of stigma applied to the police department. The more involved the newspaper was in the conflict over police organizational goals, the more the decisions seemed to be made in the direction of stigmatizing the police. Where the newspaper was least involved in the organizational goal conflict (New York), the tone, conclusions, and follow-up stories were the most restrained. Where the newspaper was involved in the conflict at the highest level of management (Oakland), the tone and conclusions were the most negative, and repetitious follow-up stories were the most frequent.

The involvement of newspaper personnel in the conflict over police organizational goals may not be a necessary condition for publication of revelations of police corruption. Other cases may be found in which there was no interest in police corruption among newspaper personnel until, for instance, zealots sought out the newspaper as a means of publishing their revelations. Merely judging from newspaper accounts, this may have been the case in Cincinnati and Albany in recent years.[24]

But in Oakland, New York, and Central City, research into the origins of the publication decisions shows that a condition common to those decisions was involvement by newspaper personnel in the conflict over whether the police department should be corrupt.

Conditions of Defense

Three of the four scandals included a public defense of the police department against the early attempts to label it corrupt, but each defense was short-lived. The condition common to the three scandals in which a defense occurred was some vulnerability in the status of the revealers.[25] In the fourth case, Newburgh, the unquestioned legitimacy of the criminal indictments was associated with almost no attempt to defend the department from the deviant label. When the Newburgh chief was suspended from duty, a group called "Concerned Citizens for the Preservation of Law and Order" was formed to organize a testimonial dinner in behalf of the police department, with a planned attendance of six hundred people. At that time, a straw poll conducted by a local newspaper showed strong public support for the police chief.[26] But after a patrolman testified in court about one of the burglaries at Sears, public opinion changed radically and the conditions of defense evaporated. The testimonial dinner was canceled, according to a spokesman, "for lack of people participation."[27] The legitimacy of the criminal process and the invulnerability of Sears as a major revealer removed the apparently necessary condition for a defense to be made. Not even the police officers themselves, let alone any other public figures, attempted to make a public defense of the department against the deviant label.

The Oakland Police Department found it difficult to make a defense against the label because one of the primary revealers of the organizational corruption was the department's superior, the city manager. The extortion victim was vulnerable to attack because he was a known inebriate, but he had only revealed allegations of individual police corruption. It was the city manager who was responsible for pointing out the organization's failure to police itself properly. The police chief remained silent, but the head of the detectives denied that any Oakland police officers could commit any criminal acts, implicitly claiming that the revealer was lying.[28] The strong role of the manager in the revelations seems to have kept any other public figures from defending the police from the deviant label.

In Central City, the active role of the young police zealots in revealing corruption seems to have favored a widely based defense of the police department against the deviant label. The defense began with the police chief claiming that the zealots were inventing their revelations because they were disgruntled by their failure to be promoted—an ironic charge, since one of the revelations was that promotions could only be obtained by paying the Republican Party several hundred dollars. Supporters of the police department on the city council also defended the department by attacking the motives of both the revealers and the newspaper. They claimed that the scandal was fabricated as a way of selling more newspapers.

The clearest attack on the status of the revealers was found in New York, where the incumbent police commissioner defended the department by labeling the sources of the revelations as "prostitutes, narcotics addicts and gamblers, and disgruntled policemen."[29] The *New York Times* responded by refuting the commissioner's claim that the revealers were of a socially or morally inferior status. An editorial note near the report of the commissioner's defense reported that no addicts or prostitutes had been interviewed for the story, but that architects, restaurant owners, contractors, social scientists, and police officers decorated for heroism had been the sources of the revelations.[30]

While the vulnerability of the revealers' status was a common condition for the appearance of a public defense, there were also other strategies for defending the police departments. One of these strategies was to attack the legitimacy of the manner in which the revelations were made, irrespective of the truth of the revelations. This strategy was an indirect attack upon the status of the revealers, implying that their methods were deviant even if their motives were not. The Central City police officials and their public supporters attacked the propriety of making criminal allegations in the press instead of in the grand jury room. Even the mayor of Central City, who generally played a dramatizer rather than a defender role, announced that anyone who had information about police corruption should present it to a grand jury. Most revealers refused to do that because of their mistrust of the prosecutor in control of the grand jury, but the symbolic invocation of the criminal justice process as the proper way to make allegations probably hurt the credibility of the revealers' claims. In New York, the methods of the Knapp Commission were denounced as a "civil liberties disaster" by a civic group usually hostile to the police, the American Civil Liberties Union. The use of hidden microphones and double agents to gather evidence, as well as the presentation of accusations in public hearings where the accused had no opportunity to defend themselves, was labeled by the civil libertarians as violations of due process.[31]

The most significant strategy for defending police departments from the deviant label was the denial of organizational deviance by the admission of individual deviance within the organization. Police officials and other defenders claimed that there are always a few rotten apples in a barrel, but that does not mean that the whole barrel is rotten. Those attempting to apply the label, of course, were claiming that the whole barrel was indeed rotten, and that the problem was organizational deviance rather than deviance by individual members of the organization. The less evidence of organizational deviance that is revealed, the more likely it may be that the "rotten apple" defense will be invoked. Even reform police executives invoked the rotten apple argument, but they generally did so after the department had already been successfully labeled as a deviant organization.

The public defense of the police departments in the three cities where it appeared failed to thwart the application of a deviant label. One key reason may have been that the defenders were for the most part closely allied to the interests of the departments they defended. Their lack of impartiality may have made their defenses unconvincing. Another reason for the failure may have been that the defenses seemed to disappear after the initial response to the publication of the revelations of organizational corruption. The continuing disclosures of organizational deviance made defenses increasingly more dangerous for the defenders' own reputations. (Where the disclosures of organizational deviance did not continue to grow, however, defenses became more frequent; a reform public safety director in Central City labeled the revelations of organizational deviance as "Mickey Mouse stuff" six months after their publication.) But perhaps the major reason for the failure of the public defenses was that the municipal executives, both mayors and managers, failed to take on a defender role. Where they have taken on that role in other cities, the defense has been successful in thwarting the deviant label.[32] That is not to say what is cause and what is effect; mayors may only defend police departments when they expect the defense will succeed. In Oakland, New York, and Central City, the municipal executives may have calculated their potential losses from defending the police as greater than their potential losses from not joining the attack on the police.

Defenses made by those too close to the control of the police department can backfire. A hasty denial of corruption charges without the appearance of a careful and thorough investigation can provide even more evidence that the police department is not interested in policing itself. While the chief in Central City was busy denying the revelations, the mayor was busy forming an "elite" police squad to investigate the revelations under his own personal direction. In New York, the police commissioner's vigorous denials of the corruption charges led to the disbanding of an investigating committee of which he was a member, and the formation of the Knapp Commission, the group ultimately responsible for the labeling of the department as deviant.

The private defense from further revelations also failed in the three cities. The little scandals of earlier years in the three cities had been successfully terminated by control of information after the initial revelations, but the information control strategies failed to work during the big scandals. Perhaps because the conflict over goals was more intense, perhaps because the news media took more interest, or perhaps because the investigative strategies were different, revelations continued to be made in the three cities after the initial revelations. The new revelations often appeared at critically important points in the development of the scandal, keeping the momentum of labeling going by providing fuel for dramatizations. The failure of covert defenses against more information leakage may have done even more harm than the absence of a continuing vigorous public defense. And as the increasing evidence gave more credibility to the revelers, the conditions of defense and the defenses themselves both disappeared.

Conditions of Dramatization

The revelations of organizational police corruption in all four cities were dramatized by various public figures. The condition common to all four dramatizations, just as for the revelations, was conflict over the organizational goals of the police department. Some dramatizers even changed sides in the conflict, publicly attacking the corrupt character of the department after having previously ignored corruption. This was true, for example, of the mayors in New York and Central City, both of whom were aiming for higher elective office at the time the revelations were first published. Once the conflict came out into the open, the numerous political figures in each city had to decide which side they would choose in the conflict. Their choices seem to have been determined by their assessment of who would win the conflict.

The mayor of New York may have sought to dramatize or to postpone the corruption issue by creating an independent investigatory commission. Whatever his intention,[23] the result was the creation of the most successful dramatizer in any of the four cities. The Knapp Commission took its dramatizer role very seriously, defining it in those terms from the very outset. Its entire purpose was to show the audience of New York City that the police department was a corrupt organization.[34] The revelations it sought out and the televised public hearing format for presenting them were all calculated to apply the deviant label to the department. The commission employed its revelations strategically in order to make the most dramatic use of them. When, for example, a city official claimed that there was no organized corruption in the police department,[35] the Knapp Commission revealed the next day that its agents had observed a large group of police officers stealing $15,000 worth of meat from a warehouse in the early hours of the morning, while the agents made repeated but unsuccessful calls to the local precinct supervisors to have them investigate the police burglary in progress.[36] The revelation refuted the defense that corruption was merely individualized, and dramatized the unwillingness of the department to police itself.

The Knapp Commission's dramatizations occurred in a community in which there had been intensive conflict over police organizational goals and conduct for a number of years. Police treatment of minority groups, police brutality, and police effectiveness in fighting crime had been major issues ever since the beginning of the then current mayoral administration in 1966. There was a large audience already receptive to the Knapp Commission's dramatizations, and the size of the audience grew after the dramatizations were made. In Oakland and Central City, however, the existing conflict over police organizational goals was quite limited. The city manager in Oakland and the zealot-revealers in Central City had to create a conflict out of an almost complete consensus that the police departments were not only adequate, but among the "finest in the country." In creating the conflict, they relied on existing support for the norms that the police had broken. The brutal nature of the extortion in Oakland and the connection of the Central City police with narcotics traffic may have been the keys to widening the conflict beyond its originators. While the communities may have been tolerant of some forms of police corruption, they were not tolerant of the particular forms that were revealed. Much the same could be said of Newburgh, although the dramatizations there occurred after the indictments of 23 percent of the department, and were somewhat superfluous by that point.

The counter examples of no dramatizations occurring where there is insufficient conflict over police organizational goals can be found in the little scandals in all four departments. The facts of corruption revealed in these precursors of the big scandals were often as serious as the facts revealed in the big scandals themselves. But without any conflict to fuel a dramatization of the facts, the little scandals did not succeed in labeling the police departments as deviant.

Conditions of Prosecution

Criminal prosecution received a great deal of publicity in the Oakland and Newburgh scandals, but not in the Central City and New York scandals. In both New York and Central City, the criminal prosecutions that did occur encompassed a very small part of the corruption that had been revealed, while in Oakland and Newburgh the criminal prosecutions encompassed virtually all of the revealed corruption.

The variation in the extent of prosecution is not consistent with the differences in the constraints upon the prosecutors. The prosecutors in Newburgh and Central City were linked to the political elite controlling the police, yet one prosecuted the police (in Newburgh) and the other did not. The prosecutors in Oakland and New York were all independent of the elected officials in control of the police, yet the Oakland prosecutor undertook extensive prosecution of police corruption and the New York prosecutors did not.

The variation in prosecution is, however, consistent with the victim or non-victim nature of the revealed corruption. Police corruption for which there is an identifiable victim to give testimony is a much easier kind of crime on which to gather evidence. As the case of Newburgh shows, it may even be impossible not to prosecute such crimes once the evidence has been gathered. But crimes without victims are much more difficult acts on which to gather evidence. It is one thing for a revealer to describe patterns of corruption in a police department; it is quite another to provide the evidence necessary for conviction of individual police officers and officials for taking bribes voluntarily offered to them, since the bribe-givers have no incentive for testifying. Prosecution may have occurred where it did because the crimes revealed produced victims. The police crimes revealed in New York and Central City were mainly victimless. Even if the prosecutors in those two cities had been eager to prosecute the large portion of the police department allegedly participating in corruption, they would have been unable to do so without a long and expensive investigation. No such time and expense was necessary in Oakland and Newburgh, where the victims provided the ready evidence needed for a speedy prosecution. Since many prosecutors seem to "contract"[37] with police departments to ignore police misconduct in exchange for police support of prosecutorial work, the presence or absence of victims seems to be the best explanation for the presence or absence of prosecution, regardless of the nature or intensity of the conflict.

Conditions of Labeling

The conditions of an audience labeling a police department as corrupt are the conditions of a successful, punitive scandal. The conditions include the appearance of the revelation, publication, and dramatization stages. Other stages are not essential. Extensive prosecution may contribute to the labeling of the department as corrupt, as it did in Oakland, or it may be virtually the sole condition for labeling the department as corrupt, as it was in Newburgh. But prosecution is not a necessary condition for labeling a police department corrupt, as the cases of New York and Central City demonstrate. The appearance of a defense in three of the cities also did not prevent the label from being applied, although more sustained defenses by more defenders might have done so.

The conditions of labeling a police department corrupt do not depend upon which stages appear so much as on what happens during each stage. A defense may backfire, a dramatization may fail to stress the organizational nature of the deviance, or a revelation may turn out to be patently untrue. Timing may also be an important factor in leading to successful labeling. The initial revelations in New York petered out into a little scandal because they were not followed by any further major revelations (although they were followed by the creation of the Knapp Commission, which provided the big scandal revelations almost two years later). A loss of momentum in the process of building a steadily more convincing case that the police department is corrupt may thwart the successful application of the label. A successful defense, a lack of dramatizations, or even a low-key approach to publication of the revelations may result in the failure of scandal to label the department as corrupt.

To the extent that general conclusions can be drawn from such limited evidence, three conditions seem to be associated with successful labeling of police departments as corrupt. One is the publication of revelations of failures of the departments to police themselves, evidence that the police organization has violated the public trust that it would exercise internal control. A second condition is that the revealers be credible, or at least endorsed by a highly credible public figure; some association of the revealers always seems to be of higher status than the police department itself, such as reporters, city managers, or blue ribbon commissions.[38] The final condition seems to be that the revelations be dramatized as serious by public figures who can claim to represent a large portion of the community. Leaders of marginal civic groups may dramatize corruption or defend the department, but their statements are not as important, for example, as those of congressmen unaffiliated with the local political elite, or of leaders of the major professional associations. To the extent that a police department can (1) demonstrate its vigor in policing corruption internally, (2) label the revealers as unreliable sources of information, and (3) escape the attacks of major public figures, it may be able to avoid being labeled as corrupt. Where a police department fails to take these steps, the conditions of successful labeling may be met, and the police department may be punished by the stigma of scandal.

Notes

1. The cities involved are New York City; Newburgh, New York; Oakland, California; and "Central City", a pseudonym for a city whose officials insisted the author disguise its identity.
2. Arnold A. Rogow and Harold Lasswell, *Power, Corruption, and Rectitude* (Englewood Cliffs, N.J.: Prentice Hall, 1963), p. 74. See also John A. Gardiner, *The Politics of Corruption* (New York: Russell Sage Foundation, 1970).
3. See Albert J. Reiss, Jr.'s discussion of fiducial roles in the foreword to Antony Simpson's *The Literature of Police Corruption: Volume 1. A Guide to Bibliography and Theory* (New York: The John Jay Press. 1977).
4. See Edward Shils, *Center and Periphery* (Chicago: University of Chicago Press, 1975); and Jack D. Douglas, "A Sociological Theory of Official Deviance and Public Concerns with Official Deviance," in *Official Deviance,* ed. Jack D. Douglas and John M. Johnson (Philadelphia: Lippincott, 1977), pp. 395–110.
5. Daniel Elazar, *American Federalism: A View from the States* (New York: Thomas Y. Crowell, 1972).
6. In the scandal over the financial affairs of President Carter's first budget director, Bert Lance, for example, the norm that a budget director should not have his personal debt service tied to the prime interest rate was proposed for the first time. See, generally, *New York Times,* August 15–October 1, 1977.
7. I am indebted to Dr. Jack Katz for both the notions of failure of self-regulation as a condition of scandal, and the division of labor in the making of scandal.
8. Harold Garfinkel, "Conditions of Successful Degradation Ceremonies," *American Journal of Sociology,* 61 (March 1956), pp. 420–24.
9. Kennedy School of Government, *The Knapp Commission and Patrick V. Murphy (B)* (Cambridge, Mass.: Harvard University, mimeo, 1977).
10. See, e.g., "Rep. Young's Wife is Apparent Suicide: Mother of 5 Found

Shot to Death—Texas Lawmaker Was Linked to Sex Scandal by Secretary," *New York Times,* Friday, July 15, 1977.

11. As another example, see the description of the Netherlands' Prince Bernhard's life a year after he was forced to resign from numerous high posts because of the collective outrage of his having taken bribes from the Lockheed Corporation. See "Bernhard, a Year after Disgrace over Lockheed, Shows No Scars," *New York Times,* July 5, 1977.

12. Television Station WHAS–TV in Louisville created a police corruption scandal in 1970–71. See Robert H. Williams, *Vice Squad* (New York: Thomas Y. Crowell, 1973), pp. 35–41.

13. Knapp Commission Report, pp. 13–15.

14. Peter Maas, *Serpico* (New York: Viking, 1973); and David Burnham, *The Role of the Media in Controlling Corruption* (New York: John Jay Press, 1976).

15. Interview with Thomas Wohlrab, deputy commissioner, Newburgh police department, February 1, 1976.

16. *Oakland Tribune,* May 5, 1952; January 16, 1953; April 7, 1953; April 10, 1953; and March 12, 1954.

17. *Oakland Tribune,* January 4, 1955.

18. Interview with Wayne Thompson, former city manager of Oakland, May 9, 1975.

19. Ibid.

20. See, e.g., Bob Woodward and Carl Bernstein, *All the President's Men* (New York: Simon and Schuster, 1974).

21. Burnham, *The Role of the Media in Controlling Corruption.*

22. Maas, *Serpico,* p. 255.

23. See, generally, Leon Sigal, *Reporters and Officials* (Lexington, Mass.: D.C. Heath and Co., 1973).

24. See, e.g., John J. McGlennon, "Bureaucratic Crisis and Executive Leadership: Corruption in Police Departments" (Ph.D. dissertation, Johns Hopkins University, 1977), pp. 133–55.

25. Albert J. Reiss, Jr., Lectures, Yale University, 1973.

26. *Newburgh Evening News,* January 25, 1972.

27. *Newburgh Evening News,* May 25, 1972.

28. *Oakland Tribune,* January 15, 1955.

29. *New York Times,* April 29, 1970, p. 1.

30. Ibid., p. 1.

31. *New York Times,* October 23, 1971, p. 21.

32. McGlennon, "Bureaucratic Crisis and Executive Leadership," pp. 139–44.

33. The district attorney of New York county, Frank Hogan, later admitted that he had nominated the "wrong man" to the mayor to head the commission. *New York Times,* October 12, 1972, p. 1.

34. Kennedy School of Government, *The Knapp Commission and Patrick V. Murphy (B).*

35. *New York Times,* February 9, 1977, p. 1.

36. *New York Times,* February 10, 1977, p. 1.

37. Reiss, Lectures.

52

Political Scandals and Corruption Issues in West Germany

Erhard Blankenburg,
Rainer Staudhammer,
and Heinz Steinert

A Labelling Approach to Corruption

Germans in the Federal Republic from the 1950s through the 1970s could pride themselves on living in a relatively corruption-free political system. Compared with the scandals that newspapers in Washington, London, or Rome reported, and compared with the endemic black market in socialist countries or the bribery in trading with Third World countries, the mostly local scandals in West German construction industries and city authorities seemed of minor magnitude and political relevance. When one appraised issues which the opposition brought up in parliament, or considered the events that occasionally forced politicians to resign, Germany did not score very high in rankings of political corruption. There seemed to be a tradition of Prussian correctness and belief in legality that kept the national political arena above influence based only on money and favoritism.

In the 1980s the self-image of legality and propriety has been tarnished. Scandals over party financing and over business failures connected to the political parties have followed one another. Figures such as the president of parliament and cabinet ministers, as well as high-ranking officials such as the cabinet's press spokesman, have had to resign because of charges such as having taken bribes on contracts, or having evaded taxes on a large scale. Networks of clientelistic relations between political parties and business corporations have been laid bare, and high officials were accused of illegal collusion.

Many of these scandals were predominantly directed against conservative politicians of the governing Christian Democratic Party (CDU and the Bavarian CSU) as well as the Liberal Party (FDP). However, there has also been some retaliation against the Social Democratic Party (SPD), especially concerning the housing cooperative "Neue Heimat," which is connected to the trade unions federation and thereby the Social Democrats. In 1985 the Neue Heimat was found to be near bankruptcy.

Thus, in the history of German democracy, the 1980s may become the period during which the Federal Republic became like other western democracies whose election campaigns and party organizations are related to a continuous stream of scandals. In a political culture like the German's, treating political opponents' personal misbehavior as public scandal has long been considered an illegitimate form of party competition. The life-styles of politicians are protected by privacy norms, and Calvinistic moralising on sex or vice is considered beyond the arena of politics. This outlook may have changed during the course of the scandals that preoccupied German politics in the 1980s. This change may also be accompanied by a related change in public attitude that is characteristic of all democracies: that mass participation is partially ritualistic, barely hiding the collusion of "all those up there who only look out for themselves."

If collusion and bribery were really all the same across political regimes, we would not have much to explain. When comparing political systems, we might assume that human tendencies to corruption are the same everywhere, and conclude that only the levels of scandalization differ from one system to the next. However, differences between political systems are more complicated than that. The degrees of corrupt practices, and of scandalizing them, do not necessarily correlate in a one-to-one relationship; both levels vary from one political system to the next, and probably they vary independently of each other. The difficulty of identifying the two phenomena lies in their relationship: because "corruption" is a socially and sometimes legally defined label used in evaluating actual patterns of behavior, corruption does not lead an existence independent of the social process of labelling. In crosscultural comparisons, therefore, we must be careful in distinguishing to what extent we compare what are simply degrees of label attribution, or to what extent we manage to grasp some indication of different levels of corruption as a behavior pattern per se.

It is one thing to identify specific patterns of illegal conduct or clientelistic behavior, while it is something else to find out whether, and under what circumstances, such behavior is being scandalized as "corruption". Party financing of all the established parties had long since been dependent on donations from foundations explicitly set up in order to evade the tax laws. As we shall try to show, the pattern of party financing that evolved in the Federal Republic since its very beginnings invites clandestine donations, allows the establishment of clientelistic relations between donors and politicians, and lends itself to outright bribery. Thus the party financing system became an objective basis of corrupt practices. However, given the recent scandals about corruption, the question is: Why did the evolution of a clientelistic financing system not become scandalized before?

In our analysis of the German Flick Corporation scandal we shall try to give an explanation for both sides of the corruption issue. While we see no way to compare the incidence of corruption per se in the Federal Republic of Germany with those of other countries, we are able to point out why financing patterns of West German political parties have evolved in a way that increases the temptation to acquire resources by illegal methods and renders the persons involved subject to scandalization. We shall try to point out why the level of corruption has increased during the history of the Federal Republic, and give some plausible suggestions why the level of scandalization has caught up in the early 1980s—and not before.

The Pattern of Party Financing

The Context of Party Financing Scandals

Party financing has become a central arena of corruption in the Federal Republic of Germany. The framework of the West German type of "party state" and, in particular, the methods of party financing have developed over some thirty years, since the German constitution *(Basic Law)* was enacted in 1949. This framework lends itself structurally to the influence of financial power on political decisionmaking. If political decisions are "bought" rather than arising from formally established rules and procedures of egalitarian institutions, no problems arise if the practice is considered legitimate. If it is not considered to be legitimate and can only be exerted covertly, then its uncovering lends itself to scandalizing. Scandals thus define what a political system considers to be "corruption." An analysis of corruption, therefore, apart from exploring the special interests and motives of the parties involved, must take into consideration the following: (1) both the legal and moral standards governing political life in a given society (and defining what is to be considered "corrupt"), (2) the institutional structures and practices giving rise to specific patterns of corruption, and (3) the institutions and people capable of scandalizing.

Scandals over political corruption may serve as an indicator of public control. They can be considered as symptomatic of the normal—rather than "pathological"—functioning of political systems; of the ways in which *economic* power is being transformed into political influence.

Theoretically, an increase in corruption may have several causes: more demanding normative standards; a decay of moral socialization; a strengthening of institutional controls, or more effective scandalization. The scandalization of corruption depends essentially on two conditions: (a) that legal or moral norms guiding public life have been violated (the graver the violation and the more publicly exposed the offender, the higher the potential for scandalization), and (b) that the institutional control mechanisms, the system of checks and balances, no longer fulfill their function for the political system: to safeguard and, if necessary, to restore "public order." Naturally, in order to set the process in motion, there also has to be someone with an interest in, and the resources for, scandalization. Someone must stand to gain politically and/or economically from shouting "scandal."

Party financing in the Federal Republic of Germany has by no means been the only field of politics in which corruption has prospered, as is evidenced by the affair of the *Neue Heimat Cooperative,* where the trade unions are highly involved, or by the series of corruption scandals haunting West Berlin, which have for a long time been the responsibility of a Social Democratic government but continued under Christian Democratic mayors. In all the latter scandals public contracts and government subsidies to the construction industry have been the chief object of bribe money; thus these constitute another, distinctive pattern of political corruption.

The "Neue Heimat" in 1985 was found to be near bankruptcy, a case which in size even surpasses that of the huge AEG electronics concern a few years ago. But while the AEG was treated as a regrettable business failure and salvaged by a joint effort of big banks and industrial corporations (since 1985 AEG has been owned by Mercedes Benz.), the "Neue Heimat" gave rise to a series of scandals on personal corruption and management incompetence of socialist politician-managers reaching back to the 1970s and even 1960s when the Social Democrats enjoyed majorities in most big city governments. The purpose of the Neue Heimat scandal as well as of the Flick Corporation is not so much that they led to scandals in the 1980s, but that they avoided scandal for so long.

As it has been by far the most prominent and spectacular, and in many ways a particularly symptomatic case of political corruption, we will concentrate in this chapter on party donations related to the Flick scandal, the affair that has coined Germany's image as a "bribable republic."[1] Of course, any look at history will reveal that the clientelistic methods of party financing that became explicit in the Flick scandal have a long tradition of dormant existence. Corruption has its structural roots in the methods of party financing; these we shall have to describe first. We shall also have to explain what has prevented this scandal from being disclosed and prosecuted earlier. The answer to both these questions lies in the oligarchic nature of the West German party system, dominated at all levels by continuously operating centralized and ideologically rather homogeneous party organizations. These organizations dispose of a wide range of resources, including foundations financed by public as well as private means, business enterprises that are partly exempt from taxes for producing public goods *(Gemeinnützigkeit),* and a set of related voluntary organizations for youth, students, and other groups.

The Party Financing Set-Up   As early as 1949, prior to the first parliamentary elections, German industrialists and business associations joined forces to set up a system of party financing that was later to be institutionalized in so-called sponsor organizations and civic associations. The sole purpose of these institutions was to collect money from the business community and to distribute it among those parties that seemed best suited to safeguard business interests, i.e., to function as financial intermediaries between business and political parties.

Thus was revived a long-standing tradition of corporate funding of political parties via donations, a tradition almost as old as the party system itself.[2] Corporate donations were regularly brought to bear on the balance of political forces—and not only during election campaigns. Indeed, the sums invested in political parties would grow considerably in size and importance whenever major social and political changes appeared on the agenda. During the early decades of this century, corporate money was mostly spent to keep left-wing parties, especially the SPD, from rising to power, and to strengthen the bourgeois center and right-wing parties. When, in the early 1930s, faced with economic depression and intense class struggle, these parties seemed less and less capable of providing a long-term solution to the crisis, a number of German industrialists searched for a viable alternative and began to pin their hopes on the Nazis. After having rescued it from imminent bankruptcy in 1933, these benefactors generously funded Hitler's NSDAP during the years to come.

This is not to suggest, however, that political parties could simply be bought and instrumentalized by "big money," nor that historical events are the result of some financial transactions, nor even that capitalists have the same interest or political option. Rather, it is to point to the historical continuity of party financing by corporate business and to recall that corporate capital has a tradition of channelling party donations as an effective (and entirely legal) instrument of wielding power and influence (cf. Heidenheimer/Langdon, 1968). As this structure has played a prominent role in dooming the Weimar Republic, party donations have remained a sensitive issue in Germany. As a means of opening doors, granting privileged access to the centers of political decisionmaking, and discreetly prearranging the political scene, party donations undeniably have their merits under authoritarian as well as democratic political regimes—although the latter aspect is usually ignored in somewhat idyllic views of pluralist interest mediation in liberal democracies (cf. Rose-Ackerman, 1978).

The system of "civic" and "sponsor" organizations, set up in the 1950s to organize the flow of funds from corporations to parties, offered contributors a number of advantages. First, it granted a high degree of anonymity to individual firms, avoiding undesired publicity. Furthermore, as these organizations were officially recognized as acting "in the public interest," contributions to them could be deducted from corporate as well as individual taxes. Last but not least, by coordinating their fund-raising activities, individual firms were kept from being played off against one another, and could bring to bear their political influence on parties by unrecognized middlemen. In sum, the "sponsoring organizations" provided an entry to political lobbying, introducing a model of pressure group influence that was both efficient and economical: they helped contributors to disguise their political influence, while at the same time exerting considerable financial control over the parties.[3]

To stabilize revenues from private donors, the first Adenauer coalition government, soon after coming to power, passed a law providing that contributions to parties should generally be tax-exempt within limits of 10 percent of personal income or 2 per mille of corporate sales, respectively. This meant that tax subsidies became a regular source of party income, almost incidentally making the state an indirect partner in the business of party financing.[4]

However, the constitutional court (Bundesverfassungsgericht, or BVG), launched into action by the Social Democrats in 1958, judged this law to be unconstitutional on two grounds. The first complaint was that the law would unduly favor parties backed by financially strong interest groups and corporations, thus distorting competition. Secondly, because the law offended the principle of equal participation of citizens, big contributors could receive greater tax benefits and would thus be granted a special premium for their participation in the political decisionmaking process.

While the 1958 constitutional court decision did not rule out private donations to political parties (whatever their amount), it did prevent those donations being deducted from taxes. After the decision, the volume of private donations declined drastically, which prompted the parties to search for, and find, new sources of financial assistance. This is where the multifaceted story of what some twenty years later came to be called the "party donation scandal" really begins.

Generally speaking, there were two main protagonists involved in the evolution of the German party financing system, both of which contribute to its becoming a "cause celebre." On the one hand, the *constitutional court,* invoking egalitarian-democratic principles of the Constitution, laid down in its 1958 and later decisions rather restrictive legal norms with regard to party financing. On the other hand, the *major political parties,* driven by ever-increasing financial desires, passed self-serving legislation. Since 1958 the history of party financing has been the history of a conflict over the division of powers and the role of political parties in a democratic state.

Party Donations: Anatomy of a Political Scandal

The Multifarious Ways of Party Financing

In the early years of the Federal Republic, membership fees and contributions from the parties' office holders still constituted around half of the parties' income (cf. Heidenheimer, 1958). Following the 1958 court decision, the German parties quickly discovered the budgets of the federal states as an alternative—and lucrative—source of funding. They began appropriating to themselves budget allocations "for the advancement of political education," an item that was soon to reach the sizeable sum of DM 38 million per party a year.

In 1966 the BVG found that this practice of state subsidization of political parties violated the constitution, as it did not consider parties to be state organs whose organizations could be publicly funded. The court conceded, however, that insofar as parties performed genuinely "public" functions, they should be reimbursed by the state for their necessary election campaign expenses. A flat sum of DM 2.50 per voter was subsequently allowed to cover these expenses, establishing public funds as a prime source of party income ever since. Additionally, the parties devised a number of indirect ways of public funding, such as making budgetary means available to the party-owned political foundations such as the Social Democratic Friedrich-Ebert-Stiftung, the Christian Democratic Konrad-Adenauer-Stiftung, and the liberal Friedrich-Naumann-Stiftung (cf. von Vieregge, 1977). Since parties continued to collect fees from their office holders, they succeeded in bringing the total share of public funds to well over 50 percent of their income. Thus, both in quantitative as well as qualitative respects, the size of German comprehensive state financing became unique among Western democracies.

Contrary to what might have been expected, however, state subsidies did not reduce the parties' eagerness to collect private donations, nor did they reduce the political influence corporate donors could exert by promising or withholding sizeable contributions. Since donations became the most variable component of party income and, accordingly, of particular strategic importance, competition for private donations increased rather than decreased.

Through the years the parties invented a considerable number of covert, indirect ways of raising donations in order to circumvent the existing legal restrictions.[5] Most frequently, money was donated to the "civic associations" or to other "public interest" tax-exempt organizations, including the parties' foundations, from where they would subsequently be diverted via hidden ways to parties' accounts or simply be transferred to the parties' treasurers in cash.

The covert practices that parties and donors resorted to not only systematically circumvented tax laws and the BVG rulings outlined above, they also violated the Party Act of 1967 as well as the constitution. These latter legal rules made it mandatory that parties publish the sources of their income and, in particular, identify their big contributors, and make party finances and the relationships between parties and corporations more transparent to the public. Almost all the big donations that the parties listed in their reports, however, were reported as coming from the "civic associations" or similar cover organizations. In general, less than 1 percent of total donations could be identified as to their real source of origin.[6] In 1976, for example, more than 80 percent of all donations (over DM 20,000) liable to publication were given by "sponsor associations" of some sort.[7]

The system of organized tax avoidance thus erected has become the central issue of the scandal about party donations. How widespread the pattern has been is illustrated by more than 1,800 cases in which preliminary proceedings had been opened since 1982, involving all major parties (except for the Green Party, founded in 1980), as well as a good part of Germany's corporate elite. So far only a few of these cases have actually been taken to court, as most of them were either dismissed or settled by fines in a plea-bargaining fashion.

In court there was insufficient evidence that the covert party donations were cases of political bribery. Thus these were rather treated as cases of tax fraud (party donations not being tax-deductible at the time, whether given to parties directly or indirectly via cover organizations), since money contributions for deputies or party functionaries do not constitute a criminal offense as does bribing public officials. The 1967 Party Act, which, of course, was worked out by the parties themselves, did not provide any legal sanctions in case of violation. Moreover, the respected persons of the economic elite who were involved in the affair argued that their donations had not been motivated by any private concerns, but had in fact served the public interest since it helped parties to fulfill their constitutional tasks. This reasoning may sound convincing to those who tend to identify party and business interests with those of democracy as a system. However, as a matter of course corporate party financing has been found to serve particular interests of parties and business corporations, rather than those of the "public at large."

Rather than any single incidence of illegal party donations, it is the overall pattern of complicity between party and business interests, as well as the close entanglement of parties, government, and private capital, that have been revealed in the course of the "party donations scandal" that seem to validate the term "corruption" in this case (cf. Schily, 1986a). Notwithstanding its strict legal regulation, party financing has actually spread in a political grey area, remote from any effective parliamentary or public control, which provided fertile ground for corruptive practices.

Whatever the final legal and political assessment of the affair, the parties' manifold attempts, both legal and illegal, at safeguarding different streams of financial revenues have no doubt evolved in a stable organizational structure. While tax revenues doubled between 1968 and 1975, party revenues almost tripled during the same period.[8] In little more than a decade, from 1969 to 1980 (both election years), total revenues of the four major parties (CDU, CSU, FDP, and SPD) climbed from DM 102 million to DM 465 million.

While parties' political activities have become more costly all over the world, the German situation is unique in at least two respects: the budgets German parties dispose of are larger, and have grown faster, than those in most countries, and the share of government subsidies they have made available to themselves is all but unequalled. Of the

DM 1.5 billion spent in the period 1977 to 1980 alone (equalling DM 34.57 per eligible voter, as compared with DM 7.65 in the United States), 31 percent had come from direct government subsidies, as compared to 19 percent in the United States.

The Rising Costs of the Party Oligopoly. No matter how imaginative and efficient the parties' efforts at fund raising may have been, the rise in revenues has always been greatly exceeded by the growth in expenses. Why? Two principal sources have caused the spiraling rise in party expenditures: Organizational costs due to the massive buildup of party organizations during the 1960s and early 1970s, and costs of advertising and election campaigns. The parties' political function, as defined by the constitution, is to "participate in forming the political will of the people." Thus, political parties have been granted constitutional status for the first time in German constitutional history, setting them apart from independent, nonparty organizations, political action groups, or grass root movements. Government subsidies and institutional privileges have evolved in an oligarchic system of interest representation, dominated by professionalized and bureaucratized party machines, whose influence on the political process and the media has become pervasive.

The Green party broke into the cartel of established parties at the beginning of the 1980s as a "system opposition," with, however, more indirect than direct effects on the other parties. Ever since the Green opposition appeared on the scene, the established parties have had difficulties in legitimizing their position. But even before this outsider broke into the oligopoly, with traditional party allegiances of the voters loosening, election campaigns (i.e., "polit-marketing") became the dominant factor in the parties' struggle for a greater share of the voter market and for political power. As a consequence, competition has grown more intense.

What is specific about the German case is the organizational oligopoly on which parties could build. The stability of this system rests, above all, on a strong interparty consensus about the basic rules of the game (including the legal/illegal ways of party financing), and on the commonly shared interest of the "established" parties—to retain their de facto monopoly of public decisionmaking and to guard it against outside forces. This common interest has in good part suspended the functioning of the checks and balances and the institutional mechanisms of control usually associated, at least in theory, with competitive party systems, replacing them with conventional patterns of tacit agreement and mutual privilege enhancement.

The Political Situation. Given the complicity of the "established" parties, neither of which had any great interest in drying up the source from which they all in good part lived, the illegal ways of party donations involved little risk. Parties were enabled to keep up with growing expenses, which was most needed by the mid-1970s when, faced with acute financial crises, parties not only were forced to resort to banking credits but also stepped up their efforts at raising private donations. Furthermore donations proved quite an effective instrument for business to make its political influence felt more directly, especially when parties were most urgently in need.

As has been revealed in the course of this scandal, corporate managers often had definite notions as to direct advantages the party donations were to serve. "Cultivating the political scene," as von Brauchitsch, Flick's former general manager put it, was designed to create a political environment conducive to business interests and business needs. Apart from lobbying for or against specific proposals (regarding, for example, tax reform or workers' codetermination), this would include a wide variety of direct or indirect interventions. These ranged from sponsoring the careers of handpicked political talents and promoting them to suitable positions, to manipulating the balance of inner-party forces by intervening in favor of those factions most staunchly committed to the ideals of free enterprise and the market economy (most notably the right wing of the FDP), and to preparing the ground for the making and unmaking of party alliances and government coalitions.

When the Liberal Democrats had shifted to the left by joining a coalition government with Social Democrats in 1969, corporate donations to the party were quickly suspended. Payments were resumed in 1972, after the Social Liberals had been confirmed in office for a second term, and business executives found it wiser to strengthen the Liberal Democrats as a counter weight against the Social Democrats.

Throughout the 1970s, with the SPD/FDP coalition still in power, business was again trying to forge a center-right coalition of CDU and FDP, staking its hopes and its money mainly on the FDP's right-wing, which eventually played a decisive role in bringing about the political change from a social-liberal to a liberal-conservative government in 1982.

However, in strategic terms it proved important and far-sighted to let all parties have "their" share of illegal donations. Thus party financing created a partial "all-party coalition," excluding only the Green party. Without their opposition to the entire system of party financing, the scandalizing attempts in the 1980s might quickly have come to a rather unspectacular close.

Coming at public expense without being in the public interest made the party donations instances of ordinary, though criminal, tax fraud. This, to be sure, is not corruption in the classical sense of the term, which implies that money is given in return for a *specific* political favor, decision, or concession (cf. Smelser, 1971). On the contrary, the long-term funding strategy of corporations was aimed at "cultivating" the political scene in such a way as to make outright corruption superfluous. Party donations, after all, are but one means to this end. In good part, this strategy may certainly be said to have succeeded.

The Chronology of Scandalization. Constitutional court rulings and legislative amendments repeatedly redefined the borderlines of legal party financing and illegal practice, as made public by the actions of a handful of active state prosecutors, especially in the local prosecutor's office in Bonn, and by the media. It surprised some that the public prosecutors, who were traditionally subservient to the hierarchical setup of their agencies, took up investigations on the practice of party financing, but they evidently enjoyed some autonomy in deciding on specific cases. The Bonn office was later followed by other prosecutors throughout the country. The fact that the capital city of Bonn lies in North Rhine Westphalia, which for long had a Social Democratic government, has been suggested as one of the facilitating factors. However, it rather looks like some of the lower-rank prosecutors asserting their authority vis-a-vis their superiors.

Courage to withstand hierarchical pressures was facilitated by outside support. Information from the files of prosecuted cases repeatedly leaked out to the press, mostly to the leading weekly magazine, *Der Spiegel*. It seems that these leaks were related to repeated pressure from politicians to silently bury allegations of corruption, under the discretionary decision of the prosecutor's office to drop indictments; however, no evidence on the culprits in the leaks has been produced so far. In any case, it is evident from the piece-meal publication of details and scandals that prosecution leaks as well as the publications of *Der Spiegel* followed a strategy of limited disclosure aptly timed to maximize the dramatic effect of "more news to come."

The scandalization strategy of *Der Spiegel* is distinctive, as German mass media do not usually engage in scandalization campaigns as does the press in more puritan cultures. During recent years *Der Speigel* has had almost a monopoly on initiating scandals, forcing the other mass media to follow. Up to 1982 the weekly magazine *Stern* could also be counted among the media capable of staging political scandals. However, *Stern* stumbled into a scandal of its own, by publishing faked

Hitler diaries and maintaining that they were true historical documents. How effectively *Der Spiegel* has staged the drama of the Flick scandal can be seen by a brief chronology:

> The publication opening the scandal was a report in issue 50/1981 (December 7, 1981) on investigations by the Bonn state prosecutors in connection with party donations and their related tax returns. The report concentrated on the plans of an all-party coalition to grant amnesty to these tax cases and the attempts to change statutory provisions relating to party donations. *Der Spiegel* followed up in the next issue with another report that effectively thwarted plans for the amnesty.

> In issue 52/1981 of *Der Spiegel* mentioned that investigations entertained suspicions of bribery. Issues concentrated on the institution of party donations. In 2/1982 there appeared a note on the clerical "mission of Steyl," which had been instrumental in "washing" money which had flowed from the Flick Corporation to the CDU.

> *Der Spiegel* also had a different scandal on its hands, involving the trade unions and the Social Democratic opposition. In its cover stories in early 1982, extensive reports blamed the union-owned corporation *Neue Heimat* for granting extensive favors.

> The Flick scandal became a major event with the cover story in issue 9/1982. This time outright bribery was at stake, with the suspicion that the ministers of finance and of economic affairs of the social-liberal coalition had unfoundedly granted generous tax exemptions to the Flick Corporation. While there has never been any sustained suspicion that the ministers involved had taken any money personally, there was an allegation that donations to their party, and sometimes explicitly to their wing of the party, had played a role.

> New information is added in issue 47/1982, in which the state prosecutor was reported to have found notes by the general manager of the Flick Corporation, von Brauchitsch, hinting at a direct relation between party donations and the tax exemption.

> By the time the coalition of Christian Democrats with the Liberal party under Chancellor Kohl had been firmly established, *Der Spiegel,* 48/1982, had a Flick cover story again giving word-by-word protocol of the interrogations by the state prosecutors. This was the starting point for a countercampaign against *Der Spiegel* and its kind of investigative journalism, amounting to the allegation of breach of privacy and anticipating condemnation of mere suspects. *Der Spiegel* answered with another cover story on Flick in 4/1983 that reported in some detail the methods and philosophy of Flick managers, which they coined "cultivating the political scene."

> Later, in 1984, another fact was added to the Flick scandal when Rainer Barzel, then president of the *Bundestag* (parliament), was reported to have indirectly been financed by the Flick Corporation and, after some hesitation, was forced to resign.

It can be said that only a combination of arenas had made possible the scope of the scandalization drama: State prosecution and judiciary, together with a news magazine that was happy to be the protagonist for scandalizing, and the presence of a small party new to the parliament, so that it had not yet benefitted from the way of party financing and could thus form an opposition against the system as a whole.

The parliamentary investigating committee concerning party donations by the Flick Corporation held hearings over a period of two years, presenting an opportune stage for the opposition. The Green Party especially used the chance, as their outstanding attorney-member Schily embarrassed the chancellor, cabinet members, and officials of all the established parties by his pointed questioning, relating to details of the multi-volume files of the entire financial system of party donations. However, the publicity effect faded quickly. The committee report, when published, aroused hardly any public interest, and none of the remedial measures that had been proposed were enacted.[11]

The court's decision of February, 1987 was also anti-climactic. The chief judge declared that the prosecution had been justified in bringing corruption charges against the defendants, but that "poor memories on the part of witnesses" had inhibited the assembling of evidence to prove the charges. So the defendants were acquitted of the corruption charges, but found guilty only on the charges of tax evasion. The two former Economics Ministers, Hans Friderichs and Otto Lambsdorff, were sentenced to pay fines of $34,000 and $100,000, respectively for their role in illegally channeling corporate donations. Eberhard von Brauchitsch, the Flick executive who distributed the contributions on which taxes were avoided, was fined $306,000 and given a two year suspended jail sentence.

The Political Handling of the Affair. The complicity of party and business interests, the close entanglement of parties, state, and corporations, the oligarchic nature of party competition, or the informal ways of behind-the-scene bargaining that have been exposed through the party donations scandal may appear as simply another variety of corruption. Together they did not constitute bribery in strictly legal terms. Rather, they are a built-in feature of representative democratic party government. "Corruption" here was systemically based on what has been called "representative absolutism."[12]

As all major parties had participated in the shady methods of detour financing (indirect payments), and were equally dependent on donations as a vital source of party income (though in varying degrees), they were obviously more interested in exploiting this source to the full than in enforcing the rule of law. Sitting in the glass house, none would dare to throw a stone.

Investigations by lower-level officials and tax-inspectors were usually stopped at an early stage by political interventions "from above." Not infrequently, ministers of finance (being responsible for the investigation of tax-fraud) were former party-treasurers (the ones who stood most to gain from illegal practices of party-financing). But in most cases it didn't even have to come to this, as public officials were usually more afraid of the political risk involved in opening such investigations than of the juridical consequences implied in their neglect of duty and would therefore shy away from taking any resolute steps anyway.[13]

Thus, it was almost by coincidence, thanks to the sense of duty of some (few) public officials, the investigative journalism and scandalizing interests of some (few) public magazines, and the rise of a non-establishment party, that the widespread practices of illegal party financing finally came to light. Although investigations had already been under way since 1975, legal proceedings on a larger scale were not taken before 1982. Only then did party financing turn into a veritable "scandal."

The established all-party-coalition reacted as might have been expected (cf. Staudhammer, 1985). To get the embarrassing affair out of the way quickly, they made several attempts at granting an amnesty to those accused of criminal offenses, arguing that none of them had pursued any private gains; instead, as Chancellor Kohl put it, they had chosen "a democratic way of supporting democratic parties," something that should not be allowed to be criminalized. Since "detour financing" had become habitual practice, it was publicly reasoned that no one could be blamed or be held responsible in particular. The attempts to grant an amnesty were doomed to failure, however, as they met with a wave of public protests, which finally prompted the Social Democrats to withdraw their support from the project.

To solve their pressing financial problems, the parties again took the offensive and passed new legislation in 1983 to establish "unequivocal" legal terms that would render the indirect ways of the past unnecessary. Apart from raising election campaign refunds to DM 5 per voter, the new law put political parties on a par with public interest organizations, which was just another way of reintroducing the tax deductibility of party donations (within a limit of 5 percent of personal income or 2 per mille of corporate sales) through the back door. This new legislation was enacted despite the fact that the constitutional court had repeatedly (in 1958, 1968, and again in 1979) ruled out this possibility, drawing repeated distinctions between public interest organizations (which do not have legislative authority or participate in the exercise of state power) and political parties (which have both of these).

Again, the new Party Act was challenged before the constitutional court. This time the parties got their way. The persistent noncompliance with existing legal rules had finally paid off. Although in its July, 1986 decision the court once again repealed the 5 percent clause on constitutional grounds for disproportionly favoring high-income earners, it established a maximum amount of DM 100,000 annually (as compared with the 600 DM it had tolerated in 1968) that could be legally tax deductible. This for all practical purposes will have much the same effect on marginal participation as those practices that were deemed unconstitutional.

Implicit in the ruling is a cynical view of "equal participation" that allows every citizen to deduct contributions up to DM 100,000 to political parties, when the average annual income of German salaried workers is around DM 40,000. Moreover, as corporations can easily multiply this sum (simply by dividing total donations among various subsidiaries), it is plain to see that the court has in fact sanctioned the practice that parties had employed illegally in the past, blatantly contradicting its own former jurisprudence. While in its earlier rulings the BVG had consistently tried to restrict the parties' omnipotence and self-privilege and to defend citizens' democratic participation against self-styled party rule, at last it submitted to the powerful realities of the "representative absolutism" and party oligopoly by adapting its jurisprudence to the parties' unconstitutional practices.

Had this ruling been in force before, there might never have been any scandal over party donations and probably no great fuss about "corruption" in the Federal Republic. With its 1986 decision, the constitutional court closed the chapter on political corruption—by legalizing the corrupt practices it had formerly judged illegal.

The Shifting Borderlines of Legality

Thanks to the Flick scandal, national politics in the Federal Republic of Germany joined the ranks of Western democracies infested by corruption scandals. The system of party financing established in the Federal Republic increased the likelihood of capital investment in the political parties, with a natural tendency to expect political favors as a return. With the help of legislation and of the constitutional court decisions, a highly vulnerable system evolved. The more detailed some of the rules regulating party finances became, the more detours were devised. The more rule-breaking became a routine pattern, the more politicians got caught in practices for which they could be scandalized and blackmailed.

A clientelistic system of party financing must on the other hand provoke some institutionalization of a "scandal industry." Remarkably few scandals on private morals of politicians have haunted the Federal Republic of Germany so far, but an increasing number of scandals on tax evasion, bribery, and favoritism preoccupied German politics ever since the beginning of the 1980s, and have severely altered its public image.

By and large, however, public reaction in the face of the "biggest scandal" in the Federal Republic's history has been characterized by indifference rather than moral indignation (cf. Enzensberger, 1983). Contrary to what might have been expected, the party donations scandal has contributed little, if anything, to a "crisis of legitimation." In part, this may be explainable with some popular knowledge or belief, corresponding to everyday experience, that a certain degree of corruption—a certain degree of bending the rules—is needed to make life bearable in a bureaucratized and highly regulated world. This view holds particularly true with regard to tax evasion, which has become a "national sport" (cf. Weinhofer/Schöler, 1986). Thus corruption within the political class would appear as nothing more than a large-scale variety of "everyday corruption."

On the other hand, and perhaps more in line with the German authoritarian state tradition, public indifference may be attributed to a view that expects politicians to be corrupt anyway. It is based on the rather popular belief that politics is a "dirty business," that power tends to corrupt, and that "those above," the rich and mighty, can do what they want to and still get away with it. Rooted in the authoritarian tradition of the German state and political culture, this view of the world and the political apathy resulting from it is part of that "civic privatism" which has been the pendant of "representative absolutism" all along (Roth, 1985b).

Notes

1. The history of political corruption in West Germany, long ignored or treated with "benign neglect" by social scientists, has yet to be written. The few studies that are available on the subject include Eschenburg 1966, 1967, 1972, Noack 1985, and Roth 1985a.

2. For the history of party financing see Heidenheimer and Langdon (1968), Kulitz 1983, Lösche 1984, and Staudhammer 1985.

3. Scholars who examined the associations in the 1950s and 1960s noted that one of their defensive goals was that of "insulating business against corruption charges." But the relative priority of this goal differed between countries. For the business sponsor associations in Japan "developing an intermediary mechanism to separate donor from recipient" and to "reduce blatant favor-buying" constituted a primary goal. But for the German sponsor associations this goal was assessed as having a much lower priority relative to more offensive ones of exerting influence on party policies. Heidenheimer/Langdon, 1968, 208–10.

4. For details, see von Arnim 1982, Lösche 1984, and Nassmacher 1984.

5. For a more detailed description of these methods see Lösche 1984 (45ff) and Kulitz 1983 (76ff); also, Wagner 1986 and de Boor et al. 1986.

6. Kaack 1978a, p. 291.

7. Troitzsch 1979, p. 486.

8. Kaack 1978a, p. 286.

9. For facts and figures regarding party finances, see Kaack 1978a, Nassmacher 1984, and Siebert 1980. While income from membership subscriptions steadily rose from DM 31 million in 1969 to 132 million in 1980, donations were highest in election years, surging from DM 37 million in 1969 to DM 89 million in 1980, after having reached a peak of 100 million in 1976. In the meantime, direct state subsidies (campaign refunds) to *all* parties, including the minor ones, soared from DM 48 million in 1969 to DM 249 million in 1979 (including elections to the European parliament being held that year). Of the DM 2.388 million parties took in from 1968 to 1978, subscriptions accounted for 743 million (31 percent), campaign-refunds for 629 million (26.3 percent), and donations for 535 million (22.4 percent).

10. Nassmacher 1984, p. 14. As regards party donations, their relative importance (as a percentage of total revenues) vary quite considerably, being highest among the bourgeois parties. On average, between 1968 and 1980 the SPD's share of donations amounted to 9 percent of party income, comparing rather unfavorably with 27 percent for the CDU, 30 percent for the CSU, and 33 percent for the FDP (Kulitz 1983, p. 87). In 1983, the first elections after the change of government, the CDU obtained 40.3 million, the CSU 17 million, the FDP 13.4 million, and the SPD 11.7 million DM in donations, highlighting capital's predilection and preferential treatment of the liberal and conservative parties, which together accounted for 86 percent of all donations that year. Much the same distributional pattern is to be found in the 1968–75 period, for instance, with the CDU/DSU receiving 66 percent of total donations, leaving 12 percent to the FDP and 22 percent to the SPD, then the senior partner in a coalition government with the FDP liberals (Kaack 1978a, p. 290).

11. In 1976 Flick sold his block of shares in Mercedes-Benz, worth almost DM 2 billion, and re-invested the money into various of the company's subsidiaries and the American Grace Corporation, respectively. Such re-investment can make proceeds from the sale of stocks tax-exempt, on condition that it is considered to be "in the interest of the national economy," the decision to be taken by the ministers of finance and of economic affairs. The two ministries did in fact decide favorably on the matter, helping Flick

to save DM 850 million in taxes. Based on material confiscated during a search at the Flick headquarters, it was suspected that the decisions had been motivated by the generous flow of illegal party donations, a good part of which coming from the corporation's "black funds" (for more detailed information, see Burchardt/Schlamp 1985, Hörster-Philipps 1985, Kilz/ Preuss 1983, Schily 1986b).

12. See Narr 1984 and Roth; also, Wassermann 1986.
13. On the role and collusion of public authorities in the affair, see Wagner 1986.

References

von Arnim, Hans Herbet 1982. *Parteienfinanzierung. Eine verfassungsrechtliche Untersuchung*. Wiesbaden.

de Boor, Wolfgang/Gerd Pfeiffer/Bernd Schünemann (Hrsg.) 1986. *Parteispendenproblematik*. Köln.

Burchardt, Rainer/Hans-Jürgen Schlamp (Hrsg.) 1985. *Flick-Zeugen. Protokolle aus dem Untersuchungsausschuschuss*. Reinbek.

Eschenburg, Theodor 1966/1967/1972. *Zur politischen Praxis in der Bundesrepublik. Kritische Betrachtungen*. München (3 vol.).

Heidenheimer, Arnold 1957. "German Party Finance: The CDU," *APSR* Vol. 51, pp. 369–85.

Heidenheimer, Arnold and Frank Langdon 1968. *Business Associations and the Financing of Political Parties*, The Hague: Nijhoff.

Hörster-Phillips, Ulrike 1985. *Im Schatten das grossen Geldes. Flick-Konzern und Politik: Weimarer Republik, Drittes Reich, Bundersrepublik*. Köln.

Kaack, Heino 1978a. "Die Finanzen der Bundestagsparteien von 1968–1975," in H. Kaack/U. Kaack (ed.), *Parteien-Jahrbuch 1975*. Meisenheim/Glan, pp. 285–312.

Kaack, Heino 1978b. "Parteiensystem und Legitimation des politischen Systems," in H. Kaack/U. Kaack (Hrsg.), *Parteien-Jahrbuch 1978*. Meisenheim/Glan, pp. 348–60.

Kilz, Hans Werner and Joachim Preuss 1983. *Flick: Die gekaufte Republik*. Reinbek.

Kulitz, Peter 1983. *Unternehmerspenden an politische Parteien*. Berlin/München.

Lösche, Peter 1984. *Wovon leben die Parteien? Uber das Geld in der Politik*. Frankfurt.

Mintzel, Alf 1975. *Die CSU Anatomie einer konservativen Partei*. Opladen.

Narr, Wolf-nieter (ed.) 1977. *Auf dem Weg zum Einparteienstaat*. Opladen.

Nassmacher, Karl-Heinz 1984. "Parteienfinanzierung im internationalen Vergleich," in *aus politik und zeitgeschichte 8–8/84*, pp. 27–45.

Noack, Paul 1985. *Korruption—die andere Seite der Macht*. München.

Rose-Ackermann, Susan 1978. *Corruption. A Study in Political Economy*. New York.

Roth, Roland 1985a. "Politische Korruption in der Bundesrepublik—Notizen zu einem verdrängten Thema," in C. Fleck/H. Kuzmics (Hrsg.), *Korruption. Zur Soziologie nicht immer abweichenden Verhaltens*. Königstein/Ts., pp. 143–59.

Roth, Roland 1985b. "Neue soziale Bewegungen in der politischen Kultur der

Bundesrepublik," in K.-W. Brand (Hrsg.), *Neue soziale Bewegungen in Westeuropa und den USA. Ein internationaler Vergleich.* Frankfurt/New York, pp. 20–82.

Schily, Otto 1986. "Wie der Flick-Konzern in Bonn Politik machte," in *Blätter für deutsche und internationale Politik* 4/1986, 436–47.

Siebert, Harald 1980. "Neuere Entwicklungstendenzen der Parteienfinanzierung," in H. Kaack/R. Roth (Hrsg.), *Handbuch des deutschen Parteiensystems, Bd. 1, Opladen, 1975–194.*

Smelser, Neil J. 1971. "Stability, Instability and the Analysis of Political Corruption," in B. Barber/A. Inkeles (eds.), *Stability and Social Change.* Boston, pp. 7–29.

Staudhammer, Rainer 1985. "Bananenrepublik Deutschland? Parteienfinanzierung im Zwielicht von Korruptionsaffären und Skandalgeschichten," in *Kriminalsoziologische Bibliographie* 46/1985, pp. 44–73.

Troitzsch, Klaus G. 1979. "Parteienfinanzierung im Wahlkampfjahr 1976," in H. Kaack/R. Roth (ed.), *Parteien-Jahrbuch 1976.* Meisenheim/Glan, pp. 483–96.

von Vieregge, Henning 1977. "Globalzuschüsse für die parteinahen Stiftungen: Parteienfinanzierung auf Umwegen?" in *Zeitschrift für Parlamentsfragen* I/1977, pp. 51–58.

Wagner, Joachim 1986. *Tatort Finanzministerium. Die staatlichen Helfer beim Spendenbetrug.* Reimbek.

Wassermann, Rudolf 1986. *Die Zuschauerdemokratie.* Düsseldorf/Wien.

Assessing Effects of Corruption: An Introduction

In our final section we consider the effects of corruption upon whole societies and political systems. A long-standing, if inconclusive, debate has been carried on for many years between those who argue that corruption impedes political and economic development while benefiting only a handful of immediate participants, and others who contend that corruption can at times be functional for development and can help build political linkages between elites and citizens. The former viewpoint has typically been labelled the "moralistic" by its critics; its adherents are often called "functionalists." But the closer we examine the question of the consequences of corruption, the more do issues break up into different levels of analysis and complex contingencies. Thus, the chapters in this final section, while hardly encompassing the full range of this debate, show us why the various schools of thought have had little trouble marshalling evidence and examples in support of their arguments, why the debate has been so difficult to resolve, and why so much further work on the issue is needed.

Gunnar Myrdal, in an excerpt from his well-known study, *Asian Drama,* sees few if any benefits flowing from corruption. Corruption, in his view, drains critical resources away from developing nations' economies and saps the vitality of their political systems. Once entrenched, corruption spreads through a society and its institutions; there are few incentives for officials and their clients to obey the formal rules. Politics can become a kind of free-for-all in which the have-nots are destined to lose while the wealthy few continue to enrich themselves. Critical developmental problems are not addressed, and societies lose their ability to defend themselves, provide basic services, and honor formal guarantees of fairness—with serious political instability the likely result.

Joseph Nye, by contrast, identifies several important contingencies bearing upon the consequences of corruption. Development, for Nye, is not one problem, but many; thus the effects of corruption will depend upon a nation's developmental situation and the particular

933

range of tasks it confronts. Cases of corruption differ as well; the level at which they occur, the kinds of stakes or inducements involved, and the seriousness of the deviation from stated norms and procedures all affect the cost-benefit calculation. Governmental capacity and the strength of national integration must also be considered. In most instances, Nye concludes, the costs of corruption will still exceed any benefits, but in some cases the reverse will more likely be true. These instances of corruption merit different judgments and responses, and Nye's categories and contingencies help us to identify such cases when they occur.

If the consequences-of-corruption debate has been inconclusive, as Michael Johnston argues, it is in part because we have been asking inappropriate questions, and because there may be several different types of corruption with their own sets of consequences. Many, but not all, kinds of corruption can be studied as processes of exchange; different types of exchanges can define varieties of corruption. And if we focus upon the ways in which these types of corrupt exchange tend to strengthen or weaken the linkages between various groups and strata within political systems, we can identify some politically important consequences of corruption without using the concept to "explain too much." Market corruption, clientelism, cronyism/nepotism, and what could be called "crisis corruption" thus emerge as important major varieties of corruption, each with a distinctive inner logic and set of political implications.

David H. Bayley argues that any realistic analysis of corruption in developing nations must recognize a mix of costs and benefits, the relative balance of which will depend upon many factors specific to the nations in question. Corruption does divert scarce resources, make more difficult the implementation of stated policy, and undercut the prestige and authority of elites. But it can also constitute an informal reward and recruitment process, bringing able people into government service who would not have been attracted by the low official salaries. Furthermore, corruption offers a way for excluded groups to buy their way back into politics—possibly forestalling more disruptive responses in the process. And Bayley also reminds us that a corruption-free government would not necessarily produce "better" policies. Analysts of corruption must therefore be very careful about the kinds of activities which they label as corrupt, and even more sensitive to the realities of developing nations as they make their judgments.

53

The Effects of Corruption in a Developing Nation

David H. Bayley

Studies of politics and administration in the developing nations, whether about Africa, Latin America, the Middle East, or South and Southeast Asia, almost invariably comment upon the prevalence of corruption on the part of both politicians and civil servants. Standards of public morality, we are told, are deplorably low. Local observers within these countries confirm this impression. Where the press is free, governmental corruption becomes a stock-in-trade of a great deal of journalistic commentary. Local authorities themselves sometimes take up the subject of venality in government in order to determine its extent and recommend measures for its eradication. Then groups within prominent political parties raise their voices in criticism, not just of politicians in other parties, but more impressively of the deteriorating standards of behavior within their own ranks. The conclusion, on the basis of all this smoke, must be that corruption certainly exists in many developing nations. It would probably not be too much to say that it forms a prominent, or at least not readily avoidable, feature of bureaucratic life in these nations.

Given its prevalence, whether as proven or assumed fact, it is surprising that so little attention has been given to its role and effects within the developing political situation. Western, as well as local, observers have generally been content with deploring its existence. This frequently involves taking rather perverse pleasure in dwelling upon the amount of corruption to be discovered and then asserting that elimination of corruption is a "must" for successful development. While most Western observers have manfully striven to avoid assum-

Source: David H. Bayley, "The Effects of Corruption in a Developing Nation," *Western Political Quarterly,* XIX, 4 (December 1966), 719–32. By permission of the author and the publisher, the University of Utah, copyright owners.

ing a moralistic posture, they have rather uncritically assumed that the presence of corruption is an important hindrance to economic growth and progressive social change. There has been a significant absence of analysis about the effects which corruption has in fact upon economic development, nascent political institutions, and social attitudes. Unless it has been determined that a social practice, such as corruption, contributes no positive benefits, condemnation of it is really a practice at rote and is no improvement upon moralism.

The purpose of this chapter is to show that corruption in developing nations is not necessarily antipathetic to the develoment of modern economic and social systems; that corruption serves in part at least a beneficial function in developing societies. In order to demonstrate this I shall present a list of the effects of corruption, *both* positive and negative. It will be necessary first to discuss the meaning of the word corruption, and then whether it makes sense to apply the category as defined in the West to behavior in non-Western countries. The focus of the essay will be entirely upon governmental corruption and not that within private agencies. The illustrative material will be taken overwhelmingly from Indian experience, for this is the country with which I am most familiar. I am sure, however, that the Indian situation is not atypical. Finally, it must be quite clear that in specifying the effects of corruption I am presenting hypotheses rather than proven conclusions. The arguments I make for asserting that an effect of a particular kind is present are often *a priori*. But I have carefully tried to frame my hypotheses in such a way as to highlight the empirical referents which must be studied in order to validate them.

The Definition of Corruption

Webster's Third New International Dictionary (1961) defines corruption as "inducement [as of a public official] by means of improper considerations [as bribery] to commit a violation of duty." A bribe is then defined as "a price, reward, gift or favor bestowed or promised with a view to pervert the judgment or corrupt the conduct esp. of a person in a position of trust [as a public official]." Bribery and corruption are intimately linked together, but they are not inseparable. A person bribed is a person corrupt; but a man may be corrupt who does not take bribes.[1] Corruption would surely include nepotism and misappropriation.[2] In both these cases there is "inducement by means of improper considerations." Corruption, then, while being tied particularly to the act of bribery, is a general term covering misuse of authority as a result of considerations of personal gain, which need not be monetary. This point has been well made in a recent Indian government report on corruption: "In its widest connotation, corruption includes improper and selfish exercise of power and influence attached to a public office or to the special position one occupies in public life."[3]

It is important to note that a person may be corrupt who does not in fact commit a violation of duty. Webster's definition only says that an individual must be induced to commit. The hero of the African novel, *No Longer at Ease,* which portrays the tension between the demands of traditional society and standards of a Western civil service, finally capitulates to the pressures upon him and accepts gratuities but salves his conscience with the thought that he only takes money from those whom he approves on their merits anyhow.[4] A variation of this is the civil servant who takes money from all applicants impartially but still goes ahead and decides the matter on merits. Rumor in India would have it that this is not an exceptional situation. Are such people corrupt? A strict application of Webster's definition would lead to an answer in the affirmative, and general Western usage would, I think, conform to the strict reading.

Corrupt behavior is behavior condemned and censured. "Corruption" is a pejorative term. However, applying the label to behavior on the part of public officials in many non-Western countries immediately poses a dilemma of intriguing dimensions. The man who in many non-Western countries is corrupt in Webster's sense is not condemned at all by his own society. Indeed, he may be conforming to a pattern of behavior his peers, family, and friends strongly support and applaud. For example, in both Africa and India the man who uses his official position to obtain jobs for his relatives is not considered immoral: in traditional terms, he is only doing what every loyal member of an extended family is expected to do. He would be censured if he did not act in this way. The point is strongly made in the fictitious musings of a Delhi businessman in these words:

> Bribery and corruption! These were foreign words, it seemed to him, and the ideas behind them were also foreign. Here in India, he thought, one did not know such words. Giving presents and gratuities to government officers was an indispensable courtesy and a respectable, civilized way of carrying on business.[5]

It not infrequently happens, then, in developing non-Western societies that existing moral codes do not agree with Western norms as to what kinds of behavior by public servants should be condemned. The Western observer is faced with an uncomfortable choice. He can adhere to the Western definition, in which case he lays himself open to the charge of being censorious and he finds that he is condemning not aberrant behavior but normal, acceptable operating procedure. On the other hand, he may face up to the fact that corruption, if it requires moral censure, is culturally conditioned. He then argues that an act is corrupt if the surrounding society condemns it.[6] This usage, however, muddies communication, for it may be necessary then to assert in the same breath that an official accepts gratuities but is not corrupt or that an official gives preference in employment to his relatives but is not corrupt. Rather tedious explanations invariably must follow and people are left with the feeling that serious violence has been done to words.

Between these two alternatives the better choice, in my view, is to preserve the Western denotative meaning of corruption. This will be the meaning employed in this paper. If the Westerner chooses the culturally relevant definition, he will either end by abandoning the term altogether or will find it necessary to define it peculiarly, perhaps differently, for every non-Western country studied. This will present serious problems of communication with colleagues. There are other reasons as well for preserving the Western meaning. As Western observers we are interested in comparative findings about behavior in our own and other cultures. We are familiar with the fact that even in the West there is some disagreement about standards of propriety in the dealings of public officials. This is particularly true of the activities of politicians on behalf of their constituents. It is not entirely curious then that one may speak of an act being corrupt and not find massive social censure. This being the case it is more felicitous to say that in many non-Western countries behavior X, which in the West is called corrupt, does not attract social condemnation. Other findings, predicated on the category corruption, will be that it is more or less prevalent than in the West, that it is or is not confined to different role players than in the West, that it serves the same or a different function, or that it is motivated by similar or rather different considerations.

The advantage of this solution is that we get rid of nonessentials, such as the element of social judgment, but keep the denotative core, i.e., the taking of bribes or employing of relatives. In this way, as the English would say, we do not throw out the baby with the bath water. Only minor adjustments are made, hence making possible comparative statements easily understood by colleagues.

There is another reason for keeping the Western denotative meaning. The intelligentsia, and especially top-level civil servants, in most underdeveloped nations are familiar with the Western label "corruption," and they apply it to their own countries. Since modernization around the world is most often Westernization, the standards the intelligentsia and opinion-leaders of these countries are trying to inculcate are Western ones. The premise of the Santhanam Committee was that "corruption," in the Western sense, should be eliminated. Similarly in Africa the conflict in the hearts of civil servants is precisely over which standard of morality should prevail, the Western or the traditional. Non-Westerners are acutely conscious of the Western meaning of corruption; they use it among themselves. And they are painfully aware that Western standards of governmental conduct condemn it. It is not unfair, therefore, to make comparative statements between West and non-West based upon Webster's definition. Such judgments will be readily understood by the nation-building elites in most developing nations.

An even more serious problem involves separating proper from improper behavior in the realm of politics whatever the country. It is easy to say that a civil servant should consider only the merits of a case. A politician, by the nature of his job, is a channel for the pressure of special groups within the country. It is an accepted part of his function that he garner public expenditures for his constituents or groups represented within his constituency; that he help them to gain access to government employment; that he influence administrators to locate a road through a town in his area rather than in an adjacent constituency. A politician is the instrument that makes government responsive to individuals. A civil servant who responded to his tribal or caste affiliation to secure jobs for young men would be accused of being nepotistic; a politician who secured government employ for the same group would be admired as an effective politician. Is there morally a difference between them? Clearly concepts of propriety, upon which the definition of corruption hinges, for the civil servant and politician are not coincidental; propriety is specific to roles to some extent. The latitude possessed by the politician is greater than that of the civil servant, and since the politician must respond to subnational pressure groups by the nature of his role, it follows that the boundary line between permissible and impermissible behavior on the part of politicians will be more hazy than that for civil servants. I shall not try to make this boundary more discernible, but will talk around the issue, realizing that even in the West there is apt to be substantial disagreement about where the duty of a politician lies as between his constituents and the larger interests of his country.

The Extent of Corruption

Estimates of the extent of corruption practices in underdeveloped countries are, expectedly, very imprecise. Rumor abounds, facts are scarce. Three observations may be made:

First: in many underdeveloped countries corruption is expected by the people as a part of everyday official life. Public cynicism on this score is colossal. As the *Times of India* has said, "People's acceptance of corruption as a fact of life and their general despondency need to be tackled first."[7]

Second: officials share this opinion of the people, and their opinions have at times been buttressed by government-sponsored investigations. The situation was considered sufficiently serious in India to warrant the appointment of an investigative committee by the central government. The result was the *Report of the Committee on Prevention of Corruption,* 1964, already referred to. Ronald Wraith and Edgar Simpkins in their book *Corruption in Developing Nations* cite several government studies of administrative procedures in West Africa, both under the British and after independence, which have discussed the widespread extent of corruption.

The Santhanam Committee reported that at a conservative estimate 5 percent of the money spent during the Second Five Year Plan for construction and purchases was lost to the exchequer through corruption.[8] In discussing the granting of export/import licenses the committee said, "It is common knowledge that *each license* fetches anything between 100 percent to 500 percent of its face-value."[9] The government of Punjab state, India, reported that in the last four years 3,000 government workers had been dismissed or punished as a result of the activities of the State Vigilance Department, which is charged with investigation of improper practices. John P. Lewis, former director of the International Development Research Center at Indiana and now A.I.D. director in India, while admitting that he cannot estimate with great accuracy the corruption at top levels in India, says that petty corruption at lower levels is immense. He also notes his impression that corruption at higher levels in India is a good deal less prevalent than in most other developing nations.[10] Read with the Santhanam Committee's assessment of the inroads corruption has made in India, this certainly does not speak well for the situation in other lands. Actually, alarming statements of the extensiveness of corrupt practices in most other developing nations could be multiplied almost indefinitely.

Wraith and Simpkins comment as follows about the African situation:

> How much is true and how much is false about corruption in high places nobody outside a small circle can ever know for certain. What *is* certain, and can be said without circumlocution, is that to wander through the corridors of power in these countries is to wander through a whispering-

gallery of gossip, in which the fact of corruption at the highest levels is taken utterly for granted, and the only interest lies in capping the latest story with one that is even more startling.[11]

The same could be said of India.

Third: corruption is not confined to only a few levels of the official hierarchy, but seems to pervade the entire structure. It should also be noted that although corruption at the top attracts the most attention in public forums, and involves the largest amount of money in separate transactions, corruption at the very bottom levels is the more apparent and obvious and in total amounts of money involved may very well rival corruption at the top.

The Effects of Corruption

Corruption comes in innumerable shapes, forms, and sizes. There are as many reasons for corrupting as there are ways in which government affects individuals; there are as many avenues for corruption as there are roles to be played in government. Corruption may be involved in the issuance of export licenses, a decision to investigate in a criminal case, obtaining of a copy of court proceedings, appointment of candidates to universities, choice of men for civil service jobs, inspection of building specifications in new housing developments, avoiding of arrest by people with defective motor vehicles, granting of contracts, and in the expediting of anything. This wealth of forms would appear to make analysis of effects formidable and perhaps impossible. The solution is to distinguish and to keep firmly in mind the essential elements of a corrupt act; that is, to establish a type-form.

Elaborating upon the definition found in Webster's, a corrupt practice will be assumed to involve the following elements: (a) a decision to depart from government-established criteria for decisions of the relevant class and (b) a monetary reward benefiting either the official directly or those related to him.

In analyzing the effects of corrupt practices two categories of generalized effects may be distinguished, apart from whether the effects are good or bad. First, there are direct, unmediated effects. These are the effects that are part of the act itself. They are the effects contained in the reasons for which the favor seeker, the corruptor, initiated the act. Second, there are indirect effects, mediated through those who perceive that an act of a certain kind—in this case a corrupt one—has taken place. There are three classes of mediating actors: the corrupted, the corruptor, and the nonparticipating audience.

In the discussion that follows I shall present the harmful factors first and the beneficial ones second. No attempt has been made explicitly to locate each effect within the analytic schema just presented, but it would be possible to do so. These lists are undoubtedly incomplete; the effects presented here are the more important.

Harmful Effects of Corrupt Acts

1. A corrupt act represents a failure to achieve the objectives government sought when it established criteria for decisions of various classes. To the extent that the objectives sought were worthwhile, corrupt acts exact a cost in nonachievement. For example, if the objective in hiring government employees is the obtaining of efficiency and ability in carrying out official tasks, then corruption in appointments produces inefficiency and waste. If the issuing of permits for domestic enterprises is designed to insure that scarce resources go to projects enjoying the highest priority in terms of facilitating long-run economic development, then corruption exacts a cost by inhibiting over-all economic development. Places in universities and opportunities for foreign educational experience are severly limited in most developing nations; if corruption is present in the awards, the country fails to obtain the best result in making use of a scarce opportunity.

2. Corruption represents a rise in the price of administration. The multiple of extra cost depends on what the market will bear. The man who is both taxpayer and also forced to submit to bribing has paid several times over for the same service. Corruption is a mechanism for allocating increased amounts of resources to the performance of a single type of function, namely, government administration.

3. If corruption takes the form of a kickback, it serves to diminish the total amount expended for public purposes. It represents a diversion of resources from public purposes to private ones. For example, a civil servant may let a contract for a certain sum, but get 10 percent back for the favor of giving the contract: 90 percent of the allocated amount goes for the public purpose, 10 percent goes into personal gains and acquisitions.

4. Corruption exerts a corrupting influence on other members of the administrative apparatus. This is a function of its persistence, its perceived rewards, and the impunity with which it is done. Corruption feeds upon itself and erodes the courage necessary to adhere to high standards of propriety. Morale declines, each man asking himself why he should be the sole custodian of morality.

5. Corruption in government, perceived by the people, lowers re-

spect for constituted authority. It undercuts popular faith in government to deal evenhandedly. The less a regime depends upon coercion in order to maintain itself, the more it must depend upon popular respect for it. One element in this process of legitimation is popular faith in government to deal fairly among competing claimants. Corruption weakens this element of support.

6. Politicians and civil servants constitute an elite. Their function is to give purpose to national effort. In so doing they cannot avoid setting an example others will emulate. If the elite is believed to be widely and thoroughly corrupt, the man-in-the street will see little reason why he too should not gather what he can for himself and his loved ones. Selig Harrison has said of contemporary India:

> The old vision is gone, and there are few signs pointing to the birth of a renewed spirit of common purpose to take its place. *The mode is increasingly one of every man for himself.* This can be felt at every turn in the impatient refusal of each sector of the population to accept the disciplines of planned development. Thus a farmer who grows more food shows more determination than ever to hoard it for a time of still greater stringency or to consume it himself rather than to free it for the market in response to pleas from New Delhi. The middleman and trader reacted to the recent food price crisis by creating artificial local scarcities to push prices up, moving operations methodically from one area to another with the police one jump behind. The low-wage consumer in the cities and towns, who has been using his increase in income in recent years to buy wheat or rice instead of coarse grains, refused to shift back during the 1964 pinch despite official exhortations. All this could also have been said of earlier food crises under Nehru, but *one detected on this occasion for the first time a role of antagonism and even of contempt toward constituted authority.*[12]

Corruption among an elite not only debases standards popularly perceived, it forces people to undertake the underhanded approach out of self-defense. They feel they must resort to corrupt practices just to get their due, not to secure inordinate returns.[13] This is a classic vicious circle.

7. An important, perhaps overwhelming, problem in those nations that have sought to develop economically within a democratic political framework has been the unwillingness of politicians to take actions which are necessary for development but unpopular with the mass of the people. Taxation is the most obvious example. A corrupt official or politician is a self-centered individual. Can such a person be expected to put country before self, to jeopardize his prospects for the sake of prosperity for the whole country in the remote future? Uncommon

political courage can hardly be maintained in an atmosphere of tolerance of corruption.

8. With erosion of belief in the evenhandedness of public officials comes the need to cultivate special contacts, to develop enough "pull" to offset the claims of others. In many underdeveloped countries the amount of time and human energy devoted to making these contacts is immense. The effort that might otherwise be spent in enhancing credentials in strengthening one's case objectively goes into the necessary task of lobbying. The loss in productive effort defies estimation.

9. Corruption, since it represents to the man-in-the-street institutionalized unfairness, inevitably leads to litigation, calumnous charges, and bitter grievances. Even the honest official may be blackmailed by the threat that unless he act unfairly he may be charged publicly with being corrupt. And there would be few to believe his disclaimer. The attention and energies of official and nonofficial alike are diverted into endless, unproductive wrangling.

10. Time is important in the making of most decisions; delays can be costly in monetary and human terms. The most ubiquitous form of corruption takes the form of what Indians call "speed money." The wheels of the bureaucratic machine must be oiled with money, and unless this is done nothing at all will be done. Corruption causes decisions to be weighed in terms of money, not in terms of human need. The poor man with an urgent and just request gets little if any sympathy.

Beneficial Effects of Corrupt Acts

In order to sustain the points that follow, I shall present arguments sufficient to show that the effects of corruption *may* be beneficial in nature. I do not pretend that they always are, simply that it would not be unreasonable to find that they are. Nor does it follow that because the effects are good the means are either desirable or blameless.

1. There is a common assumption that corrupt acts produce effects worse than those which would have followed from an untainted decision. This assumption is only true to the extent that the government-established—or system-established—criteria for choice are better than those served by corruption. Governments have no monopoly upon correct solutions; governments are simply one among many bureaucratic institutions which may do stupid things. Both the ends and the means served by government-constricted choices may be worse than those freely chosen and finding expression through corruption. Corruption may serve as a means for impelling better choices, even in terms of

government's expressed goals. Nor do I think it necessary to say that corruption only occasionally, and by chance, operates in this direction. It could systematically do so, not perhaps across the board in all decisions but certainly in all decisions of a certain kind. For example, government may desire to build a strong fertilizer industry and toward this end may have established certain requirements for the selection of firms to receive the concession. If government economists have not selected the proper indicators of efficiency, it is not farfetched to assume that ability to offer massive bribes—bribes at least bigger than anyone else's—could be correlated with entrepreneurial efficiency. Bribes represent a peculiar element of cost, applying to all competing firms; the ability to meet it may not be unrelated to efficiency.

Corruption, then, is not an inherently defective means of arriving at decisions among competing claimants. The satisfactoriness of the inducement offered may correlate with features among claimants government would choose if it had better information or greater expertise in selecting criteria for decision-making. In order to demonstrate the effect of departing from established decisionmaking criteria, two general types of cases need to be analyzed, those in which the inducement is solely monetary and those in which it is something besides money such as loyalty to family, caste, tribe, and so forth. One must then ask if, for any particular group of decisions made, the absence of the extra ingredient would have made the result of the decision better? In many cases the decision probably would be unaltered; in some it might be better; but in some it could very easily have been worse. Even in the case of nonmonetary inducements, it would be necessary to determine that bias across the group of decisionmakers, for a particular class of choices, acted to favor persons or firms less able to carry out what government intended. It could happen that groups within a society successful in penetrating the civil service in efficient numbers to influence decisions might for this very reason have qualities instrumental for the accomplishment of activities government wants carried out. Therefore nepotistic favoritism would lead government to rely on just those groups most capable of shouldering responsibility. In underdeveloped countries the tangle of popular pressures involving traditionally antagonistic groups frequently causes government to award contracts, scholarships, privileges, and jobs according to mechanical quota systems. Since talent and ability are very often unevenly distributed through these societies, this policy is not in the direction of optimum efficiency. Corruption of the monetary and nonmonetary kind might very well offset this pervasive influence.

2. Corruption, whether in the form of kickbacks or of payments

originating with the briber, may result in increased allocations of resources away from consumption and into investment. Contrary to common expectations, it may be a supplemental allocative mechanism compatible with the goals of economic development. The key elements in this determination are the marginal propensities of the corrupted and the corruptor to consume and invest. In the case of kickbacks, for example, if the kickback comes from funds designed for projects contributing little to the sum total of capital investment, then diversion of some of these to an individual who will use them for investment in productive enterprises actually results in a net accretion to the stock of capital goods. This would be the case with funds diverted from famine relief or inefficient cottage industries into the hands of civil servants backing firms manufacturing tires or machine tools. A similar instance is a bribe financed by the briber himself. His marginal propensity to consume may be greater than that of the bribed. It may even be that government servants as a whole, especially at the upper levels, representing an educated elite with unique access to information about prospects for economic development, may have a greater propensity to invest in productive enterprises of a modern kind than do a cross-section of the people who seek to bribe them. It is not indubitable, then, that corruption represents a net drain from investment into consumption or even from the modern sector of enterprise into the traditional.

3. The opportunity for corruption may actually serve to increase the quality of public servants. If wages in government service are insufficient to meet a talented man's needs, and he has an alternate choice, he will be tempted to choose the other. On the other hand, a man anxious to serve his country through government service might opt away from non-government employment if he knew that means existed to supplement a meager salary. Even for the man with no alternative prospects for employment, security in meeting his unavoidable obligations may enhance his willingness to serve ably and loyally.

The corrupt are not always unable; nor are they always unpatriotic. These propositions seem especially true of underdeveloped countries where the rewards for government service are so piteously low. Where corruption is often necessary to provide basic necessities of life to oneself and one's family, it becomes a necessary means of ensuring a supply of able and willing public servants. Furthermore, in developing nations it is an indispensable means of reconciling insufficient wage rates with the claims of traditional society operating through extended family and clan ties. The civil servant cannot wish away these obligations. Through corruption he taxes society with preserving an important element of social continuity.

4. Nepotism in government hiring, which swells the ranks of the civil service, can be looked upon as a substitute for a public works system. It provides employment for the otherwise unemployed and by making them dependent upon government may secure a measure of support for government. Inflated civil service rolls become the price for relieving intolerable political pressure due to unemployment. To be sure, the quality of performance in government service may certainly suffer from the injection of the public works objective. The goals of each may be incompatible: relief on the one hand, efficiency in government operations on the other. But, granting the incompatibility, it is incumbent upon us to admit that to the extent that a public works program is needed corruption in hiring may serve the same end.

It is well known, for example, that in many underdeveloped countries there is a growing army of half-educated unemployed. The revolutionary potential of this mass is considerable; they gravitate to the political extremes in much greater proportions than members of other groups. In countries where the absorptive capacity of private agencies is not great enough to provide employment for the educated or half-educated, government service obtained by means of illicit considerations may provide a safety valve of considerable importance.

5. Corruption provides a means of giving those persons or groups potentially disaffected as a result of exclusion from power a stake in the system. The degree to which they can be tied to the system in this way depends upon their ability and willingness to capitalize upon the opportunities for corruption. A person with money who is ideologically opposed to the regime or who dislikes the personnel at the top, may nonetheless be able to make the repugnant system work for him by means of illicit influence. He is not entirely alienated.

6. In traditional societies struggling to be Western, corruption may make the new system human in traditional terms. Corruption is an understandable means of influence in most traditional societies. A transitional people may have more faith in a system they can influence in some degree through personal action than one they do not know how to manipulate by means of the institutional mechanisms provided. The human contact provided in a corrupt act may be a necessary transitional device to insure the loyalty to the new of a tradition-bound people. Perhaps it is better that people in developing nations misuse modern agencies to their own ends than that they reject the new because they cannot work the handles. This argument particularly

applies to countries trying to implant democratic institutions. The successor to the rejected democratic forms will not be hallowed traditional ones, whatever the people may wish, but a modern, impersonal system less subject to rejection.

7. Corruption provides a means for reducing the harshness of an elite-conceived plan for economic and social development. It supplements the political system by allowing the introduction of political considerations at the administrative level. Such access may be essential to the stability of the system. When political channels are clogged, corruption provides non-violent entry into government affairs and administration.

8. Among politicians corruption may act as a solvent for uncompromisable issues of ideology and/or interest. Where potential schisms based upon the claims of caste, tribe, region, religion, or language are manifold, common interest in spoils may provide cement for effective political unity, especially within a single dominant party. In general, corruption should damp doctrinairism, no matter how predicated. It is the disheartened politician, cut off from power or perquisites, who is more likely to repair to the standard of factional rigidity or ideological extremism.

9. In developing nations, particularly where there is comparatively free play of political forces, there is often tension between the civil service and the politicians. The bureaucracy may develop considerable *esprit de corps* and feel impatient with the activities of politicians whose only thought seems to be to truckle to mass whims, hampering the orderly progress of the bureaucratic nation-building machine. Politicians, on the other hand, may find the civil service unresponsive, proud, and aloof, without the slightest understanding of the importance of the role politicians must play. Politicians accuse the bureaucrats of running a closed corporation; bureaucrats argue that politicians divert attention and resources from essential tasks.[14] The practice of corruption may lessen this potentially crippling strain. It is one means of increasing the responsiveness of bureaucrats to individual and group needs. It also links the bureaucrat and the politician in an easily discerned network of self-interest. There may be a principle here: in countries where agreement upon proper relative functions has not been fixed between bureaucrats and politicians, the less amenable planning is to political pressures—due perhaps to rigid adherence to "rational" planning criteria—the greater may be the functional importance of corruption in preserving a working relationship between civil servants and popular leaders. An alternative means to the same end could be

found in the imposition of sanctions by an agency capable of disciplining both sides. In this case agreement upon functions is enforced.

Conclusion

Because so many incommensurables are involved in the effects of corrupt practices, it is impossible to determine firmly and precisely how the positive and negative effects combine to produce an over-all thrust along either dimension. It is clear though, that corruption is an accommodating device. Its benefits are to be seen primarily in the realm of politics. But the analysis has also shown that the net effects of corrupt practices upon economic development are not always, or necessarily, of a baneful nature. There are serious negative effects, to be sure, and these may be assessed either in terms of economic costs or of dysfunctional attitudes being formed throughout the developing society. But even if a final balance sheet cannot be constructed, it is still abundantly clear that corruption is a social practice about which there is very little accurate theoretical analysis and even less empirical research.

Research into corruption will be difficult, but ingenuity should be able to overcome many seemingly insurmountable obstacles. Analysis of indirect or mediated effects of corruption will be easier than analysis of direct effects. Mediated effects are those which depend upon someone's perceiving that an act of this particular kind has occurred. Surveys designed to touch all three acting groups—corrupted, corruptor, audience—should be able to establish, among other things, each group's opinion about improper behavior among the other groups' concept of role in society, morale, and values operating to restrain or impel behavior of various kinds. Studies of this kind yield considerable information about the mediated effects of corruption found or believed found in others. Research into the direct, unmediated effects is more difficult because it requires knowledge of how many of which kinds of people are doing what in various circumstances. Precise knowledge of actors and situations is essential. By and large the researcher will have to depend upon the results of official studies; he will not have the resources, nor would it be discreet, to undertake such a survey himself—although the researcher, especially the foreign one, may find that people are distressingly willing to speak about practices engaged in by themselves which the researcher considers corrupt but the respondents do not. This is particularly true of people still substantially enmeshed in a traditional world, with little modern education, and hence unlettered in Western standards of propriety. Generally the key to unlocking tongues is to seek information about how politics works, the amount of influence various role players possess, their tactics of maneuver, and their concept of function, carefully refraining from describing behavior in pejorative terms. It must be admitted, even so, that most knowledge will be about forms of corruption and less about extent. Nonetheless, it is still possible to analyze many of the effects of corruption. Making assumptions about who corrupts and who is corrupted, describing these actors by membership in socially defined groups, one can then collect data about consumption patterns, family size, social obligations, level of remuneration, values with respect to achievement and striving, and so forth, and thereby determine either the reasons for which corruption is undertaken or the ways in which gains from it will be utilized. Moreover, it should be possible to arrive at a description of the human predicament impelling corruption. A study of this kind would underscore the root factors in corruption and thereby provide a means of gauging its function in society.

That corruption is an accommodating device has important implications. It indicates that corrupt practices are a human response to circumstances, conditioned, to be sure, by moral codes. But it also means that corruption is to some extent a creation of the very circumstances defining political and economic underdevelopment. It becomes apparent, therefore, that considerably more than exhortation may be needed in order to eliminate venality in government. It also indicates that removal of all vestiges of corruption may not be a good thing. There are three strategies that can be employed in a transitional situation to reduce corrupt practices. First, a policy may be adopted of containing the grosser forms of corruption while waiting for changing circumstance to remove the functional utility of such practices. This strategy is essentially a passive one and may be fatally flawed by the implicit assumption that corruption will not exert such harmful consequences as to jeopardize progress to a less unstable level. Second, corruption may be rooted out without hesitancy or remorse, counting upon the power of the state to contain repercussions. Coercion is used to offset the discontinuity in social accommodation which the removal of corruption may occasion. Third, the climate of opinion may be remolded so that the temptation to corruption on the part of both briber and bribed is substantially reduced. The building of a sense of national purposefulness, sacrifice, and dedication may cause the corruptor to be shunned and the potentially corrupted to be strong. This strategy relies upon psychological change and represents the substitution of one set of operational values for another. Its defect is that unless buttressed by real social change, it quickly loses force and wastes precipitously.

These three strategies are not mutually exclusive. None of them would be employed by itself. The mix of the three depends upon the character of the regime and it should also depend upon knowledge of the function corruption plays in the particular society. Corrupt practices may be more easily eradicated by exhortation and revived national morale than many suppose; corruption may also be more resistant than realized and not yield readily to such tactics. The point is that the knowledge necessary to make this judgment is now almost wholly lacking. This situation should be rapidly transformed. And this essay has sought to provide a first step, primarily by demonstrating that corruption wears two faces and not simply one. Corruption may play a useful role in transitional societies, a role which is sufficiently important that if it was not played by this device must be played by another or the consequences might severely undermine the pace, but more importantly the character, of the development effort.

Notes

1. In this respect there has been a change in the relation between "bribery" and "corruption" from *Webster's New International Dictionary* (2d ed., 1958). In the earlier edition the definition of corruption explicitly mentioned bribery and the definition of bribery explicitly referred to corruption.
2. *Webster's Third New International Dictionary* defines (a) nepotism: "favoritism shown to nephews and other relatives (as by giving them positions because of their relationship rather than on their merits)"; (b) to misappropriate: "to appropriate dishonestly for one's own use: embezzle."
3. *Report of the Committee on Prevention of Corruption* (New Delhi: Government of India, 1964), p. 5. Known as the Santhanam Committee report, after its chairman.
4. Chinua Achebe, *No Longer at Ease* (New York: Ivan Obolensky, 1960).
5. Prawer Jhabvala, *The Nature of Passion* (New York: Norton, 1956), p. 56. Novels are often a forgotten key to the human problems of traditional society, and since few scholars portray social problems in intimate, biographical terms, they are indispensable sources of information to those who would seek to understand the human, motivational problems involved.
6. This is the solution adopted by Ronald Wraith and Edgar Simpkins in *Corruption in Developing Nations* (London: G. Allen, 1963), pp 34–35. They even go farther and say that the actor must also be afflicted with a sense of guilt. The last condition, especially, seems unduly restricting. A man may act wrongly even though he is not conscious of acting wrongly. His lack of guilt feelings may have a bearing upon his guilt in law but surely

does not affect society's definition of what constitutes improper or illicit action.

7. May 10, 1964, p. 6, editorial.
8. Santhanam Committee, p. 18.
9. Santhanam Committee, p. 18, emphasis added.
10. See *Quiet Crisis in India* (New York: Doubleday, 1964), p. 145.
11. Wraith and Simpkins, pp. 15–16.
12. "Troubled India and Her Neighbors," *Foreign Affairs*, January 1965, p. 314. Emphasis added.
13. For an excellent description of this attitude see William and Charlotte Wiser, *Behind Mud Walls: 1930–1960* (Berkeley: University of California Press. 1963), pp. 128–29.
14. For an excellent discussion of this problem in one country, Burma, see Lucien Pye's *Politics, Personality, and Nation Building* (New Haven, Conn.: Yale University Press, 1962).

54

Corruption: Its Causes and Effects

Gunnar Myrdal

One of the opportunistic rationalizations of the neglect of research on the problem of corruption is its alleged unimportance—or even its alleged usefulness in development under the conditions prevailing in South Asia. We believe that these unproved assumptions are totally wrong, and that corrupt practices are highly detrimental from the point of view of the value premises applied in the present study, namely, the modernization ideals.

The remnants of precapitalist society referred to in the preceding section represent deterrents to development. This applies to the afore-mentioned contrasts with Western mores and behavior patterns— namely, while markets are nonexistent or grossly imperfect in South Asia and profit motives less effective in the economic sphere, those who have public responsibility and power are more apt to use their position for private benefit. As these contrasting conditions are complementary and sustain each other to a certain extent, the prevalence of corruption provides strong inhibitions and obstacles to development.

We have referred to the fragmentation of loyalties in South Asian societies. Development efforts must attempt to modernize people's attitudes by mitigating this fragmentation, yet in a general way corruption counteracts the strivings for national consolidation, decreases respect for and allegiance to the government, and endangers political stability.[1] . . . no South Asian government can be firmly in control unless it can convince its articulate groups that effective measures are being taken to purge corruption from public life.

From another point of view, corruption is one of the forces that help to preserve the "soft-state" with its low degree of social discipline.

Source: Gunnar Myrdal, "Corruption—Its Causes and Effects," in *Asian Drama: An Enquiry into the Poverty of Nations*, Vol. II. New York: The Twentieth Century Fund, 1968, pp. 951–58. By permission of the publisher.

Not only are politicians and administrators affected by the prevalence of corruption, but also businessmen and, in fact, the whole population. Corruption introduces an element of irrationality in plan fulfillment by influencing the actual course of development in a way that is contrary to the plan or, if such influence is foreseen, by limiting the horizon of the plan. Of particular importance is the fact that the usual method of exploiting a position of public responsibility for private gain is by threat of obstruction or delay. Where corruption is widespread, inertia and inefficiency, as well as irrationality, impede the process of decision-making and plan fulfillment. "It was the unanimous opinion of all witnesses who appeared before us," the Santhanam Committee noted, "that administrative delays are one of the major causes of corruption. We agree with this view. We have no doubt that quite often delay is deliberately contrived so as to obtain some kind of illicit gratification."[2] The influence of corruption in slowing down the wheels of administration is particularly damaging in South Asia, where the administrative system largely retains the impediments to speed and efficiency inherited from colonial times.[3]

The Santhanam Committee report speaks of "speed money":

> It is believed that the procedures and practices in the working of Government offices are cumbersome and dilatory. The anxiety to avoid delay has encouraged the growth of dishonest practices like the system of speed money. "Speed money" is reported to have become a fairly common type of corrupt practice particularly in matters relating to grant of licenses, permits, etc. Generally the bribe giver does not wish, in these cases, to get anything done unlawfully, but wants to speed up the process of the movement of files and communications relating to decisions. Certain sections of the staff concerned are reported to have got into the habit of not doing anything in the matter till they are suitably persuaded. It was stated by a Secretary that even after an order had been passed, the fact of the passing of such order is communicated to the person concerned and the order itself is kept back till the unfortunate applicant has paid appropriate gratification to the subordinate concerned. Besides being a most objectionable corrupt practice, this custom of speed money has become one of the most serious causes of delay and inefficiency.[4]

The popular notion, occasionally expressed by Western students of conditions in South Asia, that corruption is a means of speeding up cumbersome administrative procedures, is palpably wrong.[5]

At the same time, when suspicion of corruption is rampant, a natural protective device is to spread and share the responsibility for decisions to the maximum extent possible. Apart from this, the most honest official will tend to shun taking personal responsibility if he works in an administrative system widely suspected of being corrupt; the present writer has often heard testimony to this effect. Paul Appleby has criticized the Indian administration for its "excessive bureaucracy," which he relates to the "timidity of public servants at all levels, making them unwilling to take responsibility for decisions, forcing decisions to be made by a slow and cumbersome process of reference and conference in which everybody finally shares dimly in the making of every decision," and he blames it for the fact that "not enough gets done and what gets done is done too slowly."[6] He accuses parliament of being "the chief citadel of opposition to delegation of powers, the need for which is the worst shortcoming of Indian administration,"[7] but he could have added the press and articulate opinion generally. A situation is created that is vividly described by an Indian author:

> To avoid direct responsibility for any major policy decision, efforts are made to get as many departments and officials associated with such decisions as is considered desirable. Again, such consultations must be in writing; otherwise there would be nothing on record. Therefore a file must move—which itself requires some time—from one table to another and from one ministry to another for comments and it is months before the decision is conveyed to the party concerned. Even where the facts make the decision obvious and involve no significant departure from the established policy, such consultations are considered necessary for "safety." The alternative is a conference of the representatives of departments or ministries concerned. As it is thought necessary that representatives of all departments which may have even a remote interest in the question should be present, sufficient notice of the meeting has to be given and dates changed to suit conveniences of important officials even where they have little direct interest in it. Generally no action is taken on the decisions at such meetings until the minutes are approved and circulated. The increasing popularity of the conference has led to senior officials spending most of their office time in such meetings, delaying, thereby, the disposal of files.[8]

The two authors cited, like everybody else who takes part in the lively discussion about the inherited faults of the Indian administrative system and the difficulties involved in improving it, avoid relating their observations to the prevalence of corruption, the frequent allegations of corruption, and the individual official's own interest in preserving cumbersome procedures—if he is dishonest they may increase his opportunities to extract a bribe, and if he is honest they may serve to protect him from suspicion. But undoubtedly there is such a relation and it is important. Authority cannot be efficiently delegated unless those in administrative positions are incorrupt and this fact is generally recognized. In a society where corruption is prevalent, circular causation with cumulative effects operates in other ways as well. When people became convinced, rightly or wrongly, that corruption is widespread, an official's incorruptibility will tend to be weakened. And should he resist corruption, he will find it difficult to fulfill his duties. This, again, contributes to inertia and inefficiency in a society.[9]

Recognition of the very serious effects of corruption in South Asian countries raises the practical problem of what can be done to eradicate it. In all South Asian countries there have from time to time been anti-corruption drives and anti-corruption legislation. In recent years there has been, in India particularly, a growing public anxiety about corruption. The Indian Home Minister, Gulzarilal Nanda, regarded the task of eradicating corruption as his "main occupation" for some time and opened his house for daily sessions to receive complaints about corruption.

The important Santhanam Committee report was an outgrowth of this movement. While restricted to general judgments about the actual facts of corruption and their causes and effects, based on the Committee members' own information and the testimony of numerous witnesses, the report is more specific when analyzing administrative procedures that create opportunities for malfeasance and making recommendations for reform. It urges simpler and more precise rules and procedures for political and administrative decisions that affect private persons and business enterprises and also closer supervision. A main theme of these proposals is that discretionary powers should, insofar as possible, be decreased: "While we recognize that it would not be possible to completely eliminate discretion in the exercise of powers it should be possible to devise a system of administration which would reduce to the minimum, even if there is a certain seeming loss of perfection, the need for exercise of personal discretion consistently with efficiency and speedy disposal of public business."[10] The remuneration of low-paid civil servants should be raised and their social and economic status improved and made more secure. The vigilance agencies, including special police departments, should be strengthened. The penal code and other laws and procedures should be changed so that punitive action against corrupt officials can be pursued more speedily and effectively. Measures should also be taken against those in the private sector who corrupt public servants. Among such measures the committee proposes that income tax reports and assessments be made public and that the practice of declaring public documents confidential be limited. The committee recognizes that ministers and legislators must be above suspicion and proposes codes of conduct for these two categories of politicians and special procedures for complaints against them. It proposes that business enterprises be forbidden to make contributions to political parties, that persons making *bona fide* complaints be protected, and that, on the other hand, newspapers be prosecuted if they make allegations without supporting evidence.

These and other proposals deserve careful study by the student of corruption in South Asia. The committee concludes that "while it is possible to deal quickly with some forms of corruption, it is in general a long-term problem which requires firm resolve and persistent endeavour for many years to come."[11] The big questions are whether the government will take action along the lines suggested,[12] and to what extent such action will be effective within a national community when what the committee refers to as "the entire system of moral values and of the socio-economic structure" has to be changed.

When considering the prospects of reform in countries where corruption is so embedded in institutional and attitudinal remnants of traditional society and where almost everything that happens increases incentives and opportunities for personal gain, the public outcry against corruption must be regarded as a constructive force. This holds true even when this reaction is basically only the envy of people who themselves would not hesitate to engage in corrupt practices had they a chance, and even though the common awareness of corruption is apt to spread cynicism. As those people who can benefit personally from corrupt practices are a tiny minority, the public outcry against corruption should support a government intent on serious reforms. What the people—and the outside observer[13]—generally demand is punishment of the offenders. Resentment stems especially from the belief that ministers and high officials go unpunished.

When discussing the practical problem of how to fight corruption, knowledgeable persons in South Asia frequently point out that one should distinguish between traditional coruption on the part of petty officials, which in many cases amounts merely to the expectation of a customary fee by a person with a very low salary (though undoubtedly it often also injects an element of unnecessary delay and arbitrariness into business activity), and the extorting of big bribes by politicians and higher officials. It is usually stressed that corruption among minor officials cannot be combatted if it is not first stamped out at higher levels; this latter problem is thus given a strategic role. In some branches of public administration there is a systematic sharing of bribes between politicians and officials at different levels of responsibility. When there is not, and each takes care of his own interests, a tacit collusion often exists nevertheless, obstructing remedial action at all levels. The conclusion that it is quite hopeless to fight corruption if there is not a high degree of personal integrity at the top levels is obviously correct.

Great Britain, Holland, and the Scandinavian countries, where corruption is now quite limited, were all rife with it 200 years ago and even later, indeed until the liberal interlude between Mercantilism (with its many vestiges of feudalism) and the modern welfare state.[14] It was during that liberal interlude that the strong state came into being. One of its characteristics was a system of politics and administration marked by a high degree of personal integrity. While the liberalization of production and trade and particularly the liquidation of the craft guild system and the arrangements protecting urban commerce, inherited from the previous era, have been closely studied, much less interest has been manifested by political and economic historians in how the corrupt state was changed into the strong, incorrupt liberal state. It was probably accomplished by a strengthening of morals, particularly in the higher strata, together with salary reforms in the lower strata, often by transforming customary bribes into legalized fees.

Undoubtedly the South Asian countries could learn something from studies of the reforms carried out a little more than a hundred years ago in these Western countries. There is, however, a fundamental difference in initial conditions. The relative integrity in politics and administration was achieved in Great Britain, Holland, and Scandinavia during a period when state activity was reduced to a minimum. When the state again intervened in the economy on a large scale, it had a political and administrative system whose high quality only needed to be protected and preserved. The South Asian countries, on the other hand, have to fight rampant corruption in an era of their history when the activities of the state are proliferating—and, . . . when preference, even beyond what is necessary, is being given to discretionary controls. Again, South Asia stands out as a third world of planning.

One problem of considerable importance requiring specific attention is the role of Western business interests in feeding corruption in South Asia. . . . From a Western point of view—and also from the point of view of most South Asian countries—one particularly damaging effect is that Western businessmen and capitalist countries generally, already stigmatized by long association with colonialism and imperialism, appear now to South Asian intellectuals to be conspiring to undermine the integrity of their politicians and higher administrators. This damaging effect is, of course, vastly strengthened when Western government aid can be viewed in the same terms.[15]

However, a Western company that tries to maintain higher standards finds itself up against the unfair competition of companies that resort to large-scale bribery. Here Western businessmen could contribute significantly to remedial action in the South Asian countries by adhering to the stricter practices they follow at home. This would constitute a very substantial "aid" to development. At the same time it would be to the advantage of Western business interests, for collectively they have much to gain by stamping out unfair competition of this type. The Western countries might even consider putting corrupt practices by their nationals in the underdeveloped countries under the same legal sanctions that are applied in the home countries. The writer, in his contacts with Western businessmen, has often proposed this problem for study and action by the International Chamber of Commerce, but has met little response, even in countries where businessmen have shown more than average interest in maintaining high moral codes at home and abroad and where business concerns must suffer most from unfair conpetition because of their generally higher standards.

Notes

1. Corruption is essentially a sign of conflicting loyalties pointing primarily to a lack of positive attachment to the government and its ideals. In so far as corruption shows that the new government with its enormous task to fulfil in the new Asian world, is not yet sufficiently integrated in society and does not evoke full sympathy, enthusiasm and unfaltering loyalty from subjects and officials, it is a sign of weakness of the present political structure, (W.F. Wertheim, *Indonesian Society in Transition* W. Ivan Hoeve Ltd., The Hague, 1956, p. 86.)
2. Santhanam Committee report, p. 44.
3. For India, see an excellent critique by Paul H. Appleby in *Re-examination of India's Administrative System,* Government of India Press, New Delhi, 1956.
4. Santhanam Committee report, pp. 9–10.
5. The London *Times* (August 5, 1964) reports: "Many of these instances of bribery are those in which the citizen pays in order to get what he is entitled to anyway, and some students of Indian affairs have argued that this is a necessary and not harmful lubricant for a cumbersome administration. One American writer, Mr. Myron Weiner, has put it like this: 'The system of corruption . . . is a highly stable one. It is a regularized relationship. Businessmen and agriculturalists often regard the payment of baksheesh to be as much a part of the application for government services as filling in a form. The rates of payment are generally based upon the rank of the officer, the character of the services being requested, and the financial means of the claimant. The rates are more or less predictable and on the whole (there are notable exceptions, however) moderate.' Mr. Weiner's conclusion is that this corruption is 'simply a way that citizens

have found of building rewards into the administrative structure in the absence of any other appropriate incentive system.' "

The reporter comments that: "As a means of accelerating the sluggish, meandering circulation of a file within a department this might be all very well; but speed money, belying the name, actually has the effect of a brake on administration, slowing it down even further. Delay will deliberately be caused in order to invite payment of a bribe to accelerate it again."

6. *Re-examination of India's Administrative System*, p. 42.
7. Appleby, p. 45.
8. A.C. Chatrapati, "Planning Through Red Tape," *The Economic Weekly*, Special Number, July, 1961, pp. 1171–173.
9. Having become friendly with the chief police officer in the district of New Delhi where he lived for a time, the writer once complained to him about the taxi drivers' habit of ignoring all traffic rules. Why didn't he order his policemen to enforce the rules? "How could I," he answered. "If one of them went up to a taxi driver, the driver might say: 'Get away, or I will tell people that you have asked me for ten rupees.' If the policeman then pointed out that he had not done it, the rejoinder of the taxi driver could be: 'Who would believe you?' "
10. Santhanam Committee report, p. 45.
11. Santhanam Committee report, p. 110.
12. "On October 29, the government of India released the text of a code it has formulated for the conduct of ministers at the center and in the states. The code requires disclosure by a person taking office as minister of the details of his and his family's assets and liabilities as well as business interests. He is also required to sever all connections with the conduct of any business." (*Indian and Foreign Review*, November 15, 1964, p. 7.) It is a hopeful sign that this was one of the proposals by the committee in regard to the implementation of which a leading article, "Guarding the Guards," in *The Economic Weekly*, April 11, 1964, had expressed deep skepticism. Later, the eagerness for reform seems to have died down. The reports are that corruption in India has recently been increasing.
13. "Nothing would do as much to increase the faith of the common people in their governments as the prosecution of a few of those whose unwholesome activities are unnoticed or connived at by the leaders. . . . If those in positions of authority are not above suspicion, who can blame the small man for committing similar offences? This kind of thing is infectious, and ordinary people tend to copy the conduct of those at the top." (Sydney D. Bailey, *Parliamentary Government in Southern Asia*, Institute of Pacific Relations, New York, 1953, p. 72.)
14. . . . the United States is still not as free from corruption, particularly on the state and city levels, as the countries mentioned in the text. The lag in the United States is due to many interrelated facts: the spoils system since President Jackson, the consequent relative lack of a firmly established and politically independent civil service, the heterogeneity of the population (in particular, the clustering in the cities of disadvantaged colored and immigrant groups), the rise of machine politics, and so on. However, for several decades there has been a development toward greater integrity among both politicians and administrators in the United States as part of the general movement toward closer national integration.

15. At the Second Afro-Asian Economic Conference in Cairo in 1960, President Nasser spoke out against "the new form of economic imperialism which is supported by the impertinent powers which are endeavoring to dominate the newly independent Asian and African countries." He pointed out that "This new imperialism is the most dangerous form of imperialism for it depends on corruption, bribes and temptation." (Quoted from *Link,* May 15, 1960, p. 20.)

55

Corruption and Political Development
A Cost-Benefit Analysis

J.S. Nye

The Study of Corruption in Less Developed Countries

Corruption, some say, is endemic in all governments.[1] Yet it has received remarkably little attention from students of government. Not only is the study of corruption prone to moralism, but it involves one of those aspects of government in which the interests of the politician and the political scientist are likely to conflict. It would probably be rather difficult to obtain (by honest means) a visa to a developing country which is to be the subject of a corruption study.

One of the first charges levelled at the previous regime by the leaders of the coup in the less developed country is "corruption." And generally the charge is accurate. One type of reaction to this among observers is highly moralistic and tends to see corruption as evil. "Throughout the fabric of public life in newly independent States," we are told in a recent work on the subject, "runs the scarlet thread of bribery and corruption . . ." which is like a weed suffocating better plants. Another description of new states informs us that "corruption and nepotism rot good intentions and retard progressive policies."[2]

Others have reacted against this moralistic approach and warn us that we must beware of basing our beliefs about the cause of coups on post-coup rationalizations, and also of judging the social consequences of an act from the motives of the individuals performing it.[3] Under some circumstances Mandeville is right that private vice can cause public benefit. Corruption has probably been, on balance, a positive

Source: J.S. Nye, "Corruption and Political Development: A Cost-Benefit Analysis." *American Political Science Review*, LXI, 2 (June 1967), 417–27. By permission of the author and the publisher, The American Political Science Association.

factor in both Russian and American economic development. At least two very important aspects of British and American political development—the establishment of the cabinet system in the eighteenth century and the national integration of millions of immigrants in the nineteenth century—were based in part on corruption. As for corruption and stability, an anthropologist has suggested that periodic scandals can sometimes "lead to the affirmation of general principles about how the country should be run, as if there were not posed impossible reconciliations of different interests. These inquiries may not alter what actually happens, but they affirm an ideal condition of unity and justice."[4] However, the "revisionists" who echo Mandeville's aphorism often underestimate tastes for moralism—concern for worthiness of causes as well as utilitarian consequences of behavior. There is always the danger for a corrupt system that someone will question what it profits to gain the world at the price of a soul. The purpose of this paper is less to settle the difference between "moralists" and "revisionists" about the general effect of corruption on development (although a tentative conclusion is presented) than to suggest a means to make the debate more fruitful. After discussing the problem in the usual general terms of possibility, we shall turn to more specific hypotheses about probability.

This chapter is concerned with the *effects* of corruption, but a word should be said about causes to dispel any impression that corruption is a uniquely Afro-Asian-Latin American problem. I assume no European or American monopoly of morals. After all, Lord Bryce saw corruption as a major American flaw and noted its outbreak in "virulent form" in the new states in Europe.[5] Yet behavior that will be considered corrupt is likely to be more prominent in less developed countries because of a variety of conditions involved in their underdevelopment—great inequality in distribution of wealth; political office as the primary means of gaining access to wealth; conflict between changing moral codes; the weakness of social and governmental enforcement mechanisms; and the absence of a strong sense of national community.[6] The weakness of the legitimacy of governmental institutions is also a contributing factor, though to attribute this entirely to the prevalence of a cash nexus or the divergence of moral codes under previous colonial governments or to the mere newness of the states concerned may be inadequate in light of the experience with corruption of older, non-colonial less developed states such as Thailand or Liberia. Regardless of causes, however, the conditions of less developed countries are such that corruption is likely to have different effects than in more developed countries.

Most researchers on developing areas gather some information on corruption, and this paper will suggest hypotheses about the costs and benefits of corruption for development that may lure some of this information into the open. However, in view of the fact that generalizations about corruption and development tend to be disguised descriptions of a particular area in which the generalizer has done field work, I will state at the outset that generalizations in this paper are unevenly based on field work in East Africa and Central America and on secondary sources for other areas.

Definitions pose a problem. Indeed, if we define political development as "rational, modern, honest government," then it cannot coexist with corruption in the same time period; and if corruption is endemic in government, a politically developed society cannot exist. "Political development" is not an entirely satisfactory term since it has an evaluative as well as a descriptive content. At least in the cases of economic development, there is general agreement on the units and scale by which to measure (growth of per capita income). In politics, however, there is agreement neither on the units nor on a single scale to measure development.[7] Emphasis on some scales rather than others tends to reflect an author's interests.

In this author's view, the term "political development" is best used to refer to the recurring problem of relating governmental structures and processes to social change. It seems useful to use one term to refer to the type of change which seems to be occurring in our age ("modernization") and another to refer to capacity of political structures and processes to cope with social change, to the extent it exists, in any period.[8] We generally assume that this means structures and processes which are regarded as legitimate by relevant sectors of the population and effective in producing outputs desired by relevant sectors of the population. I assume that legitimacy and effectiveness are linked in the "long run" but can compensate for each other in the "short run."[9] What constitutes a relevant sector of the population will vary with the period and with social changes within a period. In the modern period we tend to assume that at least a veneer of broad participation is essential for establishing or maintaining legitimacy. In other words, in the current period, political development and political modernization may come close to involving the same things.

In this paper, political development (or decay) will mean growth (or decline) in the capacity of a society's governmental structures and processes to maintain their legitimacy over time (i.e., presumably in the face of social change). This allows us to see development as a moving equilibrium and avoid some of the limitations of equating development and modernization. Of course, this definition does not solve all the concept's problems. Unless we treat development entirely ex post facto, there will still be differences over evaluation (legitimate in whose eyes?) and measurement (national integration, administrative capacity, institutionalization?) as well as what constitutes a "long" and "short" run. Thus we will find that forms of corruption which have been beneficial effects on economic development may be detrimental for political development; or may promote one form of political development (i.e., defined one way or measured along one scale) but be detrimental to another. We shall have to continue to beware of variations in what we mean by political development. (Alternatively, those who reject the term "political development" can still read the chapter as relating corruption to three problems of change discussed below.)

The definition of corruption also poses serious problems. Broadly defined as perversion or a change from good to bad, it covers a wide range of behavior from venality to ideological erosion. For instance, we might describe the revolutionary student who returns from Paris to a former French African country and accepts a (perfectly legal) over-paid civil service post as "corrupted." But used this broadly the term is more relevant to moral evaluation than political analysis. I will use a narrower definition which can be made operational. Corruption is behavior which deviates from the formal duties of a public role because of private-regarding (personal, close family, private clique) pecuniary or status gains; or violates rules against the exercise of certain types of private-regarding influence.[10] This includes such behavior as bribery (use of a reward to pervert the judgment of a person in a position of trust); nepotism (bestowal of patronage by reason of ascriptive relationship rather than merit); and misappropriation (illegal appropriation of public resources for private-regarding uses). This definition does not include much behavior that might nonetheless be regarded as offensive to moral standards. It also excludes any consideration of whether the behavior is in the public interest, since building the study of the effects of the behavior into the definition makes analysis of the relationship between corruption and development difficult. Similarly, it avoids the question of whether non-Western societies regard the behavior as corrupt, preferring to treat that also as a separate variable. To build such relativism into the definition is to make specific behavior which can be compared between countries hard to identify. Moreover, in most less developed countries, there are two standards regarding such behavior, one indigenous and one more or less Western, and the formal duties and rules concerning most public roles tend to be expressed in terms of the latter.[11] In short, while this definition of corruption is not entirely satisfactory in terms of inclusiveness of behavior and the handling of relativity of standards, it has the merit of denoting specific behavior generally called corrupt by Western standards (which are at least partly relevant in most developing countries) and thus allowing us to ask what effects this specific behavior has under different conditions.

Possible Benefits and Costs

Discussion of the relation of corruption to development tends to be phrased in general terms. Usually the argument between moralists and revisionists tends to be about the possibility that corruption (type unspecified) *can* be beneficial for development. Leaving aside questions of probability, one can argue that corruption can be beneficial to political development, as here defined, by contributing to the solution of three major problems involved: economic development, national integration, and governmental capacity.

Economic Development

If corruption helps promote economic development which is generally necessary to maintain a capacity to preserve legitimacy in the face of social change, then (by definition) it is beneficial for political development.

There seem to be at least three major ways in which some kinds of corruption might promote economic development.

Capital Formation. Where private capital is scarce and government lacks a capacity to tax a surplus out of peasants or workers openly, corruption may be an important source of capital formation. There seems to be little question about the effectiveness of this form of taxation—Trujillo reputedly accumulated $500 million and Nkrumah and relatives probably more than $10 million.[12] The real question is whether the accumulated capital is then put to uses which promote economic development or winds up in Swiss banks.

Cutting Red Tape. In many new countries the association of profit with imperialism has led to a systematic bias against the market mechanism. Given inadequate administrative resources in most new states, it can be argued that corruption helps to mitigate the consequences of ideologically determined economic devices which may not be wholly appropriate for the countries concerned.[13] Even where the quality of bureaucrats is high, as in India, some observers believe that "too much checking on corruption can delay development. Trying to run a development economy with triple checking is impossible."[14] Corruption on the part of factory managers in the Soviet Union is sometimes credited with providing a flexibility that makes central planning more effective.

Entrepreneurship and Incentives. If Schumpeter is correct that the entrepreneur is a vital factor in economic growth and if there is an ideological bias against private incentives in a country, then corruption may provide one of the major means by which a developing country can make use of this factor. This becomes even more true if, as is often the case, the personal characteristics associated with entrepreneurship have a higher incidence among minority groups. Corruption may provide the means of overcoming discrimination against members of a minority group, and allow the entrepreneur from a minority to gain access to the political decisions necessary for him to provide his skills. In East Africa, for instance, corruption may be prolonging the effective life of an important economic asset—the Asian minority entrepreneur—beyond what political conditions would otherwise allow.

National Integration

It seems fair to assume that a society's political structures will be better able to cope with change and preserve their legitimacy if the members share a sense of community. Indeed, integration is sometimes used as one of the main scales for measuring political development.

Elite Integration. Corruption may help overcome divisions in a ruling elite that might otherwise result in destructive conflict. One observer believes that it helped bridge the gap between the groups based on power and those based on wealth that appeared in the early nationalist period in West Africa and allowed the groups to "assimilate each other." Certainly in Central America, corruption has been a major factor in the succession mechanism by integrating the leaders of the new coup into the existing upper class. Whether this is beneficial for political development or not is another question involving particular circumstances, different evaluation of the importance of continuity, and the question of the relevant period for measurement.

Integration of Non-Elites. Corruption may help to ease the transition from traditional life to modern. It can be argued that the man who has lived under "ascriptive, particularistic and diffuse" conditions cares far less about the rational impartiality of the government and its laws than he does about its awesomeness and seeming inhumanity. The vast gap between literate official and illiterate peasant which is often characteristic of the countryside may be bridged if the peasant approaches the official bearing traditional gifts or their (marginally corrupt) money equivalent. For the new urban resident, a political machine based on corruption may provide a comprehensible point at which to relate to government by other than purely ethnic or tribal means. In McMullan's words, a degree of low-level corruption can "soften relations of officials and people" or in Shils' words it "humanizes government and makes it less awesome."[15]

However, what is integrative for one group may be disintegrative for another. The "traditional" or "transitional" man may care far more that he has a means to get *his* son out of jail than that the system as a whole be incorruptible, but for "modern" groups such as students and middle classes (who have profited from achievement and universalism) the absence of honesty may destroy the legitimacy of the system. Finally, it is worth noting again Gluckman's statement that the scandals associated with corruption can sometimes have the effect of strengthening a value system as a whole.

Governmental Capacity

The capacity of the political structures of many new states to cope with change is frequently limited by the weakness of their new institutions and (often despite apparent centralization) the fragmentation of power in a country. Moreover, there is little "elasticity of power"— i.e., power does not expand or contract easily with a change of man or situation.[16]

To use a somewhat simplified scheme of motivations, one could say that the leaders in such a country have to rely (in various combinations) on ideal, coercive or material incentives to aggregate enough power to govern. Legal material incentives may have to be augmented by corrupt ones. Those who place great faith in ideal incentives (such as Wraith and Simpkins) see the use of corrupt material incentives as destructive ("these countries depend considerably on enthusiasm and on youthful pride of achievement . . .")[17] of governmental capacity. With a lower evaluation of the role of ideal incentives, however, corrupt material incentives may become a functional equivalent for violence. In Mexico, for instance, Needler has described the important role which corruption played in the transition from the violent phases of the revolution to its institutionalized form.[18] At the local level, Greenstone notes that while patronage and corruption was one factor contributing to an initial decline in governmental capacity in East Africa, corrupt material incentives may provide the glue for reassembling sufficient power to govern.[19]

Governmental capacity can be increased by the creation of supporting institutions such as political parties. Financing political parties
tends to be a problem in developed as well as less developed countries,
but it is a particular problem in poor countries. Broad-based mass
financing is difficult to maintain after independence.[20] In some cases the
major alternatives to corrupt proceeds as a means of party finance are
party decay or reliance on outside funds. Needless to say, not all such
investments are successful. The nearly $12 million diverted from
Nigeria's Western Region Marketing Board into Action Group coffers
from 1959–1962 (and probably equivalent amounts in other regions)[21]
seem to have been wasted in terms of institution-building; but on the
other hand, investment in India's Congress party or Mexico's *Partido
Revolucionario Institucional* has been more profitable for political
development.

Those who dispute the possible benefits of corruption could argue
that it involves countervailing costs that interfere with the solution of
each of the three problems. They could argue that corruption is
economically wasteful, politically destabilizing, and destructive of
governmental capacity.

Waste of Resources

Although corruption may help promote economic development, it
can also hinder it or direct it in socially less desirable directions.

Capital Outflow. As we mentioned above, capital accumulated by
corruption that winds up in Swiss banks is a net loss for the developing
country. These costs can be considerable. For instance, one source
estimates that from 1954–1959, four Latin American dictators (Peron,
Perez, Jimenez, and Batista) removed a total of $1.15 billion from their
countries.[22] It is no wonder that another source believes that economic
development in some Latin American countries has been "checked"
by corruption.[23]

Investment Distortions. Investment may be channeled into sectors
such as construction not because of economic profitability, but because
they are more susceptible to hiding corrupt fees through cost-plus
contracts and use of suppliers' credits. This was the case, for instance,
in Venezuela under Perez Jimenez and in Ghana under Nkrumah.

Waste of Skills. "If the top political elite of a country consumes its
time and energy in trying to get rich by corrupt means, it is not likely
that the development plans will be fulfilled."[24] Moreover, the costs in
terms of time and energy spent attempting to set some limits to
corruption can also be expensive. For instance, in Burma, U Nu's

creation of a Bureau of Special Investigation to check corruption actually reduced administrative efficiency.[25]

Aid Foregone. Another possible wastage, the opportunity costs of aid foregone or withdrawn by outside donors because of disgust with corruption in a developing country could be a serious cost in the sense that developing countries are highly dependent on external sources of capital. Thus far, however, there has not been a marked correlation between honesty of governments and their per capita receipt of aid. If corruption is a consideration with donors (presumably it weighs more heavily with multilateral institutions), it is not yet a primary one.

Instability

By destroying the legitimacy of political structures in the eyes of those who have power to do something about the situation, corruption can contribute to instability and possible national disintegration. But it is not clear that instability is always inimical to political development.

Social Revolution. An argument can be made that a full social revolution (whatever its short-run costs) can speed the development of new political structures better able to preserve their legitimacy in the face of social change. Thus, in this view if corruption led to social revolution, this might be a beneficial effect for political development. But it is not clear that corruption of the old regime is a primary cause of social revolution. Such revolutions are comparatively rare and often depend heavily on catalytic events (such as external wars).

Military Takeovers. If corruption causes a loss of legitimacy in the eyes of those with guns, it may be a direct cause of instability and the disintegration of existing political institutions. But the consequences for political development are again ambiguous. Much depends on differing evaluations of the ability of military regimes (which tend to comprise people and procedures oriented toward modernity) to maintain legitimacy in a democratic age either by self-transformation into political regimes or by being willing and able to foster new political institutions to which power can be returned. To the extent that this tends to be difficult, then if corruption leads to military takeover, it has hindered political development.[26]

The degree to which corruption is itself a major cause of military takeovers is, however, open to some question. Despite its prominence in post-coup rationalizations, one might suspect that it is only a secondary cause in most cases. Perhaps more significant is military leaders' total distaste for the messiness of politics—whether honest or not—and a tendency to blame civilian politicians for failures to meet overly optimistic popular aspirations which would be impossible of fulfillment even by a government of angels.[27] Indeed, to the extent that corruption contributes to governmental effectiveness in meeting these aspirations, it may enhance stability.

Crozier sees "revulsion against civilian incompetence and corruption" as a major cause of coups in several Asian countries including Burma, but he also states that the main cause of Ne Win's return to power was the Shan demand for a federal rather than unitary state.[28] Similarly, corruption is sometimes blamed for the first coup in Nigeria, but the post-electoral crisis in the Western region and the fear of permanent Northern domination was probably a more important and direct cause. In Ghana, corruption may have played a more important role in causing the coup, but not so much because of revulsion at dishonesty, as the fact that corruption had reached an extent where it contributed to an economic situation in which real wages had fallen. Nonetheless, its impact in relation to other factors should not be overestimated.[29]

Upsetting Ethnic Balances. Corruption can sometimes exacerbate problems of national integration in developing countries. If a corrupt leader must be fired, it may upset ethnic arithmetic as happened in both Kenya and Zambia in 1966. Of course this can be manipulated as a deliberate political weapon. In Western Nigeria in 1959, an anti-corruption officer was appointed but his jurisdiction was subject to approval by the cabinet, which meant that no case could be investigated "unless the party leader decided that a man needed to be challenged."[30] But as a weapon, charging corruption is a risky device. Efforts by southern politicians in Uganda to use it in 1966 precipitated a pre-emptive coup by the northern prime minister in alliance with the predominantly northern army.

Reduction of Governmental Capacity

While it may not be the sole or major cause, corruption can contribute to the loss of governmental capacity in developing countries.

Reduction of Administrative Capacity. Corruption may alienate modern-oriented civil servants (a scarce resource) and cause them to leave a country or withdraw or reduce their efforts. In addition to the obvious costs, this may involve considerable opportunity costs in the form of restriction of government programs because of fears that a new program (for instance, administration of new taxes) might be ineffective in practice. While this is a real cost, it is worth noting that efficient bureaucracy is not always a necessary condition for economic or political development (at least in the early stages), and in some cases can even hinder it.[31]

Loss of Legitimacy. It is often alleged that corruption squanders the most important asset a new country has—the legitimacy of its government. This is a serious cost but it must be analyzed in terms of groups. As we have seen, what may enhance legitimacy for the student or civil servant may not enhance it for the tradition-oriented man. It is interesting, for instance, that there is some evidence that in Tanganyika petty corruption at low levels seems to have increased during the year following the replacement of an "illegitimate" colonial regime by a "legitimate" nationalist one.[32] Loss of legitimacy as a cost must be coupled with assessment of the power or importance of the group in whose eyes legitimacy is lost. If they are young army officers, it can be important indeed.

Probabilities

Thus far I have been discussing *possible* benefits and costs. I have established that under some circumstances corruption can have beneficial effects on at least three major development problems. I have evaluated the importance of a number of frequently alleged countervailing costs. It remains to offer hypotheses about the *probabilities* of benefits outweighing costs. In general terms, such probabilities will vary with at least three conditions: (1) a tolerant culture and dominant groups; (2) a degree of security on the part of the members of the elite being corrupted; (3) the existence of societal and institutional checks and restraints on corrupt behavior.

1. Attitudes toward corruption vary greatly. In certain West African countries, observers have reported little widespread sense of indignation about corruption.[33] The Philippines, with its American colonial heritage of corruption, and appreciation of the politics of compromise, seems able to tolerate a higher level of corruption than formerly-Dutch Indonesia. According to Higgins, the Indonesian attitude to corruption (which began on a large scale only in 1954) is that it is sinful. He attributes the civil war of 1958 to corruption and argues that in the Philippines, "anomalies" are taken more for granted.[34] Not only is the general level of tolerance of corruption relevant; variations of attitude within a country can be as important (or more so) than differences between countries. Very often, traditional sectors of the populace are likely to be more tolerant of corruption than some of the modern sectors (students, army, civil service). Thus the hypothesis must take into account not only the tolerant nature of the culture, but also the

relative power of groups representing more and less tolerant sub-cultures in a country. In Nigeria, tolerance was by many accounts considerable among the population at large, but not among the young army officers who overthrew the old regime.

2. Another condition which increases the probability that the benefits of corruption will outweigh the costs is a degree of security (and perception thereof) by the members of the elites indulging in coup practices. Too great insecurity means that any capital formed by corruption will tend to be exported rather than invested at home. In Nicaragua, for instance, it is argued that the sense of security of the Somoza family encouraged them in internal investments in economic projects and the strengthening of their political party, which led to impressive economic growth and diminished direct reliance on the army. In contrast are the numerous cases of capital outflow mentioned above. One might add that this sense of security, including the whole capitalist ethic, which is rare in less developed countries today, makes comparison with capital formation by the "robber barons" of the American nineteenth century of dubious relevance to less developed countries today.

3. It is probable that for the benefits of corruption to outweigh the costs depends on its being limited in various ways, much as the beneficial effects of inflation for economic growth tends to depend on limits. These limits depend upon the existence of societal or institutional restraints on corruption. These can be external to the leaders, e.g., the existence of an independent press, and honest elections; or internalized conceptions of public interest by a ruling group such as Leys argues that eighteenth century English aristocrats held.[35] In Mandeville's words, "Vice is beneficial found when it's by Justice lopt and bound."[36]

Given the characteristics of less developed countries, one can see that the general probability of the presence of one or more of these conditions (and thus of benefits outweighing costs) is not high. But to conclude merely that the moralists are more right than wrong (though for the wrong reasons) is insufficient because the whole issue remains unsatisfactory if left in these general terms. Though corruption may not prove beneficial for resolution of development problems in general, it may prove to be the only means to solution of a particular problem. If a country has some overriding problem, some "obstacle to development"—for instance, if capital can be formed by no other means, or ethnic hatred threatens all legal activities aimed at its alleviation—then it is possible that corruption is beneficial for development despite the high costs and risks involved. While there are dangers in identifying "obstacles to development,"[37] and while the corruption that is beneficial to the solution of one problem may be detrimental to another, we need to get away from general statements which are difficult to test and which provide us with no means of ordering the vast number of variables involved. We are more likely to advance this argument if we distinguish the roles of different types of corruption in relation to different types of development problems.

The matrix in Table 55.1 relates three types of corruption to three types of development problems, first assuming favorable and then assuming unfavorable conditions described above. Favorable conditions (F) means a tolerant culture or dominance of more tolerant groups, relative security of the elite corrupted, and societal/institutional checks. Unfavorable conditions (U) means intolerant culture or groups, insecure elite, and few societal/institutional checks. The development problems are those discussed above: economic development, national integration, and governmental capacity. The scores are a priori judgments that the costs of a particular type of corruption are likely to outweigh the benefits for a particular development problem or subproblem. They represent a series of tentative hypotheses to be clarified or refuted by data. Under economic development, the specific sub-problems discussed are whether capital accumulation is promoted (benefit) without capital flight (cost); whether cutting bureaucratic red tape (benefit) outweighs distortion of rational criteria (cost); whether the attraction of unused scarce skills such as entrepreneurship (benefit) is greater than the wastage of scarce skills of, say, politicians and civil servants (cost).

Under the problem of national integration are the sub-problems of whether a particular type of corruption tends to make the elite more cohesive (benefit) or seriously splits them (cost); and whether it tends to humanize government and make national identification easier for the non-elites (benefit) or alienates them (cost). Under the problem of governmental capacity are the sub-problems of whether the additional power aggregated by corruption (benefit) outweighs possible damage to administrative efficiency (cost); and whether it enhances (benefit) or seriously weakens the governmental legitimacy (cost).

Level of Beneficiary

Shils argues that "freedom from corruption at the highest levels is a necessity for the maintenance of public respect of Government . . ." whereas a modicum of corruption at lower levels is probably not too injurious.[38] On the other hand, McMullan reports that West Africans

Table 55.1
CORRUPTION COST-BENEFIT MATRIX

Types of Corruption	Political Conditions	1. Economic development			2. National integration		3. Governmental capacity		General Probability that Costs Outweigh Benefits
		a. capital	b. bureaucracy	c. skills	d. elite	e. non-elite	f. effectiveness	g. legitimacy	
1. Level									
top	F	low	uncertain	uncertain/low	low	uncertain	low	low	low/uncertain
bottom	F	high	uncertain	uncertain/high	uncertain	low	high	low	high
top	U	high	high	uncertain/low	high	high	low	high	high
bottom	U	high	uncertain	uncertain/high	little relevance	high	high	high	high
2. Inducements									
modern	F	low	uncertain	uncertain/low	low	low	low/uncertain	uncertain	low/uncertain
traditional	F	high/uncertain	uncertain	high	high	uncertain	high	uncertain	high
modern	U	high	uncertain	uncertain/low	high	high	low/uncertain	high	high
traditional	U	high/uncertain	uncertain	high	high	uncertain	high	high	high
3. Deviation									
extensive	F	uncertain	high	uncertain	uncertain	low	uncertain/low	uncertain/high	high
marginal	F	uncertain	low	uncertain/low	low	low	low	low	low
extensive	U	uncertain	high	uncertain	high	high	uncertain	high	high
marginal	U	uncertain	low	uncertain/low	high	high	low	high	high

NOTES:
F   favorable political conditions (cultural tolerance, elite security, checks).
U   unfavorable political conditions
High   high probability that costs exceed benefits
Low   low probability that costs exceed benefits
Uncertain   little relationship or ambiguous relationship

show little sense of indignation about often fantastic stories of corruption by leaders, and impressions from Mexico indicate that petty corruption most saps morale.[39] In India, Bayley notes that "although corruption at the top attracts the most attention in public forums, and involves the largest amount of money in separate transactions, corruption at the very bottom levels is the more apparent and obvious and in total amounts of money involved may very well rival corruption at the top."[40]

The matrix in the exhibit suggests that under unfavorable conditions neither type of corruption is likely to be beneficial in general, although top level corruption may enhance governmental power more than it weakens administrative efficiency. It also suggests that under favorable conditions, top level corruption may be beneficial but bottom level corruption probably is not (except for non-elite integration). If these judgments are accurate, it suggests that countries with favorable conditions, like India, which have considerable bottom level corruption but pride themselves on the relative honesty of the higher levels may be falling between two stools.

The rationale of the scoring is as follows.

(A) Capital. Bottom level corruption with smaller size of each inducement will probably increase consumption more than capital formation. While top level corruption may represent the latter, whether it is invested productively rather than sent overseas depends on favorable political conditions.

(B) Bureaucracy. Other factors seem more important in determining whether expediting is more important than distortion; except that those with the power of the top levels will probably distort investment criteria considerably in conditions of uncertainty—witness the alleged selling of investment licenses under a previous government in Guatemala.

(C) Skills. Whether top level corruption permits the use of more skills than it wastes depends upon their supply. Where they exist, as with Asians in East Africa or "Turcos" in Honduras, it is probably beneficial. Corruption of those at lower levels of power may be more likely to waste energies than to be important in permission of use of new skills simply because their power is limited.

(D) Elite Integration. It is difficult to see a clear relation between bottom level corruption and elite integration. At the higher levels under unfavorable conditions, e.g., a powerful intolerant part of the elite such as students or army, corruption would probably have a more divisive than cohesive effect. Under favorable conditions it might be more cohesive.

(E) Non-elite Integration. Under unfavorable conditions it seems likely that both types of corruption would tend to alienate more than enhance identification, whereas under favorable conditions corruption by the lower levels that the populace deals with most frequently might have the humanizing effect mentioned above, and alienation would be slight in the tolerant culture. Top level corruption might have the same effect though the connection is less clear because of the lesser degree of direct contact.

(F) Effectiveness. Bottom level corruption is more likely to disperse rather than aggregate power by making governmental machinery less responsive than otherwise might be the case; whereas at top levels the ability to change the behavior of important power holders by corrupt inducements is likely to outweigh the loss of efficiency, even under unfavorable conditions.

(G) Legitimacy. Whether corruption enhances or reduces governmental legitimacy depends more on unfavorable conditions than on level of corruption. Much depends on another factor, visibility of corrupt behavior, which does not always have a clear relationship to level of corruption.

Inducements

Another distinction which can be made between types of corruption is the nature of the inducement used, for instance the extent to which they reflect the values of the traditional society or the values of the modern sector. A traditional inducement such as status in one's clan or tribe may be more tolerable to those who share the ascriptive affinity, but others outside the ascriptive relationship would prefer the use of money which would give them equality of access to the corruptee. Weiner writes of India that "from a political point of view, equal opportunity to corrupt is often more important than the amount of corruption, and therefore . . . an increase in *bakshish* is in the long run less serious than an increase in corruption by ascriptive criteria."[41]

As scored here, our matrix suggests that under favorable political conditions (e.g., India?) Weiner's hypothesis is probably correct but would not be correct under unfavorable conditions.

(A) Capital. Modern inducements (i.e., money) probably lead to capital formation (at top levels) which may be invested under favorable conditions or be sent abroad under unfavorable conditions. Traditional inducements (kin status) do not promote capital formation (and may even interfere with it) but probably have little effect on capital flight.

(B) Bureaucracy. What edge modern inducements may have in expediting procedure may be offset by distortion of criteria, so the relation between type of inducement and this problem is scored as uncertain.

(C) Skills. Assuming the existence of untapped skills (as above), modern inducements increase the access to power while traditional ones decrease it.

(D) Elite Integration. Under favorable conditions modern inducements are unlikely to divide elites more than make them cohere, but traditional inducements tend to preserve and emphasize ethnic divisions in the elites. Under unfavorable conditions, both types of inducements tend to be divisive.

(E) Non-elite Integration. Whether modern inducements promote identification or alienation varies with political conditions in the expected way, but the effect of traditional inducements is more ambiguous and probably varies from positive to negative according to the prevalence of traditional as against modern values in the particular country in question.

(F) Effectiveness. Modern inducements probably give the government greater range to aggregate more sources of power than traditional inducements do. The probabilities will vary not only with political conditions but also by the opportunity costs—whether there is an efficient administrative machine to be damaged or not.

(G) Legitimacy. Under favorable conditions whether traditional or modern inducements will decrease legitimacy more than they enhance it remains uncertain because it will vary with the (above mentioned) degree of existence of modern and traditional values in a society. Under unfavorable conditions, both will likely have higher costs than benefits.

Deviation

We can also distinguish types of corruption by whether the corrupt behavior involves extensive deviation from the formal duties of a public role or marginal deviation. This is not the same thing as a scale of corrupt inducements, since the size of the inducements may bear little relation to the degree of deviation. For instance, it is alleged that in one Central American country under an insecure recent regime, a business could get the government to reverse a decision for as little as $2,000, whereas in a neighboring country the mere expediting of a decision cost $50,000. Such a distinction between types of corruption by extent of deviation is not uncommon among practitioners who use terms like "speed-up money" or "honest graft" in their rationalizations.[42]

(A) Capital. It is difficult to see that the extensiveness of the deviation (except insofar as it affects the scale of inducement) has much to do with the probabilities of capital formation or flight.

(B) Bureaucracy. On the other hand, marginal deviations (by definition) are unlikely to involve high costs in distortion of criteria and even under unfavorable conditions may help expedite matters. Extensive deviations are likely to have high costs in terms of national criteria regardless of conditions.

(C) Skills. It is not clear that extensive deviations call forth more unused skills than they waste administrative skills; nor is the matter completely clear with marginal deviations, though the costs of administrative skills wasted may be lower because the tasks are simpler.

(D) Elite Integration. Under unfavorable conditions, the effects of corruption on elite cohesiveness are likely to be negative regardless of the extent of deviations, though they might be less negative for marginal deviations. Under favorable conditions, marginal deviations are likely to have low costs, but the effect of extensive deviations will be uncertain, varying with other factors such as existing cohesiveness of the elite and the nature of the extensive deviations.

(E) Non-elite Integration. Under unfavorable conditions, corruption is likely to have more alienative than identification effects regardless of the nature of the deviations. Under favorable conditions, marginal deviation will not have high costs in terms of alienation, and extensive deviation may have special appeal to those who are seeking human and "reversible" government more than impartial or "rational" government.

(F) Effectiveness. It is difficult to see that extensive deviations alone would increase governmental power more than weaken administrative efficiency, but with marginal deviation, the extent of the latter would be sufficiently small that the benefits would probably outweigh the costs.

(G) Legitimacy. Under unfavorable conditions either type of corruption would be more likely to weaken than to enhance legitimacy, but under favorable conditions the lesser challenge to rationality might make marginal corruption less detrimental than extensive—though this would depend on the proportion and dominance of groups in society placing emphasis on modern values.

Conclusion

The scoring of the matrix suggests that we can refine the general statements about corruption and political development to read "it is probable that the costs of corruption in less developed countries will exceed its benefits except for top level corruption involving modern inducements and marginal deviations and except for situations where corruption provides the only solution to an important obstacle to development." As our matrix shows, corruption can provide the solution to several of the more limited problems of development. Whether this is beneficial to development as a whole depends on how important the problems are and what alternatives exist. It is also interesting to note that while the three conditions we have identified seem to be necessary for corruption to be beneficial in general terms, they are not necessary for it to be beneficial in the solution of a number of particular problems.

At this point, however, not enough information is at hand to justify great confidence in the exact conclusions reached here. More important is the suggestion of the use of this or a similar matrix to advance the discussion of the relationship between corruption and development. The matrix can be expanded or elaborated in a number of ways if the data seem to justify it. Additional development problems can be added, as can additional types of corruption (e.g., by scale, visibility, income effects, and so forth). The above categories can be made more precise by adding possibilities; for instance intermediate as well as top and bottom levels of corruption, or distinctions between politicians and civil servants at top, bottom, and intermediate levels.

Despite the problems of systematic field research on corruption in developing countries mentioned above, there is probably much more data on corruption and development gleaned during field work on other topics than we realize. What we need to advance the study of the problem is to refute and replace *specific* a priori hypotheses with propositions based on such data rather than with the generalities of the moralists. Corruption in developing countries is too important a phenomenon to be left to moralists.

Notes

1. C.J. Friedrich, *Man and His Government* (New York, 1963), p. 167. See also "Political Pathology," *The Political Quarterly,* 37 (January–March 1966), 70–85.
2. Ronald Wraith and Edgar Simpkins, *Corruption in Developing Countries* (London, 1963), pp. 11, 12. K.T. Young, Jr., "New Politics in New States," *Foreign Affairs,* 39 (April 1961), at p. 498.
3. See, for example: Nathaniel Leff, "Economic Development Through Bureaucratic Corruption," *The American Behavioral Scientist,* 8 (November, 1964), 8:14; David H. Bayley, "The Effects of Corruption in a Developing Nation," *The Western Political Quarterly,* 19 (December 1966), 719–32; J.J. Van Klaveren in a "Comment" in *Comparative Studies*

in Society and History, 6 (January 1964), at p. 195, even argues that "recent experience in the so-called underdeveloped countries has most vividly brought home the fact that corruption is not a mass of incoherent phenomena, but a political system, capable of being steered with tolerable precision by those in power."

4. Max Gluckman, *Custom and Conflict in Africa* (Oxford, 1955), p. 135.

5. James Bryce, *Modern Democracies* (New York, 1921), Vol. II, p. 509.

6. Colin Leys, "What is the Problem About Corruption?" *Journal of Modern African Studies,* 3, 2 (1965), 224–25; Ralph Braibanti, "Reflections on Bureaucratic Corruption," *Public Administration,* 40 (Winter 1962), 365–71.

7. Nor, by the nature of the subject, is there likely to be. In Pye's words, "no single scale can be used for measuring political development": Lucian Pye (ed.), *Communications and Political Development* (Princeton, 1963). See also Lucian Pye, "The Concept of Political Development." *The Annals,* 358 (March 1965), 1–19; Samuel Huntington, "Political Development and Political Decay," *World Politics,* 17 (April 1965), 386–430; Robert Packenham, "Political Development Doctrines in the American Foreign Aid Program," *World Politics,* 18 (January 1966), 194–235.

8. See Huntington, 389.

9. S.M. Lipset, *Political Man* (New York, 1959), 72–75.

10. The second part of the definition is taken from Edward C. Banfield, *Political Influence* (New York: Free Press, 1961), p. 315.

11. See, for example: M.G. Smith. "Historical and Cultural Conditions of Political Corruption Among the Hausa," *Comparative Studies in Society and History,* 6 (January 1964), at p. 194; Lloyd Fallers, "The Predicament of the Modern African Chief: An Instance from Uganda," *American Anthropologist,* 57 (1955), 290–305. I agree with Bayley on this point: 720–22.

12. A. Terry Rambo, "The Dominican Republic," in Martin Needler (ed.), *Political Systems of Latin America* (Princeton, 1964), p. 172; New York Times, March 5, 1966. Ayeh Kumi's quoted statement has almost certainly greatly underestimated his own assets.

13. On the economic problems of "African socialism," see Elliot Berg, "Socialism and Economic Development in Tropical Africa," *Quarterly Journal of Economics,* 78 (November 1964), 549–73.

14. Barbara Ward, addressing the Harvard Center for International Affairs, Cambridge, Mass., March 3, 1966.

15. M. McMullan, "A Theory of Corruption," *The Sociological Review* (Keele), 9 (July 1961), at p. 196; Edward Shils, *Political Development in the New States* (The Hague, 1962), p. 385.

16. See Herbert Werlin, "The Nairobi City Council: A Study in Comparative Local Government," *Comparative Studies in Society and History,* 7 (January 1966), at p. 185.

17. Wraith and Simpkins, p. 172.

18. Martin Needler, "The Political Development of Mexico," *American Political Science Review,* 55 (June 1961), at pp. 310–11.

19. J. David Greenstone, "Corruption and Self Interest in Kampala and Nairobi," *Comparative Studies in Society and History,* 7 (January 1966), 199–210.

20. See J.S. Nye, "The Impact of Independence on Two African Nationalist Parties," in J. Butler and A. Castagno (eds.), *Boston University Papers on Africa* (New York, 1967), 224–45.
21. Richard L. Sklar, "Contradictions in the Nigerian Political System," *Journal of Modern African Studies,* 3, 2 (1965), at p. 206.
22. Edwin Lieuwen, *Arms and Politics in Latin America* (New York, 1960), p. 149.
23. F. Benham and H.A. Holley, *A Short Introduction to the Economy of Latin America* (London, 1960), p. 10.
24. Leys, at p. 229.
25. Brian Crozier, *The Morning After: A Study of Independence* (London, 1963), p. 82.
26. In Pye's words, the military "can contribute to only a limited part of national development," *Aspects of Political Development* (Boston, 1966), p. 187.
27. "Have no fear," General Mobutu told the Congo people, "My government is not composed of politicians." Mobutu alleged that political corruption cost the Congo $43 million: *East Africa and Rhodesia,* January 13, 1966; *Africa Report,* January 1966, 23.
28. Crozier, pp. 62, 74.
29. For two interpretations, see Martin Kilson, "Behind Nigeria's Revolts"; Immanuel Wallerstein, "Autopsy of Nkrumah's Ghana," *New Leader,* January 31, 9–12; March 14, 1966, 3–5.
30. Henry Bretton, *Power and Stability in Nigeria* (New York, 1962), p. 79.
31. Bert Hoselitz, "Levels of Economic Performance and Bureaucratic Structures," in Joseph LaPalombara (ed.), *Bureaucracy and Political Development* (Princeton, 1963), 193–95. See also Nathaniel Leff, 8–14.
32. See *Tanganyika Standard,* May 15, 1963.
33. McMullan, p. 195.
34. Benjamin Higgins, *Economic Development* (New York, 1959), p. 62.
35. Leys, p. 227. See also Eric McKitrick, "The Study of Corruption," *Political Science Quarterly,* 72 (December 1957), 502–15, for limits on corruption in urban America.
36. Bernard Mandeville, *The Fable of the Bees,* Vol. I (Oxford: Clarendon Press, by F.B. Kaye, 1924), p. 37.
37. See Albert O. Hirschman, "Obstacles to Development: A Classification and a Quasi-Vanishing Act," *Economic Development and Cultural Change,* 13 (July 1965), 385–93.
38. Shils, p. 385.
39. McMullan, p. 195; Oscar Lewis, *The Children of Sanchez* (New York, 1961).
40. Bayley, p. 724.
41. Myron Weiner, *The Politics of Scarcity* (Chicago: University of Chicago Press, 1962), p. 236.
42. Cf. William Riordan, *Plunkitt of Tammany Hall* (New York, 1948), p. 4.

56

The Political Consequences of Corruption: A Reassessment

Michael Johnston

An Inconclusive Debate

Disagreement continues over the political consequences of corruption. . . . While the debate has produced many useful studies of particular cases, its overall findings have been contradictory. In one sense, the debate has been curiously asymmetrical, with moralists arguing that corruption is harmful[1] while revisionists reply that it *can* be beneficial.[2] Moralistic analyses also suffer, at times, from an a priori assumption that corruption is a bad thing (or that "legitimate" policies are inherently preferable to those produced corruptly) and tend to blame corruption for a disproportionate share of a society's problems. Revisionists, for their part, often rely too much upon anecdotal evidence, hypothetical cases, and speculative linkages between corruption and social outcomes.

This chapter is an attempt to refocus the debate by calling attention to two recurring problems. First, I will argue that we have tended to focus upon overly broad (and at times unanswerable) questions. Before we can attribute general systemic trends and problems to corruption, we need to understand its more specific political effects. Second, I will suggest that we can reconcile seemingly contradictory findings if we recognize that corruption can come in many forms wtih differing consequences. Most forms of corruption, I will argue, can be studied as processes of exchange whose internal logic differs from one form to another. This approach will be used to define four common types of

Source: Michael Johnston, "The Political Consequences of Corruption: A Reassessment," *Comparative Politics,* 18, 4 (July 1986), 459–77. © The City University of New York. By permission of the publisher.

corruption and to point out the political consequences of each. These will be "micro" consequences, specifically the extent to which each tends to solidify or weaken linkages among people and groups at various strata of political systems.

This analysis is not intended to produce global generalizations about the implications of corruption for such systematic processes as economic or political development. Rather, it will propose categories which will allow us to employ the concept of corruption more precisely in our study of political systems and which will facilitate comparisons across systems and over time. A full test of these ideas is beyond the scope of this analysis, but I will discuss cases which illustrate some of the major characteristics and consequences of each of the categories and identify important questions for further research.

Definitions

Definitions of corruption have been a matter of considerable debate in their own right.[3] A definition incorporating all of the perceptual and normative subtleties is probably unattainable; perhaps for this reason, scholars have tended recently to avoid "over-defining" the phenomenon.[4] At its most basic level, corruption is the abuse of public roles and resources for private benefit. "Abuse," in this sense, can be initiated by people who hold public positions or by those who seek to influence them. But by what standards can we identify "abuse"? Public norms and opinions represent one possibility; the "public interest" is another. But both are seriously deficient.[5] The former rests on standards which are shifting, vague, and often contradictory, while the latter posits a standard which, in most issues and settings, does not exist.

A more stable and precise standard is the law or formal regulations. Laws change, but, unless we seek a single ultimate standard, this is an advantage, not a problem: contrasts or changes in laws allow us to compare the political processes and value conflicts involved in setting rules of behavior. Hence, the definition I will employ is based upon formal-legal norms and was formulated by J.S. Nye. Corruption is "behavior which deviates from the formal duties of a public role (elective or appointive) because of private-regarding (personal, close family, private clique) wealth or status gains: or (which) violates rules against the exercise of certain types of private-regarding influence."[6]

Problems of Analysis

Analysts of corruption, whatever their outlook, encounter a number of problems. The most difficult is a pervasive lack of data, for those who know of corrupt transactions often have an interest in maintaining secrecy. There are also problems of comparability, across systems and over time. Moreover, by its very nature as wrongdoing, corruption arouses strong emotions, simultaneously posing normative and positive questions which are difficult to disentangle. The term "corruption" itself compounds the latter problem: Moodie contends that confusion over the nature of corruption persists in part "because writers have been loathe to sacrifice the element of moral disapproval inseparable from the word itself."[7]

Two problems, however, have been particularly significant. First, we have not carefully defined our basic questions about the political consequences of corruption. Indeed, some of the most frequently posed questions cannot be answered at all, while others lead to circular arguments *post hoc.* Second, we have often tried to generalize about corruption as though it were a single unified phenomenon. Many proposed distinctions among types of corruption (high-level versus low-level, or bureaucratic versus other, often unspecified kinds) refer more to the location of corrupt processes than to their internal dynamics. I will suggest that categories defined by the internal logic of processes of exchange can enable us not only to distinguish among forms of corruption, but also to spell out some of their differing political consequences.

Asking Appropriate Questions

To identify the consequences of corruption, we must first decide what kinds of effects we are looking for and where we might expect to find them. Too often, we have posed questions which are overly broad or even unanswerable.

Summary Judgments. It makes little sense to ask whether corruption is inherently good or bad. For some, the fact that it is a departure from established rules is sufficient to make it harmful by definition. But this is precisely the reason why we cannot reach an absolute verdict, for judgment requires comparison with the rules or procedures being broken. As Leys asks, "What is the alternative?"[8] And in making these comparisons, we must judge official procedures by their actual content and consequences, not by stated goals or by the formal missions of the institutions involved. Unless we are willing to grant automatic approval to all policies and activities of the powers that be, we must acknowledge that corruption could at times create de facto policies less objectionable than their "legitimate" alternatives. "Normative statements about corruption," writes Rose-Ackerman, "require a point of view, a standard of 'goodness,' and a model of how corruption works in particular instances. . . . One does not condemn a Jew for bribing his way out of a concentration camp."⁹

Corruption and Development. A more focused question frequently posed is that of effects upon a system's development. This concern is a natural outgrowth of the fact that corruption is an overt part of political life in many developing nations (although openness is not in itself proof that corruption is necessarily more common or politically significant).¹⁰ Also, to the extent that development involves making the most of scarce resources, corruption again becomes a matter of concern as one influence upon the distribution and use of such resources.

But however tempting it is to explain trends in development in terms of corruption, here too there are problems. We have yet to sort out basic causal relationships: is corruption an influence upon development¹¹ or a *product* of development?¹² And what do we mean by "development"? Nye reminds us that development is not one problem, but many.¹³ Related to this is the need for "mediated" explanation, in which causal linkages are traced through the behavior of people and groups whose political roles are well-understood.¹⁴ Without such linkages, we may be limited to circular arguments¹⁵ "explaining" development by fitting evidence of corruption to past trends. This approach will very likely overstate the importance of corruption. Moreover, Ben-Dor argues that studies of developing nations do not add up to a theory, or even to a comprehensive set of observations; corruption and development may interact in very different ways in more advanced settings.¹⁶ Relationships between corruption and development are clearly worth careful study, but our understanding of them will depend upon what we learn by looking at many more limited political processes.

The Functionality Issue. Finally, there is the frequently posed question of whether or not corruption is functional, aiding in the survival or successful adaptation of a regime, economy, or political system. This approach does at least invite comparisons between corruption and its realistic alternatives, but we may be posing questions which cannot be answered.

First, we must be clear on the meaning of "functional." The concept is well-defined in theory,¹⁷ but its applications at times seem to imply that "functional" really means "beneficial." Such a proposition begs the same questions as assertions that corruption is inherently bad or good: again we must ask, "compared to what?" In any event, whole systems will rarely stand or fall because of corruption alone. We can apply functional concepts to more specific elements, such as a system's regime, aspects of its economy, or a particular accommodation among ethnic factions. But answers to functionality questions will then depend upon the particular aspects we choose for analysis: in Morocco, for example, Waterbury suggests that corruption in land reform policy was functional for the survival of the regime, but dysfunctional for economic growth.[18] This in turn raises the question of short- versus long-term effects. In the Moroccan case, will enhanced regime stability eventually aid economic growth? Or will the marginal reduction in growth attributable to corruption come to theaten the regime? And—perhaps most difficult—is there an answer beyond "wait and see"?

Even where corruption helps a regime or other structure to persist, it does not leave that structure unchanged. Because corruption is an alternative to other processes of influence and allocation, its significant presence means that the system is different, to some degree, from what would otherwise have been observed. As Waterbury contends,

> It is illusory to think that we can actually measure the costs and benefits of corruption. . . . Either one is dealing with a country in which some level of corruption is apparent or with a country in which, at least for the sake of argument, no corruption is apparent. On the one hand, a discussion of the benefits of corruption would oblige the observer to make a purely hypothetical guess as to how the system would function without corruption, and on the other, how a noncorrupt system would function with corruption. One can convincingly and legitimately analyze only what actually is going on and what the costs and benefits seem to be. It is very difficult to suggest what the costs and benefits of some hypothetical process might be.[19]

Perhaps we can, at times, make intelligent estimates of possible political alternatives. Still, the basic point remains: we cannot really say whether or not corruption helps a system to survive. At best, we can discuss its role as a process operating within that system *as altered by corruption.*

Multiple Forms of Corruption

Most systems will experience several sorts of corruption at any given time. Even if most of that corruption is politically inconsequential—as will often be the case—the important cases will very likely have differing implications for politics.

I have commented elsewhere at some length about a number of factors which affect the types and amounts of corruption to be found within political systems.[20] These include social attachments and customs, such as political culture, popular attachment (or lack of it) to government, and social customs (such as kinship) which pose norms and obligations contrary to official rules; attributes of the policy process, including its speed, patterns of access and exclusion, and anticorruption laws and their enforcement; and economic characteristics, such as level of development and relative size of the public sector. These have a bearing upon the kinds of behavior which will be legally and socially defined as corrupt, upon the frequency and pervasiveness of corruption, and upon popular and official responses (or nonresponses) to that corruption which comes to light. The importance of these characteristics means that a full discussion of the implications of corruption in any given system must be constructed in the context of system-specific factors. The existence of ethnic factions among elites, the extent to which kinship norms mean that citizens and/or officials take a different view of patronage practices than does the law, or the exclusion of certain economic interests from decisionmaking processes, for example, can all be critical parts of the corruption story in specific settings.

As a consequence, our comparisons of the political consequences of corruption must begin at a general level. But we can still draw significant distinctions among varieties of corruption, and explore their distinctive political consequences, if we define our types of corruption in terms of their characteristics as processses of exchange.[21] In most instances of corruption, things change hands. Money, jobs, contracts, licenses, building materials, favorable decisions: the list is as long and varied as the range of activities of government itself. Exchanges, in turn, imply some sort of relationship between people or groups, and these relationships can vary markedly from one form of exchange to another. Some corrupt exchanges may take place on more or less equal terms, while others amount to extortion. "Partners in the relationship may be linked continuously or sporadically," as Dowse has pointed out.[22] Other kinds of corrupt exchange may be marked by the kinds of people and groups they exclude. Thus, if we understand the internal logic of various forms of corrupt exchange, we can begin to compare their political consequences by exploring the kinds of relationships among people and groups which each will tend to create.

One way to compare varieties of corrupt exchange—which will be the focus of much of the rest of this analysis—is to distinguish between integrative and disintegrative corruption. Integrative corruption links people and groups into lasting networks of exchange and shared interest. Disintegrative corruption does not; indeed, it may well produce divisions and conflict, both among those involved in a corrupt enterprise and between those who are included and those left out. A related, but not identical, concern is the internal stability or instability of a form of corrupt exchange. Some varieties of integrative corruption will be less stable and lasting than others, while some types of disintegrative corruption may be relatively stable internally, even though they may strongly alienate those who are left out of the spoils.

Integration and disintegration, stability and instability are posited here as characteristics of forms of corruption, not of the systems within which they occur. Integrative, stable corruption will not necessarily bring about a stable system if its effects are outweighed by other factors, nor will disintegrative corruption necessarily produce an unstable system. Moreover, "integrative" and "stable" do not necessarily mean "beneficial" or "just"; an integrative form of corruption could solidify the power of an authoritarian regime, while disintegrative corruption could help make way for welcome political changes. Nor, finally, do these categories merely bring back functionality by another name. As we shall see, integrative and disintegrative forms of corruption can be identified by their characteristics as processes of exchange, not by their results. We need not know, or await, macro outcomes in order to categorize a form of corruption. Instead, these categories direct our attention to characteristic forms of interaction among people and groups within systems. If we do wish to consider wider trends and events, we can incorporate our understanding of these specific consequences of corruption into our more general knowledge of the system.

Varieties of Corrupt Exchange

In attempting to distinguish integrative from disintegrative forms of corrupt exchange, we have many possible bases of comparison. One is price: do the corrupt prices of contracts or jobs, for example, remain fairly constant, or do they fluctuate wildly? Another aspect is repetition: black market purchases in the *gastronoms* of Moscow are a routine and repeated event for both buyer and seller,[23] while persons seeking kickbacks from major defense contracts might have to wait for years. Price and repetition interact: those engaging in repeated transactions may settle for moderate prices and profits on each transaction, while persons trading in the extraordinary may push prices as high as possible since similar opportunities may be unlikely to recur any time soon. An exchange may be relatively equal (a bribe in exchange for a permit) or unequal and coercive (the Nixon campaign's threats of regulatory harassment against corporations unless they contributed to the reelection effort).[24] Some exchanges might be open to most who wish to participate (black market dealings, again), or closed to all but a privileged few. In the latter connection, corruption can often become a process of exclusion whereby one denies resources, influence, or opportunities to one's rivals. Finally, the stakes of exchange may be tangible or intangible, durable or nondurable. The point is that an exchange perspective allows us to classify forms of corruption (and legitimate dealings, if we wish) by their internal dynamics, rather than by the places they occur or by their popular labels.[25]

Two factors, however, best set integrative forms of corruption apart from disintegrative forms: the number of suppliers dispensing corrupt benefits (many versus few or one), and the degree to which the stakes of exchange are routine or extraordinary. "Routine" stakes are of modest scale and, while often in short supply, are at least available on a continuing basis, such as the small favors dispensed by political machines (although they are obviously not *completely* routine, or else no one could use them to extract significant illegitimate returns). "Extraordinary" stakes are unusually valuable and/or scarce: windfall profits on foreign exchange markets, perhaps, or very large construction contracts are examples of extraordinary stakes. I leave undefined for now the precise distinctions between few and many suppliers and between routine and extraordinary stakes; these may vary from system to system and will in any event involve subjective estimates on the part of participants.

These two factors relate to several other dimensions of exchange. Routine stakes imply repeated exchanges and will likely command relatively consistent prices. A large number of suppliers should, in most instances, moderate prices as well and also mark the presence of repeated exchanges. Where suppliers are few, by contrast, transactions can be tightly controlled, and corruption aimed at exclusion will be more common. Exchanges involving routine stakes should encourage frequent contacts and linkages between suppliers and clients; this integrative effect can become pervasive if routine stakes are available from many suppliers. When stakes are extraordinary or suppliers few, on the other hand, such linkages would be less likely to develop. Indeed, these sorts of exchanges may lead to alienation or conflict between suppliers and clients, or between those included in the exchanges and those left out. While numbers of suppliers and types of stakes do not directly address the demand side of corrupt exchanges, I assume a level of demand which substantially exceeds the supply of stakes available through legitimate channels; this after all is a major reason why corruption occurs in the first place.[26] The degree to which demand exceeds supplies available through *illegitimate* channels is reflected, at least crudely, in the distinction between routine and extraordinary stakes.

Together, these two variables—number of suppliers and routine versus extraordinary stakes—point to four common types of corruption which vary significantly in their integrative or disintegrative effects. These types, and some representative examples, are shown in Table 56.1.

Some comments are in order here as to just what Table 56.1 does and does not represent. The cell entries are examples of corruption within systems, not whole systems themselves; thus, the terms "stable," "disintegrative," and the like refer to the patterns of corrupt activity, not to the politics of entire nations. Second, since most systems experience more than one form of corruption at a time, nations may appear in more than one cell, as in the case of Mexico. Third, corruption is not proposed here as necessarily explaining macro outcomes in these systems, such as the fall of the Shah in Iran (cell 3),

Table 56.1

VARIETIES OF CORRUPTION AS DEFINED BY TYPES OF STAKES AND NUMBER OF SUPPLIERS

		STAKES	
		Routine	**Extraordinary**
	Many	1. Market Corruption (Black markets, *pripiska* in USSR) Integrative Very stable	4. Crisis Corruption (Bolivia; Mexico during oil boom; "rapacious individualism" in 19th-century New York) Disintegrative Very unstable
SUPPLIERS	*Few*	2. Patronage organizations, patron-client networks (urban machines; PRI in Mexico) Integrative Stable	3. Cronyism, Nepotism (Sukarno's Indonesia; Iran mid 70s) Internally integrative Externally disintegrative Somewhat unstable

even though the role of corruption in such events is worth study. Fourth, while the examples included in Table 56.1 all involve corruption as defined under the formal rules of the nations in question, I am not labeling *all* patronage, informal markets, or dealings among cronies as necessarily corrupt. That judgment, as Nye's definition implies, will depend upon the laws in a given setting. Finally, Table 56.1 is not proposed as a final answer to the consequences-of-corruption debate. Some forms of corruption, such as those not taking the form of exchanges, may not fit these categories at all. Instead, the idea is to show how a focus on varieties of corrupt exchange can help us to understand the various political consequences of corruption.

Market Corruption

Market corruption is perhaps best exemplified by the black markets, *na levo* transactions, and false reporting practices (*pripiska*) which are so much a part of life and commerce in much of the USSR.[27] These transactions range from a clerk's demanding extra payments or favors in exchange for choice consumer goods, to the widespread illegal bartering and reporting of false data among business enterprises struggling to meet their planned quotas. Katsenelinboigen has described a number of "coloured markets" in the USSR which vary in their legal and political status and in their modes of exchange.[28]

In other settings, many of these activities would not be corruption as Nye has defined it, for they would not involved public roles or resources. But in the USSR the reach of laws and of the planning apparatus is so extensive that many otherwise private roles and transactions are defined as public.

> The very broad scope of criminal regulation reflects the primacy of state property in Soviet law and the "total" character of political management over organizational life.
>
> Anybody with authority in any recognized organization in the Soviet Union is a "servant of the state," even if the organization (say a trade union) is not officially regarded as a state organization. Any holder of office is responsible to the political authority and his or her obligations to the state are defined by criminal law as well as administrative rules. The list of possible abuses is, then, a long one.[29]

Thus, the black market dealings of a functionary in a Moscow *gastronom* and the *pripiska* maneuverings of a factory clerk are just as surely corruption as the misappropriation of construction supplies by a government official. In fact, all three would likely be prosecuted under the same section of Soviet law ("crimes against socialist property"). Market corruption, of course, is not limited to Soviet-style systems; agencies elsewhere in which a number of functionaries demand small payments in exchange for routine services, such as the issuance of business permits or ration documents, fit the market corruption model as well.

Market corruption draws buyers and sellers into networks of mutual self-interest which can become quite large and pervasive. Simis contends, for example, that because of the rigidity of planned quotas *pripiska* practices are "necessary and useful not only to the party doing the cheating but also to the party that is being cheated."[30] The more routine the stakes and repetitive the transactions—purchases of basic raw materials by a factory, for example—the stronger this integrative effect is likely to be. Market corruption is relatively stable internally as well: competition among suppliers and the probability that transactions will be repeated should produce relatively constant prices and terms of exchange. There will be little incentive to "gouge" regular clients on any one exchange.

Given its stability and integrative nature, it is not surprising that in the Soviet case, for example, authorities often "wink" at market corruption.[31] It can help planners and producers alike to finesse—or at least conceal—production bottlenecks and is far less disruptive than facing up to actual economic problems and mounting serious reforms. Official toleration of market corruption in turn allows its integrative effects to extend well beyond the ranks of immediate participants themselves.

These integrative effects do have their limits: market corruption, like any other market, can be disrupted by external developments, especially to the extent that they make routine stakes scarce (and thus extraordinary, at least temporarily) or significantly reduce the number of suppliers. Moreover, the problems of imperfect information which occur in any market can be all the more serious here, for the illegitimate nature of market corruption means that participants often must communicate by word of mouth rather than more overtly. Even where discreet market corruption is tolerated, authorities may be forced to intervene once it crosses some threshold of visibility. Finally, there are questions of consumers' perceptions. I do not assume that consumers *like* market corruption (they very likely will not), but rather that they perceive it as the most workable way of obtaining things they want or need. This perception may be gradually undermined by rising prices, for example, or dashed more abruptly if consumers come to believe that underlying scarcities are artificially contrived or that more desirable alternative processes are really possible. When either of these things happens, market corruption networks can be severely disrupted.

Still, market corruption is a stable and integrative pattern of corrupt exchange, so much that regimes attempting to eradicate it often encounter great difficulty. Even when corrupt markets have been disrupted, there typically remain significant imbalances of supply and demand which must be addressed by one mechanism or another. These may range from the creation of legitimate alternative markets to stepped-up coercion, but the result may well be the reemergence of market corruption.

Patronage Networks and Machines

When routine stakes of corrupt exchange are held in fewer hands, they can be used to build and maintain extended patron-client networks. These centralized networks of benefit and obligation can be found in many forms. In traditional patron-client systems relationships tend to be "multiplex"[32] and diffuse, involving several overlapping and reinforcing kinds of ties (such as kinship, region, and political party). In other instances, such as urban political machines, relationships may be more specific and obligations more limited: loyal voting may be enough payment for political "help" in a scrape with the police. Corrupt transactions, as defined by Nye, make up only a part of the overall pattern of patron-client exchange, particularly in cases of traditional, "multiplex" systems.

Patronage organizations can be integrative and stable, as the very term "machine" implies.[33] Centralized control over things people need and the organization of action and supervision along clear-cut hierarchical lines can draw large numbers of people into extended networks of personal and political obligation. These in turn can be employed for disciplined political action, such as winning elections, or for more generalized forms of cooptation. An example of the latter sort was Morocco's "planned corruption," as analyzed by Waterbury: there, the corrupt distribution of small plots of land by land reform agencies became a form of patronage "manipulated, guided, planned and desired by the regime itself."[34]

But these networks are somewhat less stable than systems of market corruption, particularly to the extent that the stakes of exchange are specific rather than multiplex and diffuse. Analysis of the internal economies of political machines, for example, reveals contradictions and sources of instability.[35] One may distribute short-lived rewards (such as food or small gifts of cash) pretty much as one likes, but once "durable" rewards such as jobs have been distributed it can be very difficult to change allocations without a fight. As a result, key subleaders and factions may command a disproportionate share of the spoils long after their political performance has entered a decline. Networks of obligation and exchange can thus become rigid and overly complex, as multiple standards of reciprocity emerge between leaders and various factions; the organization may adapt poorly to changing circumstances or fall victim to factional disputes. In a sense, a patronage organization can "age" in ways which more internally fluid systems of market corruption do not.

Patronage organizations will also be less integrative than market corruption. While patronage networks can become quite large, they still link fewer people together than do entrenched cases of market corruption: even the largest pool of rewards will stretch only so far. Moreover, while market corruption typically revolves around frequently repeated transactions serving the short-term interests of both buyer and seller, some kinds of patronage (jobs, for example, or important contracts) change hands less often. Opportunities to call in the debts may be infrequent as well, with return "payments" proving difficult to extract over time.[36] Perhaps for this reason, a political proverb has it that a patron who has one available job and ten followers will end up with "nine enemies and one ingrate."

Finally, to be most effective at integration, those who control the stakes must enjoy as close to a monopoly as possible. If one's clients have somewhere else to turn, one must offer them more and expect less in return; the resulting organization will be the smaller and more unreliable as a result. Shefter has described a phase in the emergence of machine politics in New York City during which an oligopoly of patronage groupings, each with its pool of public spoils, competed for power.[37] Compared to the "rapacious individualism" of the era immediately preceding, these organizations were relatively integrative and stable. But for most of the 1870s and 1880s, none was able to dominate the city; thus, patrons could not monopolize rewards, or impose effective discipline. It was not until Tammany Hall defeated its rivals that New York experienced machine politics at its most disciplined and integrative. The most advantageous monopoly, almost by definition, is control of a government. But even then integration has its limits, for beyond a certain point further inclusiveness dilutes the already limited pool of spoils while yielding few new advantages; moreover, the very presence and power of a monopoly machine can give the excluded an issue around which to organize.

Cronyism and Nepotism

The essence of cronyism and nepotism is the control of extraordinary stakes of exchange by one or a few persons, "Extraordinary" refers to the scale or scarcity of the stakes of exchange; it does not imply that cronyism or nepotism themselves are necessarily extraordinary occurrences. Extraordinary stakes might include lucrative business concessions, appointments to key positions, unusually generous buyouts of private businesses by a nationalizing authority, or access to large supplies of hard currency, to name but a few examples. Control over such valuable stakes creates both opportunities and incentives to distribute them in a corrupt manner. But one would hardly distribute them directly to a mass following, for not only are they too few in number, they are also much too valuable. Better to distribute them among a small group of elites or family members, who could be expected to do more in return, and who in any case would not be satisfied with petty favors.

Cronyism and nepotism are thus small group affairs, at least as compared to market corruption and patronage organizations, and the complex and ambivalent consequences noted in Table 56.1 derive from this fact. Cronyism and nepotism are to a limited degree internally integrative, drawing participants into relationships of obligation and reward and fostering collective interests in maintaining secrecy and in excluding outsiders. Internal integration is weakened, however, by the fact that cronyism and nepotism are somewhat unstable. Extraordinary stakes do not lend themselves to repeated exchange; thus, the constant intersections of self-interest and reminders of obligation characterizing market corruption and patronage are not as strongly present. In cases of nepotism, these internal weaknesses can be minimized somewhat by the binding force of kinship; but even then there may be relatively infrequent exchanges which will differ markedly from one instance to the next or may even be unique. Thus, terms of exchange may have to be worked out from the beginning in each case, instead of being fixed by routine expectations. Partners in market corruption transactions and clients receiving a patron's routine favors know fairly well what is expected of them and know that terms will not differ markedly from one time to the next. By contrast, an elite who has an import concession, a key appointment, and a construction contract to hand out among cronies or relatives has few obvious rules of reciprocity to go by. The various potential recipients will likely possess different kinds of political currency (money, expertise, or a mass following), and a transaction which cannot soon be repeated contains built-in incentives to maximize returns, without much regard for evenhandedness. At the very least, such a situation encourages rivalries among potential recipients; indeed, it may well lead to factional conflict, to limited and grudging commitments from the winners and resentments among the losers. . . .

Cronyism and nepotism may be somewhat integrative for those directly involved, but for the wider political system they will likely be disintegrative. Unless the political stratum is exceedingly small, many more politically active people will be excluded from the benefits than are included. Exclusion can in turn hand opposing groups significant issues and grievances, made all the more powerful by the important nature of the stakes. . . .

Crisis Corruption

Finally, we are left with crisis corruption: many suppliers trading in extraordinary stakes. On its face, this would seem an impossibility: if the stakes are truly extraordinary, how can there be many suppliers? The answer is linked to the very unstable nature of this form of corruption. In a system undergoing a crisis of institutionalization,[39] for example, private parties may have so thoroughly penetrated the public realm that most public goods and decisions are up for sale. In such a case, extraordinary stakes of many sorts might be constantly coming into the market. Alternatively, a system might experience an extraordinary influx of illicit resources from without, under the control of many entrepreneurs (say, money from numerous drug dealers). The term "crisis" is perhaps overly vivid, but it does convey an important double meaning. First, it reflects the scale and significance of this form of corruption; and second, it suggests that, because of its instability and disintegrative effects, crisis corruption will be a temporary phase. It could revert to another of our forms of corruption, or the unusual conditions which permit its emergence might pass from the scene. Or, though by no means inevitably, crisis corruption could contribute to sweeping political change. Whatever the scenario, crisis corruption is unlikely to become a permanent condition.

Crisis corruption can emerge in the form of new networks of influence and exchange or may transform the old, at least temporarily. An example of the first sort was the case of cocaine-related corruption in Bolivia. There, Alexander reports, "[w]ith the seizure of power in 1980 by General Luis Garcia Meza, the country's drug smugglers took over the government."[40] The stakes of the cocaine trade—over $2 billion in 1981—were truly extraordinary for a poor nation. Within a year of the Meza coup, at least three major drug-smuggling rings had emerged.

> Drug smuggling mushroomed into an activity that overshadowed all other aspects of the economy. . . . The predominance of the drug smugglers has also greatly aggravated a problem that Bolivia has always had—that of corruption. Since the drug trade was practiced by the highest officials of the Bolivian government, the effect was to make corruption in the government service all but universal.[41]

Disintegrative consequences were visible, in the short term, in the form of disrupted government functions and the general scramble of the elite for drug-related wealth. Long-term effects may still be unfolding: Alexander speculated in 1981 that the regime might become vulnerable to the reactions of those appalled by the "international disgrace" of Bolivia's corruption.[42] This is just what occurred; in 1982, Meza's regime was ousted in favor of a civilian government. The new government, however, has been weak and internally divided and has had little success in dealing with the chaos left behind from the Meza years. The disintegrative effects of drug-related crisis corruption in Bolivia were quite persuasive.

Mexico presents a case in which, by contrast, an influx of extraordinary resources—in this case, rapidly growing oil revenues—transformed existing alignments. Key figures in PEMEX (the state oil corporation), the Oil Workers' Union, and the dominant political party (PRI) had long enjoyed a number of politically significant and mutually profitable corrupt arrangements. But when oil revenues began to grow rapidly in 1977, this corruption became particularly flagrant and disruptive.[43] Old "arrangements" in the oil industry gave way to intense competition over shares of the new wealth. The new abuses became matters of considerable controversy, and PEMEX, PRI, and union figures came under political attack from several quarters.[44] For a number of reasons—not the least of which was the strength of PRI's "extended political family"—this episode did not upset the entire system. But by 1982, when the oil boom had run its course, "it was evident that the nation had been 'sacked' by more than one set of actors. . . . According to the government's own admission the oil boom had whetted unsavory appetites in the nation and had spawned a substantial increase in the level of corruption throughout the nation."[45]

Growth of oil revenues had thus placed extraordinary resources in many hands, transforming formerly integrative forms of corruption into disintegrative crisis corruption. When Presient Miguel de la Madrid took office in 1982, "a system that had never worked smoothly without corruption was no longer working smoothly because of excessive corruption."[46]

Crisis corruption is internally unstable: the proliferation of suppliers will not produce stable prices through competition if suppliers deal in different commodities, and in any event the extraordinary nature of the stakes encourages the extraction of maximum immediate returns. Crisis corruption is politically disintegrative as well, and not merely because of the macro trends which can make it possible. Corrupt exchanges will not draw people and groups together into networks of mutual interest and obligation. Instead, at the elite level the pattern may be one of disconnected cases of extortion, in which transactions are made because access to extraordinary stakes on exploitative terms is better than no access at all. Nonelites will likely be excluded altogether for lack of sufficient resources; for them, crisis corruption may well be experienced in terms of disrupted markets and political disorder.

But crisis corruption is not inevitably a final stage of political disintegration. A leveling off in the influx of resources might make the stakes of corruption more predictable, and thus less extraordinary, with improved chances of repeated profits over longer periods of time serving to moderate prices and to regulate terms of exchange. Mexico's oil industry had gone through earlier phases of rapid growth and flagrant corruption, reverting to more accustomed forms of corruption during periods of more stable revenues.[47] . . .

Conclusion

The debate over the consequences of corruption thus has not one answer, but many. I have discussed four types of corruption, as defined by their internal logic as processes of exchange, and have characterized them in terms of their politically integrative and disintegrative effects. Some kinds of corruption will be difficult to categorize, and other dimensions of the exchange process, such as the consumption of the stakes of exchange,[48] may merit examination as well. But this analysis does offer a way to identify important similarities and contrasts among the diverse settings, practices, and vocabularies encountered in the study of corruption.

The effects of corruption, however, do not necessarily extend throughout a political system. Indeed, in an earlier section I warned against using the concept to explain too much. The impact of corruption upon systemic trends and events is mediated by long chains of linkages and contingencies and must in any event be balanced off against other casual factors. Quick generalizations will thus prove both difficult and risky to make.

Political reactions to corruption will also figure into the story. Often, reactions to corruption are more important than the actual wrongdoing itself, and these reactions are a complex matter in their own right. If we presume that those with a stake in corrupt exchanges are less likely to react against them than are the excluded, then analysis of the integrative or disintegrative consequences of particular forms of corruption can help us to understand political responses. Exclusion from corruption by no means guarantees a negative response, however, or indeed any response at all. The excluded may be unaware of corruption or may not believe the allegations they hear; if they do perceive the existence of corruption, their reactions may include apathy, tolerance, amusement, suprise, and/or anger, or attempts to get into the game themselves. These reactions will hinge upon the type and extent of corruption involved, people's perceptions of their own gains or losses from it, and their beliefs about the nature of right and wrong, to name but a few factors. Clearly, the presence and activities of counterelites in publicizing, explaining, and interpreting news and allegations of corruption will be most important in influencing political responses.

In a sense, though, each form of corruption creates a particular pattern of shared interests and cleavages in the society around it. Thus, we might begin to link corruption to more general trends and events by considering factors which might make these effects more or less pervasive. Clearly, the more corruption a society experiences, the more important its political effects are likely to be. But I am concerned here with a somewhat different issue: given a certain level of corruption, how pervasive will its integrative or disintegrative effects become?

Two propositions relating to this question have to do with the general setting of corruption. First, the larger the stakes involved in a given form of corrupt exchange relative to the overall size of the economy, and second, the fewer (or less attractive) the alternative opportunities to win political or economic advantage, the more pervasive the integrative or disintegrative consequences of corruption will be. For integrative forms of corruption, high stakes or the existence of few alternatives will increase the incentive for outsiders to attempt to join in the spoils. In cases of disintegrative corruption, these circumstances affect included and excluded parties in different ways. For the included, high stakes and few alternatives are likely to increase the costs and risks of corrupt transactions, while reducing their predictability and the degree of bargaining power one is likely to possess. For the excluded, these circumstances increase the political and economic costs of exclusion, which in turn is likely to increase the intensity of their reactions to corruption.

For integrative forms of corruption, inclusiveness or ease of joining is important. A Soviet consumer can enter into some kinds of market corruption simply by cultivating trust and friendships at a neighborhood market. A political machine, by contrast, is more difficult to join. Not only is its pool of resources more limited, but because the stakes are tightly controlled one may have to endure a lengthy probation period before being cut into the spoils. Thus, I would suggest that the easier it is for outsiders to enter into an integrative form of corruption, the more pervasive its effects will be.

Exclusion, rather than inclusion, is more likely to be an important factor in cases of disintegrative corruption. Most people are likely to be closed out of cronyism or nepotism and will not possess the table stakes needed to buy into the crisis corruption game. Therefore, it is important to compare the lines of exclusion to existing divisions in society. The more the boundaries of a disintegrative form of corruption correspond with existing class, racial, ethnic, and factional cleavages in society, the more pervasive its political effects will be. Where this correspondence is close, corruption is likely to become yet another issue in intergroup conflict, perhaps serving as the "justification" for reprisals or coups.

Although these comments are of necessity general, they may at least serve to illustrate the complexities inherent in linking corruption to systemic political trends and events. Applying these ideas to particular cases will require a knowledge of the systems involved and of the extent to which the linkages and divisions fostered by corruption correspond with the more basic fault lines of society. But this is no more than to observe that the more general consequences of particular forms of corruption, like those of any other kind of political behavior, will depend in part upon the setting in which it occurs.

Notes

An earlier version of this analysis was presented to the International Political Science Association Research Roundtable on Political Finance and Political Corruption, Pembroke College, Oxford, England, March 1984. I am greatly indebted to Douglas Ashford, R.C. Crook, Arnold J. Heidenheimer,

Christopher Hood, Joseph LaPalombara, Graeme Moodie, Daniel Regan, Bert Rockman, Dorothy Solinger, Stephen White, and two anonymous reviewers for their most helpful comments and suggestions.

1. See, for example, Stanislav Andreski, "Kleptocracy: or, Corruption as a System of Government," in Stanislav Andreski, ed., *The African Predicament: A Study in the Pathology of Modernization* (London: Michael Joseph, 1968), pp. 92–109; George C.S. Benson, Steven A. Maaranen, and Alan Heslop, *Political Corruption in America* (Lexington: D.C. Heath, 1978); Gunnar Myrdal, "Corruption: Its Causes and Effects," in Gunnar Myrdal, *Asian Drama: An Enquiry into the Poverty of Nations*, vol. 2 (New York: Twentieth Century, 1968), pp. 937–58; Ronald Wraith and Edgar Simpkins, *Corruption in Developing Nations* (London: Allen and Unwin, 1963).

2. See, for example, Jose V. Abueva, "The Contribution of Nepotism, Spoils and Graft to Political Development," *East-West Center Review*, 3 (1966), 45–54; David H. Bayley, "The Effects of Corruption in a Developing Nation," *Western Political Quarterly*, 19 (December 1966). 719–32; Nathaniel H. Leff, "Economic Development through Bureaucratic Corruption," *American Behavioral Scientist*, 8 (November 1964), 8–14; Colin Leys, "What Is the Problem about Corruption?," *Journal of Modern African Studies*, 3 (August 1965), 215–30.

3. Arnold J. Heidenheimer, "The Context of Analysis," in Arnold J. Heidenheimer, ed., *Political Corruption: Readings in Comparative Analysis* (New Brunswick: Transaction Books, 1978), pp. 3–28.

4. Anne Deysine, "Political Corruption: A Review of the Literature," *European Journal of Political Research*, 8 (December 1980), 447–62.

5. Michael Johnston, *Political Corruption and Public Policy in America* (Monterey: Brooks-Cole, 1982), chap. 1: Scott, pp. 3–9.

6. Nye, p. 416; the final clause of the definition is from Edward C. Banfield, *Political Influence* (New York: Free Press, 1961), p. 315.

7. Moodie, p. 214.

8. Leys, p. 220.

9. Susan Rose-Ackerman, *Corruption: A Study in Political Economy* (New York: Academic Press, 1978), p. 9.

10. John Waterbury, "Endemic and Planned Corruption in a Monarchical Regime," *World Politics*, 25 (July 1973), 534.

11. Abueva, pp. 45–54; Leff, pp. 8–14; Myrdal, pp. 937–58; Nye, pp. 417–27; Gabriel Ben-Dor, "Corruption, Institutionalization, and Political Development: The Revisionist Theses Revisited," *Comparative Political Studies*, 7 (April 1974), 63–83; John Waterbury, "Corruption, Political Stability and Development: Comparative Evidence from Egypt and Morocco," *Government and Opposition*, 11 (Autumn 1976), 426–45.

12. Huntington, pp. 59–71.

13. Nye, pp. 418–19.

14. David R. Cameron, "Toward a Theory of Political Mobilization," *Journal of Politics*, 36 (February 1974), 139–40.

15. Nye, p. 419.

16. Ben-Dor, p. 68.

17. Robert K. Merton, *Social Theory and Social Structure* (Glencoe: The Free Press, 1957).

18. Waterbury, "Endemic and Planned Corruption."
19. Ibid., p. 542.
20. Johnston, *Political Corruption,* chap. 2.
21. Robert Dowse, "Conceptualizing Corruption," review of Robert M. Price, *Society and Bureaucracy in Contemporary Ghana* (Berkeley: University of California Press, 1975), in *Government and Opposition,* 12 (Summer 1977), 244–54; Johnston, *Political Corruption,* chap. 1.
22. Dowse, p. 244.
23. Konstantin Simis, *USSR: The Corrupt Society* (New York: Simon and Schuster, 1982), chaps. 6, 8; John M. Kramer, "Political Corruption in the USSR," *Western Political Quarterly,* 30 (June 1977), 213–24; Hedrick Smith, *The Russians* (New York: Random House, 1976), chap. 3.
24. J. Anthony Lukas, *Nightmare: The Underside of the Nixon Years* (New York: Bantam, 1977), pp. 187–89.
25. Gerald Mars has used an analogous approach to define categories of workplace crime. See Gerald Mars, *Cheats at Work: An Anthropology of Workplace Crime* (London: George Allen and Unwin, 1982).
26. Johnston, *Political Corruption,* chap. 2; Robert O. Tilman, "Emergence of Black-Market Bureaucracy: Administration, Development, and Corruption in the New States," *Public Administration Review,* 28 (September–October 1968), 439–41.
27. Simis, chap. 6; Kramer, pp. 215–20; Smith, chap. 3.
28. A. Katsenelinboigen, "Coloured Markets in the Soviet Union," *Soviet Studies,* 29 (January 1977); see also Istvan Kemeny, "The Unregistered Economy in Hungary," *Soviet Studies,* 34 (July 1982).
29. Nick Lampert, "Law, Order and Power in the USSR," paper presented to the annual conference of the National Association for Soviet and East European Studies, Fitzwilliam College, Cambridge, England, March 1984, p. 3 (quoted by permission).
30. Simis, p. 128.
31. Kramer, p. 220.
32. Robert Springborg, "Sayed Bei Marei and Political Clientelism in Egypt," *Comparative Political Studies,* 12 (October 1979), 260–61.
33. See, for American machines, James Q. Wilson, "The Economy of Patronage," *Journal of Political Economy,* 69 (August 1961), 369–80; Milton L. Rakove, *Don't Make No Waves—Don't Back No Losers: An Insider's Analysis of the Daley Machine* (Bloomington: Indiana University Press, 1975). For machines in other settings, see Scott, *Comparative Political Corruption,* chaps. 7–9; Paul Martin Sacks, *The Donegal Mafia: An Irish Political Machine* (New Haven: Yale University Press, 1976); Judith Chubb, "The Social Bases of an Urban Political Machine: The Case of Palermo," *Political Science Quarterly,* 96 (April 1981), 107–25.
34. Waterbury, "Corruption, Political Stability, and Development," p. 534.
35. Michael Johnston, "Patrons and Clients, Jobs and Machines: A Case Study of the Uses of Patronage," *American Political Science Review,* 73 (June 1979), 385–98.
36. For an example, see Wolfinger's account of the problems the boss of the New Haven Democratic machine had in getting his political clients to perform routine political duties. Raymond E. Wolfinger, *The Politics of Progress* (Englewood Cliffs: Prentice-Hall, 1974), p. 81.

37. Martin Shefter, "The Emergence of the Political Machine: An Alternative View," in Willis D. Hawley et al., *Theoretical Perspectives on Urban Politics* (Englewood Cliffs: Prentice-Hall, 1976), pp. 25–33.
38. Scott, p. 84.
39. Huntington.
40. Robert J. Alexander, *Bolivia: Past, Present, and Future of its Politics* (New York: Praeger, 1982), p. 24.
41. Ibid., pp. 139–40.
42. Ibid., p. 140.
43. George W. Grayson, *The Politics of Mexican Oil* (Pittsburgh: University of Pittsburgh Press, 1980), pp. 93, 97.
44. Judith Gentleman, *Mexican Oil and Dependent Development* (New York: Peter Lang, 1984), p. 224; Alan Riding, *Distant Neighbors: A Portrait of the Mexicans* (New York: Alfred A. Knopf, 1985), pp. 168–79.
45. Gentleman, p. 223.
46. Riding, p. 133.
47. Grayson, p. 101.
48. I am indebted to Christopher Hood for his comments on this point.

Selected Bibliography

Compiled by Okun Attah

This bibliography includes publications on political corruption published in the major languages since 1970. It augments the bibliography and references that were published in *Political Corruption: Readings in Comparative Analysis* (1970, 1978). Titles included as selections in the present volume are not included; nor has an attempt been made to include all items listed in the reference notes of those chapters.

General

Clarke, Michael (ed.), 1983. *Corruption: Causes, Consequences, and Control*. New York: St. Martin's Press.

Deysine, Anne, 1980. "Political Corruption: A Review of the Literature," *European Journal of Political Research*, VII: 447–462.

Doig, Alan, 1983. "Watergate, Poulson and the Reform of Standards of Conduct," *Parliamentary Affairs*, XXXVI (3): 316–333.

Etzioni-Halevy, Eva, 1979. *Political Manipulation and Administrative Power*. Boston: Routledge and Kegan Paul.

Fleck, Christian and Helmut Kuzmics (ed.), 1985. *Korruption*. Königstein: Athenäum.

Henriques, Diana B., 1986. *The Machinery of Greed: Public Authority Abuse and What to do About It*. Lexington, MA: Lexington Books.

Jacoby, Neil H. Peter Nehekis, and Richard Eells, 1977. *Bribery and Extortion in the Business World: A Study of Corporate Payments Abroad*. New York: Macmillan.

Noonan, John T., Jr., 1984. *Bribes*. New York: Macmillan

Reisman, W. Michael, 1979. *Folded Lies: Bribery, Crusades, and Reforms*. New York: Free Press.

Rose-Ackerman, Susan, 1978. *Corruption: A Study in Political Economy*. New York: Academic Press.

Schuller, Wolfgang (ed.), 1982. *Korruption im Altertum*. Munich: Oldenbourg.

Schuller, Wolfgang, 1977. "Probleme Historischer Korruptionsforschung." In: *Der Staat*. Berlin: Dunker und Humblot, Jg. 16, pp. 373–392.

Scott, James C., 1972. *Comparative Political Corruption*. Englewood Cliffs, NJ: Prentice-Hall.

Werner, Simcha, 1983. "New Directions in the Study of Administrative Corruption," *Public Administration Review*, 43, 2: 146–54.

Theoretical

Banfield, E. C., 1975. "Corruption as a Feature of Governmental Organization," *Journal of Law and Economics*, XVIII (3): 587–605.

Beenstock, Michael, 1979. "Corruption and Development," *World Development*, VII (January): 15–24.

Ben-Dor, Gabriel, 1974. "Corruption, Institutionalization, and Political Development: The Revisionist Theses Revisited," *Comparative Political Studies*, 7: 63–68.

Benson, Bruce and John Baden, 1985. "The Political Economy of Governmental Corruption—The Logic of Underground Government," *Journal of Legal Studies*, 14 (2): 391–410.

Darby, Michael R. and Edi Karni, 1973. "Free Competition and the Optimal Amount of Fraud," *Journal of Law and Economics*, 16 (April) 67–88.

Dobel, J. Patrick, 1978. "The Corruption of a State," *American Political Science Review*, 72 (3): 958–78.

Nas, Tevfik, Albert C. Price, and Charles T. Weber, 1986. "A Policy-Oriented Theory of Corruption," *American Political Science Review*, 80, (1, March): 107–19.

Rakumar, R., 1976. "Political Corruption: A Review of the Literature," *West African Journal of Sociology and Political Science*, 1 (2): 177–85.

Shackleton, J. R., 1978. "Corruption: An Essay in Economic Analysis," *Political Quarterly*, IL, 1 (January–March): 25–37.

Van Roy, Edward, 1971. "On the Theory of Corruption," *Economic Development and Cultural Change*, XIX (October): 86–110.

North America

Amick, George, 1976. *The American Way of Graft*. Princeton, NJ: Center for Analysis of Public Issues.

Atkinson, Michael M. and Maureen Mancuso 1985. "Do we Need a Code of Conduct for Politicians? The Search for an Elite Political Culture of Corruption in Canada," *Canadian Journal of Political Science*, XVIII, 3: 459–80.

Basche, James R., Jr., 1976. *Unusual Foreign Payments: A Survey of the Policies of US Companies*, New York: The Conference Board.

Beard, Edmund and Stephen Horn, 1975. *Congressional Ethics: The View from the House*, Washington: Brookings Institution.

Benson, George C. S., 1978. *Political Corruption in America*. Lexington, MA: Lexington Books.

Berg, Larry L., Harlan Hahn, and John R. Schmidhauser, 1976. *Corruption in the American Political System*. Morristown, NJ: General Learning Press.

Bollens, John and Henry Schmandt, 1979. *Political Corruption: Power, Money and Sex*, Pacific Palisades, CA: Palisades Publishers.

Burnham, David, 1976. *The Role of the Media in Controlling Corruption*, New York: John Jay Press.

Caiden, Gerald E. and Naomi J. Caiden, 1977. "Administrative Corruption," *Public Administration Review*, 37, 3 (May/June): 301–309.

Carson, Thomas L., 1985. "Bribery, Extortion, and 'The Foreign Corrupt Practices Act'," *Philosophy and Public Affairs*, 14, 1 (Winter): 66–90.

Chambliss, William J., 1971. "Vice, Corruption, Bureaucracy, and Power," *Wisconsin Law Review*, 4: 50–73.

Chemerinsky, Erwin, 1981. "Fraud and Corruption Against the Government: A Proposed Statute to Establish a Taxpayer Remedy," *Journal of Criminal Law and Criminology*, 72, 4 (Winter): 1482–1521.

Douglas, Jack D. and John M. Johnson (eds.), 1977. *Official Deviance: Readings Malfeasance, Misfeasance, and Other Forms of Corruption.* Philadelphia: J. B. Lippincott.

Dunham, Roger G. and Armand L. Mauss, 1976. "Waves from Watergate: Evidence Concerning the Impact of the Watergate Scandal Upon Political Legitimacy and Social Control," *Pacific Sociological Review*, 19: 4 (October): 469–90.

Eisenstadt, Abraham S., Ari Hoogenboom, and Hans L. Trefousse (eds.), 1978. *Before Watergate: Problems of Corruption in American Society.* Brooklyn, NY: Brooklyn College Press.

Erskine, Hazel, 1973–74. "The Polls: Corruption in Government," *Public Opinion Quarterly*, 37: 4 (Winter), 628–44.

Etzioni, A., 1984. *Capital Corruption: The New Attack on American Democracy*, New York: Harcourt Brace Jovanovich.

Gardiner, J. and D. Olson (eds.), 1974. *Theft of the City*, Bloomington: Indiana University Press.

Gardiner, John A. and Theodore R. Lyman, 1978. *Decisions for Sale: Corruption in Local Land-Use and Building Regulation.* New York: Praeger.

Gibbons, Kenneth and Donald Rowat (eds.), 1976. *Political Corruption in Canada.* Toronto: McClelland and Stewart.

Halpern, Paul J., (ed.), 1975. *Why Watergate?* Pacific Palisades, CA: Palisades Publishers.

Heller, Morton, 1978. "Corruption in America: Continuity and Change." In *Before Watergate: Problems of Corruption in American Society* ed. Abraham E. Eisenstadt, Ari Hogenboom, and Hans L. Trefousse. New York: Brooklyn College Press.

Hutchison, John, 1972. *The Imperfect Union: A History of Corruption in American Trade Unions*, New York: Dutton.

Johnston, Michael, 1979. "Patrons and Clients, Jobs and Machines: A Case Study of the Uses of Patronage," *American Political Science Review*, 73: 2 (June), 385–98.

Johnston, Michael, 1982. *Political Corruption and Public Policy in America.* Monterey, CA: Brooks/Cole Publishing Company.

Johnston, Michael, 1983. "Corruption and Political Culture: An Empirical Perspective," *Publius*, 13, 1 (Winter): 19–39.

Lowi, Theodore J., 1981. "An Intelligent Person's Guide to Political Corruption," *Public Affairs* (September): 1–6.

Maas, Peter, 1973. *Serpico: The Cop Who Defied the System*, New York: Viking.

McKinney, Jerome B. and Michael Johnston (eds.), 1986. *Fraud, Waste and*

Abuse in Government, Philadelphia: Institute for the Study of Human Issues.

New York City, Knapp Commission, 1973. *The Knapp Commission Report on Police Corruption*, New York: George Braziller.

Nice, David C., 1983. "Political Corruption in the American States," *American Politics Quarterly*, 11, 4 (October): 507–517.

Peters, John G. and Susan Welch, 1978. "Politics, Corruption, and Political Culture: A View From the State Legislature," *American Politics Quarterly*, VI, 3 (July): 345–56.

Rakove, Milton, 1975. *Don't Make No Waves, Don't Back No Losers: An Insider's Analysis of the Daley Machine*, Bloomington: Indiana University Press.

Reed, Jean D., 1980. "Corporate Self-Investigations Under the Foreign Corrupt Practices Act," *University of Chicago Law Review*, 47, 4 (Summer): 803–23.

Roberts, Donald E., 1975. "Watergate and Political Socialization: The Inescapable Event," *American Politics Quarterly*, 3, 4 (October): . . .

Rundquist, Barry S., Gerald S. Strom and John G. Peters, 1977. "Corrupt Politicans and Their Electoral Support: Some Experimental Observations," *American Political Science Review*, 71 (September): 954–63.

Shefter, Martin, 1976. "The Emergence of the Political Machine: An Alternative View," in W. D. Hawley *et. al.*, *Theoretical Perspectives on Urban Politics*, Englewood Cliffs, N. J.: Prentice-Hall.

Sherman, Lawrence W., 1978. *Scandal and Reform: Controlling Police Corruption*. Berkeley, CA: University of California.

Steck, Henry, 1976. "Watergate and the American Political System" Paper prepared for delivery at the Edinburg IPSA Congress, August 16–21.

Stern, Herbert J., 1971. "Prosecutions of Local Political Corruption under the Hobbs Act: The Unnecessary Distinction Between Bribery and Extortion," *Seton Hall Law Review*, 3, 1 (Fall): 1–17.

Weeks, Joseph R., 1986. "Bribes, Gratuities and the Congress." *Journal of Legislation,* 13:2, 123–48.

Western Europe

Becquart-Leclercq, Jeanne, 1986. "Du reseau relationel a la corruption politique, *Annee universitaire 1985–6.*

Brünner, Christian (ed.), 1981. *Korruption und Kontrolle*. Vienna: Böhlaus.

Cars, Thorsten, 1979. *Mutor och Bestickning. En Presentation av den nya lagstiftningen*. Stockholm: Liber Forlag.

Chibnall, Steven and Peter Saunders, 1977. "Worlds Apart: Notes on the Social Reality of Corruption," *British Journal of Sociology*, 28, 2 (June): 138–54.

Doig, A., 1984. *Corruption and Misconduct in Contemporary British Politics*. Harmondsworth: Penguin Books.

Fennell, Phillip and Philip Thomas, 1983. "Corruption in the United Kingdom: A Historical Analysis," *International Journal of the Sociology of Law*, 11: 167–89.

Frognier, A-P., 1986. "Corruption and Consociational Democracy: First

Thoughts on the Belgian Case." *Corruption and Reform*. 1:2, 143–148.

Harding, Robert, 1981. "Corruption and the Moral Boundaries of Patronage in the Renaissance," in Guy Fitch Lyttle and Stephen Orgle, eds, *Patronage in the Renaissance*. Princeton: Princeton University Press.

Hurstfield, Joel, 1975. "The Politics of Corruption in Shakespeare's England," *Shakespearean Survey*. 28: 15–28.

Hurstfield, J., 1973. *Freedom, Corruption, and Government in Elizabethan England*. Cambridge: Harvard University Press.

Johnston, Michael and Douglas Wood, 1985. "Right and Wrong in Public and Private Life," in Roger Jowell and Sharon Witherspoon (eds.), *British Social Attitudes: The 1985 Report*, London: Gower.

Joutsen, Matti, 1975. "The Potential for Corruption," Oikenspoliittisen tutkimuslaitoksen julkaisuja, No. 6. Research Institute of Legal Policy, Helsinki, Finland.

Padioleau, J. G., 1975. "De La corruption dans les oligarchies pluralistes," *Revue Francaise de Sociologie*, XVI, 1: 33–58.

Peck, Linda Levy, 1980. "Corruption at the Court of James I: The Undermining of Legitimacy." In *After the Reformation: Reapprovals in Honor of J. H. Hexter*, ed. Barbara C. Maloment, Philadelphia: University of Philadelphia Press.

Pinto-Duschinsky, Michael, 1977. "Corruption in Britain: The Royal Commission on Standards of Conduct in Public Life," *Political Studies*, XXV, 2 (June): 274–84.

Sacks, Paul Martin, 1976. *The Donegal Mafia: An Irish Political Machine*. New Haven: Yale University Press.

Williams, Sandra, 1985. *Conflict of Interest: The Ethical Dilemma in Politics*, London: Gower.

Worm, Alfred, 1981. "Der Skandal—AKH: Story, Analyse, Dokumente—*Europas grösster Krankenhausbau*. Wien: Orac-Pietsch.

Communist Systems

Grossman, Gregory, 1977. "The 'Second Economy' of the USSR," *Problems of Communism*, XXVI (September) 40.

Jowitt, Ken, 1983. "Soviet Neotraditionalism: The Political Corruption of a Leninist Regime," *Soviet Studies*, 35, 3 (July): 275–97.

Katsenelinboigen, Aron, 1983. "Corruption in the USSR: Some Methodological Notes." In Michael Clarke, ed. *Corruption: Causes, Consequences and Control*, New York: St. Martin's Press.

Lampert, Nicholas, 1985. *Whistleblowing in the Soviet Union*. New York: Schocken.

Los, Maria, 1982. "Corruption in a Communist Country: A Case Study of Poland." Paper at the International Sociological Congress.

Ostergaard, C. S., 1986. "Explaining China's Recent Corruption," *Corruption and Reform*, 1:3, 209–34.

Schwartz, Charles A., 1979. "Corruption and Political Development in the U.S.S.R.," *Comparative Politics*, XII, 4 (July): 425–43.

Simis, Konstantin M., 1982. *USSR: The Corrupt Society*. Translated by Jacqueline Edwards and Mitchell Schneider. New York: Simon and Schuster.

Smith, Hedrick, 1976. *The Russians*. New York: Ballantine Books.
Staats, S. J., 1972. "Corruption in the Soviet System," *Problems of Communism*, 1: 40–47.

Asia and the Pacific

Agrawala, S. K., 1980. "Public Servants' Offence of Corruption and Sentencing by the Supreme Court of India," *Indian Journal of Public Administration*, 26, 4 (October–December): 937–86.
Bautista, Victoria A., 1982. "The Nature, Causes, and Extent of Corruption: A Review of Literature," *Philippine Journal of Public Administration*, XXVI (3–4): 235–70.
Bhambhri, C. P. and M. B. Nair, 1971. "Corruption in Pakistan Civil Service: An Analytical Survey," *South Asian Studies*, VI, 2: 30–40.
Carino, L. V., 1985. "The Politicalization of the Philippine Bureaucracy: Corruption or Commitment?," *International Review of Administrative Sciences*, 51, 1: 13–18.
Dixon, K., 1977. "Japan's Lockheed Scandal: 'Structural Corruption'," *Pacific Community*, VIII (2): 340–62.
Fuduka, Kanichi, 1976. "Parliamentary Democracy and Political Corruption," *Japan Interpreter*, XI, 2: 159–66.
Gopinath, P. Krishna, 1982. "Corruption in Political and Public Offices: Causes and Cure," *Indian Journal of Public Administration*, XXVIII, 4 (October–December): 897–918.
Gould, David H., 1980. *Bureaucratic Corruption and Underdevelopment in the Third World: The Case of Zaire*. New York: Pergamon.
Gould, David J. and Jose A. Amero-Reyes, 1983. "The Effects of Corruption on Administrative Performance," World Bank Staff Working Papers No. 580, Management and Development Series 7. Washington, D.C.
Hager, L. M., 1973. "Bureaucratic Corruption in India: Legal Control of Maladministration," *Comparative Political Studies*, VI, 2: 197–219.
Hay, P. R., 1977. "Factors Conducive to Political Corruption: The Tasmanian Experience," *Political Science*, 29, 2 (December): 115–30.
Hoctjes, B. J. S., 1976. "Politics and Government: A Background to Corruption in Public Administration in Developing Countries," *The Netherlands Journal of Sociology*, XII: 47–77.
Hope, Kempe Ronald, 1985. "Politics, Bureaucratic Corruption, and Maladministration in the Third World," *International Review of Administrative Sciences*, 51, 1: 1–6.
Iga, Mamoru and Morton Auerbach, 1977. "Political Corruption and Social Structure in Japan," *Asian Survey*, XVII, 6 (June): 556–64.
Imazu, H., 1976. "Power Mosaic: Hotbed of the Lockheed Case," *Japan Quarterly*, 23 (3): 228–37.
Jabbra, Joseph G., 1976. "Bureaucratic Corruption in the Third World: Causes and Remedy," *The Indian Journal of Public Administration*, XXII (October–December), 673–91.
Jain, R. B., 1983. "Fighting Political Corruption: The Indian Experience," *Indian Political Science Review*, XVII, 2 (July): 215–28.
Jones, Edwin, 1985. "Politics, Bureaucratic Corruption and Maladministration

in the Third World: Some Commonwealth Caribbean Considerations," *International Review of Administrative Sciences*, L1, 1: 19–23.

Klitgaard, Robert, 1984. "Managing the Fight Against Corruption: A Case Study," *Public Administration and Development*, 4, 77–98.

Kohli, Sureh (ed.), 1975. *Corruption in India*. New Delhi: Chetana Publications.

Lee, Rance P. L., 1981. "The Folklore of Corruption in Hong Kong," *Asian Survey*, 21, (3), 355–68.

Marican, Y. Mansoor, 1979. "Combating Corruption: The Malaysian Experience," *Asian Survey*, XIX (6), 597–610.

Morell, David, 1976. "The Functions of Corruption in Thai Politics". *Asian Affairs*, 3, (3), 151–84.

Neher, Clark D., 1977. "Political Corruption in a Thai Province," *Journal of Developing Areas*, XI, 4 (July): 479–92.

Palmier, Leslie H., 1985. *The Control of Bureaucratic Corruption*. New Delhi: Allied Publishers.

Quah, Jon S. T., 1982. "Bureaucratic Corruption in the ASEAN Countries: A Comparative Analysis of Their Anti-corruption Strategies," *Journal of Southeast Asian Studies*, 13, 1 (March): 153–83.

Seidman, Robert B., 1978. "Why Do People Obey the Law? The Case of Corruption in Developing Countries," *British Journal of Law and Society*, V, (1), 45–68.

Sivalingam, G., 1983. "Bureaucratic Corruption in Malaysia: The Incongruence Between Social and Legal Norms," *Philippine Journal of Public Administration*, 27, 4 (October): 418–35.

Somjee, A. H., 1974. "Social Perspectives on Corruption in India," *Political Science Review*, XIII, (1–4): 180–86.

Varma, S. P., 1974. "Corruption and Political Development in India," *Political Science Review*, XII, (1–4): 157–79.

Wade, Robert, 1982. "The System of Administrative and Political Corruption: Canal Irrigation in South India," *Journal of Development Studies*, 18, 3 (April): 287–328.

Zahedi, Shamsosadat, 1978. "Corruption in Developing Countries: The Iranian Case," *Administrative Change*, V, (2), 141–50.

Africa and Latin America

Aina, S., 1982. "Bureaucratic Corruption in Nigeria: The Continuing Search for Causes and Cures," *International Review of Administrative Sciences*, 48, 1, 70–76.

Brownsberger, William N., 1983. "Development and Governmental Corruption—Materialism and Political Fragmentation in Nigeria," *Journal of Modern African Studies*, XXI, 2, 215–33.

Bunker, Stephen G. and Lawrence E. Cohen, 1983. "Collaboration and Competition in Two Colonization Projects: Toward a General Theory of Official Corruption," *Human Organization*, 42, 2, 106–14.

Correa, Hector, 1985. "A Comparative Study of Bureaucratic Corruption in Latin America and the U.S.A.," *Socio-Economic Planning Sciences*, 19, 1: 63–80.

Eker, Varda, 1981. "On the Origins of Corruption: Irregular Incentives in Nigeria," *Journal of Modern African Studies*, XIX, I, 173–82.

Ekpo, Monday U. (ed.), 1977. *Bureaucratic Corruption in Sub-Saharan Africa: Toward a Search for Causes and Consequences*. Washington, DC: University Press of America.

Gould, David J., 1980. *Bureaucratic Corruption and Underdevelopment in the Third World: The Case of Zaire*. New York: Pergamon.

Grayson, George M., 1984. "An Overdose of Corruption: The Domestic Politics of Mexican Oil," *Caribbean Review*, XIII, 3, 22–24, 46–49.

Hayward, Fred M., 1971. "Ghana Experiment with Civic Education," *Africa Report* (May), 24–27.

Hope, Kempe Ronald, 1985. "Politics, Bureaucratic Corruption, and Maladministration in the Third World," *International Review of Administrative Sciences*, LI, I, 1–6.

Le Vine, Victor T., 1975. *Political Corruption: The Ghana Case*. Stanford, CA: Hoover Institution Press.

Medard, J. F., 1986. "Public Corruption in Africa: A Comparative Perspective," *Corruption and Reform,* 1:2, 115–32.

Morris, Stephen D., 1987. "Corruption and the Mexican Political System," *Corruption and Reform,* 2:1, 3–16.

Nzeribe, Francis Arthur, 1985. *Nigeria: Another Hope Betrayed*, Bungay, Suffolk: The Chaucer Press.

Offiong, Daniel A., 1984. "The Prevalence and Repercussions of Corruption in Nigeria," *The Indian Political Science Review*, XVIII (January), 59–72.

Olowu, Dele, 1983. "The Nature of Bureaucratic Corruption in Nigeria," *International Review of Administrative Sciences*, 1L, 3, 291–96.

Riley, Stephen, 1982. "The Land of Waving Palms': Political Economy, Corruption Inquiries and Politics in Sierra Leone." In Clarke, ed. *Corruption: Causes, Consequences and Control*. New York: St. Martin's Press.

Werlin, H. H., 1972. "The Roots of Corruption—The Ghanaian Inquiry," *Journal of Modern African Studies*, X, 2, 247–66.

Werlin, H. H., 1973. "The Consequences of Corruption: The Ghanaian Experience," *Political Science Quarterly*, 88, 1, 71–85.

Woldring, Klaas, 1983. "Corruption and Inefficiency in Zambia—A Survey of Recent Inquiries," *Africa Today*, 30, 3, 51–74.

About the Contributors

Ulrich von Alemann is Professor of Political Science at the Fernuniversitaet, Hagen, West Germany.

David H. Bayley is a Professor in The Graduate School of International Studies at the University of Denver, Colorado.

Jeanne Becquart-Leclercq teaches Sociology and Political Science at the University of Lille II, France.

Erhard Blankenburg is Professor of the Sociology of Law in the Law Faculty of the Free University of Amsterdam, Netherlands.

Jeremy Boissevain is Professor of Anthropology at the University of Amsterdam, Netherlands.

J.K. Campbell is an anthropologist at St. Antony's College, Oxford, England.

Wayne DiFranceisco is a graduate student in the political science department of the University of Michigan, Ann Arbor.

Abraham S. Eisenstadt is Professor of History at Brooklyn College, Brooklyn, New York.

Eva Etzioni-Halevy teaches in the Sociology Department of the Australian National University, Canberra.

Samuel E. Finer is Gladstone Professor of Government Emeritus at Oxford University.

Carl J. Friedrich was Professor of Political Science at Harvard and Heidelberg Universities.

John A. Gardiner is Professor of Political Science at the University of Illinois, Chicago.

Kenneth M. Gibbons is an Assistant Professor of Political Science at the University of Winnipeg, Canada.

Zvi Gitelman is Professor of Political Science at the University of Michigan, Ann Arbor.

Margaret Goodman taught political science at the City University of New York.

Bruce E. Gronbeck is an Associate Professor in the Department of Communication Studies at the University of Iowa, Iowa City.

Peter Harris is Professor of Political Science at the University of Hong Kong.

Arnold J. Heidenheimer is Professor of Political Science at Washington University, St. Louis, Missouri.

Samuel P. Huntington is Eaton Professor of the Science of Government at Harvard University.

Michael Johnston is Associate Professor of Political Science at Colgate University, Hamilton, New York.

V.O. Key, Jr. taught in the government department at Harvard University.

John P. King is a teacher in Newbury, Berkshire, England.

Jacob van Klaveren is Emeritus Professor of Economic History at the University of Frankfurt, West Germany.

John M. Kramer is Associate Professor of Political Science at Mary Washington College, Fredericksburg, Virginia.

Nathaniel H. Leff is Professor of Business at Columbia University, New York City.

Victor T. LeVine is Professor of Political Science at Washington University, St. Louis, Missouri.

Colin Leys is Professor of Political Science at Queens University, Kingston, Ontario, Canada.

Walter Lippmann was a distinguished author and publicist.

Alan P.L. Liu is Professor of Political Science at the University of California, Santa Barbara.

Daniel Lowenstein is Professor of Law at the University of California, Los Angeles.

Theodore R. Lyman is Associate Director of the Center for Economic Competitiveness of SRI International, Menlo Park, California.

Graeme C. Moodie is Professor of Political Science at the University of York, England.

Gunnar Myrdal was Professor of International Economics at Stockholm University.

Joseph S. Nye is Professor of Government at Harvard University.

Bruce L. Payne is a lecturer in the Institute of Policy Sciences and Public Affairs at Duke University, Durham, North Carolina.

Linda Levy Peck is Associate Professor of History at Purdue University, Lafayette, Indiana.

John G. Peters is Professor of Political Science at the University of Nebraska, Lincoln.

Jon S.T. Quah is Senior Lecturer in the Political Science Department of the National University of Singapore.

Susan Rose-Ackerman is Professor of Law and Political Economy at Columbia Law School, New York City.

Michael Rosenthal is a student at the Law School of the University of Michigan, Ann Arbor.

Charles F.C. Ruff is a partner in the law firm of Covington and Burling, Washington, D.C.

James C. Scott is Professor of Political Science at Yale University.

Lawrence W. Sherman is a Professor in the Department of Criminology, University of Maryland.

Theodore M. Smith is a consultant to the Rockefeller Foundation and to the World Bank.

Rainer Staudhammer is a research fellow in political science at the University of Frankfurt, West Germany.

Heinz Steinert is Professor of Sociology at the University of Frankfurt and Director of the Institut fuer Rechts und Kriminalsoziologie in Vienna, Austria.

Koenraad W. Swart held a professorship in Dutch history at the University of London.

John Waterbury is Professor of Politics at Princeton University.

Susan Welch is Professor of Political Science at the University of Nebraska, Lincoln.

Simcha Werner is a lecturer in the political science department of Tel Aviv University, Israel.

Laurence Whitehead is a Fellow of Nuffield College, Oxford University.

James Q. Wilson is Shattuck Professor of Government at Harvard University.

June